MODERN CONSTITUTIONAL THEORY

A READER

Third Edition

By

John H. Garvey
Professor of Law
Notre Dame Law School

and

T. Alexander Aleinikoff
Professor of Law
University of Michigan Law School

AMERICAN CASEBOOK SERIES®

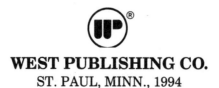

WEST PUBLISHING CO.
ST. PAUL, MINN., 1994

American Casebook Series, the key symbol appearing on the front
cover and the WP symbol are registered trademarks of West Publishing
Co. Registered in the U.S. Patent and Trademark Office.

COPYRIGHT © 1989, 1991 WEST PUBLISHING CO.

COPYRIGHT © 1994 By WEST PUBLISHING CO.
                    610 Opperman Drive
                    P.O. Box 64526
                    St. Paul, MN 55164–0526
                    1–800–328–9352

Library of Congress Cataloging-in-Publication Data
Modern constitutional theory : a reader / [edited] by John H. Garvey
    and T. Alexander Aleinikoff. — 3rd ed.
        p.   cm.
    Includes bibliographical references.
    ISBN 0-314-03718-7
        1. United States—Constitutional law.   I. Garvey, John H., 1948–
  . II. Aleinikoff, Thomas Alexander, 1952–   .
    KF4549.M63   1994
    342.73—dc20
    [347.302]   94–15806
                                                                        CIP

ISBN 0–314–03718–7

PRINTED WITH
SOY INK™

PREFACE

The teaching of Constitutional Law has changed a good deal recently. One cause of the change has been the explosive growth in the dimensions of the subject. Not very long ago, casebooks treated the Bill of Rights as a unitary whole. The Fourth, Fifth, and Sixth Amendments were taught alongside the First Amendment. Now they provide enough material for a course in Criminal Procedure. The same process of fission is evident in other parts of the curriculum. The First Amendment has grown like the tax code, and is generally taught in a separate course. Family Law has absorbed much of the Due Process and Equal Protection Clauses. Federal Courts courses are devoted to Article III problems. Separation of powers provides material for courses in Administrative Law, the Congress, and the Presidency. Taxation of interstate commerce has split off and been ignored.

The reaction to this growth has been to teach less law, not more. That response is not as paradoxical as it seems. There is not enough space for all the details of doctrine, and many of them are more efficiently taught elsewhere in the curriculum. But there is a greater need than before to explore the foundations that support and unify the doctrinal structure. Constitutional Law now tries to go down rather than out.

This emphasis on depth in lieu of breadth has another cause. The enormous growth and change in the coverage of the law have been accompanied by a proliferation of theories about the ideology of law. These include, most prominently, the law and economics movement (and the related development of public choice theory), the critical legal studies movement, critical race theory, and feminist jurisprudence. To these we might add the revival of interest in various philosophical theories (natural rights, utilitarianism, and positivism), in the civic republicanism of the 18th century, and in a liberalism concerned with the political process. We are now more self-consciously concerned with asking whose purposes the law serves, what values it should promote, and even whether law is a meaningful constraint on human behavior. Courses in Constitutional Law cannot ignore this ferment. If there is widespread disagreement about fundamental premises, we cannot make much progress in ironing out doctrinal details.

This book is designed with these problems in mind. It can be used as a supplement to introductory courses in Constitutional Law, or as a text for a course in Constitutional Theory. We begin in Chapter 1 with a look at some of the currently influential theories of the constitution. Is there an ideology that governs this area of the law? Is it a good one? We then turn in Chapter 2 to the document itself, and examine various proposals for interpreting it. It is often said that a written constitution embodies fixed principles that are beyond the reach of ideological manipulation. Here we inquire whether this is so. In Chapter 3 we take up the closely allied problem of judicial review. How we should interpret the constitution is a different question than who should interpret it. In the United States we usually assign that job to the courts. Are we right to do so?

Thereafter we have organized the book to correspond with the major topics covered in casebooks on Constitutional Law. We have, however, omitted treatment of the First Amendment. It is not addressed in most first-year classes, and is often the subject of a separate upper-level course. For that reason, and because an adequate treatment would require a vast amount of material, we thought it should be covered in a separate volume.

Although the chapters are organized according to doctrinal categories, the readings they contain are not an elaboration (or condensation) of doctrine such as one would find in a hornbook. They seek to go deeper than a restatement of the law, to ask what and whose purposes are served by existing rules, and to inquire whether some other organization is preferable. Not all the readings address these questions from the same point of view. The selections take opposing positions on each subject, in order to make students aware of the existing conflict and to facilitate class discussion of the materials.

Most of the selections have been edited. We have indicated the deletion of sentences and paragraphs by ellipses. We have not drawn attention to omitted footnotes, but have used the original numbering of those retained. Our own footnotes, added for editorial purposes, are numbered alphabetically.

JOHN H. GARVEY

T. ALEXANDER ALEINIKOFF

April, 1994

Acknowledgments

We would like to thank the authors and copyright holders of the following works, who permitted their inclusion in this book:

Bruce A. Ackerman, Beyond Carolene Products. Reprinted with permission of Bruce A. Ackerman.

Bruce A. Ackerman, We The People, volume I: Foundations. Reprinted with permission of Bruce A. Ackerman and the publishers from We The People: Foundations by Bruce Ackerman, Cambridge, Mass.: Harvard University Press. Copyright © 1991 by the President and Fellows of Harvard College.

Larry Alexander & Paul Horton, Whom Does the Constitution Command? Reprinted with permission of Larry Alexander, Paul Horton, and Greenwood Publishing Group, Inc., Westport, CT. Copyright © 1988.

T. Alexander Aleinikoff, A Case for Race-Consciousness. This article originally appeared at 91 Colum.L.Rev. 1060 (1991). Reprinted by permission.

T. Alexander Aleinikoff, Constitutional Law in the Age of Balancing. Reprinted by permission of The Yale Law Journal Company and Fred B. Rothman & Company from The Yale Law Journal, Vol. 96, pp. 943 ff.

Akhil Reed Amar & Daniel Widawsky, Child Abuse as Slavery: A Thirteenth Amendment Response to DeShaney. Reprinted with permission of Akhil Reed Amar, Daniel Widawsky, and the Harvard Law Review Association. Copyright © 1992 by the Harvard Law Review Association.

Derrick Bell, And We Are Not Saved. Copyright © 1987 by Basic Books, Inc. Reprinted by permission of BasicBooks, a division of HarperCollins Publish-ers, Inc.

Raoul Berger, Government By Judiciary. Reprinted by permission of the Harvard University Press. Copyright © 1977 by the President and Fellows of Harvard College.

Alexander M. Bickel, The Least Dangerous Branch (1962). Reprinted with permission of Josephine A. Bickel.

Charles L. Black, Jr., The People and the Court (1960). Reprinted with permission of Macmillan Publishing Company. Copyright © 1960 by Charles L. Black, Jr.

Philip C. Bobbit, Constitutional Interpretation. Reprinted with permission of Philip C. Bobbit and Blackwell Publishers.

Robert H. Bork, Neutral Principles and Some First Amendment Problems. Reprinted with permission of the Indiana Law Journal and Fred B. Rothman & Company.

Paul A. Brest, The Misconceived Quest for the Original Understanding. Reprinted with permission of Paul A. Brest and the Boston University Law Review.

Paul Brest, In Defense of the Antidiscrimination Principle. Copyright © 1976 by the Harvard Law Review Association.

Stephen L. Carter, The Political Aspects of Judicial Power: Some Notes on the Presidential Immunity Decision, 131 U.Pa.L.Rev. 1341 (1983). Copyright © 1983 by the University of Pennsylvania.

Erwin Chemerinsky, Rethinking State Action. Reprinted with permission of Erwin Chemerinsky and Northwestern University School of Law, Volume 80, Issue 3, Northwestern University Law Review, (1985), pp. 503.

Jesse H. Choper, Thoughts on State Action: The "Government Function" and "Power Theory" Approaches. Reprinted with permission of Jesse H. Choper and the Washington University Law Quarterly. This article originally appeared at 1979 Wash.U.L.Q. 757.

Edward S. Corwin, The Steel Seizure Case: A Judicial Brick Without Straw. Copyright © 1953 by the Directors of the Columbia Law Review Association, Inc. All rights reserved. This article originally appeared at 53 Colum.L.Rev. 53 (1953). Reprinted by permission.

Kimberlé W. Crenshaw, Race, Reform, and Retrenchment: Transformation and Legitimation in Antidiscrimination Law. Reprinted by permission of Kimberlé W. Crenshaw and the Harvard Law Review Association. Copyright © 1988 by the Harvard Law Review Association.

David P. Currie, The Distribution of Powers After Bowsher, 1986 Sup.Ct.Rev. 19. Copyright © 1987 by The University of Chicago. All rights reserved.

Noel T. Dowling, Interstate Commerce and State Power. Reprinted with permission of the Virginia Law Review and Fred B. Rothman & Company.

Ronald Dworkin, The Right to Death. Reprinted with permission from The New York Review of Books. Copyright © 1991 Nyrev, Inc.

Ronald Dworkin, Taking Rights Seriously. Reprinted with permission of Ronald Dworkin and the publishers from Taking Rights Seriously by Ronald Dworkin, Cambridge, Mass.: Harvard University Press. Copyright © 1977, 1978 by the President and Fellows of Harvard College.

Frank Easterbrook, Substance and Due Process, 1982 Sup.Ct.Rev. 85. Copyright © 1983 by The University of Chicago. All rights reserved.

John Hart Ely, Democracy and Distrust. Reprinted by permission of the Harvard University Press. Copyright © 1980 by the President and Fellows of Harvard College.

John Hart Ely, The Wages of Crying Wolf: A Comment on Roe v. Wade. Reprinted with permission of John Hart Ely.

Richard A. Epstein, Lucas v. South Carolina Coastal Council: A Tangled Web of Expectations, 45 Stan.L.Rev. 1369 (1993). Reprinted with permission of Richard A. Epstein, the Stanford Law Review, and Fred B. Rothman & Co. Copyright ©1993 by the Board of Trustees of the Leland Stanford Junior University.

Daniel A. Farber, State Regulation and the Dormant Commerce Clause. Reprinted with permission of Constitutional Commentary.

Louis Fisher, Constitutional Conflicts Between Congress and the President. Copyright © 1985 Princeton University Press. Excerpt, pp. 60-70, reprinted by permission of Princeton University Press.

Owen M. Fiss, Groups and the Equal Protection Clause, Philosophy & Public Affairs 5, no. 2 (Winter 1976). Copyright © 1976 Princeton University Press. Excerpts reprinted with permission by Princeton University Press.

Charles Fried, Metro Broadcasting, Inc. v. FCC: Two Concepts of Equality. Copyright © 1990 by the Harvard Law Review Association.

John H. Garvey, Freedom and Representation, from Kindred Matters, ed. Diana Meyers, Kenneth Kipnis, and Cornelius Murphy (1993). Reprinted by permission of the Cornell University Press.

Ruth Gavison, Feminism and the Public/Private Distinction. Reprinted by permission of Ruth Gavison, the Stanford Law Review, and Fred B. Rothman & Co. Copyright © 1992 by the Board of Trustees of the Leland Stanford Junior University.

Ruth Bader Ginsburg, Some Thoughts on Autonomy and Equality in Relation to Roe v. Wade. Reprinted by permission of the Honorable Ruth Bader Ginsburg and the North Carolina Law Review.

Neil Gotanda, A Critique of "Our Constitution is Color-Blind." Reprinted by permission of Neil Gotanda.

Kent Greenawalt, Judicial Scrutiny of "Benign" Racial Preference in Law School Admissions. Copyright © 1975 by the Directors of the Columbia Law Review Association, Inc. All rights reserved. This article originally appeared at 75 Colum.L.Rev. 557. Reprinted by permission.

Thomas C. Grey, Do We Have an Unwritten Constitution?, 27 Stan.L.Rev. 703 (1975). Reprinted with permission of the Stanford Law Review and Fred B. Rothman & Co. Copyright © 1975 by the Board of Trustees of the Leland Stanford Junior University.

viiiACKNOWLEDGMENTS

GeraldGunther, Judicial Hegemony and Legislative Autonomy: The
Nixon Case and the Impeachment Process. Reprinted with permission of
the UCLA Law Review and Fred B. Rothman & Company.

Learned Hand, The Bill of Rights. Reprinted by permission of the
Harvard University Press. Copyright © 1958 by the President and
Fellows of Harvard College.

Harold W. Horowitz, The Misleading Search for "State Action" Under
the Fourteenth Amendment, 30 S.Cal.L.Rev. 208-213 (1957), reprinted
with permission of Harold W. Horowitz and the Southern California Law
Review.

Lewis B. Kaden, Politics, Money, and State Sovereignty: The Judicial
Role. Copyright © 1979 by the Directors of the Columbia Law Review
Association, Inc. All rights reserved. This article originally appeared at
54 Colum.L.Rev. 543 (1954). Reprinted by permission.

Yale Kamisar, When Is There A Constitutional "Right to Die"? When Is
There No Constitutional "Right to Live"? Reprinted by permission of
Yale Kamisar and the Georgia Law Review.

Richard S. Kay, Adherence to the Original Intentions in Constitutional
Adjudication: Three Objections and Responses. 82 Nw.U.L.Rev. 226
(1988). Copyright © 1988 by Northwestern University.

Richard S. Kay, The State Action Doctrine, the Public-Private
Distinction, and the Independence of Constitutional Law. Reprinted by
permission of Richard S. Kay and Constitutional Commentary.

Harold Hongju Koh, The Coase Theorem and the War Power: A
Response. Reprinted by permission of Harold Hongju Koh and the Duke
Law Journal.

Charles S. Lawrence, III, The Id, the Ego, and Equal Protection:
Reckoning with Unconscious Racism. Copyright © 1987 by the Board of
Trustees of the Leland Stanford Junior University.

Sanford Levinson, Law as Literature. Published originally in 60 Texas
Law Review 373 (1982). Copyright © 1982 by the Texas Law Review.
Reprinted by permission.

Catharine A. MacKinnon, Difference and Dominance: On Sex
Discrimination, from Feminism Unmodified: Discourses on Life and
Law (1987). Reprinted by permission of Rowman & Littlefield
Publishers.

Thurgood Marshall, Reflections on the Bicentennial of the United States
Constitution. Copyright © 1987 by the Harvard Law Review Association.

William P. Marshall, Diluting Constitutional Rights: Rethinking
"Rethinking State Action." Reprinted by permission of William P.
Marshall and The Northwestern University Law Review.

Jerry L. Mashaw, The Supreme Court's Due Process Calculus for Administrative Adjudication in Mathews v. Eldridge: Three Factors in Search of a Theory of Value, 44 U.Chi.L.Rev. 28 (1976). Copyright © 1977 by The University of Chicago. All rights reserved.

Robert G. McCloskey, Economic Due Process and the Supreme Court: An Exhumation and Reburial. Reprinted with permission of the University of Chicago Press.

Thomas W. Merrill, The Economics of Public Use, 72 Cornell L.Rev. 61 (1986). Copyright © 1986 by Cornell University. All rights reserved.

Frank I. Michelman, Property, Utility, and Fairness: Comments on the Ethical Foundations of "Just Compensation" Law. Copyright © 1967 by the Harvard Law Review Association.

Henry P. Monaghan, Our Perfect Constitution. Reprinted by permission of Henry P. Monaghan.

Henry P. Monaghan, The Protective Power of the Presidency. This article originally appeared at 93 Colum.L.Rev. 1 (1993). Reprinted by permission.

Henry P. Monaghan, Stare Decisis and Constitutional Adjudication. This article originally appeared at 88 Colum.L.Rev. 723 (1988). Reprinted by permission.

Robert F. Nagel, The Legislative Veto, the Constitution, and the Courts. Reprinted with permission of Constitutional Commentary.

John T. Noonan, Jr., The Root and Branch of Roe v. Wade. Reprinted with permission of the Nebraska Law Review.

Richard D. Parker, The Past of Constitutional Theory — And its Future. Reprinted by permission of Richard D. Parker and the Ohio State Law Journal.

Michael J. Perry, Modern Equal Protection: A Conceptualization and Appraisal. Copyright © 1979 by the Directors of the Columbia Law Review Association, Inc. All rights reserved. This article originally appeared at 79 Colum.L.Rev. 1023 (1979). Reprinted by permission.

Richard A. Posner, Economic Analysis of Law (3rd ed. 1986). Reprinted with permission of Richard A. Posner.

Richard A. Posner, The DeFunis Case and the Constitutionality of Preferential Treatment of Racial Minorities, 1974 Sup.Ct.Rev. 1. Copyright © 1975 by The University of Chicago. All rights reserved.

H. Jefferson Powell, The Oldest Question of Constitutional Law. Reprinted with permission of H. Jefferson Powell, the Virginia Law Review Association, and Fred B. Rothman & Co.

Andrzej Rapaczynski, From Sovereignty to Process: The Jurisprudence of Federalism After Garcia, 1985 Sup.Ct.Rev. 341. Copyright © 1986 by The University of Chicago. All rights reserved.

Donald H. Regan, The Supreme Court and State Protectionism: Making Sense of the Dormant Commerce Clause. Reprinted with permission of the Michigan Law Review Association.

Nancy K. Rhoden, Litigating Life and Death. Copyright © 1988 by the Harvard Law Review Association.

Carol M. Rose, Mahon Reconstructed: Why the Takings Issue Is Still a Muddle, 55 S.Cal.L.Rev. 561 (1984). Reprinted by permission of the Southern California Law Review.

Jed Rubenfeld, The Right of Privacy. Copyright © 1989 by the Harvard Law Review Association.

Michael J. Sandel, Moral Argument and Liberal Toleration: Abortion and Homosexuality. Copyright © 1989 by Michael J. Sandel.

Joseph L. Sax, Takings and the Police Power. Reprinted with permission of the Yale Law Journal.

Frederick Schauer, Easy Cases, 58 S.Cal.L.Rev. 399 (1985). Reprinted with permission of the Southern California Law Review.

Suzanna Sherry, Civic Virtue and the Feminine Voice in Constitutional Adjudication. Reprinted with permission of the Virginia Law Review.

J. Gregory Sidak, To Declare War. Reprinted with permission of J. Gregory Sidak and the Duke Law Journal.

Rodney A. Smolla, The Reemergence of the Right-Privilege Distinction in Constitutional Law: The Price of Protesting Too Much, 35 Stanford L.Rev. 69 (1982). Copyright © 1982 by the Board of Trustees of the Leland Stanford Junior University.

Girardeau A. Spann, Pure Politics. Reprinted with permission of Girardeau A. Spann and the Michigan Law Review Association.

David A. Strauss, Abortion, Toleration, and Moral Uncertainty, 1992 Sup.Ct.Rev. 1. Copyright © 1992 by The University of Chicago. All rights reserved.

Peter L. Strauss, The Place of Agencies in Government: Separation of Powers and the Fourth Branch. Reprinted with permission of the Columbia Law Review.

Cass R. Sunstein, The Partial Constitution. Reprinted with permission of Cass R. Sunstein and the publishers from The Partial Constitution by Cass Sunstein, Cambridge, Mass.: Harvard University Press. Copyright © 1993 by the President and Fellows of Harvard College.

Kendall Thomas, Beyond the Privacy Principle. This article originally appeared at 92 Colum.L.Rev. 1431 (1992). Reprinted by permission.

Judith Jarvis Thomson, A Defense of Abortion, Philosophy & Public Affairs 1, no. 1 (Fall 1971). Copyright © 1971 by Princeton University Press. Excerpts reprinted with permission of Princeton University Press.

Laurence H. Tribe, "In What Vision of the Constitution Must the Law Be Color-Blind?" Reprinted with permission of the John Marshall Law Review.

Laurence H. Tribe, The Puzzling Persistence of Process-Based Constitutional Theories. Reprinted by permission of the Yale Law Journal Company and Fred B. Rothman & Company from the Yale Law Journal, Vol. 89, pp. 1064-1080.

Mark V. Tushnet, Following the Rules Laid Down: A Critique of Interpretivism and Neutral Principles. Copyright © 1983 by the Harvard Law Review Association.

William W. Van Alstyne, The Second Death of Federalism. Reprinted with permission of William W. Van Alstyne and the Michigan Law Review Association.

William W. Van Alstyne, Rites of Passage: Race, the Supreme Court, and the Constitution. Reprinted with permission of William W. Van Alstyne and the University of Chicago Law Review.

Richard A. Wasserstrom, Racism and Sexism. From Philosophy and Social Issues by Richard A. Wasserstrom. Copyright © 1980 by the University of Notre Dame Press. Reprinted by permission.

Herbert Wechsler, The Political Safeguards of Federalism: The Role of the States in the Composition and Selection of the National Government. Copyright © 1954 by the Directors of the Columbia Law Review Association, Inc. All rights reserved. This article originally appeared at 54 Colum.L.Rev. 543 (1954). Reprinted by permission.

Herbert Wechsler, Toward Neutral Principles of Constitutional Law. Copyright © 1959 by the Harvard Law Review Association.

Robin L. West, Constitutional Skepticism. Reprinted by permission of Robin L. West and the Boston University Law Review.

Joan C. Williams, Deconstructing Gender. Reprinted by permission of Joan C. Williams and the Michigan Law Review Association.

Patricia J. Williams, Metro Broadcasting, Inc. v. FCC: Regrouping in Singular Times. Copyright © 1990 by the Harvard Law Review Association.

Wendy W. Williams, The Equality Crisis: Some Reflections On Culture, Courts, and Feminism. Reprinted with permission of the Women's Rights Law Reporter.

*

Summary of Contents

Table of Contents

*

MODERN CONSTITUTIONAL THEORY

A READER

Third Edition

*

Chapter I

THEORIES OF THE CONSTITUTION

In these first three Chapters, we examine three overarching theoretical questions: (1) Does the Constitution have a theme? (2) How do we interpret its various provisions? and (3) Why is it the business of the Supreme Court to answer these questions? It should be apparent that these are related questions, and authors addressing one issue frequently make explicit or implicit claims about the other issues. For example, if one believes that the Constitution is largely about specifying a fair process by which political decisions ought to be reached, one might justify judicial review by charting a role for the Supreme Court of ensuring an open and well-functioning political process; such a perspective might take a dim view of attempts by the Court to read substantive values into the document (such as a right to decide whether or not to terminate a pregnancy). Or, if one believes that judicial review can be justified in a democracy only if the Court is enforcing decisions by "the people" to constitutionalize certain values, one might support interpretative strategies aimed at uncovering the "original meaning" of the text's provisions. Many other possible linkages are imaginable. What interpretative methods, for example, might be favored by a theorist who believes that the Supreme Court can contribute to the moral growth of our polity, or by a theorist who understands the Constitution as primarily concerned with ensuring deliberative decision-making by our elected officials? In short, as you read a selection in one of the first three Chapters, keep asking yourself how the author might answer the questions raised in the other two Chapters.

THEORIES AND CRITIQUES

Is the Constitution a collection of provisions directed at topical concerns of the late 18th century, a compromise among competing regional and economic interests? Or is there a political theory that lies behind the specific bits of text, supplying a unifying theory to the whole? Assuming we can identify an animating theory of the Constitution, is our Constitution, so understood, a good constitution? These are the issues addressed by the selections in this first Chapter.

1

In *Democracy and Distrust* (probably the most influential book on constitutional law in the past few decades), John Hart Ely argues that the Constitution is primarily concerned with process and structure—not the identification and preservation of specific substantive values. He suggests that the open-ended provisions of the document—such as the Fourteenth Amendment—be read to further process-based goals. Exercised in this way, judicial review can be seen as enhancing, rather than frustrating, democratic governance. Laurence Tribe's review of Ely's book—*The Puzzling Persistence of Process-Based Constitutional Theories*—is skeptical of a reading of the document simply in "process" terms. Indeed, he argues, even Ely's approach ultimately requires a commitment to substantive values (such as a theory of which groups need special protection in the political process).

To many Americans, the Constitution is primarily about guaranteeing individuals rights against a potentially oppressive majority that is exercising the levers of government. Ronald Dworkin's essay *Constitutional Cases* is a leading example of a rights-based theory of the Constitution. He argues that it is wrong to understand our liberal democratic political system as committed to pure majoritarianism, and that the Court can and should consult moral theory in explicating the fundamental values underlying the Constitution. Henry Monaghan's ironically entitled article *Our Perfect Constitution* takes issue with liberal constitutional theorists who read into the document all the equality and autonomy values they believe a decent modern political system ought to protect. He suggests that perhaps the Constitution "guarantees only representative democracy, not perfect government."

We next include an excerpt from the first volume of Bruce Ackerman's massive revisionist study of constitutional history. Ackerman argues for a "dualist" understanding of the Constitution. This two-track model distinguishes between constitutional decisions made by the People and ordinary political decisions reached by the People's elected representatives. Judicial review, from this perspective, presents no "counter-majoritarian difficulty" to the extent it is enforcing a prior higher-track decision by the People against a lower-track decision of the People's agents.

According to Cass Sunstein, central to our constitutional system is an "impartiality principle": the idea that government is prohibited from acting on the basis of pure self-interest, power, or whim. Judicial review in service of the impartiality principle furthers the framers' plan to create a system of government—a "deliberative democracy"—that would counteract the dangers of the legacy of monarchy, self-interested representation, and majority tyranny.

The Chapter concludes with three "critical perspectives" on the Constitution and constitutionalism. Justice Thurgood Marshall casts a dissenting vote on the Constitution's 1987 Bicentennial celebration. He argues that the constitutional system constructed in Philadelphia was "defective from the start" because of its unwillingness to condemn slavery and other abridgments of fundamental rights. Richard Parker, taking aim at process-theorists (including John Ely), suggests that such theories are based on the (faulty) assumptions that the political system is basically healthy and that the Court need step in only to ensure that the interests of "discrete and insular" groups are adequately represented. To Parker, this rendering dramatically understates the degree to which the mass of citizens are politically quiescent, thereby making problematic the description of the system as "democratic." Robin West's article notes the absence of "an explicitly normative debate about the Constitution's value." She argues that the combined claims of the "constitutional faithful" (liberal theorists who urge that the Constitution can be read to achieve liberal ends) and the "constitutional sceptics" (who maintain that the text is indeterminate) have impeded the development of a "progressive constitutional faith" (which challenges a constitutional tradition that fails to condemn unjust concentrations of private power).

A. PROCESS–BASED THEORIES

JOHN HART ELY, POLICING THE PROCESS OF REPRESENTATION: THE COURT AS REFEREE

Democracy and Distrust 73–84, 86–95, 97–101 (1980).

[In earlier chapters, Professor Ely discusses "interpretivism" and "noninterpretivism"—"the former indicating that judges deciding constitutional issues should confine themselves to enforcing norms that are stated or clearly implicit in the written Constitution, the latter the contrary view that courts should go beyond that set of references and enforce norms that cannot be discovered within the four corners of the document." He argues that "clause-bound interpretivism" (the claim that constitutional phrases be given content solely on the basis of their language and surrounding legislative history) is both impossible and unwise; yet "noninterpretivism" appears to invite judicial value imposition.]

All this seems to leave us in a quandary. An interpretivist approach—at least one that approaches constitutional provisions as self-contained units—proves on analysis incapable of keeping faith with the evident spirit of certain of the provisions. When we search for an external source of values with which to fill in the Constitution's open texture, however—one that will not simply end up constituting the Court a council of legislative revision—we search in vain. Despite the usual assumption that these are the only options, however, they are not, for value imposition is not the only possible response to the realization that we have a Constitution that needs filling in. A quite different approach is available, and to discern its outlines we need look no further than to the Warren Court.

That Court's reputation as "activist" or interventionist is deserved. A good deal of carping to the contrary notwithstanding, however, that is where its similarity to earlier interventionist Courts, in particular the early twentieth-century Court that decided *Lochner v. New York* and its progeny, ends. For all the while the commentators of the Warren era were talking about ways of discovering fundamental values, the Court itself was marching to a different drummer. The divergence wasn't entirely self-conscious, and the Court did lapse occasionally into the language of fundamental values: it would be surprising if the thinking of earlier Courts and the writings of the day's preeminent commentators hadn't taken some toll. The toll, however, was almost entirely rhetorical: the constitutional decisions of the Warren Court evidence a deep structure significantly different from the value-oriented approach favored by the academy.

Many of the Warren Court's most controversial decisions concerned criminal procedure or other questions of what judicial or administrative process is due before serious consequences may be visited upon individuals—process-oriented decisions in the most ordinary sense. But a concern with process in a broader sense—with the process by which the laws that govern society are made—animated its other decisions as well. Its unprecedented activism in the fields of political expression and association obviously fits this broader pattern. Other Courts had recognized the connection between such political activity and the proper functioning of the democratic process: the Warren Court was the first seriously to act upon it. That Court was also the first to move into, and once there seriously to occupy, the voter qualification and malapportionment areas. These were certainly interventionist decisions, but the interventionism was fueled not by a desire on the part of the Court to vindicate particular substantive values it had determined were important or fundamental, but rather by a desire to ensure that the political process—which is where such values *are* properly identified, weighed, and accommodated—was open to those of all viewpoints on something approaching an equal basis.

Finally there were the important decisions insisting on equal treatment for society's habitual unequals: notably racial minorities, but also aliens, "illegitimates," and poor people. But rather than announcing that good or value X was so important or fundamental it simply had to be provided or protected, the Court's message here was that insofar as political officials had chosen to provide or protect X for some people (generally people like themselves), they had better make sure that everyone was being similarly accommodated or be prepared to explain pretty convincingly why not. Whether these two broad concerns of the Warren Court—with clearing the channels of political change on the one hand, and with correcting certain kinds of discrimination against minorities on the other—fit together to form a coherent theory of representative government, or whether, as is sometimes suggested, they are actually inconsistent impulses, is a question I shall take up presently. But however that may be, it seems to be coming into focus that the pursuit of these "participational" goals of broadened access to the processes and bounty of representative government, as opposed to the more traditional and academically popular insistence upon the provision of a series of particular substantive goods or values deemed fundamental, was what marked the work of the Warren Court. Some condemn and others praise, but at least we're beginning to understand that something different from old-fashioned value imposition was for a time the order of the day.[1]

The Carolene Products Footnote

The Warren Court's approach was foreshadowed in a famous footnote in *United States v. Carolene Products Co.,* decided in 1938. Justice Stone's opinion for the Court upheld a federal statute prohibiting the interstate shipment of filled milk, on the ground that all it had to be was "rational" and it assuredly was that. Footnote four suggested, however, that mere rationality might not always be enough:

> There may be narrower scope for operation of the presumption of constitutionality when legislation appears on its face to be within a specific prohibition of the Constitution, such as those of the first ten amendments, which are deemed equally specific when held to be embraced within the Fourteenth * * *.

> It is unnecessary to consider now whether legislation which restricts those political processes which can ordinarily be expected to bring about repeal of undesirable legislation, is to be subjected to more exacting judicial scrutiny under the general prohibitions of the Fourteenth Amendment than are most other types of legislation * * *.

> Nor need we enquire whether similar considerations enter into the review of statutes directed at particular religious * * * or national * * * or racial minorities * * *; whether prejudice against discrete and insular minorities may be a special condition, which tends seriously to curtail the operation of those political processes

---

1. Participation itself can obviously be regarded as a value, but that doesn't collapse the two modes of review I am describing into one. As I am using the terms, value imposition refers to the designation of certain goods (rights or whatever) as so important that they must be insulated from whatever inhibition the political process might impose, whereas a participational orientation denotes a form of review that concerns itself with how decisions effecting value choices and distributing the resultant costs and benefits are made. I surely don't claim that the words have to be used thus. (There is even doubt that "participational" deserves to be recognized as a word at all.) I claim only that that is how I am using them, and that so used they are not synonyms.

If the objection is not that I have not distinguished two concepts but rather that one might well "value" certain decision procedures for their own sake, of course it is right: one might. And to one who insisted on that terminology, my point would be that the "values" the Court should pursue are "participational values" of the sort I have mentioned, since those are the "values" (1) with which our Constitution has preeminently and most successfully concerned itself, (2) whose "imposition" is not incompatible with, but on the contrary supports, the American system of representative democracy, and (3) that courts set apart from the political process are uniquely situated to "impose."

ordinarily to be relied upon to protect minorities, and which may call for a correspondingly more searching judicial inquiry.[7]

* * *

For all its notoriety and influence, the *Carolene Products* footnote has not been adequately elaborated. Paragraph one has always seemed to some commentators not quite to go with the other two. Professor Lusky, who as Stone's law clerk was substantially responsible for the footnote, has recently revealed that the first paragraph was added at the request of Chief Justice Hughes. Any implied substantive criticism seems misplaced: positive law has its claims, even when it doesn't fit some grander theory. It's true, though, that paragraphs two and three are more interesting, and it is the relationship between those two paragraphs that has not been adequately elaborated. Popular control and egalitarianism are surely both ancient American ideals; indeed, dictionary definitions of "democracy" tend to incorporate both. Frequent conjunction is not the same thing as consistency, however, and at least on the surface a principle of popular control suggests an ability on the part of a majority simply to outvote a minority and thus deprive its members of goods they desire. Borrowing Paul Freund's word, I have suggested that both *Carolene Products* themes are concerned with participation: they ask us to focus not on whether this or that substantive value is unusually important or fundamental, but rather on whether the opportunity to participate either in the political processes by which values are appropriately identified and accommodated, or in the accommodation those processes have reached, has been unduly constricted. But the fact that two concepts can fit under the same verbal umbrella isn't enough to render them consistent either, and a system of equal participation in the processes of government is by no means self-evidently linked to a system of presumptively equal participation in the benefits and costs that process generates; in many ways it seems calculated to produce just the opposite effect. To understand the ways these two sorts of participation join together in a coherent political theory, it is necessary to focus more insistently * * * on the American system of representative democracy.

Representative Government

Representative democracy is perhaps most obviously a system of government suited to situations in which it is for one reason or another impractical for the citizenry actually to show up and personally participate in the legislative process. But the concept of representation, as understood by our forebears, was richer than this. Prerevolutionary rhetoric posited a continuing conflict between the interests of "the rulers" on the one hand, and those of "the ruled" (or "the people") on the other.[10] A solution was sought by building into the concept of representation the idea of an association of the interests of the two groups. Thus the representatives in the new government were visual-

7. 304 U.S. 144, 152–53 n. 4 (1938) (citations omitted).

10. L. Lusky, By What Right? 110–11 (1975).

ized as "citizens," persons of unusual ability and character to be sure, but nonetheless "of" the people. Upon conclusion of their service, the vision continued, they would return to the body of the people and thus to the body of the ruled. In addition, even while in office, the idea was that they would live under the regime of the laws they passed and not exempt themselves from their operation: this obligation to include themselves among the ruled would ensure a community of interest and guard against oppressive legislation. The framers realized that even visions need enforcement mechanisms: "some force to oppose the insidious tendency of power to separate * * * the rulers from the ruled" was required.[17] The principal force envisioned was the ballot: the people in their self-interest would choose representatives whose interests intertwined with theirs and by the critical reelection decision ensure that they stayed that way, in particular that the representatives did not shield themselves from the rigors of the laws they passed.

Actually it may not matter so much whether our representatives are treating themselves the way they treat the rest of us. Indeed it may be precisely because in some ways they treat themselves better, that they seem so desperately to want to be reelected. And it may be that desire for reelection, more than any community of interest, that is our insurance policy. If most of us feel we are being subjected to unreasonable treatment by our representatives, we retain the ability—irrespective of whether they are formally or informally insulating themselves—to turn them out of office. What the system, at least as described thus far, does *not* ensure is the effective protection of minorities whose interests differ from the interests of most of the rest of us. For if it is not the "many" who are being treated unreasonably but rather only some minority, the situation will not be so comfortably amenable to political correction. Indeed there may be political pressures to *encourage* our representatives to pass laws that treat the majority coalition on whose continued support they depend in one way, and one or more minorities whose backing they don't need less favorably. Even assuming we were willing and able to give it teeth, a requirement that our representatives treat themselves as they treat most of the rest of us would be no guarantee whatever against unequal treatment for minorities.

This is not to say that the oppression of minorities was a development our forebears were prepared to accept as inevitable. The "republic" they envisioned was not some "winner-take-all" system in which the government pursued the interests of a privileged few or even of only those groups that could work themselves into some majority coalition, but rather—leaving slavery to one side, which of course is precisely what they did—one in which the representatives would govern in the interest of the whole people. Thus every citizen was said to be entitled to equivalent respect, and equality was a frequently mentioned republican concern. Its place in the Declaration of Independence, for example,

---

17. [Buel, "Democracy and The American Revolution: A Frame of Reference," 21   Wm. & M.Q. 165, 184 (1964).]

could hardly be more prominent. When it came to describing the actual mechanics of republican government in the Constitution, however, this concern for equality got comparatively little explicit attention.   This seems to have been largely because of an assumption of "pure" republican political and social theory that we have brushed but not yet stressed: that "the people" were an essentially homogenous group whose interests did not vary significantly. Though most often articulated as if it were an existing reality, this was at best an ideal, and the fact that wealth redistribution of some form—ranging from fairly extreme to fairly modest proposals—figured in so much early republican theorizing, while doubtless partly explainable simply in terms of the perceived desirability of such a change, also was quite consciously connected to republicanism's political theory. To the extent that existing heterogeneity of interest was a function of wealth disparity, redistribution would reduce it. To the extent that the ideal of homogeneity could be achieved, legislation in the interest of most would necessarily be legislation in the interest of all, and extensive further attention to equality of treatment would be unnecessary.

The key assumption here, that everyone's interests are essentially identical, is obviously a hard one for our generation to swallow, and in fact we know perfectly well that many of our forebears were ambivalent about it too. Thus the document of 1789 and 1791, though at no point explicitly invoking the concept of equality, did strive by at least two strategies to protect the interests of minorities from the potentially destructive will of some majority coalition. The more obvious one may be the "list" strategy employed by the Bill of Rights, itemizing things that cannot be done to anyone, at least by the federal government (though even here the safeguards turn out to be mainly procedural). The original Constitution's more pervasive strategy, however, can be loosely styled a strategy of pluralism, one of structuring the government, and to a limited extent society generally, so that a variety of voices would be guaranteed their say and no majority coalition could dominate. As Madison—pointedly eschewing the approach of setting up an undemocratic body to keep watch over the majority's values—put it in *Federalist* 51:

> It is of great importance in a republic not only to guard the society against the oppression of its rulers, but to guard one part of the society against the injustice of the other part * * *. If a majority be united by a common interest, the rights of the minority will be insecure. There are but two methods of providing against this evil: the one by creating a will in the community independent of the majority * * * the other, by comprehending in the society so many separate descriptions of citizens as will render an unjust combination of a majority of the whole very improbable, if not impracticable. The first method prevails in all governments possessing an hereditary or self-appointed authority. This, at best, is but a precarious security; because a power independent of the society may as well espouse the unjust views of the major, as the rightful interests of the

minor party, and may possibly be turned against both parties. The second method will be exemplified in the federal republic of the United States.

The crucial move from a confederation to a system with a stronger central government was so conceived. Madison has been conspicuously attacked for not understanding pluralist political theory, but in fact there is reason to suppose he understood it rather well. His theory, derived from David Hume and spelled out at length in *The Federalist,* was that although at a local level one "faction" might well have sufficient clout to be able to tyrannize others, in the national government no faction or interest group would constitute a majority capable of exercising control. The Constitution's various moves to break up and counterpoise governmental decision and enforcement authority, not only between the national government and the states but among the three departments of the national government as well, were of similar design.

It is a rightly renowned system, but it didn't take long to learn that from the standpoint of protecting minorities it was not enough. Whatever genuine faith had existed at the beginning that everyone's interests either were identical or were about to be rendered so, had run its course as the republic approached its fiftieth birthday. Significant economic differences remained a reality, and the fear of legislation hostile to the interests of the propertied and creditor classes—a fear that of course had materialized earlier, during the regime of the Articles of Confederation, and thus had importantly inspired the constitutional devices to which we have alluded—surely did not abate during the Jacksonian era, as the "many" began genuinely to exercise political power. * * *

Also relevant was the persistence of the institution of slavery. So long as blacks could conveniently be regarded as subhuman, they provided no proof that some people were tyrannizing others. Once that assumption began to blur, there came into focus another reason for doubting that the protection of the many was necessarily the protection of all.

Simultaneously we came to recognize that the existing constitutional devices for protecting minorities were simply not sufficient. No finite list of entitlements can possibly cover all the ways majorities can tyrannize minorities, and the informal and more formal mechanisms of pluralism cannot always be counted on either. The fact that effective majorities can usually be described as clusters of cooperating minorities won't be much help when the cluster in question has sufficient power and perceived community of interest to advantage itself at the expense of a minority (or group of minorities) it is inclined to regard as different, and in such situations the fact that a number of agencies must concur, and others retain the right to squawk, isn't going to help much either. If, therefore, the republican ideal of government in the interest of the whole people was to be maintained, in an age when faith in the republican tenet that the people and their interests were essentially homogeneous was all but dead, a frontal assault on the problem of majority tyranny was needed. The existing theory of representation had to be extended so as to ensure not simply that the representative would not sever his interests from those of a majority of his constituency but also that he would not sever a majority coalition's interests from those of various minorities. Naturally that cannot mean that groups that constitute minorities of the population can never be treated less favorably than the rest, but it does preclude a refusal to *represent* them, the denial to minorities of what Professor Dworkin has called "equal concern and respect in the design and administration of the political institutions that govern them." [34] The Fourteenth Amendment's Equal Protection Clause is obviously our Constitution's most dramatic embodiment of this ideal. Before that amendment was ratified, however, its theory was understood, and functioned as a component—even on occasion as a judicially enforceable component—of the concept of representation that had been at the core of our Constitution from the beginning.

It's ironic, but the old concept of "virtual representation" is helpful here. The actual term was anathema to our forefathers, since it was invoked to answer their cries of "taxation without representation." But the concept contained an insight that has survived in American political theory and in fact has informed our constitutional thinking from the beginning. The colonists' argument that it was wrong, even "unconstitutional," to tax us when we lacked the privilege of sending representatives to Parliament was answered on the British side by the argument that although the colonies didn't actually elect anyone, they were "virtually represented" in Parliament. * * *

Although the term understandably has not been revived, the protective device of guaranteeing "virtual representation" by tying the interests of those without political power to the interests of those with it, was one that importantly influenced both the drafting of our original Constitution and its subsequent interpretation. Article IV's Privileges and Immunities Clause was intended and has been interpreted to mean that state legislatures cannot by their various regulations treat out-of-staters less favorably than they treat locals. "It was designed to insure to a citizen of State A who ventures into State B the same privileges which the citizens of State B enjoy." [37] Article IV conveys no set of substantive entitlements, but "simply" the guarantee that whatever entitlements those living in a state see fit to vote themselves will generally be extended to visitors. An ethical ideal of equality is certainly working here, but the reason inequalities against nonresidents and not others were singled out for prohibition in the original document is obvious: nonresidents are a paradigmatically powerless class politically. And their protection proceeds by what amounts to a system of virtual representation: by constitutionally tying the fate of outsiders to the fate of those possessing political power, the framers insured that their interests would be well looked after. The Commerce Clause of Article I, Section 8 provides simply that Congress shall have the power to regulate

34. R. Dworkin, Taking Rights Seriously 180 (1977).

37. Toomer v. Witsell, 334 U.S. 385, 395 (1948).

commerce among the states. But early on the Supreme Court gave this provision a self-operating dimension as well, one growing out of the same need to protect the politically powerless and proceeding by the same device of guaranteed virtual representation. Thus, for example, early in the nineteenth century the Court indicated that a state could not subject goods produced out of state to taxes it did not impose on goods produced locally. By thus constitutionally binding the interests of out-of-state manufacturers to those of local manufacturers represented in the legislature, it provided political insurance that the taxes imposed on the former would not rise to a prohibitive or even an unreasonable level.

These examples involve the protection of geographical outsiders, the literally voteless. But even the technically represented can find themselves functionally powerless and thus in need of a sort of "virtual representation" by those more powerful than they. From one perspective the claim of such groups to protection from the ruling majority is even more compelling than that of the out-of-stater: they are, after all, members of the community that is doing them in. From another, however, their claim seems weaker: they do have the vote, and it may not in the abstract seem unreasonable to expect them to wheel and deal as the rest of us (theoretically) do, yielding on issues about which they are comparatively indifferent and "scratching the other guy's back" in order to get him to scratch theirs. "[N]o group that is prepared to enter into the process and combine with others need remain permanently and completely out of power." [41] Perhaps not "permanently and completely" if by that we mean forever, but certain groups that are technically enfranchised *have* found themselves for long stretches in a state of persistent inability to protect themselves from pervasive forms of discriminatory treatment. Such groups might just as well be disenfranchised.

* * * Whatever may have been the case before, the Fourteenth Amendment quite plainly imposes a judicially enforceable duty of virtual representation of the sort I have been describing. My main point in using the examples has been to suggest a way in which what are sometimes characterized as two conflicting American ideals—the protection of popular government on the one hand, and the protection of minorities from denials of equal concern and respect on the other—in fact can be understood as arising from a common duty of representation. * * *

* * * [C]ontrary to the standard characterization of the Constitution as "an enduring but evolving statement of general values," * * * the selection and accommodation of substantive values is [in fact] left almost entirely to the political process and instead the document is overwhelmingly concerned, on the one hand, with procedural fairness in the resolution of individual disputes (process writ small), and on the other, with what might capaciously be designated process writ large—with ensuring broad participation in the processes and distributions of

---

41. A. Bickel, The Supreme Court and the Idea of Progress 37 (1970).

government. An argument by way of *ejusdem generis* seems particularly justified in this case, since the constitutional provisions for which we are attempting to identify modes of supplying content, such as the Ninth Amendment and the Privileges or Immunities Clause, seem to have been included in a "we must have missed something here, so let's trust our successors to add what we missed" spirit. On my more expansive days, therefore, I am tempted to claim that the mode of review developed here represents the ultimate interpretivism.[48] Our review will tell us something else that may be even more relevant to the issue before us—that the few attempts the various framers *have* made to freeze substantive values by designating them for special protection in the document have been ill-fated, normally resulting in repeal, either officially or by interpretative pretense. This suggests a conclusion with important implications for the task of giving content to the document's more open-ended provisions, that preserving fundamental values is not an appropriate constitutional task.

* * *

THE NATURE OF THE UNITED STATES CONSTITUTION

Many of our colonial forebears' complaints against British rule were phrased in "constitutional" terms. Seldom, however, was the claim one of deprivation of some treasured good or substantive right: the American colonists, at least the white males, were among the freest and best-off people in the history of the world, and by and large they knew it. "Constitutional" claims thus were often jurisdictional—that Parliament lacked authority, say, to regulate the colonies "internal commerce"—the foundation for the claim being generally that we were not represented in Parliament. (Obviously the colonists weren't any crazier about being taxed than anyone else is, but what they damned as tyrannical was taxation *without representation*.) Or they were arguments of inequality: claims of entitlement to "the rights of Englishmen" had an occasional natural law flavor, but the more common meaning was that suggested by the words, a claim for equality of treatment with those living in England. Thus the colonists' "constitutional" arguments drew on the two participational themes we have been considering: that (1) their input into the process by which they were governed was insufficient, and that (partly as

---

48. As I've indicated, I don't think this terminological question is either entirely coherent or especially important. Obviously the approach recommended is neither "interpretivist" in the usual sense (of treating constitutional clauses as self-contained units) nor "noninterpretivist" in the usual sense (of seeking the principal stuff of constitutional judgment in one's rendition of society's fundamental values rather than in the document's broader themes). What counts is not whether it is "really" a broad interpretivism or rather a position that does not fall entirely in either camp, but whether it is capable of keeping faith with the document's promise in a way I have argued that a clause-bound interpretivism is not, and capable at the same time of avoiding the objections to a value-laden form of noninterpretivism, objections rooted most importantly in democratic theory. In that regard the two arguments that close this chapter, those addressed explicitly to consistency with democratic theory and the relative institutional capacities of legislatures and courts, seem at least as important as the argument from the nature of the Constitution (which given the complexity of the document must be a qualified one in any event).

a consequence) (2) they were being denied what others were receiving. The American version of revolution, wrote Hannah Arendt, "actually proclaims no more than the necessity of civilized government for all mankind; the French version * * * proclaims the existence of rights independent of and outside the body public * * *."[53]

* * *

I don't suppose it will surprise anyone to learn that the body of the original Constitution is devoted almost entirely to structure, explaining who among the various actors—federal government, state government; Congress, executive, judiciary—has authority to do what, and going on to fill in a good bit of detail about how these persons are to be selected and to conduct their business. Even provisions that at first glance might seem primarily designed to assure or preclude certain substantive results seem on reflection to be principally concerned with process. Thus, for example, the provision that treason "shall consist only in levying War against [the United States], or in adhering to their Enemies, giving them Aid and Comfort," appears at least in substantial measure to have been a precursor of the First Amendment, reacting to the recognition that persons in power can disable their detractors by charging disagreement as treason. The prohibitions against granting titles of nobility seem rather plainly to have been designed to buttress the democratic ideal that all are equals in government. The Ex Post Facto and Bill of Attainder Clauses prove on analysis to be separation of powers provisions, enjoining the legislature to act prospectively and by general rule (just as the judiciary is implicitly enjoined by Article III to act retrospectively and by specific decree). And we have seen that the Privileges and Immunities Clause of Article IV, and at least in one aspect—the other being a grant of congressional power—the Commerce Clause as well, function as equality provisions, guaranteeing virtual representation to the politically powerless.

* * *

* * * [M]y claim is * * * that the original Constitution was principally, indeed I would say overwhelmingly, dedicated to concerns of process and structure and not to the identification and preservation of specific substantive values. Any claim that it was exclusively so conceived would be ridiculous (as would any comparable claim about any comparably complicated human undertaking). And indeed there are other provisions in the original document that seem almost entirely value-oriented, though my point, of course, is that they are few and far between. Thus "corruption of blood" is forbidden as a punishment for treason. Punishing people for their parents' transgressions is outlawed as a substantively unfair outcome: it just can't be done, irrespective of procedures and also irrespective of whether it is done to the children of all offenders. The federal government, along with the states, is precluded from taxing articles exported from any state. Here too an outcome is

53. H. Arendt, [On Revolution] 147 [(1963)].

simply precluded; what might be styled a value, the economic value of free trade among the states, is protected. This short list, however, covers just about all the values protected in the original Constitution—save one. And a big one it was. Although an understandable squeamishness kept the word out of the document, *slavery* must be counted a substantive value to which the original Constitution meant to extend unusual protection from the ordinary legislative process, at least temporarily. Prior to 1808, Congress was forbidden to prohibit the slave trade into any state that wanted it, and the states were obliged to return escaping slaves to their "homes."

The idea of a bill of rights was not even brought up until close to the end of the Constitutional Convention, at which time it was rejected. The reason is not that the framers were unconcerned with liberty, but rather that by their lights a bill of rights did not belong in a constitution, at least not in the one they had drafted. As Hamilton explained in *Federalist* 84, "a minute detail of particular rights is certainly far less applicable to a Constitution like that under consideration, which is merely intended to regulate the general political interests of the nation * * *." Moreover, the very point of all that had been wrought had been, in large measure, to preserve the liberties of individuals. "The truth is, after all the declamations we have heard, that the Constitution is itself, in every rational sense, and to every useful purpose, *a Bill of Rights*." "The additional securities to republican government, to liberty, and to property, to be derived from the adoption of the plan under consideration, consist chiefly in the restraints which the preservation of the Union will impose on local factions * * * in the prevention of extensive military establishments * * * in the express guarantee of a republican form of government to each [state]; in the absolute and universal exclusion of titles of nobility * * *." [72]

Of course a number of the state ratifying conventions remained apprehensive, and a bill of rights did emerge. Here too, however, the data are unruly. The expression-related provisions of the First Amendment—"Congress shall make no law * * * abridging the freedom of speech, or of the press; or the right of the people peaceably to assemble, and to petition the Government for a redress of grievances"—were centrally intended to help make our governmental processes work, to ensure the open and informed discussion of political issues, and to check our government when it gets out of bounds. We can attribute other functions to freedom of expression, and some of them must have played a role, but the exercise has the smell of the lamp about it: the view that free expression per se, without regard to what it means to the process of government, is our preeminent right has a highly elitist cast. Positive law has its claims, and I am not suggesting that such other purposes as are plausibly attributable to the language should not be attributed: the amendment's language is not limited to political speech and it should not be so limited by construction (even assuming someone could come up

---

72. The Federalist no. 85, at 542 (B. Wright ed. 1961) (Hamilton).

with a determinate definition of "political"). But we are at present engaged in an exploration of what sort of document our forebears thought they were putting together, and in that regard the linking of the politically oriented protections of speech, press, assembly, and petition is highly informative.

The First Amendment's religious clauses—"Congress shall make no law respecting an establishment of religion, or prohibiting the free exercise thereof"—are a different matter. Obviously part of the point of combining these cross-cutting commands was to make sure the church and the government gave each other breathing space: the provision thus performs a structural or separation of powers function. But we must not infer that because one account fits the data it must be the only appropriate account, and here the obvious cannot be blinked: part of the explanation of the Free Exercise Clause has to be that for the framers religion was an important substantive value they wanted to put significantly beyond the reach of at least the federal legislature.

* * *

Amendments five through eight tend to become relevant only during lawsuits, and we tend therefore to think of them as procedural—instrumental provisions calculated to enhance the fairness and efficiency of the litigation process. That's exactly what most of them are: the importance of the guarantees of grand juries, criminal and civil petit juries, information of the charge, the right of confrontation, compulsory process, and even the assistance of counsel inheres mainly in their tendency to ensure a reliable determination. Unconcerned with the substance of government regulation, they refer instead to the ways in which regulations can be enforced against those they cover.

* * *

On first reading, the Fifth Amendment's requirement that private property not be taken for public use without just compensation may appear simply to mark the substantive value of private property for special protection from the political process (though, on the face of the document, from only the state political process). Again, though, we must ask why. Because property was regarded as unusually important? That may be part of the explanation, but note that property is not shielded from condemnation by this provision. On the contrary, the amendment assumes that property will sometimes be taken and provides instead for compensation. Read through it thus emerges—and this account fits the historical situation like a glove—as yet another protection of the few against the many, "a limit on government's power to isolate particular individuals for sacrifice to the general good." [87] Its point is to "spread the cost of operating the governmental apparatus throughout the society rather than imposing it upon some small segment

87. L. Tribe, [*American Constitutional Law* 463 (1978).]

of it." [88]   If we want a highway or a park we can have it, but we're all going to have to share the cost rather than imposing it on some isolated individual or group.

With one important exception, the Reconstruction Amendments do not designate substantive values for protection from the political process. The Fourteenth Amendment's Due Process Clause, we have seen, is concerned with process writ small, the processes by which regulations are enforced against individuals. Its Privileges or Immunities Clause is quite inscrutable, indicating only that there should exist some set of constitutional entitlements not explicitly enumerated in the document: it is one of the provisions for which we are seeking guides to construction. The Equal Protection Clause is also unforthcoming with details, though it at least gives us a clue: by its explicit concern with equality among the persons within a state's jurisdiction it constitutes the document's clearest, though not sole, recognition that technical access to the process may not always be sufficient to guarantee good-faith representation of all those putatively represented. The Fifteenth Amendment, forbidding abridgment of the right to vote on account of race, opens the process to persons who had previously been excluded and thus by another strategy seeks to enforce the representative's duty of equal concern and respect. The exception, of course, involves a value I have mentioned before, slavery. The Thirteenth Amendment can be forced into a "process" mold—slaves don't participate effectively in the political process—and it surely significantly reflects a concern with equality as well. Just as surely, however, it embodies a substantive judgment that human slavery is simply not morally tolerable. Thus at no point has the Constitution been neutral on this subject. Slavery was one of the few values the original document singled out for protection from the political branches; *non*slavery is one of the few values it singles out for protection now.

What has happened to the Constitution in the second century of our nationhood, though ground less frequently plowed, is most instructive on the subject of what jobs we have learned our basic document is suited to. There were no amendments between 1870 and 1913, but there have been eleven since. Five of them have extended the franchise: the Seventeenth extends to all of us the right to vote for our Senators directly, the Twenty–Fourth abolishes the poll tax as a condition of voting in federal elections, the Nineteenth extends the vote to women, the Twenty–Third to residents of the District of Columbia, and the Twenty–Sixth to eighteen-year-olds. Extension of the franchise to groups previously excluded has therefore been the dominant theme of our constitutional development since the Fourteenth Amendment, and it pursues both of the broad constitutional themes we have observed from the beginning: the achievement of a political process open to all on an equal basis and a consequent enforcement of the representative's duty of equal concern and respect to minorities and majorities alike. Three other amend-

88. Sax, "Takings and the Police Power," 74 Yale L.J. 36, 75–76 (1964)[.]

ments—the Twentieth, Twenty–Second, and Twenty–Fifth—involve Presidential eligibility and succession. The Sixteenth, permitting a federal income tax, adds another power to the list of those that had previously been assigned to the central government. That's it, save two, and indeed one of those two did place a substantive value beyond the reach of the political process. The amendment was the Eighteenth, and the value shielded was temperance. It was, of course, repealed fourteen years later by the Twenty–First Amendment, precisely, I suggest, because such attempts to freeze substantive values do not belong in a constitution. In 1919 temperance obviously seemed like a fundamental value; in 1933 it obviously did not.

What has happened to the Constitution's other value-enshrining provisions is similar, and similarly instructive. Some surely have survived, but typically because they are so obscure that they don't become issues (corruption of blood, quartering of troops) or so interlaced with procedural concerns they seem appropriate in a constitution (self-incrimination, double jeopardy). Those sufficiently conspicuous and precise to be controvertible have not survived. The most dramatic examples, of course, were slavery and prohibition. Both were removed by repeal, in one case a repeal requiring unprecedented carnage. Two other substantive values that at least arguably were placed beyond the reach of the political process by the Constitution have been "repealed" by judicial construction—the right of individuals to bear arms, and freedom to set contract terms without significant state regulation. Maybe in fact our forebears did not intend very seriously to protect those values, but the fact that the Court, in the face of what must be counted at least plausible contrary arguments, so readily read these values out of the Constitution is itself instructive of American expectations of a constitution. Finally, there is the value of religion, still protected by the Free Exercise Clause. Something different has happened here. In recent years that clause has functioned primarily to protect what must be counted as discrete and insular minorities, such as the Amish, Seventh Day Adventists, and Jehovah's Witnesses. Whatever the original conception of the Free Exercise Clause, its function during essentially all of its effective life has been one akin to the Equal Protection Clause and thus entirely appropriate to a constitution.

Don't get me wrong: our Constitution has always been substantially concerned with preserving liberty. If it weren't, it would hardly be worth fighting for. The question that is relevant to our inquiry here, however, is how that concern has been pursued. The principal answers to that, we have seen, are by a quite extensive set of procedural protections, and by a still more elaborate scheme designed to ensure that in the making of substantive choices the decision process will be open to all on something approaching an equal basis, with the decision-makers held to a duty to take into account the interests of all those their decisions affect. (Most often the document has proceeded on the assumption that assuring access is the best way of assuring that someone's interests will be considered, and so in fact it usually is. Other provisions, however—centrally but not exclusively the Equal Protection Clause—reflect a realization that access will not always be sufficient.) The general strategy has therefore not been to root in the document a set of substantive rights entitled to permanent protection. The Constitution has instead proceeded from the quite sensible assumption that an effective majority will not inordinately threaten its own rights, and has sought to assure that such a majority not systematically treat others less well than it treats itself—by structuring decision processes at all levels to try to ensure, first, that everyone's interests will be actually or virtually represented (usually both) at the point of substantive decision, and second, that the processes of individual application will not be manipulated so as to reintroduce in practice the sort of discrimination that is impermissible in theory. [There are] a few provisions that do not comfortably conform to this pattern. But they're an odd assortment, the understandable products of particular historical circumstances—guns, religion, contract, and so on—and in any event they are few and far between. To represent them as a dominant theme of our constitutional document one would have to concentrate quite single-mindedly on hopping from stone to stone and averting one's eyes from the mainstream.

The American Constitution has thus by and large remained a constitution properly so called, concerned with constitutive questions. What has distinguished it, and indeed the United States itself, has been a process of government, not a governing ideology. Justice Linde has written: "As a charter of government a constitution must prescribe legitimate processes, not legitimate outcomes, if like ours (and unlike more ideological documents elsewhere) it is to serve many generations through changing times." [95]

LAURENCE H. TRIBE, THE PUZZLING PERSISTENCE OF PROCESS–BASED CONSTITUTIONAL THEORIES
59 Yale L.J. 1063, 1065–73, 1075–1077 (1980).

I. THE CONSTITUTION'S OPENLY SUBSTANTIVE COMMITMENTS

One difficulty that immediately confronts process theories is the stubbornly substantive character of so many of the Constitution's most crucial commitments: commitments defining the values that we as a society, acting politically, must respect. Plainly, the First Amendment's guarantee of religious liberty and its prohibition of religious establishment are substantive in this sense. So, too, is the Thirteenth Amendment, in its abolition of slavery and repudiation of the Constitution's earlier, ostensibly procedural, protections of that institution.

In many of its parts, the Constitution also evinces a substantive commitment to the institution of private property and to the contractual expectations that surround it. The just compensation clause of the Fifth Amendment is an obvious example. The contracts clause of article I,

---

95. Linde, "Due Process of Lawmaking," 55 Neb.L.Rev. 197, 254 (1975).

section 10 is another. The old substantive due process, which is obviously an important part of our constitutional history and thus significant for our understanding of what the Constitution is about, also served to protect the transactions and expectations to which the institution of private property gives rise. Whatever our views of the substantive due process heyday, most of us would readily concede that the framers of the 1787 Constitution adopted a federal system of government organization in order to, among other goals, help secure the institution of private property. When Madison, in his theory of faction, suggested that shifting the legislative responsibility for certain problems from the state to the national level could help assure that majorities would not trample minority rights, the problems he had in mind were largely economic; the minority rights the federal system would protect were, for the most part, rights of property and contract.

Religious freedom, antislavery, private property: much of our constitutional history can be written by reference to just these social institutions and substantive values. That the Constitution has long addressed such matters, and often with beneficial effect, ought to surprise no one. What is puzzling is that anyone can say, in the face of this reality, that the Constitution is or should be predominantly concerned with *process* and *not* substance.

But our constitutional reality poses even deeper problems for process theorists. Even the Constitution's most procedural prescriptions cannot be adequately understood, much less applied, in the absence of a developed theory of fundamental rights that are secured to persons against the state—a theory whose derivation demands precisely the kinds of controversial substantive choices that the process proponents are so anxious to leave to the electorate and its representatives.

II. THE SUBSTANTIVE ROOTS OF PROCEDURAL NORMS

Much of the Constitution does indeed appear to address matters of procedure. Sometimes the subject is *adjudicative* process—the process due to individuals who become defendants in criminal or civil litigation or targets of administrative actions. Elsewhere, the Constitution focuses on *representative* process—including the process that governs the election of Congress, of the President, or of state representative bodies. That the *subject* in all these cases is procedure, however, is not to say that the *meaning* and *purpose* of the Constitution's prescriptions on each such subject are themselves merely procedural. There is no reason to suppose that "constitutive" rules—rules defining the basic structure of political and legal relations—can or should be essentially neutral on matters of substantive value.

The very dichotomy just drawn—between adjudicative and representative process—would prove incoherent without a substantive theory. How do we decide which *form* of participation the complaining individual may claim: the right to be heard as a litigant, or the right to be counted as a voter? The question whether individuals may insist on being heard by rulemakers, for whom they have already (directly or indirectly) voted, has bedeviled administrative law since the turn of the century. How the government chooses to deal with individuals—as individuals or *en masse*—cannot be dispositive. For, at least sometimes, government action that purports to deal with groups is unconstitutional precisely because it does *not* deal with individuals as such: the conclusive presumption decisions and the mandatory death penalty cases, however opaque they might otherwise be, establish this much, as does Justice Powell's opinion in *Regents of the University of California v. Bakke.* Conversely, in at least some circumstances, there is no constitutional infirmity in relying only on representative, or even directly democratic, processes to deal with individuated grievances: individual zoning variances may be made the subject of local referendum; and unions, as delegatees of federal power, may bind members of bargaining units to the terms of wage bargains or, indeed, of individual grievance negotiations, even though the unions do not act as representatives of individuals *as individuals.*

The question of whether adjudicative or representative process is required in a given context simply cannot be analyzed in terms of how fairly and accurately various participatory processes reflect the interests and inputs of those governed by them. Deciding what *kind* of participation the Constitution demands requires analysis not only of the efficacy of alternative processes but also of the character and importance of the interest at stake—its role in the life of the individual as an individual. That analysis, in turn, requires a theory of values and rights as plainly substantive as, and seemingly of a piece with, the theories of values and rights that underlie the Constitution's provisions addressing religion, slavery, and property.

Once one has decided whether the Constitution requires adjudicative or representative process in a particular setting, one must again rely on substantive values in elaborating the requirements of either procedural form. Consider first the problem of adjudicative process. Certainly the Fifth Amendment's self-incrimination and double jeopardy clauses embody concerns for protecting individual dignity in the criminal process. A substantive concern for individual "privacy" necessarily underpins the Fourth Amendment. Other superficially procedural provisions of the Constitution, such as the rights to counsel, confrontation, bail, and jury trial, echo similar themes; they function, often at some cost to the efficiency and accuracy of fact-finding, to prevent the government from treating individuals in the criminal process as though they were objects.

Even outside the criminal context, elaborating rights of adjudicative process requires recourse to a substantive theory. Procedural due process rights are not simply means of protecting whatever "entitlements" happen to be conferred by legislation or administrative regulation. Otherwise, the drafters of an entitlement could frame it in the procedural terms of their choice, and the constitutional guarantee would be reduced to a right to receive whatever process the drafters had defined as due. But that view has been repeatedly rejected by the Supreme Court, which has never fully embraced a purely positivist theory of procedural due process. The only alternative theories, however, are ones that posit a right to individual dignity, or some similarly substantive norm, as the base on which conceptions of procedural fairness are constructed.

If process is constitutionally valued, therefore, it must be valued not only as a means to some independent end, but for its intrinsic characteristics: being heard is part of what it means to be a person. Process itself, therefore, becomes substantive. There is a curious irony here. One who holds that constitutional law should aim chiefly to perfect process is apparently unable to treat process as *itself* valuable. For, to see why process would itself be valuable—intrinsically so—is to see why the Constitution is inevitably substantive. Instead, the process-perfecter must treat process as ultimately instrumental, as but a means to other ends, and thus must regard as secondary what he would at the same time celebrate as primary.

* * *

III.   The Quandary of Whom to Protect

For those who would fill the gaps left by the Constitution's ambiguities and silences with representation-reinforcing principles, perhaps the core "process value" is the value of protecting certain minorities from perennial defeat in the political arena. The theme was anticipated by John Marshall;[44] it assumed a central role for Harlan Fiske Stone;[45] it signally motivated Earl Warren;[46] and it has been elaborated by numerous scholars, most powerfully in the work of John Ely. The idea seems as simple as it sounds reasonable: governmental action that burdens groups effectively excluded from the political process is constitutionally suspect. In its most sophisticated form, the resulting judicial scrutiny is seen as a way of invalidating governmental classifications and distributions that turn out to have been motivated either by prejudiced hostility or by self-serving stereotypes.

It all sounds pretty good—until we ask how we are supposed to distinguish such "prejudice" from principled, if "wrong," disapproval. Which groups are to count as "discrete and insular minorities"? Which are instead to be deemed appropriate losers in the ongoing struggle for political acceptance and ascendancy?

* * *

44. *See* McCulloch v. Maryland, 17 U.S. (4 Wheat.) 316, 435–36 (1819) (state has no power to tax federal instrumentality because it would thereby act on national population, not represented in its legislature).

45. United States v. Carolene Prods. Co., 304 U.S. 144, 152 n. 4 (1938) (strict judicial review for statutes that are directed against "discrete and insular minorities"); South Carolina State Highway Dep't v. Barnwell Bros., 303 U.S. 177, 184 n. 2 (1938) (commerce clause may prohibit legislation burdening political outsiders).

46. *See* Ely, *The Chief,* 88 Harv.L.Rev. 11, 12 (1974) (Warren sought to ensure that machinery of democratic process does not become self-serving organ of privileged class).

Consider several illustrations. Burglars are subject to widespread hostility: indeed, the activity that defines the group is everywhere legislatively prohibited. Are burglars therefore a "suspect class"? Of course not. Suspect status is unthinkable—but only because of the substantive value we attach to personal security, and the importance for us of the system of private property and its rules of transfer, which the burglary prohibition preserves. If we speak of burglars as a class, we do so as a way of giving form to our view that burglary *is* a "different" activity, different not so much because burglars visibly define a group as because we disapprove of the activity, deny it any claim to protection as a right.

Homosexuals, too, are subject to widespread hostility; legislation penalizing homosexuals and homosexual practices is common. Homosexuals often do not identify themselves by sexual preference when acting politically, and generally do not "come out of the closet" to refute the traditional stereotypes. But even if they did, legislation might be unaltered. Coming out of the closet could dispel ignorance, but it may not alter belief. Legislators may see homosexuals as "different" not out of ignorance, but on principle—on the basis of a morality that treats certain sexual practices as repugnant to a particular view of humanity, and thus regards people who engage in those practices as "other." Such legislation can be rejected only on the basis of a principle that is equally substantive: a view of what it means to be a person, and to have a sexual identity. Process and prejudice thus seem profoundly beside the point. Any constitutional distinction between laws burdening homosexuals and laws burdening exhibitionists, between laws burdening Catholics and laws burdening pickpockets, must depend on a substantive theory of which groups are exercising fundamental rights and which are not.

Indeed, even laws putting blacks and women "in their place"— banning racial intermarriage, say, or excluding women from combat— are likely to reflect neither simple hostility nor self-serving blindness but *a substantive vision of proper conduct*—a vision that no amount of attention to flaws in the political process could condemn or correct. Accordingly, the idea of blacks or women as properly segregated beings can be rejected *only* by finding a constitutional basis for concluding that, in our society, such hierarchical visions are substantively out of bounds, at least as a justification for government action. And such a finding would in turn entail a theory of unenumerated substantive rights, rights at best *suggested* by constitutional text and history, rights whose necessarily controversial elaboration the process theorists seek to eschew.

The crux of any determination that a law unjustly discriminates against a group—blacks, or women, or even men—is not that the law emerges from a flawed process, or that the burden it imposes affects an independently fundamental right, but that the law is part of a pattern that denies those subject to it a meaningful opportunity to realize their humanity. Necessarily, such an approach must look beyond process to identify and proclaim fundamental substantive rights. Whatever difficulties this may entail, it seems plain that important aspects of constitutional law, including the determination of which groups deserve special protection, can be given significant content in no other way. Thus it is puzzling indeed that process-based approaches—designed to deny the need for, and legitimacy of, any such substantive theory—should nonetheless continue to find such articulate proponents and persist in attracting such perceptive adherents.

B. RIGHTS–BASED APPROACHES

RONALD DWORKIN, CONSTITUTIONAL CASES
Taking Rights Seriously 132–37, 140–42, 144, 146–49 (1977).

The constitutional theory on which our government rests is not a simple majoritarian theory. The Constitution, and particularly the Bill of Rights, is designed to protect individual citizens and groups against certain decisions that a majority of citizens might want to make, even when that majority acts in what it takes to be the general or common interest. Some of these constitutional restraints take the form of fairly precise rules, like the rule that requires a jury trial in federal criminal proceedings or, perhaps, the rule that forbids the national Congress to abridge freedom of speech. But other constraints take the form of what are often called "vague" standards, for example, the provision that the government shall not deny men due process of law, or equal protection of the laws.

This interference with democratic practice requires a justification. The draftsmen of the Constitution assumed that these restraints could be justified by appeal to moral rights which individuals possess against the majority, and which the constitutional provisions, both "vague" and precise, might be said to recognize and protect.

The "vague" standards were chosen deliberately, by the men who drafted and adopted them, in place of the more specific and limited rules that they might have enacted. But their decision to use the language they did has caused a great deal of legal and political controversy, because even reasonable men of good will differ when they try to elaborate, for example, the moral rights that the due process clause or the equal protection clause brings into the law. They also differ when they try to apply these rights, however defined, to complex matters of political administration, like the educational practices that were the subject of the segregation cases.

The practice has developed of referring to a "strict" and a "liberal" side to these controversies, so that the Supreme Court might be said to have taken the "liberal" side in the segregation cases and its critics the "strict" side. * * * But the distinction is in fact confusing, because it runs together two different issues that must be separated. Any case that arises under the "vague" constitutional guarantees can be seen as posing two questions: (1) Which decision is required by strict, that is to say faithful, adherence to the text of the Constitution or to the intention of those who adopted that text? (2) Which decision is required by a political philosophy that takes a strict, that is to say narrow, view of the moral rights that individuals have against society? Once these questions are distinguished, it is plain that they may have different answers. The text of the First Amendment, for example, says that Congress shall make *no* law abridging the freedom of speech, but a narrow view of individual rights would permit many such laws, ranging from libel and obscenity laws to the Smith Act.

In the case of the "vague" provisions, however, like the due process and equal protection clauses, lawyers have run the two questions together because they have relied, largely without recognizing it, on a theory of meaning that might be put this way: If the framers of the Constitution used vague language, as they did when they condemned violations of "due process of law", then what they "said" or "meant" is limited to the instances of official action that they had in mind as violations, or, at least, to those instances that they would have thought were violations if they had had them in mind. If those who were responsible for adding the due process clause to the Constitution believed that it was fundamentally unjust to provide separate education for different races, or had detailed views about justice that entailed that conclusion, then the segregation decisions might be defended as an application of the principle they had laid down. Otherwise they could not be defended in this way, but instead would show that the judges had substituted their own ideas of justice for those the constitutional drafters meant to lay down.

This theory makes a strict interpretation of the text yield a narrow view of constitutional rights, because it limits such rights to those recognized by a limited group of people at a fixed date of history. It forces those who favor a more liberal set of rights to concede that they are departing from strict legal authority, a departure they must then seek to justify by appealing only to the desirability of the results they reach.

But the theory of meaning on which this argument depends is far too crude; it ignores a distinction that philosophers have made but lawyers have not yet appreciated. Suppose I tell my children simply that I expect them not to treat others unfairly. I no doubt have in mind examples of the conduct I mean to discourage, but I would not accept that my "meaning" was limited to these examples, for two reasons. First I would expect my children to apply my instructions to situations I had not and could not have thought about. Second, I stand ready to admit that some particular act I had thought was fair when I spoke was in fact unfair, or vice versa, if one of my children is able to convince me of that later; in that case I should want to say that my instructions covered the case he cited, not that I had changed my instructions. I might say that I meant the family to be guided by the *concept* of fairness, not by any specific *conception* of fairness I might have had in mind.

This is a crucial distinction which it is worth pausing to explore. Suppose a group believes in common that acts may suffer from a special moral defect which they call unfairness, and which consists in a wrongful division of benefits and burdens, or a wrongful attribution of praise or blame. Suppose also that they agree on a great number of standard cases of unfairness and use these as benchmarks against which to test other, more controversial cases. In that case, the group has a concept of unfairness, and its members may appeal to that concept in moral instruction or argument. But members of that group may nevertheless differ over a large number of these controversial cases, in a way that suggests that each either has or acts on a different theory of *why* the standard cases are acts of unfairness. They may differ, that is, on which more fundamental principles must be relied upon to show that a particular division or attribution is unfair. In that case, the members have different conceptions of fairness.

If so, then members of this community who give instructions or set standards in the name of fairness may be doing two different things. First they may be appealing to the concept of fairness, simply by instructing others to act fairly; in this case they charge those whom they instruct with the responsibility of developing and applying their own conception of fairness as controversial cases arise. That is not the same thing, of course, as granting them a discretion to act as they like; it sets a standard which they must try—and may fail—to meet, because it assumes that one conception is superior to another. The man who appeals to the concept in this way may have his own conception, as I did when I told my children to act fairly; but he holds this conception only as his own theory of how the standard he set must be met, so that when he changes his theory he has not changed that standard.

On the other hand, the members may be laying down a particular conception of fairness; I would have done this, for example, if I had listed my wishes with respect to controversial examples or if, even less likely, I had specified some controversial and explicit theory of fairness, as if I had said to decide hard cases by applying the utilitarian ethics of Jeremy Bentham. The difference is a difference not just in the *detail* of the instructions given but in the *kind* of instructions given. When I appeal to the concept of fairness I appeal to what fairness means, and I give my views on that issue no special standing. When I lay down a conception of fairness, I lay down what I mean by fairness, and my view is therefore the heart of the matter. When I appeal to fairness I pose a moral issue; when I lay down my conception of fairness I try to answer it.

Once this distinction is made it seems obvious that we must take what I have been calling "vague" constitutional clauses as representing appeals to the concepts they employ, like legality, equality, and cruelty. The Supreme Court may soon decide, for example, whether capital punishment is "cruel" within the meaning of the constitutional clause that prohibits "cruel and unusual punishment". It would be a mistake for the Court to be much influenced by the fact that when the clause was adopted capital punishment was standard and unquestioned. That would be decisive if the framers of the clause had meant to lay down a particular conception of cruelty, because it would show that the conception did not extend so far. But it is not decisive of the different question the Court now faces, which is this: Can the Court, responding to the framers' appeal to the concept of cruelty, now defend a conception that does not make death cruel?

Those who ignore the distinction between concepts and conceptions, but who believe that the Court ought to make a fresh determination of whether the death penalty is cruel, are forced to argue in a vulnerable way. They say that ideas of cruelty change over time, and that the Court must be free to reject out-of-date conceptions; this suggests that the Court must change what the Constitution enacted. But in fact the Court can enforce what the Constitution says only by making up its own mind about what is cruel, just as my children, in my example, can do what I said only by making up their own minds about what is fair. If those who enacted the broad clauses had meant to lay down particular conceptions, they would have found the sort of language conventionally used to do this, that is, they would have offered particular theories of the concepts in question.

Indeed the very practice of calling these clauses "vague", in which I have joined, can now be seen to involve a mistake. The clauses are vague only if we take them to be botched or incomplete or schematic attempts to lay down particular conceptions. If we take them as appeals to moral concepts they could not be made more precise by being more detailed.[1]

The confusion I mentioned between the two senses of "strict" construction is therefore very misleading indeed. If courts try to be faithful to the text of the Constitution, they will for that very reason be forced to decide between competing conceptions of political morality. So it is wrong to attack the Warren Court, for example, on the ground that it failed to treat the Constitution as a binding text. On the contrary, if we wish to treat fidelity to that text as an overriding requirement of constitutional interpretation, then it is the conservative critics of the Warren Court who are at fault, because their philosophy ignores the direction to face issues of moral principle that the logic of the text demands.

I put the matter in a guarded way because we may *not* want to accept fidelity to the spirit of the text as an overriding principle of constitutional adjudication. It may be more important for courts to decide constitutional cases in a manner that respects the judgments of

---

1. It is less misleading to say that the broad clauses of the Constitution "delegate" power to the Court to enforce its own conceptions of political morality. But even this is inaccurate if it suggests that the Court need not justify its conception by arguments showing the connections be- tween its conception and standard cases, as described in the text. If the Court finds that the death penalty is cruel, it must do so on the basis of some principles or groups of principles that unite the death penalty with the thumbscrew and the rack.

other institutions of government, for example. Or it may be more important for courts to protect established legal doctrines, so that citizens and the government can have confidence that the courts will hold to what they have said before. But it is crucial to recognize that these other policies compete with the principle that the Constitution is the fundamental and imperative source of constitutional law. They are not, as the "strict constructionists" suppose, simply consequences of that principle.

* * *

There is one very popular argument in favor of [a] policy of deference, which might be called the argument from democracy. It is at least debatable, according to this argument, whether a sound conception of equality forbids segregated education or requires measures like busing to break it down. Who ought to decide these debatable issues of moral and political theory? Should it be a majority of a court in Washington, whose members are appointed for life and are not politically responsible to the public whose lives will be affected by the decision? Or should it be the elected and responsible state or national legislators? A democrat, so this argument supposes, can accept only the second answer.

But the argument from democracy is weaker than it might first appear. The argument assumes, for one thing, that state legislatures are in fact responsible to the people in the way that democratic theory assumes. But in all the states, though in different degrees and for different reasons, that is not the case. In some states it is very far from the case. I want to pass that point, however, because it does not so much undermine the argument from democracy as call for more democracy, and that is a different matter. I want to fix attention on the issue of whether the appeal to democracy in this respect is even right in principle.

The argument assumes that in a democracy all unsettled issues, including issues of moral and political principle, must be resolved only by institutions that are politically responsible in the way that courts are not. Why should we accept that view of democracy? To say that that is what democracy means does no good, because it is wrong to suppose that the word, as a word, has anything like so precise a meaning. Even if it did, we should then have to rephrase our question to ask why we should have democracy, if we assume that is what it means. Nor is it better to say that that view of democracy is established in the American Constitution, or so entrenched in our political tradition that we are committed to it. We cannot argue that the Constitution, which provides no rule limiting judicial review to clear cases, establishes a theory of democracy that excludes wider review, nor can we say that our courts have in fact consistently accepted such a restriction. * * *

So the argument from democracy is not an argument to which we are committed either by our words or our past. We must accept it, if at all, on the strength of its own logic. In order to examine the arguments more closely, however, we must make a further distinction. The argument as I have set it out might be continued in two different ways: one might argue that judicial deference is required because democratic institutions, like legislatures, are in fact likely to make *sounder* decisions than courts about the underlying issues that constitutional cases raise, that is, about the nature of an individual's moral rights against the state.

Or one might argue that it is for some reason *fairer* that a democratic institution rather than a court should decide such issues, even though there is no reason to believe that the institution will reach a sounder decision. * * *

I shall start with the second argument, that legislatures and other democratic institutions have some special title to make constitutional decisions, apart from their ability to make better decisions. One might say that the nature of this title is obvious, because it is always fairer to allow a majority to decide any issue than a minority. But that, as has often been pointed out, ignores the fact that decisions about rights against the majority are not issues that in fairness ought to be left to the majority. Constitutionalism—the theory that the majority must be restrained to protect individual rights—may be a good or bad political theory, but the United States has adopted that theory, and to make the majority judge in its own cause seems inconsistent and unjust. So principles of fairness seem to speak against, not for, the argument from democracy.

* * *

We must therefore turn to the other continuation of the argument from democracy, which holds that democratic institutions, like legislatures, are likely to reach *sounder* results about the moral rights of individuals than would courts. * * *

There is a weak version of this claim * * *. This version argues that no political principle establishing rights can be sound, whatever abstract arguments might be made in its favor, unless it meets the test of social acceptance in the long run; so that, for example, the Supreme Court cannot be right in its views about the rights of black children, or criminal suspects, or atheists, if the community in the end will not be persuaded to recognize these rights.

This weak version may seem plausible for different reasons. It will appeal, for instance, to those who believe both in the fact and in the strength of the ordinary man's moral sense, and in his willingness to entertain appeals to that sense. But it does not argue for judicial restraint except in the very long run. On the contrary, it supposes what lawyers are fond of calling a dialogue between the judges and the nation, in which the Supreme Court is to present and defend its reflective view of what the citizen's rights are, much as the Warren Court tried to do, in the hope that the people will in the end agree.

We must turn, therefore, to the strong version of the claim. This argues that the organic political process will secure the genuine rights of men more certainly if it is not hindered by the artificial and rationalistic intrusion of the courts. On this view, the rights of blacks, suspects, and atheists will emerge through the process of political institutions responding to political pressures in the normal way. If a claim of right cannot succeed in this way, then for that reason it is, or in any event it is likely to be, an improper claim of right. But this bizarre proposition is only a disguised form of the skeptical point that there are in fact no rights against the state.

Perhaps, as Burke and his modern followers argue, a society will produce the institutions that best suit it only by evolution and never by radical reform. But rights against the state are claims that, if accepted, require society to settle for institutions that may not suit it so comfortably. The nerve of a claim of right, even on the demythologized analysis of rights I am using, is that an individual is entitled to protection against the majority even at the cost of the general interest. Of course the comfort of the majority will require some accommodation for minorities but only to the extent necessary to preserve order; and that is usually an accommodation that falls short of recognizing their rights.

Indeed the suggestion that rights can be demonstrated by a process of history rather than by an appeal to principle shows either a confusion or no real concern about what rights are. A claim of right presupposes a moral argument and can be established in no other way. * * *

* * *

This has been a complex argument, and I want to summarize it. Our constitutional system rests on a particular moral theory, namely, that men have moral rights against the state. The difficult clauses of the Bill of Rights, like the due process and equal protection clauses, must be understood as appealing to moral concepts rather than laying down particular conceptions; therefore a court that undertakes the burden of applying these clauses fully as law must be an activist court, in the sense that it must be prepared to frame and answer questions of political morality.

* * *

The issue at the heart of the academic debate might be put this way. If we give the decisions of principle that the Constitution requires to the judges, instead of to the people, we act in the spirit of legality, so far as our institutions permit. But we run a risk that the judges may make the wrong decisions. Every lawyer thinks that the Supreme Court has gone wrong, even violently wrong, at some point in its career. If he does not hate the conservative decisions of the early 1930s, which threatened to block the New Deal, he is likely to hate the liberal decisions of the last decade.

We must not exaggerate the danger. Truly unpopular decisions will be eroded because public compliances will be grudging, as it has been in the case of public school prayers, and because old judges will die or retire and be replaced by new judges appointed because they agree with a

President who has been elected by the people. The decisions against the New Deal did not stand, and the more daring decisions of recent years are now at the mercy of the Nixon Court. Nor does the danger of wrong decisions lie entirely on the side of excess; the failure of the Court to act in the McCarthy period, epitomized by its shameful decision upholding the legality of the Smith Act in the *Dennis* case, may be thought to have done more harm to the nation than did the Court's conservative bias in the early Roosevelt period.

Still, we ought to design our institutions to reduce the risk of error, so far as this is possible. But the academic debate has so far failed to produce an adequate account of where error lies. For the activists, the segregation decisions were right because they advanced a social goal they think desirable, or they were wrong because they advanced a social goal they dislike. For the advocates of restraint they were wrong, whether they approve or disapprove that social goal, because they violated the principle that the Court is not entitled to impose its own view of the social good on the nation.

Neither of these tests forces lawyers to face the special sort of moral issue I described earlier, the issue of what moral rights an individual has against the state. The activists rest their case, when they argue it at all, on the assumption either that their social goals are self-evidently good or that they will in the long run work for the benefit of everybody; this optimism exposes them to [the] argument that this is not necessarily so. Those who want restraint argue that some principle of legality protects constitutional lawyers from facing any moral issues at all.

Constitutional law can make no genuine advance until it isolates the problem of rights against the state and makes that problem part of its own agenda. That argues for a fusion of constitutional law and moral theory, a connection that, incredibly, has yet to take place. It is perfectly understandable that lawyers dread contamination with moral philosophy, and particularly with those philosophers who talk about rights, because the spooky overtones of that concept threaten the graveyard of reason. But better philosophy is now available than the lawyers may remember. Professor Rawls of Harvard, for example, has published an abstract and complex book about justice which no constitutional lawyer will be able to ignore.[1] There is no need for lawyers to play a passive role in the development of a theory of moral rights against the state, however, any more than they have been passive in the development of legal sociology and legal economics. They must recognize that law is no more independent from philosophy than it is from these other disciplines.

1. *A Theory of Justice,* 1972.

HENRY P. MONAGHAN, OUR PERFECT CONSTITUTION

56 N.Y.U.L.Rev. 353, 353–56, 358–67, 391–96 (1981).

THE PERFECTIONIST CULTURE THEME

Some lawyers, many judges, and perhaps most academic commentators view the constitution as authorizing courts to nullify the results of the political process on the basis of general principles of political morality not derived from the constitutional text or the structure it creates. The supreme court is plainly committed to such an endeavor in the sex-marriage-children area, where some fifty written opinions order these relationships ostensibly in the name of securing due process and equal protection. Indeed, the court seems well on its way to "constitutionalizing" the entire subject of family law, which two short decades ago was bereft of constitutional restraints.

The court's efforts at developing a constitutional *lex non scripta* are modest when compared with those of its admiring academic commentators. For well over twenty years these commentators have been industriously formulating substantive limits on the political process in the name of equal protection of the laws. More recently, these commentators have been "taking rights seriously"—so seriously in fact that they outdo one another in urging the imposition of constitutional constraints on the basis of "rights" whose origins cannot be traced to either the constitutional text or the structure it creates. The current academic emphasis on rights, rather than equality, has two sources: the general perception that concerns over political morality are not exhausted by, and cannot be reduced to, concepts of equality; and a more focused concern for according protection to those specified areas of individual autonomy that are most highly esteemed by the commentators. Thus, the commentators eagerly defend limitations on government based upon the rights of "personhood,"[8] "intimate association,"[9] and "personal lifestyles."[10] Quite plainly, the old fear of substantive due process is dead; it has been succeeded by a confidence that "good" and "bad" varieties of substantive due process can be distinguished.

Some commentators would go still further. Mixing concepts of rights and equality, they would hold government to an affirmative constitutional duty to satisfy the "just wants" of its citizens.[12] In their view, government is constitutionally obliged to provide "adequate" levels of food, housing, education, and whatever other "goods" the commentators deem necessary to a decent existence.

Academic commentary of this character is more than simply intriguing. It vividly highlights a core issue in modern constitutional theo-

---

8. L. Tribe, American Constitutional Law ch. 15 (1978) ("rights of privacy and personhood").

9. Karst, [*The Freedom of Intimate Association,* 89 Yale L.J. 624, 629–52 (1980)].

10. Wilkinson & White, *Constitutional Protection for Personal Lifestyles,* 62 Cornell L.Rev. 563, 611–25 (1977) ("constitutional lifestyle right").

12. Professor Michelman originally advanced this idea under the concept of equal protection, while suggesting that substantive due process would have been a more appropriate vehicle. Michelman, The Supreme Court, 1968 Term—Foreword: *On Protecting the Poor Through the Fourteenth Amendment,* 83 Harv.L.Rev. 7, 11–13, 16–18 (1969)[.]

ry—the legitimacy of judicial review under (in the characterization of a former student) the "due substance clauses": substantive due process and substantive equal protection. Most commentators welcome "due substance" review in some form, proclaim that it is "here to stay," [14] and admonish that further resistance is "unwise" and "hopeless." [15] The fun, for them, begins in seeking to domesticate their creations. Since the meaning of the constitution is not to be found in its history or in judicial precedent, but in current social consensus—or, as now seems the fashion, in Kant, Rawls,[16] or Nozick [17]—the commentator's initial task is the selection of a preferred source from which to extract concepts of equality and justice. Next, the substance of political activity is expressed and weighed in scales, or even calibrated on charts. Finally, the commentator concludes, usually after the most meticulous and detailed comparison of the "interests at stake," that certain political outcomes are simply prohibited. No matter how "fair" or "open" the underlying political process, these outcomes must be set aside because they conflict with some ideal normative pattern "out there" that circumscribes the permissible distribution of governmental benefits or burdens.

"Due substance" methodology is profoundly different from one premised on a view that (in general) the constitution legitimately sanctions inquiry only into the openness and fairness of the political process. Professor Ely's process-oriented *Democracy and Distrust* is, I think, the classic affirmation in our time for those recalcitrants who, like me, oppose any further extension of an approach that tests political outcomes for their consistency with some external, ideal pattern of distributive justice. And since we recalcitrants are, as yet, unwilling to yield the battlefield, one can expect that this controversy will occupy the center of constitutional debate for some time to come.

My concern here is with an aspect of the controversy that in this context has escaped notice. Virtually every adherent to the "due substance" school of judicial review shares in whole or in large part a critical culture theme, to borrow a phrase from cultural anthropology: that of "Our perfect Constitution."

* * *

* * * One cannot read the works of Professors Tribe, Karst, Michelman, and a whole host of other due substance theorists without a profound feeling that, however much they might otherwise disagree, for them the constitution is essentially perfect in one central respect: *properly construed, the constitution guarantees against the political order most equality and autonomy values which the commentators think a twentieth century Western liberal democratic government ought to guar-*

14. Karst, Intimate Association, supra note 9, at 665.

15. A. Cox, The Role of the Supreme Court in American Government 113 (1976).

16. J. Rawls, A Theory of Justice (1971).

17. R. Nozick, Anarchy, State and Utopia (1974). * * *

antee to its citizens. For these commentators, the constitution is not Perfect with a capital "P"; it is, however, perfect in the more limited sense that a necessary link is asserted between the constitution and currently "valid" notions of rights, equality and distributive justice. The constitution is, in sum, "perfect" with a small "p."

Of course, I overstate my point. Few due substance commentators hold a "perfection" premise fully. Nevertheless, each commentator can be fairly described as "perfectionist." Each asserts that there is a clear and substantial connection between the constitution and *current* conceptions of political morality, a linkage *not* exhausted by any assumed constitutional guarantee of a fair political process. To be sure, the commentators display important differences among themselves in terms of the relative weight each places upon historical tradition, current sociological formulations, and political philosophy in defining the content of political morality. But the important fact is that they share a distinctive and controversial underlying premise: the "outputs" of even a fairly structured political process must satisfy some core substantive notions of political morality.

For example, in "an avowed effort to construct a more just constitutional order," [37] Professor Tribe elaborates a wide range of equality and autonomy claims.[38] His colleague Professor Michelman has devoted much of his academic career to cementing a union between the distributional patterns of the modern welfare state and the federal constitution.[39] Professor Karst would guarantee a whole range of nontextually based rights against government to ensure "the dignity of full membership in society," which, he asserts, inheres in the "right of equal citizenship." [40] Professor Fiss argues that the courts should give "concrete meaning and application" to those values that "give our society an identity and inner coherence [and] its distinctive public morality." [41] Professor Dworkin charges the courts with enforcing our "constitutional morality," namely, the moral principles "presupposed by the law and institutions of the community." [42] Professor Perry sees the court as having a "prophetic" role in developing moral standards in a "dialectical relationship" with congress, from which he sees emerging a "more mature" political morality.[43] Professor Richards urges that the court apply the contractarian moral theory of Professor Rawls' *A Theory of Justice* to constitu-

37. L. Tribe, American Constitutional Law iii (1978).

38. E.g., id. chs. 15–17.

39. See note [12] supra.

40. Karst, *The Supreme Court, 1976 Term—Foreword: Equal Citizenship Under the Fourteenth Amendment,* 91 Harv.L.Rev. 1, 5 (1977) [hereinafter Karst, Equal Citizenship].

41. Fiss, *The Supreme Court, 1978 Term—Foreword: The Forms of Justice,* 93 Harv.L.Rev. 1, 9, 11 (1979).

42. R. Dworkin, Taking Rights Seriously 126 (1977). Professor Dworkin argues "for a fusion of constitutional law and moral theory," a connection, he asserts, "that, incredibly, has yet to take place." Id. at 149.

43. Perry, *Noninterpretive Review in Human Rights Cases: A Functional Justifi-*

tional questions.[44] * * *

* * *

In this article I analyze the general structure of the arguments advanced by the commentators to support their marriage of the constitution with external concepts of political morality, and then examine the principal consequences of this union for the various modes of constitutional interpretation. I write from the perhaps "puerile" bias[53] that original intent is the proper mode of ascertaining constitutional meaning, although important concessions must now be made to the claims of stare decisis. From my perspective, these interpretational premises are wholly incompatible with the perfectionist culture theme.

The Justifications for Perfectionism

Most commentators agree that analyses grounded either in the constitutional text or in the structure it creates constitute valid modes of reasoning about constitutional "meaning." But what justifies looking outward to current or emerging conceptions of political morality as an acceptable interpretive mode? * * *

The Two–Clause Theory

The two-clause theory—or, to be more precise, the "two types of clauses" theory—has provided and continues to provide the most commonly invoked general justification for imposing "due substance" review on the workings of the political process. Professor Corwin expresses the theory in these terms:

> [I]t will be generally found that words [in the Constitution] which refer to governing institutions, like "jury," "legislature," "election" have been given their strictly historical meaning [by the Supreme Court], while words defining the subject-matter of power or of rights like "commerce," "liberty," "property," have been deliberately moulded to the views of contemporary society.[57]

This theory possesses considerable power. It provides at least a general account of what the supreme court has been doing, although discovery of constitutional provisions whose content is now controlled by a "strictly historical meaning" is becoming increasingly difficult. But this qualification does not impeach the general validity of the two-clause theory. Its central premise is that at least some constitutional clauses were *intended* to be "moulded to the views of contemporary society." This view has won considerable judicial and academic acceptance. If sound, it

cation, 56 N.Y.U.L.Rev. 278, 291–92, 307–10 (1981).

44. D. Richards, [The Moral Criticism of Law 45–49 (1977)]; Richards, *Commercial Sex and the Rights of the Person: A Moral Argument for the Decriminalization of Prostitution*, 127 U.Pa.L.Rev. 1195, 1228–31 (1979); Richards, *Sexual Autonomy and the Constitutional Right to Privacy: A Case*

Study in Human Rights and the Unwritten Constitution, 30 Hastings L.J. 957, 970–72 (1979).

53. Miller, *Book Review*, 32 Fla.L.Rev. 369, 370 (1980). * * *

57. Corwin, *Judicial Review in Action*, 74 U.Pa.L.Rev. 639, 659–60 (1926).

quite plainly offers considerable promise for linking the constitution with current conceptions of political morality.

The two-clause theory is, however, fundamentally unhelpful for the perfectionist. The root difficulty is that it must be advanced as a theory of the original intention of the Framers. So understood, it is far too fragile to support the weight of perfectionist concerns for distributive justice. Specifically, it will not support elaboration in the name of the constitution of a strong set of nontextually based privacy, autonomy, and economic equality rights.

I begin with the observation that no convincing evidence exists that the Framers intended a constitution with two sets of provisions, some of which are controlled by a "strictly historical meaning" and some of which are "deliberately moulded to the views of contemporary society." At the risk of considerable oversimplification, I suggest that the constitutional clauses range from the most particularized, bright-line demarcations to a set of provisions characterized by the need for ongoing interpretation and application not to the "views of contemporary society," *but to the contemporary manifestations of problems identified by the Framers.* Limitation of the presidency to persons of age thirty-five or more is an easy illustration of a particularized provision. Although the Framers' general concern may well have been for maturity and experience in the chief executive, their choice of a bright-line standard evinces a clear intention to avoid the uncertainty (and the risk of corrupt decisions) that a judicial determination of a candidate's "maturity" would surely entail. At the other end are the power-conferring grants of article 1, section 8, and at least some of the limiting provisions of the bill of rights. These provisions are rightly applied to *"the sorts of evils* against which the provisions were directed and to * * * their contemporary counterparts." [65] The first amendment, for example, encompasses subjects presumably out of the Framers' specific contemplation but within their general purpose. But I do not understand this to be the equivalent of saying that the amendment can rightly be molded to the views of contemporary society, irrespective of the sorts of evils that concerned the Framers.

The heart of the difficulty for perfectionists, however, lies elsewhere. Even if one assumes that some constitutional provisions were intended to be molded to contemporary needs, these provisions are plainly bounded by their language. The establishment clause, for instance, manifests concern with the evils flowing from certain relationships between secular and religious institutions. It would, I submit, violate the rules of our constitutional grammar to abstract the clause to a level so general that it will encompass all relationships in which government seeks to provide aid to centers of concentrated, highly influential private power, such as the Chrysler Corporation.

65. J. Ely, [Democracy and Distrust 13 (1980).] * * * Professor Ely suggests a distinction between the first and eighth amendments here, the latter calling for a more avowedly contemporary approach. [Id. at 13–14.] The distinction seems to me more asserted than demonstrated, and I reject it.

The linguistic boundaries of the specific guarantees do not deter the two-clause perfectionists. To fill in the open spaces, these theorists historically have relied most heavily upon the assertedly "open texture" of the due process and equal protection clauses, investing them with a sponge-like quality capable of absorbing any subject matter analytically outside the boundaries of other constitutional limitations. But any such absorptive quality in these clauses is not in their design. It is, rather, a post-ratification invention first employed by conservative lawyers and judges to stave off the evils of socialism,[69] and subsequently borrowed by liberal commentators to protect a different set of values. Viewed in terms of original intent, the due process clauses are appropriately bounded by a concern for fair adjudicatory procedures, even if the concept of fairness, in that context, is capable of growth. These clauses cannot fairly be relied upon by perfectionists in their quest for an original intent for fashioning open-ended substantive principles of distributive justice.

Nor can the equal protection clause. The historical evidence is overwhelming that the core concern of this clause and of its companion, the fifteenth amendment, was the protection of blacks from at least some forms of discriminatory political decisions. Taken together, these amendments extended the principle of political equality to blacks. Perhaps the general language of the equal protection clause must be taken to include discriminations closely analogous to racial discrimination as well. So viewed, the clause would demand some general judicial concern with the integrity of the political process to assure that it takes account of the interests of all citizens. This, in turn, would call for careful review of certain types of discriminatory political outcomes, not because those outcomes transgress unwritten substantive norms, but because they do not usually occur unless there has been a violation of the process norm of political equality. There is, however, no warrant in the historical origins of the equal protection clause for invalidating the outcomes of a fairly structured political process simply because those outcomes violate some ideal substantive "antidiscrimination" norms.

As a constitutional concept, equality demands no more than the *inclusion* of groups into the political process. What is at stake in the perfectionist quest is quite different: it is the measuring of political outcomes against norms of distributive justice—the kinds of problems which now usually surface under the label of substantive due process. My objection is thus the same as before. How do "two-clause" perfectionists justify the use of any clause to permit general judicial concern with the *outputs* of a fair political process?

For some commentators the ninth amendment and the privileges or immunities clause accomplish just that. These commentators argue that the ninth amendment was intended to create a broad range of nontextual rights against the national government, and that the "debates in

---

69. E.g., Coppage v. Kansas, 236 U.S. 1, 10–14, 21–23 (1915); Lochner v. New York, 198 U.S. 45, 64 (1905). On the influential role of the bar in this respect, see B. Twiss, Lawyers and the Constitution 18–173 (1942).

Congress on the [fourteenth] amendment leave one in little doubt of the intention of its framers to nationalize civil liberty in the United States" [82] through the privileges or immunities clause. For these commentators, ascribing a substantive content to due process and equal protection is defensible. While one can regret the technically unsatisfying use of the "wrong" clauses, little of substance turns on the fact that the due process and equal protection clauses, rather than the ninth amendment and the privileges or immunities clause, are employed to ensure "due substance."

The foregoing argument has force. However, I would emphasize that any invocation of either the ninth amendment or the privileges or immunities clause by two-clause perfectionists necessarily rests upon several troublesome premises. The initial assumption is that the content of the two clauses is identical. But this is hardly self-evident. Indeed, like the guaranty clause, the ninth amendment seems to me entirely empty, supplying no ascertainable direction to the courts. It is, accordingly, far too indefinite to provide any judicial authority for the development of substantive rights against the political process. But even if both amendments are appropriate repositories for an external schedule of rights, *a showing is necessary that this was not understood to be a list closed as of 1791 or 1868.* No relevant evidence on the ninth amendment and very little with respect to the privileges or immunities clause supports an inference that either was intended to have a dynamic character. If I am correct in that view, neither clause, viewed through the lens of original intent, provides support for the scope of judicial due substance review as it *now* exists in the sex-children-family area, to say nothing of the scope of due substance review advocated by the perfectionists.

* * *

The Common Law Mode of Adjudication

The perfectionists' discomfort with interpretative modes grounded in original intent and precedent is offset by their enthusiasm for viewing constitutional law as similar in method and substance to the common law of torts. Thus, Professor Brest proposes to derive and elaborate constitutional principles from "custom, social practices, conventional morality, and precedents." [219] Other commentators rely more explicitly on insights derived from currently fashionable philosophical or economic concepts to generate both common law and constitutional principles.[220] Application of common law approaches to the constitutional law area has

82. E. Corwin, Liberty Against Government 118 (1948).

219. Brest, [*The Misconceived Quest for the Original Understanding,* 60 B.U.L.Rev. 204, 228–29 (1980).]

220. E.g., B. Ackerman, Private Property and the Constitution 182–83 (1977) ("Ordinary observing" amenable to Rawlsian, Benthamite or pareto-optimal approaches to evaluation of legal rules); R. Dworkin, Taking Rights Seriously ch. 5 (building on Rawls' concept-conception distinction); id. ch. 9 (building on Mill's internal-external preference distinction) (1977); R. Posner, Economic Analysis of Law 491–551 (2d ed. 1977).

important consequences for interpretation. First, it invites the extraction of quite general political principles from the specific constitutional guarantees. Second, and more important, the common law method encourages the elaboration of supplemental, nontextually grounded principles of political morality to fill in any gaps. So supplemented, the constitution manifests a unified, coherent conception of political justice, and not simply a series of separate and incompletely related provisions which, taken together, are insufficiently expressive of the substantive values of a twentieth-century liberal democracy.

The common law approach is particularly congenial to professors of law, whose training and experience heavily emphasize this technique. The advantages of transplanting the common law method to the constitutional arena are obvious. The tedious labor associated with the historical search for original intent is eliminated. With the concerns of the past out of the way, attention may be focused exclusively on present realities. Armed with the insights of current social, political, and economic thinking, these commentators can "reason" about contemporary needs and the public good in much the same way that they would reason about tort problems—with interest balancing providing the solution to every constitutional problem, just as it purports to do for the creative common law judge. The constitutional values themselves become one set of interests—important ones to be sure, but in the end only interests—to be weighed against competing social values.

Our constitutional origins suggest a different perspective: the constitution as a superstatute. Like important statutes, the constitution emerged as a result of compromises struck after hard bargaining. In addition, its intellectual underpinnings invite a statutory perspective. The dominant conceptions of popular sovereignty and limited government realized by the device of a social compact suggest that the constitution be construed as a compact whose contents could not be altered by any organ of government. That is a great deal more like the way statutes are construed than the way common law is made. These origins make plausible, even if they do not compel, a conclusion that constitutional interpretation should be assimilated to the process of statutory interpretation. While I do not wish to overstate the differences between common law development and statutory interpretation, important interpretational consequences do flow from viewing the constitution as a statute (a super one, to be sure) rather than as declaration of common law. Statutory interpretation involves a blend of emphases upon original intention and historical context, and a full recognition of the unprincipled, and imperfect, nature of an enactment produced by compromise. By contrast, the common law method, if applied to either a statute or a constitution, tends to obscure the compromise character of the enactment, and thus renders opaque its "imperfect" quality when measured against ideal norms.

Candor requires that one recognize that the common law approach, and not the statutory approach, best describes the development of constitutional law under the bill of rights. Substantive elaboration of the bill of rights has increasingly followed the incremental, case-by-case method employed by common law judges. Viewed retrospectively, this was perhaps inevitable. Courts have had to cope with the relative paucity and indeterminacy of the underlying historical materials, as well as the difficulty of relating ancient norms to a world radically different from that of the Framers. Not surprisingly, as the text got older and interpretative materials accumulated, "the focus of professional and judicial attention * * * [shifted] from the * * * text and history to the * * * norm[s] to be derived by analysis and synthesis of the judicial precedents.[230] More importantly, adoption of the method of the common law, with its emphasis on precedent (albeit without the constraining influence of stare decisis) and analogical reasoning, brought with it a belief that the *substance* of the judicial task in each sphere is similar: balancing the interests at stake, with the constitutional guarantees assessed in functional, rather than historical, terms. At least in bill of rights cases, therefore, there is considerable force in Professor Brest's observation that reliance upon original intent "has played a very small role compared to the elaboration of the Court's own precedents. It is rather like having a remote ancestor who came over on the Mayflower."[232]

Thus, the perfectionist has much on which to rely in drawing upon a common law approach to the development of civil liberties—but not nearly enough to justify the perfectionists' central need to legitimate the existence of a *supplemental,* nontextually based list of autonomy, privacy, and equality claims that are assertable against the political organs of government. One could, after all, argue that elaboration of the specific guarantees of the bill of rights exhibits characteristics of both common law and statutory interpretation: common law because their content is worked out in the manner of the analogical and precedential reasoning characteristic of the common law courts; statutory because, so far as is practicable, emphasis has been and still should be placed on historical setting and original intent. A supplemental list of nontextual rights lacks the latter characteristics by definition.

* * *

OUR "IMPERFECT" CONSTITUTION

The "antidemocratic" charge levelled against the constitution by progressivist historians has always struck me as unconvincing. Viewed in its historical setting, the original document was remarkably "democratic." Moreover, the amendments—ignored by these critics—present in their entirety a consistently democratic theme, one that made the constitution "a far more democratic document than the one [we] inherited from [the Framers]."[238] Both in origin and line of growth, therefore,

---

230. Jones, *The Brooding Omnipresence of Constitutional Law,* 4 Vt.L.Rev. 1, 28 (1979).

232. Brest, Misconceived Quest, supra note [219] at 234. * * *

238. A. Grimes, Democracy and the Amendments to the Constitution xi (1978).

the constitution of the United States deserves the appellation "democratic." The constitution established a framework of government suitable to meet the middle distance needs of the nation at the end of the eighteenth century and, with the Civil War amendments, the nation's needs at the turn of the twentieth century. Perhaps, although I am less sure, the governmental framework is even adequate to meet the general needs of our times. But the constitution is not "perfect" in the sense we have been considering. If original intent be our guide, the constitution did not authorize judges to insulate from the political process most of the individual rights asserted in current conceptions of political morality.

This is not to say that our constitution sacrificed any concern for political justice. The important point is that the constitution is flexible enough to *permit* the political organs of the government to advance a large and expanding range of equality and autonomy claims. I part company, however, with those who believe the constitution *mandates* protection of such claims, including, for example, the "right" of vendors to sell contraceptives to minors.[239] I simply do not understand how such judicial activism can be reconciled with the original intent of the Framers of either the 1789–1791 text or 1868–1870 amendments. To be sure, the constitution embodies an ideology, but it is a limited one. As Dean Casper observes, "there have been historical developments [in American society] to which the Constitution had very few ideas to contribute; for example, the revolutionary changes in the structure and regulation of the American economy."[240] Similarly, the constitution has "very few ideas to contribute" to the social equality, privacy, and autonomy claims now pressed by perfectionist commentators. The ideology contained in the constitution is significantly less embracing in scope than the ideology of the American way of life at the end of the twentieth century. It is, therefore, fundamentally wrong to believe that one can ascertain the meaning of the constitution by asking: "Is this what America stands for?"

My review of the various efforts made by perfectionist commentators to overcome the discrepancy between the ideology fairly ascribable to the constitution and that dominant in our nearly twenty-first century, postindustrial liberal democracy leaves me with a conviction that those efforts are seriously flawed. The perfectionism of our constitution, if it has that quality, inheres in its guarantee of an open and fairly structured political process. Perhaps that is enough. Perhaps as "a charter of government a constitution must prescribe legitimate processes, not legitimate outcomes, if like ours (and unlike more ideological documents elsewhere) it is to serve many generations through changing times."[242] In short, perhaps the constitution guarantees only representative democracy, not perfect government.

239. Carey v. Population Servs. Int'l, 431 U.S. 678, 717 (1977) (Rehnquist, J., dissenting).

240. Casper, *Guardians of the Constitution,* 53 So.Cal.L.Rev. 773, 778–79 (1980).

242. Linde, *Due Process of Lawmaking,* 55 Neb.L.Rev. 197, 254 (1976).

C. "DUALIST" CONSTITUTIONALISM

BRUCE ACKERMAN, WE THE PEOPLE, VOLUME 1: FOUNDATIONS

6–14, 16–17, 40–44, 47–50 (1991).

DUALIST DEMOCRACY

THE BASIC IDEA

Above all else, a dualist Constitution seeks to distinguish between two different decisions that may be made in a democracy. The first is a decision by the American people; the second, by their government.

Decisions by the People occur rarely, and under special constitutional conditions. Before gaining the authority to make supreme law in the name of the People, a movement's political partisans must, first, convince an extraordinary number of their fellow citizens to take their proposed initiative with a seriousness that they do not normally accord to politics; second, they must allow their opponents a fair opportunity to organize their own forces; third, they must convince a majority of their fellow Americans to support their initiative as its merits are discussed, time and again, in the deliberative fora provided for "higher lawmaking." It is only then that a political movement earns the enhanced legitimacy the dualist Constitution accords to decisions made by the People.

Decisions made by the government occur daily, and also under special conditions. Most importantly, key officials must be held accountable regularly at the ballot box. In addition, they must be given incentives to take a broad view of the public interest without the undue influence of narrow interest groups. Even when this system of "normal lawmaking" is operating well, however, the dualist Constitution prevents elected politicians from exaggerating their authority. They are not to assert that a normal electoral victory has given them a mandate to enact an ordinary statute that overturns the considered judgments previously reached by the People. If they wish to claim this higher form of democratic legitimacy, they must take to the specially onerous obstacle course provided by a dualist Constitution for purposes of higher lawmaking. Only if they succeed in mobilizing their fellow citizens and gaining their repeated support in response to their opponents' counterattacks may they finally earn the authority to proclaim that *the People* have changed their mind and have given their government new marching orders.

Such a brief statement raises many more questions than answers. One set involves issues of institutional design. First, we must consider the design of a good higher lawmaking system: How to organize a process that will reliably mark out the rare occasions when a political movement rightly earns the special recognition accorded the outcomes of mobilized deliberation made in the name of We the People? Second, there is the question of normal lawmaking: How to create incentives for regularly elected officials to engage in public-spirited deliberation despite the pressures of special interests? Third, there is the design of preservation mechanisms: How to preserve the considered judgments of the mobilized People from illegitimate erosion by the statutory decisions of normal government?

And then there are the ultimate issues that transcend institutional mechanics: Is dualist democracy a good form of government for America? The best? If not, what's better?

This chapter does not aim for final answers. It simply describes how the very questions provoked by dualist democracy suggests inquiries different from those now dominant in the academy. Although each academic competitor differs from dualism in a different way, it may help to begin with the one thing they have in common. For all their luxuriant variety, they ignore the special importance dualists place upon *constitutional politics:* the series of political movements that have, from the Founding onward, called upon their fellow Americans to engage in acts of citizenship that, when successful, culminates in the proclamation of higher law in the name of We the People.

But let me be more specific.

Monistic Democracy

Of the modern schools, the monistic democrats have the most impressive pedigree: Woodrow Wilson,[1] James Thayer,[2] Charles Beard,[3] Oliver Wendell Holmes,[4] Robert Jackson,[5] Alexander Bickel,[6] John Ely.[7] These, and many other distinguished thinkers and doers, have made monism dominant amongst serious constitutionalists over the course of the last century. As with all received opinions, complexities abound. But, at its root, monism is very simple: Democracy requires the grant of plenary lawmaking authority to the winners of the last general election—so long, at least, as the election was conducted under free and fair ground rules and the winners don't try to prevent the next scheduled round of electoral challenges.

This idea motivates, in turn, a critical institutional conclusion: during the period between elections, all institutional checks upon the electoral victors are presumptively antidemocratic. For sophisticated monists, this is only a presumption. Perhaps certain constitutional checks may prevent the victors from abrogating the next scheduled election; perhaps others might be justified once one considers the deeper

1. Woodrow Wilson, Congressional Government (1885); Woodrow Wilson, Constitutional Government in the United States (1907).

2. James Thayer, 'The Origin and Scope of the American Doctrine of Constitutional Law,' 7 Harv.L.Rev. 129 (1893).

3. Charles Beard, An Economic Interpretation of the Constitution of the United States (1913).

4. Lochner v. New York, 198 U.S. 45, 74 (1905) (Holmes, J., dissenting).

5. Robert Jackson, The Struggle for Judicial Supremacy (1941); Railway Express Co. v. New York, 336 U.S. 106, 111 (Jackson, J., concurring).

6. Alexander Bickel, The Least Dangerous Branch (1962).

7. John Ely, Democracy and Distrust: A Theory of Judicial Review (1980).

ways normal elections fail to satisfy our ideals of electoral fairness. While these exceptions may have great practical importance, monists refuse to let them obscure the main point: when the Supreme Court, or anybody else, invalidates a statute, it suffers from a "countermajoritarian difficulty" which must be overcome before a good democrat can profess satisfaction with this extraordinary action.

In the work of this school, the brooding omnipresence is (an idealized version of) British parliamentary practice. For more than a century now, the Prime Minister has won her office after a relatively fair and square election, and except in truly exceptional circumstances the House of Commons has given its unswerving support to the proposals of Her Majesty's Government. If the people of Great Britain don't like what's going on, they will return the Opposition at the next election. Until that time, neither the House of Lords, nor the Queen, nor the courts seriously undermine the legislative decisions made by a majority of the Commons.

So far as the monist is concerned, the British design captures the essence of democracy. The problem posed by America is its failure to follow the trans-Atlantic model. Rather than granting a power monopoly to a single, popularly elected House of Representatives, Americans tolerate a great deal of insubordination from branches whose electoral connection is suspect or nonexistent. While the Senate gets its share of the lumps, the principal object is the Supreme Court. Whoever gave Nine Old Lawyers authority to overrule the judgments of democratically elected politicians?

There are monistic answers to this question—which try to reconcile judicial review with the fundamental premises of monistic democracy. Thus, constitutional conservatives like Alexander Bickel,[10] centrists like John Ely,[11] and progressives like Richard Parker[12] have proposed roles for the Supreme Court that operate within monistic premises. For present purposes, it is the monistic question, not the proliferating number of answers, that needs critical scrutiny.

The monist begs a big question when he asserts that the winner of a fair and open election is entitled to rule with the full authority of We the People. It is much better, of course, for electoral winners to take office rather than suffer an authoritarian putsch by the losers. But it does not follow that all statutes gaining the support of a legislative majority in Washington, D.C., represent the considered judgment of a mobilized majority of American citizens. Instead, the dualist sees a profoundly democratic point to many of the distinctive practices that baffle the monist. For her, they express our Constitution's effort to require elected politicians to operate within a two-track system. If politicians hope to win normal democratic legitimacy for an initiative, they are

---

10. See Alexander Bickel, supra n. 6; Alexander Bickel, The Supreme Court and the Idea of Progress (1970).

11. John Ely, supra n. 7.

12. Richard Parker, The Past of Constitutional Theory—And Its Future, 42 Ohio St.L.J. 223 (1981).

directed down the normal lawmaking path and told to gain the assent of the House, Senate, and President in the usual ways. If they hope for higher lawmaking authority, they are directed down a specially onerous lawmaking path—whose character and historical development will be the subject of the next chapter. Only if a political movement successfully negotiates the special challenges of the higher lawmaking system can it rightfully claim that its initiative represents the constitutional judgment of We the People.

Once the two-track character of the system is recognized, the Supreme Court appears in a different light. Consider that all the time and effort required to push an initiative down the higher lawmaking track would be wasted unless the Constitution prevented future normal politicians from enacting statutes that ignored the movement's higher law achievement. If future politicians could so easily ignore established higher law, why would any mass movement take the trouble to overcome the special hurdles placed on the higher lawmaking track?

To maintain the integrity of higher lawmaking, all dualist constitutions must provide for one or more institutions to discharge a preservationist function. These institutions must effectively block efforts to repeal established constitutional principles by the simple expedient of passing a normal statute and force the reigning group of elected politicians to move onto the higher lawmaking track if they wish to question the judgments previously made by We the People. Only after negotiating this more arduous obstacle course can a political elite earn the authority to say that We the People have changed our mind.

It follows, then, that the dualist will view the Supreme Court from a very different perspective than the monist. The monist treats every act of judicial review as presumptively antidemocratic and strains to save the Supreme Court from the "countermajoritarian difficulty" by one or another ingenious argument. In contrast, the dualist sees the discharge of the preservationist function by the courts as an essential part of a well-ordered democratic regime. Rather than threatening democracy by frustrating the statutory demands of the political elite in Washington, the courts serve democracy by protecting the hard-won principles of a mobilized citizenry against erosion by political elites who have failed to gain broad and deep popular support for their innovations.

This is not to say that any particular decision by the modern Supreme Court can be justified in preservationist terms. The key point is that dualists cannot dismiss a good-faith effort by the Court to interpret the Constitution as "antidemocratic" simply because it leads to the invalidation of normal statutes; this ongoing judicial effort to look backward and interpret the meaning of the great achievements of the past is an indispensable part of the larger project of distinguishing the will of We the People from the acts of We the Politicians.

RIGHTS FOUNDATIONALISTS

In confronting monism, the dualist's main object is to break the tight link monists construct between two distinct ideas: "democracy" on the one hand and "parliamentary sovereignty" on the other. Like monists, dualists are democrats—they believe that the People are the ultimate authority in America. They disagree only about the easy way in which normally elected politicians claim to legislate with the full authority of the People.

In contrast, the primacy of popular sovereignty is challenged by a second modern school. While none of these theorists completely denies a place for democratic principles, their populist enthusiasms are constrained by deeper commitments to fundamental rights. Unsurprisingly, members of this school differ when it comes to identifying the rights that are fundamental. Conservatives like Richard Epstein emphasize the foundational role of property rights;[13] liberals like Ronald Dworkin emphasize the right to equal concern and respect;[14] collectivists like Owen Fiss, the rights of disadvantaged groups.[15] These transparent differences should not blind us to the idea that binds them together. Whatever rights are Right, all agree that the American constitution is concerned, first and foremost, with their protection. Indeed, the whole point of having rights is to trump decisions rendered by democratic institutions that may otherwise legislate for the collective welfare. To emphasize this common thread, I shall group these thinkers together by calling them *rights foundationalists.*

As with the monists, this school is hardly a trendy creation of yesterday. There is, however, an interesting difference in the intellectual lineage they construct for themselves. While monists refer to a series of Americans from Wilson and Thayer to Frankfurter and Bickel, foundationalists favor philosophical writers further removed in time and space—with Kant (via Rawls)[16] and Locke (via Nozick)[17] presently serving as the most important sources of inspiration. Right now, I am not interested in these internal debates. My aim is to describe how foundationalists as a group differ from more democratic schools.

Begin with the monists. It is fair to say that they are hostile to rights, at least as foundationalists understand them. Indeed, it is just when the Supreme Court begins to invalidate statutes in the name of fundamental rights that the monist begins to worry about the "counter-majoritarian difficulty" that renders judicial review presumptively illegitimate.

This "difficulty" does not seem so formidable to the foundationalist. Instead, she is more impressed by the fact that a democratic legislature might endorse any number of oppressive actions—establish a religion, or

---

13. Richard Epstein, Takings: Private Property and the Power of Eminent Domain (1985).

14. Ronald Dworkin, Taking Rights Seriously, ch. 5 (1978); Ronald Dworkin, Law's Empire, chs. 10–11 (1986).

15. Owen Fiss, *Groups and the Equal Protection Clause,* 5 J.Phil. & Pub.Aff. 107 (1976).

16. John Rawls, *Kantian Constructivism in Moral Theory,* 77 J.Phil. 515 (1980).

17. Robert Nozick, Anarchy, State, and Utopia (1974).

authorize torture, or * * *. When such violations occur, the foundationalist demands judicial intervention despite the breach of democratic principle. Rights trump democracy—provided, of course, that they're the Right rights.

And there's the rub. Indeed, it is their anxiety over the arbitrary definition of rights that induces thoughtful foundationalists to recur to great philosophers like Kant and Locke in an effort to understand the Constitution. If judges are to avoid arbitrariness in defining fundamental rights, shouldn't they take advantage of the most profound reflections on the subject available in the Western tradition?

For the monist, this turn to the Great Books is yet another symptom of the foundationalist's antidemocratic disease. Whatever its philosophical merits, the foundationalist's discourse is invariably esoteric—involving encounters with authors and doctrines that most college-educated people successfully avoided during their most academic moments. This exalted talk of Kant and Locke only emphasizes the elitism involved in removing fundamental questions from the democratic process.

These objections hardly convince the foundationalist. They serve only to generate further anxieties about the ease with which monistic democracy can be swept by demagogic irrationality. And so the debate proceeds, with the two sides talking past one another: democracy versus rights versus democracy versus—point and counterpoint, with all the talk changing few minds.

How does the introduction of dualism change the shape of this familiar conversational field? By offering a framework which allows both sides to accommodate some—if not all—of their concerns. The basic mediating device is the dualist's two-track system of democratic lawmaking. It allows an important place for the foundationalist's view of "rights as trumps" without violating the monist's deeper commitment to the primacy of democracy. To grasp the logic of accommodation, suppose that a rights-oriented movement took to the higher lawmaking track and successfully mobilized the People to endorse one or another Bill of Rights. Given this achievement, the dualist can readily endorse the judicial invalidation of later statutes that undermine these rights, even when they concern matters, like the protection of personal freedom or privacy, that have nothing much to do with the integrity of the electoral process so central to monistic democrats. As we have seen, the dualist believes that the Court furthers the cause of democracy when it preserves constitutional rights against erosion by politically ascendant elites who have yet to mobilize the People to support the repeal of previous higher lawmaking principles. Thus, unlike the monist, she will have no trouble supporting the idea that rights can properly trump the conclusions of normal democratic politics. She can do so, moreover, without the need for non-democratic principles of the kinds proffered by the rights foundationalist. Thus, the dualist can offer a deeper reconciliation of democracy and rights to those who find a certain amount of truth in both sides of the debate.

This reconciliation will not, of course, prove satisfactory to all members of the previously contending schools. The problem for the committed foundationalist, unsurprisingly, is the insufficiently deep foundations the dualist has built for the protection of rights. Granted, concedes the foundationalist, the dualist will applaud the judicial protection of rights if a warrant can be found in prior higher lawmaking activity. But that is an awfully big "if." What if the People have not adopted the right Bill of Rights? Should the Constitution then be construed in ways that allow the statutory perpetration of injustice?

It is their different answers to this question that continue to distinguish dualist from committed foundationalist. For the dualist, judicial protection of rights does depend on a prior democratic affirmation on the higher lawmaking track. In this sense, the dualist's Constitution is democratic first, rights-protecting second. The committed foundationalist reverses this priority: the Constitution is first concerned with protecting rights; only then does it authorize the People to work their will on other matters. Having isolated this disagreement, we must next see whether it can be resolved. Are there very general arguments that indicate whether the American Constitution has been built on dualist or foundationalist lines?

My answer is yes. Once again, the decisive consideration is drawn from the distinctive character of two-track lawmaking. My argument against foundationalism focuses on the fact that our Constitution has never (with two exceptions I will consider shortly) explicitly entrenched existing higher law against subsequent revision by the People. While the original Constitution gave higher law protection to slavery, at least it did not try to make it unconstitutional for Americans of later generations to reconsider the question; similarly, when Americans of the early twentieth century enacted Prohibition into higher law, they did not seek to make the amendment unamendable. In these two cases, of course, the People have exercised their right to change their mind. And few among us would say that we were the worse for repeal. Foundationalists, however, must acknowledge the general availability of repeal with embarrassment. For this open-ended practice allows constitutional amendments of a kind that most modern foundationalists would consider morally disastrous.

* * *

The clash between monists and foundationalists dominates the present field of constitutional debate and has moved beyond the classroom to the courtroom. The sharp split between the two schools mimics the split between plaintiff and defendant in the typical lawsuit—the plaintiff insisting that a statute has violated her fundamental rights, the defendant responding that courts should defer to the democratic authority of Congress. Little wonder that thoughtful judges and citizens are drawn to reflections about democracy and rights—creating an audience for the work of the two competing schools.

Dualism expresses a more hopeful possibility. Perhaps the conflict between plaintiff and defendant is not a sign of unremitting conflict between the democratic and rights-oriented aspects of our tradition. Instead, both the enactment of normal statutes *and* the judicial protection of constitutional rights are part of a larger practice of dualist democracy. This abstract synthesis, of course, is hardly enough to decide concrete cases. But it points in a particular direction—toward a reflective study of the past to determine when the People have spoken and what they have said during their historic moments of successful constitutional politics.

* * *

THE SHAPE OF THE CONSTITUTIONAL PAST

When modern lawyers and judges look to the deep past, they tell themselves a story that has a distinctive structure. Though special problems may lead them to appreciate the relevance of one or another aspect of America's constitutional history, three historical periods stand out from the rest. These eras have a pervasive significance: the lessons a judge draws from each of them organizes her entire approach to concrete cases. The first of these jurisgenerative [2] eras is the Founding itself—the framing of the original Constitution and the Bill of Rights, the Supreme Court's initial assertion of judicial review in *Marbury v. Madison*. A second great period occurs two generations later, with the bloody struggles that ultimately yield the Reconstruction amendments. Then there is another pause of two generations before a third great turning point. This one centers on the 1930's and the dramatic confrontation between the New Deal and the Old Court that ends in the constitutional triumph of the activist welfare state.

This three-part story defines the legal meaning of modernity: All of us live in the modern era that begins with the Supreme Court's "switch in time" in 1937, in which an activist, regulatory state is finally accepted as an unchallengeable constitutional reality. For a modern judge, one of the worst insults is that she is reenacting the sin originally committed by the pre-New Deal Court in cases like *Lochner v. New York*. Of course, different moderns define the nature of original sin differently. What is important is not the competing diagnoses but the universal recognition that the constitutional world before the Roosevelt era was profoundly different from our own.

In contrast, today's lawyers and judges experience no similar estrangement in dealing with more recent history: the New Deal Court that digs itself out of the wreckage of laissez-faire jurisprudence in the late 1930's is recognizably *our* Court. Just as it struggled to define a new conception of individual rights in a burgeoning bureaucratic state, so do modern constitutionalists. While the New Deal Court's early confrontations with these questions differ from more recent encounters,

---

2. I borrow this term from Robert Cover, *The Supreme Court 1982 Term—Fore-* word: *Nomos and Narrative*, 97 Harv. L.Rev. 4, 11 (1983).

we still think we can learn from these early cases in very positive ways. Rather than functioning as negative precedents like *Lochner,* these early decisions of the New Deal Court mark the very dawning of the modern world.

So much, I think, is shared by all competent constitutional lawyers, regardless of their more particular political or philosophical convictions. I believe, moreover, that the profession's selective concentration upon these three historical turning points is fundamentally sound. Though other periods have contributed a lot to the modern practice of American government, lawyers and judges are right to look upon the Founding, Reconstruction, and the New Deal as decisive moments at which deep changes in popular opinion gained authoritative constitutional recognition. The problem comes only when we consider the way the profession has transformed this selective chronology into a meaningful narrative that roots the modern age in the deep past.

* * *

The problem is this: the stories lawyers tell about each of the three turning points do not invite them to reflect upon the common features of these great transformative exercises. Instead, each of these three juris-generative events is cabined by a set of lawyerly categories that emphasize how different one episode is from the next.

Of the three, the Founding is treated as if it were the most radical break with the past. Modern lawyers are perfectly prepared to admit that the Constitutional Convention was acting illegally in proposing its new document in the name of We the People. The Founding Federalists, after all, were not prepared to follow the ratification procedures set out in the Articles of Confederation that had been solemnly accepted by all thirteen states only a few years before. The Articles required the unanimous consent of all thirteen state legislatures before any new amendment could come into effect. In contrast, the Federalists blandly excluded state legislatures from *any* role in ratification, and went on to assert that the approval of special constitutional conventions meeting in only nine of the thirteen states would suffice to validate the Convention's effort to speak for the People.

Illegalities like these may not be among the first things that surface in the legal mind, but modern lawyers show no great resistance coming to terms with them. Indeed, there is a conceptual sense in which our very identification of the Founding as a Founding presupposes that the Philadelphia Convention acted without legal warrant under the preexisting Articles. If this were not the case, the *real* Founders of our Republic were the folks who wrote and ratified the Articles of Confederation; the Philadelphia Convention simply gained the ratification of some sweeping "amendments" to the Founding document. Since modern lawyers do not trace the origin of the Republic to the Articles of Confederation but to *the* Constitution of 1787, the discovery of some Founding illegalities confirms, rather than denies, their sense of the overall shape of our constitutional past.

Things are different when the subject turns to the constitutional amendments enacted after the Civil War. Here modern law-talk exhibits a sharp dichotomy between substance and procedure. Substantively, everybody recognizes that these three amendments profoundly transformed preexisting constitutional principles. But if we turn to the process by which they became part of our higher law, a remarkable silence descends on the legal community. While it has no trouble admitting the dubious legality of the Founding, professional talk contains no hint that Reconstruction might be similarly tainted. If asked to explain why the Civil War amendments are part of the Constitution, the modern American lawyer or judge would almost certainly point to the rules for constitutional amendment contained in Article Five of the 1787 Constitution. According to received opinion, the Civil War amendments are just that: ordinary amendments which, like all the others, owe their legality to their conformity with the formal rules for constitutional revision established by the Federalists in the 1787 Constitution. To put this point in a formula: while the professional narrative insists that Reconstruction was *substantively creative,* it supposes that it was *procedurally unoriginal.*

Even this much originality is denied the New Deal. While all lawyers recognize that the 1930's mark the definitive constitutional triumph of activist national government, they tell themselves a story which denies that anything deeply creative was going on. This view of the 1930's is obtained by imagining a Golden Age in which Chief Justice Marshall got things right for all time by propounding a broad construction of the national government's lawmaking authority. The period between Reconstruction and the New Deal can then be viewed as a (complex) story about the fall from grace—wherein most of the Justices strayed from the path of righteousness and imposed their laissez-faire philosophy on the nation through the pretext of constitutional interpretation. Predictably, these acts of judicial usurpation increasingly set the judges at odds with more democratic institutions, which acutely perceived the failure of laissez-faire to do justice to an increasingly interdependent world.

The confrontation between the New Deal and the Old Court climaxes this traditional morality play of decline, fall, and resurrection. Only Justice Roberts's "switch in time," and the departure of the worst judicial offenders, permitted the Court to expiate its countermajoritarian sins without permanent institutional damage. If only the Justices had not strayed from Marshall's original path, perhaps all this unpleasantness could have been avoided!

As always, this basic story line invites countless disagreements about the precise character of the Marshallian vision, the precise scope of the latter-day aberrations during the *Lochner* period of laissez-faire. For present purposes, the critical point is simple enough: in contrast to the first two turning points, modern lawyers do not describe either the substantive or the procedural aspects of the New Deal by telling themselves a tale of constitutional creation. The triumph of activist national government is mediated by a myth of rediscovery—as if the Founding Federalists had foreseen the works of Franklin Delano Roosevelt and would have been surprised to learn that the great struggles of the 1930's were necessary to gain the welfare state's constitutional legitimation.

Founding Federalists → Illegal Constitution; Reconstruction Republicans → Formal Amendments; New Deal Democrats → Judicial Rediscovery of Ancient Truths: this schema suggests a subtle but unmistakable decline in the constitutionally generative capacities of the American people. Apparently, We the People have never again engaged in the sweeping kind of critique and creation attempted by the Founding Federalists. We have made substantive revisions in the original structure of the Constitution, but we have never gone so far as to revise the very process of constitutional revision. A similar loss is implied by a comparison between the nineteenth and twentieth centuries: while the Reconstruction Republicans gained the consent of the American people to fundamental changes in governing principles, the sweeping transformations won by the New Deal Democrats represent nothing more than a return to the wisdom of the early Founders.

* * *

My counterthesis: Like the Reconstruction Republicans, the New Deal Democrats relied on the national separation of powers between Congress, President, and Court to create a new institutional framework through which the American People might define, debate, and finally decide their constitutional future. The key institutional difference between the two periods involves the Presidency. Franklin Roosevelt remained at the helm of the reformist coalition throughout the Democrats' period of constitutional transformation, whereas Lincoln's assassination deprived Republican reformers of Presidential support during the critical struggle over the Fourteenth Amendment. Roosevelt's long tenure had fundamental, if unsurprising, implications for the Presidency's role in the process of higher lawmaking. While the Republicans successfully experimented with Presidential leadership in the process of legitimating the Thirteenth Amendment, they could not build on this experience once Andrew Johnson declared war on the Fourteenth Amendment. In contrast, the Democrats were in a position to develop the power of the Presidency in a far more incisive fashion.

When due allowances are made for the defection of President Johnson from the Republican coalition, however, it will be possible to identify remarkable similarities in the way in which the separation of powers tested, and finally legitimated, the constitutional revisions proposed by nineteenth-century Republicans and twentieth-century Democrats. Each higher lawmaking exercise began with the reformers in control of only part of the national government—in the case of the Republicans, it was Congress that took on the mantle of reform leadership with Johnson's defection; in the case of the Democrats, the Presidency was the leading reform branch. In both cases, the constitutional reformers' proposals were exposed to an initial period of incisive critique by conservative branches, which publicly appealed to the People to decisively reject the dangerous innovations proposed by the reformers. In the case of the Republicans, the leading conservative branch was the Presidency; for the Democrats, it was the Supreme Court.

These institutional differences were important, of course, in explaining the different dynamics of constitutional debate and decision. But it is even more important to see the deeper similarities. In both cases, the institutional deadlock in Washington forced both sides to mobilize their supporters in the country at large. These remarkable efforts at popular mobilization, in turn, gave extraordinary constitutional meaning to the next regularly scheduled election. If one or another side could win a decisive victory at the polls, it would try to use its popular support to break the institutional impasse.

This process of interbranch struggle and popular mobilization made the elections of 1866 and 1936 decisive events in constitutional history. On both occasions, the reformers returned to Washington with a clear victory at the polls. They proceeded to proclaim that the election results gave them a "mandate from the People," and that the time had come for the conservative branches to end their constitutional resistance.

This demand by the electorally victorious reformers inaugurated the period of ratification—in which the conservative branches considered whether to continue their resistance or to recognize that the People had indeed given their fixed support to the reformist movement. In both cases, this decision was not made in silent contemplation but in response to a challenge by the reformist branches to the conservatives' continued legitimacy. During Reconstruction, the reformist Congress finally threatened President Johnson with impeachment if he continued to use his office to sabotage ratification of the Fourteenth Amendment. During the New Deal, it was the reformist President's threat of packing the Court that provoked the conservative Justices to consider the wisdom of continued resistance. In both cases, however, the question was very much the same: Should the conservatives in the dissenting branches finally recognize that *the People had spoken?*

In both cases, the conservatives' answer was the same. Rather than escalating the constitutional crisis further, they decided, with evident reluctance, that further resistance would endanger too many of the very values they held fundamental. They made the "switch in time": Johnson called off his effort to prevent the formal ratification of the Fourteenth Amendment; the Supreme Court repudiated its doctrinal defense of laissez-faire capitalism and began to build new constitutional foundations for activist national government.

In turn, the victorious reformers responded in the same way. The Republicans refused to convict the President, allowing Johnson to remain in office to proclaim the validity of the Fourteenth Amendment; the Democrats called off the threat of court-packing, allowing the Old Court to proclaim that activist New Deal government was constitutionally legitimate.

As a consequence of these "switches in time," all three branches emerge from the period of democratic testing once again united, and the separation of powers remains intact for use by the next constitutional regime. But it is now in the service of the new constitutional solution that had previously been so controversial.

Interbranch Impasse→Decisive Election→Reformist Challenge to Conservative Branches→Switch in Time: This separation of powers schema will require lots of elaboration before it can gain legal credibility. There is no way to avoid the hard historical work required to appreciate the functional similarities between President Johnson's veto of Congress's Civil Rights Act and the Supreme Court's veto of the NIRA; between the critical election of 1866 and the critical election of 1936; between the Republican effort to impeach the President and the Democratic effort to pack the Court; between the final ratification of the Fourteenth Amendment by Johnson's Secretary of State and the final ratification of the welfare state by the New Deal Court; and so forth. Fortunately, many of these fascinating events have attracted the sustained attention of generations of historians; and I will try to make use of their insights as best I can. An even more formidable challenge will be to set each particular episode into the larger context of higher lawmaking—and thereby grasp the evolving constitutional process through which the separation of powers first forced the contending parties to refine their constitutional vision and counter-vision, then presented the key issues in dramatic form to a mobilized electorate, and then provided a further period during which thoughtful conservatives could consider whether the time had not come to recognize that the People had indeed spoken.

In elaborating these striking parallels between Reconstruction and the New Deal, I shall be building upon the insights of the protagonists of the 1930's. Time and again, the New Dealers invoked Reconstruction precedents in their efforts to build a modern model of Presidential leadership in the higher lawmaking process. The challenge is to *listen* to these voices, not insist upon viewing the New Deal reformers as if they were exhausted epigones, capable only of returning to the forgotten wisdom of the Founders.

D. THE CONSTITUTION'S PROMISE OF A "DELIBERATIVE DEMOCRACY"

CASS R. SUNSTEIN, A REPUBLIC OF REASONS
The Partial Constitution 18–34, 38–39 (1993).

MONARCHY, SELF-INTEREST, FACTIONS

The framers of the American Constitution sought to create a system of government that would simultaneously counteract three related dangers: the legacy of monarchy; self-interested representation by government officials; and the power of faction, or "majority tyranny." The impartiality principle was part of the attempt to respond to all these problems.

* * *

The impartiality principle is conspicuously connected with the desire, traceable to the early period of the founding, to limit the potential arbitrariness of the king and indeed of everything entailed by the institutions of monarchy. The Constitution should be understood against the backdrop set by prerevolutionary America, which had been pervaded by monarchial characteristics, including well-entrenched patterns of deference and hierarchy. In the prerevolutionary period, many of these patterns were attributed to nature itself. These included not merely the institution of slavery but also existing family structures, relations between employers and employees, occupational categories, education, the crucial concept of the gentleman, and of course the structures of government. Indeed, those very structures were thought to be modeled on the family and to grow out of the same natural sources.

A large element in the American Revolution consisted of a radical rebellion against the monarchical legacy. The rebellion operated with special force against the traditional belief in a "natural order of things." Thus the Americans insisted, in direct opposition to their English inheritance, that "culture" was "man-made." In America, social outcomes had to be justified not by reference to nature or to traditional practices, but instead on the basis of reasons.

The American framers were alert not only to the legacy of monarchy, but also to the general risk that public officials would act on behalf of their own self-interest rather than the interests of the public as a whole. Actual corruption in government was the most dramatic illustration of this danger. But self-interested representation could be found in many places in which officials seek to aggrandize their own powers and interests at the expense of the people as a whole. The responsibility of the public official was to put personal interest entirely to one side. The impartiality principle, requiring public officials to invoke public-regarding reasons on behalf of their actions, was a check on self-interested representation.

Finally, the framers sought to limit the power of self-interested private groups, or "factions," over governmental processes. For Madison, this was the greatest risk in America: "[I]n our Governments the real power lies in the majority of the Community, and the invasion of private rights is chiefly to be apprehended, not from acts of Government contrary to the sense of its constituents, but from acts in which the Government is the mere instrument of the major number of the constituents." [3] Hence majority rule was, for the framers, a highly ambiguous good. On their view, even an insistent majority should not have its way, if power was the only thing to be invoked on its behalf.

3. Madison to Jefferson, Oct. 17, 1788, in 11 J. Madison, *The Papers of James* *Madison* 298 (R. Rutland & C. Hobson eds. 1977).

It is relevant here that the framers operated in the light of their experiences under the Articles of Confederation. Under the Articles, powerful private groups appeared to dominate state and local government, obtaining measures that favored them but no one else, and that could be explained only by reference of private self-interest. The new Constitution was intended to limit this risk.

Above all, the American Constitution was designed to create a deliberative democracy. Under that system, public representatives were to be ultimately accountable to the people; but they would also be able to engage in a form of deliberation without domination through the influence of factions. A law based solely on the self-interest of private groups is the core violation of the deliberative ideal.

The minimal condition of deliberative democracy is a requirement of reasons for governmental action. We may thus understand the American Constitution as having established, for the first time, a republic of reasons. A republic of this sort is opposed equally to outcomes grounded on self-interest and to those based solely on "nature" or authority. Where the monarchical system saw government as an outgrowth of a given or natural order, the founding generation regarded it as "merely a legal man-made contrivance having little if any natural relationship to the family or to society." [5]

Founding Institutions

The general commitment to deliberative democracy, and the belief in a republic of reasons, echo throughout the founding period. In *The Federalist* No. 10—James Madison's most outstanding contribution to political thought—the system of national representation is defended as a mechanism with which to "refine and enlarge the public views by passing them through the medium of a chosen body of citizens, whose wisdom may discern the true interest of their country and whose patriotism and love of justice will be least likely to sacrifice it to temporary or partial considerations." On this view, national officials, selected from a broad territory, would be uniquely positioned to operate above the fray of private interests.

In their aspirations for deliberative government, the framers modernized the classical republican belief in civic virtue. The antifederalists, critics of the proposed Constitution, had invoked traditional republican ideas in order to challenge the Madisonian belief that a large territory was compatible with true republicanism. In the antifederalist view, a genuine republic required civic virtue, or commitment to the public good. Civic virtue, they insisted, could flourish only in small communities united by similar interests and by a large degree of homogeneity.

The framers fully accepted the goal; but they firmly rejected the prescription. For the framers, as for those in the classical tradition, virtue was indispensable; and the framers continued to understand

---

5. Gordon Wood, *The Radicalism of the American Republic* 167 (1992).

virtue as a commitment to the general good rather than to self-interest or the interest of private factions. Thus Hamilton urged that the "aim of every political constitution is, or ought to be, first to obtain for rulers men who possess most wisdom to discern, and most virtue to pursue the common good of the society; and in the next place, to take the most effectual precautions for keeping them virtuous whilst they continue to hold their public trust." [7] But for the framers, a large republic would be more, rather than less, likely to serve republican aspirations. It would do so precisely because in a large republic, national representatives would be in an unusually good position to engage in the deliberative tasks of government. A small republic, as history had shown, would be buffeted about by the play of factions. In a large republic, the various factions would offset each other.

In recent years, there has been an extraordinary revival of interest in republican thought. The revival is directed above all against two groups: people who think that the Constitution is designed only to protect a set of identified "private rights," and people who treat the document as an effort to provide the rules for interest-group struggles among selfish private groups.

The framers' aspirations were far broader. They attempted to carry forward the classical republican belief in virtue—a word that appears throughout the period—but to do so in a way that responded realistically, not romantically, to likely difficulties in the real world of political life. They continued to insist on the possibility of a virtuous politics. They tried to make a government that would create such a politics without indulging unrealistic assumptions about human nature. We might understand the Constitution as a complex set of precommitment strategies, through which the citizenry creates institutional arrangements to protect against political self-interest, factionalism, failures in representation, myopia, and other predictable problems in democratic governance.

The commitment to these ideas explains many of the founding institutions. It helps explain why, in the original system, the Senate and the President were to be chosen by deliberative representatives rather than directly elected by the people. It helps with the mystery of the Electoral College, which was, at the inception, to be a deliberative body, one that would discuss who ought to be President, rather than simply register votes. It helps explain why the framers favored long terms of service and large election districts. All these ideas about government structure were designed to accomplish the same goals, that is, to promote deliberation and to limit the risk that public officials would be mouthpieces for constituent interests. It was in this vein that Madison attacked Congress in 1787 as "advocates for the respective interests of their constituents" and complained of "the County representatives, the members of which are everywhere observed to lose sight of the aggregate interests of the Community, and even to sacrifice them to

---

7. *The Federalist* No. 63.

the interests or prejudices of their respective constituents." [10]   The new Constitution was designed to reduce this risk.   The framers designed a system in which representatives would have the time and temperament to engage in a form of collective reasoning.

These general aspirations also explain two of the crucial decisions in the early period: the rejection of the "right to instruct" and the closing from public view of the Constitutional Convention.   In the first Congress, the representatives rejected a proposal to give citizens, as part of the Bill of Rights, a "right to instruct" their officials.   A right to instruct was thought to be inconsistent with the point of meeting, which was deliberation.   Roger Sherman's statement was especially clear: "[T]he words are calculated to mislead the people, by conveying an idea that they have a right to control the debates of the Legislature.   This cannot be admitted to be just, because it would destroy the object of their meeting.   I think, *when the people have chosen a representative, it is his duty to meet others from the different parts of the Union, and consult, and agree with them to such acts as are for the general benefit of the whole community.   If they were to be guided by instructions, there would be no use in deliberation * * *.*" [11]

The point casts light as well on the closing of the Constitutional Convention, a decision that Jefferson denounced as an "abominable * * * precedent" based on "ignorance of the value of public discussions." [12]   On Madison's view, it was best "to sit with closed doors, because opinions were so various and at first so crude that it was necessary they should be long debated before any uniform system of opinion could be formed.   Meantime the minds of the members were changing, and much was to be gained by a yielding and accommodating spirit.   * * * [B]y secret discussion no man felt himself obliged to retain his opinions any longer than he was satisfied of their propriety and truth, and was open to the force of argument." [13]

These remarks about the right to instruct and the closing of the convention are extremely revealing.   Above all, they show an important feature of political deliberation as it was originally understood.   In the process of discussion, there is no effort simply to aggregate existing private preferences, or to treat them as a given.   Representatives should not mechanically translate the desires of their constituents into law.   Nor should they treat their own beliefs and desires as fixed.   The point of the process is not only to protect a given category of rights.   Those involved in the process should always maintain "a yielding and accommodating spirit."

10. Letter to Jefferson, Oct. 3, 1785, reprinted in 8 *The Papers of James Madison* 374 (Robert Rutland & William Rachal eds. 1975); Remarks on Mr. Jefferson's Draft of a Constitution, in *The Mind of the Founder* 35 (Marvin Meyers rev. ed. 1981).

11. 1 *Annals of Cong.* 733–745 (Joseph Gales ed. 1789) (emphasis added).

12. Letter from Jefferson to John Adams, Aug. 1, 1787, reprinted in 1 *The Adams–Jefferson Letters* 194, 196 (Lester J. Cappon ed. 1959).

13. 3 Max Farrand, *The Records of the Federal Convention of 1787,* 479 (1911).

Even desires, or current beliefs about what courses of action are best, should not be frozen. The framers insisted that existing views might be a product of partial perspectives, of limited experience, or of incomplete information. People engaged in democratic discussion should thus "meet others from the different parts of the Union, and consult." People should be "open to the force of argument." They should be prepared to give up their initial views when shown "the general benefit of the whole community."

The basic institutions of the resulting Constitution were intended to encourage and to profit from deliberation, thus understood. The system of checks and balances—the cornerstone of the system—was designed to encourage discussion among different governmental entities. So too with the requirement of bicameralism, which would bring different perspectives to bear on lawmaking. The same goals accounted for the notion that laws should be presented to the President for his signature or veto; this mechanism would provide an additional perspective. The federal system would ensure a supplemental form of dialogue, here between states and the national government.

Judicial review was intended to create a further check. Its basic purpose was to protect the considered judgments of the people, as represented in the extraordinary law of the Constitution, against the ill-considered or short-term considerations introduced by the people's mere agents in the course of enacting ordinary law. As we will see, many of the original individual rights can be understood as part of the idea of deliberative democracy. Indeed, the goals of protecting rights and of promoting deliberation were understood to march hand in hand. The special status of property rights was an effort to ensure against precipitous, short-sighted, or ill-considered intrusions into the private sphere. Deliberative government and limited government were, in the framers' view, one and the same.

I have said that the framers' belief in deliberative democracy drew from traditional republican thought, and that it departed from the tradition in the insistence that a large republic would be better than a small one. It departed even more dramatically in its striking and novel rejection of the traditional republican idea that heterogeneity and difference were destructive to the deliberative process. For the framers, heterogeneity was beneficial, indeed indispensable; discussion must take place among people who were different. It was on this score that the framers responded to the antifederalist insistence that homogeneity was necessary to a republic.

Drawing on the classical tradition, the antifederalist "Brutus," complaining of the theory behind the proposed nationalist Constitution, wrote, "In a republic, the manners, sentiments, and interests of the people should be similar. If this be not the case, there will be a constant clashing of opinions; and the representatives of one part will be continually striving against those of the other." [16] Hamilton, by contrast,

16. 2 *The Complete Antifederalist* 369
(Herbert Storing ed. 1980).

thought that heterogeneity, as part of the deliberative process, could be a creative and productive force.   Thus he suggested that the "differences of opinion, and the jarrings of parties in [the legislative] department * * * often promote deliberation * * *." [17]   As the framers saw it, the exchange of reasons in the public sphere was a condition for this process.

IMPARTIALITY, THE REPUBLIC OF REASONS, AND INTEREST-GROUP PLURALISM

Read against this background, the principle of impartiality requires government to provide reasons that can be intelligible to different people operating from different premises.   The requirement might be understood in this respect as a check on government by fiat, helping to bar authoritarianism generally.   Drawing from our founding aspirations, we might even define authoritarian systems as all those that justify government outcomes by reference to power or will rather than by reference to reasons.   At the heart of the liberal tradition and its opposition to authoritarianism lies a requirement of justification by reference to public-regarding explanations that are intelligible to all citizens.   The principle of impartiality is the concrete manifestation of this commitment in American constitutional law.

Described in this way, the impartiality requirement might seem trivial and therefore uncontroversial.   But the requirement turns out to be in severe tension with one of the most influential approaches to both modern government and American constitutionalism: interest-group pluralism.   There are many different forms of pluralism, but the unifying pluralist claim is that laws should be understood not as a product of deliberation, but on the contrary as a kind of commodity, subject to the usual forces of supply and demand.   Various groups in society compete for loyalty and support from the citizenry.   Once groups are organized and aligned, they exert pressure on political representatives, also self-interested, who respond to the pressures thus imposed.   This process of aggregating and trading off interests ultimately produces law, or political equilibrium.

Whether pluralist ideas accurately describe current American politics is a subject of much dispute.   There can be little doubt that the American framers were not pluralists.   Some people also think that contemporary real-world government outcomes actually reflect reasons and justifications, and that those outcomes diverge from legislative and constituent self-interest (unless the concept of self-interest is understood so broadly as to be trivialized—as in the idea that altruism reflects self-interest, because altruists are interested in altruism).   As we will see, interest-group pluralism is not an attractive political ideal.   But if interest-group pluralism does describe contemporary politics, a requirement of impartiality, understood as a call for public-regarding justifications for government outcomes, is inconsistent with the very nature of government.   It imposes on politics a requirement that simply cannot be met.

17.   *The Federalist* No. 70.

In the discussion to follow, I explore the relationship between the principle of impartiality and contemporary constitutional law. I show the extraordinary persistence of the principle across many generations and many constitutional provisions. I do not defend the requirement here; my purpose is descriptive. I claim only that the antiauthoritarian impulse, understood as a requirement of reasons, lies at the heart of American constitutional law.

THE BAN ON NAKED PREFERENCES

Judicial interpretation of many of the most important clauses of the Constitution reveals a remarkably common theme. Although the clauses have different historical roots and were originally directed at different problems, they appear to be united by a concern with a single underlying evil: the distribution of resources or opportunities to one group rather than to another solely on the ground that those favored have exercised the raw political power to obtain what they want. I will call this underlying evil—a violation of the impartiality requirement—a *naked preference*.

The commerce clause, for example, allows one state to discriminate against commerce from another state only if that discrimination is a means of promoting some goal unrelated to helping self-interested insiders. The privileges and immunities clause prohibits a state from preferring its citizens over outsiders, unless the preference is supported by reasons independent of protecting the insiders. The equal protection clause permits laws treating two classes of people differently only if there is a good connection between the distinctions and legitimate public purposes. The due process clause requires all government action to be justified by reference to some public purpose. The contract clause allows government to break or modify a contract only if the action is intended to promote a general public goal and does not reflect mere interest-group power. The eminent domain clause protects private property against self-interested private groups, both by demanding that a "public use" be shown to justify a taking of private property and by distinguishing between permissible exercises of the government power and prohibited takings.

The prohibition of naked preferences therefore underlies a wide range of constitutional provisions. The prohibition is connected with the original idea that government must be responsive to something other than private pressure, and with the associated notion that politics is not the reconciling of given interests but instead the product of some form of deliberation about the public good. As it operates in current constitutional law, the prohibition of naked preferences—like Madison's approach to the problem of factionalism—focuses on the motivations of legislators, not of their constituents. The prohibition therefore embodies a particular conception of representation. Under that conception, the task of legislators is not to respond to private pressure but instead to select values through deliberation and debate.

The notion that governmental action must be grounded in something other than political power is of course at odds with pluralism. Naked preferences are common fare in the pluralist conception; interest-group politics invites them. The prohibition of naked preferences stands as a repudiation of theories claiming that the judicial role is only to police the processes of representation to ensure that all affected interest groups may participate. In this respect, the prohibition of naked preferences reflects a distinctly substantive value and cannot easily be captured in procedural terms. Above all, it presupposes that constitutional courts will serve as critics of the pluralist vision, not as adherents striving only to "clear the channels" for political struggle.[23] And if a judicial role seems odd here, we should recall that the founding generation itself regarded courts as an important repository for representation and preservation of republican virtue, standing above the play of interests.

The Basic Framework

We might distinguish between two bases for treating one group or person differently from another. The first is a naked preference. For example, state A may treat its own citizens better than those of state B—say, by requiring people of state B to pay for the use of the public parks in state A—simply because its own citizens have the political power and want better treatment. Or a city may treat blacks worse than whites—say, by denying them necessary police and fire protection—because whites have the power to restrict government benefits to themselves. In these examples, the political process is a mechanism by which self-interested individuals or groups seek to obtain wealth or opportunities at the expense of others. The task of the legislator is to respond to the pressures imposed by those interests.

Contrast with this a political process in which outcomes are justified by reference not to raw political power, but to some public value that they can be said to serve. For the moment we can define a public value extremely broadly, as any justification for government action that goes beyond the exercise of raw political power. (I describe later how the Constitution limits permissible public values.) For example, a state may relieve a group of people from a contractual obligation because the contract called for an act—say, the sale of heroin—that violated a public policy. Or state A may treat its own citizens better than those of state B—say, by limiting welfare payments to its own citizens—because it wants to restrict social spending to those who in the past have made, or in the future might make, a contribution to state revenues. In these examples, the role of the representative is to deliberate rather than to respond mechanically to constituent pressures. If an individual or group is to be treated differently from others, it must be for a reason that can be stated in public-regarding terms.

---

23. On this question, the influential treatment in John Hart Ely, *Democracy and* *Distrust* (1980), is untrue to the original constitutional structure or to current law.

These competing portraits of the political process are of course caricatures of a complex reality. It is rare that government action is based purely on raw political power. Losers in the political process may have lost for a very good reason that has little to do with the power of their adversaries. Belief that an action will promote at least some conception of the public good almost always plays at least some role in government decisions. Sometimes people motivated to vote for certain legislation cannot easily disentangle the private and public factors that underlie the decision.

It is also rare for government action to be based on a disembodied effort to discern and implement public values, entirely apart from considerations of private pressure. Representatives are almost always aware of the fact that their vote will have electoral consequences. What emerges is therefore a continuum of government decisions, ranging from those that are motivated primarily by interest-group pressures to those in which such pressures play a very minor role. In any particular case, it may well be difficult to see which of these is dominant. But the occasional or even frequent difficulty should not be taken to obscure the existence of a real distinction. There is all the difference in the world between a system in which representatives try to offer some justification for their decisions, and a system in which political power is the only thing that is at work.

If naked preferences are a legitimate basis for government action, it is sufficient that a particular group has been able to assemble the political power to obtain what it seeks. Might makes right. If naked preferences are forbidden, however, and the state is forced to invoke some public value to justify its conduct, government behavior becomes constrained. The extent of the constraint will depend on two considerations. The first involves the content of the public values that courts will accept as a legitimate basis for government action. The constraint would be strengthened if, for example, the government were barred from relying on disfavored ideas about women or members of minority groups.

The second consideration relates to the devices developed to ensure that public values do in fact account for legislation. If courts are willing to make up a public value as the basis for government action, and if they do not require a close fit between the public value and the measure under review, all or almost all government action will be upheld. By contrast, if courts require a good reason to believe that a naked preference was not at work, many laws will be invalidated.

Let us assume that the content of public values is subject to no limitations and that courts do not carefully scrutinize either the process or the outcome to ensure that a public value was at work. These assumptions generate a "weak version" of the prohibition of naked preferences. The weak version places only a trivial constraint on government action, for it is nearly always possible to justify an action on grounds other than the raw exercise of political power. For example, the Court has upheld a statute prohibiting opticians, but not ophthalmologists, from selling eyeglasses on the ground that the prohibition protected consumers from fraud and deception.[25]　In the circumstances of the case, the justification looked specious.　The statute was far more plausibly understood as a reflection of the political power of well-organized ophthalmologists.

But because the weak version does require some justification that goes beyond raw political power, it cannot be dismissed as entirely meaningless.　It forces those who seek to obtain government assistance to invoke some justification as a basis for assistance.　In so doing, even the weak version strikes familiar constitutional chords.　By requiring that some reason justify the exercise of governmental power, it acts as a check on the tyranny of factionalism—a core Madisonian evil.　The weak version also reflects the idea that the role of government is to engage in a form of deliberation about governing values rather than to implement or trade off preexisting private interests.　On this view, the fact that a majority is in favor of a particular measure is not, standing alone, a sufficient reason for it.

The weak version accounts for much of modern constitutional law. So-called rationality review is the prime example.　Courts have interpreted the due process and equal protection clauses to impose a requirement that government action be "rational."　This requirement simply means that public measures must be a minimally reasonable effort to promote some public value.　Modern rationality review is characterized by two principal features.　First, the category of legitimate ends is extremely broad.　Second, the Supreme Court demands only the weakest link between a public value and the measure in question, and it is sometimes willing to hypothesize legitimate ends not realistically motivating to the legislature.　As a result, few statutes fail rationality review.

As described thus far, the weak version is minimal indeed.　One might, for example, support preferential treatment of the poor on the ground that they have a special need for assistance; preferential treatment of the rich might be justified as an incentive for more work and investment.　Everything, in short, is potentially lawful.　To develop a more vigorous set of constraints on government, it is necessary to go beyond the weak version described thus far.

The constitutional text, read in light of its history, unambiguously provides a few—but only a few—of the elements of a more robust set of constraints.　Under the privileges and immunities and commerce clauses, a preference for in-staters at the expense of out-of-staters is impermissible.　Under the equal protection clause, the same is true for discrimination against blacks.　As a constitutional matter, both out-of-staters and blacks are entitled to special protection from discrimination; discrimination against either group cannot be understood as a public value.

25. Williamson v. Lee Optical, 348 U.S. 483 (1955).

Even within this narrow area of protectionism and discrimination against blacks, however, the Constitution is ambiguous. What if a state justifies discrimination against out-of-staters on the ground that they have been the main factor contributing to in-state unemployment, or discrimination against blacks on the ground that, when blacks are jailed with whites, the likelihood of violence is dramatically increased? Outside these areas, the inquiry is even more open-ended. In such cases, how do courts enforce the prohibition of naked preferences? In answering this question, two devices have been of special importance.

Heightened Scrutiny

The first device involves careful judicial review of governmental claims that a public value is being served by the measure under review. When courts apply "heightened scrutiny," they examine with unusual suspicion a government's argument that a public value motivates its actions. Here we see active judicial policing of politics in the interest of deliberative democracy.

Heightened scrutiny involves two principal elements. The first is a requirement that the government show a close connection between the asserted justification and the means that the legislature has chosen to promote it. If a sufficiently close connection cannot be shown, there is reason for skepticism that the asserted value in fact accounted for the legislation. The second element is a search for less restrictive alternatives—ways in which the government could have promoted the public value without harming the group or interest in question. The availability of such alternatives also suggests that the public value justification is a facade.

Heightened scrutiny is triggered by a concern that in the circumstances it is especially likely that the measure under review reflects a naked preference. The most familiar example is review of racial discrimination under the equal protection clause. Review of statutes that discriminate against noncitizens under the privileges and immunities clause falls into the same category. In both cases, heightened scrutiny is justified by a perception that the groups in question lack the political power to protect themselves against factional tyranny.

By contrast, more lenient scrutiny—typified by rationality review—reflects a strong presumption that a public value is at work. That presumption is conventionally supported by reference to considerations of judicial competence and legitimacy. The underlying idea is, first, that courts lack the capacity to review the factual determinations of other branches of government and, second, that vigorous judicial scrutiny would be inconsistent with the constitutional commitment to representative democracy.

Theory of Impermissible Ends

A second device in a more rigorous version of the prohibition on naked preferences consists of theories designed to distinguish between legitimate and illegitimate bases for government action. The courts attempt to root such theories in the text or history of the Constitution. Such an approach could of course accommodate a wide range of ideas about what government may do. * * * Modern equal protection doctrine reflects the development of [one] such theory: courts have come to refuse to recognize government ends that involve the subordination of women, aliens, illegitimates, and members of racial minority groups. * * *

* * *

The equal protection clause, part of the Fourteenth Amendment, forbids a state to deny to any person "the equal protection of the laws." The clause is not concerned solely with the special case of discrimination between in-staters and out-of-staters. Its prohibition is far broader. Indeed, in many respects the clause may be understood as a generalization of the central concerns of the dormant commerce and privileges and immunities clauses, applying to all classifications their prohibition of naked preferences at the behest of in-staters. In this way, the basic requirement of impartiality is applied to everything.

Disadvantaged groups, impermissible ends, and heightened scrutiny. Discrimination against blacks, the central evil at which the clause was aimed, is the equal protection analogue of discrimination against out-of-staters under the commerce and privileges and immunities clauses. When a statute discriminates on its face against blacks, the Court applies a strong presumption of invalidity. One reason for heightened scrutiny is a belief that when a statute discriminates on its face against members of racial minority groups, a naked preference is almost certainly at work. Here a familiar idea—the relative political powerlessness of members of minority groups—helps to account for that belief. The central notion is that the ordinary avenues of political redress are much less likely to be available to minorities. The danger that such statutes will result from an exercise of (what is seen as) raw political power is correspondingly increased.

Current equal protection law also treats a number of government ends as impermissible. Notably, these prohibited ends involve a wide range of justifications that do not involve the exercise of raw political power in the ordinary sense. The point becomes clearest in cases involving classifications drawn on the basis of gender, alienage, and legitimacy. For example, when a statute provides that the spouses of male workers automatically qualify for social security benefits, but that spouses of female workers must show dependency, the classification hardly reflects an exercise of raw political power—narrowly understood—but instead embodies certain conceptions about the nature of female participation in the labor market. Invalidation of such statutes cannot be explained only on the basis of the minimal requirement that classifications rest on something other than raw power. Although the Court has not provided a clear rationale for its decisions here, the central ideas seem to be that the relevant groups are politically weak and that the traditional justifications for discrimination both reflect and perpetuate existing injustice.

* * *

[T]here can be no question that current legal doctrines reject interest-group pluralism as a constitutional creed. They point instead to a conception of politics that demands a measure of deliberation from government representatives, deliberation that has some autonomy from private pressures. Many provisions of the Constitution are thus aimed at a single evil: the distribution of resources to one person or group rather than to another on the sole ground that those benefited have exercised political power in order to obtain government assistance.

To be sure, the prohibition rarely results in invalidation. But the cases are strikingly unanimous in their version of the prohibited end. In this way, the impartiality principle lies at the core of American constitutional law.

E. CRITICAL PERSPECTIVES

THURGOOD MARSHALL, REFLECTIONS ON THE BICENTENNIAL OF THE UNITED STATES CONSTITUTION
101 Harv.L.Rev. 1, 1–5 (1987).

The year 1987 marks the 200th anniversary of the United States Constitution. A Commission has been established to coordinate the celebration. The official meetings, essay contests, and festivities have begun.

The planned commemoration will span three years, and I am told 1987 is "dedicated to the memory of the Founders and the document they drafted in Philadelphia."[1] We are to "recall the achievements of our Founders and the knowledge and experience that inspired them, the nature of the government they established, its origins, its character, and its ends, and the rights and privileges of citizenship, as well as its attendant responsibilities."[2]

Like many anniversary celebrations, the plan for 1987 takes particular events and holds them up as the source of all the very best that has followed. Patriotic feelings will surely swell, prompting proud proclamations of the wisdom, foresight, and sense of justice shared by the framers and reflected in a written document now yellowed with age. This is unfortunate—not the patriotism itself, but the tendency for the celebration to oversimplify, and overlook the many other events that have been instrumental to our achievements as a nation. The focus of this celebra-

---

1. Commission on the Bicentennial of the United States Constitution, Preparation for a Commemoration: First Full Year's Report 6 (Sept. 1986).

2. Commission on the Bicentennial of the United States Constitution, First Report 6 (Sept. 17, 1985).

tion invites a complacent belief that the vision of those who debated and compromised in Philadelphia yielded the "more perfect Union" it is said we now enjoy.

I cannot accept this invitation, for I do not believe that the meaning of the Constitution was forever "fixed" at the Philadelphia Convention. Nor do I find the wisdom, foresight, and sense of justice exhibited by the framers particularly profound. To the contrary, the government they devised was defective from the start, requiring several amendments, a civil war, and momentous social transformation to attain the system of constitutional government, and its respect for the individual freedoms and human rights, that we hold as fundamental today. When contemporary Americans cite "The Constitution," they invoke a concept that is vastly different from what the framers barely began to construct two centuries ago.

For a sense of the evolving nature of the Constitution we need look no further than the first three words of the document's preamble: "We the People." When the Founding Fathers used this phrase in 1787, they did not have in mind the majority of America's citizens. "We the People" included, in the words of the framers, "the whole Number of free Persons." [3] On a matter so basic as the right to vote, for example, Negro slaves were excluded, although they were counted for representational purposes—at three-fifths each. Women did not gain the right to vote for over a hundred and thirty years. [4]

These omissions were intentional. The record of the framers' debates on the slave question is especially clear: the Southern states acceded to the demands of the New England states for giving Congress broad power to regulate commerce, in exchange for the right to continue the slave trade. The economic interests of the regions coalesced: New Englanders engaged in the "carrying trade" would profit from transporting slaves from Africa as well as goods produced in America by slave labor. The perpetuation of slavery ensured the primary source of wealth in the Southern states.

Despite this clear understanding of the role slavery would play in the new republic, use of the words "slaves" and "slavery" was carefully avoided in the original document. Political representation in the lower House of Congress was to be based on the population of "free Persons" in each state, plus three-fifths of all "other Persons." [5] Moral principles against slavery, for those who had them, were compromised, with no explanation of the conflicting principles for which the American Revolutionary War had ostensibly been fought: the self-evident truths "that all men are created equal, that they are endowed by their Creator with certain unalienable Rights, that among these are Life, Liberty and the pursuit of Happiness."

3. U.S. Const. art. I, § 2, cl. 3.   5. *Id.* art. I, § 2, cl. 3.
4. *See id.* amend. XIX (ratified in 1920).

It was not the first such compromise. Even these ringing phrases from the Declaration of Independence are filled with irony, for an early draft of what became that declaration assailed the King of England for suppressing legislative attempts to end the slave trade and for encouraging slave rebellions. The final draft adopted in 1776 did not contain this criticism. And so again at the Constitutional Convention eloquent objections to the institution of slavery went unheeded, and its opponents eventually consented to a document which laid a foundation for the tragic events that were to follow.

Pennsylvania's Gouverneur Morris provides an example. He opposed slavery and the counting of slaves in determining the basis for representation in Congress. At the Convention he objected that

> the inhabitant of Georgia [or] South Carolina who goes to the coast of Africa, and in defiance of the most sacred laws of humanity tears away his fellow creatures from their dearest connections and damns them to the most cruel bondages, shall have more votes in a Government instituted for protection of the rights of mankind, than the Citizen of Pennsylvania or New Jersey who views with a laudable horror, so nefarious a practice.[8]

And yet Gouverneur Morris eventually accepted the three-fifths accommodation. In fact, he wrote the final draft of the Constitution, the very document the bicentennial will commemorate.

As a result of compromise, the right of the Southern states to continue importing slaves was extended, officially, at least until 1808. We know that it actually lasted a good deal longer, as the framers possessed no monopoly on the ability to trade moral principles for self-interest. But they nevertheless set an unfortunate example. Slaves could be imported, if the commercial interests of the North were protected. To make the compromise even more palatable, customs duties would be imposed at up to ten dollars per slave as a means of raising public revenues.[9]

No doubt it will be said, when the unpleasant truth of the history of slavery in America is mentioned during this bicentennial year, that the Constitution was a product of its times, and embodied a compromise which, under other circumstances, would not have been made. But the effects of the framers' compromise have remained for generations. They arose from the contradiction between guaranteeing liberty and justice to all, and denying both to Negroes.

The original intent of the phrase, "We the People," was far too clear for any ameliorating construction. Writing for the Supreme Court in 1857, Chief Justice Taney penned the following passage in the *Dred Scott* case,[10] on the issue of whether, in the eyes of the framers, slaves were

---

8. The Records of the Federal Convention of 1787, at 222 (M. Farrand rev. ed. 1966).

9. U.S. Const. art. I, § 9, cl. 1.

10. Dred Scott v. Sandford, 60 U.S. (19 How.) 393 (1857).

"constituent members of the sovereignty," and were to be included among "We the People":

> We think they are not, and that they are not included, and were not intended to be included * * *.
>
>   * * *
>
> They had for more than a century before been regarded as beings of an inferior order, and altogether unfit to associate with the white race * * *; and so far inferior, that they had no rights which the white man was bound to respect; and that the negro might justly and lawfully be reduced to slavery for his benefit * * *.
>
>   * * *
>
> * * * [A]ccordingly, a negro of the African race was regarded * * * as an article of property, and held, and bought and sold as such * * *. [N]o one seems to have doubted the correctness of the prevailing opinion of the time.[11]

And so, nearly seven decades after the Constitutional Convention, the Supreme Court reaffirmed the prevailing opinion of the framers regarding the rights of Negroes in America. It took a bloody civil war before the thirteenth amendment could be adopted to abolish slavery, though not the consequences slavery would have for future Americans.

While the Union survived the civil war, the Constitution did not. In its place arose a new, more promising basis for justice and equality, the fourteenth amendment, ensuring protection of the life, liberty, and property of *all* persons against deprivations without due process, and guaranteeing equal protection of the laws. And yet almost another century would pass before any significant recognition was obtained of the rights of black Americans to share equally even in such basic opportunities as education, housing, and employment, and to have their votes counted, and counted equally. In the meantime, blacks joined America's military to fight its wars and invested untold hours working in its factories and on its farms, contributing to the development of this country's magnificent wealth and waiting to share in its prosperity.

What is striking is the role legal principles have played throughout America's history in determining the condition of Negroes. They were enslaved by law, emancipated by law, disenfranchised and segregated by law; and, finally, they have begun to win equality by law. Along the way, new constitutional principles have emerged to meet the challenges of a changing society. The progress has been dramatic, and it will continue.

The men who gathered in Philadelphia in 1787 could not have envisioned these changes. They could not have imagined, nor would they have accepted, that the document they were drafting would one day be construed by a Supreme Court to which had been appointed a woman and the descendent of an African slave. "We the People" no longer

---

11. *Id.* at 405, 407–08.

enslave, but the credit does not belong to the framers. It belongs to those who refused to acquiesce in outdated notions of "liberty," "justice," and "equality," and who strived to better them.

And so we must be careful, when focusing on the events which took place in Philadelphia two centuries ago, that we not overlook the momentous events which followed, and thereby lose our proper sense of perspective. Otherwise, the odds are that for many Americans the bicentennial celebration will be little more than a blind pilgrimage to the shrine of the original document now stored in a vault in the National Archives. If we seek, instead, a sensitive understanding of the Constitution's inherent defects, and its promising evolution through 200 years of history, the celebration of the "Miracle at Philadelphia" will, in my view, be a far more meaningful and humbling experience. We will see that the true miracle was not the birth of the Constitution, but its life, a life nurtured through two turbulent centuries of our own making, and a life embodying much good fortune that was not.

Thus, in this bicentennial year, we may not all participate in the festivities with flag-waving fervor. Some may more quietly commemorate the suffering, struggle, and sacrifice that has triumphed over much of what was wrong with the original document, and observe the anniversary with hopes not realized and promises not fulfilled. I plan to celebrate the bicentennial of the Constitution as a living document, including the Bill of Rights and the other amendments protecting individual freedoms and human rights.

RICHARD DAVIES PARKER, THE PAST OF CONSTITUTIONAL THEORY— AND ITS FUTURE

42 Ohio State L.Rev. 223, 240–46, 252–57 (1981).

This is an appeal to my generation. Specifically, this is an appeal to people in the "generation of the 1960s" who are now doing constitutional law. We are, as a group, in a better position today than we have been before or probably shall be again to think about how we want to do constitutional law. On one hand, still relatively new to the teaching or practice of the law, we can think about it free, for now, of self-imposed orthodoxy. On the other hand, by now more or less established, we are in a position to think for ourselves, free of orthodoxy imposed by others—if only we will.

My appeal is this: Our elders have brought constitutional theory to a crossroads. Out of their experience of life in our polity, they have conceived the problems of its constitution in their own way. As a generation, we have had a rather different experience of life in our polity. Therefore, it is given to us to conceive the problems of its constitution in a new way.

The books by Jesse Choper and John Ely [1] provide an occasion for my appeal. Both authors work with a constitutional theory—a "process-oriented" theory—that has dominated the field for a long time. Both work inside that theory, revising it in similar ways and, I believe, perfecting it. In so doing, they take us to the crossroads at which we confront our present choice. We may continue along the line that they have followed. Or we may turn in a new direction. Their books indicate, in my view, that further elaboration of their lines of speculation can only lead us into a fog. The reason is not that they speculate too much about the quality of the political process and too little about substantive values. Nor is it that their speculations are blindered by a focus on what the Court has already done. Nor is it that, hampered by a conventional theory, they cannot say anything new. Both of them innovate—indeed, Ely does so brilliantly. Rather, the reason is that, in doing it, they bring to the surface deeply rooted assumptions of conventional "process-oriented" theory that seem, or ought to seem, starkly implausible in light of the experience of our generation.

* * *

TENETS

Look carefully * * * at the two most basic, explicit tenets of the "process-oriented" conception of our political life as set forth by Choper and Ely. * * *

    (1) In operation, our process of representative democracy *normally functions well enough.*

        (a) Government decisionmakers, being responsible to the people at periodic elections, are *generally responsive* to the interests of majorities.

        (b) Majorities are not stable through time or across issues. They are *shifting coalitions* formed in a process of *basically fair and open competition among "minority" interests.*

        (c) Because majorities are shifting, government decisionmakers cannot afford completely to ignore minority interests on any particular issue for fear that those interests might be necessary to form a majority later. Thus, generally, they will *take all interests into fair account* with respect to particular decisions.

        (d) Individuals and groups generally can be counted on to *recognize and promote their own interests* through exercise of their voice and vote.

    (2) This process, though, is subject to *occasional, systemic malfunctions.*

        (a) Acting in their own self-interest, those "in" power may try to *restrict* the *voice and vote* of some of those who are "out"

---

1. J. Choper, Judicial Review and the National Political Process (1980) [hereinafter cited as Choper]; J. Ely, Democracy and Distrust (1980) [hereinafter cited as Ely].

of power, thereby distorting the process of fair interest competition.

(b) In cases of *majority prejudice against certain minorities,* the process of formation of shifting majority coalitions may be distorted. So, government decisionmakers may disregard or under-value the interests of such minorities.

Two things about these prescriptive-descriptive tenets stand out: our political process *works well enough as it is,* and it is given (only) to rather *discrete* sorts of malfunction. Now, look at how Choper and Ely justify their adherence to the tenets.

First, in assessing the normal functioning of the process, their standard for concluding that it works well enough turns out to be surprisingly low. For instance, Choper acknowledges that a great number of citizens do not vote, take no significant part in our political life (i.e., by using their "voice") and are "almost totally uninformed" on "both major questions of public policy and minor matters of detail."[67] Yet, according to Choper, that might not "be as incompatible with majority rule as it is made to sound." He weakly opines that "a great many" issues "do not concern large numbers of voters and probably should not."[68] By the same token, both authors acknowledge that legislatures very often are not responsive to majority coalitions seeking passage of new legislation or a repeal of old legislation. Politically effective minorities, they concede, often undermine representative democracy. But they insist that so long as such minorities can only block legislation—and not pass their own legislation without majority support—that is good enough.[69] Finally, Choper insists that the majority (of those who vote) can sometimes affect policies on "fundamental" issues in an election "if they feel strongly enough about them."[70] Still, as a day-to-day matter—when the mass of citizens do not "feel strongly enough," or are not well informed or simply do not take any significant part in political activity—Choper concedes that our political process works through the "Burkean trusteeship" of our representatives, informed by the influence of regularly active minority interest groups.[71] The "trusteeship," he notes, is constrained mainly by a fear that the usually passive, uninformed bulk of citizens might, *in extremis,* be driven to " 'outrage' " and, at long last, break form, wake up, and mobilize themselves for the next election.[72] Nonetheless, he maintains that this system does "comport with democracy, albeit somewhat murkily and imprecisely."[73] Despite "surface blemishes," he insists, there is an "unshrinking core of popular responsibility" in our political process.[74]

---

67. Choper, *supra* note 1, at 15.

68. *Id.* at 31.

69. *Id.* at 26–27; Ely, *supra* note 1, at 67.

70. Choper, *supra* note 1, at 30.

71. *Id.* at 31.

72. *Id.* at 33. *See* Ely, *supra* note 1, at 129.

73. Choper, *supra* note 1, at 45.

74. *Id.* at 48.

Contained in all of this, quite plainly, is a relatively simple assumption. The standard by which Choper and Ely determine the normal functioning of our political process to be good enough is not simply low. It is skewed against concern for potential majorities—the mass of people who are not now politically active and whose interests can be most routinely blocked by more effective interests. At bottom, both authors assume that our process of interest competition and representation works well enough even when the bulk of citizens take no very significant, regular part in it.

Turn, secondly, to their identification and discussion of instances in which the political process malfunctions. The sorts of instances they identify are, I have mentioned, fairly discrete. That follows from the tenet that in general the process functions adequately. But the instances of malfunctioning are not just discrete. They are also skewed. And, again, they are skewed against concern for potential majorities, who take no significant part in the process of political interest competition. Just as the routine non-participation of such citizens is not treated as detracting from the adequate functioning of the political process, so too it is not treated as an indication that the process is malfunctioning.

Choper and Ely do not see any indication of malfunctioning there because of another, related but deeper assumption. As they see it, people who are not minority victims of prejudice and have the opportunity to use their voice and vote, and yet take no part in our political life, do not have anything important to complain about from the standpoint of constitutional order. Such citizens presumably choose their own passivity; they may be satisfied with governmental decisions on the whole, or they may simply prefer to do other things with their time.[75] Presumably, such citizens can also "trust" government decisionmakers to take their interests into account and serve them adequately since perception of their interests is not distorted by majority prejudice.[76] These articles of faith of "process-oriented" theory are blind to the likelihood that the "choice" of political passivity by inactive citizens and service of their interests by the government may be significantly undermined by inequalities of power, wealth, status, and education. The fact is that the theory depends, at bottom, on the assumption that such inequalities afflicting the mass of citizens—not members of a "discrete and insular" minority—need not be taken into consideration for purposes of evaluating the functioning and malfunctioning of our system of representative democracy.

To give some idea of the controversialism and bias of this assumption, I shall note a few concerns that "process-orientation" should consider but does not. In order to avoid the usual charge that only "radicals" could regard it as an implausible assumption, I shall rely on

75. *See id.* at 30–31.

76. This notion would follow from the belief of both authors that officials tend to "disregard" only the interests of minority victims of prejudice.

the recent books by two "mainstream" scholars and sometime collaborators: Robert Dahl and Charles Lindblom.[77]

First of all, the "choice" by citizens to remain politically quiescent appears substantially less than "free." Dahl describes it in terms of a "cycle of defeat" by which "low resources," "weak political incentives," and "inadequate skills" reinforce each other.[78] "[O]f all the factors that social scientists have used to account for differences in political participation, *differences in social and economic status are the most important,*" he reports.[79] While "skills and incentives are to some extent independent of resources," he notes that "they do tend to run together in the United States."[80] And he adds:

> What is more, it must come as a shock to many Americans to learn that the effects on political participation of these differences in social and economic status appear to be greater in the United States than in other democracies. In one comparison, only in India were the differences in participation greater![81]

Yet such general barriers to political participation do not figure in the evaluation of our political life by Choper and Ely.

Second, the extent to which the inactive, less well-to-do citizens can count on government officials to give their interests "equal concern and respect" is open to substantial question. Dahl observes that "[t]hose who are better off participate more, and by participating more they exercise more influence on government officials."[82] And, as to those with lower resources, "[d]ecisions * * * are likely to be made, therefore, without taking their preferences into account."[83] Lindblom carries the point farther. He contends that business has a "privileged position" in our political process. Business interests, he asserts, are not simply capable of blocking a majority will; they are also assured of special treatment.[84] For Choper and Ely, none of this need be taken very seriously.

Choper does consider the role of interest groups in politics. He observes that there "is a sizable literature" on the problem—and cites a book published in 1951.[85] He says that "our knowledge" on the matter is "far from complete"—and cites a book published in 1963.[86] Citing an article also published in 1963—and a book published in 1928—he dons his rose-colored glasses and claims:

---

77. Dahl is one of the political scientists that Choper and Ely most like to cite. *See* Choper, *supra* note 1, at 488; Ely, *supra* note 1, at 264. And many of Dahl's ideas were developed with Lindblom in R. Dahl & C. Lindblom, Politics, Economics, and Welfare (1953). * * *

78. R. Dahl, Democracy in the United States 488 (3d ed. 1976).

79. *Id.* at 450.

80. *Id.* at 488.

81. *Id.* at 451.

82. *Id.* at 449.

83. *Id.* at 493.

84. C. Lindblom, Politics and Markets 170–200 (1977).

85. Choper, *supra* note 1, at 23.

86. *Id.*

the several studies undertaken suggest that the various interest groups tend to fill existing gaps—or serve as effective links—between voters and representatives, especially between elections; that legislators tend to respond initially by seeking to determine whether the urgings of pressure groups reflect a generally held constituent view, are opposed by a majority of their electorates, or involve a matter that is of no special concern to most of the voters in their district; and that the lawmakers then exercise that degree of judgment with which they feel empowered—but almost always with the next election in mind.[87]

He concludes by quoting Alexander Bickel's view—vintage 1962—that *"no one has claimed"* pressure groups are able to "capture" government without "combining in some fashion, and thus capturing or constituting * * * a majority."[88] Needless to say, such a claim *has* been made in the intervening eighteen years—for instance by Lindblom.[89] But Choper appears oblivious to the fact.[90] He does quote Dahl—from a book published in 1956—to the effect that the process of "minorities rule" works within a "consensus set by the important values of the politically active members of the society."[91] Yet he seems not to know (or perhaps care) about Dahl's more recent analysis of the effect of inequality on *which* members of society become "politically active."[92]

Third, if any one of the tenets of the "process-oriented" conception of our political process is the most fundamental, it is the tenet that citizens are able to recognize and articulate their own interests. They clearly will not have the capacity to promote their interests through political participation and thereby ensure that government officials take their interests into account unless they have that prior ability. Yet even this tenet is questionable if social and economic inequalities are considered. Dahl contends that "opportunities for discovering what one wants [and] for communicating to others what one wants" are impaired by inequalities in education.[93] And, once again, Lindblom goes farther. He explores a phenomenon of "circularity" in our political process. He argues that business interests "mold" the "volitions" of the mass of

---

87. *Id.* at 45.

88. *Id.* (emphasis added).

89. I shall stick with Dahl and Lindblom and resist offering a massive string citation of the literature Choper slights. But it may be worth noting that even introductory political science texts could be cited. *E.g.,* E. Greenberg, The American Political System (2d ed. 1980); M. Parenti, Democracy for the Few (3d ed. 1980). So could contemporary political science "classics." *E.g.,* H. Kariel, The Decline of American Pluralism (1961); T. Lowi, The End of Liberalism (1969); G. McConnell, Private Power and American Democracy (1966); E. Schattschneider, The Semi–Sovereign People (1960).

90. Perhaps I am being too hard on Choper here. After all, Ely is just about as

oblivious to noncentrist and/or recent political science writing. But the fact is that Choper, more than Ely, purports to rest his argument on political science research.

91. Choper, *supra* note 1, at 45.

92. For Dahl's even more recent writing on political inequality, *see* Dahl, *On Removing Certain Impediments to Democracy in the United States,* 92 Pol.Sci.Q. 1 (1977); Dahl, *Pluralism Revisited,* 10 Comp. Politics 191 (1978); Dahl, *What is Political Equality?,* Dissent 363 (Summer 1979); Dahl, *A Reply to Richard Krouse,* Dissent 456 (Fall 1980).

93. R. Dahl, Democracy in the United States 491 (3d ed. 1976).

citizens at least on "grand issues" of social and economic structure.[94] Ely does comment briefly on this question of "false consciousness." He recognizes that "sufficiently pervasive prejudice" against some minorities may distort their perceptions of their self-interests.[95] And, earlier, in dismissing "consensus" as a basis for identifying constitutional values, he entertains the view that a "consensus" is "likely to reflect only the domination of some groups by others." [96] But, when it comes to evaluating the functioning and malfunctioning of our political process, neither he nor Choper bothers to examine the likelihood that political interest competition is systemically distorted by a similar domination rooted in general social and economic inequalities.

In at least these three respects, then, process-oriented theory is oblivious to the effect that inequalities afflicting the bulk of quiescent citizens may have on the systemic quality of our political life—thus its bias against the interests of potential majorities. The malfunctions on which this theory focuses have to do, rather, with the concerns of "discrete and insular" minorities. Yet, even then, "process-oriented" theorists resist recognition of social and economic inequalities. Their resistance invites a last insight into the assumptions underlying the tenets of the theory.

Choper and Ely identify "discrete and insular" minorities—and thus political malfunctioning—strictly by searching for the existence of prejudice. They both believe that prejudice distorts the "empathy" that decisionmakers otherwise may feel for citizens.[97] But, if it is clear that prejudice is crucial in "process-oriented" theory, it has never been clear exactly what is supposed to be the root of prejudice, the malady that the theory, at bottom, is meant to address. Consequently, it has never been clear exactly what is supposed to be the cure for prejudice. Ely investigates the issue. He recognizes that merely affording a minority group access to the political process cannot, by itself, cure prejudice; so, he argues, the process may malfunction even if it is open to all minorities.[98] But, he says, there is a cure. The cure is "social intercourse." [99] And, he implies, the malady is a lack of such "social intercourse." If all minorities enjoyed both access to the political process and "social intercourse" with the rest of us, there would be no reason to be concerned any longer about any malfunctioning of the process. For, says Ely, "[t]he more we get to know people who are different in some ways, the more we will begin to appreciate the ways in which they are not, which is the beginning of political cooperation." [100]

94. C. Lindblom, Politics and Markets 201–13 (1977).

95. Ely, *supra* note 1, at 165.

96. *Id.* at 63.

97. *Id.* at 160–61; Choper, *supra* note 1, at 65.

98. Ely, *supra* note 1, at 151.

99. *Id.* at 161.

100. *Id.* The banal, sentimental character of this statement of Ely's central assumption contrasts curiously with the sharp, witty verbal pyrotechnics that run through less central portions of his argument.

Now, there is something peculiar about this. I would think that "social intercourse" is unlikely to cure prejudice so long as the parties concerned are substantially unequal in power or status. It is said, after all, that slave owners enjoyed close and regular association with their slaves. If Ely complains that that was not the *right kind* of "social intercourse," we are entitled to ask him: why not? Not long ago, it was said that if only whites and blacks were integrated, racial prejudice would disappear. Now, that view seems naîve. If Ely objects that, so far, integration has not produced the *right kind* of "social intercourse," we ought to ask: how so? If inequalities of power and status have something to do with it, why obfuscate them with vague talk of "social intercourse"?

It is possible, at this point, that Ely will concede that inequalities have a lot to do with it.[101] But the concession would discredit the theory. It would grant that prejudice is not really the most fundamental barrier to full participation in our politics by minority groups. It would grant that most minority groups are, roughly, in a position similar to that of the mass of nonminority citizens afflicted by inequalities—and hence that the theory is, at bottom, almost as oblivious to the plight of one as the other.

In other words, such a concession would entitle us to ask: If inequalities have a good deal to do with the malfunctioning of the political process vis-à-vis most "discrete and insular" minorities, is it not probable that inequalities afflicting other citizens also spoil the quality of our political life—and of our constitutional order? At that point, if I know "process-oriented" theory, Ely is unlikely to make any more concessions.

* * *

Apologetics

Now, we are in a position to figure out what to make of "process-oriented" constitutional theory. * * * One conclusion * * * cannot be avoided: the theory is the manifesto of one political faith. Whether we accept it turns, in the end, on whether we are adherents of that political faith.

What political faith? As perfected by Choper and Ely, the theory embodies the ideology of what, for some time, has amounted to the center in American politics. And so it enjoys the typical protective coloring of most centrist beliefs. It hardly seems to embody a political faith at all. Instead, urging the integration of minorities into the political process, it appears to represent nothing more and nothing less than "sound judgment and good sense." When closely examined, however, it turns out, also, to be an exercise in apologetics. Proceeding from the conventional assumption that our polity may sometimes malfunction, but is otherwise basically sound, it obscures our biased, withered politics in a fog of apologetic rhetoric. It consecrates the domination of our

101. *See id.* at 135.

polity by the politically effective few and the reduction of the rest to more or less passive consumers of the ministrations of government. The theory represents, at bottom, the fundamental political faith of the administrators of our enlightened, liberal welfare state.

The language of "process-oriented" theory is primarily a language of democracy—which is to say, a language of political equality, political freedom, and popular sovereignty. This is the language Choper and Ely use to urge marginal, although undeniably important, reforms of our political process. Yet this too is the language with which they praise the process. In their hands, the rhetoric of democracy serves to shield the political process from being held very rigorously to account to the ideals of democracy.

Consider, first, the "process-oriented" definition of the central problem of constitutional law: majority rule. And notice that, as "process-oriented" theorists see it, the central problem is not *whether* a majority of citizens (actually) rules, but *that* a majority of citizens (supposedly) rules. Thus, the primary worry of such theorists—the concern around which their theory pivots—is that "majorities" may disregard or undervalue the interests of "minorities." If they even acknowledge the opposite concern—that powerful minorities can get the state to act in ways that disregard or undervalue interests of nonmobilized majorities and that, in any event, legislative majorities often fail to champion the interests of passive popular majorities—they tend abruptly to dismiss it. They do not dignify it with serious consideration. Choper offers brief, bland assurances that majorities do, in fact, "rule."[122] Ely puts down the opposite view with a flippant crack.[123] To them, majority rule is not a democratic ideal against which to measure our polity. Rather, it is something to be taken as given. It is the stuff of a rhetoric, suffusing their theory, with which they consecrate our polity as already fundamentally majoritarian.

Consider, next, the language they employ to depict the process by which majorities (supposedly) are formed. Choper and Ely agree that, with its political "channels" kept "unclogged" or "cleared," with the right to "voice and vote" fully guaranteed, the process is a "democratic" one.[124] They both invoke the language of political equality to portray that process. Choper equates protection of "voice and vote" with "affording *all* participants in the democratic process a full and fair opportunity to influence the promulgation and alteration of policies affecting them."[125] And Ely describes such protection as insurance that the process is "open to those of *all* viewpoints on something approaching an *equal* basis."[126] As I have already shown, however, both of them are blind to the real world of political inequality. They may well be aware

---

122. Choper, *supra* note 1, at 44–45.

123. Ely, *supra* note 1, at 130 n. *.

124. Of course, they insist on more than just "open channels"; but the mere "openness" of the channels counts for them as "democracy."

125. Choper, *supra* note 1, at 71 (emphasis added).

126. Ely, *supra* note 1, at 74 (emphasis added).

that, in the view of many political scientists, it confuses the concept of "democracy" to apply it to a polity in which the resources crucial for effective participation are so unequally distributed. But neither of them deems it necessary to so much as mention that view. For them, the reality of political inequality and the conditions for effective participation are not of much importance—because, for them, the talk about political equality and "democracy" serves an essentially rhetorical purpose, not to critique the political process but to depict it as in need only of marginal reform.

Consider, finally, the main sort of reform they urge and the way they advocate it. Here, I must focus on Ely since Choper only adumbrates his view.[128] Ely's most important contribution is not his discussion of rights to "voice and vote"—the rights of citizens as active participants in government. Instead, his main contribution—and, it would seem, his predominant interest—involves rights of citizens as consumers of government. He notes that minority victims of prejudice often may be unable to "protect" their own interests, much less affirmatively promote them, through active participation in the political process. Hence, he proposes a conception of representative government by which officials would be obliged at least to "take into account" the interests of those who are unable to "protect themselves." [130] His proposal envisions an ideally rational welfare state, responsive to the groups which effectively promote their interests in the political process, but guarding the others against oppression, assessing their interests with a clear-eyed view of "reality" not "distorted" by prejudice.[131] The proposal, as far as it goes, is admirable enough. But Ely is determined to clothe its protection of groups, whose situation as politically ineffective consumers of government he takes as given, in the rhetoric of an ideal democracy. Thus, again, he employs the language of democracy not to insist on the realization of democracy, but as an apology for acceptance of something much less.

First, he warps the democratic ideals of "participation" and "representation"—which usually connote a polity founded on an active, effective citizenry—to dress up his conception of a polity in which citizens doomed to political ineffectiveness rely on officials to take their interests "into account." He portrays official attention to the concerns of the "functionally powerless" in the notorious old language—"anathema to our forefathers"—of "virtual representation." [132] Like the colonial authorities, he twists the ideal of "representation" to imply that it is possible to be represented in government without being able effectively to participate in government. Then, he twists the ideal of "participation" as well, suggesting that if officials "take into account" the interests of the powerless in allocating burdens and benefits, the power-

---

128. Choper, *supra* note 1, at 70–79.

130. Ely, *supra* note 1, at 82–84.

131. *Id.* at 153.

132. *Id.* at 82–84. His emphasis on "trust"—like Choper's emphasis on representatives as "trustees"—also sugar-coats political passivity.

less may then be said to "participate" in "the bounty of government." [133]
To tout "participation" in governmental "bounty," divorced from effective participation in government itself, is to use a word that implies action to sanctify mere consumption.

Second, Ely invokes the rhetoric of political equality to insist that when officials take account of the interests of those unable to "protect themselves," they must show "equal concern and respect" for such interests. This language has a democratic ring. But, as Ely applies it, it denotes the most minimal "equality" of protection. It simply means that when government responds to the requests of politically effective groups to serve their interests, it must have a rationale that does not denigrate the interests of the politically ineffective groups. It is not clear what, if anything, "equal" then adds to the requirement of "concern and respect." But it is certain that the requirement does not afford, as Ely suggests,[135] *equality of representation*. It allows officials affirmatively to *promote* the interests of more powerful citizens while, at best, it obliges them to *protect* the interests of "functionally powerless" citizens. Incantation of egalitarian language may obscure this fact but will not change it.

Third, Ely manipulates the republican political theory of the eighteenth and nineteenth centuries to provide his conception of representative government—responsive to powerful groups but taking account of the interests of politically ineffective groups—an imprimatur of history. He defines the central principle of the theory as government "in the interest of the whole people." [136] He notes that the theory was based on a notion of "the people" as "an essentially homogenous group," and he even acknowledges that republicans insisted that their polity be based on a more or less equal redistribution of wealth.[137] But, then, zipping through the nineteenth century, he states that "faith in the republican tenet that the people ... were essentially homogeneous was all but dead." In light of this perceived heterogeneity, he says, "the theory of representation had to be extended" to ensure that representatives would respond not only to the "majority" but also take account of the interests of "minorities." [138] Thus, from the central principle of republicanism, he derives his own conception. This historical account (for all its superficiality; it takes only a few pages in his book) is compelling rhetorically. But it obfuscates at least two important things. First, Ely swiftly sweeps under the carpet the republican belief that the polity should rest on a relatively equal distribution of wealth. He equates it with faith in social homogeneity—hardly a necessary equation—and then hastens to observe—as though it dealt with the problem—that that faith was "dead" by the nineteenth century. He moves the shells pretty fast. But, examined closely, the derivation of his conception of representative government from republican theory is too obviously flawed to have much

133. *Id.* at 74.

135. Ely, *supra* note 1, at 82.

136. *Id.* at 79.

137. *Id.* (misspelling of "homogeneous" in original).

138. *Id.* at 82.

value as anything more than rhetoric. Second, the derivation is also flawed in its premise. In stating what he treats as the central principle of republicanism—government in the interest of the whole people—Ely flatly ignores an equally vital republican principle: that the polity rests upon the virtue of, and the vigilant attention to public affairs by, the people.[139] In republican theory, citizenship is taken seriously. It is seen as necessarily active. In fact, *maintenance* of government in the interest of the people is said to *depend* on active involvement of the people in political life.[140] Ely, however, not only suppresses the republican concern for social equality, he suppresses as well this republican tenet of an active citizenry. He thereby enables himself to use republicanism to cloak his radically different conception of representative government, which takes inequality and the passivity of the bulk of citizens for granted.

The political faith embodied in "process-oriented" theory, as perfected by Choper and Ely, is in many respects laudable. In calling for the integration of minority groups into a polity that is assumed to be otherwise basically sound, it is resonant of the most advanced liberal thought of the late 1950s, the period when Choper and Ely grew up. Much of its program was achieved—in part by the Warren Court—during the 1960s. Now, it is mostly a matter of defending those achievements. And in the next decade they will need defending. To the extent that the books by Choper and Ely build needed defenses, they deserve our applause.

Nevertheless, they do not deserve our emulation. In his criticism of another constitutional theory, Ely complains that it is marred by a "systematic bias * * * in favor of the values of the upper-middle, professional class from which most lawyers and judges * * * are drawn." [143] So is his "process-oriented" theory. It seeks the integration of minorities into a polity that is biased against citizens who lack the resources needed to be politically effective, a polity therefore in which masses of citizens sink into political passivity as clients dependent on the minimal protection provided by the welfare state, a polity which consequently is dominated by the "upper-middle professional class." "Process-oriented" theory is not just uncritical of that polity. It constitutes an apology for it.

* * *

"People understandably think that what is important to them is important, and people like us are no exception," proclaims Ely.[144] Nor are people like us. Like our elders, who elaborated and have now perfected "process-oriented" constitutional theory, we are in the "upper-middle professional class." That—along with myriad other things, in-

---

139. *See* G. Wood, The Creation of the American Republic 52–70 (1969).

140. *See id.* at 52–56. The best of the now voluminous writing on republicanism is J. Pocock, The Machiavellian Moment (1975).

143. *Id.* at 59.

144. *Id.*

cluding caution—may incline us simply to pursue the line of inquiry laid out by our predecessors, adding filigree to their conceptions of the functioning and malfunctioning of the political process, perhaps extending their proposals for marginal reform, but embracing, as they have embraced, and apologizing, as they have apologized, for the status quo, further obfuscating its deep injustice. But that need not be our fate. We grew up in an era when it was virtually impossible to feel comfortable with the status quo, an era when it was not so easy to dismiss a "radical" critique with a clubbish word of derision, an era when hope for a newer world came naturally. It is open to us, as it was not open to our predecessors, to imagine a political life far different—far more democratic—than the one we know now. It is given to us to re-explore the constitutional theory of our polity.

ROBIN L. WEST, CONSTITUTIONAL SCEPTICISM
72 B.U.L.Rev. 765, 765–70, 774–79 (1992).

CONSTITUTIONAL MEANING AND VALUE

Interpretive constitutional debate over the last few decades has centered on two apparently linked questions: whether the Constitution can be given a determinate meaning, and whether the institution of judicial review can be justified within the basic assumptions of liberalism. Two groups of scholars have generated answers to these questions. The "constitutional faithful" argue that meaning can indeed be determinately affixed to constitutional clauses, by reference to the plain meaning of the document, the original intent of the drafters,[2] evolving political and moral norms of the community,[3] or the best political or moral philosophical theory available[4] and that, because of that determinacy, judicial review can indeed be brought within the rubric of liberalism. Taking issue with the constitutional faithful is a group who might be called "constitutional sceptics." Scholars in this group see, in every constitutional phrase or doctrine, the possibility of multiple interpretations, and in the application of every constitutional method the possibility of multiple outcomes. It follows from this indeterminacy that judicial review cannot be easily justified by reference to liberal assumptions,

---

2. For examples of originalist interpretation and defenses of originalism, see Raoul Berger, Federalism: The Founder's Design (1987) (advocating the doctrine of original intent for constitutional interpretation); * * * Robert H. Bork, *The Constitution, Original Intent, and Economic Rights,* 23 San Diego L.Rev. 823 (1986) (arguing that framers' intent is the only legitimate basis for constitutional decisionmaking and binds judges); Antonin Scalia, *Originalism: The Lesser Evil,* 57 U.Cin.L.Rev. 849 (1989) (asserting that framers' intent is the necessary method by which to interpret the Constitution).

3. For an example of "consensualist" interpretation, see Penry v. Lynaugh, 492 U.S. 302 (1989) (holding that interpretation of Cruel and Unusual Punishment Clause depends upon community consensus).

4. Those adopting this view include Bruce Ackerman, Ronald M. Dworkin, and John H. Ely. See generally Bruce Ackerman, * * * We The People (1991); Ronald M. Dworkin, Taking Rights Seriously (1977); John H. Ely, Democracy and Distrust: A Theory of Judicial Review (1980).

because the power of the interpreting judge irreparably compromises the stability and rationality of the "Rule of Law" so central to liberal ideals.[5]

As important as the debate over constitutional determinacy may be, its prominence in modern constitutional theory over the last thirty years has carried with it serious opportunity costs. Specifically, the prominence of the debate over the Constitution's meaning, whether it can be said to have one, and the implications for the coherence of liberalism that these questions of interpretation seem to raise, has pushed to the background an older and possibly more important debate about the Constitution's value. By asking relentlessly whether the Constitution's meaning can be made sufficiently determinate to serve the Rule of Law—by focusing almost exclusively on whether constitutionalism is possible within liberal theory and whether liberalism is possible, given an indeterminate Constitution—we have neglected to ask whether our Constitution is desirable. Does it further the "good life" for the individuals, communities, and subcommunities it governs?

We might pose these evaluative questions in any number of ways. Has the Constitution or the Bill of Rights well served the communities and individuals they are designed to protect? Are the visions of individualism, community, and human nature on which the Bill of Rights rests, and the balances it strikes between rights and responsibilities, or civic virtue and freedoms, noble conceptions of social life, true accounts of our being, hospitable to societal and individual attempts to live the good life? More specifically, does the First Amendment, for example, well serve its core values of free expression, individual actualization, and open political debate? Assuming that it does, are those values good values to have? Are they worth the damage to our social cohesion, our fragile sense of fraternity with others, and our attempts at community that they almost undeniably cause? Are the Fourteenth Amendment's sweeping and majestic guarantees of "liberty" and "equal protection of the law," appearances notwithstanding, in fact unduly stingy? Do they simply, and cruelly, fail to guarantee a liberty that would meaningfully protect against the most serious constraints on peoples' liberties, or an equality that would even begin to address the grotesque material inequities at the very heart of our social and economic life? Do those guarantees perversely protect, rather than guarantee against, those constraints and inequities? Similarly, but from a quite different political orientation, are Fourth Amendment guarantees simply not worth their cost in law enforcement? Is it unwise to let eighteen-year-olds vote? Is the Second Amendment the height of foolishness?

5. See, e.g., Mark Tushnet, Red, White, and Blue: A Critical Analysis of Constitutional Law 6–11 (1988) (contrasting some of the main elements of the liberal and republican traditions); Paul Brest, *The Misconceived Quest for the Original Understanding*, 60 B.U.L.Rev. 204, 224–37 (1980) (rejecting originalism and defending nonoriginalist adjudication, which accords presumptive weight to the text and original history, but does not treat them as authoritative or binding). For an impassioned argument against the "indeterminacy thesis" on this ground, see Owen Fiss, *Objectivity and Interpretation*, 34 Stan.L.Rev. 739, 742–62 (1982) (arguing against a new nihilism that insists that objectivity is impossible and that interpretation is based on the judge's own values).

These questions—about the value, wisdom, decency, or sensibility of constitutional guarantees—do of course receive some attention in contemporary legal scholarship, but nevertheless, it seems fair to say that in spite of the legal academy's supposed obsession with "normativity," normative questions about the Constitution have not been at the heart of constitutional discourse of the last thirty years. By contrast, normative questions of precisely this sort constitute the great bulk of scholarship in other areas of law. Scholars question the value of the holder in due course doctrine in commercial transactions, the negligence doctrine or strict liability in tort law, the rules governing acceptance of unilateral contracts in contract law, and insanity defenses in criminal law. But normative questions are neither the subject of constitutional "grand theory" nor, more revealingly perhaps, the subject of doctrinal constitutional scholarship. Instead, while theoretical constitutional scholarship centers on questions about the meaningfulness of the Constitution and its implications for the possibility or impossibility of liberalism, doctrinal constitutional scholarship centers on questions of the Constitution's meaning, rather than questions of its value. Thus, for example, rather than debate whether the First or the Fourteenth Amendment is a good idea, doctrinalists debate what the First Amendment or the Fourteenth Amendment means, and theorists debate whether they have any meaning and what it means to assert that they do or do not have meaning. In short, neither theoretical nor doctrinal constitutional scholarship places the value, rather than either the meaningfulness or the meaning, of the Constitution at the heart of constitutional analysis.

That we lack an explicitly normative debate about the Constitution's value might be evidenced by the visible effects of that absence in our substantive constitutional arguments. Let me cite a few examples, simply to convey the flavor of what I suggest is missing. One debate between constitutional scholars arising over the last few years, and of great interest to political progressives, concerns the constitutionality under the First Amendment of the attempts made by some cities and universities to control, through disciplinary sanctions, the intimidation and subordination of racial, ethnic, and sexual minorities by use of "hate speech." Those contributing to the small explosion of scholarly writing on this topic have generally taken one of two polar positions: one group of scholars and litigators (generally liberal) argues that hate speech regulations are simply unconstitutional under the First Amendment[6] while a second, more or less minority (and generally progressive), position argues that they are constitutional, either by virtue of the similarity between hate speech regulations and traditionally accepted limits on the First Amendment, or because of limits we should imply into that amendment through the "penumbral" and balancing, or counterbalanc-

---

6. See, e.g., George P. Fletcher, *Constitutional Identity,* 14 Cardozo L.Rev. 1, 26–27 (1992)[;] Suzanna Sherry, *Speaking of Virtue: A Republican Approach to Universi-* *ty Regulation of Hate Speech,* 75 Minn. L.Rev. 933 (1991)[;] Nadine Strossen, *Regulating Racist Speech on Campus: A Modest Proposal,* 1990 Duke L.J. 484[.]

ing, effect of the Fourteenth Amendment's equality clause.[7] The position that seems to have no adherents is that hate speech regulations are desirable, for progressive reasons, but are nevertheless unconstitutional, but shouldn't be, and that this shows that, at least from a progressive perspective, the First Amendment is morally flawed. But again, this position seems to have no adherents. Instead, those who think hate speech regulations are a good idea generally think they are constitutional while those who think they are not a good idea generally find them unconstitutional. No one seems to find them both desirable and unconstitutional, and hence exemplary of a problem with the First Amendment. No one, in other words, is led by a commitment to the desirability of hate speech regulations and a fair reading of the Constitution to take a progressive and morally sceptical stance toward the Constitution.

A second and structurally similar example involves the constitutionality of anti-pornography ordinances. Despite the wide range of conflicting feminist and libertarian positions on this issue, no one advances the apparently logical, and initially plausible, position that these ordinances are eminently desirable, but unconstitutional, revealing a serious problem with the First Amendment. Instead, those who view these ordinances as unconstitutional generally view them as objectionable,[8] while those who view the ordinances as desirable generally find them constitutional as well.[9] Again, no one is led by a commitment to the value of anti-pornography regulations and a fair reading of the Constitution to take a morally sceptical stance toward the Constitution, or at least toward the First Amendment.

Although this paper focuses primarily on the absence of progressive sceptical arguments about the Constitution's value, the same point holds regarding the absence of sceptical stances toward the Constitution reflective of other political or moral commitments. Thus, one finds few people arguing that the Constitution does indeed protect a woman's right to an abortion and, therefore, over-protects privacy, because abortion rights are morally unjustifiable. Few argue that the Constitution protects the individual's choice of sexual lifestyle and, therefore, over-protects individual choice, because homosexuality is an immoral way to live. No one seems led by a conservative commitment to the value of regulating private morality and a fair reading of the Constitution as prohibiting that regulation to the conclusion that the Constitution is morally and politically flawed. On the other hand, no one seems to believe that the Constitution does indeed fail to protect reproductive or gay rights, but

7. J. Peter Byrne, *Racial Insults and Free Speech Within the University,* 79 Geo. L.J. 399 (1991)[;] Richard Delgado, *Campus Antiracism Rules: Constitutional Narratives in Collision,* 85 Nw.U.L.Rev. 343 (1991)[;] Charles Lawrence, *If He Hollers, Let Him Go: Regulating Racist Speech on Campus,* 1990 Duke L.J. 431[;] Mari Matsuda, *Public Response to Racist Speech: Considering the Victim's Story,* 87 Mich. L.Rev. 2320 (1989)[.]

8. See Ronald Dworkin, Liberty and Pornography, 38 N.Y.Rev. Books, Aug. 15, 1991, at 12; Barry W. Lynn, *"Civil Rights" Ordinances and the Attorney General's Commission: New Developments in Pornography Regulation,* 21 Harv.C.R.–C.L.L.Rev. 27, 48–56 (1986)[.]

9. Catharine MacKinnon, Pornography: On Morality and Politics, in Toward A Feminist Theory of the State 195–214 (1989)[.]

that these rights should be granted, and that this shows the Constitution's inadequacy. Again, those who view abortion rights as desirable generally view them as constitutionally protected, and those who view them as unprotected generally view them as undesirable. No one seems led by virtue of their political views on abortion or sexuality combined with a fair reading of the Constitution to the conclusion that the Constitution is flawed.

The absence of these arguments in the legal literature evidences the more basic privation noted above: there is no general tradition, at least in the legal literature, of normatively sceptical constitutionalism from a liberal, progressive, conservative, or any other developed political or moral perspective. Regardless of political viewpoint, constitutional scholars are peculiarly reluctant to see either the Constitution or a particular constitutional guarantee as being at odds with our political or moral ideals, goals, or commitments. We tend to see the Constitution as an inappropriate object of criticism, and this may be even more true today than it was thirty, forty, or fifty years ago. Even in post-critical, post-modern, post-structuralist, post-feminist times, we lack a developed body of legal scholarship that takes a morally critical stance toward the Constitution and the rights it purports to protect.

* * *

PROGRESSIVE CONSTITUTIONAL SCEPTICISM

Progressives have both substantive and methodological reasons to be sceptical about the Constitution's value. I define "progressivism," in part, by its guiding ideal: progressives are loosely committed to a form of social life in which all individuals live meaningful, autonomous, and self-directed lives, enriched by rewarding work, education, and culture, free of the disabling fears of poverty, violence, and coercion, nurtured by life-affirming connections with intimates and co-citizens alike, and strengthened by caring communities that are both attentive to the shared human needs of its members and equally mindful of their diversity and differences. Much of this guiding ideal, however, is shared by liberals. What distinguishes progressives from liberals is that while liberals tend to view the dangers of an over-oppressive state as the most serious obstacle to the attainment of such a world, progressives, while agreeing that some obstacles emanate from the state, argue that for the most part the most serious impediments emanate from unjust concentrations of private power—the social power of whites over blacks, the intimate power of men over women, the economic power of the materially privileged over the materially deprived. From a progressive perspective, it is those concentrations of private power, not state power, that presently riddle social life with hierarchic relationships of mastery and subjection, of sovereignty and subordination. Hence, it is those concentrations of private power that must be targeted, challenged, and reformed by progressive political action. That action, in turn, will often involve state intervention into the private spheres within which hierarchies of private power are allowed to thrive, and that simple fact will commonly pit the progressive strategy of ending private domination against the liberal goal of minimizing the danger of an oppressive state.

This difference between progressives and liberals largely accounts for the degree of conflict between their respective analyses and goals. For example, liberals and progressives generally agree, and lament, that the freedom of gays and lesbians to form and maintain nurturing intimate relationships is threatened by discriminatory state action. At the same time, progressives, far more than liberals, are sensitive to the degree to which that freedom is threatened by the continuing and seemingly unshakable hegemonic rage of an intolerant, abusive, and often violent minority of heterosexual private citizens. That hegemonic rage, not just state action, must somehow be challenged and transformed if gays and lesbians are to thrive. Similarly, liberals and progressive feminists agree, and lament, that the freedom of women to engage simultaneously in well-compensated work, in public life, and in a rewarding home and family life is threatened by discriminatory state law. Still, the dramatic and well-publicized split between liberal feminists and progressive feminists reflects the extent to which progressive feminists, unlike liberal feminists, realize that women's lives and freedom may be endangered more by private, intimate, economic, and social systems of power and control than by pernicious or discriminatory state action: by, for example, a family structure that saps women's time, energy, and self-esteem with unequal distributions of demanding and unpaid domestic labor; the social acceptability of private sexual violence and coercion in marriage and intimacy that threatens women's safety and drains women's sense of self-possession and self-will; and the prevalence of unequal compensation for work of comparable responsibility and difficulty that deprives women of material security, self-esteem, and independence. If we call these systems of private coercion, intimate violence, and economic disempowerment "patriarchy," then it seems that patriarchy exists and perpetuates itself to a considerable degree independent of "state action," discrimination or otherwise. Awareness of, and concern about, that social fact distinguishes progressive from liberal feminists.

Similarly, from a progressive perspective, African Americans and other ethnic minorities are hindered in their search for meaningful freedom and full civic equality, not so much by discriminatory state laws or actions as by the continuing and escalating presence of a virulent white racism in virtually all spheres of private, social, and economic life. Awareness of, and concern about, that complex social fact in large part distinguishes progressive "critical race theorists" from their one-time liberal allies. To take one final example, the poor in this society are hurt not nearly so much by pernicious or discriminatory state actions as by concentrations of private economic power. Again, concern over the centrality of this social fact distinguishes progressive from liberal politics on issues of class. Generally, what defines a progressive political perspective is simply the awareness that the greatest obstacles to enjoyment of the good life valued by liberals and progressives alike are not actions of any sort taken by states or state officials, but concentrations of private power, whether of a patriarchal, racist, homophobic, or capitalist sort.

If that progressive insight is basically correct, then at least two problems exist with the scheme of individual rights and liberties protected by the Constitution. First, the Constitution does not prohibit the abuse of private power that interferes with the equality or freedom of subordinated peoples. The Constitution simply does not reach private power, and therefore cannot possibly prohibit its abuse. Even the most far reaching liberal interpretations of the Reconstruction Amendments— the only amendments that seemingly reach private power—refuse or fail to find either a constitutional prohibition of private societal racism, intimate sexual violence, or economic coercion or a constitutional imperative that the states take affirmative action to eradicate it. Justice Harlan's famous liberal dissent in Plessy v. Ferguson, for example, makes painfully clear that, even on his reading of the amendment (which, of course, would have outlawed Jim Crow laws), the Fourteenth Amendment does not challenge the sensed or actual cultural and social superiority of the white race. More recently, Justices Brennan and Marshall's argument in their dissent in City of Richmond v. J.A. Croson Co.,[20] that the state may remedy private discrimination if failure to do so would enmesh the state in those discriminatory practices, did not suggest that the Constitution requires the state to address private discrimination. Similarly, virtually no liberal judges or commentators have read the Constitution and the Reconstruction Amendments to require that states take affirmative action to address the unconstitutional maldistribution of household labor, with its serious, well-proven, and adverse effects on women's liberty and equality. No liberal court or commentator reads the Constitution to require that states or Congress take action to protect against homophobic violence and rage, or to protect against the deadening, soul-murdering, and often life-threatening effects of homelessness, hunger, and poverty. The Constitution apparently leaves untouched the very conditions of subordination, oppression, and coercion that relegate some to "lesser lives" of drudgery, fear, and stultifying self-hatred. For that reason alone, the Constitution appears to be fundamentally at odds with progressive ideals and visions.

The incompatibility, however, of progressivism and the Constitution goes deeper. Not only does the Constitution fail to prohibit subordinating abuses of private power, but, at least a good deal of the time, in the name of guaranteeing constitutional protection of individual freedom, it also aggressively protects the very hierarchies of wealth, status, race, sexual preference, and gender that facilitate those practices of subordination. Thus, the Constitution seemingly protects the individual's freedom to produce and consume hate speech, despite its propensity to contribute to patterns of racial oppression. It also clearly protects the individual's right to practice religion, despite the demonstrable incompatibility of the

---

20. 488 U.S. 469, 528 (1989) (Marshall, J., joined by Brennan & Blackmun, JJ., dissenting) (arguing that the program setting aside a percentage of contracts for minorities is constitutional).

religious tenets central to all three dominant mainstream religions with women's full civic and political equality.   It protects the individual's freedom to create and use pornography, despite the possible connection between pornography and increases in private violence against women. It protects the privacy and cultural hegemony of the nuclear family, despite the extreme forms of injustice that occur within that institution and the maldistribution of burdens and benefits visited by that injustice upon women and, to a lesser degree, children.   Finally, it protects, as a coincidence of protecting the freedom and equal opportunities of individuals, both the system of "meritocracy" and the departures from meritocracy that dominate and constitute the market and economy, despite the resistance of those systems to full participation of African Americans and hence despite the subordinating effects of those "markets" upon them. * * *

Finally, this incompatibility of the Constitution with progressive ideals is neither momentary nor contingent.   It is not a product of false or disingenuous interpretation by a particular court or Justice hostile to progressive politics.   Rather, the Constitution's incompatibility with progressive ideals stems from at least two theoretical and doctrinal sources that lie at the heart of our constitutional structure: first, the conception of liberty to which the Constitution is committed and, second, its conception of equality.

First, as is often recognized, the Constitution protects a strong and deeply liberal conception of what Isaiah Berlin has termed the "negative liberty" [21] of the individual to speak, think, choose, and labor within a sphere of noninterference from social, community, or state authority. As is less often recognized, however, the Constitution creates and protects these spheres of noninterference not only in preference to, but also at the cost of, the more positive conceptions of freedom and autonomy necessary for progressive change.   The cultural, intimate, private, and economic spheres of noninterference protected by the Constitution are the very spheres of private power, control, and coercion within which the positive liberty of subordinated persons to live lives of meaning is most threatened.   Thus, the Constitution protects the rights of producers and consumers of racial hate speech and pornography so as to protect the negative liberty of those speakers and listeners.   By doing so, it not only fails to protect, but also actively threatens, the positive freedom of women and African Americans to develop lives free from fear for one's safety, the seeds of racial bitterness, the "clouds of inferiority," [22] the interference with one's movements, and the crippling incapacities to participate fully in public life occasioned by the constitutionally protected cultures of racism and misogyny.   The negative liberty of the individual heralded and celebrated by liberalism is not only inconsistent with,

---

21. Sir Isaiah Berlin, Two Concepts of Liberty, in Four Essays on Liberty 118 (1969) (distinguishing the "negative" liberty to do as one pleases within a designated sphere from the "positive" liberty to live a particular kind of life).

22. Martin Luther King, Jr., Why We Can't Wait 83 (1963) (describing the impact of racism on the self image of African American children).

but also hostile to the positive liberty central to progressivism, simply because protection of "negative liberty" necessarily creates the sphere of noninterference and privacy within which the abuse of private power can proceed unabated. The Constitution is firmly committed to this negative rather than positive conception of liberty, and is thus not only not the ally, but also a very real obstacle, to progressive ideals.

Second, the Fourteenth Amendment's mandate of equality, rather than being a limit to the Constitution's celebration of liberty, is also a bar to progressive progress, the heroic efforts of progressive litigators, judges, and commentators to prove the contrary notwithstanding. The "equal protection of the laws" guaranteed by the Fourteenth Amendment essentially guarantees that one's membership in a racially or sexually defined group will not adversely affect one's treatment by the state. As such, the mandate powerfully reinforces the liberal understanding that the only attributes that matter to the state are those shared universally by all members of the community: the possession of equal dignity, the power to form one's own plan of life, and the universal aspirations to autonomy and so forth. Precisely this understanding of equality, grounded in the liberal claim and promise of universality and equal treatment, however, renders the Equal Protection Clause an obstacle to progressive progress. The need to acknowledge and compensate for the individual's membership in profoundly non-universal subordinate groups—whether racially, sexually, or economically defined—is what distinguishes the progressive political impulse from the liberal. It is precisely that membership in non-universal groups, and the centrality of the non-universal attributes that distinguish them, that both liberalism and the liberally defined constitutional mandate of equality are poised not simply to ignore, but also to oppose. It is, then, both unsurprising and inevitable that the Fourteenth Amendment's Equal Protection Clause is understood as not requiring, and indeed forbidding, the state and public interventions into private, intimate, and economic spheres of life needed to interrupt the patterns of domination, subordination, and inequality that continue to define the lives of those within these protected private realms.

Methodologically, the Constitution is also hostile to political and moral progressivism, simply because it elevates one set of moral values above others, relegating non-constitutional ideals or visions to the sphere of the "merely political." The Constitution's peculiar status as a bridge between liberal morality and aspirations and positive law, although much heralded by liberal philosophers and constitutionalists, poses a triple danger to progressive ideals. First, because the Constitution is indeed law, and law in the ordinary as well as extraordinary sense, it imprints upon the liberalism on which it rests the imprimatur of positive legal authority. One set of political convictions hence receives not only the persuasive authority derived from its merits, but also the political, willed authority of the extant, empowered, positive sovereign. These ideals simply are, as well as ought to be; and they are in a way that makes compliance mandatory. Second, because the Constitution is law in the extraordinary as well as ordinary sense, the positive political authority imprinted upon the liberal morality of the Constitution is of a higher, permanent, and constitutive sort. It severely constrains moralities and aspirations with which it is inconsistent in the name of the community from which it purportedly draws its sovereign authority. Thus, it is not just "the law" that is hostile to non-liberal moral aspirations, such as progressivism. It is also, more deeply and meaningfully, "we the people"—all of us, the inter-generational community of citizens—for whom the Constitution speaks and from whom it draws its authority that is hostile to the ideals with which it is inconsistent. Third, because the Constitution is also undeniably a moral as well as legal document, the authority it embodies is exercised not only coercively—telling us who we must be—but also instructively—telling us who we ought to be. It defines and confines not just our options—as does any law, higher or lower—but our aspirations as well. For all three reasons, the Constitution is not just a peculiarly authoritarian legal document, but is also authoritarian in a peculiarly parental way. Like a parent's authority over the identity of his or her children, the Constitution both persuades us to be a certain way and it constitutes us in a certain way. It creates us as it defines a morality to which we will and should subscribe.

For all of these reasons, the Constitution is methodologically as well as substantively hostile to progressive politics. The moral authoritarianism at its core is in many ways conducive to the reverence for the individual and distrust of the mass so central to liberalism, but it is inimical to the egalitarian, inclusive, and largely communitarian methods—the grass roots politics at the local level and the participatory democracy at the national and state level—that must form the foundation of genuine progressive change. Effective political challenges to the subordination of some groups by others must rest on a fundamental change of human orientation in both the dominated and oppressing groups: the dominated must come to see their interests as both shared with each other and opposed to the interests of the stronger; and the stronger must come to embrace empathetically the subordinated as sufficiently close to their own identities to be "of their concern." Neither progressive end—the mounting of sufficient power within the ranks of the subordinated through cross-group organizing or the challenge to the received self-identity of the strong—is attainable through the legal, coercive imposition of a particular moral paradigm that characterizes constitutional methodology. In fact, the moral and legal authoritarianism at the heart of our constitutional method will almost invariably frustrate it.

BIBLIOGRAPHY

General

Amar, *The Bill of Rights as a Constitution,* 100 Yale L.J. 1131 (1991).

Balkin, *What is a Post–Modern Constitutionalism?,* 90 Mich.L.Rev. 1966 (1992).

Chang, *A Critique of Judicial Supremacy*, 36 Vill.L.Rev. 281 (1991).

Symposium, *Contemporary Perspectives on Constitutional Interpretation*, 72 B.U.L.Rev. 681–799 (1992).

Symposium—*One Hundred Years of Judicial Review: The Thayer Centennial Symposium*, 88 Nw.U.L.Rev. 1–461 (1993).

Process–Based Theories

Klarman, *The Puzzling Resistance to Political Process Theory*, 77 Va. L.Rev. 747 (1991).

Sager, *The Incorrigible Constitution*, 65 N.Y.U.L.Rev. 893 (1990).

Symposium—*Judicial Review versus Democracy*, 42 Ohio St.L.J. 1–434 (1981).

Tushnet, *Darkness on the Edge of Town: The Contributions of John Hart Ely to Constitutional Theory*, 89 Yale L.J. 1037 (1980).

Rights–Based Theories

Brest, *The Fundamental Rights Controversy: The Essential Contradictions of Normative Constitutional Scholarship*, 90 Yale L.J. 1063 (1981).

D. Richards, TOLERATION AND THE CONSTITUTION (1986).

Schauer, *A Comment on the Structure of Rights*, 27 Ga.L.Rev. 415 (1993).

Schneider, *The Dialectic of Rights and Politics: Perspectives from the Women's Movement*, 61 N.Y.U.L.Rev. 589 (1986).

Symposium—*Individual Rights and the Powers of Government*, 27 Ga. L.Rev. 343–501 (1993).

Tushnet, *An Essay on Rights*, 62 Tex.L.Rev. 1363 (1984).

Dualist Theories

Klarman, *Constitutional Fact/Constitutional Fiction: A Critique of Bruce Ackerman's Theory of Constitutional Moments*, 44 Stan.L.Rev. 759 (1992).

Sandalow, *Abstract Democracy: A Review of Ackerman's We the People*, 9 Const.Commentary 309 (1992).

Schauer, *Deliberating About Deliberation* [reviewing B. Ackerman, WE THE PEOPLE (1991)], 90 Mich.L.Rev. 1187 (1992).

Deliberative Democracy

J. Appleby, LIBERALISM AND REPUBLICANISM (1992).

J. Diggins, THE LOST SOUL OF AMERICAN POLITICS (1986).

Elhauge, *Does Interest Group Theory Justify More Intrusive Judicial Review?*, 101 Yale L.J. 31 (1991).

Fallon, *What is Republicanism, and is it Worth Reviving?*, 102 Harv. L.Rev. 1695 (1989).

Michelman, *Foreword: Traces of Self–Government,* 100 Harv.L.Rev. 4 (1986).

Michelman, *Law's Republic,* 97 Yale L.J. 1493 (1988).

T. Pangle, THE SPIRIT OF MODERN REPUBLICANISM (1988).

Pope, *Republican Moments: The Role of Direct Popular Power in the American Constitutional Order,* 139 U.Pa.L.Rev. 287 (1990).

Sherry, *Civic Virtue and the Feminine Voice in Constitutional Adjudication,* 72 Va.L.Rev. 543 (1986).

Sunstein, *Beyond the Republican Revival,* 97 Yale L.J. 1539 (1988).

Sunstein, *Interest Groups in American Public Law,* 38 Stan.L.Rev. 29 (1986).

Critical Perspectives

Barnes, *Theoretically a Dangerous Liaison* [reviewing S. Carter, REFLECTIONS OF AN AFFIRMATIVE ACTION BABY (1991), and P. Williams, THE ALCHEMY OF RACE AND RIGHTS (1991)], 101 Yale L.J. 1631 (1992).

Becker, *The Politics of Women's Wrongs and The Bill of "Rights": A Bicentennial Perspective,* 59 U.Chi.L.Rev. 453 (1992).

Bell, *Racial Realism,* 24 Conn.L.Rev. 363 (1992).

D. Bell, FACES AT THE BOTTOM OF THE WELL: THE PERMANENCE OF RACISM (1992).

Cook, *Beyond Critical Legal Studies: The Reconstructive Theology of Dr. Martin Luther King, Jr.,* 103 Harv.L.Rev. 985 (1990).

Culp, *Toward a Black Legal Scholarship: Race and Original Understandings,* 1991 Duke L.J. 39.

Farber and Sherry, *Telling Stories Out of School: An Essay on Legal Narratives,* 45 Stan.L.Rev. 807 (1993).

Matsuda, *Looking to the Bottom: Critical Legal Studies and Reparations,* 22 Harv.C.R.–C.L.L.Rev. 323 (1987).

Peller, *Race Consciousness,* 1990 Duke L.J. 758.

M. Tushnet, RED, WHITE, AND BLUE (1988).

P. Williams, THE ALCHEMY OF RACE AND RIGHTS (1991).

Chapter II

METHODS OF CONSTITUTIONAL INTERPRETATION

Constitutional lawyers have traditionally employed a variety of methods to interpret the Constitution. They have consulted the plain or historical meaning of the language in the text; the intent of the drafters of the constitutional provision at issue; the structure of the Constitution as a whole; the purposes sought to be accomplished by the constitutional provision; precedent; and deeply held values or notions of social policy. Philip Bobbitt describes six such methods in the opening selection of this chapter. We then explore theoretical justifications for a number of these interpretive methods.

Interpretivism/Non-interpretivism: Putting to one side the difficult moral issues central to the abortion debate, *Roe v. Wade* poses troubling questions for constitutional interpretation. According to many of *Roe*'s detractors, the Court's opinion (and substantive due process analysis in general) is illegitimate because it is based on norms and values not found in the language or structure of the Constitution. Proponents of the abortion and privacy decisions assert that it is permissible for the Court to rely on values external to the document in interpreting the Constitution. Thomas Grey distinguishes these two views, labelling the four-corners approach "interpretivism" and the external approach "non-interpretivism." Grey contends that throughout our constitutional history, the Court has enforced principles of liberty and justice not traceable to the language of the Constitution. To reject these decisions, he maintains, would be to radically alter prevailing constitutional doctrine. Robert Bork, in an article widely referred to during his (non)confirmation hearing, condemns non-interpretive judicial review. He contends that the Court's identification and imposition of "fundamental values" not found in the document cannot be squared with the presuppositions of a democratic society.

Text: Frederick Schauer suggests that there are far more "easy cases" in constitutional adjudication than one might suppose from reading casebooks and Supreme Court opinions. He contends that language (either from the constitutional text or from a rule in a case or a series of cases) can be a significant, even if unappreciated, constraint on constitutional interpretation. Sanford Levinson turns Schauer's claim on its head. He argues that texts don't constrain interpretation; rather, interpretation creates texts. Drawing on modern literacy criticism, Levinson doubts that one can sensibly talk about extracting a "true" or "correct" meaning from a constitutional provision.

In evaluating the arguments of Schauer and Levinson, you may wish to consider the great opinions of Chief Justice Marshall in *Marbury, Gibbons,* and *McCulloch.* In these cases, was the Court substantially limited by the text of the Constitution, or did the Chief Justice "create" the text in the process of writing his opinions? Perhaps it would be fairer to Schauer to think about a case where the textual language looks controlling. Is it possible that the Supreme Court could conclude that a mature 33 year-old is eligible to run for the Presidency?

Original Intent: A familiar claim in constitutional law is that the original intent of the framers ought to control constitutional interpretation. Paul Brest offers both a practical and a normative critique of this view. Richard Kay provides responses to the prevailing criticisms of original intentions adjudication (that is, that it is impossible and that it is normatively objectionable). How would the arguments of Brest and Kay apply in the interpretation of the Equal Protection Clause? Can one reasonably ascertain the "original understanding" of the Clause? Should it be read to cover gender discrimination? Indeed, is the decision in *Brown v. Board of Education* consistent with "original intent"? Does it matter if it is not?

Stare Decisis: Can precedent oblige us to interpret the Constitution in ways that we once accepted, and now reject? Henry Monaghan's article analyzes these questions. He suggests that the primary justification for a principle of stare decisis is that it legitimates the constitutional order, including the practice of judicial review.

"Neutral Principles": Herbert Wechsler's famous article argues that constitutional decisions, to be legitimate, must be "genuinely principled"—that is, they must rest on reasons that transcend the immediate result of the case and that the judge is willing to apply in similar cases. Mark Tushnet critiques several understandings of "neutral principles." He contends that no version of Wechsler's concept can significantly constrain judicial interpretation of the Constitution.

Wechsler contends at the end of his article that he cannot discover a neutral principle that would justify the *Brown* decision. How might Tushnet think about *Brown?* How would you respond to Wechsler?

Balancing: It is commonplace to think that resolution of a constitutional issue requires a court to "balance" the interests at stake. T. Alexander Aleinikoff identifies "balancing" as a dominant element of modern constitutional reasoning and offers a number of critiques of a balancing methodology. Would it make sense not to balance when considering cases arising under the First Amendment, the Due Process Clause, or the Fourth Amendment? Are there sensible alternatives to balancing, or is all constitutional interpretation, at bottom, an exercise in balancing?

A. A TYPOLOGY OF CONSTITUTIONAL ARGUMENTS

PHILIP BOBBITT, THE MODALITIES OF CONSTITUTIONAL ARGUMENT
Constitutional Interpretation 12–22 (1991).

I will be speaking of *constitutional modalities*—the ways in which legal propositions are characterized as true from a constitutional point of view. * * * [The] six modalities of constitutional argument are: the historical (relying on the intentions of the framers and ratifiers of the Constitution); textual (looking to the meaning of the words of the Constitution alone, as they would be interpreted by the average contemporary "man on the street"); structural (inferring rules from the relationships that the Constitution mandates among the structures it sets up); doctrinal (applying rules generated by precedent); ethical (deriving rules from those moral commitments of the American ethos that are reflected in the Constitution); and prudential (seeking to balance the costs and benefits of a particular rule). Now let us look at some examples, and a somewhat more formal statement of each form of argument.

Consider the question whether a state may validly enforce a law that makes it a crime to procure an abortion. An *historical* modality may be attributed to constitutional arguments that claim that the framers and ratifiers of the Fourteenth Amendment intended, or did not intend, or that it cannot be ascertained whether it was their intention, to protect pregnant women from a state's coercion, through threats of fines and imprisonment, to bear children. Similarly, an historical modality might approach the abortion question as: did the framers and ratifiers of the Fourteenth Amendment intend to countenance, or to overturn by means of the Amendment, or are their intentions unclear as to the effect of the Amendment regarding, those state laws that existed at the time of ratification that prohibited abortions?

Oftentimes this modality is confused with textual argument since both can have reference to the specific text of the Constitution. Historical, or "originalist" approaches to construing the text, however, are distinctive in their reference back to what a particular provision is thought to have meant to its ratifiers. Thus, when Justice Taney in the *Dred Scott* case was called upon to construe the scope of the diversity jurisdiction in Article III, which provides for suits "between citizens of the several states," so that he might decide whether a slave could seek his freedom in a diversity suit before a federal court, he wrote:

It becomes necessary to determine who were the citizens of the several states when the constitution was adopted. And in order to do this we must recur to the governments and institutions of the colonies. We must inquire who at the time were recognized as citizens of the states, whose rights and liberties [had been] outraged by the English government and who declared their independence and assumed the powers of government to defend their rights [by force] of arms. We refer to these historical facts for the purpose of showing the fixed opinions concerning the Negro race upon which the statesmen of that day spoke and acted.[7]

Now consider the same question—who are the "citizens" of the phrase that provides for suits in federal court "between citizens of different states" ("diversity" suits)—from another point of view. A *textual* modality may be attributed to arguments that the text of the Constitution would, to the average person, appear to declare, or deny, or be too vague to say whether, a suit between a black American citizen resident in a state and a white American citizen resident in another state, is a "controversy between citizens of different states." I would imagine that the contemporary meaning of these words is rather different than that which Taney found them to mean to the framers and ratifiers of 1789. One should not be tempted to conclude, however, that textual approaches are inevitably more progressive than originalist approaches. Sometimes the text can be a straitjacket, confining the judge to language that would have been different if its drafters had foreseen later events. Thus consider whether wiretapping is prohibited by the Fourth Amendment, which guarantees "the right of the people to be secure in their persons, houses, papers and effects against unreasonable searches and seizures." Here is Chief Justice Taft in a case in which incriminating information was largely obtained by federal prohibition officers intercepting messages on the telephones of the conspirators:

> The amendment itself [he says] shows that the search is to be of material things—the person, the house, his papers or his effects. The amendment does not forbid what was done here for there was no seizure. The evidence was secured by the sense of hearing and that only. There was not entry of the houses. The language of the amendment cannot be extended and expanded.[9]

By contrast, a later court had no trouble finding that wiretapping came within the Amendment. It simply relied upon historical argument—the intentions that animated the adoption of the amendment—and concluded that:

> The purpose of the ... Fourth Amendment [is] to keep the state out of constitutionally protected areas until it has reason to believe that a specific crime has been or is being committed.[10]

Consider another constitutional question: can a court issue a subpoena (or should it enjoin some other subpoena) for the disclosure of the

---

7. Dred Scott v. Sandford, 60 U.S. (19 How.) 393, 407 [, 409] (1856).

9. Olmstead v. United States, 277 U.S. 438, 464 (1928).

10. Berger v. New York, 388 U.S. 41, 59 (1967).

President's working notes and diaries? To say that the institutional relationships promulgated by the Constitution require or are incompatible with or tolerate a particular answer to this question is to use a *structural* mode of argument. There are many recent, celebrated examples of this form of argument to be found in the cases of the US Supreme Court; indeed the 1980s were particularly notable for the Court's focus on structural issues. But structural argument is hardly a recent invention. *McCulloch v. Maryland,* the principal foundation case for constitutional analysis, relies almost wholly on structural approaches. In determining whether a Maryland tax on the Federal Bank of the United States could be enforced, Chief Justice Marshall studiedly refuses to specify the particular text that supports his argument, and explicitly rejects reliance on historical arguments, preferring instead to state the rationale on inferences for the structure of federalism. Such a structure could not be maintained, he concluded, if the states, whose officials are elected by a state's constituency, could tax the agencies of the federal government present in a state and thereby tax a nationwide constituency. The constitutional structure would not tolerate such a practice.

* * *

Structural arguments are a little less intuitively obvious than arguments from the text or history of the Constitution, so perhaps it would be well to briefly outline their characteristic form. Usually, arguments in this modality are straightforward: first, an uncontroversial statement about a constitutional structure is introduced [for example, * * * the statement that the right to vote for a member of Congress is provided for in the Constitution]; second, a relationship is inferred from this structure [that this right, for example, gives rise to the federal power to protect it and is not dependent on state protection]; third, a factual assertion about the world is made [that, if unprotected, the structure of federal representation would be at the mercy of local violence]. Finally a conclusion is drawn that provides the rule in the case. * * *

Consider whether the state can require mandatory testing for the AIDS virus antibodies. To say that it is wise, or unwise, or simply unclear on the present facts whether or not it is wise to permit such testing is to propose an evaluation from a *prudential* point of view. In the first half of this century, this mode of constitutional argument was principally associated with doctrines that sought to protect the political position of the courts. But the dramatic national crises of depression and world war soon provided ample reason to introduce the practical effects of constitutional doctrine into the rationales underpinning doctrine. For example, one such case arose when, in the depths of the midwestern farm depression, the Minnesota legislature passed a statute providing that anyone who was unable to pay a mortgage could be granted a moratorium from foreclosure. On its face such a statute not only appeared to realize the fears of the framers that state legislatures would compromise the credit market by enacting debtor relief statutes, but also plainly to violate the Contracts Clause that was the textual outcome of such concerns. Moreover, the structure of national economic union strongly counseled against permitting states to protect their constituents by exploding a national recovery program that depended on restoring confidence to banking operations. Nevertheless the Supreme Court upheld the statute, observing that:

> An emergency existed in Minnesota which furnished a proper occasion for the exercise of the reserved power of the state to protect the vital interests of the community.[16]

Very simply, the Court recognized the political expediency of the legislature's action and acquiesced in it. * * *

[P]rudential argument * * * is by no means confined to the extremes a nation undergoes in emergencies. Of course in such circumstances prudential arguments are likeliest to be decisive. But, as one of prudentialism's most eloquent practitioners argued, such an approach has a place in every decision:

> The accomplished fact, affairs and interests that have formed around it, and perhaps popular acceptance of it—these are elements * * * that may properly enter into a decision * * *; and they may also enter into the shaping of the judgment, the applicable principle itself.[18]

Prudential argument is actuated by facts, as these play into political and economic policies as to which the Constitution is itself agnostic. The legal rule to be applied is derived from a calculus of costs and benefits, when the facts are taken into account. Accordingly, this often gives rise to a "balancing test" (the balance being a scales, not a tightrope.)

By contrast, when we say that a neutral, general principle derived from the caselaw construing the Constitution should apply, does not apply or may apply, we make an appeal in a *doctrinal* mode. * * *

To familiarize oneself with this form of argument, let us take up this question: to what extent can a state constitutionally aid parochial schools? Suppose, for example, that parochial school students whose schools are not on the route of free public school buses are given a cash allowance by the state to provide for their transportation. Does this offend the Establishment Clause of the First Amendment because the state is bearing the burdens of costs that would otherwise be borne by churchmembers, in much the way that the government in Great Britain, a country that has an established church, provides funds to supplement the income of the Church of England? A judge confronting such a case would probably begin, not by reading the text of the First Amendment which states a rule in rather general terms but by turning to precedent to find similar cases in which authoritative decisions would govern the present one. Not surprisingly, in the area of Establishment jurisprudence there is a great deal of constitutional doctrine, developed in many

---

16. Home Building and Loan Assoc. v. Blaisdell, 290 U.S. 398, 444 (1934).

18. A. Bickel, The Least Dangerous Branch (1962), 116.

cases. The standards these cases develop and apply can be stated as legal rules; the case "on point"—that is, whose facts are similar in those aspects that are relevant to the legal question being posed—is probably *Everson v. Board of Education,* which sustained the power of local authorities to provide free transportation for children attending church schools. In *Everson* the Supreme Court treated the provision of transportation as a form of public welfare legislation, noting that it was being extended by the state "to all its citizens without regard to their religious belief." The Court wrote:

> It is undoubtedly true that children are helped to get to church schools. There is even a possibility that some of the children might not be sent to the church schools if the parents were compelled to pay their children's bus fares out of their pockets when transportation to a public school would have been paid for by the State.[21]

Transportation, however, benefited the child in the same way as did police protection at crossings, fire protection, connections for sewage disposal, public highways, and sidewalks. Based on this rationale, subsequent cases have developed a three-pronged test: does the state program have a secular purpose; is its principal effect neither to advance nor inhibit religion; does its administration excessively entangle the state in religious affairs?[22]

Applying this test to the question above, the judge might write: "*Everson* must be distinguished from the instant case because the program in *Everson* provided transportation common to all students, whereas here only some students—the parochial ones—are given cash allowances. While we do not question that the legislature had a secular purpose in mind, we think the evidence indicated that the effect of these allowances was in fact to make the parochial schools more attractive to parents than their secular counterparts, and thereby advance the cause of religious institutions. Moreover, the oversight required of the state to ensure that the allowances are in fact spent on providing a system of parochial school transportation intrudes the administrative apparatus of the state into the affairs of the church schools. This can only lead to the interference with budgets and an insistence on allocations for transportation that will excessively entangle the state in the administration of church affairs. Accordingly the program must be held unconstitutional."

Or a judge might write: "*Everson,* which also involved public transportation to parochial school students, governs this case. Here as there, the state's program provides aid to students and their parents, and not—as in cases that have applied *Everson* and struck down state assistance in this area—direct assistance to church-related schools. Its secular purpose, to provide school transportation at greater efficiency and less cost to the state than expanding its own bus fleets, is apparent. Like school lunches, public health services, and secular textbooks, the

---

21. [330 U.S. 1, 17 (1947).]

22. Lemon v. Kurtzman, 403 U.S. 602 (1971).

transportation provided here confers a benefit on the parochial student that is at parity with what the secular student receives. Thus its effect is neither to advance nor inhibit religion, but rather to avoid exacting a penalty from the parochial student. Finally, whatever state management is required to administer the program will be limited to the oversight of transportation; such involvement as there may be need not, therefore, excessively entangle the state in those religious matters with regard to which it has no role.''

In either case, the hypothetical judge has applied a rule derived from the relevant caselaw. The rule is neutral as to the parties; that is, it applies equally to Catholics and Jews and atheist claimants and does not vary depending on who is bringing or defending the suit. And the rule is general, that is, it applies to all cases in which the state is arguably giving assistance to religious institutions, and is not confined to the facts of the original case that gave birth to the rule. One more point, however, should be made about this modality: its operation is not confined to the application of *stare decisis,* that is, the strict adherence to previously decided cases. On the contrary, in the American system one of the principles of doctrinalism is that the Supreme Court may reverse the relevant precedent. This would appear to follow from the family of modalities—that provide alternative legal rules—and the supremacy of the Constitution to the acts of government (including, of course, the judicial branch). The Court is entitled, indeed obligated, to overrule itself when it is persuaded that a particular precedent was wrongly decided and should not be applied.

Finally, let us consider the modality of ethical argument. This form of argument denotes an appeal to those elements of the American cultural ethos that are reflected in the Constitution. The fundamental American constitutional ethos is the idea of limited government, the presumption of which holds that all residual authority remains in the private sphere. Thus when we argue that a particular constitutional conclusion is obliged by, or permitted, or forbidden by the American ethos that has allocated certain decisions to the individual or to private institutions, we are arguing in an *ethical* mode.

Ethical arguments arise as a consequence of the fundamental constitutional arrangement by which rights, in the American system, can be defined as those choices beyond the power of government to compel. Thus structural and ethical arguments share some similarities, as each is essentially an inferred set of arguments. Like structural arguments, ethical arguments do not depend on the construction of any particular piece of text, but rather on the necessary relationships that can be inferred from the overall arrangement expressed in the text. Structural argument infers rules from the powers granted to governments; ethical argument, by contrast, infers rules from the powers denied to government. The principal error one can make regarding ethical argument is to assume that any statute or executive act is unconstitutional if it causes effects that are incompatible with the American cultural ethos.

This equates ethical argument, a constitutional form, with moral argument generally.

Let us review a hypothetical example that shows the basic pattern of ethical argument. Note that while the American cultural ethos may encompass cheeseburgers, rock and roll, and a passion for Japanese electronics, the American *constitutional* ethos is largely confined to the reservation of powers not delegated to a limited government.

It was recently reported that a state judge in South Carolina had given the choice of thirty-year prison sentences or castration to three convicted sex offenders. Suppose a convicted man accepted the bargain and was released on probation terms that incorporated this pledge (as by drug-induced impotence). Then suppose that he ceased taking the prescribed drug. If his probation were revoked, a constitutional challenge to the terms of his probation might take this form:

1. The reservation to the individual of the decision to have children is deeply rooted in the American notion of autonomy; there is no express constitutional power to implement a program of eugenics.

2. Moreover, such programs are not a conventionally appropriate means to any express power.

3. Those means denied the federal government are also denied the states.

4. The South Carolina sentence amounted to ordering a man to comply with a eugenics scheme that deemed him ineligible to procreate.

The element of the American ethos at stake is the reservation to individuals and families of the freedom to make certain kinds of decisions. Similar sorts of arguments are to be found in cases in which a state attempted to bar schools from teaching foreign languages; [26] in which a state passed a compulsory education act requiring every school-age child to attend public school (that is, implicitly outlawing private schools); [27] in which a local zoning ordinance was applied to prohibit a grandmother from living with her grandchildren; [28] in which a hospital sought authority to amputate a gangrenous limb from an elderly man who refused his consent; [29] in which a man allegedly suffering from delusions (but concededly harmless) was confined to a mental hospital for almost twenty-five years without treatment.[30] One may test one's mastery of this form of argument by taking each of these examples and stating an ethical argument to resolve it, e.g., (1) There is no express constitutional power to monopolize education; (2) moreover, a statute

26. *Meyer v. Nebraska,* 262 U.S. 390 (1923).

27. *Pierce v. Society of Sisters,* 268 U.S. 510 (1925).

28. *Moore v. City of East Cleveland,* 431 U.S. 494 (1977).

29. *In re Quackenbush,* 156 N.J.Super. 282, 383 A.2d 785 (1978).

30. *O'Connor v. Donaldson,* 422 U.S. 563 (1975).

outlawing private education is not an appropriate means to any express power (such as regulating commerce or providing for armed forces); (3) The decision to educate one's children privately or parochially or publicly is reserved to the family; (4) A statute compelling attendance exclusively at public schools amounts to a scheme to coerce families into a particular educational choice and destroy private educational options.

These then are the six modalities of constitutional argument in the United States. [E]ach of these forms of argument can be used to construct an ideology, a set of political and practical commitments whose values are internally consistent and can be distinguished, externally, from competing ideologies. * * * [T]he reader should not conclude that, because of this relationship—because, for example, some persons may believe that one particular modality represents the only legitimate means of interpreting the Constitution (e.g., historical argument) since it is verifiable by a resort to materials (e.g., the intentions of the ratifiers) that are mandated according to a particular political theory of interpretation (e.g., "originalism")—the modalities of argument are no more than instrumental, rhetorical devices to be deployed in behalf of various political ideologies. The modalities of constitutional argument are the ways in which law statements in constitutional matters are assessed; standing alone they assert nothing about the world. But they need only stand alone to provide the means for making constitutional argument.

There is no constitutional legal argument outside these modalities. Outside these forms, a proposition about the U.S. constitution can be a fact, or be elegant, or be amusing or even poetic, and although such assessments exist as legal statements in some possible legal world, they are not actualized in our legal world.

B. INTERPRETIVISM/NON–INTERPRETIVISM

THOMAS C. GREY, DO WE HAVE AN UNWRITTEN CONSTITUTION?
27 Stan.L.Rev. 703, 703–717 (1975).

In reviewing laws for constitutionality, should our judges confine themselves to determining whether those laws conflict with norms derived from the written Constitution? Or may they also enforce principles of liberty and justice when the normative content of those principles is not to be found within the four corners of our founding document? Excluding the question of the legitimacy of judicial review itself, that is perhaps the most fundamental question we can ask about our fundamental law.

I. THE PURE INTERPRETIVE MODEL

For many years this most basic question has not much engaged the explicit attention of constitutional scholars or of the courts or judges themselves, with at least one important exception. That exception was Mr. Justice Black. Throughout his long and remarkable career on the bench, the most consistently reiterated theme of his constitutional jurisprudence was the need for fidelity to the constitutional text in judicial review, and the illegitimacy of constitutional doctrines based on sources other than the explicit commands of the written Constitution.[1]

It now appears that as a final mark of Mr. Justice Black's achievement, his jurisprudential view of constitutional adjudication may be returning to favor. In the last few years, distinguished commentators on constitutional law have begun to echo Mr. Justice Black's central theme, criticizing constitutional developments in terms that have scarcely been heard in the scholarly community for a generation.

* * *

The truth is that the view of constitutional adjudication that [these commentators] share with Mr. Justice Black is one of great power and compelling simplicity. That view is deeply rooted in our history and in our shared principles of political legitimacy. It has equally deep roots in our formal constitutional law; it is, after all, the theory upon which judicial review was founded in *Marbury v. Madison.*

The chief virtue of this view is that it supports judicial review while answering the charge that the practice is undemocratic. Under the pure interpretive model (as I shall henceforth call the view in question), when a court strikes down a popular statute or practice as unconstitutional, it may always reply to the resulting public outcry: "We didn't do it—you did." The people have chosen the principle that the statute or practice violated, have designated it as fundamental, and have written it down in the text of the Constitution for the judges to interpret and apply. The task of interpretation of the people's commands may not always be simple or mechanical; there is no warrant to condemn Mr. Justice Black or his allies with the epithet "mechanical jurisprudence." But the task remains basically one of interpretation, the application of fixed and binding norms to new facts.[9]

II.   BEYOND INTERPRETATION

The contrary view of judicial review, the one that I espouse and that seems to me implicit in much of the constitutional law developed by the

1. *See, e.g., In re* Winship, 397 U.S. 358, 377 (1970) (Black, J., dissenting); Griswold v. Connecticut, 381 U.S. 479, 507 (1965) (Black, J., dissenting); Rochin v. California, 342 U.S. 165, 174 (1952) (Black, J., concurring); Adamson v. California, 332 U.S. 46, 68 (1947) (Black, J., dissenting).

9. The pure interpretive model should not be confused with *literalism* in constitutional interpretation, particularly with "narrow" or "crabbed" literalism. The interpretive model, at least in the hands of its sophisticated exponents, certainly contemplates that the courts may look through the sometimes opaque text to the purposes behind it in determining constitutional norms. Normative inferences may be drawn from silences and omissions, from structures and relationships, as well as from explicit commands. Thus I do not see the sort of constitutional reasoning described by Professor Charles Black in his Structure And Relationship In Constitutional Law (1969) as necessarily going beyond the interpretive model.

What distinguishes the exponent of the pure interpretive model is his insistence that the only norms used in constitutional adjudication must be those inferable from the text—that the Constitution must not be seen as licensing courts to articulate and apply contemporary norms not demonstrably expressed or implied by the framers.

courts, does not deny that the Constitution is a written document, expressing some clear and positive restraints upon governmental power. Nor does it deny that part of the business of judicial review consists of giving effect to these explicit commands.

Where the broader view of judicial review diverges from the pure interpretive model is in its acceptance of the courts' additional role as the expounder of basic national ideals of individual liberty and fair treatment, even when the content of these ideals is not expressed as a matter of positive law in the written Constitution. It must at once be conceded that such a role for our courts is more difficult to justify than is the role assigned by the pure interpretive model. Why, one asks, are the courts better able to discern and articulate basic national ideals than are the people's politically responsible representatives? And one recalls Learned Hand's remark that he would find it "most irksome to be ruled by a bevy of Platonic Guardians, even if I knew how to choose them, which I assuredly do not." [10]

These grave difficulties no doubt explain, although they do not excuse, the tendency of our courts—today as throughout our history—to resort to bad legislative history and strained reading of constitutional language to support results that would be better justified by explication of contemporary moral and political ideals not drawn from the constitutional text. Of course, this tendency of the courts in no way helps to establish the legitimacy of noninterpretive judicial review. Indeed, standing alone it tends to establish the opposite; for if judges resort to bad interpretation in preference to honest exposition of deeply held but unwritten ideals, it must be because they perceive the latter mode of decisionmaking to be of suspect legitimacy.

However, the tendency to slipshod history and text-parsing does not stand alone. The courts do not only effectuate unwritten ideals and values covertly. Rather, in a very large proportion of their important constitutional decisions, they proceed in a mode that is openly noninterpretive. If this assertion seems at first glance surprising, it may be so partly because of the way in which constitutional law is taught in our law schools.

In the academic teaching of constitutional law, the general question of the legitimacy of judicial review is addressed largely through the vehicle of *Marbury v. Madison*. Students examine the arguments made for judicial review by Chief Justice Marshall, and perhaps contrast them with some of the counterarguments of later judges or commentators. The discussion concludes with the point that, whatever the validity of those arguments as an original matter, history has firmly decided in favor of judicial review. Thereafter, debates about judicial review focus on the question of how "activist" or how "deferential" *it* should be. *It* is always assumed to be the single unitary practice established and justified in *Marbury*.

10. L. Hand, The Bill of Rights 73 (1958).

This seems to me a seriously misleading way of proceeding. *Marbury* defends (and its detractors attack) what I have here called the pure interpretive model of judicial review. The case itself involves the close interpretation of a technical and explicit constitutional provision, which is found, upon conventional linguistic analysis, to conflict with a statute. The argument for judicial review as a general matter is made in terms appropriate to that sort of case. Chief Justice Marshall's stress is on the *writtenness* of the Constitution, and on its supremacy in cases of clear conflict with ordinary law.[11] His heuristic examples all involve obvious conflicts between hypothetical (and unlikely) statutes on the one hand, and particularly explicit constitutional commands on the other.[12]

All this makes *Marbury* a most atypical constitutional case, and an inappropriate paradigm for the sort of judicial review that has been important and controversial throughout our history, from *Dred Scott* [13] to the *Legal Tender Cases* [14] to *Lochner* [15] to *Carter Coal* [16] and on to *Brown v. Board of Education*,[17] *Baker v. Carr*,[18] and the Death Penalty [19] and Abortion [20] cases in our own day. In the important cases, reference to and analysis of the constitutional text plays a minor role. The dominant norms of decision are those large conceptions of governmental structure and individual rights that are at best referred to, and whose content is scarcely at all specified, in the written Constitution—dual federalism, vested rights, fair procedure, equality before the law.

The question of the legitimacy of this very different sort of judicial review is scarcely addressed, much less concluded, by the arguments of *Marbury v. Madison*. To approach that question, we might better examine the debate between Justice Chase and Iredell in *Calder v. Bull*.[21] And if exposure to the matchless rhetoric of John Marshall is

---

11. 5 U.S. (1 Cranch) 137, 176–78 (1803). Although the argument proceeds in terms of instances of purely interpretive judicial review, the underlying principle—that the courts must give precedence to constitutional law over ordinary law—is not itself found in or easily inferred from the text. Nevertheless, the argument for that principle still seems to be in the interpretive mode, based as it is on the intentions inferable from the framers' adoption of a written constitution.

12. For example, Marshall asks rhetorically whether the courts should enforce a statute generally imposing a duty on exports from a state, or an avowed bill of attainder or ex post facto law. *Id.* at 179.

13. Dred Scott v. Sanford, 60 U.S. (19 How.) 393 (1857).

14. 79 U.S. (12 Wall.) 457 (1871).

15. Lochner v. New York, 198 U.S. 45 (1905).

16. Carter v. Carter Coal Co., 298 U.S. 238 (1936).

17. 347 U.S. 483 (1954).

18. 369 U.S. 186 (1962).

19. Furman v. Georgia, 408 U.S. 238 (1972).

20. Roe v. Wade, 410 U.S. 113 (1973), Doe v. Bolton, 410 U.S. 179 (1973).

21. 3 U.S. (3 Dall.) 386 (1798). Chase: "I cannot subscribe to the omnipotence of a state legislature, or that it is absolute and without control, although its authority should not be expressly restrained by the Constitution, or fundamental law of the State .... There are certain vital principles in our free republican governments, which will determine and overrule our apparent and flagrant abuse of legislative power ...." *Id.* at 387–88 (majority opinion).

Iredell: "It is true, that some speculative jurists have held, that a legislative act against natural justice must, in itself, be void; but I cannot think, that under such a government, any court of justice would possess a power to declare it so ....

"[T]he ideas of natural justice are regulated by no fixed standard; the ablest and desired, *Fletcher v. Peck*[22] provides an excellent example. In that case, the Georgia statute is struck down on two alternative grounds. The first is a strained interpretation of the contract clause, comparable in flimsiness to some of the poorer interpretive efforts of the Warren Court. The second ground is expressed in the Court's conclusion that the statute violates "general principles which are common to our free institutions"—in particular, the principle of the inviolability of vested rights. Conspicuously absent is a dissent arguing that this principle is nowhere stated in the constitutional text. Indeed, the other opinion in the case—that of Justice Johnson—expresses agreement with the result on the ground of "general principles," but disavows the strained reading of the contract clause.

The parallel between *Fletcher* and most contemporary judicial review is striking. Today, the Court will formally invoke one of the majestic generalities of the Constitution, typically the due process or equal protection clause, as the textual basis for its decision. Even this much specificity is not always vouchsafed us. Thus we are told of the constitutional "right to travel" that the Court has "no occasion to ascribe the source of this right to * * * a particular constitutional provision."[25] And in the Abortion Cases, the Court's reference to the textual cover for the "right of privacy" is strikingly casual:

> This right of privacy, whether it be founded in the Fourteenth Amendment's concept of personal liberty and restrictions upon state action, as we feel it is, or, as the District Court determined, in the Ninth Amendment's reservation of rights to the people, is broad enough to encompass a woman's decision whether or not to terminate her pregnancy.[26]

It should be clear that in these cases the Court is quite openly *not* relying on constitutional text for the content of the substantive principles it is invoking to invalidate legislation. The parallel reliance on the ninth amendment and the due process clause in the Abortion Cases is instructive on the point. The ninth amendment on its face has no substantive content. It is rather a license to constitutional decisionmakers to look beyond the substantive commands of the constitutional text to protect fundamental rights not expressed therein. In this case at least, the due process clause is being used in the same way.

Much of our substantive constitutional doctrine is of this kind. Where it arises "under" some piece of constitutional text, the text is not invoked as the source of the values or principles that rule the cases.

the purest men have differed upon the subject; and all that the court could properly say, in such an event, would be, that the legislature, possessed of an equal right of opinion, had passed an act which, in the opinion of the judges, was inconsistent with the abstract principles of natural justice." *Id.* at 398–99 (concurring opinion).

22. 10 U.S. (6 Cranch) 87 (1810).

25. Shapiro v. Thompson, 394 U.S. 618, 630 (1969) (footnote omitted).

26. Roe v. Wade, 410 U.S. 113, 153 (1973). Students of the aesthetics of pseudo-interpretation may debate whether or not this formulation is preferable to the Court's celebrated shuffle in Griswold v. Connecticut, 381 U.S. 479 (1965), through the "emanations" and "penumbras" of the Bill of Rights.

Rather the broad textual provisions are seen as sources of legitimacy for judicial development and explication of basic shared national values. These values may be seen as permanent and universal features of human social arrangements—natural law principles—as they typically were in the 18th and 19th centuries. Or they may be seen as relative to our particular civilization, and subject to growth and change, as they typically are today. Our characteristic contemporary metaphor is "the living Constitution"—a constitution with provisions suggesting restraints on government in the name of basic rights, yet sufficiently unspecific to permit the judiciary to elucidate the development and change in the content of those rights over time.

This view of constitutional adjudication is at war with the pure interpretive model. As Mr. Justice Black said often and forcefully enough, he had no truck with the notion of changing, flexible, "living" constitutional guarantees.[28] The amendment process was the framers' chosen and exclusive method of adopting constitutional values to changing times; the judiciary was to enforce the Constitution's substantive commands as the framers meant them.

This is not to say that the interpretive model is incompatible with one limited sense of the concept of a "living" constitution. The model can contemplate the application of the framers' value judgments and institutional arrangements to new or changed *factual* circumstances. In that sense, its proponents can endorse Chief Justice Marshall's view of the Constitution as "intended to endure for ages to come, and consequently, to be adapted to the various crises of human affairs."[30]

But the interpretive model cannot be reconciled with constitutional doctrines protecting unspecified "essential" or "fundamental" liberties, or "fair procedure," or "decency"—leaving it to the judiciary to give moral content to those conceptions either once and for all or from age to age. That sort of "interpretation" would drain from the interpretive model its animating strength. Once it was adopted, the courts could no longer honestly defend an unpopular decision to a protesting public with the transfer of responsibility: "We didn't do it—you did." No longer would the Court's constitutional role be the technical and professional one of applying *given* norms to changing facts; instead the Court would assume the large and problematic role of discerning a society's most basic contemporary values.

III. THE IMPLICATIONS OF THE PURE INTERPRETIVE MODEL

Let me now give some examples, confined to the area of individual rights, of the numerous and important substantive constitutional doctrines which seem to me unjustified under a consistently applied pure interpretive model of judicial review. First and most obvious is virtually the entire body of doctrine developed under the due process clauses of the 5th and 14th amendments. If those clauses can be seen as having

28. *See, e.g.,* Harper v. Virginia Bd. of Elections, 383 U.S. 663, 670 (1966) (Black, J., dissenting).

30. McCulloch v. Maryland, 17 U.S. (4 Wheat.) 415, 427 (1819).

any specific normative content attributable to their framers, it is probably only that given to them by Mr. Justice Black.[31] In his view, due process requires only that deprivations of life, liberty or property be authorized by law duly enacted, rather than carried out by arbitrary executive action. A slightly more ambitious, though highly implausible, narrow interpretation is that adopted by the pre-Civil War Supreme Court—that the clause prohibits departures from the settled course of procedure familiar in the English courts in 1791.[32]

On the interpretive model, then, all the rest of due process doctrine must go. First, what many regard as the core of due process doctrine—its flexible requirement of "fundamentally fair" procedures in criminal and civil proceedings—cannot be reconciled with the interpretive model. These doctrines are developments of the "living constitution" concept *par excellence*.[33] In addition, everything that has been labeled "substantive due process" would be eliminated. It is these doctrines on which the proponents of the interpretive model have most often focused their attacks. Much of the force behind their position derives from the deeply felt opposition to the constitutionalization of laissez-faire economics epitomized by *Lochner v. New York*,[34] and they typically unite in opposition to contemporary doctrinal developments that remind them too much of *Lochner*.[35]

A striking point often overlooked by contemporary interpretivists is that the demise of substantive due process must constitutionally free the federal government to engage in explicit racial discrimination. There is no textual warrant for reading into the due process clause of the fifth amendment any of the prohibitions directed against the states by the

---

31. *See In re* Winship, 397 U.S. 358, 377–85 (1970) (dissenting opinion). As Mr. Justice Black notes in that opinion, his separate position that the 14th amendment incorporates the Bill of Rights is not based on construction of the due process clause alone, but on "the language of the entire first section of the Fourteenth Amendment, as illuminated by the legislative history surrounding its adoption." *Id.* at 382 n. 11.

32. Murray's Lessee v. Hoboken Land & Improvement Co., 59 U.S. (18 How.) 272, 277 (1856).

33. *See, e.g., In re* Winship, 397 U.S. 358, 377 (1970) (Black, J., dissenting); Goldberg v. Kelly, 397 U.S. 254 (1970) (Black, J., dissenting).

34. 198 U.S. 45 (1905).

35. It now seems that the ultimate punchline in the criticism of a constitutional decision is to say that it is "like *Lochner*." Professor Ely has even minted a generic term, "to *Lochner*," to describe whatever-it-was-so-awful-the-Court-did-in-*Lochner*. Ely, [*The Wages of*

Crying Wolf: A Comment on Roe v. Wade, 82 Yale L.J. 920, 944 (1973).]

Lochner is only one of thousands of decisions in the history of the Court that invoke a noninterpretive mode of constitutional adjudication; if it was a bad decision, as I think it was, it by no means follows that the general mode of adjudication it represents is illegitimate. There are many bad decisions in the mode of pure interpretation.

It is an often overlooked point that Mr. Justice Holmes in his classic *Lochner* dissent did not use the case as an occasion to reject noninterpretive adjudication generally, or even substantive due process as such; quite the contrary: "I think that the word liberty in the Fourteenth Amendment is perverted when it is held to prevent the natural outcome of a dominant opinion, *unless it can be said that a rational and fair man necessarily would admit that the statute proposed would infringe fundamental principles as they have been understood by the traditions of our people and our law*." 198 U.S. at 76 (emphasis added).

equal protection clause.[36]

Equally strikingly, the application of the provisions of the Bill of Rights to states cannot be justified under an interpretive model—unless one strains to accept, as the Court clearly has declined to do, the flimsy historical evidence that the framers of the 14th amendment intended this result.[37] Freedom of speech, freedom of religion, and the requirement of just compensation in the taking of property, as well as the procedural provisions of the fourth, fifth, sixth, and eighth amendments must then no longer be seen as federal constitutional restraints on state power.

All of the "fundamental interests" that trigger "strict scrutiny" under the equal protection clause would have to be discarded, if the interpretive model were to control constitutional adjudication. Most obviously, the large body of doctrine that has grown up around the interests in the franchise and in participation in the electoral process could not stand. If the values implicit in the equal protection clause are limited only to those that its framers intended at the time of enactment, the clause clearly does not speak to questions of eligibility for the franchise or of legislative apportionment.[38]

Thus far, it seems to me there is little room for disagreement that the premises of the pure interpretive model would require the conclusions I have drawn from it. For those who have not yet had enough, and coming to slightly more doubtful matters, there is serious question how much of the law prohibiting state racial discrimination can survive honest application of the interpretive model. It is clear that the equal protection clause was meant to prohibit *some* forms of state racial discrimination, most obviously those enacted in the Black Codes. It is equally clear from the legislative history that the clause was *not* intended to guarantee equal political rights, such as the right to vote or to run

36. *See* Bolling v. Sharpe, 347 U.S. 497, 499 (1954). Since *Bolling*, the Court has often applied equal protection doctrine to the federal government "under" the fifth amendment due process clause. *See, e.g.,* Shapiro v. Thompson, 394 U.S. 618 (1969), in which the Court invalidated a District of Columbia statute as a violation of due process, while relying upon the equal protection clause to invalidate similar state statutes. Since *Bolling*—at least as far as I have been able to discover—the Court has never even seriously discussed the possibility that the fifth amendment due process clause might not fully incorporate the requirements progressively imposed on the states under the equal protection clause.

37. The Court's refusal to adopt the "incorporation" theory is clear both from its refusal to apply the requirements of grand jury indictment and civil jury trial to the states, and from its statements in "selective incorporation" cases. *See, e.g.,* Duncan v. Louisiana, 391 U.S. 145, 149 (1968), which held that due process required the states to provide jury trial in serious criminal cases *because* "trial by jury in criminal cases is fundamental to the American scheme of justice * * *." For the controversy over the intent of the framers, *compare* Fairman, *Does the Fourteenth Amendment Incorporate the Bill of Rights?*, 2 Stan. L.Rev. 5 (1949), *with* Adamson v. California, 332 U.S. 46, 68 (1947) (Black, J., dissenting).

38. The numerous dissenting opinions of Mr. Justice Harlan in voting and reapportionment cases put the point beyond doubt. *See, e.g.,* Carrington v. Rash, 380 U.S. 89, 97 (1965) (Harlan, J., dissenting); Reynolds v. Sims, 377 U.S. 533, 589 (1964) (Harlan, J., dissenting).

for office, and perhaps including the right to serve on juries.[39]

It is at least doubtful whether the clause can fairly be read as intending to bar any form of state-imposed racial segregation, so long as equal facilities are made available. Professor Bickel's careful study of the legislative history revealed little evidence of intent to prohibit segregation, which at the time was widespread in the North.[40] Professor Bickel did conclude that the original understanding of the amendment was consistent with the decision in the School Segregation Cases, but only in the sense that the general language of the clause *licensed* the courts (and Congress) to enforce evolving ideals of racial justice.[41] Yet this is a classic invocation of the notion of the "living constitution," and as such is not permitted by the interpretive model.

Finally, under the interpretive model, modern applications of the provisions of the Bill of Rights based on their capacity to grow or develop with changing social values would have to be discarded. Prominent among the discarded doctrines would be the prevailing view that the eighth amendment's prohibition of cruel and unusual punishments must be "interpreted" in light of society's "evolving standards of decency." [42] It is doubtful that much of modern first amendment doctrine could be defended on the basis of value choices attributable to the framers,[43] and similar doubts must cast a shadow on some of the law of the fourth amendment.[44] The doctrine that the sixth amendment guarantees appointed counsel for indigent defendants [45] is likewise in serious jeopardy, if historically intended meaning must be the only legitimate guide in constitutional adjudication.[46]

39. *See generally* Bickel, *The Original Understanding and the Segregation Decision,* 69 Harv.L.Rev. 1 (1955).

40. *Id.* at 58.

41. *Id.* at 62–65.

42. *See, e.g.,* Trop v. Dulles, 356 U.S. 86, 101 (1958).

43. *See generally* L. Levy, Legacy of Suppression (1960).

44. *See, e.g.,* Katz v. United States, 389 U.S. 347 (1967), in which the Court extended fourth amendment coverage to the recording of oral statements by electronic devices. Justice Black filed a lone dissent arguing—from an interpretive stance— "[s]ince I see no way in which the words of the Fourth Amendment can be construed to apply to eavesdropping, that closes the matter for me * * *. I will not distort the words of the Amendment in order to 'keep the Constitution up to date' or 'to bring it into harmony with the times.' " *Id.* at 373 (dissenting opinion).

45. Johnson v. Zerbst, 304 U.S. 458 (1938).

46. The instances of noninterpretive judicial review I have mentioned fall into three general groups. First are those instances where the courts have created (or found) independent constitutional rights with almost no textual guidance. Examples are the contemporary right of privacy, and the older liberty of contract. Second are those instances where the courts have given general application to norms that the constitutional text explicitly applies in a more limited way. Examples are the application of equal protection and contract clause principles to the federal government, and the application of the Bill of Rights to the states—"under" the conveniently all-embracing due process clauses. The third type is the extension or broadening of principles stated in the Constitution beyond the normative content intended for them by the framers. Examples are the School Segregation Cases, and the extension of the fourth amendment to cover eavesdropping.

Most of the ire of proponents of the pure interpretive model has been directed against the first of these types of noninterpretive review. However the other two types are equally illegitimate, given the logic of the interpretive model. The advantage of placing a controverted case in the

While one might disagree with this rough catalogue on points of detail, it should be clear that an extraordinarily radical purge of established constitutional doctrine would be required if we candidly and consistently applied the pure interpretive model. Surely that makes out at least a prima facie practical case against the model. Conservatives ought to be cautious about adopting any abstract premise which requires so drastic a change in accepted practice, and liberals presumably will be dismayed by the prospect of any major diminution in the courts' authority to protect basic human rights.

IV. BEYOND INTERPRETATION: A PROGRAM OF INQUIRY

The uncomfortable results of adopting the interpretive model do not by themselves make a wholly satisfying argument for judicial review that goes beyond interpretation. Constitutional adjudication going beyond the norms implicit in text and original history requires its own affirmative justification. In this short Essay, I can only suggest the several levels on which this inquiry might proceed, and hint at some of the directions it might take.

A. The Question of Practical Wisdom

First, one must consider the question of the wisdom and prudence of putting—or more accurately *leaving*—in the hands of judges the considerable power to define and enforce fundamental human rights without substantial guidance from constitutional text and history. How one views this question depends largely on how one evaluates the practical results, over the long run, of the exercise of this power. Arguments about institutional competence and the general propensities of judges become relevant here. Familiar in this context is the argument made in varying forms by constitutional commentators from Alexander Hamilton to Alexander Bickel that it makes some sense to give the final—or nearly final—say over the barrier between state and individual to the "least dangerous branch," the one that possesses neither purse nor sword.[47] But much can be said the other way, particularly through assignment in the name of popular sovereignty, and through allusion to *Lochner* and its ilk.

B. The Jurisprudential Question

Second, one can ask the jurisprudential question whether as a general matter the defining and enforcing of basic rights without external textual guidance is essentially a judicial task. Judges may be fine folk, but if what they are doing when they engage in judicial review on the basis of changing and unwritten moral principles is not adjudication,

---

third rather than the first grouping is that it is usually possible to argue, with at least a shadow of plausibility, that extension of a specific constitutional prohibition really involves only the application of old norms to changed facts, and not a change in the norms themselves. *See, e.g.,* the majority opinion in Griswold v. Connecticut, 381 U.S. 479 (1965), for an implausible attempt to base a non-textual right of marital privacy on an "interpretation" of various provisions of the Bill of Rights—thus converting a Type 1 case into a "less suspect" Type 3 case.

47. *See* The Federalist No. 78, at 504–05 (E. Earle ed.) (A. Hamilton); A. Bickel, The Least Dangerous Branch 23–28 (1962).

then they are sailing under false colors. For they have consistently told us that judicial review is genuinely incident to their traditionally assigned task of deciding litigated cases according to law.

A rigorously positivist jurisprudence would hold that judicial decision not directed by the articulate command of a determinate external sovereign is not truly adjudication. Rather it is a species of legislation. But this sort of positivist also views the entirely traditional judicial task of common law development through case-by-case decision as a form of legislation.[48] If common law development is an appropriate judicial function, falling within the traditionally accepted judicial role, is not the functionally similar case-by-case development of constitutional norms appropriate as well? Granted that the supremacy of constitutional law over legislation, when contrasted with the formally inferior status of common law, makes a great difference. But the difference is in the hierarchical status of the judicial decision—which turns on a question of *authority*—and not in the intrinsic nature of the task.

C.   The Question of Lawful Authority

The question of authority is the third level of inquiry into the justification for noninterpretive judicial review. Even if this mode of judicial review produces good results in the eyes of some beholders, and even if it is not intrinsically unjudicial, there remains the question whether in our Constitution we have actually granted this large power to our judges.

In resolving this issue of legal authority, there seems to me only one plausible method of inquiry. We must apply the conventional and accepted categories of legal argument—original understanding, judicial precedent, subsequent history, and internal consistency—and see if they support judicial review that goes beyond interpretation.

I believe that when these tests are applied, constitutional adjudication of the sort objected to by Mr. Justice Black and the other proponents of the pure interpretive model will be seen to be a lawful and legitimate feature of our system of judicial review. Full development of the argument must await another occasion; it necessarily requires lengthy and detailed historical documentation. But a brief sketch may be useful here.[49]

---

48. I do not endorse this positivist analysis. It seems to me that traditional common law decision and constitutional decision according to the noninterpretive mode both can be seen as decision of cases according to law. The law in question consists of the generally accepted social norms applied in the decision of the cases, norms that are—contrary to the positivists' position— best seen as "part of the law," quite independent of their promulgation through defined lawmaking procedures. *See* Dworkin, *The Model of Rules,* 35 U.Chi.L.Rev. 14 (1967); Wellington, *Common Law Rules and Constitutional Double Standards:*

Some Notes on Adjudication, 83 Yale L.J. 221 (1973).

49. I have set out my sketch as a simple narrative, lacking the detail, the qualifications, and the analysis of conflicting evidence that the full argument requires. I have also left out any documentation, on the theory that incomplete and necessarily misleading citation of sources is worse than none at all. [For a] full-scale development of the historical argument sketched here [, see Grey, *Origins of The Unwritten Constitution: Fundamental Law in American Revolutionary Thought,* 30 Stan.L.Rev. 843 (1978)].

For the generation that framed the Constitution, the concept of a "higher law," protecting "natural rights," and taking precedence over ordinary positive law as a matter of political obligation, was widely shared and deeply felt. An essential element of American constitutionalism was the reduction to written form—and hence to positive law—of some of the principles of natural rights. But at the same time, it was generally recognized that written constitutions could not completely codify the higher law. Thus in the framing of the original American constitutions it was widely accepted that there remained unwritten but still binding principles of higher law. The ninth amendment is the textual expression of this idea in the federal Constitution.

As it came to be accepted that the judiciary had the power to enforce the commands of the written Constitution when these conflicted with ordinary law, it was also widely assumed that judges would enforce as constitutional restraints the unwritten natural rights as well. The practice of the Marshall Court and of many of its contemporary state courts, and the writings of the leading constitutional commentators through the first generation of our national life, confirm this understanding.

A parallel development during the first half of the 19th century was the frequent attachment of unwritten constitutional principles to the vaguer and more general clauses of the state and federal constitutions. Natural-rights reasoning in constitutional adjudication persisted up to the Civil War, particularly with respect to property and contract rights, and increasingly involving "due process" and "law of the land" clauses in constitutional texts. At the same time, an important wing of the antislavery movement developed a natural-rights constitutional theory, built around the concepts of due process, of national citizenship and its rights, and of the human equality proclaimed in the Declaration of Independence.

Though this latter movement had little direct effect on pre-Civil War judicial decisions, it was the formative theory underlying the due process, equal protection, and privileges and immunities clauses of the 14th amendment. Section 1 of the 14th amendment is thus properly seen as a reaffirmation and reenactment in positive law of the principle that fundamental human rights have constitutional status.

The late 19th century saw the most controversial phase in our history of unwritten constitutional law, with the aggressive development by state and federal judges of constitutional principles protecting "liberty of contract" against labor regulation, and restraining taxation and the regulation of prices charged by private business. The reaction to this tendency marked the beginning of sustained intellectual and political attack on the whole concept of unwritten constitutional principles.

Politically, emergent and eventually dominant social forces continued to press for the legislation that was being invalidated under these constitutional principles. Intellectually, the 18th–century philosophical framework supporting the concept of immutable natural rights was eroded with the growth of legal positivism, ethical relativism, pragmatism, and historicism.

Under the combined assault of these social and intellectual forces, the courts retreated from the doctrines of "economic due process," abandoning them in the 1930's. However, although the more sweeping attack on the whole tradition of unwritten constitutional principles gained some important adherents within the judiciary and still more among academic critics, it did not ultimately prevail.

For at almost the same time as the doctrines protecting the laissez-faire economy were passing out of constitutional law, the judiciary began the active development of new civil libertarian constitutional rights whose protection was deemed "essential to the concept of ordered liberty"—for example, rights against state governments of freedom of speech and religion, rights to "fundamentally fair" proceedings, and rights to familial autonomy in childrearing and education.

The last generation has seen further development of constitutional rights clearly—and sometimes avowedly—not derived by textual interpretation, notably the right of privacy, the right to vote, the right to travel, and generally the rights resulting from application of "equal protection of the laws" to the federal government. The intellectual framework against which these rights have developed is different from the natural-rights tradition of the founding fathers—its rhetorical reference points are the Anglo–American tradition and basic American ideals, rather than human nature, the social contract, or the rights of man. But it is the modern offspring, in a direct and traceable line of legitimate descent, of the natural-rights tradition that is so deeply embedded in our constitutional origins.

To summarize, there was an original understanding, both implicit and textually expressed, that unwritten higher law principles had constitutional status. From the very beginning, and continuously until the Civil War, the courts acted on that understanding and defined and enforced such principles as part of their function of judicial review. Aware of that history, the framers of the 14th amendment reconfirmed the original understanding through the "majestic generalities" of section 1. And ever since, again without significant break, the courts have openly proclaimed and enforced unwritten constitutional principles.

ROBERT H. BORK, NEUTRAL PRINCIPLES AND SOME FIRST AMENDMENT PROBLEMS
47 Ind.L.J. 1, 1–11 (1971).

The subject of the lengthy and often acrimonious debate about the proper role of the Supreme Court under the Constitution is one that preoccupies many people these days: when is authority legitimate? I find it convenient to discuss that question in the context of the Warren

Court and its works simply because the Warren Court posed the issue in acute form. The issue did not disappear along with the era of the Warren Court majorities, however. It arises when any court either exercises or declines to exercise the power to invalidate any act of another branch of government. The Supreme Court is a major power center, and we must ask when its power should be used and when it should be withheld.

Our starting place, inevitably, is Professor Herbert Wechsler's argument that the Court must not be merely a "naked power organ," which means that its decisions must be controlled by principle.[1] "A principled decision," according to Wechsler, "is one that rests on reasons with respect to all the issues in a case, reasons that in their generality and their neutrality transcend any immediate result that is involved."[2]

Wechsler chose the term "neutral principles" to capsulate his argument, though he recognizes that the legal principle to be applied is itself never neutral because it embodies a choice of one value rather than another. Wechsler asked for the neutral application of principles, which is a requirement, as Professor Louis L. Jaffe puts it, that the judge "sincerely believe in the principle upon which he purports to rest his decision." "The judge," says Jaffe, "must believe in the validity of the reasons given for the decision at least in the sense that he is prepared to apply them to a later case which he cannot honestly distinguish."[3] He must not, that is, decide lawlessly. But is the demand for neutrality in judges merely another value choice, one that is no more principled than any other? I think not, but to prove it we must rehearse fundamentals. This is familiar terrain but important and still debated.

The requirement that the Court be principled arises from the resolution of the seeming anomaly of judicial supremacy in a democratic society. If the judiciary really is supreme, able to rule when and as it sees fit, the society is not democratic. The anomaly is dissipated, however, by the model of government embodied in the structure of the Constitution, a model upon which popular consent to limited government by the Supreme Court also rests. This model we may for convenience, though perhaps not with total accuracy, call "Madisonian."[4]

A Madisonian system is not completely democratic, if by "democratic" we mean completely majoritarian. It assumes that in wide areas of life majorities are entitled to rule for no better reason [than] that they are majorities. We need not pause here to examine the philosophical underpinnings of that assumption since it is a "given" in our society; nor need we worry that "majority" is a term of art meaning often no more than the shifting combinations of minorities that add up to temporary majorities in the legislature. That majorities are so constitut-

---

1. H. Wechsler, *Toward Neutral Principles of Constitutional Law,* in Principles, Politics, and Fundamental Law 3, 27 (1961)[.]

2. *Id.*

3. L. Jaffe, English and American Judges as Lawmakers 38 (1969).

4. *See* R. Dahl, A Preface to Democratic Theory 4–33 (1956).

ed is inevitable. In any case, one essential premise of the Madisonian model is majoritarianism. The model has also a counter-majoritarian premise, however, for it assumes there are some areas of life a majority should not control. There are some things a majority should not do to us no matter how democratically it decides to do them. These are areas properly left to individual freedom, and coercion by the majority in these aspects of life is tyranny.

Some see the model as containing an inherent, perhaps an insoluble, dilemma.[5] Majority tyranny occurs if legislation invades the areas properly left to individual freedom. Minority tyranny occurs if the majority is prevented from ruling where its power is legitimate. Yet, quite obviously, neither the majority nor the minority can be trusted to define the freedom of the other. This dilemma is resolved in constitutional theory, and in popular understanding, by the Supreme Court's power to define both majority and minority freedom through the interpretation of the Constitution. Society consents to be ruled undemocratically within defined areas by certain enduring principles believed to be stated in, and placed beyond the reach of majorities by, the Constitution.

But this resolution of the dilemma imposes severe requirements upon the Court. For it follows that the Court's power is legitimate only if it has, and can demonstrate in reasoned opinions that it has, a valid theory, derived from the Constitution, of the respective spheres of majority and minority freedom. If it does not have such a theory but merely imposes its own value choices, or worse if it pretends to have a theory but actually follows its own predilections, the Court violates the postulates of the Madisonian model that alone justifies its power. It then necessarily abets the tyranny either of the majority or of the minority.

This argument is central to the issue of legitimate authority because the Supreme Court's power to govern rests upon popular acceptance of this model. Evidence that this is, in fact, the basis of the Court's power is to be gleaned everywhere in our culture. We need not canvass here such things as high school civics texts and newspaper commentary, for the most telling evidence may be found in the U.S. Reports. The Supreme Court regularly insists that its results, and most particularly its controversial results, do not spring from the mere will of the Justices in the majority but are supported, indeed compelled, by a proper understanding of the Constitution of the United States. Value choices are attributed to the Founding Fathers, not to the Court. The way an institution advertises tells you what it thinks its customers demand.

This is, I think, the ultimate reason the Court must be principled. If it does not have and rigorously adhere to a valid and consistent theory of majority and minority freedoms based upon the Constitution, judicial supremacy, given the axioms of our system, is, precisely to that extent, illegitimate. The root of its illegitimacy is that it opens a chasm

---

5. *Id.* at 23–24.

between the reality of the Court's performance and the constitutional and popular assumptions that give it power.

I do not mean to rest the argument entirely upon the popular understanding of the Court's function. Even if society generally should ultimately perceive what the Court is in fact doing and, having seen, prove content to have major policies determined by the unguided discretion of judges rather than by elected representatives, a principled judge would, I believe, continue to consider himself bound by an obligation to the document and to the structure of government that it prescribes. At least he would be bound so long as any litigant existed who demanded such adherence of him. I do not understand how, on any other theory of judicial obligation, the Court could, as it does now, protect voting rights if a large majority of the relevant constituency were willing to see some groups or individuals deprived of such rights. But even if I am wrong in that, at the very least an honest judge would owe it to the body politic to cease invoking the authority of the Constitution and to make explicit the imposition of his own will, for only then would we know whether the society understood enough of what is taking place to be said to have consented.

Judge J. Skelly Wright, in an argument resting on different premises, has severely criticized the advocates of principle. He defends the value-choosing role of the Warren Court, setting that Court in opposition to something he refers to as the "scholarly tradition," which criticizes that Court for its lack of principle.[6] A perceptive reader, sensitive to nuance, may suspect that the Judge is rather out of sympathy with that tradition from such hints as his reference to "self-appointed scholastic mandarins."[7]

The "mandarins" of the academy anger the Judge because they engage in "haughty derision of the Court's powers of analysis and reasoning."[8] Yet, curiously enough, Judge Wright makes no attempt to refute the charge but rather seems to adopt the technique of confession and avoidance. He seems to be arguing that a Court engaged in choosing fundamental values for society cannot be expected to produce principled decisions at the same time. Decisions first, principles later. One wonders, however, how the Court or the rest of us are to know that the decisions are correct or what they portend for the future if they are not accompanied by the principles that explain and justify them. And it would not be amiss to point out that quite often the principles required of the Warren Court's decisions never did put in an appearance. But Judge Wright's main point appears to be that value choice is the most important function of the Supreme Court, so that if we must take one or the other, and apparently we must, we should prefer a process of selecting values to one of constructing and articulating principles. His argument, I believe, boils down to a syllogism. I. The Supreme Court

---

6. Wright, *Professor Bickel, The Scholarly Tradition, and the Supreme Court,* 84 Harv.L.Rev. 769 (1971)[.]

7. *Id.* at 777.

8. *Id.* at 777–78.

should "protect our constitutional rights and liberties." II. The Supreme Court must "make fundamental value choices" in order to "protect our constitutional rights and liberties." III. Therefore, the Supreme Court should "make fundamental value choices."

The argument displays an all too common confusion. If we have constitutional rights and liberties already, rights and liberties specified by the Constitution, the Court need make no fundamental value choices in order to protect them, and it certainly need not have difficulty enunciating principles. If, on the other hand, "constitutional rights and liberties" are not in some real sense specified by the Constitution but are the rights and liberties the Court chooses, on the basis of its own values, to give to us, then the conclusion was contained entirely in the major premise, and the Judge's syllogism is no more than an assertion of what it purported to prove.

If I am correct so far, no argument that is both coherent and respectable can be made supporting a Supreme Court that "chooses fundamental values" because a Court that makes rather than implements value choices cannot be squared with the presuppositions of a democratic society. The man who understands the issues and nevertheless insists upon the rightness of the Warren Court's performance ought also, if he is candid, to admit that he is prepared to sacrifice democratic process to his own moral views. He claims for the Supreme Court an institutionalized role as perpetrator of limited coups d'etat.

Such a man occupies an impossible philosophic position. What can he say, for instance, of a Court that does not share his politics or his morality? I can think of nothing except the assertion that he will ignore the Court whenever he can get away with it and overthrow it if he can. In his view the Court has no legitimacy, and there is no reason any of us should obey it. And, this being the case, the advocate of a value-choosing Court must answer another difficult question. Why should the Court, a committee of nine lawyers, be the sole agent of change? The man who prefers results to processes has no reason to say that the Court is more legitimate than any other institution. If the Court will not listen, why not argue the case to some other group, say the Joint Chiefs of Staff, a body with rather better means for implementing its decisions?

* * *

It follows that the choice of "fundamental values" by the Court cannot be justified. Where constitutional materials do not clearly specify the value to be preferred, there is no principled way to prefer any claimed human value to any other. The judge must stick close to the text and the history, and their fair implications, and not construct new rights. The [*Griswold* case[a]] illustrates the point. The *Griswold* decision has been acclaimed by legal scholars as a major advance in constitutional law, a salutary demonstration of the Court's ability to protect fundamental human values. I regret to have to disagree, and my

---

a. Griswold v. Connecticut, 381 U.S. 479 (1965).

regret is all the more sincere because I once took the same position and did so in print.[15] In extenuation I can only say that at the time I thought, quite erroneously, that new basic rights could be derived logically by finding and extrapolating a more general principle of individual autonomy underlying the particular guarantees of the Bill of Rights.

The Court's *Griswold* opinion, by Justice Douglas, and the array of concurring opinions, by Justices Goldberg, White and Harlan, all failed to justify the derivation of any principle used to strike down the Connecticut anti-contraceptive statute or to define the scope of the principle. Justice Douglas, to whose opinion I must confine myself, began by pointing out that "specific guarantees in the Bill of Rights have penumbras, formed by emanations from those guarantees that help give them life and substance."[16] Nothing is exceptional there. In the case Justice Douglas cited, *NAACP v. Alabama,*[17] the State was held unable to force disclosure of membership lists because of the chilling effect upon the rights of assembly and political action of the NAACP's members. The penumbra was created solely to preserve a value central to the first amendment, applied in this case through the fourteenth amendment. It had no life of its own as a right independent of the value specified by the first amendment.

But Justice Douglas then performed a miracle of transubstantiation. He called the first amendment's penumbra a protection of "privacy" and then asserted that other amendments create "zones of privacy."[18] He had no better reason to use the word "privacy" than that the individual is free within these zones, free to act in public as well as in private. None of these penumbral zones—from the first, third, fourth or fifth amendments, all of which he cited, along with the ninth—covered the case before him. One more leap was required. Justice Douglas asserted that these various "zones of privacy" created an independent right of privacy,[19] a right not lying within the penumbra of any specific amendment. He did not disclose, however, how a series of specified rights combined to create a new and unspecified right.

The *Griswold* opinion fails every test of neutrality. The derivation of the principle was utterly specious, and so was its definition. In fact, we are left with no idea of what the principle really forbids. Derivation and definition are interrelated here. Justice Douglas called the amendments and their penumbras "zones of privacy," though of course they are not that at all. They protect both private and public behavior and so would more properly be labelled "zones of freedom." If we follow Justice Douglas in his next step, these zones would then add up to an independent right of freedom, which is to say, a general constitutional right to be free of legal coercion, a manifest impossibility in any imaginable society.

15. Bork, *The Supreme Court Needs a New Philosophy,* Fortune, Dec., 1968, at 170.

16. 381 U.S. at 484.

17. 357 U.S. 449 (1958).

18. 381 U.S. at 484.

19. *Id.* at 485, 486.

Griswold, then, is an unprincipled decision, both in the way in which it derives a new constitutional right and in the way it defines that right, or rather fails to define it. We are left with no idea of the sweep of the right of privacy and hence no notion of the cases to which it may or may not be applied in the future. The truth is that the Court could not reach its result in *Griswold* through principle. The reason is obvious. Every clash between a minority claiming freedom and a majority claiming power to regulate involves a choice between the gratifications of the two groups. When the Constitution has not spoken, the Court will be able to find no scale, other than its own value preferences, upon which to weigh the respective claims to pleasure. Compare the facts in *Griswold* with a hypothetical suit by an electric utility company and one of its customers to void a smoke pollution ordinance as unconstitutional. The cases are identical.

In *Griswold* a husband and wife assert that they wish to have sexual relations without fear of unwanted children. The law impairs their sexual gratifications. The State can assert, and at one stage in that litigation did assert, that the majority finds the use of contraceptives immoral. Knowledge that it takes place and that the State makes no effort to inhibit it causes the majority anguish, impairs their gratifications.

The electrical company asserts that it wishes to produce electricity at low cost in order to reach a wide market and make profits. Its customer asserts that he wants a lower cost so that prices can be held low. The smoke pollution regulation impairs his and the company's stockholders' economic gratifications. The State can assert not only that the majority prefer clean air to lower prices, but also that the absence of the regulation impairs the majority's physical and aesthetic gratifications.

Neither case is covered specifically or by obvious implication in the Constitution. Unless we can distinguish forms of gratification, the only course for a principled Court is to let the majority have its way in both cases. It is clear that the Court cannot make the necessary distinction. There is no principled way to decide that one man's gratifications are more deserving of respect than another's or that one form of gratification is more worthy than another.[20] Why is sexual gratification more worthy than moral gratification? Why is sexual gratification nobler than economic gratification? There is no way of deciding these matters other than by reference to some system of moral or ethical values that has no objective or intrinsic validity of its own and about which men can and do differ. Where the Constitution does not embody the moral or ethical choice, the judge has no basis other than his own values upon which to set aside the community judgment embodied in the statute. That, by definition, is an inadequate basis for judicial supremacy. The issue of the community's moral and ethical values, the issue of the

20. The impossibility is related to that of making interpersonal comparisons of utilities. *See* L. Robbins, The Nature and Significance of Economic Science, ch. 4 (2d ed. 1969); P. Samuelson, Foundations of Economic Analysis 243–52 (1965).

degree of pain an activity causes, are matters concluded by the passage and enforcement of the laws in question. The judiciary has no role to play other than that of applying the statutes in a fair and impartial manner.

One of my colleagues refers to this conclusion, not without sarcasm, as the "Equal Gratification Clause." The phrase is apt, and I accept it, though not the sarcasm. Equality of human gratifications, where the document does not impose a hierarchy, is an essential part of constitutional doctrine because of the necessity that judges be principled. To be perfectly clear on the subject, I repeat that the principle is not applicable to legislatures. Legislation requires value choice and cannot be principled in the sense under discussion. Courts must accept any value choice the legislature makes unless it clearly runs contrary to a choice made in the framing of the Constitution.

It follows, of course, that broad areas of constitutional law ought to be reformulated. Most obviously, it follows that substantive due process, revived by the *Griswold* case, is and always has been an improper doctrine. Substantive due process requires the Court to say, without guidance from the Constitution, which liberties or gratifications may be infringed by majorities and which may not. This means that *Griswold's* antecedents were also wrongly decided, *e.g., Meyer v. Nebraska,*[21] which struck down a statute forbidding the teaching of subjects in any language other than English; *Pierce v. Society of Sisters,*[22] which set aside a statute compelling all Oregon school children to attend public schools; *Adkins v. Children's Hospital,*[23] which invalidated a statute of Congress authorizing a board to fix minimum wages for women and children in the District of Columbia; and *Lochner v. New York,*[24] which voided a statute fixing maximum hours of work for bakers. With some of these cases I am in political agreement, and perhaps *Pierce's* result could be reached on acceptable grounds, but there is no justification for the Court's methods. In *Lochner,* Justice Peckham, defending liberty from what he conceived as a mere meddlesome interference, asked, "[A]re we all * * * at the mercy of legislative majorities?"[25] The correct answer, where the Constitution does not speak, must be "yes."

C. THE ROLE OF THE TEXT

FREDERICK SCHAUER, EASY CASES
58 S.Cal.L.Rev. 399, 414–423, 430–31 (1985).

* * * [It is] clear that there *are* easy cases in constitutional law— lots of them. The parties concerned know, without litigating and without consulting lawyers, that Ronald Reagan cannot run for a third term; that the junior Senator from Virginia, who was elected in 1982,

---

21. 262 U.S. 390 (1922).

22. 268 U.S. 510 (1925).

23. 261 U.S. 525 (1923).

24. 198 U.S. 45 (1905).

25. *Id.* at 59.

does not have to run again in 1984 or 1986 even though the Representative from the First Congressional District does; that bills receiving less than a majority of votes in either the House or the Senate are not laws of the United States; that the Equal Rights Amendment, the District of Columbia Representation in the Senate Amendment, and the Balanced Budget Amendment are not now part of the Constitution; and that a twenty-nine year-old is not going to be President of the United States. I have equivalent confidence that I will not receive a notice in the mail informing me that I must house members of the armed forces in my spare bedroom; that criminal defendants in federal courts cannot be denied the right to be represented by a qualified lawyer for whom they are willing to pay; and that the next in line to succeed to the Presidency in the event of the President's death is the Vice–President, and not the Secretary of the Interior, the Congressman from Wyoming, or the quarterback for the Philadelphia Eagles.

The foregoing is only a small sample of the legal events that are "easy" constitutional cases. Once free from the lawyer's preoccupation with close cases—those in which the lawyer *qua* lawyer is a necessary actor in the play [39]—we begin to comprehend the enormous quantity of instances in which the legal results are commonly considered obvious. But why is this? What makes the easy case easy?

In searching for the sources of easiness, it is perhaps best to look for the sources of hardness, and then define easy cases as those without any of the characteristics of hard cases. Such definition by exclusion is not the only approach, but it seems particularly appropriate because it is the exception, the hard case, that most commonly commands our attention.

Prototypically, a vague, ambiguous, or simply opaque linguistic formulation of the relevant rule generates a hard case. Such a linguistic phenomenon may be caused by questions about the result announced by a clearly applicable rule, questions about which rule, if any, is in fact relevant, or both. Regardless of the cause, the result is the same: one cannot find the answer to a question (which is not the same as a controversy) by a straightforward reading of rules.

To the extent that one *can* find an answer to a question by a straightforward reading of rules, other factors may make a case hard. A case that seems linguistically easy may be hard if the result announced by the language is inconsistent with the "purpose" of the rule. In such cases the tension between the plain meaning of the words and the reason for using those words creates a hard case, in much the same way that linguistic imprecision creates a hard case.

Even if a rule seems plainly applicable, and even if that application is consistent with the purpose behind a rule, it may be that two or more rules, dictating different results, will be applicable. If one rule suggests

---

39. Part of the problem, of course, is that legal theory in general is undertaken largely by those who train lawyers. We will have made considerable strides when we recognize that not only hard cases, but also all litigation and all lawyers, are in important respects epiphenomenal.

answer *A* to the question, and another suggests answer *B*, then it is as if no answer had been provided. In the calculus of rules, too many rules are no better than none at all.

Finally, and perhaps most importantly, there may be only one relevant rule, it may be quite straightforwardly applicable, and its application would be consistent with its purpose. Yet it may still be morally, socially, or politically hard, however, in the sense of *hard* to swallow. * * *

There may very well be other sources of hardness, but this sample seems sufficiently large. With these types of hard cases in mind, we can tentatively define an easy case as one having *none* of these characteristics of hardness, one in which a clearly applicable rule noncontroversially generates an answer to the question at hand, and one in which the answer so generated is consistent both with the purpose behind the rule and with the social, political, and moral climate in which the question is answered.

There is clearly more involved than merely describing an easy case. Perhaps easy cases are like unicorns, quite capable of definition and description, but not to be found in the real world. Thus, my list of seemingly easy cases purported to fill this argumentative gap, to show that easy cases not only can be imagined, but in fact exist if we only know where to look. And, as should be apparent from the particular examples offered, my thesis here is that language is a significant and often underappreciated factor in the production of easy cases. I am *not* claiming that only language can generate easy cases. Various other legal, cultural, and historical phenomena can create those shared understandings that will clarify a linguistically vague regulation, statute, or constitutional provision. And, as the foregoing taxonomy of hard cases was designed to demonstrate, language alone is insufficient to generate an easy case. Neither of these qualifications, however, is inconsistent with my central claim that language is significantly important in producing easy cases—that language can and frequently does speak with a sufficiently clear voice such that linguistically articulated norms themselves leave little doubt as to which results are consistent with that command.

One way of supporting the claim that language is important in producing easy cases is to engage in an extended and most likely incomprehensible discussion of numerous theories of meaning, attempting to demonstrate by some collage of philosophical and behavioral arguments the way in which the use of certain artificially created symbols can and does enable us to communicate with each other. In this context, however, and indeed in most others, such an excursus seems to ignore the most significant piece of evidence supporting a claim about meaning, which is that even the discussion of meaning would take place in English. The discussion itself would thus irrefutably prove the very hypothesis at issue, just as this Article is right now doing the same thing.

When Wittgenstein remarked that "[l]anguage must speak for itself," [47] he was not claiming that language existed in a vacuum, or that meaning could be disassociated from context. Rather, he was pointing out that the ability of language to function ought to be self-evident, and that the inability to explain all or even any of the sources of this phenomenon does not detract from the conclusion that language does function. Thus, to demonstrate that language works with a typical-looking argument would be possible only because of the conclusion of that very argument. If language didn't "work," the world would be so different from the world in which we live as to be beyond both description and comprehension. Regardless of how understandable this Article may be, it is certainly more understandable to this audience than it would be if it were written in Hungarian, in Chinese, or in semaphore signals. Whether our ability to understand each other in language is biological, behavioral, sociological, or some combination of these is less important than the fact that we can do it.

This is not meant to be the end of an argument, but only the beginning of one. Because law operates with language, understanding the way in which law works requires starting with the proposition that language works. In many instances, some of which I will deal with presently, it may be important to know *why* or *how* language works. In many other instances, however, it is sufficient to do less thinking and more looking, and at least take certain observable facts about language as a possible starting point in the analysis.

It is thus worthwhile to note that the Constitution is, even if nothing else, a use of language. By virtue of being able to speak the English language, we can differentiate between the Constitution and a nursery rhyme, between the Constitution and a novel, and between the Constitution and the Communist Manifesto. Let us construct a simple thought experiment involving a person who is fluent in English (even the English of 1984, and not necessarily the English of 1787 or 1868), but who knows nothing of the history, politics, law, or culture of the United States. If we were to show this person a copy of the Constitution, would that person glean from that collection of marks on a piece of paper alone at least some rudimentary idea of how *this* government works and of what types of relationships exist between the central government and the states, between the different branches of government, and between individuals and government? Although the understanding would be primitive and significant mistakes would be made, it still seems apparent that the answer to the question would be, "Yes." However sketchy and distorted the understanding might be, it would still exceed the understanding produced by a document written in a language not understood by our hypothetical reader, and surpass as well the understanding gained from no information at all.

This general intelligibility of language enables us to understand immediately the mandate of numerous constitutional provisions without

47. L. Wittgenstein, Philosophical Grammar 40 (1974).

recourse to precedent, original intent, or any of the other standard interpretive supplements. We need not depart from the text to determine the rudiments of how a bill becomes a law, the age and other qualifications for various federal offices, the permissible and impermissible limits on the franchise, the number of terms that may be served by the President, the basic procedure for amending the Constitution, the mechanics of admitting a new state, the number of witnesses necessary in a trial for treason, and the permissibility of calling the defendant as a prosecution witness in a federal criminal case.

In some of these and other instances, some noncontroversial technical knowledge may be necessary for understanding. In order to appreciate the clarity of some of the requirements of the fourth, fifth, and sixth amendments, for example, one must understand what a trial is, how it is conducted, and so on. In order to understand some of the structural provisions, it is useful to have at least some preconstitutional understanding of what a state is. These shared background understandings, however, virtually a part of understanding *this* language, do not make the notion of a clear meaning implausible. Words themselves are nothing other than marks or noises, transformed into vehicles for communication by virtue of those rules of language that make it possible for the listener to understand the speaker in most cases. But these rules are not contained in a set of maroon volumes, the linguistic equivalent to the United States Code. These rules are made and continuously remade by the society that uses the language, and different rules may prevail in different segments of that society at different times.

Thus, language cannot be divorced from its context, because meanings become clear if and only if certain understandings are presupposed. Language cannot and does not transcend completely the culture of which it is a part. It is not something that has been delivered packaged, assembled, and ready-to-use to a previously nonlinguistic culture. Language and society are part and parcel of each other; understanding a language, even at its clearest, requires some understanding of the society that has generated it.

But what does this tell us? Certainly not that the notion of plain meaning is worthless, or that questions of interpreting language collapse completely into questions about a culture. That a rosebush springs from and cannot exist without earth, sun, and water does not mean that the notion of a rosebush is not distinguishable from the concepts earth, sun, and water. Similarly, that language requires context does not mean that language *is* context. Language operates significantly because of and as a system of rules that enable people within a shared context to understand each other. At times these rules may be vague, and thus may produce hard cases, but at other times the rules can and do operate to produce the very kinds of "easy" cases I have been describing.

* * *

I am * * * quite willing to concede that it is impossible to have an entirely clear constitutional clause, for the same reason that it is impossible to have an absolutely airtight legal provision of any kind, or an absolutely airtight definition in any field. This is merely a recasting of the well-known message that all terms and all laws have fringe as well as core applications.[60] That there are fringe meanings of words, or fringe applications of laws, for which one can make a reasonable argument for either inclusion or exclusion, does not mean that there are no core cases in which an argument on one side would be almost universally agreed to be compelling, and an argument on the other side would be almost universally agreed to be specious. That I am unsure whether rafts and floating motorized automobiles are "boats" does not dispel my confidence that rowboats and dories most clearly are boats, and that steam locomotives, hamburgers, and elephants equally clearly are not.

This is not to deny that determining the contents of the core, the fringe, and what is wholly outside are contextually and culturally contingent. I can imagine a world in which "elephant" is a fringe (or core) example of a boat, and I can imagine a set of circumstances in *this* world in which a floating hamburger might legitimately present us with a definitional problem vis-à-vis the class "boats." The mere possibility of such circumstances does not eliminate our ability to make sense out of the words as standardly applied, however. If it did, we would have no way of communicating with each other.

The lesson of open texture, then, is that every use of language is potentially vague * * *. The precision of language is necessarily limited by the lack of omniscience of human beings, and thus any use of language is bounded by the limitations of human foresight. The *non sequitur,* however, is the move from the proposition that language is not perfectly precise to the proposition that language is useless. * * *

Although linguistic nihilism seems scarcely comprehensible as a general statement about language, nihilistic tendencies have had a surprising vitality in legal and constitutional theory. The attractions of nihilism seem to be largely attributable, however, to a crabbed view of the legal world, a view that focuses almost exclusively on those hard cases that wind up in court. If we focus only on the marginal cases, only on the cases that a screening process selects largely because of their very closeness, it should come as no surprise that we would have a skeptical view of the power of language to draw distinctions. The cases that wind up in court are not there solely because they lie at the edge of linguistic distinctions, but this is at least a significant factor. Thus the cases that are in court are hardly a representative sample of the effects of legal language. But if we focus instead on easy as well as hard cases, and thus take into our comprehension the full legal world, we see that the cases at the margin are but a small percentage of the full domain of legal

60. *See* Hart, *Scandinavian Realism,* 17 Cambridge L.J. 233, 239 (1959); Williams, *Language and the Law—II,* 61 Law Q.Rev. 179 (1945); *see generally* M. Black, *Reasoning with Loose Concepts,* in Margins of Precision: Essays in Logic and Language 1 (1970); I. Scheffler, Beyond the Letter: A Philosophical Inquiry into Ambiguity, Vagueness, and Metaphor in Language (1979).

events; the bulk of the remaining cases are those in which we can answer questions by consulting the articulated norm. * * *

* * *

The perspective described above views linguistically articulated rules as excluding wrong answers rather than pointing to right ones. From this perspective, there is no longer any justification to view the specific and the general clauses in the Constitution as fundamentally different in kind. Since no clause can generate a uniquely correct answer, at least in the abstract rather than in the context of a specific question, the best view of the specific clauses is that they are merely less vague than the general clauses. The language of a clause, whether seemingly general or seemingly specific, establishes a boundary, or a frame, albeit a frame with fuzzy edges. Even though the language itself does not tell us what goes within the frame, it does tell us when we have gone outside it.

It is best to view the role of language in setting the size of the frame as presumptive rather than absolute. Factors other than the language of the text, or the language of a specifically articulated rule in a case or series of cases, often influence the size and shape of the frame of permissible argument. The language of the text itself is still, however, commonly not only the starting point, but also a constant check long after leaving the starting point. When we look at an uninterpreted clause (in the sense of a series of authoritative judicial interpretations), we commonly focus quite closely on the text. Even in those cases in which an established body of precedent exists, reference to the text is never considered illegitimate.

The language of the text, therefore, remains perhaps the most significant factor in setting the size of the frame. Those clauses that look quite specific are those where the frame is quite small, and thus the range of permissible alternatives is equivalently small. Those clauses that look much more general are those with a substantially larger frame, giving a much wider range of permissible alternatives. This, however, is a continuum and not a dichotomy. Those clauses that seem specific differ from those that seem general in that the former exclude as wrong a larger number of answers than do the latter. * * *

* * * If we consider the text to be informative about boundaries, or limits, rather than about centers, or cores, then the text appears far less irrelevant than is commonly assumed. The text presumptively constrains us, or should, from overstepping what are admittedly pretheoretical and almost intuitive linguistic bounds, and thus serves as one constraint on constitutional interpretation.

We can thus view these linguistic frames as telling an interpreter, *for example* the Supreme Court, which areas are legitimately within the province of interpretation, which subjects are properly the business of the interpretation. An interpretation is legitimate (which is not the same as correct) only insofar as it purports to interpret some language of the document, and only insofar as the interpretation is within the boundaries at least suggested by that language.

SANFORD LEVINSON, LAW AS LITERATURE
60 Tex.L.Rev. 373, 376–89 (1982).

I

* * *

Constitutions, of the written variety especially, are usefully viewed as a means of freezing time by controlling the future through the "hardness" of language encoded in a monumental document, which is then left for later interpreters to decipher. The purpose of such control is to preserve the particular vision held by constitutional founders and to prevent its overthrow by future generations. The very existence of written constitutions with substantive limitations on future conduct is evidence of skepticism, if not outright pessimism, about the moral caliber of future citizens; else why not simply enjoin them to "be good" or "do what you think best"? Writers of constitutions must have a very high confidence in the ability of language both to "harden" and to control.

* * *

Any writer, including a framer of constitutions, presumably imagines the following relationship between text and reader: "The reader sets himself to make out what the author has designed and signified through putting into play a linguistic and literary expertise that he shares with the author. By approximating what the author undertook to signify the reader understands what the language of the work means."[14] And, of course, in the case of those particular texts called legal, by understanding the meaning the conscientious adjudicator-reader becomes authorized to enforce it.

The remark just quoted comes from an essay vigorously attacking certain strains of contemporary literary criticism that Abrams finds insufficiently respectful of determinate meanings allegedly generated by disciplined study of texts. The disputes currently raging through literary criticism precisely mirror some of the central problems facing anyone who would take law seriously; the basis of this parallelism is the centrality to law of textual analysis.[15] If we consider law as literature,

---

14. Abrams, *How to Do Things with Texts,* 46 Partisan Rev. 566 (1979). I owe my familiarity with this comment to Richard Rorty. *See* R. Rorty, *Nineteenth–Century Idealism and Twentieth–Century Textualism,* in Consequences of Pragmatism 139 (1982), *reprinted from* 64 Monist 155 (1981).

15. The best short treatment of these disputes is Culler, *Issues in Contemporary American Critical Debate,* in American Criticism in the Poststructuralist Age 1–18 (I.

Konigsberg ed. 1981). A very illuminating book-length study is F. Lentricchia, After the New Criticism (1980). The commonality of some of the problems of law and literary analysis are touched on in Abraham, *Three Fallacies of Interpretation: A Comment on Precedent and Judicial Decision,* 23 Ariz.L.Rev. 771 (1981); Abraham, *Statutory Interpretation and Literary Theory: Some Common Concerns of an Unlikely Pair,* 32 Rutgers L.Rev. 676 (1980); Michaels, *Against Formalism: The Autonomous Text in Legal and Literary Interpreta-*

then we might better understand the malaise that afflicts all contemporary legal analysis, nowhere more severely than in constitutional theory.

II

* * *

Two classic approaches to understanding a written constitution involve emphasizing either the allegedly plain words of the text or the certain meaning to be given those words through historical reconstruction. I think it fair to say that these particular approaches are increasingly without defenders, at least in the academic legal community. Even so capable an analyst as Professor Monaghan, who is eager to return to the confines of a knowable "originalist" Constitution, admits that he has no way of handling the authority of judicial precedents that (he argues) violate initial understandings.[19]

There is not time in this essay to canvass the problems of originalism. Suffice it to say that the plain meaning approach inevitably breaks down in the face of the reality of disagreement among equally competent speakers of the native language. Intentionality arguments, on the other hand, face not only the problem of explaining why intentions of long-dead people from a different social world should influence us, but also, perhaps more importantly, the problem of extracting intentions from the collectivity of individuals and institutions necessary to give legal validity to the Constitution. Even literary critics most committed to the existence of objective meaning through recovery of authorial intent, like E.D. Hirsch, admit that their approach applies only to individually authored works, and therefore cannot be used to analyze a document like the Constitution.[22]

As Richard Rorty has pointed out, however, there are at least two options open to critics who reject the two approaches outlined above but who, nonetheless, remain interested in interpreting the relevant texts. The first option involves the use of an allegedly more sophisticated method to extract the true meaning of the text. Thus Rorty refers to "the kind of textualist who claims to have gotten the secret of the text, to have broken its code," as a "weak" textualist,[23] where the term is

---

tion, 1 Poetics Today 23 (1979), *reprinted with minor changes as* Michaels, *Against Formalism: Chickens and Rocks,* in The State of the Language 410 (1980); and Yeazell, *Convention, Fiction, and Law,* 13 New Literary Hist. 89 (1981).

19. Monaghan, *Our Perfect Constitution,* 56 N.Y.U.L.Rev. 353, 382 (1981). Like Raoul Berger, *see* R. Berger, Government by Judiciary 412–13 (1977), Monaghan does not really counsel turning back the clock by instantly overruling all putatively misdecided cases. Both offer what might uncharitably be regarded as an "adverse possession" approach to constitutional interpretation, whereby precedents that should at one time have been properly overruled (as

wrongly decided) become entitled to recognition as authoritative after the passage of enough time and after the citizenry has come to rely on them. Neither offers the slightest guidance for recognizing the terms of such possession. To be fair, no other theorist of precedent does any better. Perhaps the central difference between law and literature is the lack in the latter of the notion of stare decisis.

22. *See* E. Hirsch, Validity in Interpretation 123 & n. 53 (1967); *see also* E. Hirsch, The Aims of Interpretation 1–13 (1976).

23. R. Rorty, *supra* note 14, at 152.

seemingly a metaphor for the power of the individual critic. Whatever pyrotechnics might come from a critic who "prides himself on not being distracted by anything which the text might previously have been thought to be about or anything its author says about it," [24] there remains the infatuation—110 years after Langdell—with the possibility of a science of criticism. A "weak" textualist "is just doing his best to imitate science—he wants a *method* of criticism and he wants everybody to agree that he has cracked the code. He wants all the comforts of consensus, even if only the consensus of readers of the literary quarterlies" (or law reviews).[25]

Perhaps the best current example of such a "weak" textualist is John Hart Ely, whose *Democracy and Distrust,* however radical some of its criticisms of so-called "interpretivism" purport to be, is merely the latest effort to crack the code of the United States Constitution and discover its true essence. As James E. Fleming pointed out in a recent review, Ely is engaged in a "quest for the ultimate constitutional interpretivism" which would in effect foreclose further debate about the genuine meaning of the Constitution.[27]

* * *

No one can read Ely and miss his anger at those who merely read their own views into the Constitution. Indeed, most of Ely's reviewers agree with him at least on this last point, even as they criticize him for reading *his* preferred views into the Constitution. What unites Ely and most of his critics, though, is the continued belief that there is something "in" the Constitution that can be extracted if only we can figure out the best method to mine its meaning.

Against such weak textualists—the decoders, whatever the fanciness of their methods of decoding—Rorty posits "strong" textualists, who reject the whole notion of questing for the essential meanings of a text. "Strong," it should be emphasized, refers to the power of the critic, not the power of the text (or of its author). According to Stanley Fish, one of the leading proponents of this approach, "Interpretation is not the art of construing but the art of constructing. Interpreters do not decode poems; they make them." [30] Fish has argued that "[t]he objectivity of the text is an illusion and, moreover, a dangerous illusion, because it is so physically convincing. The illusion is one of self-sufficiency and completeness. A line of print or a page is so obviously *there* ... that it seems to be the sole repository of whatever value and meaning we associate with it." [31]

* * *

24. *Id.* at 151–52.

25. *Id.* at 152 (emphasis in original).

27. Fleming, *A Critique of John Hart Ely's Quest for the Ultimate Constitutional Interpretivism of Representative Democracy* (Book Review), 80 Mich.L.Rev. 634 (1982).

30. S. Fish, Is There a Text in This Class? 327 (1980) * * *.

31. [*Id.*] at 43. * * *

The view endorsed by Fish regards "human beings as at every moment creating the experimental spaces into which a personal knowledge flows." [35] Meaning is created rather than discovered, though the source of creative energy is the particular community within which one finds him- or herself. Critics more Emersonian in their inspiration, like Harold Bloom, are willing to credit individual acts of creativity, though Bloom's emphasis on the ubiquity of "misreadings," rather than "truthful" renderings of what is inside texts, links him to Rorty's "strong" textualists.[36] All such readers could well join the Whitmanian anthem, where all readings, whether of life or of texts, become songs of oneself.

The patron saint of all strong textualists is Nietzsche:

> [W]hatever exists, having somehow come into being, is again and again reinterpreted to new ends, taken over, transformed, and redirected by some power superior to it; all events in the organic world are a subduing, a *becoming master,* and all subduing and becoming master involves a fresh interpretation, an adaptation through which any previous "meaning" and "purpose" are necessarily obscured or even obliterated.[37]

And the argument of Fish, Bloom, and other strong textualists, whether American or continental, is *not* that they prefer to do their thing as an alternative to the more banal work of "truthseekers" like Abrams or Hirsch, but rather that the project of ultimate truth-seeking is based on philosophical error. At the very least it presumes a privileged foundation for measuring the attainment of truth, and it is precisely this foundation that Nietzsche and most of the more radical literary theorists deny. Like Rorty, they do not substitute a new candidate for a winning method of how to recognize literary truth when one sees it; rather, they reject the very search for finality of interpretation.

To be sure, none of the radical critics defend the position that any interpretation is just as good as any other. Stanley Fish, for example, notes that he genuinely believes in the validity of any given view that he happens to hold, and he can present reasons for rejecting the views of his opponents on the interpretation of a given text.[38] In this regard Fish seems similar to Ronald Dworkin, who views judging as including the phenomenological experience of feeling oneself to have achieved the uniquely correct solution even to a hard case.[39] But Fish, more candid than Dworkin on this point, admits that his own conviction of rightness will provide no answer at all to anyone who happens to disagree with him, and that there is no way to resolve the dispute. It is at this point that he retreats to his Kuhnian [40] emphasis on communities of understanding and shared conventions. It may be true that these communi-

35. [*Id.*] at 94. * * *

36. *See, e.g.,* H. Bloom, A Map of Misreading (1975).

37. F. Nietzsche, On the Geneology of Morals 77 (W. Kaufmann trans. 1967) (emphasis in original).

38. S. Fish, *supra* note 30, at 338–71.

39. *See* R. Dworkin, Taking Rights Seriously 279–90 (1977) * * *.

40. *See* T. Kuhn, The Structure of Scientific Revolutions (2d ed. 1970).

ties will share, at any given moment, a sense of what distinguishes "on the wall" from "off the wall" arguments, but Fish is acutely aware of the contingency of such judgments. They describe only our own temporal sense of what is currently acceptable, rather than anything genuinely mirroring the essential characteristics of the texts being discussed.

III

Presumably only those professionally interested in literature are forced to wrestle with the issues presented by Abrams * * * and Fish regarding poetics or the interpretation of fiction. But if law is, in some meaningful sense, a branch of literature, then the problems discussed above take on new and bothersome implications. And nowhere is this more true within our own culture than in constitutional interpretation and its emphasis on writtenness.

The role of our Constitution is not only to enable us to pretend that past linguistic acts can control future action. It is also presumably to prevent the rise of Nietzschean "masters." Nietzsche seems to suggest, however, that a massive exercise in social deception is necessary if we are not to recognize the way that "interpretation" inevitably implies a struggle for mastery in the formation of political consciousness. For a Nietzschean reader of constitutions, there is no point in searching for a code that will produce "truthful" or "correct" interpretations; instead, the interpreter, in Rorty's words, "simply beats the text into a shape which will serve his own purpose." [43]

* * * If one takes seriously the views articulated by Nietzsche, Rorty, and Fish (among others), one must give up the search for principles and methods of constitutional interpretation. Instead, one assesses the results of an interpretive effort by something other than the criterion of adherence to an inner essence of the text being interpreted * * *.

To put it mildly, there is something disconcerting about accepting the Nietzschean interpreter into the house of constitutional analysts, but I increasingly find it impossible to imagine any other way of making sense of our own constitutional universe. For some years I have organized my own courses in constitutional interpretation around the central question, "But did the Court get it right?", as if one could grade any given opinion by whether or not it measured up to the genuine command of the Constitution. Answering such a question, of course, requires the development of a full set of "principles and methods of correct interpretation," and my courses have involved a search for such principles and methods.

I still spend a great deal of time examining various approaches, ranging from the linguistic to the historical, from the structural to what my colleague Philip Bobbitt calls the "ethical," [46] but I have less and less confidence that this is a sensible enterprise. At the very least there is

---

43. R. Rorty, *supra* note 14, at 151.   **46.** See P. Bobbitt, Constitutional Fate (1982) * * *.

no reason to believe that the community of persons interested in constitutional interpretation will coalesce around one or another of these approaches. Moreover, insofar as one accepts the plausibility of an analysis like Rorty's, there is no reason to regret this, for it is the result of a genuine plurality of ways of seeing the world, rather than of the obdurate recalcitrance of those who refuse to bend to superior argument.

Yet there are obvious difficulties in adopting Rorty's metaphor of the conversation (rather than the argument), for the principal social reality of law is its coercive force vis-à-vis those who prefer to behave other than as the law "requires." As Chairman Mao pointed out, a revolution is not a tea party, and the massive disruption in lives that can be triggered by a legal case is not a conversation. The legal system presents a conversation from which there may be no exit, and there are certainly those who would define hell as the vision of their least favorite constitutional interpreter, whether the Court or a benighted law professor.

What does one do, then, when studying opinions, if one gives up the enterprise of determining whether or not they are "correct"? Are cases simply historical fragments which should be studied for insight into the ideology of the time? [48] One no longer would say, for example, that *Dred Scott* [49] or *Lochner v. New York*, [50] or any other case, was "wrongly" decided, for that use of language presupposes belief in the knowability of constitutional essence. One *can* obviously show that constitutional tastes and styles shift over time, but this retreat into historicism has nothing to do with the legal science so desperately sought by Langdell and his successors.

* * *

Consider * * * the way we treat the innovative judges of our legal tradition, particularly as they appear in law school courses. Do we really wish to argue that John Marshall or Earl Warren (or the most recent dynamic innovator, William Rehnquist) got the essence right in their interpretations of the Constitution, or do we recognize instead the extent to which we have been subdued by their political visions?

Perhaps the most significant example of this dilemma is John Marshall himself, or rather I should say our response to Marshall. I have little trouble stating that I consider his major opinions to run the gamut from the intellectually dishonest [60] to the majestically visionary, [61]

---

48. This seems to be the approach taken by some of the most fruitful practitioners of "critical legal studies." *See, e.g.,* M. Horwitz, The Transformation of American Law, 1780–1860 (1977); M. Tushnet, The American Law of Slavery 1810–1860 (1981).

49. Dred Scott v. Sandford, 60 U.S. (19 How.) 393 (1856).

50. 198 U.S. 45 (1905). There is obviously not space here to consider in depth the complexity of our responses to these two cases. One might begin, though, by

asking whether Taney's or Peckham's arguments in the two cases are really "off-the-wall" in terms of the conventions of American legal discourse; it seems clear that the answer is no.

60. *See* Marbury v. Madison, 5 U.S. (1 Cranch) 137 (1803) (presentation and construction of § 13 of the Judiciary Act of 1789).

61. See note 61 on page 135.

and rarely to contain the only (or even the most) plausible rendering of the Constitution. Yet there is also a profound irrelevance to such a criticism. Not only does it assume the existence of a privileged discourse that allows me to dismiss Marshall as "untruthful" rather than merely different, it also ignores the fundamental fact that John Marshall is as much a "founder" of the American legal system as those who wrote the Constitution he purported to interpret. He is, perhaps, the great Nietzschean judge of our tradition.

D. ORIGINAL INTENT

PAUL BREST, THE MISCONCEIVED QUEST FOR THE ORIGINAL UNDERSTANDING
60 B.U.L.Rev. 204, 204–09, 214–24, 231–34 (1980).

By "originalism" I mean the familiar approach to constitutional adjudication that accords binding authority to the text of the Constitution or the intentions of its adopters.[1] At least since *Marbury,* in which Chief Justice Marshall emphasized the significance of our Constitution's being a written document, originalism in one form or another has been a major theme in the American constitutional tradition. The most widely accepted justification for originalism is simply that the Constitution is the supreme law of the land. The Constitution manifests the will of the sovereign citizens of the United States—"we the people" assembled in the conventions and legislatures that ratified the Constitution and its amendments. The interpreter's task is to ascertain their will. Originalism may be supported by more instrumental rationales as well: Adherence to the text and original understanding arguably constrains the discretion of decisionmakers and assures that the Constitution will be interpreted consistently over time.

The most extreme forms of originalism are "strict textualism" (or literalism) and "strict intentionalism." A strict textualist purports to construe words and phrases very narrowly and precisely. For the strict intentionalist, "the whole aim of construction, as applied to a provision of the Constitution, is * * * to ascertain and give effect to the intent of its framers and the people who adopted it."[2]

Much of American constitutional interpretation rejects strict originalism in favor of what I shall call "moderate originalism." The text of

---

61. *See* McCulloch v. Maryland, 17 U.S. (4 Wheat.) 316 (1819) (invocation of American nationalism).

1. John Ely uses the term "interpretivism" to describe essentially the same concept. J.H. Ely, Democracy and Distrust: A Theory of Judicial Review, chs. 1–2 (1980). At the cost of proliferating neologisms I have decided to stick with "originalism." Virtually all modes of constitutional decisionmaking, including those endorsed by Professor Ely, require interpretation. The differences lie in what is being interpreted, and I use the term "originalism" to describe the interpretation of text and original history as distinguished, for example, from the interpretation of precedents and social values.

2. Home Bldg. & Loan Ass'n v. Blaisdell, 290 U.S. 398, 453 (1934) (Sutherland, J., dissenting).

the Constitution is authoritative, but many of its provisions are treated as inherently open-textured. The original understanding is also important, but judges are more concerned with the adopters' general purposes than with their intentions in a very precise sense.

Some central doctrines of American constitutional law cannot be derived even by moderate originalist interpretation, but depend, instead, on what I shall call "nonoriginalism." The modes of nonoriginalist adjudication defended in this article accord the text and original history presumptive weight, but do not treat them as authoritative or binding. The presumption is defeasible over time in the light of changing experiences and perceptions.

* * *

PART ONE: THE CONCEPTS AND METHODS OF ORIGINALISM

* * *

I. *Textualism*

Textualism takes the language of a legal provision as the primary or exclusive source of law (a) because of some definitional or supralegal principle that only a written text can impose constitutional obligations, or (b) because the adopters intended that the Constitution be interpreted according to a textualist canon, or (c) because the text of a provision is the surest guide to the adopters' intentions. The last of these, probably the central rationale for an originalist-based textualism, is sometimes stated as a preamble to textualist canons. For example:

> It is a cardinal rule in the interpretation of constitutions that the instrument must be so construed as to give effect to the intention of the people, who adopted it. This intention is to be sought in the Constitution itself, and the apparent meaning of the words employed is to be taken as expressing it, except in cases where that assumption would lead to absurdity, ambiguity, or contradiction.[8]

Implicit in the preceding quotation is a canon of interpretation paradigmatic of textualism—the so-called "plain meaning rule." Chief Justice Marshall invoked this canon in *Sturges v. Crowningshield:*

> [A]lthough the spirit of an instrument, especially of a constitution, is to be respected not less than its letter, yet the spirit is to be collected chiefly from its words * * *. [I]f, in any case, the plain meaning of a provision, not contradicted by any other provision in the same instrument, is to be disregarded, because we believe the framers of that instrument could not intend what they say, it must be one in which the absurdity and injustice of applying the provision to the case, would be so monstrous that all mankind would, without hesitation, unite in rejecting the application.[9]

8. H. Black, Handbook on the Construction and Interpretation of the Laws 20 (1911).

9. 17 U.S. (4 Wheat.) 202–03 (1819).

The plain meaning of a text is the meaning that it would have for a "normal speaker of English" under the circumstances in which it is used. Two kinds of circumstances seem relevant: the linguistic and the social contexts. The linguistic context refers to vocabulary and syntax. The social context refers to a shared understanding of the purposes the provision might plausibly serve.

A tenable version of the plain meaning rule must take account of both of these contexts. The alternative, of applying a provision according to the literal meanings of its component words, misconceives the conventions that govern the use of language. Chief Justice Marshall argued this point eloquently and, I think, persuasively, in *McCulloch v. Maryland*,[13] decided the same year that he invoked the plain meaning rule in *Sturges*. The state had argued that the necessary and proper clause authorized only legislation "indispensable" to executing the enumerated powers. Marshall responded with the observation that the word "necessary," as used "in the common affairs of the world, or in approved authors, * * * frequently imports no more than that one thing is convenient, or useful, or essential to another."[14] He continued:

> Such is the character of human language, that no word conveys to the mind, in all situations, one single definite idea; and nothing is more common than to use words in a figurative sense. Almost all compositions contain words, which, taken in their rigorous sense, would convey a meaning different from that which is obviously intended. It is essential to just construction that many words which import something excessive, should be understood in a more mitigated sense—in that sense which common usage justifies * * *. This word, then, like others, is used in various senses; and, in its construction, the subject, the context, the intention of the person using them, are all to be taken into view.[15]

As Marshall implied, to attempt to read a provision without regard to its linguistic and social contexts will either yield unresolvable indeterminacies of language or just nonsense. Without taking account of the possible purposes of the provisions, an interpreter could not, for example, decide whether singing, flag-waving, flag-burning, picketing, and criminal conspiracy are within the protected ambit of the first amendment's "freedom of speech," or whether the "writings" protected by the copyright clause include photographs, paintings, sculptures, performances, and the contents of phonograph records. She would not know whether the phrase, "No person except a natural born Citizen * * * shall be eligible to the Office of President," disqualified persons born abroad or those born by Caesarian section. We understand the range of plausible meanings of provisions only because we know that some interpretations respond to the kinds of concerns that the adopters' society might have while others do not.

---

13. 17 U.S. (4 Wheat.) 316 (1819).

14. *Id.* at 413.

15. *Id.* at 414–15.

That an interpreter must read a text in the light of its social as well as linguistic context does not destroy the boundary between textualism and intentionalism. Just as the textualist is not concerned with the adopters' idiosyncratic use of language, she is not concerned with their subjective purposes. Rather, she seeks to discern the purposes that a member of the adopters' society would understand the provision to encompass.

Suppose that phrases such as "commerce among the several states," or "freedom of speech," or "equal protection of the laws," have quite different meanings today than when they were adopted. An originalist would hold that, because interpretation is designed to capture the original understanding, the text must be understood in the contexts of the society that adopted it: "The meaning of the constitution is fixed when it is adopted, and it is not different at any subsequent time when a court has occasion to pass upon it." [21]

When a provision is interpreted roughly contemporaneously with its adoption, an interpreter unconsciously places the provision in its linguistic and social contexts, which she has internalized simply because she is of that society. But she cannot assume that a provision adopted one or two hundred years ago has the same meaning as it had for the adopters' society today. She must immerse herself in their society to understand the text as they understood it. Although many provisions of the Constitution may pose no serious interpretive problems in this respect, the textualist interpreter cannot be sure of this without first understanding the ordinary usage at the time of adoption. Did "commerce" include manufacture as well as trade? Did the power to "regulate" commerce imply the power to prohibit it? Did the power to "regulate commerce among the several states" include the power to regulate intrastate transactions which affected interstate commerce? With what absoluteness did 18th century Americans understand the prohibitions against "impairing" contractual obligations and "abridging the freedom of speech?" What did the words "privileges," "immunities," "due process," "equal protection of the laws," "citizen," and "person" mean to those who adopted the fourteenth amendment in 1868?

Despite the differences between textualism and intentionalism, placing a constitutional provision in its original contexts calls for a historical inquiry quite similar to the intentionalist interpreter's. * * *

II. Intentionalism

By contrast to the textualist, the intentionalist interprets a provision by ascertaining the intentions of those who adopted it. The text of the provision is often a useful guide to the adopters' intentions, but the text does not enjoy a favored status over other sources. * * *

* * *

21. T.M. Cooley, A Treatise on the Constitutional Limitations Which Rest Upon the Legislative Power of the States of The American Union 124 (Carrington's 8th ed. 1927) (n.p. 1868). * * *

1. Who Are the Adopters?

The adopters of the Constitution of 1787 were some portion of the delegates to the Philadelphia Convention and majorities or supermajorities of the participants in the ratifying conventions in nine states. For all but one amendment to the Constitution,[35] the adopters were two-thirds or more of the members of each House of Congress and at least a majority of the legislators in [three-fourths] of the state legislatures.

For a textual provision to become part of the Constitution, the requisite number of persons in each of these bodies must have assented to it. Likewise, an intention can only become binding—only become an institutional intention—when it is shared by at least the same number and distribution of adopters. (Hereafter, I shall refer to this number and distribution as the "adopters.")

If the only way a judge could ascertain institutional intent were to count individual intention-votes, her task would be impossible even with respect to a single multimember law-making body, and a fortiori where the assent of several such bodies were required. Therefore, an intentionalist must necessarily use circumstantial evidence to educe a collective or general intent.

Interpreters often treat the writings or statements of the framers of a provision as evidence of the adopters' intent. This is a justifiable strategy for the moderate originalist who is concerned with the framers' intent on a relatively abstract level of generality—abstract enough to permit the inference that it reflects a broad social consensus rather than notions peculiar to a handful of the adopters. It is a problematic strategy for the strict originalist.

As the process of adoption moves from the actual framers of a constitutional amendment to the members of Congress who proposed it to the state legislators who ratified it, the amount of thought given the provision surely diminishes—especially if it is relatively technical or uncontroversial, or one of several of disparate provisions (e.g., the Bill of Rights) adopted simultaneously. This suggests that there may be instances where a framer had a determinate intent but other adopters had no intent or an indeterminate intent. For example, suppose that the framers of the commerce clause considered the possibility that economic transactions taking place within the confines of a state might nonetheless affect interstate commerce in such a way as to come within the clause, and that they intended the clause to cover such transactions. But suppose that most of the delegates to the ratifying conventions did not conceive of this possibility and that either they "did not intend" that the clause encompass such transactions or else their intentions were indeterminate. Under these circumstances, what is the institutional intent, i.e., the intent of the provision?

If the intent of the framers is to be attributed to the provision, it must be because the other adopters have in effect delegated their

35. The twenty-first amendment was ratified by state conventions.

intention-votes to the framers.   Leaving aside the question whether the adopters-at-large had any thoughts at all concerning this issue of delegation, consider what they might have desired if they had thought about it. Would they have wanted the framers' intentions to govern without knowing what those intentions were?   The answers might well differ depending on whether the adopters had "no intent" or "indeterminate intent."

A delegate to a ratifying convention might well want his absence of intention (*i.e.,* "no-intent") regarding wholly intrastate transactions to be treated as a vote against the clause's encompassing such transactions (*i.e.,* "intent-not"): Since no-intent is the intentionalist equivalent of no-text, to accede to the framers' unknown intentions would be tantamount to blindly delegating to them the authority to insert textual provisions in the Constitution.

Where the framers intend that the activity be covered by the clause, and the adopters' intentions are merely indeterminate, the institutional intent is ambiguous.   One adopter might wish his indeterminate intent to be treated as "no intent."   Another adopter might wish to delegate his intention-vote to those whose intent is determinate.   Yet another might wish to delegate authority to decisionmakers charged with applying the provision in the future.   Without knowing more about the mindsets of the actual adopters of particular constitutional provisions, one would be hard-pressed to choose among these.

2.   The Adopters' Interpretive Intent

The intentionalist interpreters' first task must be to determine the interpretive intentions of the adopters of the provision before her—that is the canons by which the adopters intended their provisions to be interpreted.   The practice of statutory interpretation from the 18th through at least the mid–19th century suggests that the adopters assumed—if they assumed anything at all—a mode of interpretation that was more textualist than intentionalist.   The plain meaning rule was frequently invoked: judicial recourse to legislative debates was virtually unknown and generally considered improper.   Even after references to extrinsic sources became common, courts and commentators frequently asserted that the plain meaning of the text was the surest guide to the intent of the adopters.

This poses obvious difficulties for an intentionalist whose very enterprise is premised on fidelity to the original understanding.

3.   The Intended Specificity of a Provision

I now turn to an issue that lies at the intersection of what I have called interpretive and substantive intent: How much discretion did an adopter intend to delegate to those charged with applying a provision? Consider, for example, the possible intentions of the adopters of the cruel and unusual punishment clause of the eighth amendment.   They might have intended that the language serve only as a shorthand for the Stuart tortures which were their exemplary applications of the clause.   Somewhat more broadly, they might have intended the clause to be understood to incorporate the principle of *ejusdem generis*—to include their exemplary applications and other punishments that they found or would have found equally repugnant.[41]

What of instances where the adopters' substantive intent was indeterminate—where even if they had adverted to a proposed application they would not have been certain how the clause should apply? Here it is plausible that—if they *had* a determinate interpretive intent—they intended to delegate to future decisionmakers the authority to apply the clause in light of the general principles underlying it. To use Ronald Dworkin's terms, the adopters would have intended future interpreters to develop their own "conceptions" of cruel and unusual punishment within the framework of the adopters' general "concept" of such punishments.[42]

What of a case where the adopters viewed a certain punishment as not cruel and unusual? This is not the same as saying that the adopters "intended not to prohibit the punishment." For even if they expected their laws to be interpreted by intentionalist canons, the adopters may have intended that their own views not always govern. Like parents who attempt to instill values in their child by both articulating and applying a moral principle, they may have accepted, or even invited, the eventuality that the principle would be applied in ways that diverge from their own views.[43] The adopters may have understood that, even as to instances to which they believe the clause ought or ought not to apply, further thought by themselves or others committed to its underlying principle might lead them to change their minds. Not believing in their own omniscience or infallibility, they delegated the decision to those charged with interpreting the provision. If such a motivation is plausible with respect to applications of the clause in the adopters' contemporary society, it is even more likely with respect to its application by future interpreters, whose understanding of the clause will be affected by changing knowledge, technology, and forms of society.

The extent to which a clause may be properly interpreted to reach outcomes different from those actually contemplated by the adopters depends on the relationship between a general principle and its exemplary applications. A principle does not exist wholly independently of its author's subjective, or his society's conventional exemplary applications, and is always limited to some extent by the applications they found conceivable. Within these fairly broad limits, however, the adopters may have intended their examples to constrain more or less. To the intentionalist interpreter falls the unenviable task of ascertaining, for each provision, how much more or less.

* * *

41. On a rather restrictive view, "would have found" means that, although the adopters did not advert to a punishment, they nonetheless intended that it be prohibited.

42. R. Dworkin, Taking Rights Seriously 135 (1977).

43. See id. at 134.

IV. The Interpreter–Historian's Task

The interpreter's task as historian can be divided into three stages or categories. First, she must immerse herself in the world of the adopters to try to understand constitutional concepts and values from their perspective. Second, at least the intentionalist must ascertain the adopters' interpretive intent and the intended scope of the provision in question. Third, she must often "translate" the adopters' concepts and intentions into our time and apply them to situations that the adopters did not foresee.

The first stage is common to originalists of all persuasions. Although the textualist's aim is to understand and apply the language of a constitutional provision, she must locate the text in the linguistic and social contexts in which it was adopted. * * * The intentionalist would ideally count the intention-votes of the individual adopters. In practice, she can at best hope to discover a consensus of the adopters as manifested in the text of the provision itself, the history surrounding its adoption, and the ideologies and practices of the time.

The essential difficulty posed by the distance that separates the modern interpreter from the objects of her interpretation has been succinctly stated by Quentin Skinner in addressing the analogous problem facing historians of political theory: [52]

> [I]t will never in fact be possible simply to study what any given classic writer has *said* * * * without bringing to bear some of one's own expectations about what he must have been saying * * *. [T]hese models and preconceptions in terms of which we unavoidably organize and adjust our perceptions and thoughts will themselves tend to act as determinants of what we think or perceive. We must classify in order to understand, and we can only classify the unfamiliar in terms of the familiar. The perpetual danger, in our attempts to enlarge our historical understanding, is thus that our expectations about what someone must be saying or doing will themselves determine that we understand the agent to be doing something which he would not—or even could not—himself have accepted as an account of what he *was* doing.

To illustrate the problem of doing original history with even a single example would consume more space than I wish to here. Instead, I suggest that a reader who wants to get a sense of the elusiveness of the original understanding study some specific areas of constitutional history, reading both works that have been well received,[54] and also the controversy surrounding some of those that have not.[55]

---

52. Skinner, *Meaning and Understanding in the History of Ideas,* 8 Hist. & Theory 3[, 6] (1969). * * *

54. *See, e.g.,* C. Fairman, Reconstruction and Reunion, 1864–88, Pt. 1 (1971); L. Levy, Origins of the Fifth Amendment (1968); L. Levy, Legacy of Suppression (1960). *See also* I. Brandt, The Life of

James Madison (1941–61); G. Wood, The Creation of the American Republic, 1776–87 (1969).

55. A recent example is Raoul Berger's Government by Judiciary: The Transformation of the Fourteenth Amendment (1977), which argues that almost of all the

The intentionalist interpreter must next ascertain the adopters' interpretive intent and the intended breadth of their provisions. That is, she must determine what the adopters intended future interpreters to make of their substantive views. Even if she can learn how the adopters intended contemporary interpreters to construe the Constitution, she cannot assume they intended the same canons to apply one or two hundred years later. Perhaps they wanted to bind the future as closely as possible to their own notions. Perhaps they intended a particular provision to be interpreted with increasing breadth as time went on. Or—more likely than not—the adopters may have had no intentions at all concerning these matters.[57]

For purposes of analytic clarity I have distinguished between (1) the adopters' interpretive intent and the intended scope of a provision and (2) their substantive intent concerning the application of the provision. If interpretive intent and intended scope can be ascertained at all, they may instruct the interpreter to adopt different canons of interpretation than she would prefer. Under these circumstances, the intentionalist interpreter may wish to ignore these intentions and limit her inquiry to the adopters' substantive intentions. Leaving aside the normative difficulty of such selective infidelity, this is a problematic strategy: To be a coherent theory of interpretation, intentionalism must distinguish between the adopters' personal *views* about an issue and their *intentions* concerning its constitutional resolution. And it is only by reference to their interpretive intent and the intended scope of a provision that this distinction can be drawn.

The interpreter's final task is to translate the adopters' intentions into the present in order to apply them to the question at issue. Consider, for example, whether the cruel and unusual punishment clause of the eighth amendment prohibits the imposition of the death penalty today. The adopters of the clause apparently never doubted that the death penalty was constitutional. But was death the same event for inhabitants of the American colonies in the late 18th century as it is two centuries later? Death was not only a much more routine and public phenomenon then, but the fear of death was more effectively contained within a system of religious belief.[60] Twentieth-century Americans have a more secular cast of mind and seem less willing to accept this dreadful, forbidden, solitary, and shameful event.[61] The interpreter must there-

---

Supreme Court's decisions under the fourteenth amendment are incorrect. *See, e.g.,* Kutler, *Raoul Berger's Fourteenth Amendment: A History or Ahistorical,* 6 Hastings Const.L.Q. 511 (1979); Murphy, Book Review, 87 Yale L.J. 1752 (1978); Soifer, Review Essay, 54 N.Y.U.L.Rev. 651 (1979). *But see* Perry, Book Review, 78 Colum.L.Rev. 685 (1978).

57. In any case, the adopters' sense of time and change—of the relationship between present and future—was almost certainly not the same as ours, which has been affected by such phenomena as the industrial revolution, theories of evolution, relativity and quantum mechanics, and the possibility of annihilation.

60. *See* P. Aries, Western Attitudes Toward Death 11–13 (1974); D. Stannard, The Puritan Way of Death 93 (1977).

61. *See* Death in American Experience 102 (A. Mack ed. 1973); P. Aries, *supra* note 60, at 85–86.

fore determine whether we view the death penalty with the same attitude—whether of disgust or ambivalence—that the adopters viewed their core examples of cruel and unusual punishment.[62]

Intentionalist interpretation frequently requires translations of this sort. For example, to determine whether the commerce clause applies to transactions taking place wholly within the boundaries of one state, or whether the first amendment protects the mass media, the interpreter must abstract the adopters' concepts of federalism and freedom of expression in order to find their analogue in our contemporary society with its different technology, economy, and systems of communication. The alternative would be to limit the application of constitutional provisions to the particular events and transactions with which the adopters were familiar. Even if such an approach were coherent, however, it would produce results that even a strict intentionalist would likely reject: Congress could not regulate any item of commerce or any mode of transportation that did not exist in 1789; the first amendment would not protect any means of communication not then known.

However difficult the earlier stages of her work, the interpreter was only trying to understand the past. The act of translation required here is different in kind, for it involves the counterfactual and imaginary act of projecting the adopters' concepts and attitudes into a future they probably could not have envisioned. When the interpreter engages in this sort of projection, she is in a fantasy world more of her own than of the adopters' making.

* * *

Even when the interpreter performs the more conventional historian's role, one may wonder whether the task is possible. There is a hermeneutic tradition, of which Hans–George Gadamar is the leading modern proponent, which holds that we can never understand the past in its own terms, free from our prejudices or preconceptions.[65] We are hopelessly imprisoned in our own world-views; we can shed some preconceptions only to adopt others, with no reason to believe that they are the conceptions of the different society that we are trying to understand. One need not embrace this essentially solipsistic view of historical knowledge to appreciate the indeterminate and contingent nature of the historical understanding that an originalist historian seeks to achieve.

None of this is to disparage doing history and other interpretive social science. It suggests, however, that the originalist constitutional historian may be questing after a chimera. The defense that "We're doing the best we can" is no less available to constitutional interpreters

---

62. *See* Granucci, *"Nor Cruel and Unusual Punishment Inflicted": The Original Meaning,* 57 Calif.L.Rev. 839 (1969).

65. *See* Hans–Georg Gadamer, Truth and Method (Eng. trans. 1975). *See also* P. Winch, The Idea of a Social Science and its Relation to Philosophy (1958); Taylor, *Interpretation and the Sciences of Man,* 25 Rev. of Metaphysics 3 (1971). For a sharply critical review of Gadamer's work, see E.D. Hirsch, Validity in Interpretation 245 (1967).

than to anyone else. But the best is not always good enough. The interpreter's understanding of the original understanding may be so indeterminate as to undermine the rationale for originalism. Although the origins of some constitutional doctrines are almost certainly established, the historical grounding of many others is quite controversial. It seems peculiar, to say the least, that the legitimacy of a current doctrine should turn on the historian's judgment that it seems "more likely than not," or even "rather likely," that the adopters intended it some one or two centuries ago.

V. Two Types of Originalism

The originalist interpreter can approach her task with different attitudes about the precision with which the object of interpretation—the text [or] intentions * * *—should be understood. In this section I describe the attitudes of "strict" and "moderate" originalism—two areas, not points, on a spectrum—and briefly survey the practices of American constitutional decisionmaking in terms of them.

I have devoted very little attention to the most extreme form of strict textualism—literalism. A thorough-going literalist understands a text to encompass all those and only those instances that come within its words read without regard to its social or perhaps even its linguistic context. Because literalism poorly matches the ways in which we speak and write, it is unable to handle the ambiguity, vagueness, and figurative usage that pervade natural languages, and produces embarrassingly silly results.

Strict intentionalism requires the interpreter to determine how the adopters would have applied a provision to a given situation, and to apply it accordingly. The enterprise rests on the questionable assumption that the adopters of constitutional provisions intended them to be applied in this manner. But even if this were true, the interpreter confronts historiographic difficulties of such magnitude as to make the aim practicably unattainable.

Strict textualism and intentionalism are not synergistic, but rather mutually antagonistic approaches to interpretation. The reader need only consider the strict textualist's and intentionalist's views of the first amendment protection of pornographic literature. By contrast, moderate textualism and intentionalism closely resemble each other in methodology and results.

A moderate textualist takes account of the open-textured quality of language and reads the language of provisions in their social and linguistic contexts. A moderate intentionalist applies a provision consistent with the adopters' intent at a relatively high level of generality, consistent with what is sometimes called the "purpose of the provision." Where the strict intentionalist tries to determine the adopters' actual subjective purposes, the moderate intentionalist attempts to understand what the adopters' purposes might plausibly have been, an aim far more readily achieved than a precise understanding of the adopters' intentions.

* * *

Strict originalism cannot accommodate most modern decisions under the Bill of Rights and the fourteenth amendment, or the virtually plenary scope of congressional power under the commerce clause. Although moderate originalism is far more expansive, some major constitutional doctrines lie beyond its pale as well.

A moderate textualist would treat almost all contemporary free speech and equal protection decisions as within the permissible ambit of these clauses, though not necessarily entailed by them. Because of our uncertainty about the original understanding, it is harder to assess the legitimacy of these doctrines from the viewpoint of a moderate intentionalist. For example, the proper scope of the first amendment depends on whether its adopters were only pursuing "representation reinforcing" goals,[70] or were more broadly concerned to promote a free marketplace of ideas or individual autonomy.[71] The level of generality on which the adopters conceived of the equal protection clause presents a similar uncertainty, but whether or not a moderate intentionalist could accept all of the "new" or "newer" equal protection,[72] she could read the clause to protect "discrete and insular minorities" besides blacks.

On the other hand, a moderate originalist, whether of textualist or intentionalist persuasion, would have serious difficulties justifying (1) the incorporation of the principle of equal protection into the fifth amendment,[73] (2) the incorporation of provisions of the Bill of Rights into the fourteenth amendment,[74] (3) the more general notion of substantive due process, including the minimal rational relationship standard,[75] and (4) the practice of judicial review of congressional legislation established by *Marbury v. Madison.*[76] * * *

* * *

70. *See* J.H. Ely, *supra* note 1, at chs. 4–6. *See also* Mills v. Alabama, 384 U.S. 214, 218–20 (1966) * * *.

71. *See, e.g.,* J.S. Mill, On Liberty (1859); Richards, *Free Speech and Obscenity Law: Toward a Moral Theory of the First Amendment,* 123 U.Pa.L.Rev. 45 (1974); Scanlon, *A Theory of Free Expression,* 1 Phil. & Pub. Affairs 204 (1972).

72. *See generally,* [P. Brest, Processes of Constitutional Decisionmaking 809–93 (1975)]; Gunther, *In Search of Evolving Doctrine on a Changing Court: A Model for a Newer Equal Protection,* 86 Harv.L.Rev. 1 (1972).

73. *See, e.g.,* Frontiero v. Richardson, 411 U.S. 677 (1973); Bolling v. Sharpe, 347 U.S. 497 (1954); Linde, *Judges, Critics, and the Realist Tradition,* 82 Yale L.J. 227, 233–34 (1972).

74. Compare Justice Black's and Justice Frankfurter's views in Adamson v. California, 332 U.S. 46 (1947). *See also* L. Levy, *The Fourteenth Amendment and the Bill of Rights* in Judgments: Essays on American Constitutional History 64 (1972); Fairman, *Does the Fourteenth Amendment Incorporate the Bill of Rights? The Original Understanding,* 2 Stan.L.Rev. 5 (1949); Morrison, *Does the Fourteenth Amendment Incorporate the Bill of Rights? The Judicial Interpretation,* 2 Stan.L.Rev. 140 (1949).

75. *See, e.g.,* R. Berger, *supra* note 55; C. Fairman, *supra,* note 54, at 1207 * * *.

76. *See* L. Boudin, Government by Judiciary (1932); A. Westin, Introduction and Historical Bibliography to C. Beard, The Supreme Court and the Constitution (1912); Judicial Review and the Supreme

Moderate originalism is a perfectly sensible strategy of constitutional decisionmaking. But its constraints are illusory and counterproductive. Contrary to the moderate originalist's faith, the text and original understanding have contributed little to the development of many doctrines she accepts as legitimate. Consider the relationship between the original understanding of the fourteenth amendment and current doctrines prohibiting gender-based classifications [103] and discriminations in the political process.[104] For the moderate originalist these may be legitimately premised on the equal protection clause. But to what extent have originalist sources *guided* the evolution of these doctrines? The text is wholly open-ended; and if the adopters had any intentions at all about these issues, their resolution was probably contrary to the Court's. At most, the Court can claim guidance from the general notion of equal treatment reflected in the provision. I use the word "reflected" advisedly, however, for the equal protection clause does not establish a principle of equality; it only articulates and symbolizes a principle defined by our conventional public morality. Indeed, because of its indeterminacy, the clause does not offer much guidance even in resolving particular issues of discrimination based on race.[105]

* * *

In sum, if you consider the evolution of doctrines in just about any extensively-adjudicated area of constitutional law—whether "under" the commerce, free speech, due process, or equal protection clauses—explicit reliance on originalist sources has played a very small role compared to the elaboration of the Court's own precedents. It is rather like having a remote ancestor who came over on the Mayflower.

RICHARD S. KAY, ADHERENCE TO THE ORIGINAL INTENTIONS IN CONSTITUTIONAL ADJUDICATION: THREE OBJECTIONS AND RESPONSES
82 Nw.U.L.Rev. 226, 228–30, 236, 242–57, 259, 284–92 (1988).

This essay will critically examine the reasons given by modern scholars for rejecting the conventional norm of judicial review—adherence to the original intentions of the Constitution's enactors. While variously phrased, their reasons may be subsumed under three general objections: 1) Adherence to the original intentions is impossible; 2) It is self-contradictory; and 3) It is wrong.

While there is some force in each of these objections, I conclude that the first two are unconvincing and the third depends on personal

Court 1–12 (Levy ed. 1967). *But see* R. Berger, Congress v. The Supreme Court (1969); E. Corwin, Court Over Constitution (1938); Corwin, *Marbury v. Madison and the Doctrine of Judicial Review,* 12 Mich. L.Rev. 538 (1914) * * *.

103. *E.g.,* Craig v. Boren, 429 U.S. 190 (1976).

104. *E.g.,* Harper v. Virginia Bd. of Elections, 383 U.S. 663 (1966).

105. *See* Brown v. Board of Educ., 347 U.S. 483, 489–91 (1954); Bickel, *The Original Understanding and the Segregation Decision,* 69 Harv.L.Rev. 1 (1955); Kelly, *The Fourteenth Amendment Reconsidered: The Segregation Question,* 54 Mich.L.Rev. 1049 (1956).

judgments ultimately not susceptible to rational resolution. My objective is to provide responses to these objections and not to make a complete affirmative case for original intentions adjudication. * * *

I also do not intend to argue that, historically, adjudicated constitutional law is in any significant way an actual reflection of the original intentions. Clearly it is not. Rather my goal is to clarify the arguments for one or another approach to constitutional adjudication as an abstract matter. Moreover, the practical consequences of accepting the propriety of original intentions adjudication may be extremely limited. The legal, social and economic impacts of judicial review cannot be wished away, nor may we want them to be. An abrupt and complete adoption of original intentions adjudication might inflict injuries that far transcend the kinds of specifically legal considerations I discuss here. I am convinced, however, that we cannot intelligently discuss these practical matters until we have a clear sense of the underlying theoretical positions and disagreements.

* * *

* * * Adherence to the conventional view of constitutional adjudication is sometimes associated with the idea that judges should be tethered to the intentions of those who enacted the relevant constitutional provisions, and sometimes with the idea that judges should be restrained by the *text itself,* independent of the particular historical intentions of those who created it. The model I discuss will require further elaboration, but, briefly put, it calls for judges to apply the rules of the written constitution *in the sense in which those rules were understood by the people who enacted them.* Probably the purest judicial exposition and application of this understanding can be found in Justice Sutherland's dissenting opinion in the Minnesota Mortgage Moratorium case.[17] He said the "aim of construction" is to "discover the meaning," that is to "ascertain and give effect to the intent of its framers and the people who adopted it." [18] The view discussed here, therefore, rejects the idea that judicial allegiance is owed only to the mere words of the Constitution.

* * *

III. First Objection: It's Impossible

* * *

A. *It's Really Impossible*

The objection that original intentions adjudication is really impossible is founded on an extreme and general proposition about the capacity of human beings to communicate a determinate meaning through the medium of language. The argument suggests that because linguistic communication is impossible, it is futile for judges to attempt to learn

---

17. Home Building & Loan Ass'n v. Blaisdell, 290 U.S. 398, 448 (1934) (Sutherland, J., dissenting).

18. *Id.* at 453.

the intentions of the constitution-makers by studying what they said or what other people said about them.

Some legal scholars have taken positions similar to this by adopting the views of writers in the fields of philosophy and literary criticism.[50]
* * *

* * *

The most glaring problem with the extreme position that interpretation according to original intentions is impossible, when applied to the use of language in general, is that it is wildly counterintuitive. It is inconsistent with the way people carry on their lives every day. We all confidently proceed on the assumption that we are capable of communicating through words a single determinate intention and that we are capable of understanding the single, determinate intentions of others. Most of the time our confidence is well-founded. We arrive at the right place for the right meetings at more or less the right time. We read and discuss articles with the impression that we are talking about the same thing. We stop at stop signs, file our tax returns, and obey subpoenas. All these commonplace experiences testify powerfully against the claim that the inference of a determinate meaning from a sequence of words uttered in a particular context is essentially, and always, impossible.
* * *

The most telling response to this objection is simply that no one really believes it, not even the writers who make the objection. If they did, they would not use language to advance the argument.   * * *

B. It's Too Hard

The more moderate form of the impossibility objection to original intentions adjudication—It's too hard—appears much more plausible. It concedes that language is sometimes capable of communicating a speaker's or writer's intentions, but holds that interpretation of the American Constitution creates peculiar problems which make the relevant original intentions inaccessible.

* * *

Before addressing [this criticism], it is necessary to explain precisely what original intentions adjudication requires of judges in the context of actual litigation. No judge is ever required to answer the abstract question: "What did the enactors intend by the phrase 'due process of law'?" Rather, judges must decide in a specific case whether or not, given the original intentions of the constitution-makers, a particular governmental action deprives someone of liberty or property without due process of law. The difference between the two questions is critically important. It is much easier to answer the second than the first because the alternatives are binary. The question can and can only be answered

---

50. *See, e.g.,* Garet, *Comparative Normative Hermeneutics: Scripture, Literature, Constitution,* 58 S.Cal.L.Rev. 35 (1985); Levinson, *Law As Literature,* 60 Tex.L.Rev. 373 (1982); Peller, *The Metaphysics of American Law,* 73 Calif.L.Rev. 1151 (1985).

"yes" or "no," and since the judge must give some answer, it follows that he need not answer with certainty. All he needs to do is decide which of the two possible answers in that case is *more likely* correct.

Defining the judge's task as that of choosing which of two outcomes is more likely consistent with original intentions is particularly important in light of criticisms that stress the impossibility of ascertaining those intentions with sufficient certainty. It is true that we can never know the original intentions with certainty, but then we can never know any speaker's or writer's intent with certainty. Nevertheless, it is almost always possible to examine the constitutional text and other evidence of intent associated with it and make a reasonable, good faith judgment about which result is more likely consistent with that intent. Of course confidence in these judgments will be different in different situations, but one answer will almost always appear better than the other. Indeed, one of the two possible responses will be obviously incorrect because, while it is theoretically possible that the lawmakers held such an intention, the available historical evidence will be overwhelmingly against it. Thus, we can be uncertain about the intended meaning of a constitutional provision at the same time we are convinced that it is not consistent with one of the two contesting positions in a lawsuit. And, given that we have only two options, that conviction will decide the case.

There is nothing extraordinary in making important decisions this way. Almost every decision we make and action we take is based on a judgment of probabilities, often as to the probable intended meaning of what we read or hear. To insist on certainty would lead to paralysis. In asking judges to make decisions in this way we demand nothing more or less than the same kinds of decisions everyone makes everyday.

1. *The Problem of Multiple Intentions.* * * * The first problem concerns the difficulty of discerning a single intention when there are multiple constitution-makers.[82]

In one sense this argument is a variant of the more extreme claim discussed above. To speak of an intention is to speak of a human mind. A joint intention cannot be the simple analog of an individual intention because we cannot easily conceive of a joint or group mind. But intent can be attributed to a group without positing the idea of a group mind. When we speak of such an intention we usually mean that each member of the group holds an identical individual intention. If a husband and wife discuss and settle on a list of invitations to a dinner party it seems perfectly proper to say that they have "an intention" about who their guests will be. This phenomenon would only be impossible if the couple

---

82. *See* R. Dworkin, [Law's Empire] 315–21 [(1986)]; Brennan, [*The Constitution of the United States: Contemporary Ratification,* 27 S.Tex.L.J. 433, 435 (1986)]; Brest, [*The Misconceived Quest for the Original Understanding,* 60 B.U.L.Rev. 204, 212–13 (1980)]; Dworkin, *The Forum of Principle,* 56 N.Y.U.L.Rev. 469, 480–81, 487–88 (1981); Radin, [*Statutory Interpretation,* 43 Harv.L.Rev. 863, 870–71 (1930)]; Saphire, *Judicial Review in the Name of the Constitution,* 8 U.Dayton L.Rev. 745, 772–80 (1983); Hancher, *Dead Letters: Wills and Poems,* 60 Tex.L.Rev. 507 (1982).

could not articulate and communicate their intentions to each other in a way that let each one know those intentions coincided. I have already discussed why I believe such communication is not only possible but common.

Nevertheless, ascertaining the intention of a group is more complicated than discovering the intention of a single person. Many individuals in different capacities were involved in making the Constitution. In investigating the original intentions of these individuals, one problem lies in identifying those people whose coincident intentions created the relevant original intent. This problem is two-fold. First, every constitutional provision is the product of consideration and approval by different groups; therefore, we must identify which groups should be counted in defining the original intention. Second, within a specific group, there will be a variety of individual intentions and we will have to decide whose intentions define the intention of the group. Each of these aspects will be considered in turn.

a. *Which groups?*—In answering the first question, it is useful to recall the reason for being concerned with intention in the first place. * * * Recourse to intention is necessary because only certain people have the authority to make law. Thus, in constitutional law, we must identify which groups could, by their approval, give the Constitution the sanction of law.

It is necessary at this point to distinguish between the original Constitution of 1787 and subsequent amendments. We ordinarily treat amendments as law because they were created in accordance with Article V. An amendment becomes law when it is ratified by the legislatures of three-fourths of the States. The intentions of these legislatures is, thus, essential. But knowing those intentions is not sufficient. According to Article V, state legislatures may only ratify amendments that have been proposed by Congress with a two-thirds majority in each House. Thus, the Senate and House of Representatives are indispensable actors in the law-making process. In sum, constitutional amendments require identical intentions in the two Houses of Congress and in thirty-eight state legislatures.

When we consider the Constitution of 1787, of course, there is no governing law analogous to Article V that informs us who must agree before the Constitution acquires the force of law. The Constitution was a clean break with prior existing law. This does not mean, however, that we have no idea whose judgments and approval gave the Constitution authority. Like any supreme law, the legal character of the Constitution will depend on political beliefs and attitudes in a society about who has the final right to make law. This is a complex matter I have addressed at some length elsewhere.[89] It is sufficient here to note that the authority of the Constitution is conventionally and popularly premised on the understanding that it was the work of "the People" in their

---

89. *See* Kay, [*Preconstitutional Rules,* 42 Ohio St.L.J. 187 (1981)]; Kay, *The Cre-* *ation of Constitutions in Canada and the United States,* 7 Can.–U.S.L.J. 111 (1984).

original, sovereign capacity. Actually, the role of "the People" was played by the special ratifying conventions in the individual states. The drafters at the Philadelphia Convention could claim no such mandate from "the people." Some supporters of the Constitution went so far as to disparage the importance of the Convention, except insofar as it was able to place a proposal before the state conventions.[91] The inquiry into original intent, therefore, should focus on the intentions of the various ratifying bodies who possessed the constituent authority.

With regard to both the body of the Constitution and its amendments, then, the only valid original intentions will be those held in common by a number of legislative bodies. This conclusion raises an obvious problem: What if we discover that, though they approved the same texts, different groups held different intentions so that no single intention can be applied to a particular question of interpretation? I will return to this question shortly.

b. *Which individuals within groups?*—The very same problem arises in answering the second question. Once we have found the authoritative groups, we must find a single intention for each group. Which individuals' intentions in, say, the Senate or in the Virginia Ratifying Convention should be considered?

The reasoning employed above can be applied to this problem. We wish to obtain the group intention because we deem it capable of establishing an authoritative rule. A given body acts when some number of its members agree to act. In the ordinary course that number is a majority. In the case of the Houses of Congress proposing amendments it is—by virtue of prior governing law—a two-thirds majority. The intention of the body, therefore, is embodied in the shared intentions of the appropriate majority of its members.

One consequence of this reasoning is that only the intentions of those voting in favor of the constitutional provision at issue will be relevant. The intentions of dissenters may be useful in illuminating the intention of the proponents, but they are not a part of the authoritative intention. Dissenters neither contributed nor were necessary to the event which made the text law and, for reasons already discussed, our concern is with the intentions of the lawmakers. Proper inquiry, therefore, is restricted to the members of the majority.

As we saw earlier when there were numerous law-making bodies, however, there may be more than one intention in the majority that approves the very same act of legislation. The difficulty will be even greater here because the number of potential intentions will be larger. When we multiply the number of possible intentions in a legislature by the number of possible intentions among legislative bodies the task of determining one original intention might appear hopeless.

91. *See* 1 M. Farrand, Records of the Federal Convention of 1787 295 (remarks of A. Hamilton), 253 (remarks of J. Wilson) (1966); The Federalist No. 40 at 247–48 (J. Madison) (C. Rossiter ed. 1961) * * *.

c. *Summing different intentions.*—The possibility of multiple, varying intentions is not, however, fatal to the enterprise of original intentions adjudication. The difficulty is intractable only if there are multiple and totally *contradictory* intentions. This could happen if, for example, a constitutional provision was created with some constitution-makers intending it to mean X and only X, while other constitution-makers intended it to mean not-X and only not-X. Such contradiction is extremely unlikely, however, because though the intentions involved are held by different people, those intentions are associated with the adoption of identical language. The use of the same language suggests a common core of meaning shared by all. Any different intentions are, therefore, likely to be overlapping not contradictory. Thus, if an ordinance prohibits "vehicles in the park," it is safe to assume that all of the enactors intended it apply to ordinary automobiles. Similarly, in a constitutional context, probably all of the enactors of the fifth and fourteenth amendments understood that incarceration would be a deprivation of liberty requiring due process of law. The differences in intention will arise in cases beyond the obvious situations suggested by the language, as that language was ordinarily used and understood. Where there is disagreement it will be with respect to the outer reach or scope of the rule. To use the terminology of some modern philosophers of language, these differences will be attributable to the vagueness, not the ambiguity, of the words adopted.[95]

Originally, I stated the problem in this section to be the combination of disparate intentions into one authoritative intention of the group with authority to make law. But, given the kind of differences likely to occur, we should be able to accumulate enough *identical* intentions to compose an authoritative lawmaker. By discerning the language's central paradigm, we can define an area of application that was intended by virtually all the relevant individuals who together constitute the lawmaker. As we move out from this core idea to somewhat less obvious applications, we can expect to find fewer individuals who intend the law to extend so far. Still, as long as it is probable that a necessary law-making majority shared a particular understanding it will be appropriate to so interpret the provision. This approach, therefore, requires the judge to ask whether the challenged action falls within a meaning intended by an authoritative lawmaker. Idiosyncratic meanings held by individuals within the majority (or by individual law-making bodies) falling outside that shared, core intention will not have the force of law because they lack such an authoritative source. They may be ignored for the same reasons that we ignore the intentions of the dissenters.

This argument assumes that individuals do not employ the same words to mean entirely opposite things, especially in circumstances where they discuss and debate the meaning of those words before adopting them. Therefore, there will almost always be some core meaning that reflects the intentions of the constitution-makers. This is

---

95. *See* W. Quine, Word and Object 125–34 (1960); Young, *Equivocation in the*   *Making of Agreements,* 64 Colum.L.Rev. 619, 626–32, 646–47 (1964). * * *

true even when there is no controlling intention with respect to other, fringe meanings.

* * *

2. *The Problem of Historical Understanding.*—Another argument against original intentions adjudication suggests that it is very difficult, if not impossible, to understand intentions formed and expressed a very long time ago.[103] * * * This claim is based on a "fatal" gap between the moment of expression and the moment of understanding. But all interpretation—contemporary as well as ancient—is historical in this sense. And, if it is conceded that some immediate communication is possible, then the difficulty is not different in kind simply because the time between speaking and listening or writing and reading is changed from minutes or days to decades or centuries.

* * *

The very breadth of this claim makes it implausible. It is essentially an attack on the possibility and validity of historical investigation. While some students of history deny the possibility of objectively correct historical conclusions, the contrary view is also widely and firmly held. Indeed, the force of the latter position is strengthened by the fact that history is a well-established discipline to which thousands of sensible people have devoted and continue to devote their energy and intelligence. These scholars proceed on the assumption that, with varying degrees of effort, it *is* possible to ascertain and adopt the viewpoint of another person, even if that other person is remote in place, culture or time.

* * *

Finally, as I noted when considering the problem of multiple intentions, original intentions adjudication only calls for decisions regarding which of two proposed interpretations is more likely to be consistent with those original intentions. In most cases, it should be possible to recapture enough of the past to make that choice.

3. *The Probabilities in Balance.*—The discussion thus far has omitted one significant possibility. A judge, after considering the evidence of the relevant intentions, could decide that neither of the contesting propositions about the original intention is more likely than the other— that is, he might conclude that the evidence exactly balances. In such cases, we might have a supplemental rule that, for example, places the burden of proof on the party claiming that constitutional rules have been violated.[115] But unless such a rule itself could be inferred from the original intentions of the enactors, this would result in cases being

---

103. *See* Brennan, *supra* note 82, at 435; Powell, *Rules for Originalists,* 73 Va. L.Rev. 659, 673–74 (1987); Tushnet, *Following the Rules Laid Down: A Critique of Interpretivism and Neutral Principles,* 96 Harv.L.Rev. 781, 793–804 (1983).

115. *See, e.g.,* Metropolitan Cas. Ins. Co. v. Brownell, 294 U.S. 580, 584 (1935) (heavy burden of proof rests on party claiming unconstitutionality of statutes); Brown v. Maryland, 25 U.S. (12 Wheat.) 419, 436 (1827) (same).

decided on grounds independent of the original intentions. There may exist, therefore, certain cases in which original intentions adjudication will yield no answer.

In practice, however, these "ties" will be exceedingly rare. This is because the available information about the creators of the constitutional rules is so plentiful. Given the usual denseness of the historical record, a competent person is unlikely to come across many cases where the evidence that the original intentions did and the evidence that it did not extend to the act in question is precisely equal. The strength of an interpreter's convictions may depend on the relative strength of the two cases, but he will almost always be able to say that one is better than the other.

* * *

* * * [S]ome things may fall outside the categories established by the constitution-makers * * * because they are so different from those the enactors knew about. In such cases, we cannot assume they made any provision for them at all. But do such cases really result in a 0–0 tie with original intentions adjudication providing no solution? I believe the Constitution, as intended by its creators, provides a decision on constitutionality for every possible action no matter how different it is from the things and circumstances the constitution-makers had in mind. Implicit in the Constitution are "back-up rules" which cover all things not provided for in the explicit rules. It must be stressed these back-up rules are *not* new constructs created in order to make original intentions adjudication feasible. Rather, they are legitimate inferences from the enactment of the constitutional text. They are an inherent part of what the constitution-makers did when they created the Constitution.

These back-up rules are a necessary consequence of the federal system of granted and residual powers established by the Constitution. The Constitution created a national government against a background of pre-existing states. That government exists *only* by virtue of the enactment of the Constitution. Therefore, we must find in the Constitution all of its features and all of its powers. There is nowhere else to look. Consequently, any action of the federal government not traceable to the enumerated institutions and powers is an exercise of power not granted to it and is contrary to the Constitution. Any truly *new* thing done by the federal government is unauthorized and therefore void.

On the other hand, the United States Constitution was enacted on the assumption that the existing states would continue to exist. The states necessarily derived their governmental institutions and powers from sources outside the new Constitution. Therefore, the absence of a reference to a state power is not equivalent to a lack of authorization. The Constitution declares itself to be and was, no doubt, intended to be supreme over the states, but only insofar as it specifically limited state powers. Any truly *new* thing done by a state must be outside of those prohibitions, and must, therefore, be constitutional.

This conclusion is itself an interpretation of the Constitution. It is, therefore, subject to rebuttal by persuasive historical evidence to the contrary. The case for it, however, is very strong. The constitution-makers differed among themselves about the appropriate scope of the powers of the new national government, but there is no serious evidence that these powers (whatever their extent) were not entirely granted by the new constitution or that state power was altered except insofar as affirmatively limited by the Constitution. The Tenth Amendment makes this explicit. The Civil War amendments significantly altered the constitutional allocation of national and state powers by enlarging federal legislative authority and especially by placing new and broad limits on state power. But it did not alter the underlying scheme of granted and residuary powers. Debate about power in the federal system, therefore, must turn on what the Constitution gave to the federal government and what it took away from the States. So long as that is true, there is an answer to the validity of every new thing. There are no omitted cases.

* * *

* * * Original intentions adjudication may not achieve [its] goals perfectly, but to conclude that it is, therefore, useless "is like saying that as a perfectly aseptic environment is impossible, one might as well conduct surgery in a sewer." [137] When honestly applied, original intentions adjudication seems to reduce the influence of the personal and idiosyncratic aspects of a judge's personality or ideology more than do alternative theories that rely on ill-defined standards of one kind or another. Such rule-governed adjudication may or may not be appealing, but, for the reasons suggested, it is possible.

* * *

IV. Second Objection: It's Self-Contradictory

The second principal objection to original intentions adjudication is that the enactors themselves did not want their intentions to govern judicial exposition on the lawfulness of certain governmental action. Proponents of this argument suggest that the constitution-makers intended judges to look elsewhere for guides to decision and (depending on the proponent) wanted judges to possess varying degrees of discretion.

* * *

[This] * * * objection assumes that the interpretative intentions of the enactors ought to control constitutional interpretation and that those intentions were that substantive intentions should not control. The latter can be reduced to a mere (although certainly difficult) question of historical fact. We know that the constitution-makers thought it was important to enact written constitutional rules. We know they took great pains to choose the terms they did and that they

---

137. C. Geertz, The Interpretation of   Solow). * * *
Cultures 30 (1973) (attributed to Robert

argued about the best language and about the merits of the proposals before them as if their decisions on these things would make a difference. We would not expect such deliberation from people who wanted their intentions to be ignored or to play a minor role in the future application of the rules they made. A strong case would seem in order from those who would impute such a desire to them. I do not contend that such a claim could never be proven. But [for reasons not included in these excerpts] it does not seem to me to have been proven yet.

V. Third Objection: It's Wrong

* * * [E]ven if [original intentions] adjudication is both possible and coherent, it must face a final objection: that [it] makes for bad government and bad law. While rarely put so bluntly, this is the most potent of the three objections that I have listed. Its power derives from the fact that, unlike the first two, refuting it requires more than simply an appeal to facts, history, or ordinary experience. This objection is the expression of a political and moral judgment about the best way for people to live in society. As such, conventional argument can take us only so far.

To evaluate this objection, we cannot consider original intentions adjudication in isolation, as we were able to do with the first two objections. The judgment here is necessarily relative: original intentions adjudication must be worse than *some other* system in which constitutional decisions are made according to some standards or processes other than fidelity to the original intentions.

* * *

* * * [This] third objection to original intentions adjudication might be put this way: limiting government by fixed rules intended by people in the more or less distant past will yield less satisfactory political and social consequences than will some other limiting technique. The exact nature of the objection depends on the proffered alternative, but most versions find similar problems with submission to the original intentions. These problems involve the incapacity of set, abstract rules to respond over time to our collective and individual well-being. * * *

* * *

* * * [A fair] response is to affirm the values inherent in "inflexibility"—the values of stability and clarity. Constitutional government exists to limit the sphere of appropriate government activity. It rests on the premise that there should be a realm of action and private decision-making immune from public coercion. The value of dividing human activity into exclusively private and potentially public zones would be severely diminished if the boundary between the two areas could be frequently and unpredictably altered. It is not merely the ability to contest, and sometimes successfully resist, government impositions that benefit those living under a constitutional government. It is, at least as much, the ability to "count on" government being constrained by certain procedures and within certain limits. Such stability permits us confidently to plan our lives, a freedom which is at the core of our capacity for self-definition. The opposite kind of existence, where we live in perpetual dread of the secret decree and the surprise order becomes, at the extreme, totalitarianism—the opposite of government under law.

This characteristic of government under law is not the only important value in the relationship of government and the individual, but it is difficult to overestimate its importance. * * * When life-plans are at stake, we are "risk-averse." Indeed, it may be the securing of a class of expectations from undefined and unpredictable interferences that is the peculiar contribution of law to society, a contribution particularly important when it is applied to the potential dangers of abuse by government.

* * *

But recognition of this value does not rebut the initial objection to original intentions adjudication that static constitutional rules are unsuitable for a constantly changing society. It is merely a counter-weight. Whether it is sufficient depends on an evaluation of the relative importance of the competing values: the value of flexibility and adaptability on the one hand, and the value of predictability and stability on the other.

Moreover, in specific cases, these concerns cannot be considered in isolation. How we view their competing advantages will be influenced by the substantive content of the constitutional rules at issue, and our regard for the individuals who, as judges, will undertake whatever revisions are allowed. Our enthusiasm for stable rules will be reduced if we think the rules protected are oppressive and unfair. Our taste for responsive and up-to-date rules will be diminished if we know they will be "improved" by people we regard as ignorant or immoral. Thus the preconstitutional decision must be largely empirical, depending on facts that may be disputed and it must, therefore, be only provisional.

Even if we could agree about the quality of the substantive rules and the credentials of the judges who would supervise their evolution, we would probably still disagree on the desirability of adhering to the original intentions because the weights we assign these competing sets of values are different. Those preferences, in turn, would depend on our confidence in the capacity of government officials, including judges, to discover and act on the public good without well-defined prior rules and on the risk that, without strict prior limits, such officials might cause suffering, unrest, and injury. Our choice of the governing norm of constitutional adjudication, then, will turn on the kinds of chances we are willing to take in living together in society, and, what comes to the same thing, on our judgment as to the kind of people we are.

E. STARE DECISIS

HENRY PAUL MONAGHAN, STARE DECISIS AND CONSTITUTIONAL ADJUDICATION

88 Colum.L.Rev. 723, 740–53 (1988).

STARE DECISIS AND CONSTITUTIONAL CHANGE

* * * Should the Court adhere to a prior controlling decision even though a majority of the Court now believes the precedent to be inconsistent with original understanding (or wrong on some other theory of what constitutes appropriate criteria for constitutional adjudication)? Put differently, for judges concerned with the process of constitutional adjudication, can stare decisis properly provide a sufficient justification for a result? * * *

A. *The Apparent Failure of Stare Decisis*

Resort to stare decisis presents formidable problems. In the common-law area, the doctrine has been the target of unremitting attack throughout this century. These attacks have generated an attitude that the law must be argued for, with the inevitable result that any simple justificatory appeal to authority possesses little innate attractiveness. If stare decisis cannot maintain a powerful grip on the common-law system that spawned it, it is not surprising that it appears to have fared still worse in the highly charged atmosphere of constitutional adjudication. There the conventional wisdom is that stare decisis should and does have only limited application.[109] The prescriptive side of this claim is usually rested on the Brandeisian assertion that "correction through legislative action is practically impossible."[110] But the argument that judicial change is the only possible means to achieve social improvement is badly overstated. Its undifferentiating character is apparent—no distinction is made among constitutional provisions, and certain applications of some are plainly less important than those of others. More significantly, the argument's central factual premise is overdrawn, at least regarding the decisions to which current commentators seem most anxious to deny binding authority: those *rejecting* autonomy or equality claims. In almost every instance, the results (if not the decisions) can be "overruled" by statute.

Descriptively, however, the conventional wisdom seems to rest on

---

109. See, e.g., United States v. Scott, 437 U.S. 82 (1978), which contains the canonical reference:

[I]n cases involving the Federal Constitution, where correction through legislative action is practically impossible, this court has often overruled its earlier decisions. The Court bows to the lessons of experience and the force of better reasoning, recognizing that the process of trial and

error, so fruitful in the physical sciences, is appropriate also in the judicial function.

Id. at 101 (quoting Burnet v. Coronado Oil & Gas Co., 285 U.S. 393, 406–08 (1932) (Brandeis, J., dissenting)).

110. *Burnet,* 285 U.S. at 406 (Brandeis, J., dissenting).

firmer ground. *Garcia v. San Antonio Metropolitan Transit Authority*[114] is only the most dramatic illustration of the view held by some commentators that the Supreme Court is largely unconstrained by its own precedents. * * * Decisions like *Garcia* have led thoughtful commentators to assert that constitutional law would be better off rid of any formal legal concept of stare decisis. To these commentators it would come as no surprise that in four cases during the last few days of its 1986 Term the Court overruled prior decisions,[121] and in only one of these did it purport to give any serious attention to the question of stare decisis.[122]

Nonetheless, some important and controversial civil liberties cases are still decided on the basis of prior authority and, perhaps, secure acceptance on that basis. But this fact further diminishes the appeal of decisions resting on stare decisis. Because a coherent rationale for the intermittent invocation of stare decisis has not been forthcoming, the impression is created that the doctrine is invoked only as a mask hiding other considerations. As a result, stare decisis seemingly operates with the randomness of a lightning bolt: on occasion it may strike, but when and where can be known only after the fact. A satisfactory theory of constitutional adjudication requires more than that.

B. The Strengths of Stare Decisis

1. *Agenda Limitation.*—Closer examination of the descriptive side of the conventional wisdom shows that, at least from an originalist's perspective, it is deeply wrong: *stare decisis plays a very large role in constitutional law.* Many constitutional issues are so far settled that they are simply off the agenda. For example, it seems clear that under the 1789 Constitution only metal could constitute legal tender. In fact, until driven to do so by the exigencies of the Civil War, the national government never attempted to impart that quality to paper. When the government did take this step the result was a series of post-Civil War decisions, collectively known as the Legal Tender Cases. While they "have [now] disappeared below the surface of American constitutional law * * * [m]easured by the intensity of the public debate at the time, [these cases raised] one of the leading constitutional controversies in

---

114. 469 U.S. 528 (1985).

121. See Welch v. Texas Dep't of Highways and Pub. Transp., 107 S.Ct. 2941 (1987) (overruling the "quasi-constitutional" holding in Parden v. Terminal Ry., 377 U.S. 184 (1964)); Solorio v. United States, 107 S.Ct. 2924 (1987) (overruling O'Callahan v. Parker, 395 U.S. 258 (1969)); Tyler Pipe Indus. v. Washington Dep't of Revenue, 107 S.Ct. 2810 (1987) (overruling General Motors Corp. v. Washington, 377 U.S. 436 (1964)); Puerto Rico v. Branstad, 107 S.Ct. 2802, 2807–10 (1987) (overruling Kentucky v. Dennison, 65 U.S. (24 How.) 66 (1861)).

122. In *Branstad*, the Court elaborated how *Dennison* was "fundamentally incompatible with more than a century of constitutional development." *Branstad*, 107 S.Ct. at 2809. While the Court in *Welch* did not address issues of stare decisis in its decision to overrule *Parden*, it was quick to rely on the force of precedent to refuse to overrule Hans v. Louisiana, 134 U.S. 1 (1890). *Welch*, 107 S.Ct. at 2948–49. Such selective reliance does little to enhance the Court's reputation as an objective or principled arbiter.

American history." [126] Following this painful conflict and one of the most widely criticized overrulings of precedent,[127] use of paper money as legal tender was sustained. Over one hundred years later, in our age of checks, credit cards and electronic banking, the issue is off the agenda: no Supreme Court would now reexamine the merits, no matter how closely wedded it was to original intent theory and no matter how certain it was of its predecessor's error.

The fourteenth amendment provides other examples. Could the Court now be persuaded even to consider the view that section 1 of the fourteenth amendment was intended to reach only "civil" [129]—not social and political—rights and therefore that *Brown* and the reapportionment decisions must be repudiated? * * *

Finally, many of the fundamental transformations in our governmental structure legitimated by the Supreme Court in this century are unquestionably above challenge. Is it conceivable that the Court would outlaw the administrative state? Certainly administrative legislation, in some substantial form, is a permanent feature of our constitutional order. And while the Court may or may not honor *Garcia* in the future, it cannot be doubted that as a constitutional matter the federal government's regulatory power is more aptly described as limitless than limited. The constitutional law, if not the political dimensions of the New Deal, is here to stay.

The operation of stare decisis in these contexts is agenda limiting in nature. The Court could not fairly look at these issues *res nova*. Regardless of whether the Court thought these issues rightly decided, consciously or unconsciously any challenge would be screened out *in limine*. History counts. The only significant question is how.

* * *

2. *Contested Matters.*—Many constitutional issues currently remain contested despite relevant, if not definitive, Supreme Court pronouncements regarding the subject. In the absence of those factors that coalesce to remove an issue from the agenda, judicial closure seems impossible. Sometimes the Court's continuing divisions simply mirror deep public rifts (abortion, busing), sometimes not (*National League of Cities* and *Garcia,* search and seizure). Of course, as the history of racial segregation itself shows, no sharp distinction can be made between the agenda-limitation and contested-matters categories: the categories are only relatively stable points on a continuum, issues move between them, and many matters not only fall in between the two points but at

---

126. See Dam, The Legal Tender Cases, 1981 Sup.Ct.Rev. 367.

127. See Knox v. Lee, 79 U.S. (12 Wall.) 457 (1871) (overruling Hepburn v. Griswold, 75 U.S. (8 Wall.) 603 (1870)). * * *

129. While a distinction between civil rights and social and political rights cannot be maintained today, to the Framers of the fourteenth amendment the distinction was all-important. The amendment was intended to apply only to "civil" rights: personal security, personal liberty (freedom from bodily restraint), and private property. R. Berger, [Government by Judiciary 23–36 (1977).]

different times can be at different ends of the continuum. Nonetheless, certain issues clearly fall within the contested category.

* * *

Suppose that the Court were composed of a solid majority who believe that *Roe* [*v. Wade*] was incorrectly decided. What *should* happen? Whether *Roe* should be overruled is a question not reducible to whether *Roe* was decided correctly. One can imagine the Court drawing precisely such a distinction and refusing to overrule *Roe*. Of course, to make this distinction one needs a general theory of constitutional interpretation that includes some account of precedent. Why, for example, is it proper to overrule *National League of Cities, Kentucky v. Dennison,*[141] and *General Motors Corp. v. Washington,*[142] but not *Roe*? Once we acknowledge *some* role for stare decisis in constitutional adjudication—in the agenda-limitation context—it becomes more plausible for an originalist to consider a more generalized role for stare decisis in constitutional adjudication. The problem then becomes explicating that role.

NOTES TOWARD A THEORY OF STARE DECISIS: JUSTIFICATION

Precedent is, of course, part of our understanding of what law is. But that acknowledgment does not resolve the question why it plays such an important role. Generally, judicial adherence to precedent is defended by pointing to the important values in decisionmaking that are promoted thereby: consistency, coherence, fairness, equality, predictability and efficiency.[144] Perhaps, as is sometimes suggested, these values are largely obtainable without any formal doctrine of stare decisis. Be that as it may, I believe that any meaningful role for stare decisis in constitutional adjudication must draw on more powerful considerations, weighty enough to predominate even when the constitutional issues involved are of the first order. For us, those considerations are bottomed upon the concept of legitimation.

John Rawls writes that "[i]n a constitutional democracy one of [political theory's] most important aims is presenting a political conception of justice that can not only provide a shared basis for the justification of political and social institutions but also helps ensure stability from one generation to the next."[146] For Rawls, these are especially vital needs given the ineradicable pluralism of American society. Such a society faces seemingly perpetual centrifugal forces undermining the socially necessary stability. Rawls' analysis is also pertinent to constitutional theory. Stability and continuity of political institutions (and of

---

141. 65 U.S. (24 How.) 66 (1861) (overruled by Puerto Rico v. Branstad, 107 S.Ct. 2802, 2809–2810 (1987)).

142. 377 U.S. 436 (1964) (overruled by Tyler Pipe Indus. v. Washington State Dep't of Revenue, 107 S.Ct. 2810, 2817 (1987)).

144. For an evaluation of how well these values are achieved by judicial adherence to precedent, see R. Wasserstrom, The Judicial Decision: Toward a Theory of Legal Justification 60–81 (1961).

146. Rawls, The Idea of an Overlapping Consensus, 7 Oxford J. Legal Stud. 1, 1 (1987).

shared values) are important goals of the process of constitutional adjudication, particularly "in a constitution intended to endure for ages to come, and consequently, to be adapted to the various *crises* of human affairs." [147] Moreover, these values are in part at least among the values that the new constitutional order was specifically designed to secure, as the Preamble to the Constitution itself makes plain. Indeed, the Federalist No. 49 even decried appeals to the people in order to "maintain[ ] the constitutional equilibrium of government." [148]

Achievement of these values depends at least in part upon ideology, particularly the idea of legitimate government. From the very beginning—indeed from pre-Revolutionary War days—Americans have been deeply concerned with the question of the legitimacy of their political institutions. Although considerable controversy exists over both the content and utility of "legitimacy" theory as a way of understanding the legal order, legitimation ideology can make certain modest claims as a valid and important construct, particularly given my narrow focus: I am not concerned with the relationship between legitimation ideology and popular culture, but only at the narrower level of elite groups, such as lawyers, public officials, and judges. For these members of the "reasoning class," [153] the Supreme Court functions as the central means "for bringing about a consensus on the legitimacy of important governmental measures." [154]

A. *System Legitimacy*

At its most general level, stare decisis operates to promote system-wide stability and continuity by ensuring the survival of governmental norms that have achieved unsurpassed importance in American society. Such norms include the freedom from racial discrimination by the government, the general reach of the commerce clause, and even the legality of paper money. Expectations, tangible and symbolic, have developed around the critical decisions; the massive destabilization following a successful attack on any of these would threaten the functioning of the federal government, if not the viability of the constitutional order itself.

But the question of criteria remains. For the Court to invoke a system-legitimacy justification to explain its use of stare decisis in any given instance, it must feel that the consequences of overruling settled precedent are quite serious. Of course, the nation's stability need not be imminently threatened every time such a system-legitimacy justification is appropriate. But this justification supports the use of stare decisis only to prevent disruption of practices and expectations so settled, or to

---

147. McCulloch v. Maryland, 17 U.S. (4 Wheat.) 316, 415 (1819). Of course, I do not claim that the values I identify are unique to constitutional law, but only that they have greater purchase there.

148. The Federalist No. 49, at 341 (J. Madison) (J. Cooke ed. 1961). The Federalist No. 50, at 343–47 (J. Madison) (J. Cooke

ed. 1961), also discourages periodic appeals to the people.

153. J. Ely, Democracy and Distrust 59 n.** (1980).

154. C. Black, The People and the Court 38, 51 (1960). * * *

avoid the revitalization of a public debate so divisive, that departure from the precedent would contribute in some perceptible way to a failure of confidence in the lawfulness of fundamental features of the political order.

Because credible justification in system-legitimacy terms for adherence to precedent is so restricted, it seems likely that this justification will roughly correspond to those issues where stare decisis performs an agenda-limitation function. Such issues are too central to our society to overrule, if not simply to question. To permit or vindicate challenges to these traditions would "incite radical and even revolutionary attacks on the legal status quo." [157] Consequently, the Court must remove the issue of constitutional validity from public debate and keep the book closed on the questions. Stare decisis performs that office: to the extent that it restricts judicial reconsideration of legitimacy questions, stare decisis operates to keep issues off the constitutional, if not the political agenda, thereby leaving open for debate only less threatening issues. Accordingly, in part at least, it seems fair to say that the stability of our legal system depends on the doctrine of stare decisis.

* * *

Of course, even when expectations or practices are not deeply entrenched, if serious public debate still surrounds an issue, departure from precedent may sometimes threaten the stability and continuity of the political order and should therefore be avoided: *Roe* provides a ready example. However, the contested area will include few cases with *Roe'* s significance. More typically the public will not be sufficiently concerned that the Court is of two minds about the matter.

Stability and continuity, however, are not the only important constitutional values, and sometimes even these values cannot be achieved without change. Thus, even this argument cannot establish the absolute priority of precedent over text. But constitutional law is in the end a matter of government, and the Court is a part of that government. Although *Brown* will forever remind us that the Supreme Court can occasionally act as a catalyst in generating profound social change, the Court also plays an important role in our government by conserving and perpetuating shared values. In that respect, the very existence of a body of precedent is a conservative, stabilizing force * * *. A practice of judicial adherence to this body of precedent will further foster conservative values. In the end, therefore, stare decisis reflects a political conception of the nature of our constitutional government, and it must be defended in those terms.

B. Legitimating Judicial Review

Focus on system legitimation convincingly underpins only some aspects of stare decisis. For example, the wisdom of judicial reconsidera-

157. Powell, Parchment Matters: A Iowa L.Rev. 1427, 1433 (1986).
Meditation on the Constitution as Text, 71

tion of a whole series of "small" constitutional questions—such as whether jeopardy attaches when a jury is sworn rather than when it actually hears evidence, or whether remittitur is consistent with the common-law trial by jury—is not determined by system-maintenance concerns. Of greater note, it seems that most issues one would consider "currently contested" are not easily disposed of by appeals to system legitimacy. There is, however, a second, and perhaps more universal justification for the application of stare decisis to contested matters, one that also arises from a rationale concerned with stability and continuity. Namely, the Court must strive to demonstrate—at least to elites—the continuing legitimacy of judicial review. A general judicial adherence to constitutional precedent supports a consensus about the rule of law, specifically the belief that all organs of government, including the Court, are bound by the law. At first blush it may seem perverse to defend the idea that the Court maintains its subservience to the fundamental law by upholding decisions that depart from that law. But this difficulty is not insurmountable. What the Constitution requires is often a matter for debate, and once having been adequately canvassed and resolved by the Court, an issue might presumptively remain at rest. Even when the prior judicial resolution seems plainly wrong to a majority of the present Court, adherence to precedent can contribute to the important notion that the law is impersonal in character, that the Court believes itself to be following a "law which binds [it] as well as the litigants." [167] In listing "the weighty considerations" supporting adherence to precedent, Justice Harlan included "the necessity of maintaining public faith in the judiciary as a source of impersonal and reasoned judgments." [168] While it is quite clear to any observer that the Court has no coherent or stable conception of the appropriate role of precedent in constitutional adjudication, Justice Harlan's theme is something of a decorative favorite, especially among dissenters who object to an overruling decision—and it is certain the theme is sensible beyond mere decoration.

To my mind, this rule of law argument does not suffer from criticism that the man in the street is unaware of the overruling of "small" precedents and that, in any event, he would expect the Constitution and not the Court's precedents to control adjudication. For me, the real focus of rule of law theories about the Supreme Court in the main is elites, at least "the reasoning classes." The concern is to contain, if not minimize, the existing cynicism that constitutional law is nothing more than politics carried on in a different forum. In a recent work, Professor Cox states that the future of judicial review turns largely on whether law is seen by the profession as only judicial policymaking, or "whether room is left for the older belief that judges are truly bound by law both as a confining force and as an ideal search for justice." [172] Perhaps it goes too

167. A Cox, the Role of the Supreme Court in American Government 50 (1976). * * *

168. Moragne v. States Marine Lines, 398 U.S. 375, 403 (1970).

172. A. Cox, [The Court and Constitution 377 (1987)].

far to tie the whole future of judicial review to this distinction, but Professor Cox's point does have merit.   My submission is that the Court's institutional position would be weakened were it generally perceived that the Court itself views its own decisions as little more than "a restricted railroad ticket, good for this day and train only." [173]   If courts are viewed as unbound by precedent, and the law as no more than what the last Court said, considerable efforts would be expended to get control of such an institution—with judicial independence and public confidence greatly weakened.

F. NEUTRAL PRINCIPLES

HERBERT WECHSLER, TOWARD NEUTRAL PRINCIPLES OF CONSTITUTIONAL LAW
73 Harv.L.Rev. 9, 11–20, 31–35 (1959).

[Are there] any criteria that both the Supreme Court and those who undertake to praise or to condemn its judgments are morally and intellectually obligated to support?

Whatever you may think to be the answer, surely you agree with me that I am right to state the question as the same one for the Court and for its critics.   An attack upon a judgment involves an assertion that a court should have decided otherwise than as it did.   Is it not clear that the validity of an assertion of this kind depends upon assigning reasons that should have prevailed with the tribunal; and that any other reasons are irrelevant?   That is, of course, not only true of a critique of a decision of the courts; it applies whenever a determination is in question, a determination that it is essential to make either way.   Is it the irritation of advancing years that leads me to lament that our culture is not rich with critics who respect these limitations of the enterprise in which they are engaged?

You may remind me that, as someone in the ancient world observed—perhaps it was Josephus—history has little tolerance for any of those reasonable judgments that have turned out to be wrong.   But history, in this sense, is inscrutable, concealing all its verdicts in the bosom of the future; it is never a contemporary critic.

I revert then to the problem of criteria as it arises for both courts and critics—by which I mean criteria that can be framed and tested as an exercise of reason and not merely as an act of willfulness or will.   Even to put the problem is, of course, to raise an issue no less old than our culture.   Those who perceive in law only the element of fiat, in whose conception of the legal cosmos reason has no meaning or no place, will not join gladly in the search for standards of the kind I have in mind.   I must, in short, expect dissent *in limine* from anyone whose view of the judicial process leaves no room for the antinomy Professor

---

173. Smith v. Allwright, 321 U.S. 649, 669 (1944) (Roberts, J., dissenting).

Fuller has so gracefully explored.[38] So too must I anticipate dissent from those more numerous among us who, vouching no philosophy to warranty, frankly or covertly make the test of virtue in interpretation whether its result in the immediate decision seems to hinder or advance the interests or the values they support.

I shall not try to overcome the philosophic doubt that I have mentioned, although to use a phrase that Holmes so often used—"it hits me where I live." That battle must be fought on wider fronts than that of constitutional interpretation; and I do not delude myself that I can qualify for a command, great as is my wish to render service. The man who simply lets his judgment turn on the immediate result may not, however, realize that his position implies that the courts are free to function as a naked power organ, that it is an empty affirmation to regard them, as ambivalently he so often does, as courts of law. If he may know he disapproves of a decision when all he knows is that it has sustained a claim put forward by a labor union or a taxpayer, a Negro or a segregationist, a corporation or a Communist—he acquiesces in the proposition that a man of different sympathy but equal information may no less properly conclude that he approves.

You will not charge me with exaggeration if I say that this type of *ad hoc* evaluation is, as it has always been, the deepest problem of our constitutionalism, not only with respect to judgments of the courts but also in the wider realm in which conflicting constitutional positions have played a part in our politics.

* * *

* * * [W]hether you are tolerant, perhaps more tolerant than I, of the *ad hoc* in politics, with principle reduced to a manipulative tool, are you not also ready to agree that something else is called for from the courts? I put it to you that the main constituent of the judicial process is precisely that it must be genuinely principled, resting with respect to every step that is involved in reaching judgment on analysis and reasons quite transcending the immediate result that is achieved. To be sure, the courts decide, or should decide, only the case they have before them. But must they not decide on grounds of adequate neutrality and generality, tested not only by the instant application but by others that the principles imply? Is it not the very essence of judicial method to insist upon attending to such other cases, preferably those involving an opposing interest, in evaluating any principle avowed?

Here too I do not think that I am stating any novel or momentous insight. But now, as Holmes said long ago in speaking of "the unrest which seems to wonder vaguely whether law and order pay," we "need education in the obvious." [46] We need it more particularly now respecting constitutional interpretation, since it has become a commonplace to

38. See Fuller, *Reason and Fiat in Case Law,* 59 Harv.L.Rev. 376 (1946).

46. Holmes, Law and the Court, in Collected Legal Papers 291, 292 (1920).

grant what many for so long denied: that courts in constitutional determinations face issues that are inescapably "political" * * * in that they involve a choice among competing values or desires, a choice reflected in the legislative or executive action in question, which the court must either condemn or condone.

* * * [W]hat is crucial, I submit, is not the nature of the question but the nature of the answer that may validly be given by the courts. No legislature or executive is obligated by the nature of its function to support its choice of values by the type of reasoned explanation that I have suggested is intrinsic to judicial action—however much we may admire such a reasoned exposition when we find it in those other realms.

Does not the special duty of the courts to judge by neutral principles addressed to all the issues make it inapposite to contend, as Judge Hand does, that no court can review the legislative choice—by any standard other than a fixed "historical meaning" of constitutional provisions [48]— without becoming "a third legislative chamber"? [49] Is there not, in short, a vital difference between legislative freedom to appraise the gains and losses in projected measures and the kind of principled appraisal, in respect of values that can reasonably be asserted to have constitutional dimension, that alone is in the province of the courts? Does not the difference yield a middle ground between a judicial House of Lords and the abandonment of any limitation on the other branches—a middle ground consisting of judicial action that embodies what are surely the main qualities of law, its generality and its neutrality? This must, it seems to me, have been in Mr. Justice Jackson's mind when in his chapter on the Supreme Court "as a political institution" he wrote [50] in words that I find stirring, "Liberty is not the mere absence of restraint, it is not a spontaneous product of majority rule, it is not achieved merely by lifting underprivileged classes to power, nor is it the inevitable by-product of technological expansion. It is achieved only by a rule of law." Is it not also what Mr. Justice Frankfurter must mean in calling upon judges for "allegiance to nothing except the effort, amid tangled words and limited insights, to find the path through precedent, through policy, through history, to the best judgment that fallible creatures can reach in that most difficult of all tasks: the achievement of justice between man and man, between man and state, through reason called law"? [51]

You will not understand my emphasis upon the role of reason and of principle in the judicial, as distinguished from the legislative or executive, appraisal of conflicting values to imply that I depreciate the duty of fidelity to the text of the Constitution, when its words may be decisive— though I would certainly remind you of the caution stated by Chief Justice Hughes: "Behind the words of the constitutional provisions are

48. [L. Hand, The Bill of Rights 65 (1958).]

49. *Id.* at 42.

50. Jackson, The Supreme Court in the American System of Government 76 (1955).

51. Frankfurter, Chief Justices I Have Known, in Of Law and Men 138 (Elman ed.

postulates which limit and control." [52]   Nor will you take me to deny that history has weight in the elucidation of the text, though it is surely subtle business to appraise it as a guide.   Nor will you even think that I deem precedent without importance, for we surely must agree with Holmes that "imitation of the past, until we have a clear reason for change, no more needs justification than appetite." [53]   But after all, it was Chief Justice Taney who declared his willingness "that it be regarded hereafter as the law of this court, that its opinion upon the construction of the Constitution is always open to discussion when it is supposed to have been founded in error, and that its judicial authority should hereafter depend altogether on the force of the reasoning by which it is supported." [54]   Would any of us have it otherwise, given the nature of the problems that confront the courts?

At all events, is not the relative compulsion of the language of the Constitution, of history and precedent—where they do not combine to make an answer clear—itself a matter to be judged, so far as possible, by neutral principles—by standards that transcend the case at hand?   I know, of course, that it is common to distinguish, as Judge Hand did, clauses like "due process," cast "in such sweeping terms that their history does not elucidate their contents," [55] from other provisions of the Bill of Rights addressed to more specific problems.   But the contrast, as it seems to me, often implies an overstatement of the specificity or the immutability these other clauses really have—at least when problems under them arise.

No one would argue, for example, that there need not be indictment and a jury trial in prosecutions for a felony in district courts.   What made a question of some difficulty was the issue whether service wives charged with the murders of their husbands overseas could be tried there before a military court. [56]   Does the language of the double-jeopardy clause or its preconstitutional history actually help to decide whether a defendant tried for murder in the first degree and convicted of murder in the second, who wins a reversal of the judgment on appeal, may be tried again for murder in the first or only murder in the second? [57]   Is there significance in the fact that it is "jeopardy of life or limb" that is forbidden, now that no one is in jeopardy of limb but only of imprisonment or fine?   The right to "have the assistance of counsel" was considered, I am sure, when the sixth amendment was proposed, a right to defend by counsel if you have one, contrary to what was then the English law. [58]   That does not seem to me sufficient to avert extension of

1956).

52.   Principality of Monaco v. Mississippi, 292 U.S. 313, 322 (1934).

53.   Holmes, Holdsworth's English Law, in Collected Legal Papers 285, 290 (1920).

54.   Passenger Cases, 48 U.S. (7 How.) 283, 470 (1849).

55.   Hand, [*supra* note 48], at 30.

56.   See Reid v. Covert, 354 U.S. 1 (1957), *reversing on rehearing* 351 U.S. 487 (1956).

57.   See Green v. United States, 355 U.S. 184 (1957).

58.   "Throughout the eighteenth century counsel were allowed to speak in cases of treason and misdemeanour only."   1 Stephen, A History of the Criminal Law of England 453 (1883).   * * *

its meaning to imply a right to court-appointed counsel when the defendant is too poor to find such aid [59]—though I admit that I once urged the point sincerely as a lawyer for the Government.[60] It is difficult for me to think the fourth amendment freezes for all time the common law of search and of arrest as it prevailed when the amendment was adopted, whatever the exigencies of police problems may now be or may become. Nor should we, in my view, lament the fact that "the" freedom of speech or press that Congress is forbidden by the first amendment to impair is not determined only by the scope such freedom had in the late eighteenth century, though the word "the" might have been taken to impose a limitation to the concept of that time—a time when, President Wright has recently reminded us, there was remarkable consensus about matters of this kind.[61]

Even "due process," on the other hand, might have been confined, as Mr. Justice Brandeis urged originally,[62] to a guarantee of fair procedure, coupled perhaps with prohibition of executive displacement of established law—the analogue for us of what the barons meant in Magna Carta. Equal protection could be taken as no more than an assurance that no one may be placed beyond the safeguards of the law, outlawing, as it were, the possibility of outlawry, but nothing else. Here too I cannot find it in my heart to regret that interpretation did not ground itself in ancient history but rather has perceived in these provisions a compendious affirmation of the basic values of a free society, values that must be given weight in legislation and administration at the risk of courting trouble in the courts.

So far as possible, to finish with my point, I argue that we should prefer to see the other clauses of the Bill of Rights read as an affirmation of the special values they embody rather than as statements of a finite rule of law, its limits fixed by the consensus of a century long past, with problems very different from our own. To read them in the former way is to leave room for adaptation and adjustment if and when competing values, also having constitutional dimension, enter on the scene.

Let me repeat what I have thus far tried to say. The courts have both the title and the duty when a case is properly before them to review the actions of the other branches in the light of constitutional provisions, even though the action involves value choices, as invariably action does. In doing so, however, they are bound to function otherwise than as a naked power organ; they participate as courts of law. This calls for facing how determinations of this kind can be asserted to have any legal quality. The answer, I suggest, inheres primarily in that they are—or are obliged to be—entirely principled. A principled decision, in the

59. See Johnson v. Zerbst, 304 U.S. 458 (1938).

60. Walker v. Johnston, 312 U.S. 275 (1941).

61. Wright, Consensus and Continuity, 1776–1787 *passim* (1958). * * *

62. "Despite arguments to the contrary which had seemed to me persuasive, it is settled that the due process clause of the Fourteenth Amendment applies to matters of substantive law as well as to matters of procedure." Whitney v. California, 274 U.S. 357, 373 (1927) (concurring opinion).

sense I have in mind, is one that rests on reasons with respect to all the issues in the case, reasons that in their generality and their neutrality transcend any immediate result that is involved. When no sufficient reasons of this kind can be assigned for overturning value choices of the other branches of the Government or of a state, those choices must, of course, survive. Otherwise, as Holmes said in his first opinion for the Court, "a constitution, instead of embodying only relatively fundamental rules of right, as generally understood by all English-speaking communities, would become the partisan of a particular set of ethical or economical opinions * * *." [63]

The virtue or demerit of a judgment turns, therefore, entirely on the reasons that support it and their adequacy to maintain any choice of values it decrees, or, it is vital that we add, to maintain the rejection of a claim that any given choice should be decreed. The critic's role, as T.R. Powell showed throughout so many fruitful years, is the sustained, disinterested, merciless examination of the reasons that the courts advance, measured by standards of the kind I have attempted to describe. I wish that more of us today could imitate his dedication to that task.

III. Some Appraisals of Review

One who has ventured to advance such generalities about the courts and constitutional interpretation is surely challenged to apply them to some concrete problems—if only to make clear that he believes in what he says. A lecture, to be sure, is a poor medium for such an undertaking, for the statement and analysis of cases inescapably takes time. Nonetheless, I feel obliged to make the effort and I trust that I can do so without trespassing on the indulgence you already have displayed.

* * *

[Consider] the school decision, which for one of my persuasion stirs the deepest conflict I experience in testing the thesis I propose. Yet I would surely be engaged in playing Hamlet without Hamlet if I did not try to state the problems that appear to me to be involved.

The problem for me, I hardly need to say, is not that the Court departed from its earlier decisions holding or implying that the equality of public educational facilities demanded by the Constitution could be met by separate schools. I stand with the long tradition of the Court that previous decisions must be subject to reexamination when a case against their reasoning is made. Nor is the problem that the Court disturbed the settled patterns of a portion of the country; even that must be accepted as a lesser evil than nullification of the Constitution. Nor is it that history does not confirm that an agreed purpose of the fourteenth amendment was to forbid separate schools or that there is important evidence that many thought the contrary; [111] the words are

63. Otis v. Parker, 187 U.S. 606, 609 (1903).

111. See Bickel, *The Original Understanding and the Segregation Decision,* 69 Harv.L.Rev. 1 (1955).

general and leave room for expanding content as time passes and conditions change. Nor is it that the Court may have miscalculated the extent to which its judgment would be honored or accepted; it is not a prophet of the strength of our national commitment to respect the judgments of the courts. Nor is it even that the Court did not remit the issue to the Congress, acting under the enforcement clause of the amendment. That was a possible solution, to be sure, but certainly Professor Freund is right [112] that it would merely have evaded the claims made.

The problem inheres strictly in the reasoning of the opinion, an opinion which is often read with less fidelity by those who praise it than by those by whom it is condemned. The Court did not declare, as many wish it had, that the fourteenth amendment forbids all racial lines in legislation, though subsequent per curiam decisions may, as I have said, now go that far. Rather, as Judge Hand observed,[113] the separate-but-equal formula was not overruled "in form" but was held to have "no place" in public education on the ground that segregated schools are "inherently unequal," with deleterious effects upon the colored children in implying their inferiority, effects which retard their educational and mental development. So, indeed, the district court had found as a fact in the Kansas case, a finding which the Supreme Court embraced, citing some further "modern authority" in its support.

Does the validity of the decision turn then on the sufficiency of evidence or of judicial notice to sustain a finding that the separation harms the Negro children who may be involved? There were, indeed, some witnesses who expressed that opinion in the Kansas case, as there were also witnesses in the companion Virginia case * * *, whose view was to the contrary. Much depended on the question that the witness had in mind, which rarely was explicit. Was he comparing the position of the Negro child in a segregated school with his position in an integrated school where he was happily accepted and regarded by the whites; or was he comparing his position under separation with that under integration where the whites were hostile to his presence and found ways to make their feelings known? And if the harm that segregation worked was relevant, what of the benefits that it entailed: sense of security, the absence of hostility? Were they irrelevant? Moreover, was the finding in Topeka applicable without more to Clarendon County, South Carolina, with 2,799 colored students and only 295 whites? Suppose that more Negroes in a community preferred separation than opposed it? Would that be relevant to whether they were hurt or aided by segregation as opposed to integration? Their fates would be governed by the change of system quite as fully as those of the students who complained.

---

112. See Freund, *Storm Over the American Supreme Court*, 21 Modern L.Rev. 345, 351 (1958).

113. Hand, [*supra* note 48], at 54.

I find it hard to think the judgment really turned upon the facts. Rather, it seems to me, it must have rested on the view that racial segregation is, in principle, a denial of equality to the minority against whom it is directed; that is, the group that is not dominant politically and, therefore, does not make the choice involved. For many who support the Court's decision this assuredly is the decisive ground. But this position also presents problems. Does it not involve an inquiry into the motive of the legislature, which is generally foreclosed to the courts?[117] Is it alternatively defensible to make the measure of validity of legislation the way it is interpreted by those who are affected by it? In the context of a charge that segregation *with equal facilities* is a denial of equality, is there not a point in *Plessy* in the statement that if "enforced separation stamps the colored race with a badge of inferiority" it is solely because its members choose "to put that construction upon it"?[118] Does enforced separation of the sexes discriminate against females merely because it may be the females who resent it and it is imposed by judgments predominantly male? Is a prohibition of miscegenation a discrimination against the colored member of the couple who would like to marry?

For me, assuming equal facilities, the question posed by state-enforced segregation is not one of discrimination at all. Its human and its constitutional dimensions lie entirely elsewhere, in the denial by the state of freedom to associate, a denial that impinges in the same way on any groups or races that may be involved. I think, and I hope not without foundation, that the Southern white also pays heavily for segregation, not only in the sense of guilt that he must carry but also in the benefits he is denied. In the days when I was joined with Charles H. Houston in a litigation in the Supreme Court, before the present building was constructed, he did not suffer more than I in knowing that we had to go to Union Station to lunch together during the recess. Does not the problem of miscegenation show most clearly that it is the freedom of association that at bottom is involved, the only case, I may add, where it is implicit in the situation that association is desired by the only individuals involved? I take no pride in knowing that in 1956 the Supreme Court dismissed an appeal in a case in which Virginia nullified a marriage on this ground, a case in which the statute had been squarely challenged by the defendant, and the Court, after remanding once, dismissed per curiam on procedural grounds that I make bold to say are wholly without basis in the law.[119]

But if the freedom of association is denied by segregation, integration forces an association upon those for whom it is unpleasant or

117. Motive is open to examination when executive action is challenged as discriminatory, but there the purpose is to show that an admitted inequality of treatment was not inadvertent. See, *e.g.,* Snowden v. Hughes, 321 U.S. 1 (1944). Even in such a case, invidious motivation alone has not been held to establish the inequality.

118. Plessy v. Ferguson, 163 U.S. 537, 551 (1896).

119. See Ham Say Naim v. Naim, 197 Va. 80, 87 S.E.2d 749, *vacated,* 350 U.S. 891 (1955), *on remand,* 197 Va. 734, 90 S.E.2d 849, *appeal dismissed,* 350 U.S. 985 (1956).

repugnant. Is this not the heart of the issue involved, a conflict in human claims of high dimension, not unlike many others that involve the highest freedoms—conflicts that Professor Sutherland has recently described.[120] Given a situation where the state must practically choose between denying the association to those individuals who wish it or imposing it on those who would avoid it, is there a basis in neutral principles for holding that the Constitution demands that the claims for association should prevail? I should like to think there is, but I confess that I have not yet written the opinion. To write it is for me the challenge of the school-segregation cases.

MARK V. TUSHNET, FOLLOWING THE RULES LAID DOWN: A CRITIQUE OF INTERPRETIVISM AND NEUTRAL PRINCIPLES
96 Harv.L.Rev. 781, 805–24 (1983).

The rule of law, according to the liberal conception, is meant to protect us against the exercise of arbitrary power. The theory of neutral principles asserts that a requirement of consistency, the core of the ideal of the rule of law, places sufficient bounds on judges to reduce the risk of arbitrariness to an acceptable level. The question is whether the concepts of neutrality and consistency can be developed in ways that are adequate for the task. My discussion examines various candidates for a definition of neutrality, beginning with a crude definition and moving toward more sophisticated ones. Yet each candidate suffers from similar defects: each fails to provide the kinds of constraints on judges that liberalism requires. Some candidates seek to limit the results judges might reach, others the methods they may use. The supposed substantive bounds that consistency imposes on judges, however, are either empty or parasitic on other substantive theories of constitutional law, and the methodological bounds are either empty or dependent on a sociology of law that undermines liberalism's assumptions about society.

A. NEUTRAL CONTENT

Robert Bork's version of neutral principles theory would require that decisions rest on principles that are neutral in content and in application.[65] Bork's formulation may be an attempt to generalize Wechsler's definition, which characterizes neutrality as judicial indifference to who the winner is. For Wechsler, such indifference was a matter of judicial willingness to apply the present case's rule in the next case as well, regardless whether the beneficiary in the later case was less attractive than the earlier winner in ways not made relevant by the rule itself.[66] Neutral content for Bork might mean a similar indifference, but now within the case: the principle governing the case should be devel-

---

120. See Sutherland, The Law and One Man Among Many 35–62 (1956).

65. Bork, *Neutral Principles and Some First Amendment Problems,* 47 Ind.L.J. 1, 6–7 (1971).

66. Wechsler, *Toward Neutral Principles of Constitutional Law,* 73 Harv.L.Rev. 1, 11–12, 15 (1959).

oped in a form that employs only general terms and that avoids any express preference for any named groups. This outcome, however, is impossible. We might coherently require that rules not use proper names, but there is no principled way to distinguish between the general terms that in effect pick out specific groups or individuals and those that are "truly" general. Any general term serves to identify some specific group; hence if the notion of content neutrality is to make any sense, it must depend on a prior understanding of which kinds of distinctions are legitimately "neutral" and which are not. The demand for neutrality in content thus cannot provide an independent criterion for acceptable decisions.

Standing alone, the theory that principles must be neutral in content cannot constrain judicial discretion. But it could be coupled with some other theory—such as interpretivism, Ely's reinforcement of representation,[a] or a moral philosophy. When coordinated with some such substantive theory, the demand for neutral principles stipulates that a decision is justified only if the principles derived from the other theory are neutrally applied. Yet to require neutral application of the principles of the other theory is merely to apply those principles in given cases; the requirement of content neutrality adds nothing.[68]

B. Neutral Method

If neutrality is to serve as a meaningful guide, it must be understood not as a standard for the content of principles, but rather as a constraint on the process by which principles are selected, justified, and applied. Thus, the remaining candidate explications of neutrality all focus on the judicial process and the need for "neutral *application*." This focus transfers our attention from the principles themselves to the judges who purport to use them.

* * *

1. Prospective Application.—What then are methodologically neutral principles? To Wechsler, such principles are identified primarily by a forward-looking aspect: a judge who invokes a principle in a specific instance commits himself or herself to invoking it in future cases that are relevantly identical. For example, a judge who justifies the holding in *Brown v. Board of Education* that segregated schools are unconstitutional by invoking the principle that the state may not take race into account in any significant policy decision is thereby also committed to holding state-developed affirmative action programs unconstitutional. The judge's interior monologue involves specifying the principle about to be invoked, imagining future cases and their proper resolution, determining whether those cases are different from the present one in any

a. J. Ely, Democracy and Distrust (1980).

68. In the larger work of which this Article will be a part, I argue that the other, substantive theories are all internally contradictory, at least beyond a narrow range of applications. If that argument is correct, neutral application is again an empty concept, for anything can be derived from a contradiction.

ways that the proposed principle itself says are relevant, and asking whether the principle yields the proper results.

There are two levels of problems with the idea that commitment to prospective neutral application constrains judicial choices. First, there are two features of our judicial institutions that dissipate any constraining force that the demand for prospective neutrality may impose. Second, there is a conceptual problem that robs the very idea of prospective neutrality of any normative force.

(a) Institutional Problems.—The first institutional problem is that Supreme Court decisions are made by a collective body, which is constrained by a norm of compromise and cooperation. Suppose that in case 1 Justices *M, N,* and *O* have taken neutral principles theory to heart and believe that the correct result is justified by principle *A.* Justices *P, Q, R,* and *S* have done likewise but believe that the same result is justified by principle *B.* Justices *T* and *V,* who also accept principle *A* but believe it inapplicable to case 1, dissent. The four-person group gains control of the writing of the opinion, and the three others who agree with the result accede to the institutional pressure for majority decisions and join an opinion that invokes principle *B.* Now case 2 arises. Justices *T* and *V* are convinced that, because case 2 is relevantly different from case 1, principle *A* should be used. They join with Justices *M, N,* and *O* and produce a majority opinion invoking principle *A.* If principle *B* were used, the result would be different; thus, there are four dissenters.

Kent Greenawalt has argued that neutral principles theory is required to acknowledge that neutrality sometimes must yield to other considerations, such as the institutional pressure for majority decisions.[78] If the norm of compromise is thought to authorize submersion of individual views in the selection of principles, we could not charge anyone with prospective nonneutrality in the handling of case 1. When case 2 subsequently arises, however, it would be odd—and ultimately destructive of the willingness to compromise—to demand that Justices *M, N,* and *O* follow principle *B* to a result that they, on principled grounds, believe wrong. But at the same time, to allow a judge criticized for nonneutrality to reply that in the particular situation neutrality had to yield to more pressing circumstances is to give the game of theory away. If we allow neutrality to yield to the institutional need here (a need that is quite weak—we all can live with fragmented Courts and decisions), a sufficiently pressing need will likely be available to justify virtually any deviation from neutrality.

A second institutional problem is that prospective neutrality involves unreasonable expectations concerning the capacities of judges. Every present case is connected to every conceivable future case, in the sense that a skilled lawyer can demonstrate how the earlier case's

---

78. Greenawalt, *The Enduring Significance of Neutral Principles,* 78 Co-   lum.L.Rev. 982, 1007–08 (1978).

principles ought to affect (although perhaps not determine) the outcome
in any later case.   In these circumstances, neutral application means
that each decision constrains a judge in every future decision; the
import of the prospective approach is that, the first time a judge decides
a case, he or she is to some extent committed to particular decisions for
the rest of his or her career.

There are two difficulties here.   First, even if we confine our
attention to cases in the same general area as the present one, this
formulation of the neutrality requirement is obviously too stringent.   We
cannot and should not expect judges to have fully elaborated theories of
race discrimination in their first cases, much less theories of gender,
illegitimacy, and other modes of discrimination as well.   Second, to the
extent that perceptions of connections vary with skill, the theory has the
curious effect of constraining only the better judges.   The less skilled
judge will not think to test a principle developed in a race-discrimination
case against gender-discrimination or abortion cases; a more skilled
judge will.

Wechsler responded to these difficulties by relaxing the requirement: the judge must test the principle against "applications that are
now foreseeable," and must either agree with the result in such applications or be able to specify a relevant difference between the cases.[83]   But
now the judge charged with nonneutrality will often be able to defend by
saying that he or she simply had not foreseen the case at hand when the
prior one was decided.   That defense may lead us to conclude that the
judge is not terribly competent, but it defeats the charge of nonneutrality.

(b) Conceptual Difficulty.—The third, largely conceptual difficulty
with the theory of neutral principles was foreshadowed by the example
of a case whose result could be justified by either of two principles.
Neutral application requires that we be able to identify *the* principle that
justified the result in case 1 in order to be sure that it is neutrally
applied in case 2.   This requirement, however, cannot be fulfilled,
because there are always a number of justificatory principles available to
make sense of case 1 and a number of techniques to select the "true"
basis of case 1.   Of course, the opinion in case 1 will articulate a
principle that purports to support the result.   But the thrust of introductory law courses is to show that the principles offered in opinions are
never good enough.   And this indefiniteness bedevils—and liberates—
not only the commentators and the lawyers and judges subsequently
dealing with the decision; it equally affects the author of the opinion.

* * * At the moment a decision is announced, we cannot identify
the principle that it embodies.   Even when we take account of the
language of the opinion, each decision can be traced to many different
possible principles, and we often learn the justifying principle of case 1

83. Wechsler, *The Nature of Judicial*   (S. Hook ed. 1964).
Reasoning, in Law and Philosophy 290, 298

only when a court in case 2 states it * * *. The theory of neutral principles thus loses almost all of its constraining force when neutrality has a prospective meaning. What is left is something like a counsel to judges that they be sincere within the limits of their ability. But this formulation hardly provides a reassuring constraint on judicial willfulness.

2. Retrospective Application.—Although Wechsler framed the neutral principles theory in prospective terms, it might be saved by recasting it in retrospective terms. The theory would then impose as a necessary condition for justification the requirement that a decision be consistent with the relevant precedents.[98] This tack links the theory to general approaches to precedent-based judicial decisionmaking in nonconstitutional areas. It also captures the natural way in which we raise questions about neutrality. The prospective theory requires that we pose hypothetical future cases, apply the principle, and ask whether the judges really meant to resolve the hypothetical cases as the principle seems to require. Because the hypothetical cases have not arisen, we cannot know the answer; we can do little more than raise our eyebrows, as Wechsler surely did, and emphasize the "really" as we ask the question in a skeptical tone.

In contrast, the retrospective theory encourages concrete criticism * * *. We need only compare case 2, which is now decided, with case 1 to see if a principle from case 1 has been neutrally applied in case 2. But if the retrospective demand is merely that the opinion in case 2 deploy some reading of the earlier case from which the holding in case 2 follows, the openness of the precedents means that the demand can always be satisfied. And if the demand is rather that the holding be derived from the principles actually articulated in the relevant precedents, differences between case 2 and the precedents will inevitably demand a degree of reinterpretation of the old principles. New cases always present issues different from those settled by prior cases. Thus, to decide a new case, a judge must take some liberties with the old principles, if they are to be applied at all. There is, however, no principled way to determine how many liberties can be taken; hence this second reading of the retrospective approach likewise provides no meaningful constraints.

The central problem here is that, given the difficulty of isolating a single principle for which a given precedent stands, we lack any criteria for distinguishing between cases that depart from and those that conform to the principles of their precedents. In fact, any case can compellingly be placed in either category. Although such a universal claim cannot be validated by example, examples can at least make the claim plausible. Therefore, the following paragraphs present several

---

98. *But cf.* Wechsler, *supra* note 66, at 31 (stipulating that neutrality is not a mat-   ter of adhering to precedents).

instances of cases that simultaneously depart from and conform to their precedents.

The first is *Griswold v. Connecticut,* in which the Supreme Court held that a state could not constitutionally prohibit the dissemination of contraceptive information or devices to married people.[100] *Griswold* relied in part on *Pierce v. Society of Sisters,*[101] which held unconstitutional a requirement that children attend public rather than private schools, and *Meyer v. Nebraska,*[102] which held that a state could not prohibit the teaching of foreign languages to young children. In *Griswold,* the Court said that these cases relied on a constitutionally protected interest, conveniently labeled "privacy," that was identical to the interest implicated in the contraceptive case.

On one view, *Griswold* tortures these precedents. Both were old-fashioned due process cases, which emphasized interference "with the calling of modern language teachers * * * and with the power of parents to control the education of their own." [103] On this view, the most one can fairly find in *Meyer* and *Pierce* is a principle about freedom of inquiry that is rather narrower than a principle of privacy. Yet of course one can say with equal force that *Griswold* identifies for us the true privacy principle of *Meyer* and *Pierce,* in the same way that the abortion funding cases identify the true principle of *Roe v. Wade.* * * * [T]he retrospective approach to neutral principles must recognize the extensive creativity exercised by a judge when he or she imputes to a precedent "the" principle that justifies both the precedent and the judge's present holding. [Other examples omitted—eds.]

3. The Craft Interpretation.—This critique of the retrospective-application interpretation points the way to a more refined version— what I will term the craft interpretation—of the calls of the neutral principles theorists for retrospective consistency. The failings of this final alternative bring out the underlying reasons that the demand for consistency cannot do the job expected of it.

The preceding discussion has reminded us that each decision re-works its precedents. A decision picks up some threads that received little emphasis before, and places great stress on them. It deprecates what seemed important before by emphasizing the factual setting of the precedents. The techniques are well known; indeed, learning them is at the core of a good legal education. But they are techniques. This recognition suggests that we attempt to define consistency as a matter of craft. When push comes to shove, in fact, adherents of neutral principles simply offer us lyrical descriptions of the sense of professionalism in lieu of sharper characterizations of the constraints on judges. Charles Black, for example, attempts to resolve the question whether law can rely on neutral principles by depicting "the art of law" living between the two poles of subjective preference and objective validation in much

100. 381 U.S. 479 (1965).

101. 268 U.S. 510 (1925).

102. 262 U.S. 390 (1923).

103. *Id.* at 401.

the same way that "the art of music has its life somewhere between traffic noise and a tuning fork—more disciplined by far than the one, with an unfathomably complex inner discipline of its own, far richer than the other, with inexhaustible variety of resource." [116] The difficulty then is to specify the limits to permissible craftiness. One limit may be that a judge cannot lie about the precedents—for example, by grossly mischaracterizing the facts. And Black adds that "decision [must] be taken in knowledge of and with consideration of certainly known facts of public life," such as the fact that segregation necessarily degrades blacks. [118] But these limits are clearly not terribly restrictive, and no one has suggested helpful others.

If the craft interpretation cannot specify limits to craftiness, another alternative is to identify some decisions that are within and some that are outside the limits in order to provide the basis for an inductive and intuitive generalization. As the following discussion indicates, however, it turns out that the limits of craft are so broad that in any interesting case any reasonably skilled lawyer can reach whatever result he or she wants. The craft interpretation thus fails to constrain the results that a reasonably skilled judge can reach, and leaves the judge free to enforce his or her personal values, as long as the opinions enforcing those values are well written. Such an outcome is inconsistent with the requirements of liberalism in that, once again, the demand for neutral principles fails in any appreciable way to limit the possibility of judicial tyranny.

The debate over the propriety of the result in *Roe v. Wade* [120] illustrates this problem. It seems to be generally agreed that, as a matter of simple craft, Justice Blackmun's opinion for the Court was dreadful. [121] The central issue before the Court was whether a pregnant woman had a constitutionally protected interest in terminating her pregnancy. When his opinion reached that issue, Justice Blackmun simply listed a number of cases in which "a right of personal privacy, or a guarantee of certain areas or zones of privacy," had been recognized. Then he said, "This right of privacy, whether it be founded in the Fourteenth Amendment's concept of personal liberty * * * or * * * in the Ninth Amendment's reservation of rights to the people, is broad enough to encompass a woman's decision whether or not to terminate her pregnancy." [122] And that was it. I will provisionally concede that this "argument" does not satisfy the requirements of the craft.

---

116. C. Black, Decision According to Law 81 (1981); *see also id.* at 21–24 (metaphorical evocation of delicate logic of law); *see* Sandalow, *Constitutional Interpretation,* 79 Mich.L.Rev. 1033 (1981) (tracing delicate balance between faithfulness to the constitutional text and accommodation to the needs of the time).

118. C. Black, *supra* note 116, at 82.

120. 410 U.S. 113 (1973).

121. *See, e.g.,* Ely, *The Wages of Crying Wolf: A Comment on* Roe v. Wade, 82 Yale L.J. 920 (1973); Epstein, *Substantive Due Process by Any Other Name: The Abortion Cases,* 1973 Sup.Ct.Rev. 159; Tribe, *The Supreme Court, 1972 Term—Foreword: Toward a Model of Roles in the Due Process of Life and Law,* 87 Harv.L.Rev. 1, 2–5 (1973).

122. Roe v. Wade, 410 U.S. at 153.

But the conclusion that we are to draw faces two challenges: it is either uninteresting or irrelevant to constitutional theory. Insofar as *Roe* gives us evidence, we can conclude that Justice Blackmun is a terrible judge. The point of constitutional theory, though, would seem to be to keep judges in line. If the result in *Roe* can be defended by judges more skilled than Justice Blackmun, the requirements of the craft would mean only that good judges can do things that bad judges cannot without subjecting themselves to professional criticism. For example, John Ely argues that, although *Roe* is beyond acceptable limits, *Griswold* is within them, though perhaps near the edge.[125] Justice Douglas' opinion for the Court in *Griswold* identified a number of constitutional provisions that in his view explicitly protected one or another aspect of personal privacy. The opinion then noted that the Court had in the past protected other interests closely related to those expressly protected. By arguing that those "penumbral" interests overlapped in the area of marital use of contraceptives, Justice Douglas could hold the challenged statute unconstitutional.

If *Griswold* is acceptable, we need only repeat its method in *Roe*. Indeed, Justice Douglas followed just that course in a brilliant concurring opinion.[126] And even if *Griswold*'s logic is rejected, skilled lawyers could still rewrite *Roe* to defend Justice Blackmun's outcome.[127] There is in fact a cottage industry of constitutional law scholars who concoct revised opinions for controversial decisions.[128] Thus, the craft interpretation of neutrality in application is ultimately uninteresting for reasons that we have already seen. At most it provides a standard to measure the competence of judges, a standard that by itself is insufficient to constrain adequately the risk of tyranny.

The other difficulty with the craft interpretation runs deeper. Craft limitations make sense only if we can agree what the craft is. But consider the craft of "writing novels." Its practice includes Trollope writing *The Eustace Diamonds,* Joyce writing *Finnegan's Wake,* and Mailer writing *The Executioner's Song.* We might think of Justice Blackmun's opinion in *Roe* as an innovation akin to Joyce's or Mailer's. It is the totally unreasoned judicial opinion. To say that it does not look like Justice Powell's decision in some other case is like saying that a Cubist "portrait" does not look like its subject as a member of the Academy would paint it. The observation is true, but irrelevant both to the enterprise in which the artist or judge was engaged and to our ultimate assessment of his product.

C. Rules and Institutions

We can now survey our progress in the attempt to define "neutral principles." Each proposed definition left us with judges who could

---

125. Ely, *supra* note 121, at 929–30.

126. Roe v. Wade, 410 U.S. at 209 (Douglas, J., concurring).

127. *See, e.g.,* Regan, [*Rewriting* Roe v. Wade, 77 Mich.L.Rev. 1569 (1979).]

128. *See, e.g.,* Henkin, Shelley v. Kraemer: *Notes for a Revised Opinion,* 110 U.Pa.L.Rev. 473 (1962); Pollak, *Racial Discrimination and Judicial Integrity,* 108 U.Pa.L.Rev. 1 (1959).

enforce their personal values unconstrained by the suggested version of the neutrality requirement. Some of the more sophisticated candidates, such as the craft interpretation, seemed plausible because they appealed to an intuitive sense that the institution of judging involves people who are guided by and committed to general rules applied consistently. But the very notions of generality and consistency can be specified only by reference to an established institutional setting. We can know what we mean by "acting consistently" only if we understand the institution of judging in our society. Thus, neutral principles theory proves unable to satisfy its demand for rule-guided judicial decisionmaking in a way that can constrain or define the judicial institution; in the final analysis, it is the institution—or our conception of it—that constrains the concept of rule-guidedness.

Consider the following multiple choice question: "Which pair of numbers comes next in the series 1, 3, 5, 7? (a) 9, 11; (b) 11, 13; (c) 25, 18." It is easy to show that any of the answers is correct. The first is correct if the rule generating the series is "list the odd numbers"; the second is correct if the rule is "list the odd prime numbers"; and the third is correct if a more complex rule generates the series.[131] Thus, if asked to follow the underlying rule—the "principle" of the series—we can justify a tremendous range of divergent answers by constructing the rule so that it generates the answer that we want. As the legal realists showed, this result obtains for legal as well as mathematical rules.[132] The situation in law might be thought to differ, because judges try to articulate the rules they use. But even when an earlier case identifies the rule that it invokes, only a vision of the contours of the judicial role constrains judges' understanding of what counts as applying the rule. Without such a vision, there will always be a diversity of subsequent uses of the rule that could fairly be called consistent applications of it.

There is, however, something askew in this anarchic conclusion. After all, we know that no test maker would accept (c) as an answer to the mathematical problem; and indeed we can be fairly confident that test makers would not include both (a) and (b) as possible answers, because the underlying rules that generate them are so obvious that they make the question fatally ambiguous. Another example may sharpen the point. The examination for those seeking driver's licenses in the District of Columbia includes this question: "What is responsible for most automobile accidents? (a) The car; (b) the driver; (c) road conditions." Anyone who does not know immediately that the answer is (b) does not understand what the testing enterprise is all about.

131. One possible rule is the following: $f(1) = 1$; for n greater than 1, if n is divisible by 5, $f(n) = n^2$; if $(n - 1)$ is divisible by 5, $f(n) = f(n - 1) - f(n - 2)$; if neither n nor $(n - 1)$ is divisible by 5, $f(n) = 2n - 1$.

132. Although I believe that the realists demonstrated this point, I acknowledge that most of them refused to press their arguments all the way to the conclusion drawn in the text. For overviews of the realist movement, see E. Purcell, The Crisis of Democratic Theory 74–94, 159–78 (1973); W. Rumble, American Legal Realism (1968).

In these examples, we know something about the rule to follow only because we are familiar with the social practices of intelligence testing and drivers' education. That is, the answer does not follow from a rule that can be uniquely identified without specifying something about the substantive practices. Similarly, although we can, as I have argued elsewhere, use standard techniques of legal argument to draw from the decided cases the conclusion that the Constitution requires socialism,[134] we know that no judge will in the near future draw that conclusion. But the failure to reach that result is not ensured because the practice of "following rules" or neutral application of the principles inherent in the decided cases precludes a judge from doing so. Rather, it is ensured because judges in contemporary America are selected in a way that keeps them from thinking that such arguments make sense. This branch of the argument thus makes a sociological point about neutral principles. Neither the principles nor any reconstructed version of a theory that takes following rules as its focus can be neutral in the sense that liberalism requires, because taken by itself, an injunction to follow the rules tells us nothing of substance. If such a theory constrains judges, it does so only because judges, before they turn to the task of finding neutral principles for the case at hand, have implicitly accepted some image of what their role in shaping and applying rules in controverted cases ought to be.

There is something both odd and important here. The theory of neutral principles is initially attractive because it affirms the openness of the courts to all reasonable arguments drawn from decided cases. But if the courts are indeed open to such arguments, the theory allows judges to do whatever they want. If it is only in consequence of the pressures exerted by a highly developed, deeply entrenched, homeostatic social structure that judges seem to eschew conclusions grossly at odds with the values of liberal capitalism, sociological analysis ought to destroy the attraction of neutral principles theory. Principles are "neutral" only in the sense that they are, as a matter of contingent fact, unchallenged, and the contingencies have obvious historical limits.

At the same time, however, the theory shows us an institution at the heart of liberalism that contains the potential for destroying liberalism by revealing the institution's inconsistencies and its dialectical instability. The neutral rule of law was Locke's solution to the Hobbesian problem of order. But the rule of law requires that preexisting rules be followed. If we accept substantive limitations on the rules that courts can adopt, we abandon the notion of rule-following as a neutral enterprise with no social content; yet if we truly allow all reasonable arguments to be made and possibly accepted, we abandon the notion of rule-following entirely, and with it we abandon the ideal of the rule of law. What is odd is that liberalism has generated an institution that reveals these irresolvable tensions.

134. Tushnet, Book Review, 78 Mich. L.Rev. 694, 696–98 (1980).

G. BALANCING

T. ALEXANDER ALEINIKOFF, CONSTITUTIONAL LAW IN THE AGE OF BALANCING
96 Yale L.J. 943, 945–46, 972–92 (1987).

I. THE DEFINITION AND FORMS OF BALANCING

A. *Definition*

The metaphor of balancing refers to theories of constitutional interpretation that are based on the identification, valuation, and comparison of competing interests. By a "balancing opinion," I mean a judicial opinion that analyzes a constitutional question by identifying interests implicated by the case and reaches a decision or constructs a rule of constitutional law by explicitly or implicitly assigning values to the identified interests. * * * [T]his definition captures most of the work that the Supreme Court does under the name of balancing.

Some commentators see balancing as any method of resolving conflicts among values.[7] * * * [But] choices may be made among values in ways that are not based on an assessment of the "weights" of the values at stake. Similarly, balancing, as I define it, differs from methods of adjudication that look at a variety of factors in reaching a decision. These would include some of the familiar multi-pronged tests[8] and "totality of the circumstances" approaches.[9] These standards ask questions about how one ought to characterize particular events. Was the confession voluntary or involuntary? Did the government action constitute a "taking"? In answering such questions, one starts with some conception of what constitutes voluntariness and involuntariness and then asks whether the particular situation shares more of the voluntary elements or the involuntary elements. Or one begins with a checklist of factors that have been used in the past to determine whether a "taking" has occurred. The reasoning is thus primarily analogical. Balancing represents a different kind of thinking. The focus is directly on the interests or factors themselves. Each interest seeks recognition on its own and forces a head-to-head comparison with competing interests.

B. *Metaphorical Forms*

The balancing metaphor takes two distinct forms. Sometimes the Court talks about one interest outweighing another. Under this view,

---

7. *See, e.g.,* Shiffrin, [*The First Amendment and Economic Regulation: Away from a General Theory of the First Amendment,* 78 Nw.U.L.Rev. 1212, 1249 (1983).] ("[B]alancing is nothing more than a metaphor for the accommodation of values.").

8. *See, e.g.,* Lemon v. Kurtzman, 403 U.S. 602 (1971). *See generally* Nagel, *The*

Formulaic Constitution, 84 Mich.L.Rev. 165 (1985) (examining constitutional formulas).

9. *See, e.g.,* Connolly v. Pension Benefit Guar. Corp., 106 S.Ct. 1018, 1026 (1986) (takings claim); Cleavinger v. Saxner, 106 S.Ct. 496, 501 (1985) (immunity from suit); Illinois v. Gates, 462 U.S. 213, 230–31 (1983) (probable cause under Fourth Amendment).

the Court places the interests on a set of scales and rules the way the scales tip. For example, in New York v. Ferber,[10] the Court upheld a statute criminalizing the distribution of child pornography because "the evil * * * restricted [by the statute] so overwhelmingly outweighs the expressive interests, if any, at stake."[11] Constitutional standards requiring "compelling" or "important" state interests also exemplify this form of the balancing metaphor.[12]

The Court employs a different version of balancing when it speaks of "striking a balance" between or among competing interests. The image is one of balanced scales with constitutional doctrine calibrated according to the relative weights of the interests. One interest does not override another; each survives and is given its due. Thus, in Tennessee v. Garner,[13] which considered the constitutionality of a state statute permitting the use of deadly force against fleeing felons, the Court ruled neither that the state interest in preventing the escape of criminals outweighed an individual's interest in life nor that the individual's interest outweighed the state's. The "balancing process"[14] recognized both interests: The Court ruled that an officer may not use deadly force unless such force is necessary to prevent escape and the officer has probable cause to believe that the suspect poses a threat of serious physical harm.[15] What unites these two types of balancing—and the reason they will be considered together—is their shared conception of constitutional law as a battleground of competing interests and their claimed ability to identify and place a value on those interests.

* * *

IV. An Internal Critique of Balancing

Despite the widespread use of balancing, the Supreme Court has spent surprisingly little time exploring the difficult analytic and operational problems the method presents. The following sections highlight a number of these issues. The first set of problems takes the balancing metaphor seriously and examines how interests are identified, valued and compared. The second set of problems raises the question of whether balancing—even if adequately performed—is a justifiable or sensible method of constitutional interpretation.

A. *The Problem of Evaluation and Comparison*

A frequent criticism of balancing is that the Court has no objective criteria for valuing or comparing the interests at stake. As Laurent Frantz has nicely put it, the judge's task is to "measur[e] the unmeasur-

---

10. 458 U.S. 747 (1982).

11. *Id.* at 763–64.

12. *See, e.g.,* Trimble v. Gordon, 430 U.S. 762 (1977); Craig v. Boren, 429 U.S. 190 (1976).

13. 471 U.S. 1 (1985).

14. *Id.* at 9.

15. *Id.* at 11.

able * * * [and] compare the incomparable." [189]

* * *

Competing interests are not, by definition, incomparable. Apples and oranges can be placed on a fruit scale or assigned a price in dollars per pound. The problem for constitutional balancing is the derivation of the scale needed to translate the value of interests into a common currency for comparison. The balancer's scale cannot simply represent the personal preferences of the balancer, lest constitutional law become the arbitrary act of will today characterized as "lochnering." Moreover, a personal scale would undermine a system of precedent and provide little guidance to lower courts, legislators, administrators, and lawyers and clients.

* * *

In the search for an external scale—for weights "out there"—the modern Court has relied upon several sources that seem sensible. It may turn to history [196] or search for a current "social consensus" [197] on the importance of an interest. Interests may also be assigned weight based on their contribution to the achievement of constitutional or nonconstitutional goals. This instrumental valuation (often expressed in quasi-empirical terms) is evident in dormant commerce clause opinions (measuring, for example, the burden a state's regulation places on interstate commerce and the safety benefits afforded by the regulation),[198] First Amendment libel cases (evaluating the impact on the news media occasioned by various sets of liability rules),[199] procedural due process cases (examining the financial burden that procedural requirements would impose on the government),[200] and exclusionary rule cases (considering the benefit of deterring unlawful police conduct against the cost of excluding probative evidence).[201] Sometimes the Court looks at actual numbers, but frequently it adopts a seat-of-the pants approach, freely speculating on the real world consequences of particular rules.[202]

Whether or not these potentially conflicting sources of value are defensible (and no balancer has developed a theory explaining which

189. Frantz, [*Is the First Amendment Law? A Reply to Professor Mendelson,* 51 Calif.L.Rev. 729, 748 (1963).]

196. *Compare* Zablocki v. Redhail, 434 U.S. 374, 383–86 (1978) (right to marriage deeply rooted in our society) *with* Bowers v. Hardwick, 106 S.Ct. 2841, 2844–46 (1986) (right to homosexual relations never recognized by society).

197. *See, e.g.,* Hudson v. Palmer, 468 U.S. 517, 528 (1984) ("[S]ociety would insist that [privacy interests] always yield to * * * the paramount interest in institutional security.").

198. *See, e.g.,* Kassel v. Consolidated Freightways Corp., 450 U.S. 662, 670 (1981) (plurality opinion).

199. *See, e.g.,* Dun & Bradstreet, Inc. v. Greenmoss Builders, Inc., 472 U.S. 749 (1985); Gertz v. Robert Welch, Inc., 418 U.S. 323, 343–48 (1974).

200. *See, e.g.,* Lassiter v. Department of Social Servs., 452 U.S. 18 (1981); Mathews v. Eldridge, 424 U.S. 319, 334–35 (1976).

201. *See, e.g.,* INS v. Lopez–Mendoza, 468 U.S. 1032, 1041–50 (1984); United States v. Leon, 468 U.S. 897, 915–22 (1984); United States v. Janis, 428 U.S. 433, 447–60 (1976).

202. *See, e.g.,* Plyler v. Doe, 457 U.S. 202, 230 (1982) (speculating on how class of illiterate illegal aliens would affect unemployment, welfare, and crime).

should prevail and why), they do not solve the "external scale" problem unless the same scale is applied to all the interests at stake in the case. It is here that the "apples and oranges" critique has real bite. We may know with a fair degree of certainty that society places a high value on procedural fairness in the deprivation of property and that the cost of providing welfare recipients pre-termination hearings is (let's say) $500 per case. But what follows? Nothing in the "external" sources offers a clue about how to compare differently derived values.

* * *

B. The Problem of a Universe of Interests

* * *

While, in theory, balancing takes an expansive view of what should count as a constitutional interest, in practice, the Court never makes a full inventory of the relevant interests. In *Goldberg v. Kelly*,[219] for example, the Court did not consider a huge range of interests that ought to bear on the question of whether there should be a hearing before welfare benefits are terminated. These might include broader societal notions of fairness; the willingness of society to continue funding the welfare program and other entitlement programs; the ripple effect of wrongful terminations on poor communities, housing stock and crime rates; the morale of the welfare bureaucracy and its views of its clients; the weakening or strengthening of political groups pressing for welfare reform. The Court no doubt recognized that including these considerations would have turned the opinion into a monograph on the welfare system. But on what basis (other than convenience) does the Court restrict its balance to just a few of the relevant interests? The point may be generalized. Taking balancing seriously would seem to demand the kind of investigation of the world that courts are unable or unwilling to undertake.

C. The Problem of Cumulation

Even if a balancer has properly identified the relevant interests and has an objective scale for their valuation, there is still the problem of *which* holders of the relevant interests should be counted. * * * [C]onsider *Youngberg v. Romeo*,[220] the case involving treatment of a mentally retarded person involuntarily committed to a state hospital. There the Court purported to weigh the individual's interest in safety and freedom from restraint against the hospital's interest in confining his movements.[221]

* * *

* * * [But] the Court did not survey other institutions in the state or around the country. It did not estimate whether the conditions in the

219. 397 U.S. 254 (1970).

220. 457 U.S. 307 (1982).

221. *Id.* at 320–21. The Court never defines the state interests, although it does give the example of protecting patients from violence. *Id.* at 320.

defendant hospital were typical or whether the cost of fewer restrictions would be less burdensome in other institutions. It did not "sum up" the individual weights of all Romeos or ask whether other similarly situated persons might have greater or lesser interests in freedom from restraint. Romeo stood for all patients and Pennhurst State Hospital for all institutions.

This problem is endemic to the balancing methodology; the alternative is an unwieldy litigation process in which the trial court would have to make a complete survey of similar institutions. Every case would demand Brandeis briefs of extraordinary complexity, and the costs of constitutional litigation would skyrocket. It is no wonder that the Justices are content to see Romeo as "all patients." However, in making balancing work, the Court has adopted a truncated form that ought not to be acceptable to the conscientious balancer.

* * *

E.   The Problem of the Individual/State Dichotomy

Balancing opinions typically pit individual against governmental interests. This characterization, however, is arbitrary. Interests may be conceived of in both public and private terms. The *individual* interest in communicating one's ideas to others may also be stated as a *societal* interest in a diverse marketplace of ideas. Time, place, and manner limitations on expressive behavior may be based on a *governmental* interest in public safety or a *private* interest in unencumbered access to public facilities.

Consider *Hudson v. Palmer*,[232] in which the Court described a search of a prisoner's cell as posing a conflict between the prisoner's Fourth Amendment interest in privacy and the government's interest in jail security. In that case, the prisoner's interest could also have been stated as a public interest. Society has a general interest in preventing unwarranted governmental intrusions. Extending the Fourth Amendment's protection of privacy in one context may contribute to, and reinforce, a social sense of personal freedom and liberty. As a collective body, we are in the cell with Palmer; the interests at stake are not his alone. Similarly, the government's interest in prison security may also be stated as a private interest. Both prisoners and guards have an individualized interest in being free from assaults and in having a governmental authority protect them. Because public and private interests appear on both sides, there is little sense in seeing the balance in terms of individual versus governmental interests.

To answer these problems, Roscoe Pound recommended that interests be compared "on the same plane,"[234] and occasionally the Court does so. But this "solution" reintroduces the incompleteness objection discussed above. In *Hudson v. Palmer,* one *could* state the conflict as the social interest in freedom from unreasonable searches versus the

232.   468 U.S. 517 (1985).

234.   Pound, [*A Survey of Social Interests,* 57 Harv.L.Rev. 1, 2 (1943).]

social interest in prison security. But this eliminates from the balance the very real private interests at stake.

* * *

V. THE EXTERNAL CRITIQUE OF BALANCING

Perhaps a Hercules of a judge (or a well-programmed computer) could balance in a manner that overcomes the preceding "internal" critique. But balancing also implicates deeper questions about the role of the Court and the nature of judicial review. This section links these concerns with the earlier discussion to argue that balancing builds upon, and fosters, an inappropriate conception of constitutional law.

A. The Role of the Court

A common objection to balancing as a method of constitutional adjudication is that it appears to replicate the job that a democratic society demands of its legislature. The legislative aspect of balancing has become quite pronounced in a number of recent opinions that have openly explored the "costs" and "benefits" of constitutional rules and appealed to empirical evidence of the effect of constitutional doctrine on societal interests. Such a methodology may be an appropriate model for common law adjudication. But balancing needs to be defended in constitutional interpretation where the decision of a court supplants a legislative decision.

What defense might be offered for an understanding of the role of the Court as replicating the legislative task? Some may view judicial balancing as a way to catch errors in the legislative calculations. Just as we do sums twice to check our addition, so we might want to rebalance interests through judicial review. But normally when our second sum is not the same as the first, we add again. Thus this defense must develop a theory that explains why we always accept the judiciary's calculation. Moreover, the structure established by the Constitution explicitly provides for an "addition-checker" in the form of bicameralism.

A better argument for the balancer is that the Court improves the balancing process by giving weight to interests that the legislature tends to ignore or undervalue. Under this view, the Court plays two important roles. First, it reinforces representation, ensuring that the interests of unpopular or underrepresented groups are counted and counted fairly. Second, it protects constitutional rights and interests that are sometimes forgotten in the hurly-burly of politics.

Both of these "thumb-on-the-scales" claims are plausible. Legislators may have difficulty crediting the interests of minority groups to which they do not belong. We might also be justifiably suspicious of the legislature's evaluation of constitutional interests that conflict with popular governmental conduct. Thus the balancer may claim that her form of constitutional interpretation provides a procedural and a substantive justification for judicial review.

While these arguments may point to troubling flaws in the legislative process, they do not alone establish a justification for the judiciary's performance of the legislative task. The argument from undervalued interests might support a model of judicial review analogous to court review of administrative decisions: If a court determines that an agency has ignored or misevaluated relevant interests, it may order the agency to go through the decisionmaking process again. Similarly, a conclusion that the legislature has wrongfully ignored certain interests might justify judicial review in the form of a "suspensive veto" [247] and a "remand." [248] But it does not warrant an evaluation and balancing of the interests by the court. Once the legislature has openly considered the values that the court tells it are at stake, what grounds are there for preferring a court's subsequent determination of the balance?

A balancer might respond that it is improper to portray judicial balancing as duplicating legislative balancing. According to this view, a balancing approach attempts not to maximize social welfare or represent voters. Its primary focus is the Constitution. It simply insists that the Constitution not be interpreted in a vacuum and that courts be aware of the social context and impact of constitutional doctrine. The court that balances, the argument might run, is really searching for a reasonable understanding of the Constitution—one that harmonizes constitutional provisions and values with important governmental interests. The balancing court does not *replicate* the legislative function or *supplant* legislative judgments of good social policy. It *uses* the legislative act as a measure of social importance and thus as a basis for calculating the degree to which the constitutional interest should be "softened." [249]

I think that this is the balancer's best case, and it does indeed supply a role for the court distinct from those of the other branches of government. The judicial role might be described as: Protect and preserve all constitutional interests, taking into account the value that the other branches place on achieving other legitimate ends. But this description raises a deep, and generally unaddressed, problem. Even if the balancing court purports to accept the value that the legislature places on its own output, it cannot simply factor the legislature's determination into a constitutional calculus. It must first convert the constitutional value and the legislative value into a common currency. How does a court decide how "important" a legislative or administrative policy is? For example, why are a "city's aesthetic interests" sufficiently "substantial" to sustain a city ordinance prohibiting political posters on utility poles,[250] but "administrative convenience" not an adequate justification for requiring servicewomen (but not servicemen) to prove the

---

247. *See* Sandalow, [*Judicial Protection of Minorities,* 75 Mich.L.Rev. 1162, 1183–93 (1977).]

248. *See* G. Calabresi, A Common Law for the Age of Statutes 17 (1982); Bickel & Wellington, *Legislative Purpose and the Judicial Process: The* Lincoln Mills *Case,* 71 Harv.L.Rev. 1, 14–35 (1957).

249. *See* C. Ducat, Modes of Constitutional Interpretation 133–34 (1978) (contrasting legislative and judicial balancing).

250. Members of the City Council v. Taxpayers for Vincent, 466 U.S. 789 (1984).

dependency of their spouses to receive housing allowances? [251]   At work here is some undisclosed scale of social value, one not obviously derived from the Constitution. Balancers must defend this inevitable aspect of balancing. They must suggest reasons why judgments assigning a social value to legislation are within the province and capacity of the courts.

B.   The Conception of Constitutional Law

For the balancer, constitutional law is comprised of principles discovered by weighing interests relevant to resolution of a particular constitutional problem. These interests may be traceable to the Constitution itself (free speech, federal regulation of commerce) or discoverable elsewhere (clean streets, law enforcement). Some interests are accorded great weight because society generally recognizes their importance, others because they are located in the Constitution. Indeed, one may understand the Constitution, from the balancer's point of view, as a document intended to ensure that judges (among others) treat particular interests with respect. It is an honor roll of interests.

Although this conception of law may have brought realism to the common law, it threatens to do real damage to constitutional law. Early critics of balancing were largely concerned about the impact of the methodology on the protection of constitutional rights. And, as Ronald Dworkin has tirelessly argued, viewing constitutional rights simply as "interests" that may be overcome by other non-constitutional interests does not accord with common understandings of the meaning of a "right." [253]

But the implications of balancing for constitutional law go far beyond strategic discussions about the best way to protect constitutional rights. (In fact, since the original critiques, balancing has proven to be a robust methodology for the creation and extension of rights). Balancing is undermining our usual understanding of constitutional law as an interpretive enterprise. In so doing, it is transforming constitutional discourse into a general discussion of the reasonableness of governmental conduct.

One can see this trend most clearly in opinions that define or describe a constitutional right and then weigh the right against competing state interests. Here, balancing appears as an extra step in constitutional interpretation. Once a court has done the hard work of explicating a constitutional provision through the usual methods of textual, precedential, and consequentialist reasoning, the result is subjected to another test—the weight of competing interests.

* * *

Not all balancing opinions add the balance at the end. Many view the underlying constitutional principle itself in balancing terms. Thus, in procedural due process cases, the constitutional requirement is deter-

---

251. Frontiero v. Richardson, 411 U.S. 677 (1973) (plurality opinion).

253. *See* R. Dworkin, Taking Rights Seriously 194, 269 (1977) * * *.

mined by comparing the weights of three interests.[262] Here the problem is that balancing does not require the Court to develop and defend a theoretical understanding of a constitutional provision. Under a balancing approach, the Court searches the landscape for interests implicated by the case, identifies a few, and reaches a reasonable accommodation among them. In so doing, the Court largely ignores the usual stuff of constitutional interpretation—the investigation and manipulation of texts (such as constitutional language, prior cases, even—perhaps—our "ethical tradition"). Balancing at its bleakest, to use Justice Brennan's phrase, is "doctrinally destructive nihilism." [264]

This revolt against theory is most troubling in cases that balance constitutional and non-constitutional interests. In these cases, the Constitution is viewed as a broom closet in which constitutional interests are stored and taken out when appropriate to be considered with other social values. Because the weight of the constitutional interest is usually assumed to be substantial, most of the Court's attention is focused on the competing state interests: How strong are they? Can they be achieved with less of an impact on the constitutional interest? In a curious way, constitutional law goes on *next to* the Constitution.

* * *

Does this transformation of constitutional law matter? Some might argue that balancing has made constitutional law more reasonable and accessible. But I believe that the transformation has important and troubling consequences. Constitutional law provides a set of peremptory norms—a checking power—that is basic to the American notion of a government of limited powers. Equally important, although less frequently noted, is constitutional law's validating function. As Charles Black noted long ago, "one indispensable ingredient in the original and continuing legitimation of a government must be its possession and use of some means for bringing about a consensus on the legitimacy of important governmental measures." [271] Constitutional cases provide a forum for the affirmation of background principles and for ratification of changes in those principles—changes the amendment process could only sporadically produce.

Balancing undermines the checking and validating functions of constitutional law. This is most apparent in opinions that adopt a legislative voice, openly weighing costs and benefits in order to maximize social welfare. If constitutional decisions and normal political decisions examine similar variables in similar ways, then constitutional answers ought not to "trump" non-constitutional answers; the constitutional process simply serves as an arithmetic "check" on the non-constitutional process. Nor can constitutional law perform its validation function if constitutional judgment is reached in the same manner as the legislative

262. Mathews v. Eldridge, 424 U.S. 319, 335 (1976).

264. New Jersey v. T.L.O., 469 U.S. 325, 369 (1985).

271. C. Black, The People and the Court 38 (1960).

judgment. The Court's agreement might only show that the Court and the legislature used the same calculator. These concerns are not alleviated even under the best account of balancing offered above (that a court does not replicate the legislative task but simply accommodates constitutional values with other social interests). That account supplies no basis for the authority or ability of a court to assign a value to the legislative output.

Claims that an interpretive strategy threatens the legitimacy of constitutional review are easy to make but hard to prove. More easily seen is the devastating impact that balancing has had on constitutional theory. Balancing opinions give one the eerie sense that constitutional law as a distinct form of discourse is slipping away. The balancing drum beats the rhythm of reasonableness, and we march to it because the cadence seems so familiar, so sensible. But our eyes are no longer focused on the Constitution. If each constitutional provision, every constitutional value, is understood simply as an invitation for a discussion of good social policy, it means little to talk of constitutional "theory."

Ultimately, the notion of constitutional supremacy hangs in the balance. For under a regime of balancing, a constitutional judgment no longer looks like a trump. It seems merely to be a card of a higher value in the same suit.

BIBLIOGRAPHY

Interpreting the Constitution: General

Bandes, *The Negative Constitution: A Critique,* 88 Mich.L.Rev. 2271 (1990).

Bennett, *Objectivity in Constitutional Law,* 132 U.Pa.L.Rev. 445 (1984).

C. Black, STRUCTURE AND RELATIONSHIP IN CONSTITUTIONAL LAW (1969).

P. Bobbitt, CONSTITUTIONAL FATE (1982).

Bork, *Styles in Constitutional Theory,* 26 S.Tex.L.J. 383 (1985).

E. Chemerinsky, INTERPRETING THE CONSTITUTION (1987).

Dworkin, *Hard Cases,* 88 Harv.L.Rev. 1057 (1957), reprinted in TAKING RIGHTS SERIOUSLY 81 (1978).

Dworkin, *The Jurisprudence of Richard Nixon,* New York Rev. Books, May 4, 1972, at 17, reprinted as Constitutional Cases, in TAKING RIGHTS SERIOUSLY 131 (1978).

Ely, DEMOCRACY AND DISTRUST: A THEORY OF JUDICIAL REVIEW (1980).

Fallon, *A Constructivist Coherence Theory of Constitutional Interpretation,* 100 Harv.L.Rev. 1189 (1987).

Fletcher, *Principlist Models in the Analysis of Constitutional and Statutory Texts,* 72 Iowa L.Rev. 891 (1987).

Greenawalt, *The Enduring Significance of Neutral Principles,* 78 Colum.L.Rev. 982 (1978).

Komesar, *Back to the Future—An Institutional View of Making and Interpreting Constitutions,* 81 Nw.U.L.Rev. 191 (1987).

Komesar, *Taking Institutions Seriously: Introduction to a Strategy for Constitutional Analysis,* 51 U.Chi.L.Rev. 366 (1984).

Lipkin, *Conventionalism, Pragmatism, and Constitutional Revolutions,* 21 U.C.Davis L.Rev. 645 (1988).

Lipkin, *Indeterminacy, Justification and Truth in Constitutional Theory,* 60 Fordham L.Rev. 595 (1992).

Michelman, *The Supreme Court, 1985 Term—Foreword: Traces of Self–Government,* 100 Harv.L.Rev. 4 (1986).

Munzer & Nickel, *Does the Constitution Mean What It Always Meant?,* 77 Colum.L.Rev. 1029 (1977).

Nagel, *The Formulaic Constitution,* 84 Mich.L.Rev. 165 (1985).

R. Nagel, CONSTITUTIONAL CULTURES: THE MENTALITY AND CONSEQUENCES OF JUDICIAL REVIEW (1989).

Post, *Theories of Constitutional Interpretation,* 30 Representations 13 (Spring 1990).

D. Richards, TOLERATION AND THE CONSTITUTION (1986).

Sager, *Review Essay: What's A Nice Court Like You Doing in a Democracy Like This?* [reviewing M. Perry, THE CONSTITUTION, THE COURTS, AND HUMAN RIGHTS], 36 Stan.L.Rev. 1087 (1984).

Sandalow, *Constitutional Interpretation,* 79 Mich.L.Rev. 1033 (1981).

Schauer, *An Essay on Constitutional Language,* 29 U.C.L.A.L.Rev. 797 (1982).

Symposium, *Interpretation,* 58 S.Cal.L.Rev. (1985).

Symposium, 6 Const.Comm. 19 (1989).

Symposium—*The Ira C. Rothgerber, Jr. Conference on Constitutional Law: Constitutional Law and the Experience of Judging,* 61 U.Colo. L.Rev. 783 (1990).

Wellington, *Common Law Rules and Constitutional Double Standards: Some Notes on Adjudication,* 83 Yale L.J. 221 (1973).

West, *Progressive and Conservative Constitutionalism,* 88 Mich.L.Rev. 641 (1990).

The Original Intent Debate

Alfange, *On Judicial Policymaking and Constitutional Change: Another Look at the "Original Intent" Theory of Constitutional Interpretation,* 5 Hastings Const.L.Q. 603 (1978).

R. Berger, GOVERNMENT BY JUDICIARY (1977).

Berger, *New Theories of "Interpretation": The Activist Flight from the Constitution,* 47 Ohio St.L.J. 1 (1986).

Dworkin, *The Forum of Principle,* 56 N.Y.U.L.Rev. 469 (1981).

Farber, *The Originalism Debate: A Guide for the Perplexed,* 49 Ohio St.L.J. 1085 (1989).

Maltz, *Some New Thoughts on an Old Problem—The Role of the Intent of the Framers in Constitutional Theory,* 63 B.U.L.Rev. 811 (1983).

Monaghan, *Our Perfect Constitution,* 56 N.Y.U.L.Rev. 353 (1981).

Winter, *Indeterminacy and Incommensurability in Constitutional Law,* 78 Cal.L.Rev. 1441 (1990).

Morton, *John Locke, Robert Bork, Natural Rights and the Interpretation of the Constitution,* 22 Seton Hall L.Rev. 709 (1992).

Nelson, *History and Neutrality in Constitutional Adjudication,* 72 Va. L.Rev. 1237 (1986).

Powell, *The Original Understanding of Original Intent,* 98 Harv.L.Rev. 885 (1985).

Powell, *Rules for Originalists,* 73 Va.L.Rev. 659 (1987).

Rotunda, *Original Intent, the View of the Framers, and the Role of the Ratifiers,* 41 Vand.L.Rev. 507 (1988).

Simon, *The Authority of the Framers of the Constitution: Can Originalist Interpretation Be Justified?,* 73 Calif.L.Rev. 1482 (1985).

Solum, *Originalism as Transformative Politics,* 63 Tulane L.Rev. 1599 (1989).

The Interpretivism/Non–Interpretivism Debate

Ackerman, *Robert Bork's Grand Inquisition* [reviewing R. Bork, THE TEMPTING OF AMERICA: THE POLITICAL SEDUCTION OF THE LAW (1990)], 99 Yale L.J. 1419 (1990).

Brest, *The Fundamental Rights Controversy: The Essential Contradictions of Normative Constitutional Scholarship,* 90 Yale L.J. 1063 (1981).

Corwin, *The "Higher Law" Background of American Constitutional Law,* 42 Harv.L.Rev. 149, 365 (1928–29).

Epstein, *A Common Lawyer Looks at Constitutional Interpretation,* 72 B.U.L.Rev. 699 (1992).

Grano, *Judicial Review and a Written Constitution in a Democratic Society,* 28 Wayne L.Rev. 1 (1981).

Grey, *Origins of the Unwritten Constitution: Fundamental Law in American Revolutionary Thought,* 30 Stan.L.Rev. 843 (1978).

MacArthur, *Abandoning the Constitution: The New Wave in Constitutional Theory,* 59 Tul.L.Rev. 280 (1984).

Nichol, *Children of Distant Fathers: Sketching an Ethos of Constitutional Liberty,* 1985 Wis.L.Rev. 1305.

M. Perry, THE CONSTITUTION, THE COURTS, AND HUMAN RIGHTS (1982).

Rehnquist, *The Notion of a Living Constitution,* 54 Tex.L.Rev. 693 (1976).

Richards, *Human Rights as the Unwritten Constitution: The Problem of Change and Stability in Constitutional Interpretation,* 4 U.Dayton L.Rev. 295 (1979).

Sherry, *The Founders' Unwritten Constitution,* 54 U.Chi.L.Rev. 1127 (1987).

Symposium—*Judicial Review and the Constitution—The Text and Beyond* [marking the publication of M. Perry, THE CONSTITUTION, THE COURTS, AND HUMAN RIGHTS], 4 U.Dayton L.Rev. 443–831 (1983).

Stare Decisis

Alexander, *Constrained by Precedent,* 63 S.Cal.L.Rev. 1 (1989).

Collier, *Precedent and Legal Authority: A Critical History,* 1988 Wis.L.Rev. 771.

Gerhardt, *The Role of Precedent in Constitutional Decisionmaking and Theory,* 60 Geo.Wash.L.Rev. 68 (1991).

Maltz, *Abortion, Precedent, and the Constitution: A Comment on Planned Parenthood of Southeastern Pennsylvania v. Casey,* 68 Notre Dame L.Rev. 11 (1992).

Schauer, *Precedent,* 39 Stan.L.Rev. 571 (1987).

Balancing

Faigman, *Reconciling Individual Rights and Government Interests: Madisonian Principles Versus Supreme Court Practice,* 78 Va.L.Rev. 1521 (1992).

Gottlieb, *Compelling Governmental Interests: An Essential But Unanalyzed Term in Constitutional Adjudication,* 68 B.U.L.Rev. 917 (1988).

Chapter III

JUSTIFICATIONS FOR JUDICIAL REVIEW

Marbury v. Madison continues to be viewed as one of the central texts in constitutional law, because it establishes the principle of judicial review. At the same time, *Marbury* is regularly subjected to scathing criticism in introductory constitutional law classes. It is commonplace to note that alternative interpretations of the Judiciary Act of 1789 and Article III of the Constitution were available to Chief Justice Marshall, interpretations that would have avoided holding the statute unconstitutional. Indeed, some suggest that John Marshall should have recused himself from the case because of his involvement in the underlying events. Finally, it is fairly easy to show that while Marshall's opinion admirably establishes the supremacy of the Constitution, it does not adequately demonstrate that the Supreme Court must be the final interpreter of what the Constitution means. (For an elaboration of these and other familiar criticisms of the opinion in *Marbury,* see Van Alstyne, *A Critical Guide to Marbury v. Madison,* 1969 Duke L.J. 1.)

Poking holes in Supreme Court opinions is the mainstay of scholarly work and classroom discussion. But finding fault with *Marbury v. Madison* is not merely sport or a demonstration of legal acuity. *Marbury* is the fount of the Supreme Court's role in explicating constitutional law. To say that the case rests on unsteady legal foundations is to undermine two centuries of judicial review.

This Chapter explores several attempts by scholars to provide a firmer foundation for judicial review than that supplied by Marshall. These justifications are "non-textual"; that is, they rely not on the specific language of the Constitution (compare Marshall's partial reliance on the Supremacy Clause and the Oath Clause [1]), but rather on the structure of government created by the Constitution, principles and purposes that underlie the Constitution, democratic theory, or functional considerations.

---

1. Herbert Wechsler also offers a largely textual justification for judicial review in *Toward Neutral Principles of Constitutional Law,* 73 Harv.L.Rev. 1, 2–5 (1959).

Learned Hand argues that the power of judicial review is neither expressly authorized nor implicit in the structure of the Constitution. He suggests that such a power may be interpolated into the text in order "to prevent defeat of the venture at hand"—that is, the successful operation of government.

Charles Black's defense of judicial review derives from the theory of limited powers that underlies our political system. In order to maintain the legitimacy of government, some institution must be authorized to decide whether or not governmental action transgresses constitutional limits. Black suggests that an independent, precedent-respecting, learned tribunal could best carry out this function. Not surprisingly, he views the Supreme Court as such an institution.

Alexander Bickel argues that, due to the counter-majoritarian nature of judicial review, the practice can be justified only if it serves a function distinct from legislative and executive activities that is consistent with the basic democratic principles upon which our system of government is based. He identifies that function as the identification and protection of "enduring values."

Girardeau Spann offers an ironic response to Bickel: he argues that judicial review is not counter-majoritarian *enough*. Paying particular attention to the treatment of racial minorities, he argues that judicial review is a way of carrying out majoritarian preferences, and that minorities might be better off engaging in the "pure politics" of legislative battles. As proof of his thesis he offers a revisionist reading of *Brown v. Board of Education.*

As you read the following excerpts, consider not only whether the author's view is sounder than the arguments put forward by Marshall, but also how well each justification stands up against alternative proposals. How, for example, might Charles Black respond to Learned Hand, or Alexander Bickel to Girardeau Spann?

LEARNED HAND, THE BILL OF RIGHTS
Pp. 3–6, 10–15 (1958).

[I begin with the premise] that all political power emanates from the people, and that the Constitution distributed among different "Departments"—as Hamilton called them—the authority of each as it was measured by the grant to it. No provision was expressly made, however, as to how a "Department" was to proceed when in the exercise of one of its own powers it became necessary to consider the validity of some earlier act of another "Department." Should the second accept the decision of the first that the act was within the first's authority, or should it decide the question *de novo* according to its own judgment? A third view prevailed, as you all know: that it was a function of the courts to decide which "Department" was right, and that all were bound to accept the decision of the Supreme Court.

The arguments of those who, like Jefferson, held that each "Department" was free to decide the issues before it regardless of how any other

"Department" had decided it, was, as I understand it, as follows: The exercise of any delegated power presupposes that the grantee believes that the grant extends to the occasion that has arisen; and it is a necessary incident of the grant itself that he shall so decide before he acts at all. He may of course be wrong; and, when he is, he will be accountable to the grantor; but he is accountable to no one else, unless it be an authority paramount to both himself and the grantor.

The federal courts themselves derive all their powers from the "People of the United States" when they "ordain[ed] and establish[ed]" the Constitution, and the same was true, *ceteris paribus,* of the state courts. One cannot find among the powers granted to courts any authority to pass upon the validity of the decisions of another "Department" as to the scope of that "Department's" powers. Indeed, it is to be understood that the three "Departments" were separate and coequal, each being, as it were, a Leibnizian monad, looking up to the Heaven of the Electorate, but without any mutual dependence. What could be better evidence of complete dependence than to subject the validity of the decision of one "Department" as to its authority on a given occasion to review and reversal by another whose own action was conditioned upon the answer to the same issue? Such a doctrine makes supreme the "Department" that has the last word.

Nor can any support for the doctrine of the supremacy of the judiciary be found in the "Supremacy Clause," which, so far as it proves anything, accords rather with the view that, when it was intended to grant courts the power to declare a statute invalid because it was in conflict with the Constitution, some express grant was thought necessary. That clause did indeed require state courts to follow federal laws and the federal constitution when the state laws or the state constitution were "to the contrary"; and that requirement no doubt presupposed that they should have jurisdiction to determine whether a conflict existed. Moreover, we may *arguendo* even admit that when the conflict is between a federal law and a state law or constitution, the state court is to determine the validity of the federal law *quoad* the federal constitution. Furthermore, we may accept Section 25 of the First Judiciary Law as valid, so that on some occasions the Supreme Court might have to decide whether a state court's construction of the Constitution was correct. However, the clause was obviously directed against the states alone to prevent their intruding upon the powers they had delegated or failing to obey limitations on their own powers that they had accepted. Such a grant cannot be stretched into a general authority to pass upon other instances of legislative conflict with the Constitution; rather we should resort to the maxim, *expressio unius, exclusio alterius,* and declare that it indicates the absence of any such authority.

* * *

There was [, then,] nothing in the United States Constitution that gave courts any authority to review the decisions of Congress; and it was a plausible—indeed to my mind an unanswerable—argument that it invaded that "Separation of Powers" which, as so many then believed, was the condition of all free government. That there were other reasons, not only proper but essential, for inferring such a power in the Constitution seems to me certain; but for the moment I am only concerned to show that the reasoning put forward [in *Marbury v. Madison*] to support the inference will not bear scrutiny.

As an approach, let us try to imagine what would have been the result if the power did not exist. There were two alternatives, each prohibitive, I submit. One was that the decision of the first "Department" before which an issue arose should be conclusive whenever it arose later. That doctrine, coupled with its conceded power over the purse, would have made Congress substantially omnipotent, for by far the greater number of issues that could arise would depend upon its prior action.

Hamilton in the 71st number of the Federalist forecast what would probably have been the result. He was speaking of what he called the "tendency of legislative authority to absorb every other." "In governments purely republican, this tendency is almost irresistible. The representatives of the people in a popular assembly seem sometimes to fancy that they are the people themselves, and betray strong symptoms of impatience and disgust at the last sign of opposition from any other quarter; as if the exercise of its rights by either the executive or the judiciary were a breach of their privilege and an outrage on their dignity. They often appear disposed to exert an imperious control over the other departments; and, as they commonly have the people on their side, they always act with such momentum as to make it very difficult for the other members of the government to maintain the balance of the Constitution."

It was unfair to ascribe to a mere lust for power this disposition of legislators to expand their powers. As Hamilton intimated, every legislator is under constant pressure from groups of constituents whom it does not satisfy to say, "Although I think what you want is right and that you ought to have it, I cannot bring myself to believe that it is within my constitutional powers." Such scruples are not convincing to those whose interests are at stake; and the voters at large will not usually care enough about preserving "the balance of the Constitution" to offset the votes of those whose interests will be disappointed.

The issues that arise are often extremely baffling, and the answers are not obvious. They demand, not only a detached approach, but a training in verbal analysis by no means general among legislators, even though they are usually lawyers. The uncertainties that so often arise are shown by the differences in the answers of the judges themselves. Take for instance the power of Congress to levy taxes in order "to pay the debts and provide for the common defense and general Welfare of the United States."

There is indeed no great difficulty in deciding whether a tax is "to pay the debts" of the United States; but at times it is hard to say whether a statute is a tax to "provide for the * * * general Welfare." An excise might be in form a tax and yet not raise enough revenue to pay for the cost of its administration. Furthermore, is the taxing power limited to raising money necessary to the exercise of some of the prescribed powers of Congress, or does it extend to whatever Congress may think beneficial to the "People"?

Again, consider the power "to regulate commerce with foreign nations and among the several States." Are all "regulations" valid so long as they impinge only upon "commerce among the States"? It is constitutional to prevent those who do not pay a minimum wage, or who employ child labor, from sending their wares across state lines; but would it be constitutional to forbid carpenters, plumbers, bakers, or brewers to do so, unless they passed a federal examination and received a federal license? Do the natural resources in land under water below low tide belong to the nation or the abutting states?

What I have called the first alternative would have meant that the interpretation of the Constitution on a given occasion would be left to that "Department" before which the question happened first to come; and such a system would have been so capricious in operation, and so different from that designed, that it could not have endured. Moreover, the second alternative would have been even worse, for under it each "Department" would have been free to decide constitutional issues as it thought right, regardless of any earlier decision of the others. Thus it would have been the President's privilege, and indeed his duty, to execute only those statutes that seemed to him to be constitutional, regardless even of a decision of the Supreme Court. The courts would have entered such judgments as seemed to them consonant with the Constitution; but neither the President, nor Congress, would have been bound to enforce them if he or it disagreed, and without their help the judgments would have been waste paper.

For centuries it has been an accepted canon in interpretation of documents to interpolate into the text such provisions, though not expressed, as are essential to prevent the defeat of the venture at hand; and this applies with especial force to the interpretation of constitutions, which, since they are designed to cover a great multitude of necessarily unforeseen occasions, must be cast in general language, unless they are constantly amended. If so, it was altogether in keeping with established practice for the Supreme Court to assume an authority to keep the states, Congress, and the President within their prescribed powers. Otherwise the government could not proceed as planned; and indeed would almost certainly have foundered, as in fact it almost did over that very issue.

However, since this power is not a logical deduction from the structure of the Constitution but only a practical condition upon its successful operation, it need not be exercised whenever a court sees, or thinks that it sees, an invasion of the Constitution. It is always a preliminary question how importunately the occasion demands an answer. It may be better to leave the issue to be worked out without authoritative solution; or perhaps the only solution available is one that the court has no adequate means to enforce.

CHARLES L. BLACK, JR., THE BUILDING WORK OF JUDICIAL REVIEW

The People and the Court 37–42, 47–53 (1960).

I start with the axiom that a government cannot attain and hold a satisfactorily definite attribution of legitimacy if its actions as a government are not, by and large, received as authorized. Despite its plausibility, this proposition doubtless rests on psychological rather than on purely logical grounds. It is barely possible, as a matter of sheer logic, to conceive of people's feeling that the government under which they lived was a rightful government, but that a great many of its most important governmental acts were usurpative and unempowered. A government, whatever might be the outcome of refined semantic analysis, is actually conceived of by its citizens as more than the sum of its actions. But I suggest that, as a matter of human psychology, it is quite unthinkable that such a tension could long maintain itself unresolved. Immediate and particular actions are what the citizen sees and feels, and if he believes these to be, in great part, unauthorized, lacking the character of authentic governmental acts, mere wrongs committed by persons in power, then I submit that he cannot long retain the feeling that the government itself is legitimate.

If this is true, then one indispensable ingredient in the original and continuing legitimation of a government must be its possession and use of some means for bringing about a consensus on the legitimacy of important governmental measures.

* * *

* * * Whatever else may be said about the intention of the Framers, there can be no question whatever that * * * they intended to found [a government of limited powers]. The powers of the branches of government were enumerated, and it would be pretty hard to see this enumeration as merely playful, or as an elaborate hoax. But if there were any doubt on this score, one might turn to the explicit limitations, worded as such, both in the constitutional text and in some of the Amendments. Perhaps more important (for we are talking about the generation of a conviction of governmental legitimacy among the people) the conception of our government as one of limited powers is and since the beginning has been at the very center of American political belief. It is an essential part of the picture the American has of his government.

* * *

Now, for a government based on the theory of limited powers the problem of the legitimation of governmental action is one of special difficulty. * * *

First, and perhaps most important, the fact of limitation itself generates doubt and debate on the legitimacy of particular actions. In Britain, no one can argue that a particular measure oversteps the bounds of Parliament's power, for the plain reason that there are no such bounds; an argument of that *form* is impossible. Where, on the other hand, limitations are built into government and into the theory underlying government, it is certain that particular interests will from time to time discern in the limitations a forbidding of some action to which they are about to be subjected. No matter what the nature of the limitations may be, such claims will always arise, for there will be a borderline somewhere. Given the theory of limitation, these claims cannot be brushed aside as political solecisms, but must be met and answered in some fashion.

Secondly, it is to be expected (and certainly is true in the case of our Constitution) that the language in which limitations on government are expressed will be broad, and hence will invite competing constructions, supported in entire good faith. This breadth of language is not accidental. It is inherent in the very concept of limitation, for, paradoxically, a limitation which is specific often fails effectively to limit. Our Bill of Rights, for example, prohibits the imposition of "cruel and unusual" punishments. It would have been possible to omit the general phrase, and to list the punishments specifically forbidden. But it is plain that such a technique would have failed to implement the purpose behind the provision, for if a government were specifically shut off from nose-docking and boiling in oil, it could surely find some punishment equally cruel that was not on the list.

To look at the matter from another side, the affirmative powers of government, to which it is confined, must also be expressed in general, and hence in vague, language. Here again there is no question of intellectual sloppiness; it is impossible to calculate or list, in advance, the concrete and specific measures which a government is to be authorized to take, and if you tried to do so you would unquestionably leave out some that were vital. So constitutional draftsmen, in granting powers as well as in limiting them, are driven, whether they like it or not, to do their work in relatively imprecise language. And it is inevitable that such language will lend itself to conflicting interpretations.

* * *

Thirdly (and this is beyond question the most delicate point), the resolution of doubts as to the legitimacy of governmental action must be undertaken, and bindingly effected, by the government itself. There is no other viable possibility. The alternatives may be briefly stated: judgment by an outsider, and individual judgment by the people and institutions subject to the exercise of the disputed power of government. There is no outsider to judge, and nobody would stand for his judging if there were. The other alternative has been seriously, even passionately put forward, in a limited form, but it seems plain (to cite the classic example) that if South Carolina is to decide whether Congress is empowered to levy a protective tariff, while Massachusetts comes to an opposite decision, we have neither a nation nor a government. Yet there is, in the referral of decision on governmental power to the government itself, a flavor of setting up a party as judge in his own cause. There must always be something of a miracle, as well as much sound political intuition and wisdom, in the overcoming of this difficulty, and what must be looked for is success in satisfactory measure, rather than complete success.

* * *

* * * I have tried to show how a government founded on the theory of limited powers faces and must solve the problem of legitimacy—it must devise some way of bringing about a feeling in the nation that the actions of government, even when disapproved of, are authorized rather than merely usurpative. There are several hopeless ways to go about this, and just one, I think, that has some hope in it.

First, the determinations of Congress and the President could simply have been made final on all questions affecting their own power. I have already indicated the chief objection to that: It is wholly incompatible with the notion of limited power. It might have been acquiesced in, after a while, and a consensus reached on a British-style legitimacy, though conflicts between the President and Congress, and between the nation and the states, would have made that process a highly problematic one. In any case, it is not what happened, and I venture to say there is nothing in the history of this country to indicate it ever could have succeeded.

Trust could have been placed in "appeal to reason"; it could have been tried whether, in the end, people could not be persuaded of the legitimacy of governmental actions by argument alone. This, we can say confidently, would have been doomed. First, there is no finite set of "constitutional questions"; each new period generates new ones, and they are always charged with emotion and tied in with deep political strivings. Secondly, there is no single "reasonable" view of any of the great questions of the Constitution, if by "reasonable" we mean "capable of being held, after mature reflection and study, by an intelligent and relevantly well-informed person." The test of this is objective. Such persons have, in fact, differed on all great constitutional questions—that is what made them questions. But even if we didn't know this as a fact, we'd know it must be so. Words, preeminently the great vague words of the Constitution, have no single fixed meaning, and had no single fixed meaning at the time of adoption. Difference of private opinion was and is inevitable.

The last expedient, the one that was partly planned and that partly happened, is the one suggested by all of human experience in dealing with disputes. Where consensus on the *merits* of a question cannot be attained, it is sometimes possible to get consensus on a procedure for submitting the question for decision to an acceptable tribunal. If this were not true, no baseball game could be played to the end.

The difficulty here, as we have already seen, is that, where the questions concern governmental power in a sovereign nation, it is not possible to select an umpire who is outside government. Every national government, so long as it is a government, must have the final say on its own power. The problem, then, is to devise such governmental means of deciding as will (hopefully) reduce to a tolerable minimum the intensity of the objection that government is judge in its own cause. Having done this, you can only hope that this objection, though theoretically still tenable, will practically lose enough of its force that the legitimating work of the deciding institution can win acceptance. Reliance here must be on the common sense of the people, who may be expected to see that all has been done that can be done, in the nature of the case, to ensure fair disposition of questions of governmental power.

I would suggest that the first step is to give such a decision-making institution a satisfactory degree of independence from the active policy-making branches of government. It is in these that controversial exercises of governmental power will originate, and the umpire on questions of power must have such measure of detachment from them as will convince those whose claims are being decided that he is not practically, even though he may be theoretically, deciding his own case.

Secondly, I should want my umpire to be a specialist in tradition— not in sudsy, out-of-focus tradition, but in tradition's concrete minutiae and accurate ground plan. I would recognize that the decisions I was asking him to make were not open-and-shut arithmetic examples, soluble on the basis of precedent alone. But I would be sure that wiser and more acceptable work in deciding would be done by someone with respect for precedent, with an instilled feeling of responsibility to precedent, with a trained skill in following precedent—and in discerning when it ought not to be followed.

I would want to assure that my institution would be manned by people who had had training in the orderly presentation of evidence and argument, and who had absorbed the habit, through professional inveteration, of sifting carefully and then deciding firmly. I would want people who were experienced in the handling of masses of data of all sorts, people who were schooled to deal with little things carefully while keeping big issues clearly in sight. I should want people who were accustomed enough to the concept of attachment to a cause that it could be expected that, having been assigned the supremely important task of decision that I proposed giving them, they would perceive with clarity that they were now attached to the cause of learned and wise constitutional exposition, in the long-range interest, as best they could see it, of the whole people.

I have been using the plural, and of course we would want more than one man. It would obviously be prudent to reduce the risk of the impact of personal idiosyncrasy by composing the tribunal of enough men to check one another, and to provide that institutional continuity through time which is vital to the establishment of independence and a sound tradition of work.

Finally, having set up these requirements, I would not be astounded, or overly disappointed, if the fact fell short sometimes of perfection. No institution can be as perfect, in men or work, as its ideal model, though the very mark of the truly living institution is that it has an ideal model which is always there nudging its elbow.

Now suppose such a body were set up, and given the task of deciding on the constitutional validity of measures taken by the active political departments. What would be the effect on the would-be violator of the navigation laws, when this body, umpiring, told him, "We have concluded that the navigation laws are a valid exercise of a power given to Congress"?

It would be touch and go. He might (like John C. Calhoun) scornfully point to the formal connection of the umpire with one of the parties, saying that nothing new had been added, that it was only proposed to validate the acts of one department of government by the decisions of another department of government. If this view prevailed, the whole device would have come to nothing, and I cannot think of another one so promising. We would have to say, "Very well, we must either give up, in effect, the notion of limited governmental power, or we must give up the thought of being a nation."

But he might, on the other hand, look to the substance and practicalities of the thing. He might say, "I see that you have done all you can to get me a right decision on my claim. I still think the decision is wrong. But the mode of decision was as fair as is humanly possible, under all the circumstances. And that is the most I can ask." Or, if he should still be a little too hot with the exaltation of battle, his friends might counsel with him, "Look, we agreed with you before. You were not getting a square shake. Like us, you were told that this is a government of limited powers, and then they tried to tell you that what that meant was that Congress was limited by its own interpretation of the limits on itself—an insult to the intelligence as well as a breach of faith. But things are different now. This is the real world. There is no way to ascertain, finally and without possibility of error, whether 'commerce' means 'navigation.' The absolute best that any government can do is to choose men learned in our traditions and history, isolated by temperament and placing from the day-by-day flare-up of issues such as this, and dependent on nobody else in government, and then to let them decide. If you ask more than that, you ask the impossible."

What makes the final difference between success and failure of such a legitimating device, between its contemptuous rejection on theoretical grounds and its acceptance as being the substantial best that can be done toward following out in practice the principle of limitation of power? Who can tell? Something clicks into place. When you have done the best you can, it may be good enough. No tree knows whether it will bear fruit; its job is to stand up tall and wait.

In our history, it did work, in sufficient measure. The institution I have described is, as you will have perceived, a court, manned by skillful lawyers steeped in the judicial tradition, and, with the added caveat of imperfection, it is our own Supreme Court. Pretty clearly, it had been foreseen by the Founders that the courts would decide "constitutional" questions where these arose in litigation. Surprising nobody, Congress and the Supreme Court early confirmed this understanding. And the Court took up the umpiring job.

Popular acceptance of this role was not a foregone conclusion. If it had not been forthcoming, no amount of theoretical or historical argument could have enabled the Court to fill this need. But acceptance did come, in sufficient amount and with sufficient reliability.

Now it will have been observed that I have described the function of the Supreme Court in a way which turns the usual account upside down. The role of the Court has usually been conceived as that of *invalidating* "hasty" or "unwise" legislation, of acting as a "check" on the other departments. It has played such a role on occasion, and may play it again in the future.

But a case can be made for believing that the prime and most necessary function of the Court has been that of *validation,* not that of invalidation. What a government of limited powers needs, at the beginning and forever, is some means of satisfying the people that it has taken all steps humanly possible to stay within its powers. That is the condition of its legitimacy, and its legitimacy, in the long run, is the condition of its life. And the Court, through its history, has acted as the legitimator of the government. In a very real sense, the Government of the United States is based on the opinions of the Supreme Court.

* * *

The power to validate is the power to invalidate. If the Court were deprived, by any means, of its real and practical power to set bounds to governmental action, or even of public confidence that the Court itself regards this as its duty and will discharge it in a proper case, then it must certainly cease to perform its central function of unlocking the energies of government by stamping governmental actions as legitimate. If everybody gets a Buck Rogers badge, a Buck Rogers badge imports no distinction. The Court may go thirty or forty years without declaring an Act of Congress unconstitutional; that means nothing, for it is scarcely to be looked for that Congress will pass any given annual or decennial quota of statutes that the Court will regard as invalid. But if it ever so much as became known—even as a matter of tacit understanding in the profession and on the Court, for such a secret could not be kept from the people—that the Court would not seriously ponder the questions of constitutionality presented to it and declare the challenged statute unconstitutional if it believed it to be so, then its usefulness as a legitimatizing institution would be gone.

ALEXANDER M. BICKEL, ESTABLISHMENT AND GENERAL JUSTIFICATION OF JUDICIAL REVIEW

The Least Dangerous Branch 16–26 (1962).

The root difficulty is that judicial review is a counter-majoritarian force in our system. There are various ways of sliding over this ineluctable reality. Marshall did so when he spoke of enforcing, in behalf of "the people," the limits that they have ordained for the institutions of a limited government. And it has been done ever since in much the same fashion by all too many commentators. Marshall himself followed Hamilton, who in the 78th *Federalist* denied that judicial review implied a superiority of the judicial over the legislative power—denied, in other words, that judicial review constituted control by an unrepresentative minority of an elected majority. "It only supposes," Hamilton went on, "that the power of the people is superior to both; and that where the will of the legislature, declared in its statutes, stands in opposition to that of the people, declared in the Constitution, the judges ought to be governed by the latter rather than the former." But the word "people" so used is an abstraction. Not necessarily a meaningless or a pernicious one by any means; always charged with emotion, but nonrepresentational—an abstraction obscuring the reality that when the Supreme Court declares unconstitutional a legislative act or the action of an elected executive, it thwarts the will of representatives of the actual people of the here and now; it exercises control, not in behalf of the prevailing majority, but against it. That, without mystic overtones, is what actually happens. It is an altogether different kettle of fish, and it is the reason the charge can be made that judicial review is undemocratic.

* * *

It is true, of course, that the process of reflecting the will of a popular majority in the legislature is deflected by various inequalities of representation and by all sorts of institutional habits and characteristics, which perhaps tend most often in favor of inertia. Yet it must be remembered that statutes are the product of the legislature and the executive acting in concert, and that the executive represents a very different constituency and thus tends to cure inequities of over– and underrepresentation. Reflecting a balance of forces in society for purposes of stable and effective government is more intricate and less certain than merely assuring each citizen his equal vote. Moreover, impurities and imperfections, if such they be, in one part of the system are no argument for total departure from the desired norm in another part. A much more important complicating factor—first adumbrated by Madison in the 10th *Federalist* and lately emphasized by Professor David

B. Truman and others [13]—is the proliferation and power of what Madison foresaw as "faction," what Mr. Truman calls "groups," and what in popular parlance has always been deprecated as the "interests" or the "pressure groups."

No doubt groups operate forcefully on the electoral process, and no doubt they seek and gain access to an effective share in the legislative and executive decisional process. Perhaps they constitute also, in some measure, an impurity or imperfection. But no one has claimed that they have been able to capture the governmental process except by combining in some fashion, and thus capturing or constituting (are not the two verbs synonymous?) a majority. They often tend themselves to be majoritarian in composition and to be subject to broader majoritarian influences. And the price of what they sell or buy in the legislature is determined in the biennial or quadrennial electoral marketplace. It may be, as Professor Robert A. Dahl has written, that elections themselves, and the political competition that renders them meaningful, "do not make for government by majorities in any very significant way," for they do not establish a great many policy preferences. However, "they are a crucial device for controlling leaders." And if the control is exercised by "groups of various types and sizes, all seeking in various ways to advance their goals," so that we have "minorities rule" rather than majority rule, it remains true nevertheless that only those minorities rule which can command the votes of a majority of individuals in the legislature who can command the votes of a majority of individuals in the electorate. In one fashion or another, both in the legislative process and at elections, the minorities must coalesce into a majority. Although, as Mr. Dahl says, "it is fashionable in some quarters to suggest that everything believed about democratic politics prior to World War I, and perhaps World War II, was nonsense," he makes no bones about his own belief that "the radical democrats who, unlike Madison, insist upon the decisive importance of the election process in the whole grand strategy of democracy are essentially correct." [14]

The insights of Professor Truman and other writers into the role that groups play in our society and our politics have a bearing on judicial review. They indicate that there are other means than the electoral process, though subordinate and subsidiary ones, of making institutions of government responsive to the needs and wishes of the governed. Hence one may infer that judicial review, although not responsible, may have ways of being responsive. But nothing can finally depreciate the central function that is assigned in democratic theory and practice to the electoral process; nor can it be denied that the policy-making power of representative institutions, born of the electoral process, is the distinguishing characteristic of the system. Judicial review works counter to this characteristic.

* * *

13. See D.B. Truman, *The Governmental Process* (New York: Knopf, 1951).

14. R.A. Dahl, *A Preface to Democratic Theory* (Chicago: University of Chicago Press, 1956), pp. 125, 132.

* * * Besides being a counter-majoritarian check on the legislature and the executive, judicial review may, in a larger sense, have a tendency over time seriously to weaken the democratic process. Judicial review expresses, of course, a form of distrust of the legislature. "The legislatures," wrote James Bradley Thayer at the turn of the century,

> are growing accustomed to this distrust and more and more readily inclined to justify it, and to shed the considerations of constitutional restraints,—certainly as concerning the exact extent of these restrictions,—turning that subject over to the courts; and what is worse, they insensibly fall into a habit of assuming that whatever they could constitutionally do they may do,—as if honor and fair dealing and common honesty were not relevant to their inquiries. The people, all this while, become careless as to whom they send to the legislature; too often they cheerfully vote for men whom they would not trust with an important private affair, and when these unfit persons are found to pass foolish and bad laws, and the courts step in and disregard them, the people are glad that these few wiser gentlemen on the bench are so ready to protect them against their more immediate representatives * * *. [I]t should be remembered that the exercise of [the power of judicial review], even when unavoidable, is always attended with a serious evil, namely, that the correction of legislative mistakes comes from the outside, and the people thus lose the political experience, and the moral education and stimulus that comes from fighting the question out in the ordinary way, and correcting their own errors. The tendency of a common and easy resort to this great function, now lamentably too common, is to dwarf the political capacity of the people, and to deaden its sense of moral responsibility. It is no light thing to do that.[18]

To this day, in how many hundreds of occasions does Congress enact a measure that it deems expedient, having essayed consideration of its constitutionality (that is to say, of its acceptability on principle), only to abandon the attempt in the declared confidence that the Court will correct errors of principle, if any? It may well be * * * that any lowering of the level of legislative performance is attributable to many factors other than judicial review. Yet there is no doubt that what Thayer observed remains observable. * * *

Finally, another, though related, contention has been put forward. It is that judicial review runs so fundamentally counter to democratic theory that in a society which in all other respects rests on that theory, judicial review cannot ultimately be effective. We pay the price of a grave inner contradiction in the basic principle of our government, which is an inconvenience and a dangerous one; and in the end to no good purpose, for when the great test comes, judicial review will be unequal to

18. [J.B. Thayer, *John Marshall* (Boston: Houghton Mifflin, 1901), pp. 103–04, 106–07.]

it. The most arresting expression of this thought is in a famous passage from a speech of Judge Learned Hand, a passage * * * "of Browning-esque passion and obscurity," voicing a "gloomy and apocalyptic view." Absent the institution of judicial review, Judge Hand said:

> I do not think that anyone can say what will be left of those [fundamental principles of equity and fair play which our constitutions enshrine]; I do not know whether they will serve only as counsels; but this much I think I do know—that a society so riven that the spirit of moderation is gone, no court *can* save; that a society where that spirit flourishes, no court *need* save; that in a society which evades its responsibility by thrusting upon the courts the nurture of that spirit, that spirit in the end will perish.[22]

* * *

Such, in outline, are the chief doubts that must be met if the doctrine of judicial review is to be justified on principle. Of course, these doubts will apply with lesser or greater force to various forms of the exercise of the power. For the moment the discussion is at wholesale, and we are seeking a justification on principle, quite aside from supports in history and the continuity of practice. The search must be for a function which might (indeed, must) involve the making of policy, yet which differs from the legislative and executive functions; which is peculiarly suited to the capabilities of the courts; which will not likely be performed elsewhere if the courts do not assume it; which can be so exercised as to be acceptable in a society that generally shares Judge Hand's satisfaction in a "sense of common venture"; which will be effective when needed; and whose discharge by the courts will not lower the quality of the other departments' performance by denuding them of the dignity and burden of their own responsibility. It will not be possible fully to meet all that is said against judicial review. Such is not the way with questions of government. We can only fill the other side of the scales with countervailing judgments on the real needs and the actual workings of our society and, of course, with our own portions of faith and hope. Then we may estimate how far the needle has moved.

The point of departure is a truism; perhaps it even rises to the unassailability of a platitude. It is that many actions of government have two aspects: their immediate, necessarily intended, practical effects, and their perhaps unintended or unappreciated bearing on values we hold to have more general and permanent interest. It is a premise we deduce not merely from the fact of a written constitution but from the history of the race, and ultimately as a moral judgment of the good society, that government should serve not only what we conceive from time to time to be our immediate material needs but also certain enduring values. This in part is what is meant by government under law. But such values do not present themselves ready-made. They have a past always, to be sure, but they must be continually derived,

22. L. Hand, "The Contribution of an Independent Judiciary to Civilization," in I. Dilliard, ed., *The Spirit of Liberty* (New York: Knopf, 1953), pp. 155–65.

enunciated, and seen in relevant application. And it remains to ask which institution of our government—if any single one in particular— should be the pronouncer and guardian of such values.

Men in all walks of public life are able occasionally to perceive this second aspect of public questions. Sometimes they are also able to base their decisions on it; that is one of the things we like to call acting on principle. Often they do not do so, however, particularly when they sit in legislative assemblies. There, when the pressure for immediate results is strong enough and emotions ride high enough, men will ordinarily prefer to act on expediency rather than take the long view. Possibly legislators—everything else being equal—are as capable as other men of following the path of principle, where the path is clear or at any rate discernible. Our system, however, like all secular systems, calls for the evolution of principle in novel circumstances, rather than only for its mechanical application. Not merely respect for the rule of established principles but the creative establishment and renewal of a coherent body of principled rules—that is what our legislatures have proven themselves ill equipped to give us.

Initially, great reliance for principled decision was placed in the Senators and the President, who have more extended terms of office and were meant to be elected only indirectly. Yet the Senate and the President were conceived of as less closely tied to, not as divorced from, electoral responsibility and the political marketplace. And so even then the need might have been felt for an institution which stands altogether aside from the current clash of interests, and which, insofar as is humanly possible, is concerned only with principle. We cannot know whether, as Thayer believed, our legislatures are what they are because we have judicial review, or whether we have judicial review and consider it necessary because legislatures are what they are. Yet it is arguable also that the partial separation of the legislative and judicial functions— and it is not meant to be absolute—is beneficial in any event, because it makes it possible for the desires of various groups and interests concerning immediate results to be heard clearly and unrestrainedly in one place. It may be thought fitting that somewhere in government, at some stage in the process of law-making, such felt needs should find unambiguous expression. Moreover, and more importantly, courts have certain capacities for dealing with matters of principle that legislatures and executives do not possess. Judges have, or should have, the leisure, the training, and the insulation to follow the ways of the scholar in pursuing the ends of government. This is crucial in sorting out the enduring values of a society, and it is not something that institutions can do well occasionally, while operating for the most part with a different set of gears. It calls for a habit of mind, and for undeviating institutional customs. Another advantage that courts have is that questions of principle never carry the same aspect for them as they did for the legislature or the executive. Statutes, after all, deal typically with abstract or dimly foreseen problems. The courts are concerned with the flesh and blood of an actual case. This tends to modify, perhaps to lengthen, everyone's view. It also provides an extremely salutary proving ground for all abstractions; it is conducive, in a phrase of Holmes, to thinking things, not words, and thus to the evolution of principle by a process that tests as it creates.

Their insulation and the marvelous mystery of time give courts the capacity to appeal to men's better natures, to call forth their aspirations, which may have been forgotten in the moment's hue and cry. This is what Justice Stone called the opportunity for "the sober second thought." [26] Hence it is that the courts, although they may somewhat dampen the people's and the legislatures' efforts to educate themselves, are also a great and highly effective educational institution. * * * The educational institution that both takes the observation to correct the dead reckoning and makes it known is the voice of the Constitution: the Supreme Court exercising judicial review. The Justices, in Dean Rostow's phrase, "are inevitably teachers in a vital national seminar." [28] No other branch of the American government is nearly so well equipped to conduct one. And such a seminar can do a great deal to keep our society from becoming so riven that no court will be able to save it. Of course, we have never quite been that society in which the spirit of moderation is so richly in flower that no court need save it.

GIRARDEAU A. SPANN, PURE POLITICS

88 Mich.L.Rev. 1971, 1975, 1990–94, 2012–17 (1990).

I. MAJORITARIAN JUDICIAL REVIEW

The traditional model of judicial review, which emanates from the Supreme Court decision in *Marbury v. Madison,* is premised upon the belief that the Court is capable of performing its adjudicatory function in a countermajoritarian manner. The viability of this countermajoritarian model ultimately rests upon the ability of doctrinal principles to constrain judicial discretion in a manner sufficient to prevent domination of the judicial process by the majoritarian preferences embodied in the socialized values of individual justices. However, the level of judicial discretion inescapably entailed in the process of principled adjudication seems to preclude continued adherence to the countermajoritarian assumption. In fact, that discretion actually implicates the Court in the majoritarian exploitation of minority interests, rather than permitting it to serve as the guardian of minority rights. * * *

* * *

Majoritarian preferences reside in the socialized attitudes and values of Supreme Court justices, and they find expression in the exercise of judicial discretion. Although a justice may be prompted by the formal safeguards of life tenure and salary protection consciously to guard

---

26. H.F. Stone, *"The Common Law in the United States,"* 50 Harvard Law Review 4, 25 (1936).

28. See E.V. Rostow, *"The Democratic Character of Judicial Review,"* 66 Harvard Law Review 193, 208 (1952).

against majoritarian influences, such efforts cannot be effective against the unconscious operation of those influences. Moreover, the operational safeguard of principled adjudication cannot guard effectively against majoritarianism because many legal principles incorporate majoritarian preferences into their meanings. In addition, the ambiguity inherent in both the selection and application of governing principles is too great to permit the principles to serve as meaningful constraints on the exercise of judicial discretion. Rather than protecting minority interests from majoritarian abrogation, as envisioned by the traditional model of judicial review, the Supreme Court appears actually to serve the function of advancing majority interests at minority expense, while operating behind the veil of countermajoritarian adjudication. Assuming that the traditional model has in fact failed, racial minorities must consider novel strategies to deal with the essentially majoritarian nature of the Court.

II. RACE AND POSITIVE POLITICS

Contemporary minority attraction to judicial review has been premised on the belief that the Framers' political safeguards against factionalism could not adequately protect the interests of racial minorities who would effectively be under-enfranchised by their discrete and insular character.[57] Moreover, the substantial dilution of the structured safeguards during the New Deal eliminated any effectiveness they may have had initially. Reexamination of these assumptions in light of the majoritarianism inherent in judicial review, however, suggests that, whatever their defects, the political safeguards hold more promise for contemporary racial minorities than continued reliance on judicial review. * * *

* * *

In a contest between competing societal interests that is ultimately to be judged by political considerations, minorities might well prefer to compete in an arena that is openly political, rather than one from which political concerns nominally have been excluded. In an overtly political process, minority interests will receive whatever degree of deference their innate strength can command, subject only to limitations in the bargaining and organizational skills of minority politicians. In a positive sense, therefore, the overt political process is pure. Outcomes are determined by counting votes, with no need to consider the reasons for which those votes were cast. The process purports to be nothing more than what it is—a pluralistic mechanism for generating binding results. Although rhetorical principles may accompany the solicitation of political support, the principles themselves are inconsequential. No one cares much about their content, and their meaning is measured only by the extent to which their rhetorical invocation proves to be effective.

For racial minorities, the overt political process has two attractions. First, the political process is definitionally immune from distortion because it has essentially no rules that can be violated. In the film

---

57. See J. Ely, [Democracy and Distrust] 77–88, 145–70 (describing representation-reinforcement theory of judicial review).

Butch Cassidy and the Sundance Kid, Butch Cassidy prevailed in a knife fight over one of his adversaries by exploiting the absence of formal rules. Butch first suggested that he and his adversary needed to clarify the rules of the knife fight. As the adversary—put off-guard by Butch's suggestion—protested that there were no such things as "rules" in a knife fight, Butch kicked the adversary very hard in a very sensitive part of his anatomy. With this one action, Butch was able both to establish the truth of the proposition being asserted by his adversary and to capitalize on that proposition in order to win the fight.

As a positive matter, the pure political process is nothing more than the process of casting and counting votes. Outcomes cannot be right or wrong, nor can they be just or unjust. They are simply the outcomes that the process produces. Although outcomes may be determined by how the issues are framed, how support for those issues is secured, and even by who is permitted to vote, minorities should not be distracted by considerations relating to whether the process is operating fairly. The process simply works the way it works. What minorities should focus on is how best to maximize their influence in that process. Minority participation in pluralist politics can, of course, take the form of voting, running for office, or making campaign contributions, but it is not limited to those forms of involvement. Minority participation can also take the form of demonstrations, boycotts and riots. Although such activities may be independently illegal, for purposes of positive politics their significance is limited to their potential for increasing or decreasing political strength. This is not to say that no rules at all govern the positive political process. Operative rules determine which strategies will increase and which will decrease political power. However, the operative rules are not only too complex and contingent to permit them to be articulated accurately, but those rules need never be articulated, because the selective responsiveness of the political process itself will promote adherence to those rules without regard to the accuracy of their formal expression. The process of positive politics—like a knife fight— cannot be distorted because it has no formal rules. In addition, the operative rules that do govern the process tend to be self-enforcing.

The second attraction of the overt political process is that it permits minorities to assume ultimate responsibility for their own interests. [T]here are inherent limits on the political strength of any interest group. Within those limits, however, positive politics gives minorities themselves control over the degree to which minority interests are advanced. Minorities determine how important it is for minorities to engage in political activity; minorities determine how much political activity is appropriate; and minorities decide what minority priorities should be in selecting among competing political objectives. Positive politics gives minorities both the credit for minority advances and the blame for minority failures. By thus promoting minority self-determination, positive politics elevates minority dignity and self-esteem in a way that is likely to be of more long-term significance than minority success in advancing any particular interest.

The politics inherent in the process of judicial review is of a different order. Where the overt political process is transparent and unassuming, the Supreme Court political process is opaque and pretentious. The Court requires its political bargaining to be conducted in the vernacular of legal principle, and its referenda to be cloaked in the mantle of reasoned deliberation. Moreover, because judicial convention requires the justices to camouflage the political preferences that ultimately govern their applications of principle, political negotiation with the Court is haphazard and imprecise. Judicial opinions must be deciphered for clues regarding the concessions for which a justice will commit his or her vote. And once a commitment is made, members of the Court are largely impervious to any leverage through which future fidelity to that commitment could be enforced. Unlike the positive political process that is effectively immune from distortion, the Supreme Court process is itself a distortion that renders the outcomes of ordinary politics uncertain. Because it is the Court rather than the pluralist process that has the final say over which of the competing political interests will prevail, it is the Court, rather than the affected minority group, that retains ultimate control over the fate of the minority group's interests.

The positive reasoning that permits one to conceive of the overt political process as immune from the possibility of distortion also makes it possible to characterize the Supreme Court political process in such terms. However, this does not undermine the reasonableness of a minority preference for a simple process that does not involve the Supreme Court over a complex process that does. Less experienced players can master more easily the skills required for effective participation in a simple process than acquire the skills demanded of a complex process. A preference for simplicity is particularly sensible if complexities are differentially beneficial to participants depending on whether they wish to maintain or to change the status quo. Supreme Court political complexity creates just such a differential benefit, working to the disadvantage of minorities who typically wish to alter rather than preserve the socioeconomic status quo.

The Supreme Court adjudicatory process is political, but its political dimensions are complex and obscure. Even though every interest group competing for Supreme Court endorsement will be burdened similarly by the complexities of the Supreme Court process, a rational minority response to those complexities nevertheless would be to prefer the candor and elegance of representative politics. Pluralist politics is, of course, no panacea. Its historical loss of favor reflects genuine grounds for concern. Nevertheless, pluralist negotiation offers more to minorities than continued reliance on judicial review. * * *

* * *

III. A POLITICAL MODEL OF THE SUPREME COURT

* * *

Brown v. Board of Education is the case typically offered in support of the countermajoritarian capacity of the Supreme Court. The desegregation of southern schools that the *Brown* Court ordered in 1954 provoked predictable massive resistance. According to the traditional wisdom, the fact that the Supreme Court was willing to disregard such high levels of majoritarian disapproval in issuing its school desegregation order reveals that the Court must possess counter-majoritarian capabilities. This conclusion is further buttressed by the post-*Brown* decisions in which the Court stuck to its convictions and ordered the lower courts to fashion novel equitable remedies such as busing to implement the *Brown* decision, again in the face of massive resistance. Notwithstanding this traditional view, *Brown* actually is better understood as an illustration of the selective political responsiveness of the veiled majoritarian Court.

The *Brown* decision is commonly viewed as having accomplished two things. As a practical matter, it required the desegregation of public schools. As a doctrinal matter, it overruled the separate-but-equal principle of *Plessy v. Ferguson,* and established the proposition that race-based classifications are inherently unequal because they inevitably operate to disadvantage the minority race. * * *

The fact that *Brown* is perceived to stand for the two propositions with which it is associated attests to the rhetorical success of the case. When needed, *Brown* is now available for citation in briefs and judicial opinions to support either the limited proposition that the Constitution requires public schools to be desegregated or the broader proposition that race-based classifications in general are unconstitutional. As an actual matter, *Brown* of course did not desegregate the schools. A third of the black students attending public school in the United States still attend all-black schools, and sixty-three percent attend schools that are at least half black. Private schools, gerrymandered district lines, unequal funding, white flight, residential housing patterns, and resegregation are among the many factors that prevented the rhetorical promise of *Brown* from ever becoming a reality. As an actual matter, *Brown* also did not terminate governmental use of race-based classifications. Although subsequent cases issued shortly after *Brown* relied upon the *Brown* decision to invalidate racial segregation in public facilities such as buses, beaches, and golf courses, the Court did not rely upon *Brown* to invalidate all racial classifications. Most notably, the Court declined to invalidate miscegenation statutes, straining to avoid any application of *Brown* that would produce this result.[139] Realistically, *Brown* had enormous rhetorical success and only partial practical success.

The combination of substantial rhetorical success and limited practical success that I have attributed to *Brown* appears to have been

---

139. *See* Naim v. Naim, 350 U.S. 891 (1955) (per curiam), *on remand,* 197 Va. 734, 90 S.E.2d 849, *appeal dismissed,* 350 U.S. 985 (1956) (per curiam). * * * The Virginia statute was finally invalidated 11 years later in Loving v. Virginia, 388 U.S. 1 (1967). At that time, only 16 states had miscegenation laws, as opposed to the time of the *Brown* decision, when more than half the states had such statutes.

precisely what the Court's durable majoritarian constituency desired. The massive resistance that accompanied *Brown* does not mean that the decision lacked majoritarian support. Indeed, the resistance was regional rather than national in scope. At the level of national politics—the level of politics at which *Brown* was decided—it is easy to imagine the existence of a national coalition that supported the *Brown* decision. Professor Bell first hypothesized that *Brown* was decided the way that it was because it marked the point of convergence for three national interests.[140] The decision advanced the international objectives of foreign policy interest groups by reducing the embarrassment and competitive disadvantage that domestic racism produced in our competition with communism for influence over third world nations. The decision also advanced the interests of disillusioned post-War blacks who seemed to be missing out on all of the equality that the United States claimed to have been fighting for in World War II. In addition, the decision advanced the interests of whites who saw segregation as an impediment to the economic maturation and development of the South.[141] Professor Dudziak, in an article entitled *Desegregation as a Cold War Imperative,*[142] further developed the idea that *Brown* was a response to national majoritarian interests, emphasizing the particular interest suggested by her arresting title.[143] Just as the victorious northern coalition was able to impose civil rights enactments on the South after the Civil War in order to advance its own political interests, a similar national coalition was able to impose *Brown* on the South in order to advance its political interests.

Not only does the existence of a national coalition provide a plausible account of the *Brown* decision, but the durability of that coalition coincides with the success that minorities have had under *Brown* and its progeny. When the first *Brown* decision was issued, the Court set the case for reargument concerning the issue of remedy. A year later, in *Brown II,* the Court ruled that although school desegregation need not be immediate, it had to be accomplished with "all deliberate speed,"

---

140. *See* Bell, Brown *and the Interest–Convergence Dilemma,* in Shades of *Brown:* New Perspectives on School Desegregation 91–106 (D.Bell ed. 1980).

141. *Id.* at 96–97. Professor Bell also suggested that moral and economic considerations might have played a role in the coalition that he was postulating. *Id.* Although he did not explicitly claim that the Supreme Court was incapable of counter-majoritarian acts, Professor Bell did offer the following "principle" to account for the *Brown* decision:

The interest of blacks in achieving racial equality will be accommodated only when it converges with the interests of whites; however, the fourteenth amendment, standing alone, will not authorize a judicial remedy providing effective racial equality for blacks where the remedy

sought threatens the superior societal status of middle- and upper-class whites.

Id. at 95 (emphasis omitted). This caused Bell to conclude that the remedies for *Brown* would be co-extensive with white support, *id.* at 98–102, something that is consistent with the present thesis.

142. Dudziak, *Desegregation as a Cold War Imperative,* 41 Stan.L.Rev. 61 (1988).

143. Professor Dudziak notes that the U.S. Department of Justice filed an amicus brief stressing the importance of a decision invalidating segregation because "[t]he United States is trying to prove to the people of the world, of every nationality, race and color, that a free democracy is the most civilized and most secure form of government yet devised by man." *Id.* at 65 (brackets in original).

thereby giving both school officials and the Court itself some latitude in implementing the decision. For the next fifteen years, most of the Supreme Court school desegregation decisions were resolved in a manner that was considered favorable to minority interests. All of those decisions involved southern school districts. In the early 1970s, when school desegregation cases involving northern cities began to reach the Court, the Court began to rule against the minority interests. This suggests that after fifteen years, the national coalition supporting *Brown* had broken down, in part because civil rights had ceased to be an important international issue, and in part because northern urban interest groups had withdrawn from the coalition after they were asked to internalize the costs of desegregation that had previously been deflected to the South. In a sense, *Brown* was the perfect veiled majoritarian decision. The majority garnered rhetorical benefits that were important at the time the decision was issued and that continue to be important today because of the manner in which they enhance the majority's self-image. Practical implementation of the decision, however, continued only as long as, and only to the extent that, *Brown* itself continued to command durable majoritarian support.

Brown and the cases implementing it can be understood as the product of a majoritarian coalition that advanced the immediate interests of racial minorities. It is unclear, however, whether membership in that coalition served to advance long-term minority interests. Professor Seidman has argued that *Brown* in fact advanced white majoritarian interests at the expense of long-term minority interests. By overruling *Plessy* and declaring that separate-but-equal treatment of racial minorities violated the Constitution, *Brown* saved the majority from a *Plessy*-based obligation actually to extend equal treatment to minorities.[147] Today, as a result of property-based tax structures and tax subsidies given to private schools, white students receive a significantly larger share of the governmental resources allocated to education than minority students receive. Ironically, this may well have been unconstitutional under *Plessy*'s separate-but-equal doctrine. *Brown,* however, makes this differential treatment constitutionally permissible. As long as a school district is not engaged in de jure segregation and has taken the requisite steps to eliminate the effects of any past de jure segregation in which it may have been engaged, its constitutional obligation has been satisfied. Because neither of these obligations entail anything resembling equal treatment, the majority is better off—and racial minorities are worse off—than would have been the case under a faithfully implemented separate-but-equal standard of constitutional law. Moreover, to the extent that *Brown* has made it constitutionally difficult for the government to rely upon race-based classifications, *Brown* has disadvantaged minorities by depriving them of effective affirmative action remedies. Race-conscious remedies, such as minority set-asides, are being invalidated by the Court on constitutional grounds with increasing frequency, and they are being invalidated for the stated reason of preventing

147. *See* L. Seidman, *Brown* and *Miranda,* 80 Cal.L.Rev. 673 (1992).

unfairness to whites.[150]   In addition, disillusionment with the results of *Brown* has caused some minority activists to advocate separate minority-controlled schools for minority children.   If one assumes that such a strategy is in the present best interests of minorities, *Brown* has again adversely affected minority interests by making that strategy constitutionally impermissible.   If one further assumes that the majority itself benefits from the preclusion of minority-controlled minority schools, *Brown* has again advanced majoritarian interests at minority expense.

BIBLIOGRAPHY

General Background on the Constitution and Judicial Review

A WORKABLE GOVERNMENT?   (B. Marshall ed. 1987).

B. Bailyn, THE IDEOLOGICAL ORIGINS OF THE AMERICAN REVOLUTION (1967).

C. Beard, AN ECONOMIC INTERPRETATION OF THE CONSTITUTION OF THE UNITED STATES (1935).

Bernstein, *Review Essay—Charting the Bicentennial,* 87 Colum.L.Rev. 1565 (1987).

BEYOND CONFEDERATION: ORIGINS OF THE CONSTITUTION AND AMERICAN NATIONAL IDENTITY (R. Beeman, S. Botein & E. Carter II eds. 1987).

R. Clinton, MARBURY v. MADISON AND JUDICIAL REVIEW (1989).

E. Corwin, CORWIN ON THE CONSTITUTION (R. Loss ed., 2 vols., 1981, 1987).

A. Cox, THE ROLE OF THE SUPREME COURT IN AMERICAN GOVERNMENT (1976).

W. Crosskey, POLITICS AND THE CONSTITUTION IN THE HISTORY OF THE UNITED STATES (1953).

D. Currie, THE CONSTITUTION IN THE SUPREME COURT: THE FIRST HUNDRED YEARS, 1789–1888 (1985).

R. Jackson, THE STRUGGLE FOR JUDICIAL SUPREMACY (1941).

M. Kammen, A MACHINE THAT WOULD GO OF ITSELF: THE CONSTITUTION IN AMERICAN CULTURE (1986).

R. McCloskey, THE AMERICAN SUPREME COURT (1960).

F. MacDonald, NOVUS ORDO SECLORUM: THE INTELLECTUAL ORIGINS OF THE CONSTITUTION (1985).

W. Rehnquist, THE SUPREME COURT: HOW IT WAS, HOW IT IS (1987).

H. Storing, THE COMPLETE ANTI–FEDERALIST (1981).

---

150.   *See, e.g.,* City of Richmond v. J.A. Croson Co., 109 S.Ct. 706, 720–23 (1989) (invalidating minority set-aside program in construction industry because of adverse impact that program had on whites).

L. Tribe, AMERICAN CONSTITUTIONAL LAW (2d ed. 1988).

C. Warren, THE SUPREME COURT IN UNITED STATES HISTORY, 3 vols. (1922–24).

G. Wills, EXPLAINING AMERICA: THE FEDERALIST (1981).

C. Wolfe, THE RISE OF MODERN JUDICIAL REVIEW: FROM CONSTITUTIONAL INTERPRETATION TO JUDGE–MADE LAW (1986).

G. Wood, THE CREATION OF THE AMERICAN REPUBLIC, 1776–1787 (1969).

Theories of Judicial Review

Ackerman, *The Storrs Lectures: Discovering the Constitution*, 93 Yale L.J. 1013 (1984).

J. Agresto, THE SUPREME COURT AND CONSTITUTIONAL DEMOCRACY (1984).

Attanasio, *Everyman's Constitutional Law: A Theory of the Power of Judicial Review*, 72 Geo.L.J. 1685 (1984).

Ball, *Don't Die Don Quixote: A Response and Alternative to Tushnet, Bobbitt, and the Revised Texas Version of Constitutional Law*, 59 Tex.L.Rev. 787 (1981).

A. Bickel, THE SUPREME COURT AND THE IDEA OF PROGRESS (1970).

Bishin, *Judicial Review in Democratic Theory*, 50 S.Cal.L.Rev. 1099 (1977).

Brest, *The Fundamental Rights Controversy: The Essential Contradictions of Normative Constitutional Scholarship*, 90 Yale L.J. 1063 (1981).

Burt, *Constitutional Law and the Teaching of Parables*, 93 Yale L.J. 455 (1984).

Carter, *Constitutional Adjudication and the Indeterminate Text: A Preliminary Defense of an Imperfect Muddle*, 94 Yale L.J. 821 (1985).

Carter, *Do Courts Matter?*, [reviewing G. Rosenberg, THE HOLLOW HOPE: CAN COURTS BRING ABOUT SOCIAL CHANGE? (1991)], 90 Mich.L.Rev. 1216 (1992).

Chang, *A Critique of Judicial Supremacy*, 36 Vill.L.Rev. 281 (1991).

Chemerinsky, *Wrong Questions Get Wrong Answers: An Analysis of Professor Carter's Approach to Judicial Review*, 66 B.U.L.Rev. 47 (1986).

Chemerinsky, *The Price of Asking the Wrong Question: An Essay on Constitutional Scholarship and Judicial Review*, 62 Tex.L.Rev. 1207 (1984).

J. Choper, JUDICIAL REVIEW AND THE NATIONAL POLITICAL PROCESS (1980).

Clor, *Judicial Statesmanship and Constitutional Interpretation*, 26 S.Tex.L.J. 397 (1985).

Corwin, *Marbury v. Madison and the Doctrine of Judicial Review*, 12 Mich.L.Rev. 538 (1914).

Dahl, *Decision–Making in a Democracy: The Supreme Court as National Policy–Maker*, 6 J.Pub.L. 279 (1975).

Deutsch, *Neutrality, Legitimacy, and the Supreme Court: Some Intersections Between Law and Political Science*, 20 Stan.L.Rev. 169 (1968).

Eisgruber, *Justice and the Text: Rethinking the Constitutional Relation Between Principle and Prudence*, 43 Duke L.J. 1 (1993).

J. Ely, DEMOCRACY AND DISTRUST: A THEORY OF JUDICIAL REVIEW (1980).

Fallon, *Of Speakable Ethics and Constitutional Law: A Review Essay* [of Perry, MORALITY, POLITICS, AND LAW], 56 U.Chi.L.Rev. 1523 (1989).

Fiss, *The Supreme Court, 1978 Term—Foreword: The Forms of Justice*, 93 Harv.L.Rev. 1 (1979).

Friedman, *Dialogue and Judicial Review*, 91 Mich.L.Rev. 577 (1993).

Graglia, *Judicial Review on the Basis of "Regime Principles": A Prescription for Government by Judges*, 26 S.Tex.L.J. 435 (1985).

Griffin, *What Is Constitutional Theory? The Newer Theory and the Decline of the Learned Tradition*, 62 S.Cal.L.Rev. 493 (1989).

Leedes, *The Supreme Court Mess*, 57 Tex.L.Rev. 1361 (1979).

Levinson, *"The Constitution" in American Civil Religion*, 1979 Sup.Ct. Rev. 123.

Lindgren, *Beyond Cases: Reconsidering Judicial Review*, 1983 Wis. L.Rev. 583.

Llewellyn, *The Constitution as an Institution*, 34 Colum.L.Rev. 1 (1934).

L. Lusky, BY WHAT RIGHT? (1975).

McCleskey, *Judicial Review in a Democracy: A Dissenting Opinion*, 3 Hous.L.Rev. 354 (1966).

McConnell, *The Role of Democratic Politics in Transforming Moral Convictions into Law*, 98 Yale L.S. 1501 (1989) [review of Perry, MORALITY, POLITICS, AND LAW].

Nelson, *Changing Conceptions of Judicial Review: The Evolution of Constitutional Theory in the United States*, 1790–1860, 120 U.Pa. L.Rev. 1166 (1972).

O'Fallon, *Marbury*, 44 Stan.L.Rev. 219 (1992).

M. Perry, THE CONSTITUTION, THE COURTS, AND HUMAN RIGHTS (1982).

M. Perry, MORALITY, POLITICS, AND LAW (1988).

Regan, *Community and Justice in Constitutional Theory,* 1985 Wis. L.Rev. 1073.

E. Rostow, THE SOVEREIGN PREROGATIVE (1962).

Rostow, *The Democratic Character of Judicial Review,* 66 Harv.L.Rev. 193 (1952).

Sager, *The Incorrigible Constitution,* 65 N.Y.U.L.Rev. 893 (1990).

Sager, *Rights Skepticism and Process–Based Responses,* 56 N.Y.U.L.Rev. 417 (1980).

Seidman, *Public Principle and Private Choice: The Uneasy Case for a Boundary Maintenance Theory of Constitutional Law,* 96 Yale L.J. 1006 (1987).

Symposium—*Judicial Review versus Democracy,* 42 Ohio St.L.J. 1–434 (1981).

Thayer, *The Origin and Scope of the American Doctrine of Constitutional Law,* 7 Harv.L.Rev. 129 (1893).

Tribe, *The Puzzling Persistence of Process–Based Constitutional Theories,* 89 Yale L.J. 1903 (1980).

M. Tushnet, RED, WHITE, AND BLUE (1988).

Tushnet, *Truth, Justice, and the American Way: An Interpretation of Public Law Scholarship in the Seventies,* 57 Tex.L.Rev. 1307 (1979).

Wellington, *The Nature of Judicial Review,* 91 Yale L.J. 486 (1982).

Wechsler, *Toward Neutral Principles of Constitutional Law,* 73 Harv. L.Rev. 1 (1959).

West, *Constitutional Skepticism,* 72 B.U.L.Rev. 765 (1992).

Wright, *Professor Bickel, The Scholarly Tradition and the Supreme Court,* 84 Harv.L.Rev. 769 (1971).

Chapter IV

FEDERALISM

Students of constitutional law look at federalism through a different lens than political scientists and politicians do. The latter ask what is wise and prudent in the allocation of lawmaking, enforcement, and interpretive authority between national and state governments. The former ask only what is permitted and what forbidden. Many of these constitutional questions are less important today than they once were, because the limits on permissible federal action have receded almost out of view. The readings in this Chapter are devoted to two areas where controversy is still lively. The first concerns permitted federal action. The question here is whether there are limits to national power when it is aimed at state governments themselves, rather than at private actors. The second concerns forbidden state action. Here the question is what lawmaking authority the Constitution takes away from the states—an issue most extravagantly litigated in connection with the Commerce Clause.

A. NATIONAL POWER: REGULATION OF STATE GOVERNMENTS

The character of federal-state relations has changed greatly since the New Deal. The proximate cause of the change has been the vast increase in regulation and spending by the federal government. It is sometimes assumed that this growth has been accompanied by a corresponding diminution in the power of state governments, as though lawmaking were a zero-sum game in which losses must always offset gains. This is not so. State and local governments too have grown enormously in absolute terms, in response to the same social and economic conditions that the federal government has tried to deal with.

But there has been a change in the locus of initiative, funding, and control of the business of government. Congress (and federal agencies) can now act whenever it is convenient to do so, and use the federal income tax to pay the bills. This authority, coupled with the Supremacy Clause, means that much of the legislative agenda is written in Washington rather than the state capitals. State governments are then asked to administer federal benefit programs (for education, welfare, health, small business), carry out federal regulation of private conduct (the environment), and comply with federal standards in their own behavior (wages, hours, safety, nondiscrimination). We can no longer think of our political system as a 'dual federalism,' with exclusive authority over particular subjects allocated to different levels of government. The appropriate metaphor is not a layer cake but a marble cake.[1]

This arrangement is still controversial. It is one thing for the federal government to preempt state law in the regulation of private conduct. It may be another for the federal government to control state governments themselves. Some fear that the assimilation of states into a predominantly federal confection will undermine important values traditionally associated with state sovereignty. These concerns have inevitably been brought to the courts. The states' role in executing federal benefit programs was reviewed in *Chas. C. Steward Machine Co. v. Davis*[2] and *South Dakota v. Dole*.[3] Their role in carrying out federal regulation of private conduct was an issue in *FERC v. Mississippi*,[4] *Hodel v. Virginia Surface Mining & Reclamation Ass'n*,[5] and *New York v. United States*.[6] Their duty to comply with federal standards in their own behavior was denied in *National League of Cities v. Usery*[7] and then upheld in *Garcia v. San Antonio Metropolitan Transit Authority*.[8] Each case asked whether there was some limit to Congress's authority to enlist (conscript?) state governments to carry out its own projects. That question in turn requires thought about a more fundamental one: what functions are served by a federal system and threatened by these uses of national power?

The readings in this Section explore these issues from several angles. Herbert Wechsler's influential article on *The Political Safeguards of Federalism*, written in the 1950's, contends that the fear of state assimilation is unfounded because of the role the states play in the composition and selection of the central government. This unique control over the federal lawmaking process is the best protection against results that might threaten state sovereignty. The Supreme Court's opinion in *Garcia* was greatly influenced by this piece.

Lewis Kaden and William Van Alstyne disagree. Kaden claims that Wechsler's assumptions are obsolete, and that it is unrealistic to suppose the states can look out for themselves in the political process at the federal level. Van Alstyne argues that *Garcia*'s tolerance for federal

---

1. Grodzins, *Centralization and Decentralization in the American Federal System,* in A NATION OF STATES 1 (R. Goldwin, ed. 1963).

2. 301 U.S. 548, 57 S.Ct. 883, 81 L.Ed. 1279 (1937).

3. 483 U.S. 203, 107 S.Ct. 2793, 97 L.Ed.2d 171 (1987).

4. 456 U.S. 742, 102 S.Ct. 2126, 72 L.Ed.2d 532 (1982).

5. 452 U.S. 264, 101 S.Ct. 2352, 69 L.Ed.2d 1 (1981).

6. __ U.S. __, 112 S.Ct. 2408, 120 L.Ed.2d 120 (1992).

7. 426 U.S. 833, 96 S.Ct. 2465, 49 L.Ed.2d 245 (1976).

8. 469 U.S. 528, 105 S.Ct. 1005, 83 L.Ed.2d 1016 (1985).

laws that threaten state sovereignty is inconsistent with *Marbury v. Madison:* it abandons the courts' function of judicial review.

The concluding pieces by Andrzej Rapaczynski and H. Jefferson Powell ask what legally enforceable meaning the concept of federalism has after *Garcia.* Rapaczynski urges that courts should continue to review such cases to make sure that states are represented in the national political process. *Garcia* assumes that states have the political wherewithal to protect their own interests; but if this were not true they might need judicial protection. And the courts should be vigilant because federalism still serves several important values. These include providing a space for participatory politics, and acting as a counterweight to a powerful central government. Powell argues that courts should exercise their power of review when Congress tries to control *state* political processes. That proposition underlies Justice O'Connor's 1992 opinion in *New York v. United States,* a decision that Powell says offers a refreshingly different theory about the modern essence of federalism.

HERBERT WECHSLER, THE POLITICAL SAFEGUARDS OF FEDERALISM: THE ROLE OF THE STATES IN THE COMPOSITION AND SELECTION OF THE NATIONAL GOVERNMENT

54 Colum.L.Rev. 543–552, 557–560 (1954).

I

Our constitution makers established a central government authorized to act directly upon individuals through its own agencies—and thus they formed a nation capable of function and of growth. To serve the ends of federalism they employed three main devices:

They preserved the states as separate sources of authority and organs of administration—a point on which they hardly had a choice.

They gave the states a role of great importance in the composition and selection of the central government.

They undertook to formulate a distribution of authority between the nation and the states, in terms which gave some scope at least to legal processes for its enforcement.

Scholarship—not only legal scholarship—has given most attention to the last of these enumerated mechanisms, perhaps because it has been fascinated by the Supreme Court and its interpretations of the power distribution clauses of the Constitution. The continuous existence of the states as governmental entities and their strategic role in the selection of the Congress and the President are so immutable a feature of the system that their importance tends to be ignored. Of the Framers' mechanisms, however, they have had and have today the larger influence upon the working balance of our federalism. The actual extent of central intervention in the governance of our affairs is determined far less by the formal power distribution than by the sheer existence of the states and their political power to influence the action of the national authority.

The fact of the continuous existence of the states, with general governmental competence unless excluded by the Constitution or valid Act of Congress, set the mood of our federalism from the start. The first Congress did not face the problem of building a legal system from the ground up; it started with the premise that the standing *corpus juris* of the country was provided by the states. * * *

National action has thus always been regarded as exceptional in our polity, an intrusion to be justified by some necessity, the special rather than the ordinary case. This point of view cuts even deeper than the concept of the central government as one of granted, limited authority, articulated in the Tenth Amendment. National power may be quite unquestioned in a given situation; those who would advocate its exercise must none the less answer the preliminary question why the matter should not be left to the states. Even when Congress acts, its tendency has been to frame enactments on an *ad hoc* basis to accomplish limited objectives, supplanting state-created norms only so far as may be necessary for the purpose. Indeed, with all the centralizing growth throughout the years, federal law is still a largely interstitial product, rarely occupying any field completely, building normally upon legal relationships established by the states. * * *

* * *

II

If I have drawn too much significance from the mere fact of the existence of the states, the error surely will be rectified by pointing also to their crucial role in the selection and the composition of the national authority. * * *

Despite the rise of national parties, the shift to popular election of the Senate and the difficulty of appraising the precise impact of such provisions on the legislative process, Madison's analysis has never lost its thrust:

> The State governments may be regarded as constituent and essential parts of the federal government; whilst the latter is nowise essential to the operation or organization of the former.[7]

> A local spirit will infallibly prevail much more in the members of Congress, than a national spirit will prevail in the legislatures of the particular States.[8]

> Even the House of Representatives, though drawn immediately from the people, will be chosen very much under the influence of

---

7. The Federalist, No. 45 at 288 (Lodge ed. 1888).   **8.** *Id.,* No. 46 at 294.

that class of men, whose influence over the people obtains for themselves an election into the State legislatures.[9]

To the extent that federalist values have real significance they must give rise to local sensitivity to central intervention; to the extent that such a local sensitivity exists, it cannot fail to find reflection in the Congress. Indeed, the problem of the Congress is and always has been to attune itself to national opinion and produce majorities for action called for by the voice of the entire nation. It is remarkable that it should function thus as well as it does, given its intrinsic sensitivity to any insular opinion that is dominant in a substantial number of the states.

III

The point is so clear in the Senate that, as Madison observed of the equality accorded to the states, it "does not call for much discussion." [11] The forty-nine votes that will determine Senate action,[a] even with full voting, could theoretically be drawn from twenty-five states, of which the combined population does not reach twenty-nine millions, a bare 19% of all state residents. The one-third plus one that will defeat a treaty or a resolution of amendment could, equally theoretically, be drawn from seventeen states with a total population little over twelve millions, less than that of New York. I say theoretically since, short of a combination to resist an effort to impair state equality within the Senate (which the Constitution purports to place beyond amendment) or to diminish the political power of the smaller states in other ways, a coalition in these terms is quite unthinkable. The fact remains that in more subtle ways the Senate cannot fail to function as the guardian of state interests as such, when they are real enough to have political support or even to be instrumental in attaining other ends. And if account is taken of the operation of seniority within the Senate, of the opportunity of Senators to marshal individual authority, not to speak of the possibility of filibuster, this power of negation, vested in the states without regard to population, multiplies in many ways. Given a controversy that has any sectional dimension, it is not long before the impact of this power is perceived.

* * *

IV

Even the House is slanted somewhat in the same direction, though the incidence is less severe. * * * [Here it stems from] the states' control of voters' qualifications, on the one hand, and of districting, on the other.

The position with respect to voters' qualifications derives from the constitutional provision that fixes the electorate of Representatives (and of Senators as well since the Seventeenth Amendment) as those persons

9. *Id.,* No. 45 at 288–89.

11. The Federalist, No. 62, at 385 (Lodge ed. 1888).

a. Alaska and Hawaii were admitted as states in 1959.

who "have the qualifications requisite for electors of the most numerous branch of the State Legislature." Subject, then, to the prohibition of the denial of franchise because of color, race or sex, embodied in the Fifteenth and Nineteenth Amendments and the radiations of the equal protection clause of the Fourteenth, the states determine—indirectly it is true—the electorate that chooses Representatives. The consequences of contracting the electorate by such devices as a poll-tax are, of course, incalculable, but they tend to buttress what traditionally dominant state interests conceive to be their special state position; that is the point of the contraction. This sentiment, reflected in the Representatives that these constituencies send to Congress, is not ordinarily conducive to support for an adventurous expansion of the national authority, though there have been exceptions, to be sure.

* * *

State control of congressional districting derives from the constitutional provision that the "times, places and manner of holding elections for Senators and Representatives, shall be prescribed in each State by the Legislature thereof." * * *

It is well known that there are great discrepancies in district size in many multi-district states, paralleling for Congress the discrepancies, to forego harsher terms, that prevail in districting for the state legislatures. A recent study estimates that in the spring of 1952, 115 of the 435 congressional districts showed variation as to size larger than 15% above or below the state average, the maximum above the average being 129.8% in Texas and, below the average, 51.3% in South Dakota (where there are only two districts). * * *

* * *

It may be said, and perhaps rightly, that the situation with respect to districting, while detracting from the equality of popular representation in the House, has little bearing on the role of Congress in preserving federalist values. I am not so sure. It is significant, for one thing, that it is the states that draw the districts; one can hardly think the district lines would be the same had they been drawn from the beginning by Congress. Beyond this, however, the general motive and tendency of district deviations has quite clearly been to reduce urban power, not in the meaning of the census classification but in the sense of the substantial cities. The tendency is so appreciable that a recent article assures the readers of a small town magazine that while cities or towns of under 10,000 coupled with the farms account for only 51% of the entire population, residents of such areas are numerically dominant in 265 of the 435 congressional districts, accounting for the choice of 61% of the House (including 18 of the 21 committee chairmen) in addition to their numerical dominance in the choice of 75% of the Senate. Traditionally, at least, a more active localism and resistance to new federal intrusion centers in this 51% of Americans than in the other 49%. I should suppose that this is likely to continue; and that the figures, therefore, have some relevancy to an understanding of why presidential programs calling for the extension of national activity, and seemingly supported by the country in a presidential election, may come a cropper notwithstanding in the House. Such hostility to Washington may rest far less on pure devotion to the principle of local government than on opposition to specific measures which Washington proposes to put forth. This explanation does not make the sentiment the less centrifugal in its effects. Federalism would have few adherents were it not, like other elements of government, a means and not an end.

V

If Congress, from its composition and the mode of its selection, tends to reflect the "local spirit" predicted by Madison, the prime organ of a compensating "national spirit" is, of course, the President—both as the Chief Executive and as the leader of his party. Without the unifying power of the highest office, derived from the fixed tenure gained by his election and the sense that the President speaks for and represents the full national constituency, it would be difficult to develop the centripetal momentum so essential to the total federal scheme. * * *

* * *

Federalist considerations * * * play an important part even in the selection of the President, although a lesser part than many of the Framers must have contemplated. A presidential candidacy must be pointed towards the states of largest population in so far as they are doubtful. It must balance this direction by attention to the other elements of the full coalition that is looked to for an electoral majority. Both major parties have a strong incentive to absorb protest movements of such sectional significance that their development in strength would throw elections to the House. Both must give some attention to the organized minorities that may approach balance of power status in important states, without, however, making promises that will outrun the tolerance of other necessary elements of their required strength. Both parties recognize that they must appeal to some total combination of allegiance, choice or interest that will yield sufficient nation-wide support to win elections and make possible effective government.

The most important element of party competition in this framework is the similarity of the appeal that each must make. This is a constant affront to those who seek purity of ideology in politics; it is the clue, however, to the success of our politics in the elimination of extremists— and to the tolerance and basic unity that is essential if our system is to work.

The President must be, as I have said above, the main repository of "national spirit" in the central government. But both the mode of his selection and the future of his party require that he also be responsive to local values that have large support within the states. And since his programs must, in any case, achieve support in Congress—in so far as they involve new action—he must surmount the greater local sensitivity of Congress before anything is done.

VI

If this analysis is correct, the national political process in the United States—and especially the role of the states in the composition and selection of the central government—is intrinsically well adapted to retarding or restraining new intrusions by the center on the domain of the states. Far from a national authority that is expansionist by nature, the inherent tendency in our system is precisely the reverse, necessitating the widest support before intrusive measures of importance can receive significant consideration, reacting readily to opposition grounded in resistance within the states. Nor is this tendency effectively denied by pointing to the size or scope of the existing national establishment. However useful it may be to explore possible contractions in specific areas, such evidence points mainly to the magnitude of unavoidable responsibility under the circumstances of our time.

It is in light of this inherent tendency, reflected most importantly in Congress, that the governmental power distribution clauses of the Constitution gain their largest meaning as an instrument for the protection of the states. Those clauses, as is well known, have served far more to qualify or stop intrusive legislative measures in the Congress than to invalidate enacted legislation in the Supreme Court.

* * *

The prime function envisaged for judicial review—in relation to federalism—was the maintenance of national supremacy against nullification or usurpation by the individual states, the national government having no part in their composition or their councils. This is made clear by the fact that reliance on the courts was substituted, apparently on Jefferson's suggestion, for the earlier proposal to give Congress a veto of state enactments deemed to trespass on the national domain. And except for the brief interlude that ended with the crisis of the thirties, it is mainly in the realm of such policing of the states that the Supreme Court has in fact participated in determining the balances of federalism.[56] This is not to say that the Court can decline to measure national enactments by the Constitution when it is called upon to face the question in the course of ordinary litigation; the supremacy clause governs there as well. It is rather to say that the Court is on weakest ground when it opposes its interpretation of the Constitution to that of Congress in the interest of the states, whose representatives control the

56. Of the great controversies with respect to national power before the Civil War, only the Bank and slavery within the territories were carried to the Court and its participation with respect to slavery was probably its greatest failure. The question of internal improvements, for example, which raised the most acute problem of constitutional construction, was fought out politically and in Congress. After the War only the Civil Rights Cases and income tax decisions were important in setting limits on national power—until the Child Labor Case and the New Deal decisions. The recasting of constitutional positions since the crisis acknowledges much broader power in the Congress—as against the states— than it is likely soon or ever to employ.

legislative process and, by hypothesis, have broadly acquiesced in sanctioning the challenged Act of Congress.

Federal intervention as against the states is thus primarily a matter for congressional determination in our system as it stands. So too, moreover, is the question whether state enactments shall be stricken down as an infringement on the national authority. For while the Court has an important function in this area, as I have noted, the crucial point is that its judgments here are subject to reversal by Congress, which can consent to action by the states that otherwise would be invalidated. The familiar illustrations in commerce and in state taxation of federal instrumentalities do not by any means exhaust the field. The Court makes the decisive judgment only when—and to the extent that— Congress has not laid down the resolving rule.[59]

LEWIS B. KADEN, POLITICS, MONEY, AND STATE SOVEREIGNTY: THE JUDICIAL ROLE
79 Colum.L.Rev. 847–858, 860–863, 865–868 (1979).

From 1936 to 1976 Congress determined the allocation of governmental power in the federal system virtually without judicial interference. The vast array of domestic programs initiated during this period signaled an expanding national attempt to promote social and economic activity, protect public health and welfare, redistribute resources, and facilitate participation in public decisionmaking. Many of these programs involved transfers of authority from the states to the national government and imposed new obligations on subnational governments to share in the costs and administrative burdens of mandated public services. The expansion of federal domestic spending has been accompanied, therefore, by even more dramatic growth in state and local government activity, much of it attributable to the requirements of federal policies. The result has been not only a sizeable expansion of the public sector, but also a vastly more complicated system of federalism characterized by shared costs, complex bureaucratic arrangements, and intersecting regulatory authority.

Except in the area of protection of individual rights, the expansion of the public sector and the attendant changes in the face of our federalism have occurred with substantial judicial approval. First anticipating and then adhering to Professor Herbert Wechsler's admonition that "the Court is on weakest ground when it opposes its interpretation of the Constitution to that of Congress in the interest of the states," the

---

59. The judicial function in relation to federalism thus differs markedly from that performed in the application of those constitutional restraints on Congress or the states that are designed to safeguard individuals. In this latter area of the constitutional protection of the individual against the government, both federal and state, subordination of the Court to Congress would defeat the purpose of judicial mediation. For this is where the political processes cannot be relied upon to introduce their own correctives—except to the limited extent that individuals or small minorities may find a champion in some important faction. See Stone, J., in United States v. Carolene Products Co., 304 U.S. 144, 152–53 n. 4 (1938).

Supreme Court regularly rejected challenges to the exercise of federal legislative power under the spending, commerce, and war clauses of the Constitution when those challenges were based upon an asserted interest in state autonomy. So long as the Constitution conferred upon Congress the power to regulate the underlying subject, the Court deemed it irrelevant whether the regulated object involved public or private activity. The courts and the country grew comfortable with the nationalization of public policy, and the states were obliged to seek vindication of their interest in autonomy through the political process. * * *

* * *

* * * [T]he proliferation of federal legislation imposing significant obligations on the states—"federalizing" the machinery of state government to serve the ends of national policy—warrants some broader measure of judicial supervision than the courts have recently supplied. The political branches in 1979 may no longer be as well suited as they once were to the task of safeguarding the role of the states in the federal system and protecting the fundamental values of federalism. Changes in both political practices and the direction and breadth of national initiatives suggest a new basis for judicial intervention. The task is to determine at what point the allocation of authority effected by Congress so imperils these values as to warrant the extraordinary intervention of the courts against the judgments of the political branches. * * *

I. STATE SOVEREIGNTY—ITS NATURE AND IMPORTANCE

A. *The Constitutional Concept of Sovereignty*

As Professor Wechsler observed, the framers of the Constitution were compelled to accept and protect the separate existence of the states—as their autonomy was the "means and the price" of forming the nation. * * *

The historical materials supply little guidance, however, about the nature of the state sovereignty that was to be preserved. Neither the concept of a state nor its intended functions were described in the Constitution. A geographic entity with a discrete territory was no doubt an element of the conception, but not a sufficient definition, since boundaries could be modified and nonstates shared the quality of territorial administration. Then, too, the framers must have assumed that states would have their separate governments, since they allocated responsibilities to the state legislatures and presupposed the existence of state executive and judicial authorities. But the pertinent sources belie a simple equation of a state with its government in eighteenth-century political theory, tending more often to center the concept of sovereignty in the ancient notion of the body politic: the community, or the aggregate of all inhabitants of the specific territory. * * *

* * *

Though the records of the Constitutional Convention and the nineteenth-century opinions by the Court supply shadowy suggestions of an original conception, they furnish little aid in defining the contemporary role of the state. As a starting point, however, it is not difficult to describe some of the attributes of sovereignty related to separate existence in the twentieth century. To function as a state, the body politic must have at least a minimum of its powers protected against outside interference, including control over the structure of government, the distribution of administrative responsibilities, the process of selecting popular agents, and the capacity to tax and spend. This is but another way to say that the characteristic integral to separate identity in contemporary terms is a power to make choices—about how to use public monies and direct public attention, and about how to vary the choices as the needs of the community change. Though the range of choices available to a state—the range of needs to which it may respond or services it may choose to provide—also varies over time, within the zone of its sovereign authority its assessments and elections as to public wants and needs must control. In short, sovereignty can have little modern significance unless within its domain a state is free to prefer health services over highways or public colleges over correctional facilities and to use its sovereign powers to effectuate those preferences. Similarly, to the extent it is not preempted by federal institutions, the state must be free to determine what kinds of constraints it will impose on private activity and what business activities it will regulate, as well as how it will regulate them and structure its regulatory agencies to implement the decisions it has made.

* * *

B.   The Importance of State Sovereignty

The search for a point at which limitation of a state's freedom of choice jeopardizes its integrity or separate existence must begin with some identification of the basic goals or values that support a federal system. * * *

1. *Improved Governmental Processes.* One clear value of the federal form resides in its potential to provide maximum opportunities for participation in government. Inevitably, governmental choices must be made through representatives, but decisionmaking in smaller units makes possible more direct public participation in both the process of representative selection and the process of policy determination by the delegates chosen. This participation is critical to any viable notion of accountability. Representative government depends upon the maintenance of the connection between the governors and the governed, not merely in the sense that elected officials will then reflect the popular will, but also because there is then some assurance that public preferences are communicated to the public officials whose own expressions help shape popular opinion. A fundamental advantage of local government is the opportunity it affords for this kind of communication. Simply put, proximity increases accountability by increasing access.

Experience also supports the traditional claim that federalism promotes variety in political choice and counters the impulse toward social and ideological homogeneity by allowing cultural differences to find expression in different places. Despite the homogenizing effects of media and mobility on twentieth-century American life, the existence of separate state and local governmental units still provides avenues for expression of the variations in style in different parts of the country. Tax burdens, public services, habits of living, and patterns of tolerance do vary as one moves from Maine to Alabama or New York to New Mexico, reflecting in part the differences in the political choices made by subnational governmental authorities. Thus one state opts for an elaborate system of subsidized postsecondary education while another spends far less on this service; one state chooses to permit the use of marijuana while others continue to prosecute for possession; and one state appeals to retired persons by supplementing the natural advantage of climate with tax preferences, while another discourages this type of migration.

The aphorism that a federal system permits the states to serve as laboratories for experimentation has also been borne out in our experience. * * * [S]tate experiments in matters as diverse as public financing of political campaigns, regulation of hospital facilities, protection of health and safety on the job, and requirements for open meetings by public agencies and public access to official records have laid the foundation for similar national legislative actions. * * *

2. *Individual Liberty.* Beyond these values of participation, accountability, diversity, and experimentation in government, however, the case for a federal form rests most fundamentally on the capacity of a federal system to enhance and protect individual liberty. * * *

The concept of liberty here at issue requires some greater specification. In one sense, of course, individual liberty is merely the absence of public or official constraint on individual action. This kind of personal liberty—liberty as license—looks not to social order, but rather to the freedom available to an individual to think and act as he pleases. The kind of liberty more pertinent to the values inherent in a federal system of government, however, is not the freedom to be left alone but the freedom to become involved in the public life of a polity. Political liberty—the freedom to participate in the community's political life—is the core of democratic government. This distinction, a staple of political philosophy since Aristotle, remains vital. * * *

The political liberty of the individual secured by our Constitution is a freedom to influence that same process of political choice that defines the essence of sovereignty. As discussed above, the effectiveness of this political participation turns on accountability, the connection between the representative and the represented. In our system, the connection is reinforced by rights that need not be absolute to be fundamental to democratic government, such as access to the voting booth and ballot, rights of expression through lobbying, and contributions of time and money. But beyond such guarantees, political liberty requires a level of awareness in the electorate. Information about the process of choice, including the range of alternatives and their probable effects, is a critical means of assuring accountability. Realistically, a legislator who supports a bill is accountable to the people he serves, both individually and through their association with others of like interest, to the extent that they know the options he discarded as well as the decision he adopted. In the press, the campaign fund, or the ballot box, the voter may or may not view the particular matter as critical to his ongoing support for the representative; he may judge an unwelcome decision outweighed by other decisions that he supports, or by the shortcomings of the available alternatives. The critical point, however, is that he must at least know whom to hold responsible.

To the extent accountability is diminished by reason of the electorate's lack of knowledge or understanding of the lines of authority, the value or effectiveness of participation is necessarily reduced, and the protection of political liberty is necessarily jeopardized. By fostering participation and accountability in the political process, a state's autonomy thus serves a primary constitutional value, and judicial protection of state sovereignty in circumstances where the political branches fail to safeguard it adequately is thus seen as an essential part of the traditional judicial assignment to protect the individual's right to liberty against majoritarian abuse.

These are some of the benefits of our federal system. In the contemporary political process, however, many factors combine to undermine the capacity of the separate states to realize these advantages. The following section illuminates some of these factors.

II. THE DECLINE OF STATES' INFLUENCE UPON THE FEDERAL GOVERNMENT

Congressional sensitivity to the states' autonomy turns not only on the external relationships between state officials and the federal government, but also on various internal factors, such as the structure of government as defined by the Constitution and the rules of procedure developed by the Congress for its own governance. Thus, the method of selecting members of Congress, the standards of voter eligibility, and the design of boundaries for election districts, as well as the rules governing selection of legislative leaders, all affect the state role in the selection and composition of the national legislature. Congressional representation of state interests is also influenced by political factors that contribute to legislative choice, including the effects of the media, campaign expenditures, seniority, incumbency, and party loyalty. In addition, the values and aspirations of the individuals who comprise the expanding bureaucracies in both the federal and state governments exert a significant influence upon federal actions.

Any examination of the extent to which a particular concern for state sovereignty is reflected in the Congress requires some examination of the impact of these forces. My argument, admittedly based more on impressions than the results of systematic empirical testing, is that recent changes in this internal political process have also diminished the likelihood that congressional action will be guided by special sensitivity to state autonomy.

* * *

In the last quarter century, many of the structural and political factors affecting sensitivity to localism in the Congress have changed dramatically, with the result that opposition to "federalization" of the state governmental process in the name of state sovereignty is less likely to prove compelling in congressional debates.

1. *The Structural Elements.* Some of the changes in the structural elements of federalism are by now familiar. Commencing with *Wesberry v. Sanders* in 1964, the Supreme Court began to limit the states' ability to control the process of congressional election districting. District lines must now be drawn to approach numerical equality among the constituencies. Neither municipal boundaries nor attempts to avoid political gerrymandering will excuse even slight deviations from mathematical equality. The courts have also scrutinized state plans to ensure contiguity and prevent use of the districting power to exclude minorities from political representation. At a minimum, the political effect of the decisions mandating substantial equality of congressional districting has been to diminish the influence of state parties on the composition of the Congress, and to shift a measure of political power from the previously overrepresented rural areas to the cities and, more recently, to the increasingly populous suburbs.

Next, the Court, the Congress, and the constitutional amendment process combined to limit state control over the qualifications of voters in elections for Congress. The first recent blow to state efforts to restrict electoral participation through this means was the decision in *Harper v. Virginia State Board of Elections,* an event that ended, in one swoop, years of fruitless congressional debate over proposals to abolish the poll tax. Soon after the *Harper* decision, the Congress widened the electorate even more drastically through the Voting Rights Act of 1965, facilitating the registration of black voters and the creation of new black voting strength throughout the South. * * * [In 1971] the twenty-sixth amendment [was ratified], guaranteeing for the eighteen-year-old the right to vote in all elections.

* * * Other changes at the state level facilitating participation in a party's primary elections without regard to a voter's prior membership or involvement in party affairs have further contributed to the decline of party control and the development of personal constituencies by successful candidates for Congress.

2. *The Political Forces.* The effects of the various structural modifications tending to erode sensitivity to state interests have been intensified by more subtle changes in the political process affecting national election campaigns and the internal workings of Congress. The last twenty-five years have brought enormous changes in the types of persons elected to the Senate and House, and in the techniques used in

their successful campaigns. The core element in this transformation has been the decline in importance of state party organizations, itself a product of several related forces—the effect of money on politics, the changing use of media in campaigns, the phenomenon of celebrity success in politics, and the substitution of welfare state programs for the community service functions of the neighborhood political organization. The consequences are varied, but clearly point in one direction. As Senators and Members of the House develop independent constituencies among groups such as farmers, businessmen, laborers, environmentalists, and the poor, each of which generally supports certain national initiatives, their tendency to identify with state interests and the positions of state officials is reduced. * * *

* * * The result is evident in the class of new Senators elected in 1978, which includes many first-time officeholders. As legislators, these persons seem less likely than their counterparts in the 1950's to respond to state concerns merely because voiced by state officials or state parties and significantly more likely to pursue an independent course. * * * Indeed, while prior state government service is still common to many members of Congress, the proportion with this background has declined significantly. In the Eightieth Congress, twenty-eight Senators had served formerly as Governor of their states, while only sixteen former Governors sat in the Ninety-fifth Senate. * * *

Once in Washington, the same characteristics that have distinguished the new Congressman from his predecessors have also contributed to changes in the internal procedures of the national legislature. These modifications in congressional rules and practices also tend to reduce the force of the proposition that the separate states generally acquiesce in acts of Congress interfering with their sovereignty. On the desirability of reelection, there is little to distinguish the contemporary Congressman. Most want to stay and their wish is seldom denied. But the same strains of independence that mark their election have also characterized the Congressmen's service in Washington. The old rule that "to get along in the House, you go along," while still of some importance, belies the increasing assertiveness of junior Members. The most notable consequence has been the rising influence of the party caucus in the House and the consequent decline of strict seniority in the selection of major committee chairmen. In 1974, three senior committee chairmen were defeated, in each case following the negative response of freshman Members to their appearances before the newcomers' caucus. In part as a result of the changes in seniority rules, there has been a trend away from southern states'-rights oriented domination of committee leadership positions. In the Ninety-fifth Congress, only five of twenty major House committee chairmen and five of fifteen Senate committee chairmen were from the South; not many years before, the ratio of southern to nonsouthern representatives in the leadership was significantly higher.

* * * The combined effects of incumbency, direct access to the electorate, and declining adherence to seniority in the Congress contrib-

ute to the relative independence of Congressmen from the state party and state officials.

3. *The Expansion of the Federal Government.* * * * The vast expansion in the scope of federal domestic programs has produced a new class of public administrators, in both Washington and state regional offices of federal agencies, commissioned to monitor state activities. The enlarged requirements of federal law and federal largesse have in turn expanded and altered the roles of the states, and stimulated a corresponding growth of state bureaucracies responsible for program implementation. As a result of the pervasive intermingling of functions and responsibilities among the different levels of government in the federal system, the "layer cake" of federalism has become increasingly "marbled," with local, state, and federal governments sharing responsibility for a multitude of public services. * * *

From these developments there has emerged a new system of representation and mutual influence in the federal system, comprised of two classes of public administrators who work closely with the interest groups and constituencies affected by the programs they administer as well as with individual legislators and committee staff. Collectively, they shape and implement legislation that imposes administrative obligations and fiscal burdens on the states in return for increased federal aid. Individuals in the federal and state administrative bureaucracies often move back and forth between them, and share common backgrounds and ambitions, most particularly the commitment to maintain and expand the public services they supervise. * * *

4. *Summary.* Taken together, the new relationship of the states and state administrators to the federal government and the new politics of congressional representation have dramatically changed the workings of the process of federalism. It is now far less likely that the states' interest in their continuing autonomy will consistently receive expression within the political branches of the federal government, or that the political process will yield dependable lines of accountability between the governed and the government. As Congress increasingly implements national policy by directing the governmental activity of the states, the people in whom sovereignty ultimately resides are left without a clear sense of the persons they may call to account—the national legislators who conceived and ordered a program, or the state officials charged with its implementation. And as the states find their resources and energies increasingly consumed in meeting obligations imposed by the national government, they confront a system of federalism more coopting than cooperative, in which the basic values of pluralism, creativity, participation, and liberty are progressively undermined.

[In the latter part of his article Kaden argues that state autonomy may need judicial as well as political protection. He offers several examples of cases where this may be true. One is the case of direct commands to the states. Congress would be justified in applying Clean Air Act standards to state activities in common with the activities of private groups. But it would go too far if it commanded the state legislature to establish a new agency to regulate labor relations in local government according to congressional standards. A second type of case involves conditions attached to federal grants. Given the pervasive nature of federal aid to state governments in the modern federal system, Congress could bring about almost any state behavior it wanted by making compliance a condition of assistance. Kaden would have courts apply a kind of intermediate scrutiny to such conditions, insisting that they be related to important federal objectives.]

WILLIAM W. VAN ALSTYNE, THE SECOND DEATH OF FEDERALISM
83 Mich.L.Rev. 1709, 1720–1725 (1985).

The *Garcia* case, with its overruling of *Usery,* attracted a fair amount of journalistic comment. Much of that comment was interesting but predictably limited to *Garcia's* immediate practical implications. *The (London) Economist,* however, was more discerning. It reported an appropriate sense of English puzzlement. It appeared to *The Economist* that the Supreme Court had partly repudiated *Marbury v. Madison,* in favor of a rule of parliamentary supremacy in respect to the boundaries of federalism. "[I]t is curious," *The Economist* observed, "that in the San Antonio case the justices explicitly overruled a decision they had made only nine years before." It then went on to note something even "more startling":

> Even more startling, though, was the view of federalism that the majority put forward to support its decision. The court could have made its ruling on a narrow technical ground. It did not. Justice Harry Blackmun, whose change of heart since 1976 was enough to shift the court, wrote in the majority opinion that the protection of the states from federal power "inhered principally in the workings of the national government itself," rather than in the constitution as interpreted by the Supreme Court. In other words, the states have some influence on congress and the president; if they do not succeed in using it to keep Washington from encroaching unduly on their powers, they should not expect the court to do the job for them by declaring federal laws unconstitutional. This view, said one of the dissenting justices, Mr. Lewis Powell, "rejects almost 200 years of the understanding of the constitutional status of federalism."

> [The Blackmun opinion] also called into question a central principle of the Supreme Court's own constitutional position. Since 1803 the court has claimed the authority ... to invalidate actions of the federal government if they conflict with the constitution. *The San Antonio decision seems to suggest that the principle of judicial review does not apply to questions of federalism when congress acts under the commerce clause.*

[T]he Supreme Court seems to have declared that judicial enforcement of the constitutional position on federalism is at an end.[56]

Is the "judicial enforcement of the constitutional position on federalism at an end" and, if it is, why? Is it because the general approach of the Court in *Usery* was improper and, if it was, what made it so? Or does *Garcia* actually insinuate a different sort of answer altogether, even as *The Economist* suggests it does—that federalism questions in general (and not merely in *Garcia*-type cases) are not for the Court, but fundamentally for *Congress*, finally to determine?

* * *

The constitutional clauses examined in *Usery* [58] and reexamined in *Garcia* have borne more of the burden of federalism litigation than any other clauses, including the spending clause. From the beginning, moreover, there has been a blurriness in their scope and an admitted uncertainty in measuring their margins, even as reflected in the tumultuous reactions to the Court's earliest decisions.

Even so, with all the ups and downs of judicial vagary, the commerce clause and the tenth amendment have not until now been read as though they declared that it was not for the Court, but rather for Congress, to determine the extent to which enumerated powers permit the displacement of state laws or the command of state governments. Rather, each has been a staple of substantive judicial review. It has been for Congress to decide what to do. It has been for the Court to say whether it was within Congress' power to do it.

The results of that judicial review have not always been consistent, but perfect consistency is not to be expected insofar as judicial attitudes must themselves vary and none is particularly entitled to control all the rest. Usually, however, even in close cases when the federalism claim has failed (as most often it has indeed failed), it has failed because the Court has yielded to an assertion of some overriding federal interest it deemed adequate to rationalize the exceptional intrusiveness of the challenged act. In *Garcia*, * * * the majority identified no such overriding interest. Rather, it deemed itself excused from this element of judicial review. It then weakly explained that it regarded the political safeguards of federalism to be the appropriate check against unconstitutional excesses by Congress.

By itself, this may do no more than to overrule *Usery*, i.e., to eliminate any requirement of justification even when Congress presumes to command the states themselves and even when it is not asserted that the states are engaging in commerce. Writ large, however, as the sources relied upon by Justice Blackmun would have us do,[62] such

---

56. *Nine for the Seesaw,* [The Economist, Mar. 2, 1985,] at 21 (emphasis added).

58. I.e., the commerce clause, the necessary and proper clause, and the tenth amendment.

62. *See, e.g.,* J. Choper, Judicial Review

alleged political safeguards of federalism may excuse the Court from answering any other question of a like kind as well. The practical choice between state action and national action generally, indeed always, in this view, is not to be judicially constrained but only politically constrained. To be sure, the Constitution may appear to have made an allocation (enumerating what may be national and homogeneous, reserving the rest to the states and protecting them in some measure from being commanded as well as preempted), but it is best not for the judiciary to say whether the constitutional plan is being adhered to. The determinations to be made are more appropriately resolved in Congress where the respective interests are able to work out the appropriate accommodations, rather than in the courts. The constitutional plan is thus not checked by an impacted litigant's standing to object as a sore loser in court; it is checked, rather, by the structural representation already amply afforded the states by the Constitution.

If, then, "the states" or "the people" do not appear to keep Congress to the plan, it may be because they do not see any real departure from that plan; alternatively, supposing they do, presumably they do not regard the departure as an undesirable rearrangement. Under these circumstances, it is scarcely for the courts to say that the Emperor, i.e., Congress, has no clothes. For the Constitution itself (under this view) relies upon the finality of federal politics, rather than judicial review, to determine the sufficiency of the national wardrobe. It is the role of the judiciary to uphold and enforce the majoritarian verdict on these questions and not to oppose it with a perception of its own.

Generally, the argument to this effect (which the *Garcia* case suggests the Court now flirts with), has been opposed principally in terms of the alleged naiveté of its political science.[63] Unquestionably that objection is well taken but, ironically, to press one's objection in such terms is in one sense to miss the point of what is being said. It puts the real objection on quite the wrong ground. Even to participate in that debate is in one sense to lose it. It implies that if, as, or when (in the Court's view) such structural safeguards *might* reasonably be seen as adequate, at least then and to that extent it would be inappropriate not to defer to them. Alternatively, it may concede even more, namely, that if it is true that the Constitution deems such safeguards adequate, the Court should not set up its opposing opinion, even if the Court finds those safeguards inadequate. In brief, if it is part of the constitutional plan that the constitutional boundaries of federalism are to be politically settled, rather than judicially maintained until altered by amendment,

and the National Political Process 175–84 (1980), *cited in* Garcia v. San Antonio Metro. Transit Auth., 105 S.Ct. 1005, 1018 n. 11 (1985). (The same footnote also cites to an article by Wechsler, urging extreme deference to Congress although not outright abdication of the judicial function. *See* Wechsler, *The Political Safeguards of Fed-* *eralism: The Role of the States in the Composition and Selection of the National Government,* 54 Colum.L.Rev. 543 (1954).)

63. [*See, e.g.,* Kaden, *Politics, Money, and State Sovereignty: The Judicial Role,* 79 Colum.L.Rev. 847 (1979).]

then the Court should, in decency, respect its assigned (non)role in such matters.

This is the strong form of what Justice Blackmun seems to have implied in the critical part of *Garcia*. And it is exactly *this* implication that raised an English eyebrow in surprise, as well it should. Stripped of its elegance, *Garcia* proposes the piecemeal repeal of judicial review. It also involves a double counting of what are in fact merely *pre*-judicial and *post*-judicial "safeguards" of the American constitutional plan, safeguards (such as they are) merely additional to, *and not in substitution of,* substantive judicial review.

The Constitution does of course notice the states other than through article III, i.e., other than in the duty of article III judges to hold an act of Congress invalid when, in an appropriate case, the government is unable to demonstrate the consistency of the act with the federalism provisions of the Constitution. It notices them in the representation formula of the Senate, with its assurance of two senators per state irrespective of size. It notices them in the Electoral College. It notices them in article V, with regard to the states' power to initiate and ratify proposed amendments, etc. How well (or ill) these constitutive provisions contrive to keep Congress and the President in check, one may measure for oneself. Unless, however, they are designed not as merely additive to the safeguards of substantive judicial review but rather as partial or whole substitutes for that review, their speculative efficacy or inefficacy is utterly without relevance in constitutional litigation. They are, with all respect, not the proper concern of the Supreme Court in the adjudication of a particular case.

Concretely, if in the Court's view the bare bones of the commerce clause are insufficient as against the particular objections fielded in the *Garcia* case, then the Court must say so. As to that question, moreover, *nothing* can be derived from references to constitutive processes. The Court may not appropriately uphold an act of Congress based on reasoning that relies even partly on some theory of renvoi to what are, at best, altogether separate possible sources of constraint. Those constraints either worked or did not work (to hold Congress within the boundaries laid down), and it is for the Court now to answer whether they did. The inputs of those features of the Constitution are now concluded. The product is at hand. The special "safeguard" of the Court's independent view of constitutional consistency is now requested. The litigant asks for the *Court's* answer.

ANDRZEJ RAPACZYNSKI, FROM SOVEREIGNTY TO PROCESS: THE JURISPRUDENCE OF FEDERALISM AFTER GARCIA
1985 Sup.Ct.Rev. 341–346, 359–360, 364–366, 380, 382, 385–390, 395–401, 404, 408–412, 414–418.

The position of federalism in our constitutional law is peculiar. On the one hand, next to separation of powers and individual rights, federalism is clearly one of the three main branches of our constitutional structure. On the other hand, judicial enforcement of any limits on national power that the concept of federalism might entail has a rather unfortunate history and, at least insofar as the limitations on national commerce power are concerned, seems to have been abandoned in the *Garcia* case in favor of what Professor Wechsler has called "the political safeguards of federalism."

More than in any other area of constitutional adjudication, the Court's attempts to impose federalism-related limitations on the national government have been, throughout history, frustrated by the political process, resulting three times in constitutional amendments. The Court's decision in the *Dred Scott* case that slavery was a municipal institution outside federal control, was "overruled" by the Civil War Amendments. The decision in *Pollock v. Farmers' Loan and Trust Co.* that "the boundary between the Nation and the States ... would have disappeared" if the national taxing power had been extended to taxing income from real estate, led to the enactment of the Sixteenth Amendment. The Court's attempts to give meaning to the Tenth Amendment by limiting national regulation of private activities under the Commerce Clause were instrumental in precipitating the "constitutional crisis" of 1937 and led to a wholesale judicial retreat. As recently as 1970, the Court's decision in *Oregon v. Mitchell,* holding that Congress lacked the power to enfranchise eighteen-year-olds in state elections, resulted in passing the Twenty–Sixth Amendment, which it took the country only three months to ratify.

It is important to inquire into the reasons for this rather dismal record of judicial intervention. The most common explanation, seemingly adopted by the *Garcia* Court, is that federalism is essentially a political arrangement and that the policing of it is, for one reason or another, unsuited to the *modus operandi* of the judicial department. The extreme version of this argument is exemplified by Professor Choper's claim that the Court is most needed and most effective in protecting individual rights against governmental encroachments and that its reservoir of legitimacy is only dissipated if the Court intervenes in the distribution of institutional competences among governmental entities.[16] Whatever merit this view may have, it is clearly not shared by the Court, which has not shied away from highly charged, controversial issues of institutional competence in the area of separation of powers, most recently in *Immigration and Naturalization Service v. Chadha.* Instead, the Court's reasoning in *Garcia* singles out the federalism-related limitations on the national power as peculiarly unsuitable for judicial resolution. We are not really told, however, what distinguishes federalism from the separation of powers in this respect: it is certainly not the absence of the "political safeguards" of the latter, for the Constitution abounds in provisions guaranteeing that at least the Congress and the

16. [J. Choper, Judicial Review and the
National Political Process (1980).]

President have ample means to protect themselves in the political arena. * * *

* * *

The most plausible explanation of the repeated frustration of judicial intervention in the area of state-national relations is the failure of judges and scholars to produce a viable theory of federalism that would help to develop workable principles for the judicial resolution of federalism-related disputes. To begin with, rather than focusing on a functional analysis of the role of the states in the federal system—an analysis that would parallel the Court's jurisprudence in the area of separation of powers—the basic intellectual inquiry has been concentrated on the concept of state sovereignty and its implications for the limitation of national authority. * * *

It is also possible that a political disinclination toward the state-rights doctrine, stemming from the Civil War divisions and the intellectual ascendancy of the New Deal, further contributed to the neglect of a theory of federalism. But the past failures should not be taken to preclude the possibility of future success. Indeed, even if the protection of the federal structure of the United States is to rest ultimately with the political process, and not the courts, the actors in that process, no less than judges, must have some idea of the basic purposes of federalism and the reasons behind their constitutional protection. A new theory of federalism is thus necessary to allow us a more comprehensive understanding of the American institutions. * * *

* * *

Process Jurisprudence: An Alternative Approach
* * *

Garcia stresses the fact that the Constitution "divested" the states of "their original powers" and that it is futile to try to "identify principled constitutional limitations on the scope of Congress' Commerce Clause powers over the States merely by relying on *a priori* definitions of state sovereignty." Instead, the decision proposes to rely primarily on the political safeguards of federalism and to ground any future judicial intervention not in a defense of state sovereignty but in the idea of compensating for possible failings in the national political process.[56]

* * *

Viewed from this perspective, the gist of *Garcia*'s holding lies not in ruling out as nonjusticiable all matters of federalism-related limitations on national power, but rather in formulating an approach to the elaboration of the judicial standards of review. This approach has much in

---

56. Garcia v. San Antonio MTA, 105 S.Ct. at 1019–20: "[A]ny substantive restraint on the exercise of Commerce Clause powers must find its justification in the procedural nature of [the] basic limitation [the Constitution imposes to protect the states], and it must be tailored to compensate for possible failings in the national political process rather than to dictate a 'sacred province of state autonomy.'"

common with the "process jurisprudence" originating in the famous footnote four of the *Carolene Products* decision [69] and subsequently elaborated in the scholarly literature.[70] The assumption of this approach is that the Constitution largely confines the outcomes of governmental action to the political process and that judicial review should, with a few exceptions related to very concrete substantive provisions in the Constitution, be directed toward preserving the integrity of the political process, keeping open the channels of political change, and so on. In elaborating this theory of judicial review, however, process jurisprudence does not limit the scope of judicial intervention to explicitly procedural remedies or to the enforcement of specifically procedural principles. * * * Thus, for example, in reviewing governmental actions that may inhibit free speech or discriminate against certain minorities, a court sympathetic to the tenets of process jurisprudence will feel free to elaborate the standards of review that will directly address the substantive issues of free speech or minority rights, but it will justify them not so much in terms of the autonomous values of speech or equality as in terms of their role in the properly functioning democratic process and will attempt to identify some distortions in that process that account for its presumably abnormal results. * * *

In the context of federalism, the process jurisprudence endorsed by *Garcia,* if I interpret it correctly, does not imply, therefore, an unconditional rejection of even the specific principle of the protection of the integrity of state governmental operations put forth by the *National League of Cities* so long as this principle is not rooted in the assumption of state sovereignty. Should it turn out, for example, on the basis of a well-grounded analysis of the significance of local politics for the proper functioning of the national political process, that certain systemic characteristics of the national government make it prone to fail to recognize the interdependence between its own health and the robustness of political life in the states, the Court might view with suspicion federal interference with the integrity of some vital governmental operations of the states, in much the same way as it applied its "strict scrutiny" analysis to governmental actions involving race-based classifications.

* * *

THE FUNCTION OF THE STATES WITHIN THE FEDERAL SYSTEM

* * *

A. *Tyranny Prevention*

* * * Perhaps the most frequently mentioned function of the federal system is the one it shares to a large extent with the separation of powers, namely, the protection of the citizen against governmental oppression—the "tyranny" that the Framers were so concerned about.

* * *

---

69. United States v. Carolene Products Co., 304 U.S. 144, 152–53 n. 4 (1938).

70. See, above all, Ely, Democracy and Distrust (1980) * * *.

There are three somewhat different scenarios of governmental oppression that the Framers seem to have had in mind when they spoke of the danger of "tyranny." First, they were clearly concerned that a small minority might be oppressed by a sufficiently homogeneous majority. Second, they were concerned with the danger that a few powerful minority interests might gain ascendancy over the political process and exploit the rest of society. And third, they were afraid that a powerful central government may itself develop its own separate interest and oppress the citizenry.

* * *

How is federalism related to the Framers' objection of preventing the three-headed specter of tyranny? Many American liberals tend to look with skepticism on the states as the protectors of individual freedom and they point to a whole host of situations in which the states, much more than the federal government, have engaged in practices violative of individual rights. Quite apart from the special problem of racial discrimination, which is historically tied to the regional character of slavery in the United States, there are in fact good reasons to believe that the states represent a more direct threat than the national authorities to the rights of small minorities and that the states have only a secondary role to play in protecting such minorities—so long as these minorities are not geographically defined. The explanation for this lies in the fact that local constituencies are much more homogeneous and cohesive than the national one, both because their members share more common interests and values and because, the constituencies being less numerous, stable majoritarian interests are more likely to exist within them and to be easier to organize. Consequently, at least insofar as the first of the Framers' scenarios of governmental oppression is concerned, state governments are more likely than the national one to be captured by powerful majoritarian interests and to oppress small minorities with little power to resist. * * *

* * * [W]hile the states are more easily captured by relatively undifferentiated majoritarian interests intent on suppressing small minorities, the federal government may be a more likely subject of capture by a set of special minoritarian interests, precisely because the majority interest of the national constituency is so large, diffuse, and enormously difficult to organize. * * *

It is quite easy to see how a system weighted in favor of local interests (either through the importance of state institutions or through a regional representation on the national level) will provide an institutional support to geographically defined groups that may be subject to exclusion or exploitation by the more powerful regions. But it is no less important to see that the existence of a strong system of local government may also modify those divisions between the potential ins and outs that are essentially social in nature (such as between the traditional and new industries, organized and unorganized labor, producers and consumers, and so on) rather than primarily geographically determined. * * *

[T]he very scale on which an organization must succeed before it gains meaningful access to the political process and can use the machine of the government to improve its position vis à vis other groups is very often decisive with respect to whether an effective collective action takes place. It is thus quite likely that an effort to exclude certain groups may be more successful on the federal than on the state level and that maintaining the domination of an already existing power elite is much more difficult on the local level. Insofar, then, as a large proportion of governmental benefits is dispensed on an independent local level or as the constellation of forces on the local level determines the influence on the national level, the danger of minoritarian oppression is significantly diminished.

* * *

But the most influential protection that the states offer against tyranny is the protection against the special interest of the government itself. For the fact that the federal government may be less likely than the states, in what we may call "normal times," to oppress small minorities whose mode of life offends a homogeneous majority does not mean that it is never likely to oppress them as well as to deprive the citizenry as a whole of their legitimate voice in running the national affairs. Should the federal government ever be captured by an authoritarian movement or assert itself as a special cohesive interest, the resulting oppression would almost certainly be much more severe and durable than that of which any state would be capable. In such a situation, both private individuals and private-interest groups prepared to defend their rights would face very grave organizational obstacles and could not provide anything even approaching in effectiveness the resistance that may be offered by a governmental institution, endowed with the power of coercing those who may lack a sufficient individual motivation to contribute (if even only financially) to the common good. It is precisely because the states are governmental bodies that break the national authorities' monopoly on coercion that they constitute the most fundamental bastion against a successful conversion of the federal government into a vehicle of the worst kind of oppression.

Viewed from this perspective, freedom from federal interference enjoyed by state governmental machinery, and especially by those of its organs that potentially provide the easiest means by which the citizenry can organize itself against a tyrannical movement on the national level, turns out to be a value quite independent from any limitation of the federal power to regulate any substantive field of private activity. While traditional liberal doctrine relied quite heavily on the exclusion of government from most private activities and hoped to guard us in this way from tyrannical overreaching, the realization of the pervasiveness of market failures in a complex, advanced society has made the doctrine of *laissez-faire* of less use under modern conditions. Similarly, the increasing interdependence of social and economic problems on the national scale makes it unrealistic to expect that the federal government can be kept away from regulating the ever increasing details of what had previously been thought to be essentially local activities. In this situation, when it is no longer an option simply to resist most forms of federal involvement in the private sector, the federalist idea of the separation of the national and local governmental institutions acquires more, and not less, significance for the prevention of governmental oppression. For the independence of the very process of state government, without seriously hampering the national authorities in regulating most private activities, assures the existence of an organizational framework, more efficient than any private institution could provide, that may always be used as an effective tool for bringing together otherwise defenseless individuals with some stakes in resisting the overreaching of the national government. The value of this organizational apparatus thus lies not so much in any of its concrete regulatory activities that the national government could not do as well (or better), as in the very fact that it eliminates the national monopoly on the power to coerce. * * *

* * *

B. Providing a Space for Participatory Politics

The value of citizen participation in governmental operations has often been stressed in legal literature and its enhancement has often been viewed as one of the most important purposes of federalism. But the objectives of citizen participation are usually seen as clustered around such things as the facilitation of the flow of information between the citizens and the government, improving the efficiency of governmental decisions, and the enhancement of the accountability of public officials or of the public acceptance of governmental decisions. Viewed in this way, citizen participation appears, above all, as a means of strengthening the representativeness of governmental institutions and enhancing the perception of its legitimacy. * * *

* * *

* * * [T]here is much truth in these observations but also much that is problematic. Even if we do not question the assumption that the interest of the "people" is ultimately identical to the interest of individuals, it is by no means clear that individuals themselves are best able to articulate the types of considerations that will most affect their interests or identify the decisions that will maximize them. In fact, one of the basic tenets of the classical theory of representation is that it is both wasteful and dangerous for the masses to busy themselves with the complex matters of policy making that may be better handled by professional politicians who choose this as their full-time occupation. * * * There are also persuasive arguments that too much electoral control may in some situations unproductively divert the efforts of the legislators or make them systematically ignore those issues that do not provide an immediate payoff at the polls—even though they may have an ultimately greater impact on the electorate's welfare. * * * Finally, it is not difficult to conceive of situations in which a competent bureaucrat,

operating in a clear hierarchical structure in which he expects to make his career, may do a much better job at serving the public than a politician directly responsible to the electorate.[141]

* * *

The model of representative politics rests on the idea that the main task of political institutions consists in providing a method of selecting a social policy that reflects in a fair and acceptable manner the preferences and interests of those groups or individuals who are members of a given political society. What is distinctive in this model is its essentially atomistic conception of society in which the basic interests of social actors do not derive from their being members of the political community and in which the government serves an essentially instrumental function of aggregating the actors' primary preferences into social policies.

Against this representative model, the model of participatory government, which goes as far back as Aristotle, views political activity not as instrumental toward achieving a proportionate share in the distribution of available resources, to be used in a variety of private pursuits, but rather as a good in itself, something essentially implicated in the very concept of human freedom. This way of thinking, which stresses the role of the community in the very shaping of the "interests" of its members and in infusing their lives with a sense of purpose, was by no means absent from the thought of the Founding Fathers. * * * [T]heir ever present concern with what they called public, civic, or "republican" virtue testifies clearly to their belief that the "good life," as Aristotle would have termed it, involves a commitment to a political community and participation in a process by which individuals shape in common the mode of life they are going to share. * * *

* * * [I]f there is some genuine room for noninstrumental participation in American political life, it can realistically exist only on the local level. There have been some efforts to devise new means, using modern communications technology, of reviewing participatory politics on a large scale, but the dominant view is that the optimum size of a political body that can afford significant citizen participation is nowhere near the size of the modern nation state or even of its main provincial subdivisions. * * *

* * *

If one of the primary functions, within the federalist framework, of state-run institutions is to provide the public space for participatory politics, then from this point of view federalism does not conceive the division between the state and national governments as a way of parceling out "sovereignty"—the control over substantive fields of regulation—but rather as a way of preserving alternative modes of decision

---

141. Lawyers often make arguments of this kind against the elective judiciary. But the problem is equally apparent in other areas and does not depend only on the need for expertise. * * *

making. Naturally, the vitality of the participatory state institutions depends in part on the types of substantive decisions that are left for the states. Should the federal government preempt them from most fields that touch directly on the life of local communities, the states would become but empty shells within which no meaningful political activity could take place. But whatever the effect of preemption, the principles of federalism provide an important and independent reason for protecting the autonomy of the political processes of local governments, and this not just in the name of democratic control (for the federal government is also subject to such control), but also in the name of protecting a different form of political space that the national government is very unlikely to provide.

* * *

C. Laboratories of Experiment

Courts as well as commentators are very fond of repeating Justice Brandeis's dictum that "[i]t is one of the happy incidents of the federal system that a single courageous state may, if its citizens choose, serve as a laboratory; and try novel social and economic experiments without risk to the rest of the country." While the context of Justice Brandeis's remark had nothing to do with protecting the states from Congressional interference and while his point concerned only an "incident" of the federal system, the claim that the states constitute "national laboratories of experiment" came to be viewed by many as a cornerstone of the federalist thinking and has quickly become one of the least examined verities of constitutional theory. Only recently has there been some scholarly effort to assess the accuracy of this claim, and the most that can be said is that the jury is still out.

The importance attached by many to the states' function as laboratories of experiment is at least in part exaggerated and, in any case, of little significance for constitutional adjudication. This is true for three reasons. First, whether a strong protection of the states' autonomy would actually contribute to the efficiency of the American government is a very complex question that does not admit of an easy answer. In fact, there are many arguments to the contrary. Second, insofar as there is something to the laboratory-of-experiment argument, a unitary government could avail itself of the same advantages by a partial delegation of authority to its local branches, so that there may be nothing in the laboratory rationale that is peculiarly related to the federal structure of American government. Finally, even if it turns out that decentralization does contribute to governmental efficiency, the analysis necessary to determine which aspects of local governance should be protected from central interference is of a very complex and largely pragmatic nature and thus unsuitable either for elevation to the constitutional level or for judicial assessment. In sum, then, in developing their federalist jurisprudence, the courts should concentrate on the other, more fundamental state functions within the federal framework:

the protection against tyranny and the provision of a space for participatory politics.

We should begin with the observation that if the laboratory-of-experiment argument were fully accepted, it would be hard to limit its conclusions to the protection of the internal mode of state governmental operations, as proposed by *National League of Cities,* and not to apply them to the states' control over the private sector. After all, to take the facts of *National League of Cities* as an example, the imposition of minimum-wage requirements for private hospitals reduces the possibility of state experimentation (to say nothing of private experimentation) in this area no less than in the case of public hospitals. Indeed, the very possibility of federal preemption of the regulation of any field of private activity decreases the possibility of state-introduced innovation. Thus, unless we are seriously prepared to consider reversing the long tradition of the Commerce Clause jurisprudence and go back to the idea of preserving some areas of exclusive state regulation, the laboratory-of-experiment argument proves too much.

On closer scrutiny, however, the laboratory-of-experiment argument may turn out to prove not too much but too little. * * * There are, in fact, a number of different considerations that have only rarely been taken into account in assessing the laboratory-of-experiment argument but without which its validity cannot be ascertained. The following list is probably incomplete, but it may suffice to force a reconsideration:

a). If, as has been argued, the states are political units that may have their justification in history but do not necessarily correspond to the economic and social realities of contemporary America, then the forces that determine the direction of local policies may be much less than ideally suited to foster the most efficient governmental solutions. A central government possessed of a power to reshuffle the boundaries and powers of its territorial subdivisions could perhaps produce much better (more efficient) local administration.

b). State regulation is often likely to have spillover effects on other states and produce inefficient solutions by ignoring the costs borne by outsiders. Again, a central government may tailor its delegations of regulatory powers to jurisdictions designed to minimize such externalities.

c). States will often compete with one another for various resources, such as capital, which can move relatively easily to those jurisdictions that offer them the most favorable conditions. As a byproduct of this rivalry, however, states may have to forego many redistributive and social programs that make the cost of doing business higher. * * * A central government capable of devising national solutions can afford to be much more innovative in such situations.

d). The costs involved in certain types of innovative regulatory activity (such as the costs of collecting and transmitting information or administering a program) may be too high for a local government to bear, but economies of scale on the national level may make regulations more cost effective. * * *

e). Related to the previous point is the question of incentives that local elective politicians may have, as compared to a professional looking to improve his career prospects in a national bureaucratic hierarchy. * * * First, unlike a competitive economic market, the federal system does not allow a local official to "sell" his product (i.e., to gain additional votes) outside his jurisdiction, and this limits his incentive to innovate. Second, the fact that beneficiaries of governmental innovation do not, as a rule, move from one jurisdiction to another, so as to find the one in which the government's willingness to take risks matches their own preferences, the politician's "portfolio" of governmental projects will tend to cater to the risk preferences of those around the population median (rather than gravitating toward more risky innovations). Third, the possibility of free riding on the innovative solutions of other jurisdictions further reduces a politician's incentive to take new and more risky paths. Compared to that, a career bureaucrat, looking to the approval of his superiors and the effects of his work in a well-designed national hierarchy of administrators may (though, of course, only may) have a system of incentives more favorable to innovation.

f). Finally, the advantages of uniformity may often outweigh the benefits of local innovation, even if some local solutions may have more intrinsic merit. Thus, for example, all states, except for Louisiana, have recognized the advantages of adopting the Uniform Commercial Code. But similar advantages to commerce could perhaps accrue from a uniformity in at least parts of tort or insurance law. Again, a central government, not subject to local political or constitutional constraints, could probably be much more efficient in this respect.

The considerations just listed do not, of course, mean that the function of the states as the laboratories of experiment is entirely illusory. They do mean, however, that the question of how to structure the division of competences among different levels of government to achieve the most desirable degree of innovation and efficiency is a very complex one and that the answer to it hinges on a variety of empirical and constantly shifting factors. It is thus quite likely that some forms of unitary government, with a flexible system of delegation that would not be limited by constitutional provisions concerning the structure of local authorities, could accommodate much better the demands of governmental efficiency than our own federal system. * * *

* * *

FUTURE DOCTRINAL DEVELOPMENTS

The outcome of my discussion is that the process-oriented analysis of the constitutional functions of federalism, endorsed but not really carried out in the *Garcia* decision, leads to a more affirmative procedural role of the states within the federal system than suggested on the face of Justice Blackmun's opinion. Also, two important functions of the states—tyranny prevention and the provision of a space for participatory politics—are likely to be endangered by the national government and warrant a close judicial scrutiny of federal interference with state and local governmental operations. To some extent, then, my analysis confirms the accuracy of the insights implicit in *National League of Cities* by showing that its insistence on the protection of the political process of local governments, rather than on a guarantee of some exclusive state controls over the private sector, responded to the most fundamental desiderata of federalism, while also showing that some of these insights need not be viewed as incompatible with the *Garcia* approach.

Nevertheless, developing a constitutional theory of federalism does not automatically translate into a clear judicial doctrine specifying a set of genuinely manageable standards of review. In fact, it is the problematic character of such standards that occupies the bulk of the Court's opinion in *Garcia* and the unmanageability of the "traditional governmental functions" test laid down by *National League of Cities* seems to have been one of the main reasons for its overruling. What needs to be seen is whether the theory of federalism I have articulated can provide more reliable guidance for judicial application.

* * * *Garcia*'s merciless critique of the criterion of tradition seems to evince a desire for watertight, mechanical tests of protected governmental functions that simply cannot be had in an area as complex as that of federalism. Constitutional adjudication is not, after all, a field in which simple standards predominate, and there can be no substitute for a painful case-by-case refinement and elaboration. Still, there are a number of ways in which the concerns of federalism may be intelligibly used as a guide for judicial review.

First, there are some state governmental functions so directly related to the federalist concern with preventing tyranny that they present rather easy cases for judicial intervention (though perhaps they are also, at this moment, the least likely to meet with serious interference). Under any approach, for example, federal interference with the agenda of the highest state legislative and executive organs is likely to undermine the overall autonomy of the political processes in the states and eliminate their constitutional role within the federal system. Similarly, an interference with the state electoral processes, insofar as it is not clearly related to the protection of individual rights but threatens to gerrymander the local districts in order to change the configuration of political forces in favor of the nationally powerful interests, would be clearly beyond the pale. A gradual subordination of state police forces to a federal command structure would cripple the states' ability to enforce their basic choices and resist tyrannical pressures from above. A radical limitation of the states' ability to tax would make their fiscal solvency a matter of federal grace and ultimately make a mockery of the federalist concerns.

It may be a little harder to come up with equally clearly unconstitutional instances of federal interference with the states' function of enhancing participation, especially since, as I have noted, it is mostly not the state governments themselves but rather their local emanations that provide the primary locus of direct citizen involvement in the political life in America. Even here, though, there may be clear enough cases. For example, given the special participatory mode in which school boards operate in most states, a federal education law that would attempt to transform those boards into an extension of the federal bureaucratic machinery would strike at the very core of participatory politics in the United States.

Furthermore, it would be a mistake to think that cordoning off some areas of state governments from federal interference is the only possible method of implementing the principles of federalism. After all, if it is not the protection of state sovereignty that is at stake here but rather the basic functions of the states within the federal system, it is quite likely that the nature of the central intervention itself should be more determinative of its constitutionality than the local activity interfered with. Thus, for example, many federal laws that depend on state governmental machinery for their implementation attempt, though usually with only very modest success, to assure that the states open the administrative process to citizen involvement. Insofar as such programs attempt to open up state politics to citizen participation, without undermining those aspects of local representative systems that may be important to preventing tyranny, they may be subject to a looser form of control than laws that have the opposite effect. Similarly, federal laws that provide reimbursements for costs imposed on local governments may be more acceptable than those that constitute a serious drain on state fiscal resources.

Finally, although *National League of Cities* concentrated exclusively on federal interference through a system of direct commands to local governments, federalist concerns also have some implications with respect to national action under the spending power. The common issue that is bound to arise in both contexts, but which was left unanalyzed by *National League of Cities* and its progeny, is the question of when the states are unconstitutionally induced by the national government into something that may impair their ability to fulfill their constitutional functions. In the context of the Commerce Clause, the question arose in *FERC v. Mississippi* as a result of Justice Blackmun's intimation that if the federal government had the power to preempt the states from the field of utility regulation, it could also condition its permission for the states to engage in the regulation of utilities on their acceptance of federally mandated standards and procedures. The ostensible explanation was that since the states were free to withdraw from the field altogether, they were not coerced by the federal requirements. Justice O'Connor's dissent in *FERC* disputed this approach but gave no real criteria for distinguishing incentives from coercion. It is this issue that becomes central when *National League of Cities'* concern with the federal coercion of the states is carried over to spending power legislation, which constitutes the national government's main tool of securing state compliance with its demands. The reason why federalist concerns are usually ignored in the judicial review of spending power legislation is primarily related to the claim that the states are free to refuse to participate in the federal spending programs and thus are not really coerced into anything.[187] Nevertheless, while emphasis on the consent given by the states to the various conditions in federal grants (often quite unrelated to the purposes of the grant itself) may comport quite well with the idea of state sovereignty, the states' consent is often likely to be free in a rather Pickwickian sense. Even apart from coercion, the emphasis on consent may sometimes raise serious questions under the process analysis developed here. Even if the states should "consent" to measures that weaken their organizational capacity to resist tyrannical pressures from the national government or their ability to protect local participatory institutions, it is not clear that the Constitution allows the federal government to undermine its own democratic character by proposing such measures.

H. JEFFERSON POWELL, THE OLDEST QUESTION OF CONSTITUTIONAL LAW

79 Va.L.Rev. 633, 634–635, 639–642, 644–646, 650–651, 665–675 (1993).

From the New Deal until the mid–1970s, the political branches of the federal government acted on the assumption, invariably confirmed by the Supreme Court, that there is no "legal substance, [no] core of constitutional right" limiting national power in the interests of federalism. When the Court undertook, in *National League of Cities v. Usery*,[3] to derive an "implied limitation on the federal powers" * * * its decision was subjected to a roar of criticism from the academy, rapid trivialization by the Court itself, and (only nine years later) explicit rejection in *Garcia v. San Antonio Metropolitan Transit Authority*.[6]

The Court's opinion in *Garcia* reinstituted and rendered explicit the New Deal rejection of federalism as a legal principle. According to the Court, "the principal means chosen by the Framers to ensure the role of the States in the federal system lies in the structure of the Federal Government itself" rather than in judicially crafted "conceptions of state sovereignty." * * * *Garcia* concluded that American federalism has a political basis but not a legal one.

It would have been surprising if *Garcia* had actually concluded the debate on what Justice Sandra Day O'Connor recently described as

---

187. This doctrine was spelled out in Steward Machine Co. v. Davis, 301 U.S. 548 (1937). Somewhat paradoxically, the Court elaborated its doctrine concerning the states' unconditional freedom at about the same time as it started to doubt the old

Lochner wisdom that regulating hours of work was an abridgement of the workers' freedom of contract.

3. 426 U.S. 833 (1976)[.]

6. 469 U.S. 528 (1985).

"perhaps our oldest question of constitutional law": the underlying basis for "the proper division of authority between the Federal Government and the States." In *New York v. United States* [12] the Supreme Court has reopened the debate. The Court's opinion, written by O'Connor, seeks to reconcile post-New Deal concepts of national power with the existence of legal limitations on that power derived from federalism. The Court noted that "[t]he Constitution ... 'leaves to the several States a residuary and inviolable sovereignty'" and concluded that "[w]hatever the outer limits of that sovereignty may be, one thing is clear: The Federal Government may not compel the States to enact or administer a federal regulatory program."

* * *

* * * The need to "discern[ ] the proper division of authority between the Federal Government and the States," as *New York v. United States* observed, is * * * a question that is often extremely difficult to answer satisfactorily. The answer Justice O'Connor proposes can be evaluated adequately only if we set it in the context of earlier attempts to solve the problems of federalism. Over the Constitution's two centuries of existence a variety of approaches to the issue have been proposed. Perhaps unsurprisingly, most of the possible options were advanced early in the Republic's history.

1. THE NATIONALISTIC REJECTION OF A LAW OF FEDERALISM

Perhaps the simplest resolution of the question of federalism is the one the Anti–Federalists claimed was implicit in the Constitution's text: The United States has no legally enforceable federal structure even if as a political matter American government is arranged in a federal manner. * * *

* * *

[F]rom the New Deal to *National League of Cities* the Supreme Court in effect accepted th[is] position by denying the existence of implied federalism limits on national power, a denial substantially revived by *Garcia*. * * *

2. THE TEXTUAL ENUMERATION OF FEDERAL POWERS

The most obvious approach to devising a meaningful law of federalism is to take seriously the Constitution's enumeration of federal powers as a definition of what the federal government may, and by implication may not, do. The relevance of the constitutional text to federalism was the centerpiece of one of the earliest pieces of sustained interpretation of the Constitution—Secretary of State Thomas Jefferson's 1791 cabinet opinion on the constitutionality of the national bank bill Congress had presented to President Washington. * * * The bank bill, Jefferson wrote, was not justified by the taxing power, the power to borrow, the commerce power, Article I's reference to "the general welfare," or the Necessary and Proper Cause.

12. [112 S.Ct. 2408 (1992).]

Jefferson characterized the claim that a national bank would be a useful means toward achieving the purposes of Congress' enumerated powers as a covert argument for congressional omnicompetence. On such reasoning any legislative choice of "means" could be justified, "for there is not one which ingenuity may not torture into a convenience in some instance or other, to some one of so long a list of enumerated powers. It would swallow up all the delegated powers and reduce the whole to one power...." A strict construction of the Constitution's textual definitions of federal power was necessary, Jefferson told Washington, to avoid rendering federalism an empty shell: "To take a single step beyond the boundaries thus specially drawn around the powers of Congress is to take possession of a boundless field of power, no longer susceptible of any definition."

* * *

* * * It might seem puzzling * * * that neither *National League of Cities* nor *New York v. United States* has proposed reviving textual construction of congressional power as a means of reviving the law of federalism. Why? The answer, I suggest, is that there are, or the Justices perceive there to be, insuperable obstacles to a repristination of the federalism of Jefferson's bank opinion[.]

* * * The whole history of the Court's use of limiting textual construction between the beginning of extensive congressional legislation and the New Deal repudiation of the enterprise was marked by rapid swings between generous and pinched readings of congressional powers. Even a sympathetic observer might well conclude that decisions about the proper scope and employment of federal powers are so inherently legislative and policy-driven that even a good-faith judicial attempt to make them inevitably collapses the judicial function into Congress'. Equally important is the social reality that virtually all political groups and persuasions want broad national powers wielded on behalf of their desired objectives. * * *

3. STATES' IMMUNITIES AS CONSTITUTIONAL RIGHTS

* * * [A] second historical strategy for articulating a viable law of federalism has been to discern in the Constitution certain immunities or "rights" protecting states from federal exercises of authority that are within the enumerated powers.

* * * The heyday of state-immunities thought as a protection for federalism was the early twentieth century, when the Court on several occasions used the Tenth Amendment or implied federalism principles to invalidate federal legislation. *United States v. Butler*[190] is a classic example of this approach to articulating a law of federalism. *Butler* involved the constitutionality of the Agricultural Adjustment Act of 1933, which provided subsidies for farmers who agreed to limit their

---

190. 297 U.S. 1 (1936), implicitly over-   U.S. 548 (1937).
ruled by Steward Machine Co. v. Davis, 301

production and thus reduce farm surpluses that it was believed were lowering farm revenues. The Court rejected the Madisonian argument that Congress' power to spend was limited to expenditures in pursuit of objects enumerated in Article I, Section 8, and the majority essentially conceded that the Act's expenditures were within the scope of the "general welfare" requirement. The Court nevertheless held the Act unconstitutional because it transgressed "another principle embedded in our Constitution[:] ... the reserved rights of the states." The power "to regulate and control agricultural production" was reserved to the states, and thus its proper sphere of operation must be immune from federal intrusion. * * *

National League of Cities was an attempt to revive the state-immunities-based law of federalism exemplified by *Butler*. The Court stated that a certain sphere of "traditional government functions" was protected from direct federal regulation—even that within the affirmative scope of the commerce power—by an immunity parallel to an individual's Fifth or Sixth Amendment rights. But *National League of Cities*, like *Butler* before it, was swiftly overruled[.]

The Supreme Court's failure to adopt and apply consistently a state-immunities approach as a legal basis of federalism results largely from the same factors that have repeatedly led it to abandon textual construction as a limit on congressional power. Judicial declarations that certain exercises of federal power run afoul of a state immunity, like decisions that hold congressional actions to lie beyond Congress' textual mandate, create a " 'sacred province of state autonomy.' " A state-immunities doctrine thus is equally contrary to the enormous political pressure to employ federal authority to address matters of concern to national political majorities. Similarly, the courts' historical record in employing state-immunities concepts gives little ground for confidence that the approach can be followed consistently or that its results can be distinguished from the imposition of judicial policy preferences. * * *

The state-immunities approach suffers from an additional problem[:] it is entirely unguided by constitutional text, and the inferences it seeks to draw from constitutional structure are equivocal. Finally, the state-immunities approach suffers from a historical association with slavery, racial segregation, and ethnic oppression that creates a legitimate concern over its potential implications. * * *

4. [THE] AUTONOMY OF PROCESS PRINCIPLE

Justice O'Connor's federalism * * * is not a contemporary restatement of the founders' views, and it does not follow either of the two historically common paths for devising a law of federalism.[a] O'Connor's approach consists primarily of two building blocks: first, that the federal government must respect state governments as the seat of autonomous legislative processes even where the federal government has the power completely to preempt state regulation; and, second, that under *M'Cul-*

---

a. The text included in this section has been relocated. [Eds.]

loch v. Maryland the judiciary has the duty to police Congressional encroachment on the autonomy of the states in obedience to the spirit of the Tenth Amendment. With *New York v. United States,* that approach has become law.

Justice O'Connor constructed the first of these building blocks in a very early opinion, her partial dissent in *FERC v. Mississippi.*[31] *FERC* involved a challenge to the constitutionality of certain provisions of the Public Utility Regulatory Policies Act of 1978. The State of Mississippi and its public utilities commission argued that several of the Act's provisions infringed federalism principles by exceeding federal power under the Commerce Clause and by violating the Tenth Amendment. These provisions mandated that state regulatory bodies in certain circumstances adjudicate disputes arising under the Act, that state utilities commissions consider specified ratemaking standards, and that the commissions follow specified notice and comment procedures in considering the proposed standards. [This was Justice O'Connor's reaction:]

> State legislative and administrative bodies are not field offices of the national bureaucracy. Nor are they think tanks to which Congress may assign problems for extended study. Instead, each State is sovereign within its own domain, governing its citizens and providing for their general welfare. While the Constitution and federal statutes define the boundaries of that domain, they do not harness state power for national purposes.

By imposing a federal agenda on state regulators, even if only as a set of mandatory considerations, the Act "conscript[s] state utility commissions into the national bureaucratic army" in violation of *National League of Cities* and "the values of federalism." Thus emerged the first building block of O'Connor's federalism: federalism requires that the federal government respect the autonomy of state governments as the possessors of independent institutional processes, even when Congress legislates in an area in which it has the constitutional authority completely to preempt state choices. This principle, which I shall call the "autonomy of process principle," functions to restrict the choices open to the federal government. Congress must choose either to bar state regulation of a field altogether, or to allow states to act as they please within the autonomy granted to them.

Justice O'Connor rested the autonomy of process principle on [four arguments:] (1) Straightforward federal preemption, O'Connor pointed out, permits states "free to exercise their power in other areas" to "devote their resources elsewhere." The Act's requirements, in contrast, absorbed state resources in the consideration of federal concerns and in adherence to federal procedures. (2) Federal "conscription" of state agencies "blurs the lines of political accountability" by making it unclear whether the state administrators were acting on their own or as servants of Congress. (3) Congressional control of state agency agendas "undermines the most valuable aspects of our federalism," the freedom

---

31. 456 U.S. 742, 775 (1982). * * *

of individual states to act as "laboratories" for governmental experimentation and as localized opportunities for participation in self-government. (4) Federal control of state governmental processes upsets "the balance of power" between federal and state authority "that buttresses our basic liberties" by diffusing power.

* * *

* * * Three years later, in her dissent in *Garcia,* O'Connor provided a justification for judicial interference, and the second building block in her conception of federalism.

* * *

Garcia implicated the autonomy of process principle of *FERC* only marginally. The federal statute at issue directly mandated congressional policy concerning wages and hours and affected the states only as employers * * *. O'Connor directed most of her attention, therefore, to the problem of reconciling the vast powers wielded by the post-New Deal federal government with a viable law of federalism. O'Connor's starting point was a clear statement of her acceptance of the "breathtaking expansion of the powers of Congress" in the modern era. As she noted, "the Framers of our Constitution intended Congress to have sufficient power to address national problems." * * *

[But, a]lthough the Constitution's goal of national empowerment renders legitimate the modern expansion of the commerce power, the expansion of the commerce power threatens to swallow up the Constitution's goal of preserving federalism. How can the Court recognize Congress' legislative discretion to address the nation's problems using the means Congress finds appropriate while at the same time fulfilling its "constitutional responsibility to oversee the Federal Government's compliance with its duty to respect the legitimate interests of the States"? To resolve the puzzle, O'Connor suggested a return to *M'Culloch v. Maryland*—the judicial "source of the recent expansion of the commerce power." In *M'Culloch,* Chief Justice Marshall wrote the famous passage "Let the end be legitimate, let it be within the scope of the constitution, and all means which are appropriate, which are plainly adapted to that end, which are not prohibited, but consist with the letter and spirit of the constitution, are constitutional." O'Connor emphasized that Marshall had qualified his sweeping endorsement of congressional discretion to legislate beyond the letter of Article I with the caveat that congressional choices must be consistent with "the letter and spirit of the constitution."

Thus, as O'Connor reads *M'Culloch,* the Necessary and Proper Clause requires the judiciary to accord substantial respect to Congress' choice of means but also provides the constitutional mandate for judicial review of the propriety of that choice. Built into the very doctrinal basis for the "judicially crafted expansion" of federal power, O'Connor argued, is the judiciary's obligation "to enforce affirmative limits on federal regulation of the States" derived from the "*spirit* of the Tenth Amendment." Her subsequent discussion of how to apply that "spirit" in construing the validity of congressional legislation that impairs state autonomy echoed the autonomy of process principle of *FERC.* * * *

* * *

In *New York,* Justice O'Connor made clear that her federalism is primarily concerned with protecting the integrity of state processes rather than with creating a substantive realm of state legislative autonomy. Justice O'Connor drew a careful distinction between Congress' "substantial powers to govern the Nation directly, including in areas of intimate concern to the States," and the prohibited "ability to require the States to govern according to Congress' instructions." She repeated and amplified her historical argument for the autonomy of process principle and insisted that the Court has "always understood that even where Congress has the authority under the Constitution to pass laws requiring or prohibiting certain acts, it lacks the power directly to compel the States to require or prohibit those acts."

* * *

The decline of federalism and the rise of the omnicompetent national government in the United States have brought with them a variety of consequences. Many of these are viewed positively across a broad spectrum of American political opinion[.] But the elimination of federalism as a legal check on national power also has had less desirable aspects. The nationalization of American government, as one of its chief side effects, has been crucial in rendering democracy increasingly formal, as democracy's traditional corollaries of citizen participation and governmental responsibility become less obviously relevant to the national political process.

Americans tend to be sentimental about "democracy" and nostalgic about earlier eras of supposedly participatory, localized government. Behind the sentiment and nostalgia, however, lurk concerns with substance. Some social and political theorists see in the elimination of mediating structures between the privatized individual and the nation-state Leviathan a profound source of psychological and social alienation and conflict. It is often argued that various forms of participatory political action, necessarily actualized at the local, community level (if not only there) are badly needed in our society to combat these problems. "Strong democracy requires unmediated self-government by an engaged citizenry. It requires institutions that will involve individuals at both the neighborhood and the national level in common talk, common decision-making and political judgment, and common action." [249]

---

249. [Benjamin R. Barber, Strong De-   Age 261 (1984).]
mocracy: Participatory Politics for a New

Meaningful local government requires the existence of the powers of "initiation" and "immunity." [250] The power of initiation is the power to develop, consider, adopt, and implement policies that regulate and structure private-sector activities. "Without such powers, local government could hardly affect any private activity," and (we might add) can be of little interest except as a sort of debating society for those with free time. The power of immunity is the authority "to act however [the local governments] wish within the limits imposed by their initiative powers." The sort of conscription of state processes with which *New York v. United States* is concerned denies to the states both initiation and immunity. As Justice O'Connor wrote in her *FERC* opinion, federal preemption of an area of legislative concern means that "the States may simply devote their resources elsewhere." As a result, the states retain the power of initiation in areas Congress has not occupied, and their deliberative processes remain immune from federal control. The imposition of a congressional agenda on state institutions, on the other hand, "drains the inventive energy of state governmental bodies" by commandeering scarce resources of time, attention, and public concern. The states thus become "less able to pursue local proposals" because their lack of immunity from federal agenda-setting increasingly denies them the practical possibility of exercising whatever powers of initiation the national government has theoretically left undisturbed.

BIBLIOGRAPHY

Background Reading on the American Federal System

Beer, *Federalism, Nationalism, and Democracy in America,* 72 Am.Pol. Sci.Rev. 9 (1978).

S. Davis, THE FEDERAL PRINCIPLE, A JOURNEY THROUGH TIME IN QUEST OF A MEANING (1978).

Diamond, *The Federalist's View of Federalism,* in ESSAYS IN FEDERALISM 21 (Institute for Studies in Federalism, 1961).

D. Elazar, THE AMERICAN PARTNERSHIP (1962).

McConnell, *Federalism: Evaluating the Founders' Design,* 54 U.Chi. L.Rev. 1484 (1987).

W. Riker, FEDERALISM (1964).

Rose–Ackerman, *Does Federalism Matter? Political Choice in a Federal Republic,* 89 J. of Pol.Econ. 152 (1981).

Scheiber, *Federalism and the Constitution: The Original Understanding,* in L. Friedman & H. Scheiber, AMERICAN LAW AND THE CONSTITUTIONAL ORDER 85 (1978).

Storing, *What the Anti–Federalists Were For,* in H Storing, ed., THE COMPLETE ANTI–FEDERALIST (1981).

250. * * * Gordon L. Clark, Judges and   67–75 (1985)[.]
the Cities: Interpreting Local Autonomy

THE FEDERALIST, Nos. 10, 14, 39, 44–46, 51.

Tullock, *Federalism: Problems of Scale,* 6 Pub.Choice 19 (1969).

Tushnet, *Federalism and the Traditions of American Political Theory,* 19 Ga.L.Rev. 981 (1985).

Federal Regulatory and Fiscal Control of State Governments

Advisory Commission on Intergovernmental Relations, REGULATORY FEDERALISM: POLICY, PROCESS, IMPACT AND REFORM (1984).

Field, Garcia v. San Antonio Metropolitan Transit Authority: *The Demise of a Misguided Doctrine,* 99 Harv.L.Rev. 84 (1985).

Grodzins, *Centralization and Decentralization in the American Federal System,* in R. Goldwin, ed., A NATION OF STATES 1 (1963).

Heineman, *The Law Schools' Failing Grade on Federalism,* 92 Yale L.J. 1349 (1983).

D. Kettl, THE REGULATION OF AMERICAN FEDERALISM (1983).

LaPierre, *The Political Safeguards of Federalism Redux: Intergovernmental Immunity and the States as Agents of the Nation,* 60 Wash. U.L.Q. 779 (1982).

Nagel, *Federalism As A Fundamental Value: National League Of Cities In Perspective,* 1981 Sup.Ct.Rev. 81.

Post, *Chief Justice William Howard Taft and the Concept of Federalism,* 9 Const.Comm. 199 (1992).

M. Reagan, THE NEW FEDERALISM (1972).

Soifer, *Truisms That Never Will Be True: The Tenth Amendment and the Spending Power,* 57 Colo.L.Rev. 793 (1986).

Stewart, *Federalism and Rights,* 19 Ga.L.Rev. 917 (1985).

B. STATE POWER: REGULATION OF COMMERCE

Questions about the extent of national and state power in our federal system have been most thoroughly explored in the context of commercial regulation. The Commerce Clause gives Congress power

To regulate Commerce with foreign Nations, and among the several States, and with the Indian Tribes[.] (Art. I, § 8, cl. 3)

The Clause is silent about state power. The traditional question here has been whether it somehow limits state authority, even in its 'dormant' state (when Congress has not acted). During the past decade this problem has engaged the Court's attention as keenly as at any other period in our history.

The issue of state power has many facets. One is the source of the constitutional restraint (if there is one) on state action. How does the silence of the Commerce Clause speak to the issue of state power? Noel Dowling's article contends that it actually doesn't—that restraints flow from Congress's failure to act—a proposition disputed by Daniel Farber and Donald Regan. This issue is related to another curious facet of Commerce Clause jurisprudence which Dowling is at pains to explain: the fact that Congress can 'overrule' Supreme Court decisions about the commerce power of the states.[1] A third problem that has arisen with increasing frequency in recent years is the proper treatment of states when they act as participants in the market.[2] And a fourth is the proper role of the Article IV Privileges and Immunities Clause, which the Court has said shares the same "vision of federalism" as the Commerce Clause.[3]

These questions are important and difficult, but in the big picture of Commerce Clause litigation they are peripheral rather than central. The most significant issue still remains: what standards do (or should) the courts use to test constitutional claims about state regulation of commerce? The readings in this section are primarily about this issue. They suggest three different approaches. Dowling proposes a balancing test, and his argument has had great influence on the Supreme Court's decisions during the past half century. The Court now balances local benefits against burdens on commerce even when local and foreign trade are treated alike.[4] But more recent scholarship evinces great dissatisfaction with both the theory and the practice of balancing. Farber and Regan both reject that approach, and propose instead that we focus on intentional discrimination. Their reasons for this shift in focus differ, though. Farber believes that the courts should intervene when the political process is not working, and discrimination against unrepresented foreign interests is a signal that that is happening. Regan argues that a process approach is overbroad, and worse, inconsistent with fundamental assumptions about our federal system. He suggests instead an anti-protectionism principle.

NOEL T. DOWLING, INTERSTATE COMMERCE AND STATE POWER
27 Va.L.Rev. 1–6, 19–24 (1940).

PRIOR THEORIES

The views which have been entertained as to the effect of the commerce clause on state power may be summarized under four heads. Each of them has been held by the Court, or a number of Justices, at one time or another, and one of them contains in substance, as I will try to show, the desirable doctrine for the future. They are:

1. See, e.g., Prudential Insurance Co. v. Benjamin, 328 U.S. 408, 66 S.Ct. 1142, 90 L.Ed. 1342 (1946); In re Rahrer, 140 U.S. 545, 11 S.Ct. 865, 35 L.Ed. 572 (1891).

2. See, e.g., South–Central Timber Development v. Wunnicke, 467 U.S. 82, 104 S.Ct. 2237, 81 L.Ed.2d 71 (1984); Reeves, Inc. v. Stake, 447 U.S. 429, 100 S.Ct. 2271, 65 L.Ed.2d 244 (1980).

3. Hicklin v. Orbeck, 437 U.S. 518, 98 S.Ct. 2482, 57 L.Ed.2d 397 (1978).

4. Pike v. Bruce Church, Inc., 397 U.S. 137, 90 S.Ct. 844, 25 L.Ed.2d 174 (1970).

1. That the clause impliedly prohibits all state regulation or taxation of interstate commerce;

2. That the clause itself prohibits nothing, the states being free to regulate and tax as they see fit unless and until they are stopped by Congressional action;

3. That the clause prohibits some, but not all, state regulation and taxation—that is, sometimes it prohibits and sometimes it does not;

4. That though the clause itself prohibits nothing an impediment may arise from the express or implied will of Congress.

The first is of historical interest as that to which the Court inclined at the beginning.   In *Gibbons v. Ogden,* counsel contended that "as the word 'to regulate' implies in its nature full power over the thing to be regulated, it excludes, necessarily, the action of all others that would perform the same operation on the same thing," and further that "regulation is designed for the entire result, applying to those parts which remain as they were, as well as to those which are altered." "Great force" was conceded to this argument by Chief Justice Marshall, and the Court was "not satisfied that it has been refuted."   But it was unnecessary in that case to decide whether the power of the states was surrendered by the mere grant to Congress, or is retained until Congress shall exercise the power, for the reason that the power had been exercised, and the regulations which Congress deemed it proper to make were in full operation.   And the narrow holding was that the Act of Congress prevailed over the inconsistent regulation of the New York statute.   As to taxation, *Brown v. Maryland* all but committed the Court to the first view.   * * *

The second view is, in substance, the one expounded by Chief Justice Taney, particularly in the *License* cases.   Though his opinion did not win the support of a full majority of the Court, there was agreement in the conclusion to which it led.   In general, this view would remove the commerce clause from judicial consideration.   * * *

The third view, a compromise between the two earlier views, represents the first definite position taken by the Court on the commerce clause; and this occurred in *Cooley v. The Board of Wardens,* in 1851. In the course of the opinion the Court undertook to explain the cause of its prior diversities of opinion, saying that they arose "from the different views taken of the nature of the power."   But when, the Court added, the nature of a power like this is spoken of, when it is said that the nature of the power requires that it should be exercised exclusively by Congress, "it must be intended to refer to the subjects of that power, and to say they are of such a nature as to require exclusive legislation by Congress."   For the power to regulate commerce, the Court observed, embraces a vast field, containing not only many, but exceedingly various subjects, quite unlike in their nature; some imperatively demanding a single uniform rule, and some as imperatively demanding that diversity which alone can meet local necessities.   * * *

The fourth view may be described as a composite of the second and third, and a limited version of it was announced by the Court in 1890. It originally covered only interstate commerce in intoxicating liquors, though it was later enlarged. This view squares with the second in the sense that no prohibition inheres in the commerce clause itself, and it preserves the results of the third in that some state action would be upheld—*e.g.,* where "matters of local concern" are involved—and some overturned. Also it calls for the same kind of inquiry as under *Cooley v. The Board,* but with this difference in result: if the subject were held "national," a congressional negative would be presumed rather than a constitutional prohibition applied. This view admitted the power of Congress to exercise complete control in both fields: to supersede state action in local matters, to permit it in national. The significant and salutary effect was to take constitutional rigidity out of the commerce clause problem and substitute the flexible and adaptable will of Congress. At the same time it recognized a definite function for the courts in the ascertainment of that will.   * * *

In the intervening period up to 1938 no distinctive theory appears to have been formulated or urged. New terminology crept into the opinions, and the Court talked increasingly of "direct" and "indirect" effects or burdens on interstate commerce, the former being held invalid and the latter valid. The "direct-indirect" test had this much at least in common with *Cooley v. The Board,* that it upheld some and overturned other state action; but it was far from satisfying since it offered so little of a criterion for determining on which side a case would fall. Quarantine laws, for example, which hit interstate commerce head-on and stopped it dead in its tracks at the border, surely would have to be classed as "direct," yet they were sustained. The oleomargarine laws of Massachusetts had a no less direct impact on traffic than did Iowa's liquor laws, but Massachusetts won and Iowa lost.   * * *

* * *

WHAT OF THE FUTURE?

From what has gone before, a doctrine can be drawn which offers, I believe, desirable and helpful guidance for the Court in the future. It is, that in the absence of affirmative consent a Congressional negative will be presumed in the courts against state action which in its effect upon interstate commerce constitutes an unreasonable interference with national interests, the presumption being rebuttable at the pleasure of Congress. Such a doctrine would free the states from any constitutional disability but at the same time would not give them license to take such action as they see fit irrespective of its effect upon interstate commerce. With respect to such commerce, the question whether the states may act upon it would depend upon the will of Congress expressed in such form as it may choose. State action falling short of such interference would prevail unless and until superseded or otherwise nullified by Congressional action.

[Several] reasons support the foregoing:

1. The congressional consent aspect of the doctrine would entail no sharp break with the past, and its adoption would constitute the acceptance of some of the best efforts of the Court. * * * I have always thought that it was implicit in *Cooley v. The Board* [.] * * * [The] doctrine was slow in taking form and did not acquire definite proportions until *Leisy v. Hardin* in 1890. The fact that the Court's arrival at this position culminated a long consideration accentuates the burden upon those who would depart from it. * * *

2. The substantive standard embodied in the doctrine, "unreasonable interference with national interests," would commit the Court to no new or untried principle. It would, to be sure, involve an avowal that the Court is deliberately balancing national and local interests and making a choice as to which of the two *should* prevail. That, as I see the matter, is a policy judgment. But the test of reasonableness in interstate commerce cases is not the same as, for example, in due process cases. Additional factors are involved. In a sense, a state law must take the hurdle of due process before it comes to the interstate barrier. The blow post law case from Georgia affords a striking illustration. The requirement that trains slow down at crossings was deemed, as well as it can be gleaned from the report and with regard to the situation in Georgia, an appropriate and permissible means for securing safety of life and property notwithstanding the inconvenience to local traffic and to the companies. At that stage the judicial scales tipped in favor of the statute. But other factors thrown into the other side of the scales—*e.g.,* convenience and economy of time in through traffic, more efficient and less expensive operation of railway systems—tipped them back against the statute.[35]

As already indicated, *Cooley v. The Board* comprehended a certain balancing of state and national interests, though the Court did not go into the subject in detail. And it was just there, in an effort to discover the relevant considerations for answering the question whether the "national interest in maintaining freedom of commerce across state lines" has been infringed, that Mr. Justice Stone tackled the problem in his *Di Santo* dissent.[a] His approach in that opinion appears to be well calculated to produce a "realistic" judgment whether any given state action constitutes an unreasonable interference with national interests. * * * He essayed no exhaustive list, nor would he exclude such factors as the desirability of uniform regulation (the principal point of *Cooley v. The Board*); or the consequences to the state if its action were disallowed—how serious and widespread the evil and what the prospect for national action; or the intangible but nevertheless real benefits to be had from giving the people of the states the satisfaction of, and stimulus to responsibility from, home government as against distant government. And in order to bring all such considerations into the judicial forum, could not the rules of evidence be made more generous and elastic? It is true that the litigation is between private parties, but the issue touches

---

35. Seaboard Air Line R.R. v. Blackwell, 244 U.S. 319 (1917).

a. Di Santo v. Pennsylvania, 273 U.S. 34, 43 (1927).

the relative jurisdictions of nation and state. After all, this is statecraft in which the courts are engaged.

3. This doctrine would provide flexibility in the adjustment and accommodation of national and state interests, at the same time preserving the judicial and amplifying the legislative function. From the judicial point of view it would preserve a role which the Court, beginning with the leadership of Marshall, has worked out for itself and which has conspicuously contributed to the functioning of the federal system. That role brings to constitutional cases the best of the common law methods in the building up of principles from specific decisions. The trial courts would operate out on the front line, where the impact of state action on interstate commerce is first felt, and they could appraise at close range the conflicting state and national interests. Furthermore, the judicial sifting of the facts would have the manifest merit of sharpening the issues and facilitating legislative efforts in the event that Congress, dissatisfied with the judicial results, should desire to take corrective action of its own.

* * *

There is no assurance that the commerce problem would be as well handled by Congress alone as where both Congress and the courts participate in its solution. I say "would", drawing a distinction between what seems likely and what is theoretically possible. Congress is a big and heavy machine to set in motion, and its progress is sometimes impeded even when national interests of the highest order are at stake. Meanwhile much damage to interstate commerce, to say nothing of the otherwise amicable relationships among the states, might be caused by unrestrained state action. * * *

Even if Congress should accept the task it would not find it an easy one. It would have to labor with much of the same evidence that would be offered in the courts, as well as other matters bearing upon various phases of policy (including sheer political pressures); and perhaps more often than not the solution would have to be stated in general terms. And then, after all that were done, it is not at all unlikely that the whole thing would be thrown into the courts for final settlement, but with this difference, that whereas formerly the courts could turn to the judicially developed principles and feel their way along, henceforth they would have to interpret and apply new and general formulas from Congress.

DANIEL A. FARBER, STATE REGULATION AND THE DORMANT COMMERCE CLAUSE
3 Con.Comm. 395–406, 410–414 (1986).

The Court's current view of the so-called "dormant" commerce clause, in a nutshell, is as follows. State regulations having a discriminatory effect on interstate commerce are subject to stringent judicial scrutiny even if the discrimination was inadvertent. On the other hand, regulations that burden interstate commerce without discriminating against it are subject to a less rigorous balancing test: a state law that burdens local and interstate commerce equally will be upheld if the law's local benefits outweigh the burden on commerce.

This doctrine is said to serve two purposes: preventing discrimination against outsiders who are not represented in the state's political process, and furthering the national interest in free trade among the states.[8] In the last decade, the Court has become increasingly aggressive in its pursuit of these goals. * * *

* * *

THE COURT'S CURRENT APPROACH

In understanding the Supreme Court's current approach, it is useful to distinguish among three types of cases. The first type involves intentional discrimination against interstate commerce. *City of Philadelphia v. New Jersey* illustrates the Court's approach to such statutes. New Jersey faced a serious shortage of landfill space. To conserve existing space as long as possible, the legislature prohibited the importation of waste from other states for disposal in New Jersey. The Supreme Court found this legislation unconstitutional on its face. "[W]hatever New Jersey's ultimate purpose, it may not be accomplished by discriminating against articles of commerce coming from outside the State unless there is some reason, apart from their origin, to treat them differently." Thus, intentional discrimination against interstate commerce is generally prohibited.

Even when discrimination is unintentional, state laws are subject to substantial scrutiny, as illustrated by *Hunt v. Washington State Apple Advertising Commission*. Federal law provided a system of grades to be used in labeling apples. North Carolina prohibited the use of any other grades on labels. The suit was brought by Washington apple growers, who contended that the Washington grading system was superior and that the ban on use of these grades impaired the marketability of their apples. The law did not on its face discriminate against interstate commerce. The discriminatory effect on Washington apples was enough, however, to subject the law to heightened scrutiny. Given this discriminatory effect, the state had the burden to "justify it both in terms of the local benefits flowing from the statute and the unavailability of nondiscriminatory alternatives adequate to preserve the local interests at stake." The state was unable to carry this burden.

Even a statute with neither a discriminatory purpose nor a discriminatory effect may be unconstitutional. The leading case on commerce

---

8. Another rationale sometimes used is that the Court is implementing what it believes to be the unexpressed will of Congress. That is, congressional silence is assumed to demonstrate an intention to place restrictions on the states. *See* Dowling, [*Interstate Commerce and State Power,* 27 Va.L.Rev. 1 (1940).] The obvious flaw in this concept is that congressional silence, in the end, means only that Congress has not decided to legislate. Interpreting what Congress means when it has spoken is often difficult enough; to determine what Congress means when it has said nothing at all is impossible.

clause review of non-discriminatory statutes is *Pike v. Bruce Church, Inc.*
Pike involved an Arizona statute governing cantaloupe packing. A state
official claimed that enforcement of this law required that the canta-
loupes be packed inside the state, which would have required the
company to build an expensive new packing shed. The Court began its
constitutional analysis with a synthesis of the previous case law:

> Although the criteria for determining the validity of state statutes
> affecting interstate commerce have been variously stated, the gener-
> al rule that emerges can be phrased as follows: Where the statute
> regulates evenhandedly to effectuate a legitimate local public inter-
> est, and its effects on interstate commerce are only incidental, it will
> be upheld unless the burden imposed on such commerce is clearly
> excessive in relation to the putative local benefits. If a legitimate
> local purpose is found, then the question becomes one of degree.
> And the extent of the burden that will be tolerated will of course
> depend on the nature of the local interest involved, and on whether
> it could be promoted as well with a lesser impact on interstate
> activities. Occasionally the Court has candidly undertaken a bal-
> ancing approach in resolving these issues, but more frequently it has
> spoken in terms of "direct" and "indirect" effects and burdens.

The state requirement under consideration in *Pike* did not survive this
balancing test. Since *Pike,* the balancing test has been applied to a
variety of subjects ranging from state corporation laws to highway safety
regulations.

The *Pike* test is to some extent rigged against the state. A state law
may create benefits as well as burdens for outsiders. The burdens are
weighed against the state, but any beneficial effect on interstate commerce is not weighed. *Pike,* in other words, establishes a judicial cost-
benefit analysis in which all of the costs of a state law are counted, but
only some of the benefits.

The Court's current approach has been subjected to strong scholarly
criticism. To begin with, results in dormant commerce clause cases are
notoriously unpredictable. This is particularly true of the *Pike* test,
which requires an ad hoc balancing based on the trial record in each
case. For example, even after a Wisconsin truck regulation was struck
down, no one could be sure of the validity of a similar Iowa regulation
until the Court ruled, since the records in the two cases differed.[29]

The more fundamental flaw in the current approach is that it places
the Court in the position of evaluating economic policy. Under *Pike,* as
Professor Kitch has observed,

> The question, in other words, is not whether the regulation or tax is
> or is not on interstate commerce. The question is whether, all
> things considered—including the national interest—the tax or regu-
> lation of commerce, interstate or not, is good or bad. This ap-

---

29. *See* [Kassel v. Consolidated Freight-   mond Motor Transp., Inc. v. Rice], 434 U.S.
ways Corp.], 450 U.S. 662 (1981); [Ray-   [429 (1978).]

proach, of course, has a close kinship with the now discredited substantive due process of cases like *Lochner v. New York,* 198 U.S. 45 (1905). The Court abandoned substantive due process in the 1930s, but the method has lived on in Commerce Clause matters * * *.

In one recent case, for example, the Court heavily stressed the virtues of the unregulated free market in allocating resources to their best use. The Court may be right, but many people share Justice Holmes's skepticism about assertions that the Constitution embodies particular economic theories. * * * Justices Black and Douglas argued cogently against a predecessor of the *Pike* test on just this ground.[34]

* * *

REFORMULATING THE JUDICIAL ROLE

* * *

Establishing the proper standard for judicial review under the dormant commerce clause requires first that the purposes of judicial review be determined. At various times, the Supreme Court has relied on two quite different justifications for judicial review under the commerce clause. One justification relates to the political process; the other relates to substantive constitutional values.

The process rationale is based on the lack of representation for non-residents in the political process. At least since *Carolene Products*[43] it has been a commonplace that judicial review is most defensible when it compensates for a defect in the political process. The paradigm is judicial protection of minority groups under the equal protection clause. Like racial minorities during much of our history, out-of-state residents lack political representation and thus the democratic process may fail fully to safeguard their interests.

This process rationale does provide some justification for reviewing at least some state legislation. In particular, it may justify review of state legislation that discriminates against interstate commerce. But it falls well short of justifying the extent of judicial review allowed under current doctrine. In particular, lack of political representation hardly justifies the *Pike* test. Under *Pike,* completely non-discriminatory legislation that burdens non-residents is subject to judicial review. Since the burden on non-residents is the same as that on residents, however, the state's political process seems to offer adequate protection.

Therefore, any justification for the Court's current approach must rely on substance rather than process. The Court has often referred to the important constitutional value of free trade. On close examination, however, this value does not justify expansive judicial review. Admittedly, concern about discriminatory state trade barriers was important in motivating the adoption of the Constitution in general and the commerce

34. Southern Pacific Co. v. Arizona, 325 U.S. 761, 784, 795 (1945). * * *

43. United States v. Carolene Products Co., 304 U.S. 144 (1938).

clause in particular. But no evidence exists that the clause was intended of its own force to institute free trade, or that the courts were authorized to supervise state legislation. Indeed, two strong arguments can be made against finding a judicially enforceable value of "free trade" in the clause.

First, to paraphrase Justice Stevens, "there is only one commerce clause." It is well settled that Congress may not only erect trade barriers of its own, but may also freely authorize the states to do so. If the clause embodied a constitutional preference for free trade, then allowing Congress to use the commerce power to restrict trade would be as perverse as using the first amendment as a basis for censorship. The breadth of congressional power long recognized by the Court seems to be in tension with the view that the clause established free trade as a substantive constitutional goal.

Second, even finding a free-trade value in the clause would not in itself justify a judicial role in enforcing that value. Various portions of article I seem directed at achieving a wide variety of goals, from national security to technological progress. Yet no one thinks these clauses create any warrant for a judge-made body of law directed at these goals. Thus, justifying current doctrine requires an explanation of why a grant of power to Congress has the effect of authorizing judicial review of state legislation, when Congress has not acted. One traditional justification is that Congress simply cannot keep up with the myriad of relatively insignificant state barriers to free trade. Even if the dubious factual premise of this argument is granted, its logic is flawed. The limitations of the other branches do not necessarily imply a correlative judicial power to fill the need. The Constitution places several express limitations on forms of state economic regulation that the framers found undesirable. Rather than place such a limitation on state incursions into free trade, the framers simply made free trade one of the many aspects of "general welfare" entrusted to Congress.

The process approach has recently received strong support from the Supreme Court in another federalism-related context. In *National League of Cities v. Usery,* the Court had taken upon itself the duty of protecting a substantive value (state sovereignty) without any express textual basis. In *Garcia v. San Antonio Metropolitan Transit Authority,* the Court overruled *National League of Cities.* As the *Garcia* Court explained, judicial intervention is proper only when the federal legislative process is inadequate to protect the interests of the states. The Court found no such flaw in the legislative process behind the extension of the federal minimum wage to state employees. If process theory is to determine the extent of judicial protection of the states, it seems equally applicable when determining judicial limitations on state powers. The teaching of *Garcia* is that, absent a textual limitation, protection for federalism-related values is to be found in the political process, with judicial intervention only when that process has broken down. By the same reasoning, the dormant commerce clause should be limited to its process rationale.

Under this interpretation, the dormant commerce clause serves a function much like that of the equal protection clause. Both protect politically disenfranchised groups. Yet the scope of protection under the two existing doctrines is quite different. Under current law, interstate businesses receive far more protection from state legislation than do racial minorities. A business can establish a prima facie claim under the commerce clause by showing either discriminatory intent, a disparate impact, or a substantial burden. But a law imposing a substantial burden on a racial minority is not considered suspect; even a disparate impact on the minority is not enough. Instead, minority groups must prove discriminatory intent.

Is this radical difference in doctrine justifiable? Since judicial action under the commerce clause is subject to congressional override, it is less undemocratic than judicial action under the equal protection clause. Arguably, therefore, a more freewheeling form of review is appropriate under the commerce clause.

While in isolation this argument may sound strong, powerful arguments can be made that review under the commerce clause is much *less* needed than protection of minorities. Typically, government actions that burden interstate commerce also adversely affect many state residents. For example, if outside firms are barred from entering a state market, consumers lose the benefit of the competition and pay higher prices. These consumers may not be as well organized politically as local business lobbies, but they are not completely lacking in political power. Furthermore, multistate firms may often be important in a state's domestic economy, giving them the opportunity to exert pressure on the government. Finally, even if they lack votes, interstate businesses have the other vital ingredient of political influence: money.

Thus, while the harm done to the democratic process by judicial review under the commerce clause is perhaps less, the justification for judicial review is also weaker. On balance, it is hard to see any justification for providing substantially greater judicial protection to interstate businesses than to racial minorities.

* * *

The contrast between equal protection law and commerce clause law is illustrated by two cases. In one, *Dean Milk v. City of Madison,* Madison passed a law forbidding the sale of milk imported from more than twenty-five miles away, and requiring pasteurization plants to be located within five miles of town. Obviously, the burden fell on Wisconsin farmers outside the Madison area as much as on out-of-state farmers. Yet the Court struck down the law as facially discriminatory. In contrast, *Personnel Administrator v. Feeney* involved a Massachusetts law giving an employment preference to veterans, who were, with few exceptions, men. Just as the Wisconsin law excluded many in-state farmers and all out-of-state farmers, the Massachusetts law excluded many men and virtually all women. But in *Feeney* the Court found no reason to subject the law to heightened scrutiny as a form of gender discrimination. After all, there was no demonstrated intent to discriminate against women, and the impact on a large group of men provided a political check on the legislature.

In *Dean,* the existence of discrimination was considered so serious as to create almost a per se finding of invalidity, while in *Feeney* there was not even enough discrimination to subject the legislation to serious judicial scrutiny. Under the approach suggested in this section, *Dean* would be decided differently. In the absence of a finding of intent to exclude non-residents from the market, the mere existence of an exclusionary effect would be irrelevant.

* * *

OVERCOMING DOCTRINAL INERTIA

* * *

* * * Even if current doctrine is weak as a matter of legal theory, it still might be worth retaining if it served an important practical function. The Court has often proclaimed the importance of the dormant commerce clause in maintaining the national economy. If indeed current doctrine were important to the health of the economy, conceptual purity might have to give way to practical necessity.

In reality, however, vigorous judicial review is probably not needed to keep states from blockading the national economy. Other powerful safeguards exist. Historically, state legislation has been judicially reviewed under the commerce clause on the basis that Congress cannot be expected to trouble itself with minor matters. This argument has lost whatever validity it may once have had, as Congress has shown itself willing and able to preempt burdensome state legislation.

Although Congress formerly met only for short sessions, and therefore may have had time only for the most pressing matters of national concern, clearly that is no longer true. In particular, burdens on commerce that are important enough to justify action by the Court are also likely to be important enough to prompt congressional action. For instance, after the Court's repeated bouts with the issue of truck length on interstate highways, Congress acted to settle the issue.[103]

Since Congress can correct judicial mistakes, what is ultimately at stake under the dormant commerce clause is the burden of inertia. Should the states or interstate businesses have the burden of getting congressional action? In allocating this burden, it is useful to consider which party is more likely to get judicial mistakes corrected. The very reason for giving the power to regulate interstate commerce to Congress, rather than to state legislatures, is that Congress is more responsive to the national interest and less responsive to parochial interests. If so, those claiming to represent the national interest should be better able to

---

103. *See Kassel,* 450 U.S. 662 (1981); *Rice,* 434 U.S. 429 (1978); *Surface Transportation Assistance Act of 1982,* Pub.L. No. 97–424, 96 Stat. 2097 (1982); *Department* *of Transportation and Related Agencies Appropriations Act, 1983,* Pub.L. No. 97–369, 96 Stat. 1965 (1982). * * *

secure congressional action than their opponents. Hence, the burden of overcoming congressional inertia should be on them.

* * *

[There are other safeguards against improper state legislation.] The market exacts its own inexorable penalties for needlessly burdensome regulations. For example, in *Pike,* Arizona imposed an apparently senseless and expensive requirement that its farmers build packing sheds inside the state. A state that makes a practice of doing such things will soon find that multistate firms like the plaintiff in *Pike* are making their investments elsewhere. Those farmers remaining in the state will suffer a competitive disadvantage compared with farmers in neighboring states. Similarly, laws that protect in-state firms from competition in local markets have the effect of raising prices, so the ultimate burden is borne by local consumers. These consumers may not be able to organize as effectively as business lobbies, but they should not be dismissed as a political force. * * *

* * *

In summary, the Court's current approach to the dormant commerce clause is badly in need of reform. The disparate impact and undue burden phases of current doctrine give the federal courts an undesirable policymaking role. Under current doctrine, courts are asked to decide whether laissez-faire is better national policy than state regulation. Such policy determinations are better left with more democratic institutions.

This article suggests [a more limited] judicial role in dormant commerce clause cases. * * * [T]he Court should only intervene when an intent to discriminate against interstate commerce can be proved. As in equal protection law, disparate impacts or undue burdens should not be enough in themselves to trigger judicial review.

DONALD H. REGAN, THE SUPREME COURT AND STATE PROTECTIONISM: MAKING SENSE OF THE DORMANT COMMERCE CLAUSE

84 Mich.L.Rev. 1091, 1094–1095, 1112–1118, 1124–1125, 1160–1166 (1986).

WHAT IS "PROTECTIONISM"?

* * *

I shall say that a state statute (or administrative regulation, or local ordinance, or whatever) is protectionist if and only if:

(a) the statute (or whatever) was adopted for the purpose of improving the competitive position of local (in-state) economic actors, just because they are local, vis-à-vis their foreign (by which I mean simply out-of-state) competitors; and

(b) the statute (or whatever) is analogous in form to the traditional instruments of protectionism—the tariff, the quota, or the outright embargo (all of which can be on imports or exports).[a]

The doctrine that states may not engage in protectionism (may not adopt protectionist legislation as I have defined it) I shall refer to as the "anti-protectionism principle."

* * *

There are three objections to state protectionism, which I shall call the "concept-of-union" objection, the "resentment/retaliation" objection, and the "efficiency" objection.

The concept-of-union objection is so obvious that it is easily overlooked. State protectionism is unacceptable because it is inconsistent with the very idea of political union, even a limited federal union. Protectionist legislation is the economic equivalent of war. It is hostile in its essence.

In saying protectionist legislation is hostile, I do not mean that the harm to the foreign victims is necessarily valued for itself. The ultimate goal may be only promotion of local well-being. But the harm to foreign interests is also not merely incidental. The immediate intended means to improvement of local well-being is the transfer of certain profitable activities from foreign to local hands. Protectionism does not merely harm some foreign interests in the process of conferring an independent local benefit. Rather, it takes away from the foreigners in order to give to local residents exactly what has been taken away. Nations under arms are often no more hostilely disposed to their enemies than this. Such behavior has no place in a genuine political union of any kind.

Notice I have not said that all legislation that distinguishes between locals and foreigners is objectionable. A state does have a special relationship to its own citizens. Alaska may provide that only Alaskans can run for governor or share in the distribution of the state's oil royalties. Such legislation is not hostile to non-Alaskans in the way protectionism is hostile. It takes nothing away from non-Alaskans that we would normally think they have as much right to as Alaskans have.

The reader might wonder whether protectionist legislation is any more hostile than ordinary competitive economic behavior. When the Coca–Cola Company introduced its new flavor of Coke, it was trying to take business away from Pepsi–Cola and transfer that business to itself. We would not normally characterize Coca–Cola's behavior as hostile. We even tend to assume behavior like this is socially valuable.

Now, states do not ordinarily compete with each other for customers in the way Coca–Cola and Pepsi–Cola compete, but states do sometimes try to help local businesses compete by what we would think of as

a. Regan states that part (b) of the definition "is necessary in part to account for the Court's recent decisions on the state-as-market-participant; but it is necessary for other reasons as well, and it has its own theoretical justification * * *. As it happens, all the state laws involved in what the reader would think of as standard cases under the dormant commerce clause satisfy part (b) of the definition * * *." Regan's full discussion of part (b) is omitted.

normal marketing techniques. Thus, the State of Michigan advertises Michigan as a vacation paradise for boaters and fishermen, hoping thereby to benefit the Michigan tourist industry, and recognizing that any benefit will come at least in part at the expense of other states' tourist industries.

Such behavior by Michigan is perfectly permissible. * * * [D]eveloping our war analogy, we might say that protectionism takes over a market share by force; it is like acquiring territory by armed conquest. Advertising, like product improvement and other standard market ploys, uses no force; it encourages a free transfer of allegiance. It is like acquiring territory by plebiscite of the inhabitants.

The next objection to protectionism is the resentment/retaliation objection. If protectionism is conceptually inconsistent with political union, it is also practically inconsistent. Protectionist impositions cause resentment and invite protectionist retaliation. If protectionist legislation is permitted at all, it is likely to generate a cycle of escalating animosity and isolation (and even of hostility in the strongest sense, where the harm to foreign interests *is* valued as such), eventually imperiling the political viability of the union itself.

* * *

The third objection to protectionism is that it is inefficient. Now, "efficiency" is a treacherous notion. Let us pause to be sure we know what we are saying. Why exactly is protectionism inefficient? The obvious answer is that tariffs, embargoes, quotas, and the like interfere with efficiency in the production of goods; they divert business from low-cost (foreign) to high-cost (local) producers.

For some purposes, the statement that protectionism is inefficient because it diverts business from low-cost (foreign) to high-cost (local) producers would be perfectly adequate. But for our purposes, it is inadequate. It tells part of the story, but not the whole story, of why classical protectionist measures seem so self-evidently objectionable on efficiency-related grounds.

The first problem with the statement as it stands is this: It suggests that *every* law which diverts business away from the producers who currently have it is necessarily diverting business from low-cost to high-cost producers and impairing efficiency. But that need not be so.

Consider the Oregon bottle law.[b] That law diverted business from can manufacturers to bottle manufacturers and, because of the increased transportation cost associated with heavier containers, from out-of-state bottlers to in-state bottlers. But there is no reason to think the Oregon bottle law impaired productive efficiency. The object of the law was to discourage a mode of production, the packaging of beverages in nonreusable and nonreturnable cans, that created costs (in the form of litter) not

---

b. In 1971 Oregon passed a law to protect the environment by discouraging the use of nonreturnable cans.

accounted for by market mechanisms. In other words, the object of the law was to improve productive efficiency by correcting an inefficiency that resulted from an external cost of the existing productive process.

* * *

Our discussion of the Oregon bottle law makes it clear that we cannot be satisfied with a statement of the efficiency objection to protectionism that suggests that every law that diverts business away from (foreign) producers who currently have it impairs productive efficiency and thus shares the evil of protectionism. How shall we reformulate the efficiency objection in order to avoid this suggestion?

We could say that protectionism is inefficient because it diverts business from producers who are the low-cost producers under the cost-assignment scheme implicit in the legal status quo, without the state's even claiming the justification, which Oregon claimed for its bottle law, that that cost-assignment scheme is defective. Or, compressing what we have just said: protectionism is inefficient because it diverts business away from presumptively low-cost producers without any colorable cost-based justification.

This reformulation of the efficiency objection is an improvement, but it is still not fully acceptable. The change we have made, focusing as it does on cost-based justification, responds too exclusively to the Oregon bottle law. We can see the need for further reformulation by considering a somewhat different case, *Exxon Corp. v. Maryland*. If we give the Maryland legislature the benefit of any doubts about its purpose, the object of the Maryland law forbidding ownership of retail service stations by producers or refiners of petroleum was to secure fairer treatment of independent service station operators. Is that a "cost-based justification" for the diversion of retail business away from vertically integrated oil refiners? There may be room for someone to argue that this fairness justification for the Maryland law is not cost-based; but if there is room, that merely shows that a formulation of the efficiency objection in terms of cost-based justification is still not the right formulation. Whether or not we regard the claimed justification for the Maryland law as cost-based, the justification prevents the law from being self-evidently and unambiguously objectionable in the way a classical tariff is. (Remember we are assuming innocent purpose.) To be certain we exclude the Maryland law from the scope of the efficiency objection, we need to state the efficiency objection to protectionism more narrowly still, if we can find a way to do so.

Here is the proper formulation: protectionism is inefficient because it diverts business away from presumptively low-cost producers without any colorable justification in terms of a benefit that deserves approval from the point of view of the nation as a whole. Or, again compressing slightly: protectionism is inefficient because it diverts business away from presumptively low-cost producers without any colorable justification in terms of a "federally cognizable benefit."

Consider once more the classical tariff, and see how this reformulated efficiency objection fits it. The classical protectionist tariff diverts business away from those producers who currently have it, and the only benefit sought by the state imposing the tariff is a transfer of welfare from foreign producers (firms or workers) to their local counterparts. This transfer is a benefit from the narrowly self-interested viewpoint of the state imposing the tariff; but by its very nature this benefit to the imposing state is balanced by an equal loss to some other state or states. From the point of view of the nation as a whole, such a bare transfer of welfare between similarly situated parties in different states creates no benefit at all.

It is clear, then, that a classical tariff aims at no federally cognizable benefit, no benefit that deserves approval from the point of view of the nation as a whole. But what about the Oregon bottle law, or the Maryland law about service stations? Must there be a national policy in favor of reducing the litter in Oregon's parks and highways, or must we be able to say there should be such a national policy, before we can say the Oregon law seeks a federally cognizable benefit? No. The states are independent entities. Part of the point of federalism is to allow states to make their own decisions about such matters as what sort of an environment they value and want to maintain. So long as there is no constitutionally stipulated policy against minimizing litter (that is, no constitutionally stipulated policy in favor of litter *as such*), the elimination of litter from Oregon's parks and highways is a good thing from the federal viewpoint if Oregon says it is. Similarly, so long as there is no constitutional policy against fairer treatment (or what Maryland views as fairer treatment) for independent service stations, securing fairer treatment for independent service stations in Maryland is a good thing from the federal viewpoint if Maryland says it is.

* * *

I have put the efficiency objection last, even though it would occur first to many constitutional scholars, because it deserves to be downplayed. The relevant sense of "efficiency" turns out to be much weaker than one might at first assume; and the objection also was not primary in the framers' thinking. The people who wrote our Constitution were by no means thoroughgoing free traders. They envisaged a mercantilist foreign trade policy for the United States as a whole. One reason they wanted to locate the power to regulate commerce with foreign nations in Congress was that independent regulation of such commerce by the states prevented the implementation of an optimal national mercantilist policy. The framers did have some efficiency-related objection to interstate protectionism. They argued that eliminating preferential state regulation of trade would encourage agriculture and industry. But that is a much narrower claim than is suggested by modern apostles of efficiency, who operate with a strong presumption in favor of total economic *laissez-faire*. The framers would have recognized many good reasons for state economic regulation, and they would have recognized that the states must be the primary judges of what are good reasons. To the extent the framers were concerned with efficiency, it seems reasonable to think of their objection as being the objection I have formulated.

The structural argument against state protectionism is now complete. It remains only to consider whether there is a textual argument as well. In my opinion, the structural argument does not need to be supported by an argument from any single short bit of text (which is what lawyers normally mean by a "textual" argument), so long as there is no short bit of text that contradicts the structural argument (and there is none). Even so, let us see what we make of the text in bits.

Does the constitutional text include any bit that prohibits state protectionism? That depends, not surprisingly, on how the bits are approached. If we ask whether there is any bit of text that, taken by itself, naturally suggests to a modern reader that the states are forbidden to engage in protectionism against other states, the answer is easy: No, there is not. But there is another question, still about bits of text, that may be of interest. Is there any bit of text that might have suggested to a reader in 1787 that state protectionism was forbidden? Or, what is almost the same question, is there any bit of text that we could reasonably take to embody a final intention of the framers to forbid state protectionism, if we have independent reason to think the framers intended to forbid it and intended the text to say so? Here, the answer is: Yes. The relevant bit of text is the words, "The Congress shall have power * * * to regulate commerce * * * among the several states * * *."

There is much evidence that the main point of this grant (unlike the grant of power over foreign commerce) was not to empower Congress, but rather to disable the states from regulating commerce among themselves. The type of commercial regulation uppermost in the framers' minds was what we might categorize generally as mercantile regulation—regulation of navigation, customs regulation, and the like. The framers wanted commerce among the states to be free of state-originated mercantilist impositions. Giving Congress the power to regulate internal commerce was one way of denying states that power, under the view, much more natural to the framers than to us, that granted regulatory powers were exclusive. I have remarked previously that as Congress' power over interstate commerce is now understood, we cannot treat that power as exclusive. But that does not mean the framers could not have regarded as exclusive the much narrower power they were thinking of. There is considerable evidence that they did so regard it.[68]

---

68. * * * Of course, if the commerce clause forbids state mercantilist legislation, then it also provides a ground for judicial review to prevent such legislation. But notice that this argument for judicial review extends only so far as state legislation is flatly prohibited, which is to say, only so far as Congress' power is exclusive. This argument provides no ground for judicial review of all state legislation which is "commercial" in the sense that it duplicates what Congress might do under its (largely nonexclusive) commerce power as presently interpreted. (It is a very natural extension of the mercantilist exclusion, however, to say the Court may suppress what is superficial-

Against the Carolene Products *Theory of the Dormant Commerce Clause and Open–Ended Private Interest Balancing*

The basic idea of the *Carolene Products* theory of the dormant commerce clause is simple enough: When states adopt economic regulations that affect out-of-state interests, those out-of-state interests are likely to be shortchanged because they are not represented in the political process that produces the regulations. But everyone who is affected ought to be represented. Therefore we have judicial review of state economic regulation that affects out-of-state interests in order to give those interests "virtual representation."

* * *

Now, in discussing the *Carolene Products* theory of the dormant commerce clause (which I shall refer to hereafter as just the "*Carolene Products* theory," leaving the limitation to the dormant commerce clause understood), the first thing we need to do is to be clear about the scope of judicial review that the theory is supposed to justify.

The *Carolene Products* theorist might argue only for judicial application of the anti-protectionism principle as I have developed it. This would put him on solid ground, but it would rob his theory of any interest. Certainly the *Carolene Products* theory entails the anti-protectionism principle as a consequence. There would be no protectionist legislation (in my sense) if foreign interests were represented equally with the local interests they compete against. However, the idea of virtual representation is not necessary to justify the anti-protectionism principle. My own argument for the anti-protectionism principle made no use of the idea of virtual representation. (The idea that one state may not behave hostilely to another is a much more limited idea, as is the idea that state regulation producing protectionist effect must aim at some federally cognizable benefit.) If virtual representation is the central idea of the *Carolene Products* theory, then the *Carolene Products* theory is not necessary to ground the anti-protectionism principle, and acceptance of the anti-protectionism principle does not commit us to the *Carolene Products* theory.

The *Carolene Products* theory is interesting only if it entails more than the anti-protectionism principle—specifically, if it entails that economic regulation that affects foreign interests should be reviewed by courts applying a balancing methodology. Open-ended private interest balancing is what virtual representation requires, and it is what most *Carolene Products* theorists have argued for.[c] (The balancing that is required is private interest balancing because it is private interests that are supposed to deserve virtual representation.)

ly ordinary commercial legislation if that legislation has a protectionist purpose.)

c. "Open-ended private interest balancing," Regan explains elsewhere, is the view "that any cost imposed by a statute on a private party can be advanced as an argument against the constitutionality of the statute[.]" Not every such cost will invalidate a law, but every cost counts in the scale used to measure validity.

Now, one problem with the *Carolene Products* theory is that if it justifies balancing at all, it requires balancing over a much broader range of cases than its proponents usually recognize.   Justice Stone, the original *Carolene Products* theorist (in the dormant commerce clause area as elsewhere), suggested that judicial review would not be necessary if there were in-state interests functionally equivalent to the damaged out-of-state interests.   * * * But if any foreigners are harmed, then representation of those foreigners in the political process of the enacting state might have shifted the political balance and prevented the adoption of the regulation.   This is true even if there are already similarly burdened local interests, and even if these local interests are more heavily burdened than the foreign.   * * *

This means the *Carolene Products* theory requires review of laws no one would normally think of as requiring judicial scrutiny.   If Minnesota adopts an advertising campaign to try to discourage smoking among its population, or if it forbids smoking in enough stores, offices, and places of public assembly to affect significantly the total number of cigarettes smoked, then the law should be judicially inspected to see that it does not unjustly harm tobacco growers in North Carolina.   If a major city adopts a rent control ordinance, judicial review is required to protect the interests of people living elsewhere who might have moved to the city except for the increased difficulty of securing housing.[131]   If a state has a stingy workmen's compensation program that attracts employers, the courts must stand ready to consider whether representation in that state's legislature of foreign workers might not have produced a program that was more generous.

My last example might elicit the response that review is not required because the foreign workers are not objecting to the program as it exists so much as they are objecting to the state's failure to have a more generous program.   This raises an interesting question about what counts as action by a state and what is a mere omission.   But even if we could make that distinction perfectly clear, it would not help the *Carolene Products* theorist.   On his theory, the courts ought to review legislative omissions as freely as they review positive legislative action.   After all, representation of foreign interests would not result only in blocking legislation.   Sometimes it would tip the balance in favor of legislation where none was otherwise forthcoming.   * * *

Overbreadth, however, is not the most fundamental problem with the *Carolene Products* theory of the dormant commerce clause.   The *Carolene Products* theory assumes that out-of-state interests really ought to be represented—the theory assumes it is a defect in our system that the system denies foreigners representation, as it is a defect if racial minorities or women are unrepresented or represented ineffectively. But that assumption is not warranted.   Nonrepresentation of foreign

---

131. This example is borrowed from Kitch [*Regulation and the American Common Market,* in Regulation, Federalism, and Interstate Commerce 31 (A. Tarlock, ed. 1981).]

interests follows from the simple fact that there are separate states; and the existence of separate states, while it might be a defect in an ideal political system, can hardly be treated as a defect in ours.

I suggest that with regard to treatment by the states of out-of-state interests, our system embodies the following compromise between unlimited state autonomy and perfect national unity. The states may not single out foreigners for disadvantageous treatment just because of their foreignness. But, provided they do not single out foreigners, the states need not attend positively to the foreign effects of laws they adopt nor to the distribution between locals and foreigners of the benefits and burdens of those laws. "Singling out" foreigners does not necessarily involve explicitness. It does involve purpose. The state legislature that simply fails to attend to foreign interests or to any local/foreign distinction may do as it pleases. This is the message of the dormant commerce clause, as it is the general message of the privileges and immunities clause of article IV.

Clearly, this is a compromise. If the states were perfectly autonomous, they would be free to single out foreigners for disadvantageous treatment. If, on the other hand, we had perfect national unity, there would be no states at all, except perhaps as administrative departments, and all interests throughout the nation would be taken into account in any significant legislative decision. Giving foreign interests virtual representation in the actual independent state legislatures may be thought of as an attempt to mimic a regime of perfect national unity. But in view of the compromise I have described, such "virtual" perfect unity is not required.

The autonomy interest of the states that we protect by not requiring virtual representation may seem like just a freedom to harm foreigners with impunity so long as it is done by inadvertence. This is not an interest one can feel much enthusiasm for. But in fact, there is more at stake.

By not requiring state lawmakers to be always looking over their shoulders for foreign interests and always calculating the proportionate incidence of benefits and burdens, we make legislation a possible task for lawmakers with less expertise and less administrative support available to them than Congress has. We also avoid a massive transfer of power to the courts, federal and state. And we avoid the tendency to homogenization of values that commitment of economic regulation to the courts, under the general supervision of the Supreme Court, would tend to bring about. It is worth remembering that states can disagree about issues with significant interstate aspects for reasons having nothing to do with hostility to, or even indifference to, foreigners as such.

BIBLIOGRAPHY

Article IV Privileges and Immunities Clause

Adler, *What States Owe Outsiders*, 20 Hastings Const. L.Q. 391 (1993).

Carpinello, *State Protective Legislation and Nonresident Corporations: The Privileges and Immunities Clause as a Treaty of Nondiscrimination,* 73 Iowa L.Rev. 351 (1988).

Eule, *Laying the Dormant Commerce Clause to Rest,* 91 Yale L.J. 425 (1982).

Varat, *State "Citizenship" and Interstate Equality,* 48 U.Chi.L.Rev. 487 (1981).

Congressional Silence; Consent to State Laws

Abel, *The Commerce Clause in the Constitutional Convention and in Contemporary Comment,* 25 Minn.L.Rev. 432 (1941).

Cohen, *Congressional Power to Validate Unconstitutional State Laws,* 35 Stan.L.Rev. 387 (1983).

Powell, *The Still Small Voice of the Commerce Clause,* Proceedings Nat. Tax Ass'n 337 (1938).

States as Market Participants

Anson & Schenkkan, *Federalism, the Dormant Commerce Clause, and State–Owned Resources,* 59 Tex.L.Rev. 71 (1980).

Coenen, *Untangling the Market–Participant Exemption to the Dormant Commerce Clause,* 88 Mich.L.Rev. 395 (1989).

Gergen, *The Selfish State and the Market,* 66 Tex.L.Rev. 1097 (1988).

Gillen, *A Proposed Model of the Sovereign/Proprietary Distinction,* 133 U.Pa.L.Rev. 661 (1985).

Manheim, *New–Age Federalism and the Market Participant Doctrine,* 22 Ariz.St.L.J. 559 (1990).

State Taxation of Interstate Commerce

Brown, *The Open Economy: Justice Frankfurter and the Position of the Judiciary,* 67 Yale L.J. 219 (1957).

J. Hellerstein, STATE TAXATION (1983).

Hellerstein, *Is "Internal Consistency" Foolish?: Reflections on an Emerging Commerce Clause Restraint on State Taxation,* 87 Mich. L.Rev. 138 (1988).

Hellerstein, *Justice Scalia and the Commerce Clause: Reflections of a State Tax Lawyer,* 12 Cardozo L.Rev. 1763 (1991).

Hellerstein, *State Taxation and the Supreme Court: Toward a More Unified Approach to Constitutional Adjudication?,* 75 Mich.L.Rev. 1426 (1977).

Hunter, *Federalism and State Taxation of Multistate Enterprises,* 32 Emory L.J. 89 (1983).

Lockhart, *A Revolution in State Taxation of Commerce?,* 65 Minn.L.Rev. 1025 (1981).

Schoettle, *Commerce Clause Challenges to State Taxes,* 75 Minn.L.Rev. 907 (1991).

Tatarowicz & Mims–Velarde, *An Analytical Approach to State Tax Discrimination Under the Commerce Clause,* 39 Vand.L.Rev. 879 (1986).

Theory and Practice of State Commerce Regulation

Black, *Perspectives on the American Common Market,* in REGULATION, FEDERALISM, AND INTERSTATE COMMERCE 59 (Tarlock ed. 1981).

Collins, *Economic Union as a Constitutional Value,* 63 N.Y.U.L.Rev. 43 (1988).

Dowling, *Interstate Commerce and State Power—Revised Version,* 47 Colum.L.Rev. 547 (1947).

F. Frankfurther, THE COMMERCE CLAUSE (1937).

Friedman, *Putting the Dormancy Doctrine Out of Its Misery,* 12 Cardozo L.Rev. 1745 (1991).

Gey, *The Political Economy of the Dormant Commerce Clause,* 17 N.Y.U.Rev.L. & Soc. Change 1 (1989).

Kitch, *Regulation and the American Common Market,* in REGULATION, FEDERALISM, AND INTERSTATE COMMERCE 9 (Tarlock ed. 1981).

Maltz, *How Much Regulation Is Too Much—An Examination of Commerce Clause Jurisprudence,* 50 Geo.Wash.L.Rev. 47 (1981).

O'Fallon, *The Commerce Clause: A Theoretical Comment,* 61 Ore.L.Rev. 395 (1982).

Regan, *Siamese Essays: (I)* CTS Corp. v. Dynamics Corp. of America *and Dormant Commerce Clause Doctrine; (ii) Extraterritorial State Legislation,* 85 Mich.L.Rev. 1865 (1987).

T. Sandalow and E. Stein, eds., COURTS AND FREE MARKETS (1982).

Sedler, *The Negative Commerce Clause As A Restriction On State Regulation And Taxation: An Analysis In Terms Of Constitutional Structure,* 31 Wayne L.Rev. 885 (1985).

Smith, *State Discriminations Against Interstate Commerce,* 74 Calif.L.Rev. 1203 (1986).

Tushnet, *Rethinking the Dormant Commerce Clause,* 1979 Wis.L.Rev. 125.

Tushnet, *Scalia and the Dormant Commerce Clause: A Foolish Formalism?,* 12 Cardozo L.Rev. 1717 (1991).

Chapter V

SEPARATION OF POWERS

Like federalism, separation of powers doctrine deals with relations among the institutions of American government. The former is sometimes said to address the "vertical" division of authority between national and state governments, the latter a "horizontal" division among the national executive, legislature, and judiciary. Lately the Supreme Court has decided to entrust many federalism issues to the political branches, on the theory that they are capable of protecting their own interests.[1] The Court seems to have made a different assumption about separation of powers: the area is one in which it now plays an unusually active supervisory role.

A. GENERAL THEORETICAL APPROACHES

We cannot deal intelligently with separation issues without first thinking about the purposes served by a division of authority within the national government. One reason ("efficiency") for creating a strong executive was that the Framers viewed legislative government—with which they had some experience under the Articles of Confederation—as too fragmented and episodic. They thought that the national government would be more efficient if they separated executive from legislative functions. A second reason for dividing power—one mentioned prominently by Madison[2]—is the prevention of tyranny. Lest one institution become too powerful the Constitution confers on others the ability to check and balance its authority. So, for example, the President can veto legislation, the Congress can impeach the President and cut his budget, and the courts can invalidate executive and legislative actions. But the objectives of tyranny-prevention and efficiency may conflict with one another (checks and balances will weaken a strong executive), and with still other functions served by separation. How they should best be reconciled is one theme taken up in the articles by David Currie and Peter Strauss.

1. Garcia v. San Antonio Metropolitan Transit Authority, 469 U.S. 528, 105 S.Ct. 1005, 83 L.Ed.2d 1016 (1985). But see New York v. United States, ___ U.S. ___, 112 S.Ct. 2408, 120 L.Ed.2d 120 (1992).

2. The Federalist No. 47.

The controversy over purposes is entwined with a second theme that is important today in all areas of constitutional law—the conflict over methods of interpreting the Constitution. One approach, labelled "formal" by its opponents, urges that the text and structure of the Constitution and the intentions of its authors provide clear answers to many conflicts about separation of powers. Currie argues that Articles I and II create separate categories of legislative and executive power that have edges sharp enough for drawing lines. Strauss takes a position that might be called "functional," by way of contrast. He contends that the categories of legislative and executive power overlap, especially in a complex administrative state. Strauss urges us to think about keeping institutional powers practically in balance rather than categorically separate.

DAVID P. CURRIE, THE DISTRIBUTION OF POWERS AFTER BOWSHER
1986 Sup.Ct.Rev. 19–36.

Article I of the Constitution entrusts the legislative power of the United States to Congress, so that democratically elected representatives will determine national policy. Article II vests the executive power in the President, in the interest of unified administration by an elected officer. Article III places the judicial power in judges appointed for life and removable only for high crimes and misdemeanors, so that cases may be decided without fear of reprisal. Above all, the distribution of these powers among three separate branches serves as a powerful check against arbitrary action, for it means that three distinct bodies must concur before the individual is effectively deprived of his liberty or property: Congress must pass a law, the President must seek to enforce it, and the courts must find a violation.

One would scarcely suspect all this from observing the current operations of the national government. Executive departments as well as independent agencies promulgate regulations that look for all the world like statutes. Violations of law are prosecuted by officials independent of presidential control. Administrators and "non-Article III judges" decide cases within the federal judicial power. Most strikingly, sometimes all three functions are combined in a single agency largely independent of all three branches and enjoying none of their attributes. The Federal Trade Commission, whose members are appointed for seven years and removable for "inefficiency, neglect of duty, or malfeasance in office," adopts regulations defining unfair methods of competition, institutes proceedings against purported offenders, and passes on the merits of its own complaints in a "quasi-judicial" proceeding.

* * *

In the last few years, however, the Court has displayed increasing concern for the distribution of powers. Despite its permissive precedents, the Court made clear in *INS v. Chadha* that Congress could not delegate lawmaking authority to one of its Houses, and there have been hints that delegations to administrators may also be scrutinized more closely. * * * [T]he Court held in *Buckley v. Valeo* that Congress could not appoint officers with executive duties. Last Term, in *Bowsher v. Synar,* the Court took another step in the same direction: Congress cannot remove such officers either.

The individual decisions have been dissected in detail elsewhere. My aim is to be neither bibliographic nor repetitive but to present a concise general view of the distribution of powers.

I. LEGISLATIVE POWER

"All legislative powers herein granted," says Article I, "shall be vested in a Congress of the United States * * *."

Historically the transfer of legislative power from monarch to representative assembly was, as Montesquieu observed, an important step toward self-government. It was also a significant means of protecting liberty and property. Long before there were limitations on the power of the state as a whole, liberty and property were safeguarded by requiring the consent of the people themselves, through their representatives, before their interests could be invaded.

* * *

* * * [T]he debate on the Constitution was replete with explanations why it was desirable to place legislative powers in a representative assembly. First was the conviction that, notwithstanding ultimate popular control of other organs of government, it was important to give some substantial role in lawmaking to a body directly elected by the people. * * *

Gerry appeared to suggest that self-government was an end in itself: "It is a maxim that the people ought to hold the purse strings." [18] Franklin and Madison saw it as a means of protecting the interests of the people, the former insisting that "those who feel, can best judge," [19] the latter that without a direct role in selection of the House "the people would be lost sight of altogether." [20] Wilson saw direct election of the House as contributing to "the confidence of the people," without which "[n]o government could long subsist." [21]

Apart from the democratic nature of the House, a second pervasive theme of the debates was the value of having legislative decisions made by a collective body in which various interests were represented. "[A] numerous legislature," wrote Hamilton, was "best adapted to deliberation and wisdom, and best calculated to conciliate the confidence of the people and to secure their privileges and interests." [22] * * *

The final theme, independent of the virtues of a particular lawmaking body, was the more general one of separation of powers: It was

18. [1 Farrand] 233.

19. *Id.* at 546.

20. *Id.* at 50.

21. *Id.* at 49. * * *

22. The Federalist, No. 70.

important to liberty that the legislative power not be in the same hands as the executive. This of course had been a central point for Montesquieu, whom Madison explicitly invoked during the Convention. "The accumulation of all powers legislative, executive, and judiciary in the same hands," Madison repeated in the Federalist Papers, "whether few or many, and whether hereditary, self appointed, or elective, may justly be pronounced the very definition of tyranny." [26]

In short, despite the fact that the new Constitution provided for indirect popular control of the executive, the Framers were insistent that it was important to entrust the legislative power to Congress. For the more democratic nature of the House, the sheer numbers and representative nature of an assembly, and the mere separation of legislative from executive power were seen as important means of strengthening self-government, protecting against ill-founded or oppressive legislation, and securing the confidence of the people.[27]

A. The Supremacy of Statutes

The first and most obvious consequence of vesting legislative authority in Congress is the supremacy of statutes validly enacted.

That congressional enactments bind the public at large is implicit in the concept of law and confirmed by history: The Framers meant to create not a debating society but a maker of public policy. * * * [T]he binding effect of statutes on other branches is indispensable to effectuation of the expressed purpose of parliamentary control of public policy and thus implicit in the grants of legislative power in Article I, reinforced by the declaration of Article VI that "laws of the United States * * * shall be the supreme law of the land" and by Article II's command that the President "take care that the laws be faithfully executed."

* * *

B. The Necessity for Legislation

The second implication of vesting legislative authority in Congress is that no other branch may legislate. With rare exceptions, moreover, the executive may act only on the basis of law.

It is clear enough that executive officers cannot make laws, and in general federal courts cannot either. The common law tradition in both England and the states does show that interstitial lawmaking by other branches subject to legislative correction is not wholly incompatible with the ultimate policymaking authority of the legislature. That tradition, however, is based on necessity; judges must decide cases whether or not the legislature has laid down a rule of decision. To extend such authority to the executive branch would poorly serve the goals of the

---

26. The Federalist, No. 47. * * *

27. Illustrative of the prevailing attitude was Hamilton's response to the objection that the proposed Constitution did not forbid standing armies: The interests of the people were adequately safeguarded by lodging the authority to raise them not in the executive but in "a popular body, consisting of the representatives of the people." The Federalist, Nos. 24, 26, 28.

Framers, for to require affirmative congressional action to undo bad laws made by others combines the weight of inertia with the certainty of interim harm.

Hamilton's insistence that placing the power to raise armies in Congress was adequate protection against its arbitrary exercise [34] makes clear the understanding that the executive could not raise them; legislative powers were given to Congress because the Framers did not want other federal officers exercising them. The absence of lawmaking power in executive officers is thus implicit both in the grant of that authority to Congress and in the limited enumeration of executive powers, as Justice Black suggested in *Youngstown:* "[T]he Constitution is neither silent nor equivocal as to who shall make laws which the President is to execute."

Apart from the Constitution's independent grants of Presidential authority in such fields as foreign affairs and defense, it follows that executive officers can act only on the basis of legislation. An undeclared executive war undermines the purposes of the Framers just as seriously as a declared one. The lesson of Hamilton's essay on armies was not only that the President could not pass laws raising them, but that he could not raise them at all. This was likewise the purport of Justice Black's opinion for the Court in the *Youngstown* case, for the executive had not professed to pass a law seizing the steel mills; he was forbidden to act without congressional authorization. Since its purpose was to assure legislative control of policy, the congressional monopoly of federal legislative power inherent in Articles I and II implies a monopoly of policymaking with respect to the subjects confided to congressional care.

C.   The Nondelegation Doctrine

The third consequence of the vesting of legislative power in Congress is that it cannot be further delegated. * * *

* * * This does not preclude Congress from leaving details to another agency, for filling gaps in applying inevitably imprecise legislation is inseparable from the executive function. But the purposes of the Framers in granting legislative power to a representative assembly cannot be attained unless the lawmakers themselves lay down, as the Supreme Court has said, a "primary standard" or an "intelligible principle."

Fifty years ago, in *Panama Refining Co. v. Ryan* and in *Schechter Poultry Corp. v. United States,* the Supreme Court found two instances in which Congress had failed to heed this important limitation. These decisions were no reactionary aberrations. Both were joined by such respected liberals as Brandeis and Stone, the second—rendered without dissent—also by Cardozo. It was obviously inconsistent with the constitutional plan to authorize the President, in *Schechter,* to require whatever was good for the economy. * * *

---

34. See note 27 *supra.*

Later decisions seemed lenient in reviewing claims that legislative power had been invalidly delegated. During the 1940s, for example, the Court upheld grants of authority to set "fair and equitable" maximum prices, to appoint receivers for national banks, and to recapture "excessive profits" from government contractors.[50] Such decisions have led some observers to the unsettling conclusion that the nondelegation doctrine is dead.

In no case, however, has the Court repudiated the principle. In the decisions just noted, for example, the Justices emphasized that there was no absence of standards to guide the exercise of delegated authority. * * * In two [recent] cases Justice Rehnquist argued that the not very sweeping authority to carry out a congressional policy of all feasible protection from certain workplace health hazards went too far.[54]

In sum, individual decisions over the years may have stretched the nondelegation doctrine; but it remains the law that delegated authority must be confined in order to preserve the responsibility of the legislature to make basic policy.

D. The Legislative Veto

It is clear enough that the directly elected House of Representatives was meant to play a central role in the lawmaking process. It is equally clear, however, that the House was not to make law on its own; Article I, § 7 provides for the enactment of laws by the concurrence of both Houses, subject to an overridable Presidential veto. Apart from the obvious safeguard against ill-considered action provided by any bicameral legislature, the history reveals a deliberate decision to give the states equal voices in one chamber and to require the consent of a body partly insulated by a six-year term from the fickle popular will. The President's veto was designed both to protect the executive from legislative encroachments and as an additional safeguard "against the enaction of improper laws."

When Congress began passing laws authorizing one or both of its Houses to block executive action, it undermined these provisions. Nowhere is Congress given power to reverse executive policy except by legislation; and Congress has only the powers given it by the Constitution. The Supreme Court recognized this in *INS v. Chadha* in 1983. It was not really a hard case.

II. EXECUTIVE POWER

"The executive Power," says Article II, "shall be vested in a President of the United States of America."

Three critical concerns underlie this provision. The first is the democratic principle that the executive should be elected and thus

---

50. Yakus v. United States, 321 U.S. 414 (1944); Fahey v. Mallonee, 332 U.S. 245 (1947); Lichter v. United States, 334 U.S. 742 (1948).

54. Industrial Union Dept. v. American Petroleum Inst., 448 U.S. 607, 671–88 (1980) (concurring); American Textile Manufacturers Inst. v. Donovan, 452 U.S. 490, 543–48 (1981) (dissenting).

responsive to the people: "It was desirable, that the sense of the people should operate in the choice of the person to whom so important a trust was to be confided." [62]   The second was once again the desire to separate the executive and legislative powers in order to reduce the risk of invasions of liberty.   * * * The third was the need to concentrate executive power in the hands of a single person.   Rutledge argued that "[a] single man would feel the greatest responsibility and administer the public affairs best"; Wilson "preferred a single magistrate, as giving most energy dispatch and responsibility to the office." [64]   "The persons * * * to whose immediate management [the administration of government is] committed," wrote Hamilton, "ought to be considered as the assistants or deputies of the chief magistrate; and, on this account, they ought to derive their offices from his appointment, or at least from his nomination, and ought to be subject to his superintendence." [65]

The consequences of vesting the executive power in a single, independent, elected President are several.

A.   Congress May Not Execute the Laws

Apart from such matters as impeachment and consent to appointments, where it functions as a check on other branches, Congress has been given only legislative powers.   The debates show that the withholding of executive authority from Congress was, among other things, a deliberate means of protecting against the dangers that arise when the same persons both make and carry out the laws.   The limited enumeration of congressional powers and the explicit vesting of the executive power in the President preclude Congress from administering spending programs, prosecuting offenses, or giving orders to armies in the field.

It follows that Congress cannot effectively control the exercise of executive power by making the tenure of those who administer the laws dependent upon congressional whim.   * * * To grant executive power to an officer removable at the discretion of Congress would undermine all the reasons for creating an independent executive.   For, as Hamilton wrote in connection with judges, "A power over a man's subsistence amounts to a power over his will." [68]

This unsurprising conclusion informs the decision in *Bowsher v. Synar* that Congress could not empower the Comptroller General to administer the Gramm–Rudman law requiring a balanced federal budget.   As the dissenters noted, Congress could discharge that official only upon a finding of "disability, * * * inefficiency, * * * neglect of duty, * * * malfeasance, * * * felony or * * * moral turpitude"; but that is a far cry from the degree of control the Framers grudgingly afforded Congress in the impeachment clauses.

Finally, for similar reasons, Congress may not appoint those who execute the laws.   As *Buckley v. Valeo* held, Article II makes this plain

---

62. The Federalist, No. 68 (Hamilton).

64. 1 Farrand at 65. See also The Federalist, Nos. 70, 74.   * * *

65. The Federalist, No. 72.

68. The Federalist, No. 79.

by authorizing Congress to vest appointing power in almost anybody except itself; and in any event the default provision for nomination by the President and confirmation by the Senate marks the degree of intended legislative control over appointments. * * *

In short, congressional execution of the laws and congressional appointment or removal of executive officers would make the executive more dependent upon the legislature than is consistent with the constitutional plan.

B. *The President Must Control Execution of the Laws*

Although the Court properly refrained from so deciding in *Bowsher,* it should be equally plain that Congress cannot deprive the President of the executive power. For the Constitution not only denies executive authority to Congress, in the interest of separation of powers; it also vests that authority in the democratically elected President, in order to concentrate executive authority in a single responsive official.

Thus the Court was plainly right in *Myers v. United States* that Congress could not forbid the President to discharge a postmaster. The aggravating circumstance that Congress had purported to give one of its Houses a veto power over removal played a minor role in the decision; the essence of the argument was that the President could not fulfill his duty to see that the laws were faithfully executed if he could not control those executing them. *Myers* was the converse of *Bowsher:* as one with power to discharge can control, one without that power cannot.

This does not mean that ordinary civil service limitations on groundless discharges are invalid; so long as the President retains authority to give orders, their disobedience will be cause for discharge. But the President has no such authority over Federal Trade Commissioners; a central purpose of the legislation was to create a body independent of Presidential control. Thus the 1935 decision in *Humphrey's Executor v. United States,* upholding the statute forbidding dismissal of such a Commissioner without cause, was grievously wrong. The filing of complaints, as the Court emphasized in *Buckley,* is an executive function; and the Constitution requires the President to control the execution of the laws.

It is no answer that, as the Court argued in *Humphrey's,* the Commission's prosecuting function is in some sense incidental to other activities that may be characterized as "quasi-legislative" or "quasi-judicial." *Buckley* makes that clear as to appointments, and it is no less true as to removal. The Constitution recognizes only three kinds of federal powers: legislative, executive, and judicial. If the power either to "fill[ ] in * * * the details" of the congressionally prescribed prohibitions or to adjudicate disputes arising under federal law can properly be lodged outside Congress and the courts, it is only on the theory that they pertain to the implementation of law; and this means that they too must be subject to Presidential control. To uphold the Commission's independence on the ground that these powers are not executive, on the other hand, is to argue that Congress may violate Article II whenever it is willing to violate Articles I and III as well. *Bowsher* should therefore have come out the same way if authority to administer the budget law had been given to an officer independent of congressional as well as Presidential control.

Finally, an examination of the reasons for lodging executive power in the President supports the Court's 1839 dictum that the clause of Article II empowering Congress to provide for the appointment of inferior officers by "the President alone, * * * the Courts of law, or * * * the Heads of Departments" permitted appointments only by "the department of the government to which the officer to be appointed most appropriately belonged." [85]   For judges to appoint their own clerks makes obvious sense; for them to appoint State Department officials would seem quite inconsistent with the Framers' notions of unified executive power. For them to appoint prosecutors, as they were authorized to do in the wake of the Nixon Administration scandals, offends the separation of powers as well by giving judges too much influence over the prosecution.[a]

PETER L. STRAUSS, THE PLACE OF AGENCIES IN GOVERNMENT: SEPARATION OF POWERS AND THE FOURTH BRANCH

84 Colum.L.Rev. 573, 577–580, 596–605, 609–620,
622–623, 625–626, 633–635, 637–639 (1984).

Three differing approaches have been used in the effort to understand issues [about the place of agencies in government]. The first, "separation of powers," supposes that what government does can be characterized in terms of the kind of act performed—legislating, enforcing, and determining the particular application of law—and that for the safety of the citizenry from tyrannous government these three functions must be kept in distinct places. Congress legislates, and it only legislates; the President sees to the faithful execution of those laws and, in the domestic context at least, that is all he does; the courts decide specific cases of law-application, and that is their sole function. These three powers of government are kept radically separate, because if the same body exercised all three of them, or even two, it might no longer be possible to keep it within the constraints of law.

"Separation of functions" suggests a somewhat different idea, grounded more in considerations of individual fairness in particular proceedings than in the need for structural protection against tyrannical government generally. It admits that for agencies (as distinct from the constitutionally named heads of government) the same body often does

---

85. U.S. Const. Art. II, § 2; In re Hennen, 13 Pet. 230, 257–59 (1839). Later Justices in Ex parte Siebold, 100 U.S. 371, 397–98 (1880), disputed this conclusion on the basis of the language of the Clause, but the Court added that no branch was more appropriate than the courts to appoint federal election supervisors.

a. This article was written before the Supreme Court's decision in Morrison v. Olson, 487 U.S. 654 (1988).

exercise all three of the characteristic governmental powers, albeit in a web of other controls—judicial review and legislative and executive oversight. As these controls are thought to give reasonable assurance against systemic lawlessness, the separation-of-functions inquiry asks to what extent constitutional due process for the particular individual(s) who may be involved with an agency in a given proceeding requires special measures to assure the objectivity or impartiality of that proceeding. The powers are not kept separate, at least in general, but certain procedural protections—for example, the requirement of an on-the-record hearing before an "impartial" trier—may be afforded.

"Checks and balances" is the third idea, one that to a degree bridges the gap between these two domains. Like separation of powers, it seeks to protect the citizens from the emergence of tyrannical government by establishing multiple heads of authority in government, which are then pitted one against another in a continuous struggle; the intent of that struggle is to deny to any one (or two) of them the capacity ever to consolidate all governmental authority in itself, while permitting the whole effectively to carry forward the work of government. Unlike separation of powers, however, the checks-and-balances idea does not suppose a radical division of government into three parts, with particular functions neatly parceled out among them. Rather, the focus is on relationships and interconnections, on maintaining the conditions in which the intended struggle at the apex may continue. From this perspective, as from the perspective of separation of functions, it is not important how powers below the apex are treated; the important question is whether the relationship of each of the three named actors of the Constitution to the exercise of those powers is such as to promise a continuation of their effective independence and interdependence.

In the pages following I argue that, for any consideration of the structure given law-administration below the very apex of the governmental structure, the rigid separation-of-powers compartmentalization of governmental functions should be abandoned in favor of analysis in terms of separation of functions and checks and balances. * * * A shorthand way of putting the argument is that we should stop pretending that all our government (as distinct from its highest levels) can be allocated into three neat parts. The theory of separation-of-powers breaks down when attempting to locate administrative and regulatory agencies within one of the three branches; its vitality, rather, lies in the formulation and specification of the controls that Congress, the Supreme Court and the President may exercise over administration and regulation.

* * *

From the perspective suggested here, the important fact is that an agency is neither Congress nor President nor Court, but an inferior part of government. Each agency is subject to control relationships with some or all of the three constitutionally named branches, and those relationships give an assurance—functionally similar to that provided by the separation-of-powers notion for the constitutionally named bodies—that they will not pass out of control.[18] Powerful and potentially arbitrary as they may be, the Secretary of Agriculture and the Chairman of the SEC for this reason do not present the threat that led the framers to insist on a splitting of the authority of government at its very top. What we have, then, are three named repositories of authorizing power and control, and an infinity of institutions to which parts of the authority of each may be lent. The three must share the reins of control; means must be found of assuring that no one of them becomes dominant. But it is not terribly important to number or allocate the horses that pull the carriage of government.

* * *

[This essay advances] three general propositions about the three theoretical approaches to understanding the place of agencies in government identified [above.] The first is that, as a textual and interpretational matter, the separation-of-powers model need and probably should be taken no further than its use for understanding the interrelationships of the three named actors (Congress, President, Court) at the very pinnacle of government. * * *

Although agencies certainly might be assigned to one or another of the executive, legislative, or judicial branches (but not more than one, if we are rigorously to pursue the separation idea), that signifies little for the functions they perform. No compelling textual or interpretive mandate requires such a formal placement to be effected.

A second proposition emerging from the cases is that considerations of individual fairness more closely associated with the idea of separation of functions often underlie the cases in which the idea of separation of powers appears to have played a significant role. * * *

Finally and perhaps most importantly, the text and particularly the context suggest a series of postulates about necessary relationships between the President and administrative agencies—relationships readily understood in checks-and-balances terms. The important constraint on Congress's ability to structure the work of law-administration lies in the need to perpetuate the tensions and interactions among the three named heads of the Constitution. Whatever arrangements are made, one must remain able to characterize the President as the unitary, politically accountable head of all law-administration, sufficiently potent in his own relationships with those who actually perform it to serve as an effective counter to a feared Congress. * * *

---

18. For example, one may understand the delegation doctrine in this functional way, rather than as an indication "where" in government rulemaking occurs. That doctrine requires both statutory authorization (a relationship with Congress) and a capacity on the part of the courts to assure legality (a relationship with the courts). The availability of at least limited judicial review, indeed, appears to be identified with increasing frequency as an essential element of the grant of rulemaking authority.

A. The Text and Context of the Constitution

The text and structure of the Constitution impose few limits on Congress's ability to structure administrative government. One scanning the Constitution for a sense of the overall structure of the federal government is immediately struck by its silences. Save for some aspects of the legislative process, it says little about how those it names as necessary elements of government—Congress, President, and Supreme Court—will perform their sanctions, and it says almost nothing at all about the unelected officials who, even in 1789, would necessarily perform the bulk of the government's work. Thus, article I describes in some detail the makeup of the House and Senate, the subjects on which they might act, and the manner in which they may effectively legislate; but even this relatively full description talks only to the authority and actions of elected officials. One finds no mention there of important aspects of Congress's work, or of most persons who now work on its behalf—committees and their staffs, the General Accounting Office, the Congressional Budget Office, the Library of Congress.

* * * Article II speaks directly only about elected officials, chiefly the President and his powers; it describes those powers in the most summary of terms. He is vested generally with "the executive Power," but what that is in the domestic context does not readily appear. Putting aside foreign relations and military authority—a very large part of the Presidency, but not the focus of this essay—he has the following powers and/or responsibilities:

> to appoint those "Officers of the United States * * * which shall be established by Law," subject to the requirement of senatorial confirmation and to the possibility that Congress might effectively limit this power to appointing "the Heads of Departments"; [90]

> to "require the Opinion, in writing, of the principal Officer in each of the executive Departments, upon any Subject relating to the Duties of their respective Offices"; [91]

> "from time to time give to the Congress Information of the State of the Union, and recommend to their Consideration" proposed legislation; [92]

> to "take Care that the Laws be faithfully executed." [93]

These provisions suggest a supervisory, perhaps even caretaker presidential role, in relationship to shadowy "executive departments" from which opinions might be sought. One is left to infer that there would be other officers possessing legal authority to act for the government, and one simply is not told whether the President or those officers are to act on those opinions.

* * * In almost all significant respects, then, the job of creating and altering the shape of the federal government was left to the future—to

---

90. U.S. Const. art. II, § 2, cl. 2.

91. U.S. Const. art. II, § 2, cl. 1.

92. U.S. Const. art. II, § 3.

93. Id.

the congressional processes suggested by Congress's authority to adopt any law "necessary and proper for carrying into Execution the foregoing Powers, and all other Powers vested by this Constitution in the Government of the United States, or in any Department or Officer thereof." [94]

If one moves outward from the text to its structure, the context in which it was drafted, the records and debates of the constitutional convention, and its initial implementation by the first Congress, one can identify a number of fundamental underlying judgments.   * * *

1. *The President is to be a Unitary, Politically Accountable Head of Government.*—Of the decisions clearly taken, perhaps none was as important as the judgment to vest the executive power in a single, elected official, the President.   * * * While it was understood that there would be departments responsible for daily administration, the Convention clearly and consciously chose a single and independent executive over a collegial body subject to legislative direction.[100]   * * *

If the Convention was clear in its choice of a single executive—and its associated beliefs that such a person might bear focused political accountability for the work of law-execution and serve as an effective political counter-weight to Congress—it was ambivalent in its expectations about the President's relations with those who would actually do the work of law-administration and desirous of the advantages of congressional flexibility in defining the structure of government within the constraints of this choice.   * * * Thus, the shadowy references to executive departments and, in particular, the opinions in writing clause, seem to be residues of propositions such as Gouvernour Morris's proposal in the final days of the Convention for a council of state composed of the Chief Justice and Secretaries of Domestic Affairs, State, Foreign Affairs, War, Marine, and Commerce and Finance.   * * *

Certainly one consideration underlying rejection of the Morris proposal was the wish to leave to successive Congresses, through the medium of the necessary and proper clause, the flexibility required for shaping the government to the demands of changing circumstances. Another consideration was to enhance the accountability—and thus the power—of the President by denying him the chance to hide behind a council's approval of his acts.   * * *

One ought not, however, mistake the drafters' possible ambivalence about presidential role and their willingness to trust the issue of governmental superstructure to future Congresses for a willingness to see the President assigned a role distinctly subordinate to Congress. In providing that Congress need not be convened until December of each year, the draftsmen plainly anticipated a substantial executive function. Congress's articulated functions lay in the passage of legislation to create the framework of government and then to set the standards and appropriate

---

94. U.S. Const. art. I, § 8, cl. 18.

100. The Federalist No. 70 (A. Hamilton), the first of the *Federalist* papers addressing the requisites of the presidency, is given over entirely to this choice, as the most important of the choices made, in its tendency to promote decisiveness and responsibility.

the funds by which the business of government would be carried on. Inevitably that legislation would be episodic—enacted without necessary care for its relationship to existing law and having to be applied to future events, not foreseen, in light of the then existing corpus of law and the exigencies of the moment. Executive authority had to provide correctives for these inherent difficulties, and it was important that the chief executive have a body of individuals, held in his confidence, with whom to consult. The responsibility of government was to be focally his; but day-to-day administration and decision, of necessity, was to be entrusted to the hands of others.

2. *The Maintenance of Tension Among the Named Bodies.*—A central, coordinating and overseeing role for the President in relation to all government "officers" is required, also, to permit that office to serve as an effective check on the otherwise to be feared authority of Congress. The framers sought both to create a more effective national government than they had previously experienced, and to make it resistant to domination by transitory majorities or those who for the moment might be the public's political representatives. To those ends, the governmental structure they created embodies both separated powers and interlocking responsibilities; the purpose was to prevent both majoritarian rashness and the governmental tyranny that could result from the conjoining of power in a single source. Maintaining conditions that would sustain the resulting tension between executive and legislature was to be the central constraint on any proposed structure for government.

The Constitutional Convention arose out of dissatisfaction with a government dominated by the legislature, a dissatisfaction on both practical and theoretical grounds. In practice, legislative government did not work; legislatures were fragmented and episodic in their attention to the affairs of state, diffusing and defeating responsibility. In theory, the joining of all government functions in one authority, unchecked by others, was an invitation to tyranny. Interpenetration of function and competition among the branches would protect liberty by preventing the irreversible accretion of ultimate power in any one. As Madison wrote in the *Federalist* papers, the essence lay in "giving to those who administer each department the necessary constitutional means and personal motives to resist encroachments of the others." [117] Madison's strategy was given form in the veto power and in Congress's authority to create the infrastructure of executive government and to exercise plenary control over the President's expenditure of funds (and thus over the size and power of the executive establishment).

* * *

Thus, while the actual text of the Constitution says little about the structure of the federal government beneath the apex, the structure and history of the Constitution make clear the framers' decisions concerning the interdependence of the three branches and the place of the agencies

117. The Federalist No. 51 * * * (J. Madison).

as subsidiary to all three. One may see the issue of balance of power among the three named branches of government as reflecting a process not an institution, with impermanence of resolution not only inevitable but desirable as an outcome. * * *

B. INTERPRETATIONS OF THE CONSTITUTIONAL CONSTRAINTS

In addition to constitutional text and context, the interpretations given the President's place in government by courts and others during the past two hundred years influence contemporary understandings of his relationship to the agencies and Congress's power to structure that relationship. * * *

* * * Congress is free to choose between placing ultimate responsibility for decision with the President and giving that responsibility to those to whom it has initially assigned the work of administration. Even within what is undoubtedly the sphere of executive influence—for example, the conduct of law enforcement—that proposition finds support in the Constitutional Convention's failure to adopt measures such as the Morris plan. The proposition seems undebatable where Congress can find circumstances, such as a need for objective decision, that warrant placing administration beyond the sphere of its own as well as the President's political influence. Yet note that neither choice effects or is a justification for presidential *exclusion*. However unserviceable rigid separation-of-powers arguments have become beneath the very top levels of government, the checks-and-balances idea retains force: congressional arrangements that threaten the viability of an independent, unitary executive capable of opposing the Congress's own assertions of power are, for that reason, suspect.

* * *

[1. The] Formal Approach to the Place of Administration [.]

* * *

Understanding of the relation between the Presidency and administration was shaped by two cases of the 1920's and 30's, *Myers v. United States* [142] and *Humphrey's Executor v. United States*.[143] Both tested the President's claim of inherent executive authority to remove presidential appointees from office in the face of statutory limitations on removal; both appeared to use a strictly formal, separation-of-powers approach to the place of agencies in government. The seemingly opposite conclusions to which they came are usually understood in terms of that approach as denying the independent regulatory commissions any determinate place in the tripartite structure of government. Yet their conclusions can also be understood in light of the checks-and-balances approach, and so understood the opinions are both readily reconciled and consistent with the constitutional scheme.

142. 272 U.S. 52 (1926).   **143.** 295 U.S. 602 (1935).

Myers concerned a postmaster appointed to a four-year term under a statute which for fifty years had required senatorial assent to both appointment and removal of these officials. The President sought to remove him before the expiration of his term, without obtaining senatorial concurrence. * * * A divided Court found that reserving congressional participation in the removal of an executive officer unconstitutionally invaded the President's executive function. The Court's opinion, written by a former President, suggested that the President enjoyed an inherent authority to remove every officer of government he was empowered to appoint (other than a judge protected by article III). It appeared to eradicate the executive/administrative distinction by establishing the President's disciplinary control as universally available. * * *

Humphrey's Executor resulted from President Roosevelt's effort, on the authority of *Myers,* to remove a commissioner of the Federal Trade Commission before the expiration of his seven-year statutory term. Here, a statute enacted before *Myers* required specification of cause for removal, but did not require senatorial concurrence. The President suggested no "cause" for Humphrey's removal beyond political incompatibility—a reason plainly insufficient under the statute. This challenge arose, however, at a time when presidential rather than congressional hegemony may have seemed the more palpable threat; it was decided on the same day that the Court invalidated the National Industrial Recovery Act, once the centerpiece of the New Deal, on the ground of excessive delegation to the President. * * * Acting scant weeks after argument, the Court unanimously repudiated the *Myers* dicta and found that Congress could validly impose a "cause" requirement on the discharge of a Federal Trade Commissioner; given the circumstances, the Court did not have to say what cause could be.

Reading both opinions, one is struck by their emphasis on a radical separation of powers within government, with a concomitant need to place agencies *in* one or another branch, maximally free from intrusion by the others. For the *Myers* Court, "the reasonable construction of the Constitution must be that the branches should be kept separate in all cases in which they were not expressly blended, and the Constitution should be expounded to blend them no more than it affirmatively requires." From placement of the Post Office Department in the executive branch and the absence of any constitutional provision for congressional participation in removal, all else followed. For the *Humphrey's Executor* Court, "[t]he fundamental necessity of maintaining each of the three general departments of government entirely free from the control or coercive influence, direct or indirect, of either of the others, has often been stressed, and is hardly open to serious question." * * * [T]he Court said the President could exercise no authority over [Federal Trade Commission] members beyond the constitutionally explicit one of appointment. Viewing both the unquestioned congressional purpose to remove the FTC from politics and the agency's particular functions, the Court described it as "an agency of the legislative or judicial department of the government," exercising in those contexts only an "executive function—as distinguished from executive power in the constitutional sense." ·

More than *Myers,* but perhaps in consequence of that decision, the reasoning of the *Humphrey's Executor* Court seems open to question. * * * [T]he opinion tells us that the agency is in *both* the legislative *and* the judicial branches, because of the functions it performs, but not how an agency can at the same moment reside in both the legislative and the judicial branches, consistent with the "fundamental necessity of maintaining each of the three general departments of government entirely free from the control or coercive influence * * * of either of the others." * * *

If the formal question where in government to place the agency is put aside, however, it is not hard to understand the Court's result. It described the FTC's functions as follows:

> (1) The FTC could direct cessation of unfair methods of competition in commerce, *after* full-dress adjudicatory hearings;

> (2) It could conduct investigations culminating in a report to the Congress with recommendations for legislation; and

> (3) It could act 'as a master in chancery' in antitrust suits brought by the Attorney General and referred to it by a district court.

Assurance of impartiality and the absence of political controls of any character are centrally important to two parts of the statutory scheme as thus described; providing information-gathering service to Congress (not the President) characterizes the remainder. So far as the Court was educated to the Commission's functions, the FTC did little as to which unified policy direction was even arguably relevant. Thus, the need to maintain tension between the named branches was not implicated. The Court was acutely conscious, however, of the extent to which the Commission acted in circumstances calling for judicial impartiality and the removal from politics that might tend to protect it. * * *

Once fairness considerations are taken into account, these cases can be seen as explained by the difference between * * * presidential power that implicates a struggle between the branches and one that does not. *Myers* can readily be limited to the issue * * * [of] senatorial concurrence in removal[.] * * * Reservation of senatorial approval for removals suggests political power struggles between President and Senate that are not connoted by a judgment that fixed tenure in office, with limitations on discharge, will be useful for the ends of public policy. * * * [Congress] has not only limited the President's ordinary political authority by imposing a "for cause" requirement, but also greatly expanded its own political authority by insisting on a voice in that determination. The latter measure defeats any claim that the measure has an apolitical end such as assuring objectivity.

Humphrey's Executor, in turn, could be understood as having turned on precisely this distinction between those limitations on removal where

Congress has retained some role and those in which it has not.   * * *
The FTC Act imposes no congressional intrusion analogous to that
presented to the Court in *Myers;* on its facts, it does not even foreclose
some presidential involvement in FTC policy formation.   * * * [T]he
Court found only that Congress could legitimately insist that one holding
the office of Federal Trade Commissioner serve on terms other than
those of a personal adviser. It did not have to say whether the President
could give the FTC Commissioners binding directives, or if so of what
sort, or what might be the consequences of any failure of theirs to honor
them.

* * *

[2.] *The Checks-and-Balances Approach to the Place of Administra-*
tion [.] [In the 1970's the Court indicated that it] might be ready to
abandon the pigeonholing of agencies as "executive," "legislative" or
"judicial" in favor of considering the impact of particular challenged
provisions respecting them on the balance of authority among the
institutions defined in articles I, II and III. * * *

* * *

This more functional inquiry assumed particular importance in
Buckley v. Valeo,[177] a case concerning the necessary character of presidential and congressional relationships to an administrative agency.
Buckley presented a series of challenges to the Federal Election Act and
to the Federal Election Commission (the Commission) the Act created
and empowered; significant for our purposes was a separation-of-powers
challenge to a provision for direct legislative appointment of some
members of the Commission. The Commission was authorized, inter
alia, both to conduct investigations—the quasi-legislative activity considered in *Humphrey's Executor* —and to engage in rulemaking, [a] quasi-
legislative activity which had not been at issue in that case. Were the
FEC only empowered to conduct investigations, the Court reasoned, the
appointment provisions would not have been objectionable; such powers
are "in the same general category as * * * Congress might delegate to
one of its own committees." But rulemaking "represents the performance of a significant governmental duty exercised pursuant to a public
law," and is *therefore* to be exercised only by officers of the United
States—by persons subject to appointment by the President (with or
without senatorial assent) or by a head of one of "the executive Departments."

* * *

When one is playing a shell game, however, it is important to
maintain the observer's confidence that one of the shells does contain
the pea, even if it is not the shell currently under examination. By
characterizing as a function having to be exercised outside the legislature just that quasi-legislative activity (rulemaking) that previously had

177. 424 U.S. 1 (1976).

been described with some uniformity as the result of a delegation of *legislative* power, the Court destroyed that illusion, breaking through any separation-of-powers notion that the powers of government generally could be neatly parcelled into three uniquely empowered entities. The Court insisted that the central issue was to be the character of the relationships between that agency and the named heads of government, and not the formal structure of the agency in question. Those conclusions could be reached without having to "put" the FEC anywhere; the claim to that power and relationship does not depend on where the agency "is," so much as the necessity of maintaining the desired sharing of authority among the named actors of the Constitution.   * * *

* * *

The checks-and-balances concerns with relationship and effective functioning thus suggested seem to be paralleled by analytic developments in other contexts in which the structural constraints of the Constitution are the central issue. Debate over the tenth amendment, for example, revived by *National League of Cities v. Usery*,[190] resolved into near unanimity in formulating the relevant inquiry (if not its application): whether a challenged measure threatens the integrity of the states in the constitutional scheme. Allocation of authority between state and nation, like that between executive and legislature, can be understood as a means of protecting individuals from overwhelming governmental power; deciding what is required to preserve that protection for citizens has characterized the recent judicial debates more than a cataloguing of activities inherently for the states qua states. The same may also be suggested for the public debate—not yet captured in litigation—whether the Constitution constrains Congress's authority to make exceptions to the appellate jurisdiction of the Supreme Court. What would "prevent the [Judicial] Branch from accomplishing its constitutionally assigned functions"[192] is widely accepted as the appropriate inquiry to be made.

Inquiry along these lines has substantial advantages. It permits the judiciary to recognize the inescapable merger of some governmental functions, and permits it, as well, to tolerate periodic changes in relative political effectiveness as between President and Congress, Congress and Court, Nation and States. Our political history has been characterized by the emergence of first one and then the other as the more forceful national political presence; even if it were desirable, it seems unlikely that courts could sustain the constant intervention that would be required to maintain a fixed relationship. Rigid molds are more easily broken; permitting growth and change makes more likely the enduring of the essential form.

* * *

190. 426 U.S. 833 (1976). [This article was written a year before the Court's decision in Garcia v. San Antonio Metropolitan Transit Authority, 469 U.S. 528 (1985), overruling National League of Cities v. Usery—eds. note.]

192. Nixon v. Administrator of General Services, 433 U.S. 425, 445 (1977).

C. SEPARATION OF FUNCTIONS AND CONSIDERATIONS OF INDIVIDUAL FAIRNESS

Much of the force apparently attached to the issue of "place" in the cases separating the President from the agencies has its source in considerations of fairness—notions more readily ascribed to the idea of separation of *functions* than separations of *powers*. Separation of powers, as a theoretical concern, has to do with the general tendency of certain governmental structures to result in (or prevent) tyrannical government—that is, a government no longer under the control of the people. Separation of functions suggests a much more atomistic inquiry, asking what combinations of functions or impacts of external influence will interfere with fair resolution of a particular proceeding. [T]he *Humphrey's Executor* Court [expressed horror] at the idea that a judge of the "legislative" Court of Claims might be subject to presidential discipline in "exercising judicial power." That the Court accepted her sitting on a *legislative* court suggests that the issue for the Court was not (or not only) one of place but one of function. Wherever she is located in government, a judge ought not to be connected with the controversy or the parties, ought not to be interested in the outcome, must learn from the parties only what they convey in the presence of each other, and— above all—ought not to be called upon to explain her decision in the political forum. External or political intervention in on-the-record decisionmaking would be regarded as inappropriate, whether done by the President or any other political figure (e.g., a legislator) * * *. These are judgments we reach wholly without regard to the balance of advantage between Congress and the White House in overseeing the day-to-day functioning of political government. Within agencies themselves * * * these judgments are reflected in the creation of officials (administrative law judges, appeal bodies, judicial officers) remarkably free of organizational responsibilities or political supervision, who perform on-the-record judging functions.

This separation-of-functions rationale provides, in effect, a politically neutral basis for supporting congressional judgments about governmental structure that might otherwise appear to threaten presidential function. Legislative judgments that certain types of decisions are preferably made in the absence of *any* political intervention tend to defeat arguments that statutory provisions for agency independence reflect the outcome of competition between Congress and President for political dominance. Acquiescing in such judgments has no strong implications for the allocation of authority between the political branches, and raises few threats to the scheme of checks and balances. The very judgment made requires that the relationship between Congress and the agency be affected equally with that between the President and the agency; where these considerations come into play, it would be inappropriate for either to intervene unless as a party. * * *

* * *

D. CONFLICT BETWEEN THE MODELS OR A RETURN TO FORMALISM?

* * *

The preceding pages should suggest that of the three approaches commonly used to describe our government's structure, the checks-and-balances model, understood in light of the fairness aspirations of the separation-of-functions principle, best describes the complexity of contemporary government in terms that permit adherence, as well, to the framers' vision. The seeming bright-line simplicity of separation of powers, never in fact fully embraced by those who wrote the Constitution, is neither necessary as a matter of text, context or past interpretation for those parts of government not named in the Constitution itself, nor possibly successful in describing that bulk of government as it is. Courts have been able to reconcile the reality of modern administrative government and the strict separation-of-powers model, as in *Humphrey's Executor,* only by blind feats of definition—internally inconsistent while at the same time effectively negating the ability of a unitary, competent President to serve as an essential check against legislative hegemony.

Yet an analysis framed in terms of interference with the capacity to maintain one's core function is more effective as a means of organizing debate than as a rule for deciding cases. It leaves more room for judicial fact-finding and the operation of judicial discretion than "bright-line" formulae such as those employed in *Humphrey's Executor* appear to. To one who takes from constitutional history, above all, a sense that the framers both intended effective government and placed our protection from overwhelming government in continuing struggle among its parts rather than rigid demarcation of function, that is not troublesome. However, the bright line has its allure for justices faced with the responsibility to decide particular cases in ways that will guide the future conduct of others, future justices included. * * *

* * *

[Consider the effect this allure had on the Court in *INS v. Chadha.*[257]] [T]he majority opinion strikingly returns to the formalities of *Humphrey's Executor* at the same time as it repudiates the particular use to which they were put in that case. Although denying any purpose to suggest that the three branches of government are "hermetically sealed," the opinion makes its dominant metaphor an expression of fear lest the "hydraulic pressures" of power-seeking burst the boundaries of each branch's appropriate function—a palpable evocation of the "airtightness" of the *Myers–Humphrey's Executor* approach. Where the *Humphrey's Executor* Court accomplished its ends by placing "quasi-adjudication" and "quasi-legislation" outside the executive branch, however, the *Chadha* majority identifies both as executive branch activities—a characterization consistent with *Buckley v. Valeo*—and thus finds a significant question whether Congress has usurped the President's power.

Note that the decision here subjected to congressional review cannot easily be characterized as the President's: it was made in the first

257. [462 U.S. 919] (1983).

instance by a civil servant strongly protected against political interference in his judgment and required by statute to decide the case before him "on the record." The difference between decisions that are explicitly presidential and those that are not is that the compartmentalization inherent in the separation-of-powers idea is an essential element of the framer's plan only for the former. * * *

* * *

Suppose the Court had been willing to dissociate the agency from the President and had focused primarily on the question of the relationships between the agency and the three named heads of constitutional authority. From that perspective the legislative veto issue might have looked rather different. The question would then be what impact the legislative veto could be expected to have on the President's own relationship with the agency and, in particular, on his claim to function as the sole head of government. A veto mechanism need not defeat such a claim; indeed, the more it seemed that the action being taken was fairly to be characterized as the President's own, the less objectionable the veto might be. From a checks-and-balances perspective, the need for cross-checking institutions of control is the more urgent where authority is to be exercised by one of the named heads of government. For example, in the reorganization context it might readily be argued that Congress could afford to confer the authority to initiate restructuring of government on the President only if it reserved the counterbalancing possibility of "legislative veto" disapproval. The President, gaining the initiative through the authorizing legislation, would hardly lose in the exchange.

Where the action clearly is not the President's, on the other hand, the legislative veto begins to appear, not as a device for sharing enlarged responsibility within government, but as a means for enhancing congressional political controls at the expense of presidential ones. At least within a certain range, we have seen that Congress readily can exclude the President from political control of regulatory outcomes. Yet the rationale for these measures, and for the apparent offense they give to the President's claim to serve as the unitary head of executive government, equally requires that Congress exclude itself from such controls. A measure that enhances Congress's political controls while isolating the President would threaten both his position as unitary head of government, and his continuing capacity to function as a political counterweight to Congress. Thus, in *Chadha,* Congress's reserved power to disapprove a proposed suspension is made even more problematic by the "on-the-record" regime within the Department that impairs direct presidential control. If the President is excluded from directing that a given rule be adopted, amended, or rejected while Congress is able to assert that authority, one has lost the intended focus of responsibility and balance.

BIBLIOGRAPHY

Brown, *Separated Powers and Ordered Liberty,* 139 U.Pa.L.Rev. 1513 (1991).

Bruff, *On the Constitutional Status of the Administrative Agencies,* 36 Am.U.L.Rev. 491 (1987).

Chemerinsky, *A Paradox Without a Principle: A Comment on the Burger Court's Jurisprudence in Separation of Powers Cases,* 60 S.Cal. L.Rev. 1083 (1987).

J. Choper, JUDICIAL REVIEW AND THE NATIONAL POLITICAL PROCESS ch. 5 (1980).

Devins, *Budget Reform and the Balance of Powers,* 31 Wm. & Mary L.Rev. 993 (1990).

THE FEDERALIST Nos. 47–48, 51 (Madison).

Feld, *Separation of Political Powers: Boundaries or Balance?,* 21 Ga. L.Rev. 171 (1986).

L. Fisher, CONSTITUTIONAL CONFLICTS BETWEEN CONGRESS AND THE PRESIDENT (1985).

L. Fisher, THE POLITICS OF SHARED POWER (1981).

W. Gwyn, THE MEANING OF THE SEPARATION OF POWERS (1965).

Krent, *Separating the Strands in Separation of Powers Controversies,* 74 Va.L.Rev. 1253 (1988).

Levi, *Some Aspects of Separation of Powers,* 76 Colum.L.Rev. 371 (1976).

Merrill, *The Constitutional Principle of Separation of Powers,* 1991 Sup.Ct.Rev. 225.

Osgood, *Governmental Functions and Constitutional Doctrine: The Historical Constitution,* 72 Cornell L.Rev. 553 (1987).

Sargentich, *The Contemporary Debate About Legislative–Executive Separation of Powers,* 72 Cornell L.Rev. 430 (1987).

Sargentich, *The Limits of the Parliamentary Critique of the Separation of Powers,* 34 Wm. & Mary L.Rev. 679 (1993).

Sharp, *The Classical American Doctrine of "The Separation of Powers",* 2 U.Chi.L.Rev. 385 (1935).

Stith, *Congress' Power of the Purse,* 97 Yale L.J. 1343 (1988).

Stith, *Rewriting the Fiscal Constitution: The Case of Gramm–Rudman– Hollings,* 76 Calif.L.Rev. 595 (1988).

Strauss, *Formal and Functional Approaches to Separation-of-Powers Questions—A Foolish Inconsistency?,* 72 Cornell L.Rev. 488 (1987).

Symposium, *Separation of Powers and the Executive Branch: The Reagan Era in Retrospect,* 57 Geo.Wash.L.Rev. 401 (1989).

Symposium, *The American Constitutional Tradition of Shared and Separated Powers,* 30 Wm. & Mary L.Rev. 209 (1989).

Symposium, *The Presidency and Congress: Constitutionally Separated and Shared Powers,* 66 Wash.U.L.Q. 485 (1990).

M.J.C. Vile, CONSTITUTIONALISM AND THE SEPARATION OF POWERS (1967).

B. THE EXECUTIVE POWER: DOMESTIC AFFAIRS

Courses in constitutional law usually deal with issues of value and method, like those discussed in Section A, in the context of particular substantive problems. For the sake of simplicity we group these problems in four categories. The first two focus on the scope of executive power. Unlike Article I of the Constitution, which states in some detail the powers given to Congress, Article II is fairly laconic about the President's authority. This generates frequent conflict about the limits of executive power in domestic affairs [1] (which we address in this Section) and foreign affairs [2] (which we take up in Section C).

Henry Monaghan and Edward Corwin discuss the scope of the President's inherent authority in domestic affairs—an issue raised by President Truman's seizure of the nation's steel mills during the Korean War. Monaghan argues that there is no such thing.[3] He asserts that the text and history of the Constitution envision only a "law enforcement" executive: except for those functions expressly named in Article II, the President gets his power to act from Congress alone. Monaghan concedes that nowadays (since the nondelegation barrier has fallen) the congressional authorization may be exceedingly broad and vague. But as the *Steel Seizure Case* illustrates, we have held fast to the idea that executive officials must have some statutory warrant for their actions. Corwin disagrees. He contends that the President has fairly broad inherent authority. He does not deny the fact of congressional supremacy: the President may not do what Congress has forbidden. But the courts should not try to enforce legal limits on the President's authority through a narrow definition of the idea of "executive power."

1. Youngstown Sheet & Tube Co. v. Sawyer, 343 U.S. 579, 72 S.Ct. 863, 96 L.Ed. 1153 (1952).

2. Dames & Moore v. Regan, 453 U.S. 654, 101 S.Ct. 2972, 69 L.Ed.2d 918 (1981); United States v. Curtiss–Wright Export Corp., 299 U.S. 304, 57 S.Ct. 216, 81 L.Ed. 255 (1936).

3. In a part of the article not reproduced here, he qualifies this point in one way. There is, he concedes, a narrow inherent executive "protective" power which gives the President authority to protect and defend the personnel, property, and instrumentalities of the United States from harm. For examples see In re Neagle, 135 U.S. 1, 10 S.Ct. 658, 34 L.Ed. 55 (1890), and In re Debs, 158 U.S. 564, 15 S.Ct. 900, 39 L.Ed. 1092 (1895).

HENRY P. MONAGHAN, THE PROTECTIVE POWER OF THE PRESIDENCY
93 Colum.L.Rev. 1, 3–5, 9–10, 12–18, 20–22 (1993).

The Constitution seemingly contemplates only a "law enforcement" Executive; that is, the President simply "executes" the will of Congress. * * * This conception recognizes little independent presidential authority, at least when presidential authority would directly interfere with pre-existing private rights. * * * *Youngstown Sheet & Tube Co. v. Sawyer (Steel Seizure)* [17] provides the classic illustration of this conception of presidential authority. There, the Supreme Court invalidated President Truman's attempt to seize the nation's steel mills in the face of a threatened strike that Mr. Truman feared would jeopardize the national defense and military operations in the Korean conflict. The Court said that "[i]n the framework of our constitution, the President's power to see that the laws are faithfully executed refutes the idea that he is to be a lawmaker." While the Court did not see the issue before it as involving in any significant way presidential authority in foreign affairs, its premise is fully applicable to presidential conduct in foreign as well as domestic affairs: no independent, free-standing presidential law-making authority exists insofar as the rights of American citizens are concerned.

Well before *Steel Seizure,* however, the reality behind the constitutional theory of the law enforcement Executive had been transformed. Alexander Hamilton wrote that "[t]he *essence of the legislative authority* is to enact laws, or in other words, *to prescribe rules for the regulation of the society.*" [22] In theory, this congressional authority was nondelegable, but—and the "but" is pretty nearly everything—the nondelegation barrier, never very sturdy, has collapsed. Only the fiction remains. The reality is that frequently executive officials shape and reshape the relevant legal rules. Congress itself is no longer required to "prescribe [the] rules for the regulation of society;" it can, instead, transfer much of that task to the executive. As *Steel Seizure* illustrates, what remains of the old constitutional jurisprudence is the quite different requirement that, from the President on down, all executive officials must exhibit some statutory warrant at least when their conduct invades the private rights of American citizens.

* * *

* * * My primary focus is the extent of presidential authority to invade the "private rights" of American citizens *absent legislative authority*—that is, presidential authority independently to alter negatively what in common legal understanding would be viewed as a prior liberty or property baseline. I do not, of course, refer to presidential invasions of constitutionally protected interests, because Congress could confer no such authorization. But the President is not Congress, and so the question persists: to what extent can the President, acting on his or her own, invade the rights of American citizens in circumstances which Congress could—but did not—authorize. As used here, the term "pri-

---

17. 343 U.S. 579 (1952).

22. The Federalist No. 75, at 504 (Alexander Hamilton) (Jacob E. Cooke ed., 1961) (emphasis added)[.]

vate rights" is conventional in nature. The point of reference is to contemporary legal understanding. * * *

* * *

SOURCES OF THE CONCEPT OF "THE EXECUTIVE POWER"

* * *

A. Historical Antecedents and Textual Sources of Executive Authority

The rich tradition out of which the concept of "The executive Power" sprang is best explored through Locke's notion of executive power, which was in place nearly a full century before ratification of the American Constitution. This vantage point provides insight into the concepts of executive that the Framers understood and transformed.

1. *John Locke's Taxonomy of Executive Power.*—Eighteenth-century English conceptions of legislative authority did not include many of the substantive powers now held wholly or partially by Congress. Moreover, English conceptions did not include the notion of a Parliament actively shaping policy so much as that of a Parliament either assenting to or rejecting policy formulated by the Executive. As St. George Tucker recognized, "the laws do in fact originate with the executive." [46] In allocating the powers of their new national government, the framers of the American Constitution clearly broke new ground; indeed, the American Constitution can be seen as a revolutionary document both in the powers it assigned to Congress and in the "active" role it contemplated for that body. In the process, the Constitution's terminology displaced that of Locke.

In 1690, John Locke described three kinds of powers possessed by the executive department,[47] powers, I should add, that were thought to be compatible with the Glorious Revolution's principle of parliamentary supremacy. First, Locke mentioned executive power in what, for us, is its "law enforcement" sense: "Execution of the Laws." Second, Locke described the federative power: "This therefore contains the Power of War and Peace, Leagues and Alliances, and all the Transactions, with all Persons and Communities without the commonwealth, and may be called Federative, if any one pleases. So the thing be understood, I am indifferent as to the name." Third, and finally, Locke referred to "prerogative" power. This term is not now common in American legal discourse because, for the founding generation, it was invariably a term of opprobrium. While prerogative is often simply a synonym for the exercise of lawfully conferred discretion, Locke posited two other troublesome formulations. Prerogative, he said, is "nothing but the Power of doing public good without a Rule," that is, without statutory authority. Indeed, he went further: "This Power to act according to discretion,

---

46. St. George Tucker, Blackstone's Commentaries with Notes of Reference to the Constitution and Laws of the Federal Government of the United States and of the Commonwealth of Virginia 324 (1970)[.]

47. See John Locke, Second Treatise of Civil Government §§ 144–148, 155–168, at 106–08, 113–25 (Gateway Editions 1955) (1690).

for the publick good, without the prescription of the Law, and sometimes even against it, is that which is called Prerogative." Three-quarters of a century later, Blackstone endorsed similar conceptions of prerogative power, although apparently not including the authority to disregard legislation.[55]

Behind the Lockean taxonomy stood important conceptions of the nature of what powers were inherent in the "Executive." With the exception of taxation, most of the great governmental powers were held by the Executive, including the legal right to make treaties, to decide on war and peace, to lay embargoes, to create offices, to raise armies and navies, to act in emergencies, and so on. And, as noted, "laws" generally originated in the Executive. Even after the Glorious Revolution, the Executive remained the dominant figure in government[.] But even advocates of a strong American Chief Executive distanced themselves from the Crown as an acceptable conception of executive authority. This is reflected in the disappearance of Lockean terminology from American legal discourse.

2. *The Constitution and the "Law Enforcement" Executive.*—In the overwhelming majority of cases, presidential conduct is defended on the straightforward ground that the President has simply "executed" identifiable congressional commands. This is the "law enforcement" President—a President who simply executes the authority (however open-ended) conferred by Congress.

When, however, no readily identifiable legislative warrant exists, and arguably the President is implementing presidential policy alone, a different constitutional vocabulary surfaces. The Vesting Clause,[59] the Take Care Clause,[60] the Presidential Oath to "preserve, protect and defend the constitution of the United States,"[61] and the President's "inherent," "implied" or "aggregate" powers are all invoked in defense of the President's conduct.

With one exception, each of these terms is simply a different formulation of the fundamental claim that the President's conduct is valid even though no statutory authority exists. Like the term "The executive Power," terms such as "inherent" and "aggregate" presidential power derive their substantive content from some external reference points, express or implied. Accordingly, one may assign all such claims of inherent, implied, or aggregate presidential power to the Vesting Clause, that is, "The executive Power." Moreover, the same seems true of both the Take Care and Oath Clauses; at bottom, they are simply expressions of the constitutional nature of "The executive Power."

* * *

55. See 1 William Blackstone, Commentaries * 243–44.

59. "The executive Power shall be vested in a President of the United States of America." U.S. Const. art. II, § 1.

60. "[H]e shall take Care that the Laws be faithfully executed." Id. § 3.

61. Id. § 1.

3. *Early American Constitutional History.*—We turn now from terminology to the substance behind the terminology. Whatever other uncertainties may exist about the founding generation's vision of the American presidency, no reasonable doubt existed on one point: the President possessed no independent law-making power. A good deal of the relevant evidence is negative in character, inferable simply from the complete absence of any claims. The silence is, however, fully consistent with what was said. Jefferson's Proposed Constitution for Virginia, drafted in 1783, contains perhaps the best statement of the limited nature of American conceptions of "executive power":

> By executive powers, we mean no reference to those powers exercised under our former government by the crown as of its prerogative, nor that these shall be the standard of what may or may not be deemed the rightful powers of the Governor. We give them those powers only, which are necessary to execute the laws (and administer the government), *and which are not in their nature either legislative or judiciary.* The application of this idea must be left to reason.

This is, of course, the "Whig" theory of executive power, one that is incompatible with the recognition of an independent executive regulatory power, or indeed with much of the modern presidency, because the modern Executive quite plainly executes laws that "are * * * in their nature * * * [both] legislative or judiciary." Jefferson went on, moreover, to reject specific substantive attributes of the Crown's federative and prerogative powers:

> We do however expressly deny him the prerogative powers of *erecting* courts, *offices,* boroughs, corporations, fairs, markets, ports, beacons, light-houses, and sea marks; of laying embargoes, of establishing precedence, of retaining within the State, or *recalling to it any citizen thereof,* and of making denizens, except so far as he may be authorized from time to time by the legislature to exercise any of those powers.

* * *

Not surprisingly, * * * the most important datum—the Constitution itself—contains no hint of an independent presidential regulatory power. The great powers of the national government are vested in Congress. Some of the Crown's important powers—to create offices, to declare war—were transferred outright to Congress; other formerly important "executive" powers, such as making appointments and treaties, were shared with the Senate. * * *

Federalist, the great canonical authority, is fully consistent with this view. Hamilton expressly disclaimed the Crown's powers as a model for the American presidency. While he emphasized that "[e]nergy in the executive is a leading character in the definition of good government," [78]

---

78. The Federalist No. 70, at 471 (Alexander Hamilton) (Jacob E. Cooke ed., 1961).

that energy largely consisted in authority to use the military, when necessary, to enforce national law and for the common defense. * * *

* * *

B. The Residuum Argument

The view that the "executive Power" lacks independent substantive content has not gone unchallenged. Implicitly taking the Crown's powers (or Locke's description) as a bench-mark, some commentators have insisted that, in 1789, "The executive Power" had a substantive content. Accordingly, unless the Constitution reallocates formerly "executive" powers to Congress generally, or to the Senate particularly, whatever power was held by the "Executive" in 1789 must have been understood to inhere in the President.

Writing as "Pacificus," Hamilton first articulated the public foundation for this "residuum" argument in June 1793 in his well-known defense of Washington's Proclamation of Neutrality in the conflict between Great Britain and France.[95] Emphasizing the language differences between the Constitution's grants of "all legislative Powers hereinafter granted" and "The executive Power," Hamilton insisted that the Constitution embodied an independent, substantive conception of executive power. Article II's subsequent "enumerations" of specific executive powers were, he insisted, only "intended by way of greater caution, to specify and regulate the principal articles implied in the definition of Executive Power."

In *Myers v. United States*,[97] Chief Justice Taft appeared to endorse the Hamiltonian conception: "The executive power was given in general terms, strengthened by specific terms where emphasis was regarded as appropriate, and was limited by direct expressions where limitation was needed." Taft attacked the notion that the subsequent grants of power to the Executive were unnecessary if the Vesting Clause possessed an independent substantive content. He insisted that much of Article II, such as the treaty and appointments powers, limited powers that otherwise would have been plenary in the Executive. Taft's endorsement was, however, limited, focusing only on presidential control over public administration, specifically on the President's power to remove subordinates he appointed. * * *

Moreover, the "legislative history" of the difference in language between the legislative powers "herein granted" and "The executive Power" provides no basis for ascribing any importance to this difference. That discrepancy occurred late in the Convention, on September 12, 1787, as a result of a Report of the Committee on Style, which had narrowed Congress' legislative powers to those "herein granted," but left unchanged "The executive Power." This change seemed designed

---

95. See Pacificus No. 1 (June 29, 1793), reprinted in 15 The Papers of Alexander Hamilton, June 1793–January 1794, at 33–43 (Harold C. Syrett et al. eds., 1969)[.]

97. 272 U.S. 52 (1926) (Taft, C.J.).

only to reflect the limits of federalism on national regulatory power, not to ratify or to recognize substantive executive power.

EDWARD S. CORWIN, THE STEEL SEIZURE CASE: A JUDICIAL BRICK WITHOUT STRAW
53 Colum.L.Rev. 53–61, 66 (1953).

President Truman's seizure of the steel industry without specific statutory warrant[1] brings to a new pitch a developing reliance on the "Executive Power" which began almost at the inception of the Federal Government. True, this development has not always proceeded at the same pace; while at times it has seemed to be arrested, during the last fifty years its maturation has been virtually uninterrupted. Moreover, the forces, interests and events which have energized the development are today more potent than ever.

The opening clause of Article II of the Constitution reads: "The executive Power shall be vested in a President of the United States of America." The records of the Constitutional Convention make it clear that the purposes of this clause were simply to settle the question whether the executive branch should be plural or single and to give the executive a title.[2] Yet, in the very first Congress to assemble under the Constitution, the opening clause of Article II was invoked by James Madison and others in order to endow the President with power to remove officers whose appointments had been made with the advice and consent of the Senate. Madison's view prevailed, and was finally ratified by the Supreme Court in 1926.[4] The same theory was invoked by Hamilton in support of President Washington's Proclamation of Neutrality upon the outbreak of war between France and Great Britain. This time the Court's acquiescence was not long delayed. Even in the act of asserting the power of the Court to pass upon the constitutionality of acts of Congress, Chief Justice Marshall said: "By the Constitution of the United States the President is invested with certain important political powers, in the exercise of which he is to use his own discretion, and is accountable only to his country in his political character, and to his own conscience."[6] Even Thomas Jefferson, cousin and congenital enemy of Marshall, had said of the executive power in an official opinion as Secretary of State in 1790: "The Executive [branch of the government], possessing the rights of self-government from nature, cannot be controlled in the exercise of them but by a law, passed in the forms of the Constitution."[7]

Throughout the last half century the theory of presidential power has recruited strength from a succession of "strong" presidents, from an

---

1. Youngstown Sheet & Tube Co. v. Sawyer, 343 U.S. 579 (1952).

2. 2 Farrand, Records of the Federal Convention 171, 185 (rev. ed. 1937).

4. Myers v. United States, 272 U.S. 52 (1926).

6. Marbury v. Madison, 1 Cranch 137, 166 (U.S.1803).

7. 5 Writings of Jefferson 209 (Ford ed. 1895).

economic crisis, from our participation in two world wars and a "cold" war, and finally from organization of the labor movement. Moreover, the constitutional basis of the doctrine has shifted somewhat since the early nineteenth century. It no longer relies exclusively, or even chiefly, on the opening clause of Article II. To the terminology of political disputation in the Jacksonian period it is indebted for such concepts as "residual," "resultant" and "inherent" powers. Thanks to Lincoln, it is able to invoke the president's duty to "take care that the laws," i.e., all the laws, "be faithfully executed," and his power as commander-in-chief of the armed forces. * * *

* * *

The Facts of the Youngstown Case. To avert a nation-wide strike of steel workers which he believed would jeopardize the national defense, President Truman, on April 8th, 1952, issued Executive Order 10340 directing the Secretary of Commerce to seize and operate most of the country's steel mills. The order cited no specific statutory authorization, but invoked generally the powers vested in the president by the Constitution and laws of the United States. Secretary Sawyer forthwith issued an order seizing the mills and directing their presidents to operate them as managers for the United States in accordance with his regulations and directions. The President promptly reported these events to Congress, conceding Congress' power to supersede his order; but Congress failed to take action either then or a fortnight later, when the President again raised the problem in a special letter. Of course, in the Defense Production Act of 1950, the Labor Management Relations (Taft–Hartley) Act of 1947 and the Selective Service Act of 1948, Congress had in fact provided other procedures for dealing with such situations; and in the elaboration of these statutory schemes it had repeatedly declined to authorize governmental seizures of property to settle labor disputes. The steel companies sued the Secretary in a federal district court, praying for a declaratory judgment and injunctive relief. The district judge issued a preliminary injunction, which the court of appeals stayed. On certiorari to the court of appeals, the Supreme Court affirmed the district court's order by a vote of six to three. Justice Black delivered the opinion of the Court in which Justices Frankfurter, Douglas, Jackson and Burton concurred * * *. The Chief Justice, speaking for himself and Justices Reed and Minton, dissented.

The Doctrine of the Opinion of the Court. The chief point urged in Justice Black's opinion is that there was no statute which expressly or impliedly authorized the President to take possession of the steel mills. On the contrary, in its consideration of the Taft–Hartley Act in 1947, Congress refused to authorize governmental seizures of property as a method of preventing work stoppages and settling labor disputes. Authority to issue such an order in the circumstances of the case was not deducible from the aggregate of the executive powers under Article II of the Constitution; nor was the Order maintainable as an exercise of the president's powers as commander-in-chief of the armed forces. The power sought to be exercised was the lawmaking power. * * *

The pivotal proposition of the opinion is, in brief, that inasmuch as Congress could have ordered the seizure of the steel mills, there was a total absence of power in the president to do so without prior congressional authorization. To support this thesis no proof in the way of past opinion, practice or adjudication is offered. * * *

The somewhat different truth of the matter is that the framers of the Constitution were compelled to defend their handiwork against the charge that it violated "the political maxim that the legislative, executive, and judicial departments ought to be separate and distinct." [27] To meet this charge Madison sought to show in the *Federalist* that the three departments ought not to be so far separated as to have no control over each other.[28] In his opinion for the Court in *Ex parte Grossman*,[29] decided 137 years later, Chief Justice Taft adopted the same point of view: the fact that when two departments both operate upon the same subject matter the action of one may cancel that of the other *affords no criterion of the constitutional powers of either.* Rather the question is what does *the pertinent historical record* show with regard to presidential action in the field of congressional power?

The Historical Record. Our history contains numerous instances in which, contrary to the pattern of departmental relationship assumed in the Black opinion, presidential action has occurred within a recognized field of congressional power and has, furthermore, fully maintained its tenancy until Congress adopted superseding legislation. And Congress' right to supersede was not contested. In brief, the mere existence in Congress of power to do something has not, of itself, excluded the president from the same field of power until Congress finally acted. But once this happened, its legislation was forthwith recognized as governing the subject and as controlling presidential action in the area.

* * *

[One] field which the President and Congress have occupied successively is extradition. In 1799 President Adams, in order to execute the extradition provisions of the Jay Treaty, issued a warrant for the arrest of one Jonathan Robbins. As Chief Justice Vinson recites in his opinion:

> This action was challenged in Congress on the ground that no specific statute prescribed the method to be used in executing the treaty. John Marshall, then a member of the House of Representatives, in the course of his successful defense of the President's action, said: "Congress, unquestionably, may prescribe the mode, and Congress may devolve on others the whole execution of the contract; but, till this be done, it seems the duty of the Executive

---

27. The Federalist, No. 47 at 245 (Everyman's ed. 1929).

28. The Federalist, No. 48 (Madison).

29. 267 U.S. 87 (1925). * * *

department to execute the contract by any means it possesses."[32] Not until 1848 did Congress enact a statute governing extradition cases and conferring on the courts, both State and Federal, the duty of handling them.

The power of the president to act until Congress acts in the same field is also shown in these instances. The first Neutrality Proclamation, issued by President Washington in 1793, was also without congressional authorization. The following year Congress enacted the first neutrality statute, and subsequent proclamations of neutrality have been based on an act of Congress governing the matter. The president may, in the absence of legislation by Congress, control the landing of foreign cables in the United States and the passage of foreign troops through American territory, and has done so repeatedly. Likewise, until Congress acts, he may govern conquered territory[37] and, "in the absence of attempts by Congress to limit his power," may set up military commissions in territory occupied by the armed forces of the United States.[38] He may determine in a manner binding on the courts whether a treaty is still in force as law of the land, although again the final power in the field rests with Congress.[39] One of the president's most ordinary powers and duties is that of ordering the prosecution of supposed offenders against the laws of the United States. Yet Congress may do the same thing under the "necessary and proper" clause.[40] On September 22, 1862, President Lincoln issued a proclamation suspending the privilege of the writ of habeas corpus throughout the Union in certain classes of cases. By an act passed March 3, 1863, Congress ratified his action and at the same time brought the whole subject of military arrests in the United States under statutory control. Conversely, when President Wilson failed in March, 1917, to obtain Congress' consent to his arming American merchant vessels with defensive arms, he went ahead and did it anyway, "fortified not only by the known sentiments of the majority in Congress but also by the advice of his Secretary of State and Attorney General."[42]

* * *

The doctrine dictated by the above considerations as regards the exercise of executive power in the field of legislative power was well stated by Mr. John W. Davis, principal counsel on the present occasion for the steel companies, in a brief which he filed nearly forty years ago as Solicitor General. The brief defended the action of the president in withdrawing certain lands from public entry, although his doing so was at the time contrary to express statute. "Ours," the brief reads, is a

32. Youngstown Sheet & Tube Co. v. Sawyer, 343 U.S. 579, 684 (1952), citing 10 Annals of Congress 619 (1948).

37. Santiago v. Nagueras, 214 U.S. 260 (1909).

38. Madsen v. Kinsella, 343 U.S. 341 (1952).

39. Charlton v. Kelly, 229 U.S. 447 (1913). See also Botiller v. Dominquez, 130 U.S. 238 (1889).

40. See Sinclair v. United States, 279 U.S. 263, 289, 297 (1929).

42. Berdahl, War Powers of the Executive in the United States 69 (1921).

self-sufficient Government within its sphere. (*Ex parte Siebold,* 100 U.S. 371, 395; *In re Debs,* 158 U.S. 56, 564, 578.) "Its means are adequate to its ends" (*McCulloch v. Maryland,* 4 Wheat. 316, 424), and it is rational to assume that its active forces will be found equal in most things to the emergencies that confront it. While perfect flexibility is not to be expected in a Government of divided powers, and while division of power is one of the principal features of the Constitution, it is the plain duty of those who are called upon to draw the dividing lines to ascertain the essential, recognize the practical, and avoid a slavish formalism which can only serve to ossify the Government and reduce its efficiency without any compensating good. The function of making laws is peculiar to Congress, and the Executive can not exercise that function to any degree. But this is not to say that all of the *subjects* concerning which laws might be made are perforce removed from the possibility of Executive influence. The Executive may act upon things and upon men in many relations which have not, though they might have, been actually regulated by Congress. In other words, just as there are fields which are peculiar to Congress and fields which are peculiar to the Executive, so there are fields which are common to both, in the sense that the Executive may move within them until they shall have been occupied by legislative action. These are not the fields of legislative prerogative, but fields within which the lawmaking power may enter and dominate whenever it chooses. This situation results from the fact that the President is the active agent, not of Congress, but of the Nation. As such he performs the duties which the Constitution lays upon him immediately, and as such, also, he executes the laws and regulations adopted by Congress. He is the agent of the people of the United States, deriving all his powers from them and responsible directly to them. In no sense is he the agent of Congress. He obeys and executes the laws of Congress, not because Congress is enthroned in authority over him, but because the Constitution directs him to do so.

Therefore it follows that in ways short of making laws or disobeying them, the Executive may be under a grave constitutional duty to act for the national protection in situations not covered by the acts of Congress, and in which, even, it may not be said that his action is the direct expression of any particular one of the independent powers which are granted to him specifically by the Constitution. Instances wherein the President has felt and fulfilled such a duty have not been rare in our history, though, being for the public benefit and approved by all, his acts have seldom been challenged in the courts.

* * *

* * * [T]he moral from all this is plain: namely, that escape must be sought from "presidential autocracy" by resort not to the judicial power, but to the legislative power—in other words, by resort to timely action by Congress and to procedures for the meeting of emergency situations so far as these can be intelligently anticipated.

And—not to give the thing too fine a point—what seems to be required at the present juncture is a new Labor Disputes Act which ordains procedures for the handling of industry-wide strikes in terms so comprehensive and explicit that the most headstrong president cannot sidestep them without manifest attaint to the law, the Constitution and his own oath of office. "Presidential autocracy," when it is justified, is an inrush of power to fill a power vacuum. Nature abhors a vacuum; so does an age of emergency. Let Congress see to it that no such vacuum occurs.

BIBLIOGRAPHY

Presidential Power

Abascal & Kramer, *Presidential Impoundment Part I: Historical Genesis and Constitutional Framework,* 62 Geo.L.J. 1549 (1974); *Part II: Judicial and Legislative Responses,* 63 Geo.L.J. 149 (1974).

Black, *Some Thoughts on the Veto,* 40 L. & Contemp.Probs. 87 (1976).

Bruff, *Judicial Review and the President's Statutory Powers,* 68 Va. L.Rev. 1 (1982).

Easterbrook, *Presidential Review,* 40 Case W.Res.L.Rev. 905 (1990).

THE FEDERALIST Nos. 67–77 (Hamilton).

Fleishman & Aufses, *Law and Orders: The Problem of Presidential Legislation,* 40 L. & Contemp.Probs. 1 (1976).

Ledewitz, *The Uncertain Power of the President to Execute the Laws,* 46 Tenn.L.Rev. 757 (1979).

Lessig & Sunstein, *The President and the Administration,* 94 Colum.L.Rev. 1 (1994).

P. Shane & H. Bruff, THE LAW OF PRESIDENTIAL POWER (1988).

Sidak, *The President's Power of the Purse,* 1989 Duke L.J. 1162 (1989).

A. Westin, THE ANATOMY OF A CONSTITUTIONAL CASE (1958).

C. THE EXECUTIVE POWER: WAGING WAR

Iraq's invasion of Kuwait in August, 1990 recalled the public's attention to an issue that has never really receded from view since the Viet Nam War. The Constitution makes the President Commander in Chief of the armed forces. But it also grants Congress the authority to declare war, to raise, support, and regulate the army and navy, and a number of related powers. Suppose, as is generally the case, that the President is more willing to commit forces to combat than Congress is. What independent authority does he have? When must he get Congress's permission before acting? And how may Congress rein him in if he acts in ways that it finds objectionable?

J. Gregory Sidak and Harold Koh debate these questions in the context of the Persian Gulf War. Sidak maintains that the procedure by which the President and Congress initiated that war was unconstitutional. When hostilities amount to "war" in the sense used in Article I, nothing less than a formal declaration of war can justify committing the United States to participate. On the other hand, Sidak is willing to allow the President a good deal of freedom to commit armed forces in engagements (offensive as well as defensive) falling short of Article I "wars." He believes that the courts are competent to distinguish between the two.

Koh, like Sidak, argues that the definition of "war" is not a political question. He too would insist that the President get formal congressional approval before committing American troops to a conflict like the Persian Gulf War. But Koh believes that Sidak's all-or-nothing rule is a mistake. A joint resolution like the one that authorized the use of force against Iraq may provide more clarity and direction than a formal declaration of war. And insisting on a more blunt statement may give Congress an excuse for shirking its responsibilities in smaller engagements.[1]

J. GREGORY SIDAK, TO DECLARE WAR
41 Duke L.J. 27, 29–32, 36, 39–40, 43–46, 48–56,
60, 62–63, 68–71, 94–95, 120–121 (1991).

Iraq invaded Kuwait on August 2, 1990. Six days later, President Bush ordered Operation Desert Shield, the deployment of the largest American combat force since the Vietnam War, to protect Saudi Arabia from an Iraqi attack. On November 8, Mr. Bush ordered a virtual doubling of the existing 230,000 American troops in the Persian Gulf, and stated that such additional strength would provide the United States "an adequate offensive military option." On November 29, at the urging of President Bush, the United Nations Security Council passed Resolution 678, which demanded that Iraq unconditionally withdraw from Kuwait by January 15, 1991. This resolution also authorized

1. The pieces by Sidak and Koh discuss constitutional aspects of the warmaking power. Since 1973 this controversy has also had a statutory aspect. In that year, as a kind of climax to the debate over the war in Viet Nam, Congress passed the War Powers Resolution over President Nixon's veto. 50 U.S.C.A. §§ 1541–1548. The Resolution tries to encourage consultation between the President and Congress when hostilities are imminent. It is also designed to require Congressional approval within 60 (or 90) days any time the President commits armed forces to real or imminent hostilities.

The Resolution has not succeeded in either aim. It is difficult to legislate a requirement of consultation. And the mechanism designed to trigger congressional approval has malfunctioned. Congress is re-

quired to act within 60 days after the President files a report under § 1543(a)(1). But Presidents Ford, Carter, Reagan, and Bush simply avoided filing such reports, so the 60–day clock never started running. The Resolution also authorizes Congress to direct the removal of forces by concurrent resolution. But the validity of that provision has been in doubt since the Supreme Court held the legislative veto invalid in INS v. Chadha, 462 U.S. 919, 103 S.Ct. 2764, 77 L.Ed.2d 317 (1983).

The upshot is that constitutional questions still take precedence over statutory questions in war power debates. We must first decide when Congress can stay the President's hand. Only then will we get compliance with rules about consultation, reporting, and termination of hostilities.

member nations to "use all necessary means" to liberate Kuwait and to achieve compliance with the eleven other Security Council resolutions passed in response to Iraq's invasion of Kuwait.

* * *

* * * On January 8, 1991, President Bush formally requested that Congress pass a resolution *supporting* (not authorizing) "the use of all necessary means" to implement Security Council Resolution 678. On January 12, three days after a meeting between Iraq's foreign minister and Secretary of State James Baker proved futile, Congress passed a joint resolution that approved the use of American military force against Iraq after January 15—once the President had determined and reported to Congress that all diplomatic avenues had been exhausted. An eleventh-hour meeting on January 13 between Iraqi President Saddam Hussein and United Nations Secretary General Javier Perez de Cuellar also failed. In the early morning of January 17, the United States and its allies unleashed Operation Desert Storm with over 1400 air sorties against Iraqi military targets. Within days, Iraq retaliated by attacking Saudi Arabia and Israel with ballistic missiles, igniting oil facilities in occupied Kuwait, and dumping millions of barrels of crude oil into the Persian Gulf. On February 24, 1991, the United States and its allies launched the land invasion of Kuwait. Three days later, President Bush announced that Kuwait had been liberated and ordered a cease-fire. Within hours, Iraq announced that it would comply with all United Nations Security Council resolutions regarding the crisis, including the resolution that declared Iraq's annexation of Kuwait null and void.

* * *

DID AMERICA'S ENTRY INTO THE PERSIAN GULF WAR
REQUIRE A PRIOR DECLARATION OF WAR?

* * *

*Is It a Political Question for the Judiciary to Issue
a Declaratory Judgment Saying Ex Ante What
Is or Will Constitute a "War"?*

President Bush's November 8 statement prompted Representative Dellums and fifty-three other members of Congress to file suit to enjoin any Presidential order of an attack on Iraqi forces.[50] Although Judge Harold Greene ultimately denied the motion for a preliminary injunction, holding that the controversy was not ripe for judicial decision, he nonetheless rejected all of the Justice Department's substantive arguments.

The Justice Department argued on behalf of President Bush that it is a political question to say what "war" is, and thus to say what it is that the War Clause grants Congress the power to declare. Quoting the familiar phrase from *Baker v. Carr*,[53] the Justice Department maintained

50. *See* Dellums v. Bush, 752 F.Supp.   **53.** 369 U.S. 186, 217 (1962).
1141 (D.D.C.1990).

that "there is 'a lack of judicially discoverable standards' for determining whether hypothetical military actions in the Persian Gulf area would constitute an 'offensive war' or an 'offensive military attack.' "   * * *

* * *

Judge Greene rejected the Justice Department's political question argument: "If the Executive had the sole power to determine that any particular offensive military operation, no matter how vast, does not constitute war-making but only an offensive military attack, the congressional power to declare war will be at the mercy of a semantic decision by the Executive." In Operation Desert Shield, he noted, "the forces involved are of such magnitude and significance as to present no serious claim that a war would not ensue if they became engaged in combat." The ferocity of the air attack on Iraq that began on January 17, 1991 vindicated Judge Greene's skepticism.

Moreover, Judge Greene noted that "courts have historically made determinations about whether this country was at war for many other purposes—the construction of treaties, statutes, and even insurance contracts." He could have added that the plain text of the Constitution would seem to presume that a federal court is competent to say what "war" is, for it would be difficult otherwise for a court to know what to make of the provision in Article III that "Treason against the United States, shall consist * * * in levying War against them[.]" [61]   * * *

* * *

The Iraq Resolution of January 12, 1991

* * *

On January 8, 1991, President Bush requested congressional "support" for the use of military force, but only, according to the New York Times, "after Congressional leaders said in recent days that he was almost certain to receive Congressional endorsement." After debate on January 10–12, 1991, Congress passed House Joint Resolution 77 [the "Iraq Resolution"], by which "[t]he President is authorized ... to use United States Armed Forces pursuant to United Nations Security Council Resolution 678 (1990) in order to achieve implementation" of the eleven Security Council resolutions passed in response to Iraq's invasion of Kuwait.[80] The votes, 52–47 in the Senate and 250–183 in the House,

---

61. U.S. Const. art. III, § 3, cl. 1.

80. Pub.L. No. 102–1, 105 Stat. 3 (1991)[.] The Iraq Resolution reads:

Whereas the Government of Iraq without provocation invaded and occupied the territory of Kuwait on August 2, 1990;

Whereas, Iraq's conventional, chemical, biological, and nuclear weapons and ballistic missile programs and its demonstrated willingness to use weapons of

mass destruction pose a grave threat to world peace;

Whereas the international community has demanded that Iraq withdraw unconditionally and immediately from Kuwait and that Kuwait's independence and legitimate government be restored;

Whereas the United Nations Security Council repeatedly affirmed the inherent right of individual or collective self-defense in response to the armed attack by

were preceded by debate described as notably eloquent and emotional.
* * *

Notwithstanding the solemnity and professed anguish over the vote on the Iraq Resolution, confusion surrounds its legal and constitutional significance. The Iraq Resolution does not purport to be a declaration of war. Section 2(a) of the Resolution simply states that "[t]he President is authorized * * * to use United States Armed Forces pursuant to United Nations Security Council Resolution 678 * * * in order to achieve implementation" of eleven enumerated Security Council resolutions regarding Iraq's conquest of Kuwait. * * *

* * *

Why Do We No Longer Declare War When We Wage War?

Why is Congress more reluctant to declare war formally than to permit the President to fight a war? After the military successes achieved on the first day of the Persian Gulf War, the political liability of voting for a declaration of war would seem slight. If we rule out that the 102d Congress simply doubted the ability of the American military when it voted on January 12, 1991, we are left groping for answers as to

Iraq against Kuwait in accordance with Article 51 of the United Nations Charter;

Whereas, in the absence of full compliance by Iraq with its resolutions, the United Nations Security Council in Resolution 678 has authorized member states of the United Nations to use all necessary means, after January 15, 1991, to uphold and implement all relevant Security Council resolutions and to restore international peace and security in the area; and

Whereas Iraq has persisted in its illegal occupation of, and brutal aggression against Kuwait: Now, therefore, be it

Resolved by the Senate and House of Representatives of the United States of America in Congress assembled,

Sec. 1. Short Title.

This joint resolution may be cited as the "Authorization for Use of Military Force Against Iraq Resolution".

Sec. 2. Authorization For Use of United States Armed Forces.

(a) Authorization.—The President is authorized, subject to subsection (b), to use United States Armed Forces pursuant to United Nations Security Council Resolution 678 (1990) in order to achieve implementation of Security Council Resolutions 660, 661, 662, 664, 665, 666, 667, 669, 670, 674, and 677.

(b) Requirement for Determination that Use of Military Force Is Necessary.—Before exercising the authority granted in subsection (a), the President shall make

available to the Speaker of the House of Representatives and the President pro tempore of the Senate his determination that—

(1) the United States has used all appropriate diplomatic and other peaceful means to obtain compliance by Iraq with the United Nations Security Council resolutions cited in subsection (a); and

(2) that those efforts have not been and would not be successful in obtaining such compliance.

(c) War Powers Resolution Requirements.—

(1) Specific Statutory Authorization.—Consistent with section 8(a)(1) of the War Powers Resolution, the Congress declares that this section is intended to constitute specific statutory authorization within the meaning of section 5(b) of the War Powers Resolution.

(2) Applicability of Other Requirements.—Nothing in this resolution supersedes any requirement of the War Powers Resolution.

Sec. 3. Reports to Congress.

At least once every 60 days, the President shall submit to the Congress a summary on the status of efforts to obtain compliance by Iraq with the resolutions adopted by the United Nations Security Council in response to Iraq's aggression.

why Congress evaded the formalism of a declaration of war. One possibility is the Cold War fear that a declaration of war against our adversary—usually a communist country—might escalate tensions between the United States and the Soviet Union, and eventually place the superpowers in direct military conflict. The absence of a declaration of war would enable both sides to back away, as in the Cuban Missile Crisis, from the danger of nuclear confrontation without the embarrassment of "losing" a war. A related possibility is that, since Hiroshima, America has suffered from a collective ennui about ever again being formally "at war," knowing that a commitment to wage total war might cause the United States once more to resort to nuclear weapons.

Another explanation of Congress's reluctance to declare war does not require such moral introspection. It is simply the predictable institutional bias of Congress to prefer and to gravitate toward parliamentary government. Congress, I suspect, would gladly trade the power to initiate war for the power to manage and direct the President's prosecution of war. Indeed, three weeks after the air attack of Operation Desert Storm began, members of Congress publicly opined on whether it was time to commence the ground war against Iraq. By not declaring war, Congress can impose conditions on the prosecution of hostilities based on the circular reasoning that, should the President permit things to get out of hand on the battlefield, the nation could be faced with a genuine "war"—which Congress alone has the power to declare. * * *

* * *

The President's War–Making Duties as Commander in Chief

* * *

[In this section Mr. Sidak discusses one source of the President's power to involve the United States in conflict without Congress's permission.] The Commander in Chief Clause does not explicitly address defending the United States against attack. But a more obscure provision in Article I does directly address defending the country against invasion: "No State shall, without the Consent of Congress, * * * engage in War, *unless actually invaded, or in such imminent Danger as will not admit of delay.*" [114] Surely the Commander in Chief would have as much constitutional authority as one of the states to engage in undeclared war in such circumstances. And * * * the records of the Constitutional Convention confirm at least this proposition relating to the war powers. James Madison and Elbridge Gerry made the famous motion "to insert 'declare,' striking out 'make' war; leaving to the Executive the power to repel sudden attacks." [116] The motion carried, 7–2, with one abstention. Moreover, to the extent that customary international law in 1787 informs the meaning of the War Clause, the treatises

114. U.S. Const. art. I, § 10, cl. 3 (emphasis added).

116. [James Madison, Notes of the Debates in the Federal Convention of 1787, at 476 (Norton 1966) (1840).]

on international law published before or contemporaneously with the Constitutional Convention uniformly espoused the view that no declaration of war was necessary in a defensive war for the defender's conduct to be legal as a matter of international law. * * *

[Indeed, it is probable that the President would have the authority to repel attacks on the United States even in the unlikely event that Congress ordered him not to.] First, the Preamble states that one elemental purpose of the Constitution and all the trappings of constitutionalism is to "provide for the common defense * * * and secure the Blessings of Liberty to ourselves and our posterity." Although the Preamble is often wrongly dismissed as constitutional window dressing, given its direct textual relevance, it is entitled to [considerable deference here. We should not] deny the President the power to save the nation, and with it, the Constitution—all for the curious cause of fidelity to the document that presently would cease to be worth the paper on which it was printed.

Second, the Guarantee Clause explicitly states that "[t]he United States shall guarantee to every state in this Union a Republican Form of Government, and shall protect each of them against Invasion." [126] This constitutional mandate, which takes precedence over any act of Congress, is sufficient by itself to dispose of [the problem.]

Third, the President's oath of office requires him to "the best of [his] Ability, *preserve,* protect, and defend the Constitution" [127]—which presumably would not be preserved, but rather discarded or substantially attenuated, under the boot of a foreign invader. * * *

Fourth, much like his oath of office, the President's Article II duty to execute faithfully the laws encompasses his faithful preservation of the Constitution and the form of republican democracy in the United States that it envisions.[129] In this respect, the duty might be regarded as a kind of Guarantee Clause on a national scale. The first and highest law is the Constitution. "This Constitution," the Framers took pains to emphasize, "shall be the supreme Law of the Land." How could that supreme law be preserved, so that future Presidents might execute it faithfully, if the President acquiesced to Congress's demand that he surrender the nation to a foreign invader?

In short * * * the Constitution for at least four reasons does demand that the good guys win—or at least go down fighting—when confronted by a foreign invader. As Justice Grier wrote in the *Prize Cases* in 1862, "if a war be made by invasion of a foreign nation, the President is not only authorized but bound to resist force by force." [132]

The same logic of self-defense would justify the President's ordering of a preemptive strike to thwart an imminent attack on the United States, just as the Framers intended the states to wage undeclared war

---

126. U.S. Const. art. IV, § 4. * * *

127. U.S. Const. art. II, § 1, cl. 8 (emphasis added). * * *

129. *See id.,* art. II, § 3. * * *

132. 67 U.S. (2 Black) 635, 668 (1862).

when faced with "such imminent Danger as will not admit of delay."
* * *

* * *

The President's power to use or threaten military force in self-defense encompasses more than actual or imminent attacks on U.S. territory or forces. * * * "The difficulty comes in working out what constitutes an offensive war that the Congress must declare and what amounts instead to an action in defense of the nation's interests that the president can undertake without prior approval." [137] There is no indication that the Framers intended to require the President to get the prior authorization of Congress before deploying armed forces to rescue or protect American citizens or to provide a counterweight, short of combat, to possible aggression that jeopardizes the national interests of the United States. Certainly recent Presidents have not considered prior congressional approval to be necessary in such cases. President Ford did not seek prior congressional authorization to use American troops to free the Mayaguez by force; nor did President Carter seek prior congressional authorization to undertake the attempt to rescue American hostages in Iran. President Reagan did not seek prior congressional authorization for the invasion of Grenada or for the ill-fated deployment of Marines to Beirut. None of these presidents was impeached.

The Specious Dichotomy Between "General War" and Undeclared "Limited War"

* * *

Professor Eugene Rostow * * * summarizes the * * * original meaning of the War Clause as follows: "Under international law, to which the relevant paragraphs of Article I refer, declarations of war are required only for the rare occasions when states engage in unlimited general war." [166] This view has been espoused by various scholars at least since World War II. Professor James Grafton Rogers concluded in 1945 that, on the basis of the historical practice since 1789, the concept of war that the Constitution empowers Congress to declare "is considered a special category in the uses of force, apparently confined to cases of great effort, to major contests designed to crush and conquer another nation." [167] Writing four decades later, after the experiences of Korea and Vietnam, Professor Joseph Bishop reaffirmed Rogers' conclusion: "If there is any historical difference between wars declared by Congress and other wars, it seems to be that the former have usually been larger in scale and have had as their goals not some more or less limited

---

137. [Stephen L. Carter, *Going to War Over War Powers*, Wash. Post, Nov. 18, 1990, at C4.]

166. [Eugene V. Rostow, *President, Prime Minister or Constitutional Monarch?*, 83 Am.J.Int'l L. 740, 744 (1989).]

167. [James Rogers, World Policing and the Constitution: An Inquiry Into the Powers of the President and Congress, Nine Wars and a Hundred Military Operations, 1789–1945, at 87 (1945).]

objective, such as rescuing American citizens or defending an ally from attack, but the total defeat of the enemy." [168]

* * *

Of course, it does not follow that because the Framers did not believe that a declaration of war was necessary "whenever American troops fought an engagement" [177] they also believed that a declaration of war would be unnecessary before the President could order an American attack on Iraq on the scale plainly suggested before January 15, 1991. * * * Early estimates after the cease-fire in the Persian Gulf War placed the death toll for Iraqi troops at 25,000 to 50,000. By May 22, 1991, the Defense Intelligence Agency estimated that between 50,000 and 150,000 Iraqi soldiers had been killed during Operation Desert Storm. Although I agree that it was in the best interests of the United States to liberate Kuwait, it requires either a peculiar indifference to human suffering or an uncommon capacity for euphemism to characterize so much killing as "limited" war. My concern * * * is that, even if we all agreed that the President can in certain circumstances order the use of military force without congressional approval, the War Clause is reduced to a nullity if Congress permits the President to initiate war, however noble its purpose, on the scale witnessed in the Persian Gulf without a formal declaration.

* * * POLITICAL ACCOUNTABILITY AS A NORMATIVE PRINCIPLE
FOR IMPLEMENTING THE SEPARATION OF POWERS

* * *

It is my premise that adherence to formalism in matters that affect the separation of powers, including the initiation of war, is more likely than constitutional informality and political improvisation to produce predictability and clarity in the specification of the responsibilities of political officials in Congress and the executive branch; to facilitate the effective monitoring of these political officials as they discharge their responsibilities; and to permit the electoral process to function as an effective means to reward fidelity, good judgment, and resourcefulness, and likewise to punish infidelity, folly, and indolence. One of the most important of all constitutional formalities is the declaration of war.

[It] is understandable why the Framers intentionally drafted the Constitution to elevate transaction costs associated with bargaining among the branches—to promote judiciousness and accountability. Although the Framers did not speak in terms of transaction cost economics or public choice theory, their intuition regarding agency costs is remarkable. The most fundamental choice that the Framers made in terms of elevating transaction costs was to reject a parliamentary system in favor of a system separating the executive from the legislature. This choice is

---

168. Joseph W. Bishop, Jr., *Declaration of War, in* 2 Encyclopedia of the American Constitution 549 (Leonard Levy et al. eds., 1986).

177. Carter, *supra* note [137], at C4.

so elemental that it scarcely can be found in the Constitution other than in a statement so grand as "The executive Power shall be vested in a President of the United States of America." Probably the second most fundamental choice conducive to elevating transaction costs was the Framers' creation of a bicameral legislature—a choice that raised the size of the coalition required for collective action, and whose practical importance was perceived to be so substantial that it occasioned the Great Compromise at the Constitutional Convention.

* * *

[The] Supreme Court in *INS v. Chadha* [222] exalted bicameralism as providing, in the case of a rather mundane immigration statute, the assurance that "the legislative power would be exercised only after opportunity for full study and debate in separate settings." Six months after the Persian Gulf War commenced, the Court proved that *Chadha* was not a fluke; instead it was made the cornerstone of the *Washington Airports* decision.[224] Surely the legislative authorization to commence war is weighty enough and infrequently invoked enough to warrant an opportunity for study and debate beyond what the Constitution requires for the most routine legislation. Consider the alternative: If no particular formalism need be obeyed by Congress when the United States decides to initiate war against another nation—the act that Justice Story called "the highest sovereign prerogative" [225]—then it is doubtful that any constitutional event could command obedience to form. In such a case, the Supreme Court's rejection of the legislative veto in *Chadha* on the grounds that it violated bicameralism and presentment would be simply pedantic.

* * *

* * * In his book, *The Strategy of Conflict,* Professor Thomas Schelling observed that a credible strategy of any sort is predicated "on the paradox that the power to constrain an adversary may depend on the power to bind oneself." [344] In 1941, Congress essentially told Japan that the President was empowered to prosecute *successfully* the war, using whatever public or private resources were necessary.[345] * * * [We can

---

222. 462 U.S. 919 (1983).

224. *See* Metropolitan Washington Airports Auth. v. Citizens for the Abatement of Aircraft Noise, Inc., 111 S.Ct. 2298, 2308–09 (1991).

225. [Joseph Story, Commentaries on the Constitution of the United States § 570, at 410 (Ronald D. Rotunda & John E. Nowak eds. 1987) (1833).]

344. Thomas Schelling, The Strategy of Conflict 22 (1960).

345. The declaration of war against Japan on December 8, 1941, S.J.Res. 116, Pub.L. No. 77–328, 55 Stat. 795 (1941), read as follows:

Whereas the Imperial Government of Japan has committed unprovoked acts of war against the Government and the people of the United States of America; Therefore be it

Resolved by the Senate and House of Representatives of the United States of America in Congress assembled, That the state of war between the United States and the Imperial Government of Japan which has thus been thrust upon the United States is hereby formally declared; and the President is hereby authorized and directed to employ the entire naval and military forces of the United States and the resources of the Govsee here] an appealing rationale for why Congress's support for the use of force should be recorded in a formal declaration of war: A credible threat of the sort found in the declaration of war on Japan represents to America's enemy as well as to its own people that the United States is willing to subordinate to the war effort all preferences for other public goods. One even finds some hint of this reasoning in the writings of Blackstone (with whom the Framers were familiar) when he wrote:

> [T]he reason * * * why according to the law of nations a denunciation of war ought always to precede the actual commencement of hostilities, is not so much that the enemy may be put upon his guard, (which is [a] matter rather of magnanimity than right) but that it may be certainly clear that the war is not undertaken by private persons, but the will of the whole community; whose right of willing is in this case transferred to the supreme magistrate by the fundamental laws of society.[348]

To Blackstone, the purpose of a declaration of war was not ceremonial, but rather "to make a war completely effectual." A declaration of war is, relative to the fine tuning of appropriations bills or the periodic congressional review of hostilities under the War Powers Resolution, difficult to reverse. And the greater the difficulty for a nation to gracefully extricate itself from a "war," the greater the incentive for that nation not to enter it—and the stronger the message to its enemy when it declares its intention to resort to war.

It has been clear since 1939—certainly in Europe, Japan, and the Soviet Union—that "total war" not only entails the mobilization of a nation's entire civilian economy, but also threatens to destroy all lives and property. * * * Perhaps one reason that the threat embodied in the declaration of war on Japan was credible was the accompanying willingness to suspend limited constitutional government in two respects: expanding the powers of the state by officially blurring the boundaries between the public and private sectors, and by expanding the powers of the President relative to the two other branches. * * *

* * *

CONCLUSION

The quick military victory over Iraq evokes the famous assessment of the Spanish–American War by John Hay, the United States Ambassador to England: "It has been a splendid little war; begun with the highest motives, carried on with magnificent intelligence and spirit, favored by that fortune which loves the brave." If, as President Bush proudly asserted, the Persian Gulf War has signaled America's awakening from the so-called Vietnam Syndrome, it has caused the nation to

---

ernment to carry on war against the Imperial Government of Japan; and, to bring the conflict to a successful termination, all of the resources of the country are hereby pledged by the Congress of the United States.

[Relocated text. Eds.]

348. 1 Blackstone, [Commentaries], at *249–250.

reassess the wisdom and efficacy of using conventional military force as a tool of American foreign policy. * * *

[But] the manner in which Congress and the President agreed to initiate war against Iraq was inattentive to constitutional duty. * * * If hostilities do not amount to "war," the President requires no prior congressional authorization to engage in them; if Congress "authorizes" the President to use offensive military force in such a situation, its action is precatory or hortatory, but legally insignificant. On the other hand, if hostilities do amount to war (as one reasonably would have expected before the war against Iraq to liberate Kuwait, and as Judge Greene so concluded in *Dellums v. Bush*), then a declaration of war by Congress is the constitutionally preferred means to authorize the initiation or continuation of the offensive use of American military forces. Both the euphemistic issuance of "limited" declarations of war, and the attempt to calibrate the intensity of warfare by adjusting appropriations, beg the antecedent question of whether America's political representatives favor or oppose the use of warfare in a particular instance. Compared to the Iraq Resolution * * * a formal declaration of war is a more politically accountable means to record these representatives' approval or rejection of war and, therefore, a more credible threat to our enemies. It is what the Constitution provides; it is what the American people should demand.

HAROLD HONGJU KOH, THE COASE THEOREM AND THE WAR POWER: A RESPONSE
41 Duke L.J. 122, 124–132 (1991).

[Harold Koh led a group of eleven law professors who filed an amicus curiae brief in support of the congressional complainants in *Dellums v. Bush*.[a] The brief argued that the Constitution gave Congress the power to declare war; that the definition of "war" was not a political question; and that the district court could enjoin the President from taking offensive military action in the Gulf until Congress expressed its approval. He responds here to the arguments made by J. Gregory Sidak in *To Declare War*.]

* * * Sidak's detailed argument reduces to a curious claim: The Constitution * * * required Congress to issue nothing less than a formal declaration of war against Iraq. Under this view, the joint resolution that Congress so agonizingly enacted had no more legal force than a letter to my mother.

* * *

Our memorandum argued, and Judge Greene later held, that the political question doctrine did not bar the federal courts from deciding issues regarding the President's authority to conduct war without con-

a. 752 F.Supp. 1141 (D.D.C.1990).

gressional approval. On this point, Sidak unambiguously sides with us, for he "agree[s] with the Koh Signatories (and disagree[s] with President Bush's lawyers in the Department of Justice) that it is a justiciable political question for a federal court to determine whether armed conflict of a certain level of ferocity constitutes 'war' for purposes of the War Clause." Similarly, we asserted (and Sidak apparently accepts) that the President may not, absent meaningful consultation with and genuine approval by Congress, order U.S. armed forces to make war. Finally, Sidak contends that in the interests of enhancing political accountability, Congress should manifest its approval for war with a high degree of formality. Far from disputing that claim, our memorandum insisted "that Congress must manifest its genuine approval through formal action, not legislative silence, stray remarks of individual Members, or collateral legislative activity that the President or a court might construe to constitute 'acquiescence' in executive acts."

Where, then, do we disagree? Sidak insists that a formal declaration of war is the only political mechanism whereby Congress may constitutionally manifest its understanding and approval for a presidential determination to make war. * * *

Sidak's [historical] argument [for this proposition] can be quickly dispatched. To argue that Congress may only approve war by formal declaration makes about as much sense these days as a claim that Congress may only approve an international commitment by a treaty ratified by two-thirds of the Senate.[24] The Necessary and Proper Clause grants Congress authority to "make all Laws which shall be necessary and proper for carrying into Execution *the foregoing [congressional] Powers, and all other Powers vested by this Constitution in the Government of the United States, or in any Department or Officer thereof.*"[25] In the face of this language, Sidak's conclusion that the resolution was a "legal nullity" seems nothing less than bizarre. Congress's joint resolution that authorized the Iraq war was a duly enacted statute, passed by both houses and signed by the President, and made for the stated purpose of authorizing use of armed forces by the government of the United States. The resolution clearly had legal force, whether one views it as carrying into execution Congress's "foregoing Power" to declare war (and hence as falling within Congress's exclusive constitutional authority), or as executing all the powers to use military force that the Constitution vests in the two political organs of the national government (and hence, as falling within Justice Jackson's famous "zone of twilight in which [the President] and Congress may have concurrent authori-

---

24. Over time, with the blessing of all three branches, the so-called "Congressional–Executive agreement"—an executive agreement that has been approved by joint resolution—has become viewed as effectively interchangeable with an Article II treaty for forging our international commitments. *See* Restatement (Third) of the Foreign Re-lations Law of the United States § 303 cmt. e (1987) ("The prevailing view is that the Congressional–Executive agreement can be used as an alternative to the treaty method in every instance.").

25. U.S. Const. art. I, § 8, cl. 18 (emphasis added).

ty" [27]).

* * *

While trumpeting the advantages of formal declarations, Sidak overlooks that "political accountability" was not the only policy value at issue in the Iraq case. Declarations of war have fallen into desuetude since World War II, partly because they have substantial policy defects. Formal declarations are blunt instruments that do not lend themselves as easily as joint resolutions to modulated uses of force. They tend to be tersely worded documents, enacted hastily in crisis situations, and with only minimal deliberation. They announce that a state of war exists with an enemy, but they neither name our allies nor detail our objectives; nor do they generally set either substantive or procedural limitations upon the authorities being granted to the President. In short, formal declarations—like meat cleavers—have their uses, but not in delicate situations that call for scalpels. To suggest that the Constitution leaves Congress no finer options for approving uses of force smacks of mindless originalism, the charge that some mistakenly leveled against our memorandum.

* * *

* * * Sidak posits that "[b]y requiring formality, the Constitution raises transaction costs and thus intentionally discourages certain bargains that otherwise could be struck between the branches of the federal government in the production of public goods." * * * On its face, the Constitution requires Congress to declare war and the President to obtain congressional approval, and hence assigns each institution "legal turf," but both sides have incentives to bargain around these initial [assignments.] Congress's notorious desire to escape responsibility for hard decisions and the President's instinct to seize the initiative will lead them to avoid, through presidential trespasses or congressional bargaining, the textual allocations of responsibility specified in the Constitution. Sidak concludes that formal declarations of war are normatively desirable because they raise transaction costs, and thus make it harder for both Congress and the President to escape their legal responsibilities through bargaining or acquiescence.

* * *

* * * If Sidak's goal is to construe the Constitution so as to raise the transaction costs of interbranch bargaining, why are formal declarations of war necessarily superior to other formal acts (like joint resolutions) in raising such costs? Once the Iraq Resolution was enacted, transaction costs to bargaining away Congress's "legal rights" became plenty high, even without taking the additional step of a formal declaration of war. Nor, as I have already suggested, did the public have any

27. Youngstown Sheet & Tube Co. v. Sawyer, 343 U.S. 579, 637 (1952) (Jackson, J., concurring).

difficulty monitoring the votes of their elected officials. Finally, the joint resolution, with its various conditions and caveats, was almost certainly more clear than a formal declaration would have been in producing Sidak's desideratum, "predictability and clarity in the specification of the responsibilities of political officials in Congress and the executive branch."

Why argue, then, that a formal declaration of war is constitutionally necessary? Sidak invokes political accountability and separation of powers, but in fact his approach could easily undermine both principles. History teaches that congressional declarations of war are extraordinarily rare. The crucial question thus becomes: Can the President use force abroad unilaterally, without any form of congressional approval, *in the absence of such a declaration* (i.e., in most circumstances)? At various points, Sidak suggests (without explicitly saying so) that the President could do so, citing the Commander in Chief power. * * *

[But if this is true, then] Sidak's rule in fact undercuts political accountability because it plays into the convergent incentives of both President and Congress to "let George do it." If rarely obtained declarations of war were the only occasions for approving wars, then the President would gain greater freedom to use force abroad without the need for congressional consent in "situations short of war," while Congress would gain yet another excuse for not going on the record regarding the President's conduct (namely, "the danger is not sufficiently clear or present to justify a declaration of war"). The irony is that in the name of protecting the original allocation of constitutional authorities, Sidak's "more formal" rule * * * would permit a major reallocation of those authorities. Thus, far from enforcing a system of separation of powers, Sidak's rule would undercut it by broadening the President's de facto authority to conduct unauthorized wars. If the goal is to prevent the President from involving us in wars without congressional approval, then the costs of obtaining congressional approval should be lowered— not raised. By insisting on a formal declaration of war Sidak would raise the costs to Congress of expressing its views, and, thus, widen the sphere of uncontrolled executive discretion.

BIBLIOGRAPHY

Foreign Affairs

Bestor, *Separation of Powers in the Domain of Foreign Affairs: The Original Intent of the Constitution Historically Examined,* 5 Seton Hall L.Rev. 527 (1974).

Casper, *Constitutional Constraints on the Conduct of Foreign and Defense Policy: A Nonjudicial Model,* 43 U.Chi.L.Rev. 463 (1976).

M. Glennon, CONSTITUTIONAL DIPLOMACY (1990).

R. Goldwin & R. Licht, FOREIGN POLICY AND THE CONSTITUTION (1990).

L. Henkin, CONSTITUTIONALISM, DEMOCRACY, AND FOREIGN AFFAIRS (1990).

L. Henkin, FOREIGN AFFAIRS AND THE CONSTITUTION (1972).

H. Koh, THE NATIONAL SECURITY CONSTITUTION (1990).

Koh, *Why the President (Almost) Always Wins in Foreign Affairs: Lessons of the Iran–Contra Affair*, 97 Yale L.J. 1255 (1988).

Symposium, *Legal and Policy Issues in the Iran–Contra Affair: Intelligence Oversight in a Democracy*, 11 Houston J.Int'l L. 1 (1988).

Symposium, *The United States Constitution in Its Third Century: Foreign Affairs*, 83 Am.J.Int'l L. 713 (1989).

War Powers

Adler, *The Constitution and Presidential Warmaking: The Enduring Debate*, 103 Pol.Sci.Q. 1 (1988).

Berger, *War–Making by the President*, 121 U.Pa.L.Rev. 29 (1972).

Bickel, *Congress, the President and the Power to Wage War*, 48 Chi.–Kent L.Rev. 131 (1971).

Biden, *The War Power at a Constitutional Impasse: A "Joint Decision" Solution*, 77 Geo.L.J. 367 (1988).

Buchanan, *A Proposed Model for Determining the Validity of the Use of Force Against Foreign Adversaries Under the United States Constitution*, 29 Hous.L.Rev. 379 (1992).

Ely, *Kuwait, the Constitution, and the Courts: Two Cheers for Judge Greene*, 8 Const. Comm. 1 (1991).

Ely, *The American War in Indochina (Parts I & II)*, 42 Stan.L.Rev. 876, 1092 (1990).

Lobel, *Covert War and Congressional Authority: Hidden War and Forgotten Power*, 134 U.Pa.L.Rev. 1035 (1986).

Lofgren, *On War–Making, Original Intent, and Ultra–Whiggery*, 21 Val.U.L.Rev. 53 (1986).

Lofgren, *War–Making Under the Constitution: The Original Understanding*, 81 Yale L.J. 672 (1972).

Note, *Congress, the President, and the Power to Commit Forces to Combat*, 81 Harv.L.Rev. 1771 (1968).

Note, *The Failure of Constitutional Controls Over War Powers in the Nuclear Age: The Argument for a Constitutional Amendment*, 40 Stan.L.Rev. 1543 (1988).

Ratner, *The Coordinated Warmaking Power—Legislative, Executive, and Judicial Roles*, 44 S.Cal.L.Rev. 461 (1971).

Reveley, *Presidential War–Making: Constitutional Prerogative or Usurpation?*, 55 Va.L.Rev. 1243 (1969).

W.T. Reveley, WAR POWERS OF THE PRESIDENT AND CONGRESS (1981).

A. Sofaer, WAR, FOREIGN AFFAIRS AND CONSTITUTIONAL POWER (1976).

Van Alstyne, *Congress, the President, and the Power to Declare War: A Requiem for Vietnam*, 121 U.Pa.L.Rev. 1 (1972).

F. Wormuth & E. Firmage, TO CHAIN THE DOG OF WAR: THE WAR POWER OF CONGRESS IN HISTORY AND LAW (1986).

War Powers Resolution

Carter, *The Constitutionality of the War Powers Resolution*, 70 Va.L.Rev. 101 (1984).

Ely, *Suppose Congress Wanted a War Powers Act That Worked*, 88 Colum.L.Rev. 1379 (1988).

Emerson, *The War Powers Resolution Tested: The President's Independent Defense Power*, 51 N.D.Lawyer 187 (1975).

Glennon, *The War Powers Resolution: Sad Record, Dismal Promise*, 17 Loyola L.A.L.Rev. 657 (1984).

Lungren & Krotoski, *The War Powers Resolution After the* Chadha *Decision*, 17 Loy.L.A.L.Rev. 767 (1984).

Rostow, *Great Cases Make Bad Law: The War Powers Act*, 50 Texas L.Rev. 833 (1972).

Rostow, *"Once More Into the Breach:" The War Powers Resolution Revisited*, 21 Val.U.L.Rev. 1 (1986).

Rubner, *The Reagan Administration, the 1974 War Powers Resolution, and the Invasion of Grenada*, 100 Pol.Sci.Q. 627 (1986).

Scigliano, *The War Powers Resolution and the War Powers*, in THE PRESIDENCY IN THE CONSTITUTIONAL ORDER 124 (J. Bessette & J. Tulis eds. 1981).

Vance, *Striking the Balance: Congress and the President Under the War Powers Resolution*, 133 U.Pa.L.Rev. 79 (1984).

D.   PRESIDENTIAL AND CONGRESSIONAL CONTROL OF ADMINISTRATIVE AGENCIES

What roles should the President and Congress play in directing administrative agencies? This is the common thread in the third set of substantive separation-of-power problems. Up until the New Deal courts were preoccupied with reconciling the delegation of power to this fourth branch of government with the institutional structure created by the Constitution.[1] Today it is generally agreed that agencies may make

---

1. A.L.A. Schechter Poultry Corp. v. United States, 295 U.S. 495, 55 S.Ct. 837, 79 L.Ed. 1570 (1935). See Mistretta v.

policy judgments—even very important ones—in the first instance. The important issue now is how to allocate control over them between Congress and the executive (and the courts). Many of the modern cases have arisen out of Congress's efforts to control the federal bureaucracy through such devices as appointment,[2] removal,[3] and the legislative veto.[4]

In both *Morrison v. Olson* and *Bowsher v. Synar* the major doctrinal issue was whether Congress could limit or displace the President's power to remove federal officials (the special prosecutor, the Comptroller General). The excerpt from Louis Fisher outlines some of the historical background of this controversy. It also suggests that we will find no clear answers in the text of the Constitution, the specific intentions of the Founders, or precedent. For a proper resolution we may have to look instead to the larger questions of purpose and method discussed in Section A.

The legislative veto procedure held unconstitutional in *INS v. Chadha* was a different kind of legislative response to the growth of the federal bureaucracy. It permitted Congress to give agencies broad and general statutory directives and then, when laws were implemented through orders and rules, to use the veto device to weed out agency action that it viewed as inconsistent with its mandates. Whether this procedure created more serious problems than the ones it solved, and whether its invalidation will prove to be a healthy tonic for Congress, are questions addressed by Robert Nagel (and to some degree by Currie and Strauss in Section A).

LOUIS FISHER, THEORY IN A CRUCIBLE: THE REMOVAL POWER

Constitutional Conflicts Between Congress and the President 60–70 (1985).

Occasionally a statement in the *Federalist Papers* is so wide of the mark, at such odds with events to come, that it has an abrupt and startling effect. So it is with the breezy claim of Alexander Hamilton, in Federalist 77, that the consent of the Senate "would be necessary to displace [public officials] as well as to approve."

The issue that Hamilton disposed of so nonchalantly produced deep divisions among the members of the First Congress. It overshadowed most of the matters that pressed upon the fledgling legislative body in 1789. From May 19 through June 24 the House of Representatives explored the removal power in all its nuances. The debate, occupying

United States, 488 U.S. 361, 109 S.Ct. 647, 102 L.Ed.2d 714 (1989).

2. Morrison v. Olson, 487 U.S. 654, 108 S.Ct. 2597, 101 L.Ed.2d 569 (1988); Buckley v. Valeo, 424 U.S. 1, 96 S.Ct. 612, 46 L.Ed.2d 659 (1976).

3. Morrison v. Olson, *supra* note 2; Bowsher v. Synar, 478 U.S. 714, 106 S.Ct.

3181, 92 L.Ed.2d 583 (1986); Wiener v. United States, 357 U.S. 349, 78 S.Ct. 1275, 2 L.Ed.2d 1377 (1958); Humphrey's Executor v. United States, 295 U.S. 602, 55 S.Ct. 869, 79 L.Ed. 1611 (1935); Myers v. United States, 272 U.S. 52, 47 S.Ct. 21, 71 L.Ed. 160 (1926).

4. INS v. Chadha, 462 U.S. 919, 103 S.Ct. 2764, 77 L.Ed.2d 317 (1983).

almost two hundred pages of the record, represents one of the most thorough expositions on the nature of implied powers. In contrast to many members of Congress today, who let constitutional issues slide by to be disposed of by the courts (if at all), the members of the First Congress faced the constitutional issue with a deep sense of responsibility.

For more than a century it has been the custom of attorneys and scholars, when discussing the removal issue in the First Congress, to write of four schools of thought: (1) the Senate, because of its role in appointments, must have equal participation; (2) removals may be made only by the constitutional process of impeachment; (3) Congress, since it creates an office, may attach to it any condition it decides proper for tenure and removal; (4) the power of removal belongs exclusively to the President as an incident of the executive power.

Those four categories, although convenient for simplicity and tidiness, fail to do justice to the wide-ranging nature of the debate, the complexity of the issues, or the shifting tide of opinion that advanced and receded each day as the deliberation continued. The debate merits close attention because of its instruction on constitutional power.[2]

THE "DECISION OF 1789"

James Madison began the debate by proposing three executive departments: Foreign Affairs, Treasury, and War. At the head of each department would be a Secretary appointed by the President with the advice and consent of the Senate "and to be removable by the President." William Smith of South Carolina immediately objected to giving the President sole power of removal. * * * If a department head were found unfit for his office "the person must remain there," Smith said, just like a member of Congress, unless guilty of some crime. * * * As the first day's debate drew to a close, the House by a "considerable majority" declared that the removal power lay with the President.

Two days later the House considered a resolution to make the heads of the three executive departments "removable by the President." Eleven members, Madison among them, were appointed to draw up a bill. When the House took up the topic on June 16, William Smith clarified his position by identifying two choices: either the Constitution gave the President the power of removal (in which case it was nugatory for Congress to repeat it) or else it was not given to him (and therefore improper for Congress to confer). He also cautioned that competent people would be reluctant to accept a position and risk their reputation if the President could remove them at will. Smith wanted the language eliminated and the question left to the judiciary. This represents a fifth

2. The House debate in 1789, on all three executive departments, appears in the Annals of Congress, I, 368–83 (May 19), 384–96 (May 20), 396 (May 21), 455–79 (June 16), 479–512 (June 17), 512–52 (June 18), 552–77 (June 19), 578–85 (June 22), 590–92 (June 24), 592–607 (June 25), 611–14 (June 27), 614–15 (June 30), and 615 (July 1).

school of thought on the removal issue and an early inclination, long before *Marbury v. Madison* (1803), of judicial review.

Madison, after taking a few days to reexamine the Constitution, conceded that it did not "perfectly correspond with the ideas I entertained of it from the first glance." Precisely how he had adjusted his opinion is not evident from his remarks. The Constitution, he said, vested the executive power in the President, subject to certain exceptions, such as the Senate's participation in the appointment process. He believed that Congress could not extend the exceptions or modify in any way the President's authority. Therefore it was improper to associate the Senate with the President in the removal process. Yet to strike the clause might imply that Congress doubted whether the President had the removal power. It was better, Madison concluded, to retain the language.

Other delegates objected to letting Congress amend the Constitution by statutory construction whenever the document was silent on a question. Congressman Samuel Livermore acknowledged that Congress had authority to create an office and to attach to it whatever limitations and restrictions it thought appropriate, but he thought it very improper to say that the power of giving birth to a creature permitted Congress to "bring forth a monster." Since he feared that a President might remove someone on mere caprice to make room for a favorite, he wanted every person "to have a hearing before he is punished." Here we have a sixth school; procedural due process.

On June 17 the House resumed debate on the motion to make the Secretary of Foreign Affairs "removable by the President." Thomas Hartley from Pennsylvania denied that officials had a property in their office and could be removed only for criminal conduct. That doctrine "may suit a nation which is strong in proportion to the number of dependents upon the Crown, but will be very pernicious in a Republic like ours." Some officers held their commissions during good behavior; others, like the Secretary, served at the pleasure of the President.

George Clymer of Pennsylvania had no doubt that the removal power belonged to the executive. Even if the Constitution had been silent on the power of appointment, he reasoned, the executive would have had that power as well. The Constitution mentioned appointment only to "give some further security against the introduction of improper men into office. But in cases of removal there is not such necessity for this check." One of the more active participants in the debate, Roger Sherman of Connecticut, said that an officer existed as a creature of Congress. Depending upon the statute creating the office, the person might hold office during good behavior, be elected every year, displaced for negligence of duty, or subjected to any other provision without calling upon the President or the Senate.

Madison abhorred this theory of government. He considered it fundamental that the Constitution vested the executive power in the President and required him to take care that the laws be faithfully executed. If the President wantonly removed a meritorious officer, that would "subject him to impeachment and removal from his own high trust." Madison wanted to protect the responsibility of the President: "Vest this power in the Senate jointly with the President, and you abolish at once that great principle of unity and responsibility in the Executive department, which was intended for the security of liberty and the public good."

Debate continued on June 18. The idea of deriving the removal power from the general nature of "executive power," as Madison had suggested, elicited a challenge from Alexander White of Virginia, who said that such a doctrine could be supported only by examples "brought from beyond the Atlantic." * * *

Still another Virginian, John Page, objected to joining the Senate with the President in the removal power. In nine cases out of ten, he predicted, where the President was confident that someone must be removed, it would be impossible to produce the necessary evidence. Could the Senate proceed without evidence? If not, should such a man "be saddled upon the President, who has been appointed for no other purpose but to aid the President in performing certain duties?" James Jackson denied that the heads of departments were necessarily dependent upon the President. The Constitution itself "specifically points them out." Benjamin Goodhue blunted the force of that argument. He explained that while Senators played an important role in confirming an officer, since they might be better acquainted with the nominee than the President, the man's *performance in office* could be judged better by the President. He would more likely learn of improper conduct by subordinates. To Livermore, Congress should not interfere with the executive departments by including language on removals: "Leave them to do their duty, and let us do ours."

June 19 arrived and the House still did not know whether to strike the words "to be removable by the President." Peter Silvester of New York helped crystallize the issue: Congress had to give its opinion either by declaration or by implication. If the Constitution lodged the removal power in the President it was useless for Congress to interfere by making an express declaration. If the Constitution did *not* leave the power with the President, could Congress give it? Although the Constitution did not expressly grant the power, neither was there anything "in contradiction to it." The problem was compounded, Sherman added, by the fact that the words "to be removable by the President" might imply that the President lacked the removal power and had to have it granted by law. The motion to strike the language was rejected, 20 to 34.

By June 22 the House was headed in the direction of treating the removal power by implication, not declaration. Benson moved that the bill provide that the chief clerk (second in command in the Foreign Affairs Department) take charge of all records whenever the Secretary "shall be removed from office" by the President. His motion avoided the problem in the phrase "to be removable by the President," which appeared to be a grant of power by Congress. The new language displeased Smith, who preferred that Congress express itself in "more candid and manly" terms by declaration, not implication, but Benson's motion carried, 30 to 18. Benson then moved to strike the phrase "to be removable by the President," to which the House agreed, 31 to 19.

When the Senate took up the bill and someone proposed to delete the President's power to remove the Secretary of Foreign Affairs, a tie vote (nine to nine) resulted. Vice President Adams broke the tie by voting against the motion. A few days later, during House action on the bill to establish a War Department, Benson offered language to give the President removal power by implication. Although the identical principle and language were at issue, his motion carried by the smaller margin of 24 to 22. On a motion in the Senate to strike the President's power to remove the Secretary of War, the effort failed by the close vote of nine to ten.

The Foreign Affairs and War Departments had been regarded as "executive departments," largely because of their origin and evolution during the Continental Congress. No such concession was made for Treasury. One would have expected Congress, jealous of its control over finances during the preceding decade, to contest the President's power to remove the Secretary of the Treasury. The challenge came from the Senate, not the House. The Senate deleted the President's power to remove the Secretary. Later on a motion that the Senate recede from its position and accept the House language, another tie vote occurred, ten to ten. Vice President Adams cast the deciding vote for the motion.

As a result of these actions, Congress passed legislation to adopt the same approach for the Departments of Foreign Affairs, War, and Treasury. The subordinate officers would have charge and custody of all records whenever the Secretary "shall be removed from office by the President of the United States."

The fact that Congress recognized the President's freedom to remove department heads did not mean that the President could remove all administrative officials. Congress did not vest the entire removal power with him. When Madison turned his attention to the tenure of the Comptroller of the Treasury, he said that it was necessary "to consider the nature of this office." Its properties were not "purely of an Executive nature," he said. "It seems to me that they partake of a Judiciary quality as well as Executive; perhaps the latter obtains in the greatest degree." Because of the mixed nature of the office, "there may be strong reasons why an officer of this kind should not hold his office at the pleasure of the Executive branch of the Government." Madison's insight would hold the attention of scholars and the courts more than a century later.

* * *

Controversies From Jackson to Cleveland

Congress has authority to create an office and specify the term of office. May it also specify the manner in which an incumbent is removed? This issue, offered here as an academic riddle, assumed solid form with Andrew Jackson in the White House.

Jackson's predecessors had used the removal power with restraint. The opportunity for removals, however, expanded considerably in 1820 when Congress passed legislation that limited a large number of federal officers to a term of four years, stipulating that they would be "removable from office at pleasure." Supported by this legislative authority and by his own philosophy favoring rotation of federal personnel, Jackson removed more officers than all of the Presidents who preceded him (252 for Jackson compared to 193 for his predecessors). These numbers, though large, are less impressive as a proportion of the growing bureaucracy and do not constitute anything near the "clean sweep" suggested by some historians.

Congressional opposition to Jackson's policy came to a head in 1833 when he removed the Secretary of the Treasury for refusing to carry out his policy toward the national bank. At issue was more than the removal power. Congress regarded Treasury with proprietary interest, often treating the Secretary as *its* agent. It had, for example, delegated to the Secretary—not the President—the responsibility for placing government funds either in national banks or state banks. The Senate responded to Jackson's action by passing a resolution of censure: "*Resolved,* That the President, in the late Executive proceedings in relation to the public revenue, has assumed upon himself authority and power not conferred by the Constitution and laws, but in derogation of both."

Jackson, outraged that the Senate should censure him on the basis of unspecified charges, without an opportunity to be heard and in circumvention of the formal constitutional procedure for impeachment, prepared a lengthy and impassioned protest. With great force he argued that the Constitution vested in the President the executive power, requiring him to take care that the laws be faithfully executed. That made him, he said, "responsible for the entire action of the executive department." Following this logic, the President had a right to employ agents of his own choice to aid him. When no longer willing to be responsible for their acts, he could remove them. Jackson regarded the Secretary of the Treasury as "wholly an executive officer." Three years later the Senate ordered its resolution of censure expunged from the record. * * *

The removal power ripened into a poisonous dispute during the administration of Andrew Johnson. Even before he took office, Congress had begun to trench upon the President's removal power. Legislation in 1863 created a Comptroller of the Currency to hold office for the term of five years "unless sooner removed by the President, by and with the advice and consent of the Senate." Two years later Congress passed legislation to permit military and naval officers, upon dismissal by the President, to apply for a trial.

Congress continued this policy in 1867 by passing the Tenure of Office Act. Every person holding civil office with the advice and consent of the Senate became entitled to hold office until the President appointed a successor, with the advice and consent of the Senate. The bill further provided that the Secretaries of State, Treasury, War, Navy, and Interior, the Postmaster General, and the Attorney General should hold office during the term of the President who appointed them, and for one month thereafter, "subject to removal by and with the advice and consent of the Senate." During Senate recess the President could suspend an official but would have to report to the Senate, upon its return, the evidence and reasons for the suspension. If the Senate concurred in his action the suspended officer would be removed. If the Senate refused to concur, the suspended officer would resume the functions of his office.

Here was a frontal challenge to presidential control over his own officers. Johnson vetoed the bill, claiming that it violated the Constitution and the construction placed upon it by the debate of 1789. His message was well reasoned and fully documented. But Congress, caught up in the fierce politics of that time, was not receptive to facts or argument. Both Houses promptly overrode his veto.

Johnson had hoped that the disruptive voice in his Cabinet, Secretary of War Edwin M. Stanton, would resign. He did not. As the months rolled by and the political crisis deepened, Johnson decided to suspend Stanton. The Senate returned from its recess and refused to concur in the suspension. Johnson upped the ante by *removing* Stanton, with the expectation that the constitutionality of the Tenure of Office Act would be tested in the courts. Yet because of the actions of Ulysses S. Grant, whom Johnson had installed as War Secretary ad interim, and Lorenzo Thomas, Grant's successor, the tactic backfired. Stanton was able to regain his office. Johnson's strategy merely fanned the fire of impeachment that had been smoldering for a year, a movement that fell one vote short in the Senate.

The political extravagance of Congress did not go unnoticed. President Grant, in his first annual message in 1869, recommended that Congress repeal the Tenure of Office Act. To him the law was inconsistent with efficient administration: "What faith can an Executive put in officials forced upon him, and those, too, whom he has suspended for reason?" Congress revised the act that year, softening the suspension section but retaining the Senate's involvement in the removal process.

Congress continued to expand the Senate's role. Legislation in 1872 required the Postmaster General and his three assistants to be appointed by the President, by and with the advice and consent of the Senate, and provided that they might be "removed in the same manner." In 1876 Congress required the Senate's advice and consent for the removal of all first-, second-, and third-class postmasters.

A new confrontation between President and Congress occurred from 1885 to 1886, after Grover Cleveland suspended several hundred officials and refused to deliver certain papers and documents to the Senate. Cleveland declared that the power to remove or suspend executive officials was vested solely in the President by the Constitution, particularly by the "executive power" and "take care" clauses. He also noted that the law governing suspensions, as amended in 1869, did not justify the Senate's request for documents. Because of this dispute, Congress repealed the Tenure of Office Act in 1887.

ROBERT F. NAGEL, THE LEGISLATIVE VETO, THE CONSTITUTION, AND THE COURTS

3 Const. Comm. 61, 65–66, 69–72 (1986).

In recent years * * * the Court's general willingness to use its power has included a growing inclination to monopolize questions of power definition at the national level. In 1969, for example, the Court overturned the exclusion of Adam Clayton Powell from the House of Representatives despite the apparent constitutional commitment of questions regarding "the qualifications of its own members" to each House of Congress.[7] The Court thus assumed for itself the power to define Congress's constitutional authority over its own operations, blandly insisting that this sort of determination "falls within the traditional role accorded courts * * *." The *Powell* decision raises the serious possibility that the Court may invade the clear authority of Congress over the impeachment process.

In 1974 the Justices rushed to judgment in the famous case involving the power of the judiciary to subpoena President Nixon's Watergate tapes. In sober second light it is now clear that this was a case for judicial caution. No specific constitutional provision was involved; the issues of whether to read a presidential power of immunity into the Constitution and how to balance such an implied power against the judiciary's authority were exceedingly difficult, certainly issues on which "human reason may pause." Nevertheless, the Supreme Court not only acted, but acted in enormous haste, deciding the case before the Court of Appeals could even hear arguments on the propriety of Judge Sirica's ruling. Meanwhile the appropriate committee of Congress was responsibly exercising its undoubted constitutional authority to investigate the possible impeachment and removal of the President. The Court's action in *Nixon* effectively aborted the investigation, further reducing the credibility of the constitutional sanction for presidential misconduct.

* * *

The *Chadha* decision must be understood within the context of the modern Court's tendency to monopolize the resolution of constitutional

---

7. Art. I, § 5 states, "Each House shall be the Judge of the Elections, Returns and   Qualifications of its own Members * * *."

issues of power distribution. The Court's willingness—indeed, eager-
ness—to strike down the legislative veto is a powerful illustration of the
recent tendency to sweep within "the judicial power" the authority to
decide organizational issues, even those that involve the operations of
another branch and are apparently committed by the Constitution to
that other branch. A decision that so profoundly trivializes the constitutional responsibilities of Congress is, to say the least, an unlikely vehicle
for injecting new vigor and integrity into the lawmaking process.

* * *

The *Chadha* opinion repeatedly invoked "the Constitutional design
for separation of powers." The theory of separation of powers came to
America from the seventeenth century Levellers, who opposed the British King's participation in lawmaking. The theory was passed through
Montesquieu, and contributed to the Jeffersonians' opposition to aristocracy and their extreme commitment to popular control over lawmaking.
As the Court noted in *Chadha,* separation of powers in its pure form
involves differentiation by function. Power is to be checked by dividing
it; each branch exercises a distinctive type of power, and none shares or
interferes with the power exercised by the others.

In the American Constitution separation of powers was combined
with a different principle—balance. Constitutional balance has its antecedents in the mixed government of Great Britain, where royalty shared
some of the lawmaking function and where the aristocracy was given
both the power to judge and the power to make laws in the House of
Lords. Balance involves sharing of power among the branches of government and active checking of one branch by another; its functions
have been to block popular control over lawmaking and to assure
representation of class interests.

It is elementary that these opposite principles, separation and balance, were strangely and successfully combined by the framers. The
Constitution divides government into three distinct branches, and the
lawmaking power is given to a popularly accountable branch. However,
the President shares the judicial function through, for instance, his
pardon power; and he shares the legislative function through his veto
power. The Senate shares the executive function, for example, by its
power to confirm appointments. And the doctrine of judicial review
permits courts to share (and check) the power of both the legislative and
executive branches.

Now, despite the Court's emphatic reliance on the theory of separation of powers, it should be plain that the legislative veto considered in
Chadha did not threaten the principle of separation. Insofar as it
violated the bicameralism requirement, the veto threatened only the
principle of balance, raising the possibility that class or regional interests
would not be adequately represented in a deportation decision accomplished by a vote of only one House of Congress. Insofar as the veto
violated the presentment requirement, it did threaten the authority of
the executive branch. But authority of what kind? The executive

authority at risk was, first, the authority of the President to veto a specific decision to suspend a deportation (the President having already had the opportunity to veto the general scheme setting up the system of legislative vetoes in deportation cases). The veto power, again, is a part of the principle of balance whereby the legislative power is shared and checked by the Executive. The second kind of presidential authority at risk was the authority to make the suspension decision itself, for the Attorney General's determination under the Immigration Act could be, and was, reversed by one House of Congress. *But this is the very decision that the Court described at length as legislative in nature.* In this respect also, then, the kind of executive authority threatened was the President's authority to share (through exceedingly broad delegation) the power of lawmaking.

The Court invalidated a device found in over 200 federal statutory provisions by invoking separation of powers when it meant, if anything, the opposite principle of constitutional balance. That the Court could misname a fundamental principle is in itself disturbing in a country where vast judicial power is justified by reference to the capacity of judges to understand and apply legal principles. More important, understanding the principle that *Chadha* does implement helps to remove the last shadows from around the decision. Although the Court spoke in terms of separation of powers and emphasized the protection of the integrity of legislative procedures, the decision in fact protected a principle, traceable to the British royalty and House of Lords, that has long been at war with popularly accountable legislatures. *Chadha* is a striking expansion of the judicial assault on the democratic values associated with the principle of separation of powers, which allocates the lawmaking function to Congress and not to the executive or judicial branch.

Once the real issue in *Chadha* is properly named, some small but bewildering aspects of the Court's opinion become understandable. Not only in its major contours but also in its detail, the opinion expresses repugnance at the legislative process. The decision is permeated by a hostility to the Congress that, once perceived, makes it obvious that the possibility of a judicially-led reinvigoration of the political process is fanciful.

In its description of the facts, the Court observed that in Chadha's case Congress waited "for reasons not disclosed" for a full year and a half to decide about his deportation. Similarly, the Court mentioned the precise date of the House's action and the termination date of the statutory time period for vetoing the suspension, making plain that if the House had waited seven more days, "Chadha's deportation proceedings would have been cancelled." Although it was relevant to nothing in the case, the Court stated that the House resolution was "not printed" and "was not made available to other members of the House [besides those in the relevant committee] prior to the vote." The Court also noted, for no apparent reason, that Chadha's case was one of a group of some 340 and that the resolution in his case passed without debate or recorded vote. And it opined (in a footnote) that "[i]t is not at all clear whether the House generally or Chairman Eilberg in particular * * * understood the relationship between the Resolution and the Attorney General's decision * * *."

In short, much of the Court's statement of the facts of the case bears little if any relationship to the legal issues involved; the Court's purpose, obviously, was to paint a grim picture of the quality of the legislative process. Whether or not this process worked as badly in Chadha's case as the Court implied, there is no doubt that legislative decisionmaking can be uninformed, cruel, and messy. This is no doubt true as well for many decisions that issue from the bowels of the bureaucracy or judiciary. The more rational procedures, often presumed to be generally available from administrators or judges, are, at any rate, a reflection of their distinct functions. To perform *their* functions, legislators must respond to felt constituent concerns and must trade across issues; the legislature's role in a democracy requires it to operate differently (and perhaps more untidily) than the other branches. If responsibilities are to be removed from the Congress whenever legislative techniques look different from judicial or administrative processes, there will be little of importance left for the Congress to contribute.

If there remains any doubt about whether *Chadha* portends a reinvigoration of the legislative process, consider that the decision also contained a long and approving discussion of congressional experience with the impracticality of special deportation bills. Thus the only congressional judgment given credence in the Court's opinion is the admission that Congress could not hope to legislate well on the individual suspension issues that much of the Court's opinion defined as inherently legislative in nature. With the legislative veto invalidated and special bills declared too cumbersome, Congress has left only the option of delegating its lawmaking authority to the other branches of government.

Chadha is justifiable, if at all, only on the ground that the judiciary, not the legislature, is the appropriate forum for deciding the practical questions that arise in the difficult, complicated effort to make the modern regulatory state democratically accountable. The significance of the decision is not that it protects the principle of separation of powers or that it offers new hope for the integrity or importance of the legislative process. Its significance is that it confirms and accelerates the drive, which until *Chadha* could be discerned but not fully appreciated, toward the judicial monopolization of crucial questions of power definition and distribution.

BIBLIOGRAPHY

Delegation

S. Barber, THE CONSTITUTION AND THE DELEGATION OF CONGRESSIONAL POWER (1975).

Brooks, *Gramm–Rudman: Can Congress and the President Pass This Buck?*, 64 Tex.L.Rev. 131 (1985).

Krent, *Fragmenting the Unitary Executive: Congressional Delegations of Administrative Authority Outside the Federal Government*, 85 Nw. U.L.Rev. 62 (1990).

T. Lowi, THE END OF LIBERALISM ch. 5 (2d ed. 1979).

Pierce, *The Role of Constitutional and Political Theory in Administrative Law*, 64 Tex.L.Rev. 469 (1985).

Schoenbrod, *The Delegation Doctrine: Could the Court Give It Substance?*, 83 Mich.L.Rev. 1223 (1985).

Appointment and Removal

Calabresi & Rhodes, *The Structural Constitution: Unitary Executive, Plural Judiciary*, 105 Harv.L.Rev. 1155 (1992).

Carter, *The Independent Counsel Mess*, 102 Harv.L.Rev. 105 (1988).

Corwin, *Tenure of Office and the Removal Power Under the Constitution*, 27 Colum.L.Rev. 353 (1927).

Entin, *The Removal Power and the Federal Deficit: Form, Substance, and Administrative Independence*, 75 Ky.L.J. 699 (1987).

Glitzenstein & Morrison, *The Supreme Court's Decision in* Morrison v. Olson: *A Common Sense Application of the Constitution to a Practical Problem*, 38 Amer.U.L.Rev. 359 (1989).

Kahn, *Gramm–Rudman and the Capacity of Congress To Control the Future*, 13 Hastings Const.L.Q. 185 (1986).

Miller, *Independent Agencies*, 1986 Sup.Ct.Rev. 41.

Shane, *Independent Policymaking and Presidential Power: A Constitutional Analysis*, 57 Geo.Wash.L.Rev. 596 (1989).

Verkuil, *The Status of Independent Agencies After* Bowsher v. Synar, 1986 Duke L.J. 779.

The Legislative Veto

Bruff, *Legislative Formality, Administrative Rationality*, 63 Texas L.Rev. 207 (1984).

Bruff & Gellhorn, *Congressional Control of Administrative Regulation: A Study of Legislative Vetoes*, 90 Harv.L.Rev. 1369 (1977).

Eskridge & Ferejohn, *The Article I, Section 7 Game*, 60 Geo.L.J. 523 (1992).

Elliott, INS v. Chadha: *The Administrative Constitution, the Constitution, and the Legislative Veto*, 1983 Sup.Ct.Rev. 125.

Javits & Klein, *Congressional Oversight and the Legislative Veto: A Constitutional Analysis*, 52 N.Y.U.L.Rev. 455 (1977).

Martin, *The Legislative Veto and the Responsible Exercise of Congressional Power*, 68 Va.L.Rev. 253 (1982).

Smolla, *Bring Back the Legislative Veto: A Proposal for a Constitutional Amendment,* 37 Ark.L.Rev. 509 (1984).

Spann, *Deconstructing the Legislative Veto,* 68 Minn.L.Rev. 473 (1984).

Strauss, *Was There a Baby in the Bathwater? A Comment on the Supreme Court's Legislative Veto Decision,* 1983 Duke L.J. 789.

L. Tribe, CONSTITUTIONAL CHOICES ch. 6 (1985).

Tribe, *The Legislative Veto Decision: A Law by Any Other Name?,* 21 Harv.J.Legis. 7 (1984).

Watson, *Congress Steps Out: A Look at Congressional Control of the Executive,* 63 Calif.L.Rev. 983 (1975).

E. EXECUTIVE PRIVILEGES AND IMMUNITIES

The fourth set of separation of powers problems concerns efforts by one branch of government to interfere in the internal affairs of another. Sometimes Congress or the courts will thrust themselves into executive affairs. Impeachment is one (serious) example; lawsuits and congressional demands for information are more typical. Sometimes the judiciary and the executive will pry into the affairs of Congress. Here the Constitution offers some explicit protection—in the Speech or Debate Clause—though its scope is uncertain.[1]

Stephen Carter and Gerald Gunther discuss interference in executive affairs, in the context of actions against former president Nixon. Does the President, like Congress, have some protection against such action? In particular, may he assert executive privileges (against production)[2] and immunities (from suit)?[3]

We sometimes forget that in these cases the proper role of the judiciary is a separation of powers question. The political question doctrine states that there are times when the courts should allow the other branches to resolve their own differences.[4] But that doctrine may be honored more in the breach than in the observance. Carter and Gunther both argue that the Supreme Court should intervene less often than it has of late. (Nagel, in Section D, makes the same point.) It is worth considering whether they are correct.

1. Hutchinson v. Proxmire, 443 U.S. 111, 99 S.Ct. 2675, 61 L.Ed.2d 411 (1979); Eastland v. United States Servicemen's Fund, 421 U.S. 491, 95 S.Ct. 1813, 44 L.Ed.2d 324 (1975); Doe v. McMillan, 412 U.S. 306, 93 S.Ct. 2018, 36 L.Ed.2d 912 (1973); Gravel v. United States, 408 U.S. 606, 92 S.Ct. 2614, 33 L.Ed.2d 583 (1972); United States v. Brewster, 408 U.S. 501, 92 S.Ct. 2531, 33 L.Ed.2d 507 (1972).

2. Nixon v. Administrator of General Services, 433 U.S. 425, 97 S.Ct. 2777, 53 L.Ed.2d 867 (1977); United States v. Nixon, 418 U.S. 683, 94 S.Ct. 3090, 41 L.Ed.2d 1039 (1974).

3. Nixon v. Fitzgerald, 457 U.S. 731, 102 S.Ct. 2690, 73 L.Ed.2d 349 (1982); Mississippi v. Johnson, 71 U.S. (4 Wall.) 475, 18 L.Ed. 437 (1866).

4. Nixon v. United States, 506 U.S. ___, 113 S.Ct. 732, 122 L.Ed.2d 1 (1993).

STEPHEN L. CARTER, THE POLITICAL ASPECTS OF JUDICIAL POWER: SOME NOTES ON THE PRESIDENTIAL IMMUNITY DECISION
131 U.Pa.L.Rev. 1341, 1353–1371 (1983).

[In the first part of his article Carter reviews the Supreme Court's decision in *Nixon v. Fitzgerald.*[a] The plaintiff in that case sued President Nixon for damages, claiming that he had been fired for exercising his right to freedom of speech. The Court held, 5–4, that the President was immune from suit for damages.]

The conclusion that the federal courts lack authority to punish the President of the United States may at first seem somewhat startling, but after a little thought, it makes more sense. One may begin by hypothesizing the contrary. Suppose a court did try to hold the President of the United States in contempt for disobeying an order addressed to him. Would federal marshals arrive at the White House, demanding that the Secret Service agents let them seize the President? Suppose the President—with the assistance of the security personnel—decided to resist arrest. Aside from a definite air of lese majesty about the whole thing, there is also the undeniable fact that should matters come to a showdown, the President has more guns at his command than a federal court does. The Supreme Court has never pretended otherwise. During the Reconstruction Era, the Court in *Mississippi v. Johnson,*[53] took explicit note of the difficulties it would encounter in trying to "force" a President to comply with an order, and dismissed a complaint against President Andrew Johnson. Earlier opinions included dicta to similar effect.[56]

The mere fact that forcing the President to pay damages might not be easy does not by itself justify a constitutional rule against trying. After all, President Nixon did turn over the Watergate tapes, even though the federal courts probably could not have enforced a contempt citation against him. Besides, resistance to judicial decrees is hardly new. Had the President not decided to send troops to Little Rock in the wake of *Cooper v. Aaron,*[60] the schools in that city might be segregated to this day. The Court's inability to enforce its order without the assistance of the executive branch did not mean that the Justices had no power to issue the order. Thus the claim that the Court lacks power to punish the President must be defended on some ground other than the Court's lack of enforcement power.

In supporting its conclusion in *Nixon v. Fitzgerald,* the majority focused on what it considered the public policy reasons militating in favor of an immunity rule. Justice White's dissent at least showed that these arguments have two sides. The malleability of public policy arguments makes the majority's reasoning suspect, but need not vitiate the result. In order to tie its decision more closely to the Constitution, the Court could have relied on something other than public policy.

a. 457 U.S. 731 (1982).
53. 71 U.S. (4 Wall.) 475 (1867).
56. *Cf.* Chisholm v. Georgia, 2 U.S. (2 Dall.) 419, 476–78 (1793) (dictum) (sover-eign immunity derives from ability to resist judicial process).
60. 358 U.S. 1 (1958).

Before suggesting some justifications that, although available, were absent from the majority opinion, it is useful to pause and recall what the case did not involve. The Court was not required to construe the Constitution's "open-ended" provisions protecting individual rights against government abuse. The dilemma whether to read those clauses as though the Constitution were a statute—or perhaps a contract—or to take them as invitations to import extra-constitutional values motivates much contemporary scholarship on constitutional theory.

Happily, determining whether a reasoned constitutional basis exists for the presidential immunity decision does not require wading into the midst of that scholarly battle. Whatever the best approach to the adjudication of claims under the clauses protecting individual rights (and it is not at all clear that there need be only one), there is no apparent reason to believe that the same interpretive approach ought to apply to other constitutional provisions. Different sections of the document have different purposes and interpreting each in light of its purpose will probably lead to drastically different approaches. Thus, it is one thing to look to extra-constitutional sources in deciding what rights are "retained by the People" or incorporated in the phrase "Privileges or Immunities;" it is something else altogether to do so when considering whether federal courts can, for example, review a presidential decision to cast a veto—or whether the President is a proper defendant in a suit seeking civil damages.

Provisions describing the functions and powers of the government may demand a different interpretive approach from provisions describing the rights of the people. A strict textual approach, focusing on the understanding of the Framers, may be a more sensible method to use in interpreting the structural clauses of the Constitution. * * *

1. THE ORIGINAL UNDERSTANDING APPROACH

* * * The original understanding—when one can be discerned—is more likely to be important in a case involving the system of checks and balances than it is in a case involving individual rights. The reason should be obvious. In protecting individuals against government mistreatment, those who drafted the 1787 Constitution and its amendments took pains to use language so broad as fairly to beg to be filled with substantive content from external sources. They used words sparingly, an approach that makes sense when one begins with a conception of rights as broad and government power as narrow. In structuring the government, however, the drafters set themselves rather a different task and used dramatically different language.

The 1787 Constitution set forth with painstaking attention to detail the powers and functions of the federal government. Despite a few glaring errors,[72] the document reflects an obsessive concern for the

---

72. A good example concerns the role of the Vice President. The Vice President serves as President of the Senate. U.S. Const. art. I, § 3. When the President of the United States is tried in the Senate following impeachment by the House of Representatives, the Chief Justice of the United States presides. *Id.* That is the minutiae of government operation. Words were used cautiously so as to leave little room for interpretation. Thus although some wanted to make the President impeachable for any reason, the delegates in Philadelphia finally voted to limit impeachable offenses to "Treason, Bribery, or other high Crimes and Misdemeanors," in the hope of limiting congressional power over him. The Constitution also does not include a requirement that members of the House of Representatives be "mature"—although maturity emerged as a major concern in the debates—but only that they be at least twenty-five years old. One can imagine a Constitution providing that elected representatives be "mature" or "of good character," but there is something disturbing, perhaps counterintuitive, about such provisions, as there would be about a provision for congressional overriding of the President's veto "by an extraordinary majority," unless the provision specified what the majority must be. These hypothetical provisions seem counterintuitive for a good reason, and that good reason probably explains their absence from the Constitution: in determining such matters as the qualifications for elected officials, the Framers were structuring a government, not setting forth rights. In the Framers' view, the former called for more precise language than did the latter. The precise wording of the structural provisions reflects an effort to define the structure of government carefully and circumscribe the powers of government narrowly. This purpose should not be ignored when construing the structural provisions of the Constitution.

It therefore makes sense to try to determine the way that the Framers hoped that the Presidency would be controlled. * * * The great weight of the historical evidence suggests the existence of a consensus at the time of ratification to the effect that those checks on presidential abuse of power expressly set forth in the document were the only checks available.

This consensus emerges from the nature of the disputes among the drafters and ratifiers over the proper functions and powers of the President. The intense debate surrounding the Presidency induced the Framers to define their views with rare precision. Those who favored a loose confederation of quasi-independent states argued that the President was too strong and not sufficiently accountable for wrongdoing; those who thought the central government should be strong argued that the President was too weak, that he was subject to too many controls and potential punishments to be able to do his job properly. Supporters of the Constitution had ready responses to each objection.

The President was not too strong, supporters contended, because he was subject to several specific checks on abuses of his authority. The supporters always listed the checks appearing in the document: the

only provision in the Constitution requiring the Vice President to turn over the gavel to another individual. Yet the Vice President himself is also impeachable, and if impeached by the House, he would be tried in the Senate. It appears, therefore, that the Vice President could preside at his own impeachment trial, should he choose to do so.

power of the purse rested with Congress, the President could be impeached, his veto could be overridden, he could make no appointments or treaties without Senate consent, he was subject to reelection every four years. Hamilton went to great lengths in *The Federalist* to assure the worried public that these provisions were adequate to control presidential misconduct.[97] At the same time, Hamilton and other supporters of ratification repeatedly warned that no additional checks should be permitted, lest the President become too weak.

The Constitution's supporters made, with slightly different emphasis, the same argument to those who thought the Constitution made the executive too weak. In reassuring those who feared presidential weakness, supporters emphasized that the limitations actually stated in the Constitution were the only limitations placed on the President, and these, the opponents were assured, would not impair the President's ability to do his job. Some provision had to be made against the possibility of presidential tyranny, supporters pointed out, and the drafters had done the best they could without limiting the Chief Executive's powers too greatly.

There is no reason to belabor this; attempts to piece together an original ''understanding'' from the fragments of history tend to end up looking silly. What is rather startling in this instance is that the same questions and answers occur again and again in the surviving records. That is why it may be safe to assume that a consensus existed. At the very least, it cannot fairly be asserted that the history points in some other direction.

2. THE STRUCTURAL APPROACH

The Constitution's relatively precise clauses describing the operation of the federal government are designed to fit together to form a coherent structure. This purpose distinguishes them from the open-ended clauses, many of which were designed to address particular problems and bear little relation to the other parts of the document. * * *

The system of checks and balances is a delicate one, and the Constitution sets forth with some degree of care the checks that each branch may apply to the others. Thus the President may nominate and, if the Senate consents, appoint Justices to the Supreme Court and judges to the lower federal courts, but only Congress, through impeachment and conviction, may remove them. Congress may propose legislation (including legislation channeling the President's discretion), but absent extraordinary majorities in both Houses, the proposals do not become law if the President objects. Congress may go through the motions of enacting legislation that violates the Constitution, but the federal courts, in a case properly brought, may strike those statutes down. Congress holds exclusive power of the purse, and Congress alone can impeach the President and remove him from office. A few other checks, mostly in the form of congressional powers, are scattered through the document.

97. * * * The Federalist No. 69 at 444–45 (A. Hamilton) (B. Wright ed. 1961)[.]

In addition, because all members of Congress as well as the President are elected, popular sentiment provides a powerful and constant check on the operation of the entire system. Outside the interplay of these powers, the Constitution provides no further express controls on misconduct.

As American society has evolved, powerful arguments have arisen that other checks—checks for which the Constitution makes no apparent provision—ought to be applied against any one of the three branches in order to control its growing power. New remedies instituted by Congress included statutes restricting the President's power to remove executive branch functionaries. The first such statutes were struck down, but later versions were sustained. A more recent example of an attempt to restrict the presidency was the congressional creation of the "legislative veto," through which Congress attempted to influence day-to-day policymaking in the executive branch and in the administrative agencies without affording the President an opportunity to exercise his constitutional prerogative by casting a veto. If the presidency has become "imperial" and if none of the existing restraints seems sufficient to rein in whatever maniac might then be occupying the Oval Office, the idea of creating a new remedy has a certain appeal. But in entrusting to any one branch of government the authority to create new checks on one or both of the others, the proponent of the new check is inviting one branch to act unilaterally to alter the delicate balance that the Constitution creates. At the risk of sounding melodramatic, those who advocate the creation of new checks are, however unintentionally, ultimately seeking to subvert the balance of powers in order to save it. It is difficult to see how the checks built into the structural provisions of the Constitution will retain their intended force if they are not tempered by a continuing balance.

The balance of powers among the three branches of the federal government is a delicate construct, and if any one of the branches is empowered to create new checks on the others that branch will be in the position to upset the very balance that it purports to protect. Thus the system requires placing the narrowest possible reading on the authority of each branch of government to act in the name of preserving that system. Attention to the original understanding and a strict view of constitutional language are both merely means to the end of maintaining the balance of power among the branches of the federal government.

* * *

The arguments set out above are arguments that the majority could have made, but failed to make in any detail, in support of the theory that the decision is constitutionally based. The arguments share a simple conclusion: in determining the role that each branch should play in the system of checks and balances, all judgments on proper policy must be subordinated to the most important policy, preserving that selfsame system of checks and balances. Permitting one branch to create fresh remedies will upset the balance. Anything that upsets the balance is wrong. That is why the federal courts cannot create a cause of action for damages running against a President or former President on the basis of misconduct in office.

Had it explained *Nixon v. Fitzgerald* that way, the Court would presumably have gone on to explain why the theory that all other interests must be subordinated to the need to preserve the system of checks and balances does not do violence to precedent. A distinction must be drawn between the two very different roles the federal courts play in the system of checks and balances. To paraphrase Felix Frankfurter, when the courts settle a dispute between the two more overtly political branches, they act as "referees at prize fights;" but when they act affirmatively to vindicate an individual claim of right against a representative of another branch, they act as "functionaries of justice." In *Nixon v. Fitzgerald,* an individual asked the Court to make him whole, and the Justices hesitated. The majority's reasoning suggests constitutional limitations on the judicial power to act as functionaries of justice by creating fresh remedies. Nothing in the decision is inconsistent with the cases in which the Court has acted as a referee.

United States v. Nixon [109] does not fall squarely into either category, but it is probably best viewed as a "court-as-referee" decision. The Justices were not settling a dispute between the other two branches, but they were also not protecting the rights of any individual against government excess. The Court was called upon instead to act as referee *within* a particular branch of government.[110] The Court accepted the task, and its resolution of the dispute required the President to comply with an order. The result in *Nixon v. Fitzgerald* suggests that had the President defied the Court's order in *United States v. Nixon,* the Justices would not have created a fresh remedy through which to try and punish him. The risk of presidential defiance, however, although much bandied-about at the time, was probably close to nil. President Nixon was politically helpless and the Justices must have known that. Had he refused to comply with the Court's "definitive" decision, he would almost certainly have been impeached and removed from office. The federal court could not, under the logic of the presidential immunity decision, have acted against him directly, but a punishment for disobedience would have been imposed all the same. The order would simply have been enforced by a branch other than the one that issued it.

That inability to act against the President directly is hardly inconsistent with other cases in which the federal courts have, in evaluating the legitimacy of presidential actions, evinced reluctance to deal with the President directly. With rare exception, the courts have reviewed presidential activities through suits naming as a defendant not the President

---

109. 418 U.S. 683 (1974).

110. Acting as a referee *within* a particular branch is a power that the Court exercised previously in 1969 when it issued its controversial decision in Powell v. McCor-

mack, 395 U.S. 486 (1969), invalidating a congressional attempt to exclude a member on grounds other than the "Qualifications" that the Court said are set forth expressly in the Constitution. * * *

himself, but some lower executive functionary. The same theory—that no punishment question was involved and the courts were merely acting as referees—may explain these results, but another theory fits them even better. The President was not a defendant, and it is only to the President himself, with his special place in the constitutional scheme and history, that immunity attaches. The Supreme Court acknowledged as much when, on the same day that it decided the presidential immunity case, it ruled in *Harlow v. Fitzgerald* that no similar immunity attaches to the President's aides.[116] Because the President almost always acts through his subordinates, a non-immune defendant will generally be available in any case brought to contest the validity of a presidential directive.

If the President's aides are not immune from suit as he is, they may be placed in an uncomfortable position when he orders them to do something that they believe to be wrong. There is a temptation to say flippantly that an executive functionary placed in that position may resign, tell his story to the *Washington Post,* and write a bestselling book. More seriously, the position may be uncomfortable, but the choice should not be difficult. The employees of the executive branch work for the United States of America, not for the person who happens to occupy the office of President. Faced with an order they believe to be illegitimate, executive functionaries should state their belief and refuse to carry the order out. They may be dismissed for that refusal, but they will have acted in accord with the requirements of the Constitution.

GERALD GUNTHER, JUDICIAL HEGEMONY AND LEGISLATIVE AUTONOMY: THE NIXON CASE AND THE IMPEACHMENT PROCESS
22 U.C.L.A.L.Rev. 30, 31–35 (1974).

To me, the most admirable feature of our recent constitutional history lies in the demonstration that the House of Representatives is capable of taking its impeachment responsibilities seriously. Despite the impatience with the slowness of the House Judiciary Committee and the deliberateness of the Doar–Jenner staff, despite the cynicism about the capacities of the supposed mediocrities in the House, the Committee proceedings moved forward thoughtfully and conscientiously, culminating in that impressive debate on the articles of impeachment.

To a regrettable extent, the triumph of the legislative branch was diminished by the Supreme Court's performance. For most of the first half of 1974, the Judiciary Committee proceedings were at center stage. That is where they belonged. The impeachment route is the most appropriate one in our Constitution for the pursuit of problems such as those raised by Watergate. The Court's action tended to push the Committee off center stage. With *United States v. Nixon,* the Supreme Court managed to overshadow the impeachment process which had been,

---

116. * * * 457 U.S. 800 (1982) * * *.

and should have continued to be, primary. That impact stemmed from two sources: the Court's timing and the Court's reasoning.

Though I think the timing to be the less important one, I find it a troublesome aspect nevertheless. The Court granted certiorari soon after review was sought in the intermediate appellate court from Judge Sirica's decision, before judgment, or indeed argument and opinions, in the Court of Appeals for the District of Columbia. Plainly, the Supreme Court took the case much earlier than it had to, and the decision came down on the very day the Judiciary Committee's public debate on proposed articles of impeachment got under way. The practical impact of the decision is clear: the impeachment process was soon aborted. Twelve days after the July 24 decision, President Nixon made public the transcript of the fateful and fatal June 23, 1972 tapes. Three days after that, he resigned. The interval between Court decision and presidential response afforded just enough time for the completion of the House Judiciary Committee debate and for the adoption of three articles of impeachment. But the turnover of the tapes compelled by the Court made floor debate in the House and trial in the Senate unnecessary; instead of running its full course, the impeachment process was short-circuited.

* * *

But was not the Court compelled to intervene? I think not—certainly not at the time it chose. I do not argue that the Court should have found itself powerless to adjudicate the case: Special Prosecutor Jaworski's subpoena claim came in a criminal proceeding; his demand was appropriately adjudicable by the courts. To me, the critical question was timing. Were there truly compelling arguments to have the Supreme Court enter the dispute as early as it did? The Special Prosecutor's claim was that the subpoena issue was an urgent one because the evidence he sought was needed for the Watergate trial then scheduled for early September. For effective relief, he argued, the Court had to act before its summer recess. Yet the scheduling of the Watergate trial and of a Senate impeachment trial were surely interdependent variables. If the impeachment process had run its normal course, and if a Senate trial had been scheduled for the fall, it seems most unlikely that the Watergate trial would have come on in September. If Watergate witnesses had been needed before the jurors in the Senate, assembling of the jurors in the courthouse would presumably have been postponed by the trial judge. A Supreme Court refusal to grant the Special Prosecutor's petition for extraordinarily expeditious review of the subpoena case would not have been the primary cause for delay of the Watergate trial. More probably, the criminal trial would have been delayed in any event because of the pendency of the Senate impeachment trial. Permitting the subpoena case to go to the court of appeals and to the Supreme Court in the normal course, in short, would have permitted the orderly progress of the impeachment process with no significant practical costs to the criminal proceedings.

Nevertheless, the Supreme Court granted certiorari before judgment in the court of appeals. Why, if the formal argument for such extraordinary speed—the criminal trial schedule—is so thin? I have no doubt that the Justices granted expeditious review in entire good faith; I suspect that they simply concluded that any other course, any consideration of the case under a more normal time schedule, would have been irresponsible. But that good faith judgment seems to me precisely the rub: it is a judgment of a Court that is more imbued than it may realize with a view that flourished in the Warren years, that somehow it is the Court's special obligation to save the nation in episodes of constitutional crisis. It is a Court response not only to that lingering self-image, but also to the concomitant public expectations generated by recent Courts' behavior. That makes it perhaps antiquarian to suggest that the nation would be better off with a somewhat diminished appetite for the judicial *deus ex machina*. That admonition seems especially appropriate in a context in which a parallel, indeed preeminent, constitutional process was in motion. The Court did not claim to decide issues of impeachment directly, to be sure. Yet its timing made an indirect impact on the impeachment process inevitable. It was an avoidable impact. And in speculating as to why it was not avoided, the aptest analogies may lie in Nevada or in medieval Europe. May it be appropriate to think of compulsive gamblers unable to resist a piece of the action, or of knights in shining armor tempted to ride to the rescue in every situation of distress?

But the Court's reasoning seems to me even more troubling than its timing. * * *

Two quite separate issues ran through the lower court proceedings in the Jaworski subpoena case, as they had in the Cox subpoena litigation in 1973. The first was presidential amenability to the judicial process. The second was the scope of executive privilege. It was possible to decide against President Nixon's claim as to the first issue and yet support his argument as to the second: it was possible to say that in subpoena efforts incident to a criminal case there is no presidential immunity from judicial process and yet conclude that the President, as a matter of constitutional interpretation of article II powers, had absolute discretion to determine the scope of executive privilege. *Marbury v. Madison* is an especially relevant source in deciding the first issue. It is far more tenuously related to the second. Respectable arguments after all have been made, and not only by President Nixon's counsel, that absolute executive immunity is a legitimate constitutional inference.

The opinion in *United States v. Nixon* tended to merge and blur those separate issues. And the linchpin in intertwining them was the excessive use of *Marbury v. Madison*. As Chief Justice Burger stated at one point:

The President's counsel, as we have noted, reads the Constitution as providing an absolute privilege of confidentiality for all presidential

communications.   Many decisions of this Court, however, have unequivocally reaffirmed the holding of [*Marbury v. Madison*] that "it
is emphatically the province and duty of the judicial department to
say what the law is."

That "however" suggests that the *Marbury* passage helps answer the
executive privilege contention: Chief Justice Burger's handling of the
issue suggests that recognizing absolute executive privilege as a matter
of constitutional interpretation would somehow be contrary to *Marbury
v. Madison* 's view of the proper judicial role.   But there is nothing in
Marbury v. Madison that precludes a constitutional interpretation which
gives final authority to another branch.

I do not believe that the Court intended to announce that every
constitutional issue requires final adjudication on the merits by the
judiciary.   As in the past, there are likely to be issues in the future
which the Court will find to have been "committed by the Constitution
to another branch of government * * *." [10]   For example, I would think
(and hope) that a conviction on impeachment would be found unreview-
able in the courts.   Nor do I mean to suggest that the Court's result was
wrong on the merits: I think checks and balances arguments make a
non-absolute view of executive privilege appropriate.   I simply suggest
that the argument for absolute executive privilege deserved a more
focused, careful, separable answer than the Court's invocation of *Marbury v. Madison* provides.

BIBLIOGRAPHY

Impeachment

R. Berger, IMPEACHMENT: THE CONSTITUTIONAL PROBLEMS
    (1973).

C. Black, IMPEACHMENT: A HANDBOOK (1974).

I. Brant, IMPEACHMENT: TRIALS AND ERRORS (1972).

Committee on Federal Legislation of the Bar Association of the City of
    New York, THE LAW OF PRESIDENTIAL IMPEACHMENT
    (1974).

Fenton, *The Scope of the Impeachment Power,* 65 Nw.U.L.Rev. 719
    (1971).

Firmage & Mangrum, *Removal of the President: Resignation and the
    Procedural Law of Impeachment,* 1974 Duke L.J. 1023.

Freedman, *The Law as King and the King as Law: Is a President
    Immune from Criminal Prosecution Before Impeachment?,* 20 Has-
    tings Const. L.Q. 7 (1992).

Garvey, *Foreword: Judicial Discipline and Impeachment,* 76 Ky.L.J. 633
    (1988).

10. Baker v. Carr, 369 U.S. 186, 211
(1962).

Gerhardt, *The Constitutional Limits to Impeachment and Its Alternatives,* 68 Texas L.Rev. 1 (1989).

HIGH CRIMES AND MISDEMEANORS (Funk & Wagnalls 1973).

Privileges, Immunities

R. Berger, EXECUTIVE PRIVILEGE: A CONSTITUTIONAL MYTH (1974).

Cox, *Executive Privilege,* 122 U.Pa.L.Rev. 1383 (1974).

Ervin, *The Gravel and Brewster Cases: An Assault on Congressional Independence,* 59 Va.L.Rev. 175 (1973).

Freund, *Foreword: On Presidential Privilege,* 88 Harv.L.Rev. 13 (1974).

Mishkin, *Great Cases and Soft Law: A Comment on United States v. Nixon,* 22 UCLA L.Rev. 76 (1974).

Peterson, *Prosecuting Executive Branch Officials for Contempt of Congress,* 66 N.Y.U.L.Rev. 563 (1991).

Shane, *Legal Disagreement and Negotiation in a Government of Laws: The Case of Executive Privilege Claims Against Congress,* 71 Minn. L.Rev. 461 (1987).

Separation and the Judicial Power

Fallon, *Of Legislative Courts, Administrative Agencies, and Article III,* 101 Harv.L.Rev. 916 (1988).

Redish, *Legislative Courts, Administrative Agencies, and the* Northern Pipeline *Decision,* 1983 Duke L.J. 197.

Symposium, *Paul Bator: Legislative and Administrative Courts Under Article III,* 65 Ind.L.J. 291 (1990).

Young, *Public Rights and the Federal Judicial Power: From* Murray's Lessee *Through* Crowell *To* Schor, 35 Buffalo L.Rev. 765 (1986).

Chapter VI

PROPERTY

A significant number of provisions in the Constitution protect "property." The list includes the Eminent Domain Clause, the Due Process Clauses, the Contract Clause, and the Equal Protection Clause, to name only the most obvious. This Chapter focuses on eminent domain and due process, since these clauses are, in modern times, the most energetically enforced.

A. THE EMINENT DOMAIN CLAUSE

The Fifth Amendment decrees that "private property [shall not] be taken for public use, without just compensation." [1] This is an important statement about the significance of property rights under our Constitution, but it says less than it seems to. Read literally it appears to mean that the government must not disturb the distribution of wealth arrived at in people's private dealings with one another. Whenever the government takes something from A it must give A equivalent compensation. [2] It also appears to forbid even equivalent exchanges unless the government is acting for a "public use."

But we cannot understand the clause so literally. First, "Government hardly could go on if to some extent values incident to property could not be diminished without paying for every such change in the general law." [3] Traffic lights divert customers away from some merchants; the placement of fire hydrants affects home insurance premiums. The government cannot be required to readjust the distribution of private wealth whenever it decides to provide such amenities. Second,

---

1. The Fifth Amendment applies only to the federal government. Its "takings" requirements have been read into the Fourteenth Amendment Due Process Clause, which applies to the states. Missouri Pac. Ry. v. Nebraska, 164 U.S. 403, 17 S.Ct. 130, 41 L.Ed. 489 (1896) (public use); Chicago, B. & Q. R.R. Co. v. Chicago, 166 U.S. 226, 17 S.Ct. 581, 41 L.Ed. 979 (1897) (just compensation).

2. This is in fact the reading given the clause in R. Epstein, Takings: Private Property and the Law of Eminent Domain (1985). Epstein's thesis is criticized in Grey, *The Malthusian Constitution*, 41 U.Miami L.Rev. 21 (1986).

3. Pennsylvania Coal Co. v. Mahon, 260 U.S. 393, 413, 43 S.Ct. 158, 159, 67 L.Ed. 322 (1922).

and more fundamentally, the existing distribution of private property is shaped by common law rules of acquisition and exchange. There is no pre-legal arrangement of goods which the Fifth Amendment freezes in place. But if the government gave yesterday what it takes away today, why should it have to pay compensation? Third, in order to make sense of the requirement that government can acquire property only for "public use," we must have a theory of the proper ends for which government can act. But the courts have all but abandoned hope of formulating such a theory in other areas of the law (*e.g.*, in establishing limits on the enumerated powers of Congress or legislative power under the Due Process Clauses), and there is little reason to think they will be more successful here.

The readings in this Section focus on these issues for the light they shed on the constitutional significance of property rights. The first four selections deal in general with the distinction between compensable takings and noncompensable regulations. This has been a most fruitful cause of litigation. The Supreme Court has addressed the problem frequently in the past twenty years, most recently in *Lucas v. South Carolina Coastal Council.*[4] And the most notable aspect of this jurisprudence is that the Court has occasionally been willing—as it seldom was between 1937 and 1970—to find a taking of property.[5] Some of these cases have involved physical invasions of the plaintiff's land, a situation where the Court has always awarded compensation. *Lucas* announced another categorical rule: a plaintiff is entitled to compensation where the government, by regulation, has prevented all economically beneficial use of his land. The Court qualified this rule by observing that all land was subject to background principles of nuisance law, and regulations that did no more than abate nuisances would not give rise to compensation regardless of their economic impact on the landowner.

Richard Epstein, a strong supporter of property rights, argues that *Lucas* is half right. He sees no sense in the Court's "total taking" rule. Partial takings should be compensated too, if what we seek is to maximize social welfare. On the other hand there is much to be said for a "nuisance" exception to the general principle of compensation. The common law does not require people affected by a nuisance to pay the offender to stop; the transaction costs of such a rule would be too high. *Lucas* rightly holds that whatever neighbors could forbid under nuisance

---

4. ___ U.S. ___, 112 S.Ct. 2886, 120 L.Ed.2d 798 (1992).

5. In addition to *Lucas* see Nollan v. California Coastal Commission, 483 U.S. 825, 107 S.Ct. 3141, 97 L.Ed.2d 677 (1987); Loretto v. Teleprompter Manhattan CATV Corp., 458 U.S. 419, 102 S.Ct. 3164, 73 L.Ed.2d 868 (1982); Kaiser Aetna v. United States, 444 U.S. 164, 100 S.Ct. 383, 62 L.Ed.2d 332 (1979). In the same period the Court has sometimes taken a generous view of what counts as "property" protected by the Eminent Domain Clause. Hodel v. Irv-ing, 481 U.S. 704, 107 S.Ct. 2076, 95 L.Ed.2d 668 (1987); Ruckelshaus v. Monsanto Co., 467 U.S. 986, 104 S.Ct. 2862, 81 L.Ed.2d 815 (1984); Webb's Fabulous Pharmacies, Inc. v. Beckwith, 449 U.S. 155, 101 S.Ct. 446, 66 L.Ed.2d 358 (1980). And in First English Evangelical Lutheran Church of Glendale v. County of Los Angeles, 482 U.S. 304, 107 S.Ct. 2378, 96 L.Ed.2d 250 (1987), the Court gave landowners a remedy for temporary takings under discontinued regulations.

law, the state can also forbid without having to pay compensation. Joseph Sax reviews and criticizes these various theories (physical invasion, nuisance, diminution of value) for drawing the line between takings and regulations.

The traditional tests certainly have their difficulties. Perhaps we have gone astray in our attempts to solve the compensation problem by focusing too much on the ideas of "taking" and "regulation." Those concepts may not be fundamental here. Morris R. Cohen once suggested that we need "[a]n adequate theory of private property [to] enable us to draw the line between justifiable and unjustifiable cases of confiscation." [6] Instead of chasing quarks we might do better to think about what property is, why we should protect it, and how.

Frank Michelman's article outlines a utilitarian approach to these issues. What the utilitarian most values is maximizing the output of satisfactions (wealth). Settled expectations about the distribution of resources (property) help produce wealth by giving people an incentive to labor and invest. Redistribution, on the other hand, reduces wealth because it is demoralizing. We can avoid this cost by compensating people when it occurs. But sometimes we can maximize wealth by not compensating. In the case of the traffic light it may cost more to identify the losers and measure their losses than it would to accept their demoralization. Here is a principle (though a very general one) for distinguishing between compensable and noncompensable takings: we should compensate when demoralization costs exceed the administrative costs of settling claims. Michelman makes this idea more specific by applying it to the test (diminution of value) most often used by the Supreme Court in takings cases.

This utilitarian account assumes that our system of private property has as its primary purpose encouraging the production of wealth. Carol Rose suggests that that may not be so. She points to a conflicting tradition in our history—one that subordinates the acquisition of wealth to the promotion of virtue. In this tradition, property is valued for its contribution to certain qualities of character. But since too much property can be corrupting, redistribution may sometimes be a good thing. Rose believes that the perennial muddle over the takings issue can be traced to the conflict between these two deep-rooted traditions.

The last selection in this Section deals with the "public use" limitation on takings. Up until the time of the New Deal the courts viewed this restriction as one they were capable of enforcing against too activist legislatures.[7] Since then it has become a dead letter.[8] There is an obvious parallel between this development and the Court's treatment

---

6. Cohen, *Property and Sovereignty,* 13 Cornell L.Q. 8, 26 (1927).

7. Cincinnati v. Vester, 281 U.S. 439, 446, 50 S.Ct. 360, 362, 74 L.Ed. 950 (1930) ("It is well established that in considering the application of the Fourteenth Amendment to cases of expropriation of private

property, the question what is a public use is a judicial one.").

8. The tide turned in United States ex rel. TVA v. Welch, 327 U.S. 546, 551, 66 S.Ct. 715, 717, 90 L.Ed. 843 (1946) ("it is the function of Congress to decide what type of taking is for a public use").

of legislative powers under Article I and the Due Process Clause. Thomas Merrill explains the reasons for this similarity. He goes on to argue that the judiciary can enforce the "public use" requirement, not (as Michelman's article suggests) by forbidding inefficient takings altogether, but by supervising the ways in which the government acquires property.

RICHARD A. EPSTEIN, *LUCAS v. SOUTH CAROLINA COASTAL COUNCIL*: A TANGLED WEB OF EXPECTATIONS

45 Stan.L.Rev. 1369–1372, 1386–1392 (1993).

Although anticipated before its arrival, last term's decision in *Lucas v. South Carolina Coastal Council* [1] has been rightly regarded as anticlimactic. To be sure, the decision represents something of a high water mark in takings jurisprudence, for a six justice majority of the Court allowed that some restrictions on land use might in principle be caught by the Takings Clause. But what the Court gave with one hand, it took away with the other. Justice Scalia held that the Takings Clause reached only those land use restrictions that deprived the owner of "all economically beneficial uses" of property. The proper status of permanent but partial restrictions on land use was not explicitly addressed, but these may now be regarded as legitimate and non-compensable exercises under the state police power. Yet even with total regulatory takings, Justice Scalia stopped short of embracing Lucas's theory that the total loss of beneficial use constitutes a per se compensable taking. Rather, he held that even for total regulatory takings a second test had to be passed as well: If the regulated activity constitutes some form of noxious use or nuisance-like activity subject to regulation at common law, then the state need not compensate the landowner for any resulting economic loss. Scalia's constitutional edifice thus rests on two critical distinctions. The first is whether the restriction on use is partial or total. If partial, then the constitutional inquiry is at its end, and the restriction is sustained. If total, then the second criterion must be evaluated: The regulation passes muster only if it restricts some nuisance-like behavior.

The question that I address in this essay is whether the two parts of this edifice can withstand theoretical scrutiny. That inquiry receives a split decision: Suitably refurbished, the nuisance/nonnuisance distinction * * * does withstand the attacks frequently leveled against it, and its invocation is indispensable for any coherent understanding of the Takings Clause. However, the first half of Scalia's edifice—his distinction between total and partial takings—is so rickety that it must fall of its own weight[.]

In order to understand why Justice Scalia's is a house divided, it is necessary to examine the idea of "reasonable expectations" (sometimes unfortunately called "investment-backed expectations") on which his

---

1. 112 S.Ct. 2886 (1992)[.]

holding so clearly depends. Neither he nor anyone else offers any telling explanation of why this tantalizing notion of expectations is preferable to the words "private property" (which are, after all, not mere gloss, but actual constitutional text). If "investment-backed expectations" is a term of art designed to convey the idea that property is protected only where it has been acquired by purchase or labor, then it is clearly inaccurate. The government cannot take property from a donee anymore than it can take it from a buyer. If the term is instead designed to stress that protection of private property is granted solely to encourage investment, then its usefulness is still limited by a failure to delineate the nature and scope of the protection, given the apparent ease with which those expectations are so often defeated by a simple appeal to the common good. All in all, we should be deeply suspicious of the phrase "investment-backed expectations" because it is not possible to identify even the paradigmatic case of its use.

Despite its inherent limitations, Justice Scalia relies on the concept of expectations (both the merely reasonable kind and the loftier, investment-backed variety) at critical points in his analysis. * * * Clearly, the expectations concept is being pressed to do an enormous amount of work in a very complex and troubled area of law. Ironically, however, as its salience increases, its major deficiency—circularity—becomes even more apparent[.]

The central difficulty with the Scalia * * * analysis is its failure to explain the relationship between expectations and entitlements, which cannot be unpacked solely by predicting how private parties will behave or how the state will regulate. Instead, defining reasonable expectations turns on a much more complicated inquiry: What set of entitlements maximizes the joint welfare of both the property holder and other affected parties? Democratic institutions are organized for instrumental reasons, the most important of which is to maximize the welfare of the citizens they govern. Therefore, the relevant question at every point should be: Does the regulation or restriction serve to maximize social welfare? If, by our choice of regulation, we can make one person better off while leaving no person worse off, then efficiency counsels us to adopt that particular strategy. Although it is often difficult to implement social reforms with this consequence, it is a mistake not even to try. And while the choice between the best and the next-best social arrangement may be difficult to make, either should be preferred over the 100th best allocation of rights, which is the arrangement that current takings law often yields us today.

The Supreme Court's inability to understand the role of reasonable expectations in generating entitlements paves the way for the rapid elimination of all perceived entitlements by simply claiming that the enactment of a single government regulation reasonably creates an expectation that further regulations will follow. With this understanding of expectations, individual property owners are considered "on notice" about the prospect of new legal restrictions on land use and cannot complain when they occur. Each round of government regulation thus provides justification for the next. In each successive case, it becomes easier to overwhelm a shattered expectation than it would have been to undo a claim of entitlement to private property. The constant refrain that the Takings Clause protects only investment-backed or reasonable expectations has thus been used by the Supreme Court to minimize the level of protection given to private property.

* * *

[T]o determine which expectations should inform constitutional discourse * * * we must understand the relationships created by private property not only between the property and its owner, but also between the owner and the rest of the world. * * * Reasonable expectations must be used to define the relationship between strangers in ways that maximize their joint welfare, a task which requires a number of steps. First, a framework of basic reciprocity must be adopted in which neither side could claim any special advantage denied to the other. But merely adopting a condition of equal right does not specify what substantive rights should be held equal; the best procedure for determining the content of those rights is to search for the rule that will maximize joint welfare. Thus the equality constraint is consistent with a world in which no one can develop property, as well as one in which each person can do whatever he wants with his own property[.] The baseline that allows all use of property is surely a better starting point than the alternative that allows none. In most cases, the right to use one's own land freely is more important than the right to veto one's neighbor's use of his land.

The initial presumption of unrestricted property rights is only the first of successive approximations. The question then arises of how land use might thereafter be limited. One obvious device is regulation by restrictive covenant, binding on both parties to the initial land transfer and their successors in title, where notice has been filed. * * * [A]ny effort in the private arena to draw the categorical distinction between total and partial restrictions on use is fruitless. Restrictive covenants are frequently partial; but whether partial or total, they are acquired by consent rather than coercion. * * *

The law of eminent domain dispenses with the need for consent when the taking is for a public use, for which public leisure and aesthetic pleasure surely qualify. But where the taking goes forward, the law of takings does not dispense with the need for compensation. Justice Scalia identified the crucial point when he stated, in a sentence that bears repetition, that

> [a] law or decree with such an effect must, in other words, do no more than duplicate the result that could have been achieved in the courts—by adjacent landowners (or other uniquely affected persons) under the State's law of private nuisance, or by the State under its complementary power to abate nuisances that affect the public generally, or otherwise.

The rationale is that people should never be allowed to take by majority vote without compensation what they would have to pay for if they acted cooperatively in their private capacities. To allow otherwise would cause a mass migration from the market and to the political process. But what Justice Scalia does not, or cannot, explain is why this concern with using political power to bypass the market arises only with total takings. * * * The distinction between the total and the partial taking does not exist in the private law of restrictive covenants. Why then should the understanding or reasonable expectations shift so dramatically when we move into the public sphere?

Justice Scalia clearly thought that the distinction made sense, although he did not say so. It seems evident that he resorted to this wholly artificial distinction to avoid having to attack zoning (not to mention rent control) head on—including the zoning that existed on the Isle of Palms when Lucas purchased his land. After all, zoning is, quite simply, a system of partial restrictions on land use, which would be routinely subject to intense constitutional scrutiny if the total/partial distinction in *Lucas* is abandoned. But there is no hint as to why a fuller examination of zoning is so far beyond the pale, given the massive abuse of the system that is commonly observed. In the private area, the price for each covenant (whether in cash or kind) increases as the scope of the covenant expands. Why should the government be subject to any different rule? It is, in general, highly unwise to give a single person the power to initiate a transaction by brute force and then to ignore its harmful consequences on other individuals. Yet, that vast power is vindicated when all partial restrictions (and we will never see another total one) are allowable after *Lucas*. The first of Justice Scalia's claims cannot be sustained by a sound appeal to reasonable expectations.

There still remains a second side to the story, that of state justification of taking without compensation under the police power. Here the initial question should be evident from the above discussion. Restrictive covenants are available to correct any misallocation arising from a landowner's unfettered use of his property. Why then worry about the law of nuisance at all? If one does not like pollution, then one could purchase a restrictive covenant forbidding it. The distinction between ordinary uses, forbidden only by restrictive covenants, and nuisances, restrictive as of right, is foreign to the analysis. Instead of a situation allowing a state to forbid all uses of land without compensation, we could easily veer to a system in which it could forbid none without payment to the affected landowner—Lucas' own indefensible position with respect to total (but not partial) takings.

There is, I think, only one escape from this conclusion. It relies on the [theory of transaction costs.] The difference between the ordinary use of land and the nuisance rests on the generalized perception of the relative shift in costs and benefits. With pollution, the net gain from its practice is normally lower than the costs it inflicts, such that a sole owner of two adjacent properties would take steps to reduce its incidence. The purpose of nuisance law is to replicate the same pattern of behavior when separate ownership * * * shifts either the costs or the benefits to a second landowner.

With nuisances, an initial allocation that affords the polluter the right to pollute will require many more corrective transactions than the alternative assignment of right in order to achieve the optimal level of pollution. It is preferable for 5 percent of the cases to involve the purchase of an easement to create a nuisance than for 95 percent to involve the purchase of a restrictive covenant to prevent one. Such an allocation properly reflects a world with positive transaction costs, rather than the zero-transaction-cost world of Ronald Coase.[59] Pick the path which reduces the transaction costs necessary to reach the optimal allocation of resources.

The entire story is, of course, more complicated than this, and further accommodations must be considered. In some instances, low level reciprocal nuisances would typically be the subject of reciprocal covenants, so the "live and let live" rule will allow them to continue as a matter of course. Conversely, in other situations, as with lateral support easements, where there would likely be restrictive covenants, the law should supply restrictions as a matter of course. Finding the path with the fewest transactional costs en route to the optimal social solution is therefore crucial to understanding the seemingly irreconcilable doctrines of nuisance law.

But can the connection to takings law be forged? Here the Supreme Court generally accepts only a *one-way* connection: Whatever land uses may be forbidden by neighbors under nuisance law without compensation may similarly be forbidden by the state without compensation. But the converse proposition, though ignored by Justice Scalia, is critical. Whatever uses the neighbors could not prohibit without compensation, the state cannot prohibit without compensation either. * * *

* * *

* * * Under Justice Scalia's opinion, which will apply at trial, the outcome should be clear. The connection between nuisance prevention (or lateral support) and the building restriction is tenuous at best. The other objectives of the legislation—the developmental retreat along the beach, the promotion of tourism and leisure time for citizens—are by no stretch of the imagination related to the state's police power. The selective imposition of these restrictions on the breaker islands, while allowing new construction in major urban centers, is analogous to creating a state park without paying for the change. The trial on these issues might be complicated by a set of needless political barriers, but on these facts at least, Lucas is entitled to an easy victory.

The more difficult questions regarding the overall state of takings law, however, remain unresolved. The present law is in chaos because of its muddled conceptual foundations. Too often the justices rely on a conception of reasonable expectations that is drained of all its explanato-

59. R.H. Coase, *The Problem of Social Cost,* 3 J.L. & Econ. 1 (1960).

ry power. Too often conceptual coherence is sacrificed because the Justices are afraid to face the broad implications of the Takings Clause. The fear arises because the clause is broad, not because its implications are mischievous. *Lucas* is a case of disappointed expectations because Justice Scalia embraced the private law analogies on the police power question when it was too late to do any good. What he should have done was make clear that the categorical distinction between partial and total takings has no parallel in private law and no place in public law.

JOSEPH L. SAX, TAKINGS AND THE POLICE POWER

74 Yale L.J. 36, 37, 46–53, 60 (1964).

Two basic approaches have been developed by the courts to distinguish takings from police power regulations. The earlier theory, articulated in the main by the first Justice Harlan, drew on traditional legal concepts for its rules. Notions such as appropriation of a proprietary interest, physical invasion giving rise to a prescriptive easement, and nuisance were its basic tools. The second approach originated with Justice Holmes in the first quarter of this century, when the expansion of governmental regulation yielded a proliferation of claims for compensation by aggrieved owners of private property. Holmes' approach denied the utility of artificial legalisms such as Harlan employed. Holmes proposed reliance on a pragmatic, case-by-case resolution of the policy-conflict which he perceived to lie at the heart of the problem—the conflict between public need and private loss. Neither of these two approaches has proved able to produce satisfactory results. Harlan's theory reduces the constitutional issue to a formalistic quibble; an airport noise case, for example, may turn on whether the planes have physically penetrated that segment of air directly above the claimant's land. The Holmesian approach has equal failings. Its central premise—that the right to compensation depends on the magnitude of loss suffered—is historically unsound, has never in fact been acceptable to the Court, and wasn't even followed by Holmes himself.

* * *

THE INVASION THEORY

* * * [I]t is obvious that whether the government takes title or possession of the subject property is merely a matter of the form in which it chooses to proceed. One of the oldest tricks of capitalizing on form is to try to depreciate the value or inhibit the development of property through zoning, so that it has a much reduced market value when the government gets around to buying it. Thus the government gets most of the value of the property without any formal "taking." New Jersey cities seem to have pioneered this technique. The city of Plainfield once zoned plaintiff's property exclusively for school, park, and playground use.[63] * * * The state courts have quite uniformly rejected these guises and required the payment of compensation.

But a similar device slipped by the U.S. Supreme Court, at least in part, because the Court applied the old invasion theory. In *United States v. Central Eureka Mining Company,*[68] the War Production Board shut down privately owned gold mines for the purpose of inducing experienced miners, who were in very short supply, to go into more essential war work. In essence what the government was doing was improving the labor situation by putting the competition out of business. In the private realm this is ordinarily done by buying the competitor. And in the ordinary situation this is what would have been done. But instead of buying the right to operate the business in question, and thus the economic power to induce a shift of labor to other industries, the government merely "regulated" the gold mines out of business without invoking the magic talisman of a physical invasion. Form prevailed over substance; the Court's opinion turned in at least some degree on its finding that "the Government did not occupy, use or in any manner take physical possession of the gold mines or of the equipment connected with them." Compensation was denied.

For constitutional questions to depend on such formalities is, as these cases demonstrate, preposterous. The formal appropriation or physical invasion theory should be rejected once and for all.

The Noxious Use Theory

Analysis will show the noxious use test to be no more adequate than the invasion test, although it has a beguiling simplicity and a perpetual appeal. Since the taking provision is undoubtedly an attempt to find some fair balance between the forces of change and the security of established interests, it has seemed particularly appropriate to believe that the compensation problem could be solved by saying that the uses which could be destroyed without compensation were those that were noxious, or wrongful, or harmful in some sense.

Of course it has long been obvious that all non-compensable uses could not be described in terms of moral obloquy such as might be appropriate for the regulation of prostitution or liquor. But a more modern version of the noxious use test has had considerable popularity, and it is this version which must be discussed. This is the "creation of the harm" test, based on the argument that while in general established economic interests cannot be diminished merely because of a resulting public benefit, that rule does not apply where the individual whose interest is to be diminished himself created the need for public regulation by his conduct. The test has been most explicitly articulated in the series of grade-separation cases which have come before the Court. In those situations a railroad track crosses a highway at street level. As highway traffic increases, the legislature determines that in the interests

---

63. Joint Meeting v. Borough of Middlesex, 69 N.J.Super. 136, 173 A.2d 785 (1961).

68. 357 U.S. 155 (1958).

of safety, a grade separation is necessary. The cost of providing the improvement is usually assessed in large part against the railroad. It has been almost universally the rule that the railroad must pay, and the justification has been that:

> Having brought about the problem, the railroads are in no position to complain because their share of the cost of alleviating it is not based solely on the special benefits accruing to them from the improvements.[72]

* * *

This test is, however, insufficient to explain a great number of other very important cases. Perhaps nuisance abatement is the best example. Zoning out of nuisances is perhaps the classic example of the non-compensable exercise of the police power. The typical nuisance situation is one in which a perfectly lawful industrial enterprise located on the outskirts of the city suddenly finds itself in the midst of a new and unforeseen residential development.[74] It can hardly be said that the industrial user created this evil which is now sought to be remedied: the patent fact is that the evil was created by the unfortunate juxtaposition of two lawful activities. Indeed that is precisely the situation in the grade crossing cases. If all we mean by "creation of the evil" is that one has located himself in a place which subsequently turns out to be inconsistent with the public interest—and that is all that can be said of the nuisance and grade crossing cases—then we must also say that the farmer who buys land in a place which is subsequently needed for a state highway has "created" the harm to be remedied and need not be given compensation.

Actually the problem is not one of noxiousness or harm-creating activity at all; rather it is a problem of inconsistency between perfectly innocent and independently desirable uses. And what is true of the nuisance and grade crossing cases is equally true of a great many cases in which the Court denies compensation.

For example, incompatibility is the essence of the famous decision in *Miller v. Schoene.*[76] There the complainant was required to destroy his red cedar trees because they produced cedar rust which was fatal to apple trees which happened to be cultivated nearby. To say that the cedar tree owner caused the harm is no more accurate than to say that the apple growers caused the harm by locating near cedar groves. If we are talking about blameworthiness, some moral wrongdoing or conscious act of dangerous risk-taking which induces us to shift the cost to a particular individual, it simply does not exist in these cases.

72. Atchison, T. & S.F. Ry. v. Public Utilities Comm'rs, 346 U.S. 346, 353 (1953).

74. Hadacheck v. Sebastian, 239 U.S. 394 (1915).

76. 276 U.S. 272 (1928).

Of course the same is true of cases like * * * *Goldblatt [v. Town of Hempstead].*[78] The users there created the harm only in the sense that they decided to mine sand and gravel in a place which subsequently became desirable for residential homesites. * * *

THE DIMINUTION OF VALUE THEORY

Since emphasis on the diminution of value is probably the most popular current approach to the taking problem, it is important to understand precisely what it comprehends: Essentially the theory appears to express two interrelated ideas: (1) that all legally acquired existing economic values are property, and (2) that while such values may be diminished somewhat without compensation, they may not be excessively diminished: the meaning of "excessive" is necessarily imprecise, but it is fairly clear under the theory that it would be unconstitutional to deprive a property of all or substantially all its economic value.

This approach, too, has tremendous appeal. It seems to bear out the oft-repeated observation that "the political ethics reflected in the fifth amendment reject confiscation as a measure of justice." This is a strong and attractive sentiment, but it has unfortunately been used to obscure the real problems of the compensation clause. The problem is much more complicated than merely identifying existing economic values, denominating them property, and providing a rule that those values may not be wholly or substantially destroyed.

The Test Presupposes a False Definition of Property

The first complication is presented by the fact that we very often permit total destruction of established values; in so doing we circumvent the diminution of value approach by an alternative analysis, which simply says that the interest affected was not property and thus not entitled to constitutional protection. This is a very common approach, used by Holmes himself on several occasions.[81] The classic formulation of the "no-compensation because no-property" approach was provided by Justice Jackson in the *Willow River Power* case:

> Only those economic advantages are "rights" which have the law back of them * * * whether it is a property right is really the question to be answered.[82]

The significance of this is that it shows the erroneous and delusive simplicity of the diminution of value approach. For every time we deny compensation on the ground that the interest affected was not really a property right, we repudiate in some measure the essence of the diminu-

---

78. 369 U.S. 590 (1962). [In this case the Court upheld a town "safety regulation" that banned mining at Goldblatt's sand and gravel pit in a suburban area.]

81. * * * It was Holmes who pointed out that "there are many things which a man might do at common law that the states may forbid" and which have never been thought to be property entitled to constitutional protection. "He might embezzle until a statute cut down his liberty." Noble State Bank v. Haskell, 219 U.S. 104, 113 (1911).

82. United States v. Willow River Power Co., 324 U.S. 499, 502 (1945).

tion of value test—the proposition that established economic values as such are entitled to constitutional protection.

In fact there are so many of these non-property situations that one must be irrevocably led to the conclusion that whatever it is that the compensation clause is preventing, it is something other than the destruction of established economic values. Changes in the common law are frequently made, and they are changes which may have very substantial economic import; yet we invariably deny compensation on the ground that there was no property interest in maintenance of the status quo. In the field of tort law, for example, such changes as abolition of the privity rule, imposition of the doctrine of products liability, or the extinguishment of charitable immunity are well known instances. The constitutionality of such laws is assumed on the ground that the economic advantage affected—like the common law right to embezzle—is not property. Similarly in the law of real property, it seems never to have been suggested that a compensable taking was involved when the courts first "took away" an easement by necessity from an unwilling grantor, although we today clearly treat an easement as a kind of interest which can give rise to a taking problem.

Similarly the legislatures are permitted to prohibit the continuance of businesses, lawful when established, with ensuing total or near total destruction of values. As that practice formerly affected lotteries, or the manufacture of liquor,[86] it proceeds apace today against debt adjustment,[87] and whatever other businesses which once "were thought useful adjuncts of the state" but have since fallen into popular disfavor. Of these crushing economic dislocations for the affected persons we merely say that there was no property interest involved.

When the legislature destroys 90% of value by prohibiting continuance of a brickyard,[89] it contents itself with saying the activity was a nuisance, and everyone knows that there is no property in a nuisance; when it imposes heavy regulation on the oil industry,[90] it says it is preventing waste, and so too, there is plainly no property interest in waste. Zoning, with losses of 75% or more of value, is similarly treated.[91]

* * *

The conclusion to be drawn from these examples, just a few among many, is clear. The diminution of value test gives a highly unreal view of the actual working of the compensation rule in American law. Destruction of recognized economic interests, on the ground that there is no property interest, is so widespread and pervasive that the policy of preventing individual economic loss as such, can hardly be said to have

---

86. Mugler v. Kansas, 123 U.S. 623 (1887).

87. Ferguson v. Skrupa, 372 U.S. 726 (1963).

89. Hadacheck v. Sebastian, 239 U.S. 394, 408–09 (1915).

90. Champlin Refining Co. v. Corporation Comm'n, 286 U.S. 210 (1932).

91. Euclid v. Ambler Realty Co., 272 U.S. 365, 384 (1926).

been given significant recognition by the courts. Nor can it be seriously argued that the foregoing examples are part of a special limited class of noxious or harmful uses; they are, like the typical taking cases, merely uses which have become inconsistent with the legislatively declared public interest. Thus, the question naturally arises as to whether or not we have been misled in thinking that the function of the compensation clause is essentially to protect and maintain established values. Certainly if we look to what the Court has done, the answer must be that in fact and in result the Court has not treated protection of values as its primary goal.

* * *

The Test Imports an Unworkable Problem of Definition

Because the diminution test turns on the degree of quantitative diminution of value, it is necessary that the property at issue be precisely defined, so that we can determine how great the impairment of value is. But this is no easy task. If the government floods 80 acres of a 640 acre farm, is that a total destruction of 80 acres, or a mere 12½ percent loss? In a case of compulsory dedication of real property by a land subdivider, the acreage given up can be treated as a total loss, or merely as a loss of a small portion of the entire tract, in which case the end result might even be seen as an increase in the value of the property because of the prospect of municipal services. In the famous *Pennsylvania Coal* case is the loss to be treated as a total taking of that quantum of coal left in the ground, or as a small fraction of the total productivity of the mine? These definitional problems are difficult; they have never been seriously treated in opinions which invariably solve them by flat and unsupported assertions as to the identity of "the" property at issue. Since degree of loss is the very essence of the test, this is a central problem. The failure to deal with the issue, and the terrible complexities of trying to do so are further evidence of the unsatisfactory nature of the diminution of value test.

* * *

[Sax goes on to propose that we solve the takings riddle by distinguishing between "enterprise" and "arbitral" functions of government. Compensation should be required when the government takes property in furtherance of its own interests as an enterprise—to maintain an army, build highways, run schools, etc. It is not due when the government decides disputes between private parties. This rule, Sax argues, would protect us against "arbitrary, unfair or tyrannical government" behavior—a real danger only in "enterprise" cases.]

———

Seven years later Sax changed his mind and proposed an even more permissive rule: the government need not pay compensation when it acts to prevent "spillover" effects (external costs of property use).

These he defined to include uses of private property that affect the health or well-being of others. *Takings, Private Property and Public Rights,* 81 Yale L.J. 149 (1971).

FRANK I. MICHELMAN, PROPERTY, UTILITY, AND FAIRNESS: COMMENTS ON THE ETHICAL FOUNDATIONS OF "JUST COMPENSATION" LAW
80 Harv.L.Rev. 1165, 1211–1218, 1224, 1229–1234 (1967).

[In the first part of this article Michelman reviews the rules of decision typically used to identify compensable takings and concludes, as Sax does, that they rest in general on illusory distinctions. He then turns to an examination of the purposes of the compensation requirement. The discussion excerpted here deals with a utilitarian justification for property rights and compensation. In the concluding portion of this excerpt that theory is applied to the diminution-of-value test announced by Justice Holmes in *Pennsylvania Coal Co. v. Mahon.*]

SOME THEORIES OF PROPERTY

A number of pre-utilitarian property theories rested * * * on behavioral premises indicating that productivity will be enhanced by pride and responsibility of office; or that productivity will be frustrated and consumption voided of satisfaction by the discord which only clear and simple rules of control can forestall; or that productivity demands planning and organization. Assumptions such as these stand independent of, though they perhaps suggest, the further assumption that a high level of productivity depends on arrangements which assure to every person who invests or labors that he will share in the fruits of his investment or labor to a predictable extent. This additional assumption * * * seems to have been definitively clarified and elaborated by Bentham. It was he who stimulated emphasis on the relevance of appearance and suggestion to the intensity of productive activity, as well as the maintenance of that state of association which itself lifts productivity to a new plateau. Bentham's emphasis is of peculiar importance for present purposes because it * * * furnish[es] the germ of a theoretically satisfying approach to compensation questions.

Property, according to Bentham, is most aptly regarded as the collection of rules which are presently accepted as governing the exploitation and enjoyment of resources.[96] So regarded, property becomes "a basis of expectations" founded on existing rules; that is to say, property is the institutionally established understanding that extant rules governing the relationships among men with respect to resources will continue in existence. The justification—Bentham regards it as a practical necessity—for adherence to such an understanding is that only through such adherence can we hope for a minimally acceptable level of productivity.

96. The statement which is usually accepted as definitive of Bentham's position is   J. Bentham, Theory of Legislation chs. 7–10 (6th ed. 1890). * * *

The human motivations which result in production are, he believes, such that they will not operate in the absence of secure expectations about future enjoyment of product. It is supposed that men will not labor diligently or invest freely unless they know they can depend on rules which assure them that they will indeed be permitted to enjoy a substantial share of the product as the price of their labor or their risk of savings.

If one agrees with Bentham that the will to labor and the will to invest depend upon reliable assurances about the future enjoyment of any product, he must agree also that any unpredictable redistribution is potentially destructive of society's material wellbeing. For a newly conceived redistribution, no matter how accomplished or to what end, is always something of a disappointment to the expectations which Bentham regards as the essence of property. And the very act of redistributing implies that society will not scruple to effect like redistributions in the future. It is this implication or suggestion—this disavowal of perfect security of expectation—which utilitarian property theory chiefly deprecates.

We thus receive from Bentham a theory of social utility which can explain why collective allocational decision making, deemed unobjectionable in and of itself, *might* be deemed impermissible if attended by capricious redistributions. And we may be encouraged to try to derive from that theory some criteria for determining which collective allocational decisions, attended by what particular distributional impacts, should be deemed impermissible unless those impacts are offset by compensation payments. Still we must recognize that, despite its obvious and direct relevance to the general compensation problem, the utilitarian theory will not show us how to discriminate among capricious redistribution cases—will not, that is, show us how to perfect our general practice, certain to be retained, of compensating in some but not all of such cases—if its only implication is a general one militating broadly against *all* capricious redistributions. Given the framework of practices within which the compensation problem actually arises in our society, the practical relevance of the utilitarian theory will [not be great] until it has been shown that the utilitarian theory * * * is translatable into pertinent questions of degree.

The problem, then, is to show that utilitarian property theory, applied with utmost consistency, does *not* require payment of compensation in every case of social action which is disappointing to justified, investment-backed expectations. * * *

The utilitarian * * * will probably be unable to avoid the conclusion that it is sometimes right for society to adopt a measure which cannot practically be purged of a capriciously redistributive effect frustrating to justified expectations: he could avoid that conclusion only if he were of the implausible view that no social measure which is visibly disappointing to expectations can possibly improve the allocational picture enough to outweigh resultant losses in productive effort.

* * * [W]e must remember that the utilitarian's solicitude for security is instrumental and subordinate to his goal of maximizing the output of satisfactions. Security of expectation is cherished, not for its own sake, but only as a shield for morale. Once admit that not all capricious redistributive effects are totally demoralizing, and utilitarian theory can tell us where to draw the line between compensable and noncompensable collective impositions. An imposition is compensable if not to compensate would be critically demoralizing; otherwise, not.

UTILITY * * * AND COMPENSATION

* * *

A strictly utilitarian argument leading to the specific identification of "compensable" occasions would have a quasi-mathematical structure. Let us define three quantities to be known as "efficiency gains," "demoralization costs," and "settlement costs." "Efficiency gains" we define as the excess of benefits produced by a measure over losses inflicted by it, where benefits are measured by the total number of dollars which prospective gainers would be willing to pay to secure adoption, and losses are measured by the total number of dollars which prospective losers would insist on as the price of agreeing to adoption. "Demoralization costs" are defined as the total of (1) the dollar value necessary to offset disutilities which accrue to losers and their sympathizers specifically from the realization that no compensation is offered, and (2) the present capitalized dollar value of lost future production (reflecting either impaired incentives or social unrest) caused by demoralization of uncompensated losers, their sympathizers, and other observers disturbed by the thought that they themselves may be subjected to similar treatment on some other occasion. "Settlement costs" are measured by the dollar value of the time, effort, and resources which would be required in order to reach compensation settlements adequate to avoid demoralization costs. Included are the costs of settling not only the particular compensation claims presented, but also those of all persons so affected by the measure in question or similar measures as to have claims not obviously distinguishable by the available settlement apparatus.

A measure attended by positive efficiency gains is, under utilitarian ethics, prima facie desirable. But felicific calculation under the definition given for efficiency gains is imperfect because it takes no account of demoralization costs caused by a capricious redistribution, or alternatively, of the settlement costs necessary to avoid such demoralization costs. When pursuit of efficiency gains entails capricious redistribution, either demoralization costs or settlement costs must be incurred. It follows that if, for any measure, both demoralization costs and settlement costs (whichever were chosen) would exceed efficiency gains, the measure is to be rejected; but that otherwise, since either demoralization costs or settlement costs must be paid, it is the lower of these two costs which should be paid. The compensation rule which then clearly emerges is that compensation is to be paid whenever settlement costs are lower than both demoralization costs and efficiency gains. * * *

Let us now focus on the problem of appraising demoralization costs. Since we are looking ultimately to the specification of practical methods for identifying compensable occasions, we may begin by saying that it obviously will not do to interview every potential compensation claimant and ask him how demoralized he expects to be if a given measure is adopted without provision for compensation. The objections to such a solution run far deeper than the obvious one about the costs of conducting such interviews. The interviewee probably will not himself know the answer to the question (putting aside the difficulty of his attaching a dollar value to his outrage and his loss of incentive even if he could appraise those subjectively) and, for strategic reasons, would not reveal the true answer if he knew it.

We are compelled, then, to frame the question about demoralization costs in terms of responses we must impute to ordinarily cognizant and sensitive members of society. Utilitarian algebra, it appears, cannot specify a sound compensation practice—the equation cannot be solved for that "value" of compensation which yields a maximum excess of efficiency gains over demoralization or settlement costs—until supposed facts about human psychology and behavior have been plugged into the equation as independent variables.

If we hypothesize a utilitarian defense of currently observable social practices pertaining to compensation, we can make some interesting deductions about the behavioral assumptions which must have entered into the utilitarian calculation. One clear characteristic of current practices is their reflection of a special urgency in the demand for publicly financed compensation when a loss has evidently been occasioned by deliberate social action. Society has not yet placed itself under any systematic discipline designed to assure people of compensation for all economic losses inflicted by forces regarded as beyond social control, such as earthquake or plague. * * *

We are thus led to inquire whether there is any reason to suppose that a visible risk of majoritarian exploitation should have any greater disincentive effect than the ever-present risk that accidents may happen, this being the only supposition which seems, on utilitarian premises, to justify a constitutional guaranty aimed specially against the former sort of risk. If I am able to mobilize my productive faculties under the general conditions of uncertainty which prevail in the universe, why should I be paralyzed by a realization that I am at the mercy of majorities?

There seems only one possible way to defend this behavioral supposition. The defense must begin with an imputation to human actors of a perception that the force of a majority is self-determining and purposive, as compared with other loss-producing forces which seem to be randomly generated. The argument must then proceed to the effect that even though people can adjust satisfactorily to random uncertainty, which can be dealt with through insurance, including self-insurance, they will remain on edge when contemplating the possibility of strategically determined losses. For when the bearing of strategy is evident, one faces the risk of being *systematically* imposed upon, which seems a risk of a very different order from the risk of occasional, accidental injury. One faces also the rational necessity of devoting a large proportion of his energies and resources to counter-strategy aimed at fending off the risk; where the possibility of loss will visibly be determined by strategy, that possibility cannot be conveniently dismissed from consciousness on the ground that, being uncontrollable, it is not worth thinking about.

Whatever the empirical verity of this behavioral picture, it does seem implicit in any attempt to rationalize current compensation practices in utilitarian (product-maximizing) terms. Accordingly, it seems in order to ask what criteria of compensability will emerge if the practice of compensating is taken to have the purpose of quieting people's unease about the possibility of being strategically exploited.

It seems obvious, to begin with, that this unease will be stirred by any spectacle of capricious redistribution which could easily have been avoided. Capricious redistributions will not be tolerated, even as accidental adjuncts of efficiency-dictated measures, when compensation settlements can be reached without much trouble, that is, when settlement costs are low. The clearer it is that the claimant has sustained an injury distinct from those sustained by the generality of persons in society, and the more obviously there appears to be some objectively satisfactory measure of his disproportionate or distinctive injury, the more compelling will his claim to compensation become.

Society, moreover, will have to avoid not only those capricious redistributions which a compensation payment could easily offset, but also those practically noncompensable ones which cannot plausibly be said to be necessitated by the pursuit of efficiency. Thus, measures whose efficiency is open to grave question will have to be rejected unless attended by compensation even though their arguable efficiency is enough to justify their adoption in some form. Payment of compensation in such cases may furnish a necessary assurance that the measure is not simply a disguised attempt to redistribute deliberately, by confirming the hypothesis that society deems the measure a "gainful" (efficient) one in the only ethically sure sense. Therefore, as the collective allocational measure approaches the limit of doubtful efficiency, the claim for compensation will become more compelling.

Other intertwined branches of a compensability inquiry could grow out of a utilitarian purpose to cater to the sense of security by preserving an illusion of long-run indiscriminateness in the distribution of social burdens and benefits. Thus the magnitude of the imposition would plainly be relevant: is it of quotidian variety, or is it once in a lifetime mayhem? But magnitude of individual burden, no matter how purposively conceived, reveals only a fragment, meaningless by itself, of the whole picture. We need additional information. For example, is the burden for which compensation is sought a rare or peculiar one, or do like burdens seem to have been widely, even though not uniformly, scattered about the community? Is there implicit in the measure some reciprocity of burdens coupled with benefits (as, for example, in a measure restricting a large area to residential development) or does it channel benefits and burdens to different persons? How likely does it seem that members of the class burdened by the measure were able to wield enough effective influence in the process leading to its adoption to have extracted some compensatory concession "in kind"?

* * *

THE RULES OF DECISION REVISITED

* * *

Diminution of Value

[Many people have] found it hard to understand why compensability should be thought to turn on a comparison of the size of the claimant's loss with the preexisting value of that spatially defined piece of property to which the loss in value seems to be specifically attached. It can now be suggested that judicial reliance on such comparisons reflects a utilitarian approach to compensability, as qualified by some special behavioral assumptions.

* * * [The] purpose of compensation is to prevent a special kind of suffering on the part of people who have grounds for feeling themselves the victims of unprincipled exploitation. [The appeal of the diminution of value test] rests ultimately in administrative expediency[: it defines a class] of cases whose numbers will (a) usually be easy to identify and (b) usually, under certain behavioral suppositions, present a particularly strong subjective need for compensation.

* * * [T]hese statements require explanation. We may begin by noticing a refinement, not mentioned earlier, which might initially seem only to deepen the mystery. It will be recalled that Justice Holmes, writing for the Court in the famous *Pennsylvania Coal* case,[111] held that a restriction on the extraction of coal, which effectively prevented the petitioner from exercising certain mining rights which it owned, was a taking of property and so could be enforced only upon payment of compensation. Holmes intimated strongly that the separation in ownership of the mining rights from the balance of the fee, prior to enactment of the restriction, was critically important to the petitioner's victory. But why should this be so? We can see that if one owns mining rights only, but not the residue of the fee, then a regulation forbidding mining totally devalues the owner's stake in "that" land. But is there any reason why it should matter whether one owns, in addition to mining rights, residuary rights in the same parcel (which may be added to the denominator so as probably to reduce the fraction of value destroyed below what is necessary for compensability) or residuary rights in some other parcel (which will not be added to the denominator)?

111. Pennsylvania Coal Co. v. Mahon, 260 U.S. 393 (1922).

The significance of this question is confirmed by its pertinency to many comparable judicial performances. There is, for example, the widespread rule requiring compensation to the owner of an equitable servitude (such as a residential building restriction) when the government destroys the servitude's value by acquiring the burdened land and then using that land in violation of the private restriction embodied in the servitude. Vis-à-vis the servitude owner, the government cannot be said in the narrow sense to have "taken" any property. It has not * * * engaged in an activity which would be an actionable eviction if privately instigated. It is not affirmatively exploiting any prerogative formerly held by the owner of the servitude. It is simply engaging in activity which, absent the servitude, might have been a nuisance; but government does not usually come under an automatic obligation to compensate whenever it maintains a nuisance. Yet many courts award compensation to persons deprived by government action of the benefits of private building restrictions, without asking any questions about how much value, or what fraction of some value, has been destroyed. Thus, government activity, on land adjacent to the complainant's, which would otherwise give rise to no claim to compensation, may support such a claim if it violates a building restriction of which the complainant is a beneficiary. If a justification exists for such a difference in treatment, it would seem to be that one's psychological commitment to his explicit, formally carved out, appurtenant rights in another's land is much more sharply focused and intense, and much nearer the surface of his consciousness, than any reliance he places on his general claim to be safeguarded against nuisances. This proposition, if valid, would not affect the "fairness" of noncompensation, but it means that a utilitarian, with his eye on the actual long term psychological effects of his decisions, will be wary of denying compensation to the affronted servitude owner.

* * *

The "fraction of value destroyed" test, to recapitulate, appears to proceed by first trying to isolate some "thing" owned by the person complaining which is affected by the imposition. Ideally, it seems, one traces the incidence of the imposition and then asks what "thing" is likely to be identified by the owner as "the thing" affected by this measure? Once having thus found the denominator of the fraction, the test proceeds to ask what proportion of the value or prerogatives formerly attributed by the claimant to that thing has been destroyed by the measure. If practically all, compensation is to be paid.

All this suggests that the common way of stating the test under discussion—in terms of a vaguely located critical point on a sliding scale—is misleading (though certainly a true representation of the language repeatedly used by Holmes). The customary labels—magnitude of the harm test, or diminution of value test—obscure the test's foundations by conveying the idea that it calls for an arbitrary pinpointing of a critical proportion (probably lying somewhere between fifty and one hundred percent). More sympathetically perceived, however, the test poses not nearly so loose a question of degree; it does not ask "how much," but rather (like the physical-occupation test) it asks "whether or not": whether or not the measure in question can easily be seen to have practically deprived the claimant of some distinctly perceived, sharply crystallized, investment-backed expectation.

The nature and relevance of this inquiry may emerge more clearly if we notice one other familiar line of doctrine—that which enjoins special solicitude, when a new zoning scheme is instituted, for "established" uses which would be violations were the scheme applied with full retrospective vigor. The standard practice of granting dispensations for such "nonconforming uses" seems to imply an understanding that simply to ban them without payment of compensation, thus seriously reducing the property's market value, would be wrong and perhaps unconstitutional. But a ban on potential uses not yet established may destroy market value as effectively as does a ban on activity already in progress. The ban does not shed its retrospective quality simply because it affects only prospective uses. What explains, then, the universal understanding that only those nonconforming uses are protected which were demonstrably afoot by the time the regulation was adopted? The answer seems to be that actual establishment of the use demonstrates that the prospect of continuing it is a discrete twig out of his fee simple bundle to which the owner makes explicit reference in his own thinking, so that enforcement of the restriction would, as he looks at the matter, totally defeat a distinctly crystallized expectation. Here, then, is a case in which functional division of spatially unitary property makes the same kind of difference it made in *Pennsylvania Coal* * * *, although the division here exists only within the eye of the beholder whose feelings we are concerned about, and is not reflected in any title papers.

The worth of this kind of analysis in a utilitarian compensation program depends on a number of assumptions which, while not void of plausibility, are surely debatable. The assumptions are (1) that one thinks of himself not just as owning a total amount of wealth or income, but also as owning several discrete "things" whose destinies he controls; (2) that deprivation of one of these mentally circumscribed things is an event attended by pain of a specially acute or demoralizing kind, as compared with what one experiences in response to the different kind of event consisting of a general decline in one's net worth; and (3) that events of the specially painful kind can usually be identified by compensation tribunals with relative ease.

* * * Of the three propositions, the second surely is the most suspect. The first seems self-evident, and the third seems probably true. Thus, the claimant in *Pennsylvania Coal*, which supposed itself to own a mining interest before the incidence of the regulation, owned nothing of consequence afterward, but a residential owner in the regulated district still had essentially what he had before (though its market value may have been reduced). * * * The zoned-out apartment house owner no longer has the apartment investment he depended on, whereas the nearby land speculator who is unable to show that he has yet formed any

specific plans for his vacant land still has a package of possibilities with its value, though lessened, still unspecified—which is what he had before.

CAROL M. ROSE, *MAHON* RECONSTRUCTED: WHY THE TAKINGS ISSUE IS STILL A MUDDLE
57 S.Cal.L.Rev. 561, 582, 586–595 (1984).

[Rose reviews the Supreme Court's decision in *Pennsylvania Coal Co. v. Mahon*,[a] where Justice Holmes held unconstitutional a law forbidding the mining of anthracite coal beneath someone else's property if that would cause a subsidence of the surface. Before the law was enacted Pennsylvania Coal had conveyed the surface above its property to Mahon's father, expressly reserving the right to remove all underlying coal. Rose asserts that the Court struck the law down because it was seen as a naked redistribution of property from one group to another, without any net social gain.]

* * * This conclusion, however, only moves the problem to a different level: what is wrong with redistribution? Why condemn a law because it transfers property from the Company to the Mahons?

* * *

Some of Holmes' remarks suggest [that] transfer is undesirable [because it] might disrupt what Holmes called the "stream of products."[126] This reasoning reflects Madison's views, as set forth in his famous statement that the "first object of government" is the protection of "[t]he diversity in the faculties of men, from which the rights of property originate."[127] Bentham's theories add a gloss to the argument: a country will accumulate wealth if it protects the ability to acquire, but that ability flourishes only where the laws assure some continuity in property expectations.[128] Acquisition of wealth requires planning, investment of time and effort, and secure knowledge of return on the investment. Continuous property transfers, though they may all eventually even out, will not encourage wealth production. In John Locke's language, "industrious and rational" persons cannot get a foothold if legislatures transfer their property rights, and force them to pool their labors with the "quarrelsom[e] and contentious."[130] Hence pure transfers should be restrained in the political market, * * * because they cause too much turmoil for wealth producing enterprise.

* * *

a. 260 U.S. 393 (1922).

126. Letter from Holmes to Harold Laski (May 8, 1917), in Holmes–Laski Letters 84 (M. Howe ed. 1953).

127. The Federalist No. 10, at 78 (J. Madison) (C. Rossiter ed. 1961).

128. J. Bentham, [The Theory of Legislation 70–73 (Oceana Publications, Inc., ed. 1975)].

130. J. Locke, Second Treatise of Government § 34 (P. Laslett ed. 1963).

THE FUNDAMENTAL TENSION: WEALTH VERSUS VIRTUE

Despite the familiarity of the stability argument, a deeper question remains: why encourage wealth? Is encouraging the production of wealth the primary purpose of our system of private property? A careful look at the American property tradition reveals that other views of the purpose of private property have coexisted with the wealth maximizing view since at least the framing of the Constitution.

Wealth, Virtue, And The American Property Tradition

Aristotle related property acquisition and spending to the virtue of generosity. On this account, one needs a certain amount of wealth in order to be magnanimous, but it does not necessarily follow that more is better. The ethical ends of generosity and magnanimity constrain wealth accumulation; pure acquisitiveness has no claim for protection unless it also promotes those virtues. Some theorists of the Middle Ages went far beyond Aristotle, arguing that true virtue required the renunciation of material possessions. In general, the premodern philosophic theorists saw wealth acquisition at best as subordinate to the promotion of the virtue of generosity, and at worst as a highly suspicious and dangerous passion.

Madison rejected this theory, as had Hobbes and Locke before him. According to Madison, human virtues are notoriously unstable and reliance upon them may easily lead to outrage, despoliation, and bloodshed.[140] Madison felt it safer to rely not on virtues, but on self-interest. Among self-interested motives, avarice, though perhaps the homeliest, is also the most constant and reliable. By splitting society into a multiplicity of property interests, avarice distracts persons from the perhaps more majestic, but certainly more predatory, endeavors of our forebears. Businesspersons slit each other's throats only symbolically; they fight no duels and make no great point of honor. Yet their successes encourage others to make money instead of strife, and may produce a surplus that strengthens the nation against outsiders. Thus, protecting acquisitive interests increases both productivity and national strength.

On this reasoning, the protection of settled expectations promotes acquisition which in turn brings internal peace as well as strength vis-à-vis outsiders. Thus, in the classic triad of life, liberty, and property, the element of property ultimately serves life by reducing strife at home and presenting the image of strength abroad.

* * *

Familiar as the wealth maximizing argument for protecting expectations may be, American governing institutions have frequently acted as if protecting acquisition does not really deliver wealth and its supposed derivatives of peace and strength. More importantly, one strand in American political thinking has consistently rejected the argument's

---

140. *See* The Federalist No. 10, at 81 (J. Madison) (C. Rossiter ed. 1961) (neither religious nor moral motives are reliable as checks upon oppression).

underlying assumptions that the *res publica* has no meaning aside from the sum of individual satisfactions, and no functions aside from smoothing over the transaction costs encountered by self-interested humans.

J.G.A. Pocock has brilliantly illustrated the manner in which thinkers from the sixteenth through the eighteenth centuries revived and transformed the Aristotelian idea that human excellence is linked with participation in the polity and that the polity in turn depends on the character or "virtue" of its members.[148] In the early years of the republic, this view coexisted with the antithetical Lockean conception of government based on and serving the desires of only discrete individuals. For those who looked to civic virtue as the safeguard of the republic (and vice versa), property functioned to foster the independence and civic participation of a morally committed citizenry. The protection of property was necessarily subordinate to that function, even at the cost of substantial redistribution.

Thus could Jefferson argue for wide distribution of agricultural property as conducive to civic character, and maintain that extreme inequalities in property would corrupt the republic.[151] Thus could the Antifederalists argue that riches and power were neither the exclusive nor the most important goals for American government. To the Antifederalists, the important issues related to the nature of the regime and the qualities that it produced in the people.[152] * * *

This eighteenth and early nineteenth century "propertarianism" sought to foster civic virtue through property—property that would encourage sturdy independence and liberty. Beyond that point of citizen independence, however, the widely espoused civic property doctrine had a strong egalitarian element, and might tolerate or even encourage redistribution.

* * *

The Continuing Tension in the American Property Tradition

Neither of these traditions has vanished. The Lockean/Madisonian/Benthamite argument for acquisition, with its concomitant denial of a polity founded on any civic qualities beyond individual satisfactions, has found an exuberant revival in neoclassical economics. On the other hand, the civic conception of property as a means of developing character and promoting republican participation also persists * * *. The constant (and, according to economists, hopeless) efforts to restrain landlords and fast talking merchants are outgrowths of the tradition that subordinated property protection to civic virtue, requiring the "haves" to treat the "have-nots" more generously—just as the medieval prohibi-

---

148. For an exposition of the development of this civic virtue school of thought, *see* J. Pocock, [The Machiavellian Moment: Florentine Political Thought and the Atlantic Republican Tradition 423–505 (1975).]

151. *See* Katz [*Thomas Jefferson and the Right to Property in Revolutionary*

America, 19 J.L. & Econ. 467, 470–74, 480–81 (1975)].

152. *See* 1 The Complete Anti–Federalist 20–23 (H. Storing ed. 1981) (republican government depends on civic virtue and devotion to fellow citizens). * * *

tions on regraters, forestallers, and engrossers attempted to suppress the exploitation of commercial advantage by some to the detriment of others.

In takings doctrine, the tradition of property's civic responsibility is embodied in a test that balances public benefits against private losses from a particular measure. This test baffles legal commentators who take a neoclassical economic approach. From a Benthamite point of view, this test might be relevant to the utility of the proposed measure, but would have no bearing at all on the issue of compensation: if the public needs property, it may acquire it, but must still pay for it. The premise of this takings test, however, is quite the reverse; that is, that citizens may be required to sacrifice and bear private losses in the face of a substantially greater public need.

Thus, the arguments about disturbing established expectations take two very different directions: one would protect the acquisitive faculties which bring wealth and strength; the other would protect the citizen independence and participation which enhance the community, but would thereafter raise no principled objections to redistribution.

Why the Takings Problem Remains

This tension between the two arguments helps explain why the takings problem is so intractable. Our traditional discourse envisions property as serving quite divergent purposes. Although these purposes frequently overlap, the two views of property ultimately suggest different characters and limits for public protection of property ownership; the disagreements over purposes are manifested in disagreements about the circumstances under which the public may regulate property without compensation.

The proacquisitive position is that individuals should be able to act on numerous fixed property expectations, and thus any involuntary and uncompensated disruption of those expectations is a wrongful taking. This view clearly has a rhetorical advantage. One of our prominent political metaphors includes a prepolitical right to property: humans supposedly bring property into the social contract, and consent to government in order to protect individual property, not diminish it.[170] This metaphor rejects redistribution of property and effectively precludes all but acquisitive abilities as appropriate objects of protection. The vocabulary of Locke, Madison, and Bentham, and not that of Aristotle, dominates the takings discourse, blurring the notion of a prepolitical property right with the political goals of strength and internal peace.

The concept of a prepolitical property right is problematic, primarily because it fails to address the question of what it means to "own" anything in the absence of the community's protection. For this and other reasons, courts have seldom recognized such a prepolitical right. Justice Chase, at a time when the Supreme Court still discussed seriously application of natural law in civil matters, denied that property

---

170. J. Locke, *supra* note 130, at §§ 25–51, 87.

existed prior to the social contract.[173] Aside from such an open reference to political theory, in takings litigation courts always veer noticeably away from the directions in which this antiredistributive theory should drive. Powerful as the theory is in many areas of American social thought, it has historically been rather frail in takings jurisprudence. *Mahon* is, after all, an exceptional case. The usual practice in takings jurisprudence is to allow political communities wide latitude in defining citizens' obligations, similar to the practice in the jurisprudence of obligation of contract. The rhetoric of protecting expectations of gain does appear in takings jurisprudence, but so does the rhetoric of civic duty.

THOMAS W. MERRILL, THE ECONOMICS OF PUBLIC USE

72 Cornell L.Rev. 61, 66–78, 80–81 (1986).

THE MEANS-ENDS PROBLEM

Drawing on Calabresi and Melamed's model,[a] one may isolate four possible rights that a citizen might have when faced with an attempted government taking. At one extreme, the citizen would have no entitlement; the government could take his property without his consent and without compensation. This is a citizen's plight when the government legitimately exercises its power to tax or its police power. A second possibility is that a liability rule would protect a citizen's property; the government could take the property without his consent, but would have to pay compensation. This describes a taking by eminent domain. A third possibility is that a property rule would protect a citizen's property; the government could take the property only with the citizen's consent, i.e., if he agreed to sell it to the government. This is the rule generally followed when government acquires chattels or employment services. Finally, a fourth possibility is that the government could not acquire a citizen's property by any means. This situation occurs if the proposed acquisition serves a purpose or end not permitted by the Constitution, for example, the purchase of votes or the services of a slave.

A clear distinction exists between the first three of these rules—no entitlement, liability rule, and property rule—and the fourth, which completely bars government acquisitions of property. The first three rules define different means of achieving permissible government ends. The fourth, however, effectively demarcates a sphere of impermissible government ends. In fact, the means-ends distinction inherent in the Calabresi–Melamed framework suggests that judges may ask two ques-

173. Calder v. Bull, 3 U.S. (3 Dall.) 386, 394 (1798).

a. Calabresi & Melamed, *Property Rules, Liability Rules, and Inalienability: One View of the Cathedral,* 83 Harv.L.Rev. 1089 (1972). "Property rules," as defined by Calabresi and Melamed, allow an owner to protect a right or entitlement from an unconsented taking by securing injunctive relief. "Liability rules" afford protection only through an ex post award of damages.

tions of any proposed government acquisition. First, the ends question: is the government acquiring the resources for a constitutionally permissible purpose? Second, the means question: if the purpose is permissible, should the government proceed by police power regulation, eminent domain, or voluntary exchange in the marketplace?

The two questions present sharply different inquiries. The ends question asks what the government plans to do once the property is obtained. This inquiry, in turn, requires a clear conception of the legitimate functions or purposes of the state. May the state promote employment by subsidizing the construction of a privately owned factory? May it own a professional football team or undertake land reform? The answers to such questions demand an exercise in high political theory that most courts today are unwilling (or unable) to undertake. The means question, by contrast, is narrower. It asks where and how the government should get property, not what it may do with it. For example, the means approach accepts that a state may own a professional football team. It then asks: how should the state acquire the team? Must it purchase the team through voluntary negotiations? Or may the state coerce a transfer by condemning the team? Or may it simply commandeer the team under its police power? The means approach, of course, is also "political" in that it concerns state actions that will advance or retard conflicting interests. Nevertheless, the means approach demands a more narrowly focused and judicially manageable inquiry than the ends approach.

In deciding public use cases, courts nearly always pose the issue in terms of ends rather than in terms of means. Perhaps the constitutional language is responsible for this focus. The fifth amendment provides, "nor shall private property be taken *for public use,* without just compensation." This phrasing suggests that the government may exercise the power of eminent domain, but only if it puts the property acquired to a public use, that is, an end that is sufficiently "public" in nature.

The focus on ends also figures into the two judicial tests most often relied upon to define "public use." Under the narrower test, public use means literal use by the public. Under this test, a taking must yield a facility physically accessible to some segment of the public. By contrast, the broader test requires only that the taking produce a public benefit or advantage. This test roughly equates public use with "public interest." Although courts have almost unanimously resolved this interpretive dispute in favor of the broader public interest view, the main point for present purposes is that both tests look to the ends of the taking, not whether eminent domain is an appropriate means to achieve those ends.

The distinction between ends and means clarifies several developments associated with the jurisprudence of public use. First, it helps explain the emergence of language of extreme judicial deference in the last thirty years. Given that courts have understood the public use doctrine to refer to the ends of government, the question naturally arises: which institution is better suited to determine permissible ends—

the courts or the legislature? In a society committed to majoritarian rule, not surprisingly the answer has been the legislature.

Here, as elsewhere, the crisis in democratic theory generated by judicial opposition to the New Deal provided the critical event. As late as 1930 the Supreme Court still clung to the position that legislative declarations of public use were subject to de novo judicial review. After a change in Court personnel produced a fundamental shift in judicial attitudes, however, the Court did an abrupt about-face and implied that the public use determination is exclusively for the legislature. This reversal ultimately produced Justice Douglas's formulation in *Berman v. Parker:* "Subject to specific constitutional limitations, when the legislature has spoken, the public interest has been declared in terms well-nigh conclusive." [29] As long as courts regard the public use doctrine as a limitation upon permissible government ends, this extreme rhetoric of deference to legislative judgments will no doubt persist.

* * *

[T]he distinction between ends and means [also] helps to explain the Supreme Court's statements equating the public use doctrine with the police power. The association originated with Justice Douglas's opinion in *Berman.* Deciding a public use challenge to a Washington, D.C., urban renewal project, Justice Douglas wrote, "We deal ... with what traditionally has been known as the police power." In recent decisions, including [*Hawaii Housing Authority v.*] *Midkiff,* the Supreme Court has reiterated this theme, declaring that "the 'public use' requirement of the Taking Clause is 'coterminous with the scope of a sovereign's police powers.' " [35] This pronouncement has dismayed commentators because the outer limit of the police power has traditionally marked the line between *noncompensable* regulation and compensable takings of property, not the line between compensable takings and the area where the constitution bars government from engaging in any sort of exchange whatever. Legitimately exercised, the police power requires no compensation. Thus, if public use is truly coterminous with the police power, a state could freely choose between compensation and noncompensation any time its actions served a "public use." This approach would seemingly overrule the entire takings doctrine in a single stroke.

The illogic of the Court's statements disappears, however, once one recognizes that the police power, like eminent domain, can also refer to the question of proper governmental ends, rather than means. This is clearly what Justice Douglas meant in *Berman* when he said that the police power "is essentially the product of legislative determinations addressed to the purposes of government, purposes neither abstractly nor historically capable of complete definition." He was not saying that government could freely employ any means of achieving slum clearance, and with it choose either compensation or noncompensation. Instead,

29. 348 U.S. 26, 32 (1954).

35. Ruckelshaus v. Monsanto Co., 467 U.S. 986, 1014 (1984) (quoting [Hawaii Housing Authority v. Midkiff, 467 U.S. 229, 240 (1984)]).

he was saying that slum clearance is a permissible end of government. The Court's recent decisions echo this notion. "Police power" is here synonymous with the extent to which government may constitutionally regulate private activity. It defines those issues with which government may properly concern itself. The Court's statements again indicate that the permissible ends principle cuts across all means of resource acquisition, and that one should, for the sake of analytical clarity, keep questions of ends and means distinct.

The most important insight to be gained from the distinction between ends and means, however, is that the public use limitation might be recast or reinterpreted to perform a different role. Rather than concerning itself with government ends, the public use limitation might serve to restrict a legislature's choice of means. I am not suggesting that it is somehow wrong, as a matter of first principles, to inquire about the ends to which government will put condemned property. Rather, the point is that the American judiciary is unlikely soon to assume the task of closely scrutinizing legislative judgments about the legitimate ends of government. Given also that the choice of means question is an analytically distinct and important inquiry, it is worth asking whether the public use limitation can be reformulated as a choice of means doctrine, and if so, whether the judiciary should have a role in reviewing the exercise of eminent domain from this perspective.

* * *

EMINENT DOMAIN AS A MEANS: AN ECONOMIC APPROACH

The literature addressing the public use issue from an economic perspective suggests three possible analytical models. I will briefly consider the first two, only to set them aside in favor of the third. Elements of the first two, however, ultimately reappear, "through the back door" as it were, under my "refined" version of the third approach.

The first economic model of public use, endorsed by Frank Michelman,[43] involves a straightforward comparison of costs and benefits. This model would have a court calculate all costs associated with an exercise of eminent domain, including the costs of compensation, and compare them with the taking's expected benefits. If the benefits exceed the costs, the court would deem the taking to serve public use; conversely, if the costs exceed the benefits, it would deem the taking to serve an unconstitutional private use.

The cost-benefit model of public use raises several problems. The first relates to measurement. How can courts accurately measure a taking's projected benefits, many of which will be intangible and speculative? A second problem involves the question of proper institutional roles. Presumably, the legislature has concluded that a taking's benefits exceed its costs. Are courts somehow better suited to make such a determination? Finally, the most telling problem, from this article's

---

43. Michelman, [*Property, Utility, and Fairness: Comments on the Ethical Foun-* dations of *"Just Compensation" Law,* 80 Harv.L.Rev. 1165, 1241 (1967).]

perspective, is that the cost-benefit calculus demands an inquiry into the ends of the taking rather than the choice of means. The cost-benefit approach explicitly adopts wealth maximization as the proper end, or at least one proper end, of government. Once again, I do not argue that the cost-benefit model is necessarily wrong. The problem is simply that the American judiciary, for reasons related to democratic theory, is not presently inclined to enforce directly any conception of limited government ends.

A second economic model of public use, recently advocated by Richard Epstein,[44] involves the public goods concept. Public goods, in their pure form, possess two properties: jointness in supply and impossibility of exclusion.[45] In particular, because of the latter attribute, the market generates fewer public goods than generally thought desirable. Hence, theorists have long viewed public goods as an appropriate object of governmental action. Under the public goods model, a court would ask whether an exercise of eminent domain is designed to procure a public good. If so, the court would deem the taking to serve a public use; if not, the court would deem the exercise an unconstitutional taking for a private use.

As with the cost-benefit approach, the public goods model presents several difficulties. First, a definitional problem: there are very few "pure" public goods—goods of a kind that consumption by one does not diminish in some measure consumption by others. With most goods, consumption by one necessarily excludes, at least partially, consumption by someone else. Moreover, one can say that any activity that generates positive externalities—keeping one's lawn mowed, for example—shares the quality of public goods. Thus, the public goods analysis can be either very restrictive or very broad, depending on how the term is defined. Again, however, the main failing of the public goods model, at least for present purposes, is that it directs attention to ends rather than means. It asks whether government will use acquired property to provide a public good, not whether nonconsensual means are necessary to acquire the property.

The third economic model of public use derives from the property rule/liability rule distinction introduced by Calabresi and Melamed. From this perspective, eminent domain provides a mechanism that allows government to convert property rules into liability rules. This model presumes that property rules work well where low transaction costs make consensual exchange of resources practical. Liability rules, on the other hand, are necessary where high transaction costs render consensual exchange difficult. Applied to eminent domain, this analysis suggests that where a functioning market for a resource exists, the

44. R. Epstein, [Takings: Private Property and the Power of Eminent Domain 166–169 (1985).]

45. * * * Jointness in supply means that consumption by one person does not diminish or otherwise affect consumption by others. Impossibility of exclusion means that once the good is supplied, no one can be prevented from consuming it. Classic examples of public goods are national defense and environmental controls.

public use doctrine should require that government use that market. In contrast, where barriers to market exchange render such acquisition problematic, the doctrine should permit government to use its power of eminent domain. Importantly, the property rule/liability rule model of public use has the virtue of addressing eminent domain as a means. The distinction focuses on the conditions of the market in which property is acquired, not on its postacquisition use.

In the remainder of this section, I use the property rule/liability rule distinction to develop a basic model of the role of courts in determining eminent domain's proper scope. I then qualify the basic model in light of three persuasive economic objections. Taken together, these qualifications yield what I call the refined economic model of the judicial role in public use cases.

A. The Basic Model

The purpose of eminent domain is analogous to that of other liability rules, in that eminent domain applies where market exchange, if not impossible to achieve, is nevertheless subject to imperfections. To illustrate the point, consider the most common situation in which we see the exercise of eminent domain: a public or private project requiring the assembly of numerous parcels of land. Suppose, for example, that an oil refining company wants to construct an underground pipeline to transport crude oil from a producing field to a refinery several hundred miles away. Suppose further that only one feasible pipeline route exists. Without an exercise of eminent domain, the company must obtain an easement from each of hundreds of contiguous property owners. Each owner would have the power to hold out, should he choose to exercise it. If even a few owners held out, others might do the same. In this way, assembly of the needed parcels could become prohibitively expensive; in the end, the costs might well exceed the project's potential gains.

* * *

The oil pipeline hypothetical illustrates the potential for rent seeking.[b] The opportunity cost of any one landowner's interest is near zero.[54] But when this interest combines with other similar interests to form a right of way for a pipeline, its potential value becomes considerable. The difference between these two sums—the property's negligible opportunity cost and its value as part of the pipeline project represents a potential economic rent to the seller.

Assembly projects, however, do not exhaust a seller's rent-seeking opportunities. For example, rent seeking can occur when a buyer wants access to land that he already owns, but which is surrounded by the

---

b. A seller gets economic rents when she is able to charge a price higher than her property's opportunity cost. This may happen in the oil pipeline case because each property owner is a monopolist who controls a resource needed to complete the project.

54. Each individual property interest—the right to use a small underground tunnel—almost certainly has little or no market value if offered for sale for any other use.

seller's land. It can also arise when a buyer needs to expand an existing site by acquiring adjacent land; when the buyer will lose undepreciated improvements if he does not acquire certain property from the seller; or when the seller owns property uniquely suited for some undertaking by the buyer, such as a promontory for a lighthouse or a narrows for a bridge. I will hereinafter refer to any situation where a seller can extract economic rents from a buyer as a "thin market." Conversely, I will call any situation where market conditions do not allow a seller to extract economic rents from a buyer a "thick market."

Whatever a thin market's source, its potential for engendering rent seeking may make it economically efficient to confer the power of eminent domain on a buyer. On the one hand, we know that eminent domain would transfer the resource to a higher-valued use, because its value in the new use exceeds its value in every existing possible use (its opportunity cost); otherwise the seller could not extract an economic rent. On the other hand, if this transaction were left to the market, monopoly pricing (or strategic bargaining) could lead to a suboptimal quantity of the resource being acquired, or could even prevent the transaction from taking place at all.

Before completing discussion of the basic model, however, we must consider another important factor. So far we have focused exclusively on what might broadly be termed the transaction costs of market exchange. But we must also consider the administrative costs of eminent domain, and compare these costs with the costs of market exchange in either thick or thin market settings.

* * *

Given what might collectively be called the "due process" costs of eminent domain—obtaining legislative authority, drafting and filing the complaint, serving process, securing a formal appraisal, the possibility of a trial and appeal, and so forth—it is safe to conclude that, in a thick market setting, eminent domain is a more expensive way of acquiring resources than market exchange. This conclusion has important implications for the basic model. In effect, it means that the decision whether to use eminent domain should be, from an economic perspective, self-regulating. In thick markets, where the model initially suggests that eminent domain is inappropriate, the acquiring party should in fact utilize market exchange because eminent domain would consume more resources. Conversely, in thin market settings, where the model suggests that it is appropriate to use eminent domain, the acquiring party should in fact use eminent domain, so long as the administrative costs are less than the costs of market exchange.

* * *

If, as the basic model suggests, the decision to use the power of eminent domain is essentially self-regulating, this holds important implications for judicial review of public use issues. Most obviously, there would seem to be little point in courts second-guessing legislative and executive determinations of public use. * * *

B. The Refined Model

Despite the basic model's appealing simplicity, with its thick market/thin market distinction and its modest conception of the judicial role, the model raises a number of troubling economic and noneconomic questions. To avoid unduly complicating the argument, I will discuss only the economic objections.

[Merrill goes on to describe several situations where the self-regulating character of eminent domain breaks down and where courts should consequently review decisions to condemn more carefully. One is the case where the condemnee suffers large subjective losses. (She has a sentimental attachment to the property or has modified it to accommodate her unique needs.) Because these are not compensated through an award of fair market value, the government will be tempted to eschew purchase in favor of eminent domain. A second is the case where a few private parties capture the political process and employ eminent domain for their own gain. Stricter application of the public use test in these cases (a tilt toward a "property" rather than a "liability" standard) would offer greater protection to condemnees.]

BIBLIOGRAPHY

In General

B. Ackerman, PRIVATE PROPERTY AND THE CONSTITUTION (1977).

Berger, *A Policy Analysis of the Taking Problem,* 49 N.Y.U.L.Rev. 165 (1974).

F. Bosselman, D. Callies, & J. Banta, THE TAKING ISSUE: AN ANALYSIS OF THE CONSTITUTIONAL LIMITS OF LAND USE CONTROL (1973).

Dunham, *Griggs v. Allegheny County in Perspective: Thirty Years of Supreme Court Expropriation Law,* 1962 Sup.Ct.Rev. 63.

Epstein, *Property, Speech, and the Politics of Distrust,* 59 U.Chi.L.Rev. 41 (1992).

Epstein, *Takings: Descent and Resurrection,* 1987 Sup.Ct.Rev. 1.

R. Epstein, TAKINGS: PRIVATE PROPERTY AND THE LAW OF EMINENT DOMAIN (1985).

Grey, *The Malthusian Constitution,* 41 U.Miami L.Rev. 21 (1986).

Levmore, *Just Compensation and Just Politics,* 22 Conn.L.Rev. 285 (1990).

Lunney, *A Critical Reexamination of the Takings Jurisprudence,* 90 U.Mich.L.Rev. 1892 (1992).

Paul, *The Hidden Structure of Takings Law,* 64 S.Cal.L.Rev. 1393 (1991).

J. Pennock & J. Chapman, NOMOS XXII: PROPERTY (1980).

Peterson, *The Takings Clause: In Search of Underlying Principles, Part I,* 77 Calif.L.Rev. 1299 (1989); *Part II,* 78 Calif.L.Rev. 53 (1990).

Rose, *Property Rights, Regulatory Regimes and the New Takings Jurisprudence—an Evolutionary Approach,* 57 Tenn.L.Rev. 577 (1990).

Symposium, *The Jurisprudence of Takings,* 88 Colum.L.Rev. 1581 (1988).

Wilkins, *The Takings Clause: A Modern Plot for an Old Constitutional Tale,* 64 Notre Dame L.Rev. 1 (1989).

What Is Property

Baker, *Property and Its Relation to Constitutionally Protected Liberty,* 134 U.Pa.L.Rev. 741 (1986).

Demsetz, *Toward A Theory of Property Rights,* 57 Am.Econ.Rev. 347 (1967).

Note, *The Origins and Original Significance of the Just Compensation Clause of the Fifth Amendment,* 94 Yale L.J. 694 (1985).

Radin, *Property and "Personhood",* 34 Stan.L.Rev. 957 (1982).

Schill, *Intergovernmental Takings and Just Compensation: A Question of Federalism,* 137 U.Pa.L.Rev. 829 (1989).

Underkuffler, *On Property: An Essay,* 100 Yale L.J. 127 (1990).

The Taking/Regulation Distinction

Ausness, *Wild Dunes and Serbonian Bogs,* 70 Denver U.L.Rev. 3 (1993).

Farber, *Public Choice and Just Compensation,* 9 Const.Comm. 279 (1992).

Krier, *The Regulation Machine,* 1 Sup.Ct.Econ.Rev. 1 (1982).

Levmore, *Takings, Torts, and Special Interests,* 77 Va.L.Rev. 1333 (1991).

Mandelker, *Investment–Backed Expectations: Is There a Taking?,* 31 Wash.U.J.Urb. & Contemp.L. 3 (1987).

Sax, *Takings, Private Property and Public Rights,* 81 Yale L.J. 149 (1971).

Symposium, *Constitutional Issues in Land Use Regulation,* 8 Hastings Const.L.Q. 449 (1981).

Symposium, *Lucas v. South Carolina Coastal Council,* 45 Stan.L.Rev. 1369 (1993).

Thompson, *Judicial Takings,* 76 Va.L.Rev. 1449 (1990).

Public Use

Berger, *The Public Use Requirement in Eminent Domain,* 57 Or.L.Rev. 203 (1978).

Comment, *The Public Use Limitation on Eminent Domain: An Advance Requiem,* 58 Yale L.J. 599 (1949).

Rubenfeld, *Usings,* 102 Yale L.J. 1077 (1993).

Just Compensation

Blume & Rubinfeld, *Compensation for Takings: An Economic Analysis,* 72 Calif.L.Rev. 569 (1984).

COMPENSATORY JUSTICE—NOMOS XXXIII (J. Chapman ed. 1991).

Costonis, *"Fair" Compensation and the Accommodation Power: Antidotes for the Taking Impasse in Land Use Controversies,* 75 Colum.L.Rev. 1021 (1975).

Kaplow, *An Economic Analysis of Legal Transitions,* 99 Harv.L.Rev. 509 (1986).

R. Posner, ECONOMIC ANALYSIS OF LAW § 3.6 (1986).

Williams, Smith, Siemon, Mandelker & Babcock, *The White River Junction Manifesto,* 9 Vt.L.Rev. 193 (1984).

B. PROPERTY AND DUE PROCESS

The Fifth and Fourteenth Amendments provide that no person shall be deprived of "life, liberty, or property, without due process." Under current doctrine, application of the Due Process Clause requires a two-step analysis. First a court must determine whether the interest being denied or impinged upon constitutes "life," "liberty," or "property" within the meaning of the Due Process Clause. If it does, the court then must determine what process the individual is entitled to.[1]

Common usage tells us much about the meaning of "property." Certainly an individual's home, land, or television set ought to constitute "property" for due process purposes. But the Supreme Court has recognized that "the property interests protected by procedural due process extend well beyond actual ownership of real estate, chattels or money."[2] Influenced by Charles Reich's classic article *The New Property,*[3] the Court has defined "property" to include "entitlements" such as government benefits and public employment.

The extension of due process protections to the deprivation of entitlements demolished the so-called "right/privilege distinction" which had characterized public benefits as "gratuities" that could be conditioned as the sovereign saw fit. Following the Supreme Court's lead in

1. To determine this, the courts use a balancing test formulated in Mathews v. Eldridge, 424 U.S. 319, 96 S.Ct. 893, 47 L.Ed.2d 18 (1976).

2. Board of Regents v. Roth, 408 U.S. 564, 572, 92 S.Ct. 2701, 2706, 33 L.Ed.2d 548 (1972).

3. 73 Yale L.J. 733 (1964).

Goldberg v. Kelly[4] and *Board of Regents v. Roth,* courts found the Due Process Clause applicable to the termination or denial of a wide range of government benefits and jobs.

But lurking within entitlement theory is a "positivist trap."[5] Since, as the Court stated in *Roth,* property interests "are created and their dimensions are defined by existing rules or understandings that stem from an independent source such as state law,"[6] the government can virtually nullify due process protection by defining benefits and jobs in ways that don't create entitlements. For example, if a state makes contracts that can be terminated at will, a court could conclude that the employee with whom it has contracted has no entitlement to continuation in the job. Similarly, it can be argued that the "property interest" created by state statute ought to be deemed to include the procedures provided by the state for the interest's vindication. This is the "bitter with the sweet" analysis pressed by Justice Rehnquist in *Arnett v. Kennedy.*[7]

In *Cleveland Board of Education v. Loudermill,*[8] the Court refused to be caught in the "positivist trap." It announced that under due process analysis "[t]he categories of substance and procedure are distinct. Were the rule otherwise, the [Due Process] Clause would be reduced to a mere tautology. 'Property' cannot be defined by the procedures provided for its deprivation any more than can life or liberty." While *Loudermill* firmly rejects the "bitter with the sweet" approach, it does so more by assertion than argument. This Section explores the implications of entitlement theory. Frank Easterbrook asserts that the process/substance distinction adopted by the Court in due process cases cannot be sustained. Accordingly, "[a] court that protects the legislative power to define substantive entitlements ought to give it control of process as well."

Rodney Smolla disagrees. While he concedes that the Court's definition of "property" has, in effect, reintroduced the rights/privilege distinction in due process analysis, he suggests that a way out of the positivist trap would be to require that conditions placed on government largess pass a "minimum rationality test"—even if the legislature has attempted to create a program without procedural protections.

Assuming we can identify a "property interest" that triggers application of the Due Process Clause, the next question is what process is due. Jerry Mashaw offers a critique of the prevailing approach announced by the Court in *Mathews v. Eldridge.*

4. 397 U.S. 254, 90 S.Ct. 1011, 25 L.Ed.2d 287 (1970).

5. See Mashaw, *Administrative Due Process: The Quest for a Dignitary Theory,* 61 B.U.L.Rev. 885, 888–93 (1981).

6. 408 U.S. at 577, 92 S.Ct. at 2709.

7. 416 U.S. 134, 148–58, 94 S.Ct. 1633, 1641–46, 40 L.Ed.2d 15 (1974) (Rehnquist, J., dissenting).

8. 470 U.S. 532, 105 S.Ct. 1487, 84 L.Ed.2d 494 (1985).

FRANK H. EASTERBROOK, SUBSTANCE AND DUE PROCESS

1982 Sup.Ct.Rev. 85, 85–90, 109–119.

The Supreme Court keeps saying that it is entitled under the Due Process Clause of the Constitution to determine what process is "due" when governmental action affects a liberty or property interest. Although the Court gives legislatures the utmost deference in specifying the particulars of a substantive right, it retains the privilege of determining what procedures must be used to evaluate claims of entitlement arising under the substantive rule.

I propose to examine the rationale of the peculiar constitutional dichotomy between substance and process in cases in which legislatures are given free rein in defining substance. It is peculiar, not only because there is no immediately apparent warrant for the distinction in the structure or history of the Constitution, but also because substance and process are two aspects of the same phenomenon. The process a legislature describes for vindicating the entitlements that it creates is a way of indicating how effective its plan should be. The more process it affords, the more the legislature values the entitlements and thus is willing to sacrifice to avoid mistakes. A court that protects the legislative power to define substantive entitlements ought to give it control of process as well.

I.   Introduction: The Substance–Process Dichotomy

* * *

Under *Logan v. Zimmerman Brush Co.,*[a] *Arnett v. Kennedy,*[b] and *Vitek v. Jones,*[c] due process analysis is a two-step routine. First the Court determines whether by statute or regulation the State has created an entitlement ("liberty or property") the existence or extent of which turns on some determinable facts. It also is enough that there is an antecedent interest in personal liberty, one the government may not extinguish except for cause. * * * Many cases stop here with a finding that the claim involves neither liberty nor property. If nothing turns on determinable facts, there is no need for a hearing, because the state's officer need not pay attention to the claimant's demands; the state may do what it pleases. A claimant turned away without either hearing or substance has lost nothing to which his claim was better than anyone else's.

Except in the case [where there is an antecedent interest in personal] liberty (or the rare case in which the Court finds the substantive rules unconstitutional), the definition of the entitlement is a question wholly within the power of the political branches to answer. Any political unit dissatisfied with the Court's resolution of entitlement questions may amend its statutes or regulations so that the decision no longer is controlled by determinable facts. No entitlement, no process. And the Supreme Court reviews substantive law under the most lenient

a.   455 U.S. 422 (1982).   c.   455 U.S. 480 (1980).

b.   416 U.S. 134 (1974).

standards. Legislation affecting economic interests, and most other interests as well, will be sustained as long as the Court can conceive of a set of facts under which the legislation would be rational.[10] If, however, the constitution, statute, or regulation creates a liberty or property interest, then the second step—determining "what process is due"—comes into play. At this step the legislative disposition gets some, but not very much, deference.

The most important of the recent cases in this line is *Mathews v. Eldridge.*[11] The Court explained that [12]

> identification of the specific dictates of due process generally requires consideration of three distinct factors: First, the private interest that will be affected by the official action; second, the risk of an erroneous deprivation of such interest through the procedures used, and the probable value, if any, of additional or substitute procedural safeguards; and finally, the Government's interest, including the function involved and the fiscal or administrative burdens that the additional or substitute procedural requirement would entail.

The Court made it clear that it would conduct the balancing itself, assigning its own weights and assessing the probabilities and interests. To be sure, it would listen to the legislature's views on these subjects, embodied in the statutes, with interest and respect, but with no need to accept the views as binding.

In cases since *Eldridge* the Court has conducted an essentially unrestrained interest balancing. In two cases it has held that judicial damages remedies for administrative error were sufficient process,[13] but in the others it has insisted on hearings, more or less elaborate, as part of an administrative procedure. The administrative procedure itself must afford an opportunity for a hearing "at a meaningful time and in a meaningful manner," [14] which sometimes varies with the identity of the affected party and the nature of his problem.[15]

* * *

The Court approaches its due process question much as an ideal legislature would, asking statute by statute, and sometimes case by case,

---

10. Schweiker v. Hogan, 102 S.Ct. 2597 (1982); Railroad Retirement Board v. Fritz, 449 U.S. 166 (1980); Vance v. Bradley, 440 U.S. 93 (1979); Usery v. Turner Elkhorn Mining Co., 428 U.S. 1 (1976). * * *

11. 424 U.S. 319 (1976).

12. *Id.* at 335.

13. Ingraham v. Wright, 430 U.S. 651 (1977); Parratt v. Taylor, 451 U.S. 527 (1981).

14. Armstrong v. Manzo, 380 U.S. 545, 552 (1965), a question-begging formula quoted most recently in Logan v. Zimmerman Brush Co., 455 U.S. 422, 437 (1982).

15. Lassiter v. Department of Social Services, 452 U.S. 18 (1981) (due process entitlement to counsel in parental rights termination matters must be evaluated case by case); Greene v. Lindsey, 102 S.Ct. 1874, 1879 (1982) (in circumstances of a particular case, notice of eviction by posting on a tenant's door is unconstitutional). More commonly, however, "procedural due process rules are shaped by the risk of error inherent in the truthfinding process as applied to the generality of cases, not the rare exceptions." Mathews v. Eldridge, 424 U.S. 319, 344 (1976). * * *

what is the optimal amount of process. The Court does not treat substantive entitlements in anything like that manner.

* * *

III. MODERN JUSTIFICATIONS OF THE SUBSTANCE–PROCESS DICHOTOMY

There are two modern justifications of the substance-process dichotomy, one that the Court offers for its decisions and one that scholars offer. The Court's justification is largely instrumental, the scholars' justification largely noninstrumental.

A. *The Instrumental Justification*

The Court's justification for specifying process once the statute has specified substance is that "any other conclusion would allow the State to destroy at will virtually any state-created property interest." [80] This would be a good argument if the Court could explain why a state may not destroy the interests it creates, at least prospectively. But the Court has never so argued. Under the Court's decisions legislatures are free to enact precatory statutes, statutes that contain no rules of decision, retroactive statutes, statutes that lack any methods of enforcement, statutes creating absolute immunities, and otherwise to have vacuous "entitlements." To use some invented numbers, If states may elect ten percent reliability in enforcement (the amount of adherence to a precatory statute), why can they not elect ninety percent (the amount obtainable from rudimentary procedures)? Why, in other words, is the expedient of enfeebling a statutory entitlement by providing "deficient" procedures out of bounds? The Court's cases contain no answers to this question because they are not consistent. There is no single view that could be respected in the name of stare decisis.

To the extent the Court supplies any explanation, it lies in the formula from the *Eldridge* decision. The formula exalts instrumental objectives. The goal of due process is to hold as low as possible the sum of two costs: the costs created by erroneous decisions, including false positives and false negatives, and the costs of administering the procedures. Holding this sum to a minimum maximizes society's wealth, and the gains may be shared among all affected persons. This, however, produces a puzzle. If the goal of the *Eldridge* formula is the maximization of society's wealth, why did the legislature not enact the preferable procedures in the first place? The legislative and executive branches have access to information about the costs and error rates produced by particular procedures. They are well aware that the accuracy of decisions may be improved by adopting more elaborate procedures. That they choose not to use these procedures is strong evidence that their costs outweigh their benefits.

Some might object that the legislative and executive branches do not make impartial decisions in this respect—that is, they are not well-motivated. Given interest group politics, their choices about the types of

---

80. Logan v. Zimmerman Brush Co., 455 U.S. 422, 432 (1982).

procedures to employ in decisions might be the result of political compromise rather than any desire to maximize society's well-being. This surely is true for many, perhaps most, statutes, but so what? The observation is equally true for substantive rules. The statute books are full of rules having little purpose other than to transfer wealth from one group to another. The regulation of taxicabs and the subsidy to tobacco farmers and northeast railroads are the rule, not the exception. Even statutes with some essential purpose other than wealth transfers will be influenced in some fashion by interest group politics.

The role of interest groups does not make legislators ill-motivated in a constitutional sense. It does not involve race, sex, or another forbidden ground of decision. Interest group statutes are upheld all the time, on the flimsiest of pretexts. And if the Constitution permits interest group politics to sway decisions and influence the goals of legislation, what principled objection can there be to legislators' achieving part of the preference for an interest group through choice of procedural rules? (One answer, that procedural rules are less visible, will not do; there are lots of poorly perceived substantive rules.)

This discussion overstates the importance of interest group politics in the choice of procedures. Even when the statute affects "weak" groups, there is little reason to think that the procedural rules will be selected on the basis of some animus against those groups that distorts the legislature's ability to make choices that enhance social well-being. Welfare benefits provide an example. Poor people have shown sufficient political power to obtain a welfare system. We know from the existence of the benefits that they have overcome whatever reticence or hostility exists, and they have obtained transfers in their favor. If they (and their altruistic allies) use their power to obtain X in money transfers and no elaborate procedures, why should anyone be entitled to complain? A claimant disappointed at the outcome of his own application would have a legitimate gripe only if due process created a personal right not to be the victim of a mistake. But the Court's recent cases are clear that due process does not create any personal right to escape the consequences of blunders. The *Eldridge* criteria focus on the welfare of the statutory beneficiaries as a group, and the Court treats errors in individual cases as a cost but not as an independent violation of the guarantee.

* * *

Substance and process are intimately related. The procedures one uses determine how much substance is achieved, and by whom. Procedural rules usually are just a measure of how much the substantive entitlements are worth, of what we are willing to sacrifice to see a given goal attained. The body that creates a substantive rule is the logical judge of how much should be spent to avoid errors in the process of disposing of claims to that right. The substantive rule itself is best seen as a promised benefit coupled with a promised rate of mistake: the legislature sets up an $X\%$ probability that a person will receive a certain boon. The Court cannot logically be reticent about revising the substantive rules but unabashed about rewriting the procedures to be followed in administering those rules.   * * *

All of this means that the Court's due process cases are incoherent unless the Court has its own view of substance.   The Court must be devising procedures that vindicate the Justices' views of the relative importance of different substantive entitlements, rather than legislators' views.   Substantive and procedural due process turn out not to be so different.   Yet the Justices leave loopholes for legislators: by abolishing private remedies or substantive standards altogether, they may escape the implications of the Justices' substantive preferences.

B.   The Noninstrumental Justifications

Scholars have suggested noninstrumental justifications for the Court's decisions.   They suggest that process may be valuable in itself, and not for the benefits it bestows indirectly.   There are two lines of noninstrumental justification, dignitary justifications and governmental structure justifications.

1.   *Dignity.*   Several have argued that process is valuable in itself because it treats each person as an equal, entitled to respect and autonomy, rather than as an object.[91]   Such dignitary considerations are exceptionally important to many people.   Nonetheless, an argument about the value of process for its own sake is not substantially different from an argument about the value of property, another kind of personal interest.   Property in law is the right, within defined limits, to dominion over things and therefore to structure one's relation with others.   Without property there is no autonomy and little dignity; property is thus an aspect of personal liberty.   Yet the Court permits the legislature the broadest possible scope in the regulation of property and, derivatively, of dignity.   The argument linking due process with dignity thus carries no force unless its proponent can show why the Constitution removes decisions about the appropriate level of dignity from the legislature only when claims to hearings are involved but otherwise allows the legislature full control.

* * *

[Neither historical analysis nor stare decisis supports the dignitary analysis.]   All that is left * * * is a play on the analysis of *Carolene Products.*[96]   It may be possible to depict dignitary considerations as fundamental values slighted by majoritarian processes.   * * * [But] [t]here is simply no reason to suppose that process values are slighted by legislatures.

91.   *E.g.,* L. Tribe, [American Constitutional Law 538–41 (1978)]; Laycock, [*Due Process and Separation of Powers: The Effort to Make the Due Process Clause Nonjusticiable,* 60 Tex.L.Rev. 875 (1982)]; Mashaw, [*Administrative Due Process: The Quest for a Dignitary Theory,* 61 B.U.L.Rev. 885 (1981)]; Michelman, [*Formal and Associational Aims in Procedural Due Process,* in NOMOS XVIII: Due Process 126 (J.R. Pennock & J. Chapman eds. 1977)].   * * *

96.   United States v. Carolene Products Co., 304 U.S. 144, 152–53 n. 4 (1938).

There is no logical reason why legislatures would underestimate the value of process. Process and substance are of a piece. Legislators frequently are lawyers or other specialists in process, not quick to forget their training (or the interests of their friends, also process providers). Process is not historically disfavored. Statutes overflow with process, sometimes to the point of choking the ability of executives to act. Consider for a moment the difficulty a supervisor faces in firing a secretary under the civil service laws. And there is no apparent relationship between the amount of process provided by law and the favor (or disfavor) legislators show for the affected people. Murderers are not an especially favored class, yet statutes provided elaborate procedural protections for murder cases long before the Court entered the due process fray. It can take a decade or more to deport an illegal alien, all because of procedural rules, created by statute, exceeding constitutional requirements. On the other hand, summary procedures under the Social Security Act principally affect lifetime wage earners, not the poor.

Hearings for claimants are a form of in-kind benefit. It is a commonplace observation that in-kind benefits (including food, housing, and other nonmoney transfers, as well as hearings) are worth less to the recipients than it costs society to provide them. Some of the difference between the cost of the benefits and their value to the recipients is simply lost to society; some of the difference is captured by those who render the benefits. It is not irrational for those affected by a program to spurn elaborate hearings and demand more concrete benefits instead. They may prefer money, which can be turned into other things, to dignity, which cannot be. The important consideration is that if people potentially eligible under the substantive terms of a statute value hearings at more than the cost of providing them, they will clamor for hearings even at the cost of lower money benefits. The contents of the legislation are the best available evidence about the value the affected people place on hearings. Surely it should come as no surprise that the usual proponents of hearings in welfare cases are middle- and upper-class lawyers, professors, and judges—the class from which bureaucrats, administrative law judges, and other process providers come.

2. *Governmental structure.* Professors Stewart and Sunstein have identified another constellation of functions served by hearings.[99] Judicial insistence on procedures might, for example, compel Congress to be more candid in identifying all dimensions of the entitlements it creates, or to deliver on its promises, or to reduce the extent of delegation to agencies. In other words, it would promote the Rule of Law, in which determinate standards rather than potentially capricious bureaucrats establish entitlements. Although these functions have instrumental overtones—less delegation might be thought "better" legislation—they are usually seen as valuable in themselves.

99. Stewart & Sunstein, *Public Programs and Private Rights*, 95 Harv.L.Rev. 1193, 1258–63 (1982).

These are weak arguments, as Stewart and Sunstein concede. The objective of "honest" legislation is more threatened by precatory laws, by "rights" without remedies, than by deficient procedures. The objection to delegation is much more forceful when the legislature passes statutes containing no substantive rules than when it enacts rules but does not provide for particularly accurate administration. These laws most subject their beneficiaries to the whims of ill-motivated bureaucrats.

The Stewart and Sunstein arguments sound odd as matters of due process. Governmental structure for the federal branches was settled by Articles I and II, not by the Bill of Rights. The nondelegation doctrine is a name without a doctrine. Improperly motivated decisions are controlled by doctrines other than due process. There is no general rule that Congress must legislate so clearly that people with grade school educations can follow; if it wants to use roundabout methods of stating its purpose, so be it. And states may delegate as they please; administrative agencies or judges may enact state laws.

Stewart and Sunstein maintain that the Court's control over process is justified only when (*a*) necessary to force Congress to make a clear statement of its aims or (*b*) necessary to enforce favored substantive rights, among which they would include welfare. Part *a* of the test is unsupportable for state governments, and even for Congress it puts the Court in the position of holding a very clear law (say, one providing that there shall be no process for firing a federal employee) unconstitutional because Congress has not been clear enough in its total package. A rule of this sort, unjustified by history or precedent, also gives the Court almost unlimited power. Any law, taken in its entirety, is unclear in some respect. Part *b* of the test, however, just returns us to a proposition presented several times before: there is not much difference between substance and process, and therefore the Court's substance-process dichotomy is unsupportable.

RODNEY A. SMOLLA, THE REEMERGENCE OF THE RIGHT–PRIVILEGE DISTINCTION IN CONSTITUTIONAL LAW: THE PRICE OF PROTESTING TOO MUCH

35 Stan.L.Rev. 69, 69–82, 102, 105–20 (1982).

The "right-privilege" distinction is a constitutional doctrine that scholars and Supreme Court opinions have long been declaring dead. Like the prematurely rumored death of Mark Twain, however, reports of the demise of the privilege doctrine have been greatly exaggerated. Since the nineteenth century, the doctrine has shown an uncanny ability to reconstitute itself in spite of the best efforts of scholars and jurists to bury it. In the last decade it has reemerged in the procedural due process area under the guise of "entitlement" theory to become one of the dominant themes of the Burger Court.

The Burger Court has applied the entitlement concept with increasing rigidity, thereby substantially circumscribing the range of interests to which constitutional due process safeguards apply. As the Court has stepped up the Draconian efficiency of entitlement theory, it has borrowed heavily from both the formal method and the underlying values that have historically sustained the privilege doctrine. At the same time, however, the Court has steadfastly clung to the fiction that the privilege doctrine has been fully and finally repudiated. The almost schizophrenic tendency of the Court to simultaneously disclaim the doctrine by name and resort to the concept in practice exists against a backdrop of almost universal scholarly hostility toward both the privilege and entitlement doctrines. Seldom have the Court and academe so completely talked past each other.

* * *

I. The Right-Privilege Distinction

The privilege doctrine is grounded in a dichotomy between "rights" (interests enjoyed "as a matter of right") and mere "privileges" (interests created by the grace of the state and dependent for their existence on the state's sufferance). Privileges can be primarily economic interests, such as public jobs, welfare benefits, or licenses, or primarily noneconomic interests, such as early release from imprisonment through pardon or parole, or permission for an alien to enter the country. According to the doctrine, governmentally created "privileges" may be initially given to recipients on the condition that they surrender or curtail the exercise of constitutional freedoms that they would otherwise enjoy. Further, those privileges may be denied to or withdrawn from recipients without affording them the procedural due process protections that would normally attach to the denial or the taking of "rights."

The entitlement doctrine is a specific application of the right-privilege concept in the context of procedural due process. The entitlement doctrine proceeds from literalist fidelity to the due process clauses of the fifth and fourteenth amendments, which guarantee due process of law only when an individual is deprived of "life, liberty or property." Individuals are entitled to this procedural protection only if they can demonstrate that a vested right or "entitlement" to an interest in "life," "liberty," or "property" is at stake. When the interest involved is state-created rather than preexisting—for example, when the interest is a welfare check or a pardon rather than personal property or the liberty of someone not in lawful custody—the individual is entitled to due process protection only if the state has made the interest a formally protected "entitlement." Such entitlements do not stem from the Constitution, but from nonconstitutional sources, such as statutes or contracts. Furthermore, under the most extreme form of entitlement theory, the nonconstitutional source of law that creates the interest may also determine what procedural protections surround the interest. This would mean that, in a fundamental sense, the procedures attached to interests in largess *are* the interests in largess, and that when a recipient accepts a public benefit he necessarily acquiesces in whatever level of procedural safeguards the legislature has built into the benefit.

In the earlier stages of the development of the entitlement doctrine, the Court avoided the forbidden terminology of "right" and "privilege." Ironically, in *Board of Regents v. Roth*,[13] one of the seminal cases in the development of the entitlement concept, the Court denounced the right-privilege doctrine as a "wooden distinction" that has been "fully and finally rejected."[14] In more recent cases, however, the Court has almost completely dropped all pretense of having abandoned the distinction.
* * *

The most basic rationale behind the privilege and entitlement doctrines is that a legal system must acknowledge a distinction between interests that are legally protected and interests that are not. Thus, Professor Kenneth Culp Davis argues that in one fundamental sense the distinction between entitlement and nonentitlement—the distinction between right and privilege—is implicit in the very existence of a legal system.[19]

A second theme underlying entitlement theory comes from the view that government largess is public charity. Just as the right-privilege distinction raised to constitutional dimension the almost homespun notion that the recipient of a gift must accept it with the strings that the giver has attached, the entitlement doctrine states that the recipient of a governmentally created interest must take the interest on the terms offered. One of those terms is the level of procedural protection that the government has decided to include as part of the entitlement "package."

A third major force behind the entitlement doctrine is the idea that a recipient of an interest in largess may contractually agree to accept limited procedural protection for the interest as part of the bargain out of which the interest is created. The contract analogy draws largely from the same values that favor freedom of contract in bargains between parties in the private sector. It finds additional support as far back as the assumption in social contract theory that rules implemented by consent are inherently less onerous than rules imposed by fiat.

A fourth underlying element, one that is a close corollary of the freedom of contract notion, is the idea that government should have greater latitude in its dealings with individuals when it acts as the proprietor of the public business rather than as the pandemic regulator. The proprietary-regulatory distinction, by assuming that restrictions are

---

13.   408 U.S. 564 (1972).

14.   *Id.* at 571.

19.   "A legal system cannot exist without a distinction between a 'right' and 'no right'." 2 K. Davis, [Administrative Law Treatise § 11:4, at 350 (2d ed. 1979).] Yet notwithstanding the logic of this distinction, Davis argues that "[h]uman activities produce interests that ought not to be treated as 'rights' but that still may deserve some sort of legal protection in some circumstances." *Id.* § 11:4, at 350–51. The principle proposed by Davis is that whenev-

er government officers "impose a grievous loss on any person, due process requires not less than whatever procedural protection is justified by a cost-benefit analysis." *Id.* at 399. Of course, at least for the time being, the Court has rejected "grievous loss" as a trigger for due process protection. *See, e.g.,* Jago v. Van Curen, 102 S.Ct. 31, 33 (1981) ("we have previously reject[ed] . . . the notion that *any* grievous loss visited upon a person by the state is sufficient to invoke the procedural protection of the Due Process Clause") (emphasis in original).

less necessary when government acts essentially as a private entity administering its internal business, frees government in that context from certain restrictions that would apply to it when it acts as a governing entity.

Clearly the strongest motive force behind entitlement theory, however, is deference to majoritarian sovereignty. In its most extreme form entitlement doctrine rejects the existence of a dichotomy between "substantive" and "procedural" aspects of an interest in largess. It is possible to treat the creation of a welfare program or a parole system as purely political affairs, as matters of legislative choice beyond the pale of judicial review, while nonetheless arguing that minimum procedural integrity in the administration of those programs is a matter of constitutional right. Entitlement theory in its purest form repudiates that division, and proceeds instead on the assumption that the procedural accoutrements that accompany an interest in largess are among the defining characteristics of the interest itself. Under this theory the level of procedural protection that surrounds a government job, for example, is a political expression of the importance of the job to the body politic; as such it is as much a matter of legislative prerogative as the level of salary assigned to that class of job holder.

II. REEVALUATING THE EVOLUTION OF THE ENTITLEMENT DOCTRINE

The Right–Nonright Distinction

* * *

* * * The orthodox view is that *Goldberg [v. Kelly,*[33]] was the high water mark for procedural protection for interests in largess, and thus the paradigmatic example of properly applied unitary analysis. That orthodoxy similarly regards *Goldberg* as one of the critical cases in the Court's rejection of the privilege doctrine. Ironically, however, *Goldberg* presaged the development of the entitlement concept, and formed the evolutionary link between the right-privilege cases that preceded it and the entitlement cases that followed.

In *Goldberg,* the Court held that a welfare recipient must be afforded an evidentiary hearing prior to the termination of benefits. Justice Brennan, writing for the Court, confronted the right-privilege distinction with the oft-quoted statement that "[i]t may be realistic today to regard welfare entitlements as more like 'property' than a 'gratuity.' Much of the existing wealth in this country takes the form of rights that do not fall within traditional common-law concepts of property." [36] Although Justice Brennan ostensibly rejected the right-privilege distinction, in actuality he perpetuated the dichotomy that lay at the heart of the privilege doctrine by retaining the operative distinction between vested and nonvested interests.

33. 397 U.S. 254 (1970) [relocated footnote].

36. *Id.* at 262 n. 8.

Justice Brennan's comparison of welfare assistance to property was influenced by the work of Charles Reich. Reich's 1964 article, *The New Property,*[37] cited by Justice Brennan,[38] traced the emergence of public benefits as a major source of wealth in contemporary American society. Reich had argued that in light of the "vast, imperial scale" on which government spews forth its jobs, welfare assistance, services, contracts, franchises, and licenses, interests in those government-created sources of wealth should be protected by the same sorts of procedural safeguards that had always attached to more conventional forms of property.[39]

The "new property" concept provided a way of extending procedural due process protection to public employment, welfare assistance, contracts, and licenses, that would be consistent with the constitutional text. The right-privilege distinction would no longer work as the stock response for defeating claims for procedural protection in largess, because largess could now be included within the rubric of right rather than of privilege. Like one's home, car, or bank account, one's government job or welfare check could be labeled property, and with that label safely attached, procedural due process protection seemed secure.

In retrospect, after the years that have elapsed since the new property idea was first proposed, one can make the harsh judgment that *Goldberg,* by its use of the new property metaphor, unwittingly abetted the development of the entitlement doctrine.   * * *

* * *

By resorting to the new property concept to generate increased procedural protection for public sector interests, the Court inevitably placed extreme definitional pressure on the term property. That pressure naturally bred preoccupation with distinguishing between interests that had vested and interests that had not. Reich himself spoke of the need for entitlements to be "vested."[54] The basic distinction between "right" and "privilege," if understood as connoting no more than a distinction between "right" and "nonright," is implicit in the term property; it is impossible to speak of property without conjuring up notions of ownership and dominion. In writing as a philosopher of welfare rather than as a legal technician, Reich wrote for the wrong audience; even the Warren Court was not willing to mechanistically transform principles of welfare philosophy into constitutional rules. Thus, in *Roth,* the Court began to tie due process analysis to notions of vested interests; it drew on the common law of property and contracts to define the interests that would qualify for the protection of the due process clause.

* * *

37. Reich, *The New Property,* 73 Yale L.J. 733 (1964).

38. 397 U.S. at 262 n. 8.

39. Reich, *supra* note 37, at 783–87.

54. Reich, *supra* note 37, at 785.

IV. LIMITATIONS ON ENTITLEMENT THEORY

There are indications that the Court is slowly moving toward limiting the harsher elements of entitlement thinking, even if it is not embracing any free-floating right to minimally fair procedures that transcend entitlements. While the Court probably always will permit governments the power to create jobs in which employees are terminable at will, it probably never will permit welfare administrators to terminate payments at their whim and pleasure or school superintendents to expel students without explanation—even if these practices are explicitly authorized by legislation. It is unlikely that there will ever be vigorous judicial scrutiny of all procedural standards for administering the public largess. But given the major competing values that exist in this sphere of constitutional law, some constraint on the excesses of entitlement theory is inevitable.

* * *

Equal Protection and Rationality

* * *

The rational basis standard under the equal protection test seems to require some "reason" in all government action. Government, the argument would go, has no interest in refusing to disclose its reasons for official action unless those reasons are impermissible. Although we talk about capricious action as if officials made decisions through random rolls of mental dice, the truth is that some reason, however spontaneous or ill-conceived, always exists. Since no public official ever really acts "for no reason," what we really mean when we talk of permitting officials to act for no reason is that they need not explain to anyone what their reasons are. As Justice Marshall stated in his *Roth* dissent, "it is not burdensome to give reasons when reasons exist * * *. It is only where the government acts improperly that procedural due process is truly burdensome." [141] Thus, under this argument, the only government "interest" served by allowing the state to fire employees at its "will and pleasure" is the preservation of license to act improperly.

The argument overstates the case, however, since the rational basis equal protection test has always been lenient enough to sustain certain administrative schemes that condone official silence. In certain situations the government may very well be able to articulate a rational basis for allowing administrative officials to exercise discretion without having to explain their actions. Despite initial appearances, unexplained and detrimental administrative actions may not violate the elemental equal protection injunction that persons similarly situated be similarly treated.

If, as far as they can be measured, the performances of two police officers are identical, the equal protection clause would seem to require that they receive identical treatment. If they are to receive different treatment, the burden should be on the government to explain why they

141. Board of Regents v. Roth, 408 U.S. at 591 (Marshall, J., dissenting).

are different. If the police chief is free to fire one and retain the other, and is obliged to tell the dismissed officer nothing more than "you're fired but I'm not going to tell you why," equal protection appears to be rendered illusory. Yet, in one sense the officers were treated alike—they were both given jobs in which the axe could fall unannounced and unexplained. It is not the administrative decision to act without explanation in any given case that must be defended with a legitimate state interest, but the systemic decision to allow certain administrators the license to act without explanation.

Zimmerman Brush

[*Logan v. Zimmerman Brush Co.*,[a] indicates that the Court is moving towards a "rationality requirement." In that case, the Supreme Court of Illinois had held that Logan's employment discrimination complaint had to be dismissed because the Illinois Fair Employment Practices Commission had failed to hold a hearing within the 120-day period required by law (even though Logan had filed his claim in a timely manner). The U.S. Supreme Court reversed, holding that Illinois had deprived Logan of a property interest (the discrimination cause of action) without due process.]

* * *

The importance of *Zimmerman* * * * is that a majority of Justices recognized that regardless of whether or not the state had created a "property" interest—i.e., an "entitlement" that cannot be removed except "for cause"—the state's attempt to permit administrators to act *with or without cause* may sometimes be so devoid of rational justification that it violates equal protection. Under the Court's analysis, the very existence of some programs, in effect, creates "entitlements" triggering minimum procedural protection, even if the legislature has attempted to create the program without procedural protection. To be *internally* rational, certain government programs must by their mere existence be entitlement programs, and further, to be internally rational some entitlement programs must carry minimum procedural safeguards against the taint of official subjectivity.

The Contractual Element in Government–Created Largess

Under the Court's *Zimmerman Brush* analysis, the enjoyment of government largess cannot be conditioned upon the fulfillment of procedures that are devoid of a rational basis. But, one must be careful not to read *Zimmerman* too broadly, for it does *not* stand for the proposition that all legislative classifications vesting "will and pleasure" discretion in public officials are constitutionally irrational. The fledgling rights recognized in *Zimmerman* become pressed to their limits when the very meaning of the term "arbitrary" is made part of the debate * * *

Certainly this is dangerous business; a powerful government might, as Justice Sutherland once warned, compel the surrender of all constitu-

---

a. 455 U.S. 422 (1982).

tional rights by taking advantage of recipients in an economically or politically weak bargaining position.[163] But when the contractual relationship between the state and the individual is free of such coercive taint, there is no obvious injustice or arbitrariness in holding the individual bound by the *procedural* strings that were voluntarily accepted. Some rights may be inalienable in some situations, just as some bargains are illegal despite mutual and uncoerced assent; but as long as courts retain their normal power to police bargains and carefully scrutinize the contractual process, the lack of meaningful procedural recourse for an individual can surely be the legitimate object of an enforceable bargain. A government without strong procedural protection for public benefits is less civilized than it ought to be, but it is not unconstitutional.

* * *

Contractual Element as a Rational Basis

* * *

All conditions placed on government largess must meet the minimum rationality requirement of *Zimmerman Brush*. The contractual element in the receipt of government benefits is relevant to the analysis because it may itself provide the rational basis for a condition. For example, when the government shifts into its proprietary capacity, it must compete with the private sector for the same workers. These employees will decide whether to accept private sector or government jobs based on the relative benefits offered, including salary as well as procedural and substantive job security. If equal protection is construed to require that government employees receive certain procedural rights before their jobs are terminated, the government will have less money available to offer as salaries, and thus will be at a competitive disadvantage with private employers who can make the allocation between salaries and procedural protection according to the wishes of employees. Thus, competition in the job market provides a rational basis for government to create positions without procedural protection. Government employment at will is not unconscionable because free market competition can be trusted to give employees the leverage to extract from government whatever additional procedural guarantees the political and economic marketplace will bear. Since such conditions do not offend basic notions of fairness in contractual bargains when measured against even the most modern sensibilities of contract law, they should not be regarded as irrational for the purposes of the fourteenth amendment.

* * *

While government employees can extract procedural protections because of competition in the job market, there is an effective government monopoly over the dispensation of benefits such as education and

---

163. *See* Frost v. Railroad Comm'n of California, 271 U.S. 583, 593–94 (1926).

welfare. Since these recipients of public largess lack the bargaining power enjoyed by prospective public sector employees, they cannot be said to have contracted away their right to procedural protection. In contract law terms, these are analogous to contracts of adhesion. Just as a modern common law court will strike down one-sided agreements that fail to give one party a fair quantum of remedy for breach—on the theory that illusory remedies have "failed of their essential purpose"— courts as a matter of constitutional law must strike down administrative programs in which the lack of procedural protection is internally inconsistent with the declared purpose of the program itself. The "contractual element" fails to provide a rational basis defense in such cases because the contractual element does not really exist.

To put the matter in Justice Rehnquist's own terms, the Court itself should take the bitter with the sweet. To the extent that the contractual element in public largess supplies a rational basis for diminished procedural protection, the absence of equal bargaining power should force the government to justify procedural limitations on other grounds.

* * *

Other Rational Bases for Diminished Procedural Protection

The contractual element in government largess is not the only conceivable rational basis for allowing officials to terminate or deny government benefits without giving reasons. In fact, there are areas in which we routinely allow government officials to exercise absolute and arbitrary discretion because it facilitates the smooth implementation of government policy. [Examples include the Supreme Court's practices regarding writs of certiorari and the President's authority to dismiss top advisors without a hearing or a statement of reasons.] * * *

* * *

In dealing with the ultimate recipients of government benefit programs, such as welfare and public school education, however, a rational basis for not extending some minimal procedural protections is difficult to imagine. Such systems generally operate with the use of relatively simple, objective qualifying criteria. In many such programs, all persons who meet these criteria are automatically "entitled" to participate. There is no rational basis for granting the administrator of these types of programs the unfettered discretion to cut off persons who meet the objective qualifications. Since, unlike in the employment context, the very purpose of public schooling or welfare is to satisfy the needs of those who qualify for the program, there is no conceivable basis for denying or terminating their benefits "at will."

Where subjective administrative judgment should play no role, recipients should be entitled to at least a statement of reasons before benefits are denied or terminated. Administrative silence in such situations can serve no permissible purpose, and thus seems far more likely to be a means for covering up a motivation outside the scope of the statutory criteria for the benefit. The lesson of *Zimmerman Brush* is that when no plausible explanation of administrative arbitrariness exists other than the government's wish to conceal its failure to follow its own declared principles of entitlement, the procedural scheme must be struck down.

JERRY L. MASHAW, THE SUPREME COURT'S DUE PROCESS CALCULUS FOR ADMINISTRATIVE ADJUDICATION IN *MATHEWS v. ELDRIDGE*: THREE FACTORS IN SEARCH OF A THEORY OF VALUE
44 U.Chi.L.Rev. 28, 46–59 (1976).

[In *Mathews v. Eldridge*,[a] the Supreme Court rejected Eldridge's claim that he was entitled, under the Due Process Clause, to a hearing before his Social Security disability benefits could be terminated. The Court announced a three-part balancing test for determining the constitutionally requisite elements of adjudicatory procedure; the calculus considers (1) the private interest at stake, (2) the risk of an erroneous deprivation of the private interest through the procedures used and the probable value of additional procedural safeguards, and (3) the Government's interest, including the fiscal and administrative burdens that additional procedures would entail.]

A VALUE-SENSITIVE APPROACH TO THE ELDRIDGE ANALYSIS OF DUE PROCESS

The Supreme Court's analysis in *Eldridge* is not informed by systematic attention to any theory of the values underlying due process review. The approach is implicitly utilitarian but incomplete, and the Court overlooks alternative theories that might have yielded fruitful inquiry. This section attempts, first, to articulate the limits of the Court's utilitarian approach, both in *Eldridge* and as a general schema for evaluating administrative procedures, and second, to indicate the strengths and weaknesses of three alternative theories—individual dignity, equality, and tradition. These theories, at the level of abstraction here presented, require little critical justification: they are widely held, respond to strong currents in the philosophic literature concerning law, politics, and ethics, and are supported either implicitly or explicitly by the Supreme Court's due process jurisprudence.

A. UTILITARIANISM

Utility theory suggests that the purpose of decisional procedures—like that of social action generally—is to maximize social welfare. Indeed, the three-factor analysis enunciated in *Eldridge* appears to be a type of utilitarian, social welfare function. That function first takes into account the social value at stake in a legitimate private claim; it discounts that value by the probability that it will be preserved through the available administrative procedures, and it then subtracts from that discounted value the social cost of introducing additional procedures. When combined with the institutional posture of judicial self-restraint,

a. 424 U.S. 319 (1976).

utility theory can be said to yield the following plausible decision-rule: "Void procedures for lack of due process only when alternative procedures would so substantially increase social welfare that their rejection seems irrational."

The utilitarian calculus is not, however, without difficulties. The *Eldridge* Court conceives of the values of procedure too narrowly: it views the sole purpose of procedural protections as enhancing accuracy, and thus limits its calculus to the benefits or costs that flow from correct or incorrect decisions. No attention is paid to "process values" that might inhere in oral proceedings or to the demoralization costs that may result from the grant-withdrawal-grant-withdrawal sequence to which claimants like Eldridge are subjected. Perhaps more important, as the Court seeks to make sense of a calculus in which accuracy is the sole goal of procedure, it tends erroneously to characterize disability hearings as concerned almost exclusively with medical impairment and thus concludes that such hearings involve only medical evidence, whose reliability would be little enhanced by oral procedure. As applied by the *Eldridge* Court the utilitarian calculus tends, as cost-benefit analyses typically do, to "dwarf soft variables" and to ignore complexities and ambiguities.

The problem with a utilitarian calculus is not merely that the Court may define the relevant costs and benefits too narrowly. However broadly conceived, the calculus asks unanswerable questions. For example, what is the social value, and the social cost, of continuing disability payments until after an oral hearing for persons initially determined to be ineligible? Answers to those questions require a technique for measuring the social value and social cost of government income transfers, but no such technique exists. Even if such formidable tasks of social accounting could be accomplished, the effectiveness of oral hearings in forestalling the losses that result from erroneous terminations would remain uncertain. In the face of these pervasive indeterminacies the *Eldridge* Court was forced to retreat to a presumption of constitutionality.

Finally, it is not clear that the utilitarian balancing analysis asks the constitutionally relevant questions. The due process clause is one of those Bill of Rights protections meant to insure individual liberty in the face of contrary collective action. Therefore, a collective legislative or administrative decision about procedure, one arguably reflecting the intensity of the contending social values and representing an optimum position from the contemporary social perspective, cannot answer the constitutional question of whether due process has been accorded. A balancing analysis that would have the Court merely redetermine the question of social utility is similarly inadequate. There is no reason to believe that the Court has superior competence or legitimacy as a utilitarian balancer except as it performs its peculiar institutional role of insuring that libertarian values are considered in the calculus of decision.

Several alternative perspectives on the values served by due process pervade the Court's jurisprudence, and may provide a principled basis for due process analysis. These perspectives can usually be incorporated into a broadly defined utilitarian formula and are therefore not necessarily antiutilitarian. But they are best treated separately because they tend to generate inquiries that are different from a strictly utilitarian approach.

B. INDIVIDUAL DIGNITY

The increasingly secular, scientific, and collectivist character of the modern American state reinforces our propensity to define fairness in the formal, and apparently neutral language of social utility. Assertions of "natural" or "inalienable" rights seem, by contrast, somewhat embarrassing. Their ancestry, and therefore their moral force, are increasingly uncertain.[65] Moreover, their role in the history of the due process clause makes us apprehensive about their eventual reach. It takes no peculiar acuity to see that the tension in procedural due process cases is the same as that in the now discredited substantive due process jurisprudence—a tension between the efficacy of the state and the individual's right to freedom from coercion or socially imposed disadvantage.

Yet the popular moral presupposition of individual dignity, and its political counterpart, self-determination, persist. State coercion must be legitimized, not only by acceptable substantive policies, but also by political processes that respond to a democratic morality's demand for participation in decisions affecting individual and group interests. At the level of individual administrative decisions this demand appears in both the layman's and the lawyer's language as the right to a "hearing" or "to be heard," normally meaning orally and in person. To accord an individual less when his property or status is at stake requires justification, not only because he might contribute to accurate determinations, but also because a lack of personal participation causes alienation and a loss of that dignity and self-respect that society properly deems independently valuable.[68]

The obvious difficulty with a dignitary theory of procedural due process lies in defining operational limits on the procedural claims it fosters. In its purest form the theory would suggest that decisions affecting individual interests should be made only through procedures acceptable to the person affected. This purely subjective standard of procedural due process cannot be adopted: an individual's claim to a "nonalienating" procedure is not ranked ahead of all other social values.

The available techniques for limiting the procedural claims elicited by the dignitary theory, however, either appear arbitrary or render the theory wholly inoperative. One technique is to curtail the class of substantive claims in which individuals can be said to have a right to

65. *See generally* Woodward, *The Limits of Legal Realism: An Historical Perspective,* 54 Va.L.Rev. 689 (1968).

68. *See generally* Summers, *Evaluating and Improving Legal Processes—A Plea for "Process Values,"* 60 Cornell L.Rev. 1 (1974).

what they consider an acceptable procedure. The "life, liberty, or property" language of the due process clause suggests such a limitation, but experience with this classification of interests has been disappointing. Any standard premised simply on pre-existing legal rights renders a claimant's request for due process, as such, either unnecessary or hopeless. Another technique for confining the dignitary theory is to define "nonalienating" procedure as any procedure that is formulated democratically. The troublesome effect of this limitation is that no procedures that are legislatively authorized can be said to encroach on individual dignity.

Notwithstanding its difficulties, the dignitary theory of due process might have contributed significantly to the *Eldridge* analysis. The questions of procedural "acceptability" which the theory poses may initially seem vacuous or at best intuitive, but they suggest a broader sensitivity than the utilitarian factor analysis to the nature of governmental decisions. Whereas the utilitarian approach seems to require an estimate of the quantitative value of the claim, the dignitary approach suggests that the Court develop a qualitative appraisal of the type of administrative decision involved. While the disability decision in *Eldridge* may be narrowly characterized as a decision about the receipt of money payments, it may also be considered from various qualitative perspectives which seem pertinent in view of the general structure of the American income-support system.

That system suggests that a disability decision is a judgment of considerable social significance, and one that the claimant should rightly perceive as having a substantial moral content. The major cash income-support programs determine eligibility, not only on the basis of simple insufficiency of income, but also, or exclusively, on the basis of a series of excuses for partial or total nonparticipation in the work force: agedness, childhood, family responsibility, injury, disability. A grant under any of these programs is an official, if sometimes grudging, stamp of approval of the claimant's status as a partially disabled worker or nonworker. It proclaims, in effect, that those who obtain it have encountered one of the politically legitimate hazards to self-sufficiency in a market economy. The recipients, therefore, are entitled to society's support. Conversely, the denial of an income-maintenance claim implies that the claim is socially illegitimate, and the claimant, however impecunious, is not excused from normal work force status.

These moral and status dimensions of the disability decision indicate that there is more at stake in disability claims than temporary loss of income.[73] They also tend to put the disability decision in a framework that leads away from the superficial conclusion that disability decisions are a routine matter of evaluating medical evidence. Decisions with

---

73. The *Eldridge* Court, in distinguishing *Goldberg [v. Kelly,* 397 U.S. 254 (1970),] largely on the ground that terminated welfare recipients were more desperate financially than terminated disability recipients, thus ignored a very substantial similarity. * * * The potential for feelings of demoralization, rejection, or simple righteous indignation seems essentially the same in both types of cases.

substantial "moral worth" connotations are generally expected to be highly individualized and attentive to subjective evidence. The adjudication of such issues on the basis of documents submitted largely by third parties and by adjudicators who have never confronted the claimant seems inappropriate. Instead, a court approaching an analysis of the disability claims process from the dignitary perspective might emphasize those aspects of disability decisions that focus on a particular claimant's vocational characteristics, his unique response to his medical condition, and the ultimate predictive judgment of whether the claimant should be able to work.

C. Equality

Justice in a formal philosophical sense is often defined as equality of treatment. In the realm of adjudicatory procedure, a widely recognized aspect of procedural fairness is equality of opportunity to be heard. Indeed, insofar as adjudicatory procedure is perceived to be adversarial and dispute resolving, the degree to which procedures facilitate equal opportunities for the adversaries to influence the decision may be the most important criterion by which fairness is evaluated.

Equality of opportunity is not, however, an exhaustive measure of procedural due process. While equality would seem to require an unbiased decision maker and identical opportunities to present evidence and argument, it has little to say concerning the manner in which evidence and argument are presented. A hearing participant might claim, for example, that oral proceedings, including cross-examination, would illuminate murky aspects of the case or produce a truer disclosure of facts; but if this participant's adversary or other participants are not accorded these procedural rights, he can hardly claim unequal treatment. Similarly, objection to the use of material obtained outside the record, but not from a party, is at most remotely connected with equality of access. A procedure that divested the directly affected parties of all control over the process of shaping issues and developing evidence, indeed that never informed the parties that it had begun, would be "unequal" only if institutionally biased.[77] Yet such a procedure would widely be perceived as "unfair."

Notions of equality can nevertheless significantly inform the evaluation of any administrative process. One question we might ask is whether an investigative procedure is designed in a fashion that systematically excludes or undervalues evidence that would tend to support the position of a particular class of parties. If so, those parties might have a plausible claim that the procedure treated them unequally. Similarly, in a large-scale inquisitorial process involving many adjudicators, the question that should be posed is whether like cases receive like attention and like evidentiary development so that the influence of such arbitrary factors as location [is] minimized. In order to take such equality issues

77. *See, e.g.,* F. Kafka, The Trial (3d ed. 1956). Kafka gained many of his impressions of administrative processes as a bureaucrat in an agency dispensing disability benefits. M. Brod, Franz Kafka 79–84 (1970).

into account, we need only to broaden our due process horizons to include elements of procedural fairness beyond those traditionally associated with adversary proceedings. These two inquiries might have been pursued fruitfully in *Eldridge*. First, is the state agency system of decision making, which is based on documents, particularly disadvantageous for certain classes of claimants? There is some tentative evidence that it is.[78] Cases such as *Eldridge* involving muscular or skeletal disorders, neurological problems, and multiple impairments, including psychological overlays, are widely believed to be both particularly difficult, due to the subjectivity of the evidence, and particularly prone to be reversed after oral hearing.

Second, does the inquisitorial process at the state agency level tend to treat like cases alike? If the GAO's study [79] is indicative, the answer is decidedly no. According to that study, many, perhaps half, of the decisions are made on the basis of records that other adjudicators consider so inadequate that a decision could not be rendered. The relevance of such state agency variance to Eldridge's claim is twofold: first, it suggests that state agency determinations are unreliable and that further development at the hearing stage might substantially enhance their reliability; alternatively, it may suggest that the hierarchical or bureaucratic model of decision making, with overhead control for consistency, does not accurately describe the Social Security disability system. And if consistency is not feasible under this system, perhaps the more compelling standard for evaluating the system is the dignitary value of individualized judgment, which * * * implies claimant participation.

D. Tradition or Evolution

Judicial reasoning, including reasoning about procedural due process, is frequently and self-consciously based on custom or precedent. In part, reliance on tradition or "authority" is a court's institutional defense against illegitimacy in a political democracy. But tradition serves other values, not the least of which are predictability and economy of effort. More importantly, the inherently conservative technique of analogy to custom and precedent seems essential to the evolutionary development and the preservation of the legal system. Traditional procedures are legitimate not only because they represent a set of continuous expectations, but because the body politic has survived their use.

The use of tradition as a guide to fundamental fairness is vulnerable, of course, to objection. Since social and economic forces are dynamic, the processes and structures that proved functional in one period will

---

78. *See* W. Popkin, Counsel in the Welfare State: A Statistical and Legal Analysis of the Role of Representation in Administrative Decision–Making Based on a Study of Five Disability Programs 34, 52–53, 59–61 (1975). (This is a draft report to the Administrative Conference Committee on Grant and Benefit Programs. It has not been approved by the Committee or the Conference and represents only the view of its author.)

79. [Staff of Subcomm. on Social Security of The House Comm. on Ways and Means, 94th Cong., 2d Sess., Disability Insurance—Legislative Issue Paper (Comm. Print.1976).]

not necessarily serve effectively in the next. Indeed, evolutionary development may as often end in the extinction of a species as in adaptation and survival. For this reason alone tradition can serve only as a partial guide to judgment.

Furthermore, it may be argued that reasoning by analogy from traditional procedures does not actually provide a perspective on the values served by due process. Rather, it is a decisional technique that requires a specification of the purposes of procedural rules merely in order that the decision maker may choose from among a range of authorities or customs the particular authority or custom most analogous to the procedures being evaluated.

This objection to tradition as a theory of justification is weighty, but not devastating. What is asserted by an organic or evolutionary theory is that *the purposes of legal rules cannot be fully known*. Put more cogently, while procedural rules, like other legal rules, should presumably contribute to the maintenance of an effective social order, we cannot expect to know precisely how they do so and what the long-term effects of changes or revisions might be. Our constitutional stance should therefore be preservative and incremental, building carefully, by analogy, upon traditional modes of operation. So viewed, the justification "we have always done it that way" is not so much a retreat from reasoned and purposive decision making as a profound acknowledgment of the limits of instrumental rationality.

Viewed from a traditionalist's perspective, the Supreme Court's opinion in *Eldridge* may be said to rely on the traditional proposition that property interests may be divested temporarily without hearing, provided a subsequent opportunity for contest is afforded. *Goldberg v. Kelly* is deemed an exceptional case, from which *Eldridge* is distinguished.

Like the Court's utilitarian analysis, this general traditionalist method seems incomplete. If the premise of that method is that traditional modes of operation are to provide guidelines, then the Court should have immediately characterized the legal issue in order to select the appropriate guidelines. But given the Court's quite sensible position that administrative functions are to be evaluated individually, how was that characterization to proceed? Presumably, disability payments fall within the general domain of social welfare claims—a domain that is also treated in the *Goldberg* decision. Assuming, however, that the Court properly distinguished *Goldberg,* analogical analysis is aborted because no other Supreme Court decision pertaining to social welfare claims seems apt. Nor could it discover guiding authority in prior administrative practice, which is based on the now discredited notion that social welfare benefits are subject to discretionary divestiture. What the *Eldridge* Court needed, then, was a more general way of thinking about the termination of property interests that might apply both to traditional and to novel forms of property.

The beginnings of such an approach might be found in Justice Black's dissent in *Goldberg*,[82] where he analogized the position of a welfare recipient to the traditional position of a creditor when his debtor refuses further performance. Normally, in that situation, the creditor is left with the inconvenience of forgoing receipt of performance while he seeks legal enforcement of an obligation that may or may not remain due. The majority opinion's implicit response to the analogy is that a welfare recipient is in a special position: he literally cannot wait because he depends upon the state's performance for survival. Given this special circumstance, the Court concludes, the traditional bearer of the risk of erroneous (or otherwise illicit) non-performance has a constitutional right to shift that risk to the state, pending hearing. Given this reading of *Goldberg,* the *Eldridge* opinion may be interpreted as concluding simply that the special *Goldberg* circumstances did not obtain. Therefore, the traditional allocation of the risk was acceptable.

Analyzing *Goldberg* and *Eldridge* by analogy to traditional contract-default remedies is valuable because it discourages the superficial classification of welfare recipients as immediately desperate and of disability recipients as having alternative resources. A court in equity faced with an analogous issue—a request for a temporary restraining order or preliminary injunction to insure performance by an obligor—would look to the particular circumstances of the case to determine whether extraordinary remedies were justified. In so doing, the court would take into account the peculiar hardship to the plaintiff of nonperformance pending a trial, the likelihood that he might prevail on the merits, and the burden on the defendant of requiring maintenance of the status quo. The Social Security Administration, as a matter of due process of law, might sensibly be required to do the same—or at least to explain its inability to do so.

A court pursuing an analysis based on traditional contract-default remedies should also focus on the limitations of that analogy. Contract remedies presume a competitive market in which alternative obligors are available. This presumption of the availability of alternatives undergirds traditional judicial reluctance to require specific performance pending trial, or indeed after trial. The party relying on state support is in a quite different position. His market alternatives have previously been determined to be foreclosed, and his attachment to a particular income-maintenance scheme suggests that others are at best not comparable, and at worst unavailable. While this difference between contract and income-maintenance claims may not be a sufficient reason for reversing the usual allocation of the risk of error pending a full hearing in all cases, it comes close to presenting an a fortiori case for requiring that the individual income-maintenance claimant, like the contract creditor, be allowed to establish (perhaps by affidavit) that his is such a case.

* * *

---

82. Goldberg v. Kelly, 397 U.S. 254, 271
(Black, J., dissenting).

The preceding discussion has emphasized the way that explicit attention to a range of values underlying due process of law might have led the *Eldridge* Court down analytic paths different from those that appear in Justice Powell's opinion. The discussion has largely ignored, however, arguments that would justify the result that the Court reached in terms of the alternative value theories here advanced. Those arguments are now set forth.

First, focus on the dignitary aspects of the disability decision can hardly compel the conclusion that an oral hearing is a constitutional necessity prior to the termination of benefits when a full hearing is available later. Knowledge that an oral hearing will be available at some point should certainly lessen disaffection and alienation. Indeed, Eldridge seemed secure in the knowledge that a just procedure was available. His desire to avoid taking a corrective appeal should not blind us to the support of dignitary values that the de novo appeal provides.

Second, arguments premised on equality do not necessarily carry the day for the proponent of prior hearings. The Social Security Administration's attempt to routinize and make consistent hundreds of thousands of decisions in a nationwide income-maintenance program can be criticized both for its failures in its own terms and for its tendency to ignore the way that disability decisions impinge upon perceptions of individual moral worth. On balance, however, the program that Congress enacted contains criteria that suggest a desire for both consistency and individualization. No adjudicatory process can avoid tradeoffs between the pursuit of one or the other of these goals. Thus a procedural structure incorporating (1) decisions by a single state agency based on a documentary record and subject to hierarchical quality review, followed by (2) appeal to de novo oral proceedings before independent administrative law judges, is hardly an irrational approach to the necessary compromise between consistency and individualization.

Explicit and systematic attention to the values served by a demand for due process nevertheless remains highly informative in *Eldridge* and in general. The use of analogy to traditional procedures might have helped rationalize and systematize a concern for the "desperation" of claimants that seems as impoverished in *Eldridge* as it seems profligate in *Goldberg;* and the absence in *Eldridge* of traditionalist, dignitary, or egalitarian considerations regarding the disability adjudication process permitted the Court to overlook questions of both fact and value—questions that, on reflection, seem important. The structure provided by the Court's three factors is an inadequate guide for analysis because its neutrality leaves it empty of suggestive value perspectives.

Furthermore, an attempt by the Court to articulate a set of values that informs due process decision making might provide it with an acceptable judicial posture from which to review administrative procedures. The *Goldberg* decision's approach to prescribing due process— specification of the attributes of adjudicatory hearings by analogy to judicial trial—makes the Court resemble an administrative engineer with an outdated professional education. It is at once intrusive and ineffectual. Retreating from this stance, the *Eldridge* Court relies on the administrator's good faith—an equally troublesome posture in a political system that depends heavily on judicial review for the protection of countermajoritarian values.

The path to a more appropriate and successful judicial role may lie in giving greater attention to the elaboration of the due process implications of the values that have been discussed. If the Court provided a structure of values within which procedures would be reviewed, it could then demand that administrators justify their processes in terms of the degree to which they support the elaborated value structure. The Court would have to be satisfied that the administrator had carefully considered the effects of his chosen procedures on the relevant constitutional values and had made reasonable judgments concerning those effects.

A decision that an administrator had not met that standard would not result in the prescription of a particular adjudicatory technique as a constitutional, and thereafter virtually immutable, necessity; but rather in a remand to the administrator. In meeting the Court's objections, the administrator (or legislature) might properly choose between specific amendment and a complete overhaul of the administrative process. Perhaps more importantly, under a due process approach that emphasized value rather than technique, neither the administrator in constructing and justifying his processes, nor the Court in reviewing them, would be limited to the increasingly sterile discussion of whether this or that particular aspect of trial-type procedure is absolutely essential to due process of law.

BIBLIOGRAPHY

The New Due Process: Entitlement Theory and Beyond

DUE PROCESS—NOMOS XVIII (J.R. Pennock & J. Chapman, eds. 1977).

Handler, *Controlling Official Behavior in Welfare Administration,* 54 Calif.L.Rev. 479 (1966).

Laycock, *Due Process and Separation of Powers: The Effort to Make the Due Process Clause Nonjusticiable,* 60 Tex.L.Rev. 875 (1982).

Mashaw, *Administrative Due Process: The Quest for a Dignitary Theory,* 61 B.U.L.Rev. 885 (1981).

Monaghan, *Of "Liberty" and "Property,"* 62 Cornell L.Rev. 401 (1977).

O'Neil, *Of Justice Delayed and Justice Denied: The Welfare Prior Hearing Cases,* 1970 Sup.Ct.Rev. 161.

Rabin, *Job Security and Due Process: Monitoring Administrative Discretion Through a Reasons Requirement,* 44 U.Chi.L.Rev. 60 (1976).

Reich, *The New Property,* 73 Yale L.J. 733 (1964).

Reich, *Individual Rights and Social Welfare: The Emerging Legal Issues,* 74 Yale L.J. 1245 (1965).

Rendleman, *The New Due Process: Rights and Remedies,* 63 Ky.L.J. 531 (1975).

Rubin, *Due Process and the Administrative State,* 72 Calif. 1044 (1984).

Simon, *Liberty and Property in the Supreme Court: A Defense of Roth and Perry,* 71 Calif.L.Rev. 146 (1983).

Symposium—*Procedural Due Process: Liberty and Justice,* 39 U.Fla. L.Rev. 217–581 (1987).

Terrell, *"Property," "Due Process," and the Distinction Between Definition and Theory in Legal Analysis,* 70 Geo.L.J. 861 (1982).

Tribe, *Structural Due Process,* 10 Harv.Civ.Rights—Civ.Lib.L.Rev. 269 (1975).

Tushnet, *The Newer Property: Suggestions for the Revival of Substantive Due Process,* 1975 Sup.Ct.Rev. 261.

Van Alstyne, *The Demise of the Right–Privilege Distinction in Constitutional Law,* 81 Harv.L.Rev. 1439 (1968).

Wilkinson, *Goss v. Lopez: The Supreme Court as School Superintendent,* 1975 Sup.Ct.Rev. 25.

Williams, *Liberty and Property: The Problem of Government Benefits,* 12 J.Legal Studies 3 (1983).

What Process Is Due

Davis, *The Requirement of a Trial-type Hearing,* 70 Harv.L.Rev. 193 (1956).

Friendly, *"Some Kind of a Hearing,"* 123 U.Pa.L.Rev. 1267 (1975).

Kadish, *Methodology and Criteria in Due Process Adjudication—A Survey and Criticism,* 66 Yale L.J. 319 (1957).

Mashaw, *The Management Side of Due Process: Some Theoretical and Litigation Notes on the Assurance of Accuracy, Fairness, and Timeliness in the Adjudication of Social Welfare Claims,* 59 Cornell L.Rev. 772 (1974).

Redish & Marshall, *Adjudicatory Independence and the Values of Procedural Due Process,* 95 Yale L.J. 455 (1986).

Saphire, *Specifying Due Process Values: Toward A More Responsive Approach to Procedural Protection,* 127 U.Pa.L.Rev. 111 (1978).

Summers, *Evaluating and Improving Legal Processes—A Plea for Process Values,* 60 Cornell L.Rev. 1 (1974).

Verkuil, *A Study of Informal Adjudication Procedures,* 43 U.Chi.L.Rev. 739 (1976).

Chapter VII

EQUALITY AND RACE

The next three Chapters are designed to explore several controversial themes concerning the Constitution's guarantee of equality. The Equal Protection Clause declares that "No State shall . . . deny to any person within its jurisdiction the equal protection of the laws." As the materials on interpretation in Chapter II suggest, there may be more than one approach to understanding those few words.

One way of interpreting the Clause might be: "The laws shall treat all persons alike." But there is surely no constitutional harm in denying drivers' licenses to persons under 16. People are different in many ways, and the law can take account of some of those differences. One problem in reading the Equal Protection Clause is deciding what differences matter. *Who* must be treated alike?

We might instead restate the Clause this way: "People who are alike (in whatever way matters) shall be treated alike by the laws." But what does it mean to be treated alike? A welfare program may treat the poor alike by giving each person what he needs—the difference between his income and some minimum standard of living. Here the end result is "equal." A medical assistance program like Medicaid may treat the poor alike by giving everyone 14 days of free medical care. (This may be less than some need to be cured.) Here the stipend is "equal." A program for granting broadcast licenses (or drafting soldiers) may treat all persons alike by picking the winners (or losers) at random. Here the process gives each person an opportunity that is "equal." Thus another problem in reading the Equal Protection Clause is deciding what *equal* protection means.

As a general matter, courts do not look too hard at legislative decisions about classification and similar treatment.[1] But there is general agreement that assuring equal treatment to blacks is a value that lies at the core of the Equal Protection Clause. Scholars tend to theorize about equal protection by generalizing from the case of blacks. But

1. New York City Transit Authority v. Beazer, 440 U.S. 568, 99 S.Ct. 1355, 59 L.Ed.2d 587 (1979).

425

what are the salient features of that case? What counts, for example, as equal treatment on the basis of race? Must we make no distinctions based on race? Why, for that matter, is treatment of blacks a core value of the Clause? Because that was the Framers' intent? Because there is something special about racial discrimination? Because blacks are an oppressed group in American society? Because the political process does not work for them? Getting the theory right on these questions is of the greatest importance if we are to get it right in other cases. The readings in this Chapter present a number of different answers.

We begin with historical treatments. Derrick Bell sends noted civil rights attorney Geneva Crenshaw (a fictional character) back in time to the Philadelphia Convention, where she gives the stunned delegates a look into the future. This literary technique permits Bell to explore the fundamental contradiction of our Constitution—that a document dedicated to freedom and self-government could not bring itself to condemn the most brutal denial of freedom and self-government: slavery. Raoul Berger focusses on the framing of the Fourteenth Amendment. He believes that those who wrote the Amendment intended the Equal Protection Clause to produce much less in the way of equal treatment than we usually suppose. It was, he contends, no more than a constitutional confirmation of the 1866 Civil Rights Act; and given the racism of Republicans and Democrats alike, Berger finds it unthinkable that Congress would have desired to go further.

The next set of selections seeks to identify the understanding of equality that animates Equal Protection analysis. Michael Perry argues that even if Berger is correct, cases interpreting the Equal Protection Clause "radiate the principle that no person is by virtue of race morally inferior to another." Perry's principle forbids all, not just some, unequal treatment of nonwhites. The reason is that the government should not attach negative significance to traits indicating nothing about a person's moral status.

Paul Brest and Owen Fiss both start from the premise that racial classifications produce special harm. But they disagree about whether we should focus on individuals or on groups in assessing the harm the Clause forbids. Brest seeks to explain the intuitive appeal of an antidiscrimination principle concerned with individual harm. He then addresses a difficult problem for devotees of that principle: what to do with laws that make no discriminatory classification but have a disparate racial impact. Fiss responds that the antidiscrimination principle, because of its focus on individual harm and the lawmaking process, cannot deal satisfactorily with the problem of disparate impact. He proposes instead that we read into the Equal Protection Clause a group-disadvantaging principle. Such a principle might, for example, invalidate civil service job tests simply because blacks failed in disproportionately high numbers.

Charles Lawrence offers a different solution to the problem of disparate impact. Many effects that we treat as innocent may result from unconscious racism, a problem that is more like a disease than a crime. It is a mistake to insist on a showing of individual responsibility before addressing these effects. But the law need not go as far as Fiss suggests in order to combat them. We can accommodate the problem of unconscious racism within the framework of a "stigma" theory like Brest's or a "process" theory like Ely's.

John Hart Ely and Bruce Ackerman disagree about whether the rule of equality is concerned with process or with some more substantive value. Ely believes that the Equal Protection Clause should be used to perfect the democratic process. As Justice Stone said in *United States v. Carolene Products Co.*,[2] "prejudice against discrete and insular minorities" can cause the political process to malfunction. Racial classifications that disadvantage minorities are a signal that that has happened.

Ackerman responds that the process-oriented approach of *Carolene Products* fails on all counts. It ignores anonymous and diffuse minorities (homosexuals and women), who are less able to protect themselves politically than discrete and insular minorities (blacks). More fundamentally, despite its focus on process and its claim to value-neutrality, it ends by imposing substantive values on the political branches of government.

The final selection of the Chapter is by Kimberlé Crenshaw, a leading Critical Race Theorist. She argues that racist ideology is a central factor in the continued subordination of African Americans; like Derrick Bell, she maintains that white race consciousness has cemented ties among whites with arguably conflicting interests by defining blacks as "other." Antidiscrimination law may have eradicated formal barriers based on race but it has done little to remedy the deteriorating material conditions of most blacks, nor has it undermined the race consciousness that makes such inequality appear unproblematic.

A. RACE AND THE CONSTITUTION IN HISTORICAL PERSPECTIVE

DERRICK BELL, THE CHRONICLE OF THE CONSTITUTIONAL CONTRADICTION
And We Are Not Saved 26–44 (1987).

AT THE END of a journey back millions of light-years, I found myself standing quietly at the podium at the Constitutional Convention of 1787. It was late afternoon, and hot in that late summer way that makes it pleasant to stroll down a shaded country lane, but mighty oppressive in a large, crowded meeting room, particularly one where the doors are closed and locked to ensure secrecy.

The three dozen or so convention delegates looked tired. They had doubtless been meeting all day and now, clustered in small groups, were

---

2. 304 U.S. 144, 152 n. 4, 58 S.Ct. 778, 783 n. 4, 82 L.Ed. 1234 (1938).

caucusing with their state delegations. So intense were their discussions that the few men who looked my way did not seem to see me. They knew this was a closed meeting, and thus could not readily take in the appearance, on what had just been an empty platform, of a tall stranger—a stranger who was not only a woman but also, all too clearly, black.

Though I knew I was protected by extraordinary forces, my hands were wet with nervous perspiration. Then I remembered why I was there. Taking a deep breath, I picked up the gavel and quickly struck the desktop twice, hard.

"Gentlemen," I said, "my name is Geneva Crenshaw, and I appear here to you as a representative of the late twentieth century to test whether the decisions you are making today might be altered if you were to know their future disastrous effect on the nation's people, both white and black."

For perhaps ten seconds, there was a shocked silence. Then the chamber exploded with shouts, exclamations, oaths. I fear the delegates' expressions of stunned surprise did no honor to their distinguished images. A warm welcome would have been too much to expect, but their shock at my sudden presence turned into an angry commotion unrelieved by even a modicum of curiosity.

The delegates to the Constitutional Convention were, in the main, young and vigorous. When I remained standing, unmoved by their strong language and dire threats, several particularly robust delegates charged toward the platform, determined to carry out the shouted orders: "Eject the Negro woman at once!"

Suddenly the hall was filled with the sound of martial music, blasting trumpets, and a deafening roll of snare drums. At the same time—as the delegates were almost upon me—a cylinder composed of thin vertical bars of red, white, and blue light descended swiftly and silently from the high ceiling, nicely encapsulating the podium and me.

* * *

"Gentlemen," I began, "delegates"—then paused and, with a slight smile, added, "fellow citizens, I—like some of you—am a Virginian, my forefathers having labored on the land holdings of your fellow patriot, the Honorable Thomas Jefferson. I have come to urge that, in your great work here, you not restrict the sweep of Mr. Jefferson's self-evident truths that all men are equal and endowed by the Creator with inalienable rights, including 'Life, Liberty and the pursuit of Happiness.'" It was, I thought, a clever touch to invoke the name of Thomas Jefferson who, then serving as American minister to France, was not a member of the Virginia delegation. But my remark could not overcome the offense of my presence.

"How dare you insert yourself in these deliberations?" a delegate demanded.

"I dare," I said, "because slavery is an evil that Jefferson, himself a slave owner and unconvinced that Africans are equal to whites, nevertheless found involved 'a perpetual exercise of the most boisterous passions, the most unremitting despotism on the one part, and degrading submissions on the other.' Slavery, Jefferson has written, brutalizes slave owner as well as slave and, worst of all, tends to undermine the 'only firm basis' of liberty, the conviction in the minds of the people that liberty is 'the gift of God.'

"Gentlemen, it was also Thomas Jefferson who, considering the evil of slavery, wrote: 'I tremble for my country when I reflect that God is just; that his justice cannot sleep forever.'"

There was a hush in the group. No one wanted to admit it, but the ambivalence on the slavery issue expressed by Jefferson obviously had meaning for at least some of those in the hall. It seemed the right moment to prove both that I was a visitor from the future and that Jefferson's troubled concern for his country had not been misplaced. In quick, broad strokes, I told them of the country's rapid growth, of how slavery had expanded rather than withered of its own accord, and finally of how its continued presence bred first suspicion and then enmity between those in the South who continued to rely on a plantation economy and those Northerners committed to industrial development using white wage workers. The entry into the Union of each new state, I explained, further dramatized the disparity between North and South. Inevitably, the differences led to armed conflict—a civil war that, for all its bloody costs, did not settle those differences, and they remain divisive even as we celebrate our two-hundredth anniversary as one nation.

"The stark truth is that the racial grief that persists today," I ended, "originated in the slavery institutionalized in the document you are drafting. Is this, gentlemen, an achievement for which you wish to be remembered?"

Oblivious to my plea, a delegate tried what he likely considered a sympathetic approach. "Geneva, be reasonable. Go and leave us to our work. We have heard the petitions of Africans and of abolitionists speaking in their behalf. Some here are sympathetic to these pleas for freedom. Others are not. But we have debated this issue at length, and after three months of difficult negotiations, compromises have been reached, decisions made, language drafted and approved. The matter is settled. Neither you nor whatever powers have sent you here can undo what is done."

I was not to be put off so easily. "Sirs," I said, "I have come to tell you that the matter of slavery will not be settled by your compromises. And even when it is ended by armed conflict and domestic turmoil far more devastating than that you hope to avoid here, the potential evil of giving priority to property over human rights will remain. Can you not address the contradiction in your words and deeds?"

"There is no contradiction," replied another delegate. "Gouverneur Morris of Pennsylvania, the Convention's most outspoken opponent of slavery, has admitted that 'life and liberty were generally said to be of more value, than property, ... [but] an accurate view of the matter would nevertheless prove that property was the main object of Society.' "

"A contradiction," another delegate added, "would occur were we to follow the course you urge. We are not unaware of the moral issues raised by slavery, but we have no response to the delegate from South Carolina, General Charles Cotesworth Pinckney, who has admonished us that 'property in slaves should not be exposed to danger under a Govt. instituted for the protection of property.' "

"Of what value is a government that does not secure its citizens in their persons and their property?" inquired another delegate. "Government, as Mr. Pierce Butler from South Carolina has maintained here, 'was instituted principally for the protection of property and was itself ... supported by property.' Property, he reminded us, was 'the great object of government; the great cause of war; the great means of carrying it on.' And the whole South Carolina delegation joined him in making clear that 'the security the Southern states want is that their negroes may not be taken from them.' "

"Your deliberations here have been secret," I replied. "And yet history has revealed what you here would hide. The Southern delegates have demanded the slavery compromises as their absolute precondition to forming a new government."

"And why should it not be so?" a delegate in the rear called out. "I do not represent the Southern point of view, and yet their rigidity on the slavery issue is wholly natural, stemming as it does from the commitment of their economy to labor-intensive agriculture. We are not surprised by the determined bargaining of the Georgia and South Carolina delegations, nor distressed that our Southern colleagues, in seeking the protection they have gained, seem untroubled by doubts about the policy and morality of slavery and the slave trade."

"Then," I countered, "you are not troubled by the knowledge that this document will be defended by your Southern colleagues in the South Carolina ratification debates, by admissions that 'Negroes were our wealth, our only resource'?"

"Why, in God's name," the delegate responded, "should we be troubled by the truth, candidly stated? They have said no less in these chambers. General Charles Cotesworth Pinckney has flatly stated that 'South Carolina and Georgia cannot do without slaves.' And his cousin and fellow planter, Charles Pinckney, has added, 'The blacks are the laborers, the peasants of the Southern states.' "

At this, an elderly delegate arose and rapped his cane on his chair for attention. "Woman, we would have you gone from this place. But if a record be made, that record should show that the economic benefits of slavery do not accrue only to the South. Plantation states provide a market for Northern factories, and the New England shipping industry and merchants participate in the slave trade. Northern states, moreover, utilize slaves in the fields, as domestics, and even as soldiers to defend against Indian raids.''

I shook my head. "Here you are then! Representatives from large and small states, slave states and those that have abolished slavery, all of you are protecting your property interests at the cost of your principles.''

* * *

I asked, "Are you not concerned with the basic contradiction in your position: that you, who have gathered here in Philadelphia from each state in the confederacy, in fact represent and constitute major property holders? Do you not mind that your slogans of liberty and individual rights are basically guarantees that neither a strong government nor the masses will be able to interfere with your property rights and those of your class? This contradiction between what you espouse and what you here protect will be held against you by future citizens of this nation.''

"Unless we continue on our present course," a delegate called out, "there will be no nation whose origins can be criticized. These sessions were called because the country is teetering between anarchy and bankruptcy. The nation cannot meet its debts. * * * ''

* * *

"Do you recognize," I asked, "that in order to gain unity among yourselves, your slavery compromises sacrifice freedom for the Africans who live amongst you and work for you? Such sacrifices of the rights of one group of human beings will, unless arrested here, become a difficult-to-break pattern in the nation's politics.''

* * *

"I expect," [said a man I decided must be James Madison,] "that many will question why I have agreed to the Constitution. And, like General Washington, I will answer: 'because I thought it safe to the liberties of the people, and the best that could be obtained from the jarring interests of States, and the miscellaneous opinions of Politicians; and because experience has proved that the real danger to America & to liberty lies in the defect of *energy & stability* in the present establishments of the United States.' ''

"Do not think," added a delegate from Massachusetts, "that this Convention has come easily to its conclusions on the matter that concerns you. Gouverneur Morris from Pennsylvania has said to us in the strongest terms: 'Domestic slavery is the most prominent feature in the aristocratic countenance of the proposed Constitution.' He warned again and again that 'the people of Pennsylvania will never agree to a representation of Negroes.'

"Many of us shared Mr. Morris's concern about basing apportionment on slaves as insisted by the Southern delegates. I recall with great sympathy his questions:

Upon what principle is it that the slaves shall be computed in the representation? Are they men? Then make them citizens & let them vote? Are they property? Why then is no other property included? * * *

The admission of slaves into the Representation when fairly explained comes to this: that the inhabitant of Georgia and S.C. who goes to the Coast of Africa, and in defiance of the most sacred laws of humanity tears away his fellow creatures from their dearest connections & damns them to the most cruel bondages, shall have more votes in a Govt. instituted for protection of the rights of mankind, then the Citizen of Pa or N. Jersey who views with a laudable horror, so nefarious a practice.

"I tell you, woman, this Convention was not unmoved at these words of Mr. Morris's only a few weeks ago."

* * *

To pierce the delegates' adamant front, I called on the oratorical talents that have, in the twentieth century, won me both praise and courtroom battles: "The real crisis you face should not be resolved by your recognition of slavery, an evil whose immorality will pollute the nation as it now stains your document. Despite your resort to euphemisms like *persons* to keep out of the Constitution such words as *slave* and *slavery,* you cannot evade the consequences of the ten different provisions you have placed in the Constitution for the purpose of protecting property in slaves.*"

* * *

* The historian William Wiecek has listed the following direct and indirect accommodations to slavery contained in the Constitution:

1. Article I, Section 2: representatives in the House were apportioned among the states on the basis of population, computed by counting all free persons and three-fifths of the slaves (the "federal number," or "three-fifths," clause);

2. Article I, Section 2, and Article I, Section 9: two clauses requiring, redundantly, that direct taxes (including capitations) be apportioned among the states on the foregoing basis, the purpose being to prevent Congress from laying a head tax on slaves to encourage their emancipation;

3. Article I, Section 9: Congress was prohibited from abolishing the international slave trade to the United States before 1808;

4. Article IV, Section 2: the states were prohibited from emancipating fugitive slaves, who were to be returned on demand of the master;

5. Article I, Section 8: Congress empowered to provide for calling up the states' militias to suppress insurrections, including slave uprisings;

6. Article IV, Section 4: the federal government was obliged to protect the states against domestic violence, including slave insurrections;

7. Article V: the provisions of Article I, Section 9, clauses 1 and 4 (pertaining to the slave trade and direct taxes) were made unamendable;

8. Article I, Section 9, and Article I, Section 10: these two clauses prohibited the federal government and the states from taxing exports, one purpose being to prevent them from taxing slavery indirectly by taxing the exported product of slave labor.

[William Wiecek, The Sources of Antislavery Constitutionalism in America: 1760–1848 (1977), pp. 62–63.]

Finally, a delegate responded to my challenge. "You have, by now, heard enough to realize that we have not lightly reached the compromises on slavery you so deplore. Perhaps we, with the responsibility of forming a radically new government in perilous times, see more clearly than is possible for you in hindsight that the unavoidable cost of our labors will be the need to accept and live with what you call a contradiction."

The delegate had gotten to his feet, and was walking slowly toward me as he spoke. "This contradiction is not lost on us. Surely we know, even though we are at pains not to mention it, that we have sacrificed the rights of some in the belief that this involuntary forfeiture is necessary to secure the rights for others in a society espousing, as its basic principle, the liberty of all."

He was standing directly in front of the shield now, ignoring its gentle hum, disregarding its known danger. "It grieves me," he continued, "that your presence here confirms my worst fears about the harm done to your people because the Constitution, while claiming to speak in an unequivocal voice, in fact promises freedom to whites and condemns blacks to slavery. But what alternative do we have? Unless we here frame a constitution that can first gain our signatures and then win ratification by the states, we shall soon have no nation. For better or worse, slavery has been the backbone of our economy, the source of much of our wealth. It was condoned in the colonies and recognized in the Articles of Confederation. The majority of the delegates to this convention own slaves and must have that right protected if they and their states are to be included in the new government."

He paused and then asked, more out of frustration than defiance, "What better compromise on this issue can you offer than that which has been fashioned over so many hours of heated debate?"

The room was silent. The delegate, his statement made, his question presented, turned and walked slowly back to his seat. A few from his state touched his hand as he passed. Then all eyes turned to me.

I thanked the delegate for his question and then said, "The processes by which Northern states are even now abolishing slavery are known to you all. What is lacking here is not legislative skill but the courage to recognize the evil of holding blacks in slavery—an evil that would be quickly and universally condemned were the subjects of bondage members of the Caucasian race. You fear that unless the slavery of blacks is recognized and given protection, the nation will not survive. And my message is that the compromises you are making here mean that the nation's survival will always be in doubt. For now in my own day, after two hundred years and despite bloody wars and the earnest efforts of committed people, the racial contradiction you sanction in this document remains and threatens to tear this country apart."

"Mr. Chairman," said a delegate near the podium whose accent indicated that he was from the deep South, "this discussion grows tiresome and I resent to my very soul the presence in our midst of this offspring of slaves. If she accurately predicts the future fate of her race in this country, then our protection of slave property, which we deem essential for our survival, is easier to justify than in some later time when, as she implies, negroes remain subjugated even without the threats we face."

"Hear! Hear!" shouted a few delegates. "Bravo, Colonel!"

"It's all hypocrisy!" the Colonel shouted, his arms flailing the air, "sheer hypocrisy! Our Northern colleagues bemoan slavery while profiting from it as much as we in the South, meanwhile avoiding its costs and dangers. And our friends from Virginia, where slavery began, urge the end of importation—not out of humanitarian motivations, as their speeches suggest, but because they have sufficient slaves, and expect the value of their property will increase if further imports are barred.

* * *

"This, Mr. Chairman, is nothing but hypocrisy or, worse, ignorance of history. We speak easily today of liberty, but the rise of liberty and equality in this country has been accompanied by the rise of slavery. The negress who has seized our podium by diabolical force charges that we hold blacks slaves because we view them as inferior. Inferior in every way they surely are, but they were not slaves when Virginia was a new colony 150 years ago. Or, at least, their status was hardly worse than the luckless white indentured servants brought here from debtors' prisons and the poverty-ridden streets of England. Neither slave nor servant lived very long in that harsh, fever-ridden clime."

The Colonel, so close to the podium, steadfastly refused to speak to me or even to acknowledge my presence.

"In the beginning," he went on, "life was harsh, but the coming of tobacco to Virginia in 1617 turned a struggling colony into a place where great wealth could be made relatively quickly. To cultivate the labor-intense crop, large numbers of mainly white, male servants, indentured to their masters for a period of years, were imported. Blacks, too, were brought to the colony, both as slaves and as servants. They generally worked, ate, and slept with the white servants.

"As the years passed, more and more servants lived to gain their freedom, despite the practice of extending terms for any offense, large or small. They soon became a growing, poverty-stricken class, some of whom resigned themselves to working for wages; others preferred a meager living on dangerous frontier land or a hand-to-mouth existence, roaming from one county to another, renting a bit of land here, squatting on some there, dodging the tax collector, drinking, quarreling, stealing hogs, and enticing servants to run away with them.

"It is not extraordinary to suggest that the planters and those who governed Virginia were caught in a dilemma—a dilemma more like the contradiction we are accused of building into the Constitution than may at first meet the eye. They needed workers to maintain production in their fields, but young men were soon rebellious, without either land of their own or women, who were not seen as fit to work the fields. Moreover, the young workers were armed and had to be armed to repel attacks from Indians by land and from privateers and petty-thieving pirates by sea.

"The worst fears of Virginia's leaders were realized when, in 1676, a group of these former servants returned from a fruitless expedition against the Indians to attack their rulers in what was called Bacon's Rebellion. Governor William Berkeley bemoaned his lot in terms that defined the problem: 'How miserable that man is that Governes a People where six parts of seaven at least are Poore Endebted Discontented and Armed.'

"The solution came naturally and without decision. The planters purchased more slaves and imported fewer English servants. Slaves were more expensive initially, but their terms did not end, and their owners gained the benefits of the slaves' offspring. Africans, easily identified by color, could not hope to run away without being caught. The fear of pain and death could be and was substituted for the extension of terms as an incentive to force the slaves to work. They were not armed and could be held in chains.

"The fear of slave revolts increased as reliance on slavery grew and racial antipathy became more apparent. But this danger, while real, was less than that from restive and armed freedmen. Slaves did not have rising expectations, and no one told them they had rights. They had lost their freedom. Moreover, a woman could be made to work and have children every two years, thereby adding to the income of her master. Thus, many more women than indentured servants were imported.

"A free society divided between large landholders and small was much less riven by antagonisms than one divided between landholders and landless, masterless men. With the freedmen's expectations, sobriety, and status restored, he was no longer a man to be feared. That fact, together with the presence of a growing mass of alien slaves, tended to draw the white settlers closer together and to reduce the importance of the class difference between yeoman farmer and large plantation owner.

"Racial fears tended to lessen the economic and political differences between rich and poor whites. And as royal officials and tax collectors became more oppressive, both groups joined forces in protesting the import taxes on tobacco which provided income for the high and the low. The rich began to look to their less wealthy neighbors for political support against the English government and in local elections.

"Wealthy whites, of course, retained all their former prerogatives, but the creation of a black subclass enabled poor whites to identify with and support the policies of the upper class. With the safe economic advantage provided by their slaves, large landowners were willing to grant poor whites a larger role in the political process."

"So, Colonel," I interrupted, "you are saying that slavery for blacks not only provided wealth for rich whites but, paradoxically, led also to greater freedom for poor whites. One of our twentieth-century historians, Edmund Morgan, has explained this paradox of slave owners espousing freedom and liberty:

> Aristocrats could more safely preach equality in a slave society than in a free one. Slaves did not become leveling mobs, because their owners would see to it that they had no chance to. The apostrophes to equality were not addressed to them. And because Virginia's labor force was composed mainly of slaves, who had been isolated by race and removed from the political equation, the remaining free laborers and tenant farmers were too few in number to constitute a serious threat to the superiority of the men who assured them of their equality.[32]

"In effect," I concluded, "what I call a contradiction here was deemed a solution then. Slavery enabled the rich to keep their lands, arrested discontent and repression of other Englishmen, strengthened their rights and nourished their attachment to liberty. But the solution, as Professor Morgan said, 'put an end to the process of turning Africans into Englishmen. The rights of Englishmen were preserved by destroying the rights of Africans.' "[33]

"Do you charge that our belief in individual liberty is feigned?" demanded a Virginian, outraged.

"It was Professor Morgan's point," I replied, "not that 'a belief in republican equality had to rest on slavery, but only that in Virginia (and probably in other southern colonies) it did. The most ardent American republicans were Virginians, and their ardor was not unrelated to their power over the men and women they held in bondage.' "[34]

And now, for the first time, the Colonel looked at me, amazed. "My thoughts on this slavery matter have confounded my mind for many years, and yet you summarize them in a few paragraphs. I must, after all, thank you." He walked back to his seat in a daze, neither commended nor condemned by his colleagues. Most, indeed, were deep in thought—but for a few delegates I noticed trying desparately to signal to passersby in the street. But I could not attend to them: my time, I knew, must be growing short.

* * *

I longed to continue the debate, but never got the chance. Apparently someone outside had finally understood the delegates' signals for help, and had summoned the local militia. Hearing some commotion beyond the window, I turned to see a small cannon being rolled up,

32. [Edmund Morgan, American Slavery, American Freedom (1975), pp. 380–81.]

33. [Edmund Morgan, "Slavery and Freedom: The American Paradox," Journal of American History 59 (1972); 1, 24.]

34. [Morgan, supra note 32, p. 381.]

pointing straight at me. Then, in quick succession, the cannoneer lighted the fuse; the delegates dived under their desks; the cannon fired; and, with an ear-splitting roar, the cannonball broke against the light shield and splintered, leaving me and the shield intact.

I knew then my mission was over, and I returned to the twentieth century.

————

GENEVA had related the Chronicle of the Constitutional Contradiction as though she were living it again—and, indeed, I felt, as she talked, as though I, too, were in that hot and humid hall arguing along with her. Now she sat back in her chair and looked toward me in anticipation * * *

* * * "I hope you have not missed the real point of the Chronicle[," she said.] "It was not a debate. The Chronicle's message is that no one could have prevented the Framers from drafting a constitution including provisions protecting property in slaves. If they believed, as they had every reason to do, that the country's survival required the economic advantage provided by the slave system, than it was essential that slavery be recognized, rationalized, and protected in the country's basic law. It is as simple as that."

"And not so simple, to judge by the Colonel's revelations," I suggested. "As a result of your aggressive advocacy, you forced him and the rest of the Convention to think through motivations for the slavery compromises that went beyond the Southern delegates' refusal to compromise on this issue."

"The Colonel's reaction surprised me," Geneva admitted, "but his insight into the political as well as the economic importance of slavery simply added more compelling reasons for recognizing and providing protection for slavery in the Constitution."

"The implications for current civil rights work are a bit too close for comfort."

"Exactly right." Geneva leaned forward in her chair to give emphasis to her words. "Even in that extraordinary setting, what struck me as I fought for their attention was how familiar it all was. You know, friend, we civil rights lawyers spend our lives confronting whites in power with the obvious racial bias in their laws or policies, and while, as you know, the litany of their possible exculpatory responses is as long as life, they all boil down to: 'That's the way the world is. We did not make the rules, we simply play by them, and you really have no alternative but to do the same. Please don't take it personally.' The Colonel's speech revealed components of those rules far more complex than ignorant prejudice."

* * *

RAOUL BERGER, GOVERNMENT BY JUDICIARY
Pp. 10–14, 22–24, 27, 30–31, 169–172, 176 (1977).

BACKGROUND

The key to an understanding of the Fourteenth Amendment is that the North was shot through with Negrophobia, that the Republicans, except for a minority of extremists, were swayed by the racism that gripped their constituents rather than by abolitionist ideology. At the inception of their crusade the abolitionists peered up at an almost unscalable cliff. Charles Sumner, destined to become a leading spokesman for extreme abolitionist views, wrote in 1834, upon his first sight of slaves, "My worst preconception of their appearance and their ignorance did not fall as low as their actual stupidity * * * They appear to be nothing more than moving masses of flesh unendowed with anything of intelligence above the brutes." Tocqueville's impression in 1831–32 was equally abysmal. He noticed that in the North, "the prejudice which repels the negroes seems to increase in proportion as they are emancipated," that prejudice "appears to be stronger in the States which have abolished slavery, than in those where it still exists."

Little wonder that the abolitionist campaign was greeted with loathing! In 1837 Elijah Lovejoy, an abolitionist editor, was murdered by an Illinois mob. How shallow was the impress of the abolitionist campaign on such feelings is graphically revealed in a Lincoln incident. A delegation of Negro leaders had called on him at the White House, and he told them,

> There is an unwillingness on the part of our people, harsh as it may be, for you free colored people to remain with us * * *. [E]ven when you cease to be slaves, you are far removed from being placed on an equality with the white man * * * I cannot alter it if I would. It is a fact.

Fear of Negro invasion—that the emancipated slaves would flock north in droves—alarmed the North. The letters and diaries of Union soldiers, [C. Vann] Woodward notes, reveal an "enormous amount of antipathy towards Negroes"; popular convictions "were not prepared to sustain" a commitment to equality. Racism, David Donald remarks, "ran deep in the North," and the suggestion that "Negroes should be treated as equals to white men woke some of the deepest and ugliest fears in the American mind."

One need not look beyond the confines of the debates in the 39th Congress to find abundant confirmation. Time and again Republicans took account of race prejudice as an inescapable fact. George W. Julian of Indiana referred to the "proverbial hatred" of Negroes, Senator Henry S. Lane of Indiana to the "almost ineradicable prejudice," Shelby M. Cullom of Illinois to the "morbid prejudice," Senator William M. Stewart of Nevada to the "nearly insurmountable" prejudice, James F. Wilson of Iowa to the "iron-cased prejudice" against blacks. These were

Republicans, sympathetic to emancipation and the protection of civil rights. Then there were the Democratic racists who unashamedly proclaimed that the Union should remain a "white man's" government. In the words of Senator Garrett Davis of Kentucky, "The white race * * * will be proprietors of the land, and the blacks its cultivators; such is their destiny." Let it be regarded as political propaganda, and, as the noted British historiographer Sir Herbert Butterfield states, it "does at least presume an audience—perhaps a 'public opinion'—which is judged to be susceptible to the kinds of arguments and considerations set before it." Consider, too, that the Indiana Constitution of 1851 excluded Negroes from the State, as did Oregon, that a substantial number of Northern States recently had rejected Negro suffrage, that others maintained segregated schools. It is against this backdrop that we must measure claims that the framers of the Fourteenth Amendment swallowed abolitionist ideology hook, line, and sinker.

* * *

The Civil Rights Act of 1866

The meaning and scope of the Fourteenth Amendment are greatly illuminated by the debates in the 39th Congress on the antecedent Civil Rights Act of 1866. As Charles Fairman stated, "over and over in this debate [on the Amendment] the correspondence between Section One of the Amendment and the Civil Rights Act is noted. The provisions of the one are treated as though they were essentially identical with those of the other." George R. Latham of West Virginia, for example, stated that "the 'civil rights bill' which is now a law * * * covers exactly the same ground as this amendment." In fact, the Amendment was designed to "*constitutionalize*" the Act, that is, to "embody" it in the Constitution so as to remove doubt as to its constitutionality and to place it beyond the power of a later Congress to repeal. An ardent advocate of an abolitionist reading of the Amendment, Howard Jay Graham, stated that "virtually every speaker in the debates on the Fourteenth Amendment—Republican and Democrat alike—said or agreed that the Amendment was designed to embody or incorporate the Civil Rights Act."

Section 1 of the Civil Rights Bill provided in pertinent part,

That there shall be *no discrimination in civil* rights or immunities * * * on account of race * * * but the inhabitants of every race * * * shall have the *same* right to make and enforce contracts, to sue, be parties, and give evidence, to inherit, purchase, lease, sell, hold and convey real and personal property, and to full and *equal benefit* of all laws and proceedings for the *security* of person and property, and shall be subject to *like* punishment * * * and no other.[14]

* * *

14. [Cong. Globe, 39th Cong., 1st Sess. 474 (1866) (emphasis added).]

The explanations of the Civil Rights Bill by the respective committee chairmen made its limited objectives entirely clear. Speaking to "civil rights and immunities," House Chairman Wilson asked,

> What do these terms mean? Do they mean that in all things, civil, social, political, all citizens, without distinction of race or color, shall be equal? By no means can they be so construed * * * Nor do they mean that all citizens shall sit on juries, or that their children shall attend the same schools. These are not civil rights and immunities. Well, what is the meaning? What are civil rights? I understand civil rights to be simply the absolute rights of individuals, such as "The right of personal security, the right of personal liberty, and the right to acquire and enjoy property." * * *

* * *

* * * [Senator Lyman] Trumbull [of Illinois] stated that the Bill "has nothing to do with the right of suffrage, or any other political rights." When Senator Willard Saulsbury, a Democrat of Delaware, sought specifically to except "the right to vote," Trumbull replied: "that is a political privilege, not a civil right. This bill relates to civil rights only." And he reiterated that the Bill "carefully avoided conferring or interfering with political rights or privileges of any kind." The views of Trumbull and Wilson were shared by fellow Republicans. The "only effect" of the Bill, said Senator Henderson, was to give the blacks the enumerated rights. "These measures did not pretend to confer upon the Negro the suffrage. They left each State to determine the question for itself." Senator Sherman said the Bill "defines what are the incidents of freedom, and says that these men must be protected in certain rights, and so careful is its language that it goes on and defines those rights, the rights to sue and be sued [etc.] * * * and other universal incidents of freedom." [Martin] Thayer [of Pennsylvania] stressed that the Bill did not "extend the right of suffrage," that suffrage was not a "fundamental right." That the purpose of the Bill was to *prevent discrimination with respect to enumerated,* fundamental *not political or social rights,* was also stated in one form or another by Cook and Moulton of Illinois, Hubbell, Lawrence, and Shellabarger of Ohio, and Windom of Minnesota.

* * *

What Was Equal Protection to Protect?

The Civil Rights Act * * * secured to blacks the *same* right to contract, to hold property, and to sue, as whites enjoyed, and the *"equal benefit of all laws for security of person and property."* "Political rights" were excluded. In describing these aims the framers interchangeably referred to "equality," "equality before the law," and "equal protection" (but always in the circumscribed context of the rights enumerated in the Bill), so that it is reasonable to infer that the framers regarded these terms as synonymous. What is required, said Moulton of Illinois, is "that each State shall provide for equality before the law, equal protection to life, liberty, and property, equal right to sue and be sued." A leading Radical, Samuel Shellabarger of Ohio, said, of the Civil Rights Bill, "whatever rights *as to each of these enumerated* civil (not political) matters the State may confer upon one race * * * shall be held by all races in equality * * *. It secures * * * *equality of protection in those enumerated civil rights* which the States may deem proper to confer upon any races." So it was understood by Senator Hendricks, an Indiana Democrat: "To recognize the civil rights of the colored people as equal to the civil rights of the white people, I understand to be as far as Senators desire to go; in the language of the Senator from Massachusetts [Sumner] to place all men upon an equality before the law; and that is proposed in regard to their civil rights." He objected that "in the State of Indiana we do not recognize the civil equality of the races." When Andrew Johnson combed the Bill for objections and vetoed it, he noted that § 1 "contains an enumeration of the rights to be enjoyed" and that "perfect equality" was sought with respect to "these enumerated rights." Thomas T. Davis, a New York Republican, expressed a widely shared feeling in stating, Negroes "must be made equal before the law, and be permitted to enjoy life, liberty, and the pursuit of happiness [property]," but he was against "the establishment of perfect equality between the colored and the white race of the South." While James W. Patterson of New Hampshire was "opposed to any law discriminating against [blacks] in the security and protection of life, liberty, person and property," "beyond this," he stated, "I am not prepared to go," explicitly rejecting "political and social equality." Windom declared that the Civil Rights Bill conferred an "equal right, nothing more * * * to make and enforce contracts," and so on, but no "social privileges." Thus, the concept of "equal protection" had its roots in the Civil Rights Bill and was conceived to be limited to the enumerated rights.

What reason is there to conclude that when the words "equal protection of the laws" were embodied in the Amendment they were freighted with a new cargo of meaning—unlimited equality across the board? The evidence points the other way. In an early version of the Amendment, provision was made for both "the same political rights and privileges and * * * equal protection in the enjoyment of life, liberty and property," an indication that "equal protection" did not include "political rights and privileges," but was confined to "life, liberty, or property." [John] Bingham [of Ohio] proposed a substitute, H.R. No. 63, that would empower Congress "to secure * * * all privileges and immunities * * * (Art. IV, Sec. 2); and * * * equal protection in the rights of life, liberty and property (5th Amendment)." "Political rights and privileges" had disappeared; in its place was "privileges and immunities." Neither "privileges and immunities," nor its antecedent, "civil rights" had included "political privileges." Bingham explained that his proposal was aimed at "confiscation statutes * * * statutes of unjust imprisonment" of the "rebel states," the objects of the Civil Rights Bill. * * *

Among the statements indicating that § 1 was considered to embody the objectives of the Civil Rights Act is that of Latham of West Virginia:

"The 'civil rights bill,' which is now a law * * * covers exactly the same ground as this amendment." [Thaddeus] Stevens [of Pennsylvania] explained that the Amendment

> allows Congress to correct the unjust legislation of the States *so far* that the law which operates upon one shall operate *equally* upon all. Whatever law punishes a white man for a crime shall punish the black man precisely in the same way * * *. Whatever law protects the white man shall afford *equal protection* to the black man. Whatever means of redress is afforded to one shall be afforded to all. Whatever law allows the white man to testify in court shall allow the man of color to do the same. These are great advantages over their present [Black] codes * * *. I need not enumerate these partial and oppressive laws * * *. Your civil rights bill secures the same thing. * * *

                              * * *

But, it may be asked, does not the differentiation in § 1 between "due process" protection of "life, liberty, and property" and "equal protection of the laws" indicate that "equal protection" was now divorced from the earlier limitation to "life, liberty, and property?" Nothing in the debates indicates such a purpose. "Equal protection of the laws" expressed the central object of the framers: to prevent *statutory* discrimination with respect to the rights enumerated in the Civil Rights Act. That purpose had been loosely expressed in Bingham's earlier formulation: "equal protection in the rights of life, liberty, and property," which he mistakenly identified with the "5th Amendment." Possibly some more perceptive lawyer restored the words "life, liberty, and property" to their Fifth Amendment association with due process, thus insuring access to the courts. At the same time, the established association of due process with judicial procedure made it necessary to block what Stevens denominated "partial and oppressive laws," a purpose succinctly expressed by "equal protection of the laws" to which reference had been made during the debate on the Civil Rights Bill.

———

A number of scholars have offered critical reviews of Berger's historical research and interpretive conclusions.[3] Historian Eric Foner argues that to reduce the aims of framers of the Fourteenth Amendment to invalidation of the Black Codes and validation of the Civil Rights Act of 1866 "is to misconstrue the difference between a statute and a constitutional amendment." The Fourteenth Amendment was a "broad [statement] of principle, giving constitutional form to the resolution of a national cris[i]s, and permanently altering American nationality":

3. *See, e.g.,* Soifer, *Review Essay—Protecting Civil Rights: A Critique of Raoul Berger's History,* 54 N.Y.U.L.Rev. 651, 657 (1979); Kutler, *Raoul Berger's Fourteenth Amendment: A History or Ahistorical?,* 6 Hast. Const.L.Q. 511 (1979); Murphy, *Book Review—Constitutional Interpretation: The Art of Historian, Magician or Statesman?,* 87 Yale L.J. 1752 (1978).

[Even moderate Republicans] understood Reconstruction as a dynamic process, in which phrases like "privileges and immunities" were subject to changing interpretation. They preferred to allow both Congress and the federal courts maximum flexibility in implementing the Amendment's provisions and combatting the multitude of injustices that confronted blacks in many parts of the South. * * *

* * * [I]t is abundantly clear that Republicans wished to give constitutional sanction to states' obligation to respect such key provisions [of the Bill of Rights] as freedom of speech, the right to bear arms, trial by impartial jury, and protection against cruel and unusual punishment and unreasonable search and seizure. The Freedmen's Bureau had already taken steps to protect these rights, and the Amendment was deemed necessary, in part, precisely because every one of them was being systematically violated in the South in 1866.[4]

B. EQUAL PROTECTION THEORIES

MICHAEL J. PERRY, MODERN EQUAL PROTECTION: A CONCEPTUALIZATION AND APPRAISAL

79 Colum.L.Rev. 1023, 1025–1032 (1979).

I. THE ORIGINAL UNDERSTANDING

* * *

To understand the text of the fourteenth amendment, a document written more than a century ago, it is necessary to understand the period in which it was written. Raoul Berger, in his recent historical inquiry into the original understanding of the fourteenth amendment,[11] presents a substantially compelling reconstruction of what the amendment meant to its framers. Berger rightly insists that in ascertaining the original understanding of the amendment, we must remember "that the North was shot through with Negrophobia, that the Republicans, except for a minority of extremists, were swayed by the racism that gripped their constituents rather than by abolitionist ideology." Consequently, the framers did not intend the fourteenth amendment to serve as a charter for the political and social equality of the freed race. Rather, concludes Berger, section one of the amendment was intended only to constitutionalize—and thereby place "beyond the power of a later Congress to repeal"—the specific protections of the Civil Rights Act of 1866. The Civil Rights Act had been designed to protect freedmen in the South from discrimination with respect to certain enumerated rights

---

4. E. Foner, Reconstruction 257–259 (1988).

11. R. Berger, Government by Judiciary: The Transformation Of The Fourteenth Amendment (1977).

without which the abolition of slavery was thought largely meaningless.
* * *

As originally understood, the privileges or immunities clause—"the central provision of the Amendment's § 1"—forbade every state to deny to any of its residents on the basis of race any "fundamental" right the state granted to its residents generally. The sorts of rights—"fundamental" rights—to which the clause, following the 1866 Act, had reference were rights pertaining to the physical security of one's person, freedom of movement, and capacity to make contracts and to acquire, hold, and transfer chattels and land—*i.e.*, "life, liberty, and property" in the original sense. The equal protection clause forbade enactment or enforcement of laws denying on the basis of race any fundamental right granted residents generally; the due process clause forbade denial on the basis of race of any judicial protections afforded residents generally for the security of their fundamental rights. Given the import of the privileges or immunities clause, the equal protection and due process clauses were, in a strict sense, superfluous. But then, as Professor Karst has noted, the framers made "no serious effort to differentiate the functions of the various clauses." [23] The framers of the fourteenth amendment simply assumed what anyone in their place would have assumed: that every state granted to its residents generally certain fundamental rights—"life, liberty, and property"—and certain avenues for the protection of those rights—"due process." Under the amendment, every state was obligated to extend those same, but only those same, rights and protections to all residents without regard to race.

Thus, the original understanding of the equal protection clause—actually, of section one in its entirety—was that it forbade every state to discriminate against any of its residents on the basis of race *with respect to certain sorts of rights* (and the protection of those rights)—those pertaining to physical security, freedom of movement, and capacity to contract and own property. Of course, by contemporary lights the original understanding of equal protection is exceedingly narrow. The modern principle of equal protection, however, is an "elaboration" of this original understanding, developed over the course of nearly a century of Supreme Court decisions. * * *

II. The Paradigm: Racial Discrimination

A. *Toward a Broader Understanding*

In 1880, in *Strauder v. West Virginia*,[25] the Supreme Court sustained the first claim of racial discrimination to come before it. The Court reversed the conviction of a black man who contended that his trial by a jury on which, under state statute, only white males were eligible to serve violated the fourteenth amendment. It seems clear that the Court was substantially faithful to the original understanding of the amend-

23. Karst, [*The Supreme Court, 1976 Term—Foreword: Equal Citizenship Under the Fourteenth Amendment,* 91 Harv.L.Rev. 1, 15 (1977).]

25. 100 U.S. 303 (1880).

ment: the statutory exclusion of blacks from juries, as the Court emphasized, denied to blacks a principal judicial protection of life and liberty granted to residents generally.[26]

But in *Strauder* the Court said something suggestive of a broader understanding of the amendment:

> The very fact that colored people are singled out and expressly denied by a statute all right to participate in the administration of the law, as jurors, because of their color, though they are citizens, and may be in other respects fully qualified, is practically a brand upon them, affixed by the law, an assertion of their *inferiority,* and a stimulant to that race prejudice which is an impediment to securing to individuals of the race that equal justice which the law aims to secure to all others.

This language suggests that *any* law constituting "a brand upon [blacks], * * * an assertion of their inferiority, * * * a stimulant to * * * race prejudice" is offensive to the amendment, *whether or not* the law denies a right, or a judicial protection of a right, pertaining to physical security, freedom of movement, or capacity to contract or own property. * * *

Sixteen years after *Strauder,* the Supreme Court decided the infamous *Plessy v. Ferguson.*[29] There the Court rejected a constitutional attack on a Louisiana statute requiring racially segregated accommodations on passenger trains and making it a crime for any passenger to go "into a coach or compartment to which by race he does not belong." In a prophetic dissent, the first Justice Harlan observed what was indisputable—that the statute was predicated on the view that "colored citizens are so inferior and degraded that they cannot be allowed to sit in public coaches occupied by white citizens." * * *

In sustaining the statute, however, the majority did not invoke the narrow original understanding of the equal protection clause. Far from rejecting Harlan's contention that *any* law predicated on the view that nonwhites are by virtue of race inferior offends equal protection, the majority, in making the wholly implausible argument that the statute was not predicated on the supposed inferiority of nonwhites, implicitly embraced his premise:

26. Raoul Berger would presumably take issue with me here. Berger, who insists that § 1 of the fourteenth amendment was intended to have *exactly* the same scope as the Civil Rights Act of 1866, quotes several sponsors of the Act to the effect that the Act would not grant blacks the right to serve on juries. * * * However, it is not unreasonable, after comparing the general language of § 1 of the amendment to the more specific language of the Act, to think that the framers meant to constitutionalize not only the particular rights enumerated in the Act, but also rights of the sort enumerated there. As Berger himself acknowl-

edges, § 1 was intended to prohibit racial discrimination not merely with respect to the definition of rights pertaining to "life, liberty, and property" in the narrow, original sense, but also with respect to judicial protections of those rights. * * * And certainly one such "judicial" protection, as the Court in *Strauder* took pains to emphasize, is having members of one's own race, especially when that race is the object of vilification, legally competent to serve on one's criminal jury.

29. 163 U.S. 537 (1896).

Laws permitting, and even requiring, [the] separation [of the races] in places where they are liable to be brought into contact do not necessarily imply the *inferiority* of either race to the other * * *. [T]he underlying fallacy of the plaintiff's argument * * * [is] the assumption that the enforced separation of the two races stamps the colored race with a badge of inferiority. If this be so, it is not by reason of anything found in the act, but solely because the colored race chooses to put that construction upon it.

Thus, early on, the Supreme Court moved, if only in its rhetoric, beyond the original understanding of equal protection toward a broader understanding, one embracing the principle that *any* law predicated on the view that one person is by virtue of race *inferior* to another offends equal protection. It was not until *Brown v. Board of Education* [35] that the Court was able, or willing, to enforce this broader understanding. *Brown* and the subsequent per curiam opinions disestablishing, with a simple citation to *Brown*, segregated beaches, buses, golf courses, and parks, plainly stand as the major vindication of the principle, implicit in the Court's thinking as early as *Strauder* and *Plessy*, that state action predicated on the supposed moral inferiority of a particular racial group is unjust. *Loving v. Virginia*,[37] in which the Court struck down an antimiscegenation law, represents another significant vindication of this principle. * * *

What precisely is this broader understanding of equal protection? What is the central guiding principle of decisions such as *Brown* and *Loving?* It is a notion of the moral equality of the races—the principle that no person is morally inferior to another by virtue of race. Because race is not a factor indicating anything about the moral worth of persons, race is morally irrelevant to state laws and policies. Therefore, state action predicated on the view that one person is by virtue of race inferior to another offends equal protection.

I should clarify at the outset the special sense in which I use this terminology. To say that one person is the moral equal of another is to say that the former is no less worthy or deserving than the latter of respect, concern, opportunity for self-fulfillment, and the like, and no more deserving of subordination to or domination by others. Even if one accepts that no person is morally inferior to another by virtue of race, obviously not every person is the moral equal, in the sense indicated, of every other person. The extent of the respect, concern, and the like that one person accords another is conventionally a function of the extent to which the former approves, disapproves, or regards with indifference the latter's choices and activities, his or her self-definition. Regrettably, the extent of the respect and concern that we accord another person is sometimes also a function of the extent to which we approve or disapprove that person's status, not as an individual, but as a depersonalized abstraction—"black," for example, or "woman." It is, of

35. 347 U.S. 483 (1954).   **37.** 388 U.S. 1 (1967).

course, our evolving sense of the justice—indeed, the rationality—vel non of this latter sort of consideration as a basis for evaluating the moral worth of another that informs the ongoing development of equal protection doctrine. This conception of equal protection as embodying a principle of moral equality does not rely on the notion, recently put forth by Ronald Dworkin and amplified by others, that every person is entitled to "equal concern and respect." [42] The distinct notion on which it does rely is this: although not every person is the moral equal of every other person, there are some traits and factors—of which race is the paradigmatic example—by virtue of which no person ought to be deemed morally inferior to any other person.

Whether the Supreme Court's elaboration of the original understanding of the equal protection clause is a persuasive one is not a particularly difficult question. The fourteenth amendment constitutionalized the proposition that it is unjust (or, if it makes a difference, wrong) to deny to nonwhites certain rights—those pertaining to physical security, freedom of movement, or capacity to contract or own property—granted to residents generally. Why is it unjust? Two different reasons might be given. First, it might be unjust because those rights are so important—*i.e.*, "fundamental"—that *even* nonwhites, though not so fully human or equal in moral worth to whites that they should enjoy the same legal status as whites in all respects, should nonetheless enjoy these rights. Second, it might be unjust because to deny these rights on the basis of race, as the Court in *Strauder* indicated, is to assert the *moral inferiority* of the aggrieved racial minority. Although some of those responsible for the fourteenth amendment, perhaps many, would have given the first reason and rejected the second, others would have given, and certainly most persons today would give, the second reason in support and explanation of the proposition. Although it once was taken seriously, the first reason is not taken seriously now. But, if it is unjust to deny certain rights on the basis of race because to do so is to assert the moral inferiority of the racial minority whose rights are denied, then to discriminate against nonwhites with respect to legal status in any respect must be unjust as well, because such discrimination is an

---

42. *See* R. Dworkin, Taking Rights Seriously 266–78 (1977) * * *. To the extent Dworkin's notion is simply a way of saying that all persons are entitled to be regarded *as persons,* that is, "as human beings who are capable of forming and acting on intelligent conceptions of how their lives should be lived," and "who are capable of suffering and frustration," * * * I have no quarrel with the notion, but I do not rely on it. In fact, in my view the notion is entirely too meager to be of much service in equal protection cases.

At times I wonder whether Dworkin's notion doesn't have a more ambitious thrust, or at least lend itself to misunderstanding. For example, Dworkin says that "the right to *treatment as an equal* * * * is the right * * * to be treated with the *same* respect and concern *as anyone else.* " * * * Surely "same" does not mean "same degree of." After all, the claim that every person, no matter what his or her self-definition, is entitled to the same degree of respect, concern, and the like as anyone else—that Hitler, for example, is entitled to the same degree of respect, etc., as Mahatma Ghandi—is wholly implausible. Such a claim, which no one so far as I am aware has made, denies the fundamental insight that the principal function of moral evaluation—of granting or withholding respect, concern, and the like—is to encourage choices and activities deemed beneficial and to discourage those deemed harmful.

assertion of moral inferiority, a denial of human equality. In this sense, the equal protection clause—or more precisely, the proposition that the clause constitutionalized—can fairly be taken to radiate the principle that no person is by virtue of race morally inferior to another, a principle under which not merely some but all hostile discriminations against nonwhites are unjust. Thus, the principle of *Brown* and *Loving*, that any law or other state action predicated on the supposed moral inferiority of a particular racial group is unjust, is a persuasive, even compelling, elaboration of the equal protection clause.

PAUL BREST, IN DEFENSE OF THE ANTIDISCRIMINATION PRINCIPLE

90 Harv.L.Rev. 1, 5–10, 22–26, 28–29, 31, 33, 43–52 (1976).

By the "antidiscrimination principle" I mean the general principle disfavoring classifications and other decisions and practices that depend on the race (or ethnic origin) of the parties affected.

* * *

I. THE ANTIDISCRIMINATION PRINCIPLE

The antidiscrimination principle rests on fundamental moral values that are widely shared in our society. Although the text and legislative history of laws that incorporate this principle can inform our understanding of it, the principle itself is at least as likely to inform our interpretations of the laws. This is especially true with respect to the equal protection clause of the fourteenth amendment. The text and history of the clause are vague and ambiguous and cannot, in any event, infuse the antidiscrimination principle with moral force or justify its extension to novel circumstances and new beneficiaries. Therefore, the argument of this section does not ultimately turn on authority, but on whether it comports with the reader's reflective understanding of the antidiscrimination principle.

Stated most simply, the antidiscrimination principle disfavors race-dependent decisions and conduct—at least when they selectively disadvantage the members of a minority group. By race-dependent, I mean decisions and conduct (hereafter, simply decisions) that would have been different but for the race of those benefited or disadvantaged by them. Race-dependent decisions may take several forms, including overt racial classifications on the face of statutes and covert decisions by officials.

A. *Rationales for the Antidiscrimination Principle*

The antidiscrimination principle guards against certain defects in the *process* by which race-dependent decisions are made and also against certain harmful *results* of race-dependent decisions. Restricting the principle to a unitary purpose vitiates its moral force and requires the use of sophisticated reasoning to explain applications that seem self-evident.

1. Defects of Process.—The antidiscrimination principle is designed to prevent both irrational and unfair infliction of injury.

Race-dependent decisions are irrational insofar as they reflect the assumption that members of one race are less worthy than other people. Not all such decisions are necessarily irrational, however. For example, if black laborers tend to be absent from work more often than their white counterparts—for whatever reason—it is not irrational for an employer to prefer white applicants for the job. If Americans of Japanese ancestry were more prone to disloyalty than Caucasians during World War II, it was not irrational for the United States government to take special precautions against sabotage and espionage by them. Regulations and decisions based on statistical generalizations are commonplace in all developed societies and essential to their functioning. And it is often rational for decisionmakers to rely on weak and even dubious generalizations. Consider, for example, a fire department's or airline's policy against employing overweight personnel, based on the rather slight probability that they will suffer a heart attack while on duty.

In short, the mere fact that most blacks are industrious and most Japanese–Americans loyal does not make the employer's or the Government's decision irrational. Indeed, if all race-dependent decisions were irrational, there would be no need for an antidiscrimination principle, for it would suffice to apply the widely held moral, constitutional, and practical principle that forbids treating persons irrationally. The antidiscrimination principle fills a special need because—as even a glance at history indicates—race-dependent decisions that are rational and purport to be based solely on legitimate considerations are likely in fact to rest on assumptions of the differential worth of racial groups or on the related phenomenon of racially selective sympathy and indifference.

Mr. Justice Black focused on the first of these dangers in *Korematsu v. United States*,[33] the case in which the Government sought to justify its policy of interning Japanese–Americans, and in which the Court first enunciated the modern "suspect classification" doctrine. He wrote for the majority:

> [A]ll legal restrictions which curtail the civil rights of a single racial group are immediately suspect * * *. [C]ourts must subject them to the most rigid scrutiny. Pressing public necessity may sometimes justify the existence of such restrictions; racial antagonism never can.

Mr. Justice Black chose the word "suspect" advisedly. For, although a court often cannot ascertain the true motives underlying a decision, our history and traditions provide strong reasons to suspect that racial classifications ultimately rest on assumptions of the differential worth of racial groups. These racial value judgments appear in forms besides "racial antagonism"—for example in paternalistic assumptions of racial inferiority.

33. 323 U.S. 214 (1944).

By the phenomenon of racially selective sympathy and indifference I mean the unconscious failure to extend to a minority the same recognition of humanity, and hence the same sympathy and care, given as a matter of course to one's own group.

Although racially selective sympathy and indifference (hereafter, just indifference) is an inevitable consequence of attributing intrinsic value to membership in a racial group, it may also result from a desire to enhance our own power and esteem by enhancing the power and esteem of members of groups to which we belong. And it may also result—often unconsciously—from our tendency to sympathize most readily with those who seem most like ourselves. Whatever its cause, decisions that reflect this phenomenon, like those reflecting overt racial hostility, are unfair; for by hypothesis, they are decisions disadvantaging minority persons that would not be made under the identical circumstances if they disadvantaged members of the dominant group. The unequal treatment could be justified only if one group were in fact more worthy than the other. This justification failing, such treatment violates the cardinal rule of fairness—the Golden Rule.

2. *Harmful Results.*—A second and independent rationale for the antidiscrimination principle is the prevention of the harms which may result from race-dependent decisions. Often, the most obvious harm is the denial of the opportunity to secure a desired benefit—a job, a night's lodging at a motel, a vote. But this does not completely describe the consequences of race-dependent decisionmaking. Decisions based on assumptions of intrinsic worth and selective indifference inflict psychological injury by stigmatizing their victims as inferior. Moreover, because acts of discrimination tend to occur in pervasive patterns, their victims suffer especially frustrating, cumulative and debilitating injuries.

* * *

Recognition of the stigmatic injury inflicted by discrimination explains applications of the antidiscrimination principle where the material harm seems slight or problematic. For example, it fully explains the harmfulness of de jure school segregation without the need to invoke controversial social science evidence concerning the effects of segregation on achievement, interracial attitudes, and the like, and thus explains the Supreme Court's casual extension of *Brown* [*v. Board of Education*] to prohibit the segregation of public beaches, parks, golf courses and buses. It also explains how present practices that are racially neutral may nonetheless perpetuate the harms of past de jure segregation.

Racial generalizations usually inflict psychic injury whether or not they are in fact premised on assumptions of differential moral worth. Although all of us recognize that institutional decisions must depend on generalizations based on objective characteristics of persons and things rather than on individualized judgments, we nonetheless tend to feel unfairly treated when disadvantaged by a generalization that is not true as applied to us. Generalizations based on immutable personal traits such as race or sex are especially frustrating because we can do nothing

to escape their operation. These generalizations are still more pernicious, for they are often premised on the supposed correlation between
the inherited characteristic and the undesirable voluntary behavior of
those who possess the characteristic—for example, blacks are less industrious, trustworthy or clean than whites. Because the behavior is
voluntary, and hence the proper object of moral condemnation, individuals as to whom the generalization is inaccurate may justifiably feel that
the decisionmaker has passed moral judgment on them.

The psychological injury inflicted by generalizations based on race is
compounded by the frustrating and cumulative nature of their material
injuries. Racial generalizations are pervasive and have traditionally
operated in the same direction—to the disadvantage of members of the
minority group. A person who is denied one opportunity because he or
she is short or overweight will find other opportunities, for in our society
height and weight do not often serve as the bases for generalizations
determining who will receive benefits. By contrast, at least until very
recently, a black was not denied *an* opportunity because of his or her
race, but denied virtually *all* desirable opportunities. As door after door
is shut in one's face, the individual acts of discrimination combine into a
systematic and grossly inequitable frustration of opportunity.

* * *

II. RACIALLY DISPROPORTIONATE IMPACT

Race-dependent decisions typically produce a racially disproportionate impact—a disproportion between the number of blacks and whites on
the voting rolls, in an employer's work force, on a jury, or in a school.
Because race-dependent decisions are so often concealed, racially disproportionate impact has customarily been offered as evidence that ostensibly nondiscriminatory decisions are in fact race-dependent. * * *

* * *

Last Term, in *Washington v. Davis*,[105] an action challenging the
verbal ability test required of applicants by the District of Columbia
Police Department, the Supreme Court held that * * * only official
conduct having a "discriminatory purpose" violates the equal protection
clause. * * *

* * *

Davis reflects both the centrality of race-dependence to the equal
protection clause and the judicial unmanageability of a general rule
requiring an extraordinary justification for practices that produce racially disproportionate effects. The following discussion identifies and evaluates five possible rationales for the disproportionate impact doctrine.
The first three are rooted in the antidiscrimination principle and involve
remedies for present, past, and future discrimination. I believe that the
disproportionate impact doctrine can continue to play a useful role, for

105. [426 U.S. 229 (1976).]

courts as well as for legislatures, in enforcing the antidiscrimination principle. The fourth rationale is concerned with remedying "race-specific harms" produced by disproportionate impact. Although legislatures may properly ameliorate race-specific harms, I argue that the Constitution provides no basis for judicial intervention. The fifth rationale embodies a theory that accords moral status to groups and holds that it is intrinsically unjust for one racial group to be appreciably worse off than others. I believe that this theory is fundamentally misconceived and should not serve as the basis of policymaking by any institution.

A. Suspected Race–Dependency

Federal courts have used the disproportionate impact doctrine to avoid the unique difficulties of dealing with discriminatory intent or motive. * * *

* * *

* * * If courts may grant relief only when plaintiffs have made a clear case [of discriminatory motivation] on the record, many instances will remain where race-dependent decisions are strongly suspected but cannot be proved. Although this is not essentially different from the difficulty facing the proponents in most litigation seeking to overturn government policies, it is especially troubling in the race area. The accumulation of suspected but unproved race-dependent conduct, such as decisions to zone out low income housing, may systematically deprive minorities of important benefits. And the very existence of a state of affairs which "everyone knows" is based on racial discrimination but no one will remedy is demoralizing and stigmatic.

The disproportionate impact doctrine thus acts as a safeguard against improper race-dependent decisions. But * * * the doctrine cannot reasonably be applied across the board. If disproportionate impact is to remain a useful device, it must be used selectively and perhaps be modified to create rebuttable rather than conclusive presumptions of discriminatory intent. * * *

B. The Effects of Past and Remote Discrimination

The effects of discrimination may attenuate over time or be submerged in superseding events. But the injuries inflicted by discrimination can place its victims at a disadvantage in a variety of future endeavors, and discrimination can also perpetuate itself by altering the social environment to harm new generations of victims. Discrimination often works its injuries through practices, not themselves race-dependent, implemented by institutions that have not themselves discriminated. Past and remote discrimination often manifest themselves in racially disproportionate impact, and the antidiscrimination principle may therefore support its amelioration or elimination.

* * *

The causal connection between past discrimination and present states of affairs has * * * received the Court's attention in school segregation litigation. *Green v. County School Board* [156] involved a small Virginia school district which, like many rural areas, was not residentially segregated. The district had only two schools, which were de jure segregated—first pursuant to state law, later by local practice. In 1965, in order to remain eligible for federal financial aid, the school board adopted a "freedom of choice" plan of desegregation, which required each pupil to choose which school to attend each year. After three years under the plan, fifteen percent of the black pupils attended the formerly all-white school; no whites attended the all-black school.

* * *

In *Green* the causal connection between past discrimination and the current racial composition of the schools was as clear as such matters ever can be. It is not plausible, and the school board did not try to argue, that the county school system would have been substantially segregated in 1968 had children never been assigned by race. * * *

* * *

C. *Preventing Future Remote Discrimination*

The disproportionate absence of minorities from certain positions— whether or not itself the result of racial discrimination—may conduce to discrimination in other areas. Such a link underlies the special legislative and judicial concern to protect the political power of minorities. * * *

The Supreme Court's constitutional doctrine concerning multimember legislative districts seems responsive to [this] concern[.] A 1966 opinion indicated that constitutional problems would arise if "designedly or otherwise, a multi-member constituency apportionment scheme * * * operate[d] to minimize or cancel out the voting strength of racial or political elements of the voting population." [201] In *White v. Regester*,[202] a unanimous Court struck down two multimember districts in Texas, on the ground that black and Mexican–American minorities were effectively excluded from political processes. Mr. Justice White's opinion assigned plaintiffs a heavy burden, but not one requiring proof of discriminatory intent:

> [I]t is not enough that the racial group allegedly discriminated against has not had legislative seats in proportion to its voting potential. The plaintiffs' burden is to produce evidence to support findings that the political processes leading to nomination and election were not equally open to participation by the group in question—that its members had less opportunity than did other

---

156. 391 U.S. 430 (1968).

201. Burns v. Richardson, 384 U.S. 73, 88 (1966). In Whitcomb v. Chavis, 403 U.S. 124 (1971), the Court scrutinized, but up-

held, multimember districts in Marion County, Indiana.

202. 412 U.S. 755 (1973).

residents in the district to participate in the political processes and to elect legislators of their choice.[203]

The Court did not imply that the multimember districts had been discriminatorily designed. It noted, however, that both counties involved had histories of discrimination in the provision of public services and that in one the major political organization had intentionally excluded minorities.

D. Race–Specific Harms

The disproportionate disadvantage or exclusion, or the segregation, of the members of a racial minority may give rise to individual and social costs produced solely because of the race of the people affected—costs that would not arise from the identical practices if their impact was random with respect to race. These "race-specific harms" can result from practices that are not race-dependent.

The disproportionate absence of minorities from juries is an example. The principle that juries should represent a cross-section of the community reflects a belief that jurors from different racial, ethnic, and socioeconomic groups tend to have different viewpoints which affect their perceptions of fact and exercise of discretion, and that the system will function most accurately and fairly if a variety of viewpoints is brought to bear on the decision. For this reason, although it would be impossible to assure the proportional representation of the many relevant social groups on jury panels, some legislatures and courts have taken measures to assure that salient groups are not systematically underrepresented. * * *

* * * [O]ther putative race-specific harms do not violate definite constitutional provisions. This is true, for example, of the harms that may result from de facto segregation and from the depressed socioeconomic status of certain minorities.

School segregation, whatever its cause, has been said to reduce the self-esteem, aspirations, motivations, and achievement of black children and to encourage racial fears, hostility, and prejudice. But although these hypotheses have been tested in hundreds of studies, none has been established or disproved to the satisfaction of disinterested social scientists. * * *

* * *

The existence, degree, and nature of these and most other race-specific harms arguably produced by non-race-dependent practices are seldom self-evident. The independent significance of race, as distinguished from poverty, will likely remain unknown for the immediate future. Assuming, however, that significant race-specific harms do exist, by what authority may they be ameliorated?

Much race-specific harm in contemporary American society may be traceable to present or past violations of the antidiscrimination principle.

203. *Id.* at 765–66.

It seems improbable that most lower-class, isolated, and intradependent minority communities would possess these vulnerable characteristics to nearly the same degree were it not for longstanding and pervasive patterns of discrimination. The antidiscrimination principle provides sufficient authority for ameliorating race-specific harms to the extent that they depend on conditions caused by discrimination.

An institution enjoying more or less plenary policymaking authority may remedy race-specific harms that are *not* traceable to violations of the antidiscrimination principle, just as it may remedy any number of other kinds of injuries wholly unrelated to race. For example, a school board might focus on the special needs of minority children today, and deal with blind and retarded children a decade later—as claims come to its attention through interest groups, social upheavals, personal experience, and the like. But where the very authority of the judiciary is based on its ability to expound and apply general principles, it cannot act on such an ad hoc basis. Apart from the antidiscrimination principle, does there exist a coherent principle that requires remedy of race-specific harms but not other equally severe injuries—a principle, for example, under which a school district must spend $X to prevent Y amount of race-specific harm by integrating the schools, but need not spend the same amount of money to prevent the same amount of harm to mentally or physically handicapped children or to white children from impoverished environments?

To be sure, race-specific harms may produce serious individual and social costs. But these costs seem neither different in kind nor of a greater order of magnitude to the individuals affected than many others that might be ameliorated by changing school assignment schemes, employment criteria, and the like. * * *

E. Justice for Racial Groups

The most pernicious feature of racial prejudice and discrimination is their underlying premise that members of some racial groups are less worthy than members of others. The antidiscrimination principle holds that this assumption is fallacious because race has no moral salience. For administrative purposes, some remedies for racial discrimination are triggered by disproportionate racial impact or treat persons according to membership in racial groups; but group membership is always a proxy for the individual's right not to be discriminated against. Similarly, remedies for race-specific harms recognize the sociological consequences of group identification and affiliation only to assure justice for individual members.

In contrast to the theories considered so far, some commentators have suggested that racial groups should be treated as moral entities, holding rights as groups to distributive and compensatory justice. The distributive theory assumes the moral permissibility of unequal distributions of welfare among individuals, but holds that it is at least prima facie unjust for one racial or ethnic group to be substantially worse off than others. Like many individual-oriented theories of distributive justice, a group theory is essentially indifferent to the history that led to the unequal distribution. For example, Owen M. Fiss proposes a noncompensatory, purely redistributive principle—a "group disadvantaging principle"—that requires relief for any group that constitutes a "perpetual underclass." He argues that "[t]he redistributive strategy could give expression to an ethical view against caste, one that would make it undesirable for any social group to occupy a position of subordination for any extended period of time." [218] * * *

The arguments supporting the theories of group distributive justice are difficult to discern. Professor Fiss states that his "group disadvantaging principle" is justified primarily by its intuitive correctness: "visions about how society should be structured may be as irreducible as visions about how individuals should be treated—for example, with dignity." * * *

If a society can be said to have an underlying political theory, ours has not been a theory of organic groups but of liberalism, focusing on the rights of individuals, including rights of distributive justice. Of course, we recognize the sociological fact that people desire to affiliate and associate with others who share common interests or characteristics. The religion and association clauses of the first amendment are responsive to such desires. But though groups and associations may benefit incidentally from these guarantees, the amendment is designed to protect the individual's freedom to associate. We grant rights to associations or treat them as fictitious persons only to protect the rights of their individual members and for other instrumental purposes. Otherwise, the rights of associations and groups are no greater than the sum of those of their members. Indeed, under our received—albeit philosophically inadequate—metaphor of the social contract, the state itself does not enjoy rights greater than those of its citizens.

To say that we generally embrace the liberal tradition is, of course, no response to the claim that we should modify the theory and restructure our institutions accordingly. But without derogating from competing political traditions, they have implications that vie with, if they are not inconsistent with, principles that we hold fundamental—including the antidiscrimination principle, which attributes no moral significance to membership in racial groups, and notions of individual autonomy. Moreover, although the practices of nations—including our own—often fall short of their aspirations, most societies in which power is formally allocated among racial and national groups are strikingly oppressive, unequal, and unstable. In view of all of this, it seems reasonable to place the burden on proponents of a theory of group racial justice to show that it is morally tenable and consistent with other values that we cherish. To my knowledge, this has not yet been done.

218. [Fiss, *Groups and the Equal Protection Clause*, 5 Phil. & Pub.Aff. 107   (1976).]

Several commentators, who concede that racial groups have no intrinsic moral salience, assert that they acquire moral rights once the members of a group have suffered racial discrimination.   * * *

[T]here need be no contradiction involved in claiming that being black is both morally irrelevant for discriminating against people and morally relevant in discriminating in favour of people to provide reparations * * *. One may hold that people have an obligation to give reparations to groups they have wronged. By using the characteristic of being black as an identifying characteristic to discriminate against people, a person has wronged the group, blacks. He thus has an obligation to make reparations to the group. Since the obligation is to the group, no specific individual has a right to reparation. However, since the group is not an organized one like a state, church, or corporation, the only way to provide reparations to the group is to provide them to members of the group.[225]

A similar view may be implicit in some judicial decisions requiring employers and unions to adopt hiring and admission quotas to compensate for their past discrimination, even though the remedies are not likely to benefit the victims.   * * *

* * *

The notion that the treatment of individuals as a group for malign purposes requires their treatment as a group for benign compensatory purposes has the superficial appeal of all such symmetries. But, unless one adopts a notion of group rights such as that examined and rejected above, the fact is that most injuries of discrimination—even indirect or secondary ones—were inflicted on particular persons and only they are entitled to compensation. Where discrimination has undermined the unity or culture of a group, it may be appropriate to characterize the injury as one to the group; but the appropriate remedy then is one that reestablishes the group, an end that is not promoted by the fiction of treating individual members as its agents.

OWEN M. FISS, GROUPS AND THE EQUAL PROTECTION CLAUSE
5 Phil. & Pub.Aff. 107, 108, 129, 141–142, 144–156 (1976).

One purpose of this essay is simply to underscore the fact that the antidiscrimination principle is not the Equal Protection Clause, that it is nothing more than a mediating principle. I want to bring to an end the identification of the Clause with the antidiscrimination principle. But I also have larger ambitions. I want to suggest that the antidiscrimination principle embodies a very limited conception of equality, one that is highly individualistic and confined to assessing the rationality of means. I also want to outline another mediating principle—the group-disadvantaging principle—one that has as good, if not better, claim to

225. Bayles, *Reparations to Wronged Groups*, 33 Analysis 182, 183 (1973).

represent the ideal of equality, one that takes a fuller account of social reality, and one that more clearly focuses the issues that must be decided in equal protection cases.

* * *

THE LIMITATIONS OF THE ANTIDISCRIMINATION PRINCIPLE

* * * The antidiscrimination principle has structural limitations that prevent it from adequately resolving or even addressing certain central claims of equality now being advanced. For these claims the antidiscrimination principle either provides no framework of analysis or, even worse, provides the wrong one. * * *

* * *

The Problem of Facially Innocent Criteria

* * * [One such] problem area arises from state conduct that does in fact discriminate among persons, but not on the basis of a suspect criterion. The discrimination is based on a criterion that seems innocent on its face and yet nonetheless has the effect of disadvantaging blacks (or other minorities). For example, when the state purports to choose employees or college students on the basis of performance on standardized tests, and it turns out that the only persons admitted or hired are white.

As originally conceived[,] * * * the antidiscrimination principle promised to evolve a small, finite list of suspect criteria, such as race, religion, national origin, wealth, sex. These would be presumptively impermissible. The great bulk of other criteria may ultimately be deemed arbitrary in some particular instances because of ill-fit, but they would be presumptively valid. For these criteria—which I call *facially innocent*—the mere rational-relation test would suffice, and the probability would be very high that the statute or administrative action incorporating or utilizing such criteria would be sustained.

In some instances the presumption of validity may be dissolved, and the contrary presumption created, through the use of the concept of the *real* criterion. The plaintiffs can charge cheating: while the state says that it is selecting on the basis of an innocent criterion (such as performance on a written test), in truth the selection is being made on the basis of a suspect criterion (race). The substantiation of this charge confronts the plaintiffs with enormous evidentiary burdens. No one can be expected to admit to charges of cheating, and rarely is the result so striking * * * as to permit only one inference—discrimination on the basis of a suspect criterion. But if the charge could be substantiated (perhaps with an assist from the reallocation of the burdens of proofs when the criterion had almost the same effect as a suspect one), then there would be no problem of using the strict-scrutiny branch of the antidiscrimination principle: the real criterion, as opposed to the stated criterion, is a suspect one, and there the court should insist upon a very tight fit between purpose and criterion. The troublesome cases arise, however, when the charge of cheating cannot be substantiated, where, for example, the court finds that in truth the jobs were allocated or students selected on the basis of academic performance. What then?

* * *

A second, and seemingly more modest way of rationalizing the judicial treatment of facially innocent criteria, is to introduce the concept of past discrimination. Strict scrutiny should be given, so the argument runs, to state conduct that perpetuates the effects of earlier conduct (it might be state or private) that was based on the use of a suspect classification. Conduct that perpetuates the effects of past (suspect-criterion) discrimination is as presumptively invalid as the present use of suspect criteria. An objective civil service test is presumptively impermissible whenever it perpetuates the past discrimination of the dual school system (the dual school system put the blacks at a competitive disadvantage and the test perpetuates that disadvantage). The use of geographic proximity is an impermissible criterion of school assignment whenever it perpetuates the past discrimination of the dual school system. The racial assignments of that school system led to the present residential segregation and account for the location and size of the school buildings, and both of these factors in turn explain why the use of geographic proximity as a criterion of assignment results in segregated patterns of school attendance today.

A ban on "the perpetuation of past arbitrary discrimination" looks like a close cousin of the ban on "arbitrary discrimination." But this tie can only be maintained at great expense to important institutional values—those that cluster around the ideal of objectivity, an ideal the antidiscrimination principle is supposed to serve. A true inquiry into past discrimination necessitates evidentiary judgments that are likely to strain the judicial system—consume scarce resources and yield unsatisfying results. It would require the courts to construct causal connections that span significant periods of time, periods greater than those permitted under any general statute of limitations (a common device used to prevent the judiciary from undertaking inquiries where the evidence is likely to be stale, fragmentary, and generally unreliable). The difficulties of these backward-looking inquiries are compounded because the court must invariably deal with aggregate behavior, not just a single transaction; it must determine the causal explanation for the residential patterns of an entire community, or the skill levels of all the black applicants.

* * *

The third move designed to deal with the problem of facially innocent criteria—the introduction of the concept of de facto discrimination (or discriminatory effect)—does not focus on the past. Instead it shifts the trigger for strict scrutiny from the *criterion* of selection to the *result* of the selection process, and the result is stated in terms of a *group* rather than an individual. What triggers the strict scrutiny is not the criterion of selection itself, but rather the result—the fact that a minority group has been especially hurt. (This special hurt is sometimes described as a "differential impact.")

This concept of de facto discrimination also involves a basic modification of the antidiscrimination principle. The trigger is no longer classification, but rather group-impact. * * * The concern with the result reveals to me that what is ultimately at issue is the welfare of certain disadvantaged groups, not just the use of a criterion, and if that is at issue, there is no reason why the judicial intervention on behalf of that group should be limited to an inquiry as to the degree of fit between a criterion and a purpose.

THE GROUP-DISADVANTAGING PRINCIPLE

* * *

In attempting to formulate another theory of equal protection, I have viewed the Clause primarily, but not exclusively, as a protection for blacks. In part, this perspective stems from the original intent—the fact that the Clause was viewed as a means of safeguarding blacks from hostile state action. The Equal Protection Clause (following the circumlocution of the slave-clauses in the antebellum Constitution) uses the word "person," rather than "blacks." The generality of the word chosen to describe those protected enables other groups to invoke its protection; and I am willing to admit that was also probably intended. But this generality of coverage does not preclude a theory of primary reference—that blacks were the intended primary beneficiaries, that it was a concern for their welfare that prompted the Clause.

* * *

Starting from this perspective, a distinctively racial one, it strikes me as odd to build a general interpretation of the Equal Protection Clause * * * on the rejection of the idea that there are natural classes, that is, groups that have an identity and existence wholly apart from the challenged state statute or practice. There are natural classes, or social groups, in American society and blacks are such a group. Blacks are viewed as a group; they view themselves as a group; their identity is in large part determined by membership in the group; their social status is linked to the status of the group; and much of our action, institutional and personal, is based on these perspectives.

I use the term "group" to refer to a social group, and for me, a social group is more than a collection of individuals, all of whom, to use a polar example, happen to arrive at the same street corner at the same moment. A social group, as I use the term, has two other characteristics. (1) It is an *entity* (though not one that has a physical body). This means that the group has a distinct existence apart from its members, and also that it has an identity. It makes sense to talk about the group (at various points of time) and know that you are talking about the same group. You can talk about the group without reference to the particular individuals who happen to be its members at any one moment.

(2) There is also a condition of *interdependence*. The identity and well-being of the members of the group and the identity and well-being of the group are linked. Members of the group identify themselves—explain who they are—by reference to their membership in the group; and their well-being or status is in part determined by the well-being or status of the group. * * *

I would be the first to admit that working with the concept of a group is problematic, much more so than working with the concept of an individual or criterion. It is "messy." For example, in some instances, it may be exceedingly difficult to determine whether particular individuals are members of the group; or whether a particular collection of persons constitutes a social group. I will also admit that my definition of a social group, and in particular the condition of interdependence, compounds rather than reduces, these classificatory disputes. But these disputes do not demonstrate the illegitimacy of this category of social entity nor deny the validity or importance of the idea. They only blur the edges. Similarly, the present reality of the social groups should not be obscured by a commitment to the ideal of a "classless society" or the individualistic ethic—the ideal of treating people as individuals rather than as members of groups. Even if the Equal Protection Clause is viewed as the means for furthering or achieving these individualistic ideals (and I am not sure why it should be), there is no reason why the Clause—as an instrument for bringing about the "good society"—must be construed as though it is itself governed by that ideal or why it should be assumed that the "good society" had been achieved in 1868, or is so now.

The conception of blacks as a social group is only the first step in constructing a mediating principle. We must also realize they are a very special type of social group. They have two other characteristics as a group that are critical in understanding the function and reach of the Equal Protection Clause. One is that blacks are very badly off, probably our worst-off class (in terms of material well-being second only to the American Indians), and in addition they have occupied the lowest rung for several centuries. In a sense, they are America's perpetual underclass. It is both of these characteristics—the relative position of the group and the duration of the position—that make efforts to improve the status of the group defensible. This redistribution may be rooted in a theory of compensation—blacks as a group were *put* in that position by others and the redistributive measures are *owed* to the group as a form of compensation. The debt would be viewed as owed by society, once again viewed as a collectivity. But a redistributive strategy need not rest on this idea of compensation, it need not be backward looking (though past discrimination might be relevant for *explaining* the identity and status of blacks as a social group). The redistributive strategy could give expression to an ethical view against caste, one that would make it undesirable for any social group to occupy a position of subordination for any extended period of time. What, it might be asked, is the justification for that vision? I am not certain whether it is appropriate to ask this question, to push the inquiry a step further and search for the justification of that ethic; visions about how society should be structured may be as irreducible as visions about how individuals should be treated—for example, with dignity. But if this second order inquiry is appropriate, a variety of justifications can be offered and they need not incorporate the notion of compensation. Changes in the hierarchical structure of society—the elimination of caste—might be justified as a means of (a) preserving social peace; (b) maintaining the community as a community, that is, as one cohesive whole; or (c) permitting the fullest development of the individual members of the subordinated group who otherwise might look upon the low status of the group as placing a ceiling on their aspirations and achievements.

It is not just the socioeconomic status of blacks as a group that explains their special position in equal protection theory. It is also their political status. The power of blacks in the political arena is severely limited. For the last two centuries the political power of this group was circumscribed in most direct fashion—disenfranchisement. The electoral strength of blacks was not equal to their numbers. That has changed following the massive enfranchisement of the Voting Rights Act of 1965, but structural limitations on the political power of blacks still persist. These limitations arise from three different sources, which can act either alternatively or cumulatively and which, in any event, are all interrelated. One source of weakness is their numbers, the fact that they are a numerical minority; the second is their economic status, their position as the perpetual underclass; and the third is that, as a "discrete and insular" minority, they are the object of "prejudice"—that is, the subject of fear, hatred, and distaste that make it particularly difficult for them to form coalitions with others (such as the white poor) and that make it advantageous for the dominant political parties to hurt them—to use them as a scapegoat.

* * *

Hence, despite recent demographic shifts in several large cities, I think it appropriate to view blacks as a group that is relatively powerless in the political arena and in my judgment that political status of the group justifies a special judicial solicitude on their behalf. When the product of a political process is a law that hurts blacks, the usual countermajoritarian objection to judicial invalidation—the objection that denies those "nine men" the right to substitute their view for that of "the people"—has little force. For the judiciary could be viewed as amplifying the voice of the powerless minority; the judiciary is attempting to rectify the injustice of the political process as a method of adjusting competing claims. The need for this rectification turns on whether the law is deemed one that harms blacks—a judgment that is admittedly hard to make when the perspective becomes a group one, for that requires the aggregation of interests and viewpoints, many of which are in conflict. It is important to emphasize, however, that the need for this rectification does not turn on whether the law embodies a classification, racial or otherwise; it is sufficient if the state law simply has the *effect* of hurting blacks. Nor should the rectification, once triggered by a harmful law, be confined to questions of fit—the judicial responsibility is more extensive than simply one of guarding against the risk of imprecise classifications by the political agencies. The relative powerlessness of blacks also requires that the judiciary strictly scrutinize the choice of ends; for it is just as likely that the interests of blacks as a group will not be adequately taken into account in choosing ends or goals. Maximizing goals such as reducing transportation costs (a goal that might account for the neighborhood-school plan) or having the most brilliant law students (a goal that might account for requiring a [high score] on the LSAT) are constitutionally permissible goals in the sense that there is no substantive constitutional provision (or implied purpose lying behind some provision) that deny them to the state. On the other hand, these maximizing goals are obviously not in any sense constitutionally compelled goals and there is a chance—a most substantial one—that they would not be chosen as *the* goals (without any modification) if the interests of the blacks as a group were adequately taken into account—if the goal-choosers paid sufficient attention to the special needs, desires, and views of this powerless group.

The injustice of the political process must be corrected, and perhaps as a last resort, that task falls to the judiciary. But this claim does not yield any basis for specifying what the corrected process would look like, or what the court should say when it amplifies the voice of the powerless minority. A just political process would be one in which blacks would have "more" of a voice than they in fact do, but not necessarily one in which they would "win." In a sense there is a remedial lacuna; a pure process claim cannot determine substantive outcomes. * * * But this processual theory focusing on the relative powerlessness of blacks in the political arena need not stand alone. The substantive standards can be supplied by the other critical characteristics of this social group— perpetual subordination. The political status of the group justifies the institutional allocations—our willingness to allow those "nine men" to substitute their judgment (about ends as well as means) for that of "the people." The socioeconomic position of the group supplies an additional reason for the judicial activism and also determines the content of the intervention—improvement of the status of that group.

I would therefore argue that blacks should be viewed as having three characteristics that are relevant in the formulation of equal protection theory: (a) they are a social group; (b) the group has been in a position of perpetual subordination; and (c) the political power of the group is severely circumscribed. Blacks are what might be called a specially disadvantaged group, and I would view the Equal Protection Clause as a protection for such groups. Blacks are the prototype of the protected group, but they are not the only group entitled to protection. There are other social groups, even as I have used the term, and if these groups have the same characteristics as blacks—perpetual subordination and circumscribed political power—they should be considered specially disadvantaged and receive the same degree of protection. What the Equal Protection Clause protects is specially disadvantaged groups, not just blacks. A concern for equal treatment and the word "person" appearing in the Clause permit and probably require this generality of coverage.

Some of these specially disadvantaged groups can be defined in terms of characteristics that do not have biological roots and that are not immutable; the Clause might protect certain language groups and aliens. Moreover, in passing upon a claim to be considered a specially disadvantaged group, the court may treat one of the characteristics entitling blacks to that status as a sufficient but not a necessary condition; indeed the court may even develop variable standards of protection—it may tolerate disadvantaging practices that would not be tolerated if the group was a "pure" specially disadvantaged group. Jews or women might be entitled to less protection than American Indians, though nonetheless entitled to some protection. Finally, these judicial judgments may be time-bound. Through the process of assimilation the group may cease to exist, or even if the group continues to retain its identity, its socioeconomic and political positions may so improve so as to bring to an end its status as specially disadvantaged.

All this means that the courts will have some leeway in identifying the groups protected by the Equal Protection Clause. I think, however, it would be a mistake to use this flexibility to extend the protection to what might be considered artificial classes, those created by a classification or criterion embodied in a state practice or statute, for example, those classes created by tax categories (those having incomes between $27,000 and $30,000, or between $8,000 and $10,000) or licensing statutes (the manufacturers of filled milk). By definition those classes do not have an independent social identity and existence, or if they do, the condition of interdependence is lacking. It is difficult, if not impossible, to make an assessment of their socioeconomic status or of their political power (other than that they have just lost a legislative battle). And, if this is true, neither redistribution nor stringent judicial intervention on their behalf can be justified. It is not that such arguments are unpersuasive, but that they are almost unintelligible. Thus, in only one sense should the group-disadvantaging strategy be viewed as conducive to "more equality": it will get more for fewer. It will get more for the specially disadvantaged groups but will not provide any protection for artificial classes, those solely created by statute or a state practice. Of course, this loss may be more formal than real. Artificial classes constitute part of the universe that the antidiscrimination principle *purports* to protect, but in truth almost never does protect given the permissibility of the minimum-scrutiny inquiry.

[In the concluding portion of his article Fiss explains how he would implement his proposal for a group-disadvantaging principle. He admits that it would reach the same results as the antidiscrimination principle in what he calls "first-order" situations—exclusion of blacks from public institutions. The choice of a principle would matter more in "second-order" cases—challenges to the use of facially innocent criteria such as test performance.   And in "third-order" cases—preferential treatment— the differences would be most evident.   The antidiscrimination principle, with its individualistic character, tends to prohibit such treatment; a focus on disadvantaged groups tends to allow (perhaps even require) it.

[Not every instance of disparate impact is a "second-order" case. A sales tax, because of its diffuse impact, may harm individuals but not aggravate the subordinate status of blacks as a group.   But in any true "second-order" case the state practice would be presumptively invalid. The state could overcome the presumption by showing that its practice was necessary to produce a compelling benefit.   It could, for example, insist on certain minimum levels of competence for its employees or students.

[In "third-order" cases Fiss's principle would require only a rational basis for preferential policies.   The reason is that the Equal Protection Clause is not concerned with fairness (e.g., to individual whites), but with group harm.   For the same reason, it would not matter that some individual beneficiaries (e.g. rich blacks) were not victims.]

CHARLES R. LAWRENCE III, THE ID, THE EGO, AND EQUAL PROTECTION: RECKONING WITH UNCONSCIOUS RACISM

39 Stan.L.Rev. 317, 321–323, 328, 331–339, 344–355 (1987).

Much of one's inability to know racial discrimination when one sees it results from a failure to recognize that racism is both a crime and a disease.[15]   This failure is compounded by a reluctance to admit that the illness of racism infects almost everyone.   Acknowledging and under- standing the malignancy are prerequisites to the discovery of an appro- priate cure.   But the diagnosis is difficult, because our own contamina- tion with the very illness for which a cure is sought impairs our comprehension of the disorder.

* * *

Americans share a common historical and cultural heritage in which racism has played and still plays a dominant role.   Because of this shared experience, we also inevitably share many ideas, attitudes, and beliefs that attach significance to an individual's race and induce nega- tive feelings and opinions about nonwhites.   To the extent that this cultural belief system has influenced all of us, we are all racists.   At the same time, most of us are unaware of our racism.   We do not recognize the ways in which our cultural experience has influenced our beliefs about race or the occasions on which those beliefs affect our actions.   In

---

15. "Immorality" and "criminality" are thought of in terms of blameworthiness. In contrast, Chester Pierce, a black psychia- trist, has described racism as a "public health problem." Pierce, *Psychiatric Prob- lems of Black Minority,* in 2 American Handbook of Psychiatry 512, 513 (G. Ca- plan 2d ed. 1974). * * *

other words, a large part of the behavior that produces racial discrimination is influenced by unconscious racial motivation.

There are two explanations for the unconscious nature of our racially discriminatory beliefs and ideas. First, Freudian theory states that the human mind defends itself against the discomfort of guilt by denying or refusing to recognize those ideas, wishes, and beliefs that conflict with what the individual has learned is good or right. While our historical experience has made racism an integral part of our culture, our society has more recently embraced an ideal that rejects racism as immoral. When an individual experiences conflict between racist ideas and the societal ethic that condemns those ideas, the mind excludes his racism from consciousness.

Second, the theory of cognitive psychology states that the culture—including, for example, the media and an individual's parents, peers, and authority figures—transmits certain beliefs and preferences. Because these beliefs are so much a part of the culture, they are not experienced as explicit lessons. Instead, they seem part of the individual's rational ordering of her perceptions of the world. The individual is unaware, for example, that the ubiquitous presence of a cultural stereotype has influenced her perception that blacks are lazy or unintelligent. Because racism is so deeply ingrained in our culture, it is likely to be transmitted by tacit understandings: Even if a child is not told that blacks are inferior, he learns that lesson by observing the behavior of others. These tacit understandings, because they have never been articulated, are less likely to be experienced at a conscious level.

I. "THY SPEECH MAKETH THEE MANIFEST": A
PRIMER ON THE UNCONSCIOUS AND RACE

* * *

Psychoanalytic Theory: An Explanation of Racism's Irrationality

The division of the mind into the conscious and the unconscious is the fundamental principle of psychoanalysis. Psychoanalytic theory explains the existence of pathological mental behavior as well as certain otherwise unexplained behavior in healthy people by postulating two powerful mental processes—the primary and the secondary—which govern how the mind works. The primary process, or Id, occurs outside of our awareness. It consists of desires, wishes, and instincts that strive for gratification. It follows its own laws, of which the supreme one is pleasure. The secondary process, or Ego, happens under conscious control and is bound by logic and reason. We use this process to adapt to reality: The Ego is required to respect the demands of reality and to conform to ethical and moral laws. On their way to gratification, the Id impulses must pass through the territory of the Ego where they are criticized, rejected, or modified, often by some defensive measure on the part of the secondary process. Defensive mechanisms such as repression, denial, introjection, projection, reaction formation, sublimation, and reversal resolve the conflicts between the primary and secondary processes by disguising forbidden wishes and making them palatable.

* * *

An examination of the beliefs that racially prejudiced people have about out-groups demonstrates their use of * * * mechanisms observed by both Freudian and nonFreudian behavioralists. For example, studies have found that racists hold two types of stereotyped beliefs: They believe the out-group is dirty, lazy, oversexed, and without control of their instincts (a typical accusation against blacks), or they believe the out-group is pushy, ambitious, conniving, and in control of business, money, and industry (a typical accusation against Jews). These two types of accusation correspond to two of the most common types of neurotic conflict: that which arises when an individual cannot master his instinctive drives in a way that fits into rational and socially approved patterns of behavior, and that which arises when an individual cannot live up to the aspirations and standards of his own conscience. Thus, the stereotypical view of blacks implies that their Id, the instinctive part of their psyche, dominates their Ego, the rationally oriented part. The stereotype of the Jew, on the other hand, accuses him of having an overdeveloped Ego. In this way, the racially prejudiced person projects his own conflict into the form of racial stereotypes.

The preoccupation among racially prejudiced people with sexual matters in race relations provides further evidence of this relationship between the unconscious and racism. Taboos against interracial sexual relations, myths concerning the sexual prowess of blacks, and obsessions with racial purity coexist irrationally with a tendency to break these taboos. Again, psychoanalytic theory provides insights: According to Freud, one's sexual identity plays a crucial role in the unending effort to come to terms with oneself. Thus, the prominence of racism's sexual component supports the theory that racial antagonism grows in large part out of an unstable sense of identity.

* * *

Thus far we have considered the role the unconscious plays in creating overtly racist attitudes. But how is the unconscious involved when racial prejudice is less apparent—when racial bias is hidden from the prejudiced individual as well as from others? Increasingly, as our culture has rejected racism as immoral and unproductive, this hidden prejudice has become the more prevalent form of racism. The individual's Ego must adapt to a cultural order that views overtly racist attitudes and behavior as unsophisticated, uninformed, and immoral. It must repress or disguise racist ideas when they seek expression.

* * *

A Cognitive Approach to Unconscious Racism

Cognitive psychologists offer a contrasting model for understanding the origin and unconscious nature of racial prejudice. This is essentially a rational model. The cognitivists acknowledge the importance of emotional and motivational factors, but they do not embrace the Freudian belief that instinctive drives dominate individuals' concepts, attitudes, and beliefs. Instead, they view human behavior, including racial prejudice, as growing out of the individual's attempt to understand his relationship with the world (in this case, relations between groups) while at the same time preserving his personal integrity. But while the ultimate goal of the cognitive process is understanding or rationality, many of the critical elements of the process occur outside of the individual's awareness. This is especially true when there is tension between the individual's desire for simplification and the complexity of the real world or conflict between an understanding of a situation that preserves the individual's self-image and one that jeopardizes a positive view of himself.

Cognitivists see the process of "categorization" as one common source of racial and other stereotypes. All humans tend to categorize in order to make sense of experience. Too many events occur daily for us to deal successfully with each one on an individual basis; we must categorize in order to cope. When a category—for example, the category of black person or white person—correlates with a continuous dimension—for example, the range of human intelligence or the propensity to violence—there is a tendency to exaggerate the differences between categories on that dimension and to minimize the differences within each category.

The more important a particular classification of people into groups is to an individual, the more likely she is to distinguish sharply the characteristics of people who belong to the different groups. Here, cognitivists integrate the observations of personality theorists and social psychologists with their own. If an individual is hostile toward a group of people, she has an emotional investment in preserving the differentiations between her own group and the "others." Thus, the preservation of inaccurate judgments about the out-group is self-rewarding. This is particularly so when prejudiced judgments are made in a social context that accepts and encourages negative attitudes toward the out-group. In these cases, the group judgment reinforces and helps maintain the individual judgment about the out-group's lack of worth.

The content of the social categories to which people are assigned is generated over a long period of time within a culture and transmitted to individual members of society by a process cognitivists call "assimilation." Assimilation entails learning and internalizing preferences and evaluations. Individuals learn cultural attitudes and beliefs about race very early in life, at a time when it is difficult to separate the perceptions of one's teacher (usually a parent) from one's own. In other words, one learns about race at a time when one is highly sensitive to the social contexts in which one lives.

* * *

Furthermore, because children learn lessons about race at this early stage, most of the lessons are tacit rather than explicit. Children learn not so much through an intellectual understanding of what their parents tell them about race as through an emotional identification with who their parents are and what they see and feel their parents do. Small children will adopt their parents' beliefs because they experience them as their own. If we do learn lessons about race in this way, we are not likely to be aware that the lessons have even taken place. If we are unaware that we have been taught to be afraid of blacks or to think of them as lazy or stupid, then we may not be conscious of our internalization of those feelings and beliefs.

* * *

Case studies have demonstrated that an individual who holds stereotyped beliefs about a "target" will remember and interpret past events in the target's life history in ways that bolster and support his stereotyped beliefs and will perceive the target's actual behavior as reconfirming and validating the stereotyped beliefs. While the individual may be aware of the selectively perceived facts that support his categorization or simplified understanding, he will not be aware of the process that has caused him to deselect the facts that do not conform with his rationalization. Thus, racially prejudiced behavior that is actually the product of learned cultural preferences is experienced as a reflection of rational deduction from objective observation, which is nonprejudicial behavior. The decisionmaker who is unaware of the selective perception that has produced her stereotype will not view it as a stereotype. She will believe that her actions are motivated not by racial prejudice but by her attraction or aversion to the attributes she has "observed" in the groups she has favored or disfavored.

* * *

II. A Tale of Two Theories
* * *

Two theories have attempted to specify the central function of suspect classification doctrine. The first, the "process defect" theory, sees the judicial intervention occasioned by strict scrutiny of suspect classifications as an appropriate response to distortions in the democratic process. The second theory cites racial stigma as the primary target of suspect classification doctrine. * * * [R]ecognizing the presence of unconscious motive furthers the central rationale of each theory.[115]

115. A third substantive theory of equal protection suggests that racial groups should be treated as moral entities with group rights to distributive and compensatory justice. It holds that it is prima facie unjust for one racial or ethnic group to be substantially worse off than another. This "group disadvantaging principle" requires relief for any group that constitutes a "per-

petual underclass" and argues that such redistribution would express an ethical view disfavoring caste. *See* Fiss, [*Groups and the Equal Protection Clause,* 5 Phil. & Pub. Aff. 107 (1976)]. This article will not discuss this approach. Fiss' theory is essentially indifferent to the motives and history that have led to unequal distribution and is, therefore, sufficiently sensitive to the cor-

The Process Defect Theory

The chief proponent of the process defect theory has been John Ely.[116] He identifies the systematic exclusion of a group from the normal workings of the political process as the harm that heightened judicial scrutiny for suspect classifications seeks to prevent or remedy.

* * *

Motive and intent are at the center of Ely's theory. The function of suspect classification doctrine is to expose unconstitutional motives that may have distorted the process. A statute that classifies by race is strictly scrutinized, because the requirement of "close fit" between end sought and means used will reveal those instances where the actual motive of the legislature was to disadvantage a group simply because of its race.

Under present doctrine, the courts look for Ely's process defect only when the racial classification appears on the face of the statute or when self-conscious racial intent has been proved * * *. But the same process distortions will occur even when the racial prejudice is less apparent. Other groups in the body politic may avoid coalition with blacks without a conscious awareness of their aversion to blacks or of their association of certain characteristics with blacks. They may take stands on issues without realizing that their reasons are, in part, racially oriented. Likewise, the governmental decisionmaker may be unaware that she has devalued the cost of a chosen path, because a group with which she does not identify will bear that cost. Indeed, because of her lack of empathy with the group, she may have never even thought of the cost at all.

Process distortion exists where the unconstitutional motive of racial prejudice has influenced the decision. It matters not that the decisionmaker's motive may lie outside her awareness. For example, in *Village of Arlington Heights v. Metropolitan Housing Development Corp.*,[127] a predominantly white, upper middle class Chicago suburb prevented the construction of a proposed housing development for low and moderate income families by refusing to rezone the projected site to allow multifamily units. The Supreme Court agreed that the decision not to rezone had racially discriminatory effects, but it rejected the black plaintiffs' equal protection claim on the ground that they had "simply failed to carry their burden of proving that discriminatory purpose was a motivating factor in the Village's decision." The Court focused on the lack of any evidence of conscious intent to discriminate on the part of either the city council in enacting the zoning ordinance that restricted use to single family homes or the planning commission in administering the ordinance.

rection of disadvantage resulting from unconscious racism without the assistance of my analysis.

116. *See* J. Ely, Democracy and Distrust 135–79 (1980). * * *

127. 429 U.S. 252 (1977).

We can envision several possible scenarios that demonstrate the possible process-distorting effects of unconscious racism on a governmental decision like that in *Arlington Heights:*

(1) The city council refused to rezone for the sole purpose of stigmatizing and denying housing to blacks. This case resembles *Plessy v. Ferguson* [131] and *Gomillion v. Lightfoot,* [132] in which the only motives were unconstitutional, and the ordinances were, therefore, per se unconstitutional.

(2) The city claims a legitimate economic or environmental purpose, but evidence shows that it sought to exclude blacks in order to achieve that purpose. This case is the same as a classification by race on the face of a statute for which a legitimate goal is claimed. It is the case Ely describes where blacks are consciously excluded from the political process and devalued in the assessment of costs and benefits. When this self-conscious motive can be proved, the resulting classification is subject to strict scrutiny under existing doctrine.

(3) The purpose of the ordinance was economic—i.e., to keep property values up by keeping poor people out—but the decisionmakers associated poverty with blacks and would have weighed the costs and benefits differently if the poor people they envisioned excluding were elderly white people on social security. This "selective sympathy or indifference" could have occurred at a conscious or unconscious level. It is more than likely that the decisionmakers knew that the poor people they were excluding were black, but they would not be likely to have known that they undervalued the cost to poor people because they thought of them as black rather than white.

(4) A constituency within Arlington Heights—for example, elderly whites—did not actively campaign for the rezoning because of aversion to blacks who might have benefited from it. This occurred despite the fact that this constituency's interest in low income housing would otherwise have outweighed its interest in property values. This inability or unwillingness to apprehend and act upon an overlapping interest is precisely the kind of process distortion through group vilification that Ely describes. It is as likely as not that these elderly voters are largely unaware of the vilification and resulting aversion that preempted their potential coalition with blacks.

(5) No one in Arlington Heights thought about blacks one way or the other—i.e., it was a fight between environmentalists and developers—but an inadvertent devaluing of black interests caused inattention to the costs blacks would have to bear. If one asked the decisionmakers how they had valued the cost to blacks of the exclusionary zoning, they might have responded, "I never thought of that." This is an example of selective indifference or misapprehension of costs that occurs entirely outside of consciousness.

131. 163 U.S. 537 (1896).   **132.** 364 U.S. 339 (1960).

The process defect theory sees suspect classification doctrine as a roundabout way of uncovering unconstitutional motive by suspecting those classifications that disadvantage groups we know to be the object of widespread vilification. But by only suspecting laws that classify by race on their face or are the result of overtly self-conscious racial motivation, the theory stops an important step short of locating and eliminating the defect it has identified. Where a society has recently adopted a moral ethic that repudiates racial disadvantaging for its own sake, governmental decisionmakers are as likely to repress their racial motives as they are to lie to courts or to attempt after-the-fact rationalizations of classifications that are not racial on their face but that do have disproportionate racial impact. Unconscious aversion to a group that has historically been vilified distorts the political process no less than a conscious decision to place race hatred before politically legitimate goals.

* * *

The Stigma Theory

A second theory posits elimination of racially stigmatizing actions as the central concern of the equal protection clause. Under this theory, racial classifications should be strictly scrutinized when they operate to shame and degrade a class of persons by labeling it as inferior. Stigmatization is the process by which the dominant group in society differentiates itself from others by setting them apart, treating them as less than fully human, denying them acceptance by the organized community, and excluding them from participating in that community as equals. * * *

The prevention of stigma was at the core of the Supreme Court's unanimous declaration in *Brown v. Board of Education* that segregated public schools are inherently unequal. In observing that the segregation of black pupils "generates a feeling of inferiority as to their status in the community," Chief Justice Warren recognized what a majority of the Court had ignored almost sixty years earlier in *Plessy v. Ferguson:* The social meaning of racial segregation in the United States is the designation of a superior and an inferior caste, and segregation proceeds "on the ground that colored citizens are * * * inferior and degraded."

Stigmatizing actions harm the individual in two ways: They inflict psychological injury by assaulting a person's self-respect and human dignity, and they brand the individual with a sign that signals her inferior status to others and designates her as an outcast. The stigma theory recognizes the importance of both self-esteem and the respect of others for participating in society's benefits and responsibilities.

* * *

The injury of stigmatization consists of forcing the injured individual to wear a badge or symbol that degrades him in the eyes of society. But in most cases the symbol is not inherently pejorative. Rather, the message obtains its shameful meaning from the historical and cultural context in which it is used and, ultimately, from the way it is interpreted by those who witness it. Thus the woman who is asked to use a separate public bathroom from her husband is unlikely to be stigmatized by that action: Our society does not ordinarily interpret sex-segregated toilet facilities as designating the inferiority of women. By contrast, the black who is asked to use a different public bathroom from that of a white companion of the same gender is stigmatized. * * * [R]acially segregated bathrooms were an important part of the system of segregation. That system's ideology held not only that blacks were less than fully human but also that they were dirty and impure. Racially segregated bathrooms ensured that blacks would not contaminate the facilities used by whites.

If stigmatizing actions injure by virtue of the meaning society gives them, then it should be apparent that the evil intent of their authors, while perhaps sufficient, is not necessary to the infliction of the injury. For example, a well-meaning if misguided white employer, having observed that her black employees usually sat together at lunch, might build a separate dining room for them with the intent of making them more comfortable. This action would stigmatize her black employees despite her best intentions. Similarly, when the city of Jackson, Mississippi closed its public pools after a federal court ordered it to integrate them, the action stigmatized blacks regardless of whether the government's purpose was racial or economic.

Given that stigma occurs whether there is racial animus or not, the answer to our initial question, "Is knowledge about the intent of the governmental actor significant to the achievement of the equal protection clause's purpose?" would seem an obvious "No." But many of the stigma theory's advocates find themselves in a quandary when faced with the question of how the Court should approach laws that are not apparently "race-dependent" but that result in disparate and stigmatizing effects. * * *

* * * Paul Brest, having persuasively argued the need to eliminate racially disproportionate impact that stigmatizes, cautions that the impact doctrine "cannot reasonably be applied across the board" and urges that the doctrine be used "selectively."[168] He warns that "remedies for disproportionate impact may impose heavy costs on institutions and individuals, and cannot be tailored narrowly to compensate all those and only those whose present situation is the result of past discrimination." Brest's reference to the overbreadth of remedies for disproportionate impact adds to the general concern about unduly limiting legislative discretion and the particular concern about the legitimacy of courts imposing costs on "blameless" individuals and conferring benefits on those who have not been directly harmed.

The consideration of unconscious intent responds to both of these concerns. Identifying stigmatizing actions that were affected by the

168. [Brest, *Foreword: In Defense of the*   L.Rev. 1 (1976).]
Antidiscrimination Principle, 90 Harv.

actor's unconscious racial attitudes achieves two benefits. First, it significantly decreases the absolute number of impact cases subject to heightened scrutiny without eviscerating the substantive content of the equal protection clause. The bridge toll, the sales tax, and the filing fee can no longer be numbered among the parade of horribles that Justice White suggested in [*Washington v.*] *Davis.*[171] At the same time, cases where racially discriminatory impact results directly from past intentional discrimination or from current but unprovable racial animus will be well within judicial reach. A law does not stigmatize blacks simply because exclusion itself is stigmatizing, and, in this instance, they are disproportionately represented among the excluded group. Instead, the stigma stems at least in part from society's predisposition to exclude blacks. The fact that unconscious racial attitudes affected a governmental action is evidence that the racially stigmatizing symbolism preexisted the present impact.

Second, consideration of unconscious motivation provides a neutral principle for judicial intervention—i.e., the identification of a process defect. This counters the argument made against the impact test that the judiciary has no principled basis for imposing a priority for the removal of racial stigma over other social goods to which the political branch might choose to give preeminence. In short, stigma often occurs regardless of the intent of those who have engaged in the stigmatizing action. Thus, it is arguable that under the stigma theory neither conscious nor unconscious intent should be considered, and heightened judicial scrutiny should apply in all cases when governmental action produces a stigmatizing effect. Nonetheless, recognizing unconscious racism provides a mechanism for effectively responding to continuing race-based inequalities while minimizing the costs of judicial overreaching.

[In the concluding portion of his article Lawrence deals with the most obvious objection to his theory: how courts can identify cases where unconscious racism is operating. He proposes that we should look not at individual actions but at the "cultural meaning" of allegedly discriminatory acts as the best evidence of the collective unconscious. This test would evaluate governmental conduct to see whether it conveys a symbolic message to which the culture attaches racial significance. If it does, the court should apply heightened scrutiny.

[For example, the building of a wall between white and black communities in *Memphis v. Greene* [a] has a cultural meaning because of the long history of whites separating themselves from blacks as a symbol of superiority. It would not matter that individual members of the city council were unconscious of their failure to empathize with how blacks felt.

[Lawrence stresses that the task of interpreting cultural meaning is not foreign to courts. In Establishment Clause cases the courts decide

---

171. [426 U.S. 229, 248 & n. 14 (1976).]   **a.** 451 U.S. 100, 101 S.Ct. 1584, 67 L.Ed.2d 769 (1981).

whether a practice advances religion by asking what meaning we attach to a practice—*e.g.* a Christmas creche. In sex discrimination cases the courts ask whether laws tend to perpetuate a "stereotyped view" of men and women—*e.g.* as breadwinners and homemakers. Lawrence argues that the task he sets for the judiciary in race cases would not be essentially different.]

JOHN HART ELY, FACILITATING THE REPRESENTATION OF MINORITIES

Democracy and Distrust 145–46, 148–61 (1980).

[In the opening part of the chapter from which this selection is drawn Ely argues that the Equal Protection Clause is primarily concerned with the process by which the government allocates various harms and benefits. This means that the constitutionality of any particular allocation will depend in part on why it was undertaken—*i.e.* on the motives of the actors involved. Ely notes, however, that the courts have generally been reluctant to inquire into legislative or administrative motivation.

[Ely then turns to the doctrine of "suspect classifications." He contends that the real point of this doctrine is to serve as a handmaiden of motivation analysis.]

The [suspect classification and motivation] doctrines support each other in this way. The goal the classification in issue is likely to fit most closely, obviously, is the goal the legislators actually had in mind. If it can be directly identified and is one that is unconstitutional, all well and good: the classification is unconstitutional. But even if such a confident demonstration of motivation proves impossible, a classification that in fact was unconstitutionally motivated will nonetheless—thanks to the indirect pressure exerted by the suspect-classification doctrine—find itself in serious constitutional difficulty. For an unconstitutional goal obviously cannot be invoked in a statute's defense. That means, where the real goal was unconstitutional, that the goal that fits the classification best will not be invocable in its defense, and the classification will have to be defended in terms of others to which it relates more tenuously. Where the requirement is simply the Court's standard call for a "rational" relation between classification and goal, that will seldom matter: even if the goal the classification fits best is disabled from invocation, there will likely be other permissible goals whose relation to the classification is sufficiently close to be called rational. The "special scrutiny" that is afforded suspect classifications, however, insists that the classification in issue fit the goal invoked in its defense more closely than any alternative classification would. There is only one goal the classification is likely to fit *that* closely, however, and that is the goal the legislators actually had in mind. If that goal cannot be invoked because it is unconstitutional, the classification will fall. Thus, functionally, special scrutiny, in particular its demand for an essentially perfect fit, turns out to be a way of "flushing out" unconstitutional motivation, one that lacks the proof problems of a more direct inquiry and into the bargain permits courts (and complainants) to be more politic, to invalidate (or attack) something for illicit motivation without having to come right out and say that's what they're doing.

* * *

During the Warren era, the Supreme Court was quite adventurous in expanding the set of suspect classifications beyond the core case of race. Laws classifying to the comparative disadvantage of aliens, persons of "illegitimate" birth, even poor people, were all at one time or another approached as suspect. The Burger Court has also paid lip service to the general idea. In fact Justice Blackmun was the first ever—apart, of course, from Justice Stone's original *Carolene Products* footnote [a]—to indicate in an Opinion of the Court that "discrete and insular" minorities are entitled to special constitutional protection from the political process. However, the Burger Court's performance on this score has not matched its rhetoric. Since he came on the Court, Justice Rehnquist has been campaigning to reduce the set of suspect classifications to race and "its first cousin," national origin, and his campaign seems to be succeeding. * * *

The reason Justice Rehnquist gives for wanting to cut the list back to race and national origin is one allegedly grounded in original intent, that those are the classifications the framers of the Fourteenth Amendment would have wanted to subject to unusual scrutiny. * * * The justice thinks he sees a family resemblance between national origin and race, but classifications aren't really the same thing as people and it takes a theory to make one classification the "first cousin" of another. It's true, only "racelike" classifications should be regarded as suspect, but we have to figure out what "racelike" should mean in this context.

It's probably because Court and commentator alike have failed here, at the level of theory, that Justice Rehnquist is steadily gaining his way. Factors are frequently mentioned in the literature that in an intuitive way do seem to have something to do with the point—and on further analysis we'll see that in oblique ways some of them do—but somehow none is quite capable of convincing us that it *is* the point. Thus, for example, it is often said that the immutability of the classifying trait ought to make a classification suspect. * * * [But] no one has bothered to * * * tell us exactly *why* we should be suspicious of legislatures that classify on the basis of immutable characteristics. Surely one has to feel sorry for a person disabled by something that he or she can't do anything about, but I'm not aware of any reason to suppose that elected officials are unusually unlikely to share that feeling. Moreover, classifi-

a. In *United States v. Carolene Products,* 304 U.S. 144, 152 n. 4 (1938), Justice Stone suggested in dictum that "prejudice against discrete and insular minorities may be a special condition, which tends seriously to curtail the operation of those political processes ordinarily to be relied upon to protect minorities, and which may call for a correspondingly more searching judicial inquiry."

cations based on physical disability and intelligence are typically accept-ed as legitimate, even by judges and commentators who assert that immutability is relevant. The explanation, when one is given, is that *those* characteristics (unlike the one the commentator is trying to render suspect) are often relevant to legitimate purposes. At that point there's not much left of the immutability theory, is there?

A number of commentaries, purporting to find support in *Brown v. Board of Education,* argue that classifications disfavoring racial minori-ties are suspect because they "will usually be perceived as a stigma of inferiority and a badge of opprobrium." This confuses two issues and thus misreads *Brown.* Feelings of opprobrium *are* relevant to determin-ing whether a classification the state claims is "harmless," such as "separate but equal" schooling, in fact inflicts harm on one or the other class. But *Brown* was unusual in that respect: the existence of compar-ative harm to one of the classes distinguished by a governmental classification is rarely an issue. Neither can the idea be that the presence of stigma is necessary in order to establish some requisite *amount* of harm. That account would make sense if the Court followed the practice of reviewing more strenuously those distinctions that hurt more, which it doesn't. A taxation distinction worth $1,000,000 receives about the same review as one worth $100—that is, virtually none.

An account that seems more to the point, one to which I've alluded several times, is that attributed to Justice Stone's *Carolene Products* footnote and recently paraphrased for the Court * * * by Justice Black-mun: "Aliens as a class are a prime example of a 'discrete and insular' minority * * * for whom * * * heightened judicial solicitude is appropri-ate * * * " [59] * * * In a sense the complainant in every case speaks for such a group: he wouldn't be in court if the class in which the legislature had placed him had not been, on at least one occasion, a political minority (they lost), both discrete (they're the ones on the disfavored side of the statutory line) and insular (they couldn't gather enough allies to defeat the legislation). But obviously that isn't what Justice Stone meant. His reference was rather to the sort of "pluralist" wheeling and dealing by which the various minorities that make up our society typically interact to protect their interests, and constituted an attempt to denote those minorities for which such a system of "mutual defense pacts" will prove recurrently unavailing.

* * *

* * * [T]hough the general idea here may be clear enough—courts should protect those who can't protect themselves politically—the justifi-cation for it isn't. In a way it is of the essence of democracy to allow the various persons and groups that make up our society to decide which others they wish to combine with in shaping legislation. We are not all the same in all respects, and on certain subjects our interests in fact do differ substantially. There is thus no way to exclude a priori—as the

59. Graham v. Richardson, 403 U.S. 365, 372 (1971).

theory as elaborated so far does—the possibility that there may exist groups or interests with which others will refuse to combine politically for perfectly respectable reasons.

An added element is therefore needed, that the minority in question be one that is barred from the pluralist's bazaar, and thus keeps finding itself on the wrong end of the legislature's classifications, for reasons that in some sense are discreditable. Standard renditions of what we think of as the *Carolene Products* approach, such as the one by Justice Blackmun quoted above, do not include this element: "discrete and insular minorities" are simply entitled to "heightened judicial solicitude." Justice Stone's original, however, was richer than this, indicating that *"prejudice against discrete and insular minorities* may be a special condition, which tends to curtail the operation of those political processes ordinarily to be relied upon to protect minorities * * *." Now "prejudice" is a mushword in its own right, one we shall have to clarify, but it does supply the element that is missing in the usual rendition. For whatever else it may or may not be, prejudice is a lens that distorts reality. We are a nation of minorities and our system thus depends on the ability and willingness of various groups to apprehend those overlapping interests that can bind them into a majority on a given issue; prejudice blinds us to overlapping interests that in fact exist. As Frank Goodman put it so well eight years ago: "Race prejudice divides groups that have much in common (blacks and poor whites) and unites groups (white, rich and poor) that have little else in common than their antagonism for the racial minority. Race prejudice, in short, provides the 'majority of the whole' with that 'common motive to invade the rights of other citizens' that Madison believed improbable in a pluralistic society." [63]

Switching the principal perspective thus, from the purely political to one that focuses more on the psychology of decision, possesses the additional virtue of relating rather directly to what we found to be the functional significance of a theory of suspect classifications, one of flushing out unconstitutional motivations. "Prejudice" has a lot to do with that; discreteness and insularity don't seem to (except derivatively, to the extent that they are likely to reflect and engender prejudiced behavior). That connection also puts us in a position to begin to specify the meanings of prejudice relevant in this context. If the doctrine of suspect classifications is a roundabout way of uncovering official attempts to inflict inequality for its own sake—to treat a group worse not in the service of some overriding social goal but largely for the sake of simply disadvantaging its members—it would seem to follow that one set of classifications we should treat as suspicious are those that disadvantage groups we know to be the object of widespread vilification, groups we know others (specifically those who control the legislative process) might wish to injure.

63. Goodman, [*De Facto School Segregation: A Constitutional and Empirical*   *Analysis,* 60 Calif.L.Rev. 275, 315 (1972).]

Note that the inquiry suggested is not whether there exists *unjustified* widespread hostility toward the group disadvantaged by the official act in issue—that would constitute a straightforward invitation to second-guess the legislative judgment—but simply whether there exists widespread hostility. There is a good deal of discretion in that inquiry too, of course, and courts must be scrupulous not simply to legislate there either. Later on I shall suggest a refinement that should help bridle the inquiry. For the moment, though, it may help to recall that all that labeling a classification "suspect" means functionally is that a prima facie case has been made out and that the inquiry into its suspiciousness should continue. If it turns out directly to pursue a substantial goal (other than the impermissible one of simply disadvantaging those it disadvantages), it will survive. Thus, for example, burglars are certainly a group toward which there is widespread societal hostility, and laws making burglary a crime certainly do comparatively disadvantage burglars. Such laws plainly should survive, however. There is so patently a substantial goal here, that of protecting our homes by penalizing those who break and enter them, and the fit between that goal and the classification is so close, that whatever suspicion such a classification might under other circumstances engender is allayed so immediately it doesn't even have time to register.

Although there is more to be said about what factors properly give rise to suspicion, we have reached a point where the appeal (and limitations) of a reference to the immutability of the classifying characteristic can begin to be put in perspective. A law making burglary a crime is not suspicious—or, if you prefer, the suspicion is immediately allayed—because the goal of making life unpleasant for burglars is immediately translatable into the goal of discouraging people from breaking into our homes. It would not make sense, however, to defend a law disadvantaging blacks on the ground that we are trying to discourage people from being black. The ability to frame the point of a classification harming (or subsidizing) a certain group in terms of a desire to discourage people from joining (or encourage people to join) that group obviously depends on the mutability of the characteristic that forms the basis of classification. We shouldn't go overboard and conclude that classification on the basis of an immutable characteristic is always suspicious: that would follow only if increasing or decreasing the incidence of the classifying characteristic were the only legitimate governmental end. Forbidding blind people to pilot airplanes will do little to encourage eyesight, but such a prohibition will obviously stand nonetheless, since the classification fits perfectly a different goal, one I need hardly argue is important. Immutability thus cannot be the talisman that some have tried to make it, but it isn't entirely irrelevant either, since classifications geared to characteristics it is not within the power of the individual to change will not be amenable to immediate and innocent explanation in terms of altering the classifying characteristic's incidence.

An account mentioned with increasing frequency, and indeed it does seem more to the point, is that classifications rooted in "stereotypes" should be regarded as suspicious. Stated this way, without elaboration, it cannot do. The dictionary tells us that a stereotype is "a fixed or conventional notion or conception, as of a person, group, idea, etc., held by a number of people, and allowing for no individuality * * *." Legislation on the basis of "stereotype" is thus legislation by generalization, the use of a classification believed in statistical terms to be generally valid without leaving room for proof of individual deviation. That, however, is the way legislation ordinarily proceeds, as in most cases it must. * * *

* * * If the concept is to provide us with anything beyond a basis for begging questions, it has to be refined, so as to separate, if you will, the acceptable stereotypes from the unacceptable. The approach that may initially seem most attractive would be to treat as suspicious those stereotypical generalizations to which there exist unusually high numbers or percentages of counterexamples. * * * It won't work, though; generalizations cannot be intelligibly evaluated simply in terms of the number or percentage of false-positives they entail. Sometimes, as in the case of capital punishment, any nontrivial incidence of counterexample would be intolerable. Other times, as where we are trying to keep those susceptible to heart attacks from piloting commercial airliners, a quite high percentage, surely sometimes more than half, is entirely appropriate. A determination of the acceptable incidence of counterexample must therefore involve, at a minimum, a comparison of the costs to those "wrongfully" excluded or included with the costs to the rest of us, sometimes in time and money but often also in increased risk, of trying to tune the system more finely. A mode of review geared to whether the incidence of counterexample is "too high" is thus indistinguishable from the unacceptable theory that courts should intervene in the name of the Constitution whenever they disagree with the cost-benefit balance the legislature has struck.

* * * The cases where we ought to be suspicious are not those involving a generalization whose incidence of counterexample is "too high," but rather those involving a generalization whose incidence of counterexample is significantly higher than the legislative authority appears to have thought it was. No matter how many considerations may have entered into the cost-benefit balance, a misapprehension regarding the incidence of counterexample (or for that matter the cost of individualized determination) will have distorted the entire decision. Just as we would want reconsidered any important decision that was made under the influence of an erroneous assumption about the relevant facts, so should we here. * * *

The rub comes in how the Court should go about identifying such situations. Just leaving it to their gestalt judgment seems obviously unacceptable, too close to simply handing over an unbridled power of substantive review. (I am not suggesting bad faith here, but a justice whose instinct is to disagree with the legislative cost-benefit balance is likely in all good faith to suppose the legislature "must have" overestimated the statistical validity of the generalization on the basis of which it appears to have acted.) The Court should therefore look not simply to the legislative product here, but to the process that generated it, to see whether it can identify some factor or factors that suggest the likelihood of such legislative misapprehension. * * *

In deciding how much presumptive credit to extend a given generalization in our everyday lives, we would want to know where it came from—who came up with it and whether it is one that serves their interests. This commonsense insight, again tempered with others, seems relevant to the constitutional inquiry as well. The choice between classifying on the basis of a comparative generalization and attempting to come up with a more discriminating formula always involves balancing the increase in fairness that greater individualization will produce against the added costs it will entail. Where the generalization involved is one that serves the interests of the decision-makers, however, certain dangers that are inherent in any balancing process are significantly intensified. Where it tangibly enhances their fortunes, the dangers may be most obvious—on the one hand that the costs of treating others as they are treating themselves are likely to be overestimated, and on the other that the validity of the generalization being proffered as the basis of classification is likely to be overestimated, thus resulting in an underevaluation of the interest in individual fairness. But even where no tangible gain can be identified, there are psychic rewards in self-flattering generalizations. * * *

Thus generalizations to the effect, say, that whites in general are smarter or more industrious than blacks, men more stable emotionally than women, or native-born Americans more patriotic than Americans born elsewhere, are likely to go down pretty easily—and in fact we know they have—with groups whose demography is that of the typical American legislature. Few will suppose there aren't counterexamples, but the overall validity of such a generalization is likely to be quite readily accepted. By seizing upon the positive myths about the groups to which they belong and the negative myths about those to which they don't, or for that matter the realities respecting some or most members of the two classes, legislators, like the rest of us, are likely to assume too readily that not many of "them" will be unfairly deprived, nor many of "us" unfairly benefited, by a classification of this type. Generalizations of the opposite sort, which attribute superiority to a group to which most legislators do not belong—say, that blacks are better basketball players or that Jews are better students—are a different matter. A generalization of this sort may occasionally find grudging acceptance, but here we can be sure that the imperfect, statistical nature of the claim will be well appreciated, and in addition that there will be explanations—in both these examples, that it has to do with "the way they are brought up"—that will prevail in the legislature to assure an individualized test or at least that the statutory presumption will be rebuttable. A statutory distinction built on a comparison of the qualifications of optometrists and opticians occupies an in-between position, since neither of the groups being compared is one to which most of the legislators belong. Such a law—and most legislative classifications are of this "they-they" contour—may lack the special safeguard that a self-deprecating generalization seems to provide, but it also lacks the unusual dangers of self-serving generalization and is consequently correctly classified as constitutionally unsuspicious.

We have seen already how the mutability of the classifying characteristic will often render a classification immediately defensible in terms of a legitimate social goal and thus allay any incipient suspicion. We are now in a position to understand how mutability (or something like it) may be relevant in another way as well, one that bears on the likelihood that the decision-maker's ability to generalize will be distorted by his or her perspective. For example it is at least arguable that the facts that all of us once were young, and most expect one day to be fairly old, should neutralize whatever suspicion we might otherwise entertain respecting the multitude of laws (enacted by predominantly middle-aged legislatures) that comparatively advantage those between, say, 21 and 65 vis-à-vis those who are younger or older. It is not quite the same thing as immutability, of course: alienage generally is an escapable condition, so in theory are poverty and perhaps even gender. But nonetheless, and it is this that seems more relevant, most legislators have never been alien, poor, or female. They all were young, though, a fact that may enhance their objectivity about just what the difference entails.

One can empathize without having been there, though, and at this point a reference to discreteness and insularity reasserts its relevance. Though theoretically indefensible in its usual free-standing form, it can quite sensibly augment and qualify an approach geared to the distorting effect of perspective. To render the concept useful, though, we have to recognize and break apart its two components, the political and the social. Political access is surely important, but (so long as it falls short of majority control) it cannot alone protect a group against the first type of prejudice we examined, out-and-out hostility, nor will it even serve effectively to correct the subtler self-aggrandizing biases of the majority. If voices and votes are all we're talking about, prejudices can easily survive (and even on occasion be exacerbated): other groups may just continue to refuse to deal, and the minority in question may just continue to be outvoted. Discreteness and insularity have a social component as well, however—of course the two will often go hand in hand—and it is that component that seems more relevant to the amelioration of cooperation-blocking prejudice. Increased social intercourse is likely not only to diminish the hostility that often accompanies unfamiliarity, but also to rein somewhat our tendency to stereotype in ways that exaggerate the superiority of those groups to which we belong. The more we get to know people who are different in some ways, the more we will begin to appreciate the ways in which they are not, which is the beginning of political cooperation.

BRUCE A. ACKERMAN, BEYOND
CAROLENE PRODUCTS
98 Harv.L.Rev. 713, 713–715, 717–739 (1985).

I. THE PROMISE OF *CAROLENE PRODUCTS*

*"[P]rejudice against discrete and insular minorities may be a special condition * * * curtail[ing] the operation of those political processes ordinarily to be relied upon to protect minorities, and [so] may call for a correspondingly more searching judicial inquiry."* [1]

These famous words, appearing in the otherwise unimportant *Carolene Products* case, came at a moment of extraordinary vulnerability for the Supreme Court. They were written in 1938. The Court was just beginning to dig itself out of the constitutional debris left by its wholesale capitulation to the New Deal a year before. With the decisive triumph of the activist welfare state over the Old Court, an entire world of constitutional meanings, laboriously built up over two generations, had come crashing down upon the Justices' heads. Indeed, the Court had been so politically discredited by its constitutional defense of laissez-faire capitalism that it was hardly obvious whether *any* firm ground remained upon which to rebuild the institution of judicial review. How, then, to begin the work of reconstruction?

* * *

* * * *Carolene* promises relief from the problem of legitimacy raised whenever nine elderly lawyers invalidate the legislative decisions of a majority of our elected representatives. The *Carolene* solution is to seize the high ground of democratic theory and establish that the challenged legislation was produced by a profoundly defective process. By demonstrating that the legislative decision itself resulted from an undemocratic procedure, a *Carolene* court hopes to reverse the spin of the countermajoritarian difficulty. For it now may seem that the original legislative decision, not the judicial invalidation, suffers the greater legitimacy deficit.

* * *

* * * I shall argue, however, that the *Carolene* formula cannot withstand close scrutiny.

* * *

To demonstrate the need for doctrinal reorientation, I shall examine separately each of *Carolene*'s four operative terms: (1) prejudice, (2) discrete, (3) insular, and (4) minorities. It is by means of these four terms that *Carolene* hopes to identify groups that have been unconstitutionally deprived of their fair share of democratic influence. * * *

----

1. United States v. Carolene Prods. Co., 304 U.S. 144, 152 n. 4 (1938). * * *

II. Discrete and Insular *Minorities?*

* * *

A.   *The Principle of Minority Acquiescence*

* * * [M]inorities are *supposed* to lose in a democratic system—even when they want very much to win and even when they think (as they often will) that the majority is deeply wrong in ignoring their just complaints.   This principle—call it the principle of minority acquiescence—is absolutely central to democratic theory.   Of course, a minority may not be denied its right to participate within a democratic framework.   Although it must acquiesce in current legislative decisions, it is fully entitled to use all its political resources to induce a future legislative majority to accede to its demands.   But *Carolene* promises minorities more than formal rights: it asserts that they are sometimes entitled to demand substantive victory now, not merely the chance of victory later.

The problem this promise raises is all the more acute because *Carolene* refuses to accept the solution that countless others have embraced.   It is easy to solve the problem of majority rule by positing the existence of minority rights that are so fundamental as to trump the value of democratic rule itself.   Indeed, as the *Carolene* Court was well aware, it is *too* easy to solve the problem in this way.   Faced with the political repudiation of *Lochner*'s natural rights jurisprudence, the Court was determined to build another foundation for the protection of minority rights: why not redefine the concept of democracy itself in a way that would support the notion that minorities *do* have a right to win some of the time?

B.   *The Pluralist Solution*

While the courts speak vaguely of "those political processes ordinarily relied upon to protect minorities," generations of American political scientists have filled in the picture of pluralist democracy presupposed by *Carolene*'s distinctive argument for minority rights.   According to this familiar view, it is a naive mistake to speak of democracy as if it involved rule by a single, well-defined majority over a coherent and constant minority.   Instead, normal American politics is pluralistic: myriad pressure groups, each typically representing a fraction of the population, bargain with one another for mutual support.

Once this picture of pluralistic politics is accepted, the stage has been set for the rehabilitation of *Carolene*'s concern with ineffective minorities.   We may now find that there is something about certain minority groups—call them *Carolene* or *C*-groups—that makes it especially difficult for them to strike bargains with potential coalition partners.   As a consequence, *C*-groups will find themselves in politically ascendant coalitions much less often than will otherwise comparable groups.   Over time, then, *C*-groups will achieve less than their "fair share" of influence upon legislation.   And it is for this reason, the pluralist concludes, that *Carolene* rightly suggests that judicial protection for *C*-groups can be defended in a manner responsive to the countermajoritarian difficulty afflicting judicial review.   By intervening on behalf of *C*-groups, a *Carolene* court merely produces the substantive outcomes that the *C*-group would have obtained through politics if it had not been so systematically disadvantaged in the ongoing process of pluralist bargaining.

* * *

* * * In the common legal understanding, *Carolene* is generally taken to imply that the same level of strict judicial scrutiny should apply to legislation affecting each and every *C*-group. But the pluralist model cannot justify such a uniform judicial approach.

Consider, for example, an American constituency that includes 12 percent blacks and .5 percent Jehovah's Witnesses among its population. Doubtless, both groups will be encouraged by the pluralist vision of democracy, since it suggests that neither group will inexorably be excluded from the pluralist bazaar. Nonetheless, it should be plain that these two groups have absolutely no reason to find the prospect of pluralist bargaining *equally* gratifying. To the contrary, the fact that blacks greatly outnumber Witnesses is bound to play an important role in any plausible bargaining theory. Thus, even if the two groups could somehow be compensated for their *Carolene* disadvantages, the Witnesses could not reasonably expect to win substantive victories nearly as often as the blacks.

To put the point more generally, a bargaining approach to *Carolene* does not suggest that each *C*-group has a right to be treated identically to all other *C*-groups in the legislative process. Instead, the decisive thought-experiment should involve the comparison of a particular *C*-group with a hypothetical minority that I shall call an unencumbered or *U*-group. In each comparison, the relevant *U*-group should be supposed to contain the same proportion of the population as the *C*-group that invokes the Court's protection; the *U*-group differs, however, in that it is unencumbered by the bargaining disadvantages that unconstitutionally burden the *C*-group. Thus, the *Carolene* question for blacks entails a comparative analysis of the bargaining expectations of a 12 percent minority unencumbered by those structural impediments that unconstitutionally impair blacks' bargaining position in the ongoing pluralist process, while the question for Jehovah's Witnesses involves a comparison with a much smaller *U*-group.

Such thought-experiments will most naturally result in a sliding scale of *Carolene* concern. On one end of the scale are groups consisting of ineffective majorities or very large minorities that find themselves disadvantaged in the political process by some constitutionally impermissible barrier to bargaining. In cases involving these "major minorities," a court can be quite confident that a comparable *U*-group would have a decisive impact on the terms of pluralistic legislation. In the middle of the *Carolene* scale are "middling minorities" in the 10 to 20 percent range. Here there is less reason for a court to expect that a *U*-group of comparable size would radically change the terms of political trade, though its influence would be very substantial in many plausible contexts. And finally, on the other end of the scale, there are groups so small as to elicit little solicitude from courts concerned with correcting the failures of democratic bargaining. When faced with "minor minorities" of .01 percent, for example, a judge might well be unmoved by the enumeration of *Carolene* factors that would generate substantial concern in the case of middling minorities, not to mention major minorities. For the fact is that a *U*-group of .01 percent has little to expect from a democratic political process, unless it is very lucky, or exceptionally adept, in the bargaining process. This point is essential to the responsible elaboration of *Carolene Products*—whose promise, be it recalled, is to permit courts to evade the thrust of the countermajoritarian difficulty by appealing over the heads of real-world legislatures to the hypothetical outcomes of a purified democratic process.

There is, then, an inevitably uneasy relationship between *Carolene*'s pluralist approach to democracy and the judicial protection of minority rights. The tension reaches the breaking point in the proverbial case of a minority of one: when the solitary citizen, having little to expect from pluralist bargaining, challenges the invasion of his fundamental rights by the normal political process.

My aim here, though, is to work out the doctrinal implications of the *Carolene* formula rather than to criticize its foundations. So let us focus our attention upon those groups, ranging from middling minorities to encumbered majorities, whose role in the bargaining process might well have a significant impact on the ongoing stream of legislative decisions. How does *Carolene* propose to determine whether a group suffers from severe enough bargaining disadvantages to merit special protection? In other words, how are we supposed to distinguish a *C*-group from a *U*-group?

III. DISCRETE AND *INSULAR* MINORITIES?

* * *

* * * Other things being equal, "discreteness and insularity" will normally be a source of enormous bargaining advantage, not disadvantage, for a group engaged in pluralist American politics. Except for special cases, the concerns that underlie *Carolene* should lead judges to protect groups that possess the opposite characteristics from the ones *Carolene* emphasizes—groups that are "anonymous and diffuse" rather than "discrete and insular." It is these groups that both political science and American history indicate are systematically disadvantaged in a pluralist democracy.

A. The Free–Rider Problem

To see my point, start with insularity and consider a thought-experiment suggested by the previous argument. Imagine two groups, *I* and *D*, of equal size (say each accounts for 12 percent of the population). The members of one group, the *I*'s, are distributed in an insular way, concentrated in a single massive island within the sea of American life; the *D*'s, on the other hand, are diffused evenly throughout the sea. Is it really so clear that, by virtue of their diffusion throughout American life, the *D*'s will gain systematic advantages over the *I*'s in the normal course of pluralist politics?

Hardly. To begin with the basics, a political interest gains a great advantage if its proponents can form a well-organized lobby to press their cause in the corridors of power. Yet the construction of a pressure group is no easy task. The main obstacle is the familiar free-rider problem. Simply because a person would find his interests advanced by the formation of a pressure group, it does not follow that he will spend his own scarce time and energy on political organization. On the contrary, from each individual's selfish viewpoint, abstaining from interest-group activity is a "heads-I-win-tails-you-lose" proposition. If only a few people adopt the do-nothing strategy, the do-nothings will free-ride on the successful lobbying effort of others. If free-riding becomes pervasive, things will not improve much if a single member of the group adds his money and time to the floundering political effort. Either way, it pays for a selfish person to remain a free rider even if he has a lot to gain from concerted lobbying. For this reason, many interests remain ineffectively organized even in pressure-group America. How, then, does a minority's insularity affect the probability that it will break through the free-rider barrier and achieve organizational effectiveness?

Far from being a patent disadvantage, insularity can help *I*-groups in at least four different ways[.] * * *

First, insularity will help breed sentiments of group solidarity. Given an *I*'s daily immersion in social realities that reaffirm his group identity, the typical *I* will conceive his *I*-ness as something much more than an incidental fact about himself. Instead, *I*-ness will serve as a fundamental feature of self-identity—one that will encourage each *I* to view the political activities of the group from a perspective that transcends the purely instrumental. Thus, when a black or a Jew gives $25 to the NAACP or the Anti–Defamation League, he is not merely, or even principally, gambling that his small bit of money will perceptibly increase his chance of enjoying the fruits of future lobbying victories. Rather, the contribution is a means by which the donor can symbolize the seriousness of his own commitment to his *I*-ness. By contributing to the group cause, I demonstrate to myself, as well as others, that I am serious about the values I profess to hold. Here, at last, is one commodity—group identification—that is immune from the free-rider problem: for if I do not give even a few dollars to the group cause, can I plausibly say, even to myself, that I take my *I*-ness seriously?

But insularity * * * also aids the *I*-group in a second way by providing it with a new range of social sanctions to impose upon would-be free riders. An *I* who refuses to contribute to his interest group cannot expect this fact to be kept secret from his fellow *I*'s—news travels fast along the grapevine in an insular community. * * * In contrast, a member of a diffuse *D*-group need not suffer such severe dislocation in order to avoid the disapproval of his fellow group members. Instead, he may insulate himself from their displeasure by assimilating into the majoritarian mainstream—undoubtedly a costly process, but typically less costly than the social stigma heaped on the free-riding *I*. * * *

B. Organizational Costs

It follows, then, that the average *I* is more likely to contribute his time and money to the group cause than is an otherwise comparable *D*. Yet this conclusion tells only half the story: not only will an *I*-group receive more resources from its constituency, but *I*'s will also find it cheaper to organize themselves for effective political action. First, the dense communications network generated by insularity dramatically reduces one of the heaviest costs involved in effective political lobbying: the cost of communicating with a mass membership. To get its messages out to its constituency, an insular political group can often avail itself of the communications channels already established by the group's churches, businesses, or labor unions. In contrast, a *D*-group must somehow locate and reach people who interact with one another much less frequently and who have fewer channels already established for the cheap transmission of *D*-group concerns.

Second, the organic character of insular life greatly reduces the costs of selecting credible political leaders. The *I*-group can draw upon a pool of people who have already earned the respect of their fellow *I*'s in other communal contexts: ministers and rabbis, successful lawyers, businessmen, union leaders. In contrast, even if *D*-group members manage to overcome the communications barrier, they must often take the risk of selecting political leaders who have not been tested and observed in other leadership settings.

C. Insularity and Congressional Influence

* * *

We have reached a point, however, where it is necessary to introduce an explicitly geographic concept of insularity into the discussion—for the simple reason that geography is of the first importance in assessing a group's influence within the American political system. For present purposes, it will suffice to restrict our speculations to two simple geographic alternatives. On the one hand, our sociologically insular minority might also be geographically insular: concentrated in a relatively small number of places in the United States. On the other hand, geographic insularity might not accompany sociological insularity. Indeed, at the limit, the *I*-group might be evenly spread over the fifty states and 435 congressional districts. For heuristic purposes, let us begin with the alternative that is empirically less common, but analytically more tractable. Suppose that an *I*-group is distributed in a geographically diffuse way: if it contains 12 percent of the national population, it accounts for 12 percent of each congressional district. Now compare this geographically diffuse *I*-group with a *D*-group that is both sociologically and geographically diffuse. Other things being equal, which group is more likely to succeed in influencing Congressmen?

The previous analysis suggests that the *I*-group will probably have greater influence. Such a group is more likely to form a political lobby peopled by credible leaders who remain in close touch with the insular constituency they represent. When such lobbyists threaten a Congressman with electoral retribution, they can expect a respectful hearing. * * * In short, even if the *I*-group is distributed evenly throughout the nation, it has a greater ability to exert political influence through the ultimate currency of democratic politics: votes on election day.

This conclusion is reinforced when we turn to the more realistic case in which the middling *I*-group is distributed very unevenly throughout the country. In this scenario, a middling minority could reasonably expect to be a local majority—or at least a decisive voting bloc—in 20 to 30 congressional districts. For the representatives of these districts, the support of the *I*-group amounts to nothing less than the stuff of political survival. In fact, for all our *Carolene* talk about the powerlessness of insular groups, we are perfectly aware of the enormous power such voting blocs have in American politics. The story of the protective tariff is, I suppose, the classic illustration of insularity's power in American history. Over the past half-century, we have been treated to an enormous number of welfare-state variations on the theme of insularity by the farm bloc, the steel lobby, the auto lobby, and others too numerous to mention. In this standard scenario of pluralistic politics, it is precisely the diffuse character of the majority forced to pay the bill for tariffs, agricultural subsidies, and the like, that allows strategically located Congressmen to deliver the goods to their well-organized local constituents. Given these familiar stories, it is really quite remarkable to hear lawyers profess concern that insular interests have too little influence in Congress. Instead, the American system typically deprives *diffuse* groups of their rightful say over the course of legislative policy. If there is anything to *Carolene Products,* then, it cannot be a minority's insularity, taken by itself—something more must be involved.

IV. *Discrete* and *Insular* Minorities?

Could that something be the "discreteness" of a *Carolene* minority?

I begin with a question because it is not obvious whether most constitutional lawyers endow the word "discrete" with independent significance in their understanding of the *Carolene* doctrine. Nonetheless, we can conceive the term in a way that adds something important to the overall formula. I propose to define a minority as "discrete" when its members are marked out in ways that make it relatively easy for others to identify them. For instance, there is nothing a black woman may plausibly do to hide the fact that she is black or female. Like it or not, she will have to deal with the social expectations and stereotypes generated by her evident group characteristics. In contrast, other minorities are socially defined in ways that give individual members the chance to avoid easy identification. A homosexual, for example, can keep her sexual preference a very private affair and thereby avoid much of the public opprobrium attached to her minority status. It is for this reason that I shall call homosexuals, and groups like them, "anonymous" minorities and contrast them with "discrete" minorities of the kind paradigmatically exemplified by blacks.

* * *

Carolene takes a straightforward position on this question. In its view, discreteness is a political liability. Once again, however, * * * this is not obvious. * * *

* * * If you are a black in America today, you know there is no way you can avoid the impact of the larger public's views about the significance of blackness. Because exit is not possible, there is only one way to do something about disadvantageous racial stereotypes: complain about them. Among efficacious forms of complaint, the possibility of organized political action will surely rank high.

This is not to say, of course, that individual blacks, or members of other discrete minorities, will necessarily lend their support to interest-group activity. They may, instead, succumb to the temptations of free-riding and thus deprive the group of vital political resources. But even if discreteness is no cure-all for selfishness, it does free a minority from the organizational problem confronting an anonymous group of comparable size. To see my point, compare the problem faced by black political organizers with the one confronting organizers of the homosexual community. As a member of an anonymous group, each homosexual can seek to minimize the personal harm due to prejudice by keeping his or her sexual preference a tightly held secret. Although this is hardly a fully satisfactory response, secrecy does enable homosexuals to "exit" from prejudice in a way that blacks cannot. This means that a homosexual group must confront an organizational problem that does not arise for its black counterpart: somehow the group must induce each anonymous homosexual to reveal his or her sexual preference to the larger public and to bear the private costs this public declaration may involve.

* * * So it would seem that *Carolene Products* is wrong again: a court concerned with pluralist bargaining power should be more, not less, attentive to the claims of anonymous minorities than to those of discrete ones.

V. PREJUDICE

But surely it is time to stop playing *Hamlet* without the Prince. The whole point of *Carolene*'s concern with "discrete and insular minorities" cannot be understood, I am sure you are thinking, without grasping the final term of the formula: prejudice. Indeed, it has been one of my aims to provoke precisely this reaction. By detailing all the ways discrete and insular minorities gain political advantage over diffuse and anonymous groups, I have meant to emphasize how heavy a burden the idea of prejudice must carry in the overall argument for *Carolene Products*. The burden is of two kinds: one empirical, the other conceptual. To take them one at a time, I shall defer all problems involved in conceptualizing prejudice so that we may first focus upon the empirical side of the matter.

A. Questions of Fact

Carolene's empirical inadequacy stems from its underinclusive conception of the impact of prejudice upon American society. It is easy to identify groups in the population that are not discrete and insular but that are nonetheless the victims of prejudice, as that term is commonly understood. Thus, the fact that homosexuals are a relatively anonymous minority has not saved the group from severe prejudice. Nor is sexism a nonproblem merely because women are a diffuse, if discrete, majority. Prejudice is generated by a bewildering variety of social conditions. Although some *Carolene* minorities are seriously victimized, they are not the only ones stigmatized; nor is it obvious that all *Carolene* minorities are stigmatized more grievously than any other non-*Carolene* group. Why should the concern with "prejudice" justify *Carolene*'s narrow fixation upon "discrete and insular" minorities?

The answer seemed easy in a world in which members of the paradigmatic *Carolene* minority group—blacks—were effectively barred from voting and political participation. Something is better than nothing: whatever the organizational problems engendered by anonymity and diffuseness, surely they are not nearly so devastating as total disenfranchisement. As we turn toward the future, however, it is far less clear that such selective perception makes constitutional sense. Nonetheless, I shall give *Carolene* the benefit of the doubt by sketching a "pariah" model of the political process in which *Carolene*'s emphasis on the fate of discrete and insular minorities will still seem empirically plausible. As we move beyond the pariah model, however, anonymous or diffuse minorities will increasingly emerge as the groups that can raise the most serious complaints of pluralist disempowerment.

1. The Pariah Model.—Assume a polity in which middling minorities—in the 10 to 20 percent range—attain majority status in a significant number of congressional districts because of the way their insularity interacts with the geographic biases of the American political system. Nonetheless, the minority representatives these groups elect are entirely ineffective in Congress—because all remaining Congressmen refuse to bargain with them in any way. * * *

Sound implausible? * * * Yet it is only by indulging in something like these strong empirical assumptions that *Carolene* can claim that the effects of prejudice *plainly* outweigh the political advantages enjoyed by minorities that are discrete and insular.

2. Beyond the Pariah Model.—Once we deny the general empirical validity of the pariah model, our assessment of the political impact of a discrete and insular group will invariably be more complex. * * *

* * * I turn to a very different approach to *Carolene* presented by John Hart Ely in his important work, *Democracy and Distrust*. Among its many virtues, the book explicitly recognizes that the conventional

Carolene wisdom about the powerlessness of discrete and insular minorities is "in need of some reexamination." Yet Dean Ely does not attempt the interest-group analysis that has thus far engaged our energies. Instead, he relies exclusively on a social-psychological approach to the legislative process. On his view, the critical thing about prejudice is the way it allows legislators to stereotype "discrete and insular" minorities. It is this legislative propensity to divide the world into "we-they" categories that, according to Ely, lies at the core of *Carolene*'s concern: "we" legislators will both overestimate the dangers posed by the "they" group and underestimate its similarities to the "we" group. As a consequence, legislation that disadvantages "they" groups will be based on an intolerably distorted perception of social reality.

Even if we were to accept a "we-they" view of legislative psychology, Ely's failure to recognize the limits of the pariah model serves as an independent ground for questioning his conclusions. Quite simply, our efforts in bargaining theory have led us to expect that "middling minorities" of the "discrete and insular" kind will elect a significant number of Representatives—say 20 to 25—who are extremely responsive to their interests. As long as these politicians are not treated like pariahs, they can become a potent legislative force—trading votes with other legislators to further the objectives of their own constituents. * * * This is more than diffuse or anonymous minorities can expect: *their* representatives may not even *be* at the bargaining table. As soon as he moves beyond the narrow confines of the pariah model, Dean Ely cannot rehabilitate *Carolene*'s exclusive focus on discrete and insular minorities through "we-they" psychology alone.

Dean Ely seems aware of all this. Although *Democracy and Distrust* does not contain a fully developed analysis of minority legislative power, it does hint at an approach different from the one I advance here. Dean Ely suggests that minority politicians may suffer from a distinctive psychological affliction: while other Congressmen act on "we-they" prejudices in favor of their own constituents, minority politicians may accept the very stereotypes they should be challenging. If this point were conceded, Ely's argument would take on a self-sealing quality: no matter how actively minority representatives participated in the bargaining process, they would only reinforce, and never challenge, prevailing prejudices.

Dean Ely shows great restraint in dealing with this suggestion of minority "false consciousness." While he says that "[t]he general idea is one that in some contexts has merit," his book does not, in fact, spend very much space defending and elaborating it. I believe, moreover, that an appeal to "false consciousness" cannot be elaborated in a way that makes constitutional sense.

The first question to ask about "false consciousness" is an empirical one: will the rising generation of minority politicians in fact passively accept debasing stereotypes? I see no reason to project such a grim image upon our future. To the contrary, the classic prejudices are under vigorous challenge by powerful voices emerging from a broad range of discrete and insular communities.   * * *

The second question is: even if some social psychologist could "prove" the existence of false consciousness, should the Supreme Court transform this social phenomenon into an assumption of constitutional law? We are dealing here not with an academic scientific inquiry, but with a question of institutional relationships. In branding minority politicians as victims of "false consciousness" on the pages of the *United States Reports,* the Supreme Court would be consigning them to a peculiarly demeaning constitutional status. Henceforth, they—and they alone—would be deemed constitutionally incapable of discharging the representative functions of democratically elected legislators. Such a declaration would make a mockery of *Carolene*'s promise. Rather than attempting to approximate the results of a perfect pluralist democracy, the Court would be protecting minority rights by emphatically impugning the capacity of these very same minorities to engage in democratic politics at all.

* * *

B. Questions of Value

But *Carolene*'s failure to recognize the political predicament of anonymous or diffuse groups that are victims of prejudice is only half the problem; the other half is more conceptual, but no less troubling. The idea of "prejudice" is simply unequal to the task assigned it within the overall *Carolene* analysis. Recall that *Carolene*'s promise is a form of argument that allows a court to say that it is purifying the democratic process rather than imposing its own substantive values upon the political branches. And yet it is just this process orientation that is at risk when a *Carolene* court undertakes to identify the prejudices that entitle a group to special protection from the vagaries of pluralist politics. One person's "prejudice" is, notoriously, another's "principle." How, then, do we identify a group for *Carolene* protection without performing the substantive analysis of constitutional values that *Carolene* hopes to avoid?

The kind of answer required is clear enough. To redeem *Carolene*'s promise, the judicial identification of a prejudice cannot depend upon the substance of the suspect view, but must turn on the way in which legislators come to hold their belief. The process-oriented argument goes something like this: although each of us cannot always expect to convince our legislators, we can at least insist that they treat our claims with respect. At the very least, they should thoughtfully consider our moral and empirical arguments, rejecting them only after conscientiously deciding that they are inconsistent with the public interest. If a group fails to receive this treatment, it suffers a special wrong, one quite distinct from its substantive treatment on the merits. And it is this purely processual kind of prejudice that constitutes the grievance *Caro-*

lene courts may endeavor to remedy without engaging in the suspect task of prescribing substantive values.

* * *

Let me propose a test case. Imagine that, after reading Herbert Wechsler's famous essay,[47] a group of conservative legalists becomes sincerely convinced that *Brown v. Board of Education* could not in fact be based on neutral principles and so does not deserve its place as a cornerstone of our constitutional law. Acting on this conviction, the group begins a campaign advocating a constitutional amendment to repeal *Brown* and generates some modest interest among conservatives across the country. Arriving in Washington, D.C., with their legal process arguments elaborately developed, the group proceeds to the lobbies of Congress. How do you think the group would be received? Would most Representatives be willing and able to confront the Wechslerian arguments with a thoughtful defense of our constitutional commitment to equality? Or would they respond in a *processually* prejudiced fashion—peremptorily brushing aside the Wechslerians' arguments with a catch-phrase or two that fails to join issue?

This is, in principle, an empirical question—though, like many others, it will never get a good empirical answer. Nonetheless, if my study of politics has taught me anything, I would not expect the agitating Wechslerians to receive a processually unprejudiced response on Capitol Hill. As far as I can tell, any large representative assembly will contain a bewildering variety of human types—from the elaborately thoughtful to the superficially unquestioning. It is simply self-congratulatory to suppose that the members of our own persuasion have reached their convictions in a deeply reflective way, whereas those espousing opinions we hate are superficial. Instead, a thoughtful judge can expect to find an abundance of stereotype-mongers and knee-jerks on *all* sides of *every* important issue—as well as many who have struggled their way to more considered judgments. Given the complexity of the human comedy, a judge is bound on a fool's errand if he imagines that the good guys and bad guys of American politics can be neatly classified according to the seriousness with which they have considered opposing points of view. Processual prejudice is a pervasive problem in the American political system.

But if this is right, *Carolene* cannot justify its concern with discrete and insular minorities without calling on judges to engage in a very different kind of judgment, one dealing with the *substance* of racial and religious prejudice. In doing so, the judge need not try to play the elaborate psychological and political guessing game required to assess the extent to which a statute is the product of a prejudiced refusal to give a respectful hearing to disfavored interests and opinions. Instead, she proceeds to a more familiar judicial inquiry into the nature of the

---

47. Wechsler, *Toward Neutral Princi-*   1 (1959).
ples of Constitutional Law, 73 Harv.L.Rev.

substantive reasons that might plausibly justify the legislature's assertion of authority. If the only plausible reasons for the statute's enactment offend substantive constitutional principles, the groups aggrieved by the statute are declared victims of "prejudice"; if not, not. Although this judicial inquiry into the rational foundations of a statute may sometimes require a focused inquiry into the data available to, or even the subjective opinions of, particular public officials, the critical legal question is of a very different kind: why are the political principles endorsed by some groups judicially recognized as vindicating the constitutionality of a statute, while others are viewed as inadmissible "prejudices" delegitimating a statute's claim to constitutionality?

If *Carolene* somehow hoped to find a shortcut around this substantive inquiry into constitutional values, its journey was fated to fail from the outset. The difference between the things we call "prejudice" and the things we call "principle" is in the end a substantive moral difference. And if the courts are authorized to protect the victims of certain "prejudices," it can only be because the Constitution has placed certain normative judgments beyond the pale of legitimacy.

KIMBERLÉ WILLIAMS CRENSHAW, RACE, REFORM, AND RETRENCHMENT: TRANSFORMATION AND LEGITIMATION IN ANTIDISCRIMINATION LAW
101 Harv.L.Rev. 1331, 1369–81 (1988).

The Context Defined: Racist Ideology and Hegemony
* * *

* * * [T]his Part examines the deep-rooted problem of racist ideology—or white race consciousness—and suggests how this form of consciousness legitimates prevailing injustices and constrains the development of new solutions that benefit Black Americans.

Racist ideology provides a series of rationalizations that suppress the contradiction between American political ideals and Black existence under white supremacy. Not only does racism legitimate the oppression of Blacks, it also helps to define and privilege membership in the white community, creating a basis for identification with dominant interests. Racism serves a consensus-building hegemonic role by designating Black people as separate, visible "others" to be contrasted in every way with all other social groups. Although not consenting to domination, Black people are seen as legitimate objects of antipathy and coercion by whites.

A. The Hegemonic Role of Racism: Establishing the "Other" in American Ideology

Throughout American history, the subordination of Blacks was rationalized by a series of stereotypes and beliefs that made their conditions appear logical and natural.[147] Historically, white supremacy

---

147. *See generally* D. Davis, The Problem of Slavery in the Age of Revolution, 1770–1823 (1975); G. Fredrickson, The Black Image in the White Mind, 1817 to has been premised upon various political, scientific, and religious theories, each of which relies on racial characterizations and stereotypes about Blacks that have coalesced into an extensive legitimating ideology. Today, it is probably not controversial to say that these stereotypes were developed primarily to rationalize the oppression of Blacks. What *is* overlooked, however, is the extent to which these stereotypes serve a hegemonic function by perpetuating a mythology about both Blacks *and* whites even today, reinforcing an illusion of a white community that cuts across ethnic, gender, and class lines.

As presented by * * * scholars [identified with Critical Legal Studies] hegemonic rule succeeds to the extent that the ruling class world view establishes the appearance of a unity of interests between the dominant class and the dominated. Throughout American history, racism has identified the interests of subordinated whites with those of society's white elite. Racism does not support the dominant order simply because all whites want to maintain their privilege at the expense of Blacks, or because Blacks sometimes serve as convenient political scapegoats. Instead, the very existence of a clearly subordinated "other" group is contrasted with the norm in a way that reinforces identification with the dominant group. Racism helps create an illusion of unity through the oppositional force of a symbolic "other." The establishment of an "other" creates a bond, a burgeoning common identity of all non-stigmatized parties—whose identity and interests are defined in opposition to the other.

According to the philosophy of Jacques Derrida, a structure of polarized categories is characteristic of Western thought:

> Western thought * * * has always been structured in terms of dichotomies or polarities: good vs. evil, being vs. nothingness, presence vs. absence, truth vs. error, identity vs. difference, mind vs. matter, man vs. woman, soul vs. body, life vs. death, nature vs. culture, speech vs. writing. These polar opposites do not, however, stand as independent and equal entities. The second term in each pair is considered the negative, corrupt, undesirable version of the first, a fall away from it * * *. In other words, the two terms are not simply opposed in their meanings, but are arranged in a hierarchical order which gives the first term *priority* * * *.[155]

Racist ideology replicates this pattern of arranging oppositional categories in a hierarchical order; historically, whites represented the dominant antinomy while Blacks came to be seen as separate and

1914 (1971) [hereinafter G. Fredrickson, The Black Image]; G. Fredrickson, White Supremacy: A Comparative Study in American and South African History (1981) [hereinafter G. Fredrickson, White Supremacy]; W. Jordan, White over Black: American Attitudes Toward the Negro, 1550–1812 (1968); I. Newby, Jim Crow's Defense: Anti–Negro Thought in America 1900–1930 (1968); J. Williamson, The Crucible of Race: Black/White Relations in the American South Since Emancipation (1984); C. Woodward, The Strange Career of Jim Crow (1958).

155. J. Derrida, Dissemination viii (B. Johnson trans. 1981) (emphasis in original). * * *

subordinate. This hierarchy is reflected in the chart below. Note how each traditional negative image of Blacks correlates with a counter-image of whites:

Historical Oppositional Dualities

WHITE IMAGES	BLACK IMAGES
Industrious	Lazy
Intelligent	Unintelligent
Moral	Immoral
Knowledgeable	Ignorant
Enabling Culture	Disabling Culture
Law–Abiding	Criminal
Responsible	Shiftless
Virtuous/Pious	Lascivious

The oppositional dynamic symbolized by this chart was created and maintained through an elaborate and systematic process. Laws and customs helped create "races" out of a broad range of human traits. In the process of creating races, the categories came to be filled with meaning—Blacks were characterized one way, whites another. Whites became associated with normatively positive characteristics; Blacks became associated with the subordinate, even aberrational characteristics. The operation of this dynamic, along with the important political role of racial oppositionalism, can be illustrated through a few brief historical references.

Edmund Morgan provides vivid illustration of how slaveholders from the seventeenth century onward created and politicized racial categories to maintain the support of non-slaveholding whites.[157] Morgan recounts how the planters "lump[ed] Indians, mulattoes, and Negroes in a single slave class," and how these categories became "an essential, if unacknowledged, ingredient of the republican ideology that enabled Virginians to lead the nation."[158] Having accepted a common interest with slaveholders in keeping Blacks subordinated, even whites who had material reasons to object to the dominance over the slaveholding class could challenge the regime only so far. The power of race consciousness convinced whites to support a system that was opposed to their own economic interests. As George Fredrickson put it, "racial privilege could and did serve as a compensation for class disadvantage."[159]

Domination through race consciousness continued throughout the post-Reconstruction period. Historian C. Vann Woodward has argued that the ruling plantocracy was able to undermine the progressive accomplishments of the Populist movement by stirring up anti-Black sentiment among poor white farmers.[160] Racism was articulated as the

---

157. *See* E. Morgan, American Slavery—American Freedom (1975).

158. *Id.* at 386.

159. G. Fredrickson, White Supremacy, *supra* note 147, at 87.

160. *See* C. Woodward, *supra* note 147, at 68–77.

"broader ground for a new democracy." [161]   As racism formed the new base for a broader notion of democracy, class differences were mediated through reference to a racial community of equality.   A tragic example of the success of such race-conscious political manipulation is the career of Tom Watson, leader of the progressive Populist movement of the 1890's.   Watson, in his attempts to educate the masses of poor farmers about the destructive role of race-based politics, repeatedly told Black and white audiences, "You are made to hate each other because upon that hatred is rested the keystone of the arch of financial despotism which enslaves you both.   You are deceived and blinded that you may not see how this race antagonism perpetuates a monetary system which beggars you both." [163]   Yet, by 1906, Watson had joined the movement to disenfranchise Blacks.   According to Woodward, Watson had "persuaded himself that only after the Negro was eliminated from politics could Populist principles gain a hearing.   In other words, the white men would have to unite before they could divide." [165]

White race consciousness also played a role in the nascent labor movement in the North.   Labor historian Herbert Hill has demonstrated that unions of virtually all trades excluded Black workers from their ranks, often entirely barring Black employment in certain fields.   Immigrant labor unions were particularly adamant about keeping out Black workers; indeed, it was for the precise purpose of assimilating into the American mainstream that immigrant laborers adopted these exclusionary policies.[168]

The political and ideological role that race consciousness continues to play is suggested by racial polarization in contemporary presidential politics.   Several political commentators have suggested that many whites supported Ronald Reagan in the belief that he would correct a perceived policy imbalance that unjustly benefited Blacks,[169] and some argue further that Reagan made a direct racist appeal to white voters.[170]   Manning Marable notes, for example, that "[a]ppeals to the 'race consciousness' of white workers were the decisive factor in Reagan's 1984 victory, especially in the South." [171]   Reagan received nearly 70% of the white vote whereas 90% of Black voters cast their ballots for Mondale.

161. *Id.* at 76. In the words of Southern Progressive Thomas P. Bailey:

> [The] *disenfranchisement of the negroes has been concomitant with the growth of political and social solidarity among the whites.* The more white men recognize sharply their kinship with their fellow whites, and the more democracy in every sense of the term spreads among them, the more the negro is compelled to "keep his place"—a place that is gradually narrowing in the North as well as in the South.

Id. (emphasis in original).

163. *See id.* at 44–45.

165. [*Id.*] at 73–74.

168. [Hill, *Race and Ethnicity in Organized Labor: The Historical Sources of Resistance to Affirmative Action,* J. Intergroup Rel., Winter 1984, at 5, 6.]

169. *See, e.g.,* M. Marable, Race and Realignment in American Politics (1985) (unpublished manuscript available in Harvard Law School library).

170. *See, e.g.,* Howell, *Electoral Politics and Racial Polarization,* 101 Christian Century 1117 (1984); Wilkins, *Smiling Racism,* 23 The Nation 437 (Nov. 3, 1984).

171. M. Marable, *supra* note 169, at 34.

Similarly, the vast majority of Blacks—82%—disapproved of Reagan's performance, whereas only 32% of whites did.

Even the Democratic Party, which has traditionally relied on Blacks as its most loyal constituency, has responded to this apparent racial polarization by seeking to distance itself from Black interests. Although it has been argued that the racial polarization demonstrated in the 1984 election does not represent a trend of white defections from the Democratic Party, it is significant that, whatever the cause of the Party's inability to attract white votes, Democratic leaders have expressed a willingness to moderate the Party's stand on key racial issues in attempts to recapture the white vote.

B. *The Role of Race Consciousness in a System of Formal Equality*

The previous section emphasizes the continuity of white race consciousness over the course of American history. This section, by contrast, focuses on the partial transformation of the functioning of race consciousness that occurred with the transition from Jim Crow to formal equality in race law.

Prior to the civil rights reforms, Blacks were formally subordinated by the state. Blacks experienced being the "other" in two aspects of oppression, which I shall designate as symbolic and material. Symbolic subordination refers to the formal denial of social and political equality to all Blacks, regardless of their accomplishments. Segregation and other forms of social exclusion—separate restrooms, drinking fountains, entrances, parks, cemeteries, and dining facilities—reinforced a racist ideology that Blacks were simply inferior to whites and were therefore not included in the vision of America as a community of equals.

Material subordination, on the other hand, refers to the ways that discrimination and exclusion economically subordinated Blacks to whites and subordinated the life chances of Blacks to those of whites on almost every level. This subordination occurs when Blacks are paid less for the same work, when segregation limits access to decent housing, and where poverty, anxiety, poor health care, and crime create a life expectancy for Blacks that is five to six years shorter than for whites.

Symbolic subordination often created material disadvantage by reinforcing race consciousness in everything from employment to education. In fact, the two are generally not thought of separately: separate facilities were usually inferior facilities, and limited job categorization virtually always brought lower pay and harder work. Despite the pervasiveness of racism, however, there existed even before the civil rights movement a class of Blacks who were educationally, economically, and professionally equal—if not superior—to many whites, and yet these Blacks suffered social and political exclusion as well.

* * *

The response to the civil rights movement was the removal of most formal barriers and symbolic manifestations of subordination. Thus, "White Only" notices and other obvious indicators of the societal policy of racial subordination disappeared—at least in the public sphere. The disappearance of these symbols of subordination reflected the acceptance of the rhetoric of formal equality and signaled the demise of the rhetoric of white supremacy as expressing America's normative vision. In other words, it could no longer be said that Blacks were not included as equals in the American political vision.

Removal of these public manifestations of subordination was a significant gain for all Blacks, although some benefited more than others. The eradication of formal barriers meant more to those whose oppression was primarily symbolic than to those who suffered lasting material disadvantage. Yet despite these disparate results, it would be absurd to suggest that no benefits came from these formal reforms, especially in regard to racial policies, such as segregation, that were partly material but largely symbolic. Thus, to say that the reforms were "merely symbolic" is to say a great deal. These legal reforms and the formal extension of "citizenship" were large achievements precisely because much of what characterized Black oppression was symbolic and formal.

Yet the attainment of formal equality is not the end of the story. Racial hierarchy cannot be cured by the move to facial race-neutrality in the laws that structure the economic, political, and social lives of Black people. White race consciousness, in a new form but still virulent, plays an important, perhaps crucial, role in the new regime that has legitimated the deteriorating day-to-day material conditions of the majority of Blacks.

The end of Jim Crow has been accompanied by the demise of an explicit ideology of white supremacy. The white norm, however, has not disappeared; it has only been submerged in popular consciousness. It continues in an unspoken form as a statement of the positive social norm, legitimating the continuing domination of those who do not meet it. Nor have the negative stereotypes associated with Blacks been eradicated. The rationalizations once used to legitimate Black subordination based on a belief in racial inferiority have now been reemployed to legitimate the domination of Blacks through reference to an assumed cultural inferiority.

* * *

White race consciousness, which includes the modern belief in cultural inferiority, acts to further Black subordination by justifying all the forms of unofficial racial discrimination, injury, and neglect that flourish in a society that is only formally dedicated to equality. In more subtle ways, moreover, white race consciousness reinforces and is reinforced by the myth of equal opportunity that explains and justifies broader class hierarchies.

Race consciousness also reinforces whites' sense that American society is really meritocratic and thus helps prevent them from questioning the basic legitimacy of the free market. Believing both that Blacks are inferior and that the economy impartially rewards the superior over the inferior, whites see that most Blacks are indeed worse off than whites are, which reinforces their sense that the market is operating "fairly and impartially"; those who should logically be on the bottom are on the bottom. This strengthening of whites' belief in the system in turn reinforces their beliefs that Blacks are *indeed* inferior. After all, equal opportunity *is* the rule, and the market *is* an impartial judge; if Blacks are on the bottom, it must reflect their relative inferiority. Racist ideology thus operates in conjunction with the class components of legal ideology to reinforce the status quo, both in terms of class and race.

To bring a fundamental challenge to the way things are, whites would have to question not just their own subordinate status, but also both the economic and the racial myths that justify the status quo. Racism, combined with equal opportunity mythology, provides a rationalization for racial oppression, making it difficult for whites to see the Black situation as illegitimate or unnecessary. If whites believe that Blacks, because they are unambitious or inferior, get what they deserve, it becomes that much harder to convince whites that something is wrong with the entire system. Similarly, a challenge to the legitimacy of continued racial inequality would force whites to confront myths about equality of opportunity that justify for them whatever measure of economic success they may have attained.

Thus, although [Critical Legal Studies scholars] have suggested that legal consciousness plays a central role in legitimating hierarchy in America, the otherness dynamic enthroned within the maintenance and perpetuation of white race consciousness seems to be at least as important as legal consciousness in supporting the dominant order. Like legal consciousness, race consciousness makes it difficult—at least for whites—to imagine the world differently. It also creates the desire for identification with privileged elites. By focusing on a distinct, subordinate "other," whites include themselves in the dominant circle—an arena in which most hold no real power, but only their privileged racial identity.

BIBLIOGRAPHY

Equal Protection Theory

Alexander, *What Makes Wrongful Discrimination Wrong? Biases, Preferences, Stereotypes, and Proxies,* 141 U.Pa.L.Rev. 149 (1992).

Cohen, *Is Equal Protection Like Oakland? Equality as a Surrogate for Other Rights,* 59 Tul.L.Rev. 884 (1985).

D'Amato, *Is Equality a Totally Empty Idea?,* 81 Mich.L.Rev. 600 (1983).

Frank & Munro, *The Original Understanding of "Equal Protection of the Laws",* 1972 Wash.U.L.Q. 421.

Loffredo, *Poverty, Democracy and Constitutional Law,* 141 U.Pa.L.Rev. 1277 (1993).

Michelman, *On Protecting the Poor Through the Fourteenth Amendment,* 83 Harv.L.Rev. 7 (1969).

Miller, *The True Story of Carolene Products,* 1987 Sup.Ct.Rev. 397.

Pennock, J. & Chapman, J., IX NOMOS: EQUALITY (1967).

Seidman, Brown *and* Miranda, 80 Calif.L.Rev. 73 (1992).

Simons, *Overinclusion and Underinclusion: A New Model,* 36 U.C.L.A.L.Rev. 447 (1989).

Sunstein, *Public Values, Private Interests, and the Equal Protection Clause,* 1982 Sup.Ct.Rev. 127.

Tussman & tenBroek, *The Equal Protection of the Laws,* 37 Calif.L.Rev. 341 (1949).

Westen, *The Empty Idea of Equality,* 95 Harv.L.Rev. 537 (1982).

Wilkinson, *The Supreme Court, The Equal Protection Clause, and the Three Faces of Constitutional Equality,* 61 Va.L.Rev. 945 (1975).

Race and the Constitution

Aleinikoff, *The Constitution in Context: The Continuing Significance of Racism,* 63 U.Colo.L.Rev. 325 (1992).

Bell, D., FACES AT THE BOTTOM OF THE WELL: THE PERMANENCE OF RACISM (1992).

Bell, D., RACE, RACISM AND AMERICAN LAW (3d ed. 1992).

Bickel, *The Original Understanding and the Segregation Decision,* 69 Harv.L.Rev. 1 (1955).

Cover, R., JUSTICE ACCUSED (1975).

Delgado, *Recasting the American Race Problem,* 79 Cal.L.Rev. 1389 (1991).

Delgado, *Storytelling for Oppositionists and Others: A Plea for Narrative,* 87 Mich.L.Rev. 2411 (1989).

Dimond, *The Anti–Caste Principle—Toward a Constitutional Standard for Review of Race Cases,* 30 Wayne L.Rev. 1 (1983).

Fairman, C., RECONSTRUCTION AND REUNION, 1864–88, Part I (1971); Part II (1987).

Flagg, *"Was Blind, But Now I See": White Race Consciousness and the Requirement of Discriminatory Intent,* 91 Mich.L.Rev. 953 (1993).

Franklin, J., FROM SLAVERY TO FREEDOM (3d ed. 1967).

Freeman, *Legitimizing Racial Discrimination Through Antidiscrimination Law: A Critical Review of Supreme Court Doctrine,* 62 Minn.L.Rev. 1049 (1978).

Higginbotham, A., IN THE MATTER OF COLOR (1978).

Hyman, H. & Wiecek, W., EQUAL JUSTICE UNDER LAW: CONSTITUTIONAL DEVELOPMENT, 1835–1875 (1982).

Kaczorowski, *Revolutionary Constitutionalism in the Era of the Civil War and Reconstruction,* 61 N.Y.U.L.Rev. 863 (1986).

Landsberg, *Race and the Rehnquist Court,* 66 Tulane L.Rev. 1267 (1992).

Maltz, *Slavery, Federalism, and the Structure of the Constitution,* XXXVI Am.J. Legal Hist. 466 (1992).

McNeil, G., GROUNDWORK: CHARLES HAMILTON HOUSTON AND THE STRUGGLE FOR CIVIL RIGHTS (1983).

Oberst, *The Strange Career of Plessy v. Ferguson,* 15 Ariz.L.Rev. 389 (1973).

Robinson, D., SLAVERY IN THE STRUCTURE OF AMERICAN POLITICS, 1765–1820 (1971).

Schmidt, *Principle and Prejudice: The Supreme Court and Race in the Progressive Era. Part I: The Heyday of Jim Crow,* 82 Colum.L.Rev. 444 (1982).

Soifer, *Protecting Civil Rights: A Critique of Raoul Berger's History,* 54 N.Y.U.L.Rev. 651 (1979).

Strauss, *The Myth of Colorblindness,* 1986 Sup.Ct.Rev. 99.

Swisher, C., THE TANEY PERIOD, 1835–64 (1974).

Symposium, *We the People: A Celebration of the Bicentennial of the United States Constitution,* 30 Howard L.J. 915 (1987).

Woodward, C., THE STRANGE CAREER OF JIM CROW (1955).

School Desegregation

Bell, *Serving Two Masters: Integration Ideals and Client Interests in School Desegregation Litigation,* 85 Yale L.J. 470 (1976).

Bell, ed., SHADES OF BROWN: NEW PERSPECTIVES ON SCHOOL DESEGREGATION (1980).

Bell, Brown v. Board of Education *and the Interest–Convergence Dilemma,* 93 Harv.L.Rev. 518 (1980).

Black, *The Lawfulness of the Segregation Decisions,* 69 Yale L.J. 421 (1960).

Brown, *Has the Supreme Court Allowed the Cure for De Jure Segregation to Replicate the Disease?,* 78 Cornell L.Rev. 1 (1992).

Chang, *The Bus Stops Here: Defining the Constitutional Right of Equal Educational Opportunity and an Appropriate Remedial Process,* 63 B.U.L.Rev. 1 (1983).

Davis, *The Quest for Equal Education in Mississippi: The Implications of* United States v. Fordice, 62 Miss.L.J. 405 (1993).

Devins, *School Desegregation Law in the 1980's: The Courts' Abandonment of* Brown v. Board of Education, 26 Wm. & Mary L.Rev. 7 (1984).

R. Diamond, BEYOND BUSING: INSIDE THE CHALLENGE TO UR-
BAN SEGREGATION (1985).

Dudziak, *Desegregation as a Cold War Imperative,* 41 Stan.L.Rev. 61
(1988).

Fiss, *School Desegregation: The Uncertain Path of the Law,* 4 Phil. &
Pub.Aff. 3 (1974).

Fiss, *The Fate of an Idea Whose Time Has Come: Antidiscrimination
Law in the Second Decade after* Brown v. Board of Education, 41
U.Chi.L.Rev. 742 (1974).

Gewirtz, *Choice in the Transition: School Desegregation and the Corrective Ideal,* 86 Colum.L.Rev. 728 (1986).

Gewirtz, *Remedies and Resistance,* 92 Yale L.J. 585 (1983).

Goodman, *De Facto School Segregation: A Constitutional and Empirical
Analysis,* 60 Calif.L.Rev. 275 (1972).

Graglia, L., DISASTER BY DECREE (1976).

Hayman & Levit, *The Constitutional Ghetto,* 1993 Wis.L.Rev. 627 (1993).

Kirp, D., JUST SCHOOLS (1982).

Kitch, *The Return of Color–Consciousness to the Constitution: Weber,
Dayton, and Columbus,* 1979 Sup.Ct.Rev. 1.

Kluger, R., SIMPLE JUSTICE (1975).

Kujovich, *Equal Opportunity in Higher Education and the Black Public
College: The Era of Separate But Equal,* 72 Minn.L.Rev. 29 (1987).

Landsberg, *The Desegregated School System and the Retrogression Plan,*
48 La.L.Rev. 789 (1988).

Liebman, *Desegregation Politics: "All–Out" School Desegregation Explained,* 90 Colum.L.Rev. 1463 (1990).

Marcus, *Learning Together: Justice Marshall's Desegregation Opinions,*
61 Fordham L.Rev. 69 (1992).

Note, *The Courts, HEW, and Southern School Desegregation,* 77 Yale
L.J. 321 (1967).

Shane, *School Desegregation Remedies and the Fair Governance of
Schools,* 132 U.Pa.L.Rev. 1041 (1984).

Tushnet, M., THE NAACP'S LEGAL STRATEGY AGAINST SEGRE-
GATED EDUCATION, 1925–1950 (1987).

Wilkinson, J., FROM BROWN TO BAKKE (1979).

Chapter VIII

EQUALITY AND GENDER

Since the early 1970's, the Supreme Court has subjected governmental actions that discriminate on the basis of gender to "heightened scrutiny"—a standard somewhere between the strict scrutiny applied to racial classifications and the rationality review applied to most economic and social legislation. This "middle tier" standard evidences the Court's view that although gender classifications are generally troubling, there may be legitimate reasons for governmental actions that take gender into account.

The readings in this Chapter seek to explore the theoretical issues that lie behind the legal doctrine. Are gender classifications as invidious as racial classifications? Does "gender equality" mean a gender-blind legal system? Or should the Equal Protection Clause tolerate gender-based laws that reflect existing differences between the sexes? Are such differences natural (biological) or are they socially created?

Richard Wasserstrom's article sets the stage for analyzing these questions by asking what role gender might play in an ideal society. He suggests that the arguments for taking gender into account based on biological and social differences are not as strong as is normally supposed.

Suzanna Sherry offers grounds for questioning Wasserstrom's assimilationist model. She examines recent feminist scholarship that suggests that women's moral development and sense of self may differ from men's. Sherry argues that law has been distorted by its reliance on a masculine perspective (that emphasizes autonomy, objectivity, and rights) and its exclusion of a feminine perspective (that would emphasize connection, subjectivity, and responsibility).

The next three excerpts examine the theoretical justifications for constitutional doctrine respecting gender discrimination. John Hart Ely contends that recently enacted gender-based classifications should not be subjected to strict judicial scrutiny.

Wendy Williams analyzes the extent to which current cultural understandings of gender roles may set limits on the work that the Equal Protection Clause can do for gender equality. She argues that the legal strategy of some feminists stressing differences and supporting programs that afford special treatment to women may unwittingly reflect and reinforce traditional cultural notions about the role of women.

Catharine MacKinnon sketches two models of sex discrimination law. The prevailing approach, she asserts, is based on the familiar idea that equality means treating likes alike and unlikes unalike. MacKinnon argues that this "sameness/difference approach" is inadequate because it sets up maleness as the standard against which sameness and difference are to be measured, and it supports dominance of women by approving of distinctions based on differences between the sexes. She proposes a "dominance approach" to gender discrimination which would recognize sex inequalities as matters of imposed status, as the subordination of women to men.

Joan Williams takes issue with "difference feminism" as it is represented in the work of Carol Gilligan (described in Sherry's article) and Catharine MacKinnon. She argues that to the extent that it is true that women are focused on relationships while men are not, it merely reflects the oppressive realities of the current gender system. The solution is neither the denial of gender differences nor the praise of a special voice or virtue of women; rather, the task is to "deconstruct gender" through a systematic refusal to institutionalize gender in any form.

RICHARD A. WASSERSTROM, RACISM AND SEXISM

Philosophy and Social Issues 23–43 (1980).

[W]hat would the good or just society make of an individual's race or sex, and to what degree, if at all, would racial and sexual distinctions ever properly be taken into account there?   * * *

* * *

[O]ne conception of a nonracist society is that which is captured by what I shall call the assimilationist ideal: a nonracist society would be one in which the race of an individual would be the functional equivalent of the eye color of individuals in our society today.[25] In our society no basic political rights and obligations are determined on the basis of eye color. No important institutional benefits and burdens are connected with eye color. Indeed, except for the mildest sort of aesthetic preferences, a person would be thought odd who even made private, social decisions by taking eye color into account.   * * *

What is a good deal less familiar is an analogous conception of the good society in respect to sexual differentiation—one in which an individual's sex were to become a comparably unimportant characteristic.

---

25. There is a danger in calling this ideal the "assimilationist" ideal. That term often suggests the idea of incorporating oneself, one's values, and the like into the dominant group and its practices and values. No part of that idea is meant to be captured by my use of the term. Mine is a stipulative definition.

An assimilationist society in respect to sex would be one in which an individual's sex was of no more significance * * * than is eye color today. There would be no analogue to transsexuality, and, while physiological or anatomical sex differences would remain, they would possess only the kind and degree of significance that today attaches to the physiologically distinct eye colors persons possess.

* * *

* * * [I]t must be acknowledged that to make the assimilationist ideal a reality in respect to sex would involve more profound and fundamental revisions of our institutions and our attitudes than would be the case in respect to race. On the institutional level we would, for instance, have to alter significantly our practices concerning marriage. If a nonsexist society is a society in which one's sex is no more significant than eye color in our society today, then laws which require the persons who are getting married to be of different sexes would clearly be sexist laws.

More importantly, given the significance of role differentiation and ideas about the psychological differences in temperament that are tied to sexual identity, the assimilationist ideal would be incompatible with all psychological and sex-role differentiation. That is to say, in such a society the ideology of the society would contain no proposition asserting the inevitable or essential attributes of masculinity or femininity; it would never encourage or discourage the ideas of sisterhood or brotherhood; and it would be unintelligible to talk about the virtues or the disabilities of being a woman or a man. In addition, such a society would not have any norms concerning the appropriateness of different social behavior depending upon whether one were male or female. There would be no conception of the existence of a set of social tasks that were more appropriately undertaken or performed by males or by females. And there would be no expectation that the family was composed of one adult male and one adult female, rather than, say, just two adults—if two adults seemed the appropriate number. To put it simply, in the assimilationist society in respect to sex, persons would not be socialized so as to see or understand themselves or others as essentially or significantly who they were or what their lives would be like because they were either male or female. And no political rights or social institutions, practices, and norms would mark the physiological differences between males and females as important.

Were sex like eye color, these kinds of distinctions would make no sense. Just as the normal, typical adult is virtually oblivious to the eye color of other persons for all significant interpersonal relationships, so, too, the normal, typical adult in this kind of nonsexist society would be equally as indifferent to the sexual, physiological differences of other persons for all significant interpersonal relationships. Bisexuality, not heterosexuality or homosexuality, would be the typical intimate, sexual relationship in the ideal society that was assimilationist in respect to sex.

To acknowledge that things would be very different is, of course, hardly to concede that they would thereby be undesirable—or desirable for that matter. But still, the problem is, perhaps, with the assimilationist ideal. And the assimilationist ideal is certainly not the only possible, plausible ideal.

There is, for instance, another one that is closely related to, but distinguishable from that of the assimilationist ideal. It can be understood by considering how religion rather than eye color tends to be thought about in our culture today and incorporated within social life today. If the good society were to match the present state of affairs in respect to one's religious identity, rather than the present state of affairs in respect to one's eye color, the two societies would be different, but not very greatly so. In neither would we find that the allocation of basic political rights and duties ever took an individual's religion into account. And there would be a comparable indifference to religion even in respect to most important institutional benefits and burdens—for example, access to employment in the desirable vocations, the opportunity to live where one wished to live, and the like. Nonetheless, in the good society in which religious differences were to some degree socially relevant, it would be deemed appropriate to have some institutions (typically those which are connected in an intimate way with these religions) which did in a variety of ways properly take the religion of members of the society into account. For example, it would be thought both permissible and appropriate for members of a religious group to join together in collective associations which have religious, educational, and social dimensions, and when it came to the employment of persons who were to be centrally engaged in the operation of those religious institutions (priests, rabbis and ministers, for example), it would be unobjectionable and appropriate explicitly to take the religion of job applicants into account. On the individual, interpersonal level, it might also be thought natural and possibly even admirable, were persons to some significant degree to select their associates, friends, and mates on the basis of their religious orientation. So there is another possible and plausible ideal of what the good society would look like in respect to a particular characteristic in which differences based upon that characteristic would be to some degree maintained in some aspects of institutional and interpersonal life. The diversity of the religious beliefs of individuals would be reflected in the society's institutional and ideological fabric in a way in which the diversity of eye color would not be in the assimilationist society. The picture is a more complex, somewhat less easily describable one than that of the assimilationist ideal.

* * *

What opponents of assimilationism and proponents of schemes of strong sexual differentiation seize upon is that sexual difference appears to be a naturally occurring category of obvious and inevitable relevance for the construction of any plausible conception of the nature of the good society. The problems with this way of thinking are twofold. To begin with, a careful and thorough analysis of the social realities would reveal, I believe, that it is the socially created sexual differences which constitute most of our conception of sex differences and which tend in fact to matter the most in the way we live our lives as persons of one sex or the other. For, it is, I think, sex-role differentiation and socialization, not the physiological and related biological differences—if there are any—that make men and women as different as they are from each other, and it is these same sex-role-created differences which are invoked to justify the necessity or the desirability of most sexual differentiation proposed to be maintained at any of the levels of social arrangements and practices described earlier.

It is important, however, not to attach any greater weight than is absolutely necessary to the truth or falsity of this causal claim about the source of the degree of sexual distinctions that exist in our or other cultures. For what is significant, although seldom recognized, is the fact that the answer to that question almost never goes very far in settling the question of what the good society should look like in respect to any particular characteristic of individuals. And the answer certainly does not go as far as many persons appear to believe it does to settle that question of the nature of the good society.

Let us suppose that there are what can be called "naturally occurring" sexual differences and even that they are of such a nature that they are in some sense of direct prima facie social relevance. It is essential to see that this would by no means settle the question of whether in the good society sex should or should not be as minimally significant as eye color. Even if there are major or substantial biological differences between men and women that are in this sense "natural" rather than socially created, this does not determine the question of what the good society can and should make of these differences— without, that is, begging the question by including within the meaning of "major" or "substantial" or "natural" the idea that these are things that ought to be retained, emphasized, or otherwise normally taken into account. It is not easy to see why, without begging the question, it should be thought that this fact, if it is a fact, settles the question adversely to anything like the assimilationist ideal. Persons might think that truths of this sort about nature or biology do affect, if not settle, the question of what the good society should look like for at least two different reasons.

In the first place, they might think the differences are of such a character that they substantially affect what would be *possible* within a good society of human persons. Just as the fact that humans are mortal necessarily limits the features of any possible good society, so, they might argue, the fact that males and females are physiologically or biologically different limits in the same way the features of any possible good society.

In the second place, they might think the differences are of such a character that they are relevant to the question of what would be *desirable* in the good society. That is to say, they might not think that the differences determine or affect to a substantial degree what is possible, but only that the differences are appropriately taken into account in any rational construction of an ideal social existence.

The second reason seems to be a good deal more plausible than the first. For there appear to be very few, if any, respects in which the ineradicable, naturally occurring differences between males and females *must* be taken into account. The industrial revolution has certainly made any of the general differences in strength between the sexes capable of being ignored by the good society for virtually all significant human activities. And even if it were true that women are naturally better suited than men to care for and nurture children, it is also surely the case that men can be taught to care for and nurture children well. Indeed, the one natural or biological fact that seems *required* to be taken into account is the fact that reproduction of the human species requires that the fetus develop *in utero* for a period of months. Sexual intercourse is not necessary, for artificial insemination is available. Neither marriage nor the nuclear family is necessary either for conception or child rearing. Given the present state of medical knowledge and what might be termed the natural realities of female pregnancy, it is difficult to see why any important institutional or interpersonal arrangements are constrained to take the existing biological differences as to the phenomenon of *in utero* pregnancy into account.

But to say all this is still to leave it a wholly open question to what degree the good society *ought* to build upon any ineradicable biological differences, or to create ones in order to construct institutions and sex roles which would thereby maintain a substantial degree of sexual differentiation. The way to answer that question is to consider and assess the arguments for and against doing so. What is significant is the fact that many of the arguments for doing so are less persuasive than they appear to be upon the initial statement of this possibility.

It might be argued, for instance, that the fact of menstruation could be used as a premise upon which to base the case for importantly different social roles for females than for males. But this could only plausibly be proposed if two things were true: first, that menstruation would be debilitating to women and hence relevant to social role even in a culture which did not teach women to view menstruation as a sign of uncleanliness or as a curse; and, second, that the way in which menstruation necessarily affected some or all women was in fact necessarily related in an important way to the role in question. But even if both of these were true, it would still be an open question whether any sexual differentiation ought to be built upon these facts. The society could still elect to develop institutions that would nullify the effect of these natural differences and it would still be an open question whether it ought to do so. Suppose, for example, what seems implausible—that some or all women will not be able to perform a particular task while menstruating, e.g., guard the border of a country. It would be possible, even easy, if the society wanted to, to arrange for substitute guards for the women who were incapacitated. We know that persons are not good guards when they are sleepy, and we make arrangements so that persons alternate guard duty to avoid fatigue. The same could be done for menstruating women, even given the implausibly strong assumptions about menstruation.

The point that is involved here is a very general one that has application in contexts having nothing to do with the desirability or undesirability of maintaining substantial sexual differentiation. It has to do with the fact that humans possess the ability to alter their natural and social environment in distinctive, dramatic, and unique ways. * * *

* * *

There are, though, several other arguments based upon nature, or the idea of the "natural" that also must be considered and assessed. First, it might be argued that if a way of doing something is natural, then it ought to be done that way. Here, what may be meant by "natural" is that this way of doing the thing is the way it would be done if culture did not direct or teach us to do it differently. It is not clear, however, that this sense of "natural" is wholly intelligible; it supposes that we can meaningfully talk about how humans would behave in the absence of culture. And few if any humans have ever lived in such a state. Moreover, even if this is an intelligible notion, the proposal that the natural way to behave is somehow the appropriate or desirable way to behave is strikingly implausible. It is, for example, almost surely natural, in this sense of "natural," that humans would eat their food with their hands, except for the fact that they are, almost always, socialized to eat food differently. Yet, the fact that humans would naturally eat this way, does not seem in any respect to be a reason for believing that that is thereby the desirable or appropriate way to eat food. And the same is equally true of any number of other distinctively human ways of behaving.

Second, someone might argue that substantial sexual differentiation is natural not in the sense that it is biologically determined nor in the sense that it would occur but for the effects of culture, but rather in the sense that substantial sexual differentiation is a virtually universal phenomenon in human culture. By itself, this claim of virtual universality, even if accurate, does not directly establish anything about the desirability or undesirability of any particular ideal. But it can be made into an argument by the addition of the proposition that where there is a widespread, virtually universal social practice or institution, there is probably some good or important purpose served by the practice or institution. Hence, given the fact of substantial sex-role differentiation in all, or almost all, cultures, there is on this view some reason to think that substantial sex-role differentiation serves some important purpose for and in human society.

This is an argument, but it is hard to see what is attractive about it. The premise which turns the fact of sex-role differentiation into any kind of a strong reason for sex-role differentiation is the premise of conservatism. And it is no more or less convincing here than elsewhere. There are any number of practices or institutions that are typical and yet upon reflection seem without significant social purpose. Slavery was once such an institution; war perhaps still is.

More to the point, perhaps, the concept of "purpose" is ambiguous. It can mean in a descriptive sense "plays some role" or "is causally relevant." Or, it can mean in a prescriptive sense "does something desirable" or "has some useful function." If "purpose" is used descriptively in the conservative premise, then the argument says nothing about the continued desirability of sex-role differentiation of the assimilationist ideal. If "purpose" is used prescriptively in the conservative premise, then there is no reason to think that premise is true.

To put it another way, the question that seems fundamentally to be at issue is whether it is desirable to have a society in which sex-role differences are to be retained in the way and to the degree they are today—or even at all. The straightforward way to think about the question is to ask what would be good and what would be bad about a society in which sex functioned like eye color does in our society; or alternatively, what would be good and what would be bad about a society in which sex functioned in the way in which religious identity does today; or alternatively, what would be good and what would be bad about a society in which sex functioned in the way in which it does today. We can imagine what such societies would look like and how they might work. It is hard to see how thinking about answers to this question is substantially advanced by reference to what has typically or always been the case. If it is true, for instance, that the sex-role-differentiated societies that have existed have tended to concentrate power and authority in the hands of males, have developed institutions and ideologies that have perpetuated that concentration, and have restricted and prevented women from living the kinds of lives that persons ought to be able to live for themselves, then this, it seems to me, says far more about what may be wrong with any strongly nonassimilationist ideal than does the conservative premise say what may be right about any strongly nonassimilationist ideal.

* * *

* * * [It remains an open question] whether a society in which sex functioned in the way in which eye color does (a strictly assimilationist society in respect to sex) would be better or worse than one in which sex functioned in the way in which religious identity does in our society (a nonoppressive, more diversified or pluralistic one). For it might be argued that especially in the case of sex and even in the case of race much would be gained and nothing would be lost if the ideal society in respect to these characteristics succeeded in preserving in a nonoppressive fashion the attractive differences between males and females and the comparably attractive differences among ethnic groups. Such a society, it might be claimed, would be less bland, less homogeneous and richer in virtue of its variety.

I do not think there is any easy way to settle this question, but I do think the attractiveness of the appeal to diversity, when sex or race are concerned, is less alluring than is often supposed. The difficulty is in part one of specifying what will be preserved and what will not, and in part one of preventing the reappearance of the type of systemic dominance and subservience that produces the injustice of oppression. Suppose, for example, that it were suggested that there are aspects of being male and aspects of being female that are equally attractive and hence desirable to maintain and perpetuate: the kind of empathy that is associated with women and the kind of self-control associated with men. It does not matter what the characteristic is, the problem is one of seeing why the characteristic should be tied by the social institutions to the sex of the individuals of the society. If the characteristics are genuinely ones that all individuals ought to be encouraged to display in the appropriate circumstances, then the social institutions and ideology ought to endeavor to foster them in all individuals. If it is good for everyone to be somewhat empathetic all of the time or especially empathetic in some circumstances, or good for everyone to have a certain degree of self-control all of the time or a great deal in some circumstances, then there is no reason to preserve institutions which distribute these psychological attributes along sexual lines. And the same is true for many, if not all, vocations, activities, and ways of living. If some, but not all persons would find a life devoted to child rearing genuinely satisfying, it is good, surely, that that option be open to them. Once again, though, it is difficult to see the argument for implicitly or explicitly encouraging, teaching, or assigning to women, as opposed to men, that life simply in virtue of their sex. Thus, while substantial diversity in individual characteristics, attitudes, and ways of life is no doubt an admirable, even important feature of the good society, what remains uncertain is the necessity or the desirability of continuing to link attributes or behaviors such as these to the race or sex of individuals. And for the reasons I have tried to articulate there are significant moral arguments against any conception of the good society in which such connections are pursued and nourished in the systemic fashion required by the existence and maintenance of sex roles.

SUZANNA SHERRY, CIVIC VIRTUE AND THE FEMININE VOICE IN CONSTITUTIONAL ADJUDICATION

72 Va.L.Rev. 543, 580–91 (1986).

New studies in a variety of academic disciplines suggest that women in fact may have a unique perspective, a world-view that differs in significant respects from that of men. Feminist scholars in such diverse fields as philosophy, history, sociology, art, and anthropology have identified peculiarly feminine perspectives in those disciplines.[167] Recent work

---

167. See R. Morgan, The Anatomy of Freedom: Feminism, Physics and Global Politics (1982); N. Noddings, [Caring: A Feminine Approach to Ethics and Moral in psychology and in literary theory is particularly illuminating. Psychological studies suggest that women's moral development and concept of self may differ from those of men. Feminist literary theory suggests that women's writing differs from men's in ways that reflect a radically different perspective. Despite the independence of the research and the differences in both topics of investigation and terms of description, the feminine perspective identified in each of these fields is, at its core, a single, common approach. That approach is captured in the tension between women's primary concern with intimacy or connection and men's primary focus on separation or autonomy.[168]

This difference between men and women may influence the manner in which they think about, write about, and practice their disciplines. Thus, it is probable that women's unique perspective on law and jurisprudence, as a function of their different world-view, extends well beyond areas traditionally seen as affecting women, and in fact encompasses all legal issues. Just as women's writing on all subjects—not just on intimacy, domesticity, or women's place in society—reflects a different cast, women's views on the law in general may provide insights and approaches that are less natural to, and therefore less available to, male lawyers and judges.

This different approach to the law makes women a potentially innovative force in the legal community. Because women have been excluded from the mainstream of legal authority and legal change, the legal system, like moral, political, and philosophical discourse, has become "a set of cultural and symbolic forms that view human experience

Education (1984)]; E. Showalter, A Literature of Their Own (1977); P. Spacks, The Female Imagination (1975); Blecki, Feminist Literary Criticism: An Introduction, *in* Feminist Literary Criticism: A Symposium 1 (K. Bordan & F. Rinn eds. 1974); Harding & Hintikka, Introduction, *in* Discovering Reality: Feminist Perspectives on Epistemology, Metaphysics, Methodology, and Philosophy of Science ix (S. Harding & M. Hintikka eds. 1983); O'Brien, Feminist Theory and Dialectical Logic, *in* Feminist Theory: A Critique of Ideology 99 (N. Keohane, M. Rosaldo, & B. Gelpi eds. 1982); Garfunkel, The Improvised Self: Sex Differences in Artistic Identity (Dissertation, Dep't of Psych. & Soc. Rel., Harv. Univ., 1984); Goodman, Women's Studies: The Debate Continues, N.Y. Times Magazine, Apr. 22, 1984, at 39; Kolbert, Scientific Ideas: Women's vs. Men's, N.Y. Times, Oct. 17, 1985, at C1, col. 1; Goleman, Psychology Is Revising Its View of Women, N.Y. Times, Mar. 20, 1984, at C1, col. 1.

168. The most persuasive explanation for the differences between men and women is based on differences between boys' and girls' development of an ego or sense of self.

Ego development occurs while the child is still quite young and is therefore significantly influenced by the child's primary caretaker. Because, in general, girls are raised by a primary caretaker of the same gender and boys are raised by a primary caretaker of the opposite gender, girls reaffirm their early attachments while boys repudiate them. Thus, women come to see themselves as fundamentally connected and men see themselves as fundamentally detached. See N. Chodorow, [The Reproduction of Mothering: Psychoanalysis and the Sociology of Gender 166–68 (1978)]; C. Gilligan, [In A Different Voice: Psychological Theory and Women's Development 5–23 (1982).] Other explanations for the differences between men and women include the socialization process, the mother's varying reaction to sons and daughters, and biological differences. See, e.g., E. Erikson, Identity, Youth and Crisis (1968); E. Janeway, Man's World, Woman's Place: A Study in Social Mythology (1971); J. Miller, Toward a New Psychology of Women (1976); Flax, The Conflict Between Nurturance and Autonomy in Mother–Daughter Relationships and Within Feminism, Fem. Stud., June 1978, at 171.

from the distorted and one-sided perspective of a single gender." [170]   This is not to suggest merely that the legal structure ignores or minimizes significant gender differences, but rather that because women have been excluded from shaping our legal structure in general, that structure reflects a distorted view of the tension between autonomy and connection and between the individual and society.

What sort of distortion has the masculine paradigm introduced into our legal system? Feminist scholars identify three primary dichotomies between men's and women's thinking: while women emphasize connection, subjectivity, and responsibility, men emphasize autonomy, objectivity, and rights. * * *

* * *

A brief caveat is in order. First, I am not contending that gender-based differences are universal, only that they are likely enough that the historical exclusion of women from the shaping of the legal system has had a profound impact, which cannot be reversed—or, to a large extent, even recognized—until women begin to participate in that enterprise. Second, I am not limiting my analysis to a feminist perspective: feminists have a particular political agenda that may or may not be shared by all women (and is shared by some men). Rather, this is an analysis of a feminine perspective that encompasses aspects of personality and relationship to the world that have nothing to do with one's political preferences. Finally, I am not suggesting that the feminine perspective is any better than the masculine perspective, just that it is different. The incorporation of a new perspective need not imply a hierarchical ranking; I am arguing merely that the law has been distorted by its one-sided focus and that the feminine perspective described here represents a move toward correcting that distortion. * * *

B. Connection and Autonomy

* * * [T]he feminine perspective views individuals primarily as interconnected members of a community. Nancy Chodorow and Carol Gilligan, in groundbreaking studies on the development of self and morality, have concluded that women tend to have a more intersubjective sense of self than men and that the feminine perspective is therefore more other-directed.[174]   Other studies tend to confirm this finding.[175] The essential difference between the male and female perspectives [is that] "[t]he basic feminine sense of self is connected to the world, the basic masculine sense of self is separate." [176]   Women thus tend to see

---

170. O'Brien, supra note 167, at 99. * * *

174. See N. Chodorow, supra note 168; C. Gilligan, supra note 168. * * *

175. For example, even at a very young age, female children tend to be more dependent on and reluctant to leave their mothers. See Goldberg & Lewis, Play Behavior in the Year–Old Infant: Early Sex Difference, 40 Child Dev. 21 (1969); Messer & Lewis, Social Class and Sex Differences in the Attachment and Play Behavior of the Year–Old Infant, 18 Merrill–Palmer Q. Behav. & Dev. 295 (1972).

176. N. Chodorow, supra note 168, at 169 * * *.

others as extensions of themselves rather than as outsiders or competitors.

Gilligan suggests that Kohlberg's description of a morally mature person—a "rational individual aware of values and rights prior to social contracts" who adopts "universal principles of justice," including "respect for the dignity of human beings as individual persons" [178]—instead describes a masculine morality.[179] That masculine perspective embodies the individualism inherent in the modern paradigm. The parallel between the classical paradigm and feminine morality, by contrast, is clearly illustrated by Gilligan's quotation of a typical female response to a moral dilemma:

> By yourself, there is little sense to things. It is like the sound of one hand clapping, the sound of one man or one woman, there is something lacking. *It is the collective that is important to me,* and that collective is based on certain guiding principles, one of which is that *everybody belongs to it,* and that you all come from it. You have to love someone else, because while you may not like them, you are inseparable from them. In a way, it is like loving your right hand. *They are part of you; that other person is part of that giant collection of people that you are connected to.*[180]

Women's emphasis on connection also suggests that the cliche that women are more cooperative and less competitive than men may have some basis in fact. Historically, women have tended to achieve their goals communally; from quilting bees to consciousness-raising sessions, women have banded together rather than striving individually. There are analogous differences between the organization and ideology underlying women's traditional dominion, the family, and men's traditional arena, the marketplace: as Frances Olsen notes, the market is based on an individualist ethic and the family on an altruistic ethic.[182]

Some of the most intriguing evidence of a feminine perspective comes from the field of literary criticism, where feminist critics are discovering characteristic differences in both style and substance between male and female authors. In seeking to identify this "uniquely female literary consciousness," [183] they are discovering indications of a similar tension between autonomy and connection. Male writers typically portray individuals as existing prior to and divorced from society. The male metaphor, and the male travail, is individualist. In contrast, women writers are less apt to focus on purely individual heroism.

---

178. Kohlberg, Moral Stages and Moralization: The Cognitive–Developmental Approach, *in* Moral Development and Behavior: Theory, Research, and Social Issues 34–35 (T. Lickona ed. 1976) (describing the post-conventional level).

179. See C. Gilligan, supra note 168, at 18–22.

180. Id. at 160 (some emphasis in original, some added).

182. Olsen, The Family and the Market: A Study of Ideology and Legal Reform, 96 Harv.L.Rev. 1497, 1505 (1983)[.] * * *

183. Showalter, Introduction, *in* The New Feminist Criticism: Essays on Women, Literature, and Theory 6 (E. Showalter ed. 1985) * * *.

Unlike the archetypal masculine "coming of age" novel, the developing feminine counterpart describes women's maturation in the context of a group of women, the definition of one "self" from among many "selves[.]"   * * *

Feminist literary critics are also beginning to identify some characteristically feminine styles, which also suggest an intersubjective perspective. For example, women writers more frequently use a technique of rotating a novel's perspective from one character to another.[186] This technique is often criticized by male critics, and it may be that women authors are more receptive to the technique because they are better able to perceive not only the relations among characters but also those between themselves and the characters they create. They almost literally "become" their characters (male and female) for the same reason that their intersubjective perspective keeps them from fully separating themselves from others. Males, on the other hand, with their emphasis on autonomy, see the technique as a violation of the ideal of separation.

C. Contextuality and Abstraction

Scholarship in literature and psychology also suggests that women are more contextual and men more abstract. Piaget, for example, found that girls playing children's games tend to treat the rules of the game as less fixed and more flexible than do boys and that girls are more likely to stop a game altogether—thus preserving friendships—if a dispute arises. For boys, development and application of fixed, abstract rules is almost as important as the object of the game itself.[188] Again, Kohlberg's description of moral development (i.e., the development of the masculine perspective) stresses a progression from context-bound judgments to abstract moral principles. Women, on the other hand, in responding to moral dilemmas, tend instead to look to circumstances rather than to abstractions: the right moral response depends on the context.[190]

This concept of feminine reliance on context is borne out in some empirical experiments. For example, the greater familiarity of even young boys with universal principles is well illustrated by a simple experiment in which boys and girls were shown pictures of everyday objects and asked to group related objects:

> [B]oys tend to bracket together objects (or pictures of objects) whose intrinsic characteristics are similar, whereas girls weight more heavily the functional and relational characteristics of the entities to be compared. For instance, boys frequently bracketed together such entities as a truck, a car, and an ambulance, while girls bracketed such entities as a doctor, a hospital bed, and an ambulance.[191]

186. See, e.g., Mellown, Character and Themes in the Novels of Jean Rhys, *in* Contemporary Women Novelists: A Collection of Critical Essays 118, 130 (P. Spacks ed. 1977).

188. See J. Piaget, The Moral Judgment of The Child 82 (1965); see also Lever, Sex Differences in the Games Children Play, 23 Social Probs. 478 (1976) (similar findings).

190. See C. Gilligan, supra note 168, at 38.

191. Hintikka & Hintikka, How Can Language Be Sexist? *in* Discovering Reality: Feminist Perspectives on Epistemology, Me-

The boys focused on the abstraction of "locomotion," seeing the objects as independent units, while the girls emphasized instead the concrete relationships among objects. Other studies confirm that males of all ages are better able to separate discrete objects from their backgrounds and relationships than are females. Males are said to be less field-dependent; that is, they have a greater "ability to overcome the influence of an embedding context." [193]

Moreover, current controversies in philosophy tend to break down along gender lines. Despite exceptions, male philosophers often endorse more abstract and less contextual theories. For example, mainstream discussions of virtue tend to assume that virtues are abstract qualities. Committing murder under dangerous circumstances, though a criminal act, may still constitute an instance of the virtue of courage. Philippa Foot, on the other hand, suggests that virtues are contextual, not abstract: the virtue of courage is exhibited only under circumstances where the act itself can be considered courageous.[194]

* * *

Literary criticism also recognizes the difference between the abstraction of men and the concreteness of women. One critic has suggested, for example, that George Eliot's *Mill on the Floss* illustrates the tension between the male notion of universal maxims and the female unwillingness to differentiate the universal from its particular applications.[199] Women's writing has also been characterized (and criticized) as less linear and unified and more fluid than men's; [200] this again suggests a focus on context rather than on abstract rules of progression. Even feminine literary criticism is more contextual: Elaine Showalter has suggested that one characteristic of feminist criticism is the rejection of (masculine) objective, non-experiential critical theories.[201]

D. RESPONSIBILITY AND RIGHTS

Until recently, the archetypal developmental continuum of individual moral sensibility was believed to be an orderly progression from self-centeredness through other-centeredness to the development of logical, independent, universal principles—rights—that depend neither on one's

taphysics, Methodology, and Philosophy of Science 139, 145 (S. Harding & M. Hintikka eds. 1983) (footnote omitted).

193. J. Sherman, On the Psychology of Women: A Survey of Empirical Studies 21 (1971) * * *.

194. See P. Foot, [Virtues and Vices and Other Essays in Moral Philosophy 15–17 (1978).]

199. Jacobus, The Question of Language: Men of Maxims and *The Mill on the Floss, in* Writing and Sexual Difference 37, 42 (E. Abel ed. 1982). Jacobus contrasts Eliot's remark, in her novel, that "the man of maxims is the popular representative of

the minds that are guided in their moral judgment solely by general rules," with the view of the central character, Maggie Tulliver—" 'to lace ourselves up in formulas is to ignore the special circumstances that mark the individual lot.' " Id. (quoting G. Eliot, Mill on the Floss 628 (A. Byatt ed. 1979)).

200. Gardiner, On Female Identity and Writing By Women, *in* Writing and Sexual Difference 177, 185 (E. Abel ed. 1982); Jacobus, supra note 199, at 39–40.

201. Showalter, Feminist Criticism in the Wilderness, supra note 183, at 244.

own needs nor on what others believe is right.[202]   Although this progression mirrors male moral development, it fails to reflect the moral growth pattern of women.[203]

Gender-based differences in moral structure, long seen as evidence of women's moral immaturity,[204] may in fact be evidence of a feminine morality that differs in its emphasis from that of males.   In her study of moral development, Carol Gilligan found that women tend to view a moral problem as "a problem of care and responsibility in relationships rather than as one of rights and rules." [205]   When faced with the moral dilemma of whether a man should steal a drug he cannot afford to save his dying wife, Gilligan found that, while men struggle with the conflicting rights of the parties, women focus on the druggist's "moral obligation to show compassion," [206] "not on the conflict of rights but on the failure of response." [207]   Although men and women may agree that the man ought to steal the drug, men justify it in terms of a resolution between conflicting rights of husband and druggist, and women in terms of the need for more compassion by the druggist in the face of the husband's compassion for his wife.[208]   Whether personal or political, the moral structure of "mature" males reflects a paradigm of independent rights, while that of females emphasizes relational responsibilities.

JOHN HART ELY, FACILITATING THE REPRESENTATION OF MINORITIES
Democracy and Distrust 164–70 (1980).

[In this section, Ely considers whether gender-based classifications that disadvantage women should be subject to close judicial scrutiny. We have reprinted Ely's general approach to equal protection in Chapter VII.   Recall that he suggests that strict scrutiny is appropriate when there is good reason to suspect that the political process that produced the statute was tainted—either because of ill-will towards the disadvantaged group ("first degree prejudice") or because the legislature is likely to have overestimated the accuracy of the generalization upon which the classification is based ("second degree prejudice").]

The case of women is timely and complicated.   Instances of first-degree prejudice are obviously rare, but just as obviously exaggerated stereotyping—typically to the effect that women are unsuited to the work of the world and therefore belong at home—has long been rampant throughout the male population and consequently in our almost exclusively male legislatures in particular.   It may all be in apparent good

---

202. See L. Kohlberg, The Philosophy of Moral Development (1981); Kohlberg, supra note 178.

203. See C. Gilligan, supra note 168, at 18–22.

204. See L. Kohlberg, supra note 202

* * *.

205. C. Gilligan, supra note 168, at 73.

206. Id. at 54 (quoting a subject of Gilligan's study).

207. Id.

208. See, e.g., id. at 29.

humor, even perceived as protective, but it has cost women dearly. Absent a strong demonstration of mitigating factors, therefore, we would have to treat gender-based classifications that act to the disadvantage of women as suspicious. If the stereotyping has been clear, however, so has the noninsularity of the group affected. The degree of contact between men and women could hardly be greater, and neither, of course, are women "in the closet" as homosexuals historically have been. Finally, lest you think I missed it, women have about half the votes, apparently more. As if it weren't enough that they're not discrete and insular, they're not even a minority!

Despite that seeming avalanche of rebuttal, there remains something that seems right in the claim that women have been operating at an unfair disadvantage in the political process, though it's tricky pinning down just what gives rise to that intuition. It is tempting to observe that although women may be a majority, they haven't in any real sense *consented* to the various instances of gender-based legislation. Voters, female and male alike, are typically confronted not with single-issue referenda but rather with packages of attitudes, packages we call candidates. Most women are not injured in any direct way by laws that classify on the basis of sex—depriving women, say, of the opportunity to tend bar, guard railroad crossings, or administer estates—and the fact that they help elect representatives who are unprepared to repeal such laws may mean only that there are other issues about which they feel more strongly. This may indeed be so, but the argument changes the rules. Once we start to shift from a focus on whether something is blocking the opportunity to correct the stereotype reflected in the legislation, to one that attempts to explain why those who have that opportunity have chosen to pursue other goals instead, we begin to lose our way, to permit our disagreement with the substantive merits of the legislation to take the place of what is *constitutionally* relevant, an inability to do anything about it. That answer triggers a more promising inquiry, though—whether it is fair to say that women have "chosen" not to avail themselves of their opportunities either by voting or by personally influencing those men with whom they come in contact, to correct the exaggerated stereotype that many men hold and on the basis of which they have often legislated. A major reason for lack of action on either of these fronts, or so at least it can plausibly be argued, has been that many women have *accepted* the overdrawn stereotype and thus have seen nothing to "correct" by vote or personal persuasion, and by their example may even have acted so as to reinforce it. That could, of course, imply that it wasn't so exaggerated a stereotype after all, but it could mean something else too, that our society, including the women in it, has been so pervasively dominated by men that women quite understandably have accepted men's stereotypes, of women as well as on other subjects.

The general idea is one that in some contexts has merit. A sufficiently pervasive prejudice can block its own correction not simply by keeping its victims "in the closet" but also by convincing even them of its correctness. In *Castaneda v. Partida,* decided in 1977, the Court held that a prima facie case of intentional discrimination against Mexican–Americans in the selection of grand jurors was not constitutionally affected by the fact that Mexican–Americans enjoyed "governing majority" status in the county involved. Concurring, Justice Marshall gave the reason why: "Social scientists agree that members of minority groups frequently respond to discrimination and prejudice by attempting to disassociate themselves from the group, even to the point of adopting the majority's negative attitudes towards the minority." [96] Nor does this insight seem relevant only to numerical minorities: slaves outnumbered masters in the antebellum South, and outnumbered whites generally in some states, but that apparently didn't keep many of them from assimilating much of the mythology used to legitimate their enslavement.

To apply all this to the situation of women in America in 1980, however, is to strain a metaphor past the breaking point. It is true that women do not generally operate as a very cohesive political force, banding together to elect candidates pledged to the "woman's point of view." Constitutional suspiciousness should turn on evidence of blocked access, however, not on the fact that elections are coming out "wrong." There is an infinity of groups that do not act as such in the political marketplace, but we don't automatically infer that they have a "slave mentality." The cause, more often, is that (sensibly or not) the people involved are not in agreement over the significance of their shared characteristic. Thus in assessing suspiciousness it cannot be enough simply to note that a group does not function as a political bloc. A further reference to the surrounding conditions must be had, to see if there are systemic bars (and I'm obviously not suggesting they need be official ones) to access. On that score it seems important that today discussion about the appropriate "place" of women is common among both women and men, and between the sexes as well. The very stereotypes that gave rise to laws "protecting" women by barring them from various activities are under daily and publicized attack, and are the subject of equally spirited defense. (That the common stereotypes are so openly described and debated, as they are not in the case of racial minorities, is itself some evidence of the comparatively free and non-threatening nature of the interchange.) Given such open discussion of the traditional stereotypes, the claim that the numerical majority is being "dominated," that women are in effect "slaves" who have no realistic choice but to assimilate the stereotypes, is one it has become impossible to maintain except at the most inflated rhetorical level. It also renders the broader argument self-contradictory, since to make such a claim in the context of the current debate one must at least implicitly grant the validity of the stereotype, that women are in effect mental infants who will believe anything men tell them to believe. Many women do seem to prefer the old stereotype to the new liberation. You and I may think that's a mistaken choice. But once we begin regarding

96. 430 U.S. 483, 503 (1977) (Marshall, J., concurring), citing G. Allport, [The Nature of Prejudice 150–53 (1954).] * * *

serious disagreement with a choice as proof that those who made it aren't in control of their minds, we've torn up the rulebook and made substantive wrongheadedness the test of unconstitutionality.

However, most laws classifying by sex weren't passed this morning or even the day before yesterday: in fact it is rare to see a gender-based classification enacted since the New Deal. In general women couldn't even *vote* until the Nineteenth Amendment was ratified in 1920, and most of these laws probably predate even that: they should be invalidated. Throughout this discussion, however, I have been concerned with factors more subtle than the lack of a vote, and it can at least be argued that until quite recently there persisted throughout America's female population a *"Castaneda-like"* acceptance of the prejudices of males, unventilated by more than token airing of their validity. Given what appropriately makes a classification suspicious, it is not necessarily a unitary question whether discrimination against a certain group should be so regarded, and the case of women seems one where the date of enactment should be important. It surely seems more helpful than anything the Court has come up with on the question of whether those who passed the law in issue were proceeding on the basis of an "archaic and overbroad generalization" or whether, say, they were genuinely trying to protect women from certain physical risks to which in statistical terms they are unusually subject, realized there were counterexamples and estimated their incidence about right, but nonetheless felt the costs of identifying the exceptions were simply too high. * * * Direct attempts to judge whether a given law was generated by an overdrawn stereotype can be dangerously subjective since the face of the statute will inevitably be consistent with either of these descriptions of the decision process, and the legislative history will inevitably be partial and subject to manipulation. The date of passage seems a somewhat more solid datum, one that can at least begin to anchor the judicial inquiry. That's an aside, however, since the date of passage seems unquestionably relevant to what our analysis has suggested is a more promising approach to the question of suspiciousness—one geared to the existence of official or unofficial blocks on the opportunities of those the law disadvantages to counter by argument or example the overdrawn stereotypes we might, from the demography of the decision-making body, otherwise suspect were operative.

The case of women can be further put in perspective by exploring what should follow from a judicial determination that the suspiciousness of a given classification has not been allayed and that it therefore is unconstitutional. Here too the answer is not unitary: we have looked at several indicia of suspiciousness, and their remedial implications differ. Where a law is suspect because of what I have been calling first-degree prejudice, or indeed where it has been infected by a subtler form of stereotyping under conditions where the negatively affected group was barred from effective access at the time of passage *and still is,* the only appropriate remedy is to void the classification and insist—if the legislature wishes to continue to classify—on a different, generally more finely tuned, test of qualification. The obvious alternative to this is to have the judiciary restrike the substantive balance, attempting not to let the prejudices that apparently influenced the legislature play a part, and invalidate the classification only if in some sense it still ends up unacceptable on its merits. You will not be surprised to learn that I regard that approach as quite inappropriate. We can cite occasions on which our judiciary has displayed a lesser susceptibility to bare-knuckled first-degree prejudice than our elected officials, but we also can cite some where it hasn't. Moreover, instances of such prejudice, for reasons it is not necessary to review, are almost invariably instances of self-serving comparison as well. Judges tend to belong to the same broad categories as legislators—most of them, for example, are white heterosexual males comfortably above the poverty line—and there isn't any reason to suppose that they are immune to the usual temptations to self-aggrandizing generalization. When in a given situation you can't be trusted to generalize and I can't be trusted to generalize, the answer, if possible, is not to generalize, which suggests that the Supreme Court has chosen wisely in insisting generally that a classification whose suspiciousness has not been allayed simply cannot be employed. Where in fact it was largely the product of a simple desire to disadvantage those disqualified, it probably will just be abandoned, which seems a desirable outcome. Where, however, a classification of some sort does seem necessary (though the one the legislature employed was constitutionally unacceptable), the remedy of flat-out disallowance will impose costs in both time and money, as it will generally necessitate a somewhat more individualized test of qualification. However, legislatures often incur those costs voluntarily, and courts on other occasions have forced them to do so where constitutionally protected interests will be threatened by an imperfectly fitting classification. The unusual dangers of distortion in situations of self-aggrandizing generalization seem also to demand that we bear the increased costs of more individualized justice.

A case like that of women, where access was blocked in the past but can't responsibly be said to be so any longer, seems different in a way that suggests that a less drastic remedy may be appropriate. In cases of first-degree prejudice, or self-serving stereotyping where the access of the disadvantaged group remains blocked, the alternative of "remanding" the question to the political processes for a "second look" would not be acceptable: we don't give a case back to a rigged jury. Here, however, such a "second look" approach seems to make sense. Technically the Court's judgment would be the same in all situations of unallayed suspiciousness: "due process of lawmaking" having been denied, the law that emerged would have to be declared unconstitutional. The difference would emerge in the event—unlikely, precisely because access is no longer blocked—that the legislature after such a declaration of unconstitutionality reconsidered and repassed the same or a similar law. The fact that due process of lawmaking was denied in 1908 or even in 1939 needn't imply that it was in 1982 as well, and consequently the new law should be upheld as constitutional. In fact I may be wrong in supposing that because women now are in a position to protect themselves they will, that we are thus unlikely to see in the future the sort of official gender discrimination that has marked our past. But if women don't protect themselves from sex discrimination in the future, it won't be because they can't. It will rather be because for one reason or another—substantive disagreement or more likely the assignment of a low priority to the issue—they don't choose to. Many of us may condemn such a choice as benighted on the merits, but that is not a constitutional argument.

WENDY W. WILLIAMS, THE EQUALITY CRISIS: SOME REFLECTIONS ON CULTURE, COURTS, AND FEMINISM
7 Women's Rights Law Rept'r 175, 176–200 (1982).

My thesis is that we (feminists) are at a crisis point in our evaluation of equality and women and that perhaps one of the reasons for the crisis is that, having dealt with the easy cases, we (feminists and courts) are now trying to cope with issues that touch the hidden nerves of our most profoundly embedded cultural values.

I will first set the stage for discussion with a brief history of women, equality, and the Supreme Court; second, I will examine what I believe to be evidence that the Supreme Court has, unbeknownst to itself, foundered upon the culturally instilled limits of its ability to dismantle male preserves; and third, I will speculate that there is also a female preserve, functioning as a hidden hand not only for the courts but for feminists as well, and that this unacknowledged influence may be causing problems for feminist legal theorists.

I. A Brief History of Gender Equality and the Supreme Court

Just before the American Revolution, Blackstone, in the course of his comprehensive commentary on the common law, set forth the fiction that informed and guided the treatment of married women in the English law courts. When a woman married, her legal identity merged into that of her husband; she was civilly dead. She couldn't sue, be sued, enter into contracts, make wills, keep her own earnings, control her own property. She could not even protect her own physical integrity—her husband had the right to chastise her (although only with a switch no bigger than his thumb), restrain her freedom, and impose sexual intercourse upon her against her will.

Beginning in the middle of the nineteenth century, the most severe civil disabilities were removed in this country by state married women's property acts. Blackstone's unities fiction was for the most part replaced by a theory that recognized women's legal personhood but which assigned her a place before the law different and distinct from that of her husband. This was the theory of the separate spheres of men and women, under which the husband was the couple's representative in the public world and its breadwinner; the wife was the center of the private world of the family. Because it endowed women with a place, role, and importance of their own, the doctrine of the separate spheres was an advance over the spousal unities doctrine. At the same time, however, it preserved and promoted the dominance of male over female. The public world of men was governed by law while the private world of women was outside the law, and man was free to exercise his prerogatives as he chose.

* * *

The separate spheres ideology was repudiated by the Supreme Court only [recently]. The engine of destruction was, as a technical matter, the more rigorous standard of review that the Court began applying to sex discrimination cases beginning in 1971.[20] By 1976 the Court was requiring that sex-based classifications bear a "substantial" relationship to an "important" governmental purpose.[21] This standard, announced in Craig v. Boren, was not as strong as that used in race cases, but it was certainly a far cry from the rational basis standard that had traditionally been applied to sex-based classifications.

As a practical matter, what the Court did was strike down sex-based classifications that were premised on the old breadwinner-homemaker, master-dependent dichotomy inherent in the separate spheres ideology. Thus, the Supreme Court insisted that women wage earners receive the same benefits for their families under military,[23] social security,[24] welfare,[25] and worker's compensation [26] programs as did male wage earners; that men receive the same child care allowance when their spouses died as women did; [27] that the female children of divorce be entitled to support for the same length of time as male children, so that they too could get the education necessary for life in the public world; [28] that the duty of support through alimony not be visited exclusively on husbands; [29] that wives as well as husbands participate in the management of the community property; [30] and that wives as well as husbands be eligible to administer their deceased relatives' estates.[31]

All this happened in the little more than a decade that has elapsed since 1971. The achievement is not an insubstantial one. Yet it also seems to me that in part what the Supreme Court did was simply to recognize that the real world outside the courtroom had already changed. Woman were in fact no longer chiefly housewife-dependents. The family wage no longer existed; for a vast number of two-parent

20. In Reed v. Reed, 404 U.S. 71, 75 (1971)[.] * * *

21. Craig v. Boren, 429 U.S. 190, 197 (1976). * * *

23. Frontiero v. Richardson, 411 U.S. 677 (1973).

24. Califano v. Goldfarb, 430 U.S. 199 (1977).

25. Califano v. Westcott, 443 U.S. 76 (1979).

26. Wengler v. Druggists Mutual Insurance Co., 446 U.S. 142 (1980).

27. Weinberger v. Wiesenfeld, 420 U.S. 636 (1975).

28. Stanton v. Stanton, 421 U.S. 7 (1975).

29. Orr v. Orr, 440 U.S. 268 (1979).

30. Kirchberg v. Feenstra, 450 U.S. 455 (1981).

31. Reed v. Reed, 404 U.S. 71 (1971).

families, two wage earners were an economic necessity. In addition, many families were headed by a single parent. It behooved the Court to account for this new reality and it did so by recognizing that the breadwinner-homemaker dichotomy was an outmoded stereotype.

II. MEN'S CULTURE: AGGRESSOR IN WAR AND SEX

Of course, not all of the Supreme Court cases involved the breadwinner-homemaker stereotype. The other cases can be grouped in several ways; for my purposes I will place them in two groups. One group is composed of the remedial or compensatory discrimination cases—the cases in which a statute treats women differently and better than men for the purpose of redressing past unequal treatment.[35] The other group, the focus of this paper, consists of the cases that don't really seem to fit into any neat category but share a common quality. Unlike the cases discussed above, they do not deal with laws that rest on an economic model of the family that no longer predominates; rather, they concern themselves with other, perhaps more basic, sex-role arrangements. They are what I would call, simply, the "hard" cases, and for the most part, they are cases in which a sex-based classification was upheld by the Court.[36] There are a number of ways one could characterize and analyze them. I want to view them from one of those possible perspectives, namely, what they tell us about the state of our culture with respect to the equality of men and women. What do they say about the cultural limits of the equality principle?

In the 1980–81 Term the Supreme Court decided three sex-discrimination cases. One was *Kirchberg v. Feenstra*,[37] a case which struck down the Louisiana statute that gave husbands total control over the couple's property. That, to my mind, was an easy case. It falls within the line of cases I have already described which dismantle the old separate spheres ideology. The other two cases were *Rostker v. Goldberg*,[38] the case which

35. *See, e.g.,* Kahn v. Shevin, 416 U.S. 351 (1974) (Florida statute granting widows but not widowers property tax exemption constitutional because intended to assist sex financially most affected by spousal loss) and Califano v. Webster, 430 U.S. 313 (1977) (Social Security Act section creating benefit calculation formula more favorable to women than men held constitutional because intended to compensate women for wage discrimination). * * *

36. *See, e.g.,* Schlesinger v. Ballard, 419 U.S. 498 (1975) (Court upheld (5–4) law that results in discharge of male officers if twice passed over for promotion, but guarantees female officers 13–year tenure before discharge for lack of promotion); Rostker v. Goldberg, 453 U.S. 57 (1981); Michael M. v. Superior Court, 450 U.S. 464 (1981); Dothard v. Rawlinson, 443 U.S. 321 (1977); Geduldig v. Aiello, 417 U.S. 484 (1974); General Electric Corp. v. Gilbert, 429 U.S. 125 (1976); Nashville Gas Co. v. Satty, 434

U.S. 136 (1977). All of these cases were authored either by Justice Stewart or by Justice Rehnquist.

Another case that belongs in this category, even though the gender-based classification was struck down, is the 5–4 decision in Caban v. Mohammed, 441 U.S. 380 (1979). In that case the Court held that a state statute that gave an unwed mother but not an unwed father the right to veto the adoption of her or his child violated the equal protection clause. The Court carefully limited its holding to adoptions of older children who had established a relationship with the father, leaving open the possibility, strongly argued by the dissent, that there were differences between mothers and fathers that would justify a different outcome with respect to the adoption of very young children. * * *

37. 450 U.S. 455 (1981).

38. 453 U.S. 57 (1981).

upheld the male-only draft registration law, and *Michael M. v. Superior Court*,[39] the case upholding the California statutory rape law. They are prime candidates for my hard-cases category.

Justice Rehnquist wrote the opinion of the Court in both *Rostker* and *Michael M.* In *Rostker,* the draft registration case, his reasoning was a simple syllogism. The purpose of the registration, he said, is to identify the draft pool. The purpose of the draft is to provide combat troops. Women are excluded from combat. Thus, men and women are not similarly situated with respect to the draft, and it is therefore constitutional to register males only. Of course, the problem with his syllogism was that one of the premises—that the purpose of the draft is exclusively to raise combat troops—was and is demonstrably false, but the manipulation of the facts of that case is not what I mean to focus on here.

In *Michael M.*, a 17½–year–old–man and a 16½–year–old woman had sexual intercourse. The 17½–year–old man was prosecuted under California's statutory rape law, which made such intercourse criminal for the man but not the woman. Rehnquist, for a plurality of the Court, accepted the utterly dubious proposition put forward by the State of California that the purpose of the statutory rape statute was to prevent teenage pregnancies. The difference in treatment under the statute is justified, he said, because men and women are not similarly situated with respect to this purpose. Because the young woman is exposed to the risk of pregnancy, she is deterred from sexual intercourse by that risk. The young man, lacking such a natural deterrent, needs a legal deterrent, which the criminal statute provides.

I think that perhaps the outcomes of these two cases—in which the sex-based statutes were upheld—were foregone conclusions and that the only question, before they were decided, was *how* the court would rationalize the outcome. This is perhaps more obvious in the draft case than the statutory rape case, but applies, I think, to both. Let me explain.

Suppose you could step outside our culture, rise above its minutiae, and look at its great contours. Having done so, speculate for a moment about where society might draw the line and refuse to proceed further with gender equality. What does our culture identify as quintessentially masculine? Where is the locus of traditional masculine pride and self-identity? What can we identify in men's cultural experience that most divides it from women's cultural experience? Surely, one rather indisputable answer to that question is "war": physical combat and its modern equivalents. (One could also answer that preoccupation with contact sports is such a difference, but that is, perhaps, just a subset of physical combat.)

Not surprisingly, the Court in *Rostker* didn't come right out and say "We've reached our cultural limits." Yet I did not find it insignificant

---

39.   450 U.S. 464 (1981).

that even the Justices who dissented on the constitutionality of the draft registration law seemed to concede the constitutionality of excluding women from combat. When Congress considered whether women should be drafted, it was much more forthright about its reasons and those reasons support my thesis. The Senate Armed Services Committee Report states:

> [T]he starting point for any discussion of the appropriateness of registering women for the draft is the question of the proper role of women in combat. The principle that women should not intentionally and routinely engage in combat *is fundamental, and enjoys wide support among our people.*

In addition, the committee expressed three specific reasons for excluding women from combat. First, registering women for assignment to combat "would leave the actual performance of sexually mixed units as an experiment to be conducted in war with unknown risk—a risk that the committee finds militarily unwarranted and dangerous." Second, any attempt to assign women to combat could "affect the national resolve at the time of mobilization." Third, drafting women would "place unprecedented strains on family life." The committee envisioned a young mother being drafted leaving a young father home to care for the family and concluded, "The committee is strongly of the view that such a result * * * is unwise and unacceptable to a large majority of our people." To translate, Congress was worried that (1) sexually mixed units would not be able to function—perhaps because of sex in the foxhole? (2) if women were assigned to combat, the nation might be reluctant to go to war, presumably because the specter of women fighting would deter a protective and chivalrous populace; and (3) the idea that mom could go into battle and dad keep the home fires burning is simply beyond the cultural pale. In short, current notions of acceptable limits on sex-role behavior would be surpassed by putting women into combat.

But what about statutory rape? Not such a clear case, you say. I disagree. Buried perhaps a bit deeper in our collective psyches but no less powerful and perhaps even more fundamental than our definition of man as aggressor in war is man as aggressor in sex. The original statutory rape laws were quite explicitly based on this view. Then, as is true even today, men were considered the natural and proper initiators of sex. In the face of male sexual initiative, women could do one of two things, yield or veto, "consent" or decline. What normal women did not, *should* not, do was to initiate sexual contact, to be the sexual aggressor. The premise underlying statutory rape laws was that young women's chastity was precious and their naivete enormous. Their inability knowingly to consent to sexual intercourse meant that they required protection by laws which made their consent irrelevant but punished and deterred the "aggressive" male.

The Court's opinion, I believe, is implicitly based on stereotypes concerning male sexual aggression and female sexual passivity, despite

Justice Rehnquist's express denial of that possibility. His recitation of the facts of the case sets the stage for the sexual gender-role pigeon-holding that follows: "After being struck in the face for rebuffing petitioner's advances, Sharon," we are told, "*submitted* to sexual intercourse with petitioner." Although, in theory, coercion and consent are relevant only to the crime of rape, not to statutory rape, we are thus provided with the details of this particular statutory rape case, details which cast Michael and Sharon as prototypes of the sexually aggressive male and the passive female.

But it is Rehnquist's description of the lower court opinion that most clearly reveals sex role assumptions that lead first the California high court and then the United States Supreme Court to uphold the legislation. He says, "Because *males alone* can 'physiologically cause the result which the law properly seeks to avoid' [pregnancy], the [California Supreme Court] further held that the gender classification was readily justified as a means of identifying *offender* and *victim*." [65] The statement is remarkable for two (related) reasons. The first and most dramatic is the strangeness of the biological concept upon which it is based. Do the justices still believe that each sperm carries a homunculus—a tiny person—who need only be planted in the woman in order to grow? Are they ignorant of ova? Or has sex-role ideology simply outweighed scientific fact? Since no one has believed in homunculi for at least a century, it must be the latter. Driven by the stereotype of male as aggressor/offender and woman as passive victim, even the facts of conception are transformed to fit the image.

The second is the characterization of man and woman as "offender" and "victim." Statutory rape is, in criminal law terms, a clear instance of a victimless crime, since all parties are, by definition, voluntary participants. In what sense, then, can Rehnquist assert that the woman is victim and the man offender? One begins to get an inkling when, later, the Justice explains that the statutory rape law is "protective" legislation: "The statute here protects women from sexual intercourse at an age when those consequences are particularly severe." His preconceptions become manifest when, finally, Rehnquist on one occasion calls the statute a "rape" statute—by omitting the word "statutory" inadvertently exposing his hidden assumptions and underlining the belief structure which the very title of the crime, "statutory rape," lays bare.

What is even more interesting to me than the Court's resolution of these cases is the problem they cause for feminist analysis. The notion that men are frequently the sexual aggressors and that the law ought to be able to take that reality into account in very concrete ways is hardly one that feminists could reject out of hand (I'm thinking here of sexual harassment and forcible rape, among other things): it is therefore an area, like the others I'm about to discuss, in which we need to pay special attention to our impulses lest we inadvertently support and give

---

65. 450 U.S. at 467 (emphasis added).

credence to the very social constructs and behaviors we so earnestly mean to oppose. Should we, for example, defend traditional rape laws on the ground that rape, defined by law as penetration by the penis of the vagina, is a sexual offense the psychological and social consequences of which are so unique, severe, and rooted in age-old power relationships between the sexes that a gender-neutral law would fail in important ways to deal with the world as it really is? Or should we insist that equality theory requires that we reorganize our understanding of sexual crime, that unwanted sexual intrusion of types other than male-female sexual intercourse can similarly violate and humiliate the victim, and that legislation which defines sexual offenses in gender-neutral terms, because it resists our segregationist urges, and affirms our common humanity, is therefore what feminists should support? These are not easy questions, but they must be answered if feminist lawyers are to press a coherent theory of equality upon the courts in these hard cases.

As for *Rostker v. Goldberg,* the conflicts among feminists were overtly expressed. Some of us felt it essential that we support the notion that a single-sex draft was unconstitutional;[76] others felt that feminists should not take such a position. These latter groups explicitly contrasted the female ethic of nurturance and life-giving with a male ethic of aggression and militarism and asserted that if we argued to the Court that single-sex registration is unconstitutional we would be betraying ourselves and supporting what we find least acceptable about the male world.[77]

To me, this latter argument quite overtly taps qualities that the culture has ascribed to woman-as-childrearer and converts them to a normative value statement, one with which it is easy for us to sympathize. This is one of the circumstances in which the feeling that "I want what he's got but I don't want to be what he's had to be in order to get it" comes quickly to the surface. But I also believe that the reflexive

---

76. See briefs *amici curiae* of the National Organization for Women, and of a group including Women's Equity Action League, Business and Professional Women, and others, in Rostker v. Goldberg, 453 U.S. 57 (1981).

77. *See, e.g., A Feminist Opposition to the Draft* (New Haven, Connecticut, 1980) (authors unidentified) in C. Mackinnon, Sexuality and Legality: Toward a Feminist Theory of the State 151–57 (unpublished materials for a course taught at the Stanford Law School, Fall 1980). At the outset, the author(s) state:

We need at the beginning to differentiate between two kinds of feminism. The one seeks to assimilate women into the traditional institutions of male society. This is the feminism of a small elite. There is another, more broadly based feminism, and this feminism carries with it a fundamental critique of the structure of power in this country.

The one kind of feminism would see the draft as a sign that we have reached equality, or as an opportunity for reaching equality. We consider this to be an extremely narrow notion of equality. We must place the draft in a wider context and see it as an instrument of American policy. The draft, then, is not the only, nor even the primary issue. The real question is what the foreign and domestic policy of this country is, and whether we can assent to it. For a number of reasons we cannot.

Among other grounds for withholding assent, the author or authors "reject the war reflex as an instance of male hysteria; in its essence, feminism is opposed to violence." *Id.* at 151.

response based on these deeper cultural senses leads us to untenable positions.

The single-sex laws upheld in *Michael M.* and *Rostker* ultimately do damage to women. For one thing, they absolve women of personal responsibility in the name of protection. There is a sense in which women have been victims of physical aggression in part because they have not been permitted to act as anything but victims. For another, do we not acquire a greater right to claim our share from society if we too share its ultimate jeopardies? To me, *Rostker* never posed the question of whether women should be forced as men now are to fight wars, but whether we, like them, must take the responsibility for deciding whether or not to fight, whether or not to bear the cost of risking our lives, on the one hand, or resisting in the name of peace, on the other. And do we not, by insisting upon our differences at these crucial junctures, promote and reinforce the us-them dichotomy that permits the Rehnquists and the Stewarts to resolve matters of great importance and complexity by the simplistic, reflexive assertion that men and women "are simply not similarly situated?"

III. WOMEN'S CULTURE: MOTHER OF HUMANITY

We have looked briefly at the male side of the cultural equation. What are the cultural limits on women's side? Step outside the culture again and speculate. If we find limits and conflicts surrounding the male role as aggressor in war and sex, what will be the trouble spots at the opposite pole? What does the culture identify as quintessentially female? Where does our pride and self-identity lie? Most probably, I think, somewhere in the realm of behaviors and concerns surrounding maternity.

I would expect the following areas to be the places where the move toward equality of the sexes might come into collision with cultural limits, both in judicial opinions and in ourselves: treatment of maternity in the workplace, the tender years presumption, and joint custody of children upon divorce. The issues surrounding pregnancy and maternity are the most difficult from a theoretical point of view and for that reason may be the best illustration of the conflict I am trying to explore.

* * *

Once the Supreme Court took on the task of dismantling the statutory structure built upon the separate spheres ideology, it had to face the question of how to treat pregnancy itself. Pregnancy was, after all, the centerpiece, the linchpin, the essential feature of women's separate sphere. The stereotypes, the generalizations, the role expectations were at their zenith when a woman became pregnant. Gender equality would not be possible, one would think, unless the Court was willing to examine, at least as closely as other gender-related rulemaking, those prescriptions concerning pregnancy itself. On the other hand, the capacity to bear a child is a crucial, indeed definitional, difference between women and men. While it is obvious that the sexes can be treated equally with respect to characteristics that they share, how would it be possible to apply the equality principle to a characteristic unique to women?

So what did the Court do? It drew the line at pregnancy. *Of course* it would take a more critical look at sex discrimination than it had in the past—but, it said, discrimination on the basis of pregnancy is not sex discrimination. Now here was a simple but decisive strategy for avoiding the doctrinal discomfort that inclusion of pregnancy within the magic circle of stricter review would bring with it. By placing pregnancy altogether outside that class of phenomena labeled sex discrimination, the Court need not apply to classifications related to pregnancy the level of scrutiny it had already reserved, in cases such as *Reed v. Reed* and *Frontiero v. Richardson,* for gender classifications. Pregnancy classifications would henceforth be subject only to the most casual review.

The position was revealed for the first time in 1974 in *Geduldig v. Aiello,*[86] a case challenging under the equal protection clause exclusion of pregnancy-related disabilities from coverage by an otherwise comprehensive state disability insurance program. The Court explained, in a footnote, that pregnancy classifications were not sex-based but were, instead, classifications based upon a physical condition and should be treated accordingly[.]

* * *

The second time the Supreme Court said pregnancy discrimination is not sex discrimination was in *General Electric Company v. Gilbert,*[88] decided in 1976. *Gilbert* presented the same basic facts—exclusion of pregnancy-related disabilities from a comprehensive disability program— but this case was brought under Title VII rather than the equal protection clause. The Court nonetheless relied on *Geduldig,* saying that when Congress prohibited "sex discrimination," it didn't mean to include within the definition of that term pregnancy discrimination.

There was, however, an additional theory available in *Gilbert* because it was a Title VII case that was not available in the equal protection case. That theory was that if an employer's rule has a disparate *effect* on women, even though there is no intent to discriminate, it might also violate Title VII. And did the Court find that the exclusion of pregnancy-related disabilities had a disparate effect on women? It did not. Men and women, said Justice Rehnquist, received coverage for the disabilities they had in common. Pregnancy was an *extra* disability, since only women suffered it. To compensate women for it would give them more than men got. So here there was no disparate effect—the exclusion of pregnancy merely insured the basic equality of the program.

The remarkable thing about this statement, like Rehnquist's later assertion in *Michael M.* that only men can "cause" pregnancy, is its

---

86. 417 U.S. 484.   **88.** 429 U.S. 125.

peculiarly blinkered male vision. After all, men received coverage under General Electric's disability program for disabilities they did not have in common with women, including disabilities linked to exclusively male aspects of the human anatomy. Thus, the only sense in which one can understand pregnancy to be "extra" is in some reverse-Freudian psychological fashion. Under Freud's interpretation, women were viewed by both sexes as inadequate men (men *minus*) because they lacked penises. In Rehnquist's view, woman is now man *plus,* because she shares all his physical characteristics except that she also gets pregnant. Under either of these extravagantly skewed views of the sexes, however, man is the measure against which the anatomical features of woman are counted and assigned value, and when the addition or subtraction is complete, woman comes out behind.

The corollary to *Gilbert* appeared in *Nashville Gas Co. v. Satty,*[94] decided in 1977. There the Court finally found a pregnancy rule that violated Title VII. The rule's chief characteristic was its gratuitously punitive effect. It provided that a woman returning from maternity leave lost all of the seniority she acquired *prior* to her leave. Here, said Rehnquist, we have a case where women are not seeking extra benefits for pregnancy. Here's a case where a woman, now back at work and no longer pregnant, has actually had something taken away from her—her pre-pregnancy seniority—and she therefore suffers a burden that men don't have to bear. This rule therefore has a disproportionate impact on women.

Roughly translated, *Gilbert* and *Satty* read together seemed to stand for the proposition that insofar as a rule deprives a woman of benefits for actual pregnancy, that rule is lawful under Title VII. If, on the other hand, it denies her benefits she had earned while not pregnant (and hence like a man) and now seeks to use upon return to her non-pregnant (male-like) status, it has a disproportionate effect on women and is not lawful.

In summary, then, the Court seems to be of the view that discrimination on the basis of pregnancy isn't sex discrimination. The Court achieves this by, on the one hand, disregarding the "ineluctable link" between gender and pregnancy, treating pregnancy as just another physical condition that the employer or state can manipulate on any arguably rational basis, and on the other hand, using woman's special place in "the scheme of human existence" as a basis for treating her claim to benefits available to other disabled workers as a claim not to equal benefits but to extra benefits, not to equal treatment but to special treatment. The equality principle, according to the Court, cannot be bent to such ends.

In reaction to *Gilbert* and, to a lesser extent, to *Satty,* Congress amended the definitions section of Title VII to provide that discrimination on the basis of pregnancy, childbirth, and related medical conditions was, for purposes of the Act, sex discrimination. The amendment, called

94.   434 U.S. 136 (1977).

the Pregnancy Discrimination Act (PDA),[99] required a rather radical change in approach to the pregnancy issue from that adopted by the Court. In effect, Title VII creates a general presumption that men and women are alike in all relevant respects and casts the burden on the employer to show otherwise in any particular case. The PDA, likewise, rejects the presumption that pregnancy is so unique that special rules concerning it are to be treated as prima facie reasonable. It substitutes the contrary presumption that pregnancy, at least in the workplace context, is like other physical conditions which may affect workers. As with gender classifications in general, it places the burden of establishing pregnancy's uniqueness in any given instance on the employer. The amendment itself specifies how this is to be done:

> [W]omen affected by pregnancy, childbirth, or related medical conditions shall be treated the same for all employment-related purposes, including receipt of benefits under fringe benefit programs, as other persons not so affected but similar in their ability or inability to work * * *.

Under the PDA, employers cannot treat pregnancy less favorably than other potentially disabling conditions, but neither can they treat it more favorably. And therein lies the crisis.

At the time the PDA was passed, all feminist groups supported it. Special treatment of pregnancy in the workplace had always been synonymous with unfavorable treatment; the rules generally had the effect of forcing women out of the work force and back into the home when they became pregnant. By treating pregnancy discrimination as sex discrimination, the PDA required that pregnant women be treated as well as other wage earners who became disabled. The degree to which this assisted women depended on the generosity of their particular employers' sick leave or disability policy, but anything at all was better than what most pregnant women had had before.

The conflict within the feminist community arose because some states had passed legislation which, instead of placing pregnant women at a disadvantage, gave them certain positive protections. Montana, for example, passed a law forbidding employers to fire women who became pregnant and requiring them to give such women reasonable maternity leave.[a] The Miller–Wohl Company, an employer in that state, had a particularly ungenerous sick leave policy. Employees were entitled to *no* sick leave in their first year of employment and five days per year thereafter. On August 1, 1979, the company hired a pregnant woman who missed four or five days over the course of the following three weeks because of morning sickness. The company fired her. She asserted her rights under the Montana statute. The company sought declaratory

---

99. 42 U.S.C. § 2000e(k) (Supp. IV 1980).

a. This article was written before the Supreme Court's decision in *California Federal Savings & Loan Ass'n v. Guerra,* 479 U.S. 272 (1987), which held that a California statute requiring employers to provide leave and reinstatement to women disabled by pregnancy was neither inconsistent with nor pre-empted by the PDA.

relief in federal court, claiming that Montana's special treatment statute was contrary to the equality principle mandated by the PDA and was therefore invalid under the supremacy clause of the constitution.

Feminists split over the validity of the Montana statute. Some of us felt that the statute was, indeed, incompatible with the philosophy of the PDA. Others of us argued that the PDA was passed to *help* pregnant women, which was also the objective of the Montana statute. Underneath are very different views of what women's equality means; the dispute is therefore one of great significance for feminists.

The Montana statute *was* meant to help pregnant women. It was passed with the best of intentions. The philosophy underlying it is that pregnancy is central to a woman's family role and that the law should take special account of pregnancy to protect that role for the working wife. And those who supported the statute can assert with great plausibility that pregnancy is a problem that men don't have, an extra source of workplace disability, and that women workers cannot adequately be protected if pregnancy is not taken into account in special ways.[110] They might also add that procreation plays a special role in human life, is viewed as a fundamental right by our society, and therefore is appropriately singled out on social policy grounds. The instinct to treat pregnancy as a special case is deeply imbedded in our culture, indeed in every culture. It seems natural, and *right,* to treat it that way.

Yet, at a deeper level, the Supreme Court in cases like *Gilbert,* and the feminists who seek special recognition for pregnancy, are starting from the same basic assumption, namely, that women have a special place in the scheme of human existence when it comes to maternity. Of course, one's view of how that basic assumption cuts is shaped by one's perspective. What businessmen, Supreme Court Justices, and feminists make of it is predictably quite different. But the same doctrinal approach that permits pregnancy to be treated *worse* than other disabilities is the same one that will allow the state constitutional freedom to create special *benefits* for pregnant women. The equality approach to pregnancy (such as that embodied in the PDA) necessarily creates not only the desired floor under the pregnant woman's rights but also the ceiling which the *Miller–Wohl* case threw into relief. If we can't have it both ways, we need to think carefully about which way we want to have it.

---

110. Some commentators have argued that treating the unique capabilities of women in a special way is not equivalent to granting special, inequitable favors to women. Perhaps the finest articulation of that view is the following passage:

> Uniqueness is a 'trap' only in terms of an analysis such as that generated in *Geduldig v. Aiello,* which assumes that maleness is the norm. 'Unique' does not necessarily mean uniquely handicapped * * *. To account for pregnancy and

breastfeeding is * * * to treat women as equals by respecting the female gender and by ceasing to impose upon women a bifurcated existence; it is to reject antiquated classifications and to restore to women the opportunity to live a continuous life, integrated with respect to career and procreation just as are the lives of men.

Scales. *Towards a Feminist Jurisprudence,* 56 Ind.L.J. 375, 435–36 (1981). * * *

My own feeling is that, for all its problems, the equality approach is the better one. The special treatment model has great costs. First, as discussed above, is the reality that conceptualizing pregnancy as a special case permits unfavorable as well as favorable treatment of pregnancy. Our history provides too many illustrations of the former to allow us to be sanguine about the wisdom of urging special treatment.

Second, treating pregnancy as a special case divides us in ways that I believe are destructive in a particular political sense as well as a more general sense. On what basis can we fairly assert, for example, that the pregnant woman fired by Miller–Wohl deserved to keep her job when any other worker who got sick for any other reason did not? Creating special privileges of the Montana type has, as one consequence, the effect of shifting attention away from the employer's inadequate sick leave policy or the state's failure to provide important protections to all workers and focusing it upon the unfairness of protecting one class of worker and not others.

Third, as our experience with single-sex protective legislation earlier in this century demonstrated, what appear to be special "protections" for women often turn out to be, at best, a double-edged sword. It seems likely, for example, that the employer who wants to avoid the inconveniences and costs of special protective measures will find reasons not to hire women of childbearing age in the first place.[115]

Fourth, to the extent the state (or employers as proxies for the state) can lay claim to an interest in women's special procreational capacity for "the future well-being of the race," as *Muller v. Oregon* put it in 1908, our freedom of choice about the direction of our lives is more limited than that of men in significant ways. This danger is hardly a theoretical one today. The Supreme Court has recently shown an increased willingness to permit restrictions on abortion in deference to the state's interest in the "potential life" of the fetus, and private employers are adopting policies of exclusion of women of childbearing capacity in order to protect fetuses from exposure to possibly hazardous substances in the workplace.

More fundamentally, though, this issue, like the others I discussed earlier, has everything to do with how, in the long run, we want to define women's and men's places and roles in society.

Implicit in the PDA approach to maternity issues is a stance toward parenthood and work that is decidedly different from that embodied in the special-treatment approach to pregnancy. For many years, the prototype of the enlightened employer maternity policy was one which provided for a mandatory unpaid leave of absence for the woman employee commencing four or five months before and extending for as long as six months after childbirth. Such maternity leaves were firmly premised on that aspect of the separate spheres ideology which assigned

---

115. Title VII does not permit such practices. As a practical matter, however, proof of such motivations is difficult. Ac-   tions based on a class sufficiently large to illuminate the hidden motivation are prohibitively expensive and complex.

motherhood as woman's special duty and prerogative; employers believed that women should be treated as severed from the labor force from the time their pregnancies became apparent until their children emerged from infancy. Maternity leave was always based upon cultural constructs and ideologies rather than upon biological necessity, upon role expectations rather than irreducible differences between the sexes.

The PDA also has significant ideological content. It makes the prototypical maternity leave policy just described illegal. In its stead, as discussed above, is a requirement that the employer extend to women disabled by pregnancy the same disability or sick leave available to other workers. If the employer chooses to extend the leave time beyond the disability period, it must make such leaves available to male as well as to female parents. Title VII requires sex neutrality with respect to employment practices directed at parents. It does not permit the employer to base policies on the separate spheres ideology. Accordingly, the employer must devise its policies in such a way that women and men can, if they choose, structure the allocation of family responsibilities in a more egalitarian fashion. It forecloses the assumption that women are necessarily and inevitably destined to carry the dual burden of homemaker and wage earner.

Statutes such as the Montana statute challenged in the *Miller–Wohl* case are rooted in the philosophy that women have a special and different role and deserve special and different treatment. Feminists can plausibly and forcibly claim that such laws are desirable and appropriate because they reflect the material reality of women's lives. We can lay claim to such accommodations based on the different pattern of our lives, our commitment to children, our cultural destiny. We can even resort to arguments based on biological imperatives and expect that at least some members of the Supreme Court might lend a sympathetic ear. Justice Stevens suggested one such approach in a footnote to his dissent in *Caban v. Mohammed*,[124] a case invalidating a law that granted to unwed mothers but denied to unwed fathers the right to withhold consent to adoption of their children. He observed:

> [T]here is some sociological and anthropological research indicating that by virtue of the symbiotic relationship between mother and child during pregnancy and the initial contact between mother and child directly after birth a physical and psychological bond immediately develops between the two that is not then present between the infant and the father or any other person. [Citations omitted.]

Justice Stevens' seductive bit of science is useful for making my point, although other illustrations might do as well. Many women who have gone through childbirth have experienced the extraordinary sense of connection to their newborn that the literature calls "bonding." It may be, as some have contended, that the monolithic role women have so long played has been triggered and sustained by this phenomenon, that the effect of this bonding has made it emotionally possible for women to

---

124. 441 U.S. 380 (1979).

submit to the stringent limitations imposed by law and culture upon the scope and nature of their aspirations and endeavors. On the other hand, it seems entirely possible that the concept of exclusive mother-infant bonding—the latest variation on "maternal instinct"—is a social construct designed to serve ideological ends.

Less than a century ago, doctors and scientists were generally of the view that a woman's intellect, her capacity for education, for reasoning, for public undertakings, was biologically limited. While men were governed by their intellect, women were controlled by their uteruses. No reputable scientist or doctor would make such claims today. But if women are now understood to share with men a capacity for intellectual development, is it not also possible that mother-infant bonding is, likewise, only half the story? What Justice Stevens overlooks is the evidence of the capacity of fathers (the exploration of whose nurturing potential is as new as their opportunity actively to participate in the birth of their children) to "bond" as well.

Again, the question is, are we clinging, without really reflecting upon it, to culturally dictated notions that underestimate the flexibility and potential of human beings of both sexes and which limit us as a class and as individuals?

IV: CONCLUSION: CONFRONTING YIN AND YANG

The human creature seems to be constructed in such a way as to be largely culture bound. We should not, therefore, be surprised that the creaky old justices on the Supreme Court and we somewhat less creaky feminists sometimes—perhaps often—respond to the same basic characterizations of male and female—although, unquestionably, the justices tend sometimes to do different things with those basic characterizations than feminists would do. At this point, we need to think as deeply as we can about what we want the future of women and men to be. Do we want equality of the sexes—or do we want justice for two kinds of human beings who are fundamentally different? If we gain equality, will we lose the special sense of kinship that grows out of experiences central to our lives and not shared by the other sex? Are feminists defending a separate women's culture while trying to break down the barriers created by men's separate culture? Could we, even if we wanted to, maintain the one while claiming our place within the other? *Michael M.*, which yokes assumptions about male sexual aggression with the conclusion that the sexes are not similarly situated because of women's pregnancy, and the Senate report on the all-male draft, which suggests that what sends men to war and leaves women at home is a fundamental trade-off by which men are assigned to battle and women to child rearing, should give us pause. I for one suspect a deep but sometimes nearly invisible set of complementaries, a yin-yang of sex-role assumptions and assignments so complex and inter-related that we cannot successfully dismantle any of it without seriously exploring the possibility of dismantling it all. The "hard cases"—cases like *Michael M., Rostker, Gilbert, Geduldig, Caban*—give us an opportunity to rethink our basic assumptions about women and men, assumptions sometimes buried beneath our consciousness. They allow us to ask afresh who we are, what we want, and if we are willing to begin to create a new order of things.

CATHARINE A. MacKINNON, DIFFERENCE AND DOMINANCE: ON SEX DISCRIMINATION
FEMINISM UNMODIFIED: DISCOURSES ON LIFE AND LAW, ch. 2 (1987).

What is a gender question a question of? What is an inequality question a question of? These two questions underlie applications of the equality principle to issues of gender, but they are seldom explicitly asked. I think it speaks to the way gender has structured thought and perception that mainstream legal and moral theory tacitly gives the same answer to them both: these are questions of sameness and difference. The mainstream doctrine of the law of sex discrimination that results is, in my view, largely responsible for the fact that sex equality law has been so utterly ineffective at getting women what we need and are socially prevented from having on the basis of a condition of birth: a chance at productive lives of reasonable physical security, self-expression, individuation, and minimal respect and dignity. Here I expose the sameness/difference theory of sex equality, briefly show how it dominates sex discrimination law and policy and underlies its discontents, and propose an alternative that might do something.

* * *

According to the approach to sex equality that has dominated politics, law, and social perception, equality is an equivalence, not a distinction, and sex is a distinction. The legal mandate of equal treatment—which is both a systemic norm and a specific legal doctrine—becomes a matter of treating likes alike and unlikes unlike; and the sexes are defined as such by their mutual unlikeness. Put another way, gender is socially constructed as difference epistemologically; sex discrimination law bounds gender equality by difference doctrinally. A built-in tension exists between this concept of equality, which presupposes sameness, and this concept of sex, which presupposes difference. Sex equality thus becomes a contradiction in terms, something of an oxymoron, which may suggest why we are having such a difficult time getting it.

Upon further scrutiny, two alternate paths to equality for women emerge within this dominant approach, paths that roughly follow the lines of this tension. The leading one is: be the same as men. This path is termed gender neutrality doctrinally and the single standard philosophically. It is testimony to how substance gets itself up as form in law that this rule is considered formal equality. Because this approach mirrors the ideology of the social world, it is considered abstract, meaning transparent of substance; also for this reason it is considered not only to be *the* standard, but *a* standard at all. It is so far the leading rule that the words "equal to" are code for, equivalent to, the words "the same as"—referent for both unspecified.

To women who want equality yet find that you are different, the doctrine provides an alternate route: be different from men. This equal recognition of difference is termed the special benefit rule or special protection rule legally, the double standard philosophically. It is in rather bad odor. Like pregnancy, which always calls it up, it is something of a doctrinal embarrassment. Considered an exception to true equality and not really a rule of law at all, this is the one place where the law of sex discrimination admits it is recognizing something substantive. Together with the Bona Fide Occupational Qualification (BFOQ), the unique physical characteristic exception under ERA policy, compensatory legislation, and sex-conscious relief in particular litigation, affirmative action is thought to live here.

The philosophy underlying the difference approach is that sex is a difference, a division, a distinction, beneath which lies a stratum of human commonality, sameness. The moral thrust of the sameness branch of the doctrine is to make normative rules conform to this empirical reality by granting women access to what men have access to: to the extent that women are no different from men, we deserve what they have. The differences branch, which is generally seen as patronizing but necessary to avoid absurdity, exists to value or compensate women for what we are or have become distinctively as women (by which is meant, unlike men) under existing conditions.

My concern is not with which of these paths to sex equality is preferable in the long run or more appropriate to any particular issue, although most discourse on sex discrimination revolves about these questions as if that were all there is. My point is logically prior: to treat issues of sex equality as issues of sameness and difference *is to take a particular approach*. I call this the difference approach because it is obsessed with the sex difference. The main theme in the fugue is "we're the same, we're the same, we're the same." The counterpoint theme (in a higher register) is "but we're different, but we're different, but we're different." Its underlying story is: on the first day, difference was; on the second day, a division was created upon it; on the third day, irrational instances of dominance arose. Division may be rational or irrational. Dominance either seems or is justified. Difference *is*.

There is a politics to this. Concealed is the substantive way in which man has become the measure of all things. Under the sameness standard, women are measured according to our correspondence with man, our equality judged by our proximity to his measure. Under the difference standard, we are measured according to our lack of correspondence with him, our womanhood judged by our distance from his measure. Gender neutrality is thus simply the male standard, and the special protection rule is simply the female standard, but do not be deceived: masculinity, or maleness, is the referent for both. Think about it like those anatomy models in medical school. A male body is the human body; all those extra things women have are studied in ob/gyn. It truly is a situation in which more is less. Approaching sex discrimination in this way—as if sex questions are difference questions and equality questions are sameness questions—provides two ways for the law to hold women to a male standard and call that sex equality.

* * *

Having been very hard on the difference answer to sex equality questions, I should say that it takes up a very important problem: how to get women access to everything we have been excluded from, while also valuing everything that women are or have been allowed to become or have developed as a consequence of our struggle either not to be excluded from most of life's pursuits or to be taken seriously under the terms that have been permitted to be our terms. It negotiates what we have managed in relation to men. Legally articulated as the need to conform normative standards to existing reality, the strongest doctrinal expression of its sameness idea would prohibit taking gender into account in any way.

Its guiding impulse is: we're as good as you. Anything you can do, we can do. Just get out of the way. I have to confess a sincere affection for this approach. It has gotten women some access to employment and education, the public pursuits, including academic, professional, and blue-collar work; the military; and more than nominal access to athletics. It has moved to change the dead ends that were all we were seen as good for and has altered what passed for women's lack of physical training, which was really serious training in passivity and enforced weakness. It makes you want to cry sometimes to know that it has had to be a mission for many women just to be permitted to do the work of this society, to have the dignity of doing jobs a lot of other people don't even want to do.

* * *

* * * As applied, the sameness standard has mostly gotten men the benefit of those few things women have historically had—for all the good they did us. Almost every sex discrimination case that has been won at the Supreme Court level has been brought by a man. Under the rule of gender neutrality, the law of custody and divorce has been transformed, giving men an equal chance at custody of children and at alimony. Men often look like better "parents" under gender-neutral rules like level of income and presence of nuclear family, because men make more money and (as they say) initiate the building of family units. In effect, they get preferred because society advantages them before they get into court, and law is prohibited from taking that preference into account because that would mean taking gender into account. The group realities that make women more in need of alimony are not permitted to matter, because only individual factors, gender-neutrally considered, may matter. So the fact that women will live their lives, as individuals, as members of the group women, with women's chances in a sex-discriminatory society, may not count, or else it is sex discrimination. The equality principle in this guise mobilizes the idea that the way to get things for women is to get them for men. Men have gotten them. Have women? We still have not got equal pay, or equal work, far less equal pay for equal work, and we are close to losing separate enclaves like women's schools through this approach.

Here is why. In reality, which this approach is not long on because it is liberal idealism talking to itself, virtually every quality that distinguishes men from women is already affirmatively compensated in this society. Men's physiology defines most sports, their needs define auto and health insurance coverage, their socially designed biographies define workplace expectations and successful career patterns, their perspectives and concerns define quality in scholarship, their experiences and obsessions define merit, their objectification of life defines art, their military service defines citizenship, their presence defines family, their inability to get along with each other—their wars and rulerships—defines history, their image defines god, and their genitals define sex. For each of their differences from women, what amounts to an affirmative action plan is in effect, otherwise known as the structure and values of American society. But whenever women are, by this standard, "different" from men and insist on not having it held against us, whenever a difference is used to keep us second class and we refuse to smile about it, equality law has a paradigm trauma and it's crisis time for the doctrine.

What this doctrine has apparently meant by sex inequality is not what happens to us. The law of sex discrimination that has resulted seems to be looking only for those ways women are kept down that have *not* wrapped themselves up as a difference—whether original, imposed, or imagined. Start with original: what to do about the fact that women actually have an ability men still lack, gestating children in utero. Pregnancy therefore is a difference. Difference doctrine says it is sex discrimination to give women what we need, because only women need it. It is not sex discrimination not to give women what we need because then only women will not get what we need.[18] Move into imposed: what to do about the fact that most women are segregated into low-paying jobs where there are no men. Suspecting that the structure of the marketplace will be entirely subverted if comparable worth is put into effect, difference doctrine says that because there is no man to set a standard from which women's treatment is a deviation, there is no sex discrimination here, only sex difference. Never mind that there is no man to compare with because no man would do that job if he had a choice, and of course he has because he is a man, so he won't.

---

18. This is a reference to the issues raised by several recent cases which consider whether states' attempts to compensate pregnancy leaves and to secure jobs on return constitute sex discrimination. California Federal Savings and Loan Assn. v. Guerra, 758 F.2d 390 (9th Cir.1985), [*aff'd*, 479 U.S. 272 (1987)]; *see also* Miller–Wohl v. Commissioner of Labor, 515 F.Supp. 1264 (D.Montana 1981), *vacated and dismissed*, 685 F.2d 1088 (9th Cir.1982). The position argued in "Difference and Dominance" here suggests that if these benefits are prohibited under Title VII, Title VII is unconstitutional under the equal protection clause.

Now move into the so-called subtle reaches of the imposed category, the de facto area. Most jobs in fact require that the person, gender neutral, who is qualified for them will be someone who is not the primary caretaker of a preschool child. Pointing out that this raises a concern of sex in a society in which women are expected to care for the children is taken as day one of taking gender into account in the structuring of jobs. To do that would violate the rule against not noticing situated differences based on gender, so it never emerges that day one of taking gender into account was the day the job was structured with the expectation that its occupant would have no child care responsibilities. Imaginary sex differences—such as between male and female applicants to administer estates or between males aging and dying and females aging and dying—I will concede, the doctrine can handle.

I will also concede that there are many differences between women and men. I mean, can you imagine elevating one half of a population and denigrating the other half and producing a population in which everyone is the same? What the sameness standard fails to notice is that men's differences from women are equal to women's differences from men. There is an *equality* there. Yet the sexes are not socially equal. The difference approach misses the fact that hierarchy of power produces real as well as fantasied differences, differences that are also inequalities. What is missing in the difference approach is what Aristotle missed in his empiricist notion that equality means treating likes alike and unlikes unlike, and nobody has questioned it since. Why should you have to be the same as a man to get what a man gets simply because he is one? Why does maleness provide an original entitlement, not questioned on the basis of *its* gender, so that it is women—women who want to make a case of unequal treatment in a world men have made in their image (this is really the part Aristotle missed)—who have to show in effect that they are men in every relevant respect, unfortunately mistaken for women on the basis of an accident of birth?

The women that gender neutrality benefits, and there are some, show the suppositions of this approach in highest relief. They are mostly women who have been able to construct a biography that somewhat approximates the male norm, at least on paper. They are the qualified, the least of sex discrimination's victims. When they are denied a man's chance, it looks the most like sex bias. The more unequal society gets, the fewer such women are permitted to exist. Therefore, the more unequal society gets, the *less* likely the difference doctrine is to be able to do anything about it, because unequal power creates both the appearance and the reality of sex differences along the same lines as it creates its sex inequalities.

The special benefits side of the difference approach has not compensated for the differential of being second class. The special benefits rule is the only place in mainstream equality doctrine where you get to identify as a woman and not have that mean giving up all claim to equal treatment—but it comes close. Under its double standard, women who stand to inherit something when their husbands die have gotten the exclusion of a small percentage of the inheritance tax, to the tune of Justice Douglas waxing eloquent about the difficulties of all women's economic situation.[22] If we're going to be stigmatized as different, it would be nice if the compensation would fit the disparity. Women have also gotten three more years than men get before we have to be advanced or kicked out of the military hierarchy, as compensation for being precluded from combat, the usual way to advance.[23] Women have also gotten excluded from contact jobs in male-only prisons because we might get raped, the Court taking the viewpoint of the reasonable rapist on women's employment opportunities.[24] We also get protected out of jobs because of our fertility. The reason is that the job has health hazards, and somebody who might be a real person some day and therefore could sue—that is, a fetus—might be hurt if women, who apparently are not real persons and therefore can't sue either for the hazard to our health or for the lost employment opportunity, are given jobs that subject our bodies to possible harm. Excluding women is always an option if equality feels in tension with the pursuit itself. They never seem to think of excluding men. Take combat. Somehow it takes the glory out of the foxhole, the buddiness out of the trenches, to imagine us out there. You get the feeling they might rather end the draft, they might even rather not fight wars at all than have to do it with us.

The double standard of these rules doesn't give women the dignity of the single standard; it also does not (as the differences standard does) suppress the gender of its referent, which is, of course, the female gender. I must also confess some affection for this standard. The work of Carol Gilligan on gender differences in moral reasoning [27] gives it a lot of dignity, more than it has ever had, more, frankly, than I thought it ever could have. But she achieves for moral reasoning what the special protection rule achieves in law: the affirmative rather than the negative valuation of that which has accurately distinguished women from men, by making it seem as though those attributes, with their consequences, really are somehow ours, rather than what male supremacy has attributed to us for its own use. For women to affirm difference, when difference means dominance, as it does with gender, means to affirm the qualities and characteristics of powerlessness.

Women have done good things, and it is a good thing to affirm them. I think quilts are art. I think women have a history. I think we create culture. I also know that we have not only been excluded from making what has been considered art; our artifacts have been excluded from setting the standards by which art is art. Women have a history all right, but it is a history both of what was and of what was not allowed to

22. Kahn v. Shevin, 416 U.S. 351, 353 (1974).

23. Schlesinger v. Ballard, 419 U.S. 498 (1975).

24. Dothard v. Rawlinson, 433 U.S. 321 (1977); *see also* Michael M. v. Sonoma

County Superior Court, 450 U.S. 464 (1981).

27. Carol Gilligan, *In a Different Voice* (1982).

be. So I am critical of affirming what we have been, which necessarily is what we have been permitted, as if it is women's, ours, possessive. As if equality, in spite of everything, already ineluctably exists.

I am getting hard on this and am about to get harder on it. I do not think that the way women reason morally is morality "in a different voice." I think it is morality in a higher register, in the feminine voice. Women value care because men have valued us according to the care we give them, and we could probably use some. Women think in relational terms because our existence is defined in relation to men. Further, when you are powerless, you don't just speak differently. A lot, you don't speak. Your speech is not just differently articulated, it is silenced. Eliminated, gone. You aren't just deprived of a language with which to articulate your distinctiveness, although you are; you are deprived of a life out of which articulation might come. Not being heard is not just a function of lack of recognition, not just that no one knows how to listen to you, although it is that; it is also silence of the deep kind, the silence of being prevented from having anything to say. Sometimes it is permanent. All I am saying is that the damage of sexism is real, and reifying that into differences is an insult to our possibilities.

So long as these issues are framed this way, demands for equality will always appear to be asking to have it both ways: the same when we are the same, different when we are different. But this is the way men have it: equal and different too. They have it the same as women when they are the same and want it, and different from women when they are different and want to be, which usually they do. Equal and different too would only be parity. But under male supremacy, while being told we get it both ways, both the specialness of the pedestal and an even chance at the race, the ability to be a woman and a person, too, few women get much benefit of either.

* * *

There is an alternative approach, one that threads its way through existing law and expresses, I think, the reason equality law exists in the first place. It provides a second answer, a dissident answer in law and philosophy, to both the equality question and the gender question. In this approach, an equality question is a question of the distribution of power. Gender is also a question of power, specifically of male supremacy and female subordination. The question of equality, from the standpoint of what it is going to take to get it, is at root a question of hierarchy, which—as power succeeds in constructing social perception and social reality—derivatively becomes a categorical distinction, a difference. Here, on the first day that matters, dominance was achieved, probably by force. By the second day, division along the same lines had to be relatively firmly in place. On the third day, if not sooner, differences were demarcated, together with social systems to exaggerate them in perception and in fact, because the systematically differential delivery of benefits and deprivations required making no mistake about who was who. Comparatively speaking, man has been resting ever since. Gender might not even code as difference, might not mean distinction epistemologically, were it not for its consequences for social power.

I call this the dominance approach, and it is the ground I have been standing on in criticizing mainstream law. The goal of this dissident approach is not to make legal categories trace and trap the way things are. It is not to make rules that fit reality. It is critical of reality. Its task is not to formulate abstract standards that will produce determinate outcomes in particular cases. Its project is more substantive, more jurisprudential than formulaic, which is why it is difficult for the mainstream discourse to dignify it as an approach to doctrine or to imagine it as a rule of law at all. It proposes to expose that which women have had little choice but to be confined to, in order to change it.

The dominance approach centers on the most sex-differential abuses of women as a gender, abuses that sex equality law in its difference garb could not confront. It is based on a reality about which little of a systematic nature was known before 1970, a reality that calls for a new conception of the problem of sex inequality. This new information includes not only the extent and intractability of sex segregation into poverty, which has been known before, but the range of issues termed violence against women, which has not been. It combines women's material desperation, through being relegated to categories of jobs that pay nil, with the massive amount of rape and attempted rape—44 percent of all women—about which virtually nothing is done;[30] the sexual assault of children—38 percent of girls and 10 percent of boys—which is apparently endemic to the patriarchal family;[31] the battery of women that is systematic in one quarter to one third of our homes;[32] prostitution, women's fundamental economic condition, what we do when all else fails, and for many women in this country, all else fails often; and pornography, an industry that traffics in female flesh, making sex inequality into sex to the tune of eight billion dollars a year in profits largely to organized crime.

These experiences have been silenced out of the difference definition of sex equality largely because they happen almost exclusively to women. Understand: for this reason, they are considered *not* to raise sex equality issues. Because this treatment is done almost uniquely to women, it is implicitly treated as a difference, the sex difference, when in fact it is the socially situated subjection of women. The whole point of women's

---

30. Diana Russell and Nancy Howell, "The Prevalence of Rape in the United States Revisited," 8 *Signs: Journal of Women in Culture and Society* 689 (1983) (44 percent of women in 930 households were victims of rape or attempted rape at some time in their lives).

31. Diana Russell, "The Incidence and Prevalence of Intrafamilial and Extrafamilial Sexual Abuse of Female Children," 7

Child Abuse & Neglect: The International Journal 133 (1983).

32. R. Emerson Dobash and Russell Dobash, *Violence against Wives: A Case against the Patriarchy* (1979); Bruno v. Codd, 90 Misc.2d 1047, 396 N.Y.S.2d 974 (Sup.Ct.1977), *rev'd,* 64 A.D.2d 582, 407 N.Y.S.2d 165 (1st Dep't 1978), *aff'd* 47 N.Y.2d 582, 393 N.E.2d 976, 419 N.Y.S.2d 901 (1979).

social relegation to inferiority as a gender is that for the most part these things aren't done to men.   Men are not paid half of what women are paid for doing the same work on the basis of their equal difference. Everything they touch does not turn valueless because they touched it. When they are hit, a person has been assaulted.   When they are sexually violated, it is not simply tolerated or found entertaining or defended as the necessary structure of the family, the price of civilization, or a constitutional right.

Does this differential describe the sex difference?   Maybe so.   It does describe the systematic relegation of an entire group of people to a condition of inferiority and attribute it to their nature.   If this differential were biological, maybe biological intervention would have to be considered.   If it were evolutionary, perhaps men would have to evolve differently.   Because I think it is political, I think its politics construct the deep structure of society.   Men who do not rape women have nothing wrong with their hormones.   Men who are made sick by pornography and do not eroticize their revulsion are not under-evolved. This social status in which we can be used and abused and trivialized and humiliated and bought and sold and passed around and patted on the head and put in place and told to smile so that we look as though we're enjoying it all is not what some of us have in mind as sex equality.

This second approach—which is not abstract, which is at odds with socially imposed reality and therefore does not look like a standard according to the standard for standards—became the implicit model for racial justice applied by the courts during the sixties.   It has since eroded with the erosion of judicial commitment to racial equality.   It was based on the realization that the condition of Blacks in particular was not fundamentally a matter of rational or irrational differentiation on the basis of race but was fundamentally a matter of white supremacy, under which racial differences became invidious as a consequence.   To consider gender in this way, observe again that men are as different from women as women are from men, but socially the sexes are not equally powerful.   To be on the top of a hierarchy is certainly different from being on the bottom, but that is an obfuscatingly neutralized way of putting it, as a hierarchy is a great deal more than that.   If gender were merely a question of difference, sex inequality would be a problem of mere sexism, of mistaken differentiation, of inaccurate categorization of individuals.   This is what the difference approach thinks it is and is therefore sensitive to.   But if gender is an inequality first, constructed as a socially relevant differentiation in order to keep that inequality in place, then sex inequality questions are questions of systematic dominance, of male supremacy, which is not at all abstract and is anything but a mistake.

If differentiation into classifications, in itself, is discrimination, as it is in difference doctrine, the use of law to change group-based social inequalities becomes problematic, even contradictory.   This is because the group whose situation is to be changed must necessarily be legally identified and delineated, yet to do so is considered in fundamental tension with the guarantee against legally sanctioned inequality. If differentiation is discrimination, affirmative action, and any legal change in social inequality, is discrimination—but the existing social differentiations which constitute the inequality are not? This is only to say that, in the view that equates differentiation with discrimination, changing an unequal status quo is discrimination, but allowing it to exist is not.

Looking at the difference approach and the dominance approach from each other's point of view clarifies some otherwise confusing tensions in sex equality debates. From the point of view of the dominance approach, it becomes clear that the difference approach adopts the point of view of male supremacy on the status of the sexes. Simply by treating the status quo as "the standard," it invisibly and uncritically accepts the arrangements under male supremacy. In this sense, the difference approach is masculinist, although it can be expressed in a female voice. The dominance approach, in that it sees the inequalities of the social world from the standpoint of the subordination of women to men, is feminist.

If you look through the lens of the difference approach at the world as the dominance approach imagines it—that is, if you try to see real inequality through a lens that has difficulty seeing an inequality as an inequality if it also appears as a difference—you see demands for change in the distribution of power as demands for special protection. This is because the only tools that the difference paradigm offers to comprehend disparity equate the recognition of a gender line with an admission of lack of entitlement to equality under law. Since equality questions are primarily confronted in this approach as matters of empirical fit—that is, as matters of accurately shaping legal rules (implicitly modeled on the standard men set) to the way the world is (also implicitly modeled on the standard men set)—any existing differences must be negated to merit equal treatment. For ethnicity as well as for gender, it is basic to mainstream discrimination doctrine to preclude any true diversity among equals or true equality within diversity.

To the difference approach, it further follows that any attempt to change the way the world actually is looks like a moral question requiring a separate judgment of how things ought to be. This approach imagines asking the following disinterested question that can be answered neutrally as to groups: against the weight of empirical difference, should we treat some as the equals of others, even when they may not be entitled to it because they are not up to standard? Because this construction of the problem is part of what the dominance approach unmasks, it does not arise with the dominance approach, which therefore does not see its own foundations as moral. If sex inequalities are approached as matters of imposed status, which are in need of change if a legal mandate of equality means anything at all, the question whether women should be treated unequally means simply whether women should be treated as less. When it is exposed as a naked power question, there is no separable question of what ought to be. The only real question is what is and is not a gender question. Once no amount of difference justifies treating women as subhuman, eliminating that is what equality law is for. In this shift of paradigms, equality propositions become no longer propositions of good and evil, but of power and powerlessness, no more disinterested in their origins or neutral in their arrival at conclusions than are the problems they address.

* * *

To summarize the argument: seeing sex equality questions as matters of reasonable or unreasonable classification is part of the way male dominance is expressed in law. If you follow my shift in perspective from gender as difference to gender as dominance, gender changes from a distinction that is presumptively valid to a detriment that is presumptively suspect. The difference approach tries to map reality; the dominance approach tries to challenge and change it. In the dominance approach, sex discrimination stops being a question of morality and starts being a question of politics.

You can tell if sameness is your standard for equality if my critique of hierarchy looks like a request for special protection in disguise. It's not. It envisions a change that would make possible a simple equal chance for the first time. To define the reality of sex as difference and the warrant of equality as sameness is wrong on both counts. Sex, in nature, is not a bipolarity; it is a continuum. In society it is made into a bipolarity. Once this is done, to require that one be the same as those who set the standard—those which one is already socially defined as different from—simply means that sex equality is conceptually designed never to be achieved. Those who most need equal treatment will be the least similar, socially, to those whose situation sets the standard as against which one's entitlement to be equally treated is measured. Doctrinally speaking, the deepest problems of sex inequality will not find women "similarly situated" to men. Far less will practices of sex inequality require that acts be intentionally discriminatory. All that is required is that the status quo be maintained. As a strategy for maintaining social power first structure reality unequally, then require that entitlement to alter it be grounded on a lack of distinction in situation; first structure perception so that different equals inferior, then require that discrimination be activated by evil minds who *know* they are treating equals as less.

I say, give women equal power in social life. Let what we say matter, then we will discourse on questions of morality. Take your foot off our necks, then we will hear in what tongue women speak. So long as sex equality is limited by sex difference, whether you like it or don't like it, whether you value it or seek to negate it, whether you stake it out as a grounds for feminism or occupy it as the terrain of misogyny, women will be born, degraded, and die. We would settle for that equal protection of the laws under which one would be born, live, and die, in a country where protection is not a dirty word and equality is not a special privilege.

JOAN C. WILLIAMS, DECONSTRUCTING GENDER
87 Mich.L.Rev. 797, 798–99, 837–43 (1989).

I start out, as have many others, from the deep split among American feminists between "sameness" and "difference." The driving force behind the mid-twentieth-century resurgence of American feminism was an insistence on the fundamental similarity of men and women and, hence, their essential equality. Betty Friedan comes to mind as an enormously influential housewife whose focus on men and women as individuals made her intensely hostile to gender stereotyping.[3]

Mid-century feminism, now often referred to somewhat derisively as assimilationism, focused on providing opportunities to women in realms traditionally preserved for men.[4] In the 1980s two phenomena have shifted feminists' attention from assimilationists' focus on how individual women are *like* men to a focus on gender *differences,* on how women as a group differ from men as a group. The first is the feminization of poverty, which dramatizes the chronic and increasing economic vulnerability of women. Feminists now realize that the assimilationists' traditional focus on gender-neutrality may have rendered women more vulnerable to certain gender-related disabilities that have important economic consequences. The second phenomenon that plays a central role in the current feminist imagination is that of career women "choosing" to abandon or subordinate their careers so they can spend time with their small children. These phenomena highlight the fact that deepseated social differences continue to encourage men and women to make quite different choices with respect to work and family. Thus, "sameness" scholars are increasingly confronted by the existence of gender differences.

Do these challenges to assimilationism prove that we should stop trying to kid ourselves and admit the "real" differences between men and women, as the popular press drums into us day after day, and as the "feminism of difference" appears to confirm? Do such phenomena mean that feminists' traditional focus on gender-neutrality is a bankrupt ideal? I will argue no on both counts, taking an approach quite different from that ordinarily taken by feminists on the sameness side of the spectrum. "Sameness" feminists usually have responded to the feminists of difference by reiterating their basic insight that individual men and women can be very similar. While true, this is not an adequate response to the basic insight of "difference" feminists: that gender exists, that men and women differ as groups. In this article, I try to speak to feminists of difference on their own terms. While I take gender seriously, I disagree with the description of gender provided by difference feminists.

* * *

3. B. Friedan, The Feminine Mystique (1963). * * *

4. *See, e.g.,* Wasserstrom, *Racism, Sexism, and Preferential Treatment: An Approach to the Topics,* 24 UCLA L.Rev. 581, 606 (1977). Wasserstrom's comparison of sex to eye color is often criticized by feminists of difference, who argue that something would be lost if sex were treated as a factor as irrelevant as eye color. * * *

A. From Gender-Neutrality to Deinstitutionalizing Gender

"Sameness" feminists' focus on the similarities between individual men and individual women led them to advocate "gender-neutral" categories that do not rely on gender stereotypes to differentiate between men and women. Recent feminists have challenged the traditional goal of gender neutrality on the grounds that it mandates a blindness to gender that has left women in a worse position than they were before the mid-twentieth-century challenge to gender roles.

This argument has been made in two different ways. Scholars such as Martha Fineman have argued that liberal feminists' insistence on gender-neutrality in the formulation of "no-fault" divorce laws has led to courts' willful blindness to the ways in which marriage systematically helps men's, and hurts women's, careers.[172] Catharine MacKinnon has generalized this argument. She argues that because women are systematically disadvantaged by their sex, properly designed remedial measures can legitimately be framed by reference to sex.[173]

MacKinnon's "inequality approach" would allow for separate standards for men and women so long as "the policy or practice in question [does not] integrally contribute[ ] to the maintenance of an underclass or a deprived position because of gender status." [174] The strongest form her argument takes is that adherence to gender roles disadvantages women: Why let liberal feminists' taboo against differential treatment of women eliminate the most effective solution to inequality?

This debate is graced by a core truth and massive confusion. The core truth is that an insistence on gender neutrality by definition precludes protection for women victimized by gender.

The confusion stems from the use of the term gender neutrality. One *could* argue that problems created by the gendered structure of wage labor, or other aspects of the gender system, should not be remedied through the use of categories that identify the protected group by reference to the gender roles that have disadvantaged them. For example, one could argue that workers whose careers were disadvantaged by choices in favor of child care should not be given the additional support they need to "catch up" with their former spouses, on the grounds that the group protected inevitably would be mostly female, and this could reinforce the stereotype that women need special protections. Yet I know of no feminist of any stripe who makes this argument, which would be the position of someone committed to gender neutrality.

Traditionally, feminists have insisted not upon a blindness to gender, but on opposition to the traditional correlation between sex and gender. MacKinnon's crucial divergence is that she accepts the use of

172. Fineman, *Implementing Equality: Ideology, Contradiction and Social Change,* 1983 Wis.L.Rev. 789, 791[.]

173. [C. MacKinnon, Sexual Harassment of Working Women—A Case of Sex Discrimination 100–41 (1979) [hereinafter Sexual Harassment]; C. MacKinnon, Feminism Unmodified 35–36 (1987).]

174. Sexual Harassment, *supra* note [173], at 117. *See* Taub, Book Review, 80 Colum.L.Rev. 1686 (1980).

sex as a proxy for gender. Thus MacKinnon sees nothing inherently objectionable about protecting workers who have given up ideal worker status [a] due to child-care responsibilities by offering protections to *women*.[175] Her inequality approach allows disadvantages produced by *gender* to be remedied by reference to *sex*. This is in effect an acceptance and a reinforcement of the societal presumption that the social role of primary caretaker is necessarily correlated with possession of a vagina.

MacKinnon's approach without a doubt would serve to reinforce and to legitimize gender stereotypes that are an integral part of the increasingly oppressive gender system. Let's focus on a specific example. Scholars have found that the abolition of the maternal presumption in child-custody decisions has had two deleterious impacts on women.[176] First, in the 90 percent of the cases where mothers received custody, mothers often find themselves bargaining away financial claims in exchange for custody of the children. Even if the father does not want custody, his lawyer often will advise him to claim it in order to have a bargaining chip with which to bargain down his wife's financial claims. Second, the abolition of the maternal preference has created situations where a father who wants custody often wins even if he was not the primary caretaker prior to the divorce—on the grounds that he can offer the children a better life because he is richer than his former wife. In these circumstances, the ironic result of a mother's sacrifice of ideal worker status for the sake of her children is that she ultimately loses the children.

While these results are no doubt infuriating, do they merit a return to a maternal presumption, as MacKinnon's approach seems to imply? No: the deconstruction of gender, by highlighting the chronic and increasing oppressiveness of the gender system, demonstrates the undesirability of the inequality approach, which would reinforce the gender system in both a symbolic way and a practical one. On a symbolic level, the inequality approach would reinforce and legitimize the traditional assumption that childrearing is "naturally" the province of women. MacKinnon's rule also would reinforce gender mandates in a very concrete way. Say a father chose to give up ideal worker status in order to undertake primary child care responsibility. MacKinnon's rule fails to help him, because the rule is framed in terms of biology, not gender. The result: a strong message to fathers that they should not deviate from established gender roles. MacKinnon's rule operates to reinforce the gender system.

a. By "ideal worker" Williams means the traditional view of an employer that an ideal employee is one without child-care responsibilities. Thus, the concept of "ideal worker" has significantly disadvantaged women in the workplace—eds.

175. Sexual Harassment, *supra* note [173], at 122–24.

176. *See* Polikoff, *Why Mothers Are Losing: A Brief Analysis of Criteria Used in Child Custody Determinations*, 7 Women's Rts.L.Rep. 235 (1982); L. Weitzman, [The Divorce Revolution] 217, 310–18 [1985].

What we need, then, is a rule that avoids the traditional correlation between gender and sex, a rule that is *sex-* but not *gender*-neutral. The traditional goal, properly understood, is really one of *sex*-neutrality, or, more descriptively, one of deinstitutionalizing gender. It entails a systematic refusal to institutionalize gender in any form. This approach mandates not an enforced blindness to gender, but rather a refusal to reinforce the traditional assumption that adherence to gender roles flows "naturally" from biological sex. Reinforcing that assumption reinforces the grip of the gender system as a whole.

For an example that highlights the distinction between gender neutrality and deinstitutionalization, let us return to our "divorce revolution" example. It is grossly unfair for courts suddenly to pretend that gender roles within marriage do not exist once a couple enters the courtroom, and the deinstitutionalization of gender does not require it. What is needed is not a gender-neutral rule but one that avoids the traditional shorthand of addressing gender by reference to sex.

This analysis shows that the traditional commitment, which is really one to deinstitutionalizing gender rather than to gender neutrality, need not preclude rules that protect people victimized by gender. People disadvantaged by gender can be protected by properly naming the group: in this case, not mothers, but anyone who has eschewed ideal worker status to fulfill child-care responsibilities. One court, motivated to clear thinking by a legislature opposed to rules that addressed gender disabilities by reference to sex, has actually framed child-custody rules in this way.[180]

The traditional goal is misstated by the term "gender neutrality." The core feminist goal is not one of pretending gender does not exist. Instead, it is to deinstitutionalize the gendered structure of our society. There is no reason why people disadvantaged by gender need to be suddenly disowned. The deconstruction of gender allows us to protect them by reference to their social roles instead of their genitals.

B. DECONSTRUCTING DIFFERENCE

How can this be done? Certainly the hardest task in the process of deconstructing gender is to begin the long and arduous process of seeing through the descriptions of men and women offered by domesticity. Feminists need to explain exactly how the traditional descriptions of men and women are false. This is a job for social scientists, for a new Carol Gilligan in reverse, who can focus the massive literature on sex stereotyping in a way that dramatizes that Gilligan is talking about metaphors, not actual people. Nonetheless, I offer some thoughts on Gilligan's central imagery: that women are focused on relationships while men are not. As I see it, to the extent this is true, it is merely a restatement of male and female gender roles under the current gender system. Beyond that, it is unconvincing.

180. *See* Garska v. McCoy, 278 S.E.2d 357, 360–63 (W.Va.1981), *cited in* Williams, *The Equality Crisis: Some Reflections on* *Culture, Courts, and Feminism,* 7 Women's Rts.L.Rep. 175, 190 n. 80 (1982).

This is perhaps easiest to see from Gilligan's description of men as empty vessels of capitalist virtues—competitive and individualistic and espousing liberal ideology to justify this approach to life. Gilligan's description has an element of truth as a description of *gender:* it captures men's sense of entitlement to ideal worker status and their gendered choice in favor of their careers when presented with the choice society sets up between child-care responsibilities and being a "responsible" worker.

Similarly, Gilligan's central claim that women are more focused on relationships reflects gender verities. It is true in the sense that women's lives are shaped by the needs of their children and their husbands—but this is just a restatement of the gender system that has traditionally defined women's social existence in terms of their husbands' need to eliminate child-care and other responsibilities that detract from their ability to function as ideal workers. And when we speak of women's focus on relationships with *men,* we also reflect the underlying reality that the only alternative to marriage for most women—certainly for most mothers—has traditionally been poverty, a state of affairs that continues in force to this day.

The kernal of truth in Gilligan's "voices," then, is that Gilligan provides a description of gender differences related to men's and women's different roles with respect to wage labor and child care under the current gender regime. Yet we see these true gender differences through glasses framed by an ideology that distorts our vision. To break free of traditional gender ideology, we need at the simplest level to see how men nurture people and relationships and how women are competitive and powerful. This is a task in which we as feminists will meet considerable resistance, both from inside and outside the feminist movement.

Our difficulty in seeing men's nurturing side stems in part from the word "nurture." Although its broadest definition is "the act of promoting development or growth," [183] the word derives from nursing a baby, and still has overtones of "something only a mother can do." Yet men are involved in all kinds of relationships in which they promote another's development in a caring way: as fathers, as mentors, as camp counselors, as boy scout leaders. These relationships may have a somewhat different emotional style and tone than do those of women and often occur in somewhat different contexts: that is the gender difference. But a blanket assertion that women are nurturing while men are not reflects more ideology than reality.

So does the related claim that women's voice involves a focus on relationships that is lacking in men. Men focus on relationships, too. How they can be said not to in a culture that deifies romantic love as much as ours does has always mystified me. Perhaps part of what resonates in the claim that men do not focus on relationships is that men *as a group* tend to have a different style than do women: whereas

183. The American Heritage Dictionary (William Morris ed. 1970).

women tend to associate intimacy with self-disclosure, men tend not to. This may be why women forget about the role that relationships play in men's lives, from work relationships, to solidarity based on spectator sports, to time spent "out with the boys." These relationships may not look intimate to women, but they are often important to men.

Ideology not only veils men's needy side, it also veils the competitive nature of many women who want power as avidly as men. "Feminists have long been fiercely critical of male power games, yet we have often ignored or concealed our own conflicts over money, control, position, and recognition * * *. It is time to end the silence."[187] The first step, as these authors note, is to acknowledge the existence of competition in women's lives. Women's desire for control may be exercised in running "a tight ship" on a small income, in tying children to apron strings, or in nagging husbands—the classic powerplay of the powerless. Note how these examples tend to deprecate women's desire for power. These are the stereotypes that come to mind because they confirm the ideology that "real" women don't need power. These are ways women's yearning for power has been used as evidence against them, as evidence they are not worthy as wives, as mothers, or as women. Feminists' taboo against competition has only reinforced the traditional view that real women don't need power. Yet women's traditional roles have always required them to be able to wield power with self-confidence and subtlety. Other cultures recognize that dealing with a two-year-old is one of the great recurring power struggles in the cycle of human life. But not ours. We are too wrapped up in viewing childrearing as nurturing, as something opposed by its nature to authoritative wielding of power, to see that nurturing involves a sophisticated use of power in a hierarchical relationship. The differences between being a boss and a mother in this regard are differences in degree as well as in kind.

Moving ever closer to the bone, we need to reassess the role of power in relationships based on romantic love. The notion that a marriage involves complex ongoing negotiations over power may seem shocking. But if we truly are committed to a deconstruction of traditional gender verities, we need to stop blinding ourselves to nurturing outside the home and to power negotiations within it.

BIBLIOGRAPHY

Feminist Jurisprudence

DuBois, Dunlap, Gilligan, MacKinnon & Menkel–Meadow, *Feminist Discourse, Moral Values, and the Law—A Conversation,* 34 Buff.L.Rev. 11 (1985).

Finley, *Transcending Equality Theory: A Way Out of the Maternity and the Workplace Debate,* 86 Colum.L.Rev. 1118 (1986).

Gibson, *Childbearing and Childrearing: Feminists and Reform,* 73 Va. L.Rev. 1145 (1987).

187. Competition: A Feminist Taboo?
1 (V. Miner & H. Longino eds. 1987).

Harris, *Race and Essentialism in Feminist Legal Theory*, 42 Stan.L.Rev. 581 (1990).

Littleton, *Reconstructing Sexual Equality*, 75 Cal.L.Rev. 1279 (1987).

Littleton, *Equality and Feminist Legal Theory*, 48 U.Pitt.L.Rev. 1043 (1987).

MacKinnon, *Feminism, Marxism, Method, and the State: An Agenda for Theory*, 7 Signs 515 (1982).

MacKinnon, *Feminism, Marxism, Method, and the State: Toward Feminist Jurisprudence*, 8 Signs 635 (1983).

C. MacKinnon, TOWARD A FEMINIST THEORY OF THE STATE (1989).

Matsuda, *When the First Quail Calls: Multiple Consciousness as Jurisprudential Method*, 11 Women's Rts.L.Rep. 7 (1989).

M. Minow, MAKING ALL THE DIFFERENCE: INCLUSION, EXCLUSION, AND AMERICAN LAW (1990).

Minow, *The Supreme Court 1986 Term—Foreword: Justice Engendered*, 101 Harv.L.Rev. 10 (1987).

Olsen, *Statutory Rape: A Feminist Critique of Rights Analysis*, 63 Tex.L.Rev. 387 (1984).

Olsen, *The Family and the Market: A Study of Ideology and Legal Reform*, 96 Harv.L.Rev. 1497 (1983).

Rhode, JUSTICE AND GENDER: SEX DISCRIMINATION AND THE LAW (1989).

Rifkin, *Toward a Theory of Law and Patriarchy*, 3 Harv.Women's L.J. 83 (1980).

Scales, *Towards a Feminist Jurisprudence*, 56 Ind.L.J. 375 (1981).

Scales, *The Emergence of a Feminist Jurisprudence: An Essay*, 95 Yale L.J. 1371 (1986).

Sunstein, *Feminism and Legal Theory* [review of MacKinnon, FEMINISM UNMODIFIED], 101 Harv.L.Rev. 826 (1988).

Symposium, *Feminist Jurisprudence*, 24 Ga.L.Rev. 759–1044 (1990).

Symposium—*Feminist Jurisprudence—The 1990 Myra Bradwell Day Panel*, 1 Colum.J.Gender & L. 5 (1991).

Taub & Schneider, Perspectives on Women's Subordination and the Role of Law, in THE POLITICS OF LAW 117 (D. Kairys ed. 1982).

West, *Jurisprudence and Gender*, 55 U.Chi.L.Rev. 1 (1988).

West, *The Difference in Women's Hedonic Lives: A Phenomenological Critique of Feminist Legal Theory*, 3 Wisc.Women's L.J. 81 (1987).

Whitman, *Law and Sex* [review of MacKinnon, FEMINISM UNMODIFIED], 86 Mich.L.Rev. 1388 (1988).

Williams, *On Being the Object of Property*, 14 Signs 5 (1988).

Wishik, *To Question Everything: The Inquiries of Feminist Jurisprudence,* 1 Berkeley Women's L.J. 64 (1985).

E. Wolgast, EQUALITY AND THE RIGHTS OF WOMEN (1980).

Gender and the Constitution

Allen, *Autonomy's Magic Wand: Abortion and Constitutional Interpretation,* 72 B.U.L.Rev. 683 (1992).

Brown, Emerson, Falk & Freedman, *The Equal Rights Amendment: A Constitutional Basis for Equal Rights for Women,* 80 Yale L.J. 871 (1971).

Colker, *Anti–Subordination Above All: Sex, Race, and Equal Protection,* 61 N.Y.U.L.Rev. 1003 (1986).

Farina, *Conceiving Due Process,* 3 Yale J.L. & Feminism 189 (1991).

Freedman, *Sex Equality, Sex Differences, and the Supreme Court,* 92 Yale L.J. 913 (1983).

Ginsburg, *Gender and the Constitution,* 44 U.Cin.L.Rev. 1 (1975).

Karst, *Woman's Constitution,* 1984 Duke L.J. 447.

Kay, *Models of Equality,* 1985 U.Ill.L.Rev. 39.

D. Kirp, M. Yudof, & M. Franks, GENDER JUSTICE (1986).

Law, *Rethinking Sex and the Constitution,* 132 U.Pa.L.Rev. 955 (1984).

Maltz, *Sex Discrimination in the Supreme Court—A Comment on Sex Equality, Sex Differences, and the Supreme Court,* 1985 Duke L.J. 177.

Sunstein, *Neutrality in Constitutional Law (With Special Reference to Pornography, Abortion, and Surrogacy),* 92 Colum.L.Rev. 1 (1992).

Wildman, *The Legitimation of Sex Discrimination: A Critical Response to Supreme Court Jurisprudence,* 63 Or.L.Rev. 265 (1984).

Sex Discrimination and the Law

Austin, *Sapphire Bound!,* 1989 Wis.L.Rev. 539.

Becker, *Obscuring the Struggle: Sex Discrimination, Social Security, and Stone, Seidman, Sunstein & Tushnet's* CONSTITUTIONAL LAW, 89 Colum.L.Rev. 264 (1989).

Becker, *Prince Charming: Abstract Equality,* 1987 Sup.Ct.Rev. 201.

Dowd, *Maternity Leave: Taking Sex Differences into Account,* 54 Ford. L.Rev. 699 (1986).

Estrich, *Rape,* 95 Yale L.J. 1087 (1986).

Frug, *Securing Job Equality for Women: Labor Market Hostility to Working Mothers,* 59 B.U.L.Rev. 55 (1979).

Krieger & Cooney, *The Miller–Wohl Controversy: Equal Treatment, Positive Action and the Meaning of Women's Equality,* 13 Golden Gate U.L.Rev. 513 (1983).

Law, *Women, Work, Welfare, and the Preservation of Patriarchy,* 131 U.Pa.L.Rev. 1249 (1983).

C. MacKinnon, SEXUAL HARASSMENT OF WORKING WOMEN: A CASE STUDY OF SEX DISCRIMINATION (1979).

Powers, *Sex Segregation and the Ambivalent Directions of Sex Discrimination Law,* 1979 Wisc.L.Rev. 55.

Scales–Trent, *Black Women and the Constitution: Finding Our Place, Asserting Our Rights,* 24 Harv.C.R.–C.L.L.Rev. 9 (1989).

Scarborough, *Conceptualizing Black Women's Employment Experiences,* 98 Yale L.J. 1457 (1989).

Schultz, *Telling Stories About Women and Work: Judicial Interpretations of Sex Segregation in the Workplace in Title VII Cases Raising the Lack of Interest Argument,* 103 Harv.L.Rev. 1750 (1990).

Symposium—*Comparable Worth,* 20 Mich.J.L.Ref. (1986).

Taub, *Keeping Women in their Place: Stereotyping Per Se as a Form of Employment Discrimination,* 21 B.C.L.Rev. 345 (1980).

Taub, *Review of MacKinnon,* SEXUAL HARASSMENT OF WORKING WOMEN, 80 Colum.L.Rev. 1686 (1980).

Williams, *Equality's Riddle: Pregnancy and the Equal Treatment/Special Treatment Debate,* 13 N.Y.U.Rev.L. & Soc.Change 325 (1985).

Chapter IX

AFFIRMATIVE ACTION

The materials in Chapter VII argue that governmental action that discriminates against racial minorities should be subjected to close judicial scrutiny under the Fourteenth Amendment. What do the justifications provided—the moral irrelevance of race, the stigma imposed on individuals or groups, the political powerlessness of blacks—say about governmental programs established to *benefit* racial minorities? This, of course, is the constitutional question raised by "affirmative action."

The readings in this Chapter analyze several different aspects of the affirmative action debate. We begin by asking whether it is ever appropriate to take account of race. Many Americans who sincerely oppose racial discrimination believe that the Constitution requires the government to be colorblind. But this is a position that rules out most forms of affirmative action. In Section A we examine the arguments for and against colorblindness; we also look at the alternative—race-consciousness. In Section B and C we deal with affirmative action programs in two different areas: admissions to universities and professional schools (the issue in *Bakke* [1]), and the award of broadcast licenses (the issue in *Metro Broadcasting* [2]).

A. COLORBLINDNESS OR RACE–CONSCIOUSNESS

Many people think that the most decent and simple solution to the problem of racial division is to ignore the fact of race. An early statement of this idea is found in Justice Harlan's dissent in *Plessy v. Ferguson:* "There is no caste here. Our Constitution is color-blind, and neither knows nor tolerates classes among citizens." [3] In modern times Alexander Bickel captured the same notion in another memorable phrase: "discrimination on the basis of race is illegal, immoral, unconsti-

---

1. Regents of the Univ. of Calif. v. Bakke, 438 U.S. 265, 98 S.Ct. 2733, 57 L.Ed.2d 750 (1978).

2. Metro Broadcasting, Inc. v. FCC, 497 U.S. 547, 110 S.Ct. 2997, 111 L.Ed.2d 445 (1990).

3. 163 U.S. 537, 559, 16 S.Ct. 1138, 1146, 41 L.Ed. 256 (1896).

tutional, inherently wrong, and destructive of democratic society." [4] We also find this idea in Justice O'Connor's plurality opinion in *Richmond v. J.A. Croson.* [5] As the decision in *Croson* shows, colorblindness rules out most affirmative action programs. That is the price we have to pay for a rule that is simple and even-handed. But there may be good reasons for paying that price.

William Van Alstyne is a strong supporter of colorblindness. It is the ideal the Supreme Court rejected in the 19th century, and embraced in *Brown v. Board of Education* [6] (and for 20 years thereafter). In treating all people alike it is self-evidently fair. And because the rule of colorblindness is clear and categorical it cannot be manipulated the way equal protection rules were after the Civil War: courts are not permitted to ask whether racial classifications are "reasonable."

Laurence Tribe reads the Court's progress from *Plessy* to *Brown* in a different way. According to Tribe the original intent of the framers of the Fourteenth Amendment tells against colorblindness. And it is not clear that *Brown* enshrines that principle either: we might better understand it as a decision against racial subjugation. That is a holding we could easily square with most kinds of affirmative action.

Tribe is concerned with legal support (in text, intent, and precedent) for the ideal of colorblindness. Neil Gotanda points to a very different kind of problem. Advocates of colorblindness assume that race is at bottom just a question of skin pigment, a sense datum that we can overlook, the way truly colorblind individuals do with shades of red and green. This is not so. Gotanda contends that race is at bottom a social construct rather than an empirical fact. The American system of racial classification incorporates assumptions about white racial purity and black enslaveability that we do not find, for example, in the West Indies or Latin America. The practice of colorblindness will allow us to cover these assumptions up, but they will not go away.

Alexander Aleinikoff makes a case for race-consciousness as an alternative to colorblindness. There is a deep humanism in seeing other races as like ourselves. But we need to go further—to see ourselves as others see us, to realize that our own culture is not a privileged point of view but just one among many. The calls for "black pride" and "black power" in the 1960's were a demand for a reorientation of this sort, and the consequences have been startling.

WILLIAM VAN ALSTYNE, RITES OF PASSAGE: RACE, THE SUPREME COURT, AND THE CONSTITUTION
46 U.Chi.L.Rev. 775, 780–784, 788–789, 792 (1979).

A. THE ORIGINAL INTERPRETATION

The first passage for the Court came with the immediate adjudication of race-related cases on the heels of the Civil War amendments.

---

4. Alexander M. Bickel, The Morality of Consent 133 (1975).

5. 488 U.S. 469, 493, 109 S.Ct. 706, 721, 102 L.Ed.2d 854 (1989). See also Shaw v. Reno, ___ U.S. ___, 113 S.Ct. 2816, 125 L.Ed.2d 511 (1993).

6. 347 U.S. 483, 74 S.Ct. 686, 98 L.Ed. 873 (1954).

With the exception of a few notable cases striking down the most egregious race regulations,[13] the Supreme Court adopted a wholly tolerant and deferential rendering of all three amendments, imputing to them only the most modest consequences.[14] Federal statutes flatly forbidding racial discrimination by commercial enterprises were held to be excessive, as acts of an unwarranted color-blind zeal. * * * The cases so disposing of this matter, decided by the Supreme Court in 1883, were ironically entitled *The Civil Rights Cases*.[15]

When regulation by race was the government's own, rather than the practice of private parties, the Court's decisions were nearly as tolerant of legislative discretion as they had been of commercial discrimination in *The Civil Rights Cases*. Allocation by race was not per se forbidden by the Constitution, the Court held, as the consideration of race might be thought by many reasonable persons as sometimes germane to a variety of important social concerns. Thus, the question was not whether political bodies regulated on the basis of race; it was the different question whether the particular regulation by race was constitutionally "reasonable."

* * *

This view of the matter steadily developed between 1873 and the twilight of the 19th century. It was cemented in 1896 in the "separate-but-equal" decision of *Plessy v. Ferguson*.[16] The decision upheld a state law requiring separate passenger cars for white and for black riders: neither was worse off than the other in the quality of accommodations to be furnished to each; neither was more or less protected than the other (rather, each was equally protected) by the racial regulation a legislative body deemed reasonable in the public interest.

There was but one dissent that took a less measured view and would have imposed upon the fourteenth amendment a more categorical imperative. Less flexible than others on the Supreme Court at the time, Justice Harlan was prepared to read into the Civil War amendments what was, to be sure, neither explicitly provided by their terms nor compelled by their compromised legislative history. Proceeding from a more basic premise than that either of these considerations necessarily controlled the matter, Harlan put his finger on the lessons of his own contemporary history. Prior to the Civil War amendments, race was the basis on which status had been determined, worth assigned, entitlements settled, and legal rights measured. It had been iniquitous from the very

13. *E.g.,* Strauder v. West Virginia, 100 U.S. 303 (1880)[.] *Cf.* Virginia v. Rives, 100 U.S. 313, 319 (1880)[;] *Ex parte* Virginia, 100 U.S. 339 (1880)[.]

14. *E.g.,* The Slaughter–House Cases, 83 U.S. (16 Wall.) 36 (1873)[.]

15. 109 U.S. 3 (1883)[.]

16. 163 U.S. 537 (1896).

beginning, and it subsequently proved to be a disaster for the entire country. He believed the enactment of the Civil War amendments should therefore be construed by the Court as altogether disallowing it. Government could not determine worth, assign entitlements, or measure legal rights by race *at all* * * *.

The point of emphasis here is fundamental. It is not that when race is used, all persons identified to each race must be as well regarded as all persons identified to some other race. The thing condemned is not that members of each race must be "equally" protected under laws distinguishing them by their race, nor that they are assigned entitlements unequally on the basis of race. The thing condemned, rather, is the assignment of entitlements by race. It is the impropriety of the *basis* of assignment, not the modicum thus assigned, that constitutes the government's offense:

> These notable additions to the fundamental law [the thirteenth, fourteenth, and fifteenth amendments] were welcomed by the friends of liberty throughout the world. *They removed the race line from our governmental systems.*

The Harlan opinion passed into history at the time, an artifact of mere dissent, discredited by the dominant view that the fourteenth amendment had not withdrawn from legislative bodies a political license to regulate by race. The outcome of the case was taken quite seriously, moreover, as legislatures enacted an ever-enlarging sprawl of race-based laws. Indeed, a half-century later, the dominant legislative response to *Brown v. Board of Education* [22] was one of fury, precisely on this account. For however the Court might phrase the apologetics of that decision, the message as it appeared from the outside was that what was not previously understood to be unconstitutional was now accused of being unconstitutional after all: the use of race to allocate—albeit equally—those facilities deemed most appropriate for persons of that race.

B. The Second Rite of Passage

In the swift consecutive series of per curiam decisions issued by the Supreme Court during the two years following *Brown,* the Court made no further use whatever—indeed, it made no inquiry—as to whether the particular race regulation disadvantaged some more than others. Neither did it ask whether the law stigmatized some more than others, or whether the law was enacted by whites and opposed by blacks, enacted by consent of some of each and opposed by many of each, or whatever. Rather, that line of per curiam decisions appeared more completely to enact Harlan's view that the Civil War amendments altogether "removed the race line from our governmental systems."

Between 1955 and 1976, moreover, virtually every other race-related decision by the Supreme Court appeared to convey this same message. To the reasonably discerning, this appeared true even in instances

---

22. 347 U.S. 483 (1954).

involving highly controversial judicial decrees that paired racially identifiable schools, redrafted attendance lines, or mandated busing. In each instance, the fulcrum of judicial leverage was an *existing governmental* race line, which the particular judicial order sought to remove. The object was thus to disestablish particular, existing uses of race, not to establish new ones. Indeed, decrees that would subsequently presume to require race-conscious decisions for any other purpose, for example, to maintain "proportions" or "balances" by race designation, were swiftly reversed.[26]

This second rite of passage was accompanied by consistent developments in the 1960s in the Supreme Court and then, encouragingly, in Congress and the executive branch as well. [Here Van Alstyne discusses the original enacted versions of Title VI and Title VII of the 1964 Civil Rights Act, Executive Order No. 11234, and several other provisions that prohibited racial discrimination period. As of this time, in short, the Court, Congress, and the Executive Branch seemed to be of a common resolve (namely, as Van Alstyne put it, that "we shall not see racism disappear by employing its own ways of classifying people and of measuring their rights [by race]").]

Even when the sole use of race by government was to suggest that race is at least an important political datum—the government itself not presuming to say of what kind of significance—the Supreme Court disallowed the mere encouragement to be "race conscious." A case that expresses that view as well as any other case was *Anderson v. Martin*,[44] decided succinctly and unanimously in 1964. The case involved a state statute that facilitated voter information respecting the racial identification of each candidate for local public office—by designating each candidate's race on each ballot, accurately and truthfully. Voters who might think that datum germane (as a white person to vote white, a black to vote black, a white to vote black, a black to vote white—as each might see a different, but steadfast significance in the idea) could hardly be kept from using it even in the absence of such specific ballot information. As the ballot designation by state law was nonetheless thought objectionable, it could not have been because any candidate was exempt from it, since all were equally subject to it. It must have been, rather, that each was being *individually* disadvantaged insofar as the state thought it appropriate to encourage voters to attribute at least *some* significance to every candidate's race—and that the morality of the Civil War amendments was opposed to the very idea of such encouragement. And this, indeed, was the foundation of the decision in *Anderson v. Martin*: not that a black candidate in particular might be victimized insofar as the state's "truth in candidacy" statute would gratuitously

---

26. *E.g.,* Pasadena City Bd. of Educ. v. Spangler, 427 U.S. 424 (1976). *See also* Dayton Bd. of Educ. v. Brinkman, 433 U.S. 406 (1977); Milliken v. Bradley, 418 U.S. 717 (1974); Keyes v. School Dist. No. 1, 413 U.S. 189 (1973).

44. 375 U.S. 399 (1964).

stimulate white bloc votes, but that the state could not thus encourage such racial disadvantaging of *anyone,* white or black.

* * *

In this twenty-year pattern of development, from 1954 to 1974, the Supreme Court's unambiguous lesson thus seemed to be that race was indeed constitutionally withdrawn from the incorrigible temptations of governmental use.

LAURENCE H. TRIBE, "IN WHAT VISION OF THE CONSTITUTION MUST THE LAW BE COLOR–BLIND?"
20 John Marshall L.Rev. 201–207 (1986).

[M]y focus today will be on the affirmative action controversy as a window into the constitutional and judicial vision—the philosophy of constitutional meaning and judicial role—of those who deem race-specific preferences for minorities to be presumptively invalid, subject only to a narrow exception for judicial relief to identified victims of proven race discrimination. I will call these the "race neutralists." My question is: Why do the race neutralists set themselves against the view, expressed by Justice Blackmun in his separate *Bakke* opinion, that "to get beyond racism, we must first take account of race * * * [a]nd * * * to treat some persons equally, we must * * * treat them differently." [7] In other words, what constitutional sources or theories can the race neutralists invoke?

To begin with, the race neutralists might invoke the notion that *all* racial classifications, the supposedly benign no less than the overtly malign, are "inherently suspect." Now that broad notion itself has a somewhat suspect source: it was given its first explicit articulation in the justly infamous 1944 decision—*Korematsu v. United States* [8]—upholding our government's forced relocation of Japanese–American citizens to concentration camps. Before announcing its result in *Korematsu,* the Supreme Court proclaimed that *"all* legal restrictions which curtail the civil rights of a single racial group are immediately suspect * * *. Courts must subject them to the most rigid scrutiny." [9] It is noteworthy that the Court was speaking there of restricting "civil rights," and *not* of allocating state-created opportunities for individual advancement. More important still, even in *Korematsu* the Supreme Court held that the *point* of strict scrutiny for racial classifications is to detect whether they reflect "[p]ressing public necessity" or merely "racial antagonism." [10] Racial antagonism, of course, is hardly the motive of today's minority set-aside programs.

---

7. Regents of Univ. of Cal. v. Bakke, 438 U.S. 265, 407 (1978) (Blackmun, J., separate opinion).

8. 323 U.S. 214 (1944).

9. *Id.* at 216 (emphasis added).

10. *Id.*

Seeking a sounder source than *Korematsu,* the race neutralists often recur to the first Justice Harlan's dissent in *Plessy v. Ferguson.*[11] Indeed, Solicitor General Charles Fried's argument in *Wygant v. Jackson Board of Education* leans heavily on *Plessy.*[12] The Solicitor General says: "Whether a Plessy is ejected from a railroad coach because he is one-eighth black or laid-off because he is seven-eighths white, the concrete wrong to him is much the same." [13] That may seem counterintuitive, however. For those "wrongs" are *not* self-evidently the same: the actual wrong to Mr. Plessy was a denigration of his moral worth, a perpetuation of slavery, and a reinforcement of his political exclusion; none of this, certainly, can be said of the hypothesized converse harm. Nonetheless, the race neutralists always offer the obligatory quotation from Justice Harlan: "Our Constitution is color-blind." Those who quote the elder Justice Harlan with such abandon should consider the context of the preceding five sentences in that justly famous dissent:

> The white race deems itself to be the dominant race in this country. *And so it is,* in prestige, in achievements, in education, in wealth and in power. So, I doubt not, it will continue to be for all time, if it remains true to its great heritage and holds fast to the principles of constitutional liberty. But in view of the Constitution, in the eye of the law, there is in this country no superior, dominant, ruling class of citizens. There is no caste here. Our Constitution is color-blind
> * * *[15]

Perhaps it is anachronistic and even unfair to stress too heavily the manifest racism in Justice Harlan's full statement. But even for this late nineteenth-century proponent of white dominance, the color-blind ideal, it turns out, was only shorthand for the concept that the Fourteenth Amendment prevents our law from enshrining and perpetuating white supremacy. To say that this particular vice is shared, automatically or presumptively, by race-specific minority set-asides strikes many as far-fetched.

So the question remains unanswered: *Why* would anyone equate laying off a white Plessy to make room for a black worker, and ejecting a black Plessy from a railroad coach to maintain white supremacy?

The race neutralists' reply to that question sometimes involves a reference to the "original intention" of the Fourteenth Amendment's Framers.[17] But that argument faces an enormous stumbling block. I

---

11. 163 U.S. 537 (1896).

12. See Brief of the United States as Amicus Curiae Supporting Petitioners, Wygant v. Jackson Bd. of Educ., 106 S.Ct. 1842 (1986).

13. *Id.* at 21.

15. [163 U.S. at 559 (Harlan, J., dissenting) (emphasis added).]

17. *E.g.,* Reynolds, *Individualism v. Group Rights: The Legacy of Brown,* 93 Yale L.J. 995, 997 (1984) ("History faithful-

ly records that the purpose of the [Thirteenth, Fourteenth and Fifteenth] Amendments was to end forever a system which determined legal rights, measured status, and allocated opportunities on the basis of race, and to erect in its place a regime of race neutrality."). *Compare* Bork, *Original Intent and the Constitution,* 7 Humanities 22 (1986) *with* Tribe, *The Holy Grail of Original Intent, id.* at 23.

am not referring to the often-noted historical fact that those same Framers created a Freedman's Bureau to assist former slaves.[18] As the Solicitor General has pointed out, those pieces of nineteenth century legislation were at least partially, if not exclusively, designed to assist *actual victims* of slavery.[19] I am referring to the fact that we know, with as much certainty as such matters ever permit, that the Framers of the Fourteenth Amendment did not think "equal protection of the laws" made *all* racial distinctions in law unconstitutional; they did not intend, for example, to outlaw racially segregated public schools.[20] It involves quite a stretch, then, to take their original intentions as an argument that all race-specific distinctions, even those designed to facilitate practical equality, are either automatically or presumptively unconstitutional.

The necessary response of the race neutralists is, of course, that the Supreme Court was right in *Brown v. Board of Education*—and that the 1954 Court saw the "original intention" more clearly than its 1896 predecessor, when *Brown* rightly held that *all* official distinctions by race are presumptively unconstitutional. But *did* it so hold? That is only the most sweeping and "activist" of at least several equally plausible readings of *Brown*. I will focus upon two such readings, identified as "*Brown*–A" and "*Brown*–B."

> *Brown*–A says that, more than a century after the Civil War, *all* race distinctions must now be banned as inherently "unequal;" in light of modern and more enlightened "values," courts must create a general Fourteenth Amendment right never to be disadvantaged by law on account of one's race, even if this *is* a right the Fourteenth Amendment's authors would not have endorsed.

> *Brown*–B says the Fourteenth Amendment's command of "equal protection of the laws" was *always* intended, at its most basic level, to ban the use of law to subjugate a racial group; we now see, as the 1896 Court did not, that racial segregation by law in public schools and other public facilities in fact subjugated blacks, despite its appearance of symmetry and equality, because it stood for white supremacy and therefore denied the minority "equal protection." Thus we are creating no *new* basic right the Fourteenth Amendment's authors would have rejected; it is not the law that has changed but only our relevant perceptions and understandings.

On the face of it, *Brown*–B seems a more modest, less radical and less strained interpretation than *Brown*–A. Especially when a national, state or local representative body adopts an affirmative action program

---

18. *See* Schnapper, *Affirmative Action and the Legislative History of the Fourteenth Amendment,* 71 Va.L.Rev. 753, 761, 772–73 (1985) (in practice, under the 1865 Act, most of the Bureau's programs applied only to black freedmen; in addition, the 1866 Act contained explicitly race-conscious measures).

19. Brief of the United States as Amicus Curiae Supporting Petitioners at 14–15, Wygant v. Jackson Bd. of Educ., 106 S.Ct. 1842 (1986).

20. *See* Bickel, *The Original Understanding and the Segregation Decision,* 69 Harv.L.Rev. 1, 56 (1955).

fully consistent with *Brown*–B, striking that program down as a violation of *Brown*–A seems hard to square with judicial deference to political majorities absent a textually or historically clear constitutional prohibition.

The difficulty deepens when instrumental reasons are added to support the race-neutral position: arguments that racism and race resentments will be exacerbated, and racial stereotypes perpetuated, unless we demand that government be race-blind are properly addressed to political bodies. For if government's actions violate no constitutional command, why are not arguments about their long-term effects best left to the political process?

I can think of only one constitutional command that the race neutralists might invoke to fill this gap and justify their choice of *Brown*–A: a command that law and government must not restrict *any* innocent individual's "liberty," broadly enough defined to include job opportunities and the like, even when such a restriction is justified by a desire to protect others who are equally innocent. And to deprive someone of a benefit, or to impose a burden, merely because of that person's race (and not because of what that specific individual did wrong) violates this command no less when the deprived individual is white than when she is black. But before anyone gravitates to this view, let me make this observation: when the government exercises its power to single out wholly innocent individuals by taking their "private property * * * for public use," the race neutralists do not object that only the *guilty* should ever have to make such focused sacrifices. Indeed, they often *endorse* such property takings outside the affirmative action context—so long as the "innocents" who have been required to make special sacrifices receive "just compensation" for their losses. In assessing the constitutionality and wisdom of affirmative action plans that impose similarly concrete and personalized costs on "innocent" white individuals—losses of seniority, for example—facing questions of just compensation would offer the race neutralists a more moderate alternative to the extremism of *Brown*–A.

So I end with a genuine puzzle: the race neutralists do not in fact put themselves forward, in other respects, as constitutional radicals. First, they purport to respect the historical intentions of the Framers, insofar as those intentions are knowable. Second, they regard basic constitutional norms as alterable only by constitutional amendment, and not by act of judicial improvization. Third, they advocate deference to political majorities when a constitutional prohibition is at best arguable rather than clear. And fourth, they are reluctant to have courts fashion new rights by generalizing, even with the help of the Ninth Amendment, beyond the Constitution's text. Yet on all four of these dimensions, the race neutralists—the constitutional opponents of affirmative action—seem to look the other way.

What has yet to be produced, then, is a cogent explanation of *why* judicial modesty and constitutional strict construction should be abandoned when the subject is affirmative action for racial minorities.

NEIL GOTANDA, A CRITIQUE OF "OUR CONSTITUTION IS COLOR–BLIND"

44 Stan.L.Rev. 1, 23–28, 32–34 (1991).

RACIAL CATEGORIES

* * *

A. American Racial Classification: Hypodescent

One way to begin a critique of the American system of racial classification is to ask "Who is Black?" This question rarely provokes analysis; its answer is seen as so self-evident that challenges are novel and noteworthy. Americans no longer have need of a system of judicial screening to decide a person's race; the rules are simply absorbed without explicit articulation.

1. The rule of hypodescent.

American racial classifications follow two formal rules:

1) *Rule of recognition:* Any person whose Black–African ancestry is visible is Black.

2) *Rule of descent:* (a) Any person with a known trace of African ancestry is Black, notwithstanding that person's visual appearance; or, stated differently, (b) the offspring of a Black and a white is Black.

Historians and social scientists have noted the existence of these rules, often summarized as the "one drop of blood" rule, in their analysis of the American system of racial classification. Anthropologist Marvin Harris suggested a name for the American system of social reproduction: "hypodescent." [95]

2. Alternatives to hypodescent.

The American legal system today lacks intermediate or "mixed race" classifications. While the establishment of self-contained Black or white racial categories may seem obvious, an examination of other classification schemes reveals that the American categories are not exhaustive.

Let us posit the two original races: one a "pure Black," the other a "pure white." As interracial reproduction occurs, a multiracial society emerges. Four historically documented examples of nonbinary schemes to categorize mixed-race offspring have evolved: Mulatto, Named Fractions, Majoritarian, and Social Continuum. All of these schemes are logically symmetrical, so, at least in theory, neither "pure race" is privileged over the other. Consider each of the schemes in detail:

1. *Mulatto:* All mixed offspring are called mulattoes, irrespective of the percentages or fractions of their Black or white ancestry.[97]

---

95. Marvin Harris, Patterns of Race in the Americas 37, 56 (1964). * * *

97. Laura Foner suggests that in Louisiana and St. Domingue (colonial Haiti),

2. *Named Fractions:* Individuals are assigned labels according to the fractional composition of their racial ancestry. Thus, a mulatto is one-half white and one-half Black. A quadroon is one-fourth Black and three-fourths white, a sambo one-fourth white and three-fourths Black, etc.[98]

3. *Majoritarian:* The higher percentage of either white or Black ancestry determines the white or Black label.[99]

4. *Social Continuum:* This is a variation on the Named Fractions scheme: Labels generally correspond to the proportion of white or Black ancestry, but social status is also an important factor in determining which label applies. The result is a much less rigid system of racial classification.[100]

It is worth repeating two observations that apply to all four schemes. First, the use of racial categories presumes that at some time "pure" races existed. Second, because these schemes are symmetrical, nothing in them suggests inequality or subordination between races. [But the] hypodescent rule when combined with color-blind constitutionalism, conveys a complex and powerful ideology that supports racial subordination. * * *

[B. Racial Subordination]

* * * Under hypodescent, Black parentage is recognized through the generations. The metaphor is one of purity and contamination: White is unblemished and pure, so one drop of ancestral Black blood renders one Black. Black ancestry is a contaminant that overwhelms white ancestry.[101] Thus, under the American system of racial classification,

there were three classifications of race: white, Black (mostly slaves), and free colored (mostly mulatto). Laura Foner, The Free People of Color in Louisiana and St. Domingue: A Comparative Portrait of Two Three–Caste Slave Societies, 3 J.Soc.Hist. 406 (1970). Likewise, Eugene Genovese had identified a "three-caste" system in the "Anglo–French Caribbean." E. Genovese, The World The Slaveholders Made [107 (1969)]. These arrangements suggest that the mulatto scheme is consistent with racial categorization techniques existing in other parts of the world.

98. This type of classification arrangement evolved in parts of the West Indies and Latin America, with additional labels for those with Indian blood. * * *

99. Ohio followed a majoritarian rule of racial classification for three decades, beginning with Gray v. Ohio, 4 Ohio 353 (1831), and ending with the adoption of the Reconstruction Amendments.

100. This is the prevailing classification scheme in several Latin American societies. Brazil's system is probably the most widely described. * * *

101. Writer and poet Langston Hughes observed in 1953:

"It's powerful," [Simple] said . . .

"That one drop of Negro blood—because just one drop of black blood makes a man colored. One drop—you are a Negro! Now, why is that? Why is Negro blood so much more powerful than any other kind of blood in the world? If a man has Irish blood in him, people will say, 'He's part Irish.' If he has a little Jewish blood, they'll say, 'He's half Jewish.' But if he has just a small bit of colored blood in him bam!—He's a Negro!' Not, 'He's part Negro.' No, be it ever so little, if that blood is black, 'He's a Negro!' Now, that is what I do not understand—why our one drop is so powerful. . . . Black is powerful. You can have ninety-nine drops of white blood in your veins down South—but if that other one drop is black, shame on you! Even if you look white, you're black. That drop is powerful."

Langston Hughes, Simple Takes a Wife 85 (1953). * * *

claiming a white racial identity is a declaration of racial purity and an implicit assertion of racial domination. The symmetry of racial categorization systems other than hypodescent brings a sense of objectivity and neutrality to these schemes, and a comparison of hypodescent to symmetrical systems exposes its nonneutral assumptions.

* * *

[C. The Mutability of Racial Categorization]

* * *

Modern ways of thinking about racial categories evolved throughout American history. In the early colonial period, racial classifications were highly fluid. Social status often depended as much on the labor status of the individual as on his place of origin. Typically, Africans were brought to the colonies as captives, and Europeans as contractual or indentured servants. * * * There was a hierarchy among those who were not slaves but were also not free. The labels for such labor varied. In Virginia and Maryland, where the English colonists were the dominant group, the various "unfree" were also described as "un-English." The term included French, Africans, and Scots. There were additional labels specific to the African laborers. While the early records are incomplete, there is clear evidence that by the middle 1600s, English colonists maintained some Africans in a status distinguishable from European indentured labor.

Sources from the 1600s variously describe Africans as "heathen," "infidel," and "negro." These terms were attempts to justify the political status of the Africans. The racial classifications differentiated Europeans from the natives of colonized and imperially exploited parts of the world. But the classifications did not indicate a clearly developed belief that slavery was an appropriate condition for Africans.

English colonists gradually came to prefer enslaved African labor over indentured Europeans. By the end of the seventeenth century, the number of slaves had increased dramatically.

As slavery became entrenched as the primary source of agricultural labor, slaveholders developed a complementary ideological structure of racial categories that served to legitimate slavery. The formal legal system was tailored to reflect these categories and enforce slave labor. In 1705, the Virginia assembly created the first recognizable slave code. Besides codifying punishment for slaves who stole or ran away, the slave code contained specific rules of descent for classifying offspring. Punishments for Blacks and mulattos differed from those for indentured servants. This institutionalization of racial classifications linked to disparate treatment marked the first formal establishment of racial categories in colonial America.

The new racial classifications offered a basis for legitimating subordination that was unlike the justifications previously employed. By keying official rules of descent to national origin the classification scheme differentiated those who were "enslaveable" from those who were not. Membership in the new social category of "Negro" became itself sufficient justification for enslaveability.

One can, therefore, do more than assert generally that race is not scientific or that race is socially constructed. One can say that our particular system of classification, with its metaphorical construction of racial purity for whites, has a specific history as a badge of enslaveability. As such, the metaphor of purity is not a logical oddity, but an integral part of the construction of the system of racial subordination embedded in American society. Under color-blind constitutionalism, when race is characterized as objective and apolitical, this history is disguised and discounted.

T. ALEXANDER ALEINIKOFF, A CASE FOR RACE–CONSCIOUSNESS
91 Colum.L.Rev. 1060, 1075–1083, 1087–1091, (1991).

A.   COLORBLINDNESS AND ANTIDISCRIMINATION LAW

* * *

The allure of colorblindness is strong. It is rooted in the dissenting opinion of the case that ratified American apartheid.[77] And it fits with liberal, individualistic principles that each person should be assessed on individual merits, not upon the basis of group membership. Color-consciousness, under this account, is irrational and immoral because it is so rarely relevant to acceptable purposes.

Colorblindness also has powerful strategic appeal. In a world of white supremacy, most classifications based on race will have the intent or effect of harming blacks. Colorblindness sweeps these away. Furthermore, since whites are likely to look after their own, insisting that blacks get precisely what whites get will materially advance black interests. Colorblindness also keeps white guilt and anxiety at an acceptable level. As Alan Freeman has noted, colorblindness designates as "wrongdoers" only those "racists" who continue to take race into account; colorblind whites are absolved even if they continue to benefit from an unequal state of affairs.[80] Finally, there is the risk that noticing race, even for a "benign" purpose, will only serve to affirm the view of racial differences that supported racial domination in the past.

The opinions in *Croson* and *Metro Broadcasting* show that four Justices believe that colorblindness should be the animating vision for antidiscrimination law. Justice O'Connor's plurality opinion in *Croson* identifies the central constitutional norm as prohibition of the use of racial classifications:

77. Plessy v. Ferguson, 163 U.S. 537, 554–55 (1896) (Harlan, J., dissenting).

80. Freeman, Legitimizing Racial Discrimination Through Antidiscrimination Law: A Critical Review of Supreme Court Doctrine, 62 Minn.L.Rev. 1049, 1054–56, 1067 (1978). * * *

The Richmond Plan denies certain citizens the opportunity to compete for a fixed percentage of public contracts based solely upon their race. To whatever racial group these citizens belong, their "personal rights" to be treated with equal dignity and respect are implicated by a rigid rule erecting race as the sole criterion in an aspect of public decisionmaking.[83]

The concurring opinions of Justices Scalia and Kennedy are equally explicit. Justice Scalia writes: "I share the view expressed by Alexander Bickel that ' * * * discrimination on the basis of race is illegal, immoral, unconstitutional, inherently wrong, and destructive of democratic society.' " [84]   Justice Kennedy agrees: "The moral imperative of racial neutrality is the driving force of the Equal Protection Clause." [85]

* * *

B.   From Colorblindness to Race–Consciousness

[We need to distinguish two varieties of colorblindness.] The first, which I will call "strong colorblindness," argues that race should truly be an irrelevant, virtually unnoticed, human characteristic. Richard Wasserstrom has described this "assimilationist ideal":

> [A] nonracist society would be one in which the race of an individual would be the functional equivalent of the eye color of individuals in our society today. In our society no basic political rights and obligations are determined on the basis of eye color. No important institutional benefits and burdens are connected with eye color. Indeed, except for the mildest sort of aesthetic preferences, a person would be thought odd who even made private, social decisions by taking eye color into account.[91]

The second type, "weak colorblindness," would not outlaw all recognition of race, but would condemn the use of race as a basis for the distribution of scarce resources or opportunities and the imposition of burdens. Under "weak colorblindness," race might function like ethnicity: an attribute that could have significance for group members, and one that society as a whole could recognize, but not one upon which legal distinctions could be based. * * * Thus, college courses on "African–American literature" might well be permissible under a weak colorblindness regime, but such a regime would not tolerate allocating places in the class based on race or allowing race to be used as a factor in the choice of an instructor. In the sections that follow, I will argue that strong colorblindness is impossible and undesirable, and that weak colorblindness—although perhaps able to be implemented as a legal strategy—is an inadequate response to current manifestations of racial inequality.

83. [City of Richmond v. J.A. Croson Co., 109 S.Ct. 706, 721 (1989).] Justices White and Kennedy joined O'Connor with respect to this part of the opinion. Id. at 712.

84. Id. at 735 (Scalia, J., concurring)[.]

85. Id. at 734 (Kennedy, J., concurring).

91. R. Wasserstrom, Philosophy and Social Issues 24 (1980)[.]

1. *Masking Race–Consciousness.*—It is apparently important, as a matter of widespread cultural practice, for whites to assert that they are strongly colorblind, in the sense that they do not notice or act on the basis of race. One can see this at work in such statements as: "I judge each person as an individual." Of course, it cannot be that whites do not notice the race of others. Perhaps what is being said is that the speaker does not begin her evaluation with any preconceived notions. But this too is difficult to believe, given the deep and implicit ways in which our minds are color-coded. To be truly colorblind in this way * * * requires color-consciousness: one must notice race in order to tell oneself not to trigger the usual mental processes that take race into account.

The denial of race-consciousness occasioned by the desire to be strongly colorblind is described in a recent study of a desegregated junior high school by psychologist Janet Schofield. She reports that teachers, apparently concerned that acknowledging racial awareness would be viewed as a sign of prejudice, claimed not to notice the race of their students. In pursuit of colorblindness, teachers rarely used the words "white" or "black," and avoided racial topics and identifications in class.[93]

This act of denial is troubling not only because it distorts reality, but also because it will make less accessible the ways in which color-consciousness influences our understanding of the world and of others. Strong colorblindness will perpetuate the white image of blacks by rendering irrelevant the kind of race-based discussion and data necessary for a serious critique of white definitions. Schofield's study documents how teachers' desires to act in a colorblind fashion harmed the educational experience by ignoring or denying race when it would have been appropriate to notice it:

> [One] teacher included George Washington Carver on a list of great Americans from which students could pick individuals to learn about but specifically decided not to mention he was black for fear of raising racial issues. In the best of all worlds, there would be no need to make such mention, because children would have no preconceptions that famous people are generally white. However, in a school where one white child was surprised to learn from a member of our research team that Martin Luther King was black, not white[!], it would seem reasonable to argue that highlighting the accomplishments of black Americans and making sure that students do not assume famous figures are white is a reasonable practice.

* * *

2. *Local Knowledge: Race–Consciousness as Cultural Critique.*— Strong colorblindness, I have argued, is unlikely to produce the result it promises—a world in which race does not matter. In this section, I

---

93. Schofield, Causes and Consequences of the Colorblind Perspective, *in* [Prejudice, Discrimination, and Racism 231 (J. Dovidio & S. Gaertner eds. 1986).]

want to make the case for race-consciousness more direct by focusing on the benefits of race-consciousness in undermining and shifting deep cultural assumptions and ultimately, perhaps, making progress in overcoming racism. In presenting these claims, I hope also to undermine the case for weak colorblindness. To be effective, strategies for attacking racism may well demand affirmative race-conscious governmental policies.

Clifford Geertz, in a collection of his essays entitled *Local Knowledge*, has stated that:

> To see ourselves as others see us can be eye-opening. To see others as sharing a nature with ourselves is the merest decency. But it is from the far more difficult achievement of seeing ourselves amongst others, as a local example of the forms human life has locally taken, a case among cases, a world among worlds, that the largeness of mind, without which objectivity is self-congratulation and tolerance a sham, comes.[101]

Colorblindness operates at Geertz's level of "merest decency." It begins and ends with the observation that there is something, under the skin, common to all human beings. I do not want to discount the deep humanism underlying this perspective. Indeed, it is a significant improvement over the racist ideologies that have been prevalent throughout United States history and that have denied the "inner" equality of the races. But Geertz clearly seeks more than this; he would reorient the usual hierarchical relationship between dominant and subordinate cultures by rotating the axis through its center point, making the vertical horizontal. This shift requires two related transformations: the first is to appreciate the contingency, the nonuniversalism of one's own culture—to view it as an example of "local knowledge;" the second is to recognize and credit the "local knowledges" of other groups. Of course, these two efforts are related. By valorizing the dominated, one is likely to cast doubts on the dominant group's characterizations or definition of the dominated group, which, in turn, tells us something new about the dominant group as well.

[R]ace-consciousness can aid in these cultural transformations. This is, to be sure, hardly a new claim. The calls for "black pride" and "black power" in the 1960s represented a reorienting demand of race-consciousness. * * *

The consequences wrought by the race-conscious advocates were startling. They were able to take the term "black"—which for more than three hundred years had symbolized degradation and stigma—and turn it into an assertion of a group's humanity and solidarity. But African–American self-pride does not necessarily penetrate white cultural norms and narratives. Indeed, a dominant culture can be relatively unconcerned with a subordinated group's definition of itself if that

---

101. C. Geertz, Local Knowledge: Further Essays in Interpretive Anthropology 16   (1983).

definition either does not get air time or can be dismissed as romantic, self-serving, or fictional.

Rotating the axis helps us to be open to other accounts and perspectives, and in doing so it reminds us of the fictional or constructed nature of "local knowledges"—including our own. Once white Americans shed the false assumption that "they know all they need to know" about African–Americans, they will begin to learn as much about themselves as about others.

* * *

[R]ecognizing race validates the lives and experiences of those who have been burdened because of their race. White racism has made "blackness" a relevant category in our society. Yet colorblindness seeks to deny the continued social significance of the category, to tell blacks that they are no different from whites, even though blacks as blacks are persistently made to feel that difference. Color-consciousness allows for recognition of the distinct and difficult difference that race has made; it facilitates white awareness of the efforts of African–Americans to describe and examine that difference. This is not simply the telling of a story of oppression. Color-consciousness makes blacks subjects and not objects, undermining the durability of white definitions of "blackness." It permits recognition of the strength and adaptive power of a black community able to survive slavery and oppression; and it acknowledges the contributions of black culture—not simply as windows on "the race question" but as distinct (if varied) voices and traditions, worthy of study in their own right.

It is difficult to improve upon Adrienne Rich's insight:

I used to envy the "colorblindness" which some liberal, enlightened, white people were supposed to possess; raised as I was, where I was, I am and will to the end of my life be acutely, sometimes bitterly, aware of color. Every adult around me in my childhood, white or black, was aware of it; it was a sovereign consciousness, a hushed and compelling secret. But I no longer believe that "colorblindness"—if it even exists—is the opposite of racism; I think it is, in this world, a form of naiveté and moral stupidity. It implies that I would look at a black woman and see her as white, thus engaging in white solipsism to the utter erasure of her particular reality.[131]

Here is the turn of the axis, the recognition of others that helps one to see one's own culture as "a world among worlds."

3. *Weak Colorblindness and Its Costs.*—It is common for advocates of affirmative action to point out that a legal strategy dedicated to "equality of opportunity" is likely to replicate deeply imbedded inequalities. The familiar metaphor is of a race between two runners, one of whom starts many yards back from the starting line, or is encumbered

131. A. Rich, [Disloyal to Civilization: Feminism, Racism, Gynephobia, *in* On Lies, Secrets, and Silence 275, 300 (1979).]

by ankle weights. Color-conscious policies are said to remove the advantage that has for several centuries been granted to whites. The simplicity of this argument should not disguise its soundness or moral power. Unfortunately, however, affirmative action programs based on the objective of overcoming past societal discrimination are deemed to run afoul of the Court's model of weak colorblindness.[134] To the extent race conscious policies help ameliorate material disadvantage due to societal discrimination, the negative injunction of weak colorblindness imposes heavy costs.

Beyond this familiar terrain in the affirmative action debate, there are other advantages to race-conscious programs that also call into question the adequacy of weak colorblindness. [T]here are a number of situations in which it seems eminently reasonable for government decision makers to take race into account. * * * Justice Powell's famous "diversity" argument in *Bakke* [137] implicitly acknowledges the reasonableness of some manner of color-conscious decision making in a world in which race has mattered and continues to matter. To the extent that weak colorblindness makes these forms of race-consciousness problematic, it is simply nearsighted social policy.

Most fundamentally, weak colorblindness sacrifices much of the cultural critique that race-consciousness can provide. If the task is to subject dominant views to scrutiny and challenge through the investigation and acceptance of nondominant perspectives, then it would appear sensible to permit decision makers to adopt facilitative programs that necessarily take notice of race. *Metro Broadcasting* [139] is a significant case in this respect. The FCC policies upheld in this case are important not only because they channel economic resources—broadcasting licenses—to African–Americans, but also because these resources both support minority cultural self-definition and provide a means for penetrating mainstream culture.[140] As the Court recognized, "[T]he benefits of [increased] diversity are not limited to the members of minority groups who gain access to the broadcasting industry by virtue of the ownership policies; rather, the benefits redound to all members of the viewing and listening audience."

* * *

To return to a previous example, universities need more than African–American literature classes; they need a diversity of students in all literature classes, and not simply to show white students that students of color can perform as well as white students, but also to help all students become more self-conscious of the underlying assumptions with which they approach the world. To be sure, there are risks. Given

---

134. See, e.g., City of Richmond v. J.A. Croson Co., 109 S.Ct. 706, 720–23 (1989); Wygant v. Jackson Bd. of Educ., 476 U.S. 267, 277–78, 293–94 (1986). * * *

137. Regents of Univ. of Cal. v. Bakke, 438 U.S. 265, 315–19 (1978).

139. Metro Broadcasting, Inc. v. FCC, 110 S.Ct. 2997 (1990).

140. See Williams, *Metro Broadcasting, Inc. v. FCC:* Regrouping in Singular Times, 104 Harv.L.Rev. 525, 537 (1990)[.]

the power of imbedded ways of thinking, new information may simply be "processed" in accordance with pre-existing views; or, white students may make the error of assuming that comments by black students express "the" black perspective. But to students and faculty open to a Geertzian moment, the intellectual rewards are enormous.

B. ADMISSIONS

In this section we take up the problem of preferential admissions policies for public educational institutions—policies that were at issue in the *DeFunis*[1] and *Bakke* cases. Kent Greenawalt identifies and evaluates the major justifications for these policies. He concludes that affirmative action programs aimed at ameliorating racial stereotypes and compensating for injuries caused by present discrimination and the continuing effects of past discrimination may withstand constitutional scrutiny.

Richard Posner criticizes the theoretical and policy justifications offered by Greenawalt in favor of affirmative action. He argues instead for colorblind admissions policies: the Fourteenth Amendment ought to be read to prohibit the distribution of benefits, no less than burdens, on the basis of race.

KENT GREENAWALT, JUDICIAL SCRUTINY OF "BENIGN" RACIAL PREFERENCE IN LAW SCHOOL ADMISSIONS
75 Colum.L.Rev. 559, 579–94 (1975).

[In the preceding section of this article, Greenawalt argues that "the courts should neither treat benign racial classifications as invalid per se nor subject them to a mere rationality test. They should ascertain if benign classifications are supported by an interest that is substantial, but should not require that the interest be undeniably urgent and paramount. They should give particularly intense scrutiny to whether a nonracial approach or a more narrowly tailored racial classification could promote the substantial interest about as well and at tolerable administrative expense."]

II. CONSTITUTIONAL EVALUATION OF JUSTIFICATIONS FOR PREFERENTIAL ADMISSIONS POLICIES

* * *

A. Redress for Unwarranted Injury

One justification for preferential admissions policies is that they redress unjust discrimination that blacks have suffered.

1. *Compensatory and Distributive Justice.* In his analysis, Professor Nickel makes use of the Aristotelian distinction between compensatory justice and distributive justice, between making a person whole for

---

1. DeFunis v. Odegaard, 416 U.S. 312, 94 S.Ct. 1704, 40 L.Ed.2d 164 (1974).

losses he has unjustly suffered and giving him the position in society he "deserves." [114] Though it may be difficult to draw a precise line between these two kinds of claims, in many contexts the distinction is clear. The newly elected public official who argues that he should be paid more makes a claim of distributive justice on society's resources. A rich alcoholic "bum" who returns to society after ten years in jail on an unjust conviction and who is presently at least as well off as he would be if he had never been convicted has a claim of compensatory justice for the pain he has suffered. In the context of preferential programs for blacks, the distinction largely collapses in practice. The claim for distributive justice, like that for compensatory justice, rests on assertions of past injustice. If blacks had never been peculiarly subject to social injustice, there might be no constitutionally adequate reason to treat them as a "class" for determining if society's benefits are justly distributed. If it just happened that few blacks had inherent aptitude for law or an interest in being lawyers, the minute percentage of black lawyers would not reflect any distributive injustice. The main reason why a claim of distributive justice has force is that it is assumed that more blacks would now enjoy high positions if their race had not been held back by social injustice. If preferential benefits were subject to precise calculation, it is possible that claims for compensation would support greater benefits than distributive claims; but for purposes of constitutional law the distinction between claims of compensatory and distributive justice is so slender that in this context we may treat them together as claims for redress of injustices.

2. *Injustices the Government May Constitutionally Redress.* The government's duty to redress injustices is clearest when the government itself causes an injury that is illegal at the time it is caused, but its power to rectify injustice is hardly limited to these situations. It may compensate for injustices that it caused, say by the laws of slavery, that were legal at the time they were inflicted; and it may compensate for injustices suffered at the hands of private individuals, whether or not those injustices amount to a general social practice. It may, in fact, "compensate" for losses that are not the fault of either the government or other individuals, as when it establishes special relief programs for earthquake and flood victims.

The Supreme Court's approval of racial classifications to correct de jure segregation [117] demonstrates that the government's interest in assuring redress of specific instances of illegal discrimination is great enough to justify some use of racial criteria. Since the government has the power to redress illegal discrimination indirectly as well as directly, and to redress injustices other than illegal discrimination, the person who claims that reliance on racial classifications in preferential admissions policies is impermissible must argue that the government's interest here

114. Nickel, *Preferential Policies in Hiring and Admissions: A Jurisprudential Approach,* 75 Colum.L.Rev. 534 (1975). * * * [Relocated footnote.]

117. Swann v. Charlotte–Mecklenburg County, 402 U.S. 1 (1971).

is less important than when it corrects illegal segregation, or that the particular hardships imposed by racially based preferential policies are unacceptable methods for redressing those injustices.

3. *Preferential Admissions and Social Injustice.* "Equal protection of the laws" would not have been denied to impoverished whites if in 1868 a state had made free land available to ex-slaves. If, instead, the state had made land available to all black adults within its borders, on the theory that few, if any, blacks had not suffered the effects of slavery or other state discriminations unique to blacks, it is hard to believe a court would have, or should have, found the program to be unconstitutional because all blacks and no whites were eligible for its benefits.

The constitutionality of modern programs to redress injustices to blacks is not as immediately apparent. I shall put aside for the moment the problem that the "burden" of many of these programs falls on excluded applicants, and assume that, as with the hypothetical grant of land, the burden falls on society generally. One or more of the three following theories might be used in support of a preference for a modern young black: (1) that he has been directly subjected to compensable discrimination; (2) that he has suffered the effects of discrimination against his forebears; or (3) that he should be compensated because of a special relationship to his forebears, whether or not he has suffered from wrongs done to them. We may deal briefly with the third possible theory as based on a dubious moral claim unlikely to be relied on extensively by thoughtful proponents of preferential admissions. Compensation to immediate survivors for harm done to others may have a place in the law of tort, since survival of actions helps to deter and penalize wrongful behavior and to compensate near kin for incalculable losses. Compensation to survivors may also be appropriate when a wrong is done to an ongoing entity like an Indian tribe, or when the perpetrators of a horrendous wrong wish to "purge" their guilt by compensating persons who have a significant relationship to the victims.[119] But when the perpetrators and victims of social injustice are both dead, it is hard to explain why the government should prefer those who happen to be descendants of the victims, unless they have been affected by the injustice. Because two much stronger arguments exist for redressing injustices to blacks we need not explore this one further.

Since widespread discrimination against blacks continues in the United States, it is plausible to suppose that most young blacks have suffered from it in various ways and that government redress is appropriate. But a preferential policy designed for that purpose that includes all blacks and excludes all whites now has much more serious defects of underinclusiveness and overinclusiveness than it would have had if adopted in 1868. It is not clear that most blacks suffer injustices significantly different in character from those inflicted on some whites.

---

119. An example would be German reparations to Israel for wrongs done to Euro- pean Jews.

And some young blacks are members of families recently arrived from other countries, or of families so well situated that they have not been sharply touched by discrimination. One might try to answer the charge of overinclusiveness with the suggestion that discrimination against blacks is so pervasive that it has touched, or will touch, all blacks significantly. A more general response to the charge of imprecise classification would be that proof of discrimination is too uncertain to be handled administratively, and, further, that it would be undesirable for law schools to decide how much discrimination individual applicants have suffered. This is a close point, but I believe that law schools could assess reasonably well whether particular members of non-preferred groups had suffered injustices similar to those imposed generally on the preferred group, and whether certain members of the preferred group had not suffered such injustices. I therefore think it doubtful that the fourteenth amendment should be interpreted to allow a straight racial preference where the only justification tendered is compensation to those directly injured by discrimination.

Benefits to young blacks may also be urged, however, on the ground that they continue to suffer the effects of discrimination against their parents and more distant forebears. Blacks victimized by discrimination have suffered educational, vocational, economic and psychological harms. Their ability to confer benefits on their children has been sharply impaired. No identifiable group of whites suffered injustice as extreme as that imposed on blacks under the American version of slavery. Not only were they deprived of virtually every kind of social good enjoyed by free men, they were also largely stripped of their culture. It would have taken several generations to wipe out the effects of slavery even if its end had meant instantaneous equal treatment. In fact, further systematic discrimination has perpetuated those effects. Most young blacks are undoubtedly still disadvantaged because of the direct effects of slavery and systematic racial discrimination against post-emancipation generations, and thus they have suffered from racial discrimination even if they have not all been personally subjected to racial bias.

It can be debated whether the young black has a greater claim on society's resources than a young white whose predecessors were equally ill-educated and destitute because they were persecuted in some other country or were lazy drunkards; but it is tenable to believe that a society has a special reason to eliminate the hardships stemming from its own injustices, and that this responsibility can survive the death of oppressors and direct victims, as long as ascertainable persons continue to suffer those hardships. This is not to say that rectifying the effects of injustice on subsequent generations is a typically desirable policy; it usually is not. It is only to say that a decision justified on that basis would not be evidently unsound.

If a reason for preference is to ameliorate the effects on this generation of injustice caused to past generations, then the use of an explicitly racial classification instead of a more individualized alternative is easier to defend than if the focus is on injustice to this generation. As to possible underinclusiveness, few whites have suffered from injustices like those inflicted on blacks by slavery and systematic discrimination, and the effects of any such injustices would be virtually impossible to trace.

Nor could possible overinclusiveness be cured by a study of black family histories to disqualify those few young blacks, if any, who may actually have benefited from slavery and the general discrimination against blacks. Neither this compensatory justification nor administrative necessity, however, would reach recent black immigrants from other countries.

We still have not faced the question whether the purpose of compensation is weighty enough to sustain a racial classification. It may be urged that society should be forward-looking in its policies, that society has survived intact despite the general failure to give government redress for injustices, and that a policy of compensation is of debatable wisdom and certainly does not reflect any paramount state interest. Proponents of preference can argue that social justice is among the most important aims of a social order, and that redress for blacks is both just and needed to relieve a sharp sense of injustice that most blacks feel. The need for redress may not be of undeniable urgency but the reasons that support compensation for most blacks reflect substantial government interests; if those reasons are accepted by legislators or administrators against competing arguments, they should be viewed by courts as important enough to sustain compensatory programs for blacks.

* * *

* * * [One] objection to preferential admissions policies * * * is the limited size of the class on whom the "burden" falls, and this is an objection that can be raised with respect to all the justifications given for preferential policies, not only the "compensatory" ones.

Unless a state expands facilities in order to accept more blacks, the burden of preferential admissions policies falls squarely on excluded white applicants, not the people who have practiced discrimination or even society as a whole. That the burden of preferential policies falls on a few individuals rather than on society at large or the educational institution granting the preference may be a reason for closer judicial scrutiny of the preference, but it is not of major constitutional relevance. No white has a vested interest in a legal education. A white with high test scores and grades from an intellectual city family would have no substantial constitutional claim if he were denied admission to a state law school that decided to admit some "less qualified" applicants who had grown up on farms. Since applicants are vulnerable to being excluded in pursuit of any one of a number of possible policies, no special constitutional difficulty is caused because the burden of racial preference falls on them. Moreover, insofar as it makes sense to assume that without discrimination many more blacks would qualify without preference, a state might assume that borderline whites who are admitted in the absence of preferential policies are indirectly "benefiting" from discrimination of which they are completely innocent. If they are excluded because of preferential policies, they may be put in the position they would have been in if the discrimination had never occurred. Expansion of facilities and resources is not always a sensible option, or an option the relevant institution has the power to choose. While there may be some injustice in casting the burden of preference on excluded whites, the need to make certain kinds of very important benefits the subject of compensation renders that unfortunate effect constitutionally acceptable.

B. Preferential Admissions and Qualifications

A different kind of argument made for preferential admissions is that ordinary admissions procedures inadequately reflect the qualifications of minority group members. * * *

1. *Qualifications for Law School Performance.* It is asserted that the law school aptitude tests and college grades do not adequately indicate the probable law school performance of blacks.[138] Of course, exact predictions of performance are impossible, and even for white students predictions based on tests and grades do not correlate neatly with actual performance, but this argument assumes that these predictions are sufficiently reliable to be a weighty factor in the admissions of whites. The contention is, however, that blacks are special because the law school aptitude tests are culturally biased and college grades also do not reflect the potential of those who are culturally disadvantaged.

One problem with this argument is that predictions of law school performance based on tests and grades are not significantly less accurate for black applicants than for other applicants. Perhaps the test is "culturally biased," but so also may be the law school program and the practice of law, in the sense that they call for skills and attitudes developed in the dominant culture. Insofar as tests and grades are especially inaccurate predictors for most blacks, plainly this is not a result of race pure and simple. Presumably these standards of likely performance are not culturally biased for blacks who have well-educated parents and whose predominant contacts at home and school have been with whites. And the standards may very well be culturally biased for poor whites who were educated in culturally disadvantaged settings and whose predominant contacts have been with poor blacks. If there are special reasons why tests and grades do not accurately predict law school performance for those from particular cultural backgrounds, it would not be very difficult administratively to make special exceptions from ordinary standards for whites from those backgrounds and not to make the exceptions for blacks who are not from those backgrounds. Given the constitutional presumption against racial classification, this more particularized approach should be required as a less onerous alternative.

138. See the testimony of the President of the University of Washington quoted in the state supreme court opinion in *DeFun-* is, 82 Wash.2d 11, 40, 507 P.2d 1169, 1174 (1973), *vacated as moot,* 416 U.S. 312 (1974).

Another reason why this qualifications argument cannot support existing preferential policies is that whatever special dispensation might be given to blacks because of the special inaccuracy of the usual bases for prediction of law school performance, no one can doubt that most law schools have gone far beyond that in their policies. They are admitting blacks who they are reasonably sure will not do as well in law school as white applicants denied admission.

2. *General Qualifications for the Legal Profession.* Only some of the skills lawyers need are tested in law school. Thus, there is a gap between qualifications for law school performance and qualifications for legal practice. As difficult as it may be to identify the skills needed for good lawyering, a state law school could properly decide to admit those who would make better lawyers in preference to those who would make better law students. Perhaps there is some correlation between being black and having qualifications for legal practice that will not be reflected in law school performance. Persons without educational advantages are much less likely to suffer with respect to some qualities lawyers need than with respect to the analytic precision and skill in written communication so important for law school success. And deficiencies in writing and analytical skills are much more likely to be overcome in the course of an entire career than in the three years of law school itself. Nevertheless, as with predicting law school performance, racial classification is much too imprecise a means if the underlying justification for preference is an attempt to gauge more accurately the general qualifications lawyers require.

3. *Job Placement and Qualifications.* Legal education fills a social need. Some legal jobs may be judged socially more important than others, and a state law school might decide to admit some "less qualified" students who are particularly likely to do socially valuable work in preference to "better qualified" applicants less likely to do such work. Again, even if one assumes that there is some correlation between being black and being likely to do socially valuable work, such as work for the poor and otherwise disadvantaged, it would be feasible administratively to make much "finer" guesses about an applicant's likely job orientation, based on his specific background, his previous activities and his expressed reasons for wishing to go to law school.

4. *Ability to Work With Blacks.* It can be argued that black lawyers are more likely to represent black people effectively because they can win their trust and understand them better. Commonality of background, vocabulary and attitude can be helpful for a lawyer's representation of his client. Of course, a rich white lawyer may do a superb job of representing a poor black defendant; and when a major legal issue is sharply presented, an expert lawyer's personal background makes little difference. But personal background may become much more important when one is counseling clients or trying to learn their story.

* * *

This "special qualifications" argument is the only form of the "qualifications" argument for preferences on explicitly racial lines that is plausibly consistent with the fourteenth amendment; my own conclusion is that even racial preferences based on this rationale should not withstand an equal protection attack. Racial identity is, at most, one small aspect of effective representation. A more talented white lawyer will usually represent blacks better than a less talented black one. Moreover, many black lawyers will find themselves in jobs where they rarely represent black clients, so a general racial preference benefits many applicants for whom this argument will prove to be irrelevant. I believe that the fourteenth amendment policy against such racial classifications is stronger in terms of this argument than with respect to the compensation argument, because a governmental assumption that black lawyers can represent blacks more effectively impliedly endorses racial ways of thought much more than a governmental assumption that blacks deserve compensation. It suggests that private citizens should take race into account in their dealings with lawyers. As Justice Douglas urged in his *DeFunis* dissent: "The purpose of the University of Washington cannot be to produce Black lawyers for Blacks, Polish lawyers for Poles, Jewish lawyers for Jews, Irish lawyers for the Irish." [148] Perhaps if law schools made a more particularized effort to determine which applicants would be most likely to work on behalf of disadvantaged groups, they could take into account the possibility that black lawyers may be more effective in helping disadvantaged blacks than white lawyers. Perhaps also this special qualifications argument, as well as the other qualifications arguments, can give slight added weight to the state's other interests in a general racial preference in admissions, but the qualifications arguments, separately or together, are not sufficient by themselves to sustain such a preference against constitutional attack.

C. Preferential Admissions and the Values of Diversity and the Amelioration of Attitudes that Hinder Equality of Opportunity

Some arguments for preferential policies are based on claimed benefits to the general society if there are more black students in law school and black members of the bar.

1. *The Integrated Law School.* As the Supreme Court pointed out many years ago,[150] * * * one of the values of a legal education is the exposure to persons of diverse backgrounds and points of view. One might add that the benefits of diversity in the student body accrue to the faculty as well as the students. In order to enrich the education of all its students, a state law school may admit persons with unusual experience, say former school teachers or policemen, in preference to those who are slightly more "qualified" but who lack the special experience.[153] Regret-

---

148. 416 U.S. at 341–42.

150. Sweatt v. Painter, 339 U.S. 629, 634 (1950).

153. Many institutions admit students from distant regions of the country on a preferential basis, in part to expose stutable though it may be, race is a crucially important aspect of most people's experience; a white student who has never talked seriously with blacks will be unlikely to understand many very important things about life in the United States. While increasing understanding, such contacts may also eliminate or blur racial stereotypes that can inhibit one's effective functioning as a lawyer, judge, or administrator. If the diversity sought is diversity of racial experience, then obviously a preference in racial terms is precisely tailored to the aim.

If preferences are necessary to get a significant number of blacks into law school, the interest in a racially diversified student body is substantial enough to justify preferences for some blacks, since race is now such an important determinant of social perceptions, and so many problems with which lawyers and officials deal concern race. But it should not be assumed that because some preferential representation of a group is permitted to encourage diversity, members of that group can be admitted on a preferential basis until they constitute the same percentage of the student body as their percentage of the general population. It is not certain, for example, that relevant communication between blacks and whites will be much greater if the student body is ten per cent black than if it is five per cent black. Of course, it may be unfair to impose on a small number of blacks the responsibility to communicate the "black experience" to a large number of whites, but a law school justifying its preferential policies in terms of law school diversity should make some effort to decide how widely applicable racial preferences should be to achieve adequate diversity.

The proper degree of judicial review of a policy supported by a diversity justification is very difficult to determine, because it is much harder for judges to second-guess decisions about how much diversity is needed and how it can best be achieved than it is for them to deal with the questions of administrability of alternative standards raised by some compensation and qualifications arguments. It is hard even to conceive of the "evidence" a school might give to support a particular percentage of black representation. Nevertheless, given the general undesirability of racial classifications and the potential broad sweep of diversity arguments, it would be a mistake for the courts to accept a diversity claim as justifying whatever number of preferential admissions law schools choose to make. The courts should at least require a reasoned explanation by administrators of why they believe the actual number of preferences given will yield the desired diversity.

2. *The Amelioration of Racial Stereotypes.* Past discrimination has made it very hard for blacks to become professionals. The widespread assumption that blacks are more suited for menial jobs has affected the attitudes of whites toward blacks and the attitude of blacks toward themselves. If young blacks are to aspire to, and work toward, high vocational positions, it is important for them to see that significant numbers of persons with whom they identify are in those positions. And

dents to others from diverse regional backgrounds.

the perception of blacks in those positions will do much to vitiate possible feelings of racial inferiority among a much wider group of blacks. If whites are going to accept blacks as equal, not only as a matter of religious or political philosophy but also on the intuitive level that so influences actual social relations, it is important that they deal with blacks as equals in the performance of social responsibilities.

A special reason why it is important to have black lawyers is that many lawyers become legislators and high administrators. Both blacks and whites need to see blacks in positions of community leadership, as well as to have a black perspective brought directly to bear on the resolution of many community problems.

Increasing the number of blacks in high vocational positions and as community leaders will not only raise the aspirations of young blacks and dissipate white racial stereotypes, but may also ameliorate some stereotypes blacks have about whites. No longer will it be so easy to distinguish "them" (the white power structure) from "us" (the black oppressed), because "them" will include many blacks. Other blacks will come more easily to see the constraints under which those with power operate and will abandon any oversimplified notion that those in responsible positions are invariably "oppressors."

Given the pervasiveness of racial stereotypes in this society and their destructive effect on the quality of life, their dissolution is undoubtedly a proper public purpose. It may be a public purpose that draws implicit support from the thirteenth and fourteenth amendments. The persistence of negative stereotypes about blacks can be argued to be an "incident" of slavery in the extended sense of a debilitating effect of slavery and also an "incident" in the narrower sense of a feature that accompanied slavery itself and continues to disadvantage blacks. As it has developed, the concept of equal protection in the fourteenth amendment implicitly condemns stereotypes based on race and class. It would be a denial of equal protection for the government purposefully to foster such stereotypes, and while attacking them may not be required, it is consistent with the spirit of the amendment.

If the purpose of preferential policies is to reduce racial stereotypes, then, of course, the racial classification fits its purpose exactly. So long as the superbly educated son of a black Senator or the recent immigrant from Africa are identified as relevantly "black" by whites and other blacks, then this purpose of the preferential policy is served by admitting them.

Opponents of preferential policies argue that racial preferences will be unnecessary and even unhelpful in eliminating stereotypes, that the opening up of opportunities to blacks without preference will produce, as it has for many immigrant groups, enough professionals in a generation or two to undercut racial stereotypes, and that admission preferences for blacks will actually confirm stereotypes.[164] I find neither contention

---

164. The argument is that if whites think blacks are in positions because of preference, or they find the blacks they deal with to be less qualified than most whites, persuasive enough to reject preferential policies; certainly neither is so evidently correct that a court should hold that a decision in favor of preferences is unsound. The average quality of black law students has increased quickly since the first years of preference, perhaps in part because law schools are now admitting many blacks who were admitted on a preferential basis to the best colleges. Most black law school graduates perform competently, and whatever "gap" may remain at graduation from a given school between some of them and most white students is likely to be reduced during their careers. The "negative" stereotypes fostered by preferential admissions will be far outweighed by the positive effect of having blacks in important professional positions. The answer to the contention that preferences are unnecessary is two-fold. Given the systematic historic discrimination against blacks and the more subtle and pervasive discriminatory attitudes that still exist and are particularly hard to eradicate because of the visibility of racial differences, genuine equality for blacks without preference may take much more than one or two generations. Second, the damage done to blacks by racial stereotypes now is so serious that any program that gives hope of altering stereotypes quickly is to be preferred to one that will work only over a longer term.

Whether the state's interest is put as the long run amelioration of racial stereotypes or the reasonably quick amelioration of these stereo-types, it is important enough to support preferential admissions policies. Whether these policies are "necessary" to achieve these results may be debatable, but the debate is not one that can comfortably be resolved by the judiciary. Legislative or administrative judgments of the need for preferential policies should be accepted; and so long as the gap between the percentage of black professionals and the percentage of blacks in the population remains enormous, this justification for racial preferences will support almost any breadth of application for the preference.

The amelioration of racial stereotypes and compensation of blacks for injuries caused by present discrimination and the lingering effects of past injustices, are the two justifications that are adequate to support outright racial preferences as extensive as those now being employed in many law schools.

RICHARD A. POSNER, THE DeFUNIS CASE AND THE CONSTITUTIONALITY OF PREFERENTIAL TREATMENT OF RACIAL MINORITIES
1974 Sup.Ct.Rev. 1, 7–12, 15–25.

II. THE REASONABLENESS OF REVERSE DISCRIMINATION

B. *Race as a Surrogate for Other, Nonracial Characteristics*

A frequently suggested basis for preferential treatment is the desire to increase the diversity of the student body in the hope of thereby enhancing the quality of the students' educational experience. * * *

then racial stereotypes will be strengthened rather than reduced. *See* Graglia, [*Special Admission of the "Culturally Deprived" to*] *Law School,* 119 U.Pa.L.Rev. 351, 355 (1970).]

For a diversity argument to be convincing, it must identify a differentiating factor that is relevant to the educational experience. It would make no sense to argue that in selecting the entering first-year class a law school should strive for diversity in the height of the students, or in their weight, pulchritude, posture, depth of voice, or blood pressure, or that it should give a preference to (or disfavor) albinos, or people with freckles or double chins. Diversity in these superficial physical respects contributes nothing of value to the legal education of the students. Race *per se*—that is, race completely divorced from certain characteristics that may be strongly correlated with, but do not inevitably accompany, it—is also, and in a similar sense, irrelevant to diversity. There are black people (and Chicanos, Filipinos, etc.) who differ only in the most superficial physical characteristics from whites— who have the same tastes, manners, experiences, aptitudes, and aspirations as the whites with whom one might compare them (here, white law school applicants). To give such people preferential treatment to the end of increasing the diversity of the student body would be equivalent to giving preferential treatment to albinos—were it not that race is frequently correlated with other attributes that are arguably relevant to meaningful diversity, and albinism is not. The average black applicant for admission is more likely than the average white to have known poverty and prejudice first hand, and his experience, communicated to his fellow students (and teachers) both inside and outside of the classroom, might enrich the educational process.

Race in this analysis is simply a proxy for a set of other attributes— relevant to the educational process—with which race, itself irrelevant to the process, happens to be correlated. The use of a racial proxy in making admissions decisions will produce some inaccuracy—blacks will be admitted who lack the attributes that contribute to genuine diversity—but this cost of using a racial proxy may be less than the cost, which is saved, of having to investigate the actual characteristics of each applicant.

The difficulty with this approach is that it closely resembles and could be viewed as imparting legitimacy to the case for regarding discrimination against racial minorities as a proper, because (generally) efficient, form of conduct. There are several possible explanations for the presence of racial and ethnic discrimination. One is sheer irrationality; another is exploitation; another the desire to limit competition. But it may be that most discrimination in today's America can be explained simply by the cost of information. Suppose that a particular racial or ethnic identity is correlated with characteristics that are widely disliked for reasons not patently exploitive, anticompetitive, or irrational. A substantial proportion of the members of the group in question may be loud, or poor, or hostile, or irresponsible, or poorly educated, or dangerously irascible, or ill-mannered, or have different tastes, values, and work habits from our own, or speak an unintelligible patois.[24] To be averse to association (in housing, recreation, schooling, or employment) with an individual because he possessed such a characteristic would not ordinarily be regarded as a sign of prejudice. To be "prejudiced" means, rather, to ascribe to the members of a group defined by a racial or similarly arbitrary characteristic[25] attributes typically or frequently possessed by members of the group without pausing to consider whether the individual member in question has that characteristic—sometimes without being willing even to consider evidence that he does not. The extreme bigot applies an irrebuttable presumption that every member of the group has the characteristic that he dislikes. The moderate bigot applies a rebuttable presumption to the same effect—and all of us are at least moderate bigots in some areas of life.

The history of this country contains examples of the unreasoning type of racial and ethnic prejudice, of exploitive discrimination—illustrated by the treatment of the American Indian in the nineteenth century and by the enslavement of the black—and of the anticompetitive sort as well (*e.g.,* exclusion of women from various occupations). But, today at least, it may be that most prejudice and discrimination are a product of the cost of making individual distinctions within racial and ethnic groups. This is a type of economically efficient conduct similar to a consumer's reluctance to try a new brand or more generally, to carry the process of searching for products beyond the point where the cost of searching is equal to its benefit in enabling a better purchase to be made. It is perfectly rational for an individual to support the exclusion of Armenians, or Jews, or blacks from his club if his experience, whether first or second hand, is that most or very many members of these groups do not have the characteristics that he likes in a social (or business) acquaintance and there is no scarcity of eligible applicants from other groups.

To say that discrimination is often a rational and efficient form of behavior is not to say that it is socially or ethically desirable. "Efficient" must never be confused with "good" or "right." Moreover, there is an important distinction to be drawn between private discrimination and discrimination that is compelled, practiced, or encouraged by the government, or that is practiced by a monopolist. But I am not interested in the normative basis of antidiscrimination policy. My purpose in noting that much discrimination may be applicable in terms of the costs of information is, rather, to suggest a doubt about the merits of the diversity justification for treating racial minorities preferentially. That justification, it will be recalled, rests on the correlation between

---

24. The proportion of the racial or ethnic group who actually possess the disfavored characteristic may, of course, be exaggerated, since obtaining accurate information about the characteristics of the average member of the group may be costly too.

25. An "arbitrary characteristic" in this sense is one whose only significance is as a proxy for some other characteristic. To dislike short people because one finds them repulsive is not prejudice; to dislike short people because one thinks that short people tend to have aggressive personalities is an example of prejudice, assuming that not all short people in fact possess such personalities.

racial identity and the possession of characteristics that promote meaningful diversity, and implicitly, therefore, on the cost of ascertaining whether a particular member of the racial group actually possesses the desired characteristic. Could not a policy against hostile discrimination be undermined by a program of benevolent discrimination rooted in the same habit of mind—that of using race or ethnic origin to establish a presumption, in the case of a racially preferential admissions program a conclusive one, that the individual possesses some other attribute as well, that is, some educationally relevant characteristic such as a background of deprivation or a cultural difference? The danger is underscored by the fact that the hostile and the well-disposed discriminators seem to be treating race as a proxy for the same set of characteristics. The characteristics that university admissions officers associate with "black" are the distinctive cultural attributes of many black people who have grown up in an urban slum or in the rural South, and these are the same characteristics that the white bigot ascribes to every black, although he uses a different terminology (*e.g.,* "lazy" rather than "unmotivated").

I am not making the familiar argument that the member of the favored minority is humiliated by being singled out for preferential treatment. He may or may not be. My point is rather that the use of a racial characteristic to establish a presumption that the individual also possesses other, and socially relevant, characteristics exemplifies, encourages, and legitimizes the mode of thought and behavior that underlies most prejudice and bigotry in modern America.

* * *

I have dwelled * * * on the diversity argument for preferential treatment because it is the one argument that seems at first glance not racialistic at all. The argument is not that one race should be preferred over another but that a racial preference will benefit all members of the student body, regardless of race, by enriching the educational experience. Yet if one looks a little more closely at the argument it turns out to rest on a premise fundamentally inconsistent with that of a policy against hostile discrimination, for such a policy, if it is to be effective, requires rejection of administrative convenience as a justification for using racial criteria to allocate benefits or impose burdens.

C. *Racial Proportional Representation*

Where * * * a racial preference is based squarely on a desire to increase the proportion of lawyers of a particular race, it is no longer possible to argue about whether the preference is a form of racial discrimination and it is more difficult to find a justification based on educational purposes, or for that matter on anything else. Four principal reasons are offered for attempting to achieve at least approximately proportional racial representation in the legal profession: (1) making amends for past discrimination against the minority group; (2) putting the group where it would have been but for the handicaps imposed on its members by past discrimination; (3) improving the level of professional service received by the group; and (4) encouraging the aspirations of its members by the provision of suitable "role models." None of these four reasons would be any more persuasive to an objective observer than the sorts of arguments that could be offered for discriminating against racial minorities.

1. The members of the minority group who receive preferential treatment will often be those who have not been the victims of discrimination while the nonminority people excluded because of the preferences are unlikely to have perpetrated, or to have in any demonstrable sense benefited from,[32] the discrimination. Indian reparations may be a distinct case, based on treaty (equivalent to contractual) obligations enforceable by the heirs of the original beneficiaries against the government; also distinguishable, though in my opinion only tenuously, is the use of racial quotas as part of a decree to remedy unlawful discrimination.[33]

2. Many groups are underrepresented in various occupations for reasons of taste, opportunity, or aptitude unrelated to discrimination. There is no basis for a presumption that but for past discrimination, * * * minorities * * * would supply [a percentage] of the nation's lawyers [proportionate to their representation in the general population.]

---

32. One could spend many profitless hours discussing whether [a white applicant to law school] is better or worse off as the result of the history of racial discrimination in this country. Perhaps he is better off because, but for a history of discrimination, there would be a larger pool of qualified black applicants for a law school education. Perhaps he is worse off because, but for the history of discrimination, fewer blacks (and members of other minorities) would be interested in becoming lawyers. Perhaps if there had never been discrimination against blacks, there would never have been slavery in the United States, and without slavery, it is possible, indeed probable, that the black population in the United States would be insignificant, in which event—perhaps—the real income of whites would be higher.

33. As for example in Swann v. Charlotte–Mecklenburg Bd. of Educ., 402 U.S. 1 (1971). These decisions are difficult to justify because the people adversely affected by the decree are in general different from those who discriminated unlawfully. The remedy does not run against the wrongdoer. A more acceptable remedy would be damages. The costs of a decree imposing a racial quota in a labor market are borne primarily by the white workers (I distinguish the case where the source of the discrimination is the workers themselves or the union representing them) or, in the case of educational discrimination, by children bused to distant or inferior schools. The cost of a damage award, in contrast, would be borne primarily by the owners of the discriminating firm or the taxpayers of the discriminating school district.

In discussions of black reparations, an analogy is frequently drawn to the payment of substantial reparations by Germany to the State of Israel in compensation for Nazi Germany's extermination of millions of European Jews. Among the distinguishing features is the fact that the cost of the German reparations was borne by the German taxpaying public as a whole, rather than by university students, schoolchildren, and members of the working class, who are being asked in this country to subsidize certain racial minorities. But the more important difference is in the degree of felt guilt. If the United States had recently exterminated several millions of blacks, we might be willing to give several billion dollars to some African state that had been established as a refuge for persecuted blacks. Some people believe that the American treatment of the black has been comparable in its enormity to Hitler's treatment of the Jews; for them the analogy to German reparations to Israel may be a compelling one. To evaluate such a belief will require more careful studies along the lines of Fogel & Engerman, Time on the Cross: The Economics of American Negro Slavery (1974).

3. There is no evidence of which I am aware that a substantial number or proportion of minority-group law school graduates will seek in their professional careers to serve the special needs of their minority group rather than follow the normal patterns of professional advancement.

4. The "role model" argument is similarly *ad hoc* and conjectural. So long as a significant number of members of a minority group enter the legal profession and succeed in it (one of the Justices of the Supreme Court is black, after all), others will know that it is not closed to them. There is no basis for requiring proportional representation.

The reasons advanced for proportional representation are unimpressive. But more disturbing than the lack of solid intellectual foundations are the implications of the underrepresentation approach for the overall structure of society. The ultimate logic of underrepresentation is that the percentage of members of each minority racial and ethnic group in each desirable occupation, and in each level of achievement within the occupation, should be raised to equality with its percentage of the total population (either of the entire nation or, in some versions, of some region or local area). The proponents of proportional representation do not as yet urge adoption of the standard of perfect equality, but there seems to be no logical stopping point short of it within the structure of their argument. This is true despite their soothing assurance that affirmative action is required only in a period of transition to a society in which, all vestiges of discrimination having been eliminated by affirmative action, society can resume a policy of color-blindness. If, as seems more likely than not, occupational preferences and abilities are not randomly distributed across all racial and ethnic groups, then governmental intervention in the labor markets (and in the educational process insofar as it affects occupational choice and success) will have to continue forever if proportional equality in the desirable occupations is to be secured. Consistently implemented, this sort of intervention would, by profoundly distorting the allocation of labor and by driving a wedge between individual merit and economic and professional success, greatly undermine the system of incentives on which a free society depends.

* * *

III. THE CONSTITUTIONAL ISSUE

A. *Previous Approaches*

Twenty-eight *amicus curiae* briefs were submitted to the Supreme Court in the *DeFunis* case,[a] and most of them, rather than provide the Court with additional information not available in the record of the case, discuss points of constitutional doctrine. Yet the variety of constitutional arguments in the multitude of briefs is not great. The briefs supporting DeFunis's position point to the undeniable fact that he was treated

---

a. *DeFunis v. Odegaard*, 416 U.S. 312 (1974) (holding moot a challenge to the University of Washington Law School's special admissions program for Blacks, Chicanos, American Indians, and Filipinos).

less favorably than he would have been if he had been a member of one of the four favored racial groups and argue from this fact that he was a victim of racial discrimination, an unconstitutional form of state action. The opposing briefs argue that racial discrimination is unlawful only when invidious and that DeFunis's treatment carried no implication that being a nonmember of one of the favored groups—*i.e.,* being a white— connotes a despised or inferior status.

Neither argument is persuasive in the form expressed. Discrimination against whites, who constitute the vast majority of our population and who never before (in this country) have, as a group, been subjected to discrimination, is not patently the same phenomenon as the sorts of discrimination involved in previous equal-protection cases involving members of racial or ethnic minorities, or women. But neither is it tenable to argue that discrimination is bad only when the circumstances of its adoption or expression connote invidiousness, exploitation, or hostility, or seek to place a stamp of inferiority on the victims of the discrimination. Suppose that New York City adopted an ordinance (supported by the Jewish members of the City Council) limiting the percentage of Jews who could be teachers in the New York City public school system, and the ordinance was based on a finding that Jews are so able that no merit-based principle of selection could keep them from dominating the school system, but that the resulting concentration of Jews in the public schools had exacerbated racial tensions and had, indeed, promoted anti-Semitism. It is difficult to believe that such an ordinance would or should be upheld against a constitutional challenge, albeit one could argue (though not, in my opinion, persuasively) that the ordinance was not "invidious," since it was premised not on the inferiority of the Jews but indeed on the reverse, and even that the ordinance was in the Jews' best interest.

A distinct argument for the constitutionality of discrimination in favor of minority groups has been made in a recent article by Professor Ely. He argues, along lines similar to those suggested earlier, that a policy of discrimination, favorable or unfavorable, might be adopted simply because the costs of individualized treatment were thought to exceed its benefits, but that when members of one racial group—such as the white majority of a state legislature—are appraising the costs and benefits of a proposed discrimination against another racial group the comparison is apt to be distorted by conscious or unconscious racial hostility.[37] Hence, he argues, discrimination against a racial minority should be suspect under the Fourteenth Amendment, but discrimination in favor of a minority should not be since it does not involve any danger of majority exploitation of a minority.

There are two fundamental objections to this argument. One—that it misconceives the nature of the political process—I defer for the

37. Ely, [*The Constitutionality of Re-* *verse Racial Discrimination,* 41 U.Chi. L.Rev. 723,] 729, 732–33 (1974).

moment. The other is that it provides a mode of justifying discrimination against racial minorities. Professor Ely accepts the legitimacy of comparing the costs of discriminating against the members of a racial or ethnic minority with the benefits from thereby avoiding the need to make individual distinctions. He only wants assurance that the balance will be accurately struck. He is suspicious that the majority will fail to take adequate account of the costs, or will exaggerate the benefits, of the discriminatory measure, but this suspicion only warrants that the reviewing court satisfy itself that the legislature has in fact assessed the costs and benefits of the discrimination accurately. Suppose the Post Office were able to demonstrate convincingly that blacks had, on average, inferior aptitudes to whites for supervisory positions, that the costs to the postal system of inadequate supervisors were very great, and that the costs of conducting the inquiries necessary to ascertain whether an individual black had the requisite aptitudes were also great in relation to the probability of discovering qualified blacks. It would seem to follow from Ely's analysis that the Post Office could adopt a rule barring blacks from supervisory positions. By condemning only inefficient discriminations, Ely reduces the scope of the Equal Protection Clause to triviality, if I am correct in arguing that most discrimination in contemporary society is caused by the costs of information rather than by irrationality, exploitation, or the suppression of competition.

B. Toward an Objective Constitutional Principle

In order to determine the constitutionality of racially preferential admissions policies, it is first necessary to derive from the Equal Protection Clause some rule, or principle, or standard for applying the constitutional formula (that no state may "deny to any person within its jurisdiction the equal protection of the laws") to racial discrimination.
* * *

* * *

[The task] is to derive from the specific purposes of the constitutional framers a rule that, while sufficiently general to avoid constant recourse to the amendment process, is sufficiently precise and objective to limit a judge's exercise of personal whim and preference. The rule I derive on this basis is that the distribution of benefits and costs by government on racial or ethnic grounds is impermissible. Even though it is frequently efficient to sort people by race or ethnic origin, because racial or ethnic identity may be a good proxy for functional classifications, efficiency is rejected as a basis for governmental action in this context. The government is required to incur the additional costs of determining the individual applicant's fitness to hold a particular job, or patronize a particular facility, or be admitted to one of its educational institutions. To permit discrimination to be justified on efficiency grounds, as would Professor Ely, would not only thwart the purpose of the Equal Protection Clause by allowing much, perhaps most, discrimination to continue, but it would give the judges the power to pick and choose among discriminatory measures on the basis of personal values, for the weighing of the relevant costs and benefits would of necessity be largely subjective.

* * *

It remains to consider whether an exception to the rule forbidding discrimination on racial or ethnic grounds can be recognized where the discrimination can be said to be in favor of a racial or ethnic minority, and the race discriminated against is the white race. The exception is inadmissible, because it requires the court not only to consider whether there is discrimination but to decide whether the discrimination harms or hurts a particular racial group, and to weigh the competing claims of different racial groups, and the additional inquiries rob the principle of its precision and objectivity. The Court had no good evidence before it in the *Brown* case that segregated education in fact harmed blacks. The questions critical to the point were not even asked: Would blacks have fared better under a system of no public education (assuming that whites would prefer such a system to integrated public education)? Under a system where students were sorted by IQ? By family income? In later cases the Court stopped asking whether segregation actually hurt the blacks. (Today, of course, some blacks favor segregation.) The antidiscrimination principle is not only more objective, but more compelling, when it is divorced from empirical inquiries into the effects of particular forms of discrimination on the affected groups. The necessary inquiries are intractable and would leave the field open to slippery conjecture. * * * [A] plausible argument could be made that various forms of discrimination nominally against Jews might actually advance the interests of the Jews as a whole, for example by reducing their prominence and visibility in certain areas where the conspicuousness of the Jews may stimulate anti-Semitism. Similar arguments could be made for various forms of conceivably well-intentioned discrimination against blacks (such as ''benign'' housing quotas, or limitations on the migration of blacks from southern to northern states). The Supreme Court would reject such arguments, but not because they are substantially less compelling than the arguments it accepts when it upholds the constitutionality of governmental action. The arguments about the proper characterization of discrimination nominally in favor of racial minorities have a similar elusiveness. Is the position of the whites in this country so unassailable that they cannot be harmed by racial quotas? Or is the impact of such quotas likely to be concentrated on particular, and perhaps vulnerable, subgroups within the white majority? Do racial quotas actually help the minorities intended to be benefited, or harm them by impairing their self-esteem or legitimating stereotypical thinking about race? Are whites entitled to claim minority status when they are a minority within the political subdivision that enacted the measure discriminating against whites? If so, then by parity of reasoning would blacks lack standing to complain about an ordinance discriminating against them enacted by Newark, New Jersey, or Washington, D.C., or other cities in which blacks are a majority of the population eligible to vote? If these are litigable issues, we do not have a constitutional principle but merely a directive that the judges uphold those forms of racial and ethnic discrimination which accord with their personal values.

C. METRO BROADCASTING

Charles Fried and Patricia Williams comment on the Court's decision in *Metro Broadcasting, Inc. v. FCC*.[1] Fried asserts that the majority was wrong to reject a "liberal, individualistic" understanding of equal protection, and that the Court's "group-rights" perspective led it to adopt a standard of review that insufficiently scrutinizes race-based policies. Williams supports the Court's decision, arguing that it provides a vehicle for a better understanding of the significance of and necessity for group claims within our legal system. *Metro Broadcasting* is an important case, she suggests, because it affirms "the desirability of diversity in all aspects of our economy and of multiculturalism in our lives."

CHARLES FRIED *, *METRO BROADCASTING, INC. v. FCC*: TWO CONCEPTS OF EQUALITY
104 Harv.L.Rev. 107–117, 119–121, 123–125 (1990).

Except for the shameful and discredited "separate but equal" doctrine of *Plessy v. Ferguson,* the Supreme Court has always adhered to a liberal, individualistic view of the equal protection guarantee. Until its decision last Term in *Metro Broadcasting, Inc. v. FCC,* the Court had not departed from the view that "[i]t is settled beyond question that the 'rights created by the first section of the Fourteenth Amendment are, by its terms, guaranteed to the individual. The rights established are personal rights.' "[3] The Court took as its premise that "[a]lthough many of the Framers of the Fourteenth Amendment conceived of its primary function as bridging the vast distance between members of the Negro race and the white 'majority,' the Amendment itself was framed in universal terms, without reference to color, ethnic origin, or condition of prior servitude."[4] From this premise, the Court concluded that:

> a more restrictive view of the Equal Protection Clause * * * hold[ing] that discrimination against members of the white 'majority' cannot be suspect if its purpose can be characterized as 'benign' [must be rejected] * * *. It is far too late to argue that the guarantee of equal protection to *all* persons permits the recognition

1. 497 U.S. 547, 110 S.Ct. 2997, 111 L.Ed.2d 445 (1990).

* Professor of General Jurisprudence, Harvard Law School. As Solicitor General, Charles Fried authorized the briefs amicus curiae of the United States in the cases that comprised Metro Broadcasting, Inc. v. FCC, 110 S.Ct. 2997 (1990), and was the principal signatory of the government briefs in City of Richmond v. J.A. Croson Co., 109 S.Ct.

706 (1989), and Wygant v. Jackson Board of Education, 476 U.S. 267 (1986), discussed in this Comment.

3. Regents of the Univ. of Cal. v. Bakke, 438 U.S. 265, 289 (1978) (Powell, J.) (quoting Shelley v. Kraemer, 334 U.S. 1, 22 (1948)).

4. *Id.* at 293 (citation omitted).

of special wards entitled to a degree of protection greater than that accorded others.[5]

This conviction, expressed in Justice Powell's controlling opinion in *Regents of the University of California v. Bakke,* was reaffirmed by a plurality in *Wygant v. Jackson Board of Education.* And two Terms ago in *City of Richmond v. J.A. Croson Co.,* Justice O'Connor was able to state this position firmly and unequivocally in an opinion for the court.

Two themes underlie this liberal, individualistic conception of equal protection. First, the liberal conception insists on the primacy of individuals, not groups, in our constitutional scheme and views the individual as the object of fundamental rights. Second, it resists a basic separation of the polity into racial groupings from which individuals cannot escape. Such racial balkanization is the opposite of what might be called the common market of the human spirit; balkanization creates, and even celebrates, barriers to trade that in the end impoverish the human race. That some degree of separation exists naturally in society is no justification for perpetuating or strengthening it through governmental policy. In keeping with the liberal premise that the public and private spheres are distinct, liberal individualism does not view the existence of discrimination and social segmentation as a sufficient reason to reproduce these in the coercive apparatus of the state.

Standing in sharp contrast to this liberal, individualistic conception of equal protection is the collectivist ("communitarian" or "republican") group-rights conception of equality,[12] generally reflected only in dissents written by Justice Marshall and Justice Brennan.[13] In *Bakke,* for example, Justice Marshall argued:

> It is unnecessary in 20th century America to have individual Negroes demonstrate that they have been victims of racial discrimination; the racism of our society has been so pervasive that none, regardless of wealth or position, has managed to escape its impact. The experience of Negroes in America has been different in kind, not just in degree, from that of other ethnic groups.[14]

The group-rights perspective sees groups—ethnic, cultural, gender— as having a status independent of and even superior to that of individual

---

5. *Id.* at 294–95 (emphasis in original).

12. Under this view, individuals are "constituted" by the groups—including national, ethnic, and religious communities— to which they belong. Sources discussing or exemplifying this outlook include D. Bell, And We Are Not Saved (1987); M. Sandel, Liberalism and the Limits of Justice (1982); Lasch, *The Communitarian Critique of Liberalism,* in Community in America 173 (C. Reynolds & R. Norman eds. 1988); and Lawrence, *The Id, the Ego, and Equal Protection: Reckoning with Unconscious Racism,* 39 Stan.L.Rev. 317 (1987). *Cf.* R. Unger, Knowledge and Politics 236–89 (1985) (positing a theory of political interaction

and a vision of "the good" based on "organic group" affiliations); Fiss, *Groups and the Equal Protection Clause,* 5 Phil. & Pub. Aff. 107 (1976) (advocating a group-oriented approach to equal protection).

13. *See* Wygant v. Jackson Bd. of Educ., 476 U.S. 267, 295 (1986) (Marshall, J., dissenting); *Bakke,* 438 U.S. at 324 (Brennan, White, Marshall, and Blackmun, JJ., concurring in the judgment in part and dissenting in part); *id.* at 400 (separate opinion of Marshall, J.).

14. *Bakke,* 438 U.S. at 400 (separate opinion of Marshall, J.).

group members. It assigns a value to the well-being of the group that is similarly independent of and perhaps superior to that of its component members. From this view it follows that governmental policy should measure benefits and burdens in terms of groups and, when equality is the issue, emphasize equality between groups as such.

* * *

The conflict between the liberal, individualistic conception and the collectivist, group-rights conception of equal protection plays out in doctrinal terms through the debate over the proper standard of review for race-based governmental action. The issue is whether government needs a "compelling" justification, one that would overcome "strict scrutiny," whenever it classifies persons by race, or whether a more relaxed standard is appropriate, at least when government favors members of groups seen or designated as disadvantaged. The level of scrutiny is an entirely appropriate, even inevitable doctrinal entailment of these contrasting visions. To the individualist, who believes that the equal protection clause requires the government to craft its laws to treat people equally, regardless of race, the government must make a showing of compelling need in order to legislate along racial lines. To the collectivist, for whom equal protection is a command to secure substantive aggregate equality for disadvantaged groups, legislation undertaken in that spirit need not be scrutinized as carefully.

It is impossible to ignore racial differences entirely—pure color-blindness is too extreme a principle.[19] The difficult question is whether government may use race to attack broad social problems and designate as beneficiaries of racial legislation individuals other than the particular persons who have been victimized. Justice Scalia, with a logic that is perhaps more rigorous than practical, argued in *Croson* that it may not. By insisting on victim-specificity, he pointed out, the government remains true to the principle of color-blindness, because government accords benefits to victims as such, not to members of a group against which there has been discrimination. By contrast, the collectivists feel that departing from victim-specificity is the only way to carry out the commands of equal protection. As Justice Blackmun put it in *Bakke,* "[i]n order to get beyond racism, we must first take account of race."

Strict scrutiny and the insistence on a "compelling governmental interest" are the appropriate and usual response of constitutional doctrine when a preeminent moral-political principle is at stake. It is so for limitations of first amendment liberties, and it should be so when government resorts to racial classifications. And although the issue is a close one, I believe strict scrutiny is satisfied by departing from victim-

---

19. If a disease, such as sickle-cell anemia or Tay–Sachs syndrome, overwhelmingly afflicts a particular ethnic group, it would be unreasonable to ignore that fact. If a criminal gang has an exclusive racial composition, it would be fanatical to require the government to ignore this fact in recruiting agents to infiltrate that gang. *See Wygant,* 476 U.S. at 314 (Stevens, J., dissenting). And in remedial circumstances, when a bigot has victimized according to race, race-based remedies seem an inescapable counter-response.

specificity when there is an identified, bigoted wrongdoer and the remedy is narrowly tailored to redress his prior discrimination. Because race is the most divisive and dubious governmental criterion for action, the instinct to resort to race for sentimental or purely political reasons must be vigilantly restrained; the requirement of a demanding and definite showing of direct remediation should be sufficient to provide the necessary discipline.

* * *

In *Metro Broadcasting,* the Court turned away from its past understandings. First, the Court applied a lenient, intermediate level of scrutiny to affirmative action measures approved by Congress and required only that the FCC's racial preferences be substantially related to an important governmental objective. Second, the Court recognized that "diversity," standing alone and unconnected to any remedial purpose, was such an important objective. Finally, the Court took a step that its past vigilance concerning discrimination had never permitted: it embraced the notion that some types of racial discrimination are "benign," based on the identity and presumed characteristics of the groups such discrimination is intended to benefit.

The law is now in an unstable condition. The distinctions and arguments offered by the majority to square this decision with the prior cases are so manifestly unsatisfactory that one wonders whether they were put forward quite seriously.

The most serious obfuscation in the opinion is its holding that the FCC's racial preferences should be judged under a standard of intermediate scrutiny. Justice Brennan wrote that a lesser standard of review for "benign" racial discrimination is appropriate when the discrimination is engaged in by Congress. Permission to employ this lenient standard of review is supposed to flow from the decision in *Fullilove v. Klutznick,* which addressed the constitutionality of a congressionally mandated ten percent set-aside for minority businesses in local public works programs receiving federal funds. Justice Brennan relied on *Fullilove* for the proposition that Congress is entitled to deference from the courts when it legislates pursuant to its express constitutional powers and when the expert agencies it has established use their expertise to enact policy. Even allowing for the lack of clarity of Chief Justice Burger's plurality opinion, *Fullilove* hardly authorizes the Court's conclusion in *Metro Broadcasting.*

Fullilove was based primarily on Congress' power under section 5 of the fourteenth amendment. Even assuming that *Metro Broadcasting* also implicated section 5,[41] still there would be no warrant for the Court's application of a lenient standard of review. There is no doubt that section 5 of the fourteenth amendment was meant to add something

---

41. Justice O'Connor argues convincingly that the policies at issue in *Metro Broadcasting* did not in fact implicate Congress' § 5 power. *See* 110 S.Ct. at 3030–31 (O'Connor, J., dissenting) (arguing that § 5 is implicated only when "Congress * * * act[s] respecting the states").

to the general standard of equal protection set out in the first section. Above all, section 5 makes clear that Congress has a power of legislation to enforce the equal protection command of section 1 against the states, a power that need not depend on the enumeration of its powers in article I, section 8. At the time the amendment was framed—when the power of Congress to reach what might have seemed purely local activities was highly controversial—this surely must have been the crucial consideration. To this function of section 5, which was instrumental in laying the constitutional foundation for the Civil Rights Act and the Voting Rights Act, the *Fullilove* plurality may be taken as proposing another: that section 5 endows Congress with special power to ascertain the facts that make a remedy appropriate, and perhaps also a special power akin to that derived from the necessary and proper clause to establish the remedies tailored to the occasion.

Regardless of the validity of *Fullilove's* reading of section 5, neither of these special powers of Congress could justify the outcome in *Metro Broadcasting*. The additional deference to which Congress is entitled when acting under its section 5 power amounts to a greater presumption that it has found the facts necessary to prove a constitutional violation and that it has the power to undertake the preferred remedy; deference to congressional fact-finding and remediation in no way alters the substantive standards that determine what does or does not violate the Constitution. * * *

[*Fullilove*] alluded to section 5 only in order to validate Congress' findings concerning the historical record of prior discrimination, not to manipulate the standard of scrutiny under which to evaluate the statute. That "a racial classification is suspect and subject to strict judicial scrutiny" [49] was not in serious doubt. Put another way, Congress is entitled to special deference in selecting the means to a constitutionally permissible end under the equal protection clause, but section 5 does not render an end that would be illegitimate if pursued by other legislative bodies constitutionally acceptable if pursued by Congress.

In the context of *Metro Broadcasting*, this means that the Court would have been well within its rights to show considerable deference to any congressional findings of past discrimination by the government in the broadcasting field and to accept that the precise form of remedy chosen was narrowly tailored to address that discrimination. But congressional and FCC findings concerning diversity, an objective that even the majority does not argue would satisfy the strict scrutiny normally applicable to racial legislation, are simply irrelevant. To argue that section 5 and *Fullilove* could justify a lower standard of substantive review, and thereby transform congressional factual findings into validations of new governmental interests cognizable under the fourteenth amendment, is a disingenuous form of bootstrapping.

Even according Congress the broadest legitimate fact-finding latitude possible, the congressional findings supporting the FCC's distress

---

49. [448 U.S.] at 507 (Powell, J., concurring).

sale and comparative licensing regimes are inadequate to establish that they were enacted in response to a violation of equal protection. Contrasting Congress' findings in *Metro Broadcasting* with its explicit statements supporting the enactment of the statute at issue in *Fullilove* makes this inadequacy clear. That the construction industry and its corresponding unions had been a locus of vicious, unashamed, and pervasive racism was notorious. Of course nothing of the sort had been, has been, or could be shown about the broadcasting industry. Not lenders, not advertisers, and certainly not the FCC have ever been accused of anything approaching explicitly exclusionary practices. Indeed, the Court specifically denied relying on a purpose to remedy past discrimination by the broadcast industry or the licensing authorities. What was clear was the practically nonexistent number of minority owners of broadcast licenses. What was equally clear was that this numerical disparity was the result of economic and social disadvantage— in other words, the societal discrimination which the Court in *Bakke, Wygant,* and *Croson* explicitly held was not a sufficient basis for official racial classification.

The legislative committee materials that announce the factual determination that minority group members own very few broadcast licenses and the conclusion that minority ownership preferences are the only practicable way of increasing diversity in programming that will serve the needs of minority communities are strictly irrelevant unless one already accepts the conclusion of *Metro Broadcasting* that diversity is a permissible goal of race-conscious legislation. And the conclusion that minority ownership preferences will produce diversity is itself questionable. Neither the Congress nor the Court attempted to define what constitutes a minority community or its needs, and neither examined how those needs might be served by a minority broadcaster. We are left with nothing more than the assumption that such racially defined communities exist, that they have distinct needs as to broadcast services, that minority license owners will best discern those racially circumscribed needs, and that minority owners will be more powerfully motivated to serve them once discerned. This is a veritable cascade of nonsequiturs and begged questions.

Fullilove's proposition that Congress has special remedial powers under section 5 is also irrelevant: the issue in *Metro Broadcasting* was not establishing the fact of past discrimination—there was no such fact—and therefore was not determining its appropriate remedy. The issue was the meaning of the substantive constitutional standard itself, the meaning of equal protection. Nothing in *Fullilove* or in common sense suggests that equal protection can mean one thing for the Congress and another thing for every other level and organ of government. Indeed, just this point was at the heart of the Court's morally inevitable, though textually difficult, conclusion in *Bolling v. Sharpe* that the Constitution must not be read to forbid racial segregation by state and local bodies but to allow it if sanctioned by federal enactment. *Bolling* is distinguishable only if we assume what is to be proven: that Congress has wider power to make racial distinctions if it does so in ways judged to be benign. Everything in the Court's jurisprudence until this case seems to assume that if the kind of diversity celebrated by the Court in *Metro Broadcasting* is insufficient to justify legislation by race, but rather constitutes prohibited "discrimination for its own sake," [58] then it should make no difference whether the discrimination is worked by an act of Congress or an ordinance of the Richmond City Council. If the Constitution rejects such a thing as "benign discrimination" and requires a compelling interest to justify all race-conscious measures, this must be true across the board. What the Court has given us is an unstable constitutional regime, one that meets the description of "checkerboard" justice coined by Ronald Dworkin in *Law's Empire*.[60]

* * *

Justice Brennan's defense of applying a lower standard of review to the federal government did not, however, rely solely on Congress' powers to enforce equal protection; indeed, he explicitly asserted that *Fullilove* rested on an "amalgam" of congressional powers and sought to justify the deferential standard of review based on "Congress' institutional competence as the national legislature." The opinion suggests that one component of this competence is the presumed expertise of administrative agencies. But this expertise no more justifies lenient constitutional review than does section 5 of the fourteenth amendment.

In the first place, it is questionable whether the FCC brought to bear any expertise upon the affirmative action policies at issue in *Metro Broadcasting*. The Court's decisions, not only in this case, but also in its previous cases on broadcast regulation, emphasize the expertise of the FCC. But the minority preference programs formally instituted by the FCC during the Carter administration were not instituted as a result of study by the "expert agency"; rather, they were forced upon the agency by the Court of Appeals for the District of Columbia Circuit.[73] It was those racial preference programs that the FCC in 1986 proposed to study, now that the broadcasting industry had several years of actual experience under them. But it was this study by the expert agency that Congress "in no uncertain terms" [74] shut down. To be sure, Congress may have had an inkling what such a study would conclude, particularly from a Commission whose members had been appointed by President Reagan; however, that is how our system is supposed to work. The Commission is, after all, an "independent" regulatory agency, which in other contexts is a device favored by Congress when it wants to put a matter beyond executive branch control.

---

58. Regents of the Univ. of Cal. v. Bakke, 438 U.S. 265, 307 (1978) (Powell, J.).

60. *See* R. Dworkin, Law's Empire 184 (1986) ("Checkerboard statutes are the most dramatic violations of the ideal of integrity * * *.").

73. *See* TV 9, Inc. v. FCC, 495 F.2d 929, 938 (D.C.Cir.1973), *cert. denied,* 419 U.S. 986 (1974). * * *

74. 110 S.Ct. at 3016 n. 29.

The claim of FCC expertise as applied to these programs is suspect for another reason as well. What is involved in these cases, as in the minority business enterprise set-aside area generally, is not employment but ownership. Ownership programs, however, confront discrimination and disadvantage less directly than do other types of programs. The broadcast industry, of course, must comply with the Civil Rights Acts and avoid not only intentional discrimination but also any employment practices that have the effect of unjustifiably denying employment opportunity on the basis of race or gender. In addition, the FCC has adopted and enforced its own antidiscrimination programs in the industries it regulates. These legal protections vindicate the rights of individual members of disadvantaged groups to be treated as individuals and to enjoy equal opportunities for employment. By comparison, the FCC's affirmative action programs for additional minority ownership of broadcast facilities would likely affect only a small minority elite. * * *

In the end, agency expertise proves no more relevant than section 5 to the very point critically at issue in *Metro Broadcasting*: whether there are race-based conceptions of both community and community needs that are appropriate for constitutional purposes. It would be silly to deny that there are many communities with distinct cultural attributes, and it would be Philistine to deny the richness their diversity lends to national life. But this happy collage takes on a sinister aspect when individuals are compulsorily assigned to groupings and communities, and are penalized or rewarded based on these assignments, by the coercive power of the state.

* * *

In *Metro Broadcasting,* the Supreme Court clearly [assumed] that there are race-based conceptions of social interaction that can serve as a legitimate basis for state intervention; this is evident from the Court's belief that some forms of racial discrimination are "benign." By putting the Supreme Court's imprimatur on the idea of "benign discrimination" for the first time—especially without providing an accompanying set of principles that could define "benignity"—*Metro Broadcasting* introduces substantial uncertainty and instability into the law. The dissent characterized the unanalyzed (and therefore unsupported) hypotheses that there is such a thing as minority need in broadcasting and that minority ownership will serve that need as issuing from the very kind of racial stereotyping that since *Brown v. Board of Education* the Court has been at pains to condemn. Indeed, there is no form of stereotyping more disturbing than that which assumes that members of racial or ethnic groups exhibit distinct ways of thinking, share particular dispositions, or display common patterns of values and behavior; such stereotyping is hardly "benign." The Court sought to salve the sting of this reasoning by saying that no findings of a distinct minority community interest or capacity to serve it was implied or necessary. Rather, such an interest and special ability to serve this interest may be assumed, so that "in the aggregate" broadcasting diversity will be enhanced. Justice Kennedy in his dissent drew the analogy between the Court's hypothesis and South African apartheid, an analogy that attracted Justice Brennan's ire. To be sure, the motivation behind the minority preferences at issue in *Metro Broadcasting* lacks the malice and ugliness of apartheid; it is this that perhaps led the Court to distinguish this race-conscious measure as "benign." Yet this is not a satisfactory response: what is needed is a legal theory to distinguish race-conscious governmental measures—measures that group people by race and assume a coincidence of values and interests within such groupings—that are benign from those that are not, a theory based on something better than the Court's "we know it when we see it" intuitions. * * *

The Court's only response to the danger of racial group stereotyping is to reiterate that diversity is an "important" governmental goal and that the FCC's policies are substantially related to that end, thus surviving something only marginally more rigorous than the least demanding standard of constitutional review, the rational basis standard. But this just repeats the problem, by asserting that very little need be shown to justify Congress' recourse to race-based classifications and approximate aggregations of ways of thinking and valuing. To justify the use of a racial category as benign more must be said: for instance, that the historic injustices against African–Americans justify special measures to amplify their presence in all sectors of national life. I am sure that something like that reasoning supports the preferences many people of good will would accord in their private dealings. But in the past, the Court has never embraced this reasoning—only Justice Marshall has done so with clarity.[98]

Reasonable persons can differ about the propriety of this reasoning when private persons—and private institutions—resort to it in their private dealings. But it is understandable that the Court has previously failed to embrace it as a basis for race-conscious governmental measures. The government's monopoly on coercive power, its unique ability to affect the conduct of private actors, its freedom from the equilibrating pressures of market competition, and its duty to represent the entire populace all justify treating its decisions to act in a race-conscious fashion differently from those of private actors. Grounding a theory of benign governmental discrimination in a particular historical injustice, as Justice Marshall argues, would make the equal protection principle of the fourteenth amendment applicable especially or only to the descendants of former slaves. To generalize it beyond African–Americans to Asian–Americans, Native Americans, Spanish-surnamed persons, and, as sometimes happens, Eskimos and Aleuts [99] requires a theory of deprivation that is quite indeterminate and infinitely manipulable. The only way to exclude, for instance, Jews or Italian–Americans is by a kind of

98. *See* Regents of the Univ. of Cal. v. Bakke, 438 U.S. 265, 395–402 (1978) (separate opinion of Marshall, J.).

99. *See, e.g.,* City of Richmond v. J.A. Croson Co., 109 S.Ct. 706, 713 (1989);

Statement of Policy on Minority Ownership of Broadcasting Facilities, 68 F.C.C.2d 979, 980 n. 8 (1978).

casual, anecdotal social engineering that few would want to entrust to government at any level.

Even if a determinate and morally adequate theory could be developed that would identify deprived groups, application of the theory would still be grossly unjust as applied to specific individuals within those groups. Application would almost certainly be both substantially overinclusive and underinclusive, granting significant benefits to many who did not need or deserve them and discriminating against many who badly merited greater solicitude. Furthermore, no matter how racial preferences are structured, the government always would be forced to contend with the unseemly practical difficulties involved in ascertaining whether a given individual does or does not satisfy the "definition" of the eligible race. These problems are inevitable concomitants of the group-rights perspective that Justices Brennan and Marshall have previously espoused in dissent and that *Metro Broadcasting* has finally endowed with some legitimacy as law. If the ultimate concern is for an "aggregate" effect, then situations of, and injustices suffered by, individuals are of secondary importance.

PATRICIA J. WILLIAMS, *METRO BROADCASTING, INC. v. FCC*: REGROUPING IN SINGULAR TIMES

104 Harv.L.Rev. 525–538, 545–546 (1990).

I. THE REAL ISSUES AT STAKE

* * *

Although the majority and the dissenters [in *Metro Broadcasting*] framed the issue in terms of disagreement about the standard of review, their underlying characterizations of the facts and weighing of the evidence were so polarized that the split probably would have remained even had they agreed on this doctrinal issue. The conflict underlying the opinions is revealed by the subtly nuanced and infinitely slippery vocabulary employed by each side. There was a covert adjectival war taking place in *Metro Broadcasting,* in which words were inflated like balloons in order to make the issue of diversity large or trivial, compelling or merely important, natural or momentary, grandly futuristic or of the local past.

The intensity of these divisions is rooted in profound differences in political philosophy about the nature of group identity, individualism, and the role of the market. Justice Brennan's analysis placed issues on a historical continuum that looks backward to our divided and ruthlessly co-optive past and forward to our long-term interest in the cooperative diversification of our airwaves and our lives. The dissenters' insistence, on the other hand, on a "guaranteed" link between diversity in ownership and diversity in programming arises from a highly individualistic notion of discriminatory action in which a court can consider little history beyond the limited confines of an arm's length commercially motivated bargain between neutrally feathered equals.

Similarly, the majority and the dissenters differed in their understandings of the very meaning of "necessity" in their respective descriptions of racial categorization as a means to desired ends. For the dissenters, necessity referred to an abstracted and absolute requirement of racial neutrality in the word of law. For the majority, necessity referred to the historically contextualized objective of media diversity, the achievement of which was constrained by a relative lack of alternative. Beyond that, the starting points of each differed: for the majority, its sense of "narrowly tailoring" race-conscious efforts to eradicate discrimination had as its referential backdrop a larger social context, while for the dissenters, the sense of the menacing, unbounded "enormity" of the very same measures arose out of their singular focus on a methodological individualism.

Finally, although the majority described its measures as "not 'remedial' in the sense of being designed to compensate victims of past governmental or societal discrimination," its reasoning is clearly framed as a corrective for historical conditions that are hardly long buried in the shroud of some long-forgotten past, but whose effects are specifically identifiable and endlessly enumerable. In the dissents, on the other hand, persistent protests about future-oriented remedies divert attention from the fact that the dissenters would not have supported the outcome even if it had involved a remedial scheme for the past. The insistence that the FCC program is " 'generalized' " with " 'no logical stopping point' "—and the concomitant refusal even to entertain any of a host of logical stopping points suggested by the majority—amounts to an insistence on not just a personal or "identifiable" injury, but one with a completely privatized locus.

* * *

In the swirl of all this, I would like to reframe some of the issues from a perspective that does not assume that simply because a problem such as discrimination is "societal" it is irremediable, nor that because a problem is individualized or privatized it is therefore effectively bounded. Whether racial imbalances are called societal or found to be the result of individualized injury, in either case there are overlooked (or underestimated) ways of looking at the problem that could provide both more latitude for courts and a clearer appreciation of the nuanced gradations that characterize judicial responses such as those in *Metro Broadcasting*.

II. Diversity and the Recognition of Groups

Broadcasting diversity is often portrayed as an attempt to propagate special interest markets or to ghettoize audiences into "mass appeal" on the one hand and minority markets on the other. Its implications, however, are more complex; a real notion of diversity includes a concept of multiculturalism. This entails a view of a market in which there are not merely isolated interest groups, of which "mass market" may be one, but in which "mass" accurately reflects the complicated variety of many peoples and connotes "interactive" and "accommodative" rather than "dominant" or even just "majoritarian."

This perspective embodies the historical connotations of the quest for diversity and the underlying intersection of race and culture. In particular, although it is true that there is no guaranteed relation between race and taste in television and radio fare, the seeming simplicity of this statement deserves some qualification. For example, the literal biological truth that blacks (or members of any other racial or ethnic groups) are not born with genetic inclination for "things black" is often used to obscure the fact that "black" (like most racial or ethnic classification) also defines a culture. Blackness as culture (perhaps more easily understood as such in the designation "African–American") usually evokes a shared heritage of language patterns, habits, history, and experience.

Although all the cultures named by the FCC are exceedingly diverse, the most generalized experience is that of battling cultural suppression if not obliteration, as well as discrimination and exclusion from the larger society.[23] If we cannot conclude absolutely that the victims of racial oppression are always the best architects of its cure, we must nevertheless assume that the best insight and inspiration for its amelioration will come from those most immediately and negatively affected. This allowance is not merely a concession in a random contest of cultures; it is a recognition central to the checking and balancing, the fine line of restraint, that distinguishes a fluidly majoritarian society from a singularly tyrannical one.

This notion of blackness, for example, as a culture and the recognition that this culture may be consistently suppressed or denigrated under the guise of neutral "mass" entertainment, may be difficult for people who identify themselves as part of the dominant culture to understand. The parallelism of "whiteness" as culture—or as any kind of unified experience—is not immediately apparent. Although remaining convinced that there is a culture of whiteness in the United States, I appreciate the extent to which its contours are vaguely or even negatively discerned, so that its assertion is most clearly delineated as "not other," and most specifically as "not black." For so many Americans for whom minority cultures are themselves peripheral, I suspect that a realization that a culture of whiteness exists is occasioned only rarely. Perhaps the argument is more easily understood as a matter of ethnic heritage; perhaps it is easier to look at immigrant communities of those whom we now call whites in order to recapture the extent to which acculturation in the United States is assimilationist in a deeply color-coded sense. It is easy to forget, for example, that the first waves of

23. I hope that readers will resist the temptation to reduce this struggle to protect one's culture and beliefs into an understanding of all black culture, for example, as merely a "culture of resistance." To be extremely explicit, battling discrimination, although a generalizable group experience, is not the same as or the whole of what I am calling culture.

Italian, Portuguese, Greek, Jewish, and Middle–Eastern immigrants to this country were frequently considered non-whites and suffered widespread discrimination.

It is therefore telling to note the degree to which we as Americans celebrate simultaneously our unity as a nation and the Ellis Island tradition of our variety. In the drive to achieve the unity to which our national mythology aspires, we frequently suppress if not undo the richness of our diversity by reconceptualizing any manifestation of it as a kind of unAmerican disunity. I think we do this by consistently, if unconsciously, underestimating ourselves as a distinct national culture and even denying outright the possibility of our power as a consuming, assimilationist force. We tend to universalize the characteristics commonly, if romantically, attributed to middle-class America—individualism, self-interest, self-assertion—so that the very force of our desire to embrace one another becomes an impediment to the necessary recognition that "we" are not the world.

What is also troubling about this tendency is precisely the tendency to universalize individualism. In eliding singular and plural to create an abstract *Über-market-mensch,* we diminish the notion of collectivity as a collection of various overlapping others in favor of a collective *self*— again, a plural singularity—that is both condensed yet general, multiple yet monolithic, self-contained yet presumed representative.

Because the pluralism in our life and laws is so frequently unacknowledged and sometimes even suppressed, it is sometimes hard to see the extent to which we are constantly engaged in not merely discussions among equal individuals, but also complex power struggles of group against group. Recently, for example, I saw a television program in which commentators with important regionless male voices talked about the lack of educational opportunity for black children in inner-city schools. They cited statistics about dropout rates, drugs, crime, teacher apathy, lack of funding, inadequate facilities (particularly for math and science study), low expectations of civic officials and school administrators, and general conditions of hopelessness. At the end of this very depressing summary, the anchor turned to four young teenagers in the studio, all black, all excellent students in a special program designed to encourage inner-city black students with an interest in science. He asked: "We've just heard that black kids aren't very good in math and science; are you here to show us that that's a lie?" The students then proceeded to try to redeem themselves from the great group of the "not very good" by setting themselves apart as ambitious, dedicated, "different" in one sense, yet "just the same as" the majority of all other kids at the same time.

It was unbearable listening to these young people try to answer this question. It put them in an impossible double bind. On the one hand, the invisible norm was the "average" (achieving) white middle-class ideal; although this was never articulated, this is what they had to prove themselves the same as. On the other hand, these were lower class kids who came from tough inner-city neighborhoods where very few of their friends could realistically entertain aspirations to become neurosurgeons or microbiologists. It was this community from which they were being cued to be different. Let me be clear: I am not faulting these young people's aspirations or goals. What concerns me is the way in which not just this commentator, but also society at large forces them and others like them to reconcile their successful status with a covert cultural standard. In a very insidious way, the commentator's question actually limited their alternatives, compromised their function as role models, and prompted explanations of their good fortune that tended to kill their sense of communal affiliation as the only way of permitting the truth of their individualism to remain intact. Although this sort of rhetoric is frequently wrapped in aspirations of racial neutrality, it in fact pits group against individual in a way that is not just racist but classist as well.

Moreover, a question that asks children whether they prove statistics to be "a lie" does not treat statistics as genuinely informative. If the actual conditions of large numbers of people can be proved a lie by the accomplishments of an exemplary few, then statistics only reinforce an exception that proves the rule. They do not represent the likely consequences of social impoverishment; they bear no lessons about the chaotic costs of the last several years of having eliminated from our social commitment the life nets of basic survival. Rather, statistics are reduced to evidence of deserved destitution and chosen despair, the numerical tracking of people who dissemble their purported deprivation.

In another program on the failure of education, the commentator asked, do the parents care enough? "The Parents," he asked. As in "The Blacks." The plural specific. The singular generality. The monolithic multiple. Again, this type of question makes it impossible to acknowledge the complexity of the reality with a simple single answer. Well, yes, some parents care. Well, no, not enough care. Neither of these answers addresses whether "the" parents care; neither of these is as insistently summarizing as the form of the question—do the parents care, yes or no.

I cite these examples because the ability to understand statistics and use them sensibly depends on the ability to understand the difference between information about group behaviors and information that explains individual actions. The Supreme Court in recent cases, perhaps most vividly in *City of Richmond v. J.A. Croson Co.,* has persistently done something with statistical evidence that is very like asking four schoolchildren if they can make into a lie the lost opportunities of countless thousands of others. Richmond had a black population of approximately 50%, yet only 0.67% of public construction expenditures went to minority contractors. The city set a 30% goal in the awarding of its construction contracts to minorities, based on its findings that local, state, and national patterns of discrimination had resulted in all but complete lack of access for minority-owned businesses. The *Croson* majority dismissed these gross underrepresentations of people of color, of blacks in particular, as potentially attributable to their lack of "desire" to be contractors. In other words, the nearly one hundred percent absence of a given population from an extremely lucrative profession was explained away as mere lack of initiative. As long as the glass is 0.67% full * * *.

The dismissiveness of the dissenters' analysis of statistical evidence in *Metro Broadcasting* parallels that of the majority's reasoning in *Croson*. In contrast, one of the remarkable and good things about the majority's decision in *Metro Broadcasting* is that it does not supplant history with individualized hypotheses about free choice, in which each self chooses her destiny even if it is destitution. Rather, the decision takes into account past and present social constraints as realistic infringements on the ability to exercise choice; it puts our destinies on a historical continuum that gives at least as much weight to the possibility that certain minority groups have not had many chances to be in charge of things as to the possibility that they just do not want to or that they just can't. As Congress and the FCC have indicated, we as a society must change if we are not to become permanently divided. Such social necessity not only may have, but must have at least some place in the Court's consideration.

III. DIVERSITY AND BROADCASTING

Given the existence of minority cultures, and not just minority individuals, the attempt by the *Metro Broadcasting* dissenters to disclaim any relation between programming and ownership becomes rooted in paradox. The dissenting opinions contest any relation between the multiculturalism of programming and the racial or ethnic background of station owners. And yet clearly there is *some* relation between programming and the beliefs of an owner. And clearly there is some relation between one's heritage and one's beliefs.

Underlying the dissenters' attempted disavowal of the connection between ownership and broadcasting content is a paradigm in which the class characteristics of good ownership are assumed to transcend racial, ethnic, or other forms of identity. As a friend of mine is fond of saying, middle-class status is nothing more than the inner conquest of any perceived racial or ethnic identity at all. The complete Young Urban Professional (or the accomplished businessperson) is one who has achieved a certain tweedy neutrality of dress, speech, mannerism, and desire. Although there is facetiousness in this depiction, there is certainly nothing too unfamiliar in it: it merely updates and caricatures the model of the rational man who dutifully delays gratification, acts in perfect self-interest, lives with one finger on the pulse of market appetite, patterns a lifestyle upon strong if shifting trends, and under no circumstances wears anything louder than oxblood, loden, or slate.

Ironically, such an identity is not an expression of individuality. It is fashion, a collective aesthetic, a species of mass behavior wrapped in the discourse of self-interest. This deeply embedded notion of the rational market actor is in fact a conformed identity, so normalized that we seem to have lost the ability to see it as such. Nor is this identity really racially or ethnically neutral. For all the brilliant cultural mixtures in art, music, and film that America has given the world, middle- and upper-classness remains deeply steeped in Western European traditions and dominated by strong Protestant values. Ninety-five percent of all corporate executives, including communications executives, are still white males, "a figure that hasn't changed since 1979." [34] * * *

Furthermore, in an era of "infomercials," the media is increasingly used simply to spread (rather than exchange) information about markets (rather than ideas). * * * The degree to which advertising alone purveys and censors information seriously threatens genuine freedom of information. The degree to which the major media, the culture-creators in our society, are owned by very few or are subsidiaries of each other's financial interests, must be confronted as a skewing of the way in which cultural information is collected and distributed.

Thus, executives in the communications industry exercise a power that is not merely concentrated but also propagandistic. They make far-reaching choices in a way that few others in our society can. They project their images of the world out into the world. They do not merely represent, but also recreate themselves and their vision of the world as desirable, salable. What they reproduce is not neutral, not without consequence. To pretend (as we all do from time to time) that film or television, for example, is a neutral vessel, or contentless, mindless, or unpersuasive, is sheer denial. It is, for better and frequently for worse, one of the major forces in the shaping of our national vision, a chief architect of the modern American sense of identity.

Even assuming that profit-seeking behavior explains all or that materialism is itself a kind of culture, if the United States is to be anything more than a loose society of mercenaries—of suppliers and demanders, of vendors and consumers—then it must recognize that other forms of group culture and identity exist. We must respect the dynamic power of these groups and cherish their contributions to our civic lives, rather than pretend they do not exist as a way of avoiding argument about their accommodation. And we must be on guard against either privileging in our law a supposedly neutral "mass" culture that is in fact highly specific and historically contingent or legitimating a supposedly neutral ethic of individualism that is really a corporate group identity, radically constraining any sense of individuality, and silently advancing the claims of that group identity.

This is not to say that all women or blacks or men see the world in the same way or only according to their cultures. I do not believe that a "pure" black or feminist or cultural identity of any sort exists, any more than I think culture is biological. I am arguing against a perceived monolithism of "universal" culture that disguises our overlapping variety and that locates non-whites as "separate," "other," even "separat-

34. Mann, *The Shatterproof Ceiling,* Wash. Post, Aug. 17, 1990, at D3, col. 5.

ist" cultures or, as in the context of *Metro Broadcasting,* that argues about whether such cultures even exist.

* * *

* * * Participation in ownership of anything, but most particularly of broadcast stations or other tools of mass communication, is the gateway to our greatest power as Americans. Ownership enables one not merely to sell to others or to offer oneself to the call of the market. It provides the opportunity to propagate oneself in the marketplace of cultural images. Participation in the privileges of ownership thus involves more than the power to manipulate property itself; it lends an ability to express oneself through property as an instrument of one's interests. We think of freedom of expression as something creative, innovative, each word like a birth of something new and different. But it is also the power to manipulate one's resources to sanction what is not pleasing. The property of the communications industry is all about the production of ideas, images, and cultural representations, but it also selectively silences even as it creates. Like all artistic expression, it is a crafting process of production and negation, in the same way that a painting may involve choices to include yellow and blue while leaving out red and green.

Translating this understanding of ownership into the context of broadcast diversification, the issue becomes not only what is sanctioned, but also who is sanctioning. It is not that minorities live in wholly separate worlds, enclaves walled in by barriers of language, flavors, and music; minorities are not languishing on electronically underserved islands, starving for the rap-marimba beat of a feminist Korean-speaking radio deejay whom only like others can understand. Nevertheless, a feminist Korean deejay is more likely to sanction insulting images of herself and more likely to choose to propagate images of herself that humanize her and her interests.[39] Likewise, it is not that white owners cannot be persuaded not to rerun old *Amos 'n' Andy* shows, in which white actors in blackface portrayed blacks in derogatory if comic ways and which reiterated the exclusive (until recently) image of blacks in the media. Rather, it is that it is much easier—and very likely not even necessary—to persuade Bill Cosby, for example, to choose to run programming that challenges and variegates the perpetual image of blacks as foolish and deviant.

---

39. It is this sanctioning dimension that is so important to the claims of underrepresented groups whose interests are not always understood as distinctive or cultural, such as women and gays. Thus, although some have dismissed the potential contributions of women, for example, as limited to programs "geared to the special biological concerns of women—menstruation, childbearing, breastfeeding, menopause, diseases of the female organs," M. Spitzer, Justifying Minority Preferences in Broadcasting 25 (Social Science Working Paper 718, Division of the Humanities and Social Sciences, California Institute of Technology, Mar. 1990) (unpublished manuscript on file at the Harvard Law School Library) (forthcoming 64 S.Cal.L.Rev. (1991)), the very flatness of imagination revealed in this description results, I think, from a general suppression of images of women as anything more than the sum of their parts.

In fact, I think that Bill Cosby's very success—as owner, producer, writer, and actor—in delivering an image of at least a certain middle-class segment of imagistic blackness into the realm of the "normal," rather than the deviant, has run him up against yet an even more complex (if instructive) level of cultural co-optation. As *The Cosby Show's* warm, even smarmy appeal has made it a staple in homes around the country, black cultural inflections that were initially quite conspicuous (speech patterns, the undercurrent of jazz music, the role of Hillman College as the fictional black alma mater of the Huxtables, hairstyles ranging from dreadlocks to "high top fades") have become normalized and invisible.

Moreover, the process of normalizing has exaggerated the extent to which the black middle class and white middle class are not merely derivative, but identical, so that *The Cosby Show* has been described as little more than a portrayal of blacks costumed in cultural whiteface. Although this "whitening" of its appeal is refined into the language of "sameness," the process devalues and even robs the program of its black content.

Thus, as black cultural contributions are absorbed into mainstream culture, they actually become seen as exclusively white cultural property, with no sense of the rich multiculturalism actually at work. Ultimately, the minority set-aside policies at issue in *Metro Broadcasting* must address this consuming, unconscious power as well. It is not enough to have one Bill Cosby or two Oprah Winfreys if overall power is so concentrated in one community that it remains inconceivable that power could have any other source.

* * *

V. CONCLUSION

The majority opinion in *Metro Broadcasting* marks an important step toward a recognition of multiculturalism and of the need to take active steps to nurture such diversity. If the holding in this case does not guarantee that minority owners will change programming in any constructive way, it does increase the likelihood. Although the dissenters implicitly insisted on a guarantee that there be some relation, a necessary connection, such a strict guarantee can never be gained without expense to the freedoms provided by the first amendment. Even diversity of employment at other levels than ownership is largely at the will and whimsy of those owners. If cultural diversity is, as even the dissenters acknowledge, an acceptable social goal, then alternative creative means for its encouragement must be employed. That relation is fostered by making more frequent and enhancing the opportunities for minority owners and producers, who are more likely to hire minority writers, sponsor programs designed to serve the needs and interests of minority communities, and perhaps most importantly, bring multiculturalism to mainstream programming.

Beyond the limited context of broadcasting, what I hope will be enduring about this opinion is the respect it gives to these pronounced social recognitions of the desirability of diversity in all aspects of our economy and of multiculturalism in our lives. A (probably too) concrete illustration may indicate the reconceptualization of equality that is so urgently needed. Imagine a glass half full (or half empty) of blue marbles. Their very hard-edged, discrete, yet identical nature makes it possible for the community of blue marbles to say to one another with perfect consistency both "we are all the same" and, if a few roll away and are lost in a sidewalk grate, "that's just their experience, fate, choice, bad luck." If, on the other hand, one imagines a glass full of soap-bubbles, with shifting permeable boundaries, expanding and contracting in size like a living organism, then it is not possible for the collective bubbles to describe themselves as "all the same." Furthermore, if one of the bubbles bursts, it cannot be isolated as a singular phenomenon. It will be felt as a tremor, a realignment, a reclustering among all.

Marbles and soap-bubbles are my crude way of elucidating competing conceptions of how to guarantee what we call "equal opportunity." One conception envisions that all citizens are equal, with very little variation from life to life or from lifetime to lifetime; even when there is differentiation among some, the remainder are not implicated in any necessary way.

The other conception holds that no one of us is the same and that although we can be grouped according to our similarities, difference and similarity are not exclusive categories but are instead continually evolving. Equal opportunity is not only about assuming the circumstances of hypothetically indistinguishable individuals, but also about accommodating the living, shifting fortunes of those who are very differently situated. What happens to one may be the repercussive history that repeats itself in the futures of us all.

BIBLIOGRAPHY

Aleinikoff, *Re–Reading Justice Harlan's Dissent in* Plessy v. Ferguson: *Freedom, Antiracism and Citizenship,* 1992 Ill.L.Rev. 961.

Bell, *In Defense of Minority Admissions Programs: A Response to Professor Graglia,* 119 U.Pa.L.Rev. 364 (1970).

H. Belz, EQUALITY TRANSFORMED: A QUARTER–CENTURY OF AFFIRMATIVE ACTION (1991).

Blasi, Bakke *as Precedent: Does Mr. Justice Powell Have A Theory?,* 67 Calif.L.Rev. 21 (1979).

Brooks, *The Affirmative Action Issue: Law, Policy and Morality,* 22 Conn.L.Rev. 323 (1990).

Bryden, *On Race and Diversity,* 6 Const.Comm. 383 (1989).

Carrington, *Diversity!,* 1992 Utah L.Rev. 1105 (1992).

Carter, REFLECTIONS OF AN AFFIRMATIVE ACTION BABY (1991).

Chang, *Discriminatory Impact, Affirmative Action, and Innocent Victims: Judicial Conservatism or Conservative Justices?*, 91 Colum.L.Rev. 790 (1991).

Cohen, *Race and the Constitution*, The Nation, Feb. 8, 1975.

Cohen, *Why Racial Preference is Illegal and Immoral*, Commentary, June 1979, at 40.

Days, *Fullilove*, 96 Yale L.J. 453 (1987).

Delgado, *Affirmative Action as a Majoritarian Device: Or, Do You Really Want to Be a Role Model?*, 89 Mich.L.Rev. 1222 (1991).

Devins, *Affirmative Action after Reagan*, 68 Tex.L.Rev. 353 (1989).

Devins, Metro Broadcasting, Inc. v. FCC: *Requiem for a Heavyweight*, 69 Tex.L.Rev. 125 (1990).

Duncan, *The Future of Affirmative Action: A Jurisprudential/Legal Critique*, 17 Harv.C.R.–C.L.L.Rev. 503 (1982).

R. Dworkin, TAKING RIGHTS SERIOUSLY ch. 9 (1977).

Eastland, *The Case Against Affirmative Action*, 34 Wm. & Mary L.Rev. 33 (1992).

Edwards & Zaretsky, *Preferential Remedies for Employment Discrimination*, 74 Mich.L.Rev. 1 (1975).

Ellis, *Victim–Specific Remedies: A Myopic Approach to Discrimination*, 13 N.Y.U.Rev.L. & Soc.Change 575 (1985).

Ely, *The Constitutionality of Reverse Racial Discrimination*, 41 U.Chi. L.Rev. 723 (1974).

Epps, *Of Constitutional Seances and Color-blind Ghosts*, 72 N.Car.L.Rev. 401 (1994).

EQUALITY AND PREFERENTIAL TREATMENT (M. Cohen, T. Nagel & T. Scanlon eds. 1977).

Fair, *Foreword: Rethinking the Colorblindness Model*, 13 Nat'l Black L.J. 1 (1993).

Fallon, *To Each according to His Ability, From None according to His Race: The Concept of Merit in the Law of Antidiscrimination*, 60 B.U.L.Rev. 815 (1980).

Fallon & Weiler, *Firefighters v. Stotts: Conflicting Models of Racial Justice*, 1984 Sup.Ct.Rev. 1.

Farber & Frickey, *Is* Carolene Products *Dead? Reflections on Affirmative Action and the Dynamics of Civil Rights Legislation*, 79 Cal. L.Rev. 685 (1991).

Foster, *Difference and Equality: A Critical Assessment of the Concept of "Diversity"*, 1993 Wis.L.Rev. 105.

R. Fullinwinder, THE REVERSE DISCRIMINATION CONTROVERSY: A MORAL AND LEGAL ANALYSIS (1980).

A. Goldman, JUSTICE AND REVERSE DISCRIMINATION (1979).

Gottesman, *Twelve Topics to Consider Before Opting for Racial Quotas,* 79 Geo.L.J. 1737 (1991).

Graglia, *Special Admission of the "Culturally Deprived" to Law School,* 119 U.Pa.L.Rev. 351 (1970).

K. Greenawalt, DISCRIMINATION AND REVERSE DISCRIMINATION (1983).

Jones, *The Origins of Affirmative Action,* 21 U.C.Davis L.Rev. 383 (1988).

Katz, *The Economics of Discrimination: The Three Fallacies of* Croson, 100 Yale L.J. 103 (1991).

Kennedy, *A Cultural Pluralist Case for Affirmative Action in Legal Academia,* 1990 Duke L.J. 705.

A. Kull, THE COLOR–BLIND CONSTITUTION (1992).

Matsuda, *Affirmative Action and Legal Knowledge: Planting Seeds in Plowed–Up Ground,* 11 Harv.Women's L.J. 1 (1988).

Matsuda, *Looking to the Bottom: Critical Legal Studies and Reparations,* 22 Harv.C.R.–C.L.L.Rev. 323 (1987).

Meltzer, *The* Weber *Case: The Judicial Abrogation of the Antidiscrimination Standard in Employment,* 47 U.Chi.L.Rev. 423 (1980).

Mishkin, *The Uses of Ambivalence: Reflections on the Supreme Court and the Constitutionality of Affirmative Action,* 131 U.Pa.L.Rev. 907 (1983).

O'Neil, *Preferential Admission: Equalizing the Access of Minority Groups to Higher Education,* 80 Yale L.J. 699 (1975).

Paulsen, *Reverse Discrimination and Law School Faculty Hiring: The Undiscovered Opinion,* 71 Texas L.Rev. 993 (1993).

Peller, *Race Consciousness,* 1990 Duke L.J. 758.

Reynolds, *Individualism vs. Group Rights: The Legacy of Brown,* 93 Yale L.J. 995 (1984).

Rosenfeld, *Affirmative Action, Justice, and Equalities: A Philosophical and Constitutional Appraisal,* 46 Ohio St.L.J. 845 (1985).

M. Rosenfeld, AFFIRMATIVE ACTION AND JUSTICE: A PHILOSOPHICAL AND CONSTITUTIONAL INQUIRY (1991).

Ross, *The Richmond Narratives,* 68 Tex.L.Rev. 381 (1989).

Rutherglen & Ortiz, *Affirmative Action Under the Constitution and Title VII: From Confusion to Convergence,* 35 U.C.L.A.L.Rev. 467 (1988).

Sandalow, *Racial Preferences in Higher Education: Political Responsibility and the Judicial Role,* 42 U.Chi.L.Rev. 653 (1975).

Scalia, *The Disease as Cure,* 1979 Wash.U.L.Q. 147.

Schiff, *Reverse Discrimination Redefined as Equal Protection: Orwellian Nightmare in the Enforcement of Civil Rights Law,* 8 Harv.J.L. & Pub.Pol. 627 (1985).

Schnapper, *Affirmative Action and the Legislative History of the Fourteenth Amendment,* 71 Va.L.Rev. 753 (1985).

Schwartz, *The 1986 and 1987 Affirmative Action Cases: It's All Over But the Shouting,* 86 Mich.L.Rev. 524 (1987).

Sedler, *Beyond Bakke: The Constitution and Redressing the Social History of Racism,* 14 Harv.C.R.–C.L.L.Rev. 133 (1979).

T. Sowell, CIVIL RIGHTS: RHETORIC OR REALITY (1987).

Symposium—*Affirmative Action,* 26 Wayne L.Rev. 1201–1362 (1980).

Symposium—*Affirmative Action,* 72 Iowa L.Rev. 255–85 (1987).

Symposium—*Bakke,* 67 Calif.L.Rev. 1–255 (1979).

Symposium—*Bakke,* 14 Harv.C.L.–C.R.L.Rev. 1–327 (1979).

Symposium—*DeFunis,* 75 Colum.L.Rev. 483–602 (1975).

Symposium—*DeFunis,* 60 Va.L.Rev. 917–1011 (1974).

Symposium—*Race Consciousness and Legal Scholarship,* 1992 U.Ill. L.Rev. 945.

M. Urofsky, A CONFLICT OF RIGHTS: THE SUPREME COURT AND AFFIRMATIVE ACTION (1991).

Wasserstrom, *Racism, Sexism and Preferential Treatment: An Approach to the Topics,* 24 U.C.L.A.L.Rev. 581 (1977).

Williams, *The Survival of Racism Under the Constitution,* 34 Wm. & Mary L.Rev. 7 (1992).

P. Williams, THE ALCHEMY OF RACE AND RIGHTS (1991).

Wright, *Color–Blind Theories and Color–Conscious Remedies,* 47 U.Chi. L.Rev. 213 (1980).

Chapter X

LIBERTY

It is customary to divide the Constitution's special protections for individuals into two categories—rights and liberties. What makes liberties (like freedom of speech) special is that they entitle a person to *act* in certain ways (to speak). Other rights (like equal protection and the privilege against self-incrimination) promise benefits or forbid harms to essentially passive right-holders. (The only act they perform is the "legal act" of claiming their rights.)[1]

The Constitution guarantees several specific liberties in the First Amendment: freedom of speech, freedom of the press, and the free exercise of religion. These are often taught as a separate course, and are beyond the scope of our subject matter. The Fifth and Fourteenth Amendments also provide that no person shall be deprived of "liberty * * * without due process of law." This brief bit of text conceals several important points. One is that the phrase "due process" has come to mean legislative as well as judicial process. Under some circumstances legislatures are forbidden to pass laws depriving people of liberty. Another is that there are grades of protected liberty. The Supreme Court has said that the term "embrace[s] the right of the citizen to be free in the enjoyment of all his faculties; to be free to use them in all lawful ways[.]"[2] In order to take away most of these liberties the government must have some reason that is not purely arbitrary or vindictive. But there are also a few freedoms picked out by the courts for special protection. In the *Lochner* era this class included freedom of contract. In our time it includes the right of privacy protected in *Roe v. Wade*.

Writings about due process liberty have stressed several important themes. The first is the issue of interpretation. By what criteria of meaning can the courts find substantive protection in a phrase like "due process?" How can they determine that some "liberties" are more important than others? And what makes *the courts* better able to answer these questions than the legislative and executive branches?

1. Garvey, *Freedom and Choice in Constitutional Law,* 94 Harv.L.Rev. 1756, 1757–1762 (1981).

2. Allgeyer v. Louisiana, 165 U.S. 578, 589, 17 S.Ct. 427, 431, 41 L.Ed. 832 (1897).

These issues are the focus of the readings on interpretation in Chapter II.

The readings in this Chapter address a different theme, one of value rather than method: have the courts given right answers and convincing reasons in the controversies about due process liberty? Are the current resolutions likely to be stable and enduring? The readings in Section A ask questions like these about so-called "economic due process." Those in Sections B–D deal with the right to privacy.

A. ECONOMIC DUE PROCESS

Between 1897[3] and 1937[4] the Supreme Court held unconstitutional a number of state and federal laws regulating wages, hours, working conditions, prices, market entry, and other business practices. Such laws, the Court often said, took away liberty (freedom of contract) guaranteed by the Due Process Clause. It is now generally agreed that the Court's intervention in these cases was a mistake.

Richard Posner's article suggests, though, that the Court may actually have been right in many of its economic due process decisions. He uses the example of *New State Ice Co. v. Liebmann*[5] to argue that the Court had a firmer grasp of economics than some of its contemporary critics. Restrictions on business entry, which the Court today tolerates, may in fact be nothing more than naked preferences that injure consumers as well as producers excluded from the market. But not all of the laws struck down during this period excluded entry into occupations. Some were designed to remedy perceived defects in economic bargaining power. *Lochner* itself is an example. Others dealt with business practices like product standards[6] or fee collection.[7] It is worth considering whether arguments like Posner's can be made in support of these statutes.

Robert McCloskey asks whether the Court has overcompensated for its mistakes in this area. He reviews the various justifications given for distinguishing economic from "personal" rights, and finds them unconvincing. Perhaps the Court should find some half-way house between its former zeal and its present tolerance that will allow it to provide some check on obvious abuses of the legislative process.

---

3. *Allgeyer v. Louisiana, supra.*

4. West Coast Hotel Co. v. Parrish, 300 U.S. 379, 57 S.Ct. 578, 81 L.Ed. 703 (1937).

5. 285 U.S. 262, 52 S.Ct. 371, 76 L.Ed. 747 (1932).

6. Jay Burns Baking Co. v. Bryan, 264 U.S. 504, 44 S.Ct. 412, 68 L.Ed. 813 (1924) (weight of bread); Weaver v. Palmer Bros. Co., 270 U.S. 402, 46 S.Ct. 320, 70 L.Ed.

654 (1926) (use of "shoddy" in manufacture of bedding).

7. Adams v. Tanner, 244 U.S. 590, 37 S.Ct. 662, 61 L.Ed. 1336 (1917) (fee collection practices of employment agencies). See generally Wonnell, *Economic Due Process and the Preservation of Competition*, 11 Hastings Const. L.Q. 91 (1983).

RICHARD POSNER, ECONOMIC DUE PROCESS
Economic Analysis of Law 589–593 (3rd ed. 1986).

For a period of 50 years ending in the late 1930s, liberty of contract was a key component of due process under the Fifth and Fourteenth Amendments to the Constitution as interpreted by the Supreme Court, and it was the ground on which the Court invalidated, although fitfully, a number of state and federal statutes regulating economic activity. Classical economic theory was thereby elevated to the status of constitutional principle, for the idea that voluntary transactions almost always promote welfare, and regulations that inhibit such transactions almost always reduce it, is a staple of classical theory. * * *

Although long viewed simply as grotesque distortions of constitutional principle, the liberty of contract decisions recently have attracted some staunch advocates as part of a growing revival of interest in classical economic principles. And although there are grave difficulties in reconciling their position with the philosophy of judicial self-restraint or the interest group theory (and reality) of government, the same can be said about the modern emphasis in constitutional law on personal liberties. The arguments for giving greater protection to personal than to economic liberties are superficial. Thus, while it is said that there was no source for a doctrine of liberty of contract in the text or history of the relevant constitutional provisions, the same criticism can be (and has been) made of the Court's decisions in a wide variety of other constitutional areas. It is also said that economic questions are more difficult for courts to decide than questions involving the rights of criminal defendants, political dissidents, or members of racial minorities—yet in fact less is known about those questions than about conventional economic problems. It is said that economic rights are less important than other rights; even if this is so * * *, it does not follow that the Court should give them no protection at all. It is said that the Court's mistake in the liberty of contract cases was to be out of step with dominant public opinion. But this was true only toward the end of the era, and is the reason why the era ended when it did. Moreover, the criticism can easily be turned into a compliment to the Court for its steadfastness in the face of contrary popular opinion. It is also said that the victims of economic controls are businessmen well able to protect themselves without the Court's help, unlike the powerless minorities typically involved in a noneconomic constitutional case. Yet as we are about to see, the brunt of the economic legislation challenged during the liberty of contract era was often borne by politically unorganized groups such as consumers. Nor is it correct that racial and religious minorities are unable to compete effectively in the political arena.

* * * [It is also] commonly believed that the liberty of contract decisions reflected a weak grasp of economics. An early criticism based on this view is found in Justice Brandeis's dissenting opinion in *New State Ice Co. v. Liebmann.*[4] The case involved the constitutionality of a

---

4. 285 U.S. 262 (1932).

state statute that required anyone who wanted to manufacture and sell ice to obtain a certificate of public convenience and necessity and that provided that a certificate would be denied if existing service was adequate. New State, which had such a certificate, sought to enjoin Liebmann, who did not, from entering the ice business in New State's territory. Liebmann's defense was that the statute was unconstitutional. The Court invalidated the statute for reasons with which most economists would concur:

> Stated succinctly, a private corporation here seeks to prevent a competitor from entering the business of making and selling ice * * *. There is no question now before us of any regulation by the state to protect the consuming public either with respect to conditions of manufacture and distribution or to insure purity of products or to prevent extortion. The control here asserted does not protect against monopoly, but tends to foster it. The aim is not to encourage competition, but to prevent it; not to regulate the business, but to preclude persons from engaging in it * * *. It is not the case of a natural monopoly, or of an enterprise in its nature dependent upon the grant of public privileges. The particular requirement before us was evidently not imposed to prevent a practical monopoly of the business, since its tendency is quite to the contrary.

The Court likened the certification provision to an attempt of one shoemaker, under state authority, "to prevent another shoemaker from making or selling shoes because shoemakers already in that occupation can make and sell all the shoes that are needed."

Justice Brandeis's economic argument begins with the proposition that the ice business may be "one which lends itself peculiarly to monopoly"; "the business is conducted in local plants with a market narrowly limited in area" because of the weight and perishability of the product. But the fact that a firm has only a local market area does not preclude competition. Brandeis's opinion reveals, moreover, that prior to the passage of the challenged statute there was competition in the ice business in many localities in the state. He argues that "even in those localities the prices of ice were ordinarily uniform," but since, as he stresses elsewhere in his opinion, the product is uniform, one would expect competitive sellers to charge the same price.

* * *

No doubt the real purpose of the statute was to foster cartelization of the Oklahoma ice industry. As Brandeis himself curiously emphasizes,

> Trade journals and reports of association meetings of ice manufacturers bear ample witness to the hostility of the industry to such competition, and to its unremitting efforts, through trade associations, informal agreements, combination of delivery systems, and in particular through the consolidation of plants, to protect markets and prices against competition of any character.

He also notes: "the ice industry as a whole in Oklahoma has acquiesced in and accepted the Act and the status which it creates."

In viewing the case as one in which Liebmann's economic rights were pitted against the interests of the poor people of Oklahoma who could not afford refrigerators, Justice Brandeis got it backwards. The right he would have vindicated was the interest of New State Ice and other established ice companies to be free from competition. The people actually wronged by the statute were the poor, who were compelled to pay more for ice; the well-to-do, as Brandeis pointed out, were more likely to have refrigerators.

If the ice business were a natural monopoly, the Brandeis position might be economically defensible, since * * * the effort of a natural monopolist to maximize his profits by establishing a monopoly price could lead to a wasteful duplication of facilities. Not only is the premise false, however, but it appears from the latter part of Brandeis's opinion that the natural monopoly language of the earlier part is a makeweight and that he was prepared to embrace the sweeping proposition that ruinous competition is a common phenomenon of economic markets and was a major factor behind the great depression of the 1930s. The case was decided in 1931, and although the Oklahoma statute predated the depression, Brandeis discusses extensively, and with apparent approval, the proposition that the philosophy embodied in the Oklahoma limitation on entry into the ice business might be a remedy of general application to the current economic crisis.

The view of the great depression as rooted in the excesses of competition and curable by reducing competition is discredited * * *. Of course, when demand declined during the depression much of the existing industrial capacity, geared as it was to supplying a larger demand, became temporarily excess. But limiting competition would not have increased purchasing power and therefore demand; it would just have impaired the efficiency of economic activity at its reduced level. * * *

Some of the statutes upheld by the Supreme Court in the period when it was guided by liberty of contract notions also were attempts to suppress competition under the guise of promoting the general welfare. In *Muller v. Oregon*,[7] for example, the Court upheld a state statute fixing a maximum work day of 10 hours for women employed in laundries. Unless the state also had a minimum wage law and the wages of women employed in laundries were not significantly higher than the minimum, the statute probably had little effect. Forced to reduce the work day, the employer would compensate by reducing the daily wage. If the employer were prevented from reducing the daily wage, he would treat the statute as having increased the cost of his labor (he gets less output for the same wage) and, under a now-familiar analysis, would adapt by buying a smaller quantity of labor, raising prices, or doing both things. The reduction in employment would harm any workers he laid off who did not have equally good alternative employment opportunities; the in-

7. 206 U.S. 412 (1908).

crease in prices would harm consumers, and by reducing his output would lead him to further reduce his labor inputs.

Since the Court's repudiation of liberty of contract, it has frequently upheld statutes designed to foster monopoly, such as a state statute that, on grounds of public health, forbade opticians to replace eyeglass frames without a prescription signed by an optometrist or an ophthalmologist [9]—although the statute could have had no purpose other than to increase the incomes of optometrists and ophthalmologists at the expense of opticians and consumers.

ROBERT G. McCLOSKEY, ECONOMIC DUE PROCESS AND THE SUPREME COURT: AN EXHUMATION AND REBURIAL
1962 Sup.Ct.Rev. 34, 45–53.

IV. THE DOUBTFUL DISTINCTION BETWEEN ECONOMIC AND CIVIL RIGHTS

* * *

The arguments for demoting economic rights to their modern lowly constitutional status—lowly when compared with "personal rights"—fall into two categories. First, there is a group of arguments based on judgments about the nature and relative importance of the rights concerned. For example, it is sometimes argued that laws limiting freedom of expression impinge on the human personality more grievously than do laws curbing mere economic liberty, and that the Court is therefore justified in protecting the former more zealously than the latter. The individual has, *qua* individual, "the right to be let alone." The right to free choice in the intellectual and spiritual realm is particularly precious to him. A major difficulty with this formulation is that there is the smell of the lamp about it: it may reflect the tastes of the judges and dons who advance it, rather than the real preferences of the commonality of mortals. Judges and professors are talkers both by profession and avocation. It is not surprising that they would view freedom of expression as primary to the free play of their personalities. But most men would probably feel that an economic right, such as freedom of occupation, was at least as vital to them as the right to speak their minds. Mark Twain would surely have felt constrained in the most fundamental sense, if his youthful aspiration to be a river-boat pilot had been frustrated by a State-ordained system of nepotism.[60] Needless to say, no disparagement of freedom of expression is here intended. But its inarguable importance to the human spirit, on the one hand, does not furnish an adequate ground for downgrading all economic rights, on the other.

9. See Williamson v. Lee Optical Co., 348 U.S. 438 (1955). For an extreme example of the Court's tolerance see Kotch v. Board of River Port Pilot Commrs., 330 U.S. 552 (1947).

60. Kotch v. Pilot Commissioners, 330 U.S. 552 (1947).

So much for a purely individual-centered justification for the disparity between economic rights and other civil liberties. Another suggested rationale looks toward the community rather than the separate individuals within it. Progress, it is said, "is to a considerable extent the displacement of error which once held sway as official truth by beliefs which in turn have yielded to other beliefs." [61] To encourage societal progress, it is important then to protect "those liberties of the individual which history has attested as the indispensable conditions of an open as against a closed society," *e.g.*, freedom of expression.

Presumably this "open society" argument would be relevant no matter how the political system was organized—even a benevolent autocracy must tolerate freedom of expression or risk stagnation. But Alexander Meiklejohn has contended that the point takes on an extra dimension when applied to popular government, to democracy as the West understands that term. In any political system, so the argument runs, the ruler must be fully informed if he is to govern well, and he cannot be fully informed when someone else is deciding what ideas he shall be allowed to hear. In a democracy the people are sovereign, and it follows that they and no one else must decide what and whom they will listen to. And it further follows that the Constitution must protect any freedoms that help the people to acquire "the intelligence, integrity, sensitivity, and generous devotion to the general welfare that, in theory, casting a ballot is assumed to express." [63] In short, the special importance of certain civil rights derives from their special relationship to the process of self-government. Other rights, including the economic, can be abridged when the legislature deems abridgment desirable.

Some such reasoning probably underlies the related point implied by Mr. Justice Stone in the first paragraph of his famous "footnote four" [64] and by Mr. Justice Frankfurter in the concluding words of the first flag-salute opinion [65] (though neither would of course have followed Professor Meiklejohn in the absolutist conclusions he drew). Stone suggested that judicial scrutiny would be especially exacting when legislation restricted "those political processes which can ordinarily be expected to bring about repeal of undesirable legislation," and Frankfurter intimated that the crucial question is whether "all the effective means of inducing political changes are left free from interference." These pronouncements may rest partly on Professor Meiklejohn's point that the governors must be fully informed; but they also seem to involve a separable idea: that a majoritarian system must, in the name of both justice and progress, preserve the right of a present minority to make its views the views of the majority. A businessman's price may be controlled by the mandate of a popularly elected legislature, but, if his right to work politically for repeal of the control law is untrammeled, the fundamen-

61. Frankfurter, J., concurring, in Kovacs v. Cooper, 336 U.S. 77 at 95.

63. Meiklejohn, *The First Amendment Is an Absolute*, [1961] Supreme Court Review 245, 255.

64. United States v. Carolene Products Co., 304 U.S. 144, 152 (1938).

65. Minersville School Dist. v. Gobitis, 310 U.S. 586, 600 (1940).

tals of a just democratic policy are still maintained and so is the fluidity of the sociopolitical order.

The whole "open society" line of argument in its various forms is convincing enough as a justification for protecting the free trade in ideas. If one feels the need to explain why the free speech guarantees are important, these explanations will do pretty well for a start. But they are rather less satisfactory as the basis for a policy of *not* protecting economic freedom, of regarding it as unimportant in a democratic system. For one thing, it is not entirely clear why liberty of economic choice is less indispensable to the "openness" of a society than freedom of expression. Few historians would deny that the growth of entrepreneurial and occupational freedom helped to promote material progress in England in the eighteenth and nineteenth centuries and in America after the Civil War (although they might of course argue that the price paid for this progress was unconscionably high). It is one thing to argue that economic liberty must be subject to rational control in the "public interest"; it is quite another to say in effect that it is not liberty at all and that the proponent of the "open society" can therefore regard it as irrelevant to progress.

As for the "political process" subthemes of the open-society argument—the Meiklejohn–Stone–Frankfurter rationales just described—they too must be queried insofar as they purport to justify a downgrading of economic rights. In fact, their basic difficulty is that, in exalting the freedoms bearing on the political process, they bypass the question of other freedoms altogether. Meiklejohn's arguments for protecting liberty of expression are cogent, but they do not on their face explain why other, "private," rights should be neglected. A decision to protect Peter does not necessarily involve the decision to abandon Paul. * * *

If Meiklejohn's argument contains the unexamined assumption that the political is primary and almost exclusive, the "Stone–Frankfurter" point described above contains this and an assumption of its own as well: the majoritarian idea in a peculiarly unqualified form. The notion seems to be that the citizen can have nothing really fundamental to complain about in a law if a free majority has enacted it and if he is protected in his right to agitate for its repeal. But this view ascribes a preponderance to the majority will that has certainly not been acknowledged by the American political tradition. In that tradition, it is not assumed that an unjust law becomes just by virtue of majority approval, not even if the victim has the theoretical right to persuade the majority to change its mind. * * *

Furthermore this argument overlooks a difficulty partly recognized by Stone himself in the *Carolene Products* footnote and invoked by him in the first flag-salute case, the problem of "discrete and insular minorities," *i.e.,* those who have no realistic chance of influencing the majority to rescind the law that does them harm. Stone was speaking specifically of religious, national, or racial minorities, and his suggestion was that prejudice against them might curtail the political processes that would ordinarily be expected to protect their rights. Prejudice against Jehovah's Witnesses for their "queerness" makes repressive governmental action more probable, and precisely because of their queerness they are not likely to be numerous enough or influential enough in any given community so that their weight will be felt in the city council. To speak of their power to defend themselves through political action is to sacrifice their civil rights in the name of an amiable fiction. Yet it is not clear why the thrust of this point should be restricted to ethnic and religious minorities. Perhaps it is true that a prosperous corporation can effectively plead its case at the bar of legislative judgment by resort to publicity and direct lobbying. Economic power may be an adequate surrogate for numerical power; no tears need be shed for helpless General Electric. But the scattered individuals who are denied access to an occupation by State-enforced barriers are about as impotent a minority as can be imagined. The would-be barmaids of Michigan [75] or the would-be plumbers of Illinois have no more chance against the entrenched influence of the established bartenders and master plumbers than the Jehovah's Witnesses had against the prejudices of Minersville School District. In fact the Witnesses may enjoy an advantage, for they are at least cohesive; and other "discrete" minorities, such as racial groups, have occasionally displayed respectable capacities to exert political leverage by virtue of their very discreteness. Not so the isolated economic man who belongs to no identifiable group at all.

V.   Judicial Capacity in the Realm of Economic Regulation

* * *

Although the policy of abdication cannot be justified in terms of an analysis of the nature and relative unimportance of the rights concerned, there is a second line of thought that merits consideration. Perhaps the decision to leave economic rights to the tender mercy of the legislative power is based on the idea that the Supreme Court is peculiarly ill-equipped to deal with this subject. No one would argue that the right enshrined in Article IV, the guarantee of a republican form of government, is unimportant. Yet the Court has refused to protect it, because of well-founded doubts about judicial competence to make effective judgments in this field. It may be that similar doubts underlie the policy of abdication in the area of economic affairs.

* * *

There are, of course, economic subjects so recondite that judicial surveillance of them would be anomalous. The choice between "historical cost" and "replacement cost" as a basis for rate making must be made by the legislature, not because it will always choose well, but because the judiciary lacks the knowledge and expertise for distinguishing good from bad in this area. But this point will carry only as far as its logic will bring it, and there are fields of economic regulation less intricate than the problem of public utility rates. To be sure, even the

---

75. Goesaert v. Cleary, 335 U.S. 464 (1948).

problems raised in these fields may not be simple. A fair evaluation of Oklahoma's need for its anti-optician law would require the Court to make judgments about a complex matter. But this can be said about most questions that reach the Supreme Court in any field. Our problem is not to identify the issues that present difficulties and then to discard them as improper subjects for judicial review. That would be to abandon judicial review in most of the fields where it is now exercised. Our problem is to determine whether economic statutes always or usually involve such extraordinary difficulties that a modest judiciary must eschew them, even though that same judiciary does claim the competence to judge other, more difficult, issues.

Is it easier for example for the Court to appraise a law empowering a board of censors to ban an "immoral" movie than a law empowering a real estate licensing board to deny a license unless the applicant is of "good moral character"? The two standards would seem to be equally vague and the possibility of arbitrary administrative action would seem to be as menacing in one situation as in the other. * * * Is it easier to see that the State corporate registration law in *N.A.A.C.P. v. Alabama* was being used to facilitate private reprisals against Association members than it is to see that State boards of plumbers, barbers, and morticians sometimes use their publicly granted powers to protect the private financial interests of present guild members to the disadvantage of non-members?

The point is * * * that [these] issues * * * stand on a common level of difficulty and that judicial scrutiny seems as feasible (or unfeasible) for one issue as for the other. And the further, related, point is that there are kinds and kinds of economic subjects and that it is difficult to fashion a generalization that applies to all. Some subjects may be so inscrutable that judicial review cannot fruitfully cope with them; but this is not a justification for avoiding other economic subjects which are no more opaque than the "personal rights" issues that are the standard coinage of judicial discourse these days.

This point likewise applies to the suggestion that the Court, as the relatively weak and non-political branch, simply lacks the power to dictate the economic order, however otherwise competent its members may be. No doubt the Court was presumptuous to imagine, before 1937, that it could hold back such waves as the wage-control movement or the demand for social security. The tide of the welfare state was flowing, and no court could have reversed it. But neither does the judiciary have the practical power to halt any major social developments backed by insistent popular demand. And this would be so whether the development involved economic questions or questions of "personal rights." It was the dimension of the issues in the anti-New Deal cases that made them incongruous for judicial decision, not the mere fact that they were economic in character. No such judicial delusions of grandeur would be implied by enforcement of the requirement that an occupational qualification must be rationally based, or by similar modest applications of substantive due process. The awful will of the sovereign people is not likely to be aroused because the Court has told the morticians of Winnemac that they cannot use State power to maintain a monopoly—or at least no more than it is aroused by other constitutional decisions that issue almost weekly during each Term.

BIBLIOGRAPHY

E. Corwin, LIBERTY AGAINST GOVERNMENT (1948).

Hovenkamp, *The Political Economy of Substantive Due Process,* 40 Stanford L.Rev. 379 (1988).

Miller, *The True Story of Carolene Products,* 1987 Sup.Ct.Rev. 397.

A. Paul, CONSERVATIVE CRISIS AND THE RULE OF LAW (1969).

B. Siegan, ECONOMIC LIBERTIES AND THE CONSTITUTION (1980).

Siegel, *Understanding the Lochner Era: Lessons from the Controversy over Railroad and Utility Rate Regulation,* 70 Va.L.Rev. 187 (1984).

Stigler, *The Theory of Economic Regulation,* 2 Bell J.Econ. & Mgmt.Sci. 3 (1971).

Tarrow, Lochner versus New York: *A Political Analysis,* 5 Lab.Hist. 277 (1964).

Wonnell, *Economic Due Process and the Preservation of Competition,* 11 Hast.Const.L.Q. 91 (1983).

B. ABORTION

In *Griswold v. Connecticut*[1] in 1965 the Supreme Court held that a state law forbidding the use of contraceptives violated the Due Process Clause of the Fourteenth Amendment. The Court did not make clear whether it was protecting a right to prevent conception (a liberty properly speaking—a right to act), or a right to privacy in the Fourth Amendment sense (a protection against government snooping). *Roe v. Wade*[2] eight years later was unequivocal. It held that "the Fourteenth Amendment's concept of personal liberty * * * encompass[ed] a woman's decision whether or not to terminate her pregnancy." Since then the courts have been plagued with issues about the scope of this liberty, not just in abortion cases, but also in cases dealing with other family affairs,[3] homosexual behavior,[4] the provision of medical care,[5] and so on.

The readings in this Section focus on *Roe,* because it is the axis around which these issues revolve. *Roe* has been particularly controver-

1. 381 U.S. 479, 85 S.Ct. 1678, 14 L.Ed.2d 510 (1965).

2. 410 U.S. 113, 153, 93 S.Ct. 705, 726, 35 L.Ed.2d 147 (1973).

3. Moore v. East Cleveland, 431 U.S. 494, 97 S.Ct. 1932, 52 L.Ed.2d 531 (1977).

4. Bowers v. Hardwick, 478 U.S. 186, 106 S.Ct. 2841, 92 L.Ed.2d 140 (1986).

5. Cruzan v. Director, Missouri Dept. of Health, 497 U.S. 261, 110 S.Ct. 2841, 111 L.Ed.2d 224 (1990).

sial for two reasons. The first is the difficulty of explaining what makes the freedom to terminate pregnancy a special liberty deserving unusual protection from the courts. The second is the unique quality of the countervailing interest in such cases: the government claims that it is protecting potential (or perhaps actual) human life by restricting abortions.

John Noonan's article asserts that the latter point should be decisive, and that the courts have shied away from confronting it. They have, he argues, dehumanized the unborn child much as nineteenth century courts dehumanized slaves, by treating the idea of a "person" as simply a juridical construct.

Rather than dispute Noonan's assertion, Judith Thomson's famous defense of abortion accepts it as true and asserts that a woman still has a right to decide what shall happen in and to her body. If the fetus is a person it has a right to live, but that is not a right to be kept alive at someone else's expense.

David Strauss points out that Thomson's argument relies on several libertarian assumptions that are hard to justify. Though the law does not usually require people to act as good samaritans, it does require parents to take care of their children. These duties of care are usually economic or emotional rather than physical (as they are for pregnant women), but it is not obvious that bodily intrusions are more of an imposition than other obligatory parental sacrifices. Strauss concludes that a successful pro-choice argument must make weaker assumptions about the status of fetal life.

John Hart Ely contends that *Roe* is misguided in identifying the right to have an abortion as a "liberty" deserving of special protection. If it were a weaker liberty (like freedom of contract) it would have to yield to the government's interest in protecting the fetus even if the fetus were *not* a person. Nothing in the text or the framers' thinking identifies the woman's action as special. And Ely argues that in this instance—where women's interests conflict with those of fetuses and not men—the political process can be trusted to reach a satisfactory result.

Ruth Bader Ginsburg parries Ely's criticism with one of her own. The real problem with the Court's opinion in *Roe v. Wade,* she charges, is that it invoked the wrong part of the Constitution in support of women's reproductive rights. She contends that the Court would have been on firmer ground, and would have invited less academic criticism and popular outrage, if it had relied upon equal protection rather than due process. In some ways Ginsburg's approach would have been more moderate than the path taken in *Roe*—a fact emphasized by some feminists who criticized her appointment to the Court. In others, though, it may have been more radical. Consider her suggestion that the government, if it is to govern impartially, must provide public funding for abortions for poor women.

JOHN T. NOONAN, JR., THE ROOT AND BRANCH OF *ROE v. WADE*
63 Neb.L.Rev. 668–669, 671–673, 675, 677–679 (1984).

Whoever has the power to define the bearer of constitutional rights has a power that can make nonsense of any particular constitutional right. That this power belongs to the state itself is a point of view associated in jurisprudence with Hans Kelsen. According to Kelsen a person is simply a construct of the law. As he expresses it in *The Pure Theory of Law,* even the apparently natural physical person is a construction of juristic thinking. In this account it appears that just as we personify a corporation for legal purposes so we personify natural physical beings. There are no independent, ontological existences to which we respond as persons. Personhood depends on recognition by the law.[2]

A corollary of that position appears to be what has always seemed to me one of the most terrifying of legal propositions: there is no kind of human behavior that, because of its nature, could not be made into a legal duty corresponding to a legal right. When one thinks of the vast variety of human behavior it is at least startling to think that every variation could be converted into legal duties and legal rights. The proposition becomes terrifying when one thinks of Orwell's *1984* or the actual conduct of the Nazi regime from which Hans Kelsen himself eventually had to flee.

There is one massive phenomenon in the history of our country that might be invoked to support Kelsen's point of view. That phenomenon is the way a very large class of human beings were treated prior to the enactment of the thirteenth and fourteenth amendments. When one looks back at the history of 200 years of slavery in the United States, and looks back at it as a lawyer observing that lawyers had a great deal to do with the classifications that made the phenomenon possible, one realizes that the law, in fact, has been used to create legal rights and legal duties in relation to human behavior that should never have been given a legal form and a legal blessing. To put it bluntly, law was the medium and lawyers were the agents responsible for turning one class of human beings into property. The result was that the property laws of the different states made it smooth and easy to transfer ownership of these human beings. The property laws resolved the questions that occurred at those critical junctions where humanity asserted itself either in the birth of a child to a slave or the death of the owner of a slave. The only question left open for argument was whether the human beings classified as property were realty or personalty. In the inheritance cases the slave child was treated like the issue of an animal, compared again and again in legal decisions to the issue of livestock.

Gross characterization of human beings in terms that reduced them to animals, or real estate, or even kitchen utensils now may seem so

2. H. Kelsen, The Pure Theory of Law 95 (M. Knight trans. 2nd ed. 1967).

unbelievable that we all can profess shock and amazement that it was ever done. Eminently respectable lawyers were able to engage in this kind of characterization—among them Thomas Jefferson, who co-authored the slave code of Virginia, and Abraham Lincoln who argued on behalf of a slave owner seeking to recover as his property a woman and her four children who had escaped to the free state of Illinois. Looking at such familiar examples and realizing how commonplace it was for lawyers to engage in this kind of fiction, we learn, I think, that law can operate as a kind of magic. All that is necessary is to permit legal legerdemain to create a mask obliterating the human person being dealt with. Looking at the mask—that is looking at the abstract category created by the law—is not to see the human reality on which the mask is imposed.

* * *

[Consider what happened in] *Scott v. Sanford.* Here the black plaintiff attempted to assert his right to freedom in the federal court. The Supreme Court held that the federal statute that should have made him free was an interference with the property rights guaranteed by the Constitution to his owner. The Court applied the due process clause of the fifth amendment—gratuitously reading into this clause a concept of substantive due process—and held the statute invalid. The property mask dropped over Dred Scott was the means by which the Constitution was brought into play. As James Buchanan, the President at the time, happily put it, the Court had achieved "the final settlement" of the question of slavery in the Territories.[12] It was a final settlement curiously like Adolph Hitler's "final solution" of "the Jewish question" in Germany.

Buchanan's description, of course, was inaccurate. The Supreme Court could not resolve an issue that so fundamentally divided the nation. The legal mask was shattered by the Civil War. The thirteenth and fourteenth amendments were adopted. The legal profession forgot about its participation in molding the mask that made slavery possible. It is only in our time that the analogy seems vital.

Kelsen's jurisprudence makes * * * *Dred Scott* a defensible decision: according to it, there is nothing intrinsic in humanity requiring persons to be legally recognized as persons. The relevance of Kelsen's reasoning was acknowledged in a modern case, *Byrn v. New York City Health and Hospital Corporation,*[13] decided a year before the Supreme Court decided *Roe v. Wade.* In *Byrn,* Robert Byrn was appointed guardian *ad litem* of an unborn child and asserted that child's constitutional right not to be aborted. His position was rejected by the majority of the Court of Appeals of New York, speaking through Judge Charles Breitel. Breitel quoted Kelsen explicitly to support his position that it was a policy

---

12. James Buchanan, *Third Annual Message to Congress,* 4 Papers of the Presidents 3085–86 (J. Richardson ed. 1913).

13. 31 N.Y.2d 194, 286 N.E.2d 887, 335 N.Y.S.2d 390 (1972), *appeal dismissed,* 410 U.S. 940 (1973).

determination of the state whether legal personality should be recognized or not. It was, Breitel stated, "not true that the legal order corresponds to the natural order." Breitel did not go as far as Kelsen's statement that natural persons were juristic creations—Breitel seemed to assume that there might be natural persons—but he left the recognition of natural persons to the legislature. As New York, at this time, had already enacted a fairly radical abortion law, he held that the legislature had conclusively made the decision that left the unborn child outside the class of recognized humanity.

* * *

Roe v. Wade itself, decided a year later, was profoundly ambivalent—indeed, to speak bluntly, it was schizoid in its approach to the power of the state to determine who was a person. The opinion was schizoid because the Court wanted to invoke rights that were not dependent on the state—the Court was trying to find a measure by which to invalidate state statutes. The precedents that the Court found to authorize it to act in this area of law were all cases that treated family rights as having a natural basis superior to the law of the state. The cases involved included *Meyer v. Nebraska* and *Pierce v. Society of Sisters,* recognizing a superior right of parents to educate their children; *Skinner v. Oklahoma,* recognizing that a man has a natural right to procreate and so cannot be arbitrarily sterilized by the state; *Loving v. Virginia,* where the natural right to marry was invoked in the course of invalidating a miscegenation statute; and *Griswold v. Connecticut,* where the rights of the married were also asserted, in this case to hold unconstitutional a statute prohibiting the use of contraceptives.

All of these cases rested on the supposition that the family rights being protected were those of persons, and that these persons could not be unmade at will by the state. The natural law fundament of these decisions was camouflaged by their being couched in constitutional language; but the constitutional content was derived from nowhere except the natural law as it had taken shape in the traditions of the United States. At the same time that it invoked such precedents in *Roe,* the Court, when treating of the unborn, felt free to impose its own notions of reality.

In one passage the Court spoke of the unborn before viability as "a theory of life," as though there were competing views as to whether life in fact existed before viability. The implication could also be found that there was no reality there in the womb but merely theories about what was there. The Court seemed to be uncertain itself and to take the position that if it were unsure, nobody else could be sure. In another passage the Court spoke of life in the womb up to birth as "potential life." This description was accurate if it meant there was existing life with a great deal of development yet to come, as one might say a 5–year–old is "potential life" meaning that he or she is only potentially what he or she will be at twenty-five. The Court's description was inaccurate if the Court meant to suggest that what was in the womb was pure potentiality, a zero that could not be protected by law. To judge from the weight the Court gave the being in the womb—found to be protectable in any degree only in the last two months of pregnancy—the Court itself must have viewed the unborn as pure potentiality or a mere theory before viability. The Court's opinion appeared to rest on the assumption that the biological reality could be subordinated or ignored by the sovereign speaking through the Court.

* * *

The progeny of *Roe* have confirmed the Kelsenite reading of *Roe* that there is no reality that the sovereign must recognize unless the sovereign, acting through the agency of the Court, decides to recognize it. This view would be psychologically incomprehensible if we did not have the history of the creation of the institution of slavery by judges and lawyers. With that history we can see that intelligent and humane lawyers have been able to apply a similar approach to a whole class of beings that they could see—that they were able to create a mask of legal concepts preventing humanity from being visible. A mask is a little easier to impose when the humanity concealed, being in the womb, is not even visible to the naked eye.

Kelsenite logic permits the judges at the apex of a system to dispense with correspondence to reality. The highest court is then free, within the limits that the society in which it functions will tolerate, to be inventive. It may, as the Supreme Court of the United States has sometimes thought, be constrained by the language of the Constitution and the purposes of its makers. Or, as has also sometimes happened, the Court, viewing itself as the final expounder of the Constitution's meaning, will exercise its inventiveness in creating new constitutional doctrine not dependent on text or purposes. Such doctrine—fantasy in the service of ideology—is "the branch" of *Roe v. Wade*. What then becomes possible was illustrated in 1983 by *Akron v. Akron Center for Reproductive Health*. In this case a whole set of constitutional requirements were created on behalf of the claims of an abortion clinic, named with Orwellian aptness, a center for "reproductive health."

* * *

Most strikingly of all, *Akron* held that there could not be a legal requirement that a woman seeking an abortion be informed that the being she wished put to death was a child, that the child was alive, and that the child was human. The Court treated this information as prejudicing the choice of whether to abort or not—as a kind of unfair interference with free choice. The ordinance was bad because it was designed "to influence the woman's informed choice between abortion and childbirth." The holding went beyond the Kelsenite jurisprudential root and any mainline theory of constitutional interpretation. It was, indeed, the invention of a kind of censorship by the Court itself.

* * *

A final provision of the Akron ordinance was that "the remains of the unborn child" be "disposed of in a humane and sanitary manner." The Sixth Circuit Court of Appeals found the word "humane" impermissibly vague in a criminal statute.[43] The ordinance could, the court said, mean to "mandate some sort of 'decent burial' of an embryo at the earliest stages of formation * * *."[44] Justice Powell quoted this analysis and agreed; humane and sanitary burial was beyond the comprehension of a reasonable doctor.

In this conclusion one can observe in the most concrete way the Court's discomfort before reality. The Court cannot uphold a requirement of humane burial without conceding that the being who is to be buried is human. A mask has been placed over this being. Even death cannot remove the mask.

The Court's denial of reality stands in contrast with what Andre Gide has written on the humane burial of an unborn child:

When morning came, "get rid of that," I said naively to the gardener's wife when she finally came to see how everything was. Could I have supposed that those formless fragments, to which I turning away in disgust was pointing, could I have supposed that in the eyes of the Church they already represented the sacred human being they were being readied to clothe? O mystery of incarnation! Imagine then my stupor when some hours later I saw "it" again. The thing which for me already had no name in any language, now cleaned, adorned, beribboned, laid in a little cradle, awaiting the ritual entombment. Fortunately no one had been aware of the sacrilege I had been about to commit; I had already committed it in thought when I had said get rid of "that." Yes, very happily that ill-considered order had been heard by no one. And, I remained a long time musing before "it." Before that little face with the crushed forehead on which they had carefully hidden the wound. Before this innocent flesh which I, if I had been alone, yielding to my first impulse, would have consigned to the manure heap along with the afterbirth and which religious attentions had just saved from the void. I told no one then of what I felt. Of what I tell here. Was I to think that for a few moments a soul had inhabited this body? It has its tomb in Couvreville in that cemetery to which I wish not to return. Half a century has passed. I cannot truthfully say that I recall in detail that little face. No. What I remember exactly is my surprise, my sudden emotion, when confronted by its extraordinary beauty.[46]

If the Court could respond to Gide and understand what humane and sanitary burial is, it might also perceive the reality of the extraordinary beauty of each human being put to death in the name of the

43. Akron Center for Reproductive Health v. City of Akron, 651 F.2d 1196, 1211 (1981).

44. Id.

46. A. Gide, Last Journals 95 (R. Stookey trans. 1979).

abortion liberty and concealed from legal recognition by a jurisprudence that substitutes a judge's fiat for the truth.

JUDITH JARVIS THOMSON, A DEFENSE OF ABORTION

1 Phil. & Pub.Aff. 47, 48–62, 65–66 (1971).

I propose * * * that we grant that the fetus is a person from the moment of conception. How does the argument go from here? Something like this, I take it. Every person has a right to life. So the fetus has a right to life. No doubt the mother has a right to decide what shall happen in and to her body; everyone would grant that. But surely a person's right to life is stronger and more stringent than the mother's right to decide what happens in and to her body, and so outweighs it. So the fetus may not be killed; an abortion may not be performed.

It sounds plausible. But now let me ask you to imagine this. You wake up in the morning and find yourself back to back in bed with an unconscious violinist. A famous unconscious violinist. He has been found to have a fatal kidney ailment, and the Society of Music Lovers has canvassed all the available medical records and found that you alone have the right blood type to help. They have therefore kidnapped you, and last night the violinist's circulatory system was plugged into yours, so that your kidneys can be used to extract poisons from his blood as well as your own. The director of the hospital now tells you, "Look, we're sorry the Society of Music Lovers did this to you—we would never have permitted it if we had known. But still, they did it, and the violinist now is plugged into you. To unplug you would be to kill him. But never mind, it's only for nine months. By then he will have recovered from his ailment, and can safely be unplugged from you." Is it morally incumbent on you to accede to this situation? * * *

In this case, of course, you were kidnapped; you didn't volunteer for the operation that plugged the violinist into your kidneys. Can those who oppose abortion on the ground I mentioned make an exception for a pregnancy due to rape? Certainly. They can say that persons have a right to life only if they didn't come into existence because of rape; or they can say that all persons have a right to life, but that some have less of a right to life than others, in particular, that those who came into existence because of rape have less. But these statements have a rather unpleasant sound. Surely the question of whether you have a right to life at all, or how much of it you have, shouldn't turn on the question of whether or not you are the product of a rape. And in fact the people who oppose abortion on the ground I mentioned do not make this distinction, and hence do not make an exception in case of rape.

Some won't even make an exception for a case in which continuation of the pregnancy is likely to shorten the mother's life; they regard abortion as impermissible even to save the mother's life. Such cases are nowadays very rare, and many opponents of abortion do not accept this extreme view. All the same, it is a good place to begin: a number of points of interest come out in respect to it.

1. Let us call the view that abortion is impermissible even to save the mother's life "the extreme view." I want to suggest first that it does not issue from the argument I mentioned earlier without the addition of some fairly powerful premises. Suppose a woman has become pregnant, and now learns that she has a cardiac condition such that she will die if she carries the baby to term. What may be done for her? The fetus, being a person, has a right to life, but as the mother is a person too, so has she a right to life. Presumably they have an equal right to life. How is it supposed to come out that an abortion may not be performed? If mother and child have an equal right to life, shouldn't we perhaps flip a coin? Or should we add to the mother's right to life her right to decide what happens in and to her body, which everybody seems to be ready to grant—the sum of her rights now outweighing the fetus' right to life?

The most familiar argument here is the following. We are told that performing the abortion would be directly killing the child, whereas doing nothing would not be killing the mother, but only letting her die. Moreover, in killing the child, one would be killing an innocent person, for the child has committed no crime, and is not aiming at his mother's death. And then there are a variety of ways in which this might be continued. (1) But as directly killing an innocent person is always and absolutely impermissible, an abortion may not be performed. Or, (2) as directly killing an innocent person is murder, and murder is always and absolutely impermissible, an abortion may not be performed. Or, (3) as one's duty to refrain from directly killing an innocent person is more stringent than one's duty to keep a person from dying, an abortion may not be performed. Or, (4) if one's only options are directly killing an innocent person or letting a person die, one must prefer letting the person die, and thus an abortion may not be performed.

Some people seem to have thought that these are not further premises which must be added if the conclusion is to be reached, but that they follow from the very fact that an innocent person has a right to life. But this seems to me to be a mistake, and perhaps the simplest way to show this is to bring out that while we must certainly grant that innocent persons have a right to life, the theses in (1) through (4) are all false. Take (2), for example. If directly killing an innocent person is murder, and thus is impermissible, then the mother's directly killing the innocent person inside her is murder, and thus is impermissible. But it cannot seriously be thought to be murder if the mother performs an abortion on herself to save her life. It cannot seriously be said that she *must* refrain, that she *must* sit passively by and wait for her death. Let us look again at the case of you and the violinist. There you are, in bed with the violinist, and the director of the hospital says to you, "It's all most distressing, and I deeply sympathize, but you see this is putting an additional strain on your kidneys, and you'll be dead within the month. But you *have* to stay where you are all the same. Because unplugging you would be directly killing an innocent violinist, and that's murder, and that's impermissible." If anything in the world is true, it is that you do not commit murder, you do not do what is impermissible, if you reach around to your back and unplug yourself from that violinist to save your life.

* * *

In sum, a woman surely can defend her life against the threat to it posed by the unborn child, even if doing so involves its death. And this shows not merely that the theses in (1) through (4) are false; it shows also that the extreme view of abortion is false, and so we need not canvass any other possible ways of arriving at it from the argument I mentioned at the outset.

* * *

3. Where the mother's life is not at stake, the argument I mentioned at the outset seems to have a much stronger pull. "Everyone has a right to life, so the unborn person has a right to life." And isn't the child's right to life weightier than anything other than the mother's own right to life, which she might put forward as ground for an abortion?

This argument treats the right to life as if it were unproblematic. It is not, and this seems to me to be precisely the source of the mistake.

For we should now, at long last, ask what it comes to, to have a right to life. In some views having a right to life includes having a right to be given at least the bare minimum one needs for continued life. But suppose that what in fact *is* the bare minimum a man needs for continued life is something he has no right at all to be given? If I am sick unto death, and the only thing that will save my life is the touch of Henry Fonda's cool hand on my fevered brow, then all the same, I have no right to be given the touch of Henry Fonda's cool hand on my fevered brow. It would be frightfully nice of him to fly in from the West Coast to provide it. It would be less nice, though no doubt well meant, if my friends flew out to the West Coast and carried Henry Fonda back with them. But I have no right at all against anybody that he should do this for me. * * *

Some people are rather stricter about the right to life. In their view, it does not include the right to be given anything, but amounts to, and only to, the right not to be killed by anybody. But here a related difficulty arises. If everybody is to refrain from killing that violinist, then everybody must refrain from doing a great many different sorts of things. Everybody must refrain from slitting his throat, everybody must refrain from shooting him—and everybody must refrain from unplugging you from him. But does he have a right against everybody that they shall refrain from unplugging you from him? To refrain from doing this is to allow him to continue to use your kidneys. It could be argued that he has a right against us that *we* should allow him to continue to use your kidneys. That is, while he had no right against us that we should give him the use of your kidneys, it might be argued that he anyway has a right against us that we shall not now intervene and deprive him of the use of your kidneys. I shall come back to third-party interventions later. But certainly the violinist has no right against you that *you* shall allow him to continue to use your kidneys. As I said, if you do allow him to use them, it is a kindness on your part, and not something you owe him.

* * *

4. There is another way to bring out the difficulty. In the most ordinary sort of case, to deprive someone of what he has a right to is to treat him unjustly. Suppose a boy and his small brother are jointly given a box of chocolates for Christmas. If the older boy takes the box and refuses to give his brother any of the chocolates, he is unjust to him, for the brother has been given a right to half of them. But suppose that, having learned that otherwise it means nine years in bed with that violinist, you unplug yourself from him. You surely are not being unjust to him, for you gave him no right to use your kidneys, and no one else can have given him any such right. But we have to notice that in unplugging yourself, you are killing him; and violinists, like everybody else, have a right to life, and thus in the view we were considering just now, the right not to be killed. So here you do what he supposedly has a right you shall not do, but you do not act unjustly to him in doing it.

The emendation which may be made at this point is this: the right to life consists not in the right not to be killed, but rather in the right not to be killed unjustly. This runs a risk of circularity, but never mind: it would enable us to square the fact that the violinist has a right to life with the fact that you do not act unjustly toward him in unplugging yourself, thereby killing him. For if you do not kill him unjustly, you do not violate his right to life, and so it is no wonder you do him no injustice.

But if this emendation is accepted, the gap in the argument against abortion stares us plainly in the face: it is by no means enough to show that the fetus is a person, and to remind us that all persons have a right to life—we need to be shown also that killing the fetus violates its right to life, i.e., that abortion is unjust killing. And is it?

I suppose we may take it as a datum that in a case of pregnancy due to rape the mother has not given the unborn person a right to the use of her body for food and shelter. Indeed, in what pregnancy could it be supposed that the mother has given the unborn person such a right? It is not as if there were unborn persons drifting about the world, to whom a woman who wants a child says "I invite you in."

But it might be argued that there are other ways one can have acquired a right to the use of another person's body than by having been invited to use it by that person. Suppose a woman voluntarily indulges in intercourse, knowing of the chance it will issue in pregnancy, and then she does become pregnant; is she not in part responsible for the presence, in fact the very existence, of the unborn person inside her? No doubt she did not invite it in. But doesn't her partial responsibility for its being there itself give it a right to the use of her body? If so, then her aborting it would be more like the boy's taking away the chocolates, and less like your unplugging yourself from the violinist—doing so would be depriving it of what it does have a right to, and thus would be doing it an injustice.

And then, too, it might be asked whether or not she can kill it even to save her own life: If she voluntarily called it into existence, how can she now kill it, even in self-defense?

The first thing to be said about this is that it is something new. Opponents of abortion have been so concerned to make out the independence of the fetus, in order to establish that it has a right to life, just as its mother does, that they have tended to overlook the possible support they might gain from making out that the fetus is *dependent* on the mother, in order to establish that she has a special kind of responsibility for it, a responsibility that gives it rights against her which are not possessed by any independent person—such as an ailing violinist who is a stranger to her.

On the other hand, this argument would give the unborn person a right to its mother's body only if her pregnancy resulted from a voluntary act, undertaken in full knowledge of the chance a pregnancy might result from it. It would leave out entirely the unborn person whose existence is due to rape. Pending the availability of some further argument, then, we would be left with the conclusion that unborn persons whose existence is due to rape have no right to the use of their mothers' bodies, and thus that aborting them is not depriving them of anything they have a right to and hence is not unjust killing.

And we should also notice that it is not at all plain that this argument really does go even as far as it purports to. For there are cases and cases, and the details make a difference. If the room is stuffy, and I therefore open a window to air it, and a burglar climbs in, it would be absurd to say, "Ah, now he can stay, she's given him a right to the use of her house—for she is partially responsible for his presence there, having voluntarily done what enabled him to get in, in full knowledge that there are such things as burglars, and that burglars burgle." It would be still more absurd to say this if I had had bars installed outside my windows, precisely to prevent burglars from getting in, and a burglar got in only because of a defect in the bars. It remains equally absurd if we imagine it is not a burglar who climbs in, but an innocent person who blunders or falls in.   * * *

It seems to me that the argument we are looking at can establish at most that there are *some* cases in which the unborn person has a right to the use of its mother's body, and therefore *some* cases in which abortion is unjust killing. There is room for much discussion and argument as to precisely which, if any. But I think we should sidestep this issue and leave it open, for at any rate the argument certainly does not establish that all abortion is unjust killing.

5. There is room for yet another argument here, however. We surely must all grant that there may be cases in which it would be

morally indecent to detach a person from your body at the cost of his life. Suppose you learn that what the violinist needs is not nine years of your life, but only one hour: all you need do to save his life is to spend one hour in that bed with him. Suppose also that letting him use your kidneys for that one hour would not affect your health in the slightest. Admittedly you were kidnapped. Admittedly you did not give anyone permission to plug him into you. Nevertheless it seems to me plain you *ought* to allow him to use your kidneys for that hour—it would be indecent to refuse.

* * *

Now some people are inclined to use the term "right" in such a way that it follows from the fact that you ought to allow a person to use your body for the hour he needs, that he has a right to use your body for the hour he needs, even though he has not been given that right by any person or act. They may say that it follows also that if you refuse, you act unjustly toward him. This use of the term is perhaps so common that it cannot be called wrong; nevertheless it seems to me to be an unfortunate loosening of what we would do better to keep a tight rein on. Suppose that box of chocolates I mentioned earlier had not been given to both boys jointly, but was given only to the older boy. There he sits, stolidly eating his way through the box, his small brother watching enviously. Here we are likely to say "You ought not to be so mean. You ought to give your brother some of those chocolates." My own view is that it just does not follow from the truth of this that the brother has any right to any of the chocolates. If the boy refuses to give his brother any, he is greedy, stingy, callous—but not unjust. I suppose that the people I have in mind will say it does follow that the brother has a right to some of the chocolates, and thus that the boy does act unjustly if he refuses to give his brother any. But the effect of saying this is to obscure what we should keep distinct, namely the difference between the boy's refusal in this case and the boy's refusal in the earlier case, in which the box was given to both boys jointly, and in which the small brother thus had what was from any point of view clear title to half.

* * *

So my own view is that even though you ought to let the violinist use your kidneys for the one hour he needs, we should not conclude that he has a right to do so—we should say that if you refuse, you are, like the boy who owns all the chocolates and will give none away, self-centered and callous, indecent in fact, but not unjust. And similarly, that even supposing a case in which a woman pregnant due to rape ought to allow the unborn person to use her body for the hour he needs, we should not conclude that he has a right to do so; we should conclude that she is self-centered, callous, indecent, but not unjust, if she refuses. The complaints are no less grave; they are just different. However, there is no need to insist on this point. If anyone does wish to deduce "he has a right" from "you ought," then all the same he must surely grant that there are cases in which it is not morally required of you that you allow that violinist to use your kidneys, and in which he does not have a right to use them, and in which you do not do him an injustice if you refuse. And so also for mother and unborn child. Except in such cases as the unborn person has a right to demand it—and we were leaving open the possibility that there may be such cases—nobody is morally *required* to make large sacrifices, of health, of all other interests and concerns, of all other duties and commitments, for nine years, or even for nine months, in order to keep another person alive.

* * *

8. My argument will be found unsatisfactory on two counts by many of those who want to regard abortion as morally permissible. First, while I do argue that abortion is not impermissible, I do not argue that it is always permissible. There may well be cases in which carrying the child to term requires only Minimally Decent Samaritanism of the mother, and this is a standard we must not fall below. I am inclined to think it a merit of my account precisely that it does *not* give a general yes or a general no. It allows for and supports our sense that, for example, a sick and desperately frightened fourteen-year-old schoolgirl, pregnant due to rape, may *of course* choose abortion, and that any law which rules this out is an insane law. And it also allows for and supports our sense that in other cases resort to abortion is even positively indecent. It would be indecent in the woman to request an abortion, and indecent in a doctor to perform it, if she is in her seventh month, and wants the abortion just to avoid the nuisance of postponing a trip abroad. The very fact that the arguments I have been drawing attention to treat all cases of abortion, or even all cases of abortion in which the mother's life is not at stake, as morally on a par ought to have made them suspect at the outset.

Secondly, while I am arguing for the permissibility of abortion in some cases, I am not arguing for the right to secure the death of the unborn child. It is easy to confuse these two things in that up to a certain point in the life of the fetus it is not able to survive outside the mother's body; hence removing it from her body guarantees its death. But they are importantly different. I have argued that you are not morally required to spend nine months in bed, sustaining the life of that violinist; but to say this is by no means to say that if, when you unplug yourself, there is a miracle and he survives, you then have a right to turn round and slit his throat. You may detach yourself even if this costs him his life; you have no right to be guaranteed his death, by some other means, if unplugging yourself does not kill him. There are some people who will feel dissatisfied by this feature of my argument. A woman may be utterly devastated by the thought of a child, a bit of herself, put out for adoption and never seen or heard of again. She may therefore want not merely that the child be detached from her, but more, that it die. Some opponents of abortion are inclined to regard this as beneath contempt—thereby showing insensitivity to what is surely a powerful source of despair. All the same, I agree that the desire for the child's death is not one which anybody may gratify, should it turn out to be possible to detach the child alive.

DAVID A. STRAUSS, ABORTION, TOLERATION, AND MORAL UNCERTAINTY
1992 Sup.Ct.Rev. 1, 10–16, 18–20 (1993).

THE GOOD SAMARITAN ARGUMENT

[O]ne well-known defense of the pro-choice position (actually, more strongly, a defense of abortion) claims to make it unnecessary to deal with the status of fetal life. The argument is that prohibiting abortion is equivalent to requiring a woman to assume duties of a Good Samaritan of an especially extraordinary form to the fetus.[23] This argument compares the responsibilities assigned to a woman by those who oppose abortion to the responsibilities of a conventional Good Samaritan. We do not require that a conventional Good Samaritan accept burdens comparable to those involved in a pregnancy even when an undoubted human life is at stake. It follows that we should not prohibit abortions even if we assume arguendo that fetal life is equivalent to human life.

[I]n my view the Good Samaritan argument does not succeed. The problem is that this argument depends on two libertarian premises: first, that obligations must be in some way commensurate with voluntary undertakings; and second, that there is a sharp distinction between bodily invasions and other impositions on individuals. These libertarian premises are not obviously true, are difficult to justify, and conflict with strongly held intuitions.

The first premise is needed to meet an obvious and superficial objection to the Good Samaritan argument—that, cases of rape and incest aside, no one becomes pregnant involuntarily. The burdens of pregnancy (it is therefore said), unlike the impositions on a Good Samaritan, are to some extent voluntarily assumed. This argument is insensitive to the many subtle forms of pressure and coercion that call into question the voluntariness of many pregnancies. But the principal answer to this argument offered by the proponents of the Good Samaritan view is that it is, in general, unrealistic and unfair to regard most pregnant women as voluntarily accepting the burdens of pregnancy in any meaningful sense.

That answer seems correct, as far as it goes. But it assumes away the possibility that there are obligations and duties that arise without any voluntary act. They arise by virtue of status or just because one happened to find oneself in a certain position. Obligations to a political community are probably an example; efforts to ground such obligations on voluntary undertakings are difficult to sustain. Obligations *to* a parent or to a sibling are also in this category; they arise, at least in

---

23. First advanced in Judith Jarvis Thomson, *A Defense of Abortion*, 1 Phil. &   Pub.Aff. 47 (1971)[.]

part, by virtue of status, not voluntary acts. One might, therefore, without taking any act of a kind that would ordinarily lead to such strong obligations, find oneself in the position of a parent who has obligations to her own unborn child that she would not have to a stranger.

It might be responded that, while not all obligations have their origin in voluntary acts, the anti-abortion position imposes unique obligations on the mother, obligations of a kind that are never the result of status alone. This response relies on the second libertarian premise, about the distinctiveness of bodily invasions. No one questions that parents have many burdensome obligations to their children, such as the obligation to provide for their economic and emotional support. Weighed just on some sort of quantitative scale (such as how much one would pay to avoid the obligation, other things equal), it is arguable that these burdens are greater than those incurred by a pregnant mother. If pregnancy is an unacceptable obligation to impose on a person, that must be because it involves a physical imposition that is qualitatively different from other parental obligations.

Obviously there is much to the point that physical invasions are peculiarly objectionable. [O]rdinarily we do not insist that people subject themselves to bodily impositions comparable to pregnancy, even when another life is at stake. The law does not require an individual to give up one kidney, for example, to save a stranger's life.

But people have stronger obligations to their children than to strangers, and it may be that parents have a moral obligation to sacrifice their physical integrity, to some degree, for the sake of their children. Parents may not refuse to give up their wealth or their labor, over an extended period, for the sake of their children. Why should a bodily intrusion, such as giving up a kidney, be regarded as necessarily more of an imposition than other parental sacrifices that are unquestionably obligatory? The implicit libertarian premise that bodily intrusion is a peculiarly unacceptable form of burden seems arbitrary.

* * *

In short, a person might have the moral duties of parenthood even though he or she has not taken any voluntary act of a sort that usually has such momentous consequences. Unless the interest in bodily integrity is given enormous significance, beyond what can be easily justified, those duties might include sacrificing one's bodily integrity to save a child's life. * * *

ABORTION AND THE REGIME OF TOLERATION

* * *

If the position that laws forbidding abortion are unconstitutional cannot easily be sustained on the assumption that fetal life is morally equivalent to human life, then that position must be reconciled with the uncertain status of fetal life. The Court in [*Planned Parenthood v.*

Casey [a]] seemed to recognize this, and it seemed also to perceive that religious toleration was a useful analogy, although it did not analyze the analogy closely.

[There are two] ways in which religious toleration is analogous to the pro-choice position. First, questions about religious belief are characterized by radical uncertainty. There is no agreed-upon way of deciding the issues with which religious belief is concerned: issues, for example, about the nature of the soul and the afterlife, about the proper spiritual development of human beings and their relationship to some transcendent power. Second, religious issues, although they are issues of the greatest importance, are resolved on the level of the individual, not the level of the state. Religious toleration is therefore a counterexample to the argument made by the dissent in *Casey* that the political process is the proper way to resolve unsettled, but important, issues.

At one time, of course, it was widely accepted that religious issues were to be decided by the state, not by individuals. Indeed, at one time it would have seemed bizarre to say that individuals' spiritual development and the fate of their souls were not among the central concerns of the state. But the development of religious toleration, one of the great advances in Western culture, consisted precisely in deciding that matters of religious belief are to be resolved not at the level of the state, but at the level of each individual.

It might be objected that decisions about religion are different from decisions about abortion because decisions about one's own religious faith do not affect other people. Religiously inspired actions, as distinguished from beliefs, can affect other individuals, and (the argument would go) that is why actions can be regulated. A guarantee of absolute liberty applies only to beliefs, because an individual's belief affects no one else. Since an individual's decision whether to have an abortion affects a being that may have a moral status comparable to that of a human, the analogy to religious toleration does not sustain the pro-choice position.

But this view of religious belief as a private matter is decidedly modern, and slightly skeptical. When the regime of religious toleration arose, the more common view was that one person's religious belief affected others in the most profound ways possible. Aquinas argued for persecution on the ground that "forgers and other malefactors are put to death" and "it is a far graver matter to corrupt the faith which is the life of the soul than to falsify money which sustains temporal life." More fundamentally, the idea that there are matters which are only one person's business is itself a modern artifact. A common justification for persecution was that the duty of love for one's neighbors required that they be saved from false belief and, therefore, from eternal damnation. It was a duty of love to destroy a heretic's body in order to save his or her soul.

a.   112 S.Ct. 2791 (1992).

These views are not prevalent today, but some people hold them, and—more important—we do not have to establish their falsehood in order to believe that religious liberty is morally imperative. That is, some people believe that we will all be eternally damned if we do not persecute heretics; and we have no basis for concluding that that belief is false. But we still believe that people have a right to decide for themselves, free from persecution, whether to hold heretical beliefs. This demonstrates that some unsettled issues are to be resolved on the level of the individual, not the level of the state, even if the resolution might affect others besides the individual in the most profound ways possible.

* * *

The question remains: why should the abortion issue be decided on the level of the individual instead of on the level of the state? This is the point at which the status of women, properly emphasized by *Casey*, becomes important. Allowing the abortion decision to be made at the political level, instead of the individual level, would create an impermissible risk of subordinating women.

* * *

First, the political process has a persistent tendency generally to undervalue the interests of women. Although the Court has not given this as a reason for its hostility to gender discrimination, this is the *Carolene Products* explanation—perhaps the most conventional explanation—for requiring a special justification for laws that single out a group. In any event, the persistence of laws and practices that discriminate against women is evidence that their interests are undervalued.

Second, women's bodily integrity, in particular, is systematically undervalued. The Court's opinion in *Casey* alluded to this aspect of women's status. The prevalence of harassment and violence against women, and the widespread social attitudes that implicitly or explicitly condone those practices—for example, the relative respectability of domestic violence and the sexualization of violence against women—are evidence of this.

Third, women are treated as people whose principal responsibility is child bearing and child rearing. They are not seen as full participants in the labor market. The pattern of laws, economic arrangements, and social customs that discourages women from entering the labor market and encourages them to be mothers is evidence that this treatment exists. It is not obvious a priori that this treatment constitutes subordination. But throughout our history—for example, in the opposition to slavery, the exaltation of freedom of contract at the turn of the century, and the centrality of employment discrimination to civil rights issues today—the right to alienate one's labor has been highly valued, and that is evidence that a person is not regarded as fully human in our society unless he or she is allowed to participate in the labor market.

* * *

The Court in *Casey* did not, however, make clear the exact connection between the status of women and the abortion issue. The connection, I believe, is this: the tendency to subordinate women in these three ways disqualifies the political process from resolving the moral uncertainty that is central to the abortion debate. There is too great a danger that if the political process decides the abortion issue, that decision will be an act of subordinating women in one or more of these ways.

JOHN HART ELY, THE WAGES OF CRYING WOLF: A COMMENT ON *ROE v. WADE*

82 Yale L.J. 920, 923–926, 933–939 (1973).

II

Let us not underestimate what is at stake: Having an unwanted child can go a long way toward ruining a woman's life. And at bottom *Roe* signals the Court's judgment that this result cannot be justified by any good that anti-abortion legislation accomplishes. This surely is an understandable conclusion—indeed it is one with which I agree—but ordinarily the Court claims no mandate to second-guess legislative balances, at least not when the Constitution has designated neither of the values in conflict as entitled to special protection. But even assuming it would be a good idea for the Court to assume this function, *Roe* seems a curious place to have begun. Laws prohibiting the use of "soft" drugs or, even more obviously, homosexual acts between consenting adults can stunt "the preferred life styles" of those against whom enforcement is threatened in very serious ways. It is clear such acts harm no one besides the participants, and indeed the case that the participants are harmed is a rather shaky one. Yet such laws survive, on the theory that there exists a societal consensus that the behavior involved is revolting or at any rate immoral. Of course the consensus is not universal but it is sufficient, and this is what is counted crucial, to get the laws passed and keep them on the books. Whether anti-abortion legislation cramps the life style of an unwilling mother more significantly than anti-homosexuality legislation cramps the life style of a homosexual is a close question. But even granting that it does, the *other* side of the balance looks very different. For there is more than simple societal revulsion to support legislation restricting abortion: Abortion ends (or if it makes a difference, prevents) the life of a human being other than the one making the choice.

The Court's response here is simply not adequate. It agrees, indeed it holds, that after the point of viability (a concept it fails to note will become even less clear than it is now as the technology of birth continues to develop) the interest in protecting the fetus is compelling. Exactly why that is the magic moment is not made clear: Viability, as the Court defines it, is achieved some six to twelve weeks after quickening. (Quickening is the point at which the fetus begins discernibly to move independently of the mother and the point that has historically been deemed crucial—to the extent *any* point between conception and birth has been focused on.) But no, it is *viability* that is constitutionally critical: the Court's defense seems to mistake a definition for a syllogism.

> With respect to the State's important and legitimate interest in potential life, the "compelling" point is at viability. This is so because the fetus then presumably has the capacity of meaningful life outside the mother's womb.

With regard to why the state cannot consider this "important and legitimate interest" prior to viability, the opinion is even less satisfactory. The discussion begins sensibly enough: The interest asserted is not necessarily tied to the question whether the fetus is "alive," for whether or not one calls it a living being, it is an entity with the potential for (and indeed the likelihood of) life. But all of arguable relevance that follows are arguments that fetuses (a) are not recognized as "persons in the whole sense" by legal doctrine generally and (b) are not "persons" protected by the Fourteenth Amendment.

To the extent they are not entirely inconclusive, the bodies of doctrine to which the Court adverts respecting the protection of fetuses under general legal doctrine tend to undercut rather than support its conclusion. And the argument that fetuses (unlike, say, corporations) are not "persons" under the Fourteenth Amendment fares little better. The Court notes that most constitutional clauses using the word "persons"—such as the one outlining the qualifications for the Presidency—appear to have been drafted with postnatal beings in mind. (It might have added that most of them were plainly drafted with *adults* in mind, but I suppose that wouldn't have helped.) In addition, "the appellee conceded on reargument that no case can be cited that holds that a fetus is a person within the meaning of the Fourteenth Amendment." (The other legal contexts in which the question could have arisen are not enumerated.)

The canons of construction employed here are perhaps most intriguing when they are contrasted with those invoked to derive the constitutional right to an abortion. But in any event, the argument that fetuses lack constitutional rights is simply irrelevant. For it has never been held or even asserted that the state interest needed to justify forcing a person to refrain from an activity, *whether or not that activity is constitutionally protected,* must implicate either the life or the constitutional rights of another person. Dogs are not "persons in the whole sense" nor have they constitutional rights, but that does not mean the state cannot prohibit killing them: It does not even mean the state cannot prohibit killing them in the exercise of the First Amendment right of political protest. Come to think of it, draft cards aren't persons either.

Thus even assuming the Court ought generally to get into the business of second-guessing legislative balances, it has picked a strange case with which to begin. Its purported evaluation of the balance that produced anti-abortion legislation simply does not meet the issue: That the life plans of the mother must, not simply may, prevail over the state's desire to protect the fetus simply does not follow from the judgment that the fetus is not a person. Beyond all that, however, the Court has no business getting into that business.

III

* * *

* * * In his famous *Carolene Products* footnote, Justice Stone suggested that the interests to which the Court can responsibly give extraordinary constitutional protection include not only those expressed in the Constitution but also those that are unlikely to receive adequate consideration in the political process, specifically the interests of "discrete and insular minorities" unable to form effective political alliances.[84] There can be little doubt that such considerations have influenced the direction, if only occasionally the rhetoric, of the recent Courts. My repeated efforts to convince my students that sex should be treated as a "suspect classification" have convinced me it is no easy matter to state such considerations in a "principled" way. But passing that problem, *Roe* is not an appropriate case for their invocation.

Compared with men, very few women sit in our legislatures, a fact I believe should bear some relevance—even without an Equal Rights Amendment—to the appropriate standard of review for legislation that favors men over women.[85] But *no* fetuses sit in our legislatures. Of

84. United States v. Carolene Products Co., 304 U.S. 144, 152 n. 4 (1938).

85. This is not the place for a full treatment of the subject, but the general idea is this: Classifications by sex, like classifications by race, differ from the usual classification—to which the traditional "reasonable generalization" standard is properly applied—in that they rest on "we-they" generalizations as opposed to a "they-they" generalization. Take a familiar example of the usual approach, Williamson v. Lee Optical Co., 348 U.S. 483 (1955). Of course few legislators are opticians. But few are optometrists either. Thus while a decision to distinguish opticians from optometrists will incorporate a stereotypical comparison of two classes of people, it is a comparison of two "they" stereotypes, *viz.* "They [opticians] are generally inferior to or not so well qualified as *they* [optometrists] are in the following respect(s), which we find sufficient to justify the classification: * * *." However, legislators traditionally have not only not been black (or female); they have been white (and male). A decision to distinguish blacks from whites (or women from men) will therefore have its roots in a comparison between a "we" stereotype and a "they" stereotype, *viz.* "They [blacks or women] are generally inferior to or not so well qualified as *we* [whites or men] are in

the following respect(s), which we find sufficient to justify the classification: * * *."

The choice between classifying on the basis of a comparative generalization and attempting to come up with a more discriminating formula always involves balancing the increase in fairness which greater individualization will produce against the added costs it will entail. It is no startling psychological insight, however, that most of us are delighted to hear and prone to accept comparative characterizations of groups that suggest that the groups to which *we* belong are in some way superior to others. (I would be inclined to exclude most situations where the "we's" used to be "they's," *cf.* Ferguson v. Skrupa, 372 U.S. 726 (1963), and would therefore agree that the unchangeability of the distinguishing characteristic is indeed relevant, though it is only part of the story.) The danger is therefore greater in we-they situations that we will overestimate the validity of the proposed stereotypical classification by seizing upon the positive myths about our own class and the negative myths about theirs—or indeed the realities respecting some or most members of the two classes—and too readily assuming that virtually the entire membership of the two classes fit the stereotypes and therefore that not many of "them" will be unfairly deprived, nor many of "us" course they have their champions, but so have women. The two interests have clashed repeatedly in the political arena, and had continued to do so up to the date of the opinion, generating quite a wide variety of accommodations. By the Court's lights virtually all of the legislative accommodations had unduly favored fetuses; by its definition of victory, women had lost. Yet in every legislative balance one of the competing interests loses to some extent; indeed usually, as here, they both do. On some occasions the Constitution throws its weight on the side of one of them, indicating the balance must be restruck. And on others—and this is Justice Stone's suggestion—it is at least arguable that, constitutional directive or not, the Court should throw *its* weight on the side of a minority demanding in court more than it was able to achieve politically. But even assuming this suggestion can be given principled content, it was clearly intended and should be reserved for those interests which, *as compared with the interests to which they have been subordinated,* constitute minorities unusually incapable of protecting themselves. Compared with men, women may constitute such a "minority"; compared with the unborn, they do not. I'm not sure I'd know a discrete and insular minority if I saw one, but confronted with a multiple choice question requiring me to designate (a) women or (b) fetuses as one, I'd expect no credit for the former answer.

Of course a woman's freedom to choose an abortion is part of the "liberty" the Fourteenth Amendment says shall not be denied without due process of law, as indeed is anyone's freedom to do what he wants. But "due process" generally guarantees only that the inhibition be procedurally fair and that it have some "rational" connection—though plausible is probably a better word—with a permissible governmental goal. What is unusual about *Roe* is that the liberty involved is accorded a far more stringent protection, so stringent that a desire to preserve the fetus's existence is unable to overcome it—a protection more stringent, I think it fair to say, than that the present Court accords the freedom of the press explicitly guaranteed by the First Amendment. What is frightening about *Roe* is that this super-protected right is not inferable from the language of the Constitution, the framers' thinking respecting the specific problem in issue, any general value derivable from the provisions they included, or the nation's governmental structure. Nor is it explainable in terms of the unusual political impotence of the group judicially protected vis-à-vis the interest that legislatively prevailed over it. And that, I believe—the predictable early reaction to *Roe* notwithstanding ("more of the same Warren-type activism")—is a charge that can responsibly be leveled at no other decision of the past twenty years. At times the inferences the Court has drawn from the values the Constitution marks for special protection have been controversial, even shaky, but never before has its sense of an obligation to draw one been so obviously lacking.

unfairly benefitted, by the proposed classification. In short, I trust your generalizations about the differences between my gang and Wilfred's more than I do your generalizations about the differences between my gang and yours.

IV

Not in the last thirty-five years at any rate. For, as the received learning has it, this sort of thing did happen before, repeatedly. From its 1905 decision in *Lochner v. New York* into the 1930's the Court, frequently though not always under the rubric of "liberty of contract," employed the Due Process Clauses of the Fourteenth and Fifth Amendments to invalidate a good deal of legislation. According to the dissenters at the time and virtually all the commentators since, the Court had simply manufactured a constitutional right out of whole cloth and used it to superimpose its own view of wise social policy on those of the legislatures. * * *

It may be objected that *Lochner et al.* protected the "economic rights" of businessmen whereas *Roe* protects a "human right." It should be noted, however, that not all of the *Lochner* series involved economic regulation; that even those that did resist the "big business" stereotype with which the commentators tend to associate them; and that in some of them the employer's "liberty of contract" claim was joined by the employee, who knew that if he had to be employed on the terms set by the law in question, he could not be employed at all. This is a predicament that is economic to be sure, but is not without its "human" dimension. Similarly "human" seems the predicament of the appellees in the 1970 case of *Dandridge v. Williams,* who challenged the Maryland Welfare Department's practice of limiting AFDC grants to $250 regardless of family size or need. * * * It may be, however—at least it is not the sort of claim one can disprove—that the "right to an abortion," or noneconomic rights generally, accord more closely with "this generation's idealization of America" than the "rights" asserted in either *Lochner* or *Dandridge*. But that attitude, of course, is *precisely* the point of the *Lochner* philosophy, which would grant unusual protection to those "rights" that somehow *seem* most pressing, regardless of whether the Constitution suggests any special solicitude for them. The Constitution has little to say about contract, less about abortion, and those who would speculate about which the framers would have been more likely to protect may not be pleased with the answer. The Court continues to disavow the philosophy of *Lochner*. Yet as Justice Stewart's concurrence admits, it is impossible candidly to regard *Roe* as the product of anything else.

RUTH BADER GINSBURG, SOME THOUGHTS ON AUTONOMY AND EQUALITY IN RELATION TO *ROE v. WADE*
63 N.C.L.Rev. 375–386 (1985).

These remarks contrast two related areas of constitutional adjudication: gender-based classification and reproductive autonomy. In both areas, the Burger Court, in contrast to the Warren Court, has been uncommonly active. The two areas are intimately related in this practical sense: the law's response to questions subsumed under these headings bears pervasively on the situation of women in society. * * *

Doctrine in the two areas, however, has evolved in discrete compartments. The High Court has analyzed classification by gender under an equal protection/sex discrimination rubric; it has treated reproductive autonomy under a substantive due process/personal autonomy headline not expressly linked to discrimination against women. The Court's gender classification decisions overturning state and federal legislation, in the main, have not provoked large controversy; the Court's initial 1973 abortion decision, *Roe v. Wade*,[2] on the other hand, became and remains a storm center. *Roe v. Wade* sparked public opposition and academic criticism,[3] in part, I believe, because the Court ventured too far in the change it ordered and presented an incomplete justification for its action. * * *

* * *

[The sex-discrimination decisions of the 1970s] had a spectacular aspect. The race cases that trooped before the Warren Court could be viewed as moving the federal judiciary onto the course set by the Reconstruction Congress a century earlier in the post-Civil War amendments. No similar foundation, set deliberately by actors in the political arena, can account for the Burger Court sex discrimination decisions. Perhaps for that reason, the Court has proceeded cautiously. It has taken no giant step. * * *

The Court's gender-based classification precedent impelled acknowledgement of a middle-tier equal protection standard of review, a level of judicial scrutiny demanding more than minimal rationality but less than a near-perfect fit between legislative ends and means. This movement away from the empty-cupboard interpretation of the equal protection principle in relation to sex equality claims largely trailed and mirrored changing patterns in society—most conspicuously, the emergence of the two-career family. The Court's decisions provoked no outraged opposition in legislative chambers. On the contrary, in a key area in which the Court rejected claims of impermissible sex-based classification, Congress indicated a different view, one more sensitive to discrimination against women.

That area, significantly in view of the Court's approach to reproductive choice, was pregnancy. In 1974 the Court * * * held that a state-operated disability income protection plan could exclude normal pregnancy without offense to the equal protection principle.[28] In a statutory setting as well, under Title VII, the Court later ruled, as it earlier had held in a constitutional context, that women unable to work due to pregnancy or childbirth could be excluded from disability coverage.[29] The classifications in these disability cases, according to the Court, were not gender-based on their face, and were not shown to have any sex-

---

2. 410 U.S. 113 (1973).

3. *See, e.g.,* Ely, *The Wages of Crying Wolf: A Comment on* Roe v. Wade, 82 Yale L.J. 920 (1973)[.]

28. Geduldig v. Aiello, 417 U.S. 484 (1974).

29. General Elec. Co. v. Gilbert, 429 U.S. 125 (1976).

discriminatory effect. All "nonpregnant persons," women along with men, the Court pointed out, were treated alike.

With respect to Title VII, Congress prospectively overruled the Court in 1978. It amended the statute to state explicitly that classification on the basis of sex includes classification on the basis of pregnancy. * * *

Roe v. Wade, in contrast to decisions involving explicit male/female classification, has occasioned searing criticism of the Court, over a decade of demonstrations, a stream of vituperative mail addressed to Justice Blackmun (the author of the opinion), annual proposals for overruling *Roe* by constitutional amendment, and a variety of measures in Congress and state legislatures to contain or curtail the decision. In 1973, when *Roe* issued, abortion law was in a state of change across the nation. There was a distinct trend in the states, noted by the Court, "toward liberalization of abortion statutes." Several states had adopted the American Law Institute's Model Penal Code approach setting out grounds on which abortion could be justified at any stage of pregnancy; most significantly, the Code included as a permissible ground preservation of the woman's physical or mental health. Four states—New York, Washington, Alaska, and Hawaii—permitted physicians to perform first-trimester abortions with virtually no restrictions. This movement in legislative arenas bore some resemblance to the law revision activity that eventually swept through the states establishing no-fault divorce as the national pattern.

The Texas law at issue in *Roe* made it a crime to "procure an abortion" except "by medical advice for the purpose of saving the life of the mother." It was the most extreme prohibition extant. The Court had in close view two pathmarking opinions on reproductive autonomy: first, a 1965 precedent, *Griswold v. Connecticut,*[38] holding inconsistent with personal privacy, somehow sheltered by due process, a state ban on the use of contraceptives even by married couples; second, a 1972 decision, *Eisenstadt v. Baird,*[39] extending *Griswold* to strike down a state prohibition on sales of contraceptives except to married persons by prescription. The Court had already decided *Reed v. Reed,*[40] recognizing the arbitrariness in the 1970s of a once traditional gender-based classification, but it did not further pursue that avenue in *Roe.*

The decision in *Roe* appeared to be a stunning victory for the plaintiffs. The Court declared that a woman, guided by the medical judgment of her physician, had a "fundamental" right to abort a pregnancy, a right the Court anchored to a concept of personal autonomy derived from the due process guarantee. The Court then proceeded to define with precision the state regulation of abortion henceforth permissible. The rulings in *Roe,* and in a companion case decided the same day, *Doe v. Bolton,*[42] were stunning in this sense: they called into

38. 381 U.S. 479 (1965)[.]   **40.** 404 U.S. 71 (1971).

39. 405 U.S. 438 (1972).   **42.** 410 U.S. 179 (1973).

question the criminal abortion statutes of every state, even those with the least restrictive provisions.

* * *

[I]n my judgment, *Roe* ventured too far in the change it ordered. The sweep and detail of the opinion stimulated the mobilization of a right-to-life movement and an attendant reaction in Congress and state legislatures. In place of the trend "toward liberalization of abortion statutes" noted in *Roe,* legislatures adopted measures aimed at minimizing the impact of the 1973 rulings, including notification and consent requirements, prescriptions for the protection of fetal life, and bans on public expenditures for poor women's abortions.

Professor Paul Freund explained where he thought the Court went astray in *Roe,* and I agree with his statement. The Court properly invalidated the Texas proscription, he indicated, because "[a] law that absolutely made criminal all kinds and forms of abortion could not stand up; it is not a reasonable accommodation of interests." [53] If *Roe* had left off at that point and not adopted what Professor Freund called a "medical approach," physicians might have been less pleased with the decision, but the legislative trend might have continued in the direction in which it was headed in the early 1970s. "[S]ome of the bitter debate on the issue might have been averted," Professor Freund believed; "[t]he animus against the Court might at least have been diverted to the legislative halls." Overall, he thought that the *Roe* distinctions turning on trimesters and viability of the fetus illustrated a troublesome tendency of the modern Supreme Court under Chief Justices Burger and Warren "to specify by a kind of legislative code the one alternative pattern that will satisfy the Constitution."

I commented at the outset that I believe the Court presented an incomplete justification for its action. Academic criticism of *Roe,* charging the Court with reading its own values into the due process clause, might have been less pointed had the Court placed the woman alone, rather than the woman tied to her physician, at the center of its attention. Professor Karst's commentary is indicative of the perspective not developed in the High Court's opinion; he solidly linked abortion prohibitions with discrimination against women.[57] The issue in *Roe,* he wrote, deeply touched and concerned "women's position in society in relation to men."

It is not a sufficient answer to charge it all to women's anatomy—a natural, not man-made, phenomenon. Society, not anatomy, "places a greater stigma on unmarried women who become pregnant than on the men who father their children." Society expects, but nature does not command, that "women take the major responsibility * * * for child care" and that they will stay with their children, bearing nurture and

---

53. Freund, *Storms over the Supreme Court,* 69 A.B.A.J. 1474, 1480 (1983)[.]

57. Karst, [*Foreward: Equal Citizenship Under the Fourteenth Amendment,* 91 Harv.L.Rev. 1, 58 (1977).]

support burdens alone, when fathers deny paternity or otherwise refuse to provide care or financial support for unwanted offspring.

I do not pretend that, if the Court had added a distinct sex discrimination theme to its medically oriented opinion, the storm *Roe* generated would have been less furious. I appreciate the intense divisions of opinion on the moral question and recognize that abortion today cannot fairly be described as nothing more than birth control delayed. The conflict, however, is not simply one between a fetus' interests and a woman's interests, narrowly conceived, nor is the overriding issue state versus private control of a woman's body for a span of nine months. Also in the balance is a woman's autonomous charge of her full life's course—as Professor Karst put it, her ability to stand in relation to man, society, and the state as an independent, self-sustaining, equal citizen.

* * *

I turn, finally, to the plight of the woman who lacks resources to finance privately implementation of her personal choice to terminate her pregnancy. The hostile reaction to *Roe* has trained largely on her.

Some observers speculated that the seven-two judgment in *Roe* was motivated at least in part by pragmatic considerations—population control concerns, the specter of coat hanger abortions, and concerns about unwanted children born to impoverished women. * * * In a set of 1977 decisions, however, the Court upheld state denial of medical expense reimbursement or hospital facilities for abortions sought by indigent women.[69] Moreover, in a 1980 decision, *Harris v. McRae*,[70] the Court found no constitutional infirmity in the Hyde Amendment, which excluded even medically necessary abortions from Medicaid coverage. After these decisions, the Court was accused of sensitivity only to the Justices' own social milieu—"of creating a middle-class right to abortion."

* * *

Financial need alone, under the Court's jurisprudence, does not identify a class of persons whose complaints of disadvantageous treatment attract close scrutiny. Generally, constitutional claims to government benefits on behalf of the poor have prevailed only when tied to another bark—a right to travel interstate, discrimination because of out-of-wedlock birth, or gender-based discrimination. If the Court had acknowledged a woman's equality aspect, not simply a patient-physician autonomy constitutional dimension to the abortion issue, a majority perhaps might have seen the public assistance cases as instances in which, borrowing a phrase from Justice Stevens, the sovereign had violated its "duty to govern impartially."

* * *

69. Poelker v. Doe, 432 U.S. 519 (1977)[;] Maher v. Roe, 432 U.S. 464 (1977)[;] Beal v. Doe, 432 U.S. 438 (1977)[.]

70. 448 U.S. 297 (1980).

Overall, the Court's *Roe* position is weakened, I believe, by the opinion's concentration on a medically approved autonomy idea, to the exclusion of a constitutionally based sex-equality perspective. I understand the view that for political reasons the reproductive autonomy controversy should be isolated from the general debate on equal rights, responsibilities, and opportunities for women and men. I expect, however, that organized and determined opposing efforts to inform and persuade the public on the abortion issue will continue through the 1980s. In that process there will be opportunities for elaborating in public forums the equal-regard conception of women's claims to reproductive choice uncoerced and unsteered by government.

BIBLIOGRAPHY

Privacy: In General

Hafen, *The Constitutional Status of Marriage, Kinship, and Sexual Privacy—Balancing the Individual and Social Interests*, 81 Mich. L.Rev. 463 (1983).

Karst, *Freedom of Intimate Association*, 89 Yale L.J. 624 (1980).

Lupu, *Untangling the Strands of the Fourteenth Amendment*, 77 Mich. L.Rev. 981 (1979).

Parent, *Privacy, Morality and the Law*, 12 Phil. & Pub.Aff. 269 (1983).

J. Pennock & J. Chapman, eds., NOMOS XIII: PRIVACY (1971).

Posner, *The Uncertain Protection of Privacy by the Supreme Court*, 1979 Sup.Ct.Rev. 173.

Wellington, *Common Law Rules and Constitutional Double Standards: Some Notes on Adjudication*, 83 Yale L.J. 221 (1973).

Wilkinson & White, *Constitutional Protection for Personal Lifestyles*, 62 Cornell L.Rev. 563 (1977).

Abortion

Brownstein & Dau, *The Constitutional Morality of Abortion*, 33 B.C.L.Rev. 689 (1992).

M. Cohen, T. Nagel, & T. Scanlon, eds., THE RIGHTS AND WRONGS OF ABORTION (1974).

R. Dworkin, LIFE'S DOMINION (1993).

Epstein, *Substantive Due Process by Any Other Name: The Abortion Cases*, 1973 Sup.Ct.Rev. 159.

Farber & Nowak, *Beyond the* Roe *Debate: Judicial Experience with the 1980's "Reasonableness" Test*, 76 Va.L.Rev. 519 (1990).

Farrell, *Revisiting* Roe v. Wade: *Substance and Process in the Abortion Debate*, 68 Ind.L.J. 269 (1993).

Farrell–Smith, *Rights–Conflict, Pregnancy, and Abortion*, in BEYOND DOMINATION 265 (C. Gould ed. 1983).

J. Garfield & P. Hennessey, eds., ABORTION: MORAL AND LEGAL PERSPECTIVES (1984).

Garvey, *The Pope's Submarine,* 31 San Diego L.Rev. —— (1993).

M. Glendon, ABORTION AND DIVORCE IN WESTERN LAW (1987).

Heymann & Barzelay, *The Forest and the Trees: Roe v. Wade and its Critics,* 53 B.U.L.Rev. 765 (1973).

Kreimer, *The Law of Choice and Choice of Law: Abortion, the Right to Travel, and Extraterritorial Regulation in American Federalism,* 67 N.Y.U.L.Rev. 451 (1992).

Law, *Abortion Compromise—Inevitable and Impossible,* 1992 U.Ill.L.Rev. 921 (1993).

Law, *Rethinking Sex and the Constitution,* 132 U.Pa.L.Rev. 955 (1984).

Maltz, *Abortion, Precedent, and the Constitution: A Comment on Planned Parenthood of Southeastern Pennsylvania v. Casey,* 68 Notre Dame L.Rev. 11 (1992).

Mensch & Freeman, *The Politics of Virtue: Animals, Theology and Abortion,* 25 Ga.L.Rev. 923 (1991).

J. Noonan, A PRIVATE CHOICE: ABORTION IN AMERICA IN THE SEVENTIES (1979).

Perry, *Abortion, the Public Morals, and the Police Power: The Ethical Function of Substantive Due Process,* 23 U.C.L.A.L.Rev. 689 (1976).

Prygoski, *Abortion and the Right to Die: Judicial Imposition of a Theory of Life,* 23 Seton Hall L.Rev. 67 (1992).

Regan, *Rewriting Roe v. Wade,* 77 Mich.L.Rev. 1569 (1979).

Rubenfeld, *On the Legal Status of the Proposition that "Life Begins at Conception",* 43 Stan.L.Rev. 599 (1991).

Siegel, *Reasoning from the Body: A Historical Perspective on Abortion Regulation and Questions of Equal Protection,* 44 Stan.L.Rev. 261 (1992).

L. Sumner, ABORTION AND MORAL THEORY (1981).

M. Tooley, ABORTION AND INFANTICIDE (1983).

L. Tribe, ABORTION, THE CLASH OF ABSOLUTES (1990).

Williams, *Gender Wars: Selfless Women in the Republic of Choice,* 66 N.Y.U.L.Rev. 1559 (1991).

C. HOMOSEXUALITY

In *Bowers v. Hardwick*[1] the Supreme Court held that the right to privacy, which earlier cases had found in the Due Process Clause of the Fourteenth Amendment, did not protect homosexual sodomy. Respondent Hardwick, an adult male, had challenged Georgia's criminal sodomy

---

1. 478 U.S. 186, 106 S.Ct. 2841, 92 L.Ed.2d 140 (1986).

law after he was arrested for committing a sexual act with another adult male in his own bedroom. The Court's brief opinion argued that text, precedent, and tradition did not support Hardwick's claim, and that it was unwilling to override legislative choices without such authority. Justice Blackmun's dissent asserted, by contrast, that the essential meaning of the right to privacy was the freedom to choose what form one's intimate sexual relationships should take.

Both sides of the Court in *Bowers* take what Michael Sandel calls the "sophisticated" approach to sodomy laws. They assume that the justice of such laws depends, not on a moral judgment about homosexual activity, but on a more general theory about democracy (the majority) or liberty (the dissent). Sandel argues for a more "naive" view. He claims that one cannot successfully defend either prohibition or toleration while bracketing the issue of morality.

Jed Rubenfeld offers an interesting response to Sandel's challenge. He does not argue that homosexual intimacy is a morally valuable practice. But he does say that laws against such behavior are especially harmful. This is not because he accepts Justice Blackmun's "personhood" thesis (the idea that people should be free to define their own identities by making choices about sexual relations). A person's identity, if there is such a thing, is formed by lots of influences besides his own choices. Rubenfeld instead argues that sodomy laws are unconstitutional because they have a pervasive standardizing effect—forcing homosexuals "into a network of social institutions and relations that will occupy their lives to a substantial degree." In that regard they are like laws forbidding private schools and laws whose consequence is compulsory child-bearing.

Kendall Thomas argues that Rubenfeld's case rests on false premises. Thomas thinks it unlikely that sodomy laws will force gays and lesbians to live lives of compulsory heterosexuality. On the contrary, most will continue to embrace a homosexual identity. But that does not make such laws any more acceptable to Thomas. He contends that sodomy statutes express a public theory of homophobia, which is enforced through private acts of violence against gays and lesbians.

MICHAEL J. SANDEL, MORAL ARGUMENT AND LIBERAL TOLERATION: ABORTION AND HOMOSEXUALITY
77 Calif.L.Rev. 521–522, 533–534, 536–538 (1989).

People defend laws against * * * homosexual sodomy in two different ways: Some argue that [it is] morally reprehensible and therefore worthy of prohibition; others try to avoid passing judgment on the morality of th[is] practice[,] and argue instead that, in a democracy, political majorities have the right to embody in law their moral convictions.

In a similar way, arguments against * * * antisodomy laws take two different forms: Some say the laws are unjust because the practices they prohibit are morally permissible, indeed sometimes desirable; others oppose these laws without reference to the moral status of the practices at issue, and argue instead that individuals have a right to choose for themselves whether to engage in them.

These two styles of argument might be called, respectively, the "naive" and the "sophisticated." The naive view holds that the justice of laws depends on the moral worth of the conduct they prohibit or protect. The sophisticated view holds that the justice of such laws depends not on a substantive moral judgment about the conduct at stake, but instead on a more general theory about the respective claims of majority rule and individual rights, of democracy on the one hand, and liberty on the other.

I shall try in this paper to bring out the truth in the naive view, which I take to be this: The justice (or injustice) of laws against * * * homosexual [practices] depends, at least in part, on the morality (or immorality) of those practices. This is the claim the sophisticated view rejects. In both its majoritarian and its liberal versions, the sophisticated view tries to set aside or "bracket" controversial moral and religious conceptions for purposes of justice. It insists that the justification of laws be neutral among competing visions of the good life.

In practice, of course, these two kinds of argument can be difficult to distinguish. In the debate over cases like * * * *Bowers v. Hardwick*,[3] both camps tend to advance the naive view under cover of the sophisticated. (Such is the prestige of the sophisticated way of arguing.) For example, those who would ban * * * [homosexual activity] out of abhorrence often argue in the name of deference to democracy and judicial restraint. Similarly, those who want permissive laws because they approve of * * * homosexuality often argue in the name of liberal toleration.

This is not to suggest that all instances of the sophisticated argument are disingenuous attempts to promote a substantive moral conviction. Those who argue that law should be neutral among competing conceptions of the good life offer various grounds for their claim, including most prominently the following:

(1) the *relativist* view says law should not affirm a particular moral conception because all morality is relative, and so there are no moral truths to affirm; (2) the *utilitarian* view argues that government neutrality will, for various reasons, promote the general welfare in the long run; (3) the *voluntarist* view holds that government should be neutral among conceptions of the good life in order to respect the capacity of persons as free citizens or autonomous agents to choose their conceptions for themselves; and (4) the *minimalist,* or pragmatic view says that, because people inevitably disagree about morality and religion, government should bracket these controversies for the sake of political agreement and social cooperation.

---

3. 478 U.S. 186 (1986).

In order to bring out the truth in the naive way of arguing, I look to the actual arguments judges and commentators have made in recent cases dealing with * * * homosexuality. Their arguments, unfailingly sophisticated, illustrate the difficulty of bracketing moral judgments for purposes of law. * * *

* * *

The Voluntarist Case for Toleration: Homosexuality

The dissenters' argument for toleration in *Bowers v. Hardwick* illustrates the difficulties with the version of liberalism that ties toleration to autonomy rights alone. In refusing to extend the right of privacy to homosexuals, the majority in *Bowers* declared that none of the rights announced in earlier privacy cases resembled the rights homosexuals were seeking: "No connection between family, marriage, or procreation on the one hand and homosexual activity on the other has been demonstrated * * *." Any reply to the Court's position would have to show some connection between the practices already subject to privacy protection and the homosexual practices not yet protected. What then is the resemblance between heterosexual intimacies on the one hand, and homosexual intimacies on the other, such that both are entitled to a constitutional right of privacy?

This question might be answered in at least two different ways—one voluntarist, the other substantive. The first argues from the autonomy the practices reflect, whereas the second appeals to the human goods the practices realize. The voluntarist answer holds that people should be free to choose their intimate associations for themselves, regardless of the virtue or popularity of the practices they choose so long as they do not harm others. In this view, homosexual relationships resemble the heterosexual relationships the Court has already protected in that all reflect the choices of autonomous selves.

By contrast, the substantive answer claims that much that is valuable in the conventional marriage is also present in homosexual unions. In this view, the connection between heterosexual and homosexual relations is not that both result from individual choice but that both realize important human goods. Rather than rely on autonomy alone, this second line of reply articulates the virtues homosexual intimacy may share with heterosexual intimacy, along with any distinctive virtues of its own. It defends homosexual privacy the way *Griswold* defended marital privacy, by arguing that, like marriage, homosexual union may also be "intimate to the degree of being sacred * * * a harmony in living * * * a bilateral loyalty," an association for a "noble * * * purpose." [74]

Of these two possible replies, the dissenters in *Bowers* relied wholly on the first. Rather than protect homosexual intimacies for the human goods they share with intimacies the Court already protects, Justice Blackmun cast the Court's earlier cases in individualist terms, and found

74. The phrases are from Griswold v. Connecticut, 381 U.S. 479, 486 (1965).

their reading applied equally to homosexuality because "much of the richness of a relationship will come from the freedom an individual has to *choose* the form and nature of these intensely personal bonds." At issue was not homosexuality as such but respect for the fact that "different individuals will make different choices" in deciding how to conduct their lives.

* * *

The * * * precedent [offered in *Bowers*] for homosexual rights [was] not *Griswold* but *Stanley v. Georgia*,[84] which upheld the right to possess obscene materials in the privacy of one's home. *Stanley* did not hold that the obscene films found in the defendant's bedroom served a "noble purpose," only that he had a right to view them in private. The toleration *Stanley* defended was wholly independent of the value or importance of the thing being tolerated.

* * *

The case for toleration that brackets the morality of homosexuality has a powerful appeal. In the face of deep disagreement about values, it seems to ask the least of the contending parties. It offers social peace and respect for rights without the need for moral conversion. Those who view sodomy as sin need not be persuaded to change their minds, only to tolerate those who practice it in private. By insisting only that each respect the freedom of others to live the lives they choose, this toleration promises a basis for political agreement that does not await shared conceptions of morality.

Despite its promise, however, the neutral case for toleration is subject to two related difficulties. First, as a practical matter, it is by no means clear that social cooperation can be secured on the strength of autonomy rights alone, absent some measure of agreement on the moral permissibility of the practices at issue. It may not be accidental that the first practices subject to the right of privacy were accorded constitutional protection in cases that spoke of the sanctity of marriage and procreation. Only later did the Court abstract privacy rights from these practices and protect them without reference to the human goods they were once thought to make possible. This suggests that the voluntarist justification of privacy rights is dependent—politically as well as philosophically—on some measure of agreement that the practices protected are morally permissible.

A second difficulty with the voluntarist case for toleration concerns the quality of respect it secures. * * * [T]he analogy with *Stanley* tolerates homosexuality at the price of demeaning it; it puts homosexual intimacy on a par with obscenity—a base thing that should nonetheless be tolerated so long as it takes place in private. If *Stanley* rather than *Griswold* is the relevant analogy, the interest at stake is bound to be

84. 394 U.S. 557 (1969).

reduced * * * to "sexual gratification." (The only intimate relationship at stake in *Stanley* was between a man and his pornography.)

The majority in *Bowers* exploited this assumption by ridiculing the notion of a "fundamental right to engage in homosexual sodomy." The obvious reply is that *Bowers* is no more about a right to homosexual sodomy than *Griswold* was about a right to heterosexual intercourse. But by refusing to articulate the human goods that homosexual intimacy may share with heterosexual unions, the voluntarist case for toleration forfeits the analogy with *Griswold* and makes the ridicule difficult to refute.

The problem with the neutral case for toleration is the opposite side of its appeal; it leaves wholly unchallenged the adverse views of homosexuality itself. Unless those views can be plausibly addressed, even a Court ruling in their favor is unlikely to win for homosexuals more than a thin and fragile toleration. * * *

* * *

Admittedly, the tendency to bracket substantive moral questions makes it difficult to argue for toleration in the language of the good. Defining privacy rights by defending the practices privacy protects seems either reckless or quaint; reckless because it rests so much on moral argument, quaint because it recalls the traditional view that ties the case for privacy to the merits of the conduct privacy protects. But as the * * * sodomy case [ ] illustrate[s,] the attempt to bracket moral questions faces difficulties of its own. [It] suggest[s] the truth in the "naive" view, that the justice or injustice of laws against * * * homosexual [practices] may have something to do with the morality or immorality of those practices after all.

JED RUBENFELD, THE RIGHT OF PRIVACY
102 Harv.L.Rev. 737, 783–787, 792–794, 797–802 (1989).

METHOD

The methodology heretofore universal in privacy analysis has begun with the question, "What is the state trying to forbid?" The proscribed conduct is then delineated and its significance tested through a pre-established conceptual apparatus: for its role in " 'the concept of ordered liberty,' " its status as a "fundamental" right, its importance to one's identity, or for any other criterion of fundamentality upon which a court can settle. Suppose instead we began by asking not what is being *prohibited,* but what is being *produced.* Suppose we looked not to the negative aspect of the law—the interdiction by which it formally expresses itself—but at its positive aspect: the real effects that conformity with the law produces at the level of everyday lives and social practices.

* * *

SUBSTANCE

Consider the three principal areas in which the right to privacy has been applied: child-bearing (abortion and contraception), marriage (miscegenation laws, divorce restrictions, and so on), and education of children (*Meyer* [a] and *Pierce* [b]). According to the prevailing method of privacy analysis, certain decisions concerning these matters cannot be proscribed because they are "fundamental." But what is fundamental about these decisions? Are they fundamental in themselves? If, for example, the right to decide whom to marry is inherently fundamental, how is it, for example, that the proscriptions against incestuous and bigamous marriage do not offend it? In fact, a "liberty of fundamental decisions" cannot serve as a constitutional principle any more than could that quite similar quantity—the "liberty of contract"—that animated the *Lochner* jurisprudence. There *is* something fundamental at stake in the privacy decisions, but it is not the proscribed conduct, nor even the freedom of decision—it is not what is being taken away.

The distinctive and singular characteristic of the laws against which the right to privacy has been applied lies in their *productive* or *affirmative* consequences. There are perhaps no legal proscriptions with more profound, more extensive, or more persistent affirmative effects on individual lives than the laws struck down as violations of the right to privacy. Anti-abortion laws, anti-miscegenation laws, and compulsory education laws all involve the forcing of lives into well-defined and highly confined institutional layers. At the simplest, most quotidian level, such laws tend to *take over* the lives of the persons involved: they occupy and preoccupy. They affirmatively and very substantially shape a person's life; they direct a life's development along a particular avenue. These laws do not simply proscribe one act or remove one liberty; they inform the totality of a person's life.

The principle of the right to privacy is not the freedom to do certain, particular acts determined to be fundamental through some ever-progressing normative lens. It is the fundamental freedom not to have one's life too totally determined by a progressively more normalizing state.

Someone might say, I suppose, that anti-abortion or anti-contraception laws do not force women to bear children because women can simply refrain from having sex. Similarly one might say that whites and blacks, confronted by laws forbidding interracial marriage, can simply decline to marry if they do not wish to live with members of their own race.

This is no answer at all. To begin with, it is no answer to the pregnant woman seeking an abortion. More fundamentally, it is no answer because it is merely another attempt to hide behind a factitious focus on the prohibitory aspect of the law. The practical consequence of obeying laws against contraception or interracial marriage is that people become pregnant or marry intraracially. Indeed these laws derive the depth of their affirmative force from the fact that they operate on drives and desires too strong or too subtle for most to resist.

    a. Meyer v. Nebraska, 262 U.S. 390 (1923).   **b.** Pierce v. Society of Sisters, 268 U.S. 510 (1925).

The danger, then, is a particular kind of creeping totalitarianism, an unarmed *occupation* of individuals' lives. That is the danger of which * * * the right to privacy is warning us: a society standardized and normalized, in which lives are too substantially or too rigidly directed. That is the threat posed by state power in our century.

This threat is not unknown to our constitutional jurisprudence. Consider first Justice Jackson's words in *West Virginia State Board of Education v. Barnette*,[187] when, in the midst of the Second World War, the Court struck down a law that required schoolchildren to salute the flag and profess their loyalty to the country:

> Struggles to coerce uniformity of sentiment in support of some end thought essential to their time and country have been waged by many good as well as by evil men * * *. As first and moderate attempts to attain unity have failed, those bent on its accomplishment must resort to an ever-increasing severity * * *. Ultimate futility of such attempts to compel coherence is the lesson of every such effort from the Roman drive to stamp out Christianity * * * down to the fast failing efforts of our present totalitarian enemies.

* * *

With this image, however, we have left West Virginia's enforced flag-salute far behind. Or rather we have imagined that flag-salute systematized and ramified into numerous aspects of the child's daily life. We have imagined an existence totally informed or occupied, rather than a single act of enforced loyalty. This distinction is critical: it explains why *Barnette* is not, after all, a right-to-privacy case but rather a first amendment case.

Because of the signal role that speech plays in political freedom and because of the express constitutional guarantee, government in this country can hardly forbid or compel citizens to utter a single opinion without violating their rights. By contrast, in privacy cases, the government must go much further before it transgresses a constitutional limit. Consider now the cases of *Meyer* and *Pierce*, which * * * may be considered the true progenitors of the privacy decisions. Like *Barnette*, *Meyer* and *Pierce* also involved laws pertaining to the education of children—laws suggestive of a nationalism heightened by war. Yet the statutes struck down in *Meyer* and especially *Pierce* differed significantly from that in *Barnette*.

In *Meyer*, the law at issue prohibited the teaching of "modern" foreign languages to elementary schoolchildren. In *Pierce*, the state had prohibited private elementary schooling altogether, requiring all children between the ages of eight and sixteen to attend public schools. In each of these statutes, the state had gone much further in the effort—using Justice Jackson's phrase—to "coerce uniformity" than had West Virginia in enacting its flag-salute law. It is not that a greater degree of coercion was present; I am not referring to the potential consequences

187. 319 U.S. 624 (1943).

of violating the law. To the contrary, it was the potential consequences of *obeying* the law that mattered. The *Meyer* Court saw the state as attempting to "foster a homogeneous people with American ideals." The Court drew in this connection on images from ancient civilization:

> For the welfare of his Ideal Commonwealth, Plato suggested a law which would provide: "That the wives of our guardians are to be common, and their children are to be common, and no parent is to know his own child, nor any child his parent * * *. The proper officers will take the offspring of the good parents to the pen or fold, and there they will deposit them with certain nurses who dwell in a separate quarter; but the offspring of the inferior, or of the better when they chance to be deformed, will be put away in some mysterious, unknown place, as they should be." In order to submerge the individual and develop ideal citizens, Sparta assembled the males at seven into barracks and intrusted [sic] their subsequent education and training to official guardians. Although such measures have been deliberately approved by men of great genius, their ideas touching the relation between individual and State were wholly different from those upon which our institutions rest; and it hardly will be affirmed that any legislature could impose such restrictions upon the people of a State without doing violence to both letter and spirit of the Constitution.

* * *

Pierce presented this threat even more starkly because there the state had prohibited all organized elementary education outside the public schools. That the Court was reacting to this threat—and not merely to a deprivation of the "liberty of contract"—cannot be doubted. In language that implicitly derived its force from the same sources on which the Court drew in *Meyer,* the Court struck down the law and held that the "fundamental theory of liberty upon which all governments in this Union repose excludes any general power of the State to *standardize its children.*"

This concept of standardization as applied in *Pierce* is critical for our purposes. It includes both quantitative and qualitative components. The law struck down in *Pierce*—like the Platonic or Spartan regimes described by the *Meyer* Court, but unlike *Barnette* 's flag-salute law—had the effect of affirmatively occupying a substantial portion of the material, day-to-day lives of those individuals subject to it. At the same time, this occupation potentially subjected these individuals to a narrowly directed existence: a regimen, a discipline, a curriculum in which the totality of their personhood or identity could be forcefully compressed into a particular mold.

These two elements—the affirmative occupation of one's time and the directedness of this occupation—are crucial in understanding why the mandatory public schooling law in *Pierce* implicated a constitutional concern, now called the right to privacy, even though no explicit constitutional guarantee could be said to forbid it. Privacy takes its stand at the outer boundaries of the legitimate exercise of state power. It is to be invoked only where the government threatens to take over or occupy our lives—to exert its power in some way over the totality of our lives.

In a few, rare instances this "totalitarian" intervention into a person's life may occur as a result of a single legal prohibition. The burden of elaborating a conception of privacy based on an anti-totalitarian principle is to perceive how a single law may operate positively to take over and direct the totality of our lives.

* * *

DISTINCTIONS

[L]aws against abortion, interracial marriage, * * * and private education all involve a peculiar form of obedience that reaches far beyond mere abstention from the particular proscribed act. It is a form of obedience in which the life of the person forced to obey is thereafter substantially filled up and informed by the living, institutional consequences of obedience. The person finds himself in a new and sharply-defined, but also broadly encompassing institutional role. Because of their affirmative direction of individuals' lives, these roles—whether as mother, spouse, student or family member—have profoundly formative effects on identity and character.

This attribute of the laws discussed above distinguishes them from other proscriptions of unquestionable constitutional validity that might otherwise appear to fall within the ambit of the principles elaborated here. Consider laws against murder. Are such laws not "standardizing" in that they compel all of us to be non-murderers? Do they not operate "on our bodies" in that they work by forbidding us, for example, to pick up a knife and use it in a certain way? And do they not "instrumentalize" us by requiring us to serve the state's interests insofar as we are made thereby to refrain from causing harm to society at large?

* * *

Laws against murder foreclose an avenue; they do not harness us to a given seat and direct us down a single, regulated road. This formulation is not so much a conclusion from logic as from practical, material realities. One may always reformulate propositions to state negatives as positives. Refraining from murder, however, does not fill up one's life in the same way as does bearing a child, attending public school, * * * or marrying only within one's race. Forcing a person to do these latter things goes much further in thrusting him into socially defined, particularized practices and institutions.

This distinction between "negative" and "affirmative" effects of legal rules will no doubt be greeted with skepticism. Yet—to repeat the point—the distinction is not a matter of propositional logic; it is essentially normative. Whether the obligation not to murder is called a negative or affirmative duty makes no difference. The question is the degree to which, and the ways in which, the law informs, shapes, directs, and occupies the actual day-to-day activities of the persons concerned. Power may be understood and experienced as a purely prohibitory force acting upon essentially independent individual lives; it may also, however, appear and act as a force producing those lives from the inside.

The same negative-affirmative distinction directly parallels the essential difference between the anti-totalitarian right to privacy elaborated here and the personhood version of that right [espoused by the dissenters in *Bowers v. Hardwick*]. Formulated propositionally, the two principles seem almost like corollaries. The anti-totalitarian right to privacy, it might be said, prevents the state from imposing on individuals a defined identity, whereas the personhood right to privacy ensures that individuals are free to define their own identities. Is the anti-totalitarian theory of privacy nothing more in reality than a restatement of the personhood idea from another angle?

On the contrary: first, when personhood speaks of the "freedom to define oneself," it speaks for the most part of a chimera. We are all so powerfully influenced by the institutions within which we are raised that it is probably impossible, both psychologically and epistemologically, to speak of defining one's own identity. The point is not to save for the individual an abstract and chimerical right of defining himself; the point is to prevent the state from taking over, or taking undue advantage of, those processes by which individuals are defined in order to produce overly standardized, functional citizens.

Second, because personhood concentrates on the fundamentality of the act or decision at stake in a given case—whether to have a child, whom to marry, and so on—it will produce a different analysis and different results from the anti-totalitarian principle. * * *

* * *

There remains a third and final differentiation to be made between personhood and the right to privacy as understood here. To speak of resisting state-imposed identities—as we have done—does not commit privacy to personhood's central premise: that each individual's defining his identity is an act of such value that it is of constitutional importance. Indeed the right to privacy as developed here may suggest a repudiation of personal identity altogether.

The concept of personal identity—that sense of a unitary, atomic self that we all tend to consider ourselves to "have"—is complex and difficult. It has an almost theological or metaphysical aspect, as if one's "identity" were a kind of hypostatic quantity underlying the multiplicity of his vastly different relations in the world and the mutability of his nature over time. * * * This conception of a unitary personal identity has been radically challenged again and again this century in various fields, including psychoanalysis,[217] literature,[218] and—most recently and surprisingly—analytic philosophy.[219]   Personhood, reflecting an essentially liberal philosophy, is obliged to embrace and valorize the idea of a unitary personal identity; the right to privacy is not.

* * *

HOMOSEXUALITY

[Let us consider] *Bowers v. Hardwick* in our new terms.   * * * The * * * privacy argument against laws forbidding homosexual sex cannot be rested on the claim that they deprive certain persons of something deeply important to them, crucial to their happiness, or even central to their identity.   Nor can such laws be attacked on the ground that * * * laws must not impose on individuals any majoritarian values impinging on their autonomy.   * * *

Yet laws against homosexual sex have an effect that most laws do not.   They forceably channel certain individuals—supposing the law is obeyed—into a network of social institutions and relations that will occupy their lives to a substantial degree.

Most fundamentally, the prohibition against homosexual sex channels individuals' sexual desires into *reproductive* outlets.   Although the prohibition does not, like the law against abortions, produce as an imminent consequence compulsory child-bearing, it nonetheless forcibly directs individuals into the pathways of reproductive sexuality, rather than the socially "unproductive" realm of homosexuality.   These pathways are further guided, in our society, into particular institutional orbits, chief among which are the nuclear family and the constellation of practices surrounding a heterosexuality that is defined in conscious contradistinction to homosexuality.   Indeed it is difficult to separate our society's inculcation of a heterosexual identity from the simultaneous inculcation of a dichotomized complementarity of roles to be borne by men and women.   Homosexual couples by necessity throw into question the allocation of specific functions—whether professional, personal, or emotional—between the sexes.   It is this aspect of the ban on homosexuality—its central role in the maintenance of institutionalized sexual identities and normalized reproductive relations—that have made its *affirmative* or *formative* consequences, as well as the reaction against these consequences, so powerful a force in modern society.

* * *

217. One of Freud's great theoretical innovations was his tripartite conception of the mind, in which the ego—the "I" of our apperception—is but one of the three strata of subjectivity within each individual. *See generally* S. Freud, New Introductory Lectures on Psychoanalysis 51–71 (J. Strachey trans. 1965) (describing the ego, the id, and the superego). * * *

218. It is a central theme of Proust's *Remembrance of Things Past* to disabuse us of the illusion of having a singular identity over time, in order (perhaps) for us to regain our past in an even more essential way. *See, e.g.,* 3 M. Proust, Remembrance of Things Past 499 (C. Moncrieff, T. Kilmartin & A. Mayor trans. 1981) [.]

219. Derek Parfit has made the most powerful arguments within analytic philosophy against the concept of a unitary "I" persisting over time. *See generally* D. Parfit, Reasons and Persons (1984) [.]

It is no answer to say that an individual interested in homosexual relations might simply remain celibate. The living force of the law is at issue, not its logical form, and the real force of anti-homosexual laws, if obeyed, is that they enlist and redirect physical and emotional desires that we do not expect people to suppress. Indeed, it is precisely the propensity of such prohibitions to operate on and put to use an individual's most elemental bodily faculties that gives the exertion of power in this area such formative force. We tend to analyze these proscriptions today in terms of the propriety of punishing people for homosexual conduct. We tend, in measuring their morality, to form an image of either the homosexual imprisoned or the homosexual forced to give up his sexual acts. We ought, however, to give up the image of "the homosexual" in the first place and measure the law instead in terms of its creation of heterosexuals (and, in a different way, of homosexuals too) within the standardized parameters of a state-regulated identity.

It should be emphasized that conceiving of the right to privacy as protecting homosexuality for the reasons just discussed is not at all to convert the right to privacy into a general protection of "sexual intimacy," as Justice Blackmun suggested. The point is this: child-bearing, marriage, and the assumption of a specific sexual identity are undertakings that go on for years, define roles, direct activities, operate on or even create intense emotional relations, enlist the body, inform values, and in sum substantially shape the totality of a person's daily life and consciousness. Laws that force such undertakings on individuals may properly be called "totalitarian," and the right to privacy exists to protect against them.

KENDALL THOMAS, BEYOND THE PRIVACY PRINCIPLE

92 Colum.L.Rev. 1431, 1476–1477, 1483, 1485–1487, 1496–1498, 1505–1508 (1992).

[A.] "KEEP YOUR LAWS OFF MY BODY": HOMOPHOBIC VIOLENCE, HOMOSEXUAL SODOMY LAWS AND THE RIGHT OF CORPORAL INTEGRITY

[O]ne of the first duties of the state is to protect the citizens from whom its powers derive against random, unchecked violence by other citizens, or by government officials.

For gay men and lesbians, the state has honored this fundamental obligation more in the breach than in the observance. [F]ew members of our body politic are more vulnerable to violent terrorist attack than the gay or lesbian citizen. This violence takes two forms. One form is violence at the hand of state officials such as the police. This official violence is an important part of the political history of the criminalization of homosexual sex. The second form of homophobic violence is that perpetrated by private individuals. Although this type of violence is of lower visibility than that committed by public officials, the available evidence suggests that it is even more extensive. * * *

* * *

State officials seem unwilling or unable to use the criminal justice system to reach crimes of homophobic violence. In this respect, the response to private violence against gays and lesbians apparently mirrors the reaction of state governments to private violations of homosexual sodomy law. [But] the practical and ideological effects of government indifference are not at all the same. This difference lies in the very nature of the crime. [Homosexual sodomy statutes express the official "theory" of homophobia; private acts of violence against gay men and lesbians "translate" that theory into brutal "practice." In other words, private homophobic violence punishes what homosexual sodomy statutes prohibit.]

* * *

I read the Eighth Amendment as a constitutional reflection of an important political principle. This principle presupposes a constitutive conceptual connection between the legitimacy of a government and the methods that government employs to enforce its commands. In other words, the reason our Constitution prohibits the infliction of cruel and unusual punishments is because we cannot countenance the practices the Eighth Amendment forbids without doing violence to the very concept of governmentality, or at least to the liberal conception of legitimate government that underlies our constitutional tradition. If we accept the view that under our political system, a state may not resort to terror or random violence as a standard tool of governmental control, a functional interpretation of the Eighth Amendment permits us to make two claims about the constitutionality of laws against homosexual sodomy. The Eighth Amendment prohibition against cruel and unusual punishments may be construed not only to forbid open and official government use of violence to enforce the criminal laws against homosexual sodomy, but also to bar a state from effecting the enforcement of these laws by instigating, encouraging, or permitting private attacks on gay men and lesbians.

* * *

B. THE ANTI-TOTALITARIAN CASE AGAINST BOWERS V. HARDWICK

In "The Right of Privacy," Jed Rubenfeld seeks to build an "anti-totalitarian" case against the constitutionality of the homosexual sodomy law upheld in *Hardwick*. * * *

* * * In Rubenfeld's view, privacy doctrine is the constitutional expression of a democratic, anti-totalitarian impulse: it seeks to check "the extent of control and direction that the state exercises over the day-to-day conduct of individual lives."

The crucial step in Rubenfeld's argument is a methodological claim. He argues that the assumptions that inform most discussions of the right of privacy "[have] invariably missed the real point." Rubenfeld contends that privacy analysis has mistakenly placed undue emphasis on

what the laws with which the doctrine is concerned forbid or prohibit.
* * *

* * *

Not unexpectedly, it is the productive rather than the prohibitive
force of the law challenged in *Bowers v. Hardwick* that makes it
constitutionally suspect for Rubenfeld. If obeyed, laws criminalizing
homosexual sex "forcibly channel" the individuals to whom they are
addressed "into a network of social institutions and relations that will
occupy their lives to a substantial degree." That is, compliance with
homosexual sodomy statutes leaves gay men and lesbians no alternative
for the expression of their sexuality other than the "reproductive outlets" of child-bearing, marriage and the compelled adoption of heterosexual identity and existence. The "living" or "real force" of these laws is
that "they enlist and redirect physical and emotional desires that we do
not expect people to suppress." Rubenfeld argues that as a political
matter, the clear and coercive "conditioning effects" of homosexual
sodomy statutes may fairly be deemed "totalitarian," since they involve
the use of state power to forcibly, affirmatively occupy and direct
individuals' lives. Understood in these terms, the criminalization of gay
and lesbian sex collides with "our commitment to democracy—to a set of
political values." For Rubenfeld, the right of privacy was designed to
protect against this totalitarian state of affairs, in which every aspect of
an individual's daily existence becomes an affair of the state. In
Rubenfeld's view, the case against Hardwick specifically, and homosexual sodomy statutes generally, derives from what he takes to be the most
fundamental precept of American constitutional democracy: namely,
that "government must exist for the people, and the people must not
become mere instruments of the state."

C. A Critique of "Pure" Politics
* * *

In my view, this characterization of the "living force" of homosexual
sodomy law is not borne out by actual experience. Close attention to the
lived experience of gays and lesbians both before and after the decision
in *Hardwick* indicates that the "real force" of the criminalization of
homosexual sodomy cuts considerably deeper into the bodies of the men
and women to whom they are addressed.

Perhaps Rubenfeld is correct to point out that compliance with the
laws against homosexual sodomy would force some individuals down the
path of compulsory conjugal heterosexuality. But this is not the only or
even most likely result of laws against homosexual sodomy. It is not
difficult to imagine or document another quite different response to the
criminalization of homosexual sex. A first step toward an alternative
account of a gay or lesbian life lived in obedience to homosexual sodomy
law would be to recognize that "there need be no necessary relationship
between sexual practice and sexual identity." The history of gay men
and lesbians offers abundant evidence that for many of the individuals

who have embraced it, homosexual identity is not primarily erotic, but social and political. Lillian Faderman, for example, has found that the actual historical record indicates that "women who identify themselves as lesbian generally do not view lesbianism as a sexual phenomenon first and foremost." [264] Similarly, in her pioneering "Compulsory Heterosexuality and Lesbian Existence," Adrienne Rich has persuasively argued that lesbian identity embraces a broad range of "woman-identified experience." [265] On Rich's argument, the central component of this "lesbian continuum" is not a determinate sexuality, but a distinctive sensibility.

I have dwelt on the disjunction between sexual acts and sexual identities, because I believe the failure to appreciate the difference between the two provides the best explanation for the curiously truncated hypothetical account Rubenfeld gives of the likely consequences that would flow from adherence to the laws against homosexual sodomy. Rubenfeld's rather speculative claim that the main result of homosexual sodomy laws is that they leave individuals no option outside of compulsory heterosexuality leads him to ignore a very different, and much more likely, scenario. As I read the actual historical record, three alternative possibilities should be considered. First, it is quite likely that something like a "homosexual" identity might continue to be embraced even by individuals who chose to obey the laws criminalizing homoerotic acts. Second, it is not unreasonable to think that the same might be said about the ascription of "homosexual" identity that figured so centrally in the facts of *Hardwick* itself. Individuals would most probably continue to be "marked" as homosexuals even if they fully complied with the proscriptions against homosexual sex. Third, there is good warrant to believe that individuals who either asserted a homosexual identity, or to whom such an identity was imputed, would continue to be vulnerable to the political terror of homophobic violence.

Rubenfeld's account of the political rights implicated by homosexual sodomy law does not help us apprehend or address the likely persistence of homophobic violence even in the face of full compliance with the statutory command. This difficulty in Rubenfeld's analysis is compounded by a limited understanding of the character of the political agency that gives homosexual sodomy laws their brutal force. As I have noted, Rubenfeld seems to think that the workings of the state exhaust the field of the political. I have argued to the contrary that the political constellation in which homosexual sodomy statutes are ensconced involves a much more complex division of labor between public officials and private citizens. It is precisely this network of power relations that forms the backdrop against which the political and constitutional meaning of both homosexual sodomy statutes and homophobic violence must be examined. Because he fails to appreciate the extent to which politics

264. Lillian Faderman, Surpassing the Love of Men 142 (1981).

265. [Adrienne Rich, Compulsory Heterosexuality and Lesbian Existence, *in* Pow-

ers of Desire: The Politics of Sexuality 192 (Ann Snitow et al., eds., 1983).]

overruns the formal boundaries of the state, Rubenfeld offers too impoverished an account of the concrete political stakes that the criminalization of homosexual sodomy entails for the bodies of real, living individuals.

Rubenfeld's overlapping conceptions of sexuality, politics, and the state lead his analysis of homosexual sodomy law into debilitating difficulties. Since he overlooks the political violence that surrounds the criminalization of homosexual sodomy, Rubenfeld places undue emphasis on the degree to which the most likely effect of the law challenged in *Hardwick* will be to force gay men and lesbians to assume heterosexual identities, as opposed to simply hiding their homosexual identities. That is, Rubenfeld's political account locates the constitutional illegitimacy of homosexual sodomy laws in the fact that they "enlist and redirect physical and emotional desires that we do not expect people to suppress." Rubenfeld would declare such laws invalid because they drive an individual into a certain "way of life." My account of the terror of homophobic violence finds these laws constitutionally invalid neither because they force gay men and lesbians into heterosexual lives, nor because they lead gay men and lesbians to cloak their homosexual lives in secrecy. My analysis finds homosexual sodomy laws constitutionally infirm in that they legitimize the violent deformation and destruction of life itself.

BIBLIOGRAPHY

Arriola, *Sexual Identity and the Constitution: Homosexual Persons as a Discrete and Insular Minority,* 10 Women's Rights L.Rep. 143 (1988).

Conkle, *The Second Death of Substantive Due Process,* 62 Ind.L.J. 215 (1987).

Delgado, *Fact, Norm, and Standard of Review—The Case of Homosexuality,* 10 U.Dayton L.Rev. 575 (1985).

P. Devlin, THE ENFORCEMENT OF MORALS (1965).

Duclos, *Some Complicating Thoughts on Same–Sex Marriage,* 1 Law & Sexuality 31 (1991).

Dunlap, *The Lesbian and Gay Marriage Debate,* 1 Law & Sexuality 63 (1991).

R. Dworkin, *Lord Devlin and the Enforcement of Morals,* 75 Yale L.J. 986 (1966).

Eskridge, *A Social Constructionist Critique of Posner's* Sex and Reason: *Steps Toward a Gaylegal Agenda,* 102 Yale L.J. 333 (1992).

Fajer, *Can Two Real Men Eat Quiche Together? Storytelling, Gender–Role Stereotypes, and Legal Protection for Lesbians and Gay Men,* 46 U.Miami L.Rev. 511 (1992).

Goldstein, *History, Homosexuality, and Political Values: Searching for the Hidden Determinants of* Bowers v. Hardwick, 97 Yale L.J. 1073 (1988).

Grey, *Eros, Civilization, and the Burger Court,* 43 L. & Contemp.Probs. 83 (1980).

H.L.A. Hart, LAW, LIBERTY AND MORALITY (1963).

Hunter, *Life after* Hardwick, 27 Harv.C.R.–C.L.L.Rev. 531 (1992).

Khan, *The Invasion of Sexual Privacy,* 23 San Diego L.Rev. 957 (1986).

Law, *Homosexuality and the Social Meaning of Gender,* 1988 Wis.L.Rev. 187.

Lewis, *Introduction*—Commonwealth v. Wasson: *Invalidating Kentucky's Sodomy Statute,* 81 Ky.L.Rev. 423 (1992).

Maroney, Bowers v. Hardwick: *A Case Study in Federalism, Legal Procedure, and Constitutional Interpretation,* 38 Syracuse L.Rev. 1223 (1987).

Note, *Developments in the Law—Sexual Orientation and the Law,* 102 Harv.L.Rev. 1508 (1989).

R. Posner, SEX AND REASON (1992).

Richards, *Unnatural Acts and the Constitutional Right to Privacy: A Moral Theory,* 45 Fordham L.Rev. 1281 (1977).

Richards, *Sexual Autonomy and the Constitutional Right to Privacy: A Case Study in Human Rights and the Unwritten Constitution,* 30 Hast.L.J. 957 (1979).

Rivera, *Our Straight–Laced Judges: The Legal Position of Homosexual Persons in the United States,* 30 Hast.L.J. 799 (1979).

Sims, *Moving Towards Equal Treatment of Homosexuals,* 23 Pac.L.J. 1543 (1992).

Stoddard, Bowers v. Hardwick: *Precedent by Personal Predilection,* 54 U.Chi.L.Rev. 648 (1987).

Sunstein, *Sexual Orientation and the Constitution: A Note on the Relationship Between Due Process and Equal Protection,* 55 U.Chi.L.Rev. 1161 (1988).

Survey on the Constitutional Right to Privacy in the Context of Homosexual Activity, 40 U.Miami L.Rev. 521 (1986).

Symposium, *Sex, Politics, & the Law: Lesbians and Gay Men Take the Offensive,* 14 N.Y.U.Rev. of L. & Soc.Change 891 (1986).

Symposium, *Law, Community, and Moral Reasoning,* 77 Calif.L.Rev. 475 (1989).

Vieira, Hardwick *and the Right of Privacy,* 55 U.Chi.L.Rev. 1181 (1988).

West, *Taking Preferences Seriously,* 64 Tulane L.Rev. 659 (1990).

D. THE RIGHT TO DIE

The right to die is quite a modern issue. When life was shorter people avoided death. Advances in medical science now enable most of us to reach old age. Machines can keep us going as our systems wear out. It is now possible for many people to live (or be kept alive) longer than they might want. Is there a point to prolonging respiration, circulation, or nutrition when a patient is in great pain and will not get better? Or when she is, as the doctors say, in a persistent vegetative state?

There are no simple answers to these questions. And the Constitution might seem an unlikely place to look for them. It comes into play because most people now die in hospitals, and state law regulates the behavior of health care providers. It may require keeping a patient alive longer than she wants, or her family wants her, to be. Does the Constitution impose a limit on what state law can require?

In *Cruzan v. Director, Missouri Dept. of Health*,[1] the Supreme Court addressed that question for the first time. It assumed, though it did not actually decide, that competent people have a constitutional right (a Fourteenth Amendment liberty) to refuse lifesaving treatment. But Cruzan herself was in a persistent vegetative state. The Court held that the state was entitled to require clear and convincing proof of her wishes before allowing treatment to be withdrawn. Absent such proof, the state was not required to accept the decision of Cruzan's family about the proper course of action.

The most obvious difficulty with talking about Cruzan's constitutional rights is that she herself is not able to exercise them. As John Garvey explains, freedom (Fourteenth Amendment liberty) is a right to act, and perhaps a right to choose. Cruzan could do neither of these things. Garvey argues that we can make sense of her right only if there is a representative to exercise it for her.

Nancy Rhoden draws a different conclusion from the same observation. She suggests that the idea of constitutional rights in this area may be both misguided and counterproductive. It leads, among other things, to difficult standards of proof like the one the Court approved in *Cruzan*. Perhaps we would do better to drop the idea of *rights* and focus instead on how to make the *right* decision.

Ronald Dworkin assumes that the question of rights is settled in Cruzan's favor, and looks at the other side of the balance. What interest does the state have in requiring that she be kept alive when her family opposes that course of action? He concludes that none of the reasons given by the Court is convincing enough to override Cruzan's right to die.

1. 497 U.S. 261, 110 S.Ct. 2841, 111 L.Ed.2d 224 (1990).

Yale Kamisar, alone among the commentators represented here, argues that it is permissible (and perhaps proper) for the state to keep Cruzan alive. As recently as three decades ago even the leaders of the euthanasia movement would have hesitated to urge termination of life support in a case like *Cruzan*. There is, of course, the obvious problem of proof about Cruzan's own wishes—the issue on which the case turned. But apart from that *Cruzan* was not a case where the patient was terminally ill. Nor was termination necessary to relieve her suffering; there was no indication that she was in any pain. Finally, the "medical procedures" that the patient's parents wanted to terminate were tubes for feeding and water, not the more sophisticated machines used to prolong respiration, heartbeat, kidney function, etc. But these facts went almost unnoticed in the discussion of the case. Kamisar finds that the most frightening aspect of current thinking about this problem. He fears that we have already gone a long way down the slippery slope from a right to die to active euthanasia.

JOHN H. GARVEY, FREEDOM
AND REPRESENTATION

In D. Meyers, K. Kipnis & C. Murphy, Kindred Matters (1993).

I. FREEDOM

Whenever we speak of freedom as a right we are referring to a relation of four variables. This 'freedom' is always the freedom of some person (X) from some constraint (y) by another person (Y) to do (or refrain from doing) some act (x). * * * [M]y constitutional right to freedom of speech means that I (X) am free from laws or other obstacles (y) imposed by the government (Y) to speak (or remain silent) (x).

* * *

Freedoms are different from other rights in this way: the term x always refers to an action. My constitutional rights (freedoms) to speak, worship, and contract allow me to do various things. My rights to counsel and to just compensation, and my privilege against self-incrimination, do not allow me to act in any special way. They promise benefits or forbid harms to me as an essentially passive right-holder. (The only act I perform here is the "legal act" of claiming my rights.)

In liberal constitutional theory freedoms are also bilateral. Whenever I am free to do x, I am also free to do not-x. My freedom of religion allows me to attend or stay away from church. My freedom of speech lets me speak or remain silent. This means that constitutional freedoms protect choices about certain kinds of actions.

* * *

These features (protection for choices, actions) create the problem I want to address. Some people are unable to make rational decisions about how to act. There is a real problem with saying that these people have a right to be free (to make choices about actions). [I am talking about children, people who are severely retarded, senile, comatose, etc.]

* * *

Everyone agrees that it is OK to help these people out by making some decisions for them. This is a weak version of paternalism. In general terms paternalism is action by one person (R = 'Representative') for the good of another (X), but contrary to X's present desires, and not justified by X's consent.[1] The weak version holds that R may interfere when X is unable to make a rational decision about some action (x), and x involves a risk of harm (or maybe a chance of good).

* * *

II. Representation

As I have said, freedoms allow us to make choices about actions: to have children, to speak, to worship, or not to do any of these things. In an obvious way X is not free to do these things when we allow paternalistic intervention. X does not choose for himself; rather, R chooses for him.

Yet there is a derivative sense in speaking of X's freedom under these circumstances. Freedom allows people to be self-governing, and in some cases of paternalism we may say that X is self-governing. The proper metaphor is not a direct democracy but a republic in which X rules through a representative (R).

In a republic the people are self-governing because they choose representatives by consent. That is not possible in most of the paternalistic relations we are concerned with, where R acts for X because X is incompetent to choose. Representatives in these cases are instead chosen because of ties of love and kinship: parents for children, spouses for one another, children for aged parents, etc. The issue we are concerned with is whether that method of selection is the functional equivalent of consent; or if that is asking too much, at least whether their paternalism can be seen as a kind of 'freedom.'

I would argue that the bonds of love and kinship embody all that is good in the relation between representative and represented. Their most important feature is the selfless character of love, which moves R to put X's interests ahead of all other considerations. As motives go that beats the desire for reelection, which is what we count on to make members of Congress consider the interests of their constituents. In addition to love there is the similarity of interests that derives from ties of kinship—what some call 'descriptive' or 'virtual' representation. We frequently rely on this fact to justify the choice of a representative. The Federal Rules of Civil Procedure do so in selecting representatives for class actions. The rules of property law allow siblings to represent the

---

1. See Brock, *Paternalism and Promoting the Good,* in R. Sartorius, ed., PATER-NALISM 237, 238 (1983).

future interests of unborn children. Finally, those who love one another and live together will be best informed about one another's actual needs and preferences.

* * *

III. FREEDOM AND THE REPRESENTATIVE

When X acts through a representative we can look at his freedom from two angles: (i) X's freedom vis à vis his representative; (ii) X's freedom vis à vis the government. Here I examine (i). There are three different ways of structuring the relation between X and R, and each presents a different issue about X's freedom.

A. Proxy

One way of understanding X's relation with R is most appropriate for decisions made on behalf of the post-competent (people who are senile, irreversibly comatose, etc.) and the temporarily incompetent. In these cases R will often be in a position to exercise a kind of proxy for X, giving consent to things that X would agree to if he were still competent. Sometimes the metaphor of a proxy is exactly right. Suppose I execute a living will (with my wife as executrix) that says I do not wish to be kept alive on a respirator if I should permanently lose my cognitive faculties. When my wife consents to turning off the respirator she simply announces the decision I have already made, just as my proxy at a corporate shareholders' meeting announces my vote. In cases like this R does not even act paternalistically toward X; she is merely his agent. Because X makes his own choices we can say that he is free vis à vis R. X cannot enforce his choice if R acts unfaithfully (since X is incompetent), so there is always a possibility that R can restrict X's freedom. But ties of love and duty constrain R to behave as a faithful agent. And in extreme cases the law may enforce X's proxy.

Suppose, though, that my wife had no living will to rely on. She might then say that I would want the respirator turned off, and that she knew this because she knew my history and personality about as well as her own. We had talked about death and hospitals, about medical costs and what made life worthwhile. And while I had never said in so many words that I didn't want to be kept alive on a respirator she knew what I would say if I could just speak for a moment. In cases like this my consent is hypothetical, not real.

What makes us comfortable with R's decision is not X's consent but the fact that R is guided by X's view of the good. R represents X like a Senator up for reelection. The Senator's votes are not guided by written instructions but by familiarity with the desires of her constituents. They do not actually consent to her actions—it has been five years since they voted for her. But if she wants to be reelected she must try hard to determine what they would say if asked.

Here too it is meaningful to speak of X's freedom vis à vis R, because R's choices on X's behalf are determined by X himself. They seek X's good as X has seen it up to the time of his incompetence. X's freedom again depends on R's faithful performance as an agent. He cannot threaten to discharge her as voters can their Senator. But as I said above, R is bound by other constraints to carry out X's wishes.

B. Trustee: The Objective View

When we cannot say with any confidence what X would choose, R must act more like a trustee than like a proxy. * * *

[There are two ways of viewing R's actions.] For lack of better terms I will call them the objective and the subjective approaches. The objective approach allows R to choose for X, and the courts to review R's performance for conformity with a standard like 'best interests' or 'reasonable person.' * * *

The objective approach is most convincing when applied to health care issues: blood transfusions for children, * * * life support systems for sub-competent [*i.e.* retarded] patients (or post-competent patients whose views are unknown). These cases assume that R has a motive (religious scruples, a desire to put down the burden of care) to choose wrongly for X. They also assume that courts can correct R's choice because there are certain primary goods (life, health, the absence of pain) that any rational person would want. In rejecting them, the argument goes, R acts irrationally on X's behalf. The government therefore intervenes to free X from the burden of R's representation.

There are problems, though, with relying on these goods to define X's 'best interests.' People value other things too, some more highly than the 'primary' goods. Suppose that I am hit by a truck and rendered irreversibly comatose. My wife might refuse treatment for me, because she believed that a dignified death and peace of mind for my family were more important for me than prolonged nonsapient life. There is nothing objectively wrong about this choice. A court could not confidently say that she ought to do otherwise. It might say that treatment was a more popular option than the one my wife had chosen. But even if that were true (and I doubt it), it is not a convincing reason for imposing it on me.

* * *

C. Trustee: The Subjective View

Given th[is] difficult[y] I see no alternative in many, perhaps most, cases to having R choose for X what R thinks is good. * * *

If we structure the relation between X and R in this way, then X is not free vis à vis R. R is not guided by X's choices as in proxy cases. * * * R simply chooses for X as R thinks best. This loss of freedom is not as serious as some people suppose. If X is [post]-competent he is incapable of acting freely except through a representative. The real question is who his representative should be—[his family] or the state. [His family], because they are tied to him by bonds of love and kinship, are more likely to understand his good * * * and to pursue it for his sake. * * *

IV. Freedom and the Government

I now want to look at X's freedom vis à vis the government. This is the kind of freedom the Constitution is concerned with. * * * I will conclude that in many cases we can quite sensibly speak about X's 'freedom.' But when the government steps into R's shoes, or when it supervises R's choices according to its own standards, then I think we should say that X is not free.

* * *

[A]. The Government as Representative

As a general matter * * * it is sensible to speak about X's freedom against the government when X is represented by R. But who R is makes a difference. Consider first the situation where X is incompetent and has no R to act for him: * * * the homeless mentally disabled, and similar unfortunates. Because they are incompetent these people cannot act and choose for themselves. Nor can they act and choose through representatives. If people who act through representatives are like self-governing citizens of a republic, these unfortunates are like slaves or aliens. They are not self-governing because they are unrepresented.

In these circumstances it is senseless to talk about freedom as a constitutional right. That freedom is a relation of four variables (X, x, Y, y), but here one variable is absent: such a person cannot do x. A comatose patient who has no family or friends cannot choose to live or die. * * * These people may have a right to considerate treatment, but they are not free.

Suppose though that the government as *parens patriae* steps into the role of R. It may initiate involuntary commitment of the mentally ill, or [provide treatment for abandoned people] in state institutions * * *. It is no condemnation of such treatment to say that it is inconsistent with freedom. These people have no other representative and would not be free in any event. But we must acknowledge that they are not free when the government represents them. There is a sense in which they can then act and choose. But their actions are not free because they are directed by the government. In terms of the symbols we have used (X, x, Y, y) we could say that x is not an independent variable. Rather, $x = y$. * * *

[B]. Government Supervision of Representatives

Suppose, though, that * * * X has [someone] (R) to represent him, and that the government intervenes only to assure that R acts in a way that is objectively good for X. I have already discussed in Part III.B. a number of cases that correspond to this model. In dealing with incompetent patients whose wishes are unclear, the Supreme Court has allowed states to give life-sustaining treatment over the [family's] objection.[2] * * *

---

2. See *Cruzan [v. Director, Missouri Dept. of Health]*, 110 S.Ct. [2841,] 2855– 2856 [(1990)]. Alternatively, states can decide to give or withhold treatment accord-

What happens in these cases is that X has a representative (R) who is not the government, and R can choose some actions (x) on X's behalf. But the range of choices open to R is restricted to what is objectively good, as defined by a 'best interests' or some similar standard. [Families] may be allowed to do x * * * but forbidden to do not-x: they may opt for continued treatment, * * * but not for death[.] Once again it becomes hard to talk about X's constitutional freedom as a relation of four variables (X, x, Y, y). By controlling R's discretion the government makes choices for X, and once again $x = y$.

* * *

V. Conclusion

I have argued that people who cannot act rationally are free in a constitutional sense when they have a representative to choose for them. It is inconsistent with the idea of freedom for the government to act as a representative or to supervise a representative's choices. The Constitution requires, as a general rule, that the government withdraw from these cases. This is not a radical proposition. It simply commits those who are not competent to the care of their families rather than the state.

I do not mean to idealize familial relations beyond the limits that the data support. I recognize, as anyone must, that there are [family members who have no love for one another], and whose choices can be callous, selfish, or downright evil. In such cases we should disqualify [them] as proper representatives and override their choices. In the terminology of the legal rules that we apply to claims about freedom, we would say of such cases that there is a compelling state interest in overriding X's claim to freedom. But that is not inconsistent with my argument. X, though better off, is not free.

NANCY K. RHODEN, LITIGATING LIFE AND DEATH

102 Harv.L.Rev. 375, 380, 384–394 (1988).

A. The Paradigm of the Incompetent's "Rights"

* * *

The legal paradigm * * * holds that the justification for stopping treatment for incompetents—self-determination—is the same as for competent patients; it merely must be implemented differently. Where incompetents are concerned, family members must prove that termination is what the patient would choose. It is easy to see why courts have taken this approach: a constitutional right of families to decide these issues has never been recognized, and without hearkening back to the patient's right to privacy, a decision to terminate treatment, no matter how reasonable, appears to lack legal justification. Nonetheless, this approach creates certain conceptual problems.

ing to their assessment of the patient's 'best interests.' *Id.* at 2848–2849; *Matter* of *Conroy,* 486 A.2d [1209,] 1231 [(N.J. 1985)].

B. Obvious Limitations of This Paradigm

Even supporters of the incompetent's "right" to choose must recognize that this approach has its limitations. A case that exceeded such limits was *Saikewicz,* in which the issue was whether Mr. Saikewicz, a sixty-seven-year-old, profoundly retarded state hospital patient with leukemia, should be given chemotherapy. Even with the proposed treatment, his prognosis was grim—a thirty to fifty percent chance of a brief remission.[46] The chemotherapy would cause pain, nausea, and vomiting, and because Mr. Saikewicz would not understand its purpose, he might perceive it as torture and would probably have to be restrained. The *Saikewicz* court reached the perfectly reasonable, albeit not uncontroversial, conclusion that even though most people would choose the chemotherapy, the treatment's severe limitations, combined with the patient's inability to understand the reason for the pain, made withholding chemotherapy appropriate. The perceived need for a rights-based justification, however, led the *Saikewicz* court to articulate the following rather remarkable statement of the standard for decision:

> In short, the decision in cases such as this should be that which would be made by the incompetent person, if that person were competent, but taking into account the present and future incompetency of the individual as one of the factors which would necessarily enter into the decision-making process of the competent person.

Criticism of this convoluted counterfactual legal standard abounds, and borders on ridicule. John Arras has called it the "bioethical equivalent of squaring the circle." In *In re Storar,*[51] another court faced with a treatment decision for a profoundly retarded, nonverbal patient said that asking what the patient would want if he could, for a miraculous moment, comprehend his plight, would be like asking, " '[I]f it snowed all summer would it then be winter?' " * * * [T]he miraculously lucid Mr. Saikewicz would not be Mr. Saikewicz at all. He would be someone else entirely—a person who could comprehend complex medical and moral dilemmas. The *Saikewicz* opinion is indeed an apt target for ridicule. It should be noted, however, that this is only because the court was following the judicial inclination to equate incompetents with competents to its logical—if incoherent—extension.

* * *

A proponent of the rights paradigm might respond that, although Mr. Saikewicz lacked capacity to choose, and thus was not exactly like competent or previously competent patients, it is still perfectly sensible to hold that a proxy may exercise Mr. Saikewicz's right of self-determination. After all, because it is generally agreed that all humans have a right to life, if someone were simply proposing to kill Mr. Saikewicz, we would correctly say that a guardian who objected was protecting Mr.

---

46. [*Superintendent of Belchertown State School v. Saikewicz,* 373 Mass. 728, 370 N.E.2d 417 (1977).]

51. 52 N.Y.2d 353, 420 N.E.2d 64 (1981).

Saikewicz's right to life. This response, however, simply does not work in cases like *Saikewicz*. Deciding whether Mr. Saikewicz should have been treated was not as simple as deciding to protect an incompetent's right to life, because the issue posed was one about which reasonable people could differ. The right in question was thus not the right to have one thing or another done, but the right to choose.

* * * A person can certainly have the right to do something she is incapable of doing successfully—such as sinking every basket she shoots—or at least can have a right to try. Yet it seems very odd, and certainly not helpful, to attribute to her a right to do something for which she lacks all capacity. The quadriplegic's freedom from external restraint against sinking baskets does not give her a meaningful right to sink them. Moreover, it is no solution to hold that a personal right requiring cognitive capacity—like a right of choice—can be exercised for the incompetent by someone else. Such a theory would make it perfectly sensible to claim that my cat has a right to choose where we live, and that I simply exercise it for her, as a caring, responsible proxy. In cases such as *Saikewicz,* it is unavoidable that a proxy must make the choice. Yet it is misleading to justify or characterize that act as proxy implementation of a right to choose, much as it would be misleading to say that a social worker assigned to bring a profoundly retarded person to some church or other is exercising the incompetent's "right" to freedom of religion. In these cases the proxy must simply decide, making the best decision she can.

C. Less Obvious Limitations of the Paradigm

Cases involving patients who never had rational, developed value systems into which proxies could delve are, of course, the ones for which the rights-paradigm seems the most implausible. Persons who were never competent are radically and inescapably unlike competent persons. Indeed, later decisions such as *In re Conroy* have admitted that the subjective test may be unworkable for such patients and that decisions made for them cannot be justified by reference to the right of self-determination.[58] The *Conroy* court, however, adhered to the view that, when there is clear proof of a formerly competent patient's probable desires, the subjective test can be seen as implementing the patient's right to self-determination. We must, however, distinguish between a proxy's acting upon a perceived preference and actually implementing an expressed choice.

Morally speaking, acting on the basis of even quite clear desires is not the same thing as obeying a living will and implementing the patient's choice. Perhaps an example will make this clear. Inmates on death row have a right to choose what they want to eat for their final dinner. Suppose inmate *A* specifically requests steak, french fries, and a chocolate shake. The prison chef, however, believes that a macrobiotic diet is far more healthful, and brings *A* his tastiest concoction of rice, wheatberries, and tofu. Despite the delicacy of the fare, *A*'s right to

---

58. [98 N.J. 321, 486 A.2d 1209 (1985).]

choose has been infringed. However, suppose inmate *B,* whose dietary inclinations and execution date are identical to *A*'s, is busy doing other things and forgets to put in his dinner request. Although the chef is well aware of *B*'s preferences, he brings him the macrobiotic dinner as well. The chef has certainly not made the most kind or considerate choice. But has he violated *B*'s rights? It seems not, inasmuch as *B* never explicitly made a choice. Moreover, had the chef brought *B* a juicy steak, we would say that he made a compassionate choice, even the right choice, but not that he satisfied *B*'s rights.

Treatment decisions are no different. The competent person who leaves no clear directives cannot claim a right that her wishes, imagined or extrapolated, be followed. * * * [A] proxy who implements a patient's prior choice exercises the patient's right to choose, whereas one who bases a decision on the patient's preferences does something that cannot be characterized in precisely the same way.

One might ask why this matters. After all, if there is clear proof of the patient's desires * * * a proxy should act upon them, even though her action is not rights-based in the same way as obeying a living will. This is true, but there are several problems with hearkening back to rights and requiring, even if only verbally, clear proof of what the patient would want. The problems all center around the fact that courts require a higher quantum of justification than is typically available, and are led to write opinions that misleadingly imply that such a justification is possible. In so doing, they again downplay the important differences between competent and incompetent patients: formerly competent patients differ from never-competent ones, but if they never expressed a choice, they also differ significantly from competent patients and from formerly competent patients who did make their choices known.

1. The Evidentiary Standard.—The *Conroy* court insisted that the subjective test requires clear proof of a formerly competent patient's desires. Ms. Conroy had made no specific statements about how she wanted to be treated. She had, however, avoided doctors, refused to sign herself into an emergency room, and expressed a desire to die in her own house. Although these facts did not satisfy the subjective test, *Conroy* erected no insuperable barriers to meeting the test when the patient has made no specific statements on the topic. Indeed, not only did the *Conroy* court permit inferences from such things as religious beliefs and prior medical practices, but it also said that Ms. Conroy's guardian should, for example, have investigated her responses to such things as the illnesses and deaths of her sisters and others.

* * * Yet the stringency of the *Conroy* court's evidentiary standard seems fundamentally incompatible with using someone's views about life, the afterlife, and the illnesses of others to prove her intent. By nature, inferences from this type of evidence cannot lead to the clear, unambiguous proof required by the *Conroy* court's subjective test. Ms. Conroy was independent, a trait various decisions have relied on to

Garvey,Mod.Const.Theory 3E—23

support their judgments that patients would have chosen to have treatment terminated. But are independent people necessarily less tenacious in clinging to life? And what if the patient was a timorous, dependent soul? Would this clearly imply a preference for nonsentient life? Suppose Claire Conroy had nursed her sisters, sadly mourned their passing, and said she wished they had not died so soon? Would this suggest she wished to linger on in her current state? Alternatively, what if she had called someone's sudden death a blessing? Would this suggest that she would also want to go quickly? Or is viewing another's rapid demise as a blessing simply too far removed from seeing your own death as one? * * * In sum, little other than explicit statements for or against termination seems more than mildly inferential in these cases. It is reassuring to believe that Ms. Conroy would view her life as being as intolerable as those around her saw it. Absent explicit prior statements, however, the problems in applying the subjective standard to formerly competent patients mirror, albeit in a milder form, the problems that arise when the patient was never competent. It seems that the stringent evidentiary standard, although reassuring, is often impossible to meet, even when available evidence points to nontreatment as a perfectly reasonable course of action.

2. *The Need for Proxy Interpretation.*—The problem of proving a patient's intent under *Conroy*'s subjective standard is closely connected to the problem of determining how relatives "know" what the patient would want in the absence of clear prior statements, and how this knowledge is influenced by the relatives' own values and beliefs. I am not expressing skepticism here about a family member's knowledge: the loving wife of forty years who says she *just knows* her husband would not want further treatment is probably right. Yet her knowledge may largely be of an intuitive, nonverbal sort that is difficult to translate into clear proof in a court of law. Moreover, the wife may, quite reasonably, be unable to view her husband as entirely separate from herself, or his interests and values as entirely independent of hers. * * *

* * *

What all this means is that, although a decision to terminate can be shown to be congruent with the patient's former values and psychological traits, it is unlikely, absent specific statements, that the family can prove to outsiders that these patient characteristics clearly mandate such a choice. Absent prior directives, decisions are not, properly speaking, rights-based. Nor are they likely to be demonstrably "right" to objective third parties unconnected to the patient. To someone who lacks intuitive knowledge of the patient, such a subjective test will seldom go further than yielding answers that seem reasonable, or perhaps more reasonable than the alternatives.

RONALD DWORKIN, THE RIGHT TO DEATH
N.Y.Rev. of Books 14–17 (Jan. 31, 1991).

[In *Cruzan v. Director, Missouri Department of Health* Justice Rehnquist] offered two different, though not clearly distinct, arguments why Missouri has a right to tip the scales in favor of keeping comatose people alive by demanding "clear and convincing" evidence that they had decided they would rather die. His first argument appealed to the best interests of incompetent people. He said that a rule requiring evidence of a formal declaration of a past decision to die, before life support can be terminated, benefits people who have become comatose because it protects them against guardians who abuse their trust, and because a decision not to terminate is always reversible if documented evidence of a formal past decision emerges later. His second argument is very different: it appeals not to the interests of comatose patients but to Missouri's supposed independent interests in keeping such patients alive.
* * *

* * *

Rehnquist devotes most of his opinion to the first argument: that the Missouri rule is in the best interests of most of the thousands of people who live in a permanent vegetative state and did not sign living wills when they could. * * *

* * *

[But] the insensate life of the permanently vegetative * * * is not valuable to anyone. Some people, no doubt, would want to be kept alive indefinitely in such a state out of religious convictions: they might think that failing to prolong life as long as possible is insulting to God, for example. But even they do not think that it is in *their* interests to live on; most such people would hope, I think, for an early death in that situation, though one in which everything had been done to prolong life. They would regard an early death as an instance of God's mercy.

* * *

Some of Rehnquist's arguments depend not on the assumption that it is normally in the interests of a permanently comatose person to continue living, but on the equally implausible assumption that continued life in those circumstances is never against such a person's interests. This is the premise of his argument, for example, that it is better to keep a comatose patient alive than to allow her to die, even if the chances of recovery are infinitesimal, because the latter decision is irreversible. He assumes that someone in Nancy Cruzan's position suffers no disadvantage in continuing to live, so that if there is only the barest conceivable possibility of some extraordinary medical discovery in the future, however remote that may seem now, it must be on balance in their interests to continue living as long as possible.

If the only things people worried about, or wanted to avoid, were pain and other unpleasant physical experiences, then of course they would be indifferent about whether, if they became permanently comatose, their bodies continued to live or not. But people care about many other things as well. They worry about their dignity and integrity, and about the view other people have of them, how they are conceived and remembered. Many of them are anxious that their relatives and friends not have to bear the burdens, whether emotional or financial, of keeping them alive. Many are appalled by the thought of resources being wasted on them that might be used for the benefit of other people, who have genuine, conscious lives to lead.

These various concerns explain the horror so many people feel at the idea of existing pointlessly for years as a vegetable. They think that a bare biological existence, with no intelligence or sensibility or sensation, is not a matter of indifference, but something bad for them, something that damages their lives considered as a whole. * * *

* * *

We must therefore turn to Rehnquist's second, much less developed, argument: that Missouri can impose evidentiary requirements, even if that is against Cruzan's interests and those of other permanently incompetent people, in order to protect its own interests in preserving life. * * *

* * *

* * * Of course government is properly concerned with the welfare and well-being of its citizens, and it has the right, for that reason, to try to prevent them from being killed or put at risk of death from disease or accident. But the state's obvious and general concern with its citizen's well-being does not give it a reason to preserve someone's life when his or her welfare would be better served by being permitted to die in dignity. So the state interest that Rehnquist has in mind, as justifying Missouri's otherwise unreasonable evidentiary rule, must be a different, less familiar, one: it must supply a reason for forcing people to accept medical treatment when they or their guardians plausibly think they would be better off dead.

* * *

* * * It might be said that keeping people alive, even when they would be better off dead, helps to protect the community's sense of the importance of life. I agree that society is better and more secure when its members share a sense that human life is sacred, and that no effort should be spared to save lives. People who lack that sense may themselves be more ready to kill, and will be less anxious to make sacrifices to protect the lives of others. That seems to me the most powerful available argument why states should be permitted to outlaw elective abortion of very late-stage fetuses, for example. But it is extremely implausible that allowing a permanently comatose patient to die, after a

solemn proceeding devoted only to her wishes and interests, will in any way erode a community's sense of the importance of life.

So a state cannot justify keeping comatose people alive on the instrumental ground that this is necessary to prevent murder or to encourage people to vote for famine relief. If Rehnquist is right that a state has a legitimate interest in preserving all human life, then this must be in virtue not of any instrumental argument but of the *intrinsic* value of such life, its importance for its own sake. Most people do believe that human life has intrinsic importance, and perhaps Rehnquist thinks it unnecessary either to clarify or to justify that idea. It is unclear, however, that they accept the idea on any ground, or in any sense, that supports his case. For some people, for example, life has intrinsic value because it is a gift of God; they believe, as I said, that it is wrong not to struggle to prolong life, because this is an insult to Him, who alone should decide when life ends. But the Constitution does not allow states to justify policy on grounds of religious doctrine; some more secular account of the intrinsic value of life would be needed to support Rehnquist's second argument.

It will be helpful to distinguish two forms that a more secular version of the claim might take. The first supposes that a human life, in any form or circumstance, is a unique and valuable addition to the universe, so that the stock of value is needlessly diminished when any life is shorter than it might be. That does not seem a convincing view. Even if we think that a conscious, reflective, engaged human life is inherently valuable, we might well doubt that an insensate, vegetative life has any value at all.

The view that all forms of life are inherently valuable is also disqualified for a different reason. On that view we would have as much reason to bring new lives into being, increasing the population, as for prolonging lives already in progress. After all, people who think that great art is inherently valuable have the same reason for encouraging the production of more masterpieces as for preserving art that now exists. But most people who think life has intrinsic significance do not think that they therefore have any general duty to procreate or to encourage procreation. In any case, the Supreme Court's decision in *Griswold,* which is now accepted by almost everyone, holds that the states have no power to prohibit contraception.

People who think that life has intrinsic value or importance, but do not think that this fact offers any reason for increasing the population, understand life's value in a second and more conditional way. They mean, I think, that once a human life has begun it is terribly important that it go well, that it be a good rather than a bad life, a successful rather than a wasted one. Most people accept that human life has inherent importance in that sense. That explains why they try not just to make their lives pleasant but to give them worth and also why it seems a tragedy when people decide, late in life, that they can take neither pride nor satisfaction in the way they have lived. Of course nothing in the idea that life has intrinsic importance in this second sense can justify a policy of keeping permanently comatose people alive. The worth of their lives—the character of the lives they have led—cannot be improved just by keeping the bodies they used to inhabit technically alive. On the contrary, that makes their lives worse, because it is a bad thing, for all the reasons I described earlier, to have one's body medicated, fed, and groomed, as an object of pointless and degrading solicitude, after one's mind is dead. Rehnquist's second argument is therefore a dramatic failure: Missouri's policy is not supported but condemned by the idea that human life is important for its own sake, on the only understanding of that idea that is available in our constitutional system.

YALE KAMISAR, WHEN IS THERE A CONSTITUTIONAL "RIGHT TO DIE"? WHEN IS THERE NO CONSTITUTIONAL "RIGHT TO LIVE"?
25 Ga.L.Rev. 1203, 1205–1211, 1219–1224 (1991).

As many good liberals have done in other settings, I shall make the "slippery slope" argument in the euthanasia context. But I shall not be content with that. I think I can do better. Three eventful decades have passed since Glanville Williams' highly influential book,[11] one that may be said to have launched the modern era of the euthanasia movement, first evoked my interest in the general subject. In that time, I think I can show, we have moved down the slippery slope a considerable distance; we have seen the slippery slope.

On rereading Williams' 1957 book recently, I was struck by the fact that with the passage of years most of the restrictions or conditions he prescribed for euthanasia have faded away. * * * Williams began his chapter on euthanasia as follows:

> Whatever opinion may be taken on the general subject of suicide, it has long seemed to some people that euthanasia, the merciful extinction of life, is morally permissible and indeed mandatory where it is performed upon [1] a dying patient [2] with his consent and [3] is the only way of relieving his suffering. According to this view, which will be accepted in the present chapter, a man is entitled to demand the release of death from hopeless and helpless pain, and a physician who gives this release is entitled to moral and legal absolution for his act.

A. RELIEVING THE PATIENT'S SUFFERING

Until recently, it could be said that "[m]ercy for the suffering patient has been the primary reason given by those [favoring] ... a limited form of euthanasia."[18] But that can no longer be said—as evidenced by the two landmark "right to die" cases of our time: *In re*

---

11. G. Williams, [The Sanctity of Life and the Criminal Law (1957).]

18. Bok, *Euthanasia and the Care of the Dying,* in The Dilemmas of Euthanasia 2 (1975).

Quinlan[19] and *Cruzan v. Director, Missouri Department of Health.*[20] There was no evidence that either Karen Ann Quinlan or Nancy Beth Cruzan was suffering any pain. (It is plain, of course, that their families did suffer considerable pain.)

* * *

B. THE REQUEST OR CONSENT OF THE PATIENT
* * *

Although the *Quinlan* case was widely reported and discussed as a "right to die" case, Karen Ann Quinlan lacked the capacity to request anything. She did not (and in her condition, of course, could not) consent to her death or ask anyone to let her die. Nor had she made a living will or executed any other directive requesting that she be allowed to die without medical intervention. Indeed—although this feature of the case went largely unreported—both the trial court and the Supreme Court of New Jersey agreed that Karen's previous conversations with friends on this general subject were so "remote and impersonal" as to lack "significant probative weight."

Nancy Cruzan's views, when still a vibrant person, on whether and when life-sustaining treatment should be withdrawn is a matter of some dispute. * * * In some conversations with friends, Nancy indicated that "if sick or injured she would not wish to continue her life unless she could live at least halfway normally," but these conversations "did not deal in terms with withdrawal of medical treatment or of hydration and nutrition."

Different people will assign different weight to Nancy's conversations with her friends. But whatever one makes of these conversations, I think it fair to say that they fall well short of the unequivocal consent or explicit request that yesteryear's proponents of voluntary euthanasia had in mind.

C. A "DYING" OR "TERMINALLY ILL" PATIENT

Recall another limitation on Glanville Williams' euthanasia proposal—that the patient be "dying" or "terminally ill." There is a good deal of confusion on this point. Many people would say—indeed, did say— that at the time of the litigation both Nancy and Karen *were* "dying" or "terminally ill." I think not—not as these terms have usually been defined.

* * *

Karen Ann Quinlan probably could have been kept alive for many years if her respirator had not been removed. Indeed, as many of you know, she stayed alive for nine years *after* the respirator was disconnected.

The view that all that was at stake was whether to drag out or cut short the "dying process" is even harder to sustain in the *Cruzan* case.

19. 70 N.J. 10, 355 A.2d 647 (1976). **20.** 110 S.Ct. 2841 (1990).

As the state supreme court, adopting many of the trial court's findings, described Nancy's condition: "She is not dead. She is not terminally ill. Medical experts testified that she could live another thirty years."

In general, living-will statutes provide that the directive only becomes operative after its maker has become "terminally ill." As many states, including Missouri, define this term, it means a condition that will shortly result in death *regardless* of the utilization of available medical treatment.

Because a "terminal illness" or "terminal condition" requirement greatly restricts the impact of living-will legislation, several states have recently adopted provisions defining a "terminal" condition as one that would cause death in the absence of medical intervention. This strikes me as going too far in the other direction. A *great many* illnesses would be "terminal" *without* medical treatment. Would anyone say that a pneumonia patient is in a "terminal" condition or that her death is "imminent" because she would die (assuming she would) *if* antibiotics were not available? I think most would respond: But antibiotics are available.

There *are* reasons to loosen or to wiggle out of the "dying" or "terminally ill" requirement. But there are also reasons to take the requirement seriously. If death is unpreventable—if the best medical treatment available can only postpone death for a short time—the interest in preserving life seems much weaker. Moreover, if life support is terminated in such a situation, it makes some sense to say that the underlying condition "caused" the death or that discontinuing life support *merely permits* death to occur or *only prevents* the "drawing out" of the death process. *Whether or not* life-sustaining procedures are utilized, the patient is going to die in a short time anyhow. When a patient, though, can be kept alive for many years it is much harder to avoid the conclusion that the removal of life support, rather than the patient's underlying illness, brought about the patient's death.

* * *

[In an] address to the British Medico–Legal Society, Glanville Williams * * * alluded to another distinction that had it origins in [Roman Catholic] tradition, that between "extraordinary" (or "heroic") and "ordinary" medical treatment.[67] What treatment *is* "extraordinary"? It soon became clear that little, if anything, turned on the *type* of medical treatment *in the abstract* but much, if not everything, turned on the condition of a given patient. * * *

* * *

The extraordinary/ordinary means distinction has been widely criticized and is now widely rejected. I agree that the terms are so spongy and unilluminating and were used so loosely and inconsistently that there is little to be said for retaining them. But in their time, I think,

67. Williams, [*Euthanasia,* 41 Medico–Legal J. 14 (1973).]

these terms did more than generate confusion. I think they provided reassurance—reassurance that only certain kinds of lifesaving measures could be, and would be, terminated; that disconnecting an unconscious patient's respirator in some vague way only constituted a "slight deviation" from our official morality[.]

Yes, the time has come to say good riddance to the extraordinary/ordinary means doctrine. But over the years these terms have done their work. Their very vagueness seduced not a few—and, if I may say so, greased the slippery slope.

[D.] THE RESPIRATOR VS. THE FEEDING TUBE

As we all know, Karen Ann Quinlan's parents sought, and eventually obtained, permission to remove their comatose daughter from the respirator. But it is worth recalling that, probably because they viewed feeding as "natural" or "basic" or "ordinary" care, Karen's parents did not request permission to remove the feeding tube that was to keep their daughter alive for another nine years. Indeed, Karen's father voiced surprise when asked when he wanted the feeding tube disconnected, replying, "Oh, no, that is her nourishment." Nor did Karen's parents object when, some months after the case was decided, the director of the nursing home where Karen had been moved told them: "I can't see pulling out a feeding tube * * * because that is not a nice way to die, starving and wasting away over a period of weeks."

If the Quinlans had sought permission to remove Karen's feeding tube, they probably would have been rebuffed—even if they could have shown by clear and convincing evidence that this was their daughter's wish. For as recently as the early 1980s the idea that fluids and nutriment might be withdrawn from a comatose patient [was rejected by most health professionals.] But the views of health professionals have changed—and the law has moved—very quickly in the decade and a half since the *Quinlan* case was decided.

In 1983, a presidential commission found "no particular treatments—including such 'ordinary' hospital interventions as parenteral nutrition or hydration * * * to be universally warranted" and maintained that "[t]he sensitivities of the family and of care giving professionals" should determine whether or not permanently unconscious patients should be provided artificial feeding.[77] In 1986, the American Medical Association Council of Ethical and Judicial Affairs took the position that withholding or withdrawing artificially or technologically supplied nutrition or hydration should be evaluated according to the same standards applicable to other kinds of life-sustaining measures.[78]

* * *

77. [President's Commission for the Study of Ethical Problems in Medicine and Biomedical and Behavioral Research, Deciding to Forego Life–Sustaining Treatment 90, 190 (1983).]

78. American Med. Ass'n, Current Opinions of the Council on Ethics and Judicial Affairs § 2.18 (1986).

* * * Chief Justice Rehnquist, who wrote the majority opinion in *Cruzan*, drew no distinction between the feeding tube and other lifesaving measures. And concurring Justice O'Connor explicitly rejected any such distinction. As she saw it, the artificial provision of nutrition and hydration implicated the same liberty interests as did other medical interventions—"the liberty guaranteed by the Due Process Clause must protect, if it protects anything, an individual's deeply personal decision to reject medical treatment, including the artificial delivery of food and water."

BIBLIOGRAPHY

Beschle, *Autonomous Decisionmaking and Social Choice: Examining the "Right to Die"*, 77 Ky.L.J. 319 (1989).

Bopp & Avila, *The Due Process "Right to Life" in* Cruzan *and Its Impact on "Right-to-Die" Law*, 53 U.Pitt.L.Rev. 193 (1991).

Buchanan, *The Limits of Proxy Decision–Making*, in R. Sartorious, ed., PATERNALISM 153 (1983).

R. Burt, TAKING CARE OF STRANGERS, ch. 7 (1979).

Burt, *The Ideal of Community in the Work of the President's Commission*, 6 Cardozo L.Rev. 267 (1984).

D. Callahan, SETTING LIMITS: MEDICAL GOALS IN AN AGING SOCIETY (1987).

Emanuel, *A Communal Vision of Care for Incompetent Patients*, 17 Hastings Center Rep. 15 (1987).

Garvey, *Freedom and Choice in Constitutional Law*, 94 Harv.L.Rev. 1756 (1981).

Kadish, *Letting Patients Die: Legal and Moral Reflections*, 80 Calif.L.Rev. 857 (1992).

Mayo, *Constitutionalizing the "Right to Die"*, 49 Md.L.Rev. 103 (1990).

A. Meisel, THE RIGHT TO DIE (1989).

Minow, *Beyond State Intervention in the Family: For Baby Jane Doe*, 18 Mich.J.L.Rev. 933 (1985).

Mooney, *Deciding Not To Resuscitate Hospital Patients: Medical and Legal Perspectives*, 1986 U.Ill.L.Rev. 1025.

Note, *Developments in the Law—Medical Technology and the Law*, 103 Harv.L.Rev. 1519 (1990).

Note, *Physician–Assisted Suicide and the Right to Die with Assistance*, 105 Harv.L.Rev. 2021 (1992).

Note, *Proxy Decisionmaking for the Terminally Ill: The Virginia Approach*, 70 Va.L.Rev. 1269 (1984).

Note, *State Natural Death Acts: Illusory Protection of Individuals' Life–Sustaining Treatment Decisions*, 29 Harv.J.Legis. 175 (1992).

Note, *Voluntary Active Euthanasia for the Terminally Ill and the Constitutional Right to Privacy,* 69 Cornell L.Rev. 363 (1984).

Rachels, *Active and Passive Euthanasia,* 292 New Eng.J.Med. 78 (1975).

Rhoden, *The Limits of Legal Objectivity,* 68 N.C.L.Rev. 845 (1990).

Roach, *Paradox and Pandora's Box: The Tragedy of Current Right-to-Die Jurisprudence,* 25 U.Mich.J.L.Ref. 133 (1991).

Robertson, Cruzan *and the Constitutional Status of Nontreatment Decisions for Incompetent Patients,* 25 Ga.L.Rev. 1139 (1991).

O. Russell, FREEDOM TO DIE (2d ed. 1977).

Schneider, *Rights Discourse and Neonatal Euthanasia,* 76 Calif.L.Rev. 151 (1988).

Symposium, *Legal Issues Relating to the Elderly,* 42 Hastings L.J. 679 (1991).

Symposium, *Privacy and the Family in Medical Decisions,* 23 J.Family L. 173 (1984–85).

The President's Commission for the Study of Ethical Problems in Medicine and Biomedical and Behavioral Research, DECIDING TO FOREGO LIFE–SUSTAINING TREATMENT (1983).

Vance, *Autonomy's Paradox: Death, Fear, and Advance Directives,* 42 Mercer L.Rev. 1051 (1991).

J. Wilson, DEATH BY DECISION (1975).

Wreen, *Breathing a Little Life Into a Distinction,* 46 Phil.Stud. 395 (1984).

Chapter XI

THE PUBLIC–PRIVATE DISTINCTION

To speak very generally, in Constitutional Law we distinguish private from public actions in two different ways. The first such distinction is one that we dealt with at length in Chapter X: it holds that some actions are private as a matter of right. They are of no concern to the general public, and the Constitution puts them beyond the government's ability to regulate. The right to privacy protected in cases like *Roe v. Wade* and claimed in cases like *Bowers v. Hardwick* and *Cruzan* is the best illustration of privacy in this sense, but it is not the only example. Many people also think of religion as a private right protected by the Free Exercise Clause, and kept out of the public sphere by the Establishment Clause.

The second public-private distinction is the principal focus of this Chapter. A very large number of actions are private in the more modest sense that they are simply not regulated by the Constitution. These are not things that we have a right (in any strong sense) to do. The government could pass laws forbidding them. But if it does not we can do them without undermining any more fundamental constitutional principle. For example, if I own a deli the Constitution lets me be very selective in hiring a cook: I can discriminate on the basis of religion, gender, or race. Of course the government could pass a law requiring me to be more open-minded, but I have at least this degree of autonomy in running my private life: the default setting (as we might call it) is for freedom of association. Take another example. Broadcasters, unlike newspapers, do not have a First Amendment right to control their own affairs. But the Constitution at least permits them to do so—they can, for example, simply refuse to cover certain issues.[1] If the government wants to it can take away this freedom by making a law or regulation.[2] But once again the default setting is for private autonomy.

---

1. Columbia Broadcasting System, Inc. v. Democratic Nat'l Committee, 412 U.S. 94, 93 S.Ct. 2080, 36 L.Ed.2d 772 (1973).

2. Red Lion Broadcasting Co. v. FCC, 395 U.S. 367, 89 S.Ct. 1794, 23 L.Ed.2d 371 (1969).

These two senses of privacy—the strong and the weak—are obviously related. Both of them protect the intimacy of close relationships, autonomy in our personal lives, our ability to be selective and uninhibited in our friendships, and so on. One gives more protection than the other, but there is an obvious family resemblance. These are points that lawyers often overlook, however, because the two ideas have different textual origins and have developed historically in very different ways. Privacy in the strong sense is protected by a list of rights expressly stated (occasionally implied) in the original Constitution, and more especially in the Bill of Rights and other amendments. Privacy in the weak sense is the negative implication of all the clauses that impose constitutional duties on public authorities but not on other people. The First Amendment says that "Congress shall make no law" prohibiting religious freedom or abridging free speech. This permits the rest of us to do as we like. The Fourteenth Amendment says:

> *No State shall make or enforce any law* which shall abridge the privileges or immunities of citizens of the United States; *nor shall any State deprive* any person of life, liberty, or property, without due process of law; *nor deny* to any person within its jurisdiction the equal protection of the laws.

This implies that private actors pursuing their own ends can (at least as far as the Constitution is concerned) treat each other in ways the state can not. This is why lawyers call privacy in the weak sense the "state action" requirement—to signify that some parts of the Constitution regulate only the action of the state, and leave private actors alone.

In addition to having different textual origins the two senses of privacy have very different histories. The history of the first idea has been one of continual expansion. We tend to think that progress in Constitutional Law consists in the perpetual recognition of more and more rights, giving us ever more protection against government invasion of our private space. The chief reason Constitutional Law books are so fat is that they have tried to keep up with this expansion. The history of the second idea, by contrast, for a long time was one of continual contraction. The courts were willing to find state action at every turn— or to put it the other way around, they used the Constitution to regulate the behavior of private actors. With a little reflection we can see the reason for this apparently wayward behavior. People only lay claim to privacy in the weak sense when their interests conflict with those of people whose rights have a better pedigree. The Constitution permits me to run my deli as I choose; but it gives prospective employees a right to equal protection. It permits broadcasters to control the content of their programming; but it gives political parties a right to freedom of speech. The weak sphere of privacy is just a negative implication from clauses granting rights in the strong sense. So if there is any reason to think that the state has a hand in the activities of deli owners and broadcasters, they are likely to lose out in competition with constitutionally more favored claimants.

Most of the early cases of this kind dealt with race discrimination: the *White Primary Cases*,[3] *Shelley v. Kraemer*,[4] the *Girard College Case*,[5] *Burton v. Wilmington Parking Authority*,[6] *Evans v. Newton* [7] and *Evans v. Abney*,[8] *Reitman v. Mulkey*,[9] and *Moose Lodge No. 107 v. Irvis*.[10] Here the challenged behavior, though arguably private in the weak sense, was also reprehensible. And the challengers, if only they could show some reason to question the integrity of the public-private distinction, had the strongest kind of right to constitutional protection—the guarantee of the Equal Protection Clause. But most of these problems have since been addressed by legislation like the 1964 Civil Rights Act and its successors, which forbid discrimination in many of the areas where the Constitution was once invoked (employment, public accommodations, housing, voting, education, etc.). Nowadays challengers more often attack the public-private distinction in order to extend their rights to due process [11] or freedom of speech.[12] The fact that they have had a lower success rate than earlier claimants reminds us that there are privacy values at stake on both sides of the litigation.

A. STATE ACTION

The articles in this section deal with the legal attack on the second public-private distinction. As we mentioned above, that distinction is embodied in various constitutional clauses that regulate public but not private actors—the so-called state action limitation. Those who want to attack the public-private distinction have drawn attention to difficulties

3. Nixon v. Herndon, 273 U.S. 536, 47 S.Ct. 446, 71 L.Ed. 759 (1927); Nixon v. Condon, 286 U.S. 73, 52 S.Ct. 484, 76 L.Ed. 984 (1932); Grovey v. Townsend, 295 U.S. 45, 55 S.Ct. 622, 79 L.Ed. 1292 (1935); Smith v. Allwright, 321 U.S. 649, 64 S.Ct. 757, 88 L.Ed. 987 (1944); Terry v. Adams, 345 U.S. 461, 73 S.Ct. 809, 97 L.Ed. 1152 (1953).

4. 334 U.S. 1, 68 S.Ct. 836, 92 L.Ed. 1161 (1948).

5. Pennsylvania v. Board of Directors of City Trusts, 353 U.S. 230, 77 S.Ct. 806, 1 L.Ed.2d 792 (1957). See also Pennsylvania v. Brown, 392 F.2d 120 (3d Cir.1968), cert. denied 391 U.S. 921, 88 S.Ct. 1811, 20 L.Ed.2d 657 (1968).

6. 365 U.S. 715, 81 S.Ct. 856, 6 L.Ed.2d 45 (1961).

7. 382 U.S. 296, 86 S.Ct. 486, 15 L.Ed.2d 373 (1966).

8. 396 U.S. 435, 90 S.Ct. 628, 24 L.Ed.2d 634 (1970).

9. 387 U.S. 369, 87 S.Ct. 1627, 18 L.Ed.2d 830 (1967).

10. 407 U.S. 163, 92 S.Ct. 1965, 32 L.Ed.2d 627 (1972).

11. See, e.g., DeShaney v. Winnebago County Dept. of Social Services, 489 U.S. 189, 109 S.Ct. 998, 103 L.Ed.2d 249 (1989); NCAA v. Tarkanian, 488 U.S. 179, 109 S.Ct. 454, 102 L.Ed.2d 469 (1988); Tulsa Professional Collection Services, Inc. v. Pope, 485 U.S. 478, 108 S.Ct. 1340, 99 L.Ed.2d 565 (1988); Lugar v. Edmondson Oil Co., 457 U.S. 922, 102 S.Ct. 2744, 73 L.Ed.2d 482 (1982); Blum v. Yaretsky, 457 U.S. 991, 102 S.Ct. 2777, 73 L.Ed.2d 534 (1982); Flagg Bros., Inc. v. Brooks, 436 U.S. 149, 98 S.Ct. 1729, 56 L.Ed.2d 185 (1978); Jackson v. Metropolitan Edison Co., 419 U.S. 345, 95 S.Ct. 449, 42 L.Ed.2d 477 (1974).

12. San Francisco Arts & Athletics v. USOC, 483 U.S. 522, 107 S.Ct. 2971, 97 L.Ed.2d 427 (1987); Rendell–Baker v. Kohn, 457 U.S. 830, 102 S.Ct. 2764, 73 L.Ed.2d 418 (1982); Hudgens v. NLRB, 424 U.S. 507, 96 S.Ct. 1029, 47 L.Ed.2d 196 (1976); CBS v. Democratic National Committee, 412 U.S. 94, 93 S.Ct. 2080, 36 L.Ed.2d 772 (1973); Lloyd Corporation v. Tanner, 407 U.S. 551, 92 S.Ct. 2219, 33 L.Ed.2d 131 (1972); Amalgamated Food Employees Union v. Logan Valley Plaza, 391 U.S. 308, 88 S.Ct. 1601, 20 L.Ed.2d 603 (1968).

with both parts of this phrase. Some of our problems center about the meaning of the word "state." Others concern the word "action." [13]

1. "STATE"

Take first the word "state." What do we mean when we say that "the state" has acted? Suppose Kentucky passes a law abolishing the tort of defamation for public figures. (This gives speakers more protection than does the First Amendment, which only abolishes defamation without malice.) And suppose now that the Lexington police chief arrests me for saying things about him that are nasty but true. Or suppose that a state trial court awards the chief damages for what I said. Who represents Kentucky in these hypotheticals—the legislature, or the police and the court? There are two good reasons for saying that the real state action is the action of the legislature. One is that state law makes the legislature the supreme authority on most questions. The police chief and the court are acting illegally under Kentucky law. If we give the state legal system a chance to work it will ultimately repudiate their actions. The other reason is that the Constitution seems to require it. The First Amendment says that "Congress shall make no law * * * abridging the freedom of speech." It is addressed to Congress, not the President or the courts. And it forbids lawmaking (the sort of thing legislatures do), not arrests or trials. If we extend this prohibition to the states (by incorporation), we should probably observe a comparable limitation there.

This is the place where the state action limitation first broke down. In 1913 the Supreme Court held that state action was not limited to lawmaking: it included all kinds of acts by government officials, even those that violated state law.[14] About fifty years later the Court held that the federal courts had not only constitutional but also statutory authority to deal with such acts. That is the meaning of *Monroe v. Pape*,[15] which lets people sue for lawless official action under 42 U.S.C. § 1983. Richard Kay argues that this extension was a mistake: the Constitution should apply only to lawmakers, not to public officials who violate the law (and certainly not to private individuals). The reason should be fairly obvious. Within our legal system every actor but one is subject to the control of ordinary law; the one exception is the lawmaker. (The term refers above all to the legislature. But it also includes the courts in their capacity as common law-makers, and the executive branch, when it is exercising constitutionally granted authority.)

Larry Alexander and Paul Horton respond that the lawmaker (or "legalist") model has several serious flaws. First, it is difficult to draw a line between "laws" and "other things." What about public officials who exercise discretion granted to them by statute? For that matter

---

13. For a fuller treatment of these points see John H. Garvey, *Private Power and the Constitution,* 10 Const.Comm. 301 (1993), from which some of this discussion is taken.

14. Home Telephone & Telegraph Co. v. City of Los Angeles, 227 U.S. 278, 33 S.Ct. 312, 57 L.Ed. 510 (1913).

15. 365 U.S. 167, 81 S.Ct. 473, 5 L.Ed.2d 492 (1961).

what about private citizens who make discretionary choices allowed to them by the law of property and contract? Second, how do we distinguish between acts that establish legal norms and acts that transgress them? Think about the trial court injunction in *Walker v. Birmingham*:[16] that order conflicted with the First Amendment, but the Supreme Court held that it had to be obeyed until it was overturned on direct appeal. These problems do not necessarily mean that we should extend the Constitution to all public officials, or to private actors. Alexander and Horton foresee other, equally serious, problems with those solutions.

Akhil Amar and Daniel Widawsky remind us that some parts of the Constitution speak directly to private actors—they have no state action limitation. One of these is the Thirteenth Amendment, which abolishes slavery. Amar and Widawsky suggest that we might invoke this rule to deal with "private" domestic violence in cases like *DeShaney v. Winnebago County Department of Social Services*.[17]

RICHARD S. KAY, THE STATE ACTION DOCTRINE, THE PUBLIC–PRIVATE DISTINCTION, AND THE INDEPENDENCE OF CONSTITUTIONAL LAW
10 Const. Comm. 329, 342–46, 351–53 (1993).

Logic, we have seen, carried to its conclusion demands that the Constitution apply to everything if it is to apply to anything.   * * *
[But] [i]t simply is not credible that the enactors of the Constitution believed that they were setting up rules to govern all human conduct. They were not interested in creating ideal conceptual categories but in a practical specification of regulated and prohibited activities. Few would argue with the general proposition that, at least in promulgating those rules of the Constitution whose text or history do not evince a broader intent, they were not concerned with every action prescribed or permitted by the state, but with the injuries that flowed from the positive employment of the unique power of the state.

It is consistent with this concern to suppose that, where its rules refer explicitly or implicitly to the state, the Constitution limits what may be called acts of *lawmaking*. I use the term "lawmaking" in a somewhat broader sense than it is usually employed. I mean acts stemming from decisions of human beings acting solely in the exercise of powers created by the Constitution or recognized by the Constitution as *already* possessing authority to prescribe rules of conduct binding on individuals. Put more concretely, in respect to the United States Constitution, this means acts of Congress and acts of the President in the attempted exercise of his constitutionally granted authority. It also means acts of the States, acting through the analogous public agents, under controlling state law.   * * *

16. 388 U.S. 307, 87 S.Ct. 1824, 18 L.Ed.2d 1210 (1967).

17. 489 U.S. 189, 109 S.Ct. 998, 103 L.Ed.2d 249 (1989).

Before elaborating the reasons that might move constitution-makers so to restrict their efforts, it might be useful to define with somewhat more detail what such a model would and would not cover. It would most obviously include statutes and explicit exercises of constitutionally vested executive powers. It would also extend to the rules promulgated by federal and state courts in the exercise of their common law powers.[49] (For reasons to be noted, however, this does not include the simple employment of *otherwise valid* rules of law by individuals.) It is fair to regard the creation of such rules as the exercise of the lawmaking power of the state. Since such rules are subject to revision and reversal by the legislature, they may, in fact, be regarded as a species of delegated legislation.

The amenability of lawmaking (as defined) to control by the rules of the Constitution carries it with the further conclusion that the actions of public officials acting pursuant to constitutionally contestable legislation is also subject to constitutional constraint. When the authorizing legislation is invalid the execution of its commands is naturally invalid. Even when the legislation merely creates a discretion that can be used in a way that violates the constitutional rules, it is reasonable to regard the authorizing legislation as invalid to the extent it provides the sole basis for the prohibited result.[50] What we are concerned with, in every case, are the *vires* of the institutions created by or recognized by the Constitution itself. That concern is implicated only by actions "having the cast of law."

The logic of this definition of the reach of the Constitution would exclude two kinds of actions often argued to be state action. First it would not extend the rules of the Constitution to actions by public officials *in violation* of ordinary law. Such actions would not be a consequence of any wrongful act by the lawmaking power, which is the sole concern of the Constitution. That lawmaking authority has been exercised in perfect conformity to constitutional rules and any relief for wrongs suffered may be addressed to the ordinary rules created by it. Those rules may or may not protect against some particular action or provide a remedy for injuries resulting from it. But if they do not, the wrong suffered, which by hypothesis arises in a regime of constitutionally perfect law, cannot implicate the special dangers to which the Constitution is addressed.

This conclusion, of course, is at odds with reasonably well established constitutional doctrine. For a brief period the Supreme Court flirted with the proposition that acts admittedly in violation of state law could not contravene the Fourteenth Amendment, not being acts "of the state." This doctrine seemed to have been announced by the Court in 1904 in *Barney v. City of New York*[53] but, after a brief period of

---

49. See, e.g., *American Fed. of Labor v. Swing*, 312 U.S. 321, 325–26 (1941).

50. See *Yick Wo v. Hopkins*, 118 U.S. 356, 366 (1886).

53. 193 U.S. 430 (1904).

indecision, was plainly, if not expressly, rejected in the 1913 decision in *Home Telephone and Telegraph Co. v. City of Los Angeles.*[54] The same view was maintained in more recent cases construing the reach of the post-Civil War civil rights statutes' specification of acts undertaken "under color of law" over dissents reiterating the reasoning of the repudiated doctrine of *Barney v. City of New York.*[55] Those dissents emphasized the danger of superimposing a more or less general federal tort and criminal jurisdiction on the law of the states. Such a result, the dissenters claimed, could be avoided by restricting the extraordinary reach of federal law, including the Constitution, to instances where the wrong had occurred as a result of the "authentic command of the State."

The second category of actions excluded from this limited class of public action subject to the rules of the Constitution would be conduct of private persons that is merely permitted by law. This category has proved to raise the most perplexing problems in testing the reach of the state action doctrine. Illustrative hypothetical cases cited in the literature include an individual, acting pursuant to common law rules of contract or property, discriminating on the basis of race in private social relations, firing an employee without notice or prohibiting speech on his or her own property.[58]

* * *

When we observe the character of a law-governed society, one in which the power of the state is principally exercised through the creation and enforcement of laws, the utility of a constitution specially designed to control lawmaking is evident. In an imagined anti-constitutional period, one where there is a legislative power but no constitution, the lawmaking power is, by definition, unlimited. The American constitution-makers lived at a time, and in a place, where the emerging view of the state was that it presented the risk of such an unlimited legislative power. Blackstone's *Commentaries,* published in the middle of the eighteenth century, cited Coke for the proposition that the jurisdiction of Parliament "is so transcendent and absolute, that it cannot be confined either for causes or persons, within any bounds." "What they [the Parliament] do," Blackstone asserted, "no authority upon earth can undo." It was, of course, the abuses of such an absolute concentration of power that spurred the colonists to revolution and they contested that omnipotence in theory as well as in arms. Although they sometimes premised the proper limits of the Parliament's authority on ideas of natural law or common law, by the time of the drafting of the Constitution the positivist conception of the state was sufficiently established

---

54. 227 U.S. 278 (1913). * * *

55. See *Screws v. United States,* 325 U.S. 91 (1945) and id. at 138 (Roberts, J., dissenting); *Monroe v. Pape,* 365 U.S. 167 (1961) and id. at 202 (Frankfurter, J., dissenting).

58. In such cases the permitted private decision might itself be called "lawmaking."

See [Larry Alexander and Paul Horton,] *Whom Does the Constitution Command?* [16 (1988).] Clearly the lawmaking to which I refer is that decisionmaking by people whose actions are immediately authorized by a constitution (state or federal) and that by people whose authority is solely traceable to such decisionmaking.

that the constitution-makers thought the lawmaking power should be controlled by the establishment and articulation of a special and superior kind of positive law, one grounded in the supreme political authority of "the People."

To a very significant extent, we share these conceptions of law and the state. For us, as for the Framers, there are no logical, inherent or pre-existing limits to the lawmaking power of the state. If this view predominates, it is plausible to see the state—in its capacity to make and enforce law—as a unique source of power and, therefore, as a unique center of danger. As an *empirical* matter, individuals may be faced with more serious threats from non-state sources, but the state as lawmaker is a source of power qualitatively different from any other in society (and, of course, the modern state is still, by any reckoning, a formidable source of worry). That is because it is by definition the only actor not subject to regulation by ordinary law. On this account it is reasonable to see the special function of the constitution as providing a law for the lawmaker, a law for that power which would otherwise be lawless.

It is for this reason that the two regimes of ordinary law and constitutional law should differ with respect to their subject matters. The ordinary law may reach any and every instance of human conduct. But, exactly because its potential reach is so extensive, the ordinary law needs to be subject to the second legal regime, that of the Constitution. It is perhaps an irony that the arguments against the limits created by the state action doctrine often focus on the fact that all ostensibly private conduct really has a public aspect since it might have been regulated by the state. It is exactly this otherwise omnipresent feature of ordinary law that demands the establishment of constitutional law for the special and limited purpose of controlling it.

The lawmaking authority is a power that stands in need of restraint. It is built into our idea of a society controlled by the rule of law that the legislature ought not be left to control itself. We presume that every human agency is subject to the defects of character that underlie the dictum of Lord Coke in *Dr. Bonham's Case* that no person may properly judge his or her own case and it is the unstated but essential premise of Marshall's judgment in *Marbury v. Madison*. Given the breadth and variety of the jurisdiction of the ordinary lawmaking regime, the injuries it might inflict are endless and, critically, the apparent justifications of public policy for such actions will often appear to have compelling force. Therefore, it makes sense to chart out with special clarity and special permanence the rules for exercising that power. The peculiar contribution a constitution makes to social well-being is the security it affords that the restless and threatening power of the state will be confined within knowable boundaries.

This picture of the relative roles of the separate regimes of ordinary and of constitutional law portrays a society in which every exercise of power but one is theoretically amenable to rule by law. For conduct generally, it is by the medium of the ordinary rules of law promulgated by lawmakers acting according to procedures, and within substantive limits, prescribed by the Constitution. For the force of lawmakers, it is by application of the rules of the Constitution especially created for that purpose. The only action not subject to legal control is the creation of the Constitution by the constituent power.

LARRY ALEXANDER & PAUL HORTON, WHOM DOES THE CONSTITUTION COMMAND?

6–7, 13–16, 19–20, 25–27, 29–30, 32–35, 89–90 (1988).

Whom does the Constitution command? Three general alternative answers to this question come immediately to mind:

1. The Constitution commands—imposes prescriptions upon—only those persons who are acting in the role of lawmakers within our federal system. (We will refer to this answer as the "Legalist model.")

2. The Constitution commands not only those persons who are acting in the role of lawmakers, but also a broader audience composed of persons who perform other governmental roles, imposing prescriptions upon them that are linked to their association with government. (We will refer to this answer as the "Governmental model.")

3. The Constitution commands more broadly still, imposing prescriptions upon each person within the jurisdiction of American law, so that each of us might sometime "violate" a constitutionally imposed prescription while acting in a purely private, nongovernmental capacity. (We will refer to this answer as the "Naturalist model.")

These three general answers may be conceived of as shown in Diagram 1.1.

DIAGRAM 1.1

THE AMBIT OF THE CONSTITUTION'S COMMANDS(?)

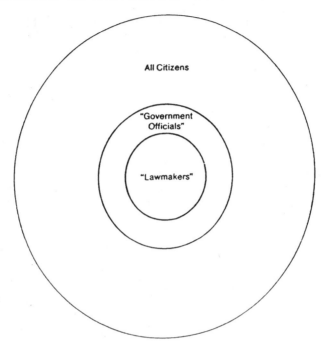

THE LEGALIST MODEL

The Legalist model is arguably in accord both with some common notions of what constitutions are about and with the assumptions of our Constitution's authors about the nature of their document. The premise of this model is that the focus of constitutional prescriptions is a sovereignty's legal regime. * * *

A "legal regime," for purposes of the Legalist model, is a sovereign's entire set of laws (excluding the Constitution itself), rather than any particular law within the set. [A] given sovereignty's legal regime includes not only the entire set of laws on its books—constitutional, statutory, administrative, judge-made—but includes as well the unwritten rules, policies, and practices by which the written laws are implemented and the resources allocated to their implementation. * * *

The characteristic of the Legalist model that is its strength is also its weakness. The Legalist model is characterized by the drawing of a solid line between "laws" (sets of laws, or legal regimes) and "other things." The line thus drawn, the model identifies the Constitution's referent to be "laws" and not "other things."

The problem, of course, is in the line drawing. What constitutes a "law" (set of laws, or legal regime) as opposed to an "other thing"? This problem reposes *within* the Legalist model itself; it must be resolved before the model can achieve cogency and internal consistency on its own terms. This central problem has many variants, some of which we briefly identify here[.]

* * *

What Counts for a "Law"?

* * *

Previously we suggested that, by referring to a government's entire legal regime, the Legalist model would incorporate within its ambit a wide variety of "laws": constitutional provisions, statutory enactments, administrative regulations, judge-made rules, and perhaps as well an indefinite array of unwritten rules, policies, and practices by which "recorded laws" are implemented. Such a broad definition of "laws," while perfectly understandable in the abstract and entirely consistent with honest employment of the Legalist model, creates havoc for the thoroughgoing Legalist's attempts at line drawing.

Suppose, for example, that a state statute gives an administrative official discretion to do either A or B as the situation warrants, and the official determines to "do A not B" in a particular situation. Is the determination to "do A not B"—or, indeed, to "do A not B in the particular situation"—to be included within, or to be excluded from, the concept of "laws" for purposes of the operation of the Legalist model?

A thoroughgoing Legalist would be concerned with such a question. If the tentative conclusion is that such exercises of administrative discretion count as "lawmaking"—and any other conclusion by a Legalist seems untenable to us—then the Legalist confronts a very basic difficulty in attempts to mark her model's boundary. Many—perhaps most—laws delegate discretion, not only to government officials, but also to private citizens. The "laws" we associate with "property" and "contract," for example, principally serve to define and channel private discretion. Is the exercise of this discretion—the "private ordering" that in its effects on others closely resembles the public ordering of law—"lawmaking"? If so, then the boundary between the Legalist and other models is seriously compromised. If not, then we need to know why not, how not, and when not; and any attempt to resolve this problem by resort to a model's need for clear boundaries is unlikely to assuage our need to know.

* * *

The Problem of "Inconsistent Laws"

* * *

In order to pretend to cogency, the Legalist model must identify the criteria by which acts by officials (or others) that *establish* legal norms are to be distinguished from acts by officials (or others) that *transgress* legal norms. Some such criteria undoubtedly will be provided within a particular legal regime: for example, by higher-level legal norms that are accepted by the officials (or others) themselves. These internal criteria comfortably will assist in the determination whether a particular act entails the establishment of a legal norm or the transgression of a preexisting legal norm. For constitutional purposes, however, the Legalist model demands its own criteria for making this determination;

otherwise unconstitutional transgressions (those that, according to the Legalist, relate to the establishment of legal norms) cannot clearly be distinguished from nonconstitutional transgressions (those that relate to the violation of legal norms that are themselves not unconstitutional). And precious little if anything within the Constitution itself, so far as we can tell, can be found to supply the Legalist with these criteria.

Consider the following examples that seem to entail this conceptual problem of characterizing acts of officials (and others) as "lawmaking" rather than as "illegal": acts that are legally proscribed and subject to sanction, but are not resistible by ordinary citizens; illegal, sanctionable, and perhaps completely resistible acts of officials who possess the "pretense" of authority for such acts; acts, such as erroneous lower court decisions, that are proscribed (by being reversible by higher authority) but are subject neither to sanction nor to resistance by ordinary citizens; acts of officials that are neither explicitly proscribed nor explicitly authorized but for which the state provides a damages remedy; acts of officials that are neither explicitly proscribed nor explicitly authorized and for which the state (permissibly) provides no damages remedy; and state laws that violate the state's own constitution (or other higher-order state laws) but that nevertheless are on the books.

* * *

The Naturalist Model

The Naturalist model produces a simple and direct answer to the question of whom the Constitution commands. Its answer is that the Constitution, which is the "supreme law of the land" in a society that draws no clear line between "law" and "other things," commands everyone within that society's jurisdiction. Such an answer, of course, avoids the difficulties that arise in attempts to create a more restricted audience for the Constitution's referent. In avoiding these difficulties, the Naturalist model poses a new set of difficulties that relate primarily to the maintenance of a federalist regime and of clear jurisdictional boundaries between state and federal governments.

According to the Naturalist model, the Constitution mandates, forbids, and permits various states of affairs, not just in the law itself, but also in the world that law governs. That is, the Constitution speaks directly to all acts, whether those acts amount to lawmaking or law applying, whether they can be acts that only governmental officials can commit, or otherwise.

According to other models for the Constitution's referent, the Constitution speaks only indirectly to acts undertaken by private citizens. That is so because the other models maintain the Constitution speaks only to the laws, or perhaps to laws and governmental officials, that in turn act on private citizens to mandate, prohibit, or permit "private acts." The Naturalist model rejects this two-step procedure. If an act, whether by an official or by a private citizen, violates a norm that the

Constitution prescribes, then the actor has engaged directly in a constitutional violation according to the Naturalist model.

Thus, if the Constitution requires that the states have laws against murder and theft, then it is so because acts of murder and theft are bad things constitutionally; and they would be bad things constitutionally regardless whether they were also made illegal under the (nonconstitutional) laws of the state. Or if the Constitution forbids that a state permit certain types of creditor repossession, then any act of creditor repossession within the constitutional prohibition, even if it happens also to be illegal under the laws of the state, amounts to a constitutional violation by the creditor.

* * *

The major difficulty with the Naturalist model lies in its conversion of every claim of illegality under state and local law into a federal constitutional claim, so long as the Constitution would proscribe a state's or local government's legalization of the act that is the subject of the claim.

Thus, suppose the contracts clause of the Constitution requires that the state must proscribe and provide a remedy for a private breach of contract, at least whenever the law of the state at the time of contracting proscribed breach and provided for a remedy. Or suppose the due process clause requires that a state must proscribe and provide a remedy for certain categories of injury-imposing acts by private citizens. On the Naturalist model, a promisor who breaches such a promise, or a private citizen who engages in such an injury-imposing act, has violated the Constitution in addition to having violated any law of the state and being subject to the state's remedial laws. On the Legalist model, by contrast, something unconstitutional has occurred only when the lawmakers have failed to proscribe and provide adequate remedies for the private acts; and it is only the lawmakers—and not the private individuals—who will be deemed to have acted unconstitutionally.

* * *

The Governmental Model
* * *

According to the Governmental model for the Constitution's referent, the Constitution is the highest level of legal norms, which operate, not just on lower-level legal norms (the Legalist model), but also on some of the nonlawmaking activities of persons who comprise "the government."

The Governmental model is distinguished from the Legalist model as follows. On the Legalist model, if all lower-level legal norms are in accord with the Constitution, then governmental officials (acting in their capacities as "lawmakers") have fulfilled their constitutional obligations; thereafter these and other governmental officials may very well act illegally, but their illegal acts do not amount to constitutional violations, since those acts are not "lawmaking." On the Governmental model, however, governmental officials perform various constitutionally relevant government functions besides simply "lawmaking"; and any act by a governmental official that [violates a law] would also be an unconstitutional act if it occurs while the official is acting within her "official capacity."

The Governmental model likewise is to be distinguished from the Naturalist model. Unlike the Naturalist model, the Governmental model maintains that an act committed by a private citizen (including a government official acting outside her "official capacity") is not an unconstitutional act, and hence not a constitutional violation[.]

* * *

What is "Acting in Official Capacity"?

Assume, for the benefit of the Governmental model, that we can stipulate who is, and who is not, a "government official." Most government officials are government officials only part of the time; the rest of the time they are spouses, parents, taxpayers, automobile drivers, Presbyterians, club and union members—in short, most of the time they are indistinguishable from "private citizens" even according to the Governmental model. According to the Governmental model, government officials may violate constitutional duties only while they are acting in their capacities as government officials; otherwise, they are ordinary folks who can only behave illegally, not unconstitutionally.

It follows that the Governmental model needs a good test by which to distinguish, not only between "government official" and "private citizen," but also between "government official acting in official capacity" and "government official not acting in official capacity." Various tests have been suggested in the case law and commentary for creating this distinction between "(unconstitutional) illegal acts by government officials (acting as government officials)" and "(nonconstitutional) illegal acts by private citizens (including government officials not acting as government officials)." These efforts all boil down to variants of three tests, none of which appears to be satisfactory in accomplishing its intended purpose.

"Pretense of authority." The first test may be labeled "pretense of authority." This test is traceable to Justice Douglas' statement in the majority opinion in *Screws v. United States* (1945): "It is clear that under 'color' of law means under 'pretense' of law."

* * *

[The fatal] problem with the "pretense" test is that its key is "pretense of authority" not "actual" even "implied" authority. The "pretense" test requires us to examine an illegal act's "officiality-hence-unconstitutionality" from the perspective of those to whom "pretense" appears—victims, onlookers, or strangers (like courts) looking back upon the transaction. The heavy implication is that government officials who are pretending to be private citizens while actually engaged in government business would not come under constitutional commands. The equally heavy implication is that nonofficials, pretending to be officials who are legally authorized to take the actions in question, *would* come under constitutional commands. After all, if "pretense" not "actual" authority is what matters for the Governmental model—as the "pretense of authority" test holds—then it would seem clearly to follow that a rapist who lures his victims by flashing a fake police badge would be the subject of constitutional commands, while a police officer who engages in illegal government surveillance while in plainclothes would be acting beyond the reach of those commands.

"Agency." The second test that has been suggested for purposes of "acting in official capacity" goes like this: A government official will be deemed to be subject to constitutional commands if her acts, despite being illegal, are within the scope of her government employment; and "scope of government employment" is defined according to the common law of agency.

One serious problem with "agency" as the measure of the Governmental model is that no principled test has yet been developed for determining when an agent who is disobeying her principal's orders is still acting on behalf of the principal. We doubt that such a test can be developed, largely because the underlying notion of a legally authorized yet illegal act is incoherent.

A second serious problem with the "agency" test is that its common law design is addressed primarily to questions of the principal's liability, not to questions whether the agent violated a command (constitutional or otherwise). By hypothesis, in most instances in which a government official has violated a constitutionally mandated law, the principal (the state) has not violated the Constitution; instead, it has enacted the law mandated by the Constitution that the agent has violated. The fact that, under agency doctrine, the state as principal might be vicariously liable on constitutional grounds does not prove—but rather assumes to be the case—that the agent was a constitutional duty bearer.

* * *

"Abuse of authority." The third test, which we shall label the "abuse of authority" test, derives from Chief Justice White's majority opinion in *Home Telephone & Telegraph Co. v. City of Los Angeles* (1913):

> [T]he settled construction of the [Fourteenth] Amendment is that it presupposes the possibility of an abuse by a state officer or representative of the powers possessed and deals with such a contingency. It provides, therefore, for a case where one who is in possession of state power uses that power to the doing of the wrongs which the Amendment forbids even though the consummation of the wrong may not be within the powers possessed if the commission of the wrong itself is rendered possible or is efficiently aided by the state

authority lodged in the wrongdoer. That is to say, the theory of the Amendment is that where an officer or other representative of a State in the exercise of the authority with which he is clothed misuses the power possessed to do a wrong forbidden by the Amendment, inquiry concerning whether the State has authorized the wrong is irrelevant and the Federal judicial power is competent to afford redress for the wrong by dealing with the officer and the result of his exertion of power.

* * *

In using the "made possible or is efficiently aided" language, Chief Justice White [was probably] asserting that acts of government officials have some presumptive legality under the law, even if those acts turn out to be illegal; and that this presumptive legality poses a special threat to constitutional values because it precludes citizens from resisting or ignoring such acts. After all, the Los Angeles ordinance at issue in *Home Telephone & Telegraph* (which set telephone rates), if in fact illegal under the California Constitution as alleged, *and if entitled to no presumption of legality,* could just as easily be ignored by the telephone company as could an "order" to lower telephone rates that was issued by a private citizen.

The problems with this form of the "abuse of authority" argument, however, are that it proves too little and proves too much. First, not all illegal acts of government officials carry some legal presumption of legality that makes them less easily resisted than ordinary illegal acts can be. Second, some illegal acts of nonofficials carry a similar legal presumption of legality.[14]

* * *

The Models Contrasted: A Prescriptive Epilogue

The purpose of this book has been primarily to *describe* the choice of models by which to answer the question of whom the Constitution commands. We have refrained, wherever possible, from attempting to *prescribe* the choice. When all is said and done, however, we can make explicit two points of comparison that carry heavy prescriptive implications:

> The Legalist model accords to the states—to their laws and to their courts—the greatest importance within the constitutional scheme, while the Naturalist model accords the least importance to the states.

> The Legalist model is a fully principled model. The Naturalist model, likewise, is a fully principled model. Choice between them is a choice of governing principles.

---

14. For example, the legal power of one wrongfully in possession to prevent self-help by the rightful owner can be viewed as analogous to the legal power of some officials to have their illegal acts treated differently from ordinary illegal acts.

The Governmental model is unprincipled; at best it represents an *ad hoc*—and ultimately unstable—compromise between the two more extreme yet principled models.

AKHIL REED AMAR AND DANIEL WIDAWSKY, CHILD ABUSE AS SLAVERY: A THIRTEENTH AMENDMENT RESPONSE TO *DeSHANEY*

105 Harv.L.Rev. 1359, 1360, 1363–1368, 1380 (1992).

In *DeShaney v. Winnebago County Department of Social Services,*[3] the Rehnquist Court held that the state of Wisconsin had no constitutional duty under the Due Process Clause of the Fourteenth Amendment to protect a young child [Joshua DeShaney] from his father's physical abuse. * * *

* * *

Joshua's attorneys did not assert a Thirteenth Amendment claim. But Justice Blackmun, in his passionate dissent in *DeShaney,* set the stage for such a claim when he compared the majority in *DeShaney* to "the antebellum judges who denied relief to fugitive slaves." The analogy between antebellum slavery and child abuse—an analogy that Justice Blackmun's provocative language invites but does not develop— seems both striking and fruitful. Consider the following preliminary analysis.

Like an antebellum slave, an abused child is subject to near total domination and degradation by another person, and is treated more as a possession than as a person. Unless the state acts to protect an abused child, the child's status bears an eerie resemblance to that of a pre-Civil War American slave. For example, if a child runs away, the state typically returns her to parental custody, just as antebellum judges returned fugitive slaves to their masters. And just as antebellum states enforced the legal rights of masters to physical control over their slaves, today's states continue to enforce the legal rights of parents to physical control over their children.

To be sure, it is unhelpful to conceptualize all children as slaves, for this conceptualization would imply that there is no difference between a free child and a slave child. But it would be equally unhelpful to categorically exempt all children from Thirteenth Amendment scrutiny, for that exemption, too, obscures the key difference between a free child and a slave child. Although virtually all children are in some form of parental "custody," custody alone should not be confused with slavery, at least when children are involved. Under ordinary circumstances, parental custody does not violate the Thirteenth Amendment because, it is presumed, the parent exercises control over the child in the interests of that child. But when a parent perverts this coercive authority by systematically abusing and degrading his ward—treating his child not as

3.   489 U.S. 189 (1989).

a person but as a chattel, acting as if he had title over the child rather than a trusteeship on behalf of the child—the parent violates the Thirteenth Amendment and should be subject to suit.

Whereas the Fourteenth Amendment applies only to state conduct, the Thirteenth applies to private conduct as well. The absence of a "state action" trigger in the Thirteenth Amendment does more than just allow the slave to bring suit against the private master; the Amendment's broad mandatory language that slavery "shall [not] exist" commands the state to affirmatively protect the child once it knows of concrete, identifiable, de facto slavery within its borders. To carry out this obligation, the state must enact and actively enforce child abuse laws within its jurisdiction. Thus, the Amendment prohibits both private action *and* state inaction whenever the state is aware of private slavery.

The state's affirmative obligation under the Amendment, however, would not unleash the parade of liability that troubled the *DeShaney* Court. Unlike a potentially unbounded substantive due process claim, a Thirteenth Amendment claim would not expose the state to liability for every private wrong. Under the Thirteenth Amendment, a state has an obligation only in concrete, identifiable cases of slavery or involuntary servitude—not in every case involving liberty or property.

* * *

But what, precisely, *is* "slavery"? For our purposes a good working definition of "slavery" is: "A power relation of domination, degradation, and subservience, in which human beings are treated as chattel, not persons." Implicit in this definition is a rejection of the idea that "slavery" depends necessarily on adulthood, biological otherness, race, forced labor, or state action. In other words, a person can be a Thirteenth Amendment "slave" whether or not she is a minor; whether or not the "master" is a blood relation of the "slave"; whether or not she has African roots; whether or not the enslavement takes the form of forced "labor"; and whether or not the enslavement is officially sanctioned by state law. Insofar as a child like Joshua is treated as chattel and subjected (legally or illegally) to domination and degradation by a parent, such a child—of any race—is guaranteed protection by both the literal terms and the underlying vision of the Thirteenth Amendment. Legislative history [and] judicial precedent * * * support this broad reading of the Amendment's letter and spirit.

A. Legislative History

The history of the Amendment makes clear that slavery was understood as intimately connected with issues of family servitude. Critics of slavery in the mid-nineteenth century repeatedly linked the "peculiar institution" with polygamy. For example, the Republican Platform of 1856 declared that "it is both the right and the imperative duty of Congress to prohibit in the Territories those twin relics of barbarism—Polygamy, and Slavery." * * *

The analogy between slavery and polygamy was neither casual nor merely an expedient political slogan designed to forge an alliance between anti-slavery and anti-Mormon voters. Rather, the analogy was a deep, almost literal, equation. Slavery in the antebellum South was itself a polygamy of sorts. As popular abolitionist tracts emphasized in graphic—almost lurid—terms, slavery gave white masters free sexual access to a virtual harem of black women slaves[.]

* * *

Thus, both supporters and opponents of slavery understood that the "peculiar institution" was tightly bound up with private and intimate relations between persons linked by sex and blood. Although such relations were centuries old, the Thirteenth Amendment broke sharply with custom insofar as custom condoned the condition of slavery. As one legislator noted, antiquity cannot justify a practice because antiquity, at one point, also practiced polygamy and cannibalism. To end slavery was thus to radically restructure this "private" sphere, and to reorder not simply the political and economic system but the social fabric as well. Accordingly, unlike virtually every earlier provision of the Constitution, the Thirteenth Amendment contained no state action requirement.

B. JUDICIAL INTERPRETATION

* * * When it first considered the Thirteenth Amendment in the *Slaughter–House Cases*,[29] the Court noted that the Amendment protects a class broader than African slaves: "[W]hile negro slavery alone was in the mind of the Congress which proposed the thirteenth article, it forbids any other kind of slavery, now or hereafter." The Court concluded that judges must look to the "pervading spirit" of the Civil War amendments when interpreting the terms "slavery" and "involuntary servitude."

The "pervading spirit" of the Thirteenth Amendment, as the Court explained a decade later, prohibits not only state action, but private action as well—private action either in conformity with or in violation of law. Thus, in the *Civil Rights Cases*,[32] the Court declared that "the Amendment is not a mere prohibition of state laws establishing or upholding slavery, but an absolute declaration that slavery or involuntary servitude shall not exist in any part of the United States." When one person enslaves another—whether or not the slavery is backed by the state—the Thirteenth Amendment's sweeping command that slavery "shall [not] exist" is violated.

* * *

Thus far, it might seem as if the Amendment creates a legal duty only on the part of the private master, and not the state. Such an

29. 83 U.S. (16 Wall.) 36 (1873).   **32.** 109 U.S. 3 (1883).

analysis overlooks the fact that the very idea of a private legal duty logically entails a governmental system to enforce that legal duty. A state must, for example, provide courts open to hear the required suits against masters. Hence, the broad command that slavery shall not exist does more than impose an absolute duty on private would-be enslavers; it also imposes a duty on the state to provide an adequate apparatus to enforce the emancipation of all persons within its jurisdiction. A state has considerable flexibility in discharging this obligation—for example, criminal punishment of enslavers is not constitutionally compelled—but the state may not simply turn a blind eye to slavery within its jurisdiction.

---

2. "ACTION"

Most efforts to break down the state action distinction have focused on the meaning of the word "action." Arguments of this kind assert that even if the Constitution applies only to state officials, we can find official influence almost anywhere, even in what we might think of as quintessentially private transactions. Two such arguments have been particularly influential. One (the "permission" argument) holds that the state acts by *allowing,* as much as by *requiring* or *forbidding,* private behavior. State action includes state inaction. This vision attributes to the state a kind of God-like omnipotence. Just as an omnipotent God should not allow the presence of evil in the world, so an omnipotent state should not allow private actors to violate one another's constitutional interests. The state of Wisconsin had reason to know that Joshua DeShaney's father was beating him senseless and permitted that action to go on. For that it is constitutionally responsible. The other argument (the "enforcement" argument) holds that in any event there is state action whenever courts enforce private common-law or statutory rights. When a judge enforces the common law of trespass to evict a Sikh from my yard, she is enforcing my private discrimination and making it her own.

Harold Horowitz uses the permission theory to show why there was state action in the *Civil Rights Cases* and in *Shelley v. Kraemer.* He adds that the existence of state action is only the first question in each case. We must then decide whether the state action is unconstitutional. In the first case it was not; in the second it was.

Jesse Choper charges that the permission and enforcement theories contradict a central feature of the Fourteenth Amendment. They take away from state authorities, and give to federal judges, the task of regulating private activity. This breaks down the public-private distinction. But it also increases the power of the federal government at the expense of the states, and so corrodes the principle of federalism.

HAROLD W. HOROWITZ, THE MISLEADING SEARCH FOR "STATE ACTION" UNDER THE FOURTEENTH AMENDMENT

30 S.Cal.L.Rev. 208–213 (1957).

The Fourteenth Amendment provides that no state shall "*deny* to any person within its jurisdiction the equal protection of the laws," nor "*deprive* any person of life, liberty, or property, without due process of law," nor "*make or enforce any law* which shall *abridge* the privileges or immunities of citizens of the United States." The principle was established in 1883, in the *Civil Rights Cases*,[2] that these provisions of the Fourteenth Amendment refer only to "state," as distinguished from "private," action. But the Supreme Court has in many situations applied the corollary principle that the constitutional restrictions on state action apply to the manner in which a state regulates legal relations between "private" persons.[3]

* * *

[W]henever, and however, a state gives legal consequences to transactions between private persons there is "state action"—*i.e.,* * * * the definition by a state of legal relations between private persons is, for the purposes of the Fourteenth Amendment, a matter of "state action." If *A* strikes *B,* and *B* sues *A* for damages, the problem is raised whether in the particular factual situation *A* had a duty not to strike *B* and *B* had a right that *A* not strike him. The law governing that right-duty relationship may perhaps be set forth in a legislative enactment, or it may be a common-law principle. The declaration of the *A–B* right-duty relationship by state statute or common law may in itself arguably constitute state action. But whether or not the mere "definition" of legal relations between *A* and *B,* before there has been a judgment of a court in a lawsuit between *A* and *B,* should be said to constitute state action, it is clear that if *B* sues *A* for damages in a state court, and wins, there has then been state action in adjudicating the legal relations between *A* and *B.* (This would be constitutional state action, for there would be no violation of any of the provisions of the Fourteenth Amendment in the creation and enforcement of this right-duty relationship.) What if it is determined in *B's* suit that because *A* was acting in self-defense *A* was therefore privileged under the circumstances to strike *B*—*i.e.,* that *A* did not have a duty not to strike *B,* that *B* did not have a right that *A* not strike him. The state court holds for *A.* Is there any less state action because *B* loses? It would seem clearly not. (And this, too, would be constitutional state action.) There is state action in the definition and enforcement of the right-duty relationship, and there is state action in adjudicating that there is no right-duty relationship. The result reached

---

2. 109 U.S. 3 (1883).

3. See, *e.g.,* Plessy v. Ferguson, 163 U.S. 537 (1896); Holden v. Hardy, 169 U.S. 366

(1898); Lochner v. New York, 198 U.S. 45 (1905); * * * Shelley v. Kraemer, 334 U.S. 1 (1948) * * *.

by the court on the merits is irrelevant insofar as the presence or absence of state action is concerned. When state law is applied to determine legal relations between private persons there is "state action."

* * *

I

The *Civil Rights Cases* set forth the basic distinction between "private" and "state" action under the Fourteenth Amendment—*i.e.*, that the Fourteenth Amendment imposes no limitations on "private" action. Because of the influence of the *Civil Rights Cases* on later decisions it is important to make clear, before turning to current problems, that there is no inconsistency between the "private"-"state" action distinction of the *Civil Rights Cases* and the often-applied principle that the Fourteenth Amendment imposes limits on the way in which a state can balance legal relations between private persons. An examination of the *Civil Rights Cases* will illustrate this point.

Congress enacted a statute which provided for civil and criminal liability of innkeepers, theatre owners, and operators of public conveyances who discriminated on the basis of race or color in the offering of their facilities to the public. The defendants in the *Civil Rights Cases* were prosecuted for violating this statute. The basis in the Constitution for this legislation was the provision of the Fourteenth Amendment empowering Congress "to enforce, by appropriate legislation, the provisions of this article." [6] The validity of the act of Congress turned on whether there was a violation of the Amendment toward which the legislation was directed. More specifically, did this legislation deal with congressional "enforcement" of the Amendment by imposing civil and criminal liability for violation of the Amendment? The Supreme Court, in the *Civil Rights Cases,* decided that the legislation was invalid, presumably because the legislation was directed only at private racial discrimination, whereas the Amendment refers only to a prohibition on a state denying a person the equal protection of the laws. But the private-state distinction does not seem to be a wholly accurate description of the reasoning of the majority of the Court in the *Civil Rights Cases.*

Why was there no violation of the equal protection clause in the racial discrimination by the defendants? Was it because they were "private" persons? The defendants carried on their racial discrimination in states in which the Court apparently assumed that under state law they were prohibited to discriminate on the basis of race in offering their facilities to the public. Compare the problem which would have been before the Court if there had been statutes in these states prohibiting the defendants from extending their facilities to Negroes. Would the federal legislation involved in the *Civil Rights Cases* have been valid if there had been such state statutes? Even though the same "private" defendants would have been involved, it would seem that in that case

---

6. U.S. Const. amend. XIV, § 5.

Garvey,Mod.Const.Theory 3E---24

appropriate corrective congressional legislation would have been valid. For in that situation very likely such state statutes would be held invalid under the equal protection clause. The reason, then, why the act of Congress was held unconstitutional in the *Civil Rights Cases* was because the legislation was not directed at correcting state action which was in violation of the equal protection clause; there could have been valid federal legislation if there had been unconstitutional state action— *e.g.*, state statutes which compelled racial discrimination by the defendants. And the reason why there was no violation of the equal protection clause in the *Civil Rights Cases* was not because there was no state action, but because there was state action which was constitutional. The defendants in the *Civil Rights Cases* were assumed by the Court to have been prohibited by state law from refusing to deal with Negroes because of their race—*i.e.*, the defendants were under a state imposed duty not to discriminate. * * *

There would certainly be no denial to the prospective Negro patron of equal protection of the laws if state law actually *prohibits* the racial discrimination—as the Court assumed in the *Civil Rights Cases*. It would be a closer question whether there would be a "denial" of equal protection of the laws if state law simply *permits* an innkeeper (as distinguished from a private homeowner) to refuse to open his premises to a Negro because of his race. But there would probably be a "denial" of equal protection of the laws if state law *compels* an innkeeper to refuse to deal with a Negro. * * *

* * *

II

An effort will now be made to apply the points made in the preceding general discussion to * * * recent problems concerning legal relations between private persons which have been decided primarily in terms of presence or absence of "state action."

* * * The decision in *Shelley v. Kraemer* was that a state court could not constitutionally enforce against a Negro buyer of land a restrictive covenant prohibiting use of the land by the Negro because of his race. Mr. Chief Justice Vinson said:

> * * * the restrictive agreements standing alone cannot be regarded as violative of any rights guaranteed to petitioners by the Fourteenth Amendment. So long as the purposes of those agreements are effectuated by voluntary adherence to their terms, it would appear clear that there has been no action by the State and the provisions of the Amendment have not been violated * * *.
>
> We hold that in granting judicial enforcement of the restrictive agreements in these cases, the States have denied petitioners the equal protection of the laws and that, therefore, the action of the state courts cannot stand.

Is this distinction drawn in Mr. Chief Justice Vinson's opinion one which properly rests on presence or absence of state action? Would not a more satisfactory explanation of the Court's conclusion * * * be found in the following analysis:

As pointed out above, there is state action in the definition and enforcement of the principle that a landowner is free, if he so wishes, to refuse to sell his land to a Negro, whether the landowner has covenanted not to sell to a Negro or if the landowner, without having entered into a covenant, simply decides that he does not wish to convey to a Negro. Under such a principle of state law, if a Negro sued a landowner because the landowner had refused to deal with the Negro because of his race the landowner would win, because he was privileged to refuse to deal with the plaintiff under those circumstances. And there is state action in the definition and enforcement of a duty on a landowner not to convey to a Negro—*i.e.*, enforcing the restrictive covenant. But it is only the latter state action which is unconstitutional, because the creation and enforcement by state law of a duty on one private person not to deal with another private person because of the latter's race is in these circumstances a "denial" of the equal protection of the laws. State action which does no more than permit a landowner to discriminate on the basis of race in selling his land is constitutional state action, for giving effect to such a privilege in the landowner does not have so great a degree of effect on the prospective Negro purchaser as to be a "denial" of the equal protection of the laws. There is involved here a question of the degree of effect of different forms of state action on a prospective Negro buyer's opportunity to purchase and use land without being discriminated against because of his race. The state does not substantially deny the Negro that opportunity by *permitting* a private person to refuse to deal with him because of his race. This would be the situation where there was "voluntary adherence" to the restrictive covenant by the landowner. But the state does to a far greater degree deny the Negro the opportunity to acquire land, because of his race, if it *compels* a landowner not to deal with the Negro. This is the situation where the state enforces the restrictive covenant after a landowner has decided not to adhere to it.

JESSE H. CHOPER, THOUGHTS ON STATE ACTION: THE "GOVERNMENT FUNCTION" AND "POWER THEORY" APPROACHES

1979 Wash.U.L.Q. 757, 760–765, 770, 776.

It has been persuasively argued that state action is a false issue. The position, put most broadly, is that there is virtually always state action because all private conduct is undertaken under the aegis of the law of the state. The point was probably first elaborated by Harold Horowitz, who contended that "whenever, and however, a state gives legal consequences to transactions between private persons there is 'state action.'"[13] * * *

13. Horowitz, *The Misleading Search for "State Action" Under the Fourteenth* *Amendment,* 30 S.Cal.L.Rev. 208, 209 (1957).

Another, only slightly qualified, statement of this position is that because the state has extensive power to regulate private individuals' conduct, all private action, except that which the state has no constitutional power to regulate, is state action because it is undertaken with either express state permission or tacit state toleration. Thus, it is not only state action when a state statute or a state executive or administrative official denies government employment on the basis of race or when a state statute requires private employers to discriminate on the basis of race. It is also state action when state common law refuses to recognize a cause of action for damages or injunctive relief in favor of a job applicant who proves that he has been denied work by a private employer on the basis of race. In all these instances, the argument proceeds, the state—acting through its legislative, executive, or judicial branches—has made an affirmative policy choice. Therefore, in all these instances—including the last, because we may assume that the defendant-private employer has no constitutional right to racially discriminate—there is state action subject to the constraints of the fourteenth amendment. As Horowitz summarizes the matter:

> There is state action in the definition and enforcement of the right-duty relationship, and there is state action in adjudicating that there is no right-duty relationship. The result reached by the court on the merits is irrelevant insofar as the presence or absence of state action is concerned. When state law is applied to determine legal relations between private persons there is "state action."

A variation of this view is that the state is responsible for the acts of private individuals when its courts intervene to render the private acts effective. This approach reads the beleaguered case of *Shelley v. Kraemer* [18] for all it is worth. Any time a court enforces a private common-law or statutory right, there is state action. By virtue of this rationale, almost any private transaction can be converted into state action if one party balks at consensual compliance and forces the other party to bring legal proceedings to enforce his alleged rights. Once the state courts are brought in, there is state action.

* * *

The difficulty with both the state permission-toleration and judicial enforcement theories of state action is * * * that they contradict a central feature of the fourteenth amendment. Although its major purpose was to augment the authority of the national government to secure certain constitutional rights, its primary thrust was to accomplish this goal by outlawing deprivations of these rights by state governments and their legal structures rather than by the impact of private choice. By effectively obliterating the distinction between state action and private action, these theories eviscerate the fourteenth amendment's restriction on the authority of the national government vis-à-vis the states regard-

18. 334 U.S. 1 (1948).

ing the regulation of the myriad relationships that occur between one individual and another. These approaches require that all private activity, except that small amount which is beyond all governmental control, conform to federal constitutional standards.

* * *

Another substantial problem common to all these theories of state action arises as a consequence of a recently clarified doctrine delineating the scope of the fourteenth amendment's guarantee of equal protection. Unlike other substantive constitutional provisions such as the first amendment's guarantees of freedom of expression and religion, which may be violated by the *effect* of state action irrespective of its purpose, the Court has held that equal protection may be violated only by *intentionally* discriminatory action.[29] * * *

* * *

Under the theories of state action that we have considered, it is obvious that state action existed in *Shelley* [*v. Kraemer*]. What is not obvious, however, is whether the conceded state action violated the equal protection clause. Indeed, because it was not shown that the state court, the state agency involved in the case, had any racially discriminatory purpose, but rather appeared to be acting in a racially neutral manner in giving effect to a private agreement, there would be no violation of the fourteenth amendment under contemporary equal protection doctrine. Although the state court certainly knew that the consequences of its action would be to effectuate the private discrimination, this knowledge alone does not meet the need to find intentional discrimination by the state.

* * *

* * * As a consequence, no matter how pervasive or profound the impact of intentional private discrimination (whether against racial or ethnic minorities, aliens, women, illegitimate children, or some other group that obtains solicitous judicial protection from invidious government action), it is not constitutionally remediable unless the state, acting through its legislative, executive, judicial, or administrative officers, has deliberately discriminated. * * *

Therefore, wholly apart from the other formidable objections to the theories that have been discussed, there may be substantial merit * * * in directing state action analysis to the question of whether certain private individuals or organizations should be held to the constitutional responsibilities of the state. This "actor-focused" inquiry would permit the federal judiciary in certain circumstances to conclude that equal protection has been denied and may be remedied, although there is no

---

29. *See* Personnel Adm'r v. Feeney, 99 S.Ct. 2282 (1979); Arlington Heights v. Metropolitan Hous. Dev. Corp., 429 U.S. 252 (1977); Washington v. Davis, 426 U.S. 229 (1976).

proof of an official discriminatory purpose, but only that the "private" actor has abridged the constitutional norm.

B. JUSTIFICATIONS

The readings in this section ask why we might want the Constitution to control only state action. To that question courts and legal scholars have usually given two kinds of answers. The first is that constitutional controls over private action are undesirable for the same reason that statutory controls are—they inhibit the conduct of intimate affairs, they restrict a person's freedom to live her own life in her own way, and so on. In some ways constitutional controls are worse than ordinary law controls. They are imposed by courts, while ordinary lawmaking is done by legislatures and agencies. (The common law is a significant exception. It, like constitutional law, is made by courts.) It is often easier to make rules through the judicial process than through legislative or administrative processes. Proposals must have more popular appeal in the latter cases; and at some points the systems are designed to make success difficult. Judges, on the other hand, need only to agree among themselves. This means that sometimes constitutional controls are more likely to be imposed in the first place. Once in place they are also harder to remove. If a court decides that the Constitution forbids deli owners to make arbitrary hiring decisions and this restriction proves very hard to live with, the only remedy is to amend the Constitution, a process that is seldom successful. By contrast, when we regulate deli employment by statute we can change the rules as easily as we made them in the first place.

The second justification given for the state action limitation is that it serves a federalist purpose. Constitutional controls on private action are, after all, federal rules enforced primarily by federal courts. If we leave the control of private action to ordinary law, this will typically (though certainly not always) be law made and enforced by the states. Abolishing the state action limitation, then, would work a substantial transfer of lawmaking authority from the states to the federal government. Many people think this would be undesirable for the same reasons that unlimited Article I power is undesirable. These reasons are discussed in the series of cases from *M'Culloch v. Maryland*[1] to *National League of Cities v. Usery*[2] and *New York v. United States*.[3] We treat these problems in Chapter IV. These federalist arguments have had little success in Article I cases during the last half century. Is there more reason for them to succeed in Fourteenth Amendment cases?[4]

1. 17 U.S. (4 Wheat.) 316, 4 L.Ed. 579 (1819).

2. 426 U.S. 833, 96 S.Ct. 2465, 49 L.Ed.2d 245 (1976).

3. ___ U.S. ___, 112 S.Ct. 2408, 120 L.Ed.2d 120 (1992).

4. If we take the Article I analogy seriously we might consider this further point. The Supreme Court has held that, although federalist concerns are important, the states do not need the protection of the courts because they are adequately represented in the political process. Garcia v. San Antonio Metropolitan Transit Authori-

Erwin Chemerinsky reviews and criticizes both of these justifications. He argues that the privacy argument looks at only half the picture. For every private actor ("violator") whose liberty is protected by the state action doctrine, there is another private actor ("victim") who suffers some harm. The doctrine protects my freedom to hire whom I please at my deli, at the expense of qualified job applicants whom I arbitrarily or discriminatorily reject. If we are really interested in maximizing the regime of private liberty, Chemerinsky says, we should look at the merits of these conflicts and hold for the party who has more at stake. As to the argument for state sovereignty, Chemerinsky claims that it has been rendered obsolete by *United States v. Darby*[5] and *Garcia v. San Antonio Metropolitan Transit Authority*.[6]

William Marshall observes that Chemerinsky's cure may be worse than the disease. If what we really want is a regime that maximizes individual liberty, we should not assume that we can get this by allowing the courts to engage in case-by-case balancing of private interests. What's more there is another, often unappreciated, danger in extending the Constitution to cover private cases. All proponents of universal coverage concede that we will have to apply the substantive rules more leniently to private actors. Marshall points out that these new exceptions may leak back into the law governing public authorities.

Ruth Gavison reviews and assesses the modern feminist critique of the public-private distinction. In part this critique is conceptual: it asserts that the distinction is illusory because nothing is really private. Child-rearing arrangements affect the lives of caretakers, not to mention the way children learn to think. And they are carried out within a framework of laws governing the creation of families, the obligations of custody, the ownership of property, and so on. In part the critique is ideological: it asserts that we should not shield arrangements traditionally characterized as "private" from public scrutiny. If we do, we will be turning a blind eye to domestic violence, sexual harassment in the workplace, and a variety of other harms against women. We should assume instead that "the personal is political." Gavison agrees with many of the assumptions behind both critiques, but she cautions against abandoning the public-private distinction altogether. After all, there are occasions when women too will want protection for their private lives.

ERWIN CHEMERINSKY, RETHINKING STATE ACTION
80 Nw.U.L.Rev. 503, 535–546, 550–553 (1985).

The Contemporary Justifications for the State Action Doctrine

* * *

Contemporary commentators all offer the same two reasons for requiring state action. First, the doctrine protects individual liberty by

ty, 469 U.S. 528, 105 S.Ct. 1005, 83 L.Ed.2d 1016 (1985). This suggests that we should accord Congress the same wide authority under § 5 of the Fourteenth Amendment as we give it under the Commerce Clause. *See* Cohen, *Congressional Power to Interpret Due Process and Equal Protection*, 27 Stan. L.Rev. 603 (1975). But maybe the federal courts should not have the same latitude.

5. 312 U.S. 100, 61 S.Ct. 451, 85 L.Ed. 609 (1941).

6. 469 U.S. 528, 105 S.Ct. 1005, 83 L.Ed.2d 1016 (1985).

defining a zone of private conduct that does not have to comply with the Constitution. Second, limiting the Constitution's protections to state action preserves state sovereignty by giving the states almost complete authority to regulate private behavior. I believe that the state action requirement is unnecessary to achieve these purposes and, in fact, is counterproductive to these goals.

A. *Preserving a Zone of Private Autonomy*

The state action doctrine frequently is defended on the ground that it "preserves an area of individual freedom by limiting the reach of federal law and federal judicial power." [180] Undoubtedly this is correct; the state action doctrine does preserve the liberty of private parties to ignore the Constitution and the limits contained within it. In considering whether the overall effect of the state action doctrine is to enhance individual liberty, however, we must remember that every time a person's freedom to violate a constitutional right is upheld, a victim's liberty is sacrificed. In each case when a question of state action arises, both the freedom of the violator and the freedom of the victim are at stake. In challenges to private racial discrimination, for example, there is the claimed liberty to discriminate, say, on freedom of association grounds, and the claimed right to be free from discrimination. No matter how a court decides, someone's liberty will be expanded and someone's liberty restricted. To assert that the state action doctrine is desirable because it preserves autonomy and liberty is to look at only one side of the equation.

Furthermore, the state action doctrine is an absurd basis for choosing between the two liberties. The concept of state action completely ignores the competing rights at stake and chooses based entirely on the identity of the actors. There is no reason to believe that the state action doctrine preserves more liberty than it denies because it does not even consider the rights involved. In fact, under the state action doctrine, the rights of the private violator always are favored over the rights of the victims. Therefore, state action enhances freedom only if it is believed that the liberty to violate the Constitution always is more important than the individual rights that are infringed.

* * *

If the goal is to protect individual freedom, then it is best to decide cases on the merits, without reference to state action. The argument that the state action requirement is necessary to preserve individual autonomy obviously is based on the premise that there is a zone of private conduct that should not be constrained by the Constitution. Accordingly, it would make the most sense to identify the precise rights in that zone and directly protect them. Consider an example frequently

---

180. Lugar v. Edmondson Oil Co., 457 U.S. 922, 936 (1982).

mentioned in the literature. It often is suggested that if there were no state action requirement, people could not exclude demonstrators from their living rooms and every dinner party would have to be racially integrated. Such a prospect is antithetical because it offends a belief in privacy and freedom of association. Therefore, the logical way to avoid the harm is to hold directly that, in such circumstances, the rights of privacy and freedom of association outweigh freedom of speech and the right not to be discriminated against. The state action doctrine adds absolutely nothing to the protection of individual liberties. The values hidden in the claim that state action is necessary to preserve personal autonomy can be made explicit and protected openly.

Thus, abandoning the concept of state action does not eliminate the distinction between the public and private realms. Surely everyone believes that there are certain private activities that should be completely uncontrolled by the state. What is suggested is eliminating state action as the dividing line between public and private activities. The state action doctrine is a totally arbitrary basis for separation; the division should be made by focusing on what is substantively desirable to keep private. The emphasis should be on defining the content of the private domain that is immune from state supervision in any form. Simply stated, if the state action requirement is jettisoned, courts will directly balance the competing liberties involved in each case. Such an approach maximizes protection of liberty, replacing the current policy of always choosing to favor the rights of the private violator over those of the victim.

At the very least, state action is unnecessary to protect individual autonomy; direct protection would be at least as effective in upholding personal liberties. In fact, I would suggest that the state action requirement is counterproductive—that individual freedom would be enhanced greatly by eliminating the state action doctrine.

First, allowing the concept of state action to determine when rights are protected undermines liberty by allowing all private invasions of rights, even when the balance completely favors the victims. For example, assume that a utility company with a state-granted monopoly refuses to provide service to blacks. If the holding of *Jackson v. Metropolitan Edison Co.* were followed, a court could not stop the discrimination because there is no state action.[199] Yet, it is hard to imagine any freedom of the utility company that outweighs the harms of the discrimination imposed. Frequently, corporations are allowed to infringe basic rights, even when their freedom is far less important than the liberties infringed.

* * *

199. 419 U.S. 345 (1975). *Jackson* involved a claim that the utility company denied due process by terminating service without providing a hearing. The Supreme Court held that there was no state action.

Second, eliminating the state action doctrine enhances protection of liberty by focusing attention directly on the valued rights. Obviously, the courts already balance somewhat in determining when state action exists. For example, the state action doctrine is applied more leniently in cases involving allegations of private racial discrimination than in situations when the challenge is to a violation of other rights. This differential approach reflects the courts' unarticulated conclusion that stopping racial discrimination is more important than protecting other rights—that in instances of discrimination the rights of the victim are more important than those of the violator. But this balancing is hidden by the courts, obscured behind the question whether there is state action.

Liberty would best be protected if the courts openly articulated the competing interests that they were balancing. This would force the courts clearly to identify and define the conflicting liberties, enhancing understanding of each of the rights at stake. In dismissing cases for want of state action, the courts fail to describe the liberties of the violators that are preserved by court abstention, and thus the zone of private autonomy protected by the state action doctrine remains undefined. If there are liberties sufficiently important to justify discrimination or infringements of freedom of speech, society is best off if these interests are articulated so that they can be applied in other situations and recognized as a part of personal freedom.

Finally, the state action doctrine does not adequately protect liberties because even if state action is found and private parties are deemed to infringe rights with the impermissible aid of the state, the court does not order the offensive conduct to stop. Rather, the court orders the state only to disengage itself from the challenged activity. Although in some cases the effect is to end the constitutional violation, in other instances the behavior continues, but without the state's involvement. Liberty would be maximized if the court could directly halt the violations of rights.

A different, stronger argument might be made that the state action requirement protects personal autonomy by creating a shield that immunizes certain conduct from any governmental review. Arguably, without a state action doctrine, individuals could be called into court to justify any behavior that interferes with another person's rights. The prospect of such government review is itself a denial of liberty and the state action doctrine is useful because it creates a zone of private activity about which the government may not even inquire.

The flaw in this argument is that it assumes that the state action requirement is necessary to create such a shield. There is no reason why laws and legal doctrines cannot directly create a shield in the absence of a state action doctrine. Balancing need not be done on a case-by-case basis by calling individuals into court in each instance to account for their actions. General rules could be formulated in some areas, where the balance in almost every case will be in a particular direction. For example, a broad rule might be articulated that the associational rights of hosts of private dinner parties always will outweigh the rights of uninvited guests not to be discriminated against. * * *

* * *

B. Preserving a Zone of State Sovereignty

A second contemporary justification for the state action requirement is that it upholds federalism by preserving a zone of state sovereignty. The *Civil Rights Cases* held that federal constitutional rights do not govern individual behavior and, furthermore, that Congress lacks authority to apply them to private conduct:[211] structuring the legal relationships of private citizens was for the state, not the national government. Thus, the state action doctrine protects state sovereignty by leaving governance of individual behavior to state political processes.

This justification for state action assumes, first, that under the Constitution there is a zone of activities completely reserved to state control. The Court in the *Civil Rights Cases* explicitly stated that the tenth amendment creates such a zone of authority, and that congressional regulation of private conduct "is repugnant to the Tenth Amendment." The regulation of private behavior, including protection of civil rights, was seen as a matter entirely of state, not federal, authority.

Thus, the *Civil Rights Cases* reflected a belief in "dual sovereignty"—that there is a domain which only the states may regulate. The doctrine of "dual sovereignty" dominated constitutional law from the late nineteenth century until 1937. Repeatedly during this era, the Supreme Court struck down congressional economic regulations, holding that they concerned activities which only the states may control.[218] But the experience of the Depression, the pressure from President Roosevelt's Court-packing plan, and the perceived need for federal government actions led to the complete demise of the concept of dual sovereignty. No longer is it believed that there is a zone of activities which only the states may regulate.[220]

In 1940, in *United States v. Darby,* the Supreme Court declared that the tenth amendment "states but a truism that all is retained which has not been surrendered."[221] In other words, under this view of the tenth amendment, Congress may legislate if it points to an enumerated power as justification for its action. If such authority exists, congressional action is valid, irrespective of the activity regulated. There are no activities that only state governments can regulate. Viewing the state action requirement as a way to protect state sovereignty, thus, is based

---

211. 109 U.S. 3, 11 (1883).

218. *See, e.g.,* Carter v. Carter Coal Co., 298 U.S. 238 (1936); A.L.A. Schechter Poultry Corp. v. United States, 295 U.S. 495 (1935); Hammer v. Dagenhart, 247 U.S. 251 (1918) (striking down congression-

al regulations as exceeding congressional power and violating state sovereignty).

220. *See* Garcia v. San Antonio Metropolitan Dist., [469 U.S. 528 (1985).]

221. 312 U.S. 100, 124 (1941). * * *

on the false assumption that there exists a zone of constitutionally reserved state authority.

Second, even if such a zone exists, there is the further assumption that a state's area of control includes determining the protection of individual rights. In particular, it is assumed that state autonomy includes the ability of the state to decide which fundamental rights will not be protected from private interference. The claim must be that under the fourteenth amendment states have the right to decide to do nothing to stop private discrimination or abridgment of free speech. Once it is established that constitutional rights should be protected from private interference, however, then why tolerate a state's refusal to provide protection? State sovereignty provides a justification only if it is believed that a state's rights are more important than individual rights—a premise consistently rejected since the Civil War.

* * *

It might be argued that although Congress has the authority to override state control of private behavior, courts do not have this power. The notion is that states have their institutional interests represented in Congress, and, therefore, the legislature can be trusted best to balance national and state interests.[232] Yet, concluding that courts may not stop private infringements of rights assumes that states have the authority to tolerate the denial of liberty and equality if Congress does not act to restrain them. States clearly have no such authority. * * * If nothing is reserved to the states, then there is no limitation on the judicial power to vindicate rights because of state sovereignty.

Furthermore, to conclude that only Congress can compel states to safeguard rights leaves protection of basic liberties to the political process. If Congress does not remedy state denials of liberty, violations of individual freedoms would be unchecked. The argument about state sovereignty is that states, through their political systems, have the authority to structure individual activities. Such deference to majoritarian politics, however, is completely inappropriate when rights are at stake. The whole idea of enshrining rights in a Constitution is to protect them from majority rule. Judicial review to prevent state denials of due process and equal protection therefore is essential.

Finally, eliminating the requirement of state action would not cause a loss of state autonomy. Although states would be compelled to protect rights, they would have great flexibility in choosing the means to be used. State laws would become a major guarantee of liberty, making detailed federal standards unnecessary. Once laws protecting the rights of individuals were well established, federal supervision would be largely

---

232. *Cf.* Garcia v. San Antonio Metropolitan Dist., 105 S.Ct. 1005 (1985) (political safeguards of federalism are sufficient to protect states' interests); * * * Wechsler, *The Political Safeguards of Federalism,* 54 Colum.L.Rev. 543 (1954) (states' interests are represented in Congress, and, therefore, federalism issues can be left to the legislature).

unnecessary. Thus, in the long term, more responsibility would shift to state governments, enhancing state sovereignty.

* * *

Doing Away With the State Action Requirement

I have argued that limiting the Constitution's protections to state action is harmful because it permits deprivations of fundamental liberties and that it is completely unnecessary because nothing valuable would be lost without it. The inescapable conclusion is that the doctrine should be banished from American law. The effect of discarding the concept of state action is that the Constitution would be viewed as a code of social morals, not just of governmental conduct, bestowing individual rights that no entity, public or private, could infringe without a compelling justification. Such an approach makes sense especially because the "Constitution was designed to embody and celebrate values and to inculcate proper acceptance of them, as much as to compel governments to abide by them." [250]

Freedom of speech, privacy, and equality are rights of the individual that must be protected from all unjustified deprivations. This does not necessarily mean that protection must come from the Constitution or the federal courts. The legislatures, federal and state, can protect rights from private interference by statute, as Congress did in the area of civil rights. State courts can protect rights through the development of the common law. When protection is afforded in this way, application of the Constitution is unnecessary and would be eliminated—not because of the application of the state action doctrine, but because there is no deprivation of rights.

Direct application of the Constitution is necessary only to see if other sources are providing adequate protection. Eliminating the state action requirement would, I hope, encourage legislatures and state courts to fulfill their roles in protecting rights. If no other redress exists, then it would be essential that the federal courts provide protection. * * *

Again, applying constitutional principles to private conduct does not mean that all individual conduct must meet the same standard as that required of the government. Courts would apply traditional principles of constitutional adjudication to determine if sufficiently important justifications exist for the challenged conduct. Essentially, the courts would balance the rights of the violator and victim in deciding the proper result. Thus, the entire inquiry as to state action would be discarded; the only question would be whether a person's rights were unjustifiably infringed.

One objection to eliminating the requirement of state action is that it seemingly would make almost every crime or tort a constitutional violation. Any action denying life, liberty, or property—meaning most

250. Franz v. United States, 707 F.2d 582, 594 n. 45 (D.C.Cir.1983).

crimes and torts—would, arguably, be actionable as a constitutional claim. This objection, however, ignores the fact that if state criminal and tort laws provide adequate remedies, then there is no denial of due process. * * *

* * *

A second objection to eliminating the state action doctrine is that there will be an undesirable increase in the power of the judiciary: if courts are able to redress all private violations of rights, they will have too much control over American society.

* * *

[But] in evaluating the claim that the courts will have too much power, the question is, "too much power compared to what?" The common-law role of the courts was to ensure the vindication of all rights that an individual possesses. Therefore, eliminating the state action doctrine merely would restore the powers that traditionally belonged to the courts. Moreover, in modern society, the most important role courts perform is the protection of rights. Through the removal of the state action requirement, courts would be given precisely the power to accomplish this task.

WILLIAM P. MARSHALL, DILUTING CONSTITUTIONAL RIGHTS: RETHINKING "RETHINKING STATE ACTION"
80 Nw.U.L.Rev. 558, 561–564, 566–569 (1985).

OF VICTIMS AND VIOLATORS: THE HARMS IN BALANCING CONSTITUTIONAL INTERESTS OF PRIVATE INDIVIDUALS

* * * *Rethinking State Action* is replete with references to constitutional "victims" and "violators." The distinction between victim and violator, however, is not as clear as Professor Chemerinsky would have us believe. In most, if not all, of the cases in which Chemerinsky criticizes the use of the state action doctrine to avoid constitutional inquiry, there are serious constitutional interests present on behalf of the defendant as well as the plaintiff. For example, in *Taylor v. St. Vincent's Hospital*,[18] the plaintiff sought to compel the defendant, a private hospital, to perform a medical procedure that it opposed on religious grounds. Similarly, in *Cook v. Advertiser Co.*,[19] the plaintiffs sought to affect the right of a newspaper to control the content of its publication. Can it rightfully be said that the plaintiffs in these cases were constitutional victims while the defendants were violators?

These are not isolated examples. In defending an eviction motivated by disagreement with a tenant's political beliefs, a landlord can assert the constitutional defenses of due process property rights and rights of

18. 523 F.2d 75 (9th Cir.1975), *cert. denied*, 424 U.S. 948 (1976).

19. 323 F.Supp. 1212 (D.Ala.1971), *aff'd on other grounds*, 458 F.2d 1119 (5th Cir. 1972). * * *

association and speech. A rule that entitles the tenant to the premises simply recharacterizes the tenant as the violator and the landlord as the victim of constitutional deprivation. Similarly, in employment cases, employers may be able to raise rights of association in defense against discrimination claims and also will be able to utilize rights of free speech if the refusal to employ is based on political considerations. If an employer loses, is he a constitutional victim?

* * *

* * * Professor Chemerinsky's solution to resolve the inevitable conflicts is that age-old constitutional standby: balancing. For Professor Chemerinsky, the way to assure that both sides receive the fullest constitutional protection is to balance the constitutional interests at stake. He argues that the state action requirement is actually implicit, "obscured" balancing and states, "Liberty would best be protected if the courts openly articulated the competing interests that they were balancing. This would force the courts clearly to identify and define the conflicting liberties, enhancing understanding of each of the rights at stake."

But is this "articulated" balancing really possible, and if possible, advisable? How does one articulate valid grounds of decision in choosing between the right of a parent to disinherit his offspring because the latter intends to marry outside of the religion, and the rights of the offspring and putative spouse to be free of religious discrimination? How does one choose between the right of a church to discriminate on religious grounds and the right of a minority seeking admission to that church to be free of discrimination? How, in cases like *St. Vincent's,* can the right to contraceptive surgery be evaluated in relation to the right of a religious hospital to practice medicine according to its theological tenets? More importantly, how are judges going to make consistent decisions with only openended balancing as a guideline?

* * * Given the extreme difficulty of choosing between competing rights in the first place, perhaps the decision to insulate private activity from constitutional scrutiny is justified as a way to avoid forcing judges to make impossible decisions.

* * *

Even more critical than the dangers of balancing itself is that the balancing foreseen by Chemerinsky will create a class of constitutional "losers." If one constitutional right is embattled against another, the protection accorded one liberty is going to be diminished. The courts would be forced to articulate priorities in constitutional liberties, with the result that certain liberties eventually might be found to possess only secondary constitutional significance. This in turn may lead to less protection being accorded these rights, even in cases involving "pure" state action.

* * *

Still another difficulty lies in the constitutional balancing process as applied to private law: It inhibits or precludes other sources of legal development. Assume a person, in renting a room in a one-family dwelling, chooses to discriminate because of political differences with the tenant and the court vindicates the landlord's interests under a balancing analysis. What if Congress or a state subsequently enacted a statute prohibiting evictions for political reasons? Because the court's earlier decision was held to be constitutionally mandated, there would be a constitutional bar to the new legislation.

In short, the effect of constitutionalizing private law is to freeze that law. Under existing doctrine, if legislative or common-law rules prove unsatisfactory, they can be changed. On the other hand, a doctrine of constitutional law that imposes judicially created parameters on private conduct places serious constraints on the ability of both the common law and legislatures to respond to social issues.

* * *

The Inevitable Dilution: Replacing State Action With Adequate State Remedies

Professor Chemerinsky's thesis also ignores a practical concern inherent in constitutional jurisprudence: The more broadly rights are drawn, the more difficult it becomes to enforce those rights stringently. In first amendment jurisprudence, for example, although everything we do may be characterized as "expressive," it is nonetheless inappropriate to consider all individual action as constitutionally protected. As Professor Karst has explained, "the danger of such a doctrinal approach is that First Amendment doctrine would become encumbered with new limits and exceptions, because some claims inevitably would be rejected. From these decisions a doctrinal infection would spread, touching even traditional First Amendment concerns."[53] The strength accorded the first amendment, in short, becomes "diluted."

Professor Chemerinsky faces a similar problem in his efforts to apply constitutional principles to private law. Some modifying principle must be adopted in order to make the constitutional protection meaningful. Chemerinsky, as we have seen, does not adopt the approach used in first amendment jurisprudence itself: the exclusion of certain types of expression from full constitutional protection by definition and categorization. Rather, his solution is more surprising.

Professor Chemerinsky argues that if the state provides an adequate remedy, a constitutional violation should not be found. Indeed, he goes so far as to suggest that it "[be assumed] state common law protects natural rights." This is a strange proposition to be advanced by one advocating civil libertarian interests.

---

53. Karst, *The Freedom of Intimate Association,* 89 Yale L.J. 624, 654–55 n. 140   (1980).

Modern civil rights law, in contrast, is predicated on the conclusion in *Monroe v. Pape*[59] that state remedies are inadequate substitutes for constitutional rights. In *Monroe*, Justice Harlan stated that "a deprivation of a constitutional right is significantly different from and more serious than a violation of a state right and therefore deserves a different remedy even though the same act may constitute both a state tort and the deprivation of a constitutional right."

* * *

The underlying policies and importance of *Monroe* require more development than can be offered here and, in any event, the significance of Professor Chemerinsky's adequate state remedy solution is not in its specifics. Rather, the point is that once constitutional principles are so broadly drawn, some limiting principle becomes necessary. Before adopting Chemerinsky's thesis, then, we must ask whether the cure offered for private infringements of constitutional rights is worth a remedy that undercuts existing constitutional protections against state officials.

RUTH GAVISON, FEMINISM AND THE PUBLIC/PRIVATE DISTINCTION
45 Stanford L.Rev. 1, 10, 14–16, 18–21, 35–38 (1992).

On the surface, many feminist challenges to the public/private distinction appear to be external, denying that any difference exists. The challenges, however, actually document the ways in which the real and pervasive differences between private and public affect the welfare of women in our society. As a result, many feminists advocate changing existing social and political structures in order to eliminate the difference between private and public in some contexts and to downplay its importance in others. Above all, such feminists urge that the distinction should not be invoked as a justification for different treatment in either legal or social realms. In this way, feminist arguments can be internal challenges, invoking the distinction and using it as a central tool of description and evaluation.

* * *

NOTHING IS REALLY PRIVATE.

* * *

Nothing is self-regarding. This challenge has become familiar from criticisms of J.S. Mill's On Liberty. A cornerstone of Mill's argument for liberty was the distinction he drew between self- and other-regarding activities. According to Mill, the former were outside the jurisdiction of society. Mill's arguments for liberty were attacked by critics who contended that, because individuals do not exist as monads, independent of all others, no significant activity can be solely self-regarding.

59. 365 U.S. 167 (1961). * * *

Some feminists sound like Mill's critics. In response to the claim that what happens within families is self-regarding, affecting only members of the family unit, feminists answer that the "private" arrangements within families affect both nonmembers and society at large in important ways. Citizens of the state are socialized within the family, and evidence shows that child-rearing arrangements affect children in profound and complex ways. Consequently, the characteristics brought by children into their adult lives will eventually affect the general norms and expectations of their society. Furthermore, child-rearing arrangements affect not only the chances of particular family members to participate fully in the public worlds of work and politics, but also the general pattern of participation of women in society (including those women not raising children).

Similarly, some feminists argue that activities that are commonly viewed as paradigmatically self-regarding, such as an individual's decision to watch pornography alone in the privacy of her home, are in fact other-regarding in important ways. According to this argument, such decisions presuppose the availability and permissibility of the activity, as well as society's toleration of the possible consequences of the choice to view pornography. A society in which such outlets not only exist, but are tolerated, is a society that permits the creation of images portraying women enjoying abuse and pain. It is also a society in which it is more likely that people will respond to pornography and abuse others.

No controversial activity can be purely self-regarding. The very fact that an activity creates a controversy indicates that it has an effect on others. Moreover, it may be true that no significant activity is completely self-regarding, because any conduct may have some effects, however remote, speculative, or diffuse, on others. Additionally, while consent, freely given, may entitle participants in an activity to noninterference in some contexts, it does not make the activity self-regarding. The real question, however, is whether we can intelligibly distinguish among activities according to the quality, magnitude, probability, and irreversibility of the effects that they may have on others. Herein lies the strength of Mill's intuition. Any individual's decision to violate a social norm in the privacy of her home may contribute to the demise of that norm (and thus may not be fully self-regarding). This conduct, however, differs from a public denial or violation of that same norm. Such public denial, in turn, is very different from conduct which harms individuals directly.

* * *

No social institution is private. Critical Legal Studies scholars took this argument about contract and property from the Realists and their mentors, and it was subsequently applied to the family.[39] This argument seeks to undermine the presumption of noninterference with private

---

39. Much literature documents the fact that the family is regulated quite heavily. *See, e.g.,* Christopher Lasch, Haven in a Heartless World (1977); Frances Olsen, *The Myth of State Intervention in the Family,* 18 U.Mich.J.L.Ref. 835 (1985).

institutions by showing that these institutions are in fact public in important respects. In doing so, the criticism demonstrates how the presumption of noninterference arises: We label property, for example, as private to signify that it depends on voluntary transactions between relatively equal private adults. When coupled with a general respect for the voluntary activities of individuals, this description creates a presumption of noninterference.

According to the criticism, contract, property, and marriage are public because they are defined and regulated by the law and social norms, both public creations. The law determines the initial endowments of property. The law confers the "private" powers of deciding whether to make a contract, to sell a piece of property, to get married, or to enter into a co-habitation agreement. The State also grants and, when necessary, enforces powers such as the prohibition on nonowners to enter, use, or sell. The implication is that the presumption of noninterference is misguided: What the public created and maintains, the public can take away. The ultimate decision about what should be private is, and should be, public.

While this important insight should be conceded and even stressed, * * * the conceded fact that what is private is determined by public norms and laws does not invalidate the presumption of noninterference with private arrangements. Although the public realm may be the final arbiter of what remains immune from interference, public norms and laws should grant private arrangements this immunity where these are transactions between full and informed individuals. This follows from the belief that it is desirable to leave individuals an area in which they can act free from governmental interference.

THE PERSONAL IS POLITICAL.

* * *

Feminists, especially radical ones, attack the classification of things into personal and political, arguing that many personal problems are deeply political. For these feminists, the slogan does not act as a mere reminder of interdependence between the public and private realms. Rather, it is used to challenge the existence of alleged differences: The "personal" should not be allowed to stop conversations, critique, or accountability; the "personal" should not be seen as an improper theme for concern and possible public interference. It is against the background of this interpretation of "personal" that the slogan identifying the personal with the political should be understood. When women are harassed in the workplace, it is not just the predicament of the individual women who are unfortunate enough to work for exceptional male employers. When women are battered at home, it is not because each particular victim has triggered an unfortunate "individual" tragedy. When women feel constrained and bored in their expensive suburban homes, with nothing to do but wait for their husbands and children so that they may cater to their needs, it is not because these women fail, as individuals, to adjust to their natural feminine roles. Social structures are involved, social structures which are not simply "natural." They are person-made, and they benefit males.[48]

Furthermore, the argument goes, dubbing certain activities or choices as "personal" is in itself part of the mechanism used to perpetuate the anomalous and unjust situation, by obscuring the injustice of the structure, and instead highlighting individual adjustments within the status quo. For this reason, feminist consciousness-raising groups, meeting to discuss the lives of their individual members, are not properly understood as an indulgence in the personal. Such groups are a way to give the experiences of women more visibility and to make women understand that their "individual" problems are actually the reflections of undesirable social structures.

One part of this argument must be valid: To effectively recognize that the structures are partly responsible for these "personal" problems, society must first identify the symptoms as part of a social problem. We should then seek to make the underlying problem visible (instead of encouraging the secrecy and shame which are too often the accepted approaches to personal inadequacies) and to mobilize individuals to regard the situation as political, enlisting the forces of political and social reform for change.

More questionable is the attempt to conclude from "the personal is political" that nothing should be immune from public scrutiny, discussion, and accountability. This is a substantive question of political morality, which should be discussed on its merits. It cannot be decided simply by identifying the effective preconditions of putting something on the public agenda and by evaluating it against its social and political background.

* * * Nothing in this claim * * * supports the conclusion that the realms of personal and political are identical or that the use of the terminology is never useful. This claim does not affect the basic intuition that our particular struggles with our activities, loves, and work are what make our lives our own. Of course we are affected and constrained by available options and social norms, and our own struggles may well help to reinforce political and social processes. But most of us feel that there are aspects of our lives which are "private" and "personal," and thus should not be accessible to others without our consent; they should not be matters dealt with by the public, be it media or politicians. This intuition presupposes some distinction between private and public, between personal and political. It is not affected by the validity of the insight that "privatization" may be, at times, a cause of invisibility and paralysis.

* * *

48. This is an important part of the reason why Betty Friedan's best-selling book The Feminine Mystique was so influential: It argued that the factors affecting women's lives were systemic rather than personal.

Domestic violence. Domestic violence is [a] frequently cited example of the bad consequences resulting from the public/private distinction. Here, the argument is that family relations are seen as paradigmatically private. In part, this is based upon the assumption that family relationships are voluntary and equal. Consequently, there is a presumption that these private relations should be free from external interference. Often people, incorrectly, jump from the accurate description of family relationships as private to the conclusion that no interference is justified, without examining the truth of the initial assumptions or contrary considerations which might defeat the presumption.

* * *

* * * The language of privacy, allegedly, masks a form of ethical confusion. Use of the language of public and private suggests that there are valid reasons for protecting the private from state regulation. But under present social conditions, and in contrast to this implication, women have no interest in such protection. For them, the intimate and the realm of family life is neither a realm of freedom, nor a haven in which the dignity of self-direction can be cultivated. To the contrary, in private, women are exploited and abused with impunity. Women should, therefore, recognize that invocations of the value of privacy are a means of perpetuating their oppression by creating the false impression that the protection of privacy is good for women, by isolating them, and by depoliticizing their struggle.

This assertion raises a substantive moral and political question. In private, women may be vulnerable in ways that are beyond the scrutiny and censure of the public. Does it follow, then, that women have no interest in the values of privacy and intimacy, or that there are no contexts in which women would want to keep the state out of their lives? Presumably, * * * the answer is no. Therefore, we must differentiate between good arguments, derived from the values associated with privacy, and bad arguments, in which reference to the same values is used to mask exploitation and abuse. This distinction is not a matter of language, but a matter of the features of the specific situations involved.

Some legal scholars may then respond that what is protected is not really privacy or intimacy, but the value of what is done within them. Intimacy, importance to self-identity, and choice are not necessary, on the one hand, to justify protecting activities which are valuable in themselves. On the other hand, when the activities in question are destructive, their inaccessibility or possible intimacy should not count as reasons for protecting them. In other words, the substance of the activity, rather than its public or private context, determines its value.

This response is misleading in two ways. First, while privacy and intimacy should not provide blanket immunity from public interference, it does not follow that we always look at the substance of the activity rather than its context. The value of privacy and inaccessibility includes not only the protection of activities which are desirable, but also some activities which are undesirable. This is especially true for activities that many regard as victimless sins, such as homosexual conduct between consenting adults. We do not want to reduce the question to a debate about the morality of the conduct. Politically, it is quite clear that such debates could result in prohibitions, even though many people who believe that this conduct is immoral may oppose criminalization due to its close relation to self-identity and physical intimacy.

Such considerations provide powerful arguments against perspectives which examine only the substantive morality of conduct. Generally, we want to afford immunity for voluntary consensual associations where consent and freedom are not illusory. If we accept that such situations exist even in our gendered, unequal society, then intimacy and privacy do operate, presumptively, to limit interference without requiring that we publicly judge all behavior on its moral merits.

We may also wish to protect the privacy or the intimacy of relationships among individuals. Some of these relationships are institutionalized, such as the family and small clubs; others provide the background against which individuals grow up and live (various affective communities). The protection of such associations and groups requires a measure of state noninterference if such associations are to provide the functions for which we value them. Small associations are protected through the restraint of external force. Interference only occurs in the case of blatant violations of members' rights, while it seeks to insure the voluntariness of the association, and the viability of exit as an option.

BIBLIOGRAPHY

"The State"

John H. Garvey, *Private Power and the Constitution,* 10 Const.Comm. 301 (1993).

Henry Monaghan, *State Law Wrongs, State Law Remedies, And The Fourteenth Amendment,* 86 Colum.L.Rev. 979 (1986).

"Action"

Lawrence A. Alexander, *Cutting the Gordian Knot: State Action And Self–Help Repossession,* 2 Hast.L.Q. 893 (1975).

Boris I. Bittker & Kenneth M. Kaufman, *Taxes and Civil Rights: "Constitutionalizing" the Internal Revenue Code,* 82 Yale L.J. 51 (1972).

Charles Black, *Foreword: "State Action," Equal Protection, and California's Proposition 14,* 81 Harv.L.Rev. 69 (1967).

William M. Burke & David J. Reber, *State Action, Congressional Power and Creditors' Rights: An Essay on the Fourteenth Amendment,* 46 S.Cal.L.Rev. 1003 (1973).

Erwin Chemerinsky, *More Is Not Less: A Rejoinder to Professor Marshall,* 80 Nw.U.L.Rev. 571 (1985).

Comment, *Tax Incentives as State Action,* 122 U.Pa.L.Rev. 414 (1973).

Henry Friendly, The Dartmouth College Case and the Public–Private Penumbra (1969).

John H. Garvey, *Another Way of Looking at School Aid,* 1985 Sup.Ct. Rev. 61.

Robert J. Glennon, Jr. & John E. Nowak, *A Functional Analysis of the Fourteenth Amendment "State Action" Requirement,* 1976 Sup.Ct. Rev. 221.

Louis Henkin, Shelley v. Kraemer: *Notes for a Revised Opinion,* 110 U.Pa.L.Rev. 473 (1962).

Harold W. Horowitz, *Fourteenth Amendment Aspects of Racial Discrimination in "Private" Housing,* 52 Calif.L.Rev. 1 (1964).

Kenneth L. Karst & Harold W. Horowitz, *Reitman v. Mulkey: A Telophase of Substantive Equal Protection,* 1967 Sup.Ct.Rev. 39.

Kenneth L. Karst & William W. Van Alstyne, *Sit–Ins and State Action— Mr. Justice Douglas, Concurring,* 14 Stan.L.Rev. 762 (1962).

Thomas P. Lewis, *The Meaning of State Action,* 60 Colum.L.Rev. 1083 (1960).

Thomas P. Lewis, *Burton v. Wilmington Parking Authority—A Case Without Precedent,* 61 Colum.L.Rev. 1458 (1961).

Thomas P. Lewis, *The Sit–In Cases: Great Expectations,* 1963 Sup.Ct. Rev. 101.

Ira Nerken, *A New Deal for the Protection of Fourteenth Amendment Rights: Challenging the Doctrinal Bases of the* Civil Rights Cases *and State Action Theory,* 12 Harv.Civ.Rts.–Civ.Lib.L.Rev. 297 (1977).

Note, *State Action: Theories for Applying Constitutional Restrictions to Private Activity,* 74 Colum.L.Rev. 656 (1974).

Frank R. Parker, *Evans v. Newton and the Racially Restricted Charitable Trust,* 13 How.L.J. 223 (1967).

Louis H. Pollak, *Racial Discrimination and Judicial Integrity: A Reply to Professor Wechsler,* 108 U.Pa.L.Rev. 1 (1959).

Thomas D. Rowe, Jr., *The Emerging Threshold Approach to State Action Determinations: Trying to Make Sense of* Flagg Brothers, Inc. v. Brooks, 69 Georgetown L.J. 745 (1981).

Maimon Schwarzschild, *Value Pluralism and the Constitution: In Defense of the State Action Doctrine,* 1988 Sup.Ct.Rev. 129.

Theodore J. St. Antoine, *Color Blindness But Not Myopia: A New Look at State Action, Equal Protection, and "Private" Racial Discrimination,* 59 Mich.L.Rev. 993 (1961).

David A. Strauss, *Due Process, Government Inaction, and Private Wrongs,* 1989 Sup.Ct.Rev. 53.

Symposium, *The Public/Private Distinction,* 130 U.Pa.L.Rev. 757 (1982).

Anthony Thompson, *Piercing the Veil of State Action: The Revisionist Theory and A Mythical Application To Self–Help Repossession*, 1977 Wis.L.Rev. 1.

Mark Tushnet, *Shelley v. Kraemer and Theories of Equality*, 33 N.Y.L.Sch.L.Rev. 383 (1988).

William W. Van Alstyne & Kenneth L. Karst, *State Action*, 14 Stan. L.Rev. 3 (1961).

William W. Van Alstyne, *Mr. Justice Black, Constitutional Review, and the Talisman of State Action*, 1965 Duke L.J. 219.

Herbert Wechsler, *Toward Neutral Principles of Constitutional Law*, 73 Harv.L.Rev. 1 (1959).

Harry H. Wellington, *The Constitution, The Labor Union, and "Governmental Action"*, 70 Yale L.J. 345 (1961).

Jerre S. Williams, *Mulkey v. Reitman and State Action*, 14 U.C.L.A.L.Rev. 26 (1966).

Jerre S. Williams, *The Twilight of State Action*, 41 Texas L.Rev. 347 (1963).

The Power of Congress

William Cohen, *Congressional Power to Interpret Due Process and Equal Protection*, 27 Stan.L.Rev. 603 (1975).

Archibald Cox, *The Role of Congress in Constitutional Determinations*, 40 U.Cin.L.Rev. 199 (1971).

Laurent B. Frantz, *Congressional Power to Enforce the Fourteenth Amendment Against Private Acts*, 73 Yale L.J. 1353 (1964).

Gary C. Leedes, *State Action Limitations on Courts and Congressional Power*, 60 N.C.L.Rev. 747 (1982).

Larry W. Yackle, *The Burger Court, "State Action," and Congressional Enforcement of the Civil War Amendments*, 27 Ala.L.Rev. 479 (1975).